GOD AND HIS PEOPLE

TEACHER'S EDITION

BJU Press Third Edition

Consultants
from the administration, faculty, and staff of Bob Jones University
Philip D. Smith, Ed.D., *Provost*
Stewart Custer, Ph.D., *Chairman, Department of Bible, School of Religion*
James R. Davis, M.A., *Director of Product Development, Bob Jones University Press*
Bryan Smith, M.A., *Secondary Authors, Bob Jones University Press*
Vicky Burr, *Elementary Authors Project Director, Bob Jones University Press*
Charlene McCall, *Grade 4 Consultant, Bob Jones Elementary School*

NOTE:
The fact that materials produced by other publishers may be referred to in this volume does not constitute an endorsement of the content or theological position of materials produced by such publishers. Any references and ancillary materials are listed as an aid to the student or the teacher and in an attempt to maintain the accepted academic standards of the publishing industry.

Bible Truths 4 for Christian Schools® Teacher's Edition
God and His People

Third Edition

Coordinating Writer
Tammie D. Jacobs

Writers
Eileen M. Berry
Peggy Davenport
Lynnae A. Hadaway
Lisa Marie Massato
Charlotta Pace
Diana C. Simms

God and His People Worktext
Nellie Ashe Cooper

Contributing Writers
Marnie Batterman
Lucille Fisher
Joanne Hall
Sharon Hambrick
Susan Jaeger
Karin Wiley
Karen Wooster

Computer Formatting
Peggy Hargis

Project Editors
Martin Grove
John Mark Steele

Project Editor-Worktext
V. Ed Myers

Typesetting
Peggy Hargis
Kelley Moore

Graphics Coordinator
Wendy Searles

Graphics
Johanna Berg
John Bjerk
Paula Cheadle
Janet Davis
Justin Gerard
Holly Gilbert
Preston Gravely
Dyke Habegger
Jim Hargis
Jenny Ho
Ellyson Kalagayan
Stephanie Kubena
Sam Laterza
Mary Ann Lumm
Keith Neely
Duane Nichols
Asher Parris
Kathy Pflug
John Roberts
Lynda Slattery
Melissa Smith
Noelle Snyder
Thompson Bros.
Stephanie True
Dawn Watkins
Cheryl L. Weikel

Photo Acquisition
Terry Latini
Cynthia R. Mauk

Cover Photo
Dawn Watkins

ISBN 1-57924-290-1

15 14 13 12 11 10 9 8 7 6 5 4

Table of Contents

God and His People

Teaching students to live the Bible as well as know the Bible

Teaches that the Bible is God's Word

- Students are taught that Bible accounts are fact.
- The Bible is used as the final authority in all guided discussions.

Aids students in recognizing their need of Christ as personal Savior

- Lessons emphasize God's dealing with His people and the need of every individual to be saved.
- Students learn how to share the plan of salvation with others.

Encourages Christlikeness in students

- Application stories teach students by example what behaviors please and displease God.
- Students learn what steps of Christian obedience follow salvation.

Instills a desire in students to know more about God

- As students learn about the Word of God, they also learn about the God of the Word.
- Discussion questions after each Bible account focus on what the account teaches.

Encourages students to apply Bible knowledge to their daily lives

- Students study the principles found in the memory verses.
- Students learn that God's Word has relevance to every part of their lives.

Provides a systematic plan for the practice of Bible skills

- The student worktext teaches skills such as using a glossary, using cross-references, and using a concordance.
- Students use their Bibles to find information and interpret meaning.

Connects Bible events with historical events

- Background information for Bible accounts provides a broader knowledge of Bible times.
- Students learn chronology of Bible events and characters by use of individual time lines.
- Students hear stories about noted Christians in history.

Correlates other subjects with Bible teaching

- Lessons are supplemented with optional connections, including history, art, science, language, writing, math, and music.
- Everyday objects are used to teach Bible truths.

Instructional Materials

Student Materials

Student Worktext

The Student Worktext is a colorful companion to the Teacher's Edition. It reviews Bible accounts, provides practice of Bible study skills, and applies Bible knowledge to the lives of students.

The Supplement provides music for each of the unit hymns, maps of Bible times, and a copy of the catechism. Activity pages correlate with a missionary biography, an application novel, and Heroes of the Faith. The glossary contains definitions of Bible terms.

Tests

The test packet includes a copy of the ten unit tests.

Student Materials Packet

Illustrated bookmarks help the student mark the locations of the memory verses studied in each unit. Bible Book Cards are used to develop Bible study skills. An individual-sized TimeLine aids the student in understanding the chronology of Bible characters and Heroes of the Faith. (*Note:* There is some disagreement in certain areas of Old and New Testament chronology. The dates in this curriculum reflect our best interpretation of the evidence. It is not uncommon, however, for dates in conservative sources to vary by a year or two. This has no effect, of course, on the reliability of the biblical record; disagreement comes from our own limitations.)

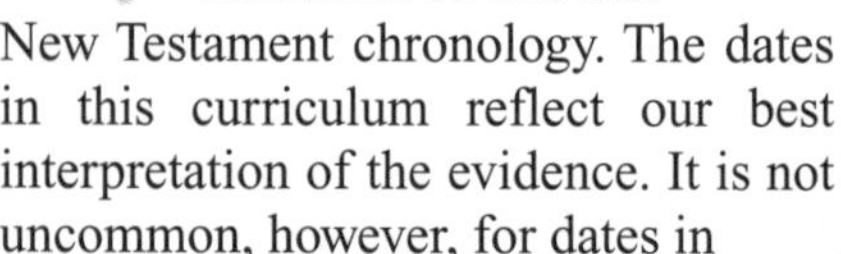

Miscellaneous School Supplies

Each student will need standard school supplies: a Bible; crayons, colored pencils, or felt-tip pens; pencils; scissors; and glue. Each student is encouraged to have a copy of the application novel *Captive Treasure* to read for the lessons in Unit 2. The teacher may choose to read the book to the students before discussing the story together.

Teacher Materials

Teacher's Edition

The Teacher's Edition is the heart of this Bible program. The daily lesson plans are divided into thirty-six parts (or weeks). Each part contains four lessons. On the fifth day of the week the students can attend chapel, do Enrichment activities from the Going Beyond section, and/or be evaluated on their knowledge of the Bible.

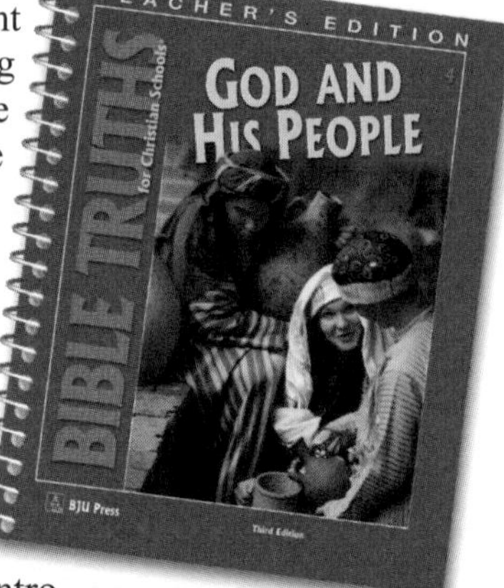

The thirty-six parts are divided into ten thematic units. The Christmas and Easter units may be moved so that they are taught at the correct time of year. Each unit begins with a Unit Overview, providing introductory information for the teacher. Each Overview offers a short personal devotional for the teacher to use in preparing himself to teach that unit. It also contains a list of special materials used to teach the lessons and a lesson plan chart. An optional bulletin board provides the teacher an additional teaching aid emphasizing the unit theme.

The Supplement provides music for the hymns taught in the lessons and two additional songs for each unit that reinforce the unit theme.

Reproducible lesson activity pages and unit review pages aid the teacher in presenting some lessons and provide a convenient way to review the unit and prepare for the optional unit test. The Supplement also includes a short Thanksgiving MiniUnit with three lesson plans, a bulletin board, and reproducible activity pages.

The glossary contains definitions and pronunciations of Bible terms. The cumulative index provides a view of the topics taught in the second, third, and fourth grades.

CD/Cassette

The recording presents the unit hymns and two songs about the books of the Bible sung by children with instrumental accompaniment. Accompaniment may be used without voices by adjusting the balance control.

Application Novel

The application novel *Captive Treasure* is used in teaching lessons in Unit 2. The students may read the chapters individually, or the teacher may read them aloud, discussing the story. Worktext pages are designed to accompany the teaching of this book.

Missionary Biography

With Daring Faith, a missionary biography about Amy Carmichael, is used in teaching lessons in Unit 7. Since the book is written above an elementary reading level, the teacher will read the chapters aloud before discussing the story with the students. Worktext pages are designed to accompany the teaching of this book.

Visual Packet

The visual packet contains twenty-one colorful InfoScenes to be used in the teaching of the lessons and classroom display. Additional charts show the divisions of the books of the Bible, the Ten Commandments, and the plagues in Egypt. The classroom-sized TimeLine enhances the students' grasp of chronology of Bible characters and heroes of church history studied on this grade level. The History of Time TimeLine is vertical and can be placed on the back of a standard door.

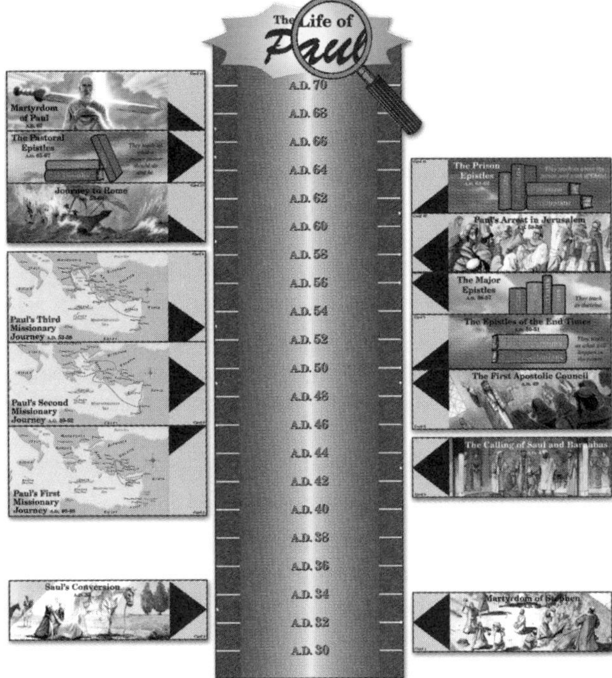

Smaller TimeLines focus on the Life of Paul and show the order of events during the end times. Also included are maps of Bible lands. (*Note:* Copies of the InfoScenes and maps are in the worktext for displaying to an individual or small group of students.) Bible Book Cards are included for studying sequence and abbreviations.

Lesson Plan Format

Preview

The *Preview* lists the *Doctrines*, as well as the *Skills and Applications* the students will work on in the four lessons.

Doctrines

This section notes the lesson number in which the teacher can point out foundational doctrines and read supporting Bible references if desired.

Skills and Applications

This section identifies practical educational skills that students accomplish in Bible class and notes specific Bible attitudes and biblical understanding that the teacher wants to develop in the students.

Lesson

Materials

This list entails specific materials needed for teaching lesson activities, including preparations necessary for the lessons. (*Note:* Standard school supplies, Bibles, and the Student Worktexts are not listed for each lesson.)

Memory Verse

Each memory verse that the students learn is accompanied by a principle and discussion questions to further develop understanding of the verse.

Hymn

The unit hymn reinforces the teaching of the unit and is aided by explanations of the text to help students sing with understanding. (*Note:* Additional songs are included in the Supplement of this book.)

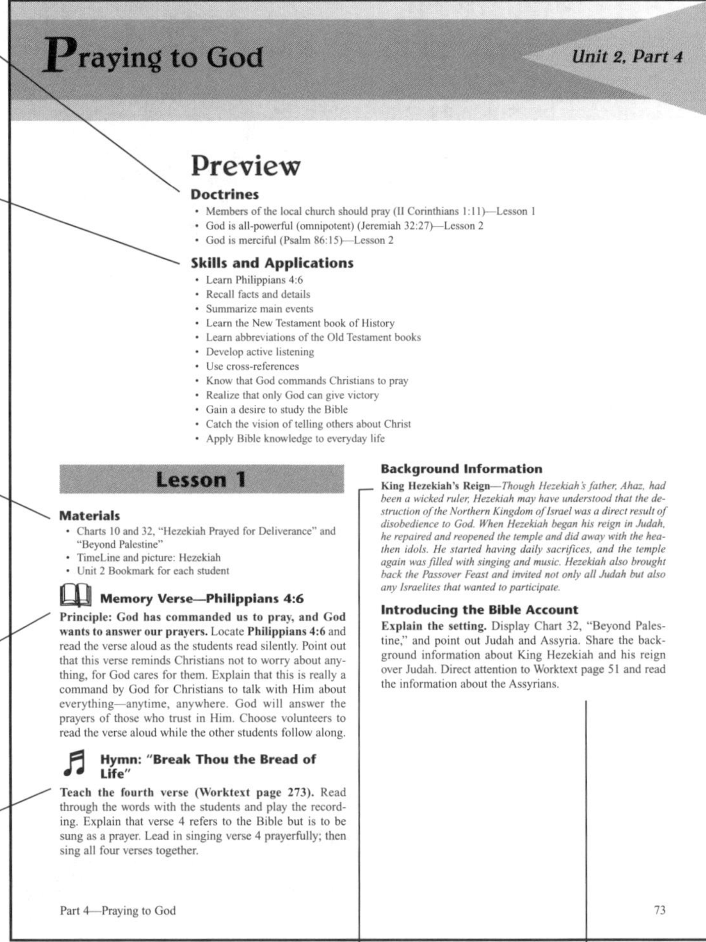

Praying to God

Unit 2, Part 4

Preview

Doctrines
- Members of the local church should pray (II Corinthians 1:11)—Lesson 1
- God is all-powerful (omnipotent) (Jeremiah 32:27)—Lesson 2
- God is merciful (Psalm 86:15)—Lesson 2

Skills and Applications
- Learn Philippians 4:6
- Recall facts and details
- Summarize main events
- Learn the New Testament book of History
- Learn abbreviations of the Old Testament books
- Develop active listening
- Use cross-references
- Know that God commands Christians to pray
- Realize that only God can give victory
- Gain a desire to study the Bible
- Catch the vision of telling others about Christ
- Apply Bible knowledge to everyday life

Lesson 1

Materials
- Charts 10 and 32, "Hezekiah Prayed for Deliverance" and "Beyond Palestine"
- TimeLine and picture: Hezekiah
- Unit 2 Bookmark for each student

Memory Verse—Philippians 4:6

Principle: God has commanded us to pray, and God wants to answer our prayers. Locate **Philippians 4:6** and read the verse aloud as the students read silently. Point out that this verse reminds Christians not to worry about anything, for God cares for them. Explain that this is really a command by God for Christians to talk with Him about everything—anytime, anywhere. God will answer the prayers of those who trust in Him. Choose volunteers to read the verse aloud while the other students follow along.

Hymn: "Break Thou the Bread of Life"

Teach the fourth verse (Worktext page 273). Read through the words with the students and play the recording. Explain that verse 4 refers to the Bible but is to be sung as a prayer. Lead in singing verse 4 prayerfully; then sing all four verses together.

Background Information

King Hezekiah's Reign—*Though Hezekiah's father, Ahaz, had been a wicked ruler, Hezekiah may have understood that the destruction of the Northern Kingdom of Israel was a direct result of disobedience to God. When Hezekiah began his reign in Judah, he repaired and reopened the temple and did away with the heathen idols. He started having daily sacrifices, and the temple again was filled with singing and music. Hezekiah also brought back the Passover Feast and invited not only all Judah but also any Israelites that wanted to participate.*

Introducing the Bible Account

Explain the setting. Display Chart 32, "Beyond Palestine," and point out Judah and Assyria. Share the background information about King Hezekiah and his reign over Judah. Direct attention to Worktext page 51 and read the information about the Assyrians.

Part 4—Praying to God

73

Background Information

The background information provides the teacher with additional information for a broader knowledge of Bible times and can often be shared with the students.

Introducing the Bible Account (or Application Story)

The introduction furnishes the teacher with questions for a discussion or directions for an activity related to the Bible account or story that follows.

Worktext

Students use the pages to review Bible accounts, practice Bible study skills, and apply Bible knowledge to their personal lives.

Bible Account or Application Story

The Bible account is a retelling from a specific passage. The application story emphasizes a specific point. Both are designed to be read aloud.

Discussion Questions

Questions aid the teacher in checking the students for understanding and in applying Bible principles to the lives of each student.

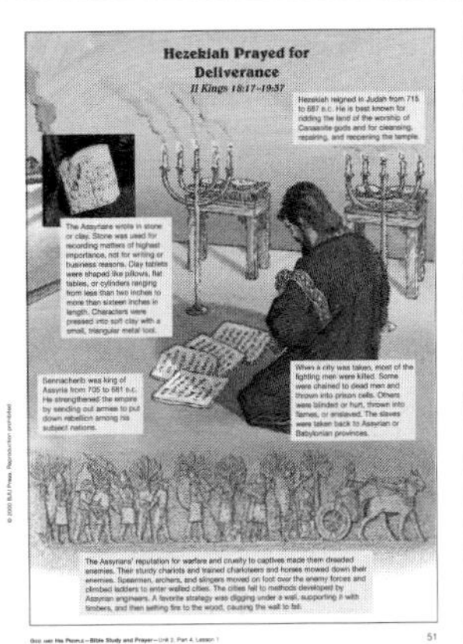

The Threatening Letter
II Kings 18:17–19:37

Name ____________

Read the directions for the three sections: People, Places, Events. While your teacher is reading or telling the Bible account, circle the correct answers.

People

When you hear one of these names in the story, circle it here.

King Nebuchadnezzar · Nehemiah · Isaiah · King Ahab · King Sennacherib · Jeremiah · Ezra · King Hezekiah

Places

When you hear one of these places in the story, circle it here.

Edom · Jerusalem · Jericho · Assyria · Egypt · Moab · Judah · Israel

Events

Circle the correct word(s) to complete each sentence.

1. King Hezekiah / King Sennacherib of Assyria / Judah sent messengers to King Sennacherib / King Hezekiah of Judah / Assyria.
2. King Hezekiah / King Sennacherib sent to the prophet Ezekiel / Isaiah for advice / money.
3. Isaiah said that King Sennacherib would hear a mighty rushing wind / hear a rumored report.
4. Isaiah said that King Hezekiah / King Sennacherib would be killed / wounded by the sword / the plague.
5. King Sennacherib / King Hezekiah laid King Sennacherib's / King Hezekiah's letter / sword before the prophet / Lord.
6. Isaiah / God gave King Hezekiah / King Sennacherib riches / victory without fighting / prayer.

52 God and His People—Bible Study and Prayer—Unit 2, Part 4, Lesson 1

Worktext page 52

Develop active listening. Point out the three sections of the page: people, places, events. Direct the students to complete the page while you read the Bible account.

Bible Account

Read the following Bible account or II Kings 18:17–19:37.

Hezekiah Prayed for Deliverance

The Assyrians had taken the Northern Kingdom of Israel into captivity 136 years earlier. Now King Sennacherib, the Assyrian king, set his eyes on the Southern Kingdom of Judah. However, the king of Judah was Hezekiah, who trusted in God.

King Sennacherib sent his messengers to tell the messengers of King Hezekiah that they and their king were trusting in the wrong thing. The messengers from King Sennacherib made fun of their dependence upon God. The messengers of King Hezekiah had been told not to answer them, so they said nothing but went back and told King Hezekiah everything King Sennacherib's men had said. Hearing this, King Hezekiah was not sure what to do.

King Hezekiah was in great turmoil, and his heart was heavy. He tore his beautiful clothes and put on sackcloth, and went into the house of God.

Then Hezekiah sent his messengers to see Isaiah, the prophet of God. After hearing all that the messengers had been told, Isaiah went to God. After talking to God, Isaiah told the messengers of King Hezekiah, "Be not afraid of the words which thou hast heard," because King Sennacherib will hear a rumor and go back to his own land. God will defend you. King Sennacherib will die by his own sword.

King Sennacherib sent a message, in the form of a letter, to King Hezekiah, saying the second time, "Let not thy God in whom thou trustest deceive thee, saying, Jerusalem, shall not be delivered into the hand of the King of Assyria."

Hezekiah laid the letter out before God and prayed by acknowledging God as the true God, the Creator of heaven and earth. He recounted how the Assyrians had destroyed the gods of other people, and how they were thinking that they could destroy the true and living God. "Now therefore, O Lord our God,

74 Unit 2—Bible Reading and Prayer

I beseech thee, save thou us out of his hand, that all the kingdoms of the earth may know that thou art the Lord God, even thou only."

Then Isaiah the prophet of God sent word to Hezekiah that God had heard Hezekiah's prayer. Isaiah told Hezekiah all that God said against King Sennacherib. God promised Hezekiah that He would defend the city and that King Sennacherib would not shoot even one arrow into Jerusalem. God said that King Sennacherib would return to his home without destroying Jerusalem.

During the night, the angel of the Lord came into the camp of the Assyrians and killed 185,000 soldiers. In the morning, the camp of the enemy contained only dead bodies. So King Sennacherib returned to his own land. One day as the evil king was in the house of his gods, worshiping his idols, his sons came in and killed him with his own sword.

InfoScene: "Hezekiah Prayed for Deliverance"
Display Chart 10 for reference throughout this unit. Review and discuss the Bible account as time permits.

➤ **What did the king of Assyria say when he told King Hezekiah he was coming to destroy Jerusalem?** *(He bragged about all the lands he had conquered and the gods he had destroyed. He said his armies were stronger than Hezekiah's God; he called God a liar, which is blasphemy.)*

➤ **After the second threat, what did Hezekiah do?** *(He took the letter he received from King Sennacherib, laid it out before God, and asked God to show the world that He is the true God.)*

➤ **What did God say He would do?** *(God said He would defend Jerusalem, and not one arrow would enter Jerusalem from Sennacherib's army. He said that Sennacherib would return home and would die by his own sword.)*

➤ **What happened?** *(God defended Jerusalem, and 185,000 men were killed. The king returned home and later was killed by his sons with his sword.)*

➤ **Why is it better to trust in God than in strong armies?** *(Many answers are acceptable, but point out the omnipotence, omniscience, and omnipresence of God.)*

➤ **What should Christians do when they have difficult situations?** *(Pray and trust God.)*

TimeLine

Place *Hezekiah* on the TimeLine. Direct the students to place *Hezekiah* onto the TimeLine at 728-686 B.C. Guide them in gluing *Hezekiah* onto their individual TimeLines.

Bible Study Skills

Review the New Testament book of History. Hold up the card for Acts. Explain that there is only one book in the division of New Testament History. Direct attention to the table of contents in the Bible.

➤ **How many books are in the division of Old Testament History from Joshua to Esther?** *(twelve)*

Review the abbreviations for the books of the Old Testament. Divide the students into three or four teams. Line up the teams. Show a card with an abbreviation to the students at the front of each line. The student who first calls out the name of the book receives a point for his team. Let the students in front go to the end of the line after their turn. Continue as time permits.

One-on-One: Show the abbreviation card to the student, who should answer with the correct name. Or give the student the Old Testament cards and the abbreviation cards, challenging him to match them correctly.

Going Beyond

Enrichment

Learn about who sang to God. Assign students to look up the following verses to read aloud. Tell the students to listen as the verse is read to decide who sang the song and why.

Verse	Who sang?	Why did they sing?
Exodus 15:1	Moses and the children of Israel	God gave them victory in crossing the Red Sea.
II Chronicles 29:28	The singers in the congregation (the people)	They were worshiping God during the burnt offering.
Ezra 3:11	The Israelites	They were praising the Lord.
Psalm 106:12	They (the Israelites)	They believed His (God's) words.
Acts 16:25	Paul and Silas	They were praising God.

Explain that these people counted their blessings and, as a result, sang to God. God gave us music so that we can glorify Him. When we get angry or sad about something, we should focus on what God has done for us, and our sadness will turn to joy. Sing several hymns, encouraging the students to sing joyfully.

Part 4—Praying to God 75

TimeLine

The TimeLine aids understanding of Bible chronology.

Bible Study Skills

Skills are taught to increase the students' ability to use their Bibles.

One-on-One

The One-on-One feature provides an alternate activity for use with the teacher and one student or an individual student at an activity center.

Going Beyond

This section of the lesson plan is optional. The activity can be completed on the fifth day of each week or can supplement one of the lessons in that part.

Teaching Tips

Classroom Use

The daily lesson plans are organized into ten thematic units that study the Old and New Testaments, usually in chronological order. The teaching order of the units may be changed if desired. Eight of the units are divided into four parts, one part to be taught each week for a total of four weeks. Unit 4, the Christmas unit, and Unit 8, the Easter unit, contain only two parts to be taught in two weeks. You may have to adjust your teaching schedule so that you can teach these units at the appropriate time of year. An optional Thanksgiving MiniUnit containing three lessons appears in the supplement of this book.

Each part contains four days of lessons. The fifth day of each week is left free for chapel. If your class does not have a chapel to attend, you may choose to do the activity in the Going Beyond section. Teachers wanting to evaluate their students' Bible knowledge may want to do this on the fifth day of the week.

Church Use

This curriculum may be adapted for Sunday school or junior church. The teacher may choose to teach one part each Sunday. Depending on the length of the class (60-90 minutes), the teacher would teach a Bible account, an application story, one activity, the memory verse, and the hymn. Following this procedure, the teacher would complete one part each Sunday (approximately one unit each month) and a grade-level curriculum in thirty-six weeks. If the teacher desires, he may spend two Sundays teaching a part, enabling him to use all of the Bible accounts and application stories and most of the activities. The teacher would use one grade-level curriculum for an entire year. If a junior church includes several grades, teachers should alternate grade levels each year, repeating the cycle after three years.

Teaching Bible

The Bible accounts in the lessons are retellings from specific passages. When reading the Bible account aloud to the students, it is good to have a Bible open to the passage to help convey the importance of the account's being from God's holy Word. Instead of reading from the lesson, you may choose to read the Scripture aloud to the students or retell it in your own words.

During a typical week, you will share two or three Bible accounts with the students. At least one doctrine is identified for each Bible account. You may choose to read the supporting Bible reference and emphasize this doctrine as desired. It is important to take time to discuss the account, to develop further understanding, and to make application of Bible principles to the students' personal lives.

Several times during the school year a lesson explains the life and teachings of a prophet. The purpose of these Prophet Focus sections is to introduce the students to the prophets and their specific ministry: warning people of God's judgment, encouraging the people, and foretelling Christ's coming.

Bible studies occur in some of the lessons. You may choose to read the verses aloud or allow students to read them aloud as you guide the discussion.

Teaching Church History

This third edition of the Bible Truths curriculum includes information about important people who have contributed to the history of the church. Referred to as Heroes of the Faith, these people were chosen because they established churches, wrote about God and His glory, and defended the faith—some to the point of death. The Christian church today still feels the effects of their ministries. These accounts help balance what students learn about the accomplishments of explorers, scientists, mathematicians, leaders of government, and sports heroes.

Students hear a story based on the life of one of these heroes in six lessons in various units. An optional page in the supplement of the Student Worktext may be used to reinforce the information on each hero. A picture of each hero accompanies the TimeLines and may be attached at the appropriate date.

Teaching Christian Living

The application stories show students what behavior pleases and displeases God through examples of children in fictionalized stories. An application novel and a missionary biography take the place of the short application stories in two of the units. Because you and your students read these books over a period of time, students will become more involved in the characters' lives. Students can identify with the characters' application of biblical principles in different situations. The application novel *Captive Treasure* teaches students that the Word of God is our greatest treasure. The missionary biography *With Daring Faith* teaches students that God's plan for our life is best and that nothing in our lives is too precious to give to Jesus. It is important that students learn how to apply Bible knowledge to their personal lives so that they can live the Bible as well as know the Bible.

Picturing the Point

Sometimes a concept (e.g., faithfulness) can be made more understandable to students by using an object to visually illustrate the point. A few such illustrations are included in the lessons.

Memorizing Bible Verses

Students need to understand the Scripture that they are memorizing. When a new verse is introduced, the teacher needs to explain it fully. The main principle of the verse is identified for the teacher and can be shared with the students. The memory verses focus on the unit themes, and the references are noted on the Bookmarks for each unit. Students should look up and read the verses from their own Bibles. Verse visuals may be made and are helpful for memorizing Scripture, but students need to read Scripture from the Bible. The Bookmark will aid students in locating the verse during the week. Students may use a highlighter to mark the memory verse. If this procedure is used throughout elementary school, the students will have a record of the verses they memorized at school.

The key to memorizing Bible verses is frequent practice. Teachers should not expect that all the necessary practice needed to memorize will take place in the students' homes. Practice time is provided during the Bible lesson. Some teachers find it helpful to draw five pictures on the chalkboard and erase one picture every time students practice. This ensures that the teacher and students remember to practice throughout the day. Memorizing verses should be pleasant and positive, not a dreaded time of drill.

You may adjust the amount of required memorization to meet the needs of the students in your class. If the Scripture is too long, emphasize only the main portion of the selection. The verse may also be adjusted to meet the abilities of a specific student.

The evaluation of Scripture memory is optional. Some teachers have students say verses aloud as a class, as small groups, or as individuals. Other teachers prepare verse quizzes with a limited number of blanks that the students complete, using words from a word bank. It is not necessary to assign a grade to this evaluation. Assigning letter grades to memory verses often requires the teacher to deviate from a strict percentage for the number of correct answers. It is more important for students to understand the meaning of the verse and to be able to use it in their own lives than to know the verse word perfect. Students should hide God's Word in their hearts—not just in their minds.

Singing

Most teachers and students have favorite songs they enjoy singing in Sunday school, Bible class, and church. Because teachers and students are familiar with these and will want to continue to sing them during Bible time, only one hymn was chosen for most of the units. Each unit hymn was selected based on its potential for continued use in worship, inspiration, and growth in the lives of the students. Some of these hymns contain adult phraseology, abstraction, and symbolism. Simple explanations are included to help you explain the meanings of these hymns. Singing with Understanding pages are included in the Worktext. Two additional songs for each unit appear with the unit hymn in the supplement of this book.

Praying

Prayer is an integral part of each school day. Use this time to teach students what prayer is and how God answers prayer. Prayer time may be a part of the Bible lesson or a part of the beginning of the school day. Invite students to share prayer requests from time to time. A colorful prayer journal is located at the back of the student worktext. Encourage students to record some of their classmates' prayer requests.

Teaching Bible Study Skills

An important aspect of teaching the Bible to students is teaching them how to use their Bibles. Time is allotted for memorizing the books that come before and after each book so students can locate verses in their Bibles easily. Students use a glossary to look up Bible terms. They learn how to use cross-references and a concordance. They study the books of the Bible and learn which book contains specific Bible accounts (e.g., Creation and the Flood in Genesis, Moses' leading the Israelites out of Egypt in Exodus, God's talking to Job in Job). Students actively use their Bibles to find information and interpret meaning.

Connecting Bible to Other Subjects

Just as the Christian teacher integrates Bible into all the subjects he is teaching, the Bible connects to all subjects. The obvious connection is between Bible and history (e.g., government at the time of Christ's birth, culture in Egypt during the Israelites' bondage). Other connections include mathematics (e.g., distance between cities), science (e.g., birds), world history (e.g., King Tutankhamen), and American history (e.g., the Oregon Trail).

Students also need to see that the skills they learn in other subjects are helpful in Bible class. The following are only a few connections made within the lessons:

- using a glossary
- reading a map
- reading a time line
- writing a creed

Combining Grade Levels

Bible instruction is free of two considerations in combining grade levels: achievement testing and preparing students for the next grade level. When combining grades, consider the age of the students as well as the span of grades, and adjust your teaching and requirements. Younger students need more explanations, less memory work, and more help in completing worktext pages. Older students can review memory verses from previous weeks, can complete worktext pages independently, and can apply the lessons further.

If you are teaching this curriculum to a group of third, fourth, and fifth graders, you will need to decide whether the third graders can easily memorize the verses. If not, assign only a phrase or choose one verse and work on it for two weeks. Both third and fourth graders need guidance in completing some of the worktext pages. Difficult pages such as those containing map skills may be omitted. Remember, the goal is to teach all students to live the Bible as well as know the Bible.

Leading a Child to the Lord

One of the greatest desires of Christian teachers is to lead their students to the Savior. To instill in each student a desire to know Christ as his personal Savior is a great responsibility and joy.

Take advantage of the opportunities that arise during the lessons for presenting the plan of salvation, relying on the Holy Spirit to reach the conscience of each student. Encourage students to talk with you individually about accepting Christ and be alert to their individual needs. You may find the following outline (based on the Romans Road) helpful.

1. **I have sinned** *(Romans 3:23).*
   - I disobey God's Word. (examples: disobeying parents, taking things that do not belong to me, saying unkind words to others)
   - My sin must be punished *(Romans 6:23).*
   - I cannot get rid of my sin by myself.
2. **Christ died for my sin** *(Romans 5:8).*
   - God is holy and cannot sin.
   - God loves me and sent Jesus Christ to die on the cross for my sins.
   - I may decide to ask Jesus to forgive me and be my Savior. It is my choice *(Romans 10:9-10).*
3. **I receive God's gift of salvation** *(Romans 10:13).*
   - If I believe Jesus died for me and ask Him to be my Savior, I become a child of God.
   - I am in God's family and will live forever in heaven with God.
   - Salvation is a gift of God *(Romans 6:23).*

When talking individually with a student, ask questions to discern sincerity or any misunderstandings. *(What is sin? Have you sinned? Why did God send Jesus?)* Read the Scripture from your Bible or the student's Bible.

- ➤ Do you choose to accept Jesus as your Savior from sin?
- ➤ If so, read *John 1:12.*

When a student shows genuine readiness, ask him to pray. Sometimes students are unsure how to pray. When you ask a student whether he would like you to pray, be sure he understands and agrees with your words.

> "Dear God, I know You love me. I know You sent Your Son Jesus to die for me. I know I am a sinner. I believe Jesus died for my sins. I ask Jesus to be my Savior from sin today. In Jesus' name I pray. Amen."

Show the student how to know from God's Word that he is in God's family *(I John 5:12-13).* Encourage the student to obey God's Word. Point out that he can have God's forgiveness when he sins again *(I John 1:9).*

Encourage the student to tell others about his salvation.

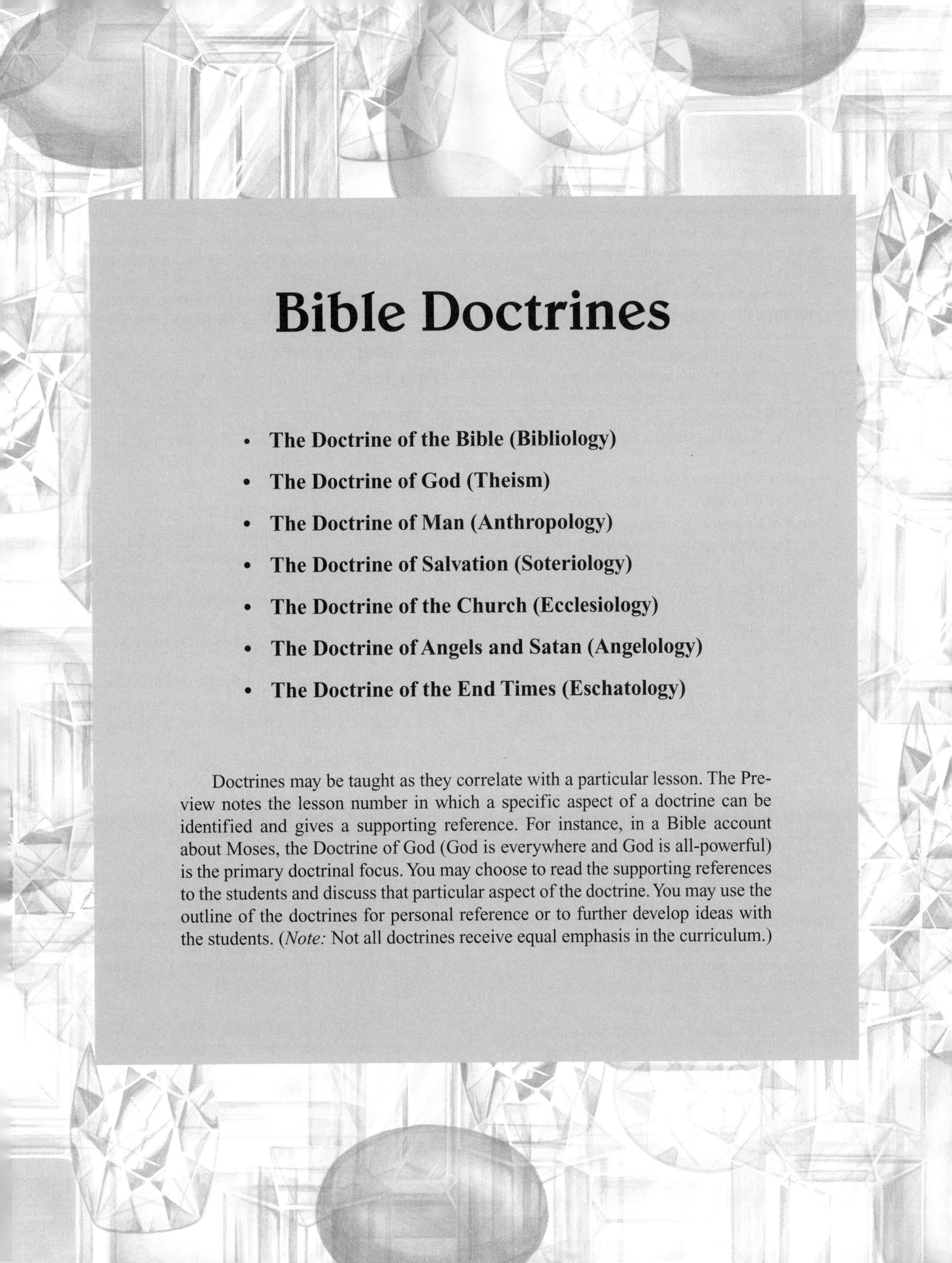

Bible Doctrines

- **The Doctrine of the Bible (Bibliology)**
- **The Doctrine of God (Theism)**
- **The Doctrine of Man (Anthropology)**
- **The Doctrine of Salvation (Soteriology)**
- **The Doctrine of the Church (Ecclesiology)**
- **The Doctrine of Angels and Satan (Angelology)**
- **The Doctrine of the End Times (Eschatology)**

Doctrines may be taught as they correlate with a particular lesson. The Preview notes the lesson number in which a specific aspect of a doctrine can be identified and gives a supporting reference. For instance, in a Bible account about Moses, the Doctrine of God (God is everywhere and God is all-powerful) is the primary doctrinal focus. You may choose to read the supporting references to the students and discuss that particular aspect of the doctrine. You may use the outline of the doctrines for personal reference or to further develop ideas with the students. (*Note:* Not all doctrines receive equal emphasis in the curriculum.)

The Doctrine of the Bible (Bibliology)

I. Inspiration

A. Definition of inspiration: the supernatural influence of the Holy Spirit upon the individual writers of the Bible. This influence of the Holy Spirit resulted in the words of the authors in the original manuscripts being the very words of God. These words are without error and are authoritative.
   1. The Holy Spirit worked in the hearts and lives of the writers of the Bible.
   2. Inspiration applies to the original writings, not translations or copies.
   3. The Bible is the Word of God.
      a. The Bible has authority over man.
      b. The Bible does not have any mistakes.

B. Proofs for inspiration
   1. The Bible says that it is inspired (II Timothy 3:16-17).
   2. The Bible cannot be destroyed.
   3. The Bible is known throughout the world.
   4. The Bible does not contradict itself.
   5. The Bible presents standards of living and a way of life that are of God.
   6. The Bible is accurate in its history.
   7. The Bible is accurate in its prophecy.
   8. The Bible provides for man's physical and spiritual needs.
   9. The Bible has the witness of the Spirit in the hearts of believers (I Corinthians 2:11-15).
   10. The Bible has been shown to be inspired by believers who have found its teachings to work (Psalm 119:97-104).

C. Details of inspiration
   1. The Bible is complete (Revelation 22:18-19).
      a. Nothing should be taken away from the Bible.
      b. Nothing should be added to the Bible.
   2. The Bible is eternal (Psalm 119:89; Matthew 24:35).

II. Canonicity

A. Definition of canonicity: the study of the way books became part of the Bible.
   1. The decision to make a book part of the Bible involved many people.
   2. The decision to make a book part of the Bible involved recognizing the book as an authoritative rule for faith and practice in the church.

B. Questions asked to determine the canonicity of the New Testament books. (All the questions had to be answered yes before the book became a part of the New Testament.)
   1. Was the book inspired? (This question was the most important.)
   2. Was the book written by an apostle or someone who was close to an apostle?
   3. Was the book's message on a high level spiritually?
   4. Was the book received by all the churches?

C. Details of canonicity
   1. All the books of the Bible were inspired and had authority when they were written. (They became part of the Bible later.)
   2. All the books of the Bible formally became part of the Bible by the fourth century.

The Doctrine of God (Theism)

I. Existence of God

A. God has shown Himself in nature (Romans 1:20).
B. God has shown Himself in the Bible (John 5:39).

II. Attributes of God

A. God is Spirit (John 4:24; I Timothy 6:16).
B. God is eternal (Psalm 90:2; I Timothy 1:17).
C. God is everywhere (omnipresent) (I Kings 8:27; Psalm 139:7-10).
D. God is all-knowing (omniscient) (Job 42:2; Psalm 94:11).
E. God is all-powerful (omnipotent) (Jeremiah 32:27; Matthew 19:26).
F. God is unchanging (immutable) (Malachi 3:6; James 1:17).
G. God is faithful (I Corinthians 1:9; II Timothy 2:13).
H. God is holy (Isaiah 6:3; I Peter 1:16).
I. God is righteous (Psalm 116:5; 145:17).
J. God is merciful (Psalm 86:15; 103:8).
K. God is love (John 3:16; I John 4:8).

III. Nature of God

A. God is one being or essence.
   1. God's being is not divided: God is one. (There is no disunity.) (Deuteronomy 6:4)
   2. God's being is not multiplied: God is the only one. (There are no other gods.) (Deuteronomy 4:35; I Timothy 2:5)

B. God is three persons.
   1. The Father, Son, and Spirit are eternally distinct (John 15:26; 17:22; Galatians 4:6).
   2. The Father, Son, and Spirit are recognized as God.
      a. The Father is God (John 6:27; I Peter 1:2).
      b. The Son is God (Titus 2:13; Hebrews 1:8).

c. The Spirit is God (Acts 5:3, 4; I Corinthians 3:16).
3. The Father, Son, and Spirit possess attributes of Deity.

	God the Father	God the Son	God the Spirit
Eternal	Psalm 90:2	Revelation 1:8, 17	Hebrews 9:14
Omnipresent	Jeremiah 23:24	Ephesians 1:23	Psalm 139:7-10
Omniscient	Jeremiah 17:10	Revelation 2:23	I Corinthians 12:11
Omnipotent	I Peter 1:5	II Corinthians 12:9	Romans 15:19
Holy	Revelation 15:4	Acts 3:14	Ephesians 4:30
Righteous	Revelation 16:7	I Corinthians 1:30	Romans 8:4
Loving	II Corinthians 13:14	I John 3:16	Romans 15:30

C. Practical points
1. The human mind cannot understand fully the fact that God is one being and yet three persons.
2. The human mind can recognize some teachings on the nature of God to be false.

The Doctrine of Man (Anthropology)

I. Original State of Man

A. God created man directly (Hebrews 11:3).
1. Man did not just happen.
2. Man did not evolve.

B. God created man for His glory (Isaiah 43:7; Colossians 1:16; Revelation 4:11).
1. God would show His glory.
2. God would receive glory.

C. God created man perfect (Genesis 1:26).
1. Man is created in the image of God (Genesis 1:27).
2. Man has personality.
a. He has intelligence (Genesis 2:20).
b. He has emotions (Genesis 3:10).
c. He has a will (Genesis 3:6; I Timothy 2:14).
3. Man had original righteousness and holiness (Ecclesiastes 7:29; Ephesians 4:24; Colossians 3:10).
4. Man has immortality (I Corinthians 15:54).
5. Man has a conscience (Romans 2:15).

II. Fall of Man

A. Temptation of man
1. Satan was the tempter (Genesis 3:1; II Corinthians 11:14).
2. Eve received the temptation (Genesis 3:1-7; II Corinthians 11:3; I Timothy 2:14).
3. Obedience to God was the principle (Genesis 2:17; 3:2-5).

B. Results to man
1. Adam and Eve experienced immediate results.
a. They experienced spiritual death (Genesis 2:17; cf. Ephesians 2:1).
b. They experienced physical punishment (Genesis 3:16-19).
2. Mankind experienced lasting results.
a. Man has a sinful nature: he lost communion with God (Romans 5:12, 19).
(1) Man's spiritual understanding has been darkened (I Corinthians 2:14; Ephesians 4:18).
(2) Man's mind and conscience have been damaged (Titus 1:15).
(3) Man's will has been debilitated (Romans 7:18-19).
(4) His body has been subject to death (Genesis 3:19; Hebrews 9:27).
b. Man is guilty before God (Leviticus 4:13, 22, 27; Romans 3:10-12).
c. Man is in a hopeless condition (Ephesians 2:12).
d. Man lives in a corrupted environment (Genesis 3:17-19; Romans 8:22).

III. Redemption of Man

A. Man's standing in Christ before God (I Corinthians 1:30)
1. Man by faith receives Christ's righteousness (Philippians 3:9).
2. Man in Christ stands perfect before God (II Corinthians 5:21; Hebrews 10:14).

B. Man's state in Christ
1. Man is saved (II Timothy 1:9).
2. Man is dead to sin (I Peter 2:24).
3. Man is a child of God (Galatians 3:26).
4. Man is a new creature (II Corinthians 5:17).
5. Man has a new nature (Romans 7:21-25).
a. He does not lose his old nature (Romans 7:21).
b. He faces a struggle between the two natures (Romans 7:23-25).
6. Man has God's favor (Ephesians 1:3).
7. Man has hope (Philippians 3:20-21).

IV. Final State of Man

A. Unredeemed man: eternal separation from God
1. He experiences the second death (Revelation 20:14).
2. He exists in the lake of fire (Revelation 20:15).
3. He has no hope (Revelation 21:8, 27).

B. Redeemed man: eternal fellowship with God
1. He experiences eternal life (Revelation 22:3-5).
2. He lives in heaven (Revelation 21:3).
3. He has security (Revelation 21:4).

The Doctrine of Salvation (Soteriology)

I. Provision of God

A. Christ became man (incarnation) (John 1:14; Philippians 2:5-8; Hebrews 2:14).
   1. Christ did not yield to temptations in His nature (John 14:30; Hebrews 4:15).
   2. Christ did not yield to temptations in His actions (John 8:29; I Peter 2:22-23).

B. Christ died for man (atonement) (I Corinthians 15:3).
   1. His death was substitutionary (Isaiah 53:6; I Peter 2:24).
   2. His death was sufficient (Hebrews 9:12-14; 10:12).

C. Christ arose from the dead (resurrection) (I Corinthians 15:3-8).
   1. His resurrection was bodily (John 20:24-29).
   2. His resurrection showed God's approval and acceptance of Christ's sacrificial death as full atonement for sin (Romans 1:4).
   3. His resurrection was followed by His ascension to heaven (Acts 1:9-11; Hebrews 10:12).

II. Reception by Man

A. Man must admit that he is a sinner and is deserving of eternal punishment in hell (Romans 3:10, 23; 6:23*a*).

B. Man must repent of his sins (Romans 2:4).

C. Man must believe that Christ died for his sins (Romans 5:6, 8; 10:10*a*).

D. Man must ask Christ to become his Savior (Romans 10:13).
   1. He must turn away from everything else, including works, for salvation (Romans 4:5; 11:6; Ephesians 2:8-9).
   2. He must turn to Christ alone for salvation (John 14:6; Romans 6:23*b*).

E. Man must confess to others that he has accepted Christ (Romans 10:10*b*-11).

III. Elements of Salvation

A. God invites men to come to the Lord Jesus Christ for salvation by grace through faith (calling) (Matthew 11:28; 22:9; Romans 8:30; II Peter 3:9).
   1. God calls men through the Bible (Romans 10:16-17).
   2. God calls men through the Holy Spirit (John 16:7-11).
   3. God calls men through men (Romans 10:14-15).
   4. God calls men through providence (Romans 2:4).

B. Man turns to God through repentance and faith (conversion) (II Corinthians 7:9-10; Ephesians 3:17).
   1. Repentance is turning away from sin (Acts 26:19-20; Romans 2:4; II Corinthians 7:9-10).
   2. Faith is turning to Christ (John 1:12; Ephesians 3:17).

C. God says that the sins of the believer are forgiven and Christ's righteousness is imputed to him by faith (justification).
   1. God forgives the believer's sins (pardon) (Acts 13:38-39; Ephesians 1:7).
   2. God restores the believer to His favor (adoption) (Romans 5:1-2; Galatians 4:4-5).
   3. God gives to the believer the righteousness of Christ (Romans 4:5-6; II Corinthians 5:21).

D. God imparts to the believer spiritual life and a new nature (regeneration) (Ephesians 2:1; Colossians 1:13).

E. God, working through the Holy Spirit, makes the believer holy in heart and behavior (sanctification) (I Corinthians 6:11; Hebrews 13:12, 21).
   1. Sanctification includes dying to sin and living to righteousness (Romans 8:13; Galatians 2:20; Colossians 3:5).
   2. Sanctification is a process.
      a. Initial sanctification takes place at the time of the new birth (I Corinthians 6:11; cf. I Corinthians 3:3).
      b. Progressive sanctification takes place throughout the Christian life (Romans 6:6; II Corinthians 5:15).
      c. Final sanctification takes place at the appearing of Christ or at death (Philippians 3:21; Hebrews 12:23).
   3. Sanctification is the work of God's Spirit which enables Christians more and more to die to sin and to live unto righteousness.

The Doctrine of the Church (Ecclesiology)

I. Definitions

A. The universal church, an organism, is the mystical body of Christ composed of all true believers (I Corinthians 12:13; Ephesians 1:22, 23).

B. The local church, an organization, is a group of professing believers gathered together for the purposes of God (Acts 2:41, 42; 16:5).

II. Organization of the Local Church

A. Membership: professing believers (Acts 2:47; I Corinthians 1:2)

B. Officers

1. The apostles served in the establishment of the church: nowhere in the New Testament is the apostolic office shown to be passed on (Ephesians 4:11).
2. The prophets serve to communicate God's truth (Ephesians 4:11).
   a. Until the Bible was completed (Revelation 22:18-19), the prophetic office involved foretelling and forth-telling (proclaiming).
   b. Since the Bible was completed (Revelation 22:18-19), the prophetic office involves forth-telling (proclaiming) only.
3. The pastor, teacher, and evangelist are given not to the world but to the church for the perfecting of the saints to the work of the ministry (Acts 21:8; Ephesians 4:11, 12; II Timothy 4:5).
4. The teachers serve to instruct the church (I Corinthians 12:28-29; Ephesians 4:11; I Timothy 2:7).
5. The pastors, bishops, and elders serve to guide, care for, and teach the church (Ephesians 4:11-12; Titus 1:5-7; Hebrews 13:17; I Peter 5:1-4).

III. Functions of the Local Church

A. Officers

1. Preach the Word (II Timothy 4:2).
2. Teach members (Ephesians 4:11-16).
3. Evangelize the lost (Matthew 28:19-20; Acts 1:8).
4. Discipline members (Matthew 18:15-17; Romans 16:17; I Corinthians 5:1-5, 11-13; I Thessalonians 5:14*a*; II Thessalonians 3:6, 14, 15).
5. Defend the Word (I Timothy 1:3-4; II Timothy 1:13; Titus 1:9-11; Jude 3).
6. Oppose sin (Ephesians 5:11; II Thessalonians 3:14; Titus 1:9-11).
7. Care for those having special needs (Acts 6:1-7; James 5:14).
8. Administer the ordinances: the Lord's Supper and Baptism (Acts 2:41-42).

B. Members

1. Exhort one another (Hebrews 10:25).
2. Pray (Acts 2:42; 12:5; II Corinthians 1:11).
3. Evangelize the lost (Matthew 22:1-14; 28:19-20).
4. Contribute financially (Romans 15:26; I Corinthians 16:1-2).
5. Fellowship (Acts 2:46).
6. Partake of the ordinances: the Lord's Supper and Baptism (Acts 8:12; 20:7).

The Doctrine of Angels and Satan (Angelology)

I. Angels

A. Characteristics

1. They are created beings (Nehemiah 9:6; Colossians 1:16).
   a. The Bible does not reveal the time of their creation.
   b. The Bible does reveal that they existed at the time of the earth's creation (Job 38:4-7).
2. They are spirit beings (Psalm 104:4; Hebrews 1:7, 14).
   a. They sometimes assume the form of man (Genesis 19:1, 5; Judges 13:16).
   b. They neither die (not subject to the corruption of the flesh) nor marry (Matthew 22:30; Luke 20:35, 36).
3. They are wiser than men (II Samuel 14:20), yet, from the church, they learn about the grace of God (I Peter 1:12).
4. They are stronger than men (Psalm 103:20).
5. They are innumerable (Matthew 26:53; Hebrews 12:22; Revelation 5:11).

B. Organization

1. There are different ranks and orders of angels (Ephesians 3:10; Colossians 1:16).
2. There are angels of God.
   a. Angels have specific titles and responsibilities.
      (1) Cherubim guard God's throne, possessions, and holiness (Genesis 3:24; Ezekiel 1:5-14; 10:1-22).
      (2) Seraphim are attendants of God who serve Him in purging men's uncleanness (Isaiah 6:2, 6).
      (3) Archangels do battle for God.
         (a) Michael, the only angel so titled, serves to defend the nation Israel and to battle against Satan (Daniel 10; Jude 9; Revelation 12:7-9).
         (b) Jewish tradition, in accord with Daniel 10:21 and Revelation 8:2, taught that there were seven archangels including Michael, Gabriel, and Lucifer.
   b. Angels do service for God.
      (1) They worship God (Revelation 5:11, 12; 8:3, 4).
      (2) They assisted at the giving of the Law (Acts 7:38, 53; Galatians 3:19).

(3) They reveal God's will to man (Genesis 19:12, 13; Luke 1:13).
(4) They exercise God's judgments (II Kings 19:35; Matthew 13:41, 42; Acts 12:23).
(5) They will accompany Christ at His return (Matthew 25:31; II Thessalonians 1:7).

c. Angels do service on behalf of man.
(1) They guard individuals (Psalm 34:7; Matthew 18:10; Hebrews 1:14) and nations (Daniel 10:13, 20; 11:1).
(2) They assist mankind (Genesis 21:17; Daniel 6:22; Acts 12:5-11).
(3) They receive believers at death (Luke 16:22).
(4) They work in nature (Matthew 28:2).

3. There are fallen angels of Satan (demons).
a. They were created sinless but later fell into sin (II Peter 2:4; Revelation 12:3-4, 7).
b. They inflict men with evil (Matthew 17:15, 18; Luke 13:11, 16; II Corinthians 12:7).
c. They will one day be judged (Matthew 25:41; Jude 6).

II. Satan

A. Characteristics

1. Satan possesses several characteristic titles.
a. He is called the Adversary (I Peter 5:8).
b. He is called the Accuser of the Brethren (Revelation 12:10).
c. He is called the Angel of Light: the deceiver of the unsuspecting and untaught (II Corinthians 11:14).
d. He is called the Enemy (Matthew 13:39).
e. He is called the Evil (One) (John 17:15).
f. He is called the Father of Lies (John 8:44).
g. He is called the Murderer (John 8:44).
h. He is called the Tempter (Matthew 4:3; I Thessalonians 3:5).
i. He is called the Wicked One (Matthew 13:19, 38).

2. Satan possesses limitations.
a. God limits him (Job 1:12; 2:6).
b. Believers may resist him (Ephesians 6:11; James 4:7; Revelation 12:11).

B. Work

1. Satan is the head of a host of evil spirits (Matthew 9:34; 12:26; Ephesians 2:2).
2. Satan can control unbelievers (Luke 22:3; John 13:27).
3. Satan turns men from the gospel (II Corinthians 4:4).
4. Satan tempts believers (I Chronicles 21:1; Zechariah 3:1; Luke 22:31).
5. Satan corrupts the church (Matthew 13:25, 36-43).

The Doctrine of the End Times (Eschatology)

I. The Rapture (instantaneous) (I Corinthians 15:52)

A. Time of the Rapture

1. It may occur at any time (Matthew 24:42, 44; 25:1-13).
2. It will be before the revelation of the Antichrist (Luke 21:36; II Thessalonians 2:6-8; Revelation 3:10).

B. Purpose of the Rapture

1. The resurrection of the dead saints will take place (I Thessalonians 4:16).
2. The translation of the living saints will take place (I Thessalonians 4:17).

II. The Tribulation (seven years) (Daniel 9:27)

A. Purpose of the Tribulation

1. The judgment of an ungodly world will take place (Isaiah 63:6; Revelation 6:15-17).
2. The conversion of a repentant Israel will take place (Jeremiah 30:7-9; Ezekiel 39:22).

B. Events in heaven

1. The judgment of rewards for Christians will take place (I Corinthians 3:12-15; II Corinthians 5:10).
2. The marriage of the Lamb will take place (Revelation 19:7-9).

C. Events on earth (These will not necessarily come in the following order; many will occur simultaneously.)

1. The Roman Empire will be revived into a ten-nation confederacy (Daniel 2:31-43; 7:7; Revelation 13:1; 17:3, 12, 13).
2. The Antichrist will rise (Daniel 7:8, 19-25; Revelation 13:1-8).
3. The Antichrist and Israel will establish a peace treaty which will lead to the rebuilding of the temple and renewal of the levitical priesthood and sacrificial system (Daniel 9:27).
4. The 144,000 Jewish evangelists and the Two Witnesses will minister publicly (Revelation 7:4-8; 11:3-12).
5. The northern coalition will attack Israel (Ezekiel 38, 39).
6. The Antichrist will be wounded, will recover, and will be worshiped (Matthew 24:15; II Thessalonians 2:4; Revelation 13:1-10).

7. The False Prophet will exalt the Antichrist (Revelation 13:11-15).
8. The world government, economic system, and religion will develop (Daniel 7:23; Revelation 13:4-18).
9. The Antichrist will break the peace treaty with Israel (Daniel 9:27).
10. Saints will be persecuted (Jeremiah 30:7; Daniel 7:25; 12:1; Zechariah 13:8, 9; Matthew 24:21; Revelation 7:9-17; 13:7-9, 15).
11. The apostate world church will be destroyed (Revelation 17:1-6).
12. The earth will experience cataclysmic judgments (Revelation 6-18).
13. The world's commercial system will collapse (Revelation 18:1-24).
14. Warfare in the Middle East will culminate in the Battle of Armageddon (Daniel 11:40-45; Revelation 16:12-16; 19:19).
15. Christ will appear gloriously (Daniel 2:44; 7:9-13; Matthew 24:27-31; Revelation 19:11-16).

D. Determination of destiny
1. There will be the judgment of the wicked (Ezekiel 20:33-38; Matthew 25:31-46; Jude 14, 15; Revelation 19:11-21; 20:1-3).
2. There will be the casting of the Antichrist and the False Prophet into the lake of fire (Revelation 19:20–20:10).
3. There will be the binding of Satan in the bottomless pit (Revelation 20:1-3).
4. There will be the resurrection of the tribulation saints (Revelation 20:4).

III. The Millennium (one thousand years) (Revelation 20:3-6)

A. Governmental changes
1. The saints will rule with Christ (Revelation 3:21; 5:10; 20:6).
2. There will be worldwide peace among men and animals (Isaiah 2:4; 11:6-8; 65:25).
3. Jerusalem will be the capital of the earth (Isaiah 60:1-22; Zechariah 14:9-15).
4. Palestine will be redivided among Israel (Ezekiel 47:13–48:29).

B. Spiritual changes
1. Satan will be bound (Revelation 20:3).
2. Worship will center at the millennial temple in Jerusalem (Ezekiel 40-48; Zechariah 14:16-21).
3. Earth will be filled with the knowledge of the Lord, although not all will be saved (Isaiah 2:3; 65:20; Revelation 20:8, 9).

C. Physical changes
1. Man will be freed from the curse and consequences of sin, including physical infirmities (Isaiah 32:3, 4; 35:5, 6).
2. The earth will be freed from the curse of sin (Isaiah 55:12, 13; 60:13).

IV. Ages to Come

A. Satan's final rebellion and final judgment
1. He will be freed from the bottomless pit (Revelation 20:7).
2. He will lead unsaved men against God (Revelation 20:8, 9).
3. He will be defeated (Revelation 20:9*b*).
4. He will be cast into the lake of fire (Revelation 20:11-13).

B. Great White Throne Judgment
1. There will be the resurrection of the unsaved (Revelation 20:12, 13).
2. There will be the judgment of sin and punishment in the lake of fire (Revelation 20:13-15).

C. New heaven and a new earth (Isaiah 65:17; Revelation 21, 22).

Teaching Catechism

Catechism means "learning God's truth by question and answer." The catechism questions and answers have been grouped by topic in this third edition of the Bible Truths curriculum. Each of the ten groups contains from five to thirty-two questions and answers. Teachers may choose to study questions and answers from one group, a few groups, or all ten groups. The following catechism section may be duplicated and sent home to parents as the class studies a particular group.

When introducing a catechism question, explain the meaning of unfamiliar words, relate the question to the Bible lessons when appropriate, and apply the truth to the students' lives. The verse references offer scriptural proofs for the answers and are to help you explain and present the catechism. To practice the catechism, repeat each question and answer several times before expecting the students to begin saying it with you. (*Note:* Answers do not have to be word perfect.) After the students become familiar with the questions and answers, a variety of games may be played for review. Learning the catechism should not be a dreaded activity. It is an optional part of this curriculum.

If an evaluation is desired, the following ideas are more valid than a fill-in-the-blank test in determining whether a student can give an answer for the Bible truths he believes.

- **Role-playing**—Example: One student asks another student why he goes to church. The student should be able to give a reply that includes that God commands Christians to fellowship and worship together. *For each situation, the student's response may vary but should reflect his understanding of the answer.*

- **Matching**—Prepare an activity sheet that includes several everyday situations that could occur in the lives of the students. Provide a list of possible answers from the catechism for the students to match the catechism answer to its appropriate situation. If desired, allow the students to use their personal copies of the catechism in their worktexts to find an appropriate answer instead of making a match.

- **Complete the story**—Share with the students a contrived story or a story based on true events. Explain to the students that they are to complete the story by applying Bible principles to the situation.

A good catechism will provide students with a strong foundation in knowing what they believe and why they believe it.

Do I Know About God?

1. **Who is God?**
   God is a spirit and does not have a body like man (John 4:24).

2. **What is God like?**
   God is infinite, eternal, and unchangeable (Psalms 139:7-10; 90:2; Malachi 3:6).

3. **Where is God?**
   God is everywhere (Psalm 139:7-12; Proverbs 15:3).

4. **Can you see God?**
   No, I cannot see God, but He always sees me (Jeremiah 23:23-24; John 1:18).

5. **Does God know all things?**
   Yes, nothing can be hidden from God (Job 34:21).

6. **Can God do all things?**
   Yes, God can do all His holy will (Matthew 19:26).

7. **Does God ever do evil?**
   No, God is always good (Exodus 34:6; Psalm 86:5).

8. **Are there more gods than one?**
   No, there is only one God (Isaiah 45:6; I Timothy 2:5).

9. **In how many persons does this one God exist?**
   God exists in three persons (Matthew 3:16-17; II Corinthians 13:14).

10. **Who are the three persons of God?**
    The three persons of God are the Father, the Son, and the Holy Spirit (Matthew 28:19).

11. **Who made God?**
    Nobody made God (Psalm 90:2).

12. **Has God ever had a beginning?**
    No, God has always been (Psalm 90:2; Revelation 4:8).

13. **Will God ever die?**
    No, God lives forever (Psalm 90:2).

14. **What is God's attitude toward us?**
    God loves us unconditionally (John 3:16; Romans 5:8).

Do I Know About God's Creation?

1. **Who made you?**
   God made me (Genesis 1:27; Job 33:4).

2. **What else did God make?**
   God made all things (Genesis 1:1-31; John 1:3).

3. **Why did God make you and all things?**
   God made me and all things for His own glory (Romans 11:36; I Corinthians 6:20).

4. **How can you glorify God?**
   I can glorify God by loving Him and doing what He commands (Micah 6:8; I John 5:3).

5. **Why ought you to glorify God?**
   I ought to glorify God because He made me and takes care of me (Psalm 146:5-10).

6. **Where do you learn how to love and obey God?**
   I learn how to love and obey God in the Bible alone (Deuteronomy 30:11-16; Joshua 1:8).

7. **Who wrote the Bible?**
   Holy men who were taught by the Holy Spirit wrote the Bible (II Peter 1:21).

8. **Who were our first parents?**
   Adam and Eve were our first parents (Genesis 2:7, 18-22).

9. **Of what were our first parents made?**
   God made the body of Adam out of the dust of the ground and formed Eve from the body of Adam (Genesis 2:7, 21-22).

10. **Whom did God make Adam to be like?**
    God made Adam after His own image (Genesis 1:27; 9:6).

11. **What did God give Adam and Eve besides bodies?**
    God gave them souls that could never die (Genesis 2:7).

12. **Do you have a soul as well as a body?**
    Yes, I have a soul that can never die (Ecclesiastes 12:7; I Thessalonians 5:23).

13. **How do you know that you have a soul?**
    God tells me so in Genesis 2:7, "And the Lord God formed man of the dust of the ground, and breathed into his nostrils the breath of life; and man became a living soul" (Genesis 2:7).

14. **In what condition did God make Adam and Eve?**
    God made them holy and happy (Genesis 1:27-31).

Do I Know What God Says About Sin?

1. **What is a covenant?**
   A covenant is an agreement between two or more persons (Genesis 9:11-17).

2. **What was Adam's part in the covenant in order to stay in the Garden of Eden?**
   Adam was required to obey God perfectly (Genesis 2:15-17).

3. **Did Adam obey God?**
   No, Adam chose to disobey God (Genesis 3:6).

4. **Did Adam's sin affect himself alone?**
   No, Adam's sin made all men lose communion with God and become sinful in nature and subject to God's wrath (Romans 5:14; 6:23; Ephesians 2:3).

5. **How did God punish Adam's disobedience?**
   Adam's punishment was death and separation from God (Genesis 3:17-24).

6. **What is sin?**
   Sin is the transgression of the law of God (I John 3:4).

7. **What is meant by transgression?**
   Transgression is failing to do what God commands or doing what God forbids (Psalm 25:6-7; Matthew 15:3-6).

8. **What was the sin of our first parents?**
   Adam and Eve disobeyed God and ate the fruit that God told them not to eat (Genesis 2:17; 3:6).

9. **Who tempted Adam and Eve to sin?**
   Satan tempted Eve, and she gave the fruit to Adam (Genesis 3:1-6).

10. **What happened to our first parents when they had sinned?**
    Instead of being holy and happy, they became sinful and miserable (Genesis 3:8-24).

11. **What effect did Adam's sin have on all mankind?**
    Because of Adam's sin, every man is born with a sinful nature that wants to do evil and has no fellowship with God (Romans 5:12).

12. **What is that sinful nature we inherit from Adam called?**
    Our corrupt nature is called original sin (Psalm 51:5; Romans 5:12).

13. **What does every sin deserve?**
    Every sin deserves the wrath and curse of God (Psalm 89:30-32; Galatians 3:10).

Do I Know About Angels and Satan?

1. **Did God make anyone before Adam and Eve?**
   Yes, God made angels (Job 38:7; Genesis 3:24).

2. **What do angels do?**
   They serve God (Hebrews 1:14).

3. **Are all angels good?**
   No, some angels are holy, while others are evil (Matthew 25:31; Revelation 12:9).

4. **Who is Satan?**
   Satan is an evil spirit who is the enemy of God and all Christians (John 8:44; I Peter 5:8).

5. **Was Satan ever good?**
   Yes, Satan was once one of God's greatest angels (Isaiah 14:12-15).

6. **What was Satan's name when he was one of God's angels?**
   Satan's name was Lucifer (Isaiah 14:12).

7. **Why is Lucifer not one of God's angels today?**
   Lucifer became jealous of God and wanted to be as great as He, so God cast him out of heaven (Isaiah 14:12-15; Revelation 12:7-9).

8. **What is Lucifer now called?**
   Lucifer is now called Satan or the Devil (Luke 10:18; I John 3:8).

9. **Who is stronger, God or Satan?**
   God is stronger (I John 3:8; 4:4).

10. **Does Satan want God's will to be done?**
    No, Satan always wants people to do the opposite of what God wants them to do (I Chronicles 21:1; Ephesians 6:11-12, 16).

Do I Know About the Work of Christ?

1. **Who can save us?**
   The only Savior of men is the Lord Jesus Christ (John 14:6; Acts 4:12).

2. **What does God require of man before he can go to heaven?**
   No one can enter heaven unless his heart is changed (John 3:3, 16; Acts 4:12).

3. **What is this change of heart called?**
   This change of heart is called regeneration (Ezekiel 36:26-27; Titus 3:5-6).

4. **Who can change a sinner's heart?**
   The Holy Spirit can change a sinner's heart (Titus 3:5).

5. **How is a heart changed?**
   A heart is changed by the Holy Spirit because of the grace of God shown in the work of Christ (Titus 3:4-7).

6. **What is grace?**
   Grace is God's kindness to us when we deserve punishment (Deuteronomy 7:6-9; Ephesians 2:8-9).

7. **What is the work of Christ?**
   The work of Christ is to keep perfectly the law of God and to suffer the penalty for our sins (II Corinthians 5:21; Hebrews 9:11-14).

8. **Can anyone be saved by his own works?**
   No one can be saved by his own works (Ephesians 2:8-9; Titus 3:4-7).

9. **Did Christ ever sin?**
   No, Christ was holy, sinless, and undefiled (II Corinthians 5:21; Hebrews 7:26).

10. **How could the Son of God suffer?**
    Christ, the Son of God, became man that He might obey and suffer in our nature (Philippians 2:7-8; Hebrews 2:9).

11. **What is meant by atonement?**
    The atonement is Christ's satisfying divine justice by His sufferings and death in the place of sinners (Romans 5:8-11).

12. **What do we gain from the work of Christ?**
    God regenerates, justifies, and sanctifies those who believe in Christ (I Corinthians 6:11; Titus 3:5-7).

13. **What is justification?**
    Justification is God's forgiving me and treating me just as if I had never sinned (Romans 3:24-25, II Corinthians 5:19, 21).

14. **How am I justified?**
    I am justified by faith in the work of Christ and on the grounds of His righteousness (Romans 3:25-28).

15. **What is sanctification?**
    Sanctification is God's making me holy in heart and behavior (I Corinthians 6:19-20).

16. **What are the two parts of sanctification?**
    The two parts of sanctification are dying to sin and living to righteousness (Romans 8:13; Galatians 2:20).

17. For whom did Christ obey and suffer?
Christ obeyed and suffered for sinners (Romans 5:8).

18. What kind of death did Christ die?
Christ died the painful and shameful death of being nailed to a cross (Luke 23:33-38; Philippians 2:8).

19. Who will be saved?
Whoever repents and believes on the Lord Jesus Christ will be saved (Isaiah 55:7; John 3:16).

20. What does it mean to repent?
To repent is to be sorry for sin and to hate and forsake it because it is displeasing to God (II Chronicles 7:14; II Corinthians 7:9).

21. What is saving faith in Christ?
Saving faith is believing that Christ died for my sins, that He was buried, and that He rose again according to the Scriptures (I Corinthians 15:1-4).

22. Can you repent and believe in Christ by your own power?
No, I cannot repent and believe in Christ without the help of God's Holy Spirit (John 3:5-6; Titus 3:5).

23. Does Christ care for little children?
Yes, for He says in Mark 10:14, "Suffer the little children to come unto me, and forbid them not: for of such is the kingdom of God" (Mark 10:14).

24. How long has it been since Christ died?
Christ died nearly 2,000 years ago.

25. How were people saved before the coming of Christ?
People were saved by believing in a Savior to come (Hebrews 11:13).

26. How did people show their faith before the coming of Christ?
People showed their faith by offering sacrifices on God's altar (Hebrews 11:4).

27. What did the sacrifices represent?
The sacrifices represented Christ, the Lamb of God, who was to die for sinners (John 1:29, 36; Hebrews 9:11-14).

28. How many offices does Christ have?
Christ has three offices (Acts 3:22; Hebrews 5:5-6; Revelation 19:16).

29. What are Christ's offices?
Christ's offices are prophet, priest, and king (Acts 3:22; Hebrews 5:5-6; Revelation 19:16).

30. How is Christ a prophet?
Christ teaches us the will of God (Luke 4:18; John 15:15).

31. How is Christ a priest?
Christ died for our sins and pleads with God for us (Romans 3:26; Hebrews 7:25-27).

32. How is Christ a king?
Christ rules over us, defends us, and will establish His kingdom on earth (Isaiah 33:22; I Corinthians 15:25).

Do I Know About the Resurrection?

1. **On which day of the week do Christians worship?**
   Christians worship on the first day of the week, called the Lord's Day (Acts 20:7; I Corinthians 16:1-2).

2. **Why is it called the Lord's Day?**
   On that day Christ rose from the dead (Matthew 28:1-6; Mark 16:1-6).

3. **How should the Lord's Day be spent?**
   The Lord's Day should be spent in prayer and praise, in hearing and reading God's Word, and in doing good to our fellow man (Luke 13:10-13; Acts 15:21; 16:13).

4. **Did Christ remain in the tomb after His crucifixion?**
   No, Christ rose bodily from the tomb on the third day after His death (Matthew 16:21; 28:1-6; I Corinthians 15:3-4).

5. **Where is Christ now?**
   Christ is in heaven, interceding for us (Acts 1:9; Ephesians 1:19-21; Hebrews 4:14-16; 7:25).

Do I Know About God's Ordinances?

1. **What is an ordinance?**
   An ordinance is a way of remembering Christ's death and resurrection (Romans 6:3-10; I Corinthians 11:23-26).

2. **How many ordinances are there in the Bible?**
   There are two ordinances in the Bible (Matthew 28:19; I Corinthians 11:23-26).

3. **What are the two ordinances?**
   The two ordinances are baptism and the Lord's Supper (Matthew 26:26-28; 28:19).

4. **Who appointed these ordinances?**
   The Lord Jesus Christ appointed them (Matthew 26:26-28; 28:18-19).

5. **Why did Christ appoint these ordinances?**
   Christ appointed these ordinances to distinguish His disciples from the world and to comfort and strengthen them (Acts 2:38-41; Romans 6:4).

6. **What sign is used in baptism?**
   The sign used in baptism is water (Matthew 3:6, 11, 14-17).

7. **What does baptism mean?**
   Baptism is an outward sign of our union with Christ and our decision to follow Him (Romans 6:3-11; Galatians 3:27).

8. **In whose name are we baptized?**
   We are baptized in the name of the Father and of the Son and of the Holy Spirit (Matthew 28:19).

9. **What is the Lord's Supper?**
   The Lord's Supper is a remembrance of Christ's death for us on the cross and a looking forward to His return (Matthew 26:26-28; I Corinthians 11:23-26).

10. **Who is to partake of the Lord's Supper?**
    All those who have trusted Christ as their Savior and are living for Him may partake of the Lord's Supper (I Corinthians 11:28, 29).

11. **What are the elements used in the Lord's Supper?**
    The elements used in the Lord's Supper are bread and the fruit of the vine (Matthew 26:26-28; Mark 14:22-25).

12. **What do the bread and fruit of the vine symbolize?**
    The bread symbolizes Christ's body, which was crucified for us, and the cup symbolizes His blood, which was shed for us (Matthew 26:26-28; Mark 14:22-25; Luke 22:17-20).

Do I Know About God's Commandments?

1. **How many commandments did God give on Mount Sinai?**
   God gave ten commandments (Exodus 20:1-17).

2. **What are the Ten Commandments sometimes called?**
   They are called the Decalogue.

3. **What does *Decalogue* mean?**
   The word *Decalogue* means "ten words."

4. **What do the first four commandments teach?**
   The first four commandments teach our duty to God (Exodus 20:1-11; Matthew 22:37-38).

5. **Is God pleased with those who love and obey Him?**
   Yes, for He says in Proverbs 8:17, "I love them that love me; and those that seek me early shall find me" (Proverbs 8:17).

6. **Is God displeased with those who do not love and obey Him?**
   Yes, for He says in Psalm 7:11, "God judgeth the righteous, and God is angry with the wicked every day" (Psalm 7:11).

7. **What is the first commandment?**
   The first commandment is "Thou shalt have no other gods before me" (Exodus 20:3).

8. **What does the first commandment teach us?**
   The first commandment teaches us to worship God alone (Matthew 4:10).

9. **What is the second commandment?**
   The second commandment is "Thou shalt not make unto thee any graven image, or any likeness of any thing that is in heaven above, or that is in the earth beneath, or that is in the water under earth" (Exodus 20:4-6).

10. **What does the second commandment teach us?**
    The second commandment teaches us to worship God in a proper manner and to avoid idolatry (Exodus 20:23; Deuteronomy 6:13-18).

11. **What is the third commandment?**
    The third commandment is "Thou shalt not take the name of the Lord thy God in vain; for the Lord will not hold him guiltless that taketh his name in vain" (Exodus 20:7).

12. **What does the third commandment teach us?**
    The third commandment teaches us to reverence God's name, Word, and works (Psalms 29:2; 107:21-22; 138:2).

13. **What is the fourth commandment?**
    The fourth commandment is "Remember the sabbath day, to keep it holy" (Exodus 20:8-11).

14. **What does the fourth commandment teach us?**
    The fourth commandment teaches us that one day of the week is God's special day (Leviticus 19:30; Deuteronomy 5:12).

15. **What do the last six commandments teach?**
    The last six commandments teach our duty to our fellow man (Exodus 20:12-17; Matthew 22:39).

16. What is the fifth commandment?

The fifth commandment is "Honour thy father and thy mother: that thy days may be long upon the land which the Lord thy God giveth thee" (Exodus 20:12).

17. What does the fifth commandment teach us?

The fifth commandment teaches us that God blesses those that love and obey their parents (Romans 13:1; Ephesians 6:1-3).

18. What is the sixth commandment?

The sixth commandment is "Thou shalt not kill" (Exodus 20:13).

19. What does the sixth commandment teach us?

The sixth commandment teaches us to avoid anger and injury to others (Genesis 9:6; I John 3:15).

20. What is the seventh commandment?

The seventh commandment is "Thou shalt not commit adultery" (Exodus 20:14).

21. What does the seventh commandment teach us?

The seventh commandment teaches us to be pure in heart, language, and conduct (I Corinthians 7:2; Ephesians 4:29; 5:3-4).

22. What is the eighth commandment?

The eighth commandment is "Thou shalt not steal" (Exodus 20:15).

23. What does the eighth commandment teach us?

The eighth commandment teaches us to respect the property of others and to be honest and industrious (Romans 12:11, 17; Ephesians 4:28; II Thessalonians 3:10-12).

24. What is the ninth commandment?

The ninth commandment is "Thou shalt not bear false witness against thy neighbour" (Exodus 20:16).

25. What does the ninth commandment teach us?

The ninth commandment teaches us to tell the truth (Proverbs 14:5; Zechariah 8:16; I Peter 3:16).

26. What is the tenth commandment?

The tenth commandment is "Thou shalt not covet thy neighbour's house, thou shalt not covet thy neighbour's wife, nor his manservant, nor his maidservant, nor his ox, nor his ass, nor any thing that is thy neighbour's" (Exodus 20:17).

27. What does the tenth commandment teach us?

The tenth commandment teaches us to be content with what we have (Galatians 5:26; Philippians 4:11).

28. Of what use are the Ten Commandments to us?

They teach us how God wants us to live and show us our need of a Savior (Joshua 1:7-8; Galatians 5:26; Philippians 4:11).

29. What commandments does God command us to obey first of all?

God commands us to obey the two great commandments (Matthew 22:37-40).

30. What is the first great commandment?

The first great commandment says in Matthew 22:37, "Thou shalt love the Lord thy God with all thy heart, and with all thy soul, and with all thy mind" (Matthew 22:37).

31. What is the second great commandment?

The second great commandment says in Matthew 22:39, “Thou shalt love thy neighbour as thyself” (Matthew 22:39).

32. Who is your neighbor?

All my fellow men are my neighbors (Luke 10:25-37; Galatians 6:10).

Do I Know About Prayer?

1. **What is prayer?**
   Prayer is talking to God (Psalm 10:17; Philippians 4:6).

2. **In whose name should we pray?**
   We should pray only in the name of Christ, our intercessor (John 16:23).

3. **What guide has Christ given us to teach us how to pray?**
   Christ has given us the Lord's Prayer (Matthew 6:9-13).

4. **How should we pray?**
   We should pray after this manner: "Our Father which art in heaven, Hallowed be thy name. Thy kingdom come. Thy will be done in earth, as it is in heaven. Give us this day our daily bread. And forgive us our debts, as we forgive our debtors. And lead us not into temptation, but deliver us from evil: For thine is the kingdom, and the power, and the glory, for ever. Amen" (Matthew 6:9-13).

5. **How many petitions are there in the Lord's Prayer?**
   There are six petitions in the Lord's Prayer (Matthew 6:9-13).

6. **What is the first petition?**
   The first petition is "Hallowed be thy name" (Matthew 6:9).

7. **What do we pray for in the first petition?**
   We tell God He is holy and we want to honor Him (Psalm 145:1-13; Romans 11:36).

8. **What is the second petition?**
   The second petition is "Thy kingdom come" (Matthew 6:10).

9. **What do we pray for in the second petition?**
   We pray that God's kingdom may be established on earth (Psalm 67:1-3; Romans 10:1).

10. **What is the third petition?**
    The third petition is "Thy will be done in earth, as it is in heaven" (Matthew 6:10).

11. **What do we pray for in the third petition?**
    We pray that the will of God be done in the life of every one on earth (Psalm 103:22; Romans 12:2).

12. **What is the fourth petition?**
    The fourth petition is "Give us this day our daily bread" (Matthew 6:11).

13. **What do we pray for in the fourth petition?**
    We pray that God would give us all things needful (Proverbs 30:8; Philippians 4:19).

14. **What is the fifth petition?**
    The fifth petition is "And forgive us our debts, as we forgive our debtors" (Matthew 6:12).

15. **What do we pray for in the fifth petition?**
    We pray that God would pardon our sins for Christ's sake and enable us to forgive those who have injured us (Psalm 51:1; Matthew 6:14-15).

16. What is the sixth petition?

The sixth petition is "And lead us not into temptation, but deliver us from evil" (Matthew 6:13).

17. What do we pray for in the sixth petition?

We pray that God will keep us from being tempted and will keep us from sin when we are tempted (Psalm 51:10, 12; Matthew 26:41).

Do I Know What God Says About the Future?

1. **Will Christ come again?**
   Yes, Christ has promised to return to take us to be with Him (John 14:1-3; Acts 1:11).

2. **When will Christ return?**
   No one knows when Christ will return (Matthew 24:42, 50; 25:13).

3. **What are the two parts of the Second Coming?**
   The Second Coming consists of the Rapture and the glorious appearing (I Corinthians 15:51-52; Revelation 19:11-16).

4. **What will happen at the Rapture?**
   At the Rapture Christ will bring to life all Christians who have died, change those who are living, and give them an incorruptible body (I Corinthians 15:51-52; I Thessalonians 4:15-17).

5. **What will happen at the glorious appearing?**
   Christ will return to earth, remove all the wicked, and establish His kingdom (II Thessalonians 1:7-10; Revelation 19:11-16).

6. **What becomes of man at death?**
   The body returns to dust, and the soul goes either to heaven or hell (Genesis 3:19; Romans 6:23).

7. **What will become of the wicked in the day of judgment?**
   The wicked will be cast into the lake of fire (Psalm 9:17; Revelation 20:11-15).

8. **What is hell?**
   Hell is a place of dreadful and endless torment (Matthew 25:41; Mark 9:43; Luke 16:19-26; Revelation 20:10, 13-15).

9. **What will become of the righteous?**
   The righteous will be taken to heaven (Matthew 5:11-12; 25:46; John 10:28; 14:1-3; Colossians 3:4).

10. **What is heaven?**
    Heaven is a glorious and happy place where the saved will be forever with the Lord.

Attributes of God

Overview

Preparing the Teacher

Your students might complete this unit and simply be able to name and define some attributes of God, or they might glimpse the wonder of one who is great beyond comprehending—perfect in all His ways, yet tenderly inclined toward sinful man. The difference is in the inclination of *your* heart as you teach these lessons. Begin your preparation by reading **Psalm 139:1-18.** Meditate on the evidences in your life of God's complete knowledge and foreknowledge of you, His presence with you everywhere, and His power to save and keep you. Examine your heart and seek God's direction, using the prayer in **Psalm 139:23-24.**

Preparing the Lessons

Part 1 Lesson 1 Materials—two small pieces of magnetic tape for each student; candle and match (optional)

Part 1 Going Beyond Materials—straw; a shoebox for each student; a container for mixing or a wading pool; mud; some extra water

Part 2 Lesson 3 Materials—encyclopedia pictures of the seven wonders of the ancient world (optional)

Part 2 Going Beyond Materials—a variety of old magazines

Part 3 Lesson 1 Materials—a variety of gospel tracts

Part 3 Lesson 3—three metal brads

Part 3 Going Beyond Materials—three metal brads for each student (optional)

Part 4 Lesson 2 Materials—a long piece of red ribbon or string (optional)

Part 4 Going Beyond Materials—a copy of *Sinners in the Hands of an Angry God* by Jonathan Edwards

UNIT 1 ATTRIBUTES OF GOD

Hymn: "I Sing the Mighty Power of God"

Part	Lesson number	Lesson pages	Worktext pages	Supplement pages	Bible Account	Application
PART 1: GOD IS OMNISCIENT, OMNIPOTENT, OMNIPRESENT	1	5	1-4		God Calls Moses (Exodus 3:1-22)	
	2	8	5-6		God Prepares Moses (Exodus 4:1-17)	
	3	10	7-8		God Sends Moses (Exodus 5:1–12:36)	
	4	13	9-10			"More Than Words" (Part 1)
PART 2: GOD IS FAITHFUL, HOLY, UNCHANGING	1	16	11-12		Victory at the Red Sea (Exodus 14:1-31)	
	2	18	13-14		God Gives the Law (Exodus 19:1–31:18)	
	3	20	15			"More Than Words" (Part 2)
	4	23	16		Who Is on the Lord's Side? (Exodus 32:1-34)	
PART 3: GOD IS MERCIFUL, LOVING	1	25	17			"More Than Words" (Part 3)
	2	26	18		The Twelve Spies (Numbers 13:1–14:45)	
	3	29	19-20	S68	The Bronze Serpent (Numbers 21:4-9)	**Hymn History Story:** "I Sing the Mighty Power of God"
	4	30	21-22	S68	King Sihon and King Og (Numbers 21:21-35)	
PART 4: GOD IS SOVEREIGN	1	33	23-24		Balaam (Numbers 22:1–24:25)	
	2	35	25		Rahab and Two Spies (Joshua 2:1-24; 6:1-27)	
	3	37	26			**Hero of the Faith:** Jonathan Edwards **Picture the Point:** Borrowing
	4	38	27-28			"More Than Words" (Part 4)

Connections	Memory Verses and Principles	Bible Doctrines	Skills/Applications
TimeLine: Moses	Psalm 103:6 *The all-powerful God protects Christians.*	**The Doctrine of God** **Existence of God:** God has shown Himself in the Bible (John 5:39). **Attributes of God:** God is eternal (Ps. 90:2). God is everywhere (omnipresent) (I Kings 8:27). God is all-knowing (omniscient) (Job 42:2). God is all-powerful (omnipotent) (Jer. 32:27). God is unchanging (immutable) (Mal. 3:6). God is faithful (I Cor. 1:9). God is holy (Isa. 6:3). God is merciful (Ps. 86:15). God is love (John 3:16). **The Doctrine of Man** **Original State of Man:** God created man for His glory (Isa. 43:7). **The Doctrine of Salvation** **Elements of Salvation:** Man turns to God through repentance and faith (conversion) (Eph. 3:17).	**Foundational:** • Realize that God is faithful and never changes • Realize that God is merciful and loving • Realize that God is eternal, omniscient, omnipresent, and omnipotent • Realize that God is sovereign • Realize that God's mercy saves believers from everlasting punishment **Practical:** • Recall facts and details • Learn the books of Moses, History, Poetry, and Major Prophets • Identify cause and effect • Read a map • Read a time line • Identify the main idea • Identify supporting details • Write a letter • Use a glossary **Personal:** • Realize that God protects Christians • Develop a Bible reading habit • Apply Bible knowledge to everyday life
History	Psalm 103:7 *The God of the Israelites is also our God.*		
TimeLine: Joshua and the Spies	Psalm 103:8-9 *God is merciful.*		
TimeLine: Jonathan Edwards Writing	Psalm 103:10 *God's mercy keeps believers from everlasting punish-ment.*		

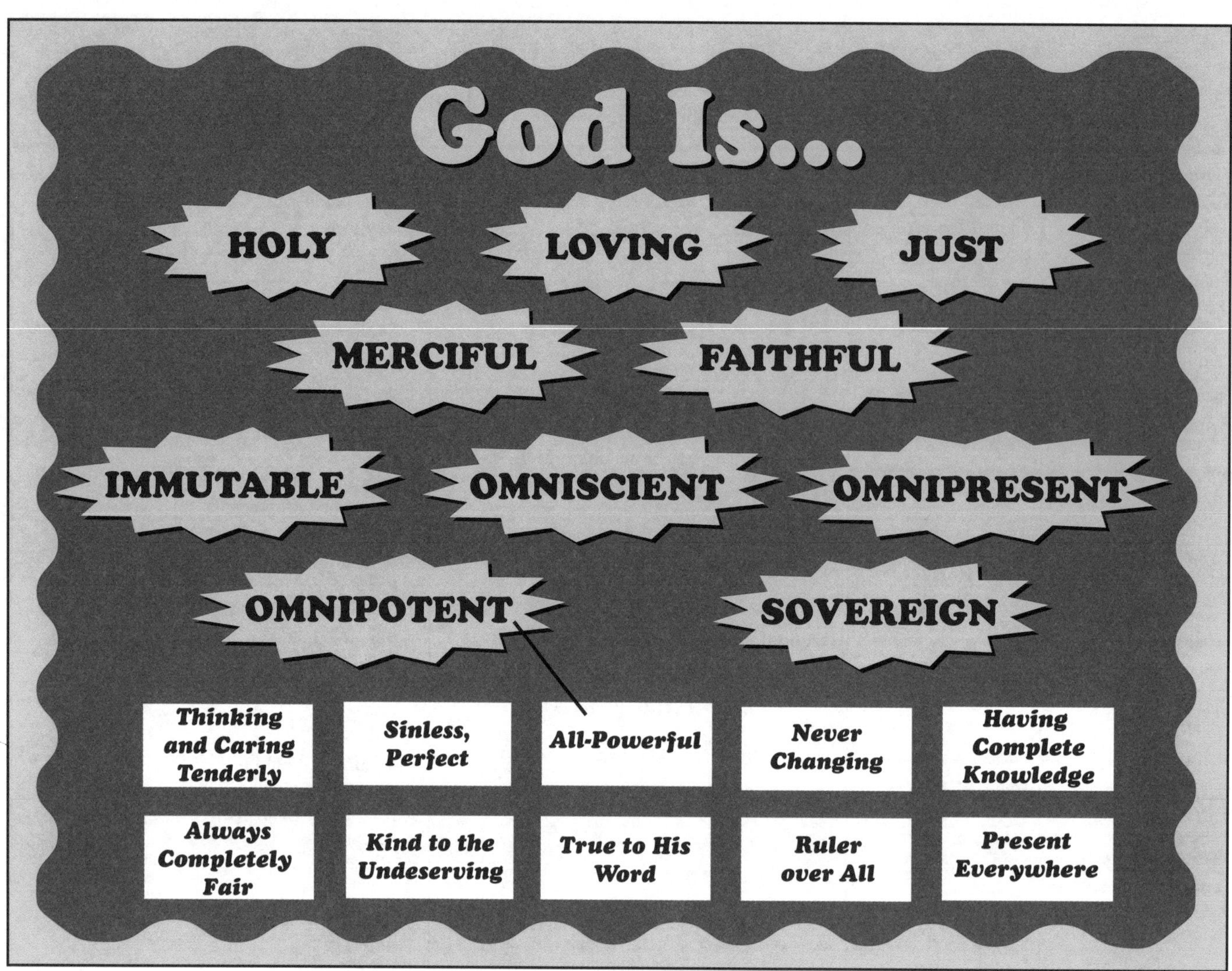

Preparing the Unit 1 Bulletin Board

Cover the bulletin board with deep blue paper and border it with gold. Title it "God Is . . . " in gold letters. Label ten gold starbursts with attributes of God. Write the meaning of each attribute on white paper. Attach one end of a long piece of yarn to each starburst. Tie the other end to a pushpin and let it hang loose. To match attributes and meanings, students will insert pushpins in the correct place. Tack an answer key facedown or place it in a card pocket in a lower corner of the bulletin board. Use the following answer key.

Attributes	Meanings
Holy	Sinless, perfect
Loving	Thinking and caring tenderly
Just	Always completely fair
Omnipotent	All-powerful
Faithful	True to His Word
Omnipresent	Present everywhere
Merciful	Kind to the undeserving
Omniscient	Having complete knowledge
Sovereign	Ruler over all
Immutable	Never changing

God Is Omniscient, Omnipotent, Omnipresent

Unit 1, Part 1

Preview

Doctrines

- God is eternal (Psalm 90:2)—Lesson 1
- God is all-knowing (omniscient) (Job 42:2)—Lesson 1
- God is everywhere (omnipresent) (I Kings 8:27)—Lessons 1-2
- God is all-powerful (omnipotent) (Jeremiah 32:27)—Lessons 1-3

Skills and Applications

- Learn Psalm 103:6
- Learn the books of Moses
- Recall facts and details
- Read a time line
- Match dialogue to the correct Bible character
- Realize that God is eternal, omniscient, omnipresent, and omnipotent
- Realize that God protects Christians
- Develop a Bible reading habit
- Apply Bible knowledge to everyday life

Lesson 1

Materials

- Chart 29, "Journey to the Promised Land"
- TimeLine and picture: *Moses*
- Song: "The Bible Reading Habit"
- Unit 1 Bookmark for each student
- Two small pieces of magnetic tape for each student
- A highlighter for each student (optional)
- Candle and match (optional)
  (Note: Bibles, worktexts, and unit hymns are standard lesson materials and will not be listed in the materials list for each lesson. Other songs will be listed when used.)

Material	Location
Charts Maps InfoScenes TimeLine TimeLine pictures Bible Book Cards	Visual Packet
Student Bookmarks Student TimeLine Student TimeLine pictures Student Bible Book Cards	Student Materials Packet
Music for teaching the grade 4 unit hymns and the books of the Bible songs is located in the supplement of this Teacher's Edition and the supplement of the Student Worktext. A recording of children singing these hymns and songs is available on the *God and His People* cassette tape or CD. Additional music located in the supplement of this Teacher's Edition provides the teacher with more hymns and songs in keeping with the theme of each unit.	

TimeLine

Explain *The History of Time* TimeLine. Point out that the time line covers history from the beginning of time (Creation) until Jesus returns. Read **Psalm 90:2** aloud and discuss God.

➤ **Who is God?** *(God is a spirit and does not have a body like man.)*

➤ **Who made God?** *(Nobody made God.)*

➤ **Has God ever had a beginning?** *(No. God has always been.)*

➤ **Will God ever die?** *(No. God lives forever.)*

Explain that God is *eternal.* He has always existed and always will exist. We cannot understand how this is possible, but we can worship God and respect Him for His great power.

Define attributes of God. Display the words *omnipotent, omnipresent,* and *omniscient.* Call on students to read the definitions of the words from their glossaries. Write the definitions *all-powerful, always present,* and *all-knowing* next to their corresponding words. Explain that *omni* means "all," *potent* means "strong," *present* is the opposite of absent, and *scient,* similar to the word *science,* means "to see or to know." All of these words describe God. They are *attributes* of God.

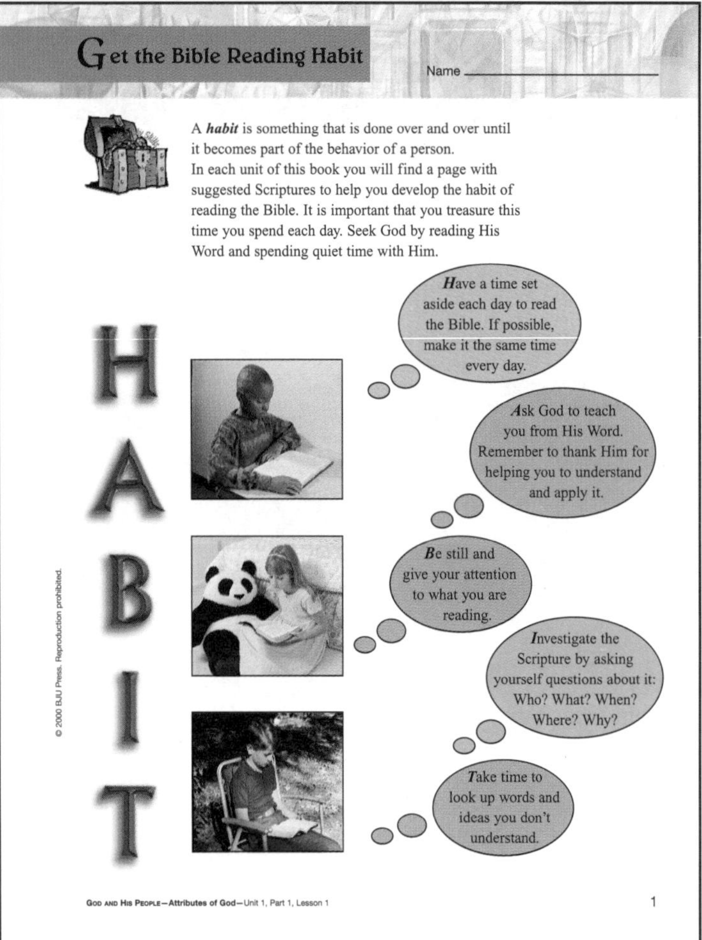

Get the Bible Reading Habit

Name ______________

A *habit* is something that is done over and over until it becomes part of the behavior of a person.
In each unit of this book you will find a page with suggested Scriptures to help you develop the habit of reading the Bible. It is important that you treasure this time you spend each day. Seek God by reading His Word and spending quiet time with Him.

Have a time set aside each day to read the Bible. If possible, make it the same time every day.

Ask God to teach you from His Word. Remember to thank Him for helping you to understand and apply it.

Be still and give your attention to what you are reading.

Investigate the Scripture by asking yourself questions about it: Who? What? When? Where? Why?

Take time to look up words and ideas you don't understand.

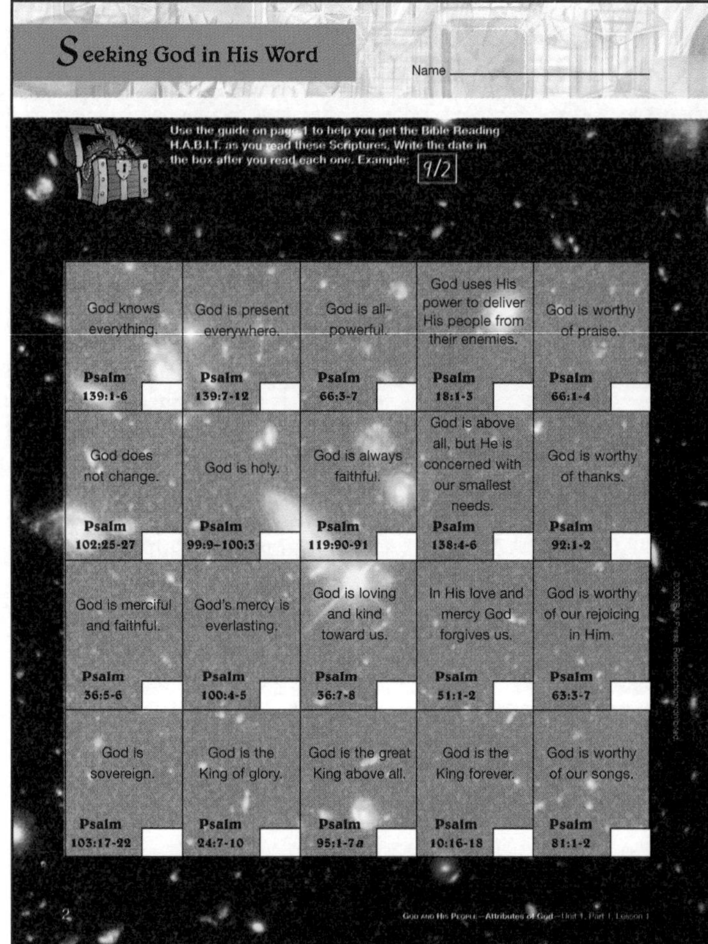

Seeking God in His Word

Name ______________

Use the guide on page 1 to help you get the Bible Reading H.A.B.I.T. as you read these Scriptures. Write the date in the box after you read each one. Example: 9/2

God knows everything. Psalm 139:1-6	God is present everywhere. Psalm 139:7-12	God is all-powerful. Psalm 66:3-7	God uses His power to deliver His people from their enemies. Psalm 18:1-3	God is worthy of praise. Psalm 66:1-4
God does not change. Psalm 102:25-27	God is holy. Psalm 99:9–100:3	God is always faithful. Psalm 119:90-91	God is above all, but He is concerned with our smallest needs. Psalm 138:4-6	God is worthy of thanks. Psalm 92:1-2
God is merciful and faithful. Psalm 36:5-6	God's mercy is everlasting. Psalm 100:4-5	God is loving and kind toward us. Psalm 36:7-8	In His love and mercy God forgives us. Psalm 51:1-2	God is worthy of our rejoicing in Him. Psalm 63:3-7
God is sovereign. Psalm 103:17-22	God is the King of glory. Psalm 24:7-10	God is the great King above all. Psalm 95:1-7a	God is the King forever. Psalm 10:16-18	God is worthy of our songs. Psalm 81:1-2

Worktext pages 1-2

Explain the importance of personal Bible reading.

- ➤ **What is a habit?**
- ➤ **Do you have any good habits?**
- ➤ **Do you have any bad habits?**

Direct attention to page 1 as you share the information given. Explain the four-week Bible reading activity on page 2. Encourage each student to complete the Bible reading. (*Note:* You may choose to have students do their reading in the morning before class begins, during class, or at a time of their own choosing.) Lead in singing "The Bible Reading Habit" song from Worktext page 271.

Background Information

Moses—*Threatened by the increasing Israelite population in the land, the new Egyptian ruler decreed that all Hebrew male children were to be killed at birth. The mother of Moses kept Moses until he could no longer be hidden. She then placed him in a waterproof basket in the river. Pharaoh's daughter found him and took him to be her own child. She named him Moses, which means "to draw from the water."*

Moses grew up in Pharaoh's palace. When Moses became a man, he left all the Egyptian splendor to identify himself with God and His people. Because he murdered an Egyptian, Moses fled to Midian. There he married a woman named Zipporah.

I AM—*When God told Moses to go in the name of "I AM," He meant to assure Moses that He was the covenant-keeping God. God always keeps His promises. God made a covenant with Abraham, Isaac, and Jacob. God said that He would make of them a great nation. They would be a blessing to the entire world. "I AM" is actually the name Jehovah.*

Introducing the Bible Account

Discuss the burning of an object. Share the background information about Moses. Light a candle and allow it to burn while you use the following questions to elicit the definition of the word *consumed* (optional).

- ➤ **What is happening to the candle?** *(It is burning, and the wax is melting.)*
- ➤ **What happens to a piece of paper or to a house that catches on fire?** *(They burn.)* Explain that these things are *consumed,* or destroyed, when they catch on fire.
- ➤ **If you saw something that was on fire but not consumed, what would you think?** *(Answers will vary.)*

Bible Account

Read the following Bible account, explaining that it is a retelling, or read Exodus 3:1-22. Display Chart 29, "Journey to the Promised Land," pointing out Egypt where Moses came from and Mount Horeb, also called Mount Sinai, where this Bible account takes place. (*Note:* To avoid confusion, you may wish to explain that the Bible refers to the Israelites as *Israel, God's chosen people, the children of Israel,* and *the Hebrews*, but they are all the same group of people.)

God Calls Moses

While Moses was living in Midian, he took care of his father-in-law's sheep. One day, he took the flock of sheep to an area of the desert near Mount Horeb [Mount Sinai]. Moses saw a bush that was burning but was not consumed. The angel of the Lord was in a flame of fire in the middle of the bush. "I will now turn aside," said Moses, "and see this great sight, why the bush is not burnt."

God called to Moses from out of the bush, "Moses, Moses."

"Here am I," said Moses. God told him not to come near the bush but to take his shoes off because he was standing on holy ground. The Lord said, "I am the God of thy father, the God of Abraham, the God of Isaac, and the God of Jacob. And Moses hid his face; for he was afraid to look upon God."

God said that He had seen His people the Israelites in slavery in Egypt. He had heard their cries and knew their sorrows. God wanted Moses to go to Pharaoh, the king of Egypt, and command that he let the Israelites go so that they could worship God in the wilderness.

"And Moses said unto God, Behold, when I come unto the children of Israel, and shall say unto them, The God of your fathers hath sent me unto you; and they shall say to me, What is his name? what shall I say unto them?"

God told Moses, "I AM THAT I AM. . . . Say unto the children of Israel, I AM hath sent me unto you." God in His omnipotence promised to be with Moses. All the power and authority of the covenant-keeping Jehovah (*I AM*) would be with him.

God gave Moses the words to say to the children of Israel. "The Lord God of your fathers, the God of Abraham, the God of Isaac, and the God of Jacob hath sent me unto you: this is my name for ever, and this is my memorial unto all generations." God told Moses to go to the elders and tell them that God would bring the Israelite slaves "out of the affliction of Egypt unto the land . . . flowing with milk and honey."

God told Moses what to do. Moses and the elders would go to Pharaoh and tell him to let them go on a three days' journey into the wilderness so that they could sacrifice to their Lord.

God, in His omniscience, knew that Pharaoh would not let them go. First, God would have to show His omnipotence by sending plagues to Pharaoh and the Egyptians. God said to Moses, "I will stretch out my hand, and smite Egypt with all my wonders . . . and after that he will let you go." Then not only would the Israelites be allowed to leave, but they would take with them jewels and clothes from the Egyptians. God promised that Moses would succeed if he obeyed.

- ➤ **What did Moses do when he saw the bush that was on fire but not consumed?** *(He went closer to see why.)*
- ➤ **Why did God tell Moses to take off his shoes?** *(because he was standing on holy ground)*
- ➤ **How do we know that God cared about the Israelite slaves in Egypt?** *(He heard their cries and was sending Moses to rescue them.)*
- ➤ **Does God hear our cries when we are in trouble?** *(yes)*
- ➤ **What did God know would have to happen before Pharaoh would let His people go?** *(God would have to show His power through the plagues.)*

TimeLine

Add *Moses* to the TimeLine. Choose a student to attach the picture of *Moses* on the large TimeLine (1525-1405 B.C.). Point out that Moses lived about one thousand years after the flood. Guide the students as they glue their picture of *Moses* onto their TimeLines.

Memory Verse—Psalm 103:6

Principle: The all-powerful God protects Christians. Locate **Psalm 103:6-10** and read it aloud as the students read silently. Explain that they will be learning this entire passage, but at this time they will learn only verse 6. Choose students to read verse 6 aloud. Explain that *oppressed* refers to those who are treated unfairly and severely by those in authority.

- ➤ **Who in today's Bible account was being oppressed?** *(the Israelites who were made slaves in Egypt)*

Remind the students that the Lord allows things in our lives to teach us to look to Him. We should always remember that He is a good God, full of mercy and grace. Allow students time to study the verse, then direct them to highlight the verse in their Bibles (optional).

Give each student a Unit 1 Bookmark. Point out the illustration of the burning bush, on the bookmark, reminding the students of God's power, presence, and knowledge. Demonstrate how to fold the bookmark on the dotted lines and how to place a small piece of magnetic tape on the

God Calls Moses
Exodus 3:1-22

Name ____________________

To spell the missing words, write the letter that comes *before* each letter.

1. God spoke to Moses from a C V S O J O H / b u r n i n g bush.
2. God told Moses that he was standing on I P M Z / h o l y ground.
3. God said that He had seen His people in T M B W F S Z / s l a v e r y.
4. Moses asked God to tell him His O B N F / n a m e.
5. God said that He should be called J / I B N / A M.
6. God promised to take His people out of F H Z Q U / E g y p t.
7. He promised them a land flowing with N J M L / m i l k and I P O F Z / h o n e y.
8. God knew that Q I B S B P I / P h a r a o h would not let His people go.
9. God would have to show His Q P X F S / p o w e r to the Egyptians.

Draw a line to match each attribute of God with the correct meaning. Use the glossary to help.

God is ***omnipotent***.	everywhere
God is ***omnipresent***.	all-knowing
God is ***omniscient***.	all-powerful

GOD AND HIS PEOPLE—Attributes of God—Unit 1, Part 1, Lesson 1 3

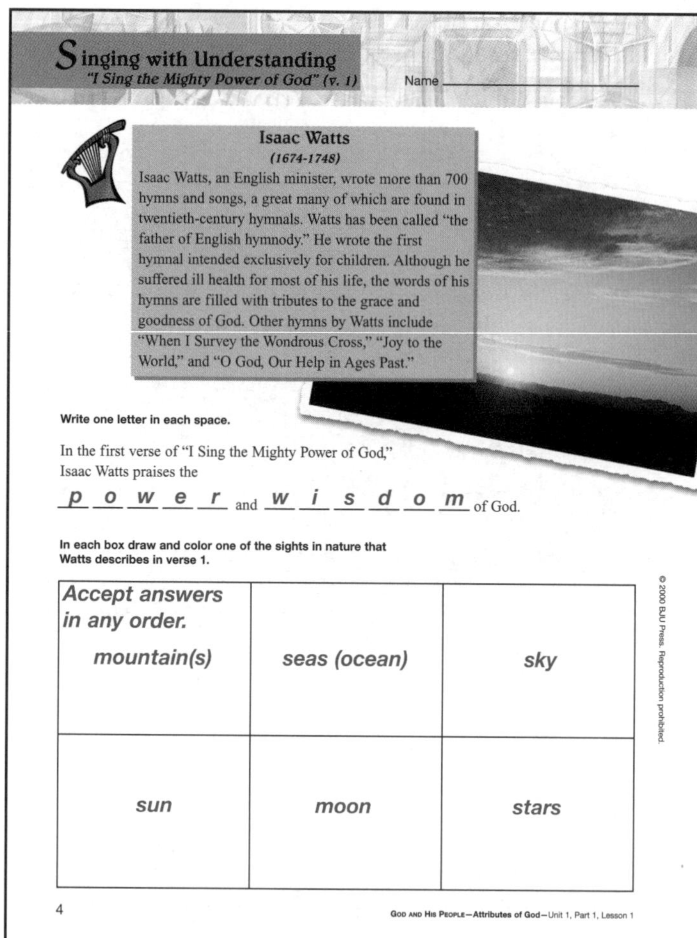
Singing with Understanding
"I Sing the Mighty Power of God" (v. 1)

Name ____________________

Isaac Watts
(1674-1748)
Isaac Watts, an English minister, wrote more than 700 hymns and songs, a great many of which are found in twentieth-century hymnals. Watts has been called "the father of English hymnody." He wrote the first hymnal intended exclusively for children. Although he suffered ill health for most of his life, the words of his hymns are filled with tributes to the grace and goodness of God. Other hymns by Watts include "When I Survey the Wondrous Cross," "Joy to the World," and "O God, Our Help in Ages Past."

Write one letter in each space.

In the first verse of "I Sing the Mighty Power of God," Isaac Watts praises the p o w e r and w i s d o m of God.

In each box draw and color one of the sights in nature that Watts describes in verse 1.

Accept answers in any order. *mountain(s)*	*seas (ocean)*	*sky*
sun	*moon*	*stars*

4 GOD AND HIS PEOPLE—Attributes of God—Unit 1, Part 1, Lesson 1

inside of the bookmark at both ends. Direct the students to place their bookmark over the page to mark the location of the memory verse.

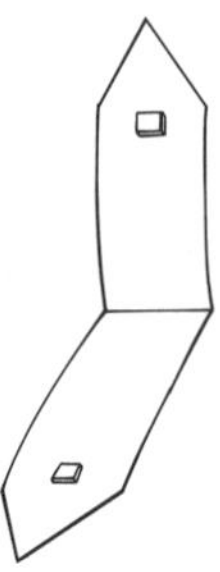

Worktext page 3

Recall details about the Bible account.

Hymn: "I Sing the Mighty Power of God"

Teach the first verse (Worktext page 272). Read the words of the first verse as the students follow along. Explain that *lofty skies* means "skies up above, the blue skies that we see and heaven, which we cannot see." *Ordained,* which sounds like *order,* means "God ordered creation into being." Only God can do this.

➤ **When did the Lord do all the things mentioned in this verse?** *(at Creation)*

➤ **What are some of the things that this verse says that God created?** *(the mountains, seas, skies, sun, moon, and stars)*

➤ **What are some other things that the Lord created?** *(Possible answers include light, animals, man, trees, and plants—God made all things.)*

Play the recording of the first verse and sing it with the students several times.

Worktext page 4

Singing with understanding, verse 1.

Lesson 2

Background Information

The Slaves—*Joseph had been taken to Egypt as a slave but became a ruler. Because of the famine in Hebron, Joseph moved his family to Egypt. Almost five hundred years later, the Israelites had multiplied into more than two million people. Each new pharaoh that took over Egypt knew less about Joseph. The ruling pharaoh, whom Moses was to confront, had made these foreigners into slaves. Pharaoh forced the people to make bricks for building—free labor that Pharaoh would not give up easily.*

Introducing the Bible Account

Review Moses. Share the background information to help the students understand the situation the slaves were in and why Moses was afraid to go to Pharaoh. Use the questions from the previous lesson to review the call of Moses with the students. Tell them that they will learn what Moses said in response to God's call.

Bible Account

Read the following Bible account or read Exodus 4:1-17.

God Prepares Moses

Moses answered the Lord with excuses for not being able to obey. "They will not believe me," said Moses. "They will say, The Lord hath not appeared unto thee."

"What is that in thine hand?" asked the Lord.

"A rod," said Moses. God told Moses to throw the rod down. When he did, the rod turned into a serpent, and Moses ran from it in fear.

The Lord told Moses, "Put forth thine hand, and take it by the tail." Moses caught the serpent, and it changed back into his rod.

God had a second task for Moses. "Put now thine hand into thy bosom," said the Lord. Moses did so, and when he took out his hand, it was white with leprosy. "Put thine hand into thy bosom again," said the Lord. When Moses pulled his hand out this time, the leprosy was gone, and his hand was like the rest of his skin. God showed Moses that He would give him power to make men believe him.

God gave Moses these miracles as tools. If the people did not believe his words, Moses had these two miracles to show them that God was all-powerful. Then God gave Moses a third miracle. "Thou shalt take of the water of the river," said the Lord. "And pour it upon the dry land: and the water . . . shall become blood."

But Moses had a second excuse for not obeying the Lord. "I am slow of speech, and of a slow tongue."

"Who hath made man's mouth?" asked the Lord. God had given Moses a voice and the ability to speak. The Lord promised to be with Moses and to give him the words to say. "I will be with thy mouth, and teach thee what thou shalt say," said the Lord. God promised to help Moses do things that were hard for him.

But Moses was afraid to let God speak through him, so he asked God to send someone else. "Is not Aaron the Levite thy brother?" asked the Lord. "I know that he can speak well. . . . Thou shalt speak unto him, and put words in his mouth: and I will be with thy mouth."

Finally convinced that he could do the job in God's strength, Moses agreed to be a spokesman for God.

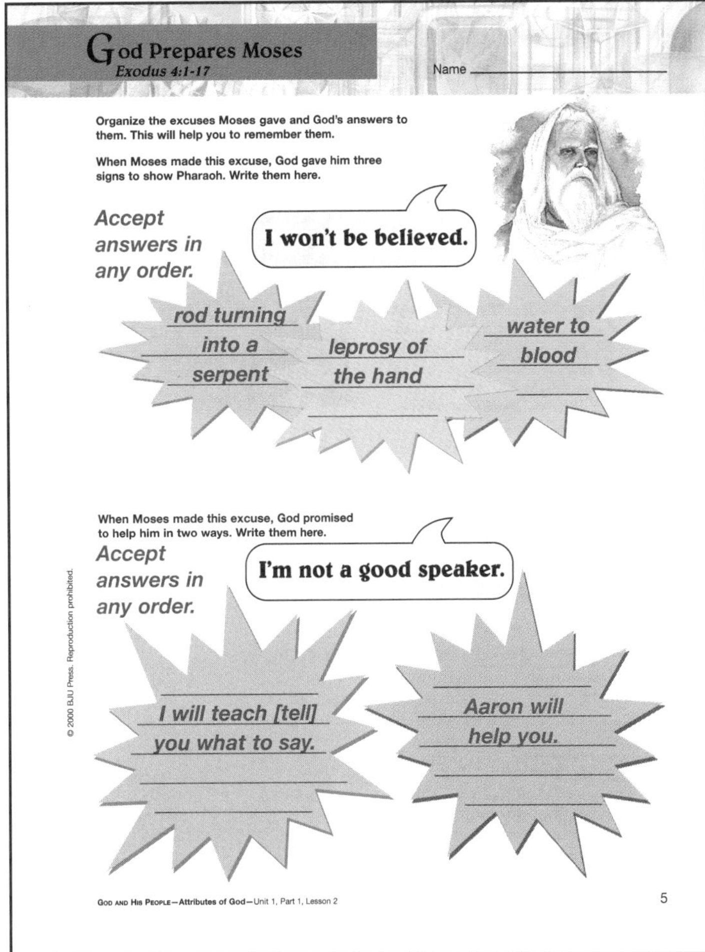

- ➤ **What reasons did Moses give for not going to Egypt?** *(No one would believe him; he was a poor speaker.)*
- ➤ **What two acts did God use to show His power to Moses?** *(He turned Moses' rod into a serpent and gave Moses temporary leprosy.)*
- ➤ **What two reasons did God give to Moses to comfort him about his speaking skills?** *(that God created his mouth and He would give him the words to say)*
- ➤ **Have you ever been afraid to tell someone about God?** *(Answers will vary.)* Allow students to tell about these situations if they wish to.
- ➤ **What should be a comfort to Christians today?** *(God created their mouths and can give them the words to say.)*

Worktext page 5

Recall God's answers to Moses' excuses.

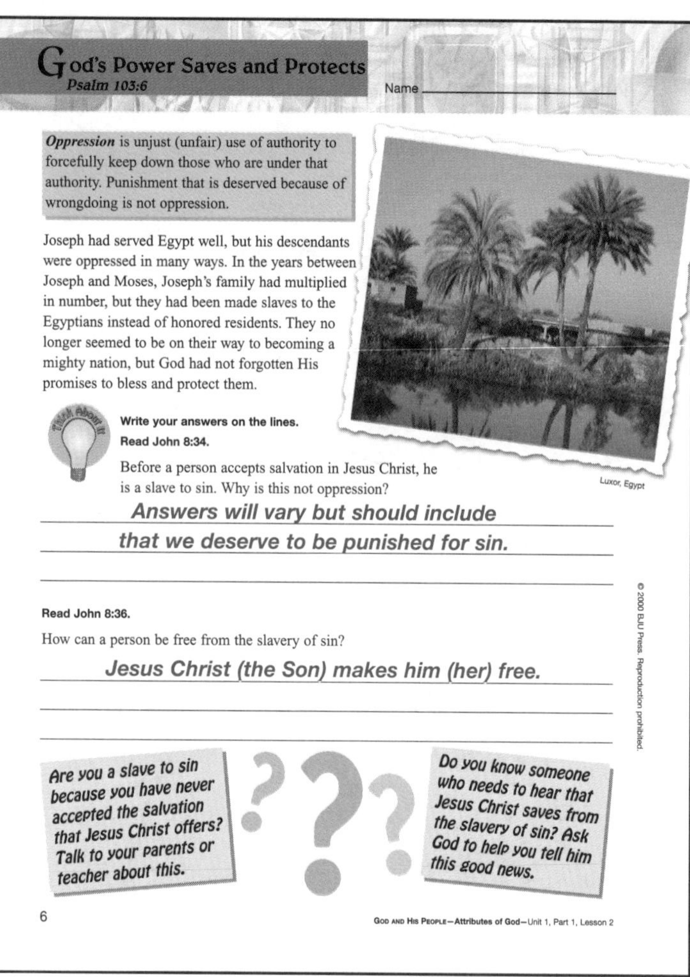

God's Power Saves and Protects
Psalm 103:6

Name ____________________

Oppression is unjust (unfair) use of authority to forcefully keep down those who are under that authority. Punishment that is deserved because of wrongdoing is not oppression.

Joseph had served Egypt well, but his descendants were oppressed in many ways. In the years between Joseph and Moses, Joseph's family had multiplied in number, but they had been made slaves to the Egyptians instead of honored residents. They no longer seemed to be on their way to becoming a mighty nation, but God had not forgotten His promises to bless and protect them.

Luxor, Egypt

Write your answers on the lines.
Read John 8:34.

Before a person accepts salvation in Jesus Christ, he is a slave to sin. Why is this not oppression?

Answers will vary but should include that we deserve to be punished for sin.

Read John 8:36.

How can a person be free from the slavery of sin?

Jesus Christ (the Son) makes him (her) free.

Are you a slave to sin because you have never accepted the salvation that Jesus Christ offers? Talk to your parents or teacher about this.

Do you know someone who needs to hear that Jesus Christ saves from the slavery of sin? Ask God to help you tell him this good news.

6 God and His People—Attributes of God—Unit 1, Part 1, Lesson 2

Hymn: "I Sing the Mighty Power of God"

Sing the first verse (Worktext page 272). Play the recording of verse 1.

➤ **Why do you think that God made the sun for the day and the moon and stars for the night?** *(God knew that man would need the day to work and the night for rest.)*

Explain that only God could decide how His creation would be made—nothing could be more perfect. God had a reason for making each one of us different—and none of us could be more perfect. God who is omniscient and omnipotent made us. Sing verse 1.

Memory Verse—Psalm 103:6

Practice the memory verse with a "verse volley." Locate **Psalm 103:6** and choose different students to read it aloud. Review the meaning of the verse.

Divide the students into two teams. Direct team 1 to read the first word (the). Direct team 2 to repeat that word and add the second word (the Lord). Continue until the entire verse is said. Repeat as desired. (*Note:* One-on-One presents an alternate activity for use with the teacher and one student or an individual student at an activity center.)

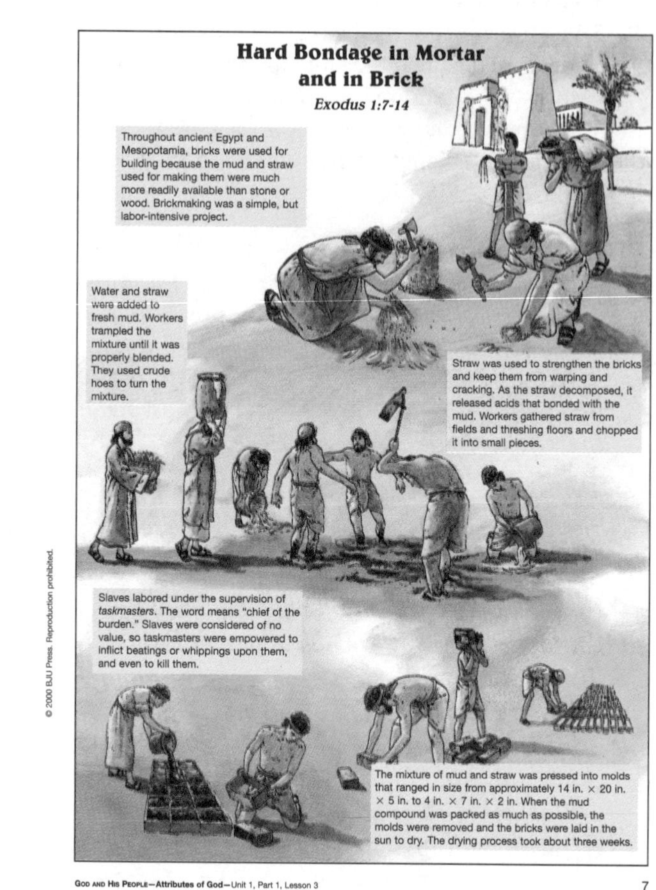

Hard Bondage in Mortar and in Brick
Exodus 1:7-14

Throughout ancient Egypt and Mesopotamia, bricks were used for building because the mud and straw used for making them were much more readily available than stone or wood. Brickmaking was a simple, but labor-intensive project.

Water and straw were added to fresh mud. Workers trampled the mixture until it was properly blended. They used crude hoes to turn the mixture.

Straw was used to strengthen the bricks and keep them from warping and cracking. As the straw decomposed, it released acids that bonded with the mud. Workers gathered straw from fields and threshing floors and chopped it into small pieces.

Slaves labored under the supervision of *taskmasters*. The word means "chief of the burden." Slaves were considered of no value, so taskmasters were empowered to inflict beatings or whippings upon them, and even to kill them.

The mixture of mud and straw was pressed into molds that ranged in size from approximately 14 in. × 20 in. × 5 in. to 4 in. × 7 in. × 2 in. When the mud compound was packed as much as possible, the molds were removed and the bricks were laid in the sun to dry. The drying process took about three weeks.

God and His People—Attributes of God—Unit 1, Part 1, Lesson 3 7

One-on-One: Follow the directions of practicing the verse, allowing the teacher to say the first word and the student to say the second word and so on.

Worktext page 6

Develop understanding of the memory verse.

Lesson 3

Materials

- Chart 7, "Hard Bondage in Mortar and in Brick," and Charts 1-2, "I Will Stretch Out My Hand and Smite Egypt"

Background Information

The First Plague—*The Nile River, which flows from south to north, is the longest river in the world. It was central to the life of ancient Egypt and most of the nearby civilization. The rugged desert territory beyond the Nile was unfit for habitation. Every year winter rain caused the Nile River to swell and overflow. When the water receded, it left a layer of sand and clay called* silt. *Farmers planted their crops in this rich soil while it remained exposed. Because of the benefits the Nile provided, the ancient Egyptians made the river one of their gods. God's first plague upon them was a strike against their worship of false gods and was the beginning of a year-long period of plagues in Egypt.*

Introducing the Bible Account

Explain brickmaking. Direct attention to Worktext page 7, reading how bricks were made in Egypt.

Bible Account

Read the following Bible account or retell Exodus 5:1–12:36 in your own words. Display Charts 1-2, "I Will Stretch Out My Hand and Smite Egypt," as you tell the account. (*Note:* Supplement page S74 may be used for displaying to a small group or an individual student.)

God Sends Moses

Moses obeyed God and went to Pharaoh. Moses said to Pharaoh, "Thus saith the Lord God of Israel, Let my people go, that they may hold a feast unto me in the wilderness." God wanted His people to go into the desert to worship and sacrifice to Him.

"And Pharaoh said, Who is the Lord, that I should obey his voice to let Israel go? I know not the Lord, neither will I let Israel go."

The oppression of the Israelites did not stop after Moses spoke to Pharaoh. Instead their suffering was made worse. Pharaoh commanded that the Israelites no longer be brought straw for brickmaking. "I will not give you straw," said Pharaoh. "Go ye, get you straw where ye can find it." The officers of the children of Israel were beaten and told that the people were not working hard enough.

The officers went to Pharaoh and said, "There is no straw given unto thy servants, and they say to us, Make brick: and, behold, thy servants are beaten." They were angry with Moses for making their work harder. Moses took the problem to the Lord. "Since I came to Pharaoh to speak in thy name," Moses said to God, "he hath done evil to this people; neither hast thou delivered thy people at all."

"Then the Lord said unto Moses, Now shalt thou see what I will do to Pharaoh." And so began the ten plagues that God used to demonstrate His power to the Egyptians and to free the Israelites. After every plague, Pharaoh had opportunity to let the people go, but it was not until after the tenth plague that the Israelites were freed.

For the first plague, God used Aaron's rod to turn all of the rivers into blood. Aaron, Moses, and Pharaoh stood by the river, and Aaron said, "The Lord God of the Hebrews hath sent me unto thee, saying, Let my people go, that they may serve me in the wilderness: and . . . thou wouldest not hear." The river was turned to blood, and all the fish in it died. The river smelled terrible, and the Egyptians could not drink it.

God sent frogs out of the river to cover the whole land for the second plague. There were frogs in every room of their houses, in their beds, in their ovens, in their clothes—everywhere. Pharaoh said to Moses and Aaron, "Intreat [beg] the Lord, that he may take away the frogs from me, and from my people; and I will let the people go, that they may do sacrifice unto the Lord." The next day, all the frogs died "out of the houses, out of the villages, and out of the fields." But when Pharaoh saw that they were gone, he hardened his heart and would not let the Israelites go.

Then God told Aaron to stretch out his rod and hit the dust of the earth. For the third plague, the dust turned into lice and got all over the people and animals. Pharaoh's magicians tried to bring forth lice, but they could not. They told Pharaoh, "This is the finger of God." Pharaoh would not listen to his own magicians who finally realized the truth.

The fourth plague brought swarms of flies that covered the land as the frogs had done. Pharaoh promised to release the slaves if God would take away the flies but took his promise back when the flies were gone.

For the fifth plague, God caused all the Egyptians' animals to sicken and die, but none of the Israelites' animals were harmed. God protected His people while punishing those who disobeyed Him.

God told Moses to sprinkle handfuls of ashes toward heaven in front of Pharaoh. For the sixth plague, the ashes turned to dust and gave boils, horrible sores that break out all over the body, to all the people and animals in Egypt.

For the seventh plague, Moses stretched his hand toward heaven, and God sent thunder, hail, and fire down on the Egyptians. People and animals were killed, and their land was destroyed. But where the Israelites were living, there was no hail.

Then Moses stretched out his rod, and the wind blew all day and all night. When it was morning, the wind brought locusts that covered the land for the eighth plague. The locusts covered the whole land so that it was dark. They ate any crops that the hail had not destroyed.

Next Moses stretched out his hand to heaven, and for the ninth plague there was thick darkness in Egypt for three days. No one could see anything. No one could leave home because it was so dark.

Then came the tenth and final plague. The Lord said to Moses, "Yet will I bring one plague more upon Pharaoh, and upon Egypt; afterwards he will let you go." The Lord told

Moses that the plague would happen "in the tenth day of this month."

"About midnight," said the Lord, "will I go out into the midst of Egypt: And all the firstborn in the land of Egypt shall die, from the firstborn of Pharaoh that sitteth upon his throne, even unto the firstborn of the maidservant . . . and all the firstborn of beasts. And there shall be a great cry throughout all the land of Egypt, such as there was none like it, nor shall be like it any more." But the children of Israel would be protected. God told them how they could escape: every Israelite family was to sacrifice a perfect lamb, put the blood of the lamb "on the two side posts and on the upper door post of the houses," and eat the flesh that night; then they were to get packed and get ready to leave Egypt. "When I see the blood," said the Lord, "I will pass over you, and the plague shall not be upon you to destroy you, when I smite the land of Egypt."

On the tenth day of the month at midnight, the Lord killed all the firstborn in Egypt. "There was a great cry in Egypt; for there was not a house where there was not one dead." Pharaoh called for Moses and Aaron and said, "Rise up, and get you forth from among my people, both ye and the children of Israel; and go, serve the Lord, as ye have said." The Israelites left that night. The Egyptians were so eager to get rid of them that they gave the Israelites clothes and jewelry to make them leave. All that God had spoken had come to pass.

InfoScene: "Hard Bondage in Mortar and in Brick"
Display Chart 7 for reference throughout this unit. Review and discuss the Bible account as time permits.

➤ **Why did God want His people freed from slavery?** *(Possible answers include His promises to Abraham, Isaac, and Jacob—His special people.)*

➤ **Why did the Israelites' work get harder when Moses came?** *(Pharaoh made them get their own straw instead of providing it for them.)*

➤ **Whom did the plagues affect?** *(only the Egyptians)*

➤ **What was the tenth plague?** *(death of the firstborn of every family—people and animals)*

➤ **Why do you think that the tenth plague became known as the Passover?** *(because the Lord said, "When I see the blood, I will pass over you")*

➤ **How was the Passover lamb like Christ?** *(The lamb was sacrificed so the blood could cover the doorpost; the Lord Jesus Christ was sacrificed on the cross to provide a way for us to be saved from our sins.)*

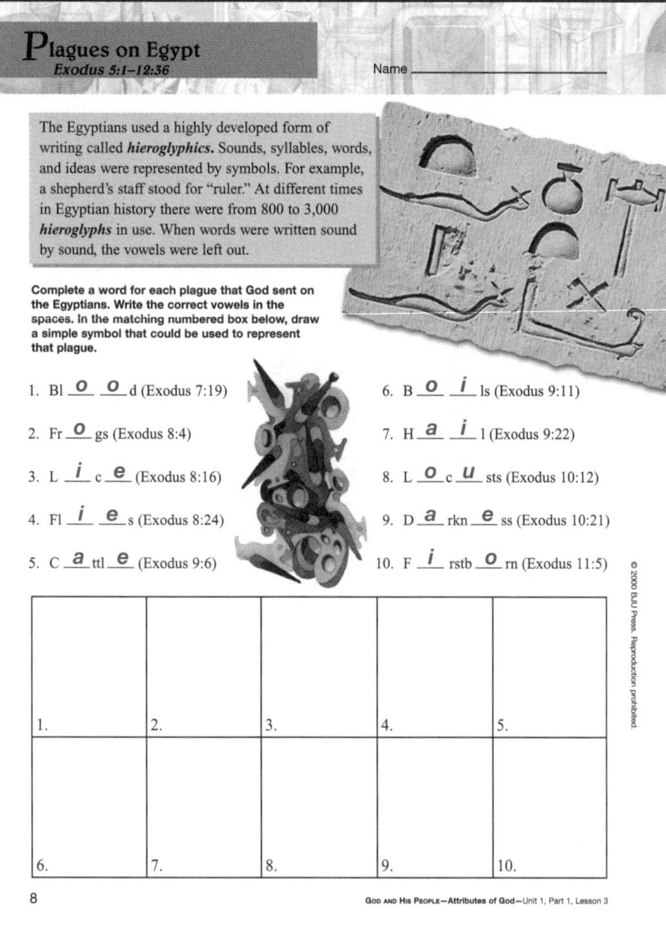

Plagues on Egypt
Exodus 5:1–12:36

Name ____________________

The Egyptians used a highly developed form of writing called ***hieroglyphics.*** Sounds, syllables, words, and ideas were represented by symbols. For example, a shepherd's staff stood for "ruler." At different times in Egyptian history there were from 800 to 3,000 ***hieroglyphs*** in use. When words were written sound by sound, the vowels were left out.

Complete a word for each plague that God sent on the Egyptians. Write the correct vowels in the spaces. In the matching numbered box below, draw a simple symbol that could be used to represent that plague.

1. Bl **o** **o** d (Exodus 7:19)
2. Fr **o** gs (Exodus 8:4)
3. L **i** c **e** (Exodus 8:16)
4. Fl **i** **e** s (Exodus 8:24)
5. C **a** ttl **e** (Exodus 9:6)
6. B **o** **i** ls (Exodus 9:11)
7. H **a** **i** l (Exodus 9:22)
8. L **o** c **u** sts (Exodus 10:12)
9. D **a** rkn **e** ss (Exodus 10:21)
10. F **i** rstb **o** rn (Exodus 11:5)

1.	2.	3.	4.	5.
6.	7.	8.	9.	10.

8 GOD AND HIS PEOPLE—Attributes of God—Unit 1, Part 1, Lesson 3

Memory Verse—Psalm 103:6

Practice the memory verse. Direct the students to locate and silently read **Psalm 103:6.**

➤ **Who were oppressed in this lesson's Bible account?** *(the Israelites)*

➤ **Why are they considered to be oppressed?** *(They were treated unfairly and with severity.)*

➤ **Who else in the Bible was oppressed?** *(Possible answers include Job, Paul, and John the Baptist.)*

Choose several volunteers to read or say Psalm 103:6 from memory.

Hymn: "I Sing the Mighty Power of God"

Sing the first verse (Worktext page 272). Play the recording and sing the first verse together. Direct the students to choose something from the Bible account that proved God is in control of nature and draw a picture of it (optional).

Worktext page 8

Recall facts about the plagues on Egypt.

Lesson 4

Materials

- Bible Book Cards: books of Moses
- Song: "Books of the Old Testament"

Song: "Books of the Old Testament"

Sing the first verse (Worktext page 287). Play the recording and sing the first verse together.

Bible Study Skills

Review the books of Moses. Distribute the books of Moses cards to five students. Direct the students to arrange themselves in the correct order at the front of the room. Display the flashcards one at a time and review the book before and after each book on the card. Invite the students to tell what each book is about or to tell an account found in each book. Possible answers include:

> **Genesis**—Creation, Adam and Eve's fall, Noah and the Flood, Abraham, Isaac, Jacob, and Joseph
>
> **Exodus**—Moses born in Egypt, flees to Midian, returns for Israelites, ten plagues, wandering in the wilderness, tabernacle built, Ten Commandments, and the golden calf
>
> **Leviticus**—directions for sacrifices, the priesthood, and laws of clean and unclean
>
> **Numbers**—Israelites numbered, Korah rebels, Balaam prophesies, and the spies are sent
>
> **Deuteronomy**—ordinances given, Joshua charged, and the death of Moses

One-on-One: Allow the student to sequence the books of Moses student cards; then challenge him to tell an account that is found in one of the books.

Memory Verse—Psalm 103:6

Practice the memory verse. Review that God wanted the Israelites to worship Him in the wilderness. Explain that the word *worship* means "to show honor, love, and respect."

➤ **Why would the Israelites want to worship God?** *(He had helped them out of slavery, kept them from the plagues, called them His chosen people, and promised to take them to the Promised Land.)*

Allow individual students or groups of students to say the verse from memory.

Introducing the Application Story

Guide a discussion about fear.

➤ **What fears did you have as a young child that you don't have now?**

➤ **How did you overcome those fears?**

➤ **What fears do you have now?**

➤ **How can you overcome these fears?**

Application Story

Read the following story to the students.

More Than Words (Part 1)

As the plane began to roll down the runway, Bryan checked his seat belt for the tenth time. As the plane picked up speed, the whoosh of the wind grew louder. Bryan pushed his head back against his head rest and closed his eyes tightly. The wheels of the plane lifted off the ground, and Bryan's stomach sank.

He clutched the arm in the next chair. "Dad, I want to get off the plane," he said.

"Too late," said Dad. He smiled. "We're in the air now."

Bryan looked around. "Where are the parachutes? Where are those bags for when I get sick? What if we crash? Will the pilot know what to do if the engine stops running? What if—"

"Hey, hey, now," said Dad. "Are you saying that you don't think God is in control of this plane?"

Bryan shrugged his shoulders. "God didn't make the plane, and the pilot is flying it."

"In school you learned that God is omniscient, right?" asked Dad. Bryan nodded. "What does that mean?"

"God is all-knowing and all-seeing," said Bryan.

"Yes," answered Dad. "But what does that mean to us right now, here in this plane?"

Bryan scratched his head. "God sees and knows us. He sees the plane, the pilot, where we're sitting—and even the food cart."

"Does God know where we came from?" asked Dad.

"Sure, even I know that. Denver," said Bryan. The plane hit an air pocket, and Bryan felt his stomach flip upside down. He pulled down the plastic window shade with one hand as he dug the fingers of his other hand into Dad's arm.

"Does God know our future?" asked Dad. "Can He see what will happen and know how it will affect us?"

Bryan paused just a moment before nodding. "He must, huh, Dad?"

"God is also omnipotent, which means he is all-powerful. Now if God can see our future, do you think that He is in control of it too?" Bryan nodded harder. "So if God knows our future and is all-powerful, can He do anything about our future?"

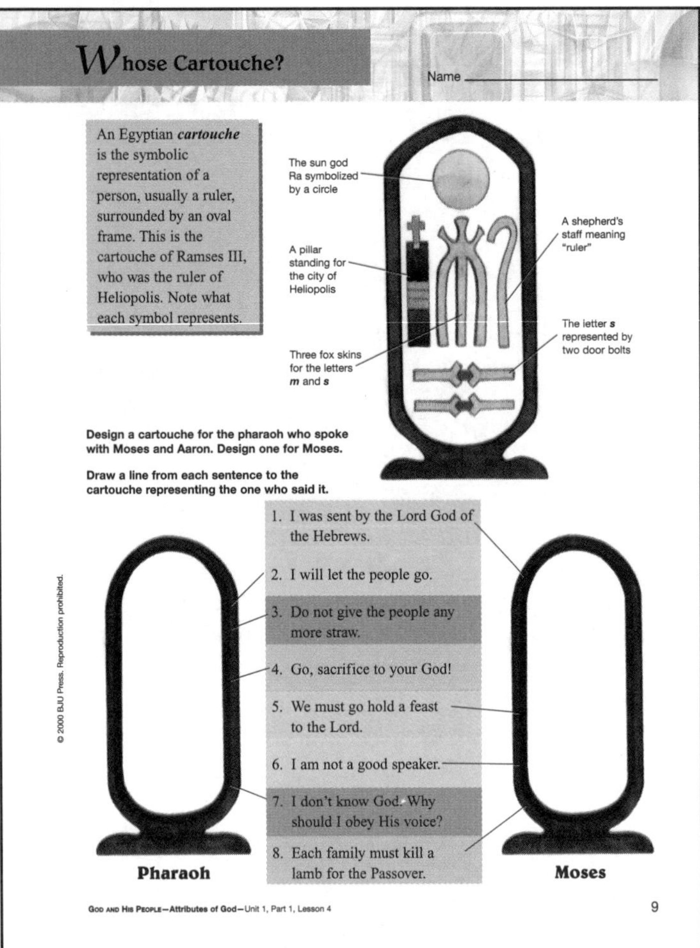

Whose Cartouche?

Name ______________

An Egyptian *cartouche* is the symbolic representation of a person, usually a ruler, surrounded by an oval frame. This is the cartouche of Ramses III, who was the ruler of Heliopolis. Note what each symbol represents.

Design a cartouche for the pharaoh who spoke with Moses and Aaron. Design one for Moses.

Draw a line from each sentence to the cartouche representing the one who said it.

1. I was sent by the Lord God of the Hebrews.
2. I will let the people go.
3. Do not give the people any more straw.
4. Go, sacrifice to your God!
5. We must go hold a feast to the Lord.
6. I am not a good speaker.
7. I don't know God. Why should I obey His voice?
8. Each family must kill a lamb for the Passover.

Pharaoh **Moses**

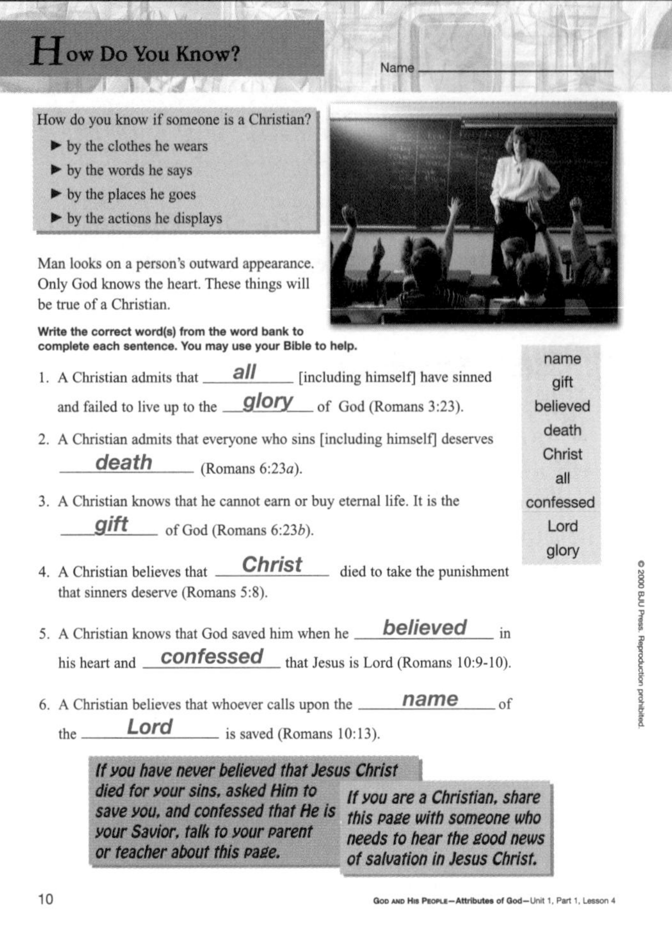

How Do You Know?

Name ______________

How do you know if someone is a Christian?
- by the clothes he wears
- by the words he says
- by the places he goes
- by the actions he displays

Man looks on a person's outward appearance. Only God knows the heart. These things will be true of a Christian.

Write the correct word(s) from the word bank to complete each sentence. You may use your Bible to help.

name, gift, believed, death, Christ, all, confessed, Lord, glory

1. A Christian admits that **all** [including himself] have sinned and failed to live up to the **glory** of God (Romans 3:23).
2. A Christian admits that everyone who sins [including himself] deserves **death** (Romans 6:23*a*).
3. A Christian knows that he cannot earn or buy eternal life. It is the **gift** of God (Romans 6:23*b*).
4. A Christian believes that **Christ** died to take the punishment that sinners deserve (Romans 5:8).
5. A Christian knows that God saved him when he **believed** in his heart and **confessed** that Jesus is Lord (Romans 10:9-10).
6. A Christian believes that whoever calls upon the **name** of the **Lord** is saved (Romans 10:13).

If you have never believed that Jesus Christ died for your sins, asked Him to save you, and confessed that He is your Savior, talk to your parent or teacher about this page.

If you are a Christian, share this page with someone who needs to hear the good news of salvation in Jesus Christ.

"He could stop the plane from crashing," said Bryan. "But it still could crash, couldn't it?"

"Only if God lets it," said Dad. "God is omnipresent. What does that mean?"

"He is always present and everywhere at once," said Bryan. He knew Dad would want more of an answer, so he continued. "That means that God is with us here in the plane, and He is up there with the pilot, and He is with Uncle Don waiting for us in North Carolina."

Dad nodded. "How do you think it makes God feel to be here with you, knowing everything about you and being all-powerful to protect you, and seeing that you're scared?"

"It probably makes Him sad. But you know what, Dad? I don't feel so afraid anymore."

"Good," said Dad. "Then you can stop squeezing my arm so hard."

- **Why was Bryan afraid?** *(Students may answer that Bryan was afraid of planes, but elicit that he was not trusting God.)*
- **Who was in the seat next to Bryan?** *(his dad)*
- **How did Bryan's dad lessen Bryan's fear?** *(He talked about God and reminded Bryan of God's presence and His promises.)* Explain that God was truly the one who comforted Bryan.

Guide a discussion about the attributes of God. Call on students to tell how the attributes of God (omniscience, omnipotence, and omnipresence) discussed in the previous lessons can be applied to their lives.

Worktext page 9

Match dialogue to the correct Bible character.

Worktext page 10

Apply Bible knowledge to everyday life. Take time to discuss the page and to read the verses. (*Note:* This is a good opportunity to present the plan of salvation to the students.)

Going Beyond

Materials

- Chart 7, "Hard Bondage in Mortar and in Brick"
- Straw
- A shoebox for each student
- A container for mixing or a wading pool
- Mud and some extra water

Enrichment

Guide a brickmaking activity. Reread the information from Chart 7, "Hard Bondage in Mortar and in Brick." Explain that brickmaking was a messy job. The Israelites would dig holes in the ground, where they would mix the mud and straw by using tools or their feet. The Israelites were required to make a certain number of bricks each day, or they would be beaten. The wooden molds for the bricks were larger (about 20" × 10" × 5") than most bricks we have today. Some pharaohs required that their seals be stamped into each brick. The bricks would be removed from the molds when they were dry, and then bake in the sun for about two weeks.

Direct the students to mix the ingredients in a container (approximately two parts dirt to one part water and one part straw); put the mixture into shoe boxes and pat it down. (*Note:* You may wish to fill a wading pool with the mud and allow the students to mix the mud with their feet.) Let the bricks dry for several days; then tear the shoe boxes away from the bricks. Create a pyramid with the finished bricks (using mud for mortar) or allow the students to take their bricks home.

Show the video, *The Printing.* Discuss the oppression that Christians in Russia and other countries have had. Discuss the freedom that you enjoy in your country. (Note: *The Printing* is available through Bob Jones University Press.)

God Is Faithful, Holy, Unchanging

Unit 1, Part 2

Preview

Doctrines

- God is all-powerful (omnipotent) (Jeremiah 32:27)—Lesson 1
- God is faithful (I Corinthians 1:9)—Lesson 1
- God is unchanging (immutable) (Malachi 3:6)—Lesson 2
- God is holy (Isaiah 6:3)—Lesson 4

Skills and Applications

- Learn Psalm 103:7
- Read a map
- Use a scale of miles
- Identify cause and effect
- Learn the Old Testament books of History
- Realize that God is faithful and never changes
- Apply Bible knowledge to everyday life

Lesson 1

Materials

- Chart 29, "Journey to the Promised Land"
- Unit 1 Bookmark for each student
- Ruler for each student
- Highlighter for each student (optional)

Background Information

The Red Sea—*There were six hundred thousand Israelite men, not counting the women and children. The Lord had to provide enough time and space for one to two million people to cross the Red Sea.*

Introducing the Bible Account

Show the setting. Point out the Red Sea on Chart 29, "Journey to the Promised Land."

Bible Account

Read the following Bible account, explaining that it is a retelling, or read Exodus 14:1-31.

Victory at the Red Sea

At last Pharaoh let the Israelites go, but then he decided he wanted to bring them back. God warned Moses that Pharaoh would change his mind and try to bring them back. Pharaoh took six hundred chariots and chased the children of Israel, who were on foot.

The Israelites had nowhere to go. The Red Sea was in front of them, and Pharaoh's army was behind them. The Israelites said to Moses, "Because there were no graves in Egypt, hast thou taken us away to die in the wilderness?" The Israelites said that they would rather have served as slaves to the Egyptians than die in the wilderness. They did not have faith that God would protect them. "Fear ye not," said Moses. "The Lord shall fight for you."

God told Moses, "Lift thou up thy rod, and stretch out thine hand over the sea, and divide it: and the children of Israel shall go on dry ground through the midst of the sea."

The angel of God had been leading the Israelites with a pillar of cloud. After the Lord spoke these words, the angel and pillar went behind the Israelites. The pillar acted as a cloud over the camp of the Egyptians but gave light to the camp of the Israelites. Neither camp came near the other one all night.

"Moses stretched out his hand over the sea; and the Lord caused the sea to go back by a strong east wind all that night." The water divided, and the sea became dry land with two giant walls of water on the left and right. The Israelites passed through the Red Sea on dry ground.

Then God lifted the cloud. When Pharaoh's army saw God's people walking on dry land across the sea, they rushed after them. But God caused the wheels of their chariots to come off.

The Lord said to Moses, "Stretch out thine hand over the sea, that the waters may come again upon the Egyptians, upon their chariots, and upon their horsemen." So Moses stretched out his hand, and the Lord caused the walls of water to come down and to cover "the chariots, and the horsemen, and all the host of Pharaoh." It was too late for the Egyptians to turn around, so they drowned.

The Lord saved Israel that day from the hand of the Egyptians. "Israel saw that great work which the Lord did upon the Egyptians: and the people feared the Lord, and believed the Lord, and his servant Moses."

➤ **How did the Israelites feel when they realized that they were trapped by the sea?** *(They were angry with Moses for taking them out of Egypt.)*

➤ **What did God tell Moses to do to divide the sea?** *(lift up his rod, and stretch out his hand over the sea)*

➤ **What other miracles had God done using Moses' rod?** *(turned it into a snake twice, used it for several of the plagues, and brought the sea back together)*

➤ **What did God use to show the Israelites that He was with them?** *(a pillar of fire and cloud)*

Direct the students to locate the word *faithful* in the glossary. Select a student to read the definition aloud.

➤ **How was God faithful to the Israelites?** *(He promised to fight for them, and He did.)*

➤ **How does God show His faithfulness to us?**

Hymn: "I Sing the Mighty Power of God"

Sing the first verse (Worktext page 272). Play the recording of the first verse and lead in singing it together.

➤ **What mighty power did God show the Israelites on the day that this account took place?** *(He held the water back with a wind and dried up the floor of the Red Sea.)*

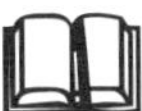

Memory Verse—Psalm 103:7

Principle: The God of the Israelites is also our God. Locate **Psalm 103:7** and read the verse aloud as the students read silently.

➤ **How did God make His ways known to Moses and the Israelites?** *(He talked to Moses from the burning bush; He showed that He was with the Israelites in a pillar of fire and cloud.)*

➤ **How does God make His ways known to us?** *(through His Word and through answers to prayer)*

➤ **What acts did God perform for the children of Israel?** *(He rescued them out of Egypt, and He parted the Red Sea for them to cross.)*

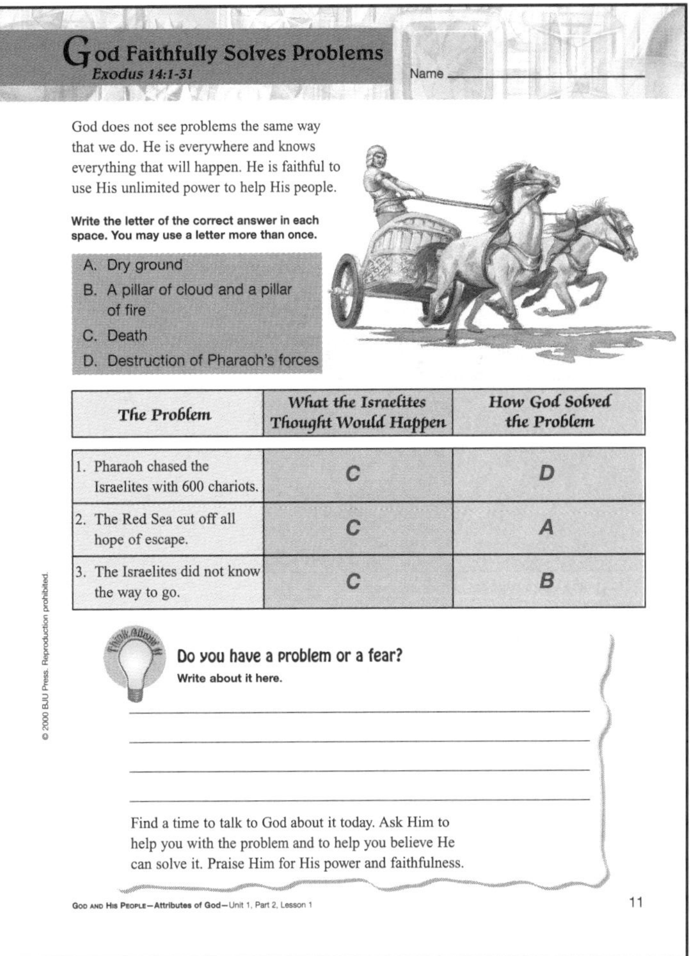

God Faithfully Solves Problems
Exodus 14:1-31

Name ____________

God does not see problems the same way that we do. He is everywhere and knows everything that will happen. He is faithful to use His unlimited power to help His people.

Write the letter of the correct answer in each space. You may use a letter more than once.

A. Dry ground
B. A pillar of cloud and a pillar of fire
C. Death
D. Destruction of Pharaoh's forces

The Problem	What the Israelites Thought Would Happen	How God Solved the Problem
1. Pharaoh chased the Israelites with 600 chariots.	C	D
2. The Red Sea cut off all hope of escape.	C	A
3. The Israelites did not know the way to go.	C	B

Think About It

Do you have a problem or a fear?
Write about it here.

Find a time to talk to God about it today. Ask Him to help you with the problem and to help you believe He can solve it. Praise Him for His power and faithfulness.

God and His People—Attributes of God—Unit 1, Part 2, Lesson 1 11

➤ **What acts has God done for us?** *(Possible answers include He provides salvation through His Son; He provides comfort and protection for Christians; and He forgives us when we sin.)*

Choose several students to read aloud **Psalm 103:6-7** several times. Direct the students to highlight verse 7 in their Bibles (optional) and to mark the location with the Unit 1 Bookmark.

Worktext page 11

Recall details about the Bible account.

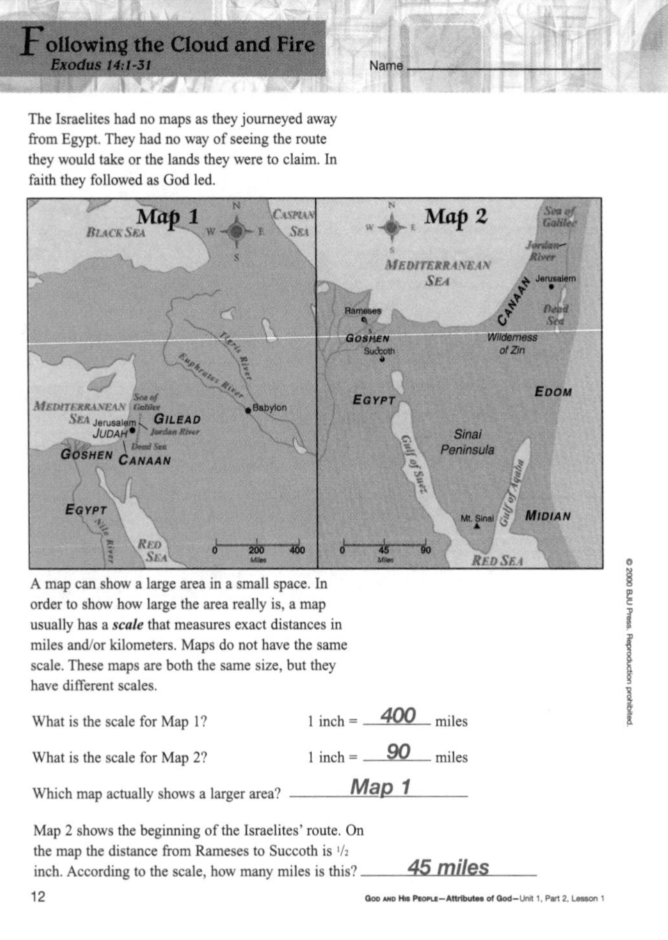

Following the Cloud and Fire
Exodus 14:1-31

Name ____________

The Israelites had no maps as they journeyed away from Egypt. They had no way of seeing the route they would take or the lands they were to claim. In faith they followed as God led.

A map can show a large area in a small space. In order to show how large the area really is, a map usually has a ***scale*** that measures exact distances in miles and/or kilometers. Maps do not have the same scale. These maps are both the same size, but they have different scales.

What is the scale for Map 1? 1 inch = 400 miles

What is the scale for Map 2? 1 inch = 90 miles

Which map actually shows a larger area? Map 1

Map 2 shows the beginning of the Israelites' route. On the map the distance from Rameses to Succoth is ½ inch. According to the scale, how many miles is this? 45 miles

12 God and His People—Attributes of God—Unit 1, Part 2, Lesson 1

Worktext page 12

Use a scale of miles. Direct the students to use their rulers to measure the distance from Goshen to Jerusalem to the nearest inch on both maps. Compare the distances.

Map 1—1 inch: 400 miles

Map 2—3 inches: 90 miles

Guide the students as they complete the page. Read **Exodus 13:17** aloud.

➤ **Why did God not lead the Israelites from Goshen to their Promised Land in Canaan by the most direct route?** *(The Israelites were not ready to go to war with the Philistines.)*

Lesson 2

Materials

- Charts 3-4 and 29: "The Ten Commandments" and "Journey to the Promised Land"

Background Information

Decalogue—*Two Greek words form to make this word.* Deka *means "ten" and* logos *means "word."* Decalogue *means "ten words" or "the Ten Commandments." The first four commandments deal with man's relationship to God. The last six deal with man's relationship to others.*

Covenant—*A covenant is a promise made between two people or between God and man. God made a covenant with Israel at Mount Sinai [Mount Horeb]. God promised to reward the Israelites' obedience with providential care, earthly blessing, and victory over their enemies.*

In the New Testament, the word covenant *is sometimes translated* testament. *The old covenant spoken of is the law. It is referred to as the old covenant because it was replaced by the new covenant. Christ brought in and established the new covenant of grace through which the righteousness of the law could now be fulfilled through the work of Christ. The new covenant existed in some form from the very beginning, for all of God's dealings with His people are through grace. God's promise of a Savior after the fall in the Garden of Eden showed His grace in providing salvation for sinful man.*

Introducing the Bible Account

Show the setting. Point to Mount Sinai [Mount Horeb] on Chart 29, "Journey to the Promised Land," to show where God gave His people the law.

Bible Account

Read the following Bible account or tell Exodus 19:1–31:18 in your own words. Encourage the students to listen for three things that God talked about when He gave the law. *(the Ten Commandments, laws specifically for the Israelites, and instructions about the tabernacle)*

God Gives the Law

God chose Israel to be His special people. He said to them, "If ye will obey my voice indeed, and keep my covenant, then ye shall be a peculiar treasure unto me above all people." God rescued the Israelites and brought them to Mount Sinai where He would give them the law through Moses.

Even before God gave the law, the Israelites told Moses, "All that the Lord hath spoken we will do." They were ready to obey after seeing God do great miracles. Moses told God what the people said, and God told them to prepare to receive the law.

Everyone was to wash his clothes. No one was allowed to climb Mount Sinai or even come near the bottom of it; anyone who tried to approach the mountain would die. For three days the people cleansed themselves.

On the morning of the third day, there was thunder and lightning, a thick cloud on the mountain, and the sound of a loud trumpet. The Lord came down to the top of Mount Sinai in a fire, making the mountain shake and surrounding it in smoke. Moses went up to meet God on the mountain top.

The law that God gave to Moses can be divided into three parts: The Ten Commandments, laws for the Israelites, and laws about the tabernacle.

Display Charts 3-4, "The Ten Commandments" for reference throughout the rest of the Bible account. (*Note:* Supplement page S75 may be used for displaying to a small group or an individual student.)

The Ten Commandments are general laws that God wrote on stone tablets. They teach us how God wants us to live and show us our need of a Savior. The first four commandments explain man's duty to God. The first commandment is "Thou shalt have no other gods before me." This teaches us to worship only God.

The second commandment is "Thou shalt not make unto thee any graven image or any likeness of any thing that is in heaven above, or that is in the earth beneath, or that is in the water under the earth." This teaches us to worship God in a proper manner and to avoid idolatry.

The third commandment is "Thou shalt not take the name of the Lord thy God in vain; for the Lord will not hold him guiltless that taketh his name in vain." This teaches us to reverence God's name, Word, and works.

The fourth commandment is "Remember the sabbath day, to keep it holy." This teaches us that one day of the week is to be set aside for special communion with God.

The remaining six commandments explain man's duty to other people. The fifth commandment is "Honour thy father and thy mother: that thy days may be long upon the land which the Lord thy God giveth thee." This teaches us that God blesses those that love and obey their parents.

The sixth commandment is "Thou shalt not kill." This teaches us to avoid anger and injury to others.

The seventh commandment is "Thou shalt not commit adultery." This teaches us to be pure in heart, language, and conduct.

The eighth commandment is "Thou shalt not steal." This teaches us to respect the property of others and to be honest and industrious.

The ninth commandment is "Thou shalt not bear false witness against thy neighbour." This teaches us to tell the truth.

The tenth commandment is "Thou shalt not covet thy neighbour's house, thou shalt not covet thy neighbour's wife, nor his manservant, nor his maidservant, nor his ox, nor his ass, nor any thing that is thy neighbour's." This teaches us to be content with what we have.

The Israelites failed to keep the law. They broke all ten commandments because they were sinners. God gave the Ten Commandments to show that all men are sinners.

- ➤ **Who can keep all of the Ten Commandments?** *(no one)*
- ➤ **Why did God give us the Ten Commandments if no one can obey them?** *(They show us that we are sinners.)*
- ➤ **How are the Ten Commandments important to Christians today?** *(Though Christians today no longer sacrifice animals for forgiveness of sin, they still should obey the Ten Commandments. The commandments show us that we are sinners and need a Savior.)*

Point out that God tells us that the law is like a school teacher to teach us that we need to trust Christ as our Savior. Read **Galatians 3:24** aloud.

- ➤ **Which two commandments do you think God says are the most important?** *(Accept any answer.)*
- ➤ Read **Matthew 22:36-40** aloud. **According to Jesus, what are the two great commandments?** *(Love the Lord with all your heart, soul, and mind; and love your neighbor as yourself.)*
- ➤ **Who is your neighbor?** *(everyone)*

God also gave specific laws about how the Israelites should live. There were laws about the Israelites' slaves, animals, land, crops, sacrifices, and marriages. These laws are not for us today though they teach us important principles. The Israelites sacrificed animals to show that they believed that Jesus Christ, God's Son, was coming to die for their sins. Jesus was the final and perfect sacrifice, which is why we do not need to sacrifice today. When Moses told the people what the Lord had said, they answered, "All the words which the Lord hath said will we do."

Then God gave laws dealing with the tabernacle and worshiping Him. He told the people exactly how they should make the tabernacle. He told them what kind of wood and metals to use, how to build the furniture, and where to put it in the tabernacle. God said who could enter the tabernacle, when and how they could enter, and what they should wear. God wanted His people to worship Him in the right way, and He gave them instructions on how to do it.

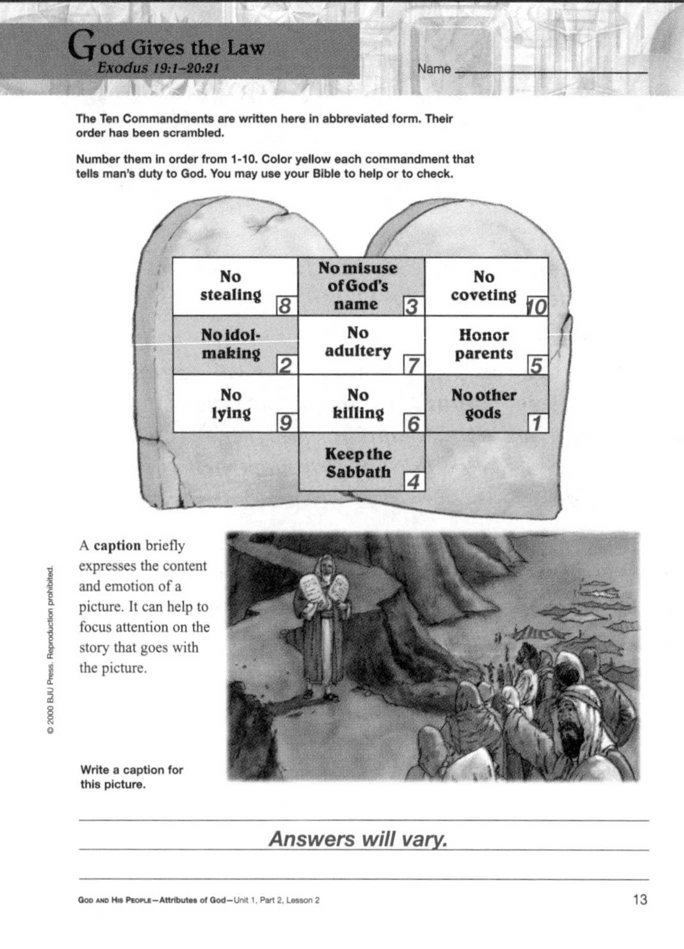
God Gives the Law
Exodus 19:1–20:21

Name ____________

The Ten Commandments are written here in abbreviated form. Their order has been scrambled.

Number them in order from 1-10. Color yellow each commandment that tells man's duty to God. You may use your Bible to help or to check.

No stealing 8	No misuse of God's name 3	No coveting 10
No idol-making 2	No adultery 7	Honor parents 5
No lying 9	No killing 6	No other gods 1
	Keep the Sabbath 4	

A **caption** briefly expresses the content and emotion of a picture. It can help to focus attention on the story that goes with the picture.

Write a caption for this picture.

Answers will vary.

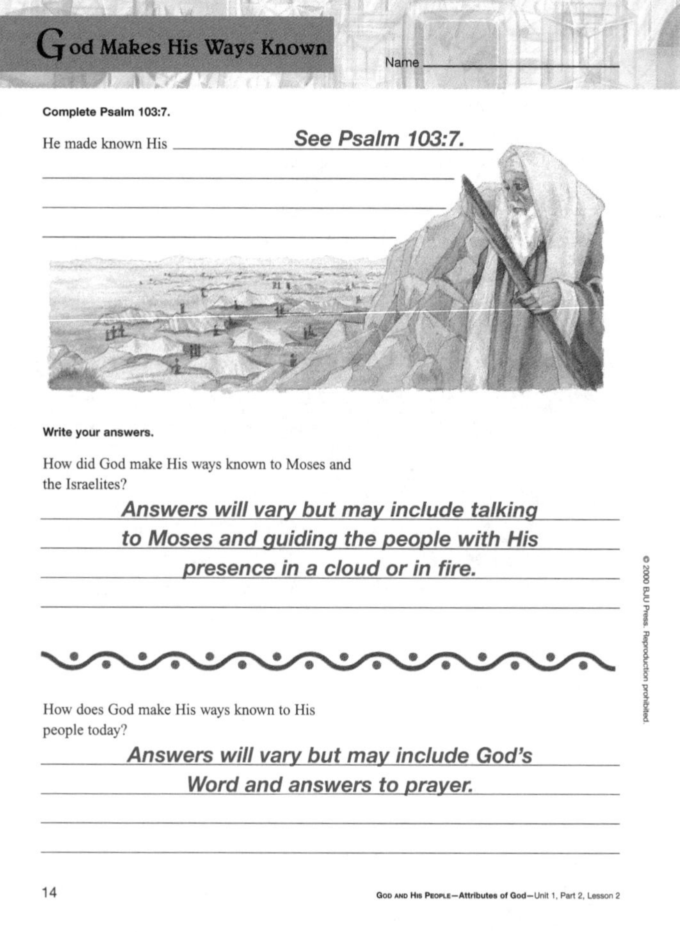
God Makes His Ways Known

Name ____________

Complete Psalm 103:7.

He made known His *See Psalm 103:7.*

Write your answers.

How did God make His ways known to Moses and the Israelites?

Answers will vary but may include talking to Moses and guiding the people with His presence in a cloud or in fire.

How does God make His ways known to His people today?

Answers will vary but may include God's Word and answers to prayer.

Worktext page 13

Sequence the Ten Commandments.

Memory Verse—Psalm 103:7

Practice the memory verse. Direct the students to locate **Psalm 103:7** and to read the verse silently. Divide the students into two groups. Direct Group 1 to read the first phrase and Group 2 to read the second phrase. Practice this way several times; then switch phrases.

One-on-One: Allow the student to read the first phrase and the teacher to read the second phrase. Practice this way several times; then switch phrases.

Worktext page 14

Develop an understanding of the memory verse.

Lesson 3

Materials

- Chart 30, "Roman Empire"
- Encyclopedia pictures of the seven wonders of the ancient world (optional) (*Note: The Seven Wonders of the World* by Ron Tagliapietra is available from Bob Jones University Press.)

Hymn: "I Sing the Mighty Power of God"

Teach the second verse (Worktext page 272). Play the recording of the second verse. Read the words aloud, pausing between lines to ask questions.

➤ **What kind of nourishment did God fill the earth with?** *(animals, plants, and water)*

➤ **When did God fill the earth with food?** *(at Creation)*

Explain that *the ground I tread* means anywhere that you walk. Guide a discussion about some of the places where you can walk and see God's creation. Sing verse 2 with the recording; then sing verses 1 and 2.

Memory Verse—Psalm 103:7

Practice the memory verse. Direct the students to locate **Psalm 103:6-7** and to read the verses silently. Write verse 7 on an erasable board and lead in reading it together. Erase a few words, directing the students to read the verse together again. Continue erasing words, reading the verse together each time until all the words have been erased and the students can say the verse from memory.

Introducing the Application Story

Review "More Than Words" (Part 1) on pages 13-14.

- ➤ **What was Bryan afraid of?** *(flying)*
- ➤ Dad reminded Bryan that God is omnipotent, omniscient, and omnipresent. **What do *omnipotent, omniscient,* and *omnipresent* mean?** *(all-powerful, all-knowing, and present everywhere)*

Explain that the following story is Part 2 of Bryan's story.

Application Story

Read the following story to the students.

More Than Words (Part 2)

Bryan jumped at the sound of the voice on the intercom. "Due to adverse weather conditions, we are forced to land. Flight attendants, please prepare for landing."

Bryan pushed up the plastic window shade. Fierce rain was hitting the side of the plane. "Dad, what's going on?" he asked.

"It's okay," said Dad. "The pilot wants to land the plane because it's gotten so awful outside."

Mom leaned forward from the chair behind Bryan. "Everything okay up there?"

"Just fine," said Dad. Bryan closed his eyes and prayed until the plane safely landed. Mom, Dad, and Bryan got off the plane and looked for a phone.

"What about our luggage?" asked Bryan.

"It left in a plane before our flight," said Mom.

They found a phone, and Dad called Uncle Don. "What about our stuff? What are we going to wear? How are we going to get to North Carolina?" Bryan questioned.

"Don't worry," said Mom. "We'll get to North Carolina—just not when we thought."

Dad hung up the phone. "Uncle Don already left for the airport. Aunt Joanne said that the weather is bad there too. She'll leave a message for him at the airport."

"But what about our stuff?" asked Bryan. "Our clothes, the presents, the toys? What are we going to eat? Are we going to sleep in the airport?"

Dad put his arm around Bryan's shoulder and motioned toward some empty seats. "Son," said Dad, "do you remember when you were scared in the plane?" Bryan nodded. "The same God that took care of us up there will take care of us now."

"As for food," said Mom, "we've never had to go without before. Do you remember in the Bible when Jesus fed more than five thousand people?" Bryan nodded.

"That was a long time ago," said Bryan.

"Here's a word for you," said Dad. "Immutable. It means changeless, always the same. Jesus calmed a storm, and God still has the same power over the weather. God who supplied needs in the Bible is the same God who will help us now. God is faithful to all believers, from the first people on earth to the last."

Bryan smiled and said, "And all of us people in between."

- ➤ **Why was Bryan upset?** *(The airplane landed because of the bad weather, and his family was stuck in an airport without their luggage.)*
- ➤ **What happened to the family's luggage?** *(It had been put on a different flight.)*
- ➤ **Where in the Bible does it tell about God's providing food for people?** *(Possible answers include Elijah's being fed by the ravens, the Israelites' being given manna and quail, and Jesus' feeding thousands of people.)*
- ➤ **Where in the Bible does it tell about God's controlling the weather?** *(Possible answers include the parting of the Red Sea, darkness at the crucifixion of Christ, and Jesus' calming of the storm.)*
- ➤ **What does the word *immutable* mean?** *(changeless; always the same)*

Guide a discussion of things about God that were true in the Bible for Adam and Eve and are still true now. (e.g., People sin; God forgives; Satan tempts.)

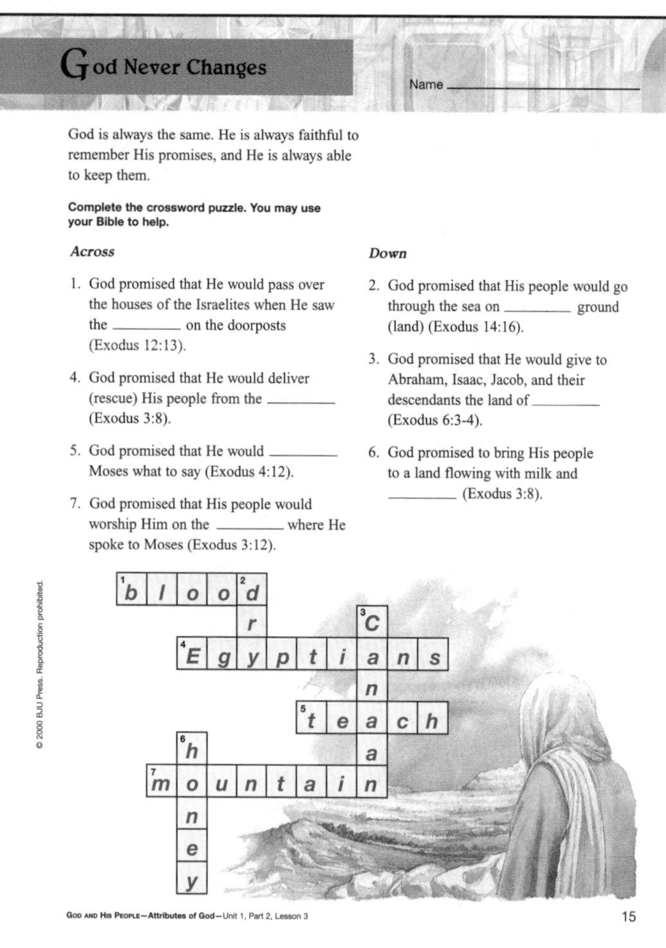

God Never Changes

Name ______________

God is always the same. He is always faithful to remember His promises, and He is always able to keep them.

Complete the crossword puzzle. You may use your Bible to help.

Across

1. God promised that He would pass over the houses of the Israelites when He saw the ________ on the doorposts (Exodus 12:13).
4. God promised that He would deliver (rescue) His people from the ________ (Exodus 3:8).
5. God promised that He would ________ Moses what to say (Exodus 4:12).
7. God promised that His people would worship Him on the ________ where He spoke to Moses (Exodus 3:12).

Down

2. God promised that His people would go through the sea on ________ ground (land) (Exodus 14:16).
3. God promised that He would give to Abraham, Isaac, Jacob, and their descendants the land of ________ (Exodus 6:3-4).
6. God promised to bring His people to a land flowing with milk and ________ (Exodus 3:8).

GOD AND HIS PEOPLE—Attributes of God—Unit 1, Part 2, Lesson 3 15

Worktext page 15

Review promises made by God.

Background Information

Egyptian Pyramids at Giza—*(2550 B.C.) Pyramids are tombs built for Egyptian pharaohs to show the glory of the kings who built them. The pharaoh's mummified body was placed in his pyramid after he died. The first and largest pyramid ever built is called the Great Pyramid and stands more than 450 feet high. It took more than one hundred thousand workers thirty years to complete the Great Pyramid since work was done only three months of each year, when the Nile flooded and no one could farm. Each of the two million blocks of limestone weighs about two and one-half tons. The Great Pyramid of Egypt is the only remaining wonder of the ancient world.*

The Hanging Gardens of Babylon—*(600 B.C.) This garden was a series of terraces connected by marble stairways about seventy-five feet above the area of the Euphrates River. Flowers, bushes, and fifty-foot-tall trees surrounded the twenty-two-foot-thick wall. Today only pieces of the wall remain.*

The Temple of Artemis at Ephesus—*(550 B.C.) This giant marble temple with a wooden roof was built for the Greek moon goddess, Artemis, twin sister of Apollo. It stood in Ephesus and had 106 columns, each measuring about fifty feet high. The temple was demolished, and only the foundation and a few statues remain today.*

The Statue of Zeus at Olympia—*(450 B.C.) This statue was built in Olympia, where the Olympic games began. The forty-foot statue portrayed Zeus, the king of the gods, sitting on his throne. This grand statue was of stone and wood with the robe and sandals of gold, the throne of jewels, and the king's flesh of ivory. A wreath of olive sprays crowned his head. In the king's right hand he held a statue of Nike, his messenger and the goddess of victory; in his left hand, a king's scepter with an eagle. The statue was destroyed.*

The Mausoleum at Halicarnassus—*(353 B.C.) As a sign of her love and dedication, the wife of the Persian ruler Mausolus had this marble tomb built. The tomb was over 130 feet high. The rectangular base of the tomb was brick covered with marble. On the base stood a temple with thirty-six columns, covered with a pyramid roof. The top of the mausoleum contained a chariot. Only pieces of the tomb remain today. The word* mausoleum *has come to mean "a tomb" because of its fame.*

The Colossus of Rhodes—*(280 B.C.) This bronze statue was built to honor the sun god, Helios, who stood with one arm raised. It took twelve years to complete the 120-foot statue. This statue is often compared to the Statue of Liberty, which stands 152 feet high. The Colossus was destroyed by an earthquake in 224 B.C. The word* colossal *has come to mean "giant" because of its fame.*

The Lighthouse at Alexandria—*(250 B.C.) This lighthouse, dedicated to Zeus, stood on the island of Pharos in Egypt. The lighthouse was of three tiers of marble, and stood over 450 feet high, making it the tallest structure of ancient times. Polished bronze mirrors served as reflectors so that the light could be seen from up to thirty-five miles away. The lighthouse was later destroyed by an earthquake. The word* pharos *has come to mean "lighthouse" because of its fame.*

History Connection (optional)

Discuss the seven wonders of the ancient world.

➤ **What is a wonder?** *(Answers will vary, but elicit that it is something fantastic.)*

Share the background information for each of the wonders as you point out their locations in Chart 30, "Roman Empire." Show pictures of these wonders (optional). (*Note:* Dates are approximate.)

Explain that these are wonders because they are magnificent examples of the work that man can do. All of these wonders have been worn down and in most cases destroyed over time. God's wonders, by contrast, are wonders because they are miracles that no man can make. God's wonders are everywhere and can never be destroyed outside of God's control.

➤ **What is the difference between wonders of man and wonders of God?** *(Man's wonders are destroyed while God's last forever; man could never do one of God's wonders.)*

Lesson 4

Materials

- Song: "Books of the Old Testament"
- Bible Book Cards: books of Moses, History

Song: "Books of the Old Testament"

Sing the first and second verses (Worktext page 287). Play the recording and lead in singing the first two verses together.

Bible Study Skills

Review the books of History. Distribute the books of History cards to eighteen students. Direct the students to arrange themselves in order at the front of the room. Say the books of History together several times; then say all the names of the Old Testament books.

Divide the students into three or four teams and tell them to line up as teams. Show a card (from the books of Moses or books of History) to the student at the front of each line. The student who first calls out the book that comes before the book shown receives a point for his team. Let each student in front go to the end of his line after his turn. (*Note:* When the card for Genesis is displayed, the game can be stopped and a winner determined, or students can call out "First Book.")

One-on-One: Give the student the books of History cards to sequence correctly. Then show a card (from the books of Moses or the books of History) for the student to identify the book that comes before.

Memory Verse—Psalm 103:7

Practice the memory verse. Locate **Psalm 103:7** and choose a volunteer to read it aloud. Give a closed Bible to a student, directing him to say the first word and to pass the Bible to another student to say the next word. Continue passing the Bible to a different student who will say the next word in the verse until each student has had a turn, and the verse has been said at least five times. Challenge the students to increase their speed each time they say the verse so that it sounds as if one person is saying the verse. Then say verses 6 and 7 from memory.

One-on-One: Say the verse responsively, passing a Bible back and forth between the student and teacher with each saying the next word in the verse. Continue until the verse has been repeated several times.

Background Information

Aaron—*Aaron, Moses' brother, was three years older than Moses. Their father was Amram the Levite, and their mother was Jochebed. Their sister, Miriam, was the oldest of the three children. God appointed Aaron spokesman for Moses in Egypt.*

Introducing the Bible Account

Define *idols.* Direct the students to locate the word *idol* in the glossary. Select a student to read the definition aloud. Explain that in the Old Testament, Egyptians worshiped many gods. They made statues and bowed down to them. When the Israelites lived in Egypt, they became familiar with how to make and use idols.

Bible Account

Read the following Bible account or read Exodus 32:1-34.

Who Is on the Lord's Side?

While Moses was receiving the law on the mountain, the Israelites became tired of waiting. Their impatience soon turned into sin. They demanded that Aaron make an idol for them.

When the Israelites left Egypt, the Egyptians had given them gold, silver, and jewels. God planned for them to use these items in building the tabernacle. Instead, the people gave gold to Aaron to make a statue of a calf. The people even broke off their gold earrings to help make the calf. When the idol was finished, Aaron said, "These be thy gods, O Israel, which brought thee up out of the land of Egypt."

God, who sees everything, knew what the Israelites were doing while He was giving Moses the law on the mountain. God was angry with the Israelites and told Moses what they were doing. God said that He would destroy all these wicked people. "I will make of thee a great nation," God told Moses. Moses had obeyed while the other Israelites had forgotten about God. God wanted to punish the wicked and reward the obedient.

Moses knew the people had sinned but asked God to be merciful. "Remember Abraham, Isaac, and Israel, thy servants," said Moses, "to whom thou swarest by thine own self, and saidst unto them, I will multiply your seed as the stars of heaven." God had promised Abraham that his descendants would become a great nation: the Israelites were that nation of people.

Moses came down from the mountain with the stone tablets of the law in his hands. These tablets "were the work of God, and the writing was the writing of God, graven upon the tables." When Moses saw the golden calf and the people dancing, he became angry. He threw the tablets to the ground and broke them. He took the golden calf and burned it with fire, ground the metal to dust, threw it into the water, and made the people drink it.

Then Moses said to Aaron, "What did this people unto thee, that thou hast brought so great a sin upon them?" Aaron told Moses that the people wanted to make gods, so they gave him their gold. Then Aaron said, "I cast it into the fire, and there came out this calf."

"Who is on the Lord's side?" Moses said to the people. "Let him come unto me." One group of people called the Levites came and stood with Moses. He commanded them to kill the idol worshipers in the camp. The Levites obeyed, and three thousand men died that day. Moses told the people, "Ye have sinned a great sin." He said that he would go to the Lord and ask Him to forgive their sin. The Lord showed mercy and forgiveness to the Israelites, but He did not take away the consequences of their sin. The Israelites were punished with plagues for their disobedience.

God had to write the Ten Commandments on stone tablets a second time. Moses made two stone tablets just like the first and brought them up to Mount Sinai. The Lord gave Moses the commandments and told him to write the words. After forty days and nights of fasting, Moses came down from the mountain with his face shining. He had to put a veil on his face because the holiness of God showed so plainly that his face was too bright to look upon.

➤ **Which commandments did the Israelites disobey by making and worshiping the golden calf?** *(1st—Worship no other god; 2nd—Make no idols.)*

➤ **How did God respond to the Israelites' sin?** *(He was angry.)*

➤ **What was the reaction of Moses when he saw what the Israelites were doing?** *(Moses was angry and threw down the stone tablets, and they broke.)*

➤ **What did Moses do with the calf?** *(He burned it, ground the metal into dust, threw it in the water, and made the people drink it.)*

➤ **What happened to people who did not turn away from their sin to God?** *(They were killed.)*

Guide a discussion about idolatry. Read **Psalm 115:4-9** to the students. If you discussed the seven wonders of the ancient world in the previous lesson, you may want to point out that the temple of Artemis, the statue of Zeus, and the lighthouse at Alexandria were structures dedicated to Greek gods and goddesses.

➤ **What is *idolatry?*** *(worshiping something besides God)*

Explain that it may sound strange to worship statues, but even some modern religions commit idolatry. Idolatry is not always about statues. An idol is anything in a Christian's life that he puts before God.

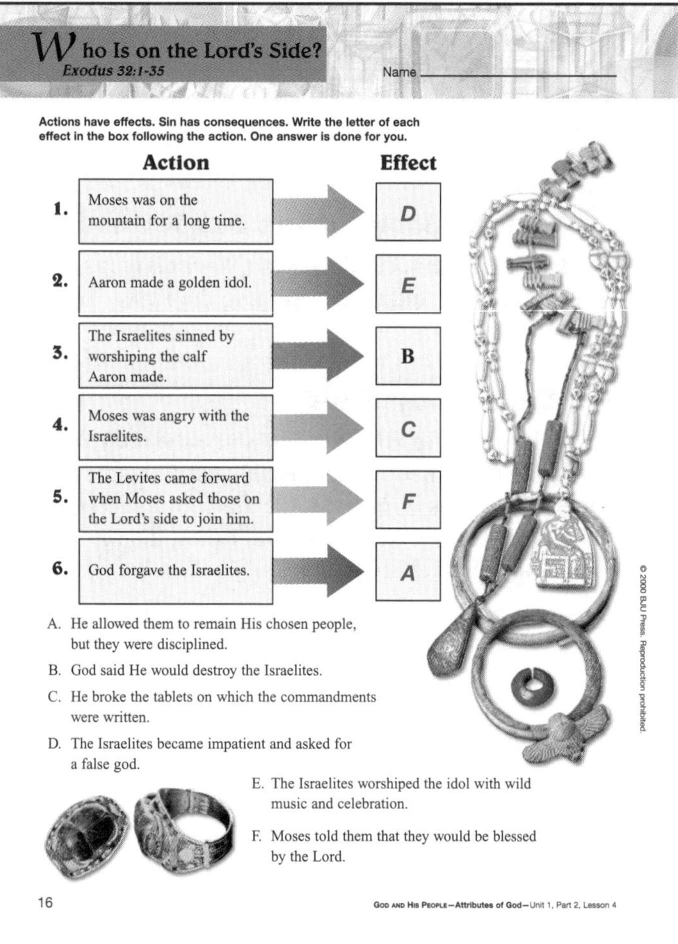

Who Is on the Lord's Side?
Exodus 32:1-35

Name ____________

Actions have effects. Sin has consequences. Write the letter of each effect in the box following the action. One answer is done for you.

	Action	Effect
1.	Moses was on the mountain for a long time.	D
2.	Aaron made a golden idol.	E
3.	The Israelites sinned by worshiping the calf Aaron made.	B
4.	Moses was angry with the Israelites.	C
5.	The Levites came forward when Moses asked those on the Lord's side to join him.	F
6.	God forgave the Israelites.	A

A. He allowed them to remain His chosen people, but they were disciplined.
B. God said He would destroy the Israelites.
C. He broke the tablets on which the commandments were written.
D. The Israelites became impatient and asked for a false god.
E. The Israelites worshiped the idol with wild music and celebration.
F. Moses told them that they would be blessed by the Lord.

16 God and His People—Attributes of God—Unit 1, Part 2, Lesson 4

➤ **What are some things that Christians could make more important than God in their lives?** *(Possible answers include any possession that might occupy their time, thoughts, and money so that they do not worship God as they should.)*

Worktext page 16

Identify cause and effect.

Going Beyond

Materials

- Various old magazines (enough for each student to have several pictures)
- Construction paper for each student

Enrichment

Illustrate God's wonders. Allow the students to cut out words or pictures from magazines that show God's wonders in nature. Tell them to glue their pictures, overlapping them with each other, onto construction paper. Challenge them to copy an appropriate verse onto their collages. Display the collages.

God Is Merciful, Loving

Preview

Doctrines

- God is merciful (Psalm 86:15)—Lesson 2
- God is love (John 3:16)—Lesson 3
- God has shown Himself in the Bible (John 5:39)—Lesson 4

Skills and Applications

- Learn Psalm 103:8-9
- Read a time line
- Read a map
- Use a glossary
- Recall facts and details
- Learn the books of Poetry
- Realize that God is merciful and loving
- Apply Bible knowledge to everyday life

Lesson 1

Materials

- A variety of gospel tracts
- Unit 1 Bookmark for each student
- Highlighter for each student (optional)

Hymn: "I Sing the Mighty Power of God"

Sing the first and second verses (Worktext page 272). Play the recording and lead in singing the first two verses.

Introducing the Application Story

Discuss gospel tracts. Show the students the tracts and call on students to share what they know about tracts. Discuss how and with whom a tract may be shared. Pass the tracts around the room and talk about their different audiences (age, gender, general, etc.).

Review the story. Call on students or review what has happened previously to Bryan in previous lessons (pages 13-14, 21).

Application Story

Read the following application story to your students.

More Than Words (Part 3)

The airport in Nashville, Tennessee, was packed with people. Bryan, Mom, and Dad waited in a long line in front of the checkout desk. Bryan could see that other people in line were angry. Some shouted into their cell phones as they stood in line; others talked to those around them about the forced landing due to terrible weather. The people in the front of the line complained to the workers at the desk, who also seemed frustrated.

At last Bryan and his parents reached the front. A man behind the counter gave them a tired smile as he looked at the tickets that Dad handed to him. "I'm afraid all the flights for this evening are canceled, sir. We can get you on a flight tomorrow morning at eight. Would you like reservations?"

"Do you have three seats near each other?"

"Yes, sir. Let me get your tickets." In a few minutes he handed Dad three tickets. "There you are, sir, and I'm sorry about the delay. Overnight kits are available at the office near the luggage claim if you'd like them."

Dad nodded. "Thank you, but does the airport provide rooms for the passengers at nearby hotels?" Dad asked.

"We normally do, but all the hotels we have agreements with are already filled this evening because of the weather."

"Okay, thanks." Bryan and his parents left the counter to pick up the overnight kits.

Bryan fidgeted while they stood in another line. "Dad, my feet hurt. And I'm tired—and hungry. Are we going to stay here? How are we going to take a shower? Where is Uncle Don?" Bryan asked.

"Settle down, Bryan. Remember how we talked about God's providing for all His people?"

"Sure I do," Bryan said.

"Well, then, we must believe that God will provide for us too. You're starting to sound like the Israelites who complained after all that God had done for them. Why don't you think about all the ways that God shows His love to you and say thank you?"

Bryan did so, and the line seemed to move much faster. At the front, a lady handed them three overnight kits. Bryan opened his as soon as he got it. Inside was a toothbrush, toothpaste, a comb, a washcloth, and a little zipper bag. Bryan tried to open the little bag, but Mom took the kit. "We also provide transportation to your hotel," the lady said to Dad.

"Well, we don't have a hotel to go to," said Dad. "The man at the counter said all the hotels are full."

The lady looked down at Bryan. "One moment," she said. She signaled another worker to take her place and used the phone behind the counter. Bryan moved to the other side of Mom so that he could hear the lady better.

"Hello, Joe," she said. "Can you put up three people in a room tonight? And give them some dinner and breakfast? Great, thanks. I'll send them over."

"Take the shuttle for Greycourt Inn. I have a friend who works there. He'll take care of you."

"Thank you so much," said Dad. "I'm sorry I have no money to give you," said Dad. "But I'd like to give you this." Dad handed the lady a tract from his wallet.

The lady smiled. "Thank you, sir. I'm a Christian too. I was saved a few years ago when a worker here told me about the Lord," she said. "But I will pass this on to someone else."

Dad thanked her again, and they walked to the shuttle. "Bryan, sometimes just your actions say something to other people about God. People can't see God, you know, but they can see His children. That's why you need to remember how wonderful God is to us. If you're thinking right about Him, you'll show it by the way you act. And you never know when you'll have an opportunity to tell someone about Him."

"Is that why you gave that lady the tract, Dad?" asked Bryan. Dad nodded. "So if she'd heard my complaining, she might not see how great God is."

God Is Merciful and Loving

Psalm 103:8-9

Name ____________________

God's mercy and love are shown in the Bible. What is another way these attributes of God may be seen?

Solve the puzzle to find out. Color the squares that have more than one letter. Write the letters that are left in order on the lines and divide them into words.

T	IA	H	CA	E	Y	HI	M	MS	NH	A
WA	Y	MT	KS	B	OK	ME	E	S	RI	MN
E	DC	MD	E	OR	N	I	N	T	MI	WA
AR	AL	H	DE	E	L	FL	GA	I	CN	MO
F	E	LA	NV	O	WV	VA	F	TN	MX	KY
A	IL	IN	C	TX	OK	H	NM	R	UK	AZ
CO	I	S	CT	VT	NJ	T	NY	UT	SA	WY
NE	I	ND	SD	WI	A	NC	PA	N	NZ	MA

THEY/MAY/BE/SEEN/IN/THE/LIFE/OF/A/CHRISTIAN

How has God shown His mercy and love to you today?

"Probably not," said Dad.

"From now on," said Bryan, "I want to show people how wonderful God is."

➤ **Why was the airline unable to put Bryan and his parents in a hotel?** *(All the hotels were full.)*

➤ **Why did Dad compare Bryan to the Israelites?** *(He complained even though God was good to him.)*

➤ **How did Bryan and his parents get a hotel?** *(A lady handing out overnight kits called someone that she knew and was able to get them a room.)*

➤ **What did Bryan's dad give to the lady?** *(a tract)*

➤ **Why do you think that he gave her the tract?** *(to tell her about God and His plan of salvation)*

Memory Verses—Psalm 103:8-9

Principle: God is merciful. Locate **Psalm 103:8-9** and read the verses aloud as the students read silently. Tell the students to use the glossary to find the definition for *grace.* Select a student to read the definition aloud. Explain that God gives us grace by blessing us with good things as well as by holding back punishment.

➤ **How did God show mercy to Bryan and his family?** *(Elicit that God shows mercy to all saved people by not sending them to hell.)*

- ➤ **How did God show grace to Bryan and his family?** *(He kept them safe in the plane; He gave them food and a place to sleep that night.)*
- ➤ **When did Dad have to scold Bryan?** *(when Bryan was scared in the plane and did not trust God, when the family's things were gone and they were stuck in the airport, and when they had to wait in lines)*

Direct the students to highlight the verses in their Bibles (optional) and to mark the location with the Unit 1 Bookmark.

Worktext page 17

Develop an understanding of the memory verses.

Lesson 2

Materials

- Chart 29, "Journey to the Promised Land"
- TimeLine and picture: *Joshua and the Spies*

Make a memory-verse visual by cutting six large circles out of purple construction paper for grapes. Write the words of **Psalm 103:8-9** on the circles, putting each attribute of God on a different circle. Make a long stick by cutting strips of brown construction paper and connecting them. Write the reference *Psalm 103:8-9* on the stick. Attach the stick to the wall, leaving room for the grapes below it.

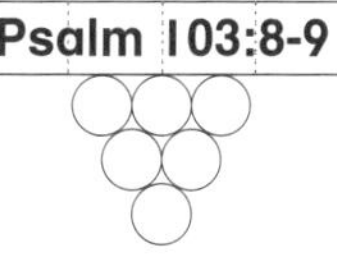

Hymn: "I Sing the Mighty Power of God"

Sing the first two verses (Worktext page 272). Divide the students into four groups and assign each group one of the four lines. Direct them to sing verses 1 and 2 by singing their assigned lines.

Memory Verses—Psalm 103:8-9

Practice the memory verses. Direct the students to locate **Psalm 103:8-9** and read the verses silently. Show the students the verse visual and explain that they are about to hear a story about men who found an extraordinarily large cluster of grapes. Display the six grapes together in random order. Read the verses and allow a student to choose the first attribute mentioned in the memory verses. Attach that grape to the stick on the wall. Repeat until all of the grapes are on the wall. Then read **Psalm 103:6-9** together.

Background Information

Canaan—*This land was also called the Promised Land and the land flowing with milk and honey—an expression used to show that the land was beautiful and overflowing with good things. God promised this land to Abraham as a place for his many descendants.*

Introducing the Bible Account

Share the background information. Explain that milk and honey were not actually flowing in the streams in Canaan.

Bible Account

Read the following Bible account or retell Numbers 13:1–14:45 in your own words. As you read the Bible account, use Chart 29, "Journey to the Promised Land," to point out the locations of the italicized places.

The Twelve Spies

God told Moses to send a man from each of the twelve tribes into the land of Canaan to see what was there. Moses told the men to find out whether the people in Canaan were strong or weak, were few or many, and lived in cities or tents. Moses also wanted to know whether the land was good or bad and whether there were trees for wood. Since it was the time of the year for the first of the grapes to ripen, Moses told them to also bring back some fruit of the land.

So the spies went up, and searched for forty days from the *Wilderness of Zin* to *Rehob,* and to *Hebron.* When they came to the *valley of Eshcol,* they found huge clusters of grapes. They cut down one cluster and needed two men to carry it between them on a stick because it was so heavy.

When the spies returned to the Israelites, they showed the huge fruit from the land and said that it was a land flowing with milk and honey, just as the Lord had said. Then they told about the people: "The Amalekites dwell in the land of the south: and the Hittites, and the Jebusites, and the Amorites, dwell in the mountains: and the Canaanites dwell by the sea, and by the coast of Jordan." Most of the spies decided that these men were too strong for them to conquer. They thought they would be like grasshoppers trying to fight giants. The cities that they lived in were surrounded by great walls. Both these things would make it difficult for the Israelites to conquer or occupy the land that God promised to them.

Only two of the twelve spies had a good report to give: Joshua and Caleb. "Let us go up at once, and possess it; for we are well able to overcome it," said Caleb. The children of Israel had a choice to make; they could believe the bad report or the good report.

Even though God had promised to give them the land, the Israelites doubted. They cried all night and complained to Moses that they were now trapped in the wilderness.

They wished that they had never left Egypt. They wanted to choose a new leader and return to Egypt. Joshua and Caleb tried to encourage the people. They had seen the land and knew how good it was. "The Lord is with us," they said, but the people rebelled.

God was angry. The children of Israel were sinning again. God told Moses the same thing He had said when the Israelites committed idolatry—that He would destroy them and raise up a nation greater and mightier than the Israelites. Moses again asked God to forgive the people.

"The Lord is longsuffering," said Moses, "and of great mercy, forgiving iniquity and transgression, and by no means clearing the guilty. . . . Pardon . . . the iniquity of this people."

God said that He would pardon the people. From the time they had left Egypt, the Israelites had sinned against God many times. Since the Israelites were afraid and did not trust God to be with them, God said that they would not have the good land.

Joshua and Caleb, the two faithful men, would enter the land and enjoy it. The rest of the Israelites would wander in the wilderness for forty years—one year for each day the spies explored the land. Everyone over the age of twenty would die and never live in Canaan.

Moses told the Israelites what God said, and they were sad. "We . . . will go up unto the place which the Lord hath promised; for we have sinned." Finally they agreed to do as God had commanded, but it was too late. God would not give them the land at this time. The Amalekites and Canaanites came down and fought the Israelites and chased them into Hormah. Then the Israelites' forty years of wandering as punishment began.

➤ **What good things and what frightening things did the spies find in the land?** *(food and beautiful land; giants and tall city walls)*

➤ **What report did the spies give?** *(Joshua and Caleb gave a good report that the Israelites should go and possess the land; the other ten spies gave a bad report that they would not be able to possess the land.)*

➤ **How did God show mercy to the Israelites?** *(He did not destroy them for their rebellion.)*

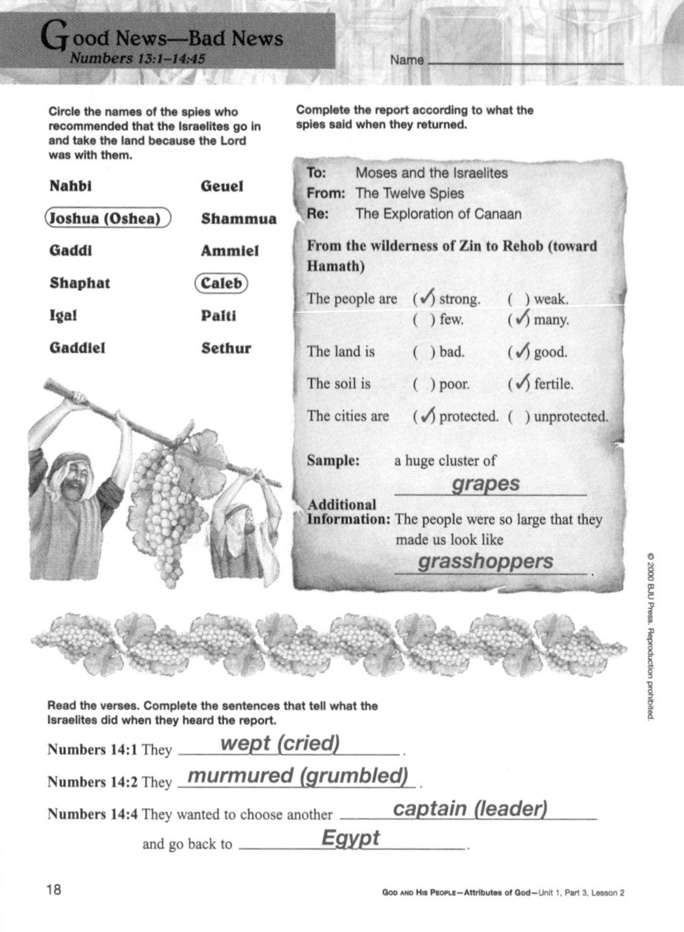

Good News—Bad News
Numbers 13:1–14:45

Name ____________

Circle the names of the spies who recommended that the Israelites go in and take the land because the Lord was with them.

Nahbi	Geuel
(Joshua (Oshea))	Shammua
Gaddi	Ammiel
Shaphat	(Caleb)
Igal	Palti
Gaddiel	Sethur

Complete the report according to what the spies said when they returned.

To: Moses and the Israelites
From: The Twelve Spies
Re: The Exploration of Canaan

From the wilderness of Zin to Rehob (toward Hamath)

The people are (✓) strong. ( ) weak. ( ) few. (✓) many.
The land is ( ) bad. (✓) good.
The soil is ( ) poor. (✓) fertile.
The cities are (✓) protected. ( ) unprotected.

Sample: a huge cluster of *grapes*

Additional Information: The people were so large that they made us look like *grasshoppers*.

Read the verses. Complete the sentences that tell what the Israelites did when they heard the report.

Numbers 14:1 They *wept (cried)*.
Numbers 14:2 They *murmured (grumbled)*.
Numbers 14:4 They wanted to choose another *captain (leader)* and go back to *Egypt*.

18 God and His People—Attributes of God—Unit 1, Part 3, Lesson 2

➤ **Why did the Lord decide the Israelites would wander for forty years?** *(He gave a year of wandering to represent each day that the spies had explored the land.)*

➤ **How did the people respond when Moses told them about their punishment?** *(First they were sad; then they decided to enter the Promised Land of Canaan in their own strength.)*

➤ **Why were the Israelites unable to win the land?** *(They tried to do it without the Lord's help.)*

➤ **How can we accomplish difficult things?** *(with the Lord's strength and in His strength)*

TimeLine

Place *Joshua and the Spies* onto the TimeLine. Call on a student to place the picture of *Joshua and the Spies* on the TimeLine at 1446 B.C. Point out that Moses was about eighty years old at this time. Guide each student in gluing the picture onto his TimeLine.

Worktext page 18

Recall facts about the Bible account.

Lesson 3

Materials

- Chart 8, "The Bronze Serpent"
- Copy of Supplement page S68 "Shape and Tell" on brown construction paper
- Three metal brads

Hymn: "I Sing the Mighty Power of God"

Sing the first two verses (Worktext page 272).

➤ **Which of God's attributes do we sing about in verse 1?** *(His power—omnipotence—and His wisdom—omniscience)*

➤ **Which attribute of God do we sing about in verse 2?** *(His goodness)*

Encourage the students to thank God for His continual power, wisdom, and goodness. Sing verses 1 and 2 together.

Hymn History Story: "I Sing the Mighty Power of God"

Read the following information about Isaac Watts.

Isaac Watts was a genius in psychology, logic, and theology and is known today as the father of English hymnody. Although Watts wrote many hymns, he did not consider himself a poet. He said of his hymn writing: "My design was not to exalt myself to the rank and glory of poets, but I was ambitious to be a servant to the churches, and a helper to the joy of the meanest Christian."

Isaac Watts wrote most of his hymns as an invalid in the home of his friend, Sir Thomas Abney. Watt's health was poor for most of his life, but his mind was healthy and active. He wrote not only hymns but essays, sermons, textbooks, catechisms, and scholarly papers on a number of different subjects.

His love for children prompted him to write a hymnal especially for them. *Divine Songs for Children* was published in 1715, and one of the hymns that appeared in it was "I Sing the Mighty Power of God."

Background Information

Brass—*When we read of* brass *in the Old Testament, it almost always refers to* bronze, *an alloy of copper and tin. Sometimes it refers to copper alone. Modern brass, an alloy of copper and zinc, was unknown in Bible times.*

Bible Account

Read the following Bible account or read Numbers 21:4-9. Use the visual from Supplement page S68, "Shape and Tell," to make an "M" when you talk about Moses, a serpent when you refer to it, and then a cross when talking about it

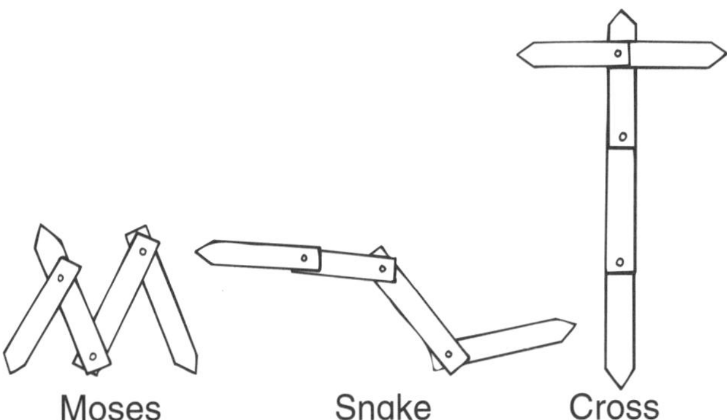

The Bronze Serpent

Even after the Israelites were forced to wander in the wilderness, they continued to sin against God. The people complained to Moses about life in the desert. "Wherefore have ye brought us up out of Egypt to die in the wilderness?" they asked Moses, "for there is no bread, neither is there any water."

As a punishment, God sent fiery serpents into the camp to destroy the complainers. Every person that a serpent bit would die. The Israelites knew that they had sinned and asked Moses to pray to the Lord that He would take the serpents away. "We have sinned," they said to Moses, "for we have spoken against the Lord, and against thee; pray unto the Lord, that he take away the serpents from us."

Moses prayed for the people. God told Moses to make a serpent of brass and to set it on a pole so that anyone who was bitten could look up at it and be saved from death.

➤ **Why were the Israelites complaining?** *(They wanted food and water.)*

➤ **How do we know that the Israelites would not have gone hungry or thirsty in the wilderness?** *(God had promised them that He would take care of their needs.)*

➤ **What would happen to the people who were bitten by the serpents?** *(They would die.)*

➤ **What did God tell Moses to do?** *(make a serpent and put it on a pole)*

➤ **Why was making a serpent not breaking the second commandment if making a golden calf was?** *(Accept any answer, but point out that the Israelites were not to worship the serpent, but to look at it in faith and to realize their sin against God.)*

➤ **What does Moses' brass serpent picture for us?** *(The serpent was a symbol of sin. When Christ died on the cross, He was made sin for us and took the punishment we deserved.)*

The Bronze Serpent

Numbers 21:4-9

Moses' making of the bronze serpent did not break the commandment against making images to worship. The Israelites did not worship it but instead looked to it as a sign of faith and repentance. It pointed ahead to the Savior who would be lifted up on a cross to offer eternal life to sinful mankind (John 3:14-15).

Symptoms of the viper's bite:

- Fiery pain at the site
- Swelling and discoloration (from white to red to purple to dark blue) at the site
- Nausea and vomiting
- Stomach cramps
- Bleeding from the nose, mouth, and eyes

Quick death from a viper's bite is rare. The victim usually weakens gradually from internal bleeding over a period of one or two days.

It is commonly held that the serpents in this account are *sand vipers*, usually called *carpet vipers* or *saw-scaled vipers*. Like most vipers, this viper has a thick body and a rather short tail. At maturity it is approximately two feet long. It is native to Middle Eastern deserts, where it lies hidden in the sand unless it is hungry or disturbed. Its venom is injected from a pair of hollow fangs in the upper jaw.

GOD AND HIS PEOPLE—Attributes of God—Unit 1, Part 3, Lesson 3 19

InfoScene: "The Bronze Serpent"

Display Chart 8 for reference throughout this unit. Review and discuss the Bible account as time permits.

Worktext page 19

Discuss the bronze serpent. Direct the students to look at Worktext page 19 as you read **John 3:14-15** aloud. Explain that when Jesus was telling Nicodemus how to be born again, He said that what happened to the Israelites was a picture of salvation. Christ took our judgment for sin when He died on the cross. Just as the Israelites could be saved from physical death by looking at the serpent, we can be saved from spiritual death (separation from God in hell) by looking to the cross. Read and discuss Worktext page 19 together.

Memory Verses—Psalm 103:8-9

Practice the memory verses. Direct the students to read **Psalm 103:8-9** silently, then to close their Bibles to quietly say the verses to themselves, and then to reread the verses as a check.

➤ **What are some ways that we can show a person we love him?** *(Answers will vary.)*

➤ **How did God show that He loved us?** *(He sent His Son to die for us.)*

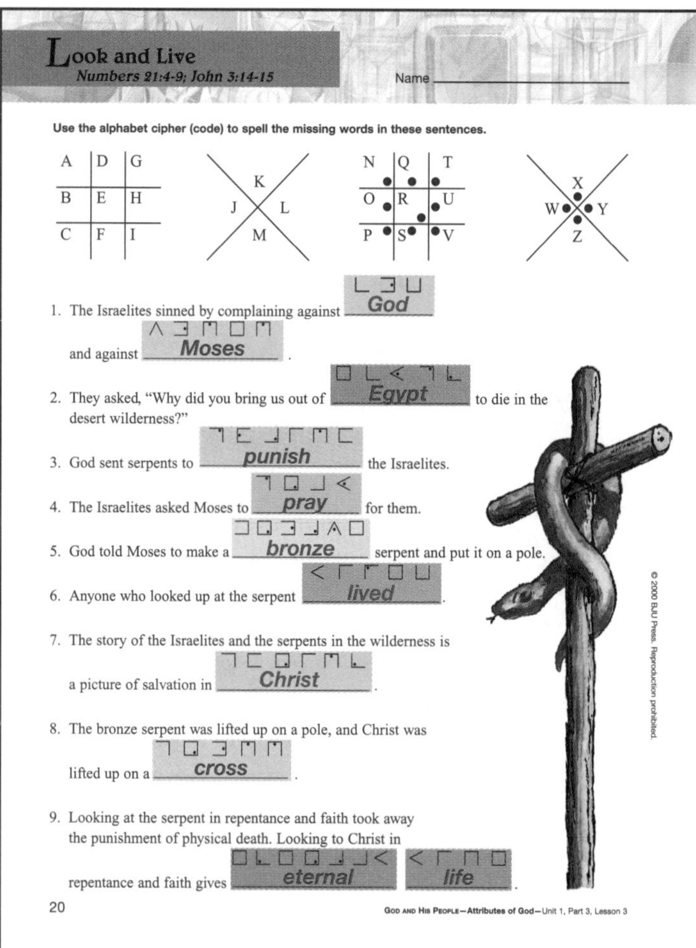

Look and Live

Numbers 21:4-9; John 3:14-15

Name ____________

Use the alphabet cipher (code) to spell the missing words in these sentences.

1. The Israelites sinned by complaining against **God** and against **Moses**.
2. They asked, "Why did you bring us out of **Egypt** to die in the desert wilderness?"
3. God sent serpents to **punish** the Israelites.
4. The Israelites asked Moses to **pray** for them.
5. God told Moses to make a **bronze** serpent and put it on a pole.
6. Anyone who looked up at the serpent **lived**.
7. The story of the Israelites and the serpents in the wilderness is a picture of salvation in **Christ**.
8. The bronze serpent was lifted up on a pole, and Christ was lifted up on a **cross**.
9. Looking at the serpent in repentance and faith took away the punishment of physical death. Looking to Christ in repentance and faith gives **eternal** **life**.

20 GOD AND HIS PEOPLE—Attributes of God—Unit 1, Part 3, Lesson 3

If students are unsure, read **John 3:16** aloud to them. Draw a cross shape throughout the day to practice saying Psalm 103:6-9 together.

Worktext page 20

Recall details about the Israelites and the bronze serpent.

Lesson 4

Materials

- Song: "Books of the Old Testament"
- Verse visual from Unit 1, Part 3, Lesson 2
- Bible Book Cards: books of Moses, History, Poetry

Memory Verses—Psalm 103:8-9

Practice the memory verses. Display the six grapes in verse order. Read the verses; then remove a grape. Continue the procedure until the students are saying the verses from memory.

God's Mercy and Love
Psalm 103:8-9

Name ______________

Fill in the missing words from Psalm 103:8-9. You may use your Bible to help.

See Psalm 103:8-9 for answers.

The Lord is ______________ and gracious,

slow to anger, and ______________ in

______________.

He will not always ______________:

______________ will He ______________ His anger for ever.

The Israelites were shown God's love and mercy again and again. How did God show His mercy and love to them? ______________

Circle these reminders of those times in the picture below.

Sword, Golden Calf, Tablets of the Law, Frog, Lamb, Serpent, Chariot, Grapes

Worktext page 21

Develop an understanding of the memory verses.

Bible Account

Read the following Bible account or read Numbers 21:21-35. Direct the students to look at the map on Worktext page 22 as they listen to the account.

King Sihon and King Og

As Israel wandered through the wilderness for the next forty years, they had to travel across lands where people already were living. When they came to the land of the Amorites, Moses sent messengers to their king, Sihon.

The messengers said, "Let me pass through thy land: we will not turn into the fields, or into the vineyards; we will not drink of the waters of the well." The Israelites wanted to pass through the area without stopping.

King Sihon would not let the Israelites pass his land. He gathered all his people together and went out to fight the Israelites in the desert. They met at *Jahaz*, where the Amorites tried to defeat God's people. The Israelites took over King Sihon's cities and drove out the Amorites who lived there.

The Israelites continued through the wilderness toward Bashan. Og, king of Bashan, along with his armies, met the Israelites at *Edrei* for battle. God said to Moses, "Fear him not: for I have delivered him into thy hand, and all his people, and his land; and thou shalt do to him as thou didst unto Sihon king of the Amorites."

The Israelites killed King Og, his sons, and all his people. They took over his land of Bashan, just as the Lord had promised. God made the Israelites wander in the wilderness as a punishment for disobedience, but He did not let them be destroyed. God had promised that they would reach the Promised Land of Canaan.

- **When would the Israelites be given the Promised Land?** *(after their punishment for doubting God was over—wandering in the wilderness for forty years.)*
- **What did Moses ask Sihon, the king of the Amorites?** *(for permission to cross his land)*
- **Why did the Israelites battle King Sihon and the Amorites?** *(He would not allow the Israelites to cross his land, and he took his people out to battle the Israelites.)*
- **Whom else did the Israelites defeat besides King Sihon?** *(King Og, his sons, and the people of Bashan)*
- **Who told Moses that the Israelites would win the battle against King Og?** *(God)*
- **How did God show His mercy and love for the Israelites in these two situations?** *(Answers will vary.)*

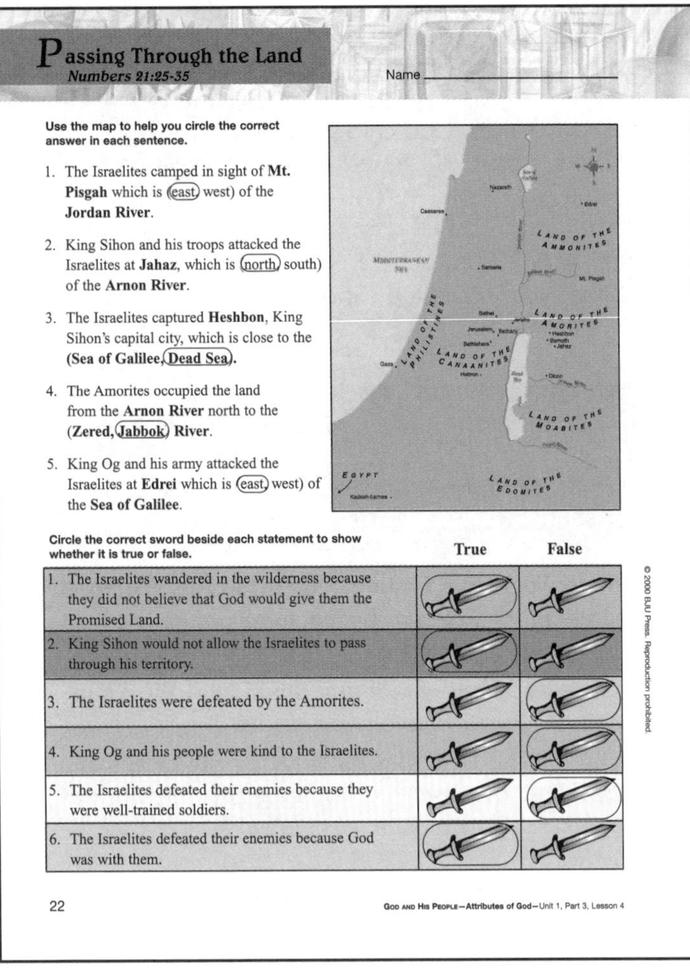

Passing Through the Land
Numbers 21:25-35

Name ____________________

Use the map to help you circle the correct answer in each sentence.

1. The Israelites camped in sight of **Mt. Pisgah** which is (east, west) of the **Jordan River**.
2. King Sihon and his troops attacked the Israelites at **Jahaz**, which is (north, south) of the **Arnon River**.
3. The Israelites captured **Heshbon**, King Sihon's capital city, which is close to the **(Sea of Galilee, Dead Sea)**.
4. The Amorites occupied the land from the **Arnon River** north to the **(Zered, Jabbok) River**.
5. King Og and his army attacked the Israelites at **Edrei** which is (east, west) of the **Sea of Galilee**.

Circle the correct sword beside each statement to show whether it is true or false.

	True	False
1. The Israelites wandered in the wilderness because they did not believe that God would give them the Promised Land.		
2. King Sihon would not allow the Israelites to pass through his territory.		
3. The Israelites were defeated by the Amorites.		
4. King Og and his people were kind to the Israelites.		
5. The Israelites defeated their enemies because they were well-trained soldiers.		
6. The Israelites defeated their enemies because God was with them.		

22 GOD AND HIS PEOPLE—Attributes of God—Unit 1, Part 3, Lesson 4

Worktext page 22

Read a map and recall facts about the Bible account.

Song: "Books of the Old Testament"

Sing the first three verses (Worktext page 287). Play the recording, singing together verses 1, 2, and 3.

Bible Study Skills

Review the books of Poetry. Distribute the cards to four students, directing them to arrange themselves in the correct order at the front of the room. Lead in saying together the books of Poetry several times; then say all of the names of the Old Testament books. Mix up the cards for the first three divisions. Display a flash card one at a time and allow the students to tell the division the card is in. If time allows, review the flash cards again and allow the students to tell the book that follows the one named by the card.

One-on-One: Give the student the books of Poetry cards to sequence correctly. Then mix up all of the division cards and have the student sequence them all, or show a card, having the student identify in which division it belongs.

Going Beyond

Materials

- Copy of Supplement page S68, "Shape and Tell," on brown construction paper for each student
- Three metal brads for each student

Enrichment

Retell a Bible account. Guide the students in making a story visual, using Supplement page S68, "Shape and Tell," to retell a Bible account. (*Note:* The students may want to practice with each other before retelling the Bible account to a young child.)

God Is Sovereign

Unit 1, Part 4

Preview

Doctrines

- God created man for His glory (Isaiah 43:7)—Lesson 1
- Man turns to God through repentance and faith (conversion) (Ephesians 3:17)—Lesson 2

Skills and Applications

- Learn Psalm 103:10
- Learn the books of the Major Prophets
- Identify the main idea
- Identify supporting details
- Recall facts and details
- Write a letter
- Realize God's mercy saves believers from everlasting punishment
- Realize that God is sovereign
- Apply Bible knowledge to everyday life

Lesson 1

Materials

- Chart 29, "Journey to the Promised Land"
- Unit 1 Bookmark for each student
- Highlighter for each student (optional)

Hymn: "I Sing the Mighty Power of God"

Teach the third verse (Worktext page 272). Play the recording of the third verse; then read the verse aloud. Explain that *glories* refers to praise and honor that all God's creation gives to Him and *tempests* means "windstorms."

➤ **Who can give life to flowers and plants?** *(only God)*

➤ **Who sits on a throne?** *(Possible answers include a king, queen, or monarch.)*

➤ **What do all these people have in common?** *(They are all rulers over something.)*

➤ **What does God rule over?** *(everything)*

Explain that because God is sovereign, He has complete rule over all. He rules over us and takes care of us. Allow students to share times when God takes care of us. Lead in singing verse 3 together; then sing all three verses.

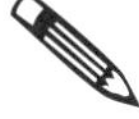

Worktext page 23

Singing with understanding, verse 3.

Bible Account

Read the following Bible account or retell Numbers 22:1–24:25 in your own words. Display Chart 29, "Journey to the Promised Land," to show the location of the Plains of Moab.

Balaam

The Israelites won the battles against all enemies who attacked them on their way to the Promised Land. Balak, ruler of the Moabites, saw what Israel had done to other kings like Sihon and Og. Balak was afraid that the same thing would happen to him and his people, so he sent a group of princes to a man named Balaam.

Balaam was a sorcerer, but he had some knowledge of God. Balak thought Balaam had the power to curse the Israelites. Balak sent messengers to Balaam to ask him to come and to put a curse on the Israelites.

Balaam told the messengers to stay the night and that he would give them an answer in the morning. That night, God came to Balaam and told him not to curse the people because they were special to the Lord.

The next morning, Balaam told the messengers that the Lord did not want him to go with them. Balak sent another group of princes, more honorable than the first group, to offer Balaam rewards if he would come and curse the Israelites.

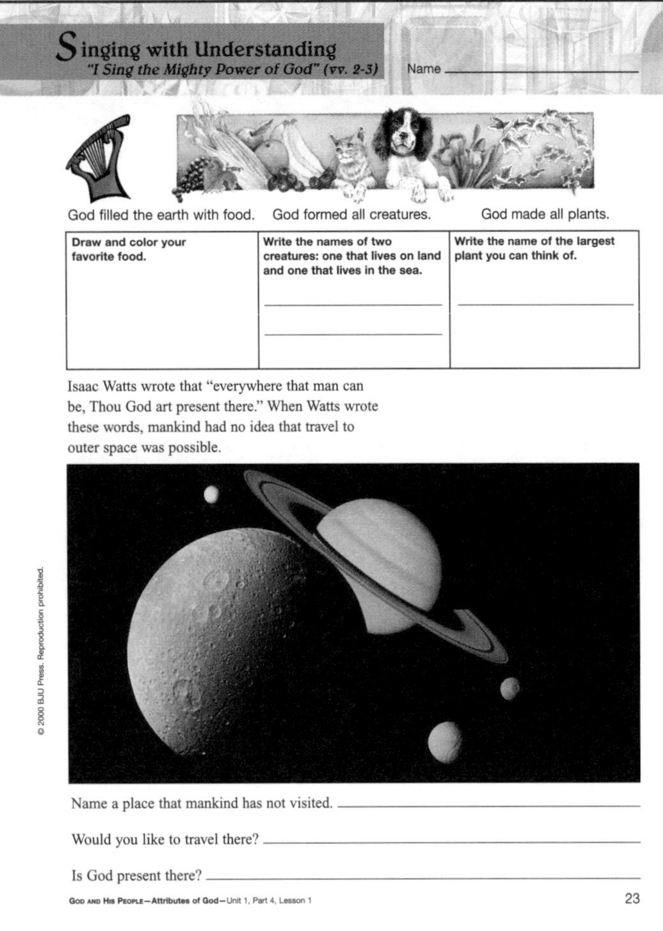

Singing with Understanding
"I Sing the Mighty Power of God" (vv. 2-3)

Name ____________

God filled the earth with food. God formed all creatures. God made all plants.

Draw and color your favorite food.	Write the names of two creatures: one that lives on land and one that lives in the sea.	Write the name of the largest plant you can think of.
	____________ ____________	____________

Isaac Watts wrote that "everywhere that man can be, Thou God art present there." When Watts wrote these words, mankind had no idea that travel to outer space was possible.

Name a place that mankind has not visited. ____________

Would you like to travel there? ____________

Is God present there? ____________

GOD AND HIS PEOPLE—Attributes of God—Unit 1, Part 4, Lesson 1 23

Balaam again asked the princes to spend the night to see what the Lord would say to him. God told Balaam that he could go, but only if he did what God told him to do.

The next morning, Balaam and his two servants went with Balak's princes of Moab. As Balaam was riding his donkey, the angel of the Lord stood in the road, holding a sword high in the air. Balaam did not see the angel, but the donkey did and tried to turn off the road.

Balaam hit the donkey and made her go straight again. As they went down the road, they came to a narrow place with walls on either side of them. The angel of the Lord was standing in the road with His sword. Again, Balaam did not see the angel, but the donkey did. When the donkey tried to turn, she crushed Balaam's foot against the wall. Balaam hit the donkey again and made her go straight.

The road became even more narrow. The angel of the Lord appeared a third time. The donkey, having no place to turn, fell down under Balaam. Balaam hit the donkey with his staff.

Then the Lord opened the mouth of the donkey, and she turned to Balaam and said, "What have I done unto thee, that thou hast smitten me these three times?" The Lord opened Balaam's eyes, and he saw the reason the donkey had kept stopping. Balaam saw the angel of the Lord in the way with His sword held high. Balaam bowed his head and fell flat on his face. "I have sinned," he said, "for I knew not that thou stoodest in the way against me." Balaam said that he would turn around and go back.

The angel of the Lord told Balaam to go with the men, and God would give him words to say when he arrived in Moab. Balaam obeyed God.

God told Balaam to build seven altars and to prepare seven oxen and seven rams for a sacrifice. Balak was then ready for Balaam to curse Israel, but Balaam instead blessed Israel. "How shall I curse whom God hath not cursed?" asked Balaam. But Balak did not give up. Twice more he took Balaam to another place, had seven altars built, prepared the oxen and rams for sacrifice, and asked him to curse Israel. And twice more Balaam blessed God's chosen people. Balak then told Balaam to go home. "I thought to promote thee unto great honour," he said, "but . . . the Lord hath kept thee back from honour."

Before Balaam left, he had one more message for Balak. Balaam spoke the words that the Lord had given him about the future. Israel, he said, would destroy Balak and his people, the Moabites. Then Balaam foretold the coming Messiah, Jesus Christ. Afterwards, he went on his way home.

- **Why was Balak, ruler over the Moabites, afraid of the Israelites?** *(because they had beaten the nations of King Sihon and King Og in battle)*
- **Why did Balak go to Balaam for help?** *(Balak believed Balaam had the power to curse Israel.)*
- **How did the Lord get Balaam's attention?** *(The angel of the Lord stood in the road, and the donkey talked to Balaam.)*
- **How many times did Balaam ask God if he should curse the Israelites?** *(twice)*
- **Why was it unnecessary for Balaam to ask the second time?** *(God would not change His mind about having an evil curse put on His chosen people.)*
- **Why did Balaam speak the words of the Lord?** *(Answers may vary.)*

Point out that God showed power and sovereignty over natural things (e.g., making the donkey speak), over someone who did not fully acknowledge Him (e.g., making Balaam bless Israel), and over other nations (e.g., defeating Bashan and Moab).

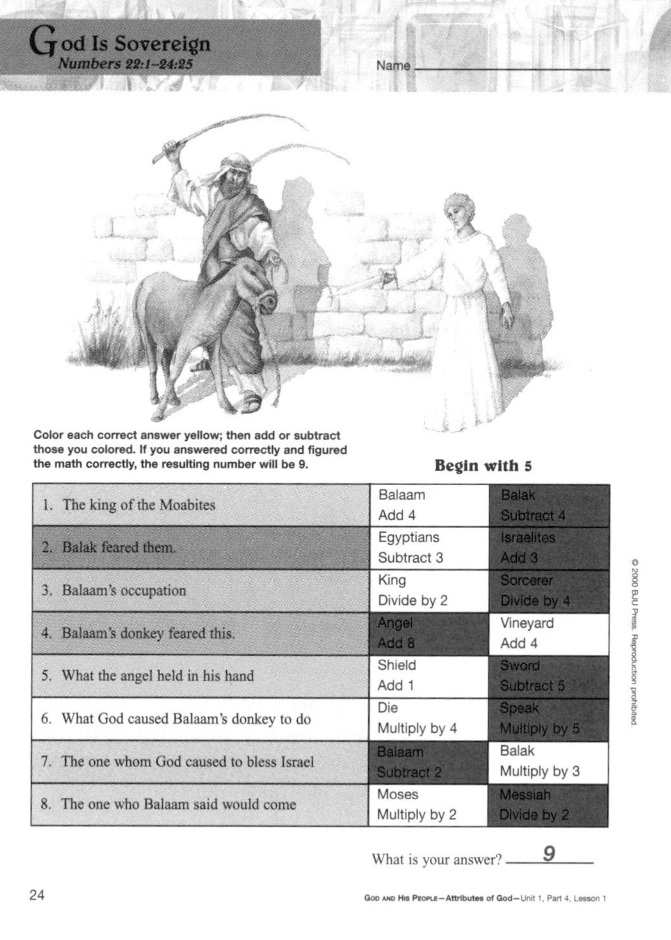

God Is Sovereign
Numbers 22:1–24:25

Name ____________________

Color each correct answer yellow; then add or subtract those you colored. If you answered correctly and figured the math correctly, the resulting number will be 9.

Begin with 5

1. The king of the Moabites	Balaam Add 4	Balak Subtract 4
2. Balak feared them.	Egyptians Subtract 3	Israelites Add 3
3. Balaam's occupation	King Divide by 2	Sorcerer Divide by 4
4. Balaam's donkey feared this.	Angel Add 8	Vineyard Add 4
5. What the angel held in his hand	Shield Add 1	Sword Subtract 5
6. What God caused Balaam's donkey to do	Die Multiply by 4	Speak Multiply by 5
7. The one whom God caused to bless Israel	Balaam Subtract 2	Balak Multiply by 3
8. The one who Balaam said would come	Moses Multiply by 2	Messiah Divide by 2

What is your answer? 9

24 God and His People—Attributes of God—Unit 1, Part 4, Lesson 1

Memory Verse—Psalm 103:10

Principle: God's mercy keeps believers from everlasting punishment. Locate **Psalm 103:10** and read it aloud as the students read silently. Explain that *iniquity* is another name for sin. You may wish to explain that the word *reward* does not always mean to receive something good; it can also mean to receive a punishment for doing evil.

➤ **What would happen if God gave us what we deserved for our sins?** *(We would be in hell.)*

➤ **How many sins do we need to commit to deserve everlasting punishment?** *(one)*

➤ **What keeps believers out of hell?** *(God's mercy)*

Choose several students to read the verse aloud; then direct the students to highlight the verse in their Bibles (optional) and to mark the location with the Unit 1 Bookmark.

Worktext page 24

Recall facts about the Bible account.

Lesson 2

Materials

- Chart 29, "Journey to the Promised Land"
- A long piece of red ribbon or string

Background Information

Scarlet Cord—*Scripture says that Rahab was saved by faith (Hebrews 11:31). She was a wicked, sinful woman and did not know much about the God of Israel, but God saved her from her sin because she believed God's message. The "scarlet cord" (Joshua 2:18) that marked her house saved her from destruction. This pictures the shed blood of the Lord Jesus Christ that saves people from their sins. The scarlet cord of redemption by Christ's blood runs throughout the Bible. Only God's grace can save a sinner and make him fit for God's heaven. God not only saved Rahab but also made her part of the Lord's family lineage. Matthew lists Rahab as an ancestor of the Lord Jesus (Matthew 1:5). Rahab was the grandmother of Boaz, Ruth's husband.*

Introducing the Bible Account

Introduce Joshua as the new Israelite leader. Explain that Joshua had helped Moses in leading the Israelites through the wilderness. Joshua was also one of the two spies who returned from Canaan with a good report. Before Moses died, God told him to make Joshua the new leader. Moses took Joshua before Eleazar the priest and the Israelites and laid his hands on him. Joshua took Moses' place.

Bible Account

Read the following Bible account or read Joshua 2:1-24; 6:1-27. Display Chart 29, "Journey to the Promised Land," pointing out where the events of the account took place.

Rahab and Two Spies

Moses was dead, and Joshua was the new leader of the Israelites. The Israelites had wandered the desert for forty years and were now in Shittim. Joshua sent out two men to see the land of Jericho in Canaan. They stayed in a house on the city wall—the home of a woman named Rahab.

Someone told the king of Jericho that two Israelite spies had sneaked into the land.

Rahab was a woman who had been known for her sinful life. She had heard about how the Israelites had crossed the Red Sea, and how they had defeated King Sihon and King Og. Rahab knew about their God and was willing to help the two men.

Rahab hid the two men on the flat roof of her house under some bundles of flax. That night, the men of Jericho came to look for the spies. Rahab waited for the king's men to leave; then she shut the gate.

Rahab knew that the Israelites would soon conquer her city, so she asked the spies to

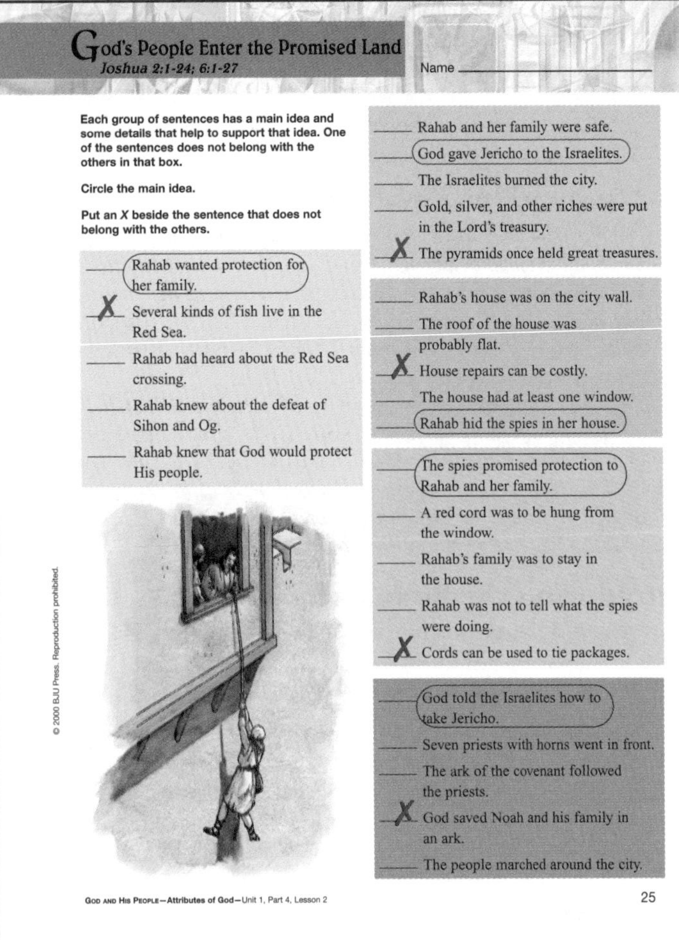

God's People Enter the Promised Land
Joshua 2:1-24; 6:1-27

Name ____________

Each group of sentences has a main idea and some details that help to support that idea. One of the sentences does not belong with the others in that box.

Circle the main idea.

Put an *X* beside the sentence that does not belong with the others.

____ (Rahab wanted protection for her family.)
__X__ Several kinds of fish live in the Red Sea.
____ Rahab had heard about the Red Sea crossing.
____ Rahab knew about the defeat of Sihon and Og.
____ Rahab knew that God would protect His people.

____ Rahab and her family were safe.
____ (God gave Jericho to the Israelites.)
____ The Israelites burned the city.
____ Gold, silver, and other riches were put in the Lord's treasury.
__X__ The pyramids once held great treasures.

____ Rahab's house was on the city wall.
____ The roof of the house was probably flat.
__X__ House repairs can be costly.
____ The house had at least one window.
____ (Rahab hid the spies in her house.)

____ (The spies promised protection to Rahab and her family.)
____ A red cord was to be hung from the window.
____ Rahab's family was to stay in the house.
____ Rahab was not to tell what the spies were doing.
__X__ Cords can be used to tie packages.

____ (God told the Israelites how to take Jericho.)
____ Seven priests with horns went in front.
____ The ark of the covenant followed the priests.
__X__ God saved Noah and his family in an ark.
____ The people marched around the city.

GOD AND HIS PEOPLE—Attributes of God—Unit 1, Part 4, Lesson 2 25

promise that they would protect the lives of her family since she had protected their lives. The spies thanked Rahab for helping them to escape and promised that if she would tie a scarlet line of thread to the window, they would make sure the house and anyone within would be safe when they conquered the city.

So Rahab took a rope and lowered the two men down the wall outside of her window. She told them to go to the mountains and hide for three days.

The Lord God gave Israel the city of Jericho. He told them to march around the city walls seven times for seven days. On the seventh day, the Lord caused the walls to fall, and the Israelites took over the city. Joshua told the people not to harm anyone in Rahab's house where the scarlet cord hung.

The two spies who hid in Rahab's house went there to bring her, her family, and her possessions out safely. Rahab did not die with the unbelievers. Gold, silver, and other riches were taken and placed in the Lord's treasury; then the Israelites burned the city.

- ➤ **What city were the Israelites trying to conquer?** *(Jericho)*
- ➤ **What kind of life was Rahab living when the spies met her?** *(a sinful life)*
- ➤ **How did God use Rahab?** *(She hid the spies and helped them get out of the city.)*

Point out that the Lord can use anyone to fulfill His will. All people—the good and the evil—are under God's sovereignty.

- ➤ **What was the symbol that showed where Rahab and her family lived?** *(the scarlet cord)* Share the background information as you wish.
- ➤ **Did Rahab become a believer?** *(yes)*

Worktext page 25

Identify the main idea and supporting details.

Memory Verse—Psalm 103:10

Practice the memory verse. Direct the students to read **Psalm 103:10** silently and then to close their Bibles and quietly say the verse to themselves and then to reread the verse as a check. Pass the red ribbon to students throughout the day to explain the significance of it in the Bible account and then practice reading or saying the memory verse.

Lesson 3

Materials

- A library book
- TimeLine and picture: *Jonathan Edwards*

Hymn: "I Sing the Mighty Power of God"

Sing the third verse (Worktext page 272). Read the words to the third verse together and discuss the meaning of line 3. Sing all the verses together.

Memory Verse—Psalm 103:10

Practice the memory verse. Pair the students with partners, directing the students to take turns reading **Psalm 103:10** to one another. Lead in saying **Psalm 103:6-10.** Display the library book throughout the day as a signal to say verses 6-10 together.

Worktext page 26

Review the attributes of God.

Introducing the Hero of the Faith

Explain the Great Awakening. Tell the students that people in the New England colonies "woke up" to their spiritual condition as sinners and saw their need to be saved. This is referred to as the Great Awakening, which took place in the 1700s in the American colonies. Jonathan Edwards was a theologian (someone who studies about

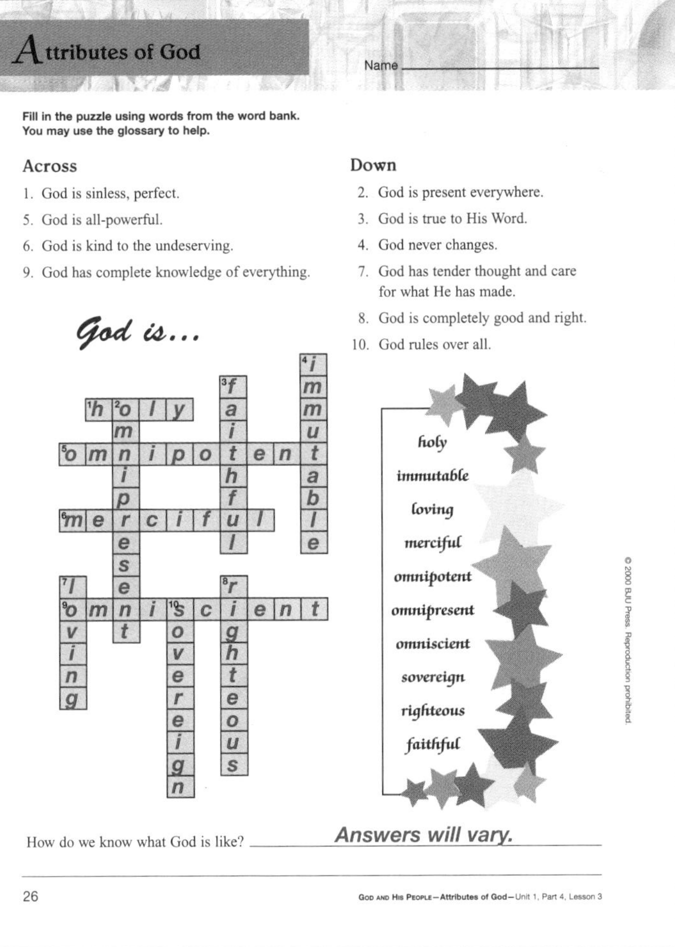

Attributes of God

Name ____________________

Fill in the puzzle using words from the word bank. You may use the glossary to help.

Across

1. God is sinless, perfect.
5. God is all-powerful.
6. God is kind to the undeserving.
9. God has complete knowledge of everything.

Down

2. God is present everywhere.
3. God is true to His Word.
4. God never changes.
7. God has tender thought and care for what He has made.
8. God is completely good and right.
10. God rules over all.

God is…

holy
immutable
loving
merciful
omnipotent
omnipresent
omniscient
sovereign
righteous
faithful

How do we know what God is like? *Answers will vary.*

26 God and His People—Attributes of God—Unit 1, Part 4, Lesson 3

God). He was also a great preacher who began preaching in 1734 and became the leader of the Awakening in New England.

Hero of the Faith

Read the story based on the life of Jonathan Edwards.

Jonathan Edwards

Imagine a hot July afternoon. You're in your good Sunday clothes in a building with no air conditioning. A preacher stands on the platform behind a pulpit, delivering a long sermon.

Imagining this scene may make you feel hot and a little sleepy, but when Jonathan Edwards preached the sermon *Sinners in the Hands of an Angry God,* people paid attention. As he spoke of the danger that sinners were in, people realized their need of the Lord Jesus Christ as their Savior.

Before Jonathan Edwards could finish his sermon, people were crying out, "What must I do to be saved?" and moaning and holding onto the pews. Some people even feared that the ground would open up and swallow them.

Years before as a youngster, Jonathan Edwards was a child genius, writing a long essay on the habits of balloon spiders. At age thirteen, he was enrolled in college at Yale University.

Later Edwards used his education and talent to become a preacher. His most famous sermon, *Sinners in the Hands of an Angry God,* was preached during the Great Awakening in New England. People turned to God when Jonathan Edwards preached.

Knowing that all men were wicked sinners, Jonathan Edwards preached about the **sovereign** pleasure of God—the only thing that keeps man from being sent to hell. He used his knowledge about spiders to show a picture of what he meant:

"Our wickedness makes us heavy as if we were about to fall into hell," said Edwards. If God were to let us go, we *would* fall into hell. We cannot depend on our good deeds to keep us from hell any more than a rock can depend on a spider web to keep it from hitting the ground. Edwards said that God holds us as you would hold some creepy, crawling insect—we are worth nothing except to be thrown into hell.

More than God's anger, Jonathan Edwards spoke of God's love. Because God loves us, He holds back his wrath and shows us mercy and grace. He wants us to come to Him as sinners and ask for forgiveness.

God used Jonathan Edwards to bring people to salvation. He was known for his love, devotion, and total dependence on God.

- ➤ **What was special about Jonathan Edwards's ability?** *(He was a genius and went to college when he was thirteen.)*
- ➤ **What was the name of Jonathan Edwards's most famous sermon?** (Sinners in the Hands of an Angry God)
- ➤ **Did Jonathan Edwards preach more about God's anger toward sinners or His love for sinners?** *(His love)*
- ➤ **According to Jonathan Edwards, what is the only thing that keeps us from going to hell?** *(the sovereign pleasure of God, God's mercy)*
- ➤ **What is the *sovereign pleasure of God?*** *(God's sovereignty is His rule over us; His pleasure is enjoying us.)*

Jonathan Edwards
(1703-1758)

Name ______________________

Imagine that it's a hot July afternoon in the mid 1700s. You are dressed in your Sunday clothes, seated in a building with no air conditioning. A preacher stands before the congregation and delivers a long sermon. Are you hot and sleepy? Are you thinking about what you will do after church? Do you wish the sermon would end?

That was usually not the case when Jonathan Edwards preached. His listeners forgot everything except what he was saying. When Edwards preached his most famous sermon, "Sinners in the Hands of an Angry God," people did not want the service to end before they were sure of their salvation. Before he had finished speaking, they were crying out, "What must I do to be saved?"

Jonathan Edwards was a gifted learner who began his education at Yale University when he was thirteen years old. The dedication of his intelligence, education, and talents to the ministry of preaching God's Word was used to point many to faith in Christ.

Answer the questions.

Why does the writer tell you to imagine being in another time and place, and ask you questions about how you feel?

Answers will vary but should include that the writer wants the reader to know how it felt to be there.

What did people think about when Jonathan Edwards preached?

Answers will vary but should include that people thought about their salvation; about how to be saved.

How did God use Jonathan Edwards's intelligence, education, and talents?

Answers will vary but should include that God used him to point many to salvation [faith] in Christ.

Jonathan Edwards
(continued)

Name ______________________

An analogy is a relationship between things that are not generally alike.

Jonathan Edwards knew that all men are sinners and deserve to be cast into hell. God has power to send them to hell. The Devil wants them in hell. But Edwards preached that the ***sovereign*** pleasure of God is the only thing that can keep sinful man out of hell. As a child, Edwards had researched and written a long essay on spiders. When he preached, he used an ***analogy*** about spiders to help people understand God's sovereignty. Sinfulness makes man heavy, said Edwards. Just as a stone falls because of its own weight, so man is always naturally falling down because of his own sin. If God were to let a person go, he ***would*** fall into hell. Good deeds cannot stop anyone from falling into hell any more than a spider's web can keep a stone from falling. Sin makes man as ugly and undesirable before the righteousness of God as an awful, creeping thing is to a person.

Jonathan Edwards did not speak only of God's anger with sin. He also told of God's great love, mercy, and grace. God does not want to let anyone fall into hell. He wants every sinner to come to Him and ask for forgiveness.

Write the correct letter beside each part of the picture below to show the analogy Jonathan Edwards used.

A. like sinful man
B. like the weight of sin
C. like good deeds

TimeLine

Place *Jonathan Edwards* on the TimeLine. Select a student to add *Jonathan Edwards* to the large TimeLine at 1703-1758. Guide the students in gluing the picture of *Jonathan Edwards* onto their individual TimeLines.

Worktext Supplement pages 303-4 (optional)

Recall facts about Jonathan Edwards, a Hero of the Faith.

Picture the Point

Illustrate borrowing life. Display the library book, showing the name of the library stamped inside to elicit that it is a library book.

➤ **To whom does the book belong?** *(the library)*
➤ **Can I keep the book forever?** *(no)*
➤ **How should I handle the book?** *(Any answer is acceptable, but elicit that you must be careful.)*
➤ **Who owns our lives?** *(God)*
➤ **Can we keep our lives forever?** *(No, we will die.)*
➤ **How should we handle our lives?** *(We should spend them loving God and doing things pleasing to Him.)*

Lesson 4

Materials

- Song: "Books of the Old Testament"
- Bible Book Cards: books of Moses, History, Poetry, and Major Prophets

Memory Verse—Psalm 103:10

Practice the memory verse. Write verse 10 on the chalkboard. Lead in reading it together several times, erasing some words each time until the students can say it from memory. Lead in saying **Psalm 103:6-10** from memory together.

Introducing the Application Story

Review the story. Call on volunteers to share what has happened to Bryan and his family in previous lessons (pages 13-14, 21 25-26).

Application Story

Read the following application story to the students.

More Than Words (Part 4)

Bryan and his parents walked into the lobby of the Greycourt Inn. A young man in a coat and loosened tie jogged over to meet them. "Good evening!" he said. "You must be the Davisons. I'm Joe Harris, the manager of this hotel." He shook Dad's hand.

"We really appreciate this," Dad said.

"Yes. It was so kind of you to put us up at the last minute like this," said Mom.

"No problem," said Joe. "Lucy, the agent you talked to, is a good friend of mine. I like to do her a favor whenever I can. Say, I'm really sorry about what happened with your plane. You must be exhausted."

Mom nodded. Bryan noticed for the first time that she *did* look tired.

Joe loosened his tie a little further. "I've had kind of a rough day myself," he said. "I was just getting ready to head across the street for a sandwich. If you'll just see Cindy at the desk there, she'll set you up with the room. It's the only vacancy we have left. You're a pretty lucky family; someone must be looking out for you."

Bryan glanced up at his father. Was this another one of those opportunities he had been talking about?

Dad cleared his throat. "Well, actually, someone is," he said. "We believe God watches over us all the time. We know He's in control of everything that happens to us and that He orders all of our affairs. Although we do appreciate your kindness, we believe it was God who arranged for us to be here tonight."

Joe's eyes were fixed on Dad's face as he talked. "Yeah, well—" he said. He paused for a moment. "Are you folks Christians?"

"Yes," said Bryan, and Mom and Dad nodded.

Joe frowned thoughtfully. "Lucy's been trying to talk to me about this Christian stuff too," he said. "It seems to really work for her."

"I'd be glad to talk to you further about what it means to be a Christian," Dad said.

Joe's eyebrows lifted. "Would you?" he asked.

Dad glanced at Mom. "As a matter of fact," he said, "if it's all right with you, I'd love to have you join our family for dinner. We haven't eaten yet either."

"Hey, that'd be great," Joe said.

"I'm hungry!" Bryan said, and everyone laughed.

"I'll just wait here while you folks get checked into your room," said Joe. "And then I'll take you to the sandwich shop across the street. No hurry," he added as they started toward the desk.

"Dad," Bryan whispered, tugging on Dad's sleeve. "Do you think he'll get saved?"

"I don't know, Bryan; he seems pretty interested. But whatever comes of our talk tonight, I think I know at least one reason God arranged the events of this trip the way He did—don't you?"

"Just so we could talk to Mr. Harris about Jesus?"

Dad nodded. "I think God had this planned from the beginning," he said quietly.

- ➤ **What was unusual about the room Mr. Harris had for Bryan and his parents?** *(It was the only one left.)*
- ➤ **What led to the opportunity to tell Mr. Harris about God's sovereignty?** *(He commented that they were "lucky" and that someone must be looking out for them.)*
- ➤ **Who had already been talking to Mr. Harris about Christ?** *(Lucy, the Christian agent from the airport)*
- ➤ **How do you know Mr. Harris was interested in knowing more about the Lord?** *(He was eager to join them for dinner so he could hear more.)*
- ➤ **What did Bryan's dad believe about the events of their trip?** *(that God had arranged them in order to allow them to meet Mr. Harris and witness to him)*
- ➤ **Has God ever arranged events in your own life so that you could tell someone else about Him?** *(Any answer is acceptable.)*

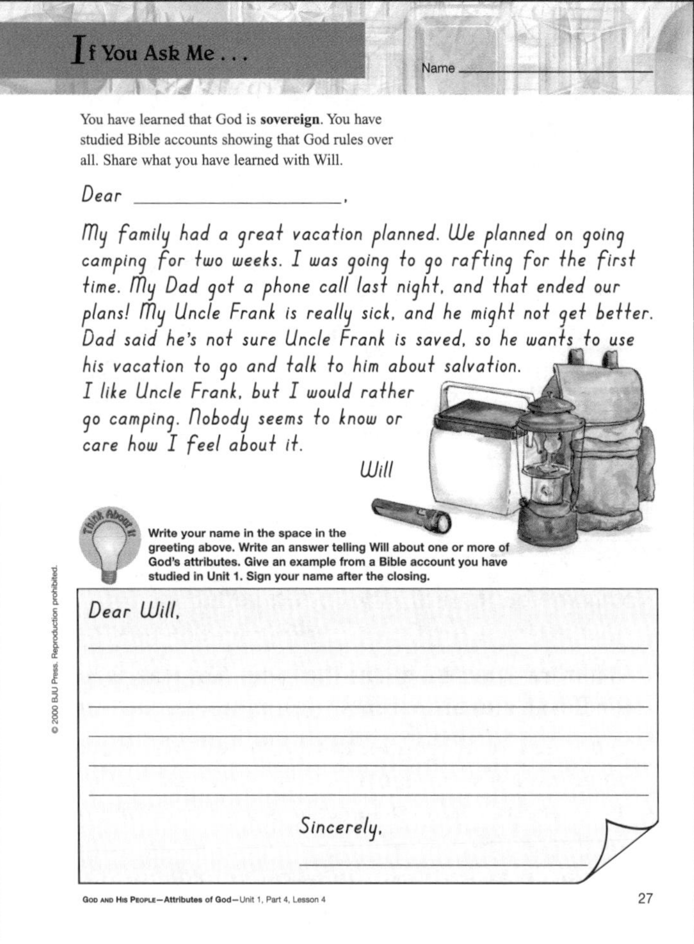

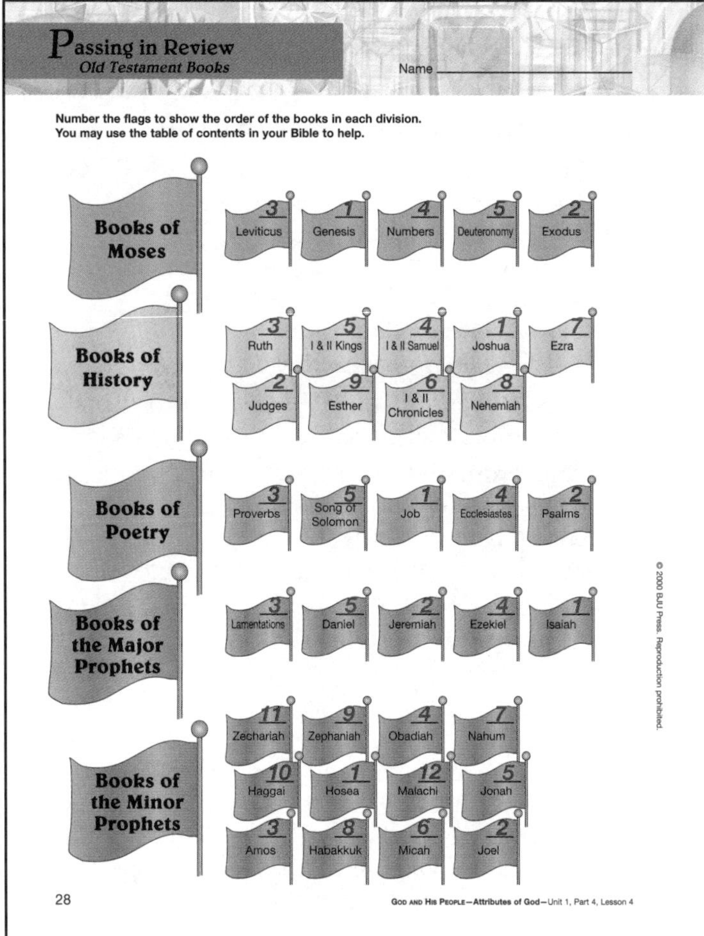

Worktext page 27

Write a letter applying Bible knowledge to everyday life.

Song: "Books of the Old Testament"

Sing the first four verses (Worktext page 287). Play the recording and lead the singing of the first four verses.

Bible Study Skills

Review the books of the Major Prophets. Distribute the Major Prophet cards to five students, directing the students to arrange themselves in the correct order at the front of the room. Say the books of the Major Prophets together several times; then say all of the names of the Old Testament books together.

Divide the students into four teams and tell them to line up as teams. Show a card (from the books of Moses, History, Poetry, or Major Prophets) to the student at the front of each line. The student who calls out the book that comes before the book shown receives a point for his team. Let each student in front go to the end of his line after his turn. (*Note:* When the card for Genesis is displayed, the game can be stopped and a winner determined, or students can call out "First Book." Play the game a second time with the students telling the book that comes after the book shown.)

One-on-One: Give the student the Major Prophet cards and tell him to sequence them correctly. Then give him the cards (from the books of Moses, History, Poetry, and Major Prophets) to organize by divisions. Finally, show the student a card, telling him to identify the book that comes next.

Bible Study Skills, Worktext page 28

Sequence the books of the Old Testament.

Going Beyond

Materials

- A copy of *Sinners in the Hands of an Angry God* by Jonathan Edwards

Enrichment

Listen to a sermon. Obtain a copy of Jonathan Edwards's sermon *Sinners in the Hands of an Angry God* to read to the students or invite your pastor to read it to the class. (*Note:* A quality excerpt and discussion questions of this sermon can be found in *AMERICAN LITERATURE for Christian Schools,* available from Bob Jones University Press.)

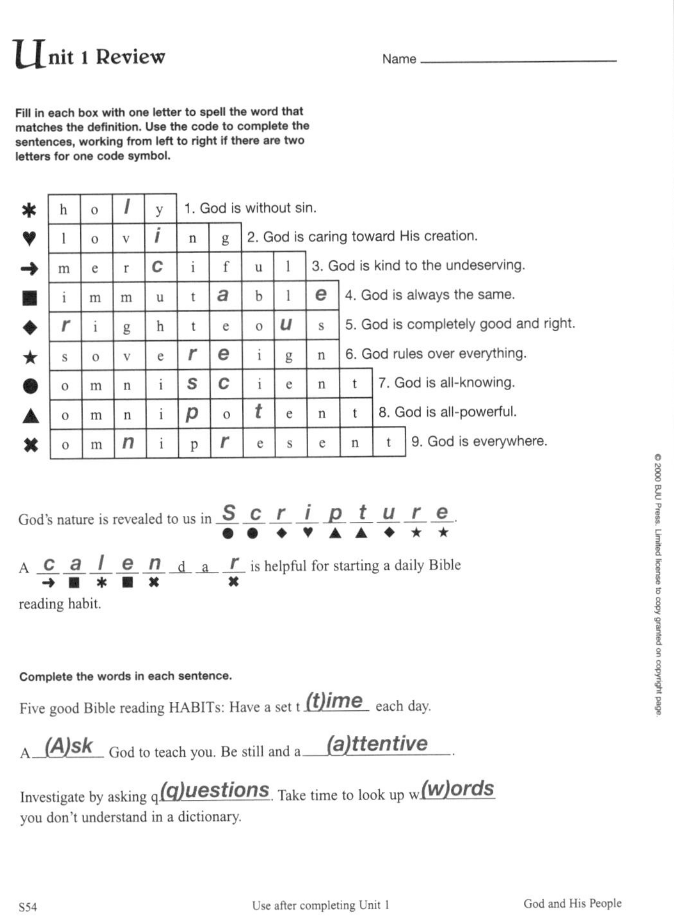

Unit 1 Review

Name ____________

Fill in each box with one letter to spell the word that matches the definition. Use the code to complete the sentences, working from left to right if there are two letters for one code symbol.

✱	h	o	*l*	y	1. God is without sin.
♥	l o v *i* n g	2. God is caring toward His creation.
➔	m e r *c* i f u l	3. God is kind to the undeserving.
■	i m m u t *a* b l *e*	4. God is always the same.
◆	*r* i g h t e o *u* s	5. God is completely good and right.
★	s o v e *r* *e* i g n	6. God rules over everything.
●	o m n i *s* *c* i e n t	7. God is all-knowing.
▲	o m n i *p* o *t* e n t	8. God is all-powerful.
✖	o m *n* i p *r* e s e n t	9. God is everywhere.

God's nature is revealed to us in *S c r i p t u r e*.
(● ● ◆ ♥ ▲ ▲ ◆ ★ ★)

A *c a l e n* d a *r* is helpful for starting a daily Bible reading habit.
(➔ ■ ✱ ■ ✖ ✖)

Complete the words in each sentence.

Five good Bible reading HABITs: Have a set t *(t)ime* each day.

A *(A)sk* God to teach you. Be still and a *(a)ttentive*.

Investigate by asking q *(q)uestions*. Take time to look up w *(w)ords* you don't understand in a dictionary.

Unit 1 Review (continued)

Name ____________

Compare the Israelites with people today. Write the letter on the line. Use each answer only one time.

Israelites		People today
B	A. Slaves to sin	*A*
C	B. Slaves to Pharaoh	*D*
	C. Moses, through God's power, frees from slavery.	
	D. Jesus Christ frees from the bondage of sin.	

Write *T* if the sentence is true and *F* if it is false. If a sentence is false, change it to make it true. Draw a line through the word that is false, and write what will make it true on the line.

T The bronze snake on the pole was a picture of what it is like to look to Jesus in faith and be saved from sin and death.

F Pharaoh let the Israelites go after the plague of ~~hail~~. *the death of the firstborn*

F The ~~last~~ four commandments teach our duty to God. *first*

Unit Review

Materials

- Copy of Supplement pages S54-55, "Unit 1 Review," for each student

Guide a review of Unit 1. Review the people and events in preparation for the Unit 1 Test (optional).

Bible Study and Prayer

Overview

Preparing the Teacher

The unchanging truth of God is the foundation for all knowledge and is our basis for Christian education. We cannot overemphasize this in a day when all truth is considered relative and integrity is lacking even in the lives of professing Christians. All knowledge must be evaluated in the light of God's Word. Since the Fall, men have sought to substitute their own desires for God's Truth. Only God's Word is absolute. Read **Isaiah 33:6** and **Psalm 19:8-9.** Meditate daily on God's Word, using it for wisdom, worship, warfare, and witnessing. Pray for your students by name; let them know you care for them by remembering their prayer requests at the throne of grace. Share with them the love and grace of the Lord with specific answers to prayers in your own life.

Preparing the Lessons

Parts 1-4—a copy of *Captive Treasure* for the teacher (optional for each student)

Part 1 Lesson 1 Materials—two small pieces of magnetic tape for each student

Part 1 Lesson 2 Materials—cedar wood (optional), uncut loaf of bread (optional) and a knife to cut the bread (optional)

Part 1 Lesson 3 Materials—United States map

Part 1 Lesson 4 Materials—a Bible with family names and important dates; the following items for each student: four small, round cookies or chocolate-covered peppermint candies; six toothpicks; a 3" × 5" index card (or construction paper); a flat chocolate snack cake about 3" long; a small rectangular foil-wrapped candy; tape; and a pretzel stick (optional)

Part 1 Going Beyond Materials—audio Bible cassette tapes or CDs

Part 2 Going Beyond Materials—computer software of the Bible

Part 3 Lesson 1 Materials—an x-ray or a picture of an x-ray (optional)

Part 3 Lesson 4 Materials—a pair of shoes (optional)

Part 4 Lesson 2 Materials—a picture of a sundial (optional); items for Science Connection for each group: a piece of plywood (approximately 12" × 14"), enough white paper to cover the board, cardboard (approximately 6" square), and thread or string (optional)

Unit 2 Bible Study and Prayer						**Hymn: "Break Thou the Bread of Life"**
Part	**Lesson number**	**Lesson pages**	**Worktext pages**	**Supplement pages**	**Bible Account**	**Application**
Part 1: **Knowing God**	1	47	29-32		David, a Man After God's Own Heart (I Samuel 16–I Kings 2)	
	2	50	33-34		Solomon Prayed for Wisdom (I Kings 3:4-28)	
	3	52	35-36, 312			**Hymn History Story:** "Break Thou the Bread of Life" **Application Novel:** *Captive Treasure*
	4	54	37-38, 313			**Application Novel:** *Captive Treasure*
Part 2: **Worshiping God**	1	58	39-40		Dedication of the Temple of God (II Chronicles 5:1–7:3)	
	2	60	41-42		Israel Worships God (II Chronicles 7:4-22)	
	3	62	43, 314			**Application Novel:** *Captive Treasure*
	4	64	44, 315			**Application Novel:** *Captive Treasure*
Part 3: **Sharing God's Word**	1	66	45-46		Jehoshaphat Lived and Shared God's Word (II Chronicles 17:1-9)	
	2	68	47-48		Judah Turns Back to God (II Chronicles 17:10-19)	
	3	69	49, 316			**Application Novel:** *Captive Treasure*
	4	71	50, 317			**Application Novel:** *Captive Treasure*
Part 4: **Praying to God**	1	73	51-52		Hezekiah Prayed for Deliverance (II Kings 18:17–19:37)	
	2	75	53-54		Hezekiah Prayed for Healing (II Kings 20:1-11, 20-21)	
	3	78	55, 318			**Application Novel:** *Captive Treasure*
	4	79	56, 319			**Application Novel:** *Captive Treasure*

Connections	Memory Verses and Principles	Bible Doctrines	Skills/Applications
TimeLine: David **TimeLine: Solomon** History Food	Psalm 119:9-11 *Studying and memorizing God's Word helps believers obey God's Word.*	**The Doctrine of the Bible** **Inspiration:** The Bible says that it is inspired (II Tim. 3:16-17). The Bible presents standards of living and a way of life that are of God (Ps. 119:1-8). The Bible is eternal (Ps. 119:89). **The Doctrine of God** **Attributes of God:** God is everywhere (omnipresent) (Ps. 139:7-10). God is all-powerful (omnipotent) (Jer. 32:27). God is unchanging (immutable) (James 1:17). God is faithful (I Cor. 1:9; II Tim. 2:13). God is merciful (Ps. 86:15). **The Doctrine of the Church** **Functions of the Local Church:** Members should pray (II Cor. 1:11).	**Foundational:** • Appreciate the attributes of God • Realize that only God can give victory • Realize that God's Word is powerful • Realize that studying and memorizing God's Word helps believers obey God's Word • Recognize prophecy foretold and prophecy fulfilled **Practical:** • Recall facts and details • Locate information in Scripture • Learn the Old Testament books, their abbreviations, and their divisions • Sequence the Old Testament books • Identify the book of the Bible where an account is located • Use cross-references • Read a map • Read a time line • Develop active listening • Identify cause and effect • Draw conclusions • Match characters and dialogue • Sequence events • Summarize main events **Personal:** • Develop a Bible reading habit • Remember that God is a Christian's help and strength • Realize that if we trust in God, He will take care of us • Catch the vision of telling others about Christ • Realize how God wants Christians to worship Him • Know that God commands Christians to pray • Apply Bible knowledge to everyday life
History	Psalm 29:2 *God wants us to worship Him.*		
Science	Hebrews 4:12 *God's Word is alive and powerful.*		
TimeLine: Hezekiah Science	Philippians 4:6 *God has commanded us to pray, and God wants to answer our prayers.*		

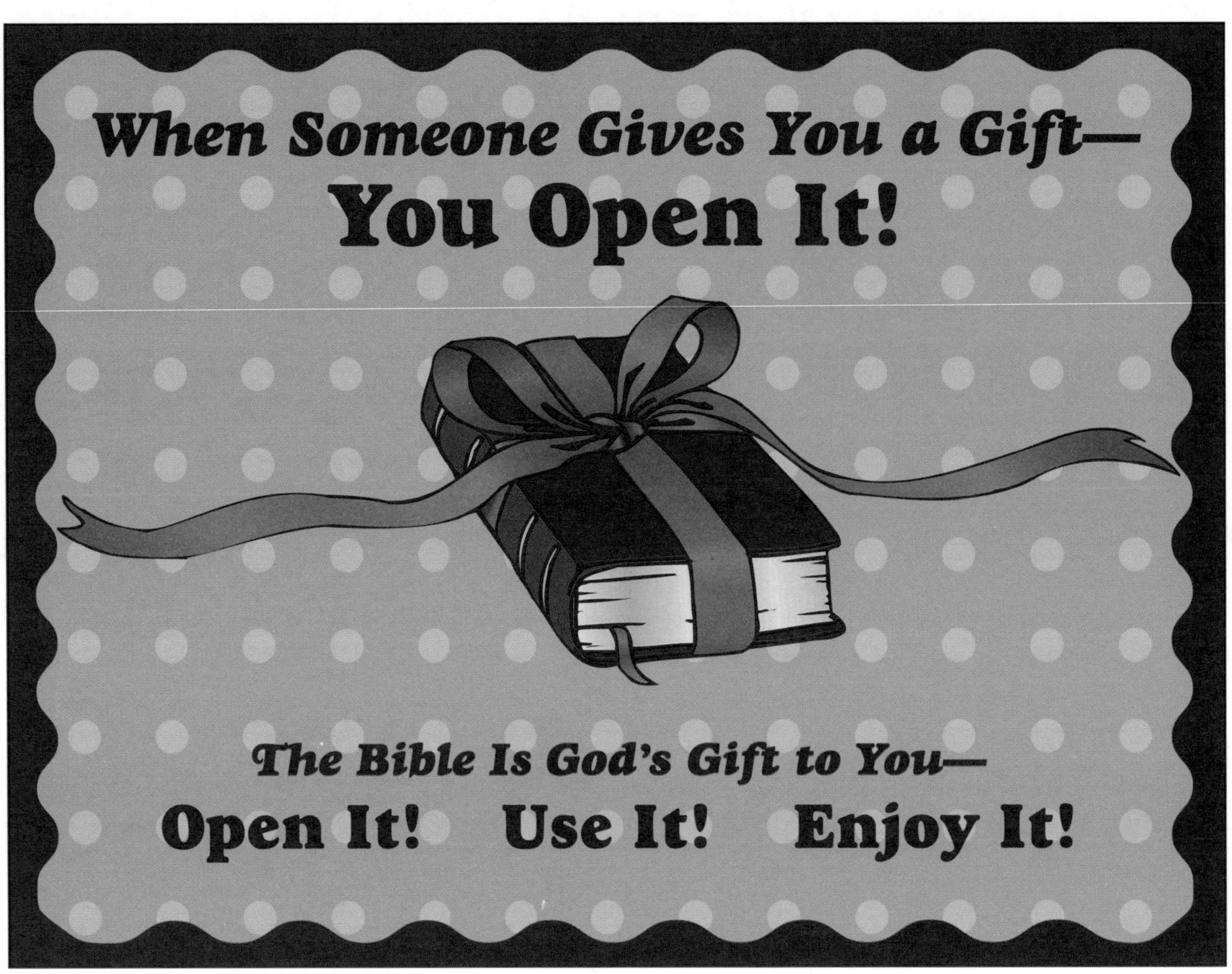

Preparing the Unit 2 Bulletin Board

Cover the bulletin board with a small-patterned gift wrap. Center a large picture of a closed Bible on the board. Wrap the Bible with wide ribbon in a complementary color, putting a gift bow on the top and allow the ends of the ribbon to fill in the open space on the board. Prepare the title and subtitle: "When Someone Gives You a Gift—You Open It!" and "The Bible Is God's Gift to You—Open It! Use It! Enjoy It!" as shown.

Knowing God

Preview

Doctrines

- God is faithful (I Corinthians 1:9)—Lesson 1
- God is everywhere (omnipresent) (Psalm 139:7-10)—Lesson 1
- God is merciful (Psalm 86:15)—Lesson 2

Skills and Applications

- Learn Psalm 119:9-11
- Learn the books of the Minor Prophets
- Recall facts and details
- Read a map
- Read a time line
- Locate information in Scripture
- Develop a Bible reading habit
- Recognize prophecy foretold and prophecy fulfilled
- Realize that studying and memorizing God's Word helps believers obey God's Word
- Apply Bible knowledge to everyday life

Lesson 1

Materials

- Chart 31, "Divided Kingdom"
- TimeLine and picture: *David*
- Song: "The Bible Reading Habit."
- Two small pieces of magnetic tape for each student
- Unit 2 Bookmark for each student
- Highlighter for each student (optional)

(Note: Bibles, worktexts, and unit hymns are standard lesson materials and will not be listed in the materials list for each lesson. Other songs will be included when necessary.)

Material	Location
Charts Maps InfoScenes TimeLine TimeLine pictures Bible Book Cards	Visual Packet
Student Bookmarks Student TimeLine Student TimeLine pictures Student Bible Book Cards	Student Materials Packet
Music for teaching the grade 4 unit hymns and the books of the Bible songs is located in the supplement of this Teacher's Edition and the supplement of the Student Worktext. A recording of children singing these hymns and songs is available on the *God and His People* cassette tape or CD. Additional music located in the supplement of this Teacher's Edition provides the teacher with more hymns and songs in keeping with the theme of each unit.	

 Memory Verses—Psalm 119:9-11

Principle: Studying and memorizing God's Word helps believers obey God's Word. Locate **Psalm 119:9-11** and read the verses aloud as the students read silently. Choose students to read the verses aloud.

➤ **What is fun about playing Hide and Seek?** *(Answers will vary.)*

➤ **How would you feel if you hid something valuable but forgot where you hid it?** *(Accept any answer.)*

Explain that in the memory verses, believers are told to hide something, but only so that it can be seen later—not so it will be hidden forever. God's Word is the believer's light.

➤ **How can a young man keep his life clean?** *(by studying God's Word and memorizing it)*

➤ **How is a believer to study God's Word?** *(with a whole or loving, enthusiastic heart)*

➤ **Why does a believer hide God's Word in his heart?** *(to keep from sinning)*

➤ **Why will just memorizing God's Word not keep us from sin?** *(We must obey it, use it in our lives, and live according to it.)*

Direct the students to highlight the verses in their Bibles (optional). Give each student a Unit 2 Bookmark, directing attention to the illustration of the Bible as a reminder for Christians to read and study God's Word. Tell the students to fold the bookmark on the dotted lines and to attach a

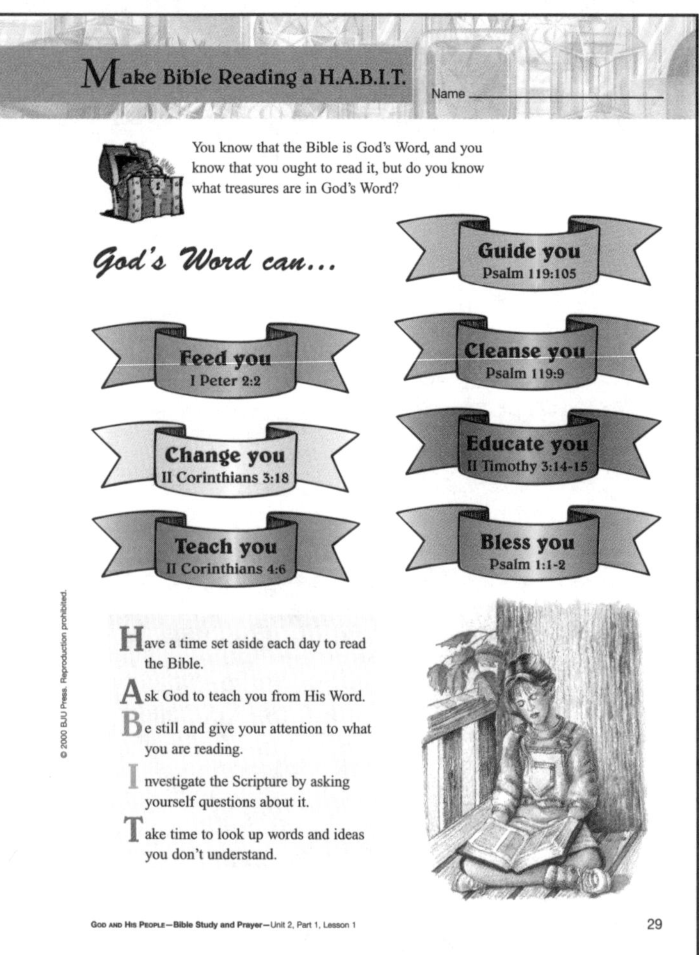

Make Bible Reading a H.A.B.I.T.

Name ______________

You know that the Bible is God's Word, and you know that you ought to read it, but do you know what treasures are in God's Word?

God's Word can...

- **Guide you** Psalm 119:105
- **Feed you** I Peter 2:2
- **Cleanse you** Psalm 119:9
- **Change you** II Corinthians 3:18
- **Educate you** II Timothy 3:14-15
- **Teach you** II Corinthians 4:6
- **Bless you** Psalm 1:1-2

Have a time set aside each day to read the Bible.

Ask God to teach you from His Word.

Be still and give your attention to what you are reading.

Investigate the Scripture by asking yourself questions about it.

Take time to look up words and ideas you don't understand.

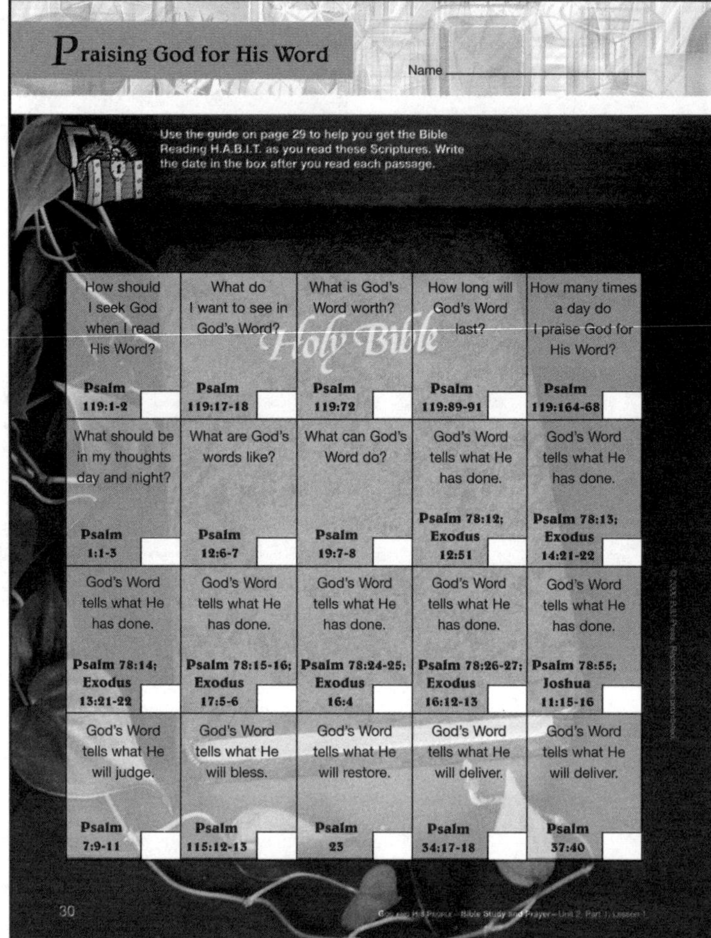

Praising God for His Word

Name ______________

Use the guide on page 29 to help you get the Bible Reading H.A.B.I.T. as you read these Scriptures. Write the date in the box after you read each passage.

How should I seek God when I read His Word? Psalm 119:1-2	What do I want to see in God's Word? Psalm 119:17-18	What is God's Word worth? Psalm 119:72	How long will God's Word last? Psalm 119:89-91	How many times a day do I praise God for His Word? Psalm 119:164-68
What should be in my thoughts day and night? Psalm 1:1-3	What are God's words like? Psalm 12:6-7	What can God's Word do? Psalm 19:7-8	God's Word tells what He has done. Psalm 78:12; Exodus 12:51	God's Word tells what He has done. Psalm 78:13; Exodus 14:21-22
God's Word tells what He has done. Psalm 78:14; Exodus 13:21-22	God's Word tells what He has done. Psalm 78:15-16; Exodus 17:5-6	God's Word tells what He has done. Psalm 78:24-25; Exodus 16:4	God's Word tells what He has done. Psalm 78:26-27; Exodus 16:12-13	God's Word tells what He has done. Psalm 78:55; Joshua 11:15-16
God's Word tells what He will judge. Psalm 7:9-11	God's Word tells what He will bless. Psalm 115:12-13	God's Word tells what He will restore. Psalm 23	God's Word tells what He will deliver. Psalm 34:17-18	God's Word tells what He will deliver. Psalm 37:40

small piece of magnetic tape on the inside of the bookmark at both ends. Direct the students to place the Unit 2 Bookmark over the page to mark the location of the verses. Practice the memory verses by reading them throughout the day.

Bible Study Skills, Worktext pages 29-30

Develop a Bible reading habit. Read the top part of the page to the students, selecting students to read the Scriptures aloud if you wish. Point out the HABIT acrostic on page 29, reading each statement for developing the habit of Bible reading. Explain the four-week Bible reading activity on page 30. Lead in singing together the song "The Bible Reading Habit" from Worktext page 271. Encourage each student to complete the daily Bible reading, dating the small boxes. (*Note:* You may choose to have students do their reading before class, during class, or at a time of their own choosing.)

Worktext page 31

Develop understanding of the memory verses.

Background Information

A King for Israel—*God was the leader of the Israelites, but the Israelites were not satisfied. They told the prophet Samuel that they wanted a king to lead them like the other nations. Samuel asked God what he should do, and God provided the people with a king. God instructed Samuel to anoint Saul as king. One time King Saul became impatient and disobeyed God by offering his own sacrifice instead of waiting for a priest to offer the sacrifice. This displeased God, and God instructed Samuel to anoint a son of Jesse to be the next king of Israel.*

Introducing the Bible Account

Share the background information. Explain how Saul became Israel's first king, and because of his disobedience, God chose another king.

Character Focus

Read the following or summarize the life of David in your own words.

David, a Man After God's Own Heart

God told the prophet Samuel that the next king would be a son of Jesse. In obedience to God, Samuel went to sacrifice in Bethlehem, and he called Jesse and his sons to the sacrifice. Jesse sent his sons, one by one, to Samuel. Each time, God indicated that this son was not to be the next king.

Samuel asked Jesse if these were all his sons. Jesse explained that his youngest son was caring for the sheep. "Send and fetch him," said Samuel. When David arrived, God told Samuel to anoint him, for David was to be the next

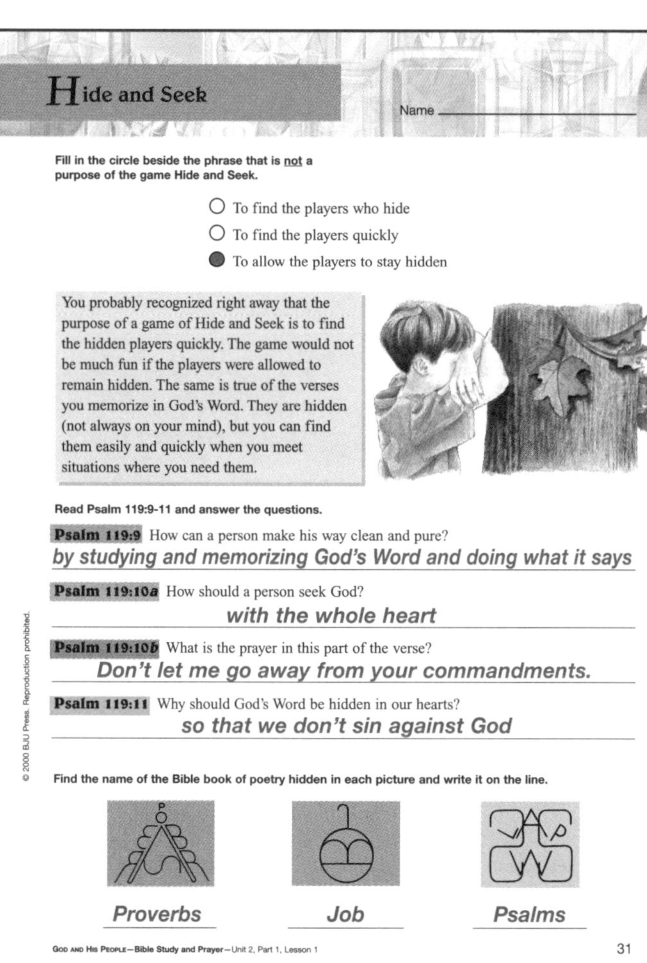

Hide and Seek

Name ____________

Fill in the circle beside the phrase that is not a purpose of the game Hide and Seek.

- ○ To find the players who hide
- ○ To find the players quickly
- ● To allow the players to stay hidden

You probably recognized right away that the purpose of a game of Hide and Seek is to find the hidden players quickly. The game would not be much fun if the players were allowed to remain hidden. The same is true of the verses you memorize in God's Word. They are hidden (not always on your mind), but you can find them easily and quickly when you meet situations where you need them.

Read Psalm 119:9-11 and answer the questions.

Psalm 119:9 How can a person make his way clean and pure?
by studying and memorizing God's Word and doing what it says

Psalm 119:10a How should a person seek God?
with the whole heart

Psalm 119:10b What is the prayer in this part of the verse?
Don't let me go away from your commandments.

Psalm 119:11 Why should God's Word be hidden in our hearts?
so that we don't sin against God

Find the name of the Bible book of poetry hidden in each picture and write it on the line.

Proverbs *Job* *Psalms*

king. "Then Samuel took the horn of oil, and anointed him in the midst of his brethren: and the Spirit of the Lord came upon David from that day forward" (I Samuel 16:1-13).

David did not become king right away. King Saul asked him to come to his palace for a time. King Saul had heard of David's skill in playing the harp. Often David would play his harp for him until Saul was refreshed. King Saul loved David and made him his armor bearer.

Before long, war broke out between the Israelites and the Philistines. King Saul led the men of Israel to battle, and David returned home to care for his father's sheep. One day David's father sent him to carry food to his brothers at the battlefield. There David saw the giant Goliath mocking the Israelites, God's chosen people. David knew that God could defeat the giant. God used David with his sling and a stone to kill the mighty Goliath (I Samuel 17).

King Saul did not allow David to return again to his home. He placed David over his men of war. David went wherever King Saul sent him, and the people accepted him and sang his praises. When King Saul realized this, he came to hate David. He knew the people liked David and that God had chosen him to be the next king. Once, King Saul tried to kill David by throwing a spear at him. But "David behaved himself wisely in all his ways; and the Lord was with him." King Saul became afraid and continued to plot how to kill David.

David fled from Saul and went into hiding. A band of about four hundred men joined him. Saul and his men pursued David wherever he went, through cities and through wilderness. More than once, David had an opportunity to kill Saul, but he refused to harm him because Saul was God's anointed king. The Lord protected David from Saul and his men. Saul finally died by purposely falling on his sword during another battle with the Philistines (I Samuel 18-31).

After the death of Saul, David was crowned king over Judah, a portion of the land of Israel. The remaining portion was ruled by Ishbosheth, a son of King Saul (II Samuel 2-4). (Show Chart 31, "Divided Kingdom," explaining how the kingdoms were divided and later united.)

At the death of Ishbosheth, David became king over all Israel. David looked to God for guidance and ruled well. God blessed Israel. Then David looked away from God and sinned. After he sinned, David tried to cover up his sin.

God sent Nathan the prophet to teach and to warn David about his sin. David confessed the evil he had done and asked God to forgive him (II Samuel 5-12).

Read **Psalm 51:1-4, 10-15** aloud, explaining that David wrote these words, a prayer to God, after he was confronted by Nathan about his sin. Tell the students that many of the Psalms are songs of prayer and praise written by David.

God forgave David's sin, but David had to endure the consequences of that sin. David's family turned against each other and against David. His son Absalom gathered some people with him and tried to take over his father's throne. King David left the city to avoid a battle with his son. Absalom's forces were defeated. God had protected King David from his enemies, but when he heard of Absalom's death, he wept (II Samuel 13-19).

God guided David throughout his life and considered him a "man after God's own heart." Only when David walked away from God did he stumble.

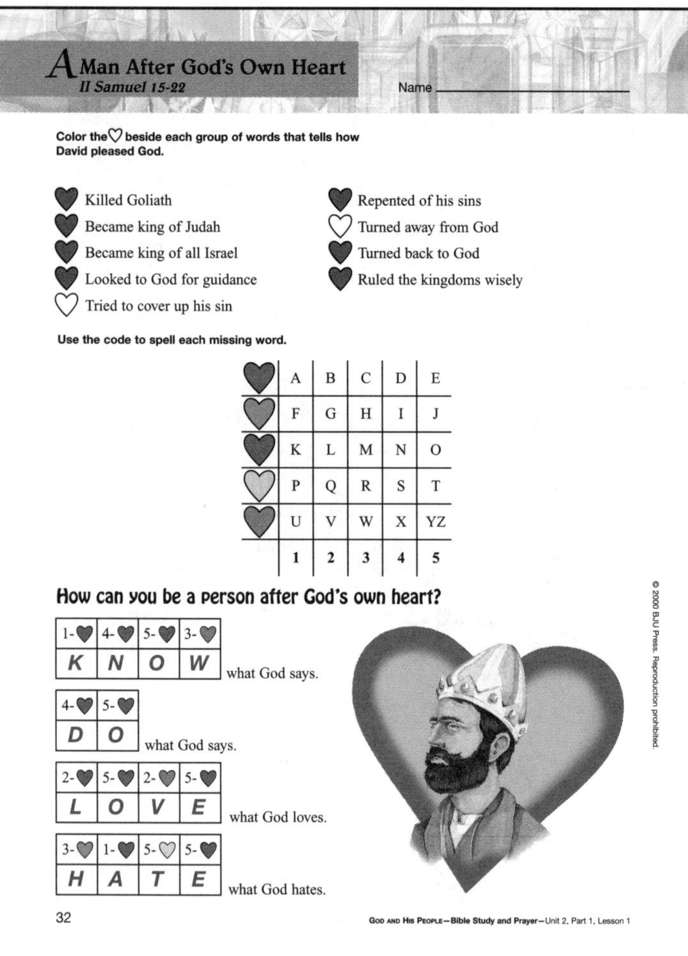

A Man After God's Own Heart
II Samuel 15-22

Name ____________

Color the ♡ beside each group of words that tells how David pleased God.

♥ Killed Goliath	♥ Repented of his sins
♥ Became king of Judah	♡ Turned away from God
♥ Became king of all Israel	♥ Turned back to God
♥ Looked to God for guidance	♥ Ruled the kingdoms wisely
♡ Tried to cover up his sin	

Use the code to spell each missing word.

♥	A	B	C	D	E
♥	F	G	H	I	J
♥	K	L	M	N	O
♡	P	Q	R	S	T
♥	U	V	W	X	YZ
	1	2	3	4	5

How can you be a person after God's own heart?

1-♥ 4-♥ 5-♥ 3-♥ — K N O W what God says.

4-♥ 5-♥ — D O what God says.

2-♥ 5-♥ 2-♥ 5-♥ — L O V E what God loves.

3-♥ 1-♥ 5-♡ 5-♥ — H A T E what God hates.

32 God and His People—Bible Study and Prayer—Unit 2, Part 1, Lesson 1

➤ **What did Saul ask David to do?** *(come live at the palace and play his harp for him)*

➤ **Why did King Saul place David over his men of war?** *(Possible answers include David killed Goliath, and he was brave.)*

➤ **Why did David need to go into hiding?** *(King Saul grew to hate David and wanted to kill him)*

➤ **How did David react to Saul's change of attitude and behavior?** *(He behaved wisely and would not harm Saul.)*

➤ **How could David be "a man after God's own heart" when he was sinful?** *(Answers will vary but should include that David had a heart of repentance toward God. David knew he had disobeyed God, was sorry for his sin, and asked God to forgive him. David had a desire to obey and please God.)*

➤ **How can a believer become a person after God's heart?** *(by reading and obeying God's Word and spending time in prayer)*

TimeLine

Place *David* on the TimeLine. Choose a student to attach the picture of *David* onto the TimeLine at 1040-970 B.C. Guide each student in gluing the picture of *David* onto his TimeLine.

Worktext page 32

Recall facts about the life of David.

Lesson 2

Materials

- Charts 3-4, and 9: "The Ten Commandments" and "God Gives Wisdom" (optional)
- TimeLine and picture: *Solomon*
- Cedar wood (optional)
- Uncut loaf of bread (optional)
- A knife to cut the bread (optional)

Prepare verse cards with key words from **Psalm 119:9-11.**

Memory Verses—Psalm 119:9-11

Practice the memory verses. Locate **Psalm 119:9-11** and read the verses aloud as the students read silently. Display the memory-verse cards and lead in saying the verses by looking at the key words.

Hymn: "Break Thou the Bread of Life"

Teach the first verse (Worktext page 273). Play the recording while the students follow along. Explain that the hymn writer is comparing the breaking of bread to opening and studying God's Word. Choose a student to help you cut a loaf of bread in half (optional). Explain that it is not until a loaf of bread is cut open that they can see what is on the inside. The same is true of the Word of God. It is not until we open it and read it that we can see and understand God. Lead in singing verse 1 several times. Allow students to eat a piece of the bread (optional).

Background Information

Solomon—*Solomon was the second son born to David and Bathsheba. (Their first son died as an infant.) As King David was about to die, he called Solomon to him and had Solomon anointed as the next king. David told Solomon to walk in the way of the Lord and to obey God. God would make Solomon prosperous if he followed after God.*

Introducing the Bible Account

Review the Ten Commandments. Share the background information with the students (optional). Explain that David told Solomon to obey God and to keep His commandments. Point out that these rules teach us the holiness of God and show us our own sinfulness. Display Charts 3-4, "The Ten Commandments," or read aloud Exodus 20:1-17 to review the commandments.

Bible Account

Read the following Bible account or read I Kings 3:4-28.

Solomon Prayed for Wisdom

Solomon knew from the teachings of his father David that he was to sacrifice a pure—not scarred, spotted, or diseased—lamb on an altar and to ask forgiveness of his sins. Solomon did this regularly. He went to the city of Gibeon many times to sacrifice in obedience to God's teaching.

One visit to Gibeon was very special. In the night, while Solomon was sleeping, God appeared to him in a dream and said, "Ask what I shall give thee." And God promised to give Solomon whatever he asked.

Solomon talked first about how God had blessed his father, King David. Then Solomon told God that all he wanted from Him was wisdom—a heart to understand and make wise decisions—not that he might be the wisest king but that he might lead and serve others. Solomon confessed to God that he did not know enough to be the king of God's people. He needed wisdom from God so he could be a wise king and make good decisions.

God was pleased with Solomon's request. God told Solomon that since he did not ask for long life, riches, or victory over his enemies, God would give him all of these things anyway. God said that, indeed, He would also give Solomon an understanding heart. He promised Solomon that he would be a king like no other king. Solomon would be the wisest king who ever lived.

Solomon awoke from his dream, went to Jerusalem, and stood before the ark of the covenant of the Lord. He offered sacrifices on an altar and praised God.

Direct the students to look at Worktext page 33. Read and explain the information. Show the cedar wood, pointing out that it has a wonderful-smelling fragrance (optional). Then continue reading the Bible account.

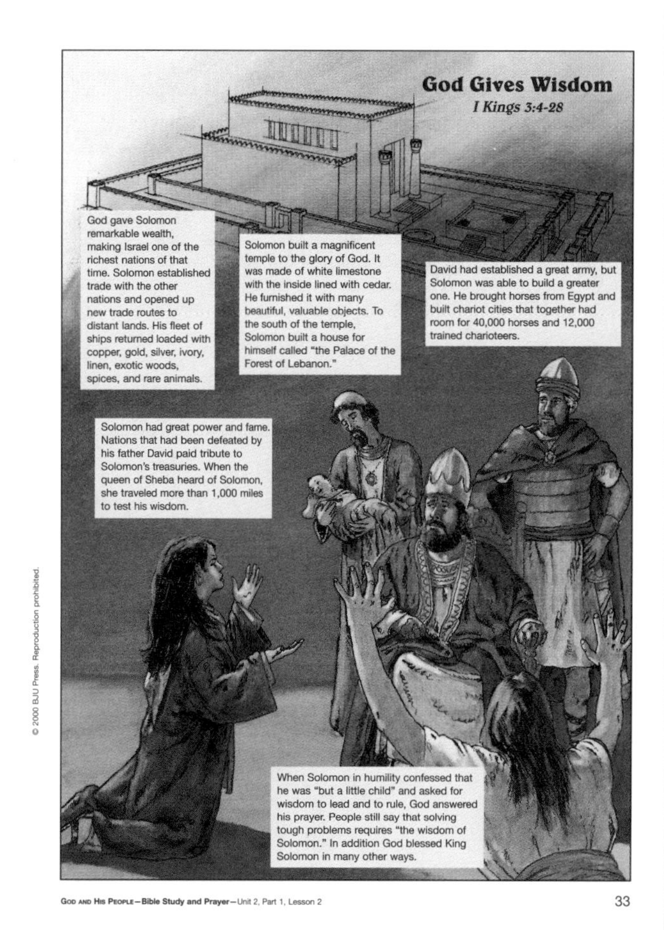

While Solomon was in Jerusalem, two women came to him with a baby. Each woman said that *she* was the mother of the child—not the other woman. They asked King Solomon to decide which of them was telling the truth and who should have the baby for her own. King Solomon explained to the women that since they both claimed to be the baby's mother, the child could be cut in half and each woman given half of the baby. He asked for a sword to cut the baby. But the baby's real mother spoke up and said, "O my lord, give her the living child, and in no wise slay it. But the other said, Let it be neither mine nor thine, but divide it." As soon as King Solomon heard their cries, he knew that the child's real mother was the woman who showed her love by being willing to give the child to the other woman in order to save the child's life. When the people of Israel heard this, "they feared the king: for they saw that the wisdom of God was in him, to do judgment."

InfoScene: "God Gives Wisdom"

Display Chart 9 for reference throughout this unit. Review and discuss the Bible account as time permits.

- ➤ **What did Solomon ask of God?** *(wisdom, an understanding heart to lead God's people rightly)*
- ➤ **How did God answer Solomon's request?** *(He said Solomon would have an understanding heart and that he would be known throughout the world for his wisdom and his greatness. Because Solomon did not ask for long life, riches, or victory over his enemies, he would have these things also.)*
- ➤ **What decision did Solomon have to make?** *(who the true mother of the child was)*

Wish Lists–Gift Lists

I Kings 3:4-28

Name ______________________

Complete Solomon's wish list and the list of gifts God gave to him.

Solomon's Wish List

(I Kings 3:9) a wise (discerning, understanding) heart

Solomon's Gift List

(I Kings 3:12) a wise heart

(I Kings 3:13) riches

(I Kings 3:13) honor

(I Kings 3:14) long life

Write your name on the top lines. Complete your own wish list, and list some of the gifts God has given to you.

__________'s Wish List

Answers will vary.

__________'s Gift List

Answers will vary.

- ➤ **How did Solomon make his decision?** *(Solomon knew that the mother of the child would not want the baby to die and would rather give it to the other woman.)*
- ➤ **Do you think Solomon asked for a good thing from God?** *(Accept any response, but discuss it.)*
- ➤ **Where can we get wisdom?** *(from the Word of God and from God Himself [James 1:5])*

TimeLine

Place *Solomon* on the TimeLine. Choose a student to attach the picture of *Solomon* onto the TimeLine at 992-931 B.C. Guide each student in gluing the picture of *Solomon* onto his TimeLine.

Worktext page 34

Locate information in Scripture and apply Bible knowledge to everyday life.

Lesson 3

Materials

- Copy of *Captive Treasure* for the teacher (and for each student [optional])
- Verse cards from the previous lesson
- United States map

Memory Verses—Psalm 119:9-11

Practice the memory verses. Locate **Psalm 119:9-11** and choose several students to read the verses aloud. Display the verse cards from the previous lesson. Lead in saying the verses by reading the key words. Remove one or two key words and say the verses together again. Repeat the procedure until no cards are displayed and the students can say the verses from memory.

Hymn History Story: "Break Thou the Bread of Life"

Read the following information to the students.

Miss Mary Artemisia Lathbury was given a writing assignment. "I need a hymn to be sung at the conference," John Vincent told her. Mr. Vincent led a Christian camp meeting in Chautauqua (shə•tô′•kwə), New York, and Miss Lathbury was his secretary.

Miss Lathbury decided to go and sit beside the quiet water of Lake Chautauqua to write her hymn. Maybe being outdoors with the beauty of God's creation all around her would give her an idea. For a while Miss Lathbury just sat still, feeling the warm breeze and watching the reflections of the white clouds floating in the lake.

She turned her thoughts to the Bible. *I wonder if it was a day like this that Jesus fed the five thousand beside the Sea of Galilee,* she said to herself. She began to pray for the Lord to guide her as she wrote. "Dear Lord, break Thou the bread of life to me as Thou didst break the loaves beside the sea."

Miss Lathbury picked up her pencil and jotted down the words she had just prayed. They were the beginning to her hymn. The rest of that verse and then another verse came to her quickly. She had finished the new hymn before sunset.

Miss Lathbury had loved to write poems even when she was young. As a girl growing up in a pastor's home, she recognized that her talent for writing poetry came from God. "Consecrate these talents to Me," she seemed to hear God saying. And she did. Miss Lathbury wrote many other hymns for the conferences at Chautauqua. She also wrote stories and books, taught art, and painted pictures of children.

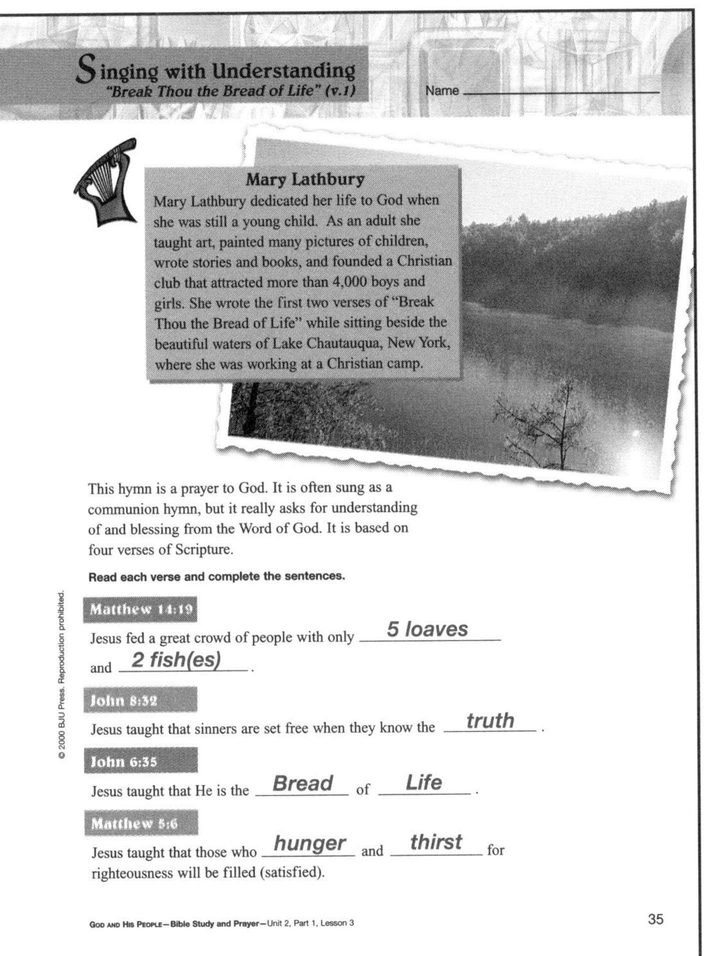

Singing with Understanding
"Break Thou the Bread of Life" (v.1)

Name ______________________

Mary Lathbury
Mary Lathbury dedicated her life to God when she was still a young child. As an adult she taught art, painted many pictures of children, wrote stories and books, and founded a Christian club that attracted more than 4,000 boys and girls. She wrote the first two verses of "Break Thou the Bread of Life" while sitting beside the beautiful waters of Lake Chautauqua, New York, where she was working at a Christian camp.

This hymn is a prayer to God. It is often sung as a communion hymn, but it really asks for understanding of and blessing from the Word of God. It is based on four verses of Scripture.

Read each verse and complete the sentences.

Matthew 14:19
Jesus fed a great crowd of people with only 5 loaves and 2 fish(es).

John 8:32
Jesus taught that sinners are set free when they know the truth.

John 6:35
Jesus taught that He is the Bread of Life.

Matthew 5:6
Jesus taught that those who hunger and thirst for righteousness will be filled (satisfied).

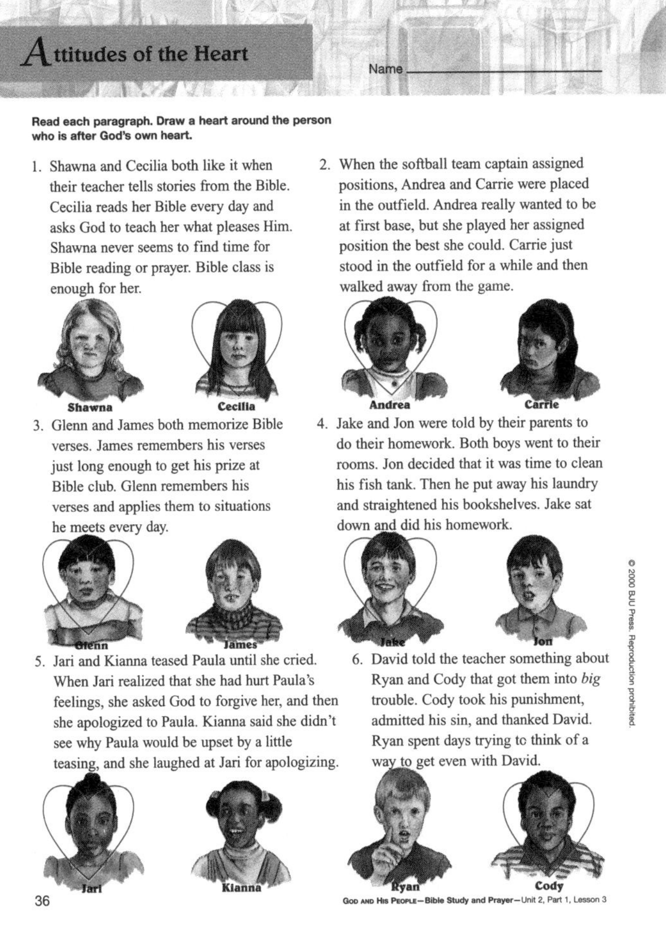

Attitudes of the Heart

Name ______________________

Read each paragraph. Draw a heart around the person who is after God's own heart.

1. Shawna and Cecilia both like it when their teacher tells stories from the Bible. Cecilia reads her Bible every day and asks God to teach her what pleases Him. Shawna never seems to find time for Bible reading or prayer. Bible class is enough for her.

2. When the softball team captain assigned positions, Andrea and Carrie were placed in the outfield. Andrea really wanted to be at first base, but she played her assigned position the best she could. Carrie just stood in the outfield for a while and then walked away from the game.

3. Glenn and James both memorize Bible verses. James remembers his verses just long enough to get his prize at Bible club. Glenn remembers his verses and applies them to situations he meets every day.

4. Jake and Jon were told by their parents to do their homework. Both boys went to their rooms. Jon decided that it was time to clean his fish tank. Then he put away his laundry and straightened his bookshelves. Jake sat down and did his homework.

5. Jari and Kianna teased Paula until she cried. When Jari realized that she had hurt Paula's feelings, she asked God to forgive her, and then she apologized to Paula. Kianna said she didn't see why Paula would be upset by a little teasing, and she laughed at Jari for apologizing.

6. David told the teacher something about Ryan and Cody that got them into *big* trouble. Cody took his punishment, admitted his sin, and thanked David. Ryan spent days trying to think of a way to get even with David.

The final two verses of her hymn, "Break Thou the Bread of Life," were added later by an Englishman named Alexander Groves. The words to this hymn weave four passages of Scripture into a beautiful prayer for nourishment from God's Word: Matthew 14:19, John 8:32, John 6:35, and Matthew 5:6.

Hymn: "Break Thou the Bread of Life"

Sing the first verse (Worktext page 273). Play the recording and lead in singing verse 1 together several times.

Worktext page 35

Singing with understanding, verse 1.

Worktext page 36

Apply Bible knowledge to everyday life.

Background Information

Historical Novel—*A historical novel is a story related to times, events, people, or places from the past. Supporting details accurately portray a specific time period in history. While the characters are believable, they may not be actual people who lived during that time.*

Setting—*The Talbot family is traveling west to be missionaries. They travel by ship to St. Joseph, Missouri, and then join a wagon train to continue the trip farther west.*

Introducing the Application Novel.

Generate interest in reading the novel. Explain that the book *Captive Treasure* will be read throughout this unit instead of your reading application stories from the Teacher's Edition. Distribute a copy of the book to each student (optional). Direct attention to the cover.

- ➤ **What is the name of the book?** *(*Captive Treasure*)*
- ➤ **Who is the author?** *(Milly Howard)*
- ➤ **What do you think the book is going to be about?** *(Accept any answer.)*

Read about the author, Milly Howard, from the back of the book. Explain the background information about a historical novel. Point to St. Joseph, Missouri, and Oregon on the map of the United States. Tell the students that many pioneers traveled west from Missouri to Oregon in the 1840s. Discuss what it would be like to travel across the country as a family during this time in history. Share the remaining background information. (*Note:* If each student has a copy of the book, you may want to arrange for them to read the chapter assignment at the beginning of the day, during the day, or for homework the previous night.)

Application Novel: *Captive Treasure*

Read and discuss Chapter 1. Direct the students to read the first chapter silently to find out what kind of ship the Talbots were aboard. *(a steamer, a steamboat)* Explain how a steamboat works: steam gives power to the engine, the engine turns the paddles, and the paddles move the boat through the water. (*Note:* If each student does not have a copy of the book, read the chapter orally.)

- ➤ **What was the nickname for St. Joseph, Missouri?** *(Saint Joe)*
- ➤ **Why did the people going west call St. Joseph, Missouri, the "jumping off place"?** *(It was the starting place for wagon trains going west.)*
- ➤ **Why was the Talbot family going west?** *(Carrie's father would help his brother at the mission.)*
- ➤ **Why was Carrie's mother worried about Carrie on the boat?** *(She was afraid that Carrie would be "swept overboard"–fall from the ship into the water.)*
- ➤ **Was Carrie's father worried? Why not?** *(No. He knew she was responsible and could take care of herself.)*
- ➤ **How did Carrie show that she was responsible in the store?** *(She cared for a lady's baby.)*

Worktext Supplement page 312

Apply Bible knowledge to everyday life.

History Connection (optional)

Read and discuss the following information.

Lewis and Clark expedition (1804-1806)—Meriwether Lewis and William Clark explored the Northwestern Territory and opened the way for the Oregon Trail. Their travel to the Pacific Northwest and back east took them over eight thousand miles in two years. Oregon became a territory in 1848. Land was offered to those who would settle in Oregon, and many people came. Some people wanted a new beginning. Others were searching for gold. Oregon later became a state in 1859.

Oregon Trail—Many wagon trains traveled westward on the California, Santa Fe, and Oregon Trails. The Oregon Trail began in Independence, Missouri, in 1841 and led to Willamette Valley in the Northwest. Since the wagon trains traveled only about fifteen miles each day, the two-thousand-mile journey took six months. The wagon trains left in early spring to avoid traveling when there would be snow in the mountains.

Plains Indians—The Plains Indians lived on the prairie westward from the Mississippi River to the Rocky Mountains. They kept a medicine bundle, a bag of items they thought had special power.

The Cheyenne, Crow, Comanche, and Sioux were some of the tribes that lived on the Plains. Each tribe had its own territory and language. Sign language became a way to

Captive Treasure
Chapter 1 Name ____

Read the verses in your Bible. Write the missing words to complete the sentences. Color the two pictures that show actions that please God.

Proverbs 15:1—Soft, kind answers will turn away __wrath__.
Hard, mean words will stir up __anger__.

Colossians 3:20— __Children__, you should obey your __parents__ in everything that you do. This will please the __Lord__.

312 God and His People—Captive Treasure—Unit 2, Part 1, Lesson 3

communicate among people of different languages. These tribes sometimes fought other tribes for food, horses, animal skins, or land. As pioneers settled into the area, the conflict for food and land intensified. (*Note:* The term *Indian* in *Captive Treasure* refers to Native Americans.)

Lesson 4

Materials

- Copy of *Captive Treasure* for the teacher (and for each student [optional])
- Song: "Books of the Old Testament"
- Old Testament Bible Book Cards
- Reading, math, history books
- A family Bible or another Bible with family names and important dates
- Food Connection items for each student: four small, round cookies or chocolate-covered peppermint candies; six toothpicks; a 3" × 5" index card (or piece of construction paper); a flat, chocolate snack cake about 3" long; a small, rectangular foil-wrapped candy; tape; and a pretzel stick (optional)

(*Note:* To adapt the Food Connection activity, use a cake prepared in a 9" × 13" pan and cut into twelve 2" × 4" pieces. Use a 4" × 6" index card with these cakes.)

Cut out a heart from red construction paper.

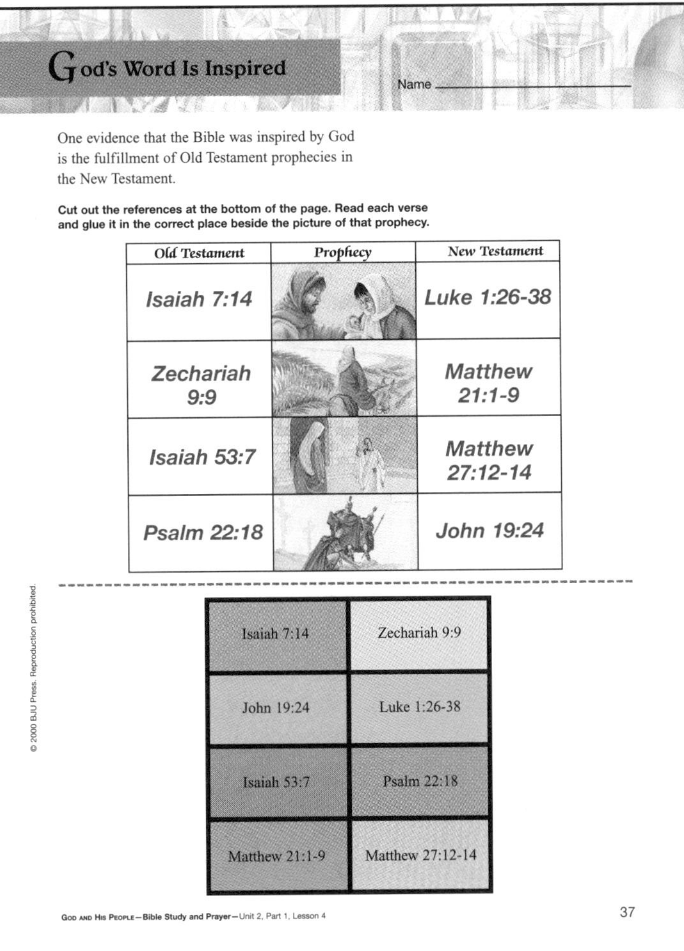

God's Word Is Inspired

Name ____________________

One evidence that the Bible was inspired by God is the fulfillment of Old Testament prophecies in the New Testament.

Cut out the references at the bottom of the page. Read each verse and glue it in the correct place beside the picture of that prophecy.

Old Testament	Prophecy	New Testament
Isaiah 7:14		Luke 1:26-38
Zechariah 9:9		Matthew 21:1-9
Isaiah 53:7		Matthew 27:12-14
Psalm 22:18		John 19:24

Isaiah 7:14	Zechariah 9:9
John 19:24	Luke 1:26-38
Isaiah 53:7	Psalm 22:18
Matthew 21:1-9	Matthew 27:12-14

GOD AND HIS PEOPLE—Bible Study and Prayer—Unit 2, Part 1, Lesson 4 37

Song: "Books of the Old Testament"

Sing all five verses (Worktext page 287). Play the recording and lead in singing verse 5; then sing all five verses together or divide the students into five groups, letting each group sing a verse.

Bible Study Skills

Review the books of the Minor Prophets. Distribute the Minor Prophet cards to twelve students. Direct the students to arrange themselves in the correct order at the front of the room. Lead in saying together the books of the Minor Prophets several times; then say all the names of the Old Testament books together.

Mix up all of the Old Testament Bible Book Cards. Display one flash card at a time and allow the students to tell the division the card is in. If time allows, review the flash cards again and allow the students to tell the book that follows the one named by the card.

One-on-One: Give the student the books of Minor Prophets cards to sequence correctly. Then mix up all of the division cards and have the student sequence them all, or show a card, challenging the student to identify to which division it belongs.

Memory Verses—Psalm 119:9-11

Practice the memory verses. Choose students to read **Psalm 119:9-11** aloud. Give the paper heart to a student. Explain that he is to say the Scripture passage from memory. If he comes to a section that he does not know, he may give the heart to someone else to finish the passage. Continue this procedure as time allows or until all students have had an opportunity.

Worktext pages 37-38

Discuss inspiration. Distribute a reading, history, and math book to three different students. Tell those three students to look up **John 3:16.** (*Note:* Allow a few seconds for the students to look in the books.)

➤ **Why can't you find the verse?** *(because it is found in the Bible, not in most reading, history, or math books)*

➤ **What makes the Bible different from all other books?** *(The Bible is God's Word, and all other books have been written by ordinary people.)*

Explain that one way we know that the Bible is God's Word is that it claims to be God's Word. Direct the students to look up the word *inspiration* in the glossary. Read **Deuteronomy 18:21-22,** explaining that God chose men who were called prophets to give the people messages and warnings from God.

Locate prophecy foretold and fulfilled in Scripture.

Introducing the Application Novel

Introduce Chapter 2. Display the family Bible. Explain that a family Bible records the history or *heritage* of a family and sometimes is passed from one generation to the next. Read some of the entries recorded.

➤ **What dates might be recorded in a family Bible?** *(salvation, birthdays, weddings, deaths)*

Application Novel: *Captive Treasure*

Read and discuss Chapter 2. Review the events of the first chapter. Read the title of Chapter 2, "Dusty Trails." Direct the students to read the chapter silently (if they have a copy of the book) or read it to them to find out what routines took place on a wagon train. *(Accept answers such as early rising, campfire meals, walking and playing alongside the wagon train, Sunday preaching, chores, and Bible memorization.)*

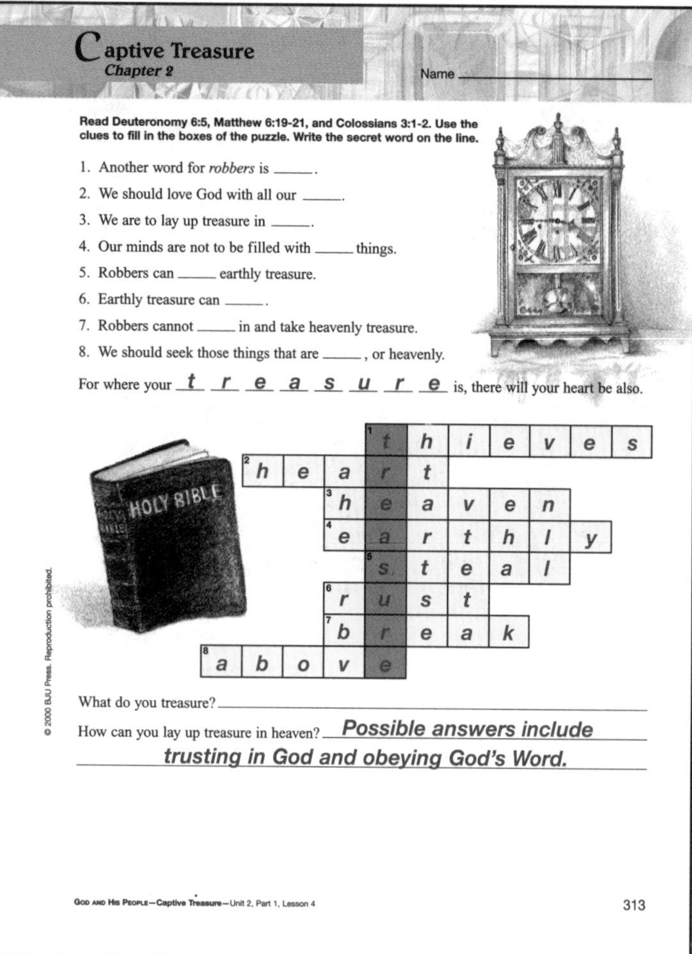

Captive Treasure
Chapter 2

Name ____________________

Read Deuteronomy 6:5, Matthew 6:19-21, and Colossians 3:1-2. Use the clues to fill in the boxes of the puzzle. Write the secret word on the line.

1. Another word for *robbers* is ______.
2. We should love God with all our ______.
3. We are to lay up treasure in ______.
4. Our minds are not to be filled with ______ things.
5. Robbers can ______ earthly treasure.
6. Earthly treasure can ______.
7. Robbers cannot ______ in and take heavenly treasure.
8. We should seek those things that are ______, or heavenly.

For where your t r e a s u r e is, there will your heart be also.

				1 t	h	i	e	v	e	s
	2 h	e	a	r	t					
			3 h	e	a	v	e	n		
			4 e	a	r	t	h	l	y	
				5 s	t	e	a	l		
			6 r	u	s	t				
			7 b	r	e	a	k			
8 a	b	o	v	e						

What do you treasure? ____________________

How can you lay up treasure in heaven? *Possible answers include trusting in God and obeying God's Word.*

God and His People—Captive Treasure—Unit 2, Part 1, Lesson 4 313

➤ **Was a wagon train the same as a railroad? How do they differ?** *(No. A wagon train was a line of moving wagons; a railroad was a line of connected train cars.)*

➤ **Where was the family Bible placed?** *(in a pocket at the front of the covered wagon)*

➤ **Why did Father say it was important to learn the sign language of the Indians that was taught by the wagon train scout?** *(They needed to know as much as possible before reaching the mission.)*

➤ **What unusual items were found along the trail? Why were they there?** *(a clock, an oak dresser; To make the wagons lighter and easier to cross over the Rocky Mountains, people often left items behind.)*

➤ **What advice did Father give to Carrie about worldly treasure?** *(Set your heart on things above.)* Read **Matthew 6:19-21** and **Colossians 3:2** aloud.

➤ **Where do you learn how to love what God loves?** *(in the Bible)*

➤ **What things do you think would be pleasing to God?** *(Possible answers include praising God; honoring parents; worshiping God; having pure thoughts, language, and conduct; being honest and content; and repenting of sin.)*

Worktext Supplement page 313

Locate information in Scripture.

Food Connection (optional)

Make wagon cakes. Display the following instructions in an activity center for the students to use, or demonstrate each step as you guide the students to make the cakes.

1. Use a toothpick as an axle to connect front wheels (small cookies or candies) to the snack cake; then connect the back wheels with another toothpick.
2. Tape two toothpicks on each 3" side of the index card.

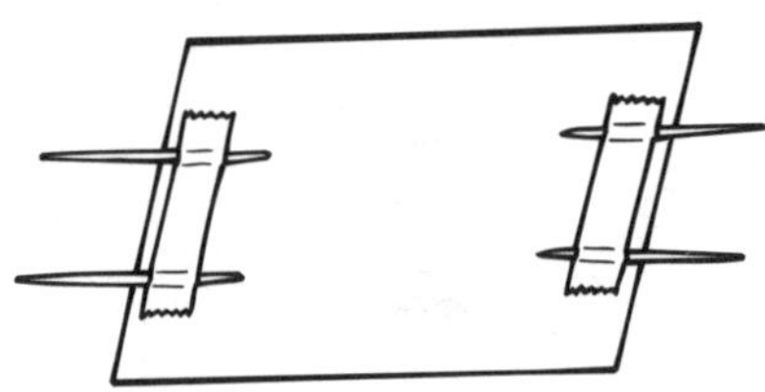

3. Poke toothpicks from one side of the index card into the top of the snack cake, slightly away from the edge of the cake. Curve the index card to place the remaining toothpicks, forming the top of the covered wagon.
4. Insert the pretzel stick into the front of the cake as the wagon tongue (optional). Place the foil-wrapped candy on the top as the wagon seat.
5. Store cakes in air-tight containers until they will be eaten.

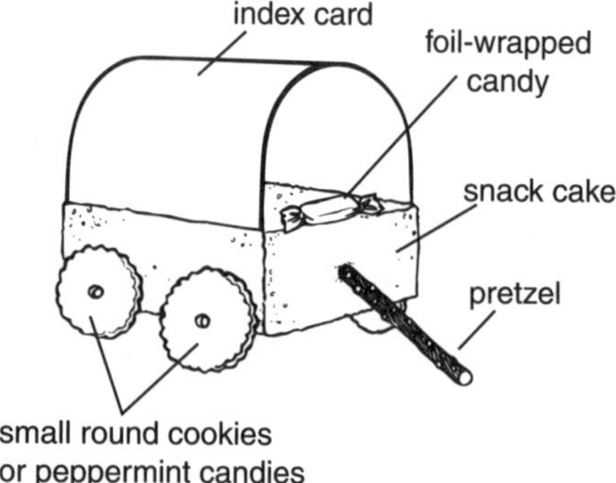

Going Beyond

Materials

- Audio Bible cassette tapes or CDs

Enrichment

Introduce the Bible in audio form. Play a cassette tape or CD of a Scripture passage for the students. (*Note:* Passage suggestion is Psalm 91.)

➤ **Why is it helpful to have an audio form of the Bible?** *(Possible answers include listening to God's Word while in a car or while working, using the recording to help you to memorize Scripture, and using the audio version if you could not see or read well.)*

Preview

Doctrines
- God is unchanging (immutable) (James 1:17)—Lesson 1
- God is faithful (II Timothy 2:13)—Lesson 2

Skills and Applications
- Learn Psalm 29:2
- Learn the Old Testament books and their divisions
- Sequence the books of the Old Testament
- Identify the books of the Bible where an account is located
- Identify cause and effect
- Recall facts and details
- Locate information in Scripture
- Realize how God wants Christians to worship Him
- Remember that God is a Christian's help and strength
- Apply Bible knowledge to everyday life

Lesson 1

Materials
- Unit 2 Bookmark for each student
- Highlighter for each student (optional)

Background Information
Building of the Temple—*King David wanted a place for the people to worship God; however, it was not God's plan for David to build the temple because David had been a man of war and had shed blood. David, under God's leading, chose the location for the temple as well as the design and collected the materials needed. After the death of David, his son Solomon started building the temple in Jerusalem on Mount Moriah. The procedures for the building of the temple were unique. The top of Mount Moriah was leveled before the building began. Because the temple was to be God's house, the construction work was not actually done in Jerusalem. Solomon negotiated contracts that called for the cutting down of trees and the quarrying of stone. The wood and stone were then prepared for the temple. Solomon would send supplies of food for the laborers. Then when the pieces were ready, everything was put together. The Bible says that no noises were heard in God's house, the temple, while it was being built (I Kings 6:7). God wanted his house to be special in every way. The building of the temple took seven and one-half years and was completed approximately 959 B.C.*

Introducing the Bible Account
Discuss worship. Explain that worship—a way of life for a believer—shows reverence and love to God's name, God's Word, and God's works. Christians express their love for God by praising Him with the words they say and the songs they sing.

➤ **Where do believers go to worship?** *(church, or the house of God)*

➤ **Where can believers worship?** *(anywhere)*

Explain the building of the temple. Read all or part of the background information to the students.

Bible Account
Read the following Bible account or read II Chronicles 5:1–7:3.

Dedication of the Temple of God

All the work for the temple was completed. The silver, gold, and all the instruments were in the treasuries. So Solomon gathered together all the elders of Israel, all the leaders of the tribes, and the princes of Israel to dedicate the temple to God.

With the people all assembled, the Levites took the ark of the covenant, which contained the stone tablets of the law and the holy vessels, out of the tabernacle and brought them into the temple. King Solomon and the people sacrificed to the Lord so many sheep and oxen that they could not be counted. Then the priests brought the ark of the covenant to the inner sanctuary, which was the most holy place of the temple. The priests placed the ark of the covenant in its permanent location. They removed the staves that had been used to carry the ark of the covenant. After the priests left the holy place, the Levites who served as temple musicians praised and thanked God. The musicians—singers, players of cymbals, psalteries, and harps, and 120 trumpeters—were dressed in white as they played their instruments and sang. Their music was as one sound of praise to the Lord, "For he is good; for his mercy endureth for ever." Then the temple was filled with a cloud, and the priests were unable to minister because the glory of the Lord had filled the house.

Solomon stood and blessed the whole congregation and praised God. He told the history of the building of the temple, how his father David wanted to build God a house. He told how God said that David's son would build it.

Then Solomon kneeled down on a platform he had built and prayed a prayer of dedication before all the congregation. Solomon praised God for who He is and for the promises He had kept. Solomon asked God to continue in the keeping of His promises to his father, David, and praised God for His goodness, which cannot be contained in a building. He asked God to hear the prayers of the people and to show favor on the temple day and night.

When Solomon stopped praying, a fire came down from heaven and consumed the burnt offerings and sacrifices, "and the glory of the Lord filled the house." When the children of Israel saw the fire, they all bowed down to the ground and praised the Lord, saying, "For he is good; for his mercy endureth forever."

➤ **Why did God allow King Solomon and not King David to oversee the building of the temple?** *(God planned the building of the temple through David, but He did not allow David to oversee the building of the temple because he was a man of war and had shed blood.)*

➤ **Why was the temple built on a high place—Mount Moriah?** *(God chose the location, and the temple could be seen from a distance.)*

➤ **What happened when all the people were assembled at the temple?** *(The Levites carried the ark of the covenant and holy vessels out of the tabernacle and into the temple. Solomon dedicated the temple to God, presented offerings and sacrifices to God, and prayed a prayer of praise and thanksgiving.)*

➤ **What does *dedication* mean?** *(a setting apart for a special or holy purpose)*

➤ **What did the people do on dedication day?** *(They praised God with instruments and voices. They made offerings and sacrifices to God. They bowed down and worshiped God.)*

➤ **What filled the temple of God?** *(the glory of the Lord, like a cloud)*

Memory Verse—Psalm 29:2

Principle: God wants us to worship him. Locate **Psalm 29:2** and read the verse aloud as the students read silently. Allow different students to read the verse aloud. Tell the students to highlight the verse in their Bibles (optional) and to mark the location with the Unit 2 Bookmark.

➤ **What is the first thing this verse tells us to do?** *(to give unto the Lord the glory that He deserves)*

➤ **How do you think you can give glory to the Lord?** *(Possible answers include avoiding sin, attending church, singing praises, witnessing, helping others, praying, reading God's Word, and relating everything in life to God.)*

➤ **What is the second thing this verse tells us to do?** *(to worship the Lord in His holiness)*

➤ **What does it mean to worship God?** *(Possible answers include showing reverence, devotion, and love through our actions, words, prayer, and songs so that God receives the glory for everything we do.)*

Explain that to worship God, a Christian should keep himself free from sin and try to be holy as God is holy. Read **Psalm 66:18** to the students.

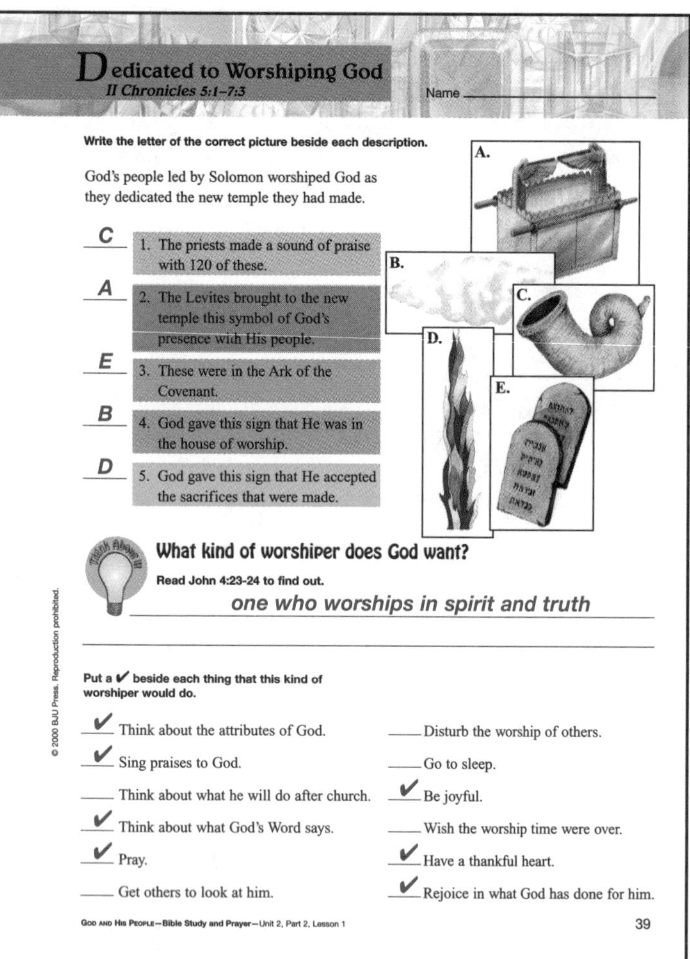

Dedicated to Worshiping God
II Chronicles 5:1–7:3

Name ____________

Write the letter of the correct picture beside each description.

God's people led by Solomon worshiped God as they dedicated the new temple they had made.

C 1. The priests made a sound of praise with 120 of these.

A 2. The Levites brought to the new temple this symbol of God's presence with His people.

E 3. These were in the Ark of the Covenant.

B 4. God gave this sign that He was in the house of worship.

D 5. God gave this sign that He accepted the sacrifices that were made.

A. B. C. D. E.

What kind of worshiper does God want?

Read John 4:23-24 to find out.

one who worships in spirit and truth

Put a ✔ beside each thing that this kind of worshiper would do.

✔ Think about the attributes of God.
✔ Sing praises to God.
___ Think about what he will do after church.
✔ Think about what God's Word says.
✔ Pray.
___ Get others to look at him.
___ Disturb the worship of others.
___ Go to sleep.
✔ Be joyful.
___ Wish the worship time were over.
✔ Have a thankful heart.
✔ Rejoice in what God has done for him.

God and His People—Bible Study and Prayer—Unit 2, Part 2, Lesson 1 39

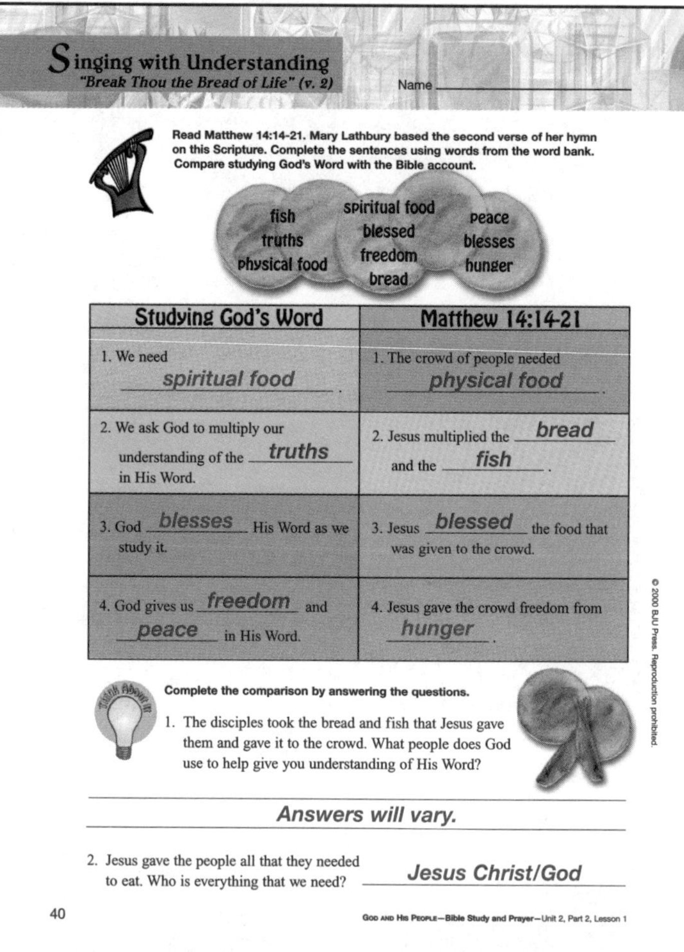

Singing with Understanding
"Break Thou the Bread of Life" (v. 2)

Name ____________

Read Matthew 14:14-21. Mary Lathbury based the second verse of her hymn on this Scripture. Complete the sentences using words from the word bank. Compare studying God's Word with the Bible account.

fish, truths, physical food, spiritual food, blessed, freedom, bread, peace, blesses, hunger

Studying God's Word	Matthew 14:14-21
1. We need *spiritual food*.	1. The crowd of people needed *physical food*.
2. We ask God to multiply our understanding of the *truths* in His Word.	2. Jesus multiplied the *bread* and the *fish*.
3. God *blesses* His Word as we study it.	3. Jesus *blessed* the food that was given to the crowd.
4. God gives us *freedom* and *peace* in His Word.	4. Jesus gave the crowd freedom from *hunger*.

Complete the comparison by answering the questions.

1. The disciples took the bread and fish that Jesus gave them and gave it to the crowd. What people does God use to help give you understanding of His Word?

Answers will vary.

2. Jesus gave the people all that they needed to eat. Who is everything that we need? *Jesus Christ/God*

40 God and His People—Bible Study and Prayer—Unit 2, Part 2, Lesson 1

Worktext page 39

Recall details about the Bible account and apply Bible knowledge to everyday life.

Hymn: "Break Thou the Bread of Life"

Teach the second verse (Worktext page 273). Explain that verse 2 reads like part of a prayer, asking God to multiply or increase our understanding of His truth just as He multiplied the bread when He fed the thousands that came to hear Him. Lead in singing the second verse; then sing together the first two verses with a prayerful heart.

Worktext page 40

Singing with understanding, verse 2.

Lesson 2

Hymn: "Break Thou the Bread of Life"

Sing the first and second verses (Worktext page 273). Divide the students into four groups, letting each group sing one phrase of the first verse. Then ask someone from each group to explain the meaning of his phrase. Repeat the procedure with the second verse.

Background Information

Feast of Tabernacles—*Through Moses, God brought His people out of the land of Egypt. While they were still in the wilderness, living in tents, God told them about memorials that they were to hold each year to celebrate what He had done for them. In Leviticus 23, God told His people to keep the* Feast of Tabernacles (Booths), *a thanksgiving feast for the final harvests of the year, as well as a remembrance of living in tents while traveling through the wilderness from Egypt to Canaan. This is the only feast of the Old Testament mentioned to be reinstituted during the Millennium.*

Introducing the Bible Account

Review the previous Bible account. Review the building and the dedication of the temple.

Bible Account

Read the following Bible account or read II Chronicles 7:4-22.

Israel Worships God

King Solomon offered a sacrifice of 22,000 oxen and 120,000 sheep to dedicate the temple and himself to God. The people also offered sacrifices to dedicate the temple and themselves to God.

The priests stood at their posts. They sounded trumpets and played the musical instruments that King David had made to praise the Lord. The Bible says that all the people stood.

King Solomon set aside the inner court for burnt offerings to be sacrificed to the Lord. Then Solomon proclaimed that the feast was to begin. During this feast, the people of Israel were to worship God by dedicating His temple or house. After the dedication of the temple, King Solomon and the people observed the Feast of the Tabernacles (Booths) for seven more days. (Share the background information about the Feast of Tabernacles.)

On the eighth day Solomon called the people together for a *solemn assembly.*

After the solemn assembly the people went away to their tents. The Israelites went with gladness and merriment in their hearts, for the goodness of the Lord had been shown unto them. After the celebrations were over, God spoke to Solomon in the night and told him that his prayer had been heard. God promised Solomon, "If my [God's] people, which are called by my name, shall humble themselves, and pray, and seek my face, and turn from their wicked ways; then will I hear from heaven, and will forgive their sin, and will heal their land." But if my [God's] people turn away from me, no longer obey my commandments, and worship other gods, I will remove them from this land. And as their enemies walk by and look up at this temple they will ask why the Lord did this to you. "And it shall be answered, Because they forsook the Lord God of their fathers."

- ➤ **During the feast celebrating the completion of the temple, what were the people to do?** *(Offer sacrifices to dedicate the temple and dedicate themselves to God.)*
- ➤ **Why did God instruct His people in the days of Moses to keep the Feast of Tabernacles every year?** *(to help them remember how God had delivered them out of slavery in Egypt and remember all that God had done for them)*

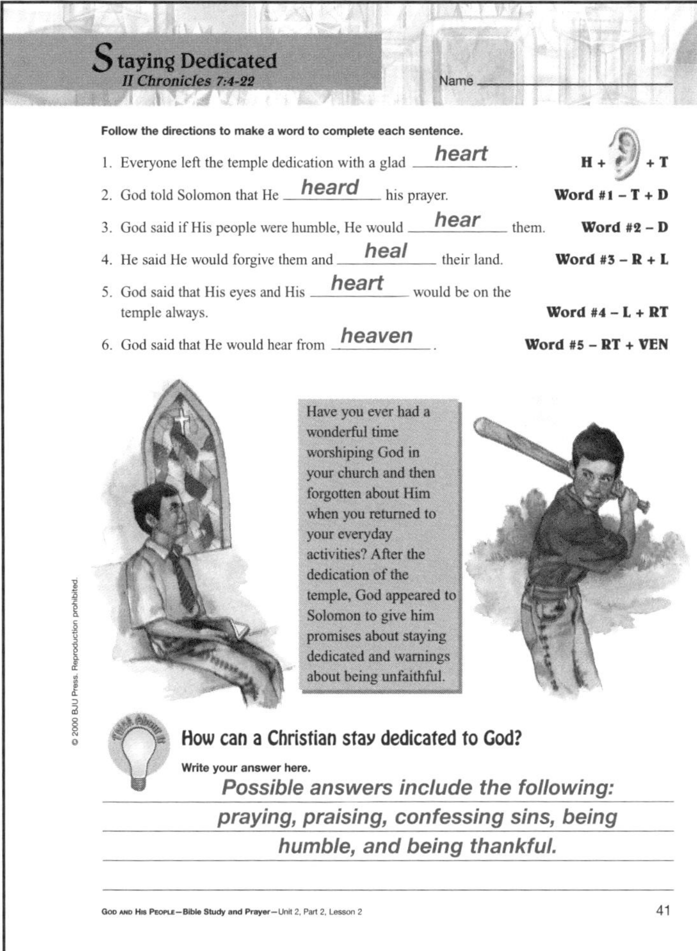

Staying Dedicated
II Chronicles 7:4-22
Name ____________

Follow the directions to make a word to complete each sentence.

1. Everyone left the temple dedication with a glad *heart*. — H + (ear) + T
2. God told Solomon that He *heard* his prayer. — Word #1 – T + D
3. God said if His people were humble, He would *hear* them. — Word #2 – D
4. He said He would forgive them and *heal* their land. — Word #3 – R + L
5. God said that His eyes and His *heart* would be on the temple always. — Word #4 – L + RT
6. God said that He would hear from *heaven*. — Word #5 – RT + VEN

Have you ever had a wonderful time worshiping God in your church and then forgotten about Him when you returned to your everyday activities? After the dedication of the temple, God appeared to Solomon to give him promises about staying dedicated and warnings about being unfaithful.

How can a Christian stay dedicated to God?
Write your answer here.
Possible answers include the following: praying, praising, confessing sins, being humble, and being thankful.

God and His People—Bible Study and Prayer—Unit 2, Part 2, Lesson 2 41

- ➤ **What did God promise Solomon?** *(God would bless His people if they stayed true to God.)*
- ➤ **What did God tell Solomon?** *(If God's people turned from Him, He would remove them from His land and make the temple an example to other nations.)*

Worktext page 41

Recall details about the Bible account.

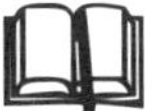

Memory Verse—Psalm 29:2

Practice the memory verse. Locate **Psalm 29:2** and read the verse aloud while the students read silently. Explain that when David wrote psalms, he wrote them as songs to be sung in praise to God. Psalm 29 is one of David's songs of praise that he might have sung or spoken in public to the people of Israel.

Direct the students to read **Psalm 29:2** as if they were telling it to someone. Demonstrate how to put expression in the voice and how to emphasize some words.

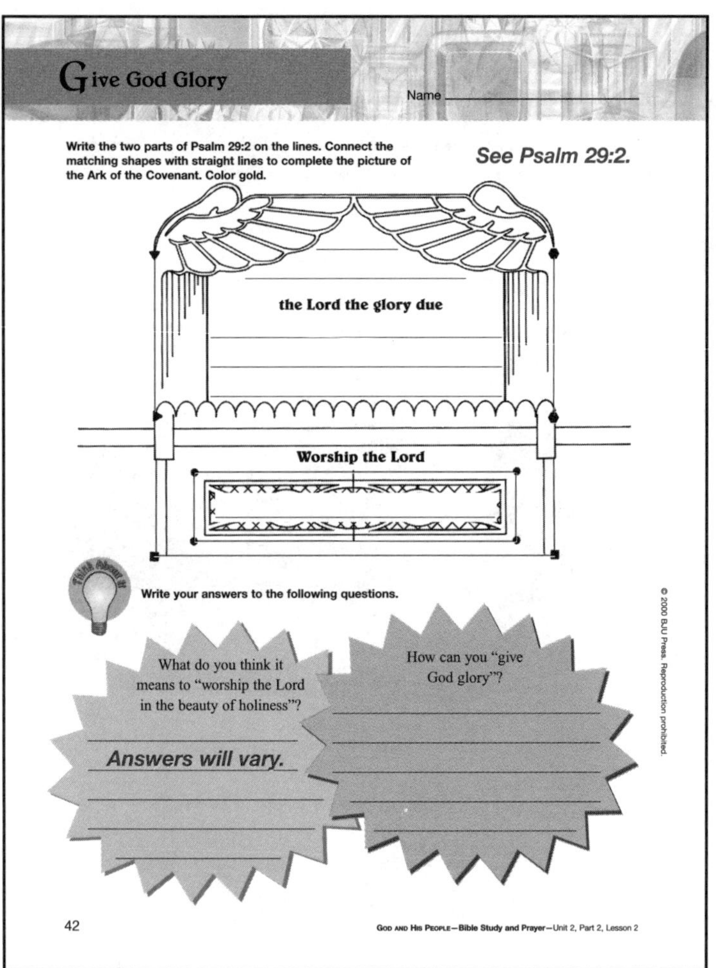

Give God Glory
Name
Write the two parts of Psalm 29:2 on the lines. Connect the matching shapes with straight lines to complete the picture of the Ark of the Covenant. Color gold.
See Psalm 29:2.
the Lord the glory due
Worship the Lord
Write your answers to the following questions.
What do you think it means to "worship the Lord in the beauty of holiness"?
Answers will vary.
How can you "give God glory"?
© 2000 BJU Press. Reproduction prohibited.
42
God and His People—Bible Study and Prayer—Unit 2, Part 2, Lesson 2

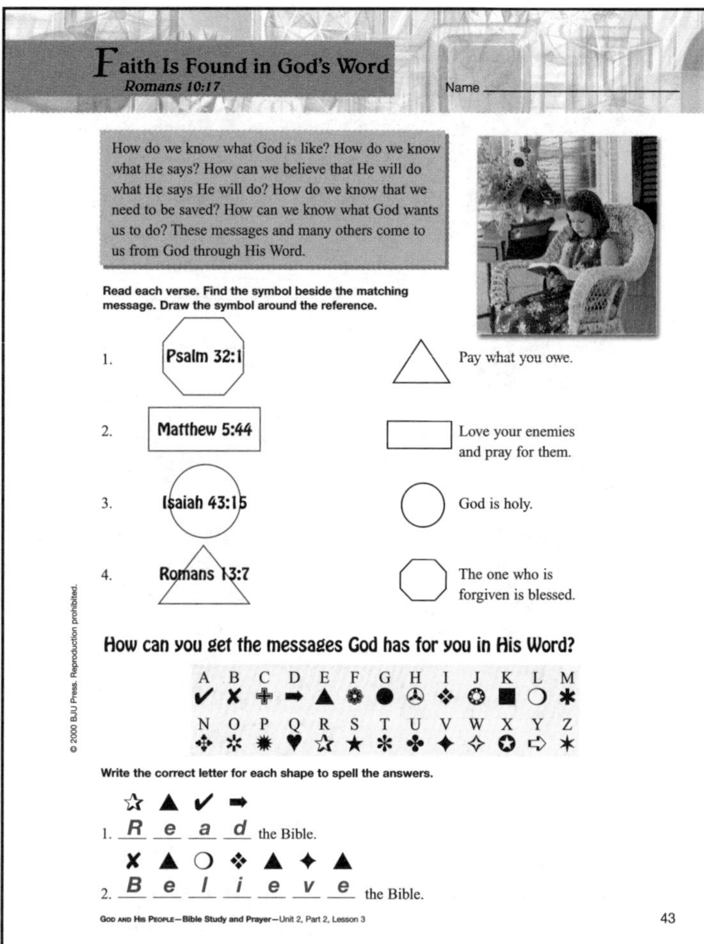

Faith Is Found in God's Word
Romans 10:17
Name
How do we know what God is like? How do we know what He says? How can we believe that He will do what He says He will do? How do we know that we need to be saved? How can we know what God wants us to do? These messages and many others come to us from God through His Word.
Read each verse. Find the symbol beside the matching message. Draw the symbol around the reference.
1. Psalm 32:1
2. Matthew 5:44
3. Isaiah 43:15
4. Romans 13:7
Pay what you owe.
Love your enemies and pray for them.
God is holy.
The one who is forgiven is blessed.
How can you get the messages God has for you in His Word?
Write the correct letter for each shape to spell the answers.
1. Read the Bible.
2. Believe the Bible.
© 2000 BJU Press. Reproduction prohibited.
God and His People—Bible Study and Prayer—Unit 2, Part 2, Lesson 3
43

Worktext page 42

Develop understanding of the memory verse.

Lesson 3

Materials

- Copy of *Captive Treasure* for the teacher (and for each student [optional])"

Hymn: "Break Thou the Bread of Life"

Sing the first and second verses (Worktext page 273). Play the recording and lead in singing the first two verses reverently like a prayer.

Memory Verse—Psalm 29:2

Practice the memory verse. Locate **Psalm 29:2.** Choose several students to read the verse aloud while the others follow along. Say the verse together from memory. Allow groups of two to practice saying the verse to each other.

Worktext page 43

Locate information in Scripture.

History Connection (optional)

Discuss the results of God's people turning away from Him. Read aloud **II Chronicles 7:19-21,** God's warning to His people.

➤ **Did God's people stay true to God?** *(No. They went their own rebellious way.)*

Tell the students that the Babylonians were one of many nations who defeated the Israelites and took captives (605-538 B.C.). During the captivity, God instructed the people through the prophets. Ezekiel and Daniel prophesied to the people while in Babylon. Jeremiah, Habakkuk, and Zephaniah also gave God's words at this time. The kingdom of Babylon was later overthrown by Cyrus, the Persian ruler, who allowed the Jews to return to their homeland (538 B.C.). Ezra and Nehemiah led the people to rebuild the temple and the walls. Today God also uses people and nations to accomplish His will.

Introducing the Application Novel

Discuss Plains Indians. Explain that the Plains Indians lived in tipis (homes made of animal skins stretched over poles) during the summer months as they followed the buffalo herds. Their **lodges** of logs and dirt provided more permanent shelter during the colder months. Many Indian tribes fought to keep their land. Sometimes raids (surprise attacks) were made for revenge or honor. It was an honorable thing to touch an enemy in battle and return to tell about it. Upon his return, a brave warrior was given a feather to add to his *coup stick.*

Application Novel: *Captive Treasure*

Read and discuss Chapter 3. Review the events that took place in Chapters 1 and 2. Direct the students to read Chapter 3 silently or read it aloud to discover what new dangers the Talbots faced. *(Indians, sickness)*

➤ **How did Mr. Talbot show thoughtfulness?** *(He saw the needs of other families and invited them to the Fourth of July celebration feast.)*

➤ **What names did the girls and Peter give for the full moon?** *(a copper penny, a silver medallion, a savory pie, a warrior's moon because Indian warriors traveled by moonlight to attack.)*

➤ **Why was cholera a danger to the wagon train?** *(Carrie and many other people got the disease, and some died.)*

➤ **Why was Peter driving the Talbot's wagon, and why did he stop the wagon?** *(Mother was caring for the Gantz family and Father was helping the wagon master, so Peter drove their wagon. He stopped to see a certain horse.)*

➤ **What happened to Carrie as the wagon rushed to safety from the Indians?** *(She reached to get the Bible from the torn pocket and fell out of the wagon.)*

➤ **What did Carrie use to protect herself from the Indian attack?** *(the Bible)*

Read and discuss Chapter 4. Direct the students to read Chapter 4 silently or listen as you read it aloud to find out what brought peace to Carrie's worries. *(remembering a Bible verse and praying)* Point out that when it is difficult to know how to pray, a believer can pray that the will of God be done.

➤ **What did the Indians call Carrie's Bible?** *(the medicine bundle)*

➤ **How did the Indians respond when they saw Carrie's Bible?** *(with reverence)*

➤ **How can you show reverence to God's Word?** *(Possible answers include handling a Bible carefully, and listening respectfully when hearing Scripture or preaching.)*

Explain that we worship God when showing reverence to God's name, Word, and works. Worship is also expressed through praise to God in song and words.

➤ **How did the Cheyenne family show kindness to Carrie by their actions?** *(They fed her, smiled at her, and motioned for her to sleep.)*

➤ **How did Carrie understand what the Cheyenne were saying?** *(She had learned some of the sign language as she traveled with the wagon train and figured out some of their signs.)*

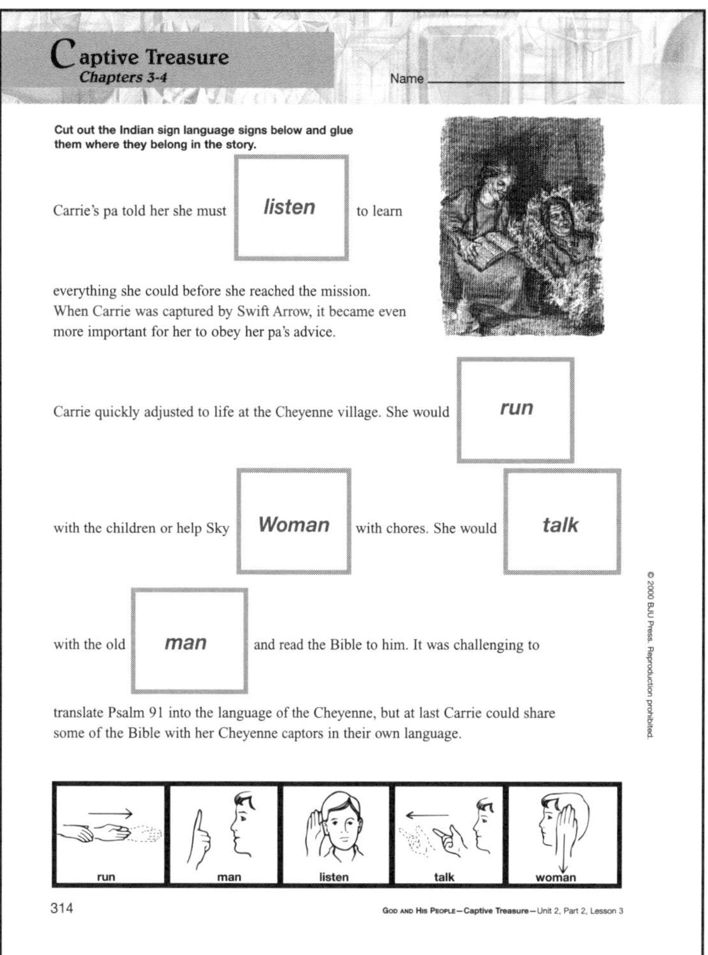

Captive Treasure
Chapters 3-4
Name ____________

Cut out the Indian sign language signs below and glue them where they belong in the story.

Carrie's pa told her she must [listen] to learn everything she could before she reached the mission. When Carrie was captured by Swift Arrow, it became even more important for her to obey her pa's advice.

Carrie quickly adjusted to life at the Cheyenne village. She would [run] with the children or help Sky [Woman] with chores. She would [talk] with the old [man] and read the Bible to him. It was challenging to translate Psalm 91 into the language of the Cheyenne, but at last Carrie could share some of the Bible with her Cheyenne captors in their own language.

run | man | listen | talk | woman

© 2000 BJU Press. Reproduction prohibited.

314 GOD AND HIS PEOPLE—Captive Treasure—Unit 2, Part 2, Lesson 3

➤ **What do you think is going to happen to Carrie?** *(Answers will vary.)*

Worktext Supplement page 314

Use sign language to convey meaning. Explain that the Cheyenne that Carrie was with used sign language to convey their messages. Demonstrate the following signs: *man, woman, listen, talk, run.* Allow the students to use the signs to communicate a message.

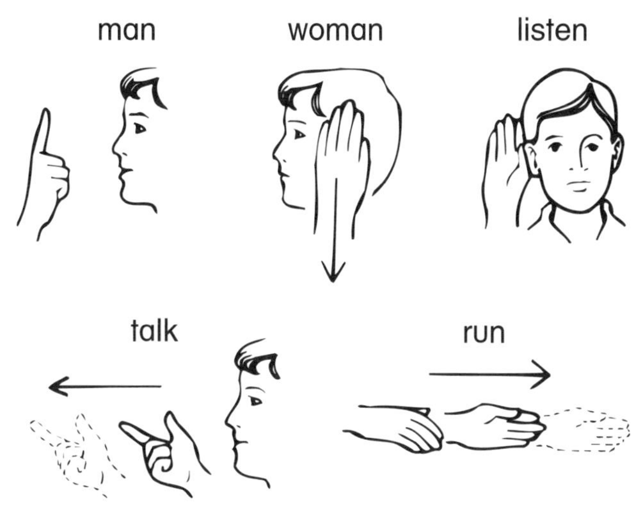

Lesson 4

Materials

- Song: "Books of the Old Testament"
- Old Testament Bible Book Cards
- Old Testament Divisions Bookmark
- Copy of *Captive Treasure* for the teacher (and for each student [optional])

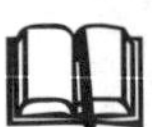

Memory Verse—Psalm 29:2

Practice the memory verse. Locate **Psalm 29:2** and read the verse aloud as the students read silently. Divide into two groups. Practice saying the verse from memory by having group 1 say the first phrase and group 2 say the second phrase. Direct the groups to switch phrases and say the verse. Allow all the students to say the verse from memory.

Song: "Books of the Old Testament"

Sing all five verses (Worktext page 287). Play the recording and lead in singing the song. Distribute the bookmarks of the Old Testament books.

Bible Study Skills

Review the order of the Old Testament books. Direct the students in saying together the names of the books of the Old Testament. Form three or four groups, and direct each group to line up. Show a Bible Book Card to the students at the front of the lines. The student who first calls out the book that comes before the book shown receives a point for his team. Direct the students in front to go to the end of their lines to allow the next players in line to have a turn. (*Note:* When the card for Genesis is displayed, the game can be stopped and a winner determined, or students can call out "first book." A variation is to have the students call out the book that comes after the book shown.)

One-on-One: The student looks at the card, says the name of the book that comes before the book on the card; then he checks his answer with the table of contents in his Bible or with his bookmark.

Bible Study Skills, Worktext page 44

Sequence the books of the Old Testament and identify the book where an account is located.

Background Information

Medicine Bundle—*The medicine bundle was a bag of items kept on a pole in the lodge. The Cheyenne Indians thought the medicine bundle had great power.*

Pemmican—*Buffalo meat was dried, ground into a powder, and then mixed with fat and sometimes berries. It was used especially when traveling.*

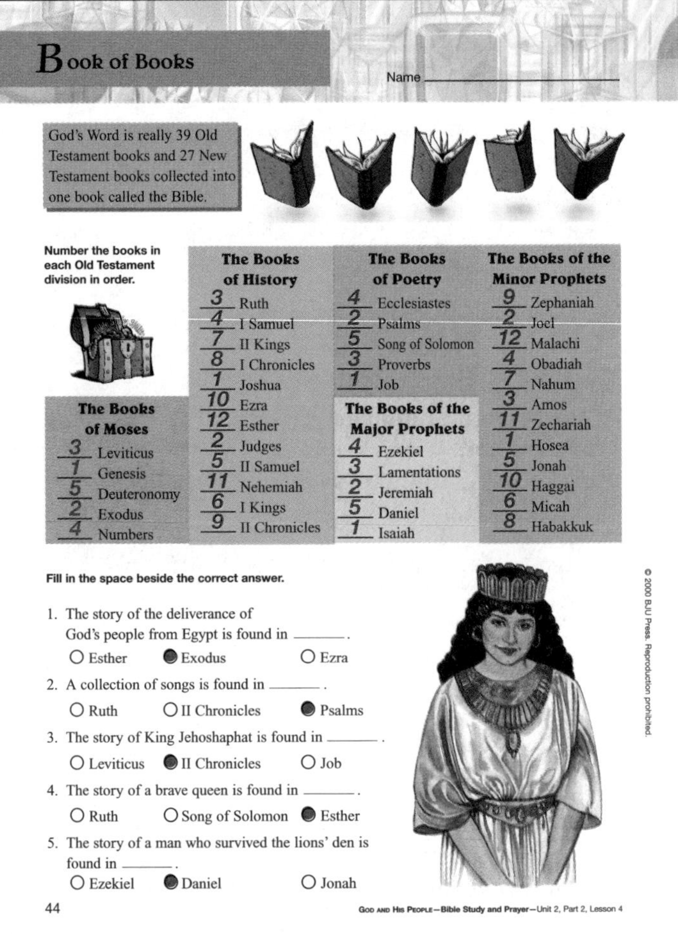

Book of Books Name ____________

God's Word is really 39 Old Testament books and 27 New Testament books collected into one book called the Bible.

Number the books in each Old Testament division in order.

The Books of Moses
3 Leviticus
1 Genesis
5 Deuteronomy
2 Exodus
4 Numbers

The Books of History
3 Ruth
4 I Samuel
7 II Kings
8 I Chronicles
1 Joshua
10 Ezra
12 Esther
2 Judges
5 II Samuel
11 Nehemiah
6 I Kings
9 II Chronicles

The Books of Poetry
4 Ecclesiastes
2 Psalms
5 Song of Solomon
3 Proverbs
1 Job

The Books of the Major Prophets
4 Ezekiel
3 Lamentations
2 Jeremiah
5 Daniel
1 Isaiah

The Books of the Minor Prophets
9 Zephaniah
2 Joel
12 Malachi
4 Obadiah
7 Nahum
3 Amos
11 Zechariah
1 Hosea
5 Jonah
10 Haggai
6 Micah
8 Habakkuk

Fill in the space beside the correct answer.

1. The story of the deliverance of God's people from Egypt is found in ______.
   ○ Esther ● Exodus ○ Ezra
2. A collection of songs is found in ______.
   ○ Ruth ○ II Chronicles ● Psalms
3. The story of King Jehoshaphat is found in ______.
   ○ Leviticus ● II Chronicles ○ Job
4. The story of a brave queen is found in ______.
   ○ Ruth ○ Song of Solomon ● Esther
5. The story of a man who survived the lions' den is found in ______.
   ○ Ezekiel ● Daniel ○ Jonah

44 God and His People—Bible Study and Prayer—Unit 2, Part 2, Lesson 4

Introducing the Application Novel

Review previous events.

➤ **What do these words remind you of from the story: horses, cholera, Fourth of July, penny, warrior's moon, and Bible?** *(Answers will vary.)*

➤ **What treasure had been captured?** *(the Bible)*

Point out that the Indians thought good things would happen to them because they had the Bible. The Bible was also a treasure to Carrie. She read and studied it to know more about God. She memorized God's Word to meditate upon during the day.

Application Novel: *Captive Treasure*

Read and discuss Chapter 5. Direct the students to read Chapter 5 silently, or read the chapter aloud to the students. Challenge them to find out how Carrie learned the Cheyenne language. *(She listened to them talk and tried to repeat the syllables.)*

➤ **How did Carrie show a good attitude toward her captors?** *(She worked and played with the children.)*

➤ **What did Carrie do to comfort herself?** *(She read the Scriptures aloud.)*

➤ **Who listened as Carrie read aloud from the Bible?** *(the grandfather)*

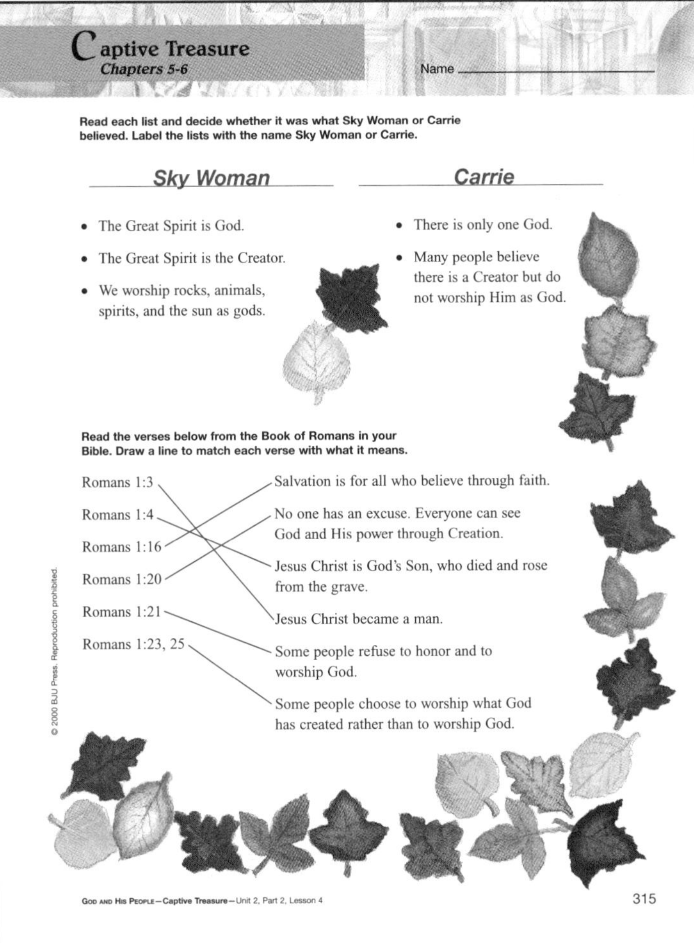
Captive Treasure
Chapters 5-6

Name ____________

Read each list and decide whether it was what Sky Woman or Carrie believed. Label the lists with the name Sky Woman or Carrie.

Sky Woman	Carrie
• The Great Spirit is God.	• There is only one God.
• The Great Spirit is the Creator.	• Many people believe there is a Creator but do not worship Him as God.
• We worship rocks, animals, spirits, and the sun as gods.	

Read the verses below from the Book of Romans in your Bible. Draw a line to match each verse with what it means.

Romans 1:3	Salvation is for all who believe through faith.
Romans 1:4	No one has an excuse. Everyone can see God and His power through Creation.
Romans 1:16	Jesus Christ is God's Son, who died and rose from the grave.
Romans 1:20	Jesus Christ became a man.
Romans 1:21	Some people refuse to honor and to worship God.
Romans 1:23, 25	Some people choose to worship what God has created rather than to worship God.

GOD AND HIS PEOPLE—Captive Treasure—Unit 2, Part 2, Lesson 4 315

➤ **How do you know that Carrie was brave?** *(She frightened a bear away from Little One.)*

➤ **How did Swift Arrow honor Carrie for her bravery?** *(He gave her an eagle feather from his coup stick.)*

➤ **Who did Carrie say was her help?** *(God)* Share the background information about the medicine bundle.

Read and discuss Chapter 6. Direct the students to read Chapter 6 silently or listen as you read it aloud to find out who these Indians worshiped. *(the Great Spirit)*

➤ **Why were the people going to the valley?** *(It was fall and their lodges in the valley gave shelter for the winter.)*

➤ **What preparations had been made for the trip?** *(Chokecherries were dried, and pemmican and hides were packed.)* Share the background information about pemmican.

➤ **What decision did Swift Arrow make?** *(The family would stay with the Keeper and join the others later.)*

➤ **What did Carrie do to help the Keeper understand the Bible?** *(translated Psalm 91 into the Cheyenne language)*

➤ **Where did Carrie find the answers to the Keeper's questions?** *(She remembered her father's lessons and studied her Bible.)*

➤ **How is it possible to have contentment?** *(Answers will vary but point out that Christians can rest peacefully, knowing that God watches over and cares for them and is with them all the time. He has the power to do anything.)*

Worktext Supplement page 315

Distinguish biblical truth from error. Discuss the differences between what Carrie and Sky Woman believed. Read aloud **Isaiah 45:5-6.**

Find information in Scripture. Point out that those who worship things in nature try to find salvation through man's ways.

Going Beyond

Materials

- Computer software of the Bible

Enrichment

Introduce the Bible in computer software form. Show the features of the program on a computer.

➤ **Why is it helpful to have Bible software?** *(Possible answers include the ease of finding verses, studying topics, and printing out verses for memory cards.)*

Allow the students to do a word search using the computer.

Preview

Doctrines

- The Bible says that it is inspired (II Timothy 3:16-17)—Lesson 1
- The Bible presents standards of living and a way of life that are of God (Psalm 119:1-8)—Lesson 2
- The Bible is eternal (Psalm 119:89)—Lesson 2

Skills and Applications

- Learn Hebrews 4:12
- Learn the Gospels
- Read a map
- Recall facts and details
- Match characters and dialogue
- Locate information in Scripture
- Draw conclusions
- Realize that God's Word is powerful
- Realize that if Christians trust in God, He will take care of them
- Appreciate the attributes of God
- Apply Bible knowledge to everyday life

Lesson 1

Materials

- Chart 31, "Divided Kingdom"
- Unit 2 Bookmark for each student
- An x-ray or a picture of an x-ray (optional)
- Highlighter for each student (optional)

Hymn: "Break Thou the Bread of Life"

Teach the third verse (Worktext page 273). Play the recording of verse 3 as the students read the words silently. Explain that another name for God's Word is the Bread of Life. In the third verse, the writer is asking God to help him love the Bread of Life more and to give him the ability to share it with others. Lead in singing verse 3 together while thinking of the meaning of the hymn; then sing verses 1-3.

Memory Verse—Hebrews 4:12

Principle: God's Word is alive and powerful. Locate **Hebrews 4:12** and read the verse aloud as the students read it silently. Explain that God's Word is able to penetrate to our innermost being and to reveal to us our sinful nature and our need of a Savior. Choose volunteers to read the verse aloud. Direct the students to highlight the verse in their Bibles (optional) and to mark the location with the Unit 2 Bookmark.

Background Information

Divided Kingdom—*After King Solomon's wonderful dedication of the temple and his reliance on God for wisdom, he began to fall into luxurious living and pride in his possessions. To support his high living, he began to raise taxes. Then Solomon died and his son, Rehoboam, took the throne. Rehoboam imposed even more taxes on the people. When the nation rebelled over taxes, it divided into a southern kingdom (Judah) and a northern kingdom (Israel). One of Solomon's officers, Jeroboam, became king over the Northern Kingdom, which included ten tribes, and Rehoboam remained king over the Southern Kingdom, with only two tribes. Many battles were fought between the two kingdoms, but the division remained.*

Northern Kingdom and Idolatry—*The separating of the Southern Kingdom from the Northern Kingdom also separated those Israelites from Jerusalem, the city of their worship. As a quick remedy, King Jeroboam set up golden calves in Bethel and Dan. The Israelites in the North no longer worshiped in Jerusalem, for King Jeroboam was worried that they might change their allegiance back to Judah. The golden calves were supposed to represent God but were worshiped as idols instead.*

Introducing the Bible Account

Explain the divided kingdoms. Display Chart 31, "Divided Kingdom" and point out the kingdom of Israel and the kingdom of Judah. Share the background information about the divided kingdoms and the Northern Kingdom and idolatry. Point out the city of Jerusalem, where the people of Judah worshiped God in the temple. Point out the cities of Bethel and Dan, where the people of Israel worshiped idols.

Bible Account

Read the following Bible account or read II Chronicles 17:1-9.

Jehoshaphat Lived and Shared God's Word

When Asa, king of Judah, died, his son Jehoshaphat reigned in his place. Jehoshaphat wanted to please the Lord. The Bible says he "strengthened himself against Israel." He made strongholds of the cities of his nation and put soldiers in those cities so that Israel could not defeat Judah in battle.

Jehoshaphat walked in the ways of his ancestor David and sought the Lord as David had.

The good king did as God commanded, tearing down the idols and high places that kings before him had built. Because of this, God made him powerful and gave him honor among his own people and the peoples of the world.

In the third year of King Jehoshaphat's rule, he sent out princes and Levites with the Word of God to all the people. These representatives went throughout Judah, teaching the people from God's Word. As a result of this teaching, the fear of the Lord fell on all the people of Jehoshaphat's kingdom. This was very pleasing to the Lord God.

➤ **How did the nation of Israel become divided?** *(Ten tribes rebelled against paying high taxes to King Rehoboam, Solomon's son.)*

➤ **Why was Jehoshaphat considered a good king?** *(He sought God, followed God, and taught the people from God's Word.)*

➤ **Which kingdom was Jehoshaphat's kingdom?** *(Judah, the Southern Kingdom)*

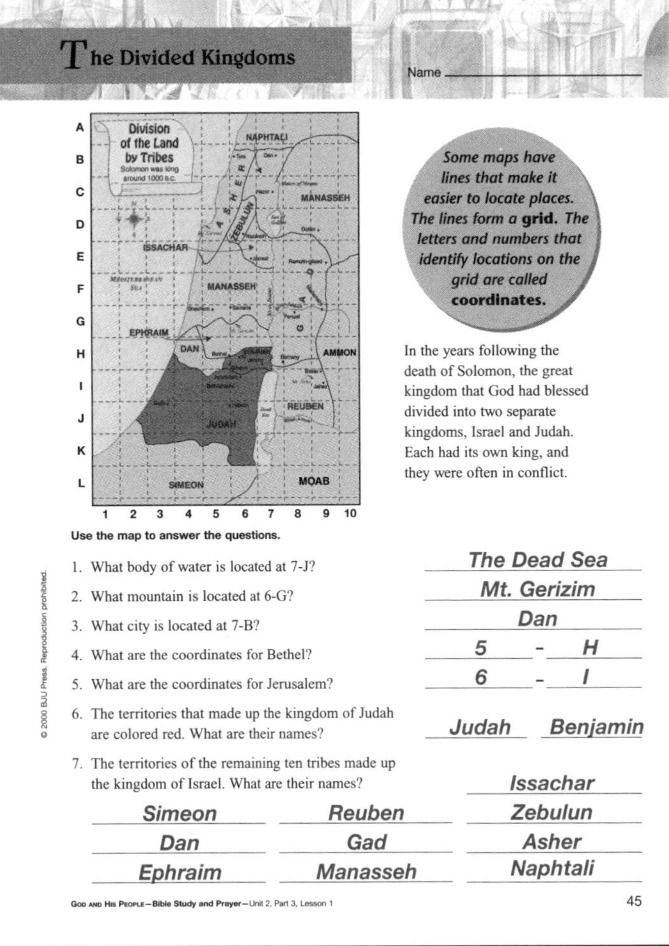

The Divided Kingdoms

Name ____________

Some maps have lines that make it easier to locate places. The lines form a **grid.** The letters and numbers that identify locations on the grid are called **coordinates.**

In the years following the death of Solomon, the great kingdom that God had blessed divided into two separate kingdoms, Israel and Judah. Each had its own king, and they were often in conflict.

Use the map to answer the questions.

1. What body of water is located at 7-J? *The Dead Sea*
2. What mountain is located at 6-G? *Mt. Gerizim*
3. What city is located at 7-B? *Dan*
4. What are the coordinates for Bethel? *5* - *H*
5. What are the coordinates for Jerusalem? *6* - *I*
6. The territories that made up the kingdom of Judah are colored red. What are their names? *Judah* *Benjamin*
7. The territories of the remaining ten tribes made up the kingdom of Israel. What are their names? *Issachar*, *Simeon*, *Reuben*, *Zebulun*, *Dan*, *Gad*, *Asher*, *Ephraim*, *Manasseh*, *Naphtali*

God and His People—Bible Study and Prayer—Unit 2, Part 3, Lesson 1 45

➤ **What else did King Jehoshaphat do for Judah?** *(He fortified the cities against the kingdom of Israel.)*

➤ **What did King Jehoshaphat do to encourage his people to live and worship God?** *(He tore down the false gods and their high places of worship and sent men around the country to teach the people from God's Word.)*

➤ **How can the life of King Jehoshaphat be a good example for you?** *(Possible answers include by obeying God, by sharing God's Word, and by living according to God's Word.)*

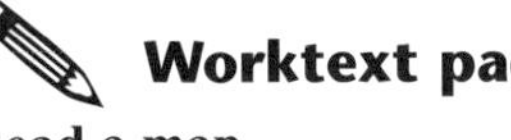

Worktext page 45

Read a map.

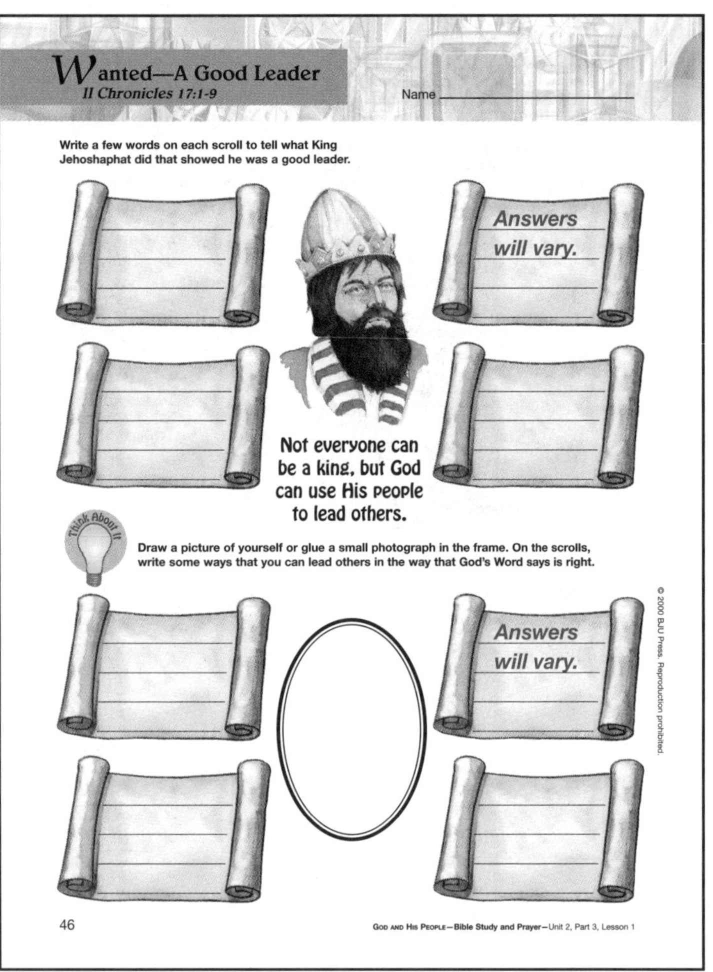
Wanted—A Good Leader
II Chronicles 17:1-9
Name ______________

Write a few words on each scroll to tell what King Jehoshaphat did that showed he was a good leader.

Answers will vary.

Not everyone can be a king, but God can use His people to lead others.

Think About It

Draw a picture of yourself or glue a small photograph in the frame. On the scrolls, write some ways that you can lead others in the way that God's Word says is right.

Answers will vary.

46 God and His People—Bible Study and Prayer—Unit 2, Part 3, Lesson 1

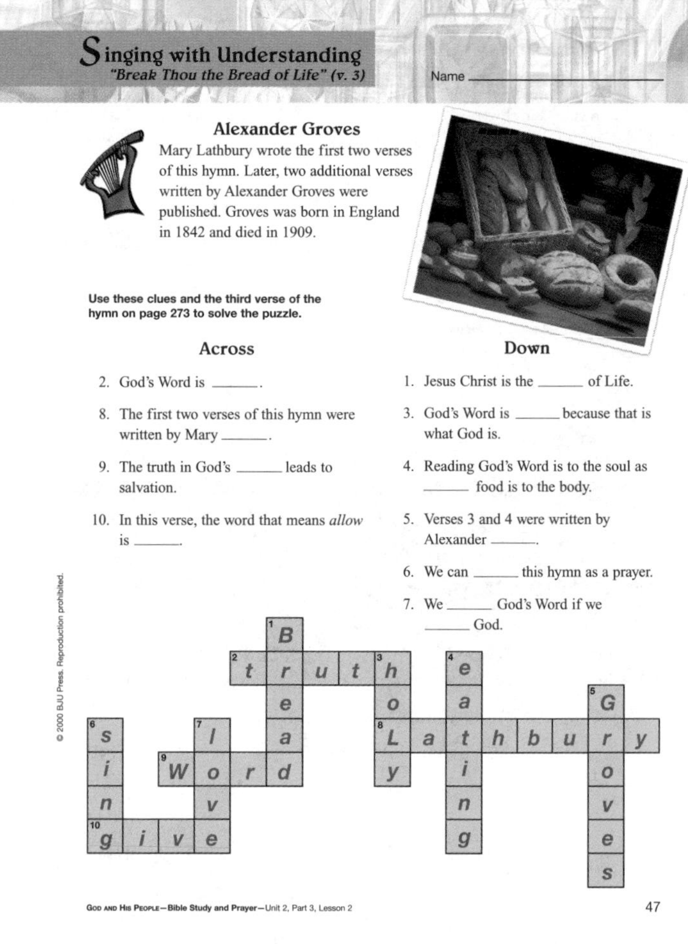
Singing with Understanding
"Break Thou the Bread of Life" (v. 3)
Name ______________

Alexander Groves
Mary Lathbury wrote the first two verses of this hymn. Later, two additional verses written by Alexander Groves were published. Groves was born in England in 1842 and died in 1909.

Use these clues and the third verse of the hymn on page 273 to solve the puzzle.

Across

2. God's Word is ______.
8. The first two verses of this hymn were written by Mary ______.
9. The truth in God's ______ leads to salvation.
10. In this verse, the word that means *allow* is ______.

Down

1. Jesus Christ is the ______ of Life.
3. God's Word is ______ because that is what God is.
4. Reading God's Word is to the soul as ______ food is to the body.
5. Verses 3 and 4 were written by Alexander ______.
6. We can ______ this hymn as a prayer.
7. We ______ God's Word if we ______ God.

Answers: 1 Bread; 2 truth; 3 holy; 4 eating; 5 Groves; 6 sing; 7 love; 8 Lathbury; 9 Word; 10 give

God and His People—Bible Study and Prayer—Unit 2, Part 3, Lesson 2 47

Worktext page 46

Apply Bible knowledge to everyday life.

Science Connection (optional)

Compare an x-ray with the Bible. Show an x-ray or a picture of an x-ray.

- ➤ **What is an x-ray?** *(a picture of the inside of something, generally a person)*
- ➤ **What might an x-ray be used for?** *(Possible answers include to reveal broken bones or tooth decay.)*
- ➤ Read **Hebrews 4:12** aloud. **How is an x-ray like the Word of God?** *(The x-ray and God's Word both reveal what is inside—inside the body for the x-ray and inside the heart for the Bible.)*
- ➤ **What are some of the differences between an x-ray and God's Word?** *(God's Word reveals the heart, soul, and spirit; whereas generally only the bones are revealed on an x-ray.)*

Lesson 2

Preparation of Materials

Write **Hebrews 4:12** on an erasable board.

Hymn: "Break Thou the Bread of Life"

Sing the first three verses (Worktext page 273). Play the recording and lead in singing the third verse; then sing together verses 1-3.

Worktext page 47

Singing with understanding, verse 3.

Introducing the Bible Account

Review the previous account. Guide a discussion about King Jehoshaphat. Explain that while King Jehoshaphat was ruler over Judah for twenty-five years, Israel, the Northern Kingdom, was ruled by evil kings. Tell the students that this Bible account continues the story about King Jehoshaphat.

Bible Account

Read the following Bible account or read II Chronicles 17:10-19.

Judah Turned Back to God

In response to the teaching of God's Word by the princes and Levites that King Jehoshaphat sent out, the fear of the Lord fell not only on the people of Judah but also on all the kingdoms around Judah. This fear of God caused these kingdoms to fear Judah, and not to war with Judah. The fear of God brought peace to Judah.

Even the hated Philistines brought presents and tributes of silver to King Jehoshaphat. The Arabians brought King Jehoshaphat flocks of birds and thousands of rams and goats. The king had God's Word taught to everyone, and he and the kingdom of Judah benefited greatly from it.

King Jehoshaphat became great and was able to build more fortresses in Judah. Thousands of brave men of war came to help defend the kingdom of Judah and to be with the king in Jerusalem.

All this happened to Judah because King Jehoshaphat loved God's law and wanted his people to learn God's Word.

- ➤ **Why did King Jehoshaphat send princes and Levites throughout the land of Judah?** *(to teach God's Word to the people)*
- ➤ **What happened because the king did this?** *(The fear of God fell on all the kingdoms around Judah.)*
- ➤ **How did the fear of God affect the kingdoms around Judah?** *(They did not war against Judah. These kingdoms brought great gifts to King Jehoshaphat and to Judah.)*
- ➤ **Did the king spread God's Word so that he could be great? Why not?** *(No. He did it because he loved God.)*
- ➤ **What did God do for King Jehoshaphat?** *(God made him great because he honored God.)*

Memory Verse—Hebrews 4:12

Practice the memory verse. Direct attention to **Hebrews 4:12** on the board. Read the verse together several times; then erase a word or phrase and reread the verse. Continue until the verse has been completely erased.

Worktext page 48

Draw conclusions and develop an understanding of the memory verse.

Sharper Than Any . . . Sword

Name ____________________

King Jehoshaphat had many brave captains who commanded thousands of soldiers, but the real defense of his kingdom was God's protection. God defended Judah because the people and their leader delighted in God's Word. The neighboring countries were fearful of challenging such a nation.

Use your Bible to help you write the rest of Hebrews 4:12 on the lines.

For the word ____________________

See Hebrews 4:12.

How is the Word of God like a sword? *Possible answers include that the Word of God can protect Christians and can open/reveal what is in someone's heart or mind.*

Put an X on each sword you find hidden in this picture. Do not forget that the Bible can be called a sword!

© 2000 BJU Press. Reproduction prohibited.

48 God and His People—Bible Study and Prayer—Unit 2, Part 3, Lesson 2

Lesson 3

Materials

- Copy of *Captive Treasure* for the teacher (and for each student [optional])

Hymn: "Break Thou the Bread of Life"

Sing the first three verses (Worktext page 273). Lead in singing verses 1-3. If time allows, divide into groups and let each group make up hand motions for words in a verse. Allow time for each group to share its hand motions with the other students.

One-on-One: Direct the student to make up hand motions for words in one verse.

Memory Verse—Hebrews 4:12

Practice the memory verse. Locate **Hebrews 4:12** and choose a student to explain what the verse means to him and then to read the verse aloud. Practice saying the verse responsively with the teacher saying the first word, students the second word, teacher the next word, and so on. Practice the verse by reading it throughout the day.

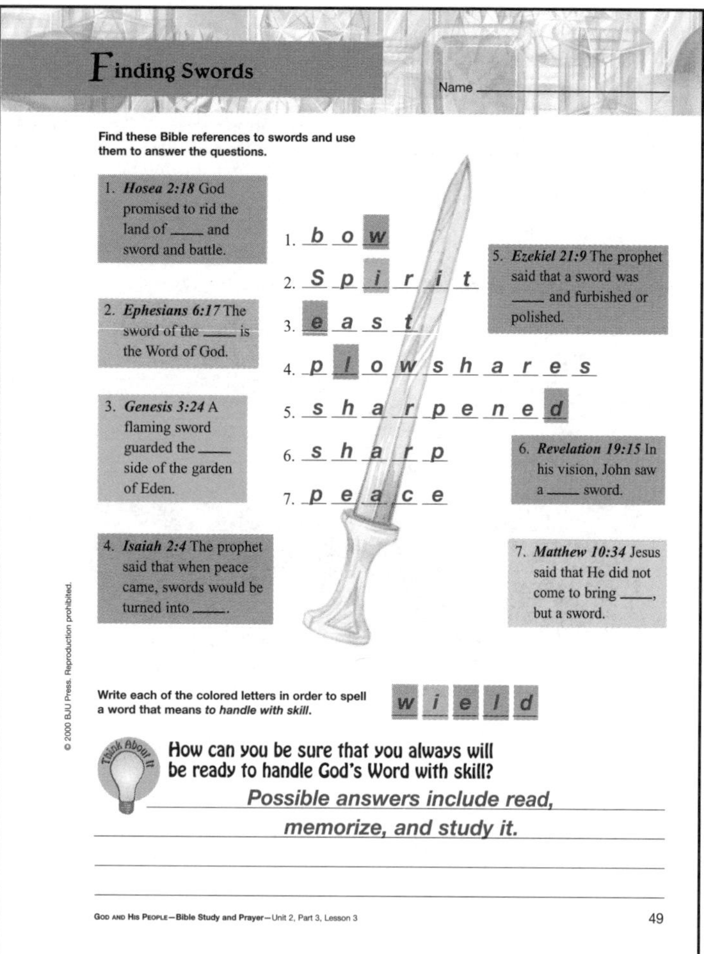

Finding Swords

Name ______________

Find these Bible references to swords and use them to answer the questions.

1. *Hosea 2:18* God promised to rid the land of ____ and sword and battle.
2. *Ephesians 6:17* The sword of the ____ is the Word of God.
3. *Genesis 3:24* A flaming sword guarded the ____ side of the garden of Eden.
4. *Isaiah 2:4* The prophet said that when peace came, swords would be turned into ____.
5. *Ezekiel 21:9* The prophet said that a sword was ____ and furbished or polished.
6. *Revelation 19:15* In his vision, John saw a ____ sword.
7. *Matthew 10:34* Jesus said that He did not come to bring ____, but a sword.

1. b o w
2. S p i r i t
3. e a s t
4. p l o w s h a r e s
5. s h a r p e n e d
6. s h a r p
7. p e a c e

Write each of the colored letters in order to spell a word that means *to handle with skill.* w i e l d

Think About It: How can you be sure that you always will be ready to handle God's Word with skill?

Possible answers include read, memorize, and study it.

© 2000 BJU Press. Reproduction prohibited.

God and His People—Bible Study and Prayer—Unit 2, Part 3, Lesson 3 49

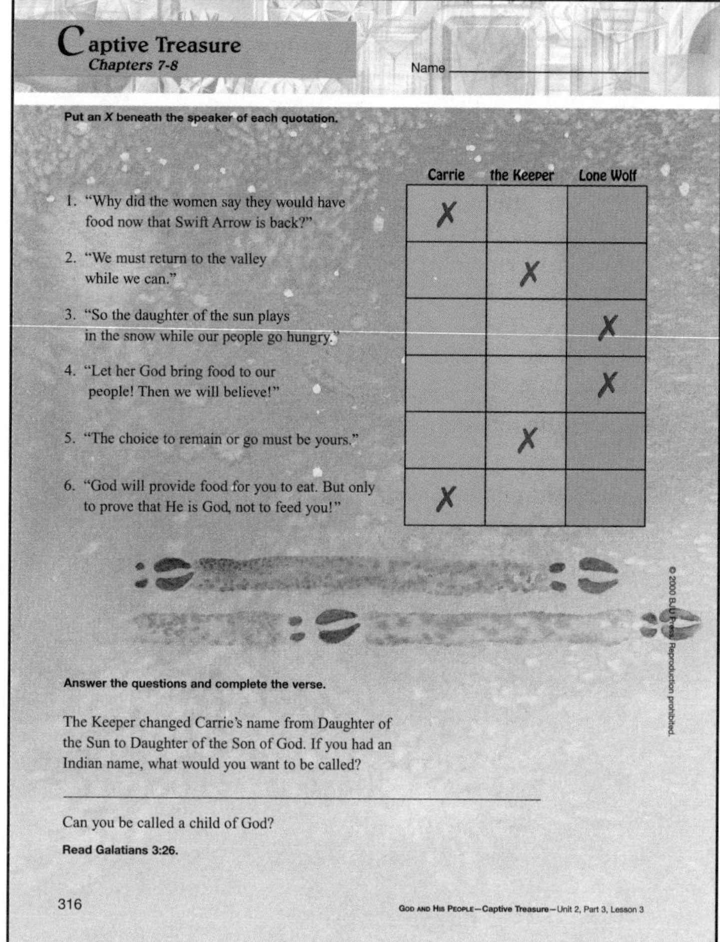

Captive Treasure
Chapters 7-8

Name ______________

Put an *X* beneath the speaker of each quotation.

Quotation	Carrie	the Keeper	Lone Wolf
1. "Why did the women say they would have food now that Swift Arrow is back?"	X		
2. "We must return to the valley while we can."		X	
3. "So the daughter of the sun plays in the snow while our people go hungry."			X
4. "Let her God bring food to our people! Then we will believe!"			X
5. "The choice to remain or go must be yours."		X	
6. "God will provide food for you to eat. But only to prove that He is God, not to feed you!"	X		

Answer the questions and complete the verse.

The Keeper changed Carrie's name from Daughter of the Sun to Daughter of the Son of God. If you had an Indian name, what would you want to be called?

____

Can you be called a child of God?

Read Galatians 3:26.

© 2000 BJU Press. Reproduction prohibited.

316 God and His People—Captive Treasure—Unit 2, Part 3, Lesson 3

Worktext page 49

Find information in Scripture.

Introducing the Application Novel

Review Elijah's challenge (I Kings 18:17-39).

When?—at a time of drought in Israel

Where?—Mount Carmel

Who?—Ahab, Elijah, people of Israel, prophets of Baal

What?—The sacrifice, consumed by fire, would show whether Baal or the Lord is God.

Result?—Elijah prayed. God sent fire to consume the sacrifice, the altar, and the water.

Why?—People acknowledged that the Lord is God.

Explain that a similar challenge is given in the novel *Captive Treasure*. Read the titles of Chapter 7, "Wolves of Hunger," and of Chapter 8, "The Challenge."

Application Novel: *Captive Treasure*

Read and discuss Chapter 7. Direct the students to read the chapter silently or listen as you read it aloud to the students. Encourage them to read to find out why Carrie said Lone Wolf would not be a good leader. *(He thought only of himself.)*

- ➤ **Why was too much snow too soon a problem?** *(There was no food for the animals, the animals died, and then there was no food for the people.)*
- ➤ **Why did the Keeper decide to make the four-day trip to the valley?** *(If they stayed, they would die.)*
- ➤ **Why were the wolves no longer following them?** *(Swift Arrow released two of the horses so the wolves would stop and eat them.)*

Read and discuss Chapter 8. Direct the students to read the chapter silently or listen as you read it aloud to find out what challenge is given. *(Lone Wolf challenges God to send food.)*

- ➤ **Why were the Indians glad to see Carrie?** *(They thought they would have food because the "medicine bundle" she carried had special power.)*
- ➤ **How had the Keeper's beliefs changed?** *(He now believed the Bible taught about God.)*
- ➤ **Why did Carrie think God sent her to the Indians?** *(to tell them about God)*

Read **Romans 8:28** aloud. Point out the importance of memorizing and meditating on God's Word. Discuss with the students opportunities they have had or might have for sharing God's Word. Stress that a Christian relies on God's power for courage and on God's love as a motivation for loving others.

➤ **Why did the Keeper change Carrie's Cheyenne name?** *(She was not Daughter of the Sun but daughter of the Son of God.)*

➤ **What did Carrie say specifically about the food God would provide?** *(They would not be able to eat it; it would come in the morning and would show God's great power.)*

➤ **How did God provide the answer to the challenge?** *(God sent a herd of deer through the camp the next morning.)*

➤ **How did Carrie know that God would answer her prayer?** *(through faith)* Read **Hebrews 11:6** aloud.

Worktext Supplement page 316

Match characters with dialogue.

Lesson 4

Materials

- Copy of *Captive Treasure* for the teacher (and for each student [optional])
- Song: "Books of the New Testament"
- Bible Book Cards: Gospels
- A pair of shoes (optional)

Memory Verse—Hebrews 4:12

Practice the memory verse. Locate and read **Hebrews 4:12** silently and out loud several times. Allow each student to choose a partner and practice saying the verse from memory.

Worktext page 50

Apply Bible knowledge to everyday life.

Song: "Books of the New Testament"

Sing the first verse (Worktext page 288). Play the recording and lead in singing verse 1 several times.

Bible Study Skills

Review the Gospels. Distribute the Bible Book Cards for the Gospels to four students, directing them to arrange themselves in the correct order at the front of the room. Display the flash cards to all the students one at a time and review the book that comes before and the book that comes after the book on the card.

One-on-One: Give the student the Gospel cards and tell him to sequence them. Then show a card, directing the student to tell which books come before and after the book on the card.

Background Information

Tallow—*The buffalos provided much more than food for the Plains Indians. The skins were used for clothing and for covering the tipi. Tools were made from the bones and horns. The animal*

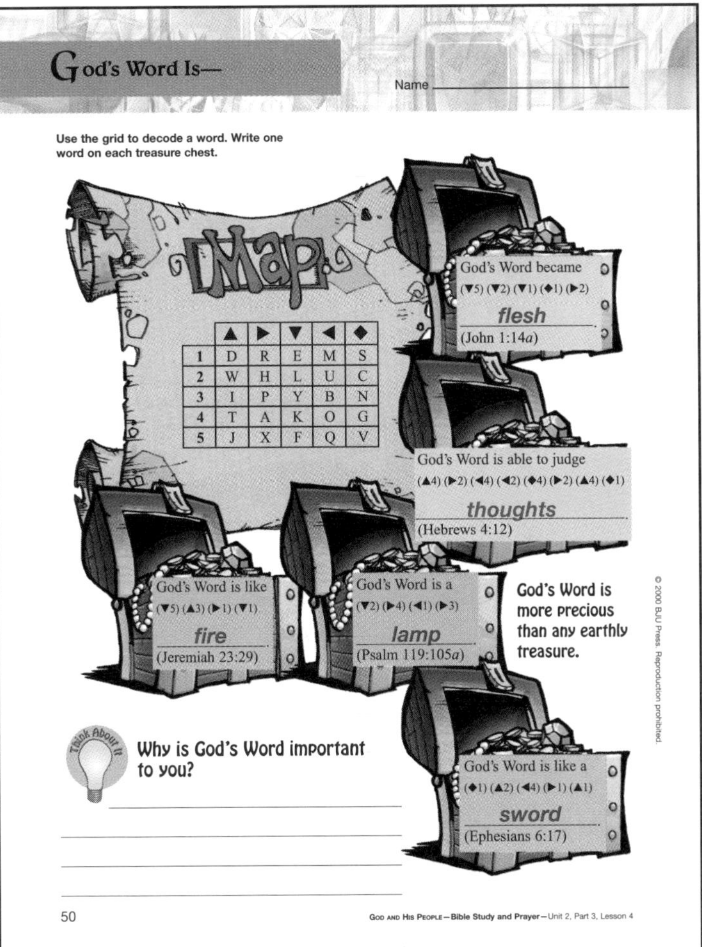

God's Word Is—

Name ____________________

Use the grid to decode a word. Write one word on each treasure chest.

Map

	▲	▶	▼	◀	◆
1	D	R	E	M	S
2	W	H	L	U	C
3	I	P	Y	B	N
4	T	A	K	O	G
5	J	X	F	Q	V

God's Word became (▼5) (▼2) (▼1) (◆1) (▶2) flesh (John 1:14*a*)

God's Word is able to judge (▲4) (▶2) (◀4) (◀2) (◆4) (▶2) (▲4) (◆1) thoughts (Hebrews 4:12)

God's Word is like (▼5) (▲3) (▶1) (▼1) fire (Jeremiah 23:29)

God's Word is a (▼2) (▶4) (◀1) (▶3) lamp (Psalm 119:105*a*)

God's Word is more precious than any earthly treasure.

God's Word is like a (◆1) (▲2) (◀4) (▶1) (▲1) sword (Ephesians 6:17)

Think About It

Why is God's Word important to you?

50 God and His People—Bible Study and Prayer—Unit 2, Part 3, Lesson 4

fat was melted to make tallow, giving oil for lamps. Today, tallow is used in shortening, soaps, detergents, tires, and plastics.

Introducing the Application Novel

Review Chapters 7 and 8.

➤ **How has Carrie shown others that she is a Christian?** *(by her words and actions, by her faith)*

➤ **How has she shared God's Word with others?** *(translated Psalm 91 into the Cheyenne language, read Scripture aloud, told Bible stories)*

Display the shoes (optional). Read aloud **Romans 10:13-15, 17.** Point out the importance of sharing the gospel that others may *hear*, *believe*, and *call* on the Lord. Read **Psalm 119:59** to the students.

Explain tallow. Share the background information about tallow if desired.

Application Novel: Captive Treasure

Read and discuss Chapter 9. Direct the students to read Chapter 9 silently or listen as you read the chapter aloud to find out what the Keeper asked of Carrie. *(He wanted her to tell him how to become a child of God.)*

➤ **Why did Carrie tell Small Bird to forgive Turtle?** *(God has forgiven us.)*

➤ **How did Carrie respond to the Keeper's request?** *(She quoted salvation verses to him.)*

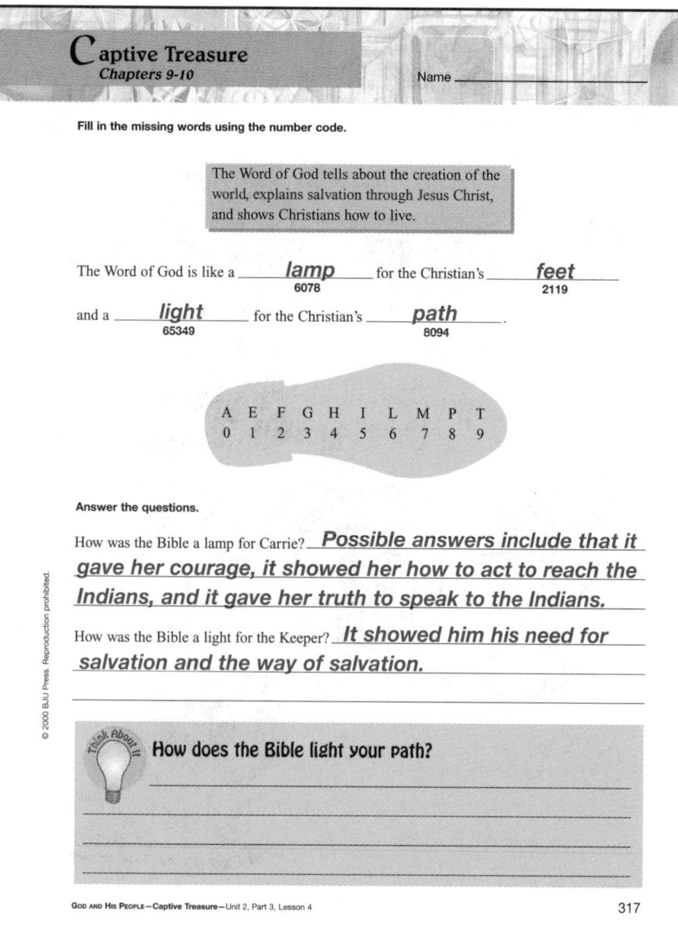

Captive Treasure
Chapters 9-10

Name ____________

Fill in the missing words using the number code.

The Word of God tells about the creation of the world, explains salvation through Jesus Christ, and shows Christians how to live.

The Word of God is like a *lamp* (6078) for the Christian's *feet* (2119) and a *light* (65349) for the Christian's *path* (8094).

A	E	F	G	H	I	L	M	P	T
0	1	2	3	4	5	6	7	8	9

Answer the questions.

How was the Bible a lamp for Carrie? *Possible answers include that it gave her courage, it showed her how to act to reach the Indians, and it gave her truth to speak to the Indians.*

How was the Bible a light for the Keeper? *It showed him his need for salvation and the way of salvation.*

Think About It: How does the Bible light your path?

GOD AND HIS PEOPLE—Captive Treasure—Unit 2, Part 3, Lesson 4 317

- ➤ **How did the Keeper respond?** *(He prayed and received Jesus as his Savior.)*
- ➤ **Whom did the Keeper tell to cut down the medicine arrows?** *(Swift Arrow)*
- ➤ **How did the tribe show respect upon the Keeper's death?** *(They moved the Indian camp.)*
- ➤ **What becomes of man at death?** *(The body returns to dust, and the soul goes either to heaven or to hell.)*

Explain that everyone is born with an earthly father and mother. Point out that every person is born with a sinful nature. Spiritually, each person is born into God's family only at salvation. Review God's plan of salvation, using page xii (optional).

Read and discuss Chapter 10. Direct the students to read the chapter silently or listen as you read it aloud to find out if Sky Woman and Swift Arrow listened as Carrie continued to read Scripture each night. *(Sky Woman did, but Swift Arrow didn't.)*

- ➤ **How did Swift Arrow change?** *(He was angry and afraid. He joined a group of Indian soldiers called the* Dog Men. *He married Windsinger.)*
- ➤ **Why did the chief call for Carrie?** *(She knew both languages and could translate for the trade between the trader and the Indians.)*
- ➤ **What news did the man have about Carrie's parents?** *(They had tried to find her. They were at the mission.)*
- ➤ **What promise did the man make to Carrie?** *(He would take her to her parents when he came back.)*
- ➤ **Who do you think took Carrie's Bible? Why?** *(Accept any responses.)*

Worktext Supplement page 317

Find information in Scripture.

Going Beyond

Materials

- Chart 28, "World Map" or globe

Enrichment

Share information about missionaries. Discuss how missionaries during the time period of the *Captive Treasure* took the message of salvation to people in the United States and to other parts of the world. Point out that God wants Christians to love Him and to love others. Sharing the Word of God is one way to show love to others. As you read the following information, point out the mission fields on a world map or globe.

Marcus (1802-1847) and Narcissa (1808-1847) Whitman—*The Whitmans were pioneer missionaries in the Pacific Northwest. Today the area where they served is known as the state of Washington. The Whitmans started part of the Oregon Trail when they traveled west in 1836. Marcus Whitman was a medical doctor and a missionary teacher. He and his wife Narcissa established a mission and school among the Cayuse Indians. The Whitmans were killed by Indians in 1847.*

D. L. Moody (1837-99)—*As a young man, Dwight went to Boston where he worked for his uncle in a shoe store. Dwight's Sunday school teacher came to witness to him at the store, and Dwight L. Moody gave his life to Christ. Then he began ministering to children in Chicago. Many Union and Confederate soldiers heard the gospel from D. L. Moody during the American Civil War. He also started schools to help teach and train people to serve the Lord better.*

J. Hudson Taylor (1832-1905)—*Hudson Taylor was a missionary, preacher, medical doctor, and writer. He sailed for China in 1853 after receiving a medical degree. Many Chinese people were won to Christ through his witness. Taylor was willing to dress in Chinese clothing and be as much like the Chinese as he could. Taylor returned to England in 1860 due to poor health, during which time he revised the Chinese New Testament. He also prayed that God would send workers to inland China. God answered the prayer when in 1866, Hudson Taylor returned to China with his family and twenty-four missionaries.*

Praying to God

Unit 2, Part 4

Preview

Doctrines

- Members of the local church should pray (II Corinthians 1:11)—Lesson 1
- God is all-powerful (omnipotent) (Jeremiah 32:27)—Lesson 2
- God is merciful (Psalm 86:15)—Lesson 2

Skills and Applications

- Learn Philippians 4:6
- Recall facts and details
- Summarize main events
- Sequence events
- Learn the New Testament book of History
- Learn abbreviations of the Old Testament books
- Develop active listening
- Use cross-references
- Know that God commands Christians to pray
- Realize that only God can give victory
- Gain a desire to study the Bible
- Catch the vision of telling others about Christ
- Apply Bible knowledge to everyday life

Lesson 1

Materials

- Charts 10 and 32, "Hezekiah Prayed for Deliverance" and "Beyond Palestine"
- Unit 2 Bookmark for each student
- Highlighter for each student (optional)

Memory Verse—Philippians 4:6

Principle: God has commanded us to pray, and God wants to answer our prayers. Locate **Philippians 4:6** and read the verse aloud as the students read silently. Point out that this verse reminds Christians not to worry about anything, for God cares for them. Explain that this is really a command by God for Christians to talk with Him about everything—anytime, anywhere. God will answer the prayers of those who trust in Him. Choose volunteers to read the verse aloud while the other students follow along. Direct the students to highlight the verse in their Bibles (optional) and to mark the location with the Unit 2 Bookmark.

Hymn: "Break Thou the Bread of Life"

Teach the fourth verse (Worktext page 273). Read through the words with the students and play the recording. Explain that verse 4 refers to the Bible but is to be sung as a prayer. Lead in singing verse 4 prayerfully; then sing all four verses together.

Background Information

King Hezekiah's Reign—*Though Hezekiah's father, Ahaz, had been a wicked ruler, Hezekiah may have understood that the destruction of the Northern Kingdom of Israel was a direct result of disobedience to God. When Hezekiah began his reign in Judah, he repaired and reopened the temple and did away with the heathen idols. He started having daily sacrifices, and the temple again was filled with singing and music. Hezekiah also brought back the Passover Feast and invited not only all Judah but also any Israelites that wanted to participate.*

Introducing the Bible Account

Explain the setting. Display Chart 32, "Beyond Palestine," and point out Judah and Assyria. Share the background information about King Hezekiah and his reign over Judah. Direct attention to Worktext page 51 and read the information about the Assyrians.

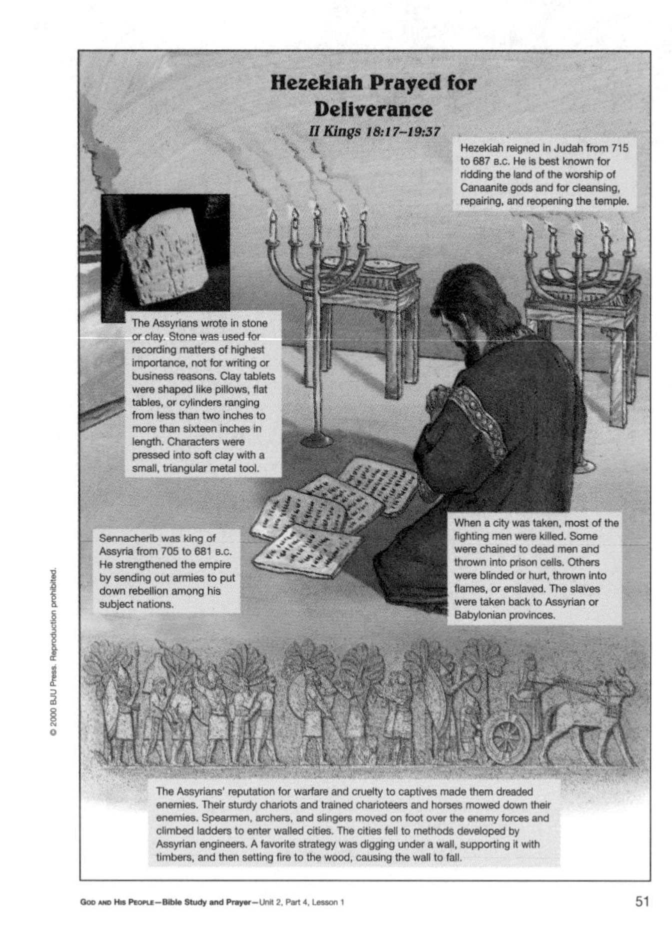

Hezekiah Prayed for Deliverance
II Kings 18:17–19:37
Hezekiah reigned in Judah from 715 to 687 B.C. He is best known for ridding the land of the worship of Canaanite gods and for cleansing, repairing, and reopening the temple.
The Assyrians wrote in stone or clay. Stone was used for recording matters of highest importance, not for writing or business reasons. Clay tablets were shaped like pillows, flat tables, or cylinders ranging from less than two inches to more than sixteen inches in length. Characters were pressed into soft clay with a small, triangular metal tool.
Sennacherib was king of Assyria from 705 to 681 B.C. He strengthened the empire by sending out armies to put down rebellion among his subject nations.
When a city was taken, most of the fighting men were killed. Some were chained to dead men and thrown into prison cells. Others were blinded or hurt, thrown into flames, or enslaved. The slaves were taken back to Assyrian or Babylonian provinces.
The Assyrians' reputation for warfare and cruelty to captives made them dreaded enemies. Their sturdy chariots and trained charioteers and horses mowed down their enemies. Spearmen, archers, and slingers moved on foot over the enemy forces and climbed ladders to enter walled cities. The cities fell to methods developed by Assyrian engineers. A favorite strategy was digging under a wall, supporting it with timbers, and then setting fire to the wood, causing the wall to fall.
© 2000 BJU Press. Reproduction prohibited.
God and His People—Bible Study and Prayer—Unit 2, Part 4, Lesson 1
51

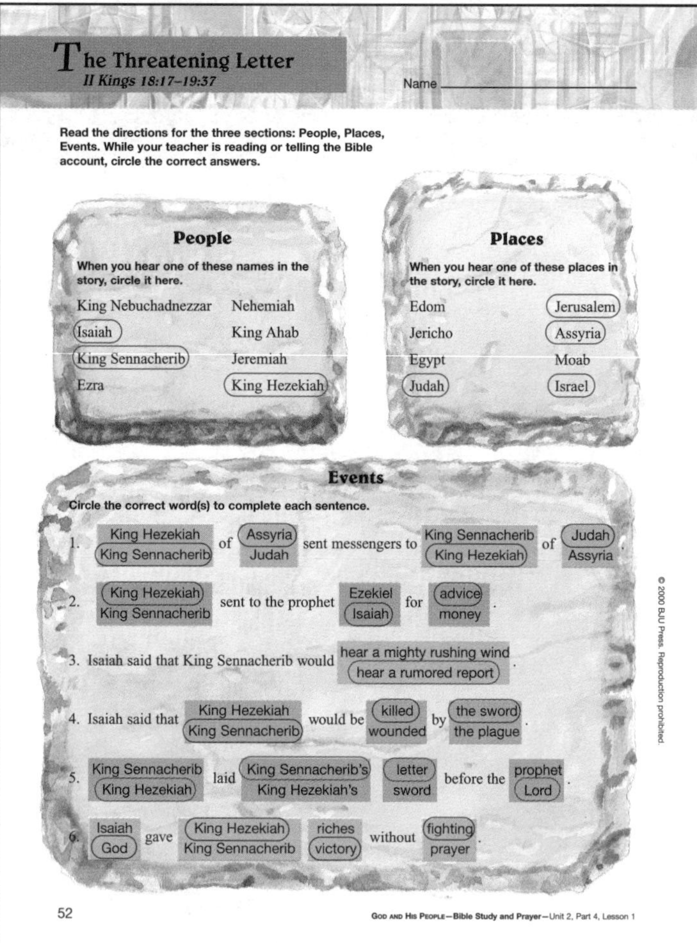

Worktext page 52

Develop active listening. Point out the three sections of the page: people, places, events. Direct the students to complete the page while you read the Bible account.

Bible Account

Read the following Bible account or II Kings 18:17–19:37.

Hezekiah Prayed for Deliverance

The Assyrians had taken the Northern Kingdom of Israel into captivity 136 years earlier. Now King Sennacherib, the Assyrian king, set his eyes on the Southern Kingdom of Judah. However, the king of Judah was Hezekiah, who trusted in God.

King Sennacherib sent his messengers to tell the messengers of King Hezekiah that they and their king were trusting in the wrong thing. The messengers from King Sennacherib made fun of their dependence upon God. The messengers of King Hezekiah had been told not to answer them, so they said nothing but went back and told King Hezekiah everything King Sennacherib's men had said. Hearing this, King Hezekiah was not sure what to do. King Hezekiah was in great turmoil, and his heart was heavy. He tore his beautiful clothes and put on sackcloth, and went into the house of God.

Then Hezekiah sent his messengers to see Isaiah, the prophet of God. After hearing all that the messengers had been told, Isaiah went to God. After talking to God, Isaiah told the messengers of King Hezekiah, "Be not afraid of the words which thou hast heard," because King Sennacherib will hear a rumor and go back to his own land. God will defend you. King Sennacherib will die by his own sword.

King Sennacherib sent a message, in the form of a letter, to King Hezekiah, saying the second time, "Let not thy God in whom thou trustest deceive thee, saying, Jerusalem shall not be delivered into the hand of the King of Assyria."

Hezekiah laid the letter out before God and prayed by acknowledging God as the true God, the Creator of heaven and earth. He recounted how the Assyrians had destroyed the gods of other people, and how they were thinking that they could destroy the true and living God. "Now therefore, O Lord our God,

I beseech thee, save thou us out of his hand, that all the kingdoms of the earth may know that thou art the Lord God, even thou only."

Then Isaiah the prophet of God sent word to Hezekiah that God had heard Hezekiah's prayer. Isaiah told Hezekiah all that God said against King Sennacherib. God promised Hezekiah that He would defend the city and that King Sennacherib would not shoot even one arrow into Jerusalem. God said that King Sennacherib would return to his home without destroying Jerusalem.

During the night, the angel of the Lord came into the camp of the Assyrians and killed 185,000 soldiers. In the morning, the camp of the enemy contained only dead bodies. So King Sennacherib returned to his own land. One day as the evil king was in the house of his gods, worshiping his idols, his sons came in and killed him with his own sword.

InfoScene: "Hezekiah Prayed for Deliverance"
Display Chart 10 for reference throughout this unit. Review and discuss the Bible account as time permits.

➤ **What did the king of Assyria say when he told King Hezekiah he was coming to destroy Jerusalem?** *(He bragged about all the lands he had conquered and the gods he had destroyed. He said his armies were stronger than Hezekiah's God; he called God a liar, which is blasphemy.)*

➤ **After the second threat, what did Hezekiah do?** *(He took the letter he received from King Sennacherib, laid it out before God, and asked God to show the world that He is the true God.)*

➤ **What did God say He would do?** *(God said He would defend Jerusalem, and not one arrow would enter Jerusalem from Sennacherib's army. He said that Sennacherib would return home and would die by his own sword.)*

➤ **What happened?** *(God defended Jerusalem, and 185,000 men were killed. The king returned home and later was killed by his sons with his sword.)*

➤ **Why is it better to trust in God than in strong armies?** *(Many answers are acceptable, but point out the omnipotence, omniscience, and omnipresence of God.)*

➤ **What should Christians do when they have difficult situations?** *(Pray and trust God.)*

Lesson 2

Materials

- TimeLine and picture: *Hezekiah*
- A picture of a sundial (optional)
- Items for Science Connection for each group: a piece of plywood (approximately 12" × 14"), enough white paper to cover the board, cardboard (approximately 6" square), and thread or string (optional)

Prepare a chart or overhead transparency of **Philippians 4:6.** Write each phrase on a line so it can be used as a choral reading.

Memory Verse—Philippians 4:6

Practice reading the verse as a choral reading. Display the copy of **Philippians 4:6,** directing the students to read the verse in a choral reading. Read through the verse several times, allowing different groups to read different phrases.

One-on-One: Alternate reading a line or phrase with the student.

Background Information

The Sundial—*A sundial is an instrument with a central projecting pointer that indicates by the shadow of the sun approximately what time of day it is in that location. Before the clock was invented, long before the discovery of electricity, the sundial was the way men measured time.*

The Dial of Ahaz—*The instrument used by Hezekiah to tell the time of day was a carefully placed staircase upon which the rays of the sun moved up and down. The time was revealed by the placement of shadows on the steps. The miracle that Hezekiah asked for was for the shadow to move back up the steps, therefore lengthening the time of daylight. The stairway is named after Hezekiah's predecessor, King Ahaz, who had it built.*

Introducing the Bible Account

Discuss how God answers prayer. Explain that God has three ways in which He answers prayer:

> **Yes**—Review Hezekiah's prayer, asking for deliverance (II Kings 19:14-19).
>
> **No**—Explain why God answered Abraham's request to spare Sodom with "no" (Genesis 18:20–19:29).
>
> **Wait**—Explain why God's will was fulfilled by Christ's waiting to raise Lazarus from the dead rather than Christ's healing him when he was sick (John 11:1-44).

Remind the students that when Christians pray, God always answers—but not always with a "yes."

Bible Account

Read the following Bible account or read II Kings 20:1-11, 20-21.

Hezekiah Prayed for Healing

King Hezekiah was sick and was near death. One day God sent the prophet Isaiah to give Hezekiah a message.

The message was, "Set thine house in order; for thou shalt die, and not live." God was giving Hezekiah a warning to get ready to die. God was also warning him to get the kingdom of Judah ready for his death.

When Hezekiah heard this, the Bible says, "He turned his face to the wall, and prayed unto the Lord." Hezekiah reminded God that he had served God and had done right in God's eyes. He cried out to God and wept.

Before Isaiah had even left the palace, God spoke to him again. He told Isaiah to go back and tell Hezekiah, "I have heard thy prayer, I have seen thy tears: behold, I will heal thee: on the third day thou shalt go up unto the house of the Lord." God also said that He would add fifteen years to Hezekiah's life, and that He would save Judah from the hands of the Assyrians. God chose to do these things for His own glory and for that of His servant David.

Then Isaiah told Hezekiah's servants to take a lump of figs, boil them, and lay them on the boil that Hezekiah had. Hezekiah's servants did as Isaiah the prophet told them.

Then Hezekiah asked for a sign that God was going to heal him. Isaiah asked Hezekiah what he wanted God to do: move the shadow ten degrees (steps) forward or ten degrees (steps) backward? Hezekiah answered by asking that the shadow on the sundial go *backward* ten degrees if he were truly to be healed. Isaiah the prophet told God what Hezekiah asked, and the Bible says, "He brought the shadow ten degrees backward, by which it had gone down."

Fifteen years later, King Hezekiah died and his son, Manasseh, reigned in his place. Before his death a son (heir to David's throne) was born to Hezekiah. He also accomplished many things—one being he had a pool and a tunnel built through which he brought water (from Spring Gihon) into the city of Jerusalem.

➤ **What did the prophet Isaiah come to tell Hezekiah?** *(that he was going to die and should make plans)*

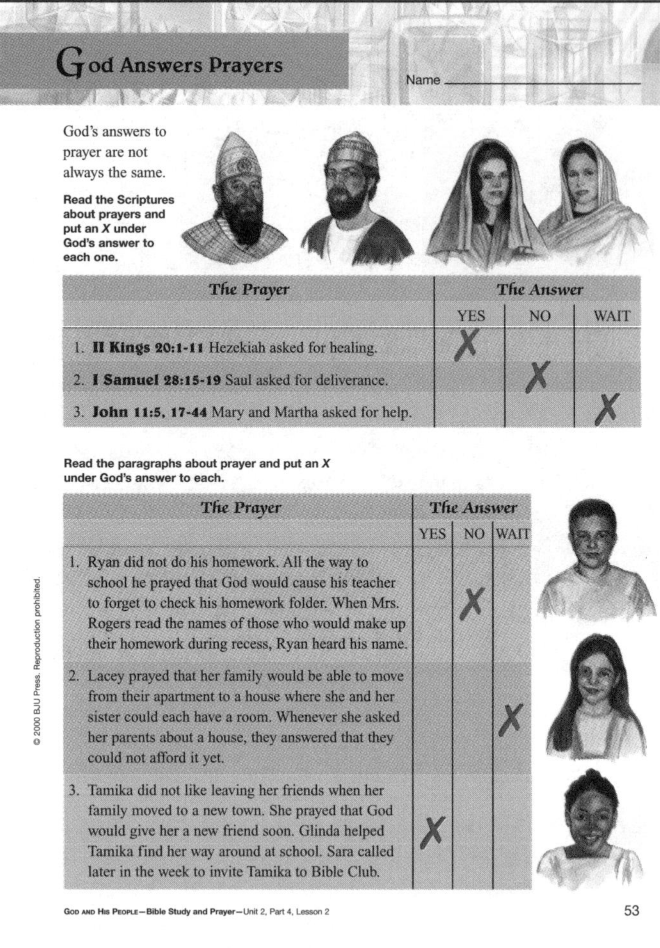

God Answers Prayers

Name ____________

God's answers to prayer are not always the same.

Read the Scriptures about prayers and put an *X* under God's answer to each one.

The Prayer	The Answer		
	YES	NO	WAIT
1. **II Kings 20:1-11** Hezekiah asked for healing.	X		
2. **I Samuel 28:15-19** Saul asked for deliverance.		X	
3. **John 11:5, 17-44** Mary and Martha asked for help.			X

Read the paragraphs about prayer and put an *X* under God's answer to each.

The Prayer	The Answer		
	YES	NO	WAIT
1. Ryan did not do his homework. All the way to school he prayed that God would cause his teacher to forget to check his homework folder. When Mrs. Rogers read the names of those who would make up their homework during recess, Ryan heard his name.		X	
2. Lacey prayed that her family would be able to move from their apartment to a house where she and her sister could each have a room. Whenever she asked her parents about a house, they answered that they could not afford it yet.			X
3. Tamika did not like leaving her friends when her family moved to a new town. She prayed that God would give her a new friend soon. Glinda helped Tamika find her way around at school. Sara called later in the week to invite Tamika to Bible Club.	X		

God and His People—Bible Study and Prayer—Unit 2, Part 4, Lesson 2 53

➤ **What did Hezekiah do when he heard this news?** *(He prayed to God and wept.)*

➤ **What did God decide to do for His own sake and for that of David's?** *(He decided to give Hezekiah fifteen more years of life during which a son was born who would become the next king.)*

➤ **How did God show that He has power over this world?** *(He changed time by changing the sun's shadow.)*

Point out that God's prolonging of Hezekiah's life was in keeping with His covenant promise to David. The Lord moved His servant to pray that his life would be spared to prove God's faithfulness. If Hezekiah had had no son, David's line would have ended.

TimeLine

Place *Hezekiah* on the TimeLine. Direct the students to place *Hezekiah* onto the TimeLine at 728-686 B.C. Guide them in gluing *Hezekiah* onto their individual TimeLines.

Worktext page 53

Apply Bible knowledge to everyday life.

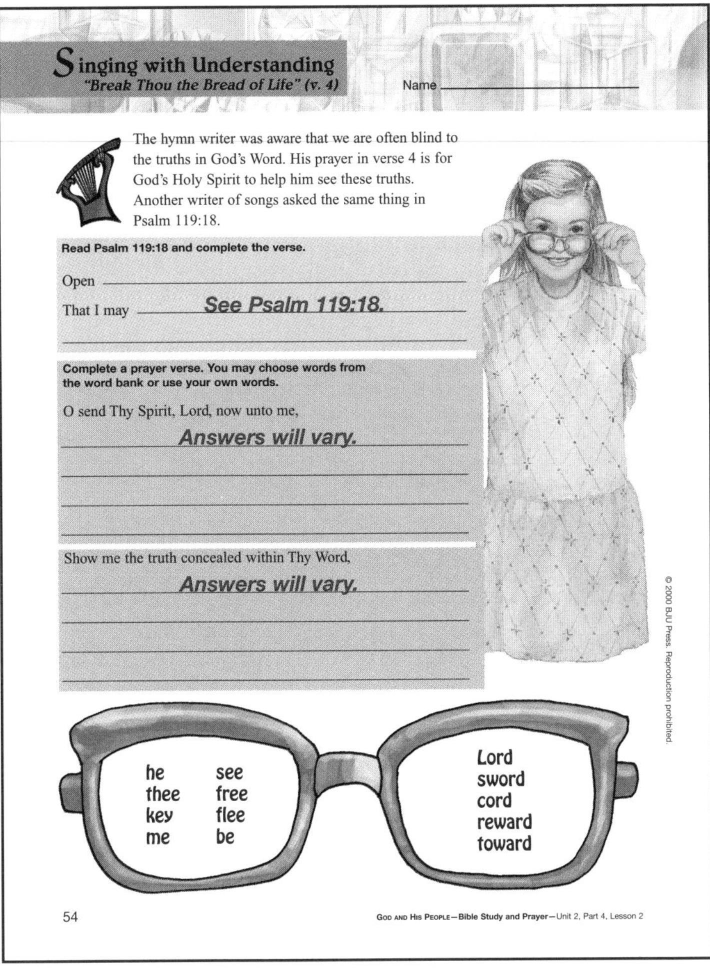

Singing with Understanding
"Break Thou the Bread of Life" (v. 4)

Name ______________________

The hymn writer was aware that we are often blind to the truths in God's Word. His prayer in verse 4 is for God's Holy Spirit to help him see these truths. Another writer of songs asked the same thing in Psalm 119:18.

Read Psalm 119:18 and complete the verse.

Open ______________________

That I may *See Psalm 119:18.*

Complete a prayer verse. You may choose words from the word bank or use your own words.

O send Thy Spirit, Lord, now unto me,

Answers will vary.

Show me the truth concealed within Thy Word,

Answers will vary.

he see
thee free
key flee
me be

Lord
sword
cord
reward
toward

54 God and His People—Bible Study and Prayer—Unit 2, Part 4, Lesson 2

Hymn: "Break Thou the Bread of Life"

Sing the hymn (Worktext page 273). Play the recording and lead in singing all the verses. Alternate singing the chorus between groups (optional).

Worktext page 54

Singing with understanding, verse 4.

Science Connection (optional)

Construct a sundial. Put the students in groups to construct sundials. Give each group a board, white paper, cardboard, and string. Direct each group to cover their board with the white paper, securing the flaps with glue or tape. Tell them to make a right-angled triangle with the cardboard, folding a flap at the base. Guide them in attaching the flap on the base, tightly tying string across it; then tell them to draw two curved lines from each corner of the base to the triangle's highest side.

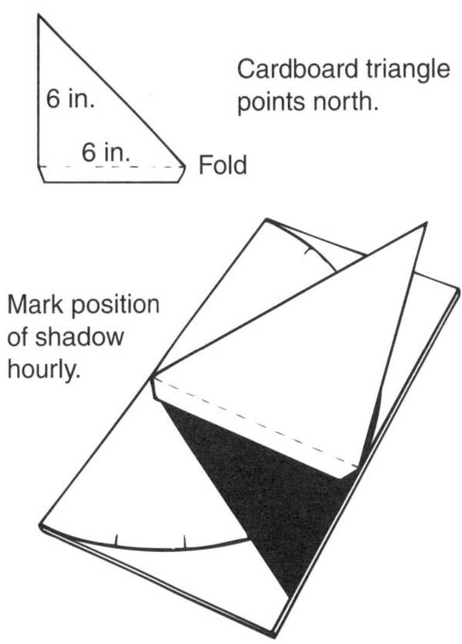

Use the sundial. Place the completed sundials where they will receive sun for most of the day. Use a compass to determine north, and place the tall point of each sundial pointing north. Check the sundial each hour throughout the day, noting the shadow that the sun casts on the cardboard. Mark and label with the time the shadow's position as it crosses the curved line. If the next day is a sunny day, you could use the sundial to tell the time. (*Note:* Seasonal changes mean that sundials are not accurate year round.)

Lesson 3

Materials

- Song: "Books of the New Testament"
- Bible Book Cards: New Testament—History division and Old Testament abbreviations
- Copy of *Captive Treasure* for the teacher (and for each student [optional])

Memory Verse—Philippians 4:6

Practice the memory verse. Allow different students to read aloud **Philippians 4:6**. Allow each student to make a list of praises and prayer requests of different students or make a list together. Encourage the students to pray for one another. If possible, take time at a later date to see how many requests can be moved to the praises column. Practice the verse by reading it throughout the day.

Worktext page 55

Develop understanding of the memory verse and apply Bible knowledge to everyday life.

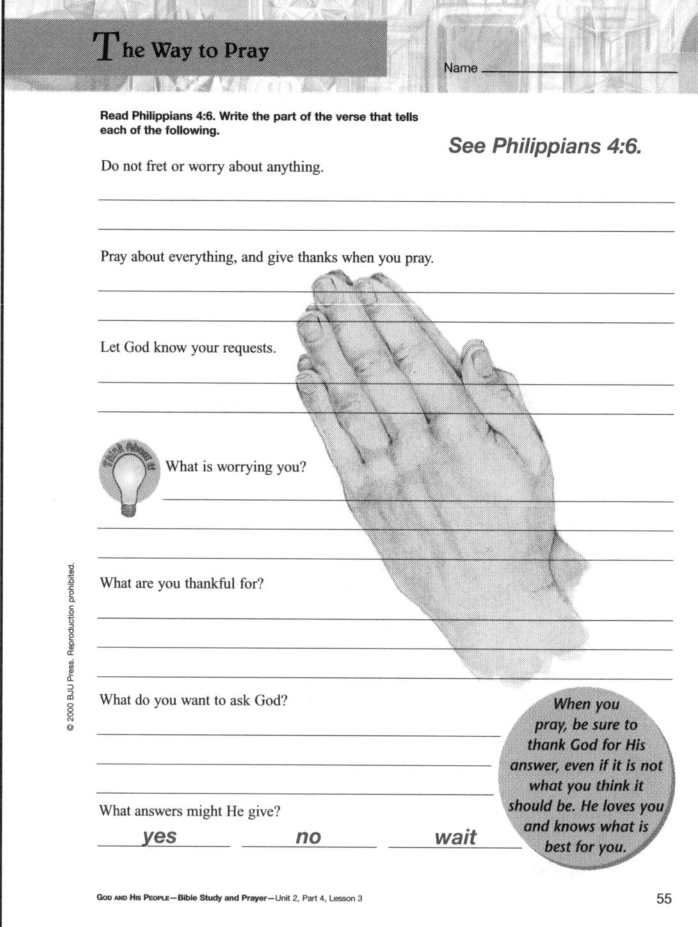

The Way to Pray

Name ____________

Read Philippians 4:6. Write the part of the verse that tells each of the following.

See Philippians 4:6.

Do not fret or worry about anything.

Pray about everything, and give thanks when you pray.

Let God know your requests.

What is worrying you?

What are you thankful for?

What do you want to ask God?

What answers might He give?

yes   no   wait

When you pray, be sure to thank God for His answer, even if it is not what you think it should be. He loves you and knows what is best for you.

God and His People—Bible Study and Prayer—Unit 2, Part 4, Lesson 3   55

Song: "Books of the New Testament"

Sing the first two verses (Worktext page 288.) Play the recording and sing the verses together.

Bible Study Skills

Review the New Testament book of History. Hold up the card for Acts. Explain that there is only one book in the division of New Testament History. Direct attention to the table of contents in the Bible.

➤ **How many books are in the division of Old Testament History from Joshua to Esther?** *(twelve)*

Review the abbreviations for the books of the Old Testament. Divide the students into three or four teams. Line up the teams. Show a card with an abbreviation to the students at the front of each line. The student who first calls out the name of the book receives a point for his team. Let the students in front go to the end of the line after their turn. Continue as time permits.

One-on-One: Show the abbreviation card to the student, who should answer with the correct name. Or give the student the Old Testament cards and the abbreviation cards, challenging him to match them correctly.

Introducing the Application Novel

Discuss the purpose of prayer.

➤ **Why do you pray?**

Elicit that prayer is more than asking for God's help when we are in trouble. Point out that prayer also includes the following:

- praising and thanking God
- seeking God's will
- asking for forgiveness
- telling God our needs or burdens
- bringing requests for others to God

Application Novel: *Captive Treasure*

Read and discuss Chapter 11. Direct the students to read Chapter 11 silently or read it to them. Encourage the students to find out who Sky Woman thinks took the Bible. *(Lone Wolf)*

➤ **What two questions did Swift Arrow ask Carrie when she witnessed to him on the prairie?** *(Why did the Keeper choose Carrie's way before he died? Why was Carrie's way right?)*

➤ **How did Carrie answer these questions and how did Swift Arrow respond to her answers?** *(She quoted Scripture verses to Swift Arrow, and he said he would think about her words.)*

Read aloud the last paragraph on page 123. Emphasize the need for studying and memorizing God's Word.

➤ **Why did the warriors plan to attack a wagon train?** *(for food, horses, wealth, and honor)*

➤ **What did Lone Wolf say would give them victory?** *(the Bible)*

➤ **What was the outcome of the raid?** *(Many men were wounded and others were killed. Lone Wolf was shot from his horse.)*

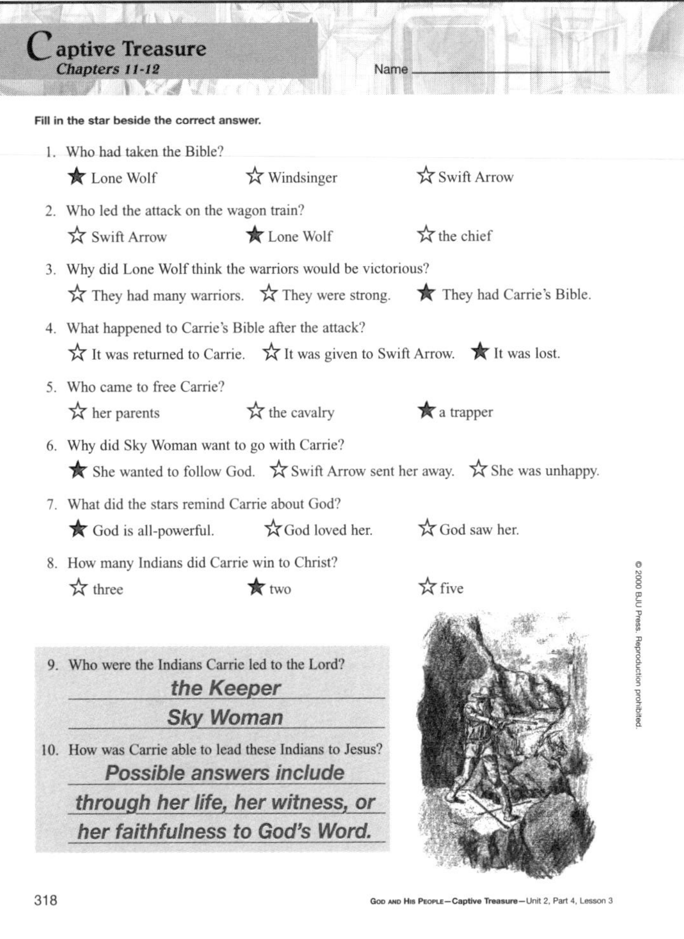
Captive Treasure
Chapters 11-12

Name ____________________

Fill in the star beside the correct answer.

1. Who had taken the Bible?
   ★ Lone Wolf ☆ Windsinger ☆ Swift Arrow
2. Who led the attack on the wagon train?
   ☆ Swift Arrow ★ Lone Wolf ☆ the chief
3. Why did Lone Wolf think the warriors would be victorious?
   ☆ They had many warriors. ☆ They were strong. ★ They had Carrie's Bible.
4. What happened to Carrie's Bible after the attack?
   ☆ It was returned to Carrie. ☆ It was given to Swift Arrow. ★ It was lost.
5. Who came to free Carrie?
   ☆ her parents ☆ the cavalry ★ a trapper
6. Why did Sky Woman want to go with Carrie?
   ★ She wanted to follow God. ☆ Swift Arrow sent her away. ☆ She was unhappy.
7. What did the stars remind Carrie about God?
   ★ God is all-powerful. ☆ God loved her. ☆ God saw her.
8. How many Indians did Carrie win to Christ?
   ☆ three ★ two ☆ five
9. Who were the Indians Carrie led to the Lord?
   the Keeper
   Sky Woman
10. How was Carrie able to lead these Indians to Jesus?
   Possible answers include through her life, her witness, or her faithfulness to God's Word.

➤ **Why did Sky Woman think that Swift Arrow would not turn to God?** *(Swift Arrow chose to follow the old ways in the sundance ceremony.)*

Explain that this was the most important religious ceremony to the Plains Indians. It was only during this ceremony that the medicine bundle was opened.

Read and discuss Chapter 12. Direct the students to read Chapter 12 silently or to listen as you read it aloud to find out God's plan for Carrie. *(Carrie was given her freedom.)*

➤ **What did the stars remind Carrie about God?** *(God is great; He is all-powerful.)*

The chief refused to trade Carrie for blankets, a pipe, and knives.

➤ **What was the final item the trapper offered the chief in exchange for Carrie?** *(a medicine arrow that had been stolen from the tribe)*

➤ **Who was to go with Carrie?** *(Sky Woman and the children)*

➤ **Why did Sky Woman want to leave?** *(She chose to follow God, and Carrie was like her own daughter.)*

➤ **Who gave permission for them to leave?** *(Swift Arrow)*

Worktext Supplement page 318

Recall facts and details.

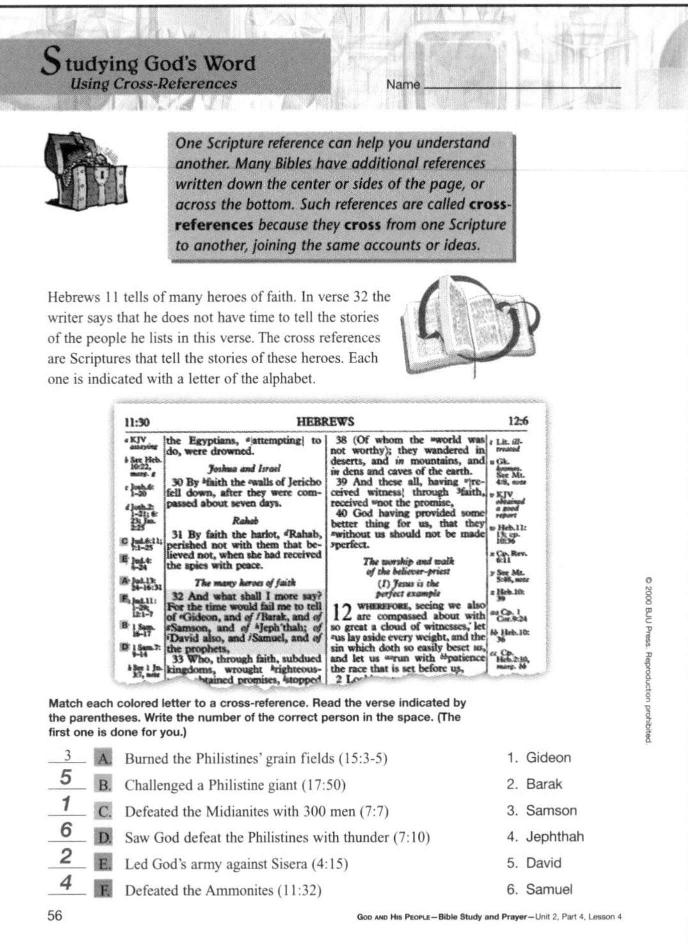
Studying God's Word
Using Cross-References

Name ____________________

One Scripture reference can help you understand another. Many Bibles have additional references written down the center or sides of the page, or across the bottom. Such references are called ***cross-references*** *because they* ***cross*** *from one Scripture to another, joining the same accounts or ideas.*

Hebrews 11 tells of many heroes of faith. In verse 32 the writer says that he does not have time to tell the stories of the people he lists in this verse. The cross references are Scriptures that tell the stories of these heroes. Each one is indicated with a letter of the alphabet.

11:30 HEBREWS 12:6

the Egyptians, attempting to do, were drowned.

Joshua and Israel

30 By faith the walls of Jericho fell down, after they were compassed about seven days.

Rahab

31 By faith the harlot, Rahab, perished not with them that believed not, when she had received the spies with peace.

The many heroes of faith

32 And what shall I more say? For the time would fail me to tell of Gideon, and of Barak, and of Samson, and of Jeph'thah; of David also, and Samuel, and of the prophets.

33 Who, through faith, subdued kingdoms, wrought righteousness, obtained promises, stopped

38 (Of whom the world was not worthy); they wandered in deserts, and in mountains, and in dens and caves of the earth.

39 And these all, having received witness through faith, received not the promise,

40 God having provided some better thing for us, that they without us should not be made perfect.

The worship and walk of the believer-priest

(1) Jesus is the perfect example

12 WHEREFORE, seeing we also are compassed about with so great a cloud of witnesses, let us lay aside every weight, and the sin which doth so easily beset us, and let us run with patience the race that is set before us,

2 L...

Match each colored letter to a cross-reference. Read the verse indicated by the parentheses. Write the number of the correct person in the space. (The first one is done for you.)

3	A.	Burned the Philistines' grain fields (15:3-5)	1. Gideon
5	B.	Challenged a Philistine giant (17:50)	2. Barak
1	C.	Defeated the Midianites with 300 men (7:7)	3. Samson
6	D.	Saw God defeat the Philistines with thunder (7:10)	4. Jephthah
2	E.	Led God's army against Sisera (4:15)	5. David
4	F.	Defeated the Ammonites (11:32)	6. Samuel

Lesson 4

Materials

- Copy of *Captive Treasure* for the teacher (and for each student [optional])

Hymn: "Break Thou the Bread of Life"

Sing the hymn (Worktext page 273). Play the recording and lead in singing the hymn. Review the meaning of the words.

Memory Verse—Philippians 4:6

Practice the memory verse. Read **Philippians 4:6** aloud while the students read silently. Choose a student or group to say the verse from memory. If you made a list of prayer requests in the previous lesson, pray for these requests at this time.

Bible Study Skills, Worktext page 56

Use cross-references. (*Note:* The abbreviations in the cross-references may differ from those on the Bible Book Cards. There are usually two or more ways to abbreviate each book.)

Background Information

Cavalry—*The cavalry was a group of soldiers sent from a fort on horses to keep peace. In the United States, the cavalry became a major fighting unit during the Civil War. The bugle (brass instrument with no keys whose sounds were made by blowing in the mouthpiece and adjusting the lips) was blown as a signal for a charge. These soldiers often broke through enemy lines, causing the enemy to flee in the opposite direction. The favorite weapon of the cavalry was the saber, a curved sword. (Note: President Harry S. Truman officially ended the U.S. Army horse cavalry in 1950. The soldiers on horses were replaced by tanks and guns.)*

Introducing the Application Story

Explain the cavalry. Read the background information to the students.

Application Novel: *Captive Treasure*

Read Chapter 13 and discuss it. Direct the students to read Chapter 13 silently (or you may read it to the students). Encourage the students to find out what danger concerned the trapper. *(a raiding party of Indians)*

- ➤ **How long would it take to reach the mission?** *(about two weeks)*
- ➤ **Who did the trapper say might be able to help them?** *(the cavalry)*
- ➤ **How long did they stay hidden in the cave?** *(several days)*
- ➤ **What was the trapper's opinion of Lone Wolf (Wolf Scar)?** *(He was a bully and a coward.)*
- ➤ **How did God answer the prayers of Carrie and Sky Woman?** *(The soldiers rescued them.)*
- ➤ **Does God always answer our prayers according to our will?** *(No. God will accomplish all His holy will. We cannot understand God's ways, for He sees the end from the beginning.)* Emphasize the goodness and greatness of God.

Read and discuss Chapter 14. Direct the students to read Chapter 14 silently or listen as you read it aloud to find out why Carrie was sad after returning home. *(She was sad that Swift Arrow and Windsinger had not accepted Christ as their Savior.)*

- ➤ **Why did the soldiers think that Carrie was Caroline Talbot?** *(She had red hair.)*
- ➤ **Why did the soldiers believe Carrie was alive?** *(They had found the Bible.)*

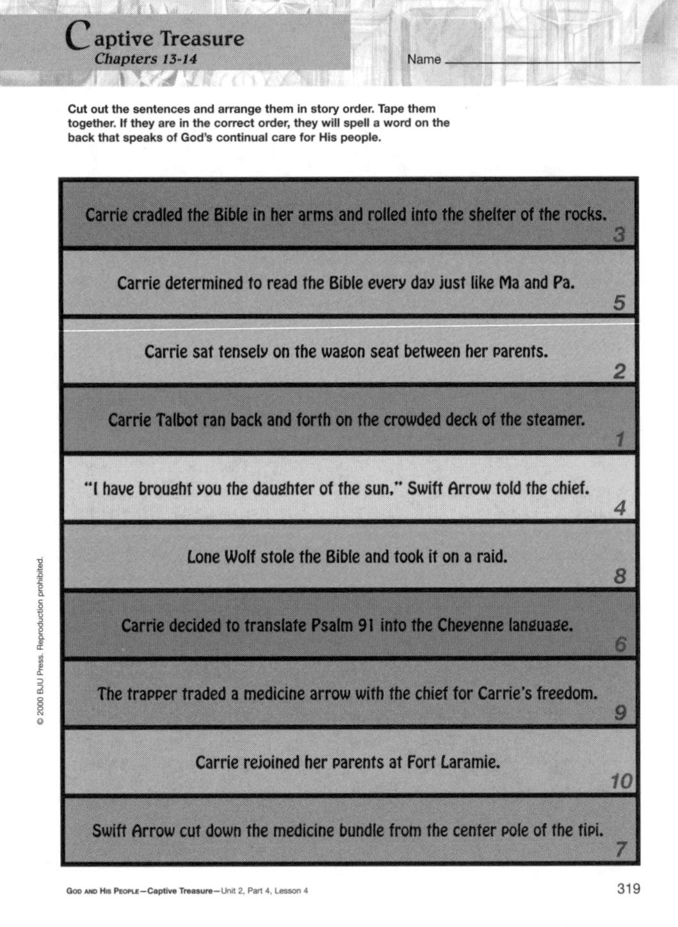

Captive Treasure
Chapters 13-14

Name ____________

Cut out the sentences and arrange them in story order. Tape them together. If they are in the correct order, they will spell a word on the back that speaks of God's continual care for His people.

Carrie cradled the Bible in her arms and rolled into the shelter of the rocks. 3

Carrie determined to read the Bible every day just like Ma and Pa. 5

Carrie sat tensely on the wagon seat between her parents. 2

Carrie Talbot ran back and forth on the crowded deck of the steamer. 1

"I have brought you the daughter of the sun," Swift Arrow told the chief. 4

Lone Wolf stole the Bible and took it on a raid. 8

Carrie decided to translate Psalm 91 into the Cheyenne language. 6

The trapper traded a medicine arrow with the chief for Carrie's freedom. 9

Carrie rejoined her parents at Fort Laramie. 10

Swift Arrow cut down the medicine bundle from the center pole of the tipi. 7

God and His People—Captive Treasure—Unit 2, Part 4, Lesson 4 319

- ➤ **Where did Carrie go to meet her parents?** *(Fort Laramie)*
- ➤ **How would Sky Woman and Carrie pray for Swift Arrow?** *(They would pray that Swift Arrow would accept Christ and lead the others.)*
- ➤ **What were some of the good results from Carrie's captivity?** *(Answers will vary, but should include her sharing the message of salvation, learning the Cheyenne language, having two mothers, and learning to know and trust God.)*
- ➤ **What verse about treasure had helped Carrie through the past year?** *(". . . for where your treasure is, there will your heart be also.")*

Worktext Supplement page 319

Sequence events.

Going Beyond

Preparation of Materials

Prepare six sentence strips for the acronym *prayer,* writing each bold sentence on an individual strip.

Enrichment

Discuss the model prayer. Read **Matthew 6:5-15,** explaining that this was a prayer the Lord Jesus prayed, and it is an example to believers. Display the sentence strips prepared for the acronym *prayer* and explain the meaning for each letter.

- **P***raise to God*—Read **Matthew 6:9** aloud, explaining that believers are to praise God. Tell the students to list ways that they can praise God.
- **R***each the lost*—Read **Matthew 6:10*a*** aloud, explaining that someday God will set up His kingdom on earth. Until that time believers are to be praying for others and doing all they can reach others with the gospel.
- **A***ccept God's plan*—Read **Matthew 6:10*b*** aloud, explaining that God has a plan for each of our lives, but that plan can be hindered if a believer has sin in his life and wants to go his own way.
- **Y***ield to God's plan*—Explain that outwardly doing what is right and avoiding outward sin is not enough. Believers are to have a proper heart attitude, praying daily for God's help to have a right attitude.
- **E***veryday needs*—Read **Matthew 6:11** aloud, explaining that God wants to provide for us and that we can ask Him for our daily needs.
- **R***elationships to others*—Read **Matthew 6:13-15** aloud, explaining that believers need God's help in keeping away from temptation that may come, as well as in how we treat and respond to others.

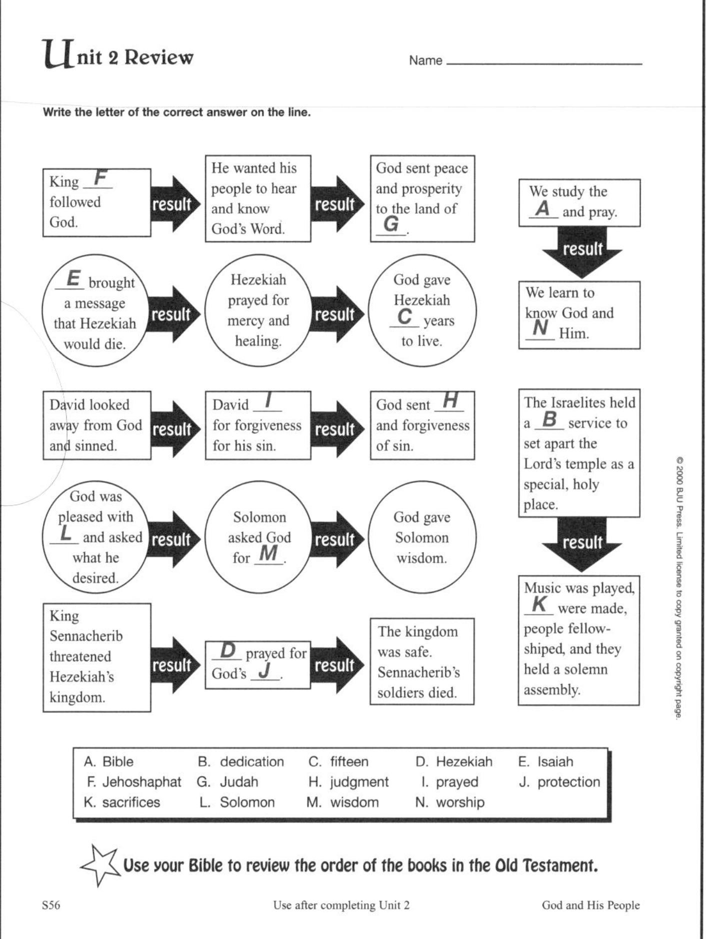

Unit 2 Review

Name ____________

Write the letter of the correct answer on the line.

King __F__ followed God. → result → He wanted his people to hear and know God's Word. → result → God sent peace and prosperity to the land of __G__.

__E__ brought a message that Hezekiah would die. → result → Hezekiah prayed for mercy and healing. → result → God gave Hezekiah __C__ years to live.

David looked away from God and sinned. → result → David __I__ for forgiveness for his sin. → result → God sent __H__ and forgiveness of sin.

God was pleased with __L__ and asked what he desired. → result → Solomon asked God for __M__. → result → God gave Solomon wisdom.

King Sennacherib threatened Hezekiah's kingdom. → result → __D__ prayed for God's __J__. → result → The kingdom was safe. Sennacherib's soldiers died.

We study the __A__ and pray. → result → We learn to know God and __N__ Him.

The Israelites held a __B__ service to set apart the Lord's temple as a special, holy place. → result → Music was played, __K__ were made, people fellowshiped, and they held a solemn assembly.

A. Bible	B. dedication	C. fifteen	D. Hezekiah	E. Isaiah
F. Jehoshaphat	G. Judah	H. judgment	I. prayed	J. protection
K. sacrifices	L. Solomon	M. wisdom	N. worship	

Use your Bible to review the order of the books in the Old Testament.

S56 Use after completing Unit 2 God and His People

Unit Review

Materials

- Copy of Supplement page S56, "Unit 2 Review," for each student

Guide a review of Unit 2. Review the people and events in preparation for the Unit 2 Test (optional).

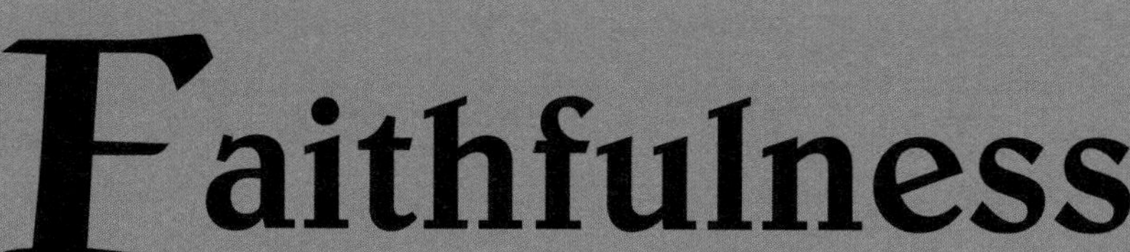

Faithfulness

Overview

Preparing the Teacher

God is faithful in His promises as well as in His judgments. Read **II Corinthians 10:5** and **Philippians 2:5-8** to see that Christians are admonished to have the mind of Christ. Since self-control is based on submissiveness to authority, we can teach our students more readily about responsibility, reliability, and faithfulness to God's Word by our own example. Yield to God daily in showing yourself faithful to Him through consistent Bible reading, prayer, and a personal testimony that glorifies the Lord.

Preparing the Lessons

Part 1 Lesson 1 Materials—two small pieces of magnetic tape for each student

Part 1 Lesson 2 Materials—a large map of the United States (optional)

Part 1 Lesson 4 Materials—a copy of a creed (optional)

Part 1 Going Beyond Materials—books about sign language

Part 2 Lesson 1 Materials—items for Art Connection; pictures of chariots; two metal brads, tagboard or poster board, and felt-tip pens for each student (optional)

Part 2 Lesson 2 Materials—a bag of wrapped candy—enough for each student to have a piece (optional)

Part 2 Lesson 3 Materials—a piece of 6" × 24" drawing paper for each student (optional)

Part 2 Lesson 4 Materials—a bunch of grapes (real or artificial); an artificial grapevine (optional)

Part 3 Lesson 2 Materials—an oil lamp (optional); one olive for each student (optional)

Part 3 Lesson 3 Materials—a small ax, ax head, or picture of an ax (optional); items for Food Connection: green olives, olive oil, parsley or oregano, bread and small bowls(optional)

Part 4 Lesson 1 Materials—picture of Stonewall Jackson or Civil War battle (optional)

Part 4 Lesson 3 Materials—a beanbag or ball (optional)

Unit 3 Faithfulness

Hymn: "I Would Be True"

Part	Lesson number	Lesson pages	Worktext pages	Supplement pages	Bible Account	Application
Part 1: God Is Faithful to Himself	1	87	57-60		Naboth's Vineyard (I Kings 21:1-26)	
	2	90	61-62			**Hymn History Story:** "I Would Be True"
	3	92	63		Jezebel's Wickedness Punished (II Kings 9:1-37)	
	4	93	64			"Lessons on the Mountain"
Part 2: God Is Faithful to His People	1	96	65-66		Elisha's Fiery Chariots (II Kings 6:8-23)	
	2	98	67-68		God Used Lepers (II Kings 6:24–7:20)	
	3	100	69-70			"Grandmother's Faith"
	4	102	71-72		**Prophet Focus:** Hosea	**Picture the Point:** Israel's Rebellion
Part 3: God's People Should Be Faithful to God	1	105	73-74			"Don't Forget Heaven"
	2	107	75-76		The Widow and the Oil (II Kings 4:1-7)	
	3	109	77-78		The Ax That Floated (II Kings 6:1-7)	
	4	110	79-80		Death in the Pot (II Kings 4:38-44)	
Part 4: God's People Should Be Faithful to Others	1	113	81-82			**Picture the Point:** Faithfulness
	2	115	83		Jehoiada Faithfully Raised Joash (II Kings 11:1-21)	
	3	117	84-86		The Temple Repaired (II Chronicles 24:1-22)	
	4	118	87-88			"Faithful in Little Things"

Connections	Memory Verses and Principles	Bible Doctrines	Skills/Applications
Language Writing	Deuteronomy 7:9 *God never changes.*	**The Doctrine of God** **Attributes of God:** God is all-powerful (omnipotent) (Jer. 32:27). God is unchanging (immutable) (Mal. 3:6). God is faithful (I Cor. 1:9). God is merciful (Ps. 86:15). **The Doctrine of Man** **Redemption of Man:** Man has hope (Phil. 3:20-21). **The Doctrine of the Church** **Functions of the Local Church:** Contribute financially (Rom. 15:26) **The Doctrine of Angels and Satan** **Organization:** Angels guard individuals and nations (Ps. 34:7).	**Foundational:** • Understand that God is unchanging • Realize that God is faithful; He keeps His promises • Realize that God is all-powerful • Realize that God protects and provides for His people • Realize that God must punish sin • Know that God rewards faithfulness • Understand that angels stand guard **Practical:** • Recall facts and details • Locate information in Scripture • Read a time line • Learn the divisions of the New Testament • Develop active listening • Complete a bar graph • Frame a story • Edit a story • Draw conclusions • Compare and contrast characters **Personal:** • Realize that Christians should be faithful to God • Realize that God wants us to be faithful to others • Realize that God wants Christians to support His work financially • Develop a Bible reading habit • Apply Bible knowledge to everyday life
TimeLine: Elisha Art Art **TimeLine: Hosea**	Joshua 1:9 *Be not afraid; God is with you.*		
History Food	Psalm 101:6 *God blesses His faithful servants.*		
History **TimeLine: Joash**	Matthew 25:23 *God rewards faithfulness.*		

Preparing the Unit 3 Bulletin Board

Cover the bulletin board with a pale yellow background. Prepare the title and subtitle in black or purple. Write the students' names on large grapes in the center. Border the board with grapevines. (*Note:* Grapevines can be made or artificial ones purchased.)

God Is Faithful to Himself

Preview

Doctrines

- God is unchanging (immutable) (Malachi 3:6)—Lesson 1
- God is faithful (I Corinthians 1:9)—Lesson 3

Skills and Applications

- Learn Deuteronomy 7:9
- Learn the books called Paul's Letters
- Recall facts and details
- Locate information in Scripture
- Compare and contrast characters
- Develop a Bible reading habit
- Understand that God is unchanging
- Realize that God must punish sin
- Realize that God is faithful; He keeps His promises
- Apply Bible knowledge to everyday life

Lesson 1

Materials

- Chart 11, "Naboth's Vineyard"
- Song: "The Bible Reading Habit"
- Two small pieces of magnetic tape for each student
- Unit 3 Bookmark for each student
- Highlighter for each student (optional)

Hymn: "I Would Be True"

Teach the first verse (Worktext page 274). Tell the students to read silently as you read the poem aloud. (*Note:* Read all three verses.) Play the recording and lead in singing the first verse.

➤ **Why will the hymn writer be true and pure?** *(There are those who trust him and care about him.)*

➤ **Why will he be strong and brave?** *(He knows he will suffer, and there will be times he will need to be daring.)*

Bible Study Skills, Worktext pages 57-58

Develop a Bible reading habit. Read the top part of page 57 to the students. Select students to read aloud the Bible reading guidelines, emphasizing that God's Word is spiritual food for Christians. Point out the HABIT acrostic and read aloud each statement for developing the habit of Bible reading. Explain the four-week Bible reading activity on page 58. Lead in singing together the song "The Bible Reading Habit" from Worktext page 271. Encourage each student to complete the daily Bible reading, coloring the fork after each day's reading. (*Note:* You may choose to have students do their reading before class, during class, or at a time of their own choosing.)

Background Information

Ahab and Jezebel—*Ahab was a wicked king who ruled Israel for twenty-two years (874-853 B.C.). Ahab's capital was the city of Samaria, but he built his royal palace in the city of Jezreel. Jezebel was Ahab's wife and more wicked than he. She was the daughter of the King of Tyre and was not an Israelite. Jezebel worshiped Baal and tried to force this worship on the Israelites.*

Vineyards—*The growing of grapes was an important industry in Israel. Grapes grew on the vines in the valleys and on the mountainous slopes. Naboth's vineyard was located in Jezreel.*

Introducing the Bible Account

Guide a discussion. Direct the students to find the word *covet* in the glossary. Select a student to read the definition aloud.

➤ **Where in the Bible have you heard the word *covet* used?** *(Possible answers include in the Ten Commandments or in the account of Achan.)*

➤ **Have you ever wanted something someone else had?**

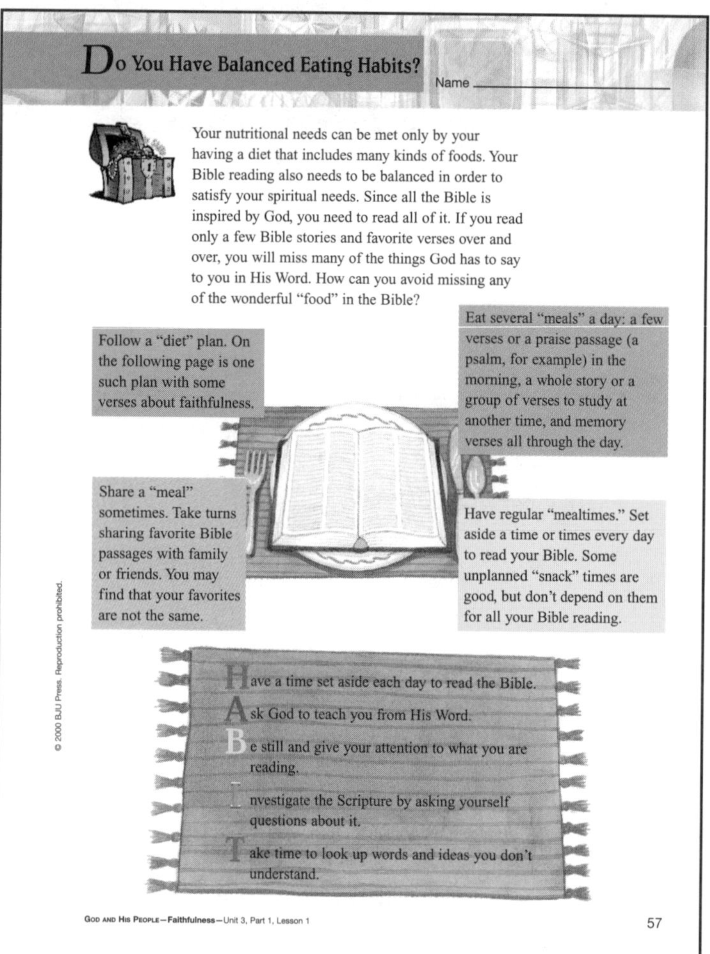

Do You Have Balanced Eating Habits?

Name ____________

Your nutritional needs can be met only by your having a diet that includes many kinds of foods. Your Bible reading also needs to be balanced in order to satisfy your spiritual needs. Since all the Bible is inspired by God, you need to read all of it. If you read only a few Bible stories and favorite verses over and over, you will miss many of the things God has to say to you in His Word. How can you avoid missing any of the wonderful "food" in the Bible?

Follow a "diet" plan. On the following page is one such plan with some verses about faithfulness.

Eat several "meals" a day: a few verses or a praise passage (a psalm, for example) in the morning, a whole story or a group of verses to study at another time, and memory verses all through the day.

Share a "meal" sometimes. Take turns sharing favorite Bible passages with family or friends. You may find that your favorites are not the same.

Have regular "mealtimes." Set aside a time or times every day to read your Bible. Some unplanned "snack" times are good, but don't depend on them for all your Bible reading.

Have a time set aside each day to read the Bible.
Ask God to teach you from His Word.
Be still and give your attention to what you are reading.
Investigate the Scripture by asking yourself questions about it.
Take time to look up words and ideas you don't understand.

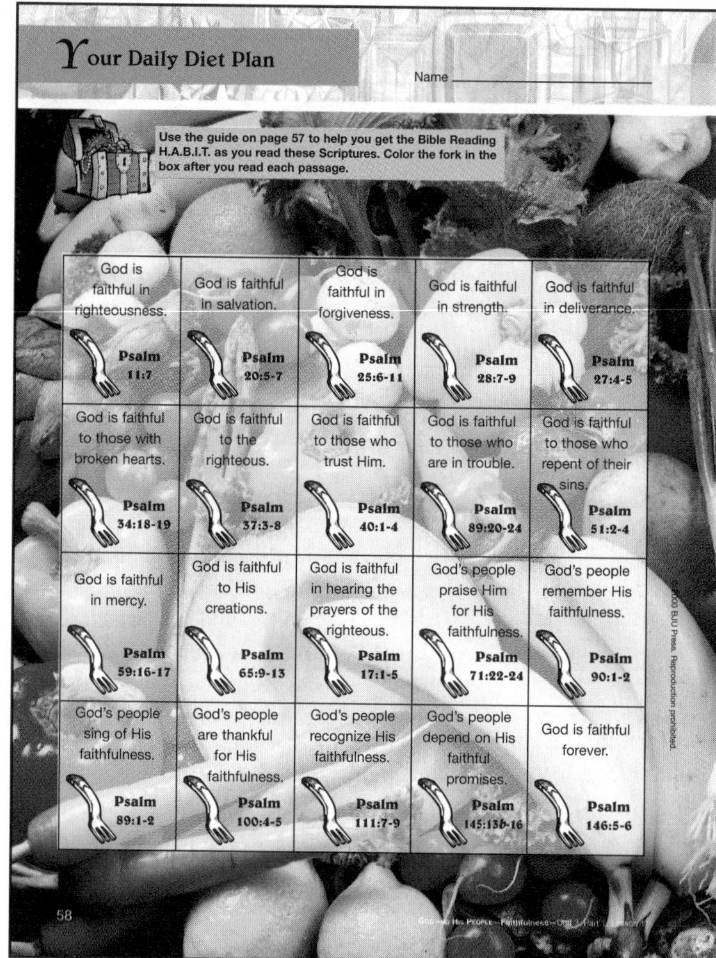

Your Daily Diet Plan

Name ____________

Use the guide on page 57 to help you get the Bible Reading H.A.B.I.T. as you read these Scriptures. Color the fork in the box after you read each passage.

God is faithful in righteousness. Psalm 11:7	God is faithful in salvation. Psalm 20:5-7	God is faithful in forgiveness. Psalm 25:6-11	God is faithful in strength. Psalm 28:7-9	God is faithful in deliverance. Psalm 27:4-5
God is faithful to those with broken hearts. Psalm 34:18-19	God is faithful to the righteous. Psalm 37:3-8	God is faithful to those who trust Him. Psalm 40:1-4	God is faithful to those who are in trouble. Psalm 89:20-24	God is faithful to those who repent of their sins. Psalm 51:2-4
God is faithful in mercy. Psalm 59:16-17	God is faithful to His creations. Psalm 65:9-13	God is faithful in hearing the prayers of the righteous. Psalm 17:1-5	God's people praise Him for His faithfulness. Psalm 71:22-24	God's people remember His faithfulness. Psalm 90:1-2
God's people sing of His faithfulness. Psalm 89:1-2	God's people are thankful for His faithfulness. Psalm 100:4-5	God's people recognize His faithfulness. Psalm 111:7-9	God's people depend on His faithful promises. Psalm 145:13b-16	God is faithful forever. Psalm 146:5-6

Bible Account

Read the following Bible account, or read I Kings 21:1-26. Direct the students to look at Worktext page 59. Read and discuss the information on the page, telling the students that the man and his wife in this Bible account coveted something that did not belong to them.

Naboth's Vineyard

Naboth was a faithful man who followed the teachings of God all his life. King Ahab's palace overlooked the vineyard that belonged to Naboth. Ahab went to Naboth and asked for the vineyard that Naboth had inherited from his father. Ahab wanted it for a vegetable garden.

Naboth reminded Ahab of the teachings of the Lord. Naboth said, "The Lord forbid it me, that I should give the inheritance of my fathers unto thee." This is the law that God commanded Moses to give to the people of Israel (Leviticus 25:23).

King Ahab offered either to give Naboth money for his vineyard or to buy him another vineyard. But Naboth would not break the law of the Lord which had been given through Moses. Naboth would not sell his vineyard to Ahab.

When Ahab went back to his palace, he pouted, lay down on his bed, and would not eat because he was so upset and angry. Ahab's wife, Jezebel, was a wicked queen who believed that she and her husband could have whatever they wanted because they were royalty. When Jezebel saw Ahab upset, she asked, "Why is thy spirit so sad, that thou eatest no bread?"

Ahab told her that Naboth would not give him what he wanted. Jezebel told Ahab that because he was king he could have anything he wanted. She said she would take care of it for him.

So Jezebel wrote letters and signed King Ahab's name to them and sealed them with King Ahab's royal seal. In the letters, she told the leaders of Jezreel to proclaim a fast and to have two men tell lies about Naboth. Jezebel told the leaders to have the liars say that Naboth blasphemed God and the king.

In Old Testament days it took two witnesses giving testimony about someone breaking the law in order for that person to be killed (or given the death penalty). According to Jezebel's plan, the two men lied about

Naboth, and the people took him out of the city and stoned him until he died.

When the news of Naboth's death reached the palace, Jezebel told King Ahab to go down and claim the vineyard of Naboth for himself because Naboth was dead. But God knew of the evil that had been done to His faithful servant Naboth. And God told Elijah the prophet to meet Ahab at the vineyard and to tell the king that God had seen the evil deed. Elijah foretold the horrible deaths of Ahab and Jezebel. Ahab would be killed in battle, wild dogs licking up his blood (I Kings 22:37-38), and Jezebel would be killed and her flesh *eaten* by wild dogs. And none of Ahab's male descendants would rule in Israel after the death of his sons.

InfoScene: "Naboth's Vineyard"
Display Chart 11 for reference throughout this unit. Review and discuss the Bible account as time permits.

➤ **How does God want us to be like Naboth?** *(God wants us to obey Him.)*

➤ **What did Ahab do when Naboth refused to sell King Ahab his vineyard?** *(He went home and pouted.)*

➤ **What should we do when we don't get our own way?** *(Possible answers include be satisfied, don't pout.)*

➤ **What did Jezebel do to fix the problem?** *(She wrote letters arranging for two men to lie saying that Naboth had blasphemed God and the king so he would be killed.)*

➤ **What did God have Elijah tell Ahab?** *(that God had seen his evil deeds, that both he and Jezebel would die horrible deaths, and that none of his ancestors would rule after him)*

➤ **What warning through God's Word does God give us about sin today?** *(He tells us that our sin deserves His wrath and curse, but that we can escape that wrath by believing in His Son, the Lord Jesus Christ, who took the punishment for our sin.)*

Memory Verse—Deuteronomy 7:9

Principle: God never changes. Locate **Deuteronomy 7:9** and read the verse aloud as the students read silently. Explain the following words: *faithful (God keeps His promises), covenant (promise), and generations (all the people born in a certain time period).*

➤ **How does God keep His promises to us?** *(He still judges sin and shows mercy to those that love Him and keep His commandments.)*

➤ **How long will God keep His promises and show mercy to those that love Him?** *(forever; to a thousand generations)*

Choose volunteers to read the verse aloud. Guide the students to highlight the verse in their Bibles (optional).

Give each student a Unit 3 Bookmark, directing attention to the illustration of the pottery, reminding the students that God is the master potter who makes and keeps us always in His care. Tell the students to fold their bookmarks on the dotted lines and to attach a small piece of magnetic tape on the inside of the bookmark at both ends. Direct them to place the Unit 3 Bookmark over the page to mark the location of the memory verse.

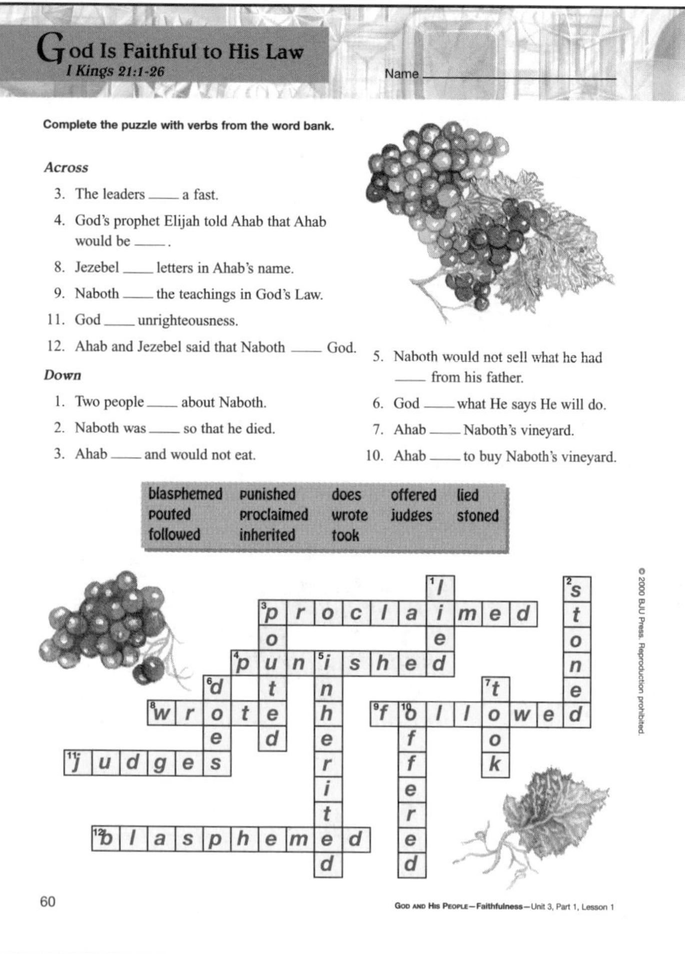

God Is Faithful to His Law
I Kings 21:1-26

Name ____________________

Complete the puzzle with verbs from the word bank.

Across

3. The leaders ____ a fast.
4. God's prophet Elijah told Ahab that Ahab would be ____.
8. Jezebel ____ letters in Ahab's name.
9. Naboth ____ the teachings in God's Law.
11. God ____ unrighteousness.
12. Ahab and Jezebel said that Naboth ____ God.

Down

1. Two people ____ about Naboth.
2. Naboth was ____ so that he died.
3. Ahab ____ and would not eat.
5. Naboth would not sell what he had ____ from his father.
6. God ____ what He says He will do.
7. Ahab ____ Naboth's vineyard.
10. Ahab ____ to buy Naboth's vineyard.

blasphemed	punished	does	offered	lied
pouted	proclaimed	wrote	judges	stoned
followed	inherited	took		

60 — God and His People—Faithfulness—Unit 3, Part 1, Lesson 1

Worktext page 60

Recall facts about the Bible account.

Lesson 2

Materials

- Song: "Books of the New Testament"
- Bible Book Cards: Gospels, History, Paul's Letters
- A large map of the United States (optional)

Hymn History Story: "I Would Be True"

Read the story about how Howard Walter came to write "I Would Be True."

"I Would be True"

When Howard Walter was twenty-three years old, he went to Japan to teach English for a year. He was sad to leave his mother alone in the United States, and he wrote to her often. She must have been afraid of the influences of the foreign culture on her son. Howard wanted to assure his mother that he would never lose the values that she had taught him while he was growing up.

He sent her a poem he had entitled, "My Creed." A *creed* is a statement of one's beliefs that he will live by. Mrs. Walter was very impressed by her son's poem. She was very pleased with the beliefs presented in the poem, and she might have been proud that her son had written them so well.

Mrs. Walter sent the poem to *Harper's Magazine,* a leading journal of that time. The publishers liked the poem too, and in 1907 they published the poem in the May issue of the magazine.

In 1909 Howard Walter showed his poem to a preacher named Joseph Yates Peek. Peek immediately started whistling a tune for the words. Although he was not an expert at putting music down on paper, Peek had a friend who could help him—Grant Colfax Tullar. Mr. Tullar was an organist, and he wrote out the tune Mr. Peek had whistled to the words Mr. Walter had written, harmonizing the music as we have it today in the hymn "I Would Be True."

Hymn: "I Would Be True"

Sing the first verse (Worktext page 274). Play the recording and lead in singing verse 1 together.

Worktext page 61

Singing with understanding, verse 1. Direct attention to the American Sign Language hand signs for the following key words; then guide the students to sign the key words as they sing verse 1 several times. (*Note:* You may want to tell students to keep Worktext page 61 as a reference throughout this unit.)

True—Touch the tip of the right index finger to the mouth, palm facing left, and move it slightly up and forward
Trust—Bring both hands slightly to the left closing them to form fists, the right one slightly below the left.
Pure—Hold left hand palm up. Wipe right hand across left hand from palm to fingertips.
Care (Love)—Fists are crossed at the wrists and pressed to the heart.
Strong—Bring the fists up with elbows bent showing strength.
Suffer—Place the thumbnail of the right fist against the lips and draw downward.
Brave—Place the fingertips of both hands high on the chest near the shoulders and bring them forward into fists.
Dare (Try)—Place both fists facing each other in front of you and push them forward with effort.

Memory Verse—Deuteronomy 7:9

Practice the memory verse. Locate **Deuteronomy 7:9** and call on a student to read the verse aloud. Review the meaning of the verse.

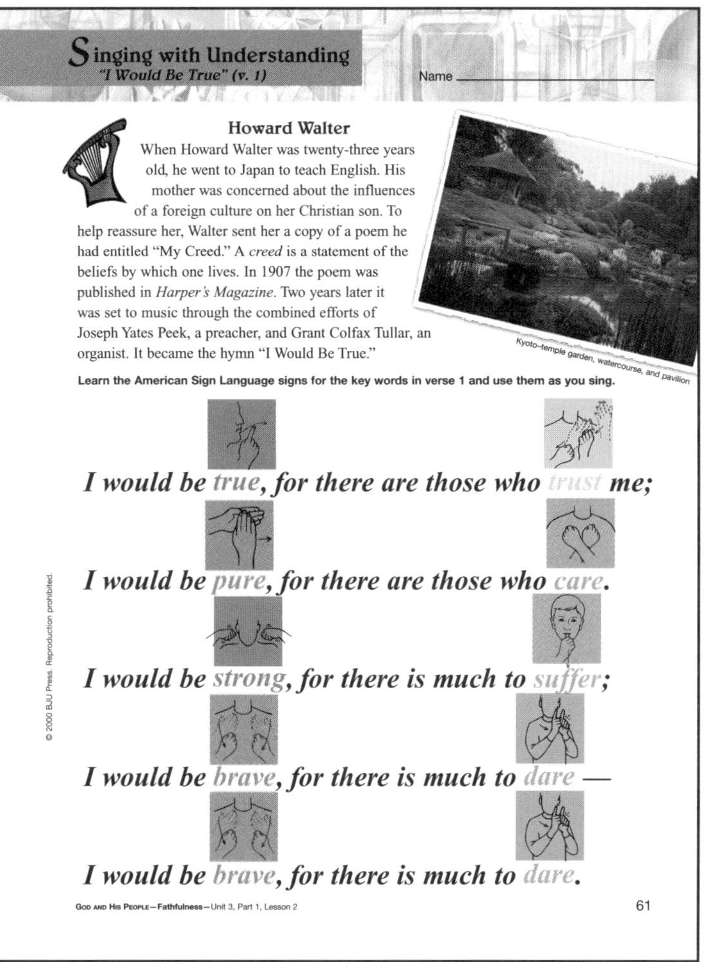

Singing with Understanding
"I Would Be True" (v. 1)

Name ____________

Howard Walter

When Howard Walter was twenty-three years old, he went to Japan to teach English. His mother was concerned about the influences of a foreign culture on her Christian son. To help reassure her, Walter sent her a copy of a poem he had entitled "My Creed." A *creed* is a statement of the beliefs by which one lives. In 1907 the poem was published in *Harper's Magazine*. Two years later it was set to music through the combined efforts of Joseph Yates Peek, a preacher, and Grant Colfax Tullar, an organist. It became the hymn "I Would Be True."

Kyoto-temple garden, watercourse, and pavilion

Learn the American Sign Language signs for the key words in verse 1 and use them as you sing.

I would be true, for there are those who trust me;
I would be pure, for there are those who care.
I would be strong, for there is much to suffer;
I would be brave, for there is much to dare —
I would be brave, for there is much to dare.

God and His People—Faithfulness—Unit 3, Part 1, Lesson 2 61

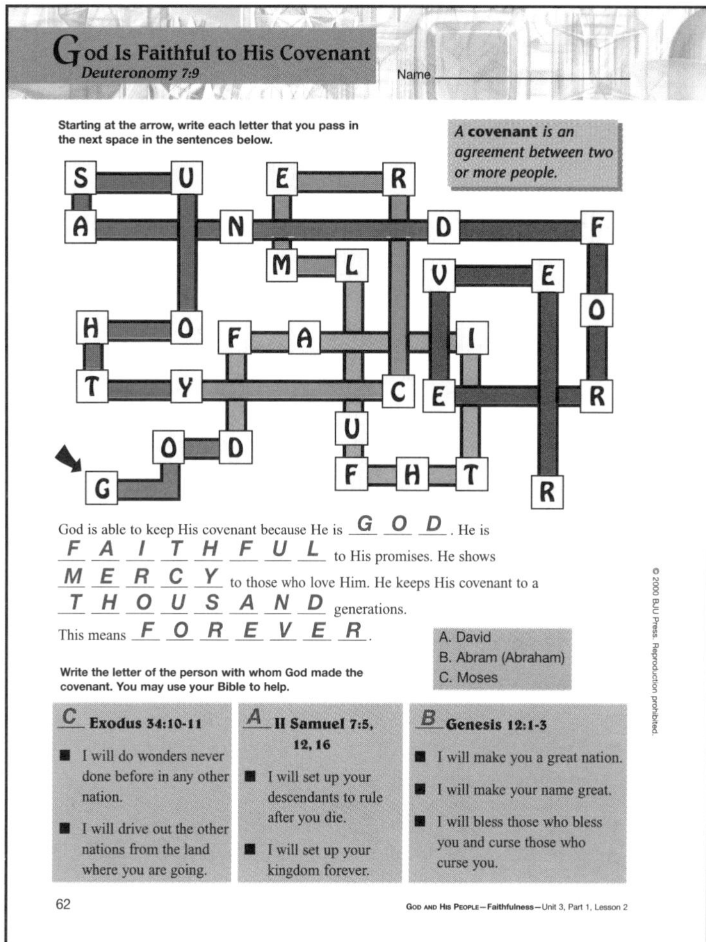

God Is Faithful to His Covenant
Deuteronomy 7:9

Name ____________

Starting at the arrow, write each letter that you pass in the next space in the sentences below.

A ***covenant*** *is an agreement between two or more people.*

God is able to keep His covenant because He is G O D. He is F A I T H F U L to His promises. He shows M E R C Y to those who love Him. He keeps His covenant to a T H O U S A N D generations. This means F O R E V E R.

Write the letter of the person with whom God made the covenant. You may use your Bible to help.

A. David
B. Abram (Abraham)
C. Moses

C **Exodus 34:10-11**	A **II Samuel 7:5, 12, 16**	B **Genesis 12:1-3**
■ I will do wonders never done before in any other nation. ■ I will drive out the other nations from the land where you are going.	■ I will set up your descendants to rule after you die. ■ I will set up your kingdom forever.	■ I will make you a great nation. ■ I will make your name great. ■ I will bless those who bless you and curse those who curse you.

62 God and His People—Faithfulness—Unit 3, Part 1, Lesson 2

➤ **How has God been faithful to you?**

➤ **How has God shown mercy to you?**

Divide the students into two groups. Direct group 1 to read the first part of the verse and group 2 to read the second part of the verse. Instruct everyone to read the last part of the verse together. Read the verse again, reversing parts.

Worktext page 62

Locate information in Scripture.

Song: "Books of the New Testament"

Sing the first three verses (Worktext page 288). Play the recording and sing verses 1-3.

Bible Study Skills

Review Paul's Letters. Distribute the cards of Paul's Letters to twelve students. Direct the students to arrange themselves in the correct order at the front of the room. Say together the names of Paul's Letters several times. Divide the students into three or four teams. Line up the teams. Show a Bible Book Card (from the first three New Testament divisions) to the student at the front of each line. The student who calls out the name of the book that comes before the book shown receives a point for his team. Let each student in front go to the end of his line after his turn. (*Note:* When the card for Matthew is displayed, the game can be stopped and a winner determined, or the student can say "Malachi" as the book that comes before since it is the last book of the Old Testament.)

One-on-One: Give the student the twelve Bible Book Cards of Paul's Letters to sequence correctly. Then mix up the cards (from the first three New Testament divisions) and show one at a time, challenging the student to identify in which division it belongs.

Language Connection (optional)

Learn about sign language. Display the United States map. Read the following sentence aloud, *signing* the underlined words instead of reading them. Allow students to guess the words you signed.

I like to <u>eat</u> pepperoni <u>pizza.</u>

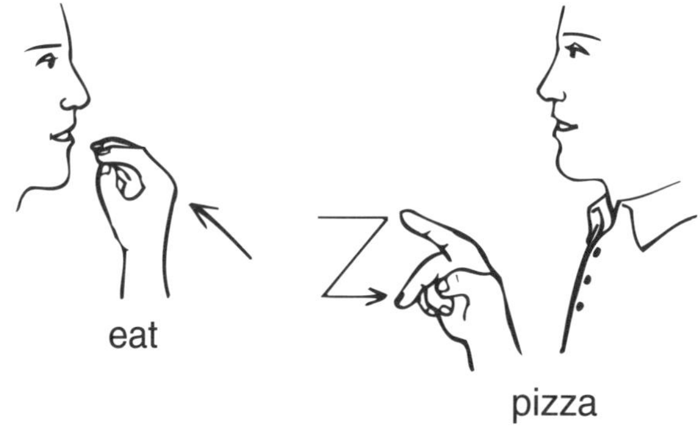

➤ **Who uses sign language?** *(deaf, hearing impaired, and people with normal hearing to communicate with the deaf and hearing impaired)*

Explain that sign language is a language that uses symbols made with the hands to communicate ideas. Sign language was introduced in America in the nineteenth century. The American language of signs is based on the French sign language. Laurent Clerc, a deaf Frenchman, was the first person to teach deaf people in the United States. Choose a student to point to the state of *Connecticut* on the map. Explain that in 1817 Mr. Clerc opened the first permanent school for the deaf in Hartford, Connecticut.

Lesson 3

Preparation of Materials

Write Deuteronomy 7:9 on an erasable board.

Hymn: "I Would Be True"

Sing the first verse (Worktext page 274). Review the signs for the key words in verse 1. (*Note:* See Worktext page 61 for the signs.) Sing the verse through several times, using the signs.

Memory Verse—Deuteronomy 7:9

Practice the memory verse. Call attention to the verse written on the board. Read the verse together several times; then call on a student to erase a few words and lead in reading the verse. Continue this procedure until the verse is completely erased and the students can say the verse from memory.

Background Information

Jehu—*He was a king of Israel from 841 to 814 B.C. He should be distinguished from Jehu the prophet (I Kings 16:1-4). In the beginning of his reign, Jehu listened to Elisha's advice but later turned from the Lord.*

Dogs—*For an Israelite a dog symbolized uncleanness and shame. Dogs were not kept as pets and were not considered "man's best friend." In contrast, Egyptians regarded dogs as one of the highest forms of life. Dogs may have been among the animals worshiped as symbols of the gods.*

Elijah—*Years had passed since Elijah was directed by God to foretell the end of Ahab and Jezebel. Elijah had been taken up in a chariot of fire, and Elisha had become the head prophet, but God had not forgotten His promise. Ahab and his house had done wickedly in the sight of the Lord, and God would punish their wickedness.*

Introducing the Bible Account

Review the prophecies made about Ahab and Jezebel.

➤ **What did Elijah prophesy would happen to Ahab and Jezebel?** *(that they would die horrible deaths)*

Read **I Kings 22:37-38.** Explain that Ahab was killed in battle and that the wild dogs licked up his blood when his chariot was being washed at a pool in Samaria.

Bible Account

Read the following Bible account or read II Kings 9:1-37. Direct the students to listen to find out what happened to Jezebel. *(She was thrown from a window and run over by a chariot; the wild dogs ate her flesh and left only bones.)*

Jezebel's Wickedness Punished

One day Elisha told one of the young prophets to take a flask of oil and to anoint a new king. Elisha said to go find Jehu, take him into a house, pour the oil on his head, and say, "Thus saith the Lord, I have anointed thee king over Israel." Then he was to open the door and flee.

The young prophet did as he was commanded and told Jehu, "Thus saith the Lord God of Israel, I have anointed thee king over the people of the Lord, even over Israel. And thou shalt smite the house of Ahab thy master, that I may avenge the blood of my servants the prophets, and the blood of all the servants of the Lord, at the hand of Jezebel." The young prophet then fled as Elisha had told him.

Jehu's servants wanted to know what the young prophet had said. Jehu told them that he had been anointed king over Israel. Then the people celebrated, blowing trumpets and proclaiming, "Jehu is king."

Jehu rode in his chariot towards Jezreel. He met Ahab's son Joram (Jehoram) and Ahaziah, Ahab's grandson and king of Judah, in the land that had belonged to Naboth. Jehu drew his bow and shot an arrow that killed Joram. Jehu then told Bidkar, his captain, to take the dead body and to throw it into Naboth's field as the Lord had said to do.

Ahaziah saw what had happened and fled, but Jehu followed him and wounded him. The injured Ahaziah fled to Megiddo and died there.

Jehu returned to Jezreel by way of the city gate. When Jezebel heard he was coming, she fixed her hair and made herself ready to see him. As Jehu saw her looking down from the window, he commanded that Jezebel be thrown down. Several servants threw her down, and she was trodden underfoot by Jehu's horses and chariot. When Jehu came in, he ate and drank, and said, "Go, see now this cursed woman, and bury her: for she is a king's daughter." When the men went to bury Jezebel, they found that the dogs had eaten her flesh. The word of the Lord, as spoken by Elijah years before, had come to pass. Judgment had come to Ahab's house.

God Is Faithful to Punish Unrighteousness
II Kings 9:1-37

Name ____________

Decide whether each statement is True or False. Circle the letter in the correct column. Write the circled letter in the square with the same number. You will spell a word that tells what God is.

Statement	True	False
1. Elisha anointed Jehu to be king.	S	(R)
2. God said He would destroy the house of Ahab.	(I)	M
3. The people cheered when they heard Jehu was king.	(G)	J
4. Joram and Ahaziah rode together in a chariot to meet Jehu.	A	(H)
5. Joram was killed and thrown on the ground that had belonged to Naboth.	(T)	N
6. Ahaziah lived on for many years and did evil.	R	(E)
7. Jezebel waited for Jehu in Jezreel.	(O)	P
8. Jehu killed Jezebel with a sword.	E	(U)
9. Wild dogs ate Jezebel's body.	(S)	T

1.	2.	3.	4.	5.	6.	7.	8.	9.
R	I	G	H	T	E	O	U	S

God and His People—Faithfulness—Unit 3, Part 1, Lesson 3 63

- ➤ **How did God keep His promise in today's Bible account?** *(He judged Ahab's and Jezebel's wickedness as He had said He would.)*
- ➤ **Whom did the young prophet anoint as king?** *(Jehu)*
- ➤ **Where did the battle with Jehu, Joram, and Ahaziah take place?** *(in the land which had belonged to Naboth)*
- ➤ **What happened to Ahaziah, Ahab's grandson and king of Judah?** *(He fled; Jehu chased him and wounded him. He then fled to Megiddo and died.)*
- ➤ **What happened to Jezebel?** *(She was thrown from the window and trodden by horses and a chariot; her flesh was eaten by wild dogs.)*
- ➤ **Does God keep His promises?** *(Yes. God is faithful in His promises to the righteous and to the unrighteous.)*

Worktext page 63

Recall details about the Bible account.

Lesson 4

Materials

- A copy of a creed (optional)

Hymn: "I Would Be True"

Sing the first verse (Worktext page 274). Review the meaning of verse 1. Review the signs for the key words as used in Lesson 2. Lead the students in singing and signing verse 1.

Memory Verse—Deuteronomy 7:9

Practice the memory verse. Read **Deuteronomy 7:9**. Direct the students to say the verse from memory in their normal voices, in a whisper, and then silently to themselves.

Introducing the Application Story

Discuss Creation. Direct the students to think back to when they studied about Creation and God as the Creator. Explain that believers know God is the Creator because of faith.

- ➤ **How does God show Himself daily?** *(Possible answers include the sun coming up in the morning, the rain watering the earth so things will grow, and our physical bodies that God gave us so we can learn and play.)*

Application Story

Read the following application story to the students.

Lessons on the Mountain

Darren and Tyrone stood at the beginning trail for Mount Mitchell. "Is Jake still coming?" Darren asked. "I thought he wanted to help us do some tracking."

"Here he comes," said Tyrone, jumping up. "What took you so long, Jake?"

"Had to find my stuff," Jake answered. He was carrying a container and a butterfly net. "Thought I might see a neat butterfly for my collection."

Tyrone slapped Jake on the back. "We *might* catch something *bigger* than a butterfly. Come on, let's go back to where we saw those tracks yesterday."

The three boys started their hike through the woods up to the top of the mountain. As the trail made a turn, Jake stopped and bent down. "Look, guys. Footprints!" The other two boys crouched to examine the footprints.

"Wow! Look at the size of those things," said Darren. They went on further, crawling on hands and knees to follow the tracks.

Suddenly Jake shoved his container into Tyrone's hand and said, "Hold that! I see a butterfly—looks like a Viceroy!" Jake chased the orange and black butterfly and returned with the trapped insect.

"Isn't that a Monarch butterfly?" asked Tyrone.

"Nope. See that dark stripe running across each lower wing? That's how you can tell it's a Viceroy," said Jake. "Fools the birds every time. Birds don't come near the Viceroy—they think it's a bitter-tasting Monarch!"

"Sure is funny how they happen to look so much alike," said Darren.

"That's how God made them," Jake said.

Darren shrugged. "My dad says that the world is just a hunk that broke off from the sun, and everything in it grew from one tiny piece of life."

Tyrone's mouth dropped open. "Your dad believes that stuff?"

Jake studied his container in silence for a moment. Then he said, "But look how the birds know exactly what to feed their babies. And look how the salmon goes hundreds of miles from the ocean to lay its eggs in the same creek where it was hatched."

Tyrone added, "And look how the birds travel for thousands of miles each fall and come back again in the spring, sometimes to the very same tree or birdhouse they lived in the year before."

Darren sighed. "Yeah, yeah. Well, we don't have all day. Let's get on with seeing what made those tracks." Tyrone and Jake glanced at each other then followed Darren through the thick brush.

The boys came out in a clearing. Grassy paths went off in two directions.

"We'll have to explore both directions till we pick up the footprints again," said Darren.

Jake went to the right, and Darren and Tyrone took the path to the left. A few moments later Darren shouted, "Here it is! We've picked up the trail again."

Tyrone bent down to see several footprints in the soft earth. He was quiet for a moment. Then he said, "This doesn't prove anything."

Darren stared at him. "What's the matter with you? There are wild animal tracks just as plain as the nose on your face."

"Yeah, I see them. But how do we know an animal made them? They might have just happened. Maybe the mud sank in the shape of footprints."

Darren frowned. "What, are you crazy?"

Tyrone grinned. "So you don't believe a footprint could just happen? A minute ago you were trying to tell me that everything in the whole world just happened. I said all along that someone had to make it." He folded his arms and watched Darren.

For a moment Darren just glared at Tyrone. Then he burst out laughing. "Okay, you win. Guess it does sound stupid to think things just happened. I'll have to tell Dad what you said."

Jake ran up. "Did you find the footprints?"

Before Darren could answer, a small rock tumbled down from the cliff above them. Three heads jerked up. High on a cliff, many yards away, stood a mountain goat staring down at them.

The boys stood frozen for a few seconds. Then Jake whistled long and low. "Wouldn't want *those* sharp horns poking me," he whispered. The next minute three boys were racing each other for home.

➤ **Where were the boys going?** *(tracking on the mountain)*

➤ **Why did the boys start talking about the way things are made?** *(because Jake was catching butterflies)*

➤ **How did Tyrone and Jake know someone had created all the many beautiful things around them?** *(they were willing to accept that by faith)*

God Is Faithful to His Creation
Psalm 139:1-3

Name ____________________

Neither you nor any other part of the earth and its contents "just happened." God created all that is. He knows all about you, even when you stand up or sit down. He even knows each heartbeat.

Read Psalm 139:1-3; then work with a partner to conduct the following procedure.

1. Tell your partner to stand up. Place the fingertips of one hand on the inside of your partner's wrist; press lightly to feel the pulse.
2. Using a watch or clock with a second hand to keep time, count the number of heartbeats in 15 seconds at each of the positions. Record numbers at each of these positions in the first column on Chart A.
3. Multiply each count by 4 to determine the pulse rate at each position.
4. Exchange places with your partner and repeat Steps 1-3, recording the information on Chart B.

A.

Body Position	Pulse beats in 15 seconds	x 4 =	Pulse Rate
Standing	Answers will vary.		
Sitting			
Lying down			

B.

Body Position	Pulse beats in 15 seconds	x 4 =	Pulse Rate
Standing	Answers will vary.		
Sitting			
Lying down			

In which position was your partner's pulse rate the fastest?
Answers will vary.

In which position was your pulse rate the fastest?
Answers will vary.

Why do you think this was so?
Answers will vary, but explain that the heart beats faster when the body has more work to do. Standing and sitting requires more work by muscles than lying down.

Spend some time thanking God for making you so wonderfully and for caring for you so faithfully.

Worktext page 64

Apply Bible knowledge to everyday life. Pair each student with a partner and guide the activity step by step, allowing time for the students to record their results.

Writing Connection (optional)

Write a simple creed. Read a creed, telling whose creed it is (e.g., personal, church, school, Boy Scout, etc.). Explain that a *creed* is a statement of one's beliefs that he pledges to live by. Guide the students as they write an individual, class, or family creed. (*Note:* The following creed is the one used at Bob Jones University. You may use it as a model, explaining unfamiliar words to the students.)

I believe in the inspiration of the Bible (both the Old and the New Testaments); the creation of man by the direct act of God; the incarnation and virgin birth of our Lord and Savior, Jesus Christ; His identification as the Son of God; His vicarious atonement for the sins of mankind by the shedding of His blood on the cross; the resurrection of His body from the tomb; His power to save men from sin; the new birth through the regeneration by the Holy Spirit; and the gift of eternal life by the grace of God.

Going Beyond

Materials

- Books about sign language

Enrichment

Expand sign language vocabulary. Provide books about sign language. Encourage the students to learn how to sign different words. You may want to provide a list of words from the Bible with a reference (e.g., *neighbor—Ephesians 4:25*). Once the student learns how to sign the word, allow him to read the verse to the other students, signing the word he learned. He may want to learn to sign several words from the same verse.

God Is Faithful to His People

Preview

Doctrines

- Angels guard individuals and nations—Lesson 1
- God is all-powerful (omnipotent) (Jeremiah 32:27)—Lesson 2

Skills and Applications

- Learn Joshua 1:9
- Read a time line
- Learn the books called General Letters
- Recall facts and details
- Locate information in Scripture
- Complete a bar graph
- Complete a flow chart
- Draw conclusions
- Realize that God is faithful
- Realize that God is all-powerful
- Understand that angels stand guard
- Apply Bible knowledge to everyday life

Lesson 1

Materials

- Chart 12, "Fiery Chariots"
- TimeLine and picture: *Elisha*
- Unit 3 Bookmark for each student
- Highlighter for each student (optional)
- Items for the optional Art Connection: pictures of chariots and two metal brads; tagboard, poster board, or construction paper; felt-tip pens for each student

Hymn: "I Would Be True"

Teach the second verse (Worktext page 274). Read the words of the second verse to the students. Explain the following words:

> **foe**—*enemy*
>
> **friendless**—*without friends*
>
> **humble**—*not proud, meek*

Discuss the phrase "I would be giving, and forget the gift." Elicit from the students that the hymn writer is saying that we should be giving ourselves to others and forgetting what we can get. Explain that the hymn encourages Christians to look to the Lord for their joy, love others as Christ loves them, and encourage one another. Play the recording and lead in singing verse 2; then sing verses 1 and 2 together.

Background Information

Chariots—*These two-wheeled vehicles were pulled by teams of horses with matched gaits and were used for fighting as well as for transportation. Chariots used for transportation were elaborately decorated, but those used in war had only the essentials. Trained teams of charioteers (a driver and a soldier with weapons) manned the chariots. Some chariots included attachments to hold weapons such as arrows, spears, and axes. Some chariots had bronze and iron fittings. During times of peace, chariot races were a favorite sport. Coins from New Testament times show reproductions of Roman chariots used for racing.*

Introducing the Bible Account

Discuss chariots. Call on students to tell what they know about *chariots.* Share the background information.

Bible Account

Read the following Bible account or read II Kings 6:8-23. Direct attention to the picture on Worktext page 65, telling the students to listen to find out how God used chariots. *(The chariots were God's heavenly army, placed on the hillside to protect Elisha and his servant.)*

Elisha's Fiery Chariots

The king of Syria wanted to capture Israel. He planned to take the nation little by little, city by city. However, each time his soldiers tried to attack a city, they found it was heavily guarded. How did the Israelite king know which city would be attacked?

The king of Syria decided he would find the man who was telling his military secrets. He called his men together and demanded to know who was giving secrets to the enemy. One of his servants spoke, "Elisha, the prophet that is in Israel, telleth the king of Israel the words that thou speakest in thy bedchamber."

The Syrian king knew he could not win the battles as long as this man of God, Elisha, was telling the Israelites his plans. He told his men, "Go and spy where he is, that I may send and fetch him."

Then the king of Syria sent a large army to Dothan to capture Elisha. The Syrian chariots and horses surrounded the city. Elisha's servant saw the armies coming from everywhere. In great fear he called to Elisha, asking what they should do. Elisha told his servant not to be afraid because they had more with them than were in the large army around them.

Elisha prayed, "Lord, I pray thee, open his eyes, that he may see." When Elisha prayed, the servant's eyes were opened, and he looked up and saw the hills *full of horses and chariots of fire*. The servant was no longer afraid; he could see that God was with them.

Elisha then asked God to smite the armies with blindness. God did this, and Elisha led them to the city of Samaria. Then God opened their eyes. The king of Samaria asked Elisha whether he should kill them. Elisha told the king not to kill them but to give them bread and water and send them on their way. The king followed Elisha's advice. He fed them well and sent them back to their own land. God had faithfully protected His people once again. He had revealed the enemy's plans to Elisha and had shown Elisha His heavenly army that was sent to protect His servant, Elisha. God struck the enemy soldiers with blindness and delivered Elisha and the nation of Israel. God showed His power to be greater than any other power.

InfoScene: "Fiery Chariots"
Display Chart 12 for reference throughout this unit. Review and discuss the Bible account as time permits.

- ➤ **Why did the King of Syria's plan to capture Israel city by city not work?** *(Elisha knew his plans, and the cities were always ready for the attack.)*
- ➤ **How did Elisha know the king's plans?** *(Elisha was God's prophet; God revealed the plans to Elisha.)*
- ➤ **Why was Elisha's servant fearful when he saw the Syrian armies?** *(He was not trusting the Lord.)*
- ➤ **When was the servant no longer afraid?** *(When God opened his eyes, he saw the chariots of fire—God's army of angels, and knew God was protecting them.)*
- ➤ **How was God faithful to the Israelites?** *(He protected them by revealing the enemies' plans to Elisha.)*
- ➤ **How is God faithful to us?** *(Answers will vary, but elicit that God promises eternal life to all who will accept Christ as their personal Savior.)*

TimeLine

Add *Elisha* to the TimeLine. Attach the picture of *Elisha* onto the TimeLine (852-790 B.C.). Explain that Elisha was a great prophet of God, whose miracles were used to bring glory to God. Guide the students as they glue the picture of *Elisha* onto their TimeLines.

Memory Verse—Joshua 1:9

Principle: Be not afraid; God is with you. Locate **Joshua 1:9** and read the verse aloud as the students read silently.

- ➤ **What does God command us to do?** *(Be strong and courageous, not fearful; don't be dismayed or lose courage.)*
- ➤ **What characters in this Bible account obeyed this verse?** *(Elisha and then later his servant)*

Surrounded!
II Kings 6:8-23

Name ____________________

Put an *X* on the word in each row that does not belong in this account.

1. Syria	~~Egypt~~	Israel
2. ~~Elijah~~	Elisha	servant
3. Samaria	~~Jerusalem~~	Dothan
4. chariots	horses	~~ships~~
5. blindness	~~plagues~~	protection

Retell the story of the fiery chariots as it might have been told by Elisha's servant Gehazi.

Elisha and I

Answers will vary but should follow the Bible account.

66 God and His People—Faithfulness—Unit 3, Part 2, Lesson 1

➤ **What are some specific times when you may want to remember this verse?** *(Possible answers include when confronted by unfriendly people, when someone in your family is ill, and when you need to take a stand against wrongdoing.)*

Allow volunteers to read the verse aloud. Direct the students to highlight the verse in their Bibles (optional) and to mark the location with the Unit 3 Bookmark.

Worktext page 66

Recall details about Elisha and the fiery chariots.

Art Connection (optional)

Make a chariot. Display pictures of chariots. Give each student two metal brads, tagboard, and felt-tip pens. Tell them to cut out, decorate, and assemble a chariot. The metal brads may be used to attach the wheels to the chariot. (*Note:* The students may cut and color paper horses to attach to their chariots if they wish.) Encourage the students to use their chariots to retell the Bible account about Elisha's fiery chariots to a relative or friend.

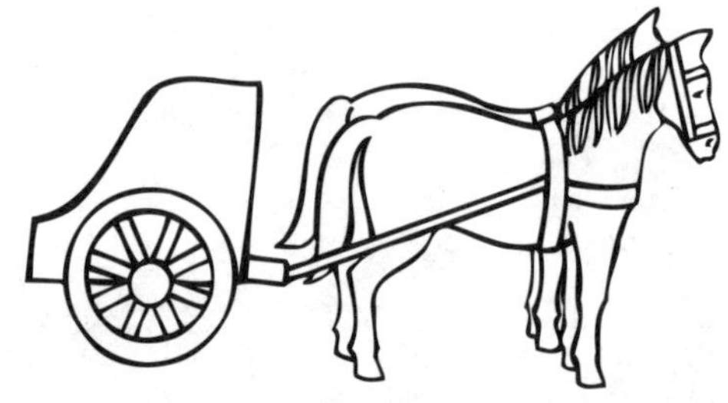

Lesson 2

Materials

- A bag of wrapped candy, one piece of candy for each student (optional)

Memory Verse—Joshua 1:9

Practice the memory verse. Locate and read aloud **Joshua 1:9** while the students read silently.

➤ **What question appears in the verse?** *(Have not I commanded thee [you]?)*

➤ **How many commands does God give?** *(three)*

Choose three students to each read or say from memory one of the commands after you read the questions. Direct the students to read together or say from memory God's promises. Read the verse throughout the day for practice.

Hymn: "I Would Be True"

Sing the first two verses (Worktext page 274). Play the recording and lead in singing verses 1 and 2.

Singing with Understanding
"I Would Be True" (v. 2)

Name ____________________

Answer each of the questions honestly. For each C answer, color a section of the Strength-o-Meter.

1. **There is a student in your class who is very unfriendly. He doesn't want anyone to come near him or talk to him. How do you react?**
   A. Ignore him.
   B. Make fun of him.
   C. Write him a note to let him know you are willing to be his friend.

2. **You give your friend a super birthday gift. What is the next thing you do?**
   A. Tell her how much it cost and how difficult it was for you to get it.
   B. Ask her again and again if she really likes it.
   C. Don't mention it.

3. **You win the Scripture memory contest for your whole school. How do you react?**
   A. Boast about winning.
   B. Say to everyone who will listen that you really are thankful that you have such a good memory.
   C. Thank God privately for His Word and His help in memorizing it.

4. **Nothing seems to be going your way today. How do you react?**
   A. Frown, whine, and complain.
   B. Pout, shout, and blame others.
   C. Smile and look for ways to encourage someone else.

God and His People—Faithfulness—Unit 3, Part 2, Lesson 2 67

Worktext page 67

Singing with understanding, verse 2.

Background Information

Lepers—*According to the laws of Moses, a person who had leprosy was to be removed from society. Lepers wore sackcloth, mourning clothes made from a coarse, dark-colored cloth, usually goat's hair. If anyone approached, the leper was to cry out "unclean" so that no one would come near. Lepers lived outside the camp, village, or city.*

Introducing the Bible Account

Play a game (optional). Hide a bag of candy. Allow the students to search for the treats. When the bag is found, elicit from the student who found it that it would please the Lord if he *shared* the treats with the other students rather than eating them all by himself. Allow the student to share the candy.

Bible Account

Read the following Bible account or read II Kings 6:24–7:20. Tell the students to listen to see who finds something valuable. *(Four lepers find the Syrian camp deserted. All their food has been left; the lepers share the food with the Israelites.)*

God Used Lepers

Ben-Hadad, king of Syria, gathered his armies and surrounded the city of Samaria. The city's food supply was cut off, and food became very scarce. The food that was available sold for very high prices. The king of Israel blamed the man of God, Elisha, for the famine. The king determined he would kill Elisha.

Elisha knew that the king of Israel was sending a man to kill him. Therefore, he told his friends, "When the messenger cometh, shut the door and hold him fast at the door; is not the sound of his master's feet behind him?"

When the king arrived, Elisha told him that at about that time the next day there would be food for all the people. There would be so much food that the prices would be very low. The king's officer did not believe Elisha's prediction. Elisha told the officer that he would see this take place and not get to taste the food because He did not believe God could do what He said He would do. The king told Elisha he would wait another day to see whether his words were true.

At that time there were four hungry lepers at the gate of the city. As they sat they reasoned: we can stay here and die of hunger, or we can go into the city and die of hunger, or we can surrender to the Syrians. The Syrians may spare our lives, give us food to eat, and we will live. Or they may kill us, but we are going to die anyway.

The four lepers decided to go into the Syrian camp. Meanwhile the Lord "had made the host of the Syrians to hear a noise of chariots, and a noise of horses, even the noise of a great host: and they said one to another, Lo, the king of Israel hath hired against us the kings of the Hittites, and the kings of the Egyptians, to come upon us." The Syrians had been terrified and had jumped up and fled, leaving their food and possessions behind.

When the four lepers came into the camp, they found no one there. They went into a tent and ate and drank; they took and hid silver, gold, and clothing. Then they went into another tent and found more and hid it. Then they remembered the people and went and told the gatekeepers that the Syrians were gone and had left food and goods behind.

When the king of Israel learned what had happened, he thought it was a trap. So he sent out some scouts to see what had happened. The messengers returned and told the king that indeed the Syrians were gone and had left all their food and belongings. The people rushed out of the city to get the food.

The officer who had not believed what Elisha had said the day before was in charge of the gate. As the people rushed to the Syrians' camp, the officer was trampled to death. He had seen what Elisha said would come to pass, but he did not taste any of the food. God used four lepers, men who were shunned by the people because of their disease. The lepers chose to do right and share what they had found. God had been faithful to his servant Elisha by protecting him from the king of Israel and by providing for Elisha and the Israelites once more.

➤ **The king blamed Elisha for the famine and came to kill him. What did Elisha tell the king?** *(that there would be food the next day for all the people)*

➤ **Who did not believe Elisha?** *(The king's officer did not believe, and the king doubted but said he would wait until the next day to see whether it would happen.)*

➤ Read **John 20:29** aloud. **Does God want us to "see" before we believe? Why not?** *(No. He would like us to have faith and believe without seeing.)*

➤ **How did God use the lepers to save the starving people?** *(They found food in the deserted Syrian camp and shared it with the others.)*

➤ **What happened to the king's officer because of his unbelief?** *(He saw the fulfillment of Elisha's prediction but was not allowed to eat the food; he was trampled to death.)*

➤ **What happens to us because of our unbelief?** *(If we are believers, we lose God's full blessing. If we are not believers, God will judge our sin; we will be separated from Him forever.)*

➤ God used the lepers, and He can use you. **How can God use you?**

Worktext page 68

Complete a flowchart about the Bible account.

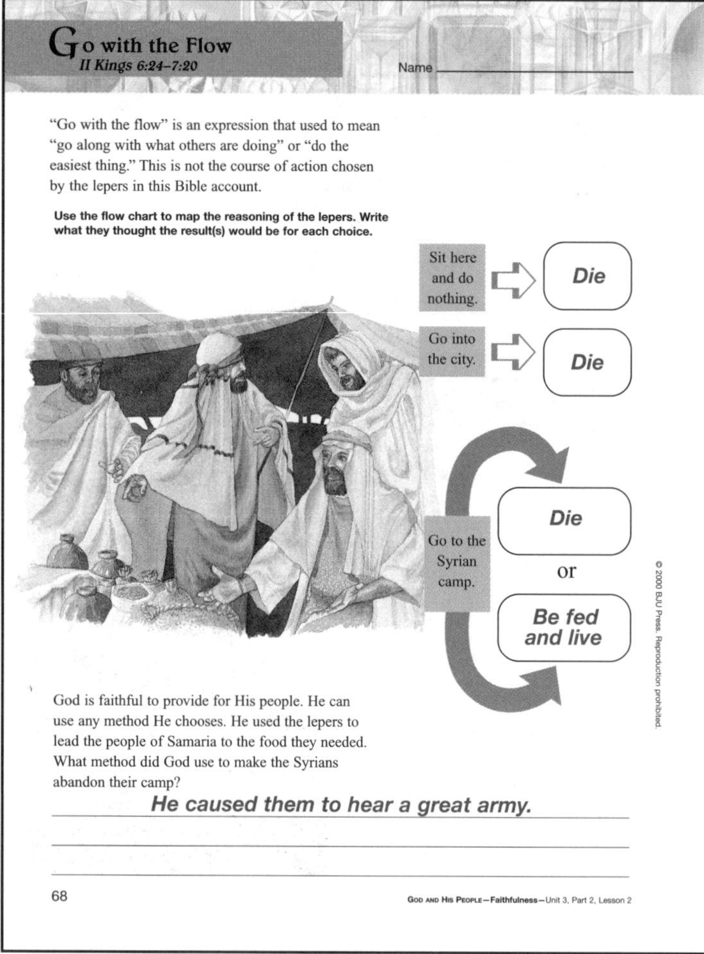

Go with the Flow
II Kings 6:24–7:20

Name ____________________

"Go with the flow" is an expression that used to mean "go along with what others are doing" or "do the easiest thing." This is not the course of action chosen by the lepers in this Bible account.

Use the flow chart to map the reasoning of the lepers. Write what they thought the result(s) would be for each choice.

Sit here and do nothing. ⇨ *Die*

Go into the city. ⇨ *Die*

Go to the Syrian camp. ⇨ *Die* or *Be fed and live*

God is faithful to provide for His people. He can use any method He chooses. He used the lepers to lead the people of Samaria to the food they needed. What method did God use to make the Syrians abandon their camp?

He caused them to hear a great army.

68 God and His People—Faithfulness—Unit 3, Part 2, Lesson 2

Lesson 3

Materials

- A piece of 6" × 24" drawing paper, folded into fourths for each student (optional)

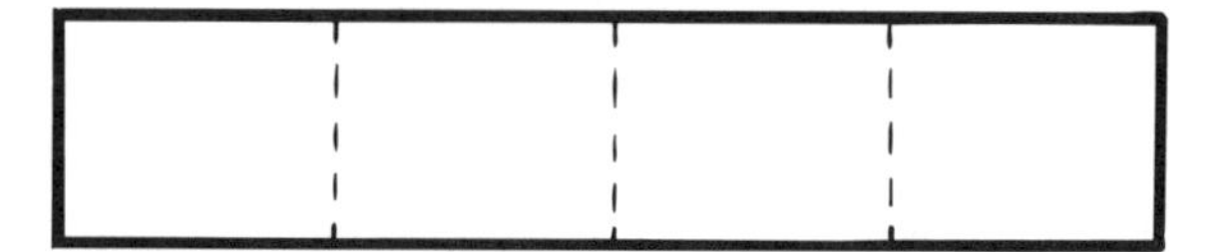

Hymn: "I Would Be True"

Sing the first two verses (Worktext page 274). Play the recording and sing together verses 1 and 2.

➤ **How are we weak?** *(Possible answers include we are sinful and need God's power to do right; we often fail to obey; sometimes we just make mistakes.)*

➤ **What is meant by "I would look up, and laugh, and love, and lift"?** *(I would look to Jesus, have His joy and love for others, and encourage others.)*

Art Connection (optional)

Illustrate a story sequentially. Distribute a piece of drawing paper, folded in fourths, to each student. Direct the students to draw and color four important events in the following application story as you read it aloud.

Introducing the Application Story

Discuss dangerous situations.

- ➤ **Have you ever been in a dangerous situation?**
- ➤ **Do you know someone who has been in a dangerous situation?**

Application Story

Read the following story to the students.

Grandmother's Faith

Many years ago, during a terrible war, an old woman and her grandson lived alone in a little house at the bottom of a hill. Enemy soldiers were in the area, and any day the woman and the boy expected soldiers to come and capture them and destroy their home. The boy watched his grandmother pray and read her Bible with a bitter scowl on his face.

"Grandmother, God won't help us," he said.

But Grandmother kept praying. "God is able," she said.

One morning they were awakened by a loud knock on the door. It was their neighbor from over the hill. "The soldiers," she said, "are in the next town and are on their way here. They'll be here by nightfall. You'd better flee while you can!"

The grandmother closed the door, and when her grandson asked what they should do, she said, "Pray."

The boy turned away and began to get his clothes ready to go. His grandmother knelt beside her bed. While she continued praying, the boy interrupted her to say that he had gathered their things together and was ready to flee from the soldiers.

She looked up quietly and said, "You may go without me. I'll stay. I have faith that God will build a wall about our house and protect us."

- ➤ **Do you think God will build a wall around the house in time for them to be protected?**
- ➤ **What do you think will happen?**

Grandmother went on praying, but the boy laughed out loud. *Imagine, God building a wall around our house!* he thought. But he would not leave his grandmother alone, and she would not go no matter how hard he begged her. It began snowing, and his grandmother kept praying. The boy decided to go to bed.

While the boy slept, his grandmother kept praying. All through the night she stayed on her knees in the darkened room.

The next morning the boy awoke and looked out the window. His eyes opened wide. He could see nothing but whiteness. He could hear nothing but the howling of the wind. The house was completely buried in snow.

That day the soldiers marched through the town on icy roads. They left the town behind and stomped over the hills through the deep snow. And when they reached the little house in the valley, the grandmother and her grandson heard their muffled footsteps marching above their heads. The soldiers passed the little house without even knowing it was there.

The boy turned to his grandmother. "Grandmother, please tell me more about your God. I want Him for my God, too. You had faith that He'd build a wall, and He did—a wall of snow!"

- ➤ **What did the boy do when his grandmother prayed and read her Bible?** *(He watched her with a scowl.)*
- ➤ **Who were in the next town and were on their way?** *(enemy soldiers)*
- ➤ **Why would the grandmother not leave?** *(She believed God would build a wall around the house to protect them.)*
- ➤ **What happened while the boy was sleeping?** *(It snowed, and the house was buried in the snow.)*
- ➤ **Why do you think the grandson wanted his grandmother's God to be his God?** *(Possible answers include her God was powerful, protective, and true.)*
- ➤ **Do you trust in a god that is powerful and protects you?**

Memory Verse—Joshua 1:9

Practice the memory verse. Locate and read aloud **Joshua 1:9**. Place the students into two groups, directing everyone to read the question, Group 1 to read God's commands, and Group 2 to read God's promise. Practice in this way several times; then exchange parts.

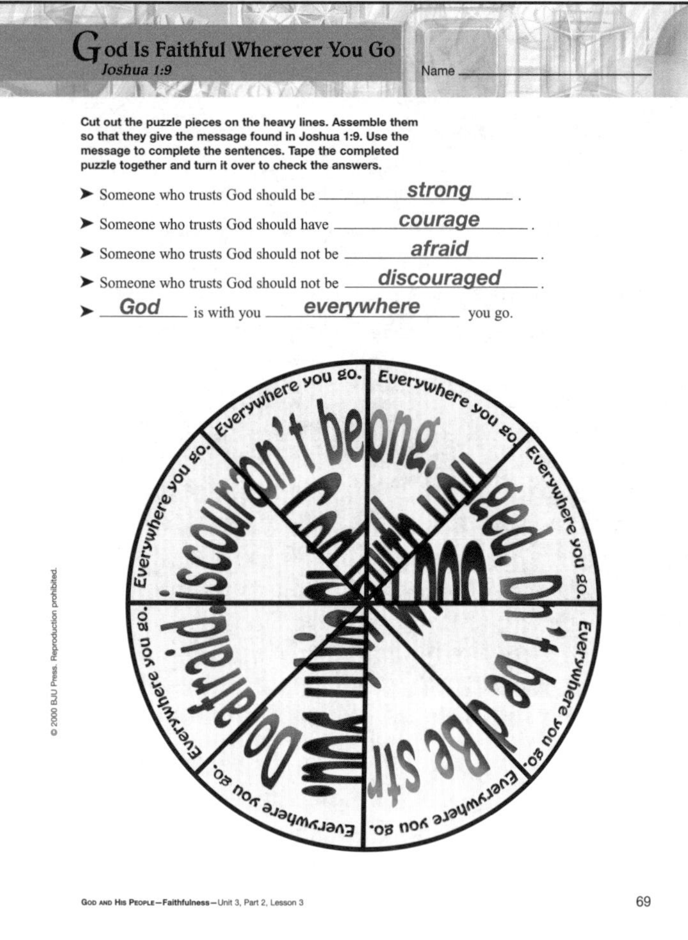

God Is Faithful Wherever You Go
Joshua 1:9

Name ____________

Cut out the puzzle pieces on the heavy lines. Assemble them so that they give the message found in Joshua 1:9. Use the message to complete the sentences. Tape the completed puzzle together and turn it over to check the answers.

- ➤ Someone who trusts God should be *strong*.
- ➤ Someone who trusts God should have *courage*.
- ➤ Someone who trusts God should not be *afraid*.
- ➤ Someone who trusts God should not be *discouraged*.
- ➤ *God* is with you *everywhere* you go.

Worktext pages 69-70

Apply the memory verse to everyday life.

Lesson 4

Materials

- Song: "Books of the New Testament"
- Bible Book Cards: Gospels, History, Paul's Letters, General Letters
- TimeLine and picture: *Hosea*
- A bunch of grapes (real or artificial)
- An artificial grapevine (optional)

Memory Verse—Joshua 1:9

Practice the memory verse. Locate and read **Joshua 1:9**. Select students to say the verse from memory. Practice reading or saying the verse throughout the day.

Song: "Books of the New Testament"

Sing the first four verses (Worktext page 288). Lead in saying the books of the New Testament together. Play the recording and lead in singing verses 1-4.

Bible Study Skills

Review the books from the division General Letters. Distribute to eight students the Bible cards for the General Letters. Challenge them to arrange themselves correctly at the front of the room. Lead in reading together the names of the General Letters; then say all the names of the New Testament books together. Divide the students into three or four teams. Line up the teams. Show a card from the first four divisions of the New Testament to the student at the front of each line. The student who calls out the name of the book that comes after the book shown receives a point for his team. Let each student in front go to the end of his line after his turn.

One-on-One: Give the student the cards for the General Letters to sequence correctly. Then mix up the first four divisions of the New Testament Bible Book Cards, challenging the student to sequence them, or you may show a card, allowing him to say the name of the book that comes after the book shown.

Background Information

Hosea—*It is the first book of the Old Testament division of Minor Prophets. The books in this division are shorter than the Major Prophets—Isaiah, Jeremiah, Lamentations, Ezekiel, and Daniel—but they are not less important. Hosea means "salvation" and emphasizes faithfulness. Hosea began to prophesy near the end of the reigns of Uzziah (king of Judah) and Jeroboam II (king of Israel) and concluded during Hezekiah's reign. Hosea prophesied at the same time as Amos, Isaiah, and Micah. He reminded Israel that God had promised to bless obedience and judge disobedience and that He was ready to judge their disobedience.*

Hosea's Family—*Hosea married Gomer. As an unfaithful wife Gomer pictured Israel, who was unfaithful to God. Their children pictured God's message to sinning Israel. Jezreel was a reminder that Ahab's blood flowed in the Valley of Jezreel; Lo-ruhamah meant God would judge Israel and not show mercy; Lo-ammi meant God had cast off the Israelites because they forsook Him for other gods. God did not forsake them forever. One day they will again be His people.*

Picture the Point

Illustrate Israel's rebellion. Display the bunch of grapes and artificial vine (optional). Elicit from the students that grapes grow in a vineyard. Tell them that the nation of Israel is like God's vineyard. Read **Psalm 80:8** and **Isaiah 5:2** aloud.

- ➤ **Who do you think the "vine" is that God brought out of Egypt?** *(the children of Israel)*
- ➤ **God wanted His vineyard to bring forth good grapes, but what kind of grapes did it bring forth?** *(wild grapes; bad fruit)*

God expected Israel to obey Him, but instead they rebelled against Him and worshiped idols. Instead of bringing forth fruit unto righteousness, they had produced "wild grapes." Elicit from the students that Christians are like Israel; God wants them to obey Him and to be faithful to Him, but many times they rebel and disobey Him. Point out that God always wants believers to return (confess their sin and accept His forgiveness) when they wander from Him.

Tell the students that in this lesson they will learn about a prophet of God named Hosea. Hosea warned the nation of Israel that God could not bless their disobedience. (*Note:* If you have used real grapes in your demonstration, you may want to give some to each student to eat.)

Prophet Focus

Read the following to the students.

> **Hosea**
>
> Hosea prophesied in Israel, the Northern Kingdom, for almost sixty years. He was called not only to *preach* his message, but also to *live* it. Hosea's wife, Gomer, was unfaithful and left him, but God told Hosea to keep loving Gomer and to bring her back home. Hosea's marriage to Gomer was a "picture" of Israel's relationship to God. Gomer's unfaithfulness to Hosea represented Israel's unfaithfulness to God. All through the land of Israel, people were worshiping idols, cursing God, lying, and murdering. Hosea told the Israelites that they were like a troop of robbers, a silly dove, and half-baked pancakes.
>
> Although the Israelites sinned and forsook God, God loved them and wanted to bring them back to Himself. At God's command Hosea took his wife back and loved her. God told Hosea to tell the people to turn from their sin and backslidings and return to Him. Hosea told the people of God's abundant love. He told them that God said, "I drew them with cords of a man, with bands of love." Hosea told them that God would not give up on His rebellious children. God was willing to forgive the Israelites' sins, heal their backslidings, and love them freely if they would return to Him. Hosea told the people that God would judge their sin if they did not turn from it.

Tell the students that just as God warned the people through Hosea, He is warning and teaching us about His ways through His Word. Call on students to read the following verses and answer the questions.

➤ Read **Hosea 5:1. What message were the priests, Israel, and the king's house to listen to?** *(Judgment was near.)*

➤ Read **Hosea 6:1** and **Hosea 14:4. What would God do if the people would return to Him?** *(He would heal them, love them freely, and turn His anger from them.)*

➤ Read **Hosea 14:9. What does Hosea say about God's ways?** *(The wise would understand God's ways. His ways are just, and the just, or righteous through salvation in Christ, will walk in them. The disobedient will stumble in God's ways.)*

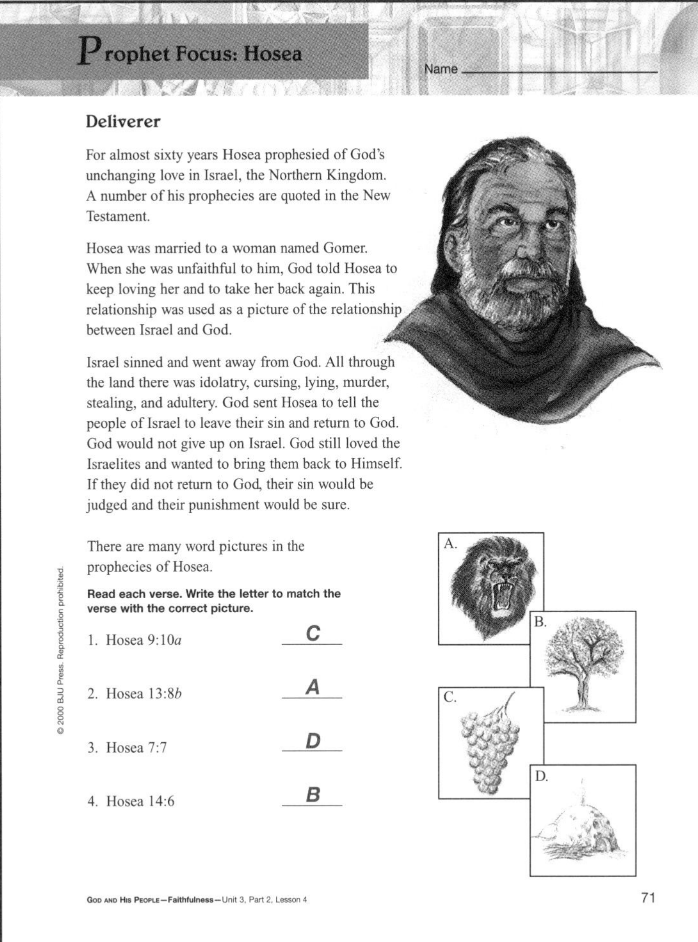

Prophet Focus: Hosea

Name ______________

Deliverer

For almost sixty years Hosea prophesied of God's unchanging love in Israel, the Northern Kingdom. A number of his prophecies are quoted in the New Testament.

Hosea was married to a woman named Gomer. When she was unfaithful to him, God told Hosea to keep loving her and to take her back again. This relationship was used as a picture of the relationship between Israel and God.

Israel sinned and went away from God. All through the land there was idolatry, cursing, lying, murder, stealing, and adultery. God sent Hosea to tell the people of Israel to leave their sin and return to God. God would not give up on Israel. God still loved the Israelites and wanted to bring them back to Himself. If they did not return to God, their sin would be judged and their punishment would be sure.

There are many word pictures in the prophecies of Hosea.

Read each verse. Write the letter to match the verse with the correct picture.

1. Hosea 9:10*a* ___C___
2. Hosea 13:8*b* ___A___
3. Hosea 7:7 ___D___
4. Hosea 14:6 ___B___

GOD AND HIS PEOPLE—Faithfulness—Unit 3, Part 2, Lesson 4 71

➤ **What did God want Israel to do after they had sinned and forsaken Him?** *(to come back to Him)*

➤ **What does God want you to do when you disobey and forsake Him?** *(to confess your sin, accept His forgiveness, and with His help, live for Him)*

Tell the students that God wanted to bless Israel but had to judge them because they did not turn from their sin. Explain that what happens to us depends upon how we respond to God. Challenge the students to make the right decisions and to choose to obey God and be faithful to Him. Read **Proverbs 10:8** aloud.

➤ **If you are wise, what will you do?** *(Receive God's commandments and obey them.)*

TimeLine

Add *Hosea* to the TimeLine. Attach the picture of *Hosea* to the TimeLine (742-724 B.C.), pointing out that he prophesied at the time of Isaiah and Micah. Guide the students as they glue the picture of *Hosea* onto their TimeLines.

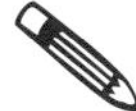

Worktext page 71

Review details about the prophet Hosea.

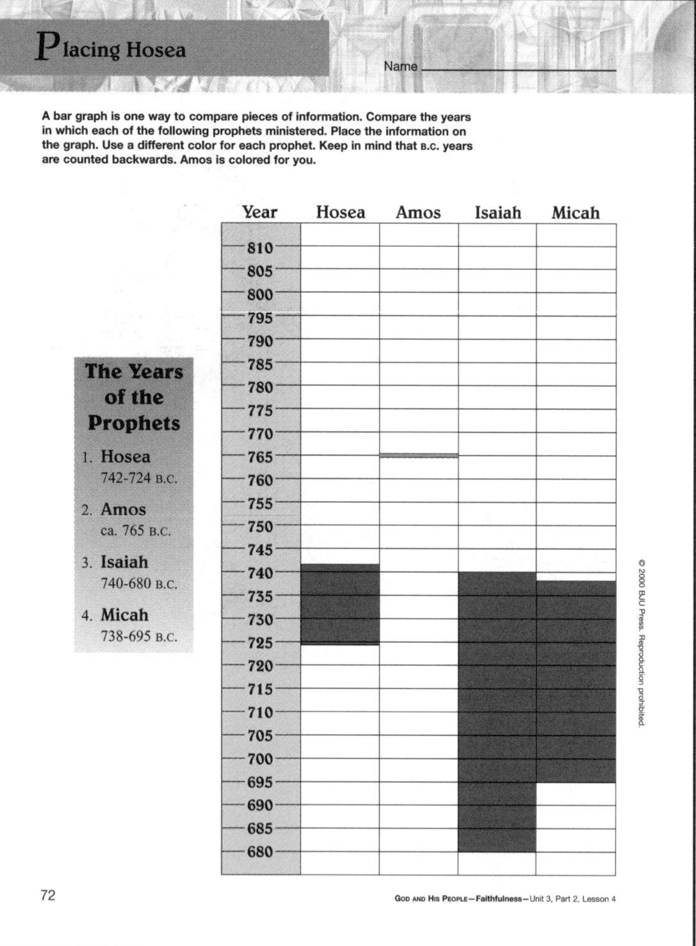

Placing Hosea

Name ________________

A bar graph is one way to compare pieces of information. Compare the years in which each of the following prophets ministered. Place the information on the graph. Use a different color for each prophet. Keep in mind that B.C. years are counted backwards. Amos is colored for you.

The Years of the Prophets

1. **Hosea** 742-724 B.C.
2. **Amos** ca. 765 B.C.
3. **Isaiah** 740-680 B.C.
4. **Micah** 738-695 B.C.

72

God and His People—Faithfulness—Unit 3, Part 2, Lesson 4

Worktext page 72

Complete a bar graph. Read the information at the top of the page, guiding the students to complete the bar graph.

Going Beyond

Enrichment

Find what God says about fear. Tell the students that the following verses remind us not to be afraid because God is with us. Remind them of the rules for conducting a Bible drill (e.g., you say the reference; they repeat the reference; you say "charge" as a signal for them to look up the verse; they stand and wait to be recognized as soon as they find the verse). Tell the student who found the verse first to stand and read the verse aloud; then discuss the verse.

Matthew 14:27	Exodus 20:20
Mark 5:36	Psalm 56:4
John 6:20	Hebrews 13:6
Psalm 27:1	Luke 12:32
Deuteronomy 1:17	Psalm 91:5
Psalm 43:5	Mark 6:50
Isaiah 14:3	Isaiah 41:10
Exodus 14:13	Psalm 118:6

God's People Should Be Faithful to God

Unit 3, Part 3

Preview

Doctrines

- Man has hope (Philippians 3:20-21)—Lesson 2
- God is all-powerful (omnipotent) (Jeremiah 32:27)—Lessons 2-3
- God is merciful (Psalm 86:15)—Lesson 3

Skills and Applications

- Learn Psalm 101:6
- Learn the book of Prophecy
- Locate information in Scripture
- Develop active listening
- Frame a story
- Edit a story
- Realize that God protects and provides for His people
- Know that God rewards faithfulness
- Realize that Christians should be faithful to God
- Apply Bible knowledge to everyday life

Lesson 1

Materials

- Unit 3 Bookmark for each student
- Highlighter for each student (optional)

Application Story

Read the following story to the students.

Don't Forget Heaven

James walked through the door and tossed his goodie bag on the kitchen table.

"How was the party?" asked Mom.

"Fine," said James. He sighed and started to walk up the steps.

"James," said Mom. "What's wrong?"

James came back down the stairs. "You wouldn't believe what Andrew got for his birthday. He got the coolest pair of basketball shoes, a pair of in-line skates, and *Basketball Championship 2*."

"Don't you have that computer game?" asked Mom.

"Not *Championship 2*," said James. "I've only got *Championship 1*."

Mom reached for her Bible, pulled a bookmark out, and laid the Bible back on the table.

"Aunt Eileen gave me this bookmark. Listen to the story that's on it," said Mom. She held the bookmark so James could see it and read the story.

"Once a preacher was invited to the home of a wealthy man in Texas. After dinner the man took him up to the roof of his house and showed him the large oil fields he owned. He said, 'Preacher, I came to this country twenty-five years ago without a penny. Now I own everything as far as you can see!' He motioned in all directions and said, 'Everything you see is mine! Once I was penniless, but now I am rich!'

"The man paused, expecting to hear the preacher praise him. But to his surprise, the praise did not come. Instead the preacher put his hand on the man's shoulder, pointed upward toward the sky and asked, 'My friend, how much do you own in *that* direction?'

"The man dropped his head in shame and said, 'I never thought of that.' "

Mom returned the bookmark to her Bible, then read Matthew 6:19 to James. (*Note:* Read the verse aloud from your Bible.) "Son, it's sad when a person lays up treasures on earth and forgets about heaven."

"So you're saying I don't need *Basketball Championship 2*," said James.

"I'm saying that even *Basketball Championship 17* isn't going to help you live for God—only for yourself."

James picked up his goodie bag. "Andrew got all that stuff," he said. "But I guess he can't take any of it to heaven, huh?"

Mom shook her head. "Remember that boy who came to visit your Sunday school class?"

"Yeah," said James. "He'd never even heard about Jesus Christ. He said I was the first person to tell him how to be saved."

"That," said Mom, "is the most precious kind of treasure you can own. Spend your time and effort on things that will last forever."

- ➤ **Why was the wealthy man proud?** *(He had come to this country penniless, and now he was rich.)*
- ➤ **What did the rich man expect the preacher to do?** *(praise him)*
- ➤ **What did the preacher do?** *(He asked the man how much he had in heaven.)*
- ➤ **What lesson did James learn from the story?** *(Answers will vary.)*
- ➤ **How can Christians be faithful to God and be laying up treasures in heaven?** *(Possible answers include witnessing, reading the Bible and praying, treating others kindly, suffering for Christ, and using time and talents wisely.)*
- ➤ **What will rewards given in heaven depend upon?** *(our faithfulness)*

Memory Verse—Psalm 101:6

Principle: God blesses His faithful servants. Locate **Psalm 101:6** and read the verse aloud as the students read silently.

- ➤ **Who are the faithful?** *(those who are true and loyal to God and trust in God)*
- ➤ **Where will the King's attention be?** *(upon the faithful)*
- ➤ **Where will the faithful dwell?** *(with the King)*
- ➤ **Who will serve the King?** *(those who are made perfect or blameless through the death of God's Son)*

Choose a volunteer to read the verse. Direct the students to highlight the verse in their Bibles (optional) and to mark the location with the Unit 3 Bookmark. Read the verse throughout the day for practice.

Help Wanted—Servants Name ________

What kind of people does God want to serve or minister for Him?

Read Psalm 101:6 in your Bible and complete the ad.

By himself, no one can meet the requirements of this advertisement. How can a person have the perfect life that makes him able to serve God?

Write a word from the word bank to complete each sentence. You may use your Bible to help you.

Christ
Christ
sin

1. Jesus Christ had no *sin* in His life (II Corinthians 5:21).
2. If a person is saved, his old sinful life has been crucified with *Christ* (Galatians 2:20).
3. *Christ*, who is perfect, lives in him (Galatians 2:20).

God and His People—Faithfulness—Unit 3, Part 3, Lesson 1 73

Worktext page 73

Develop understanding of the memory verse.

Hymn: "I Would Be True"

Teach the third verse (Worktext page 274). Play the recording and lead in singing the third verse. Then sing verses 1-3.

- ➤ **What is the hymn writer emphasizing in the first part of verse 3?** *(being in fellowship with God through praying and reading His Word)*
- ➤ **What does the last part of verse 3 mean?** *(He desires to have faith to follow Christ, living as He lived.)*

Singing with Understanding
"I Would Be True" (v. 3)

Name ____________________

One of God's attributes is that He is omnipresent. He is the only one who can be with us every moment of every day. We need times when we pray alone in a quiet place, but verse 3 of the hymn reminds us that we can talk and listen to God anywhere, anytime. We are commanded to pray this way in Philippians 4:6 and I Thessalonians 5:17.

Write Philippians 4:6 or I Thessalonians 5:17 on a card or small piece of paper and keep it with you as a reminder. Complete the following record of the prayers in your day. The first row is a sample.

Time	Activity	Thank God for—	Ask God for—
	Getting dressed for school	Another day to serve Him, clothes, opportunity to go to school.	Help to remember spelling words I studied, opportunities to show His love.

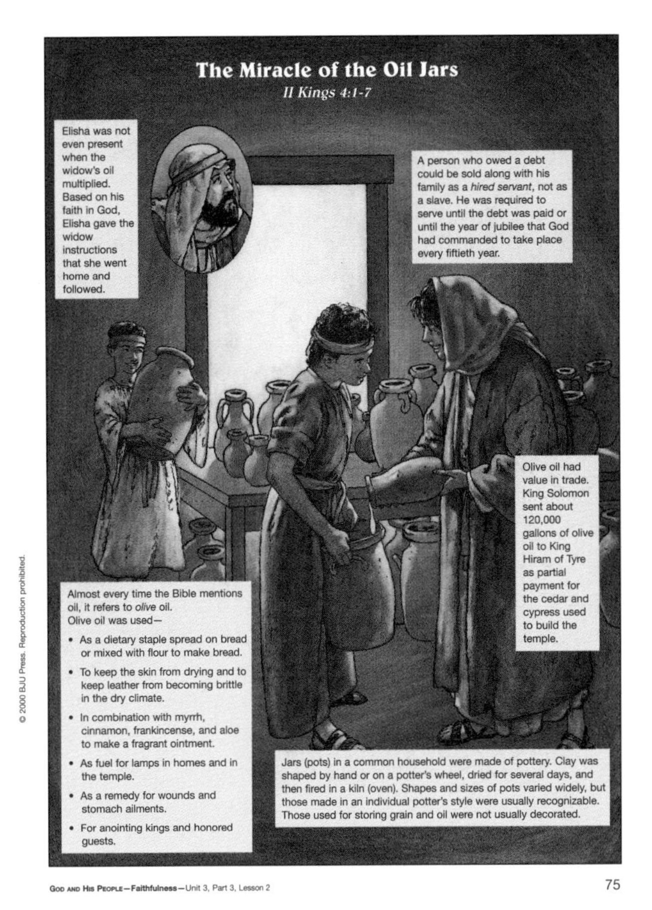

Worktext page 74

Singing with understanding, verse 3.

Lesson 2

Materials

- Charts 13 and 28: "The Miracle of the Oil Jars" and "World Map" or a map of Europe and the Mediterranean Sea (optional)
- Olives (one for each student) (optional)
- An oil lamp (optional)

Hymn: "I Would Be True"

Sing the hymn (Worktext page 274). Play the recording and lead in singing all the verses.

Introducing the Bible Account

Guide a discussion. Display the oil lamp. Elicit from the students that this type of lamp is not used in most homes today as a main source of light because we have electricity. Explain that a lamp with a wick and oil was used to light homes in Bible times. The wick usually soaked in small clay bowls of olive oil.

Bible Account

Read the following Bible account or read II Kings 4:1-7. Direct the students to look at the picture on Worktext page 75. Read aloud the information about olive oil. Explain that in this Bible account they will see how God used olive oil to help a faithful servant.

The Widow and the Oil

One day a widow, the young wife of a prophet who had died, came to Elisha. She told Elisha that her husband, a faithful servant and man who feared God, had died. The widow explained that her husband had had a debt that she must now pay, but she did not have the money to pay it. The man she owed wanted to make her sons servants in payment for the money she owed. (Read aloud about hired servants from Worktext page 75.)

Elisha wanted to help the widow. He asked her what she had in her house. She told Elisha that she had nothing except one jar of oil. Elisha told her to borrow as many empty jars as she could from her neighbors. Elisha told the widow, "And when thou art come in, thou shalt shut the door upon thee and upon thy sons, and shalt pour out into all those vessels, and thou shalt set aside that which is full."

(Read aloud about jars from Worktext page 75.)

The widow did not question Elisha about how this was going to help her. She trusted Elisha, the man of God. She went into her house and shut the door. Her sons were there with all the empty jars they had collected. The widow took her one jar of oil and began pouring it into the empty jars. As she continued to pour, the oil kept flowing. She filled jar after jar. Finally, she said, "Bring me yet a vessel."

Her son replied, "There is not a vessel more." Then the oil stopped flowing from her jar. She and her sons had just witnessed a miracle!

The widow was excited and hurried to tell Elisha what had happened. Elisha told her, "Go, sell the oil, and pay thy debt, and live thou and thy children of the rest." The widow had great faith. She collected many jars and had much oil to sell. She had enough money to pay the debt, with enough left over for her and her sons to live on—as Elisha had said. (Read aloud about Elisha.)

InfoScene: "The Miracle of the Oil Jars"
Display Chart 13 for reference throughout this unit. Review and discuss the Bible account as time permits.

- ➤ **Why do you think the widow went to Elisha for help?** *(Elisha was a man faithful to God, and she knew that he would be able to help her.)*
- ➤ **What would happen if the widow did not pay the debt?** *(Her sons would be taken as servants.)*
- ➤ **Why did Elisha tell the widow to borrow many vessels?** *(Elisha knew God's power is unlimited and that God could provide above what she needed to pay the debt. Elisha had great faith.)*
- ➤ **What can you say about the widow's faith?** *(She had great faith because she did not question Elisha but believed and obeyed what he told her to do, knowing that God would be faithful to her and her family.)*
- ➤ **What happened after the widow filled many jars?** *(When there were no more jars to fill, the oil stopped flowing.)*
- ➤ **Why do you think God provided for the widow?** *(Answers may vary, but point out that the widow's husband had been a faithful servant of the Lord, and God was rewarding his faithfulness by providing for his wife and sons.)*

Worktext page 76

Solve measurement problems.

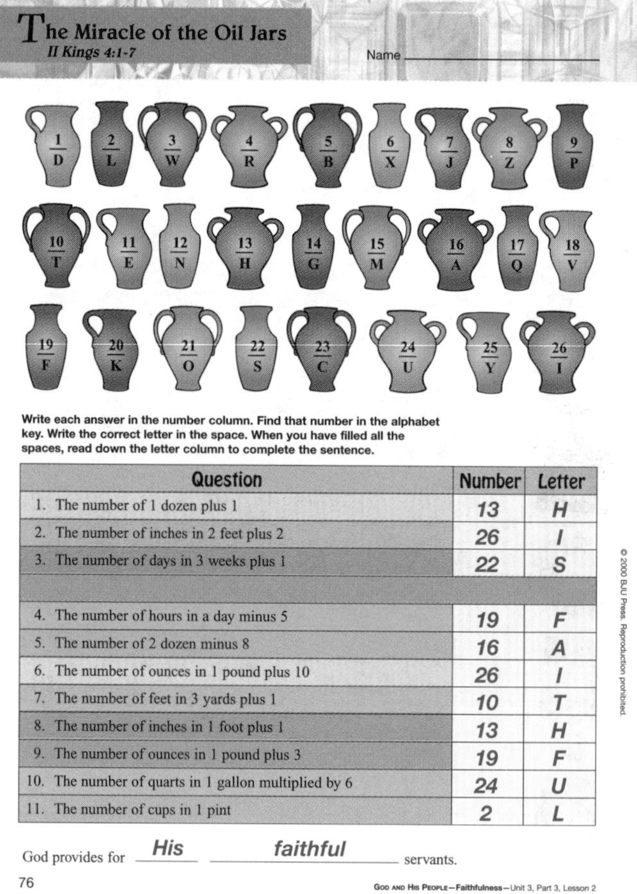

The Miracle of the Oil Jars
II Kings 4:1-7

Name ____________________

Write each answer in the number column. Find that number in the alphabet key. Write the correct letter in the space. When you have filled all the spaces, read down the letter column to complete the sentence.

Question	Number	Letter
1. The number of 1 dozen plus 1	13	H
2. The number of inches in 2 feet plus 2	26	I
3. The number of days in 3 weeks plus 1	22	S
4. The number of hours in a day minus 5	19	F
5. The number of 2 dozen minus 8	16	A
6. The number of ounces in 1 pound plus 10	26	I
7. The number of feet in 3 yards plus 1	10	T
8. The number of inches in 1 foot plus 1	13	H
9. The number of ounces in 1 pound plus 3	19	F
10. The number of quarts in 1 gallon multiplied by 6	24	U
11. The number of cups in 1 pint	2	L

God provides for *His* *faithful* servants.

Memory Verse—Psalm 101:6

Practice the memory verse. Locate **Psalm 101:6** and read the verse aloud while students read silently.

- ➤ **What will those who walk in a perfect way do?** *(They will serve God.)*
- ➤ **How can Christians have God's blessing in their lives?** *(Be faithful to Him.)*

Direct the students to read the first part of the verse in a normal voice, the second part in a whisper, and the third part silently.

History Connection (optional)

Discuss olives. Display Chart 28, "World Map," or a map of Europe and the Mediterranean Sea (optional). Explain that *olives* and *oil* are important items of commerce even today. Give each student an olive to examine and to eat. Elicit from the students that there is oil in both the flesh and the pit of the olive. Direct a student to point out the Mediterranean Sea on the map. Explain that most of the world's olives are grown along the Mediterranean Sea.

- ➤ **What kind of climate do you think olives grow best in?** *(hot and dry; a moderate supply of water)*
- ➤ **What countries do you think produce olives as a chief crop?** Direct the students to point to the countries on the map. *(Portugal, Italy, Spain, and Greece)*

➤ **Where in the United States do you think olive trees grow?** *(California)* (*Note:* Olives were brought to California in 1769.)

Elicit from the students that Americans use olive oil primarily for salad dressing and as a cooking oil.

Lesson 3

Materials

- A small ax, ax head, or picture of an ax (optional)
- Items for the optional Food Connection: resealable bags, green olives, olive oil, parsley or oregano, bread, small bowls

Write the memory verse on an erasable board.

Hymn: "I Would Be True"

Sing the hymn (Worktext page 274). Allow students to sing a verse as soloists or in a small group if they choose.

➤ **What do we need to do, even when we are very busy?** *(keep in touch with the Lord through prayer and Bible reading.)*

➤ **How can we be "tuned to hear His [God's] slightest whisper"?** *(We should have our hearts right by knowing we are saved, confessing our sins daily, and being willing to follow Christ.)*

Memory Verse—Psalm 101:6

Practice the memory verse. Call attention to the verse written on the board. Read the verse together several times; then call on a student to erase several words and lead in reading the verse. Continue this procedure until the verse is completely erased, and the students can say the verse from memory.

Background Information

Ax—*In Old Testament times an ax head was made of copper, bronze, or iron. An ax was used to cut trees and stone. Carpenters used it for carving and cutting. It was also used in hand-to-hand combat during battle. Kings would carry battle-axes richly decorated with gold, ivory, and jewels.*

Introducing the Bible Account

Discuss axes. Display an ax, an ax head, or a picture of an ax (optional).

➤ **How do you use this tool?**

➤ **Do you have an ax at your home?**

➤ **Have you ever seen someone use an ax?**

Worktext page 77

Develop active listening by illustrating a Bible account. Direct the students to listen carefully as you read the title and the following Bible account. Explain that they are to illustrate the account as you read it aloud. (*Note:* This activity is given to promote active listening by "taking notes" with illustrations. You may choose to encourage each student to listen to a sermon at his church and to illustrate the main ideas. Invite them to show you their illustrations and to explain the main ideas. Do not make the church activity a required assignment, since some parents may not allow their children to draw in church and other students may have progressed to the stage of taking notes.)

Listen and Learn
II Kings 6:1-7

Name __________

Listen as your teacher tells or reads the Bible account; then follow the directions for each part below.

Circle the word in the title that you hear in the account.

The Boat (Ax) River That Floated

Draw the people and objects necessary to complete each picture.

Our meeting place is too small. Come with us.

I will.

Oh no, master! It was borrowed!

Where did it fall?

Elisha cut a stick and threw it into the water.

Lift it out.

© 2000 BJU Press. Reproduction prohibited.

God and His People—Faithfulness—Unit 3, Part 3, Lesson 3 77

Bible Account

Read the following Bible account or read II Kings 6:1-7.

The Ax That Floated

The young prophets whom Elisha taught had a problem. They had outgrown their school, and their living quarters were too small. Elisha's ministry was growing. The prophets wanted to build new living quarters near the Jordan River.

The prophets wanted Elisha to go with them to cut the wood.

Elisha answered them, "I will go."

Elisha and the men went to the Jordan River and began cutting wood for their new home along the banks of the river. While they were working, an iron ax head flew off its handle and dropped into the water. The man using the ax was horrified, because the ax was borrowed. He could go to prison or be taken as a servant because he had no money to pay for the borrowed ax head. He cried out to Elisha, "Alas, Master! for it was borrowed."

Elisha asked where the ax head sunk.

The prophet showed Elisha where the ax head had fallen. Elisha cut a stick and threw it into the water where the ax head had fallen. Immediately, the ax head floated to the top. Elisha said, "Take it up to thee." The prophet reached out and retrieved the ax head. Elisha, in God's power, performed a miracle. God had met the faithful prophet's need through his faithful servant, Elisha.

➤ **Why did the prophets go to the Jordan River to cut wood?** *(to build themselves a new home)*

➤ **Why was the prophet upset about the lost ax head?** *(It was borrowed; he could be sent to prison or taken as a servant because he could not pay for it.)*

➤ **How did Elisha respond when the prophet cried out?** *(He asked where the ax had fallen.)*

➤ **How was Elisha able to retrieve the ax?** *(God miraculously caused the ax head to float to the top when Elisha threw the stick into the water.)*

➤ **How did God reward faithfulness in this lesson?** *(He met the need of a prophet who had been serving Him; He used Elisha, who was faithful to Him, to perform the miracle.)*

➤ **How does God reward your faithfulness?** *(Answers will vary.)*

Worktext page 78

Frame the Bible account.

Food Connection (optional)

Make Eastern "butter." Place the students in groups of four to six. Give each group a resealable bag with some olives. Tell them to roll and press the olives until some juice is extracted. (*Note:* Throw away the pressed olives.) Tell the students to mix the juice from the olives with the olive oil and either parsley or oregano in a bowl to make Eastern "butter." (*Note:* This Eastern "butter" will not have consistency of butter as we know it; it will be the consistency of oil.) Give each student a piece of bread and tell them to dip a corner at a time carefully in the Eastern "butter" to eat and enjoy.

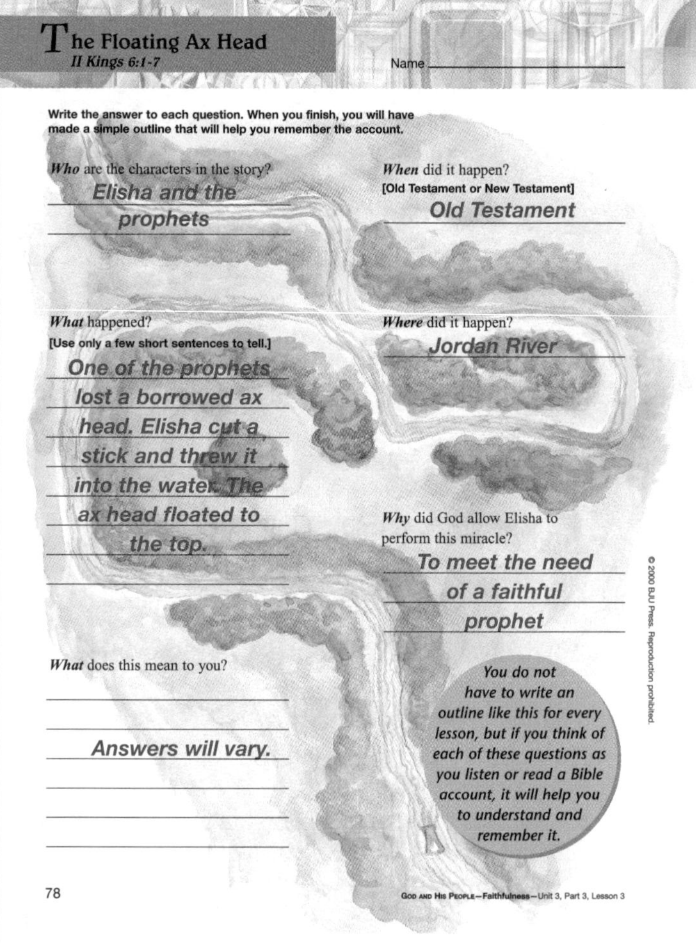

The Floating Ax Head
II Kings 6:1-7

Name ____________

Write the answer to each question. When you finish, you will have made a simple outline that will help you remember the account.

Who are the characters in the story?
Elisha and the prophets

When did it happen?
[Old Testament or New Testament]
Old Testament

What happened?
[Use only a few short sentences to tell.]
One of the prophets lost a borrowed ax head. Elisha cut a stick and threw it into the water. The ax head floated to the top.

Where did it happen?
Jordan River

Why did God allow Elisha to perform this miracle?
To meet the need of a faithful prophet

What does this mean to you?
Answers will vary.

You do not have to write an outline like this for every lesson, but if you think of each of these questions as you listen or read a Bible account, it will help you to understand and remember it.

78 God and His People—Faithfulness—Unit 3, Part 3, Lesson 3

Lesson 4

Materials

- Song: "Books of the New Testament"
- New Testament Bible Book Cards

Memory Verse—Psalm 101:6

Practice the memory verse. Locate **Psalm 101:6** and call on students to read the verse aloud. Choose students to say the verse from memory. Instruct the students to say the verse together from memory.

Background Information

Famine—*This is a time when there is very little food throughout the land. Many different things caused famines in Bible times. Sometimes there was not enough rain for crops to grow. Sometimes locusts ate the crops. Hailstorms or wars could destroy the grain.*

Introducing the Bible Account

Discuss favorite foods.

➤ **What are your favorite foods?**

➤ **Have you ever eaten a specific food and gotten sick?**

Share the background information about famine.

Bible Account

Read the following Bible account or read II Kings 4:38-44.

Death in the Pot

Elisha was visiting the sons of the prophets in Gilgal during the time of a famine in the land. Elisha told his servant to make a large pot ready to cook some food for the visitors.

One of the men went out to gather herbs to put in the pot. He found a wild vine and gathered some wild gourds. When he returned, he cut them up and put them in the pot.

The men were very hungry and began to eat. All of a sudden the prophets cried out, "O thou man of God, there is death in the pot." They realized the gourds were poisonous and that they should not be eating the stew!

Elisha asked for some meal (flour) to be brought to him. He threw it into the pot and said, "Pour out for the people that they may eat." Now the stew was safe for them to eat. They would not get sick if they ate it. Everyone happily began to eat the food that God through Elisha had made safe for them.

This was not the only time God performed a miracle through Elisha in order to feed the prophets. Shortly after this, God provided more food for the prophets through a man who brought his firstfruits to Elisha. He brought twenty loaves of bread and some grain, but Elisha's servant did not think it was enough to feed one hundred men. Elisha ordered the food to be given out, saying that the Lord had said they would have plenty to eat, and there would be food left over! The food was distributed, and God's promise was fulfilled! God is good. First He used His faithful servant Elisha to meet the need of the prophets, and then He used a man who brought his firstfruits to Elisha to meet the prophets' needs.

➤ **What was Elisha going to do for the prophets?** *(provide a meal for them with the things they would gather)*

➤ **What did the prophets cry out as they were eating the stew?** *(There was death in the pot.)*

➤ **What did Elisha do about the problem?** *(threw some meal [flour] in the pot)*

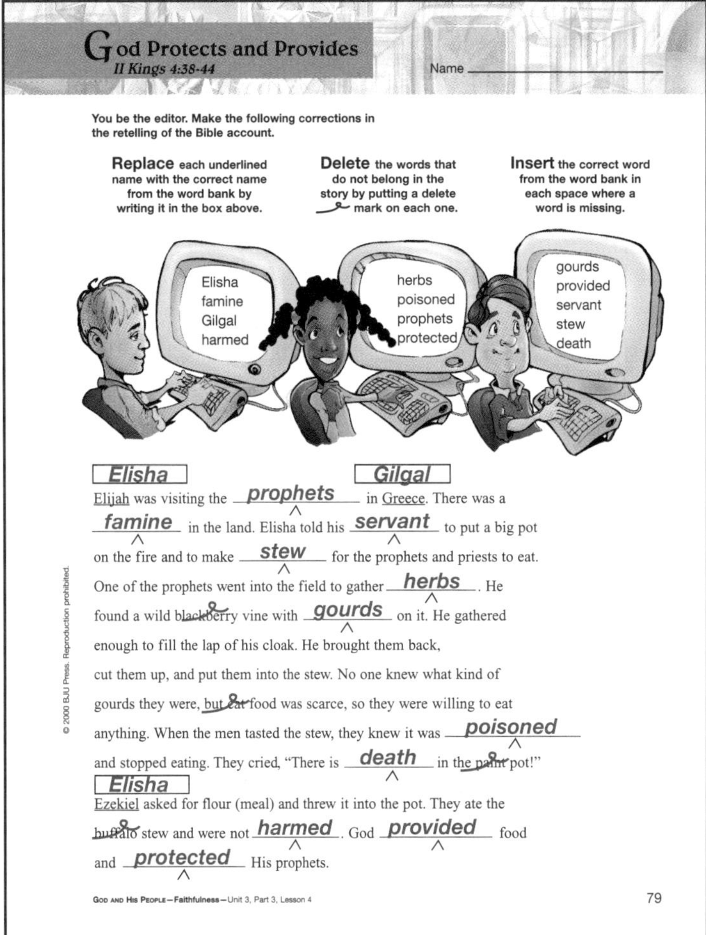

God Protects and Provides

II Kings 4:38-44

Name ____________

You be the editor. Make the following corrections in the retelling of the Bible account.

Replace each underlined name with the correct name from the word bank by writing it in the box above.

Delete the words that do not belong in the story by putting a delete mark on each one.

Insert the correct word from the word bank in each space where a word is missing.

[Elisha] Elijah was visiting the *prophets* in [Gilgal] Greece. There was a *famine* in the land. Elisha told his *servant* to put a big pot on the fire and to make *stew* for the prophets and priests to eat. One of the prophets went into the field to gather *herbs*. He found a wild ~~blackberry~~ vine with *gourds* on it. He gathered enough to fill the lap of his cloak. He brought them back, cut them up, and put them into the stew. No one knew what kind of gourds they were, but ~~eat~~ food was scarce, so they were willing to eat anything. When the men tasted the stew, they knew it was *poisoned* and stopped eating. They cried, "There is *death* in the ~~paint~~ pot!" [Elisha] Ezekiel asked for flour (meal) and threw it into the pot. They ate the ~~buffalo~~ stew and were not *harmed*. God *provided* food and *protected* His prophets.

God and His People—Faithfulness—Unit 3, Part 3, Lesson 4 79

➤ **Did the meal remove the poison? How was it removed?** *(No. God performed a miracle through Elisha.)*

➤ **How did God use the man's twenty loaves of bread that he brought to Elisha?** *(He performed a miracle and caused the food to feed one hundred men and there was food left over.)*

➤ **How can you be like Elisha?** *(Elicit from the students that they cannot perform miracles, but they can faithfully trust God the way Elisha did, and they can serve others as Elisha did.)*

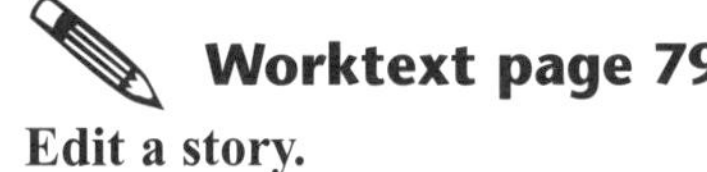

Worktext page 79

Edit a story.

Worktext page 80

Apply Bible knowledge to everyday life.

Song: "Books of the New Testament"

Sing the song (Worktext page 283). Play the recording, directing the students to sing all the verses.

Bible Study Skills

Review the book of Prophecy. Display the Revelation card, explaining that many books in the Bible contain some prophecy of the end times, but Revelation is an entire book written about the end times. Lead in saying all the names of the New Testament books together. Divide the students into teams. Line up the teams. Show a New Testament Bible Book Card to the student at the front of each line. The student who calls out the name of the book that comes *before* and the name of the book that comes *after* the book shown receives two points for his team. Let each student in front go to the end of his line after his turn. (*Note:* When the card for Matthew is displayed, the game can be stopped and a winner determined, or the student can say "Malachi" as the book that comes before and "Mark" as the book that comes after.)

One-on-One: Review Revelation, the book of Prophecy. Give the student the New Testament Bible Book Cards to sequence correctly. Then mix up the cards and show one at a time, challenging the student to name the book that comes before and after.

Going Beyond

Enrichment

Guide a role-playing activity. Divide the students into three groups. Assign a Bible account from this unit to each group. Provide time for the groups to practice role-playing the Bible account before presenting it to the class.

One-on-One: Challenge the student to select a Bible account to illustrate or to make puppets of the characters for retelling the account to family members or friends.

God's People Should Be Faithful to Others

Unit 3, Part 4

Preview

Doctrines

- God is faithful (I Corinthians 1:9)—Lesson 2
- God's people should contribute financially (Romans 15:26)—Lesson 3

Skills and Applications

- Learn Matthew 25:23
- Use prefixes and suffixes to make words
- Learn the divisions of the New Testament
- Read a time line
- Recall facts and details
- Locate information in Scripture
- Realize that God wants us to be faithful to others
- Realize that God wants Christians to support His work financially
- Know that God rewards faithfulness
- Apply Bible knowledge to everyday life

Lesson 1

Materials

- Unit 3 Bookmark for each student
- A picture in a picture frame
- Picture of Stonewall Jackson or Civil War battle (optional)
- Highlighter for each student (optional)

Hymn: "I Would Be True"

Sing the hymn (Worktext page 274). Review the meaning of the hymn. Allow the students to sing and sign the key words in verse 1. (*Note:* Refer to Worktext page 61 for the signs.) Play the recording and sing verses 1-3.

Picture the Point

Illustrate the meaning of faithfulness. Display the picture in the picture frame.

➤ **What is the purpose of the picture frame?** *(to hold the picture in place so that it can be displayed)*

➤ **How long can you leave a picture in a frame?** *(for a very long time)*

➤ **Can you depend on a picture frame to hold your picture in place?** *(Yes. Under normal circumstances it will hold your picture for a very long time.)*

➤ **Can you depend on God's promises to you?** *(yes)*

➤ Read **Psalm 89:33** aloud. **What does God say about His faithfulness?** *(It will not fail us.)*

Review with the students what they have learned about how God is faithful to Himself and to His people. Elicit from the students that God wants Christians to be faithful to Him. He should be able to depend upon them to obey, serve, and love Him. He wants them to be faithful to others also. The people Christians come in contact with each day should be able to trust them and depend upon them. Christians should be people who will do what they say they will do. They should be punctual (on time) and responsible.

God has given each person a talent that he or she should use to bring people to Him. Encourage the students to *think about* how they would answer the following questions, but do not have them answer the questions aloud.

➤ **Can you be depended upon to turn in your homework on time?**

➤ **Can your parents depend upon you to do your chores each day?**

➤ **Can your friends depend upon you to be loving and kind to them?**

➤ **Can your Sunday school teacher and pastor depend upon you to attend Sunday school and church faithfully?**

➤ **Can the Lord depend upon you to listen to His Word and hide it in your heart so that it can help you to do the right thing in the time of temptation?**

➤ **Can the Lord depend upon you to witness to others when He gives you the opportunity to do so?**

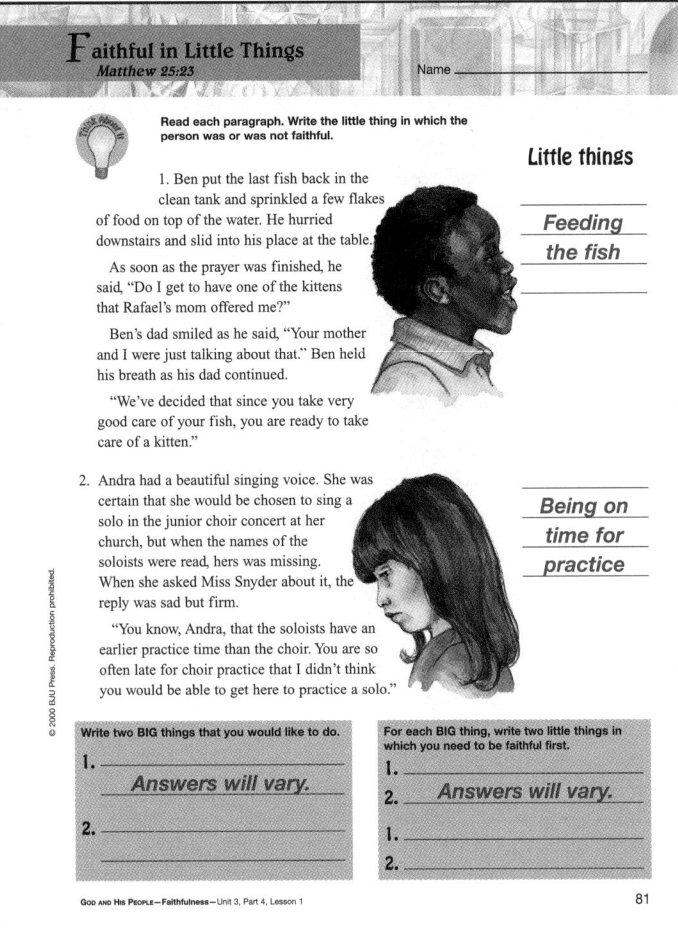

Faithful in Little Things
Matthew 25:23

Name ____________

Read each paragraph. Write the little thing in which the person was or was not faithful.

Little things

1. Ben put the last fish back in the clean tank and sprinkled a few flakes of food on top of the water. He hurried downstairs and slid into his place at the table.

As soon as the prayer was finished, he said, "Do I get to have one of the kittens that Rafael's mom offered me?"

Ben's dad smiled as he said, "Your mother and I were just talking about that." Ben held his breath as his dad continued.

"We've decided that since you take very good care of your fish, you are ready to take care of a kitten."

Feeding the fish

2. Andra had a beautiful singing voice. She was certain that she would be chosen to sing a solo in the junior choir concert at her church, but when the names of the soloists were read, hers was missing. When she asked Miss Snyder about it, the reply was sad but firm.

"You know, Andra, that the soloists have an earlier practice time than the choir. You are so often late for choir practice that I didn't think you would be able to get here to practice a solo."

Being on time for practice

Write two BIG things that you would like to do.	For each BIG thing, write two little things in which you need to be faithful first.
1. *Answers will vary.*	1.
	2. *Answers will vary.*
2.	1.
	2.

GOD AND HIS PEOPLE—Faithfulness—Unit 3, Part 4, Lesson 1 81

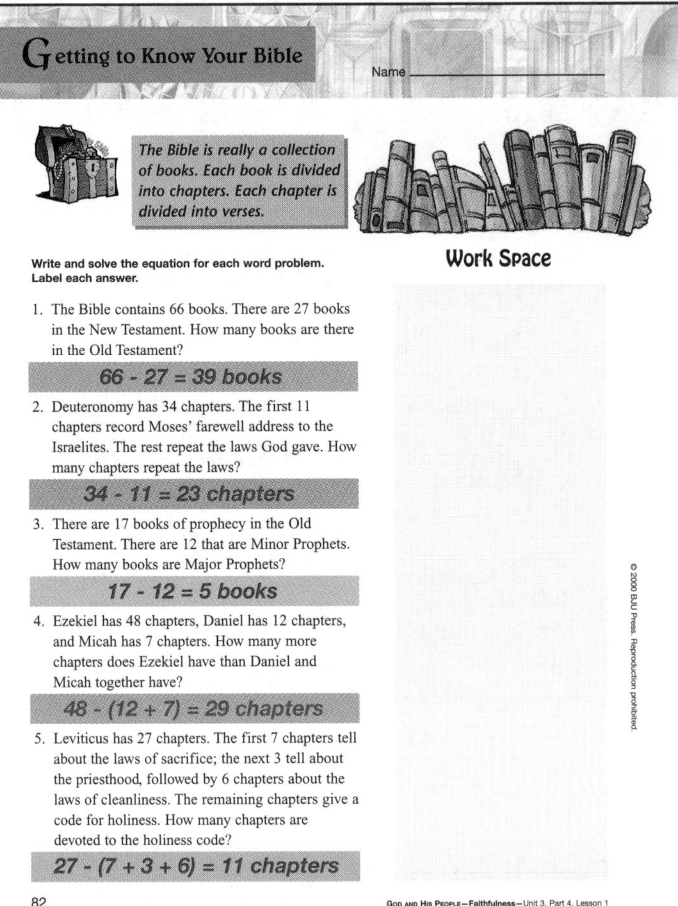

Getting to Know Your Bible

Name ____________

The Bible is really a collection of books. Each book is divided into chapters. Each chapter is divided into verses.

Write and solve the equation for each word problem. Label each answer.

Work Space

1. The Bible contains 66 books. There are 27 books in the New Testament. How many books are there in the Old Testament?

66 - 27 = 39 books

2. Deuteronomy has 34 chapters. The first 11 chapters record Moses' farewell address to the Israelites. The rest repeat the laws God gave. How many chapters repeat the laws?

34 - 11 = 23 chapters

3. There are 17 books of prophecy in the Old Testament. There are 12 that are Minor Prophets. How many books are Major Prophets?

17 - 12 = 5 books

4. Ezekiel has 48 chapters, Daniel has 12 chapters, and Micah has 7 chapters. How many more chapters does Ezekiel have than Daniel and Micah together have?

48 - (12 + 7) = 29 chapters

5. Leviticus has 27 chapters. The first 7 chapters tell about the laws of sacrifice; the next 3 tell about the priesthood, followed by 6 chapters about the laws of cleanliness. The remaining chapters give a code for holiness. How many chapters are devoted to the holiness code?

27 - (7 + 3 + 6) = 11 chapters

82 GOD AND HIS PEOPLE—Faithfulness—Unit 3, Part 4, Lesson 1

Memory Verse—Matthew 25:23

Principle: God rewards faithfulness. Locate **Matthew 25:23** and read the verse aloud as the students follow along. Explain that *lord* here means "master," and that the master is speaking to his faithful servant.

➤ **How do you know the master was pleased?** *(The master told the servant he had done a good job.)*

➤ **What had the servant been faithful in?** *(He had been faithful and trustworthy with a few things.)*

➤ **What was the servant's reward?** *(He would be trusted with more.)*

➤ **What will be the result of the servant's being faithful and being trusted with more?** *(He will be invited to share the joy of a job well done.)*

➤ **How does God reward faithful servants?** *(He will make them to be happy, joyous Christians.)*

Read the verse several times to the students. Direct them to highlight the verse in their Bibles (optional) and to mark the location with the Unit 3 Bookmark. Read the verse throughout the day for practice.

Worktext page 81

Apply the memory verse to everyday life.

Worktext page 82

Learn about the Bible.

History Connection (optional)

Guide a discussion about Thomas "Stonewall" Jackson.

➤ **What are qualities that are needed to be a great leader?** *(Possible answers include courage, good judgment, quick thinking, and organization.)*

Show the picture of Stonewall Jackson or a Civil War battle (optional), explaining that Thomas Jackson was a Confederate general during the Civil War. He had a genuine love for his men and a faithful Christian testimony. All his life he worked hard and wanted to do his best. He knew it would be wrong and others would suffer if he allowed himself to be lazy. Thomas Jackson was faithful to finish any job he was given.

➤ **How do you think Thomas Jackson got the name *Stonewall*?** *(Accept any answer.)*

Tell the students that during the first big battle of the Civil War, the First Battle of Bull Run, the Southern army was outnumbered. They were being defeated, and some of the Southern officers feared their men would panic and run. In the middle of the battle another Southern general was desperate; his men were hurt and scared. Through the smoke he saw Jackson calm and brave on his horse, his soldiers standing firm. "Look!" called out the general. "There is Jackson and his brigade of men like a stone wall." It was at this time that Thomas Jackson was first called "Stonewall," and his brigade of men were known as the "Stonewall Brigade." Jackson was wounded, and many of his men died, but they were not driven back. Jackson's line of soldiers held like a stone wall, and they won the battle.

➤ **How was Stonewall Jackson faithful?** *(Although his troops were outnumbered, they did not run away or give up. He and his men stood firm and won the battle.)*

➤ **Why would it have been easy for General Jackson to give up?** *(because he was outnumbered)*

➤ Read **Psalm 36:5** aloud. General Jackson was a faithful servant of God. **How faithful is God to us?** *(God's faithfulness reaches to the sky.)*

➤ **How can we be faithful to others?** *(Possible answers include by keeping our promises, by obeying, by putting others before ourselves.)*

Explain to the students that General Jackson gave God the credit for his victories. When asked once about his unusual bravery, Jackson replied, "My religious belief teaches me to feel as safe in battle as I feel in bed. God knows the time for my death; I do not concern myself about that but to always be ready no matter where it would overtake me." Stonewall Jackson read his Bible faithfully every day and prayed throughout the day. Before a battle he would pray with his other officers. Thomas "Stonewall" Jackson was a faithful soldier and servant of God.

Lesson 2

Materials

- TimeLine and picture: *Joash*

Label three index cards or pieces of paper, each with a number: *1, 2,* or *3.*

Hymn: "I Would Be True"

Sing the hymn (Worktext page 274). Place the students in three groups. Place the three numbered cards face down or fold the papers and place in a container. Allow a member of each group to select a card or paper. Explain that the number on it is the number of the verse of the hymn that their group will sing. Play the recording with each group singing its selected verse.

Memory Verse—Matthew 25:23

Practice the memory verse. Locate **Matthew 25:23** and read the verse aloud as the students read silently. Allow pairs of students to read the phrases with each other, or read the first phrase of the verse and then call on a student to read the words that tell what the master said to the servant. Continue as time permits.

Background Information

Athaliah—*She was the only woman ruler of Judah, ruling from 838 to 835 B.C. Athaliah was a wicked queen like her mother, Jezebel.*

Baal Worship—*Baal was the prominent false god worshiped by the Canaanites. God did not want His people defiled with the wicked, ungodly religions of Canaan. Baal worship was introduced to Israel by Ahab. Joash followed Jehoiada the priest, eliminating Baal worship while Jehoiada was alive.*

Mosaic Law—*This was the law given to Moses on Mt. Sinai. Generally the law can be divided into three parts. The first are the commandments given to express the righteous will of God. The second are the judgments given to govern social life in Israel. The third and final part are the ordinances given to govern the religious life of Israel.*

Introducing the Bible Account

Discuss responsibilities of parents and guardians.

➤ **Why has God given you parents (or guardians)?** *(to watch over me, love and protect me, and instruct me in the ways of the Lord)*

➤ **What are some ways in which your parents (or guardians) are obeying God in the way they are raising you?** *(Answers will vary, but point out that instructing children in the way of the Lord is one responsibility God has given them.)*

Bible Account

Read the following Bible account or read II Kings 11:1-21.

Jehoiada Faithfully Raised Joash

When Athaliah realized that her son, Ahaziah, had been killed, she saw her opportunity to seize the throne. Athaliah wanted to be the queen so much that she ordered members of the royal family—including her own grandchildren—to be killed.

Athaliah did not know that one of her grandsons had been taken and safely hidden by Jehosheba, Ahaziah's sister. Jehosheba had taken baby Joash and his nurse and had hidden them in the bedroom. Jehoiada, the high priest, and his wife Jehosheba raised Joash in the temple of the Lord until he was seven years old.

Jehoiada had a plan to crown Joash king. He knew that it was God's will for a descendant of David to rule Judah and that Athaliah was not a rightful heir to the throne. Jehoiada called for the military officials (rulers, captains, and guards) to meet in the temple. He made a covenant with them as he showed them Ahaziah's son, seven-year-old Joash.

Jehoiada spoke to the crowd and told them what to do on the Sabbath: a third of them were to watch at the king's house, a third were to watch at the gate Sur, and a third were to watch at the gate behind the guard. Jehoiada told them to watch that the king's house not be broken down and that the king not be harmed. He told them to have their weapons ready and to kill anyone who came too close to the king whether in the house or outside.

The people supported Jehoiada and did as he commanded. Jehoiada gave the captains King David's spears and shields which were in the temple. Joash was crowned king, anointed, and given a copy of the Mosaic law. The people clapped their hands and shouted, "God save the king."

➤ **Why did Athaliah order her grandchildren to be killed?** *(She wanted to be the queen.)*

➤ **Who faithfully raised Joash?** *(Jehoiada, the high priest, and his wife, Jehosheba)*

➤ **How did Joash become king at the age of seven?** *(Jehoiada had a plan that the people supported.)*

➤ **How do you know the Mosaic law (God's law) was valued?** *(Joash was given a copy of the Mosaic law when he was made king.)* Share the background information about Mosaic law (optional).

The crowd was celebrating. Joash was king! Athaliah heard the noise and went to the temple, where she saw the people running, playing instruments, and praising the king. She looked and saw Joash standing by the pillars with the princes and trumpeters all around. The people continued to rejoice and blow the trumpets.

Athaliah tore her clothes and cried, "Treason, Treason." Jehoiada ordered the captains to seize Athaliah, take her to the horse gate, and kill her with the sword. Then Jehoiada made a covenant between the Lord, the king, and the people that they would be the Lord's people. Baal's altars and images were broken down. Mattan, the priest of Baal, was killed.

Jehoiada appointed officers to guard the house of the Lord. Joash was taken to the king's house and was seated on the throne. The people of the land rejoiced. Joash was their king, and he reigned in Jerusalem for forty years. As long as Jehoiada was alive to instruct Joash, he did that which was right in God's eyes.

➤ **When Athaliah arrived at the temple, what did she find?** *(Joash had been crowned king, and the people were celebrating.)*

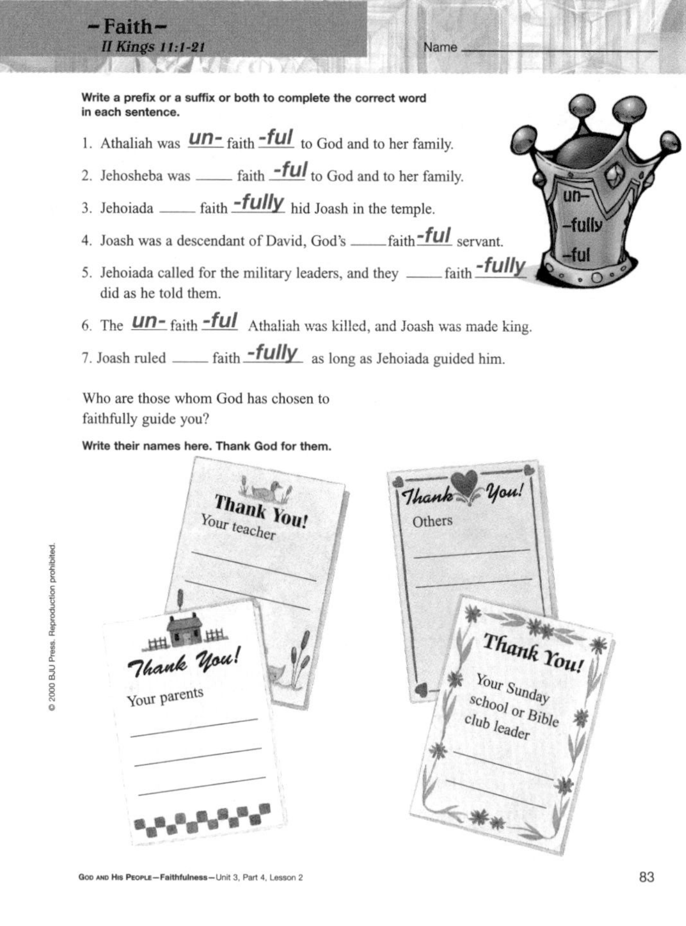
– Faith –
II Kings 11:1-21

Name ______________

Write a prefix or a suffix or both to complete the correct word in each sentence.

1. Athaliah was **un-** faith **-ful** to God and to her family.
2. Jehosheba was ____ faith **-ful** to God and to her family.
3. Jehoiada ____ faith **-fully** hid Joash in the temple.
4. Joash was a descendant of David, God's ____ faith **-ful** servant.
5. Jehoiada called for the military leaders, and they ____ faith **-fully** did as he told them.
6. The **un-** faith **-ful** Athaliah was killed, and Joash was made king.
7. Joash ruled ____ faith **-fully** as long as Jehoiada guided him.

Who are those whom God has chosen to faithfully guide you?

Write their names here. Thank God for them.

➤ **What happened to Athaliah?** *(She was put to death as her mother, Jezebel, had been.)*

➤ **What did Jehoiada and the others vow to the Lord?** *(that they would be the Lord's people)*

➤ **What was one of the first things the people did?** *(They tore down the altars of Baal and killed Mattan, the priest of Baal.)*

➤ **How long did Joash reign in Jerusalem?** *(forty years)*

➤ **Do you think Joash was a successful king when he obeyed God?** *(Accept any answer.)*

TimeLine

Add *Joash* to the TimeLine. Attach the picture of *Joash* to the TimeLine (835-796 B.C.), reminding the students that with Jehoiada's help, Joash became king at the age of seven. Guide the students as they glue the picture of *Joash* onto their TimeLines.

Worktext page 83

Use prefixes and suffixes to complete words. Review what prefixes and suffixes are before directing students to complete the words in the sentences. Tell them to write the names of those who faithfully guide them.

Lesson 3

Materials

- A beanbag or a ball (optional)

Write **Matthew 25:23** with the reference for display.

Hymn: "I Would Be True"

Sing the hymn (Worktext page 274). Select students to come to the front and sign the key words (*Note:* See Worktext page 61.) Play the recording and lead the singing of the first verse; then sing verses 2 and 3.

Memory Verse—Matthew 25:23

Practice the memory verse with a Beanbag Toss (optional). Call attention to the verse on display. Choose a student to read it aloud; then toss the beanbag to a student, who reads the reference. Instruct the student to toss the beanbag to another student, who should say the first word of the verse. Continue this procedure until the verse is said and the reference is repeated. Continue as time permits.

Introducing the Bible Account

Review the previous Bible account.

➤ **Who reigned in Jerusalem for forty years?** *(Joash)* Point out that Joash was faithful to the Lord and to Jehoiada while Jehoiada was alive.

Bible Account

Read the following Bible account or read II Chronicles 24:1-22.

The Temple Repaired

Athaliah's sons had broken up the temple and had used the dedicated furnishings in the temple for Baal worship. King Joash, with Jehoiada, decided to restore the temple of the Lord. Joash gathered the priests and Levites together and said, "Go out unto the cities of Judah, and gather of all Israel money to repair the house of your God from year to year, and see that ye hasten the matter."

However, the Levites did not do this quickly as Joash had commanded. Joash called Jehoiada to him and asked him why the money to repair the temple had not yet been collected.

King Joash commanded that a chest be made and be set outside by the gate of the house of the Lord. All the people rejoiced at this and brought their money and put it in the chest until it was full. The money chest was emptied and the chest returned to the gate so that the people could continue to contribute daily to the repair of the temple. A large amount of money was collected.

Joash and Jehoiada gave the money to the workmen, who hired masons and carpenters to do the work of repairing the temple. Men who worked in bronze and iron were hired. The workers labored faithfully, building and strengthening the temple according to its original design. The extra money was made into utensils for the house of the Lord. Dishes and other objects of silver and gold were made. The Bible tells us that burnt offerings were offered "in the house of the Lord continually all the days of Jehoiada."

When Jehoiada was 130 years old, he died. King Joash now listened to the advice given to him from the officials of Judah. He turned from the Lord and no longer remembered Jehoiada's faithfulness. Soon Judah and Jerusalem began worshiping idols again. God sent Jehoiada's son Zechariah to warn the people, "Thus saith God, Why transgress ye the commandments of the Lord, that ye cannot prosper? because ye have forsaken the Lord, he hath also forsaken you." However, the people did not listen, and Joash had Zechariah stoned to death.

➤ **How were the temple furnishings used under Athaliah's reign?** *(in Baal worship)*

➤ **What did King Joash command the Levites to do?** *(He told them to quickly gather money, which was to be used to rebuild the temple.)*

➤ **What plan did Joash have since the Levites did not quickly carry out his command?** *(He had a chest made and placed outside the gate by the temple.)*

➤ **How did the people react to the placing of the money box outside the gate by the temple?** *(They rejoiced and gave generously.)*

➤ **What happened after Jehoiada died?** *(King Joash was no longer faithful to the Lord or to those the Lord had put him in charge of. He led the people in worshiping idols again and even had Jehoiada's son Zechariah, a prophet of God, killed.)*

➤ **What can Christians learn from the life of King Joash?** *(Answers will vary, but point out that a Christian can become unfaithful if he is not careful to follow God's way and accept only godly advice.)*

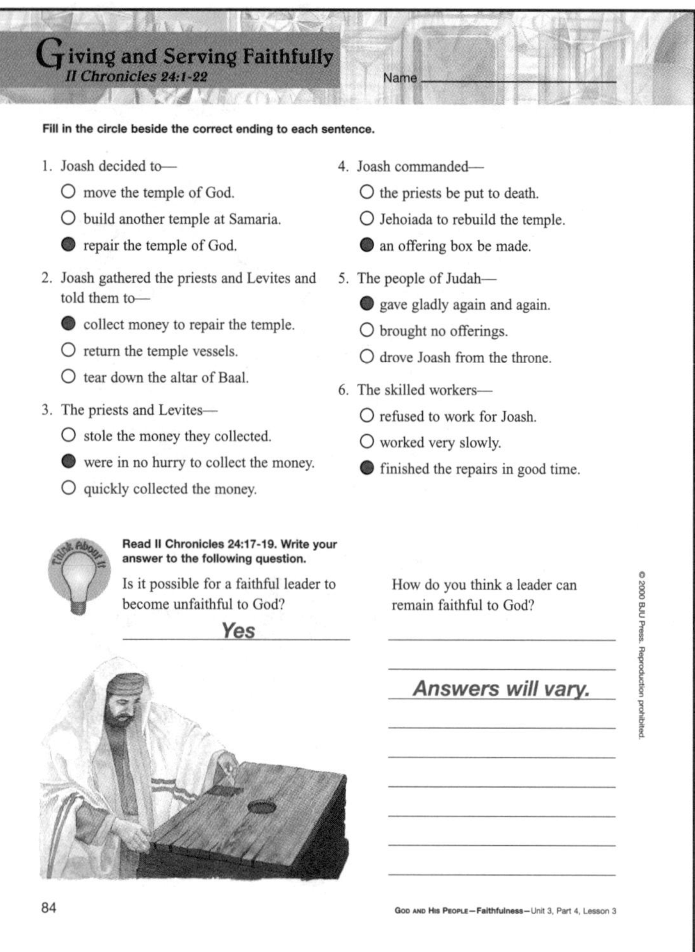

Giving and Serving Faithfully
II Chronicles 24:1-22

Name ____________________

Fill in the circle beside the correct ending to each sentence.

1. Joash decided to—
   - ○ move the temple of God.
   - ○ build another temple at Samaria.
   - ● repair the temple of God.
2. Joash gathered the priests and Levites and told them to—
   - ● collect money to repair the temple.
   - ○ return the temple vessels.
   - ○ tear down the altar of Baal.
3. The priests and Levites—
   - ○ stole the money they collected.
   - ● were in no hurry to collect the money.
   - ○ quickly collected the money.
4. Joash commanded—
   - ○ the priests be put to death.
   - ○ Jehoiada to rebuild the temple.
   - ● an offering box be made.
5. The people of Judah—
   - ● gave gladly again and again.
   - ○ brought no offerings.
   - ○ drove Joash from the throne.
6. The skilled workers—
   - ○ refused to work for Joash.
   - ○ worked very slowly.
   - ● finished the repairs in good time.

Think About It

Read II Chronicles 24:17-19. Write your answer to the following question.

Is it possible for a faithful leader to become unfaithful to God?

Yes

How do you think a leader can remain faithful to God?

Answers will vary.

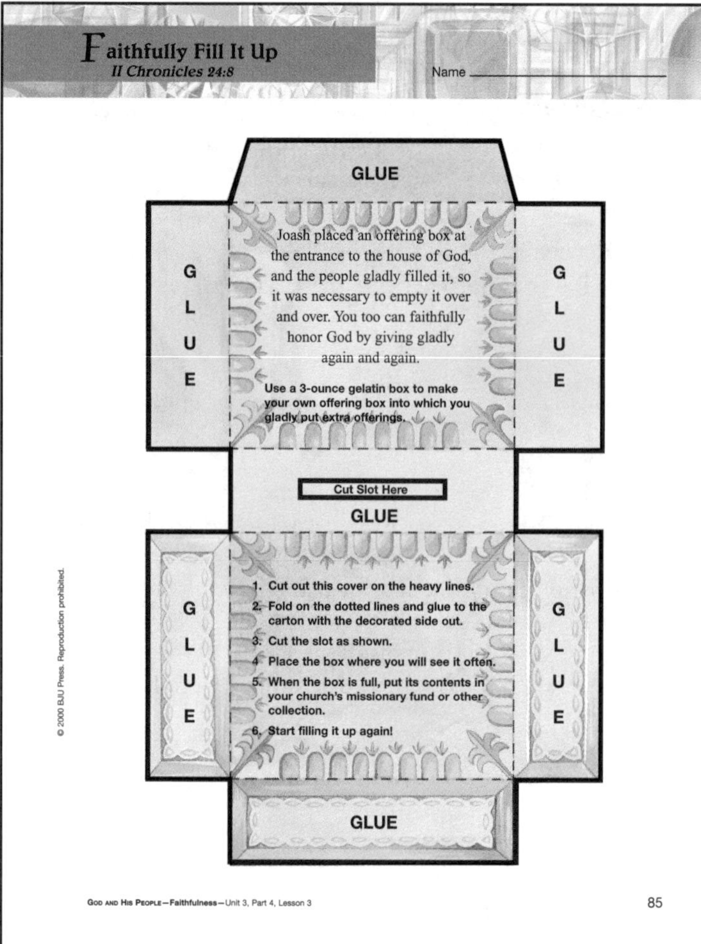

Faithfully Fill It Up
II Chronicles 24:8

Name ____________________

GLUE

Joash placed an offering box at the entrance to the house of God, and the people gladly filled it, so it was necessary to empty it over and over. You too can faithfully honor God by giving gladly again and again.

Use a 3-ounce gelatin box to make your own offering box into which you gladly put extra offerings.

GLUE

GLUE

Cut Slot Here

GLUE

1. Cut out this cover on the heavy lines.
2. Fold on the dotted lines and glue to the carton with the decorated side out.
3. Cut the slot as shown.
4. Place the box where you will see it often.
5. When the box is full, put its contents in your church's missionary fund or other collection.
6. Start filling it up again!

GLUE

GLUE

GLUE

Worktext page 84

Recall facts about the Bible account.

Worktext pages 85-86

Make an offering box.

Lesson 4

Materials

- Song: "Books of the New Testament"
- New Testament Bible Book Cards
- New Testament Divisions Bookmark

Memory Verse—Matthew 25:23

Practice the memory verse. Choose volunteers to read **Matthew 25:23.** As you practice saying the verse from memory, hold your hands as if you were going to clap. Instruct the students to say the memory verse loudly when your hands are wide apart and softer if they are close together.

Introducing the Application Story

Discuss jobs.

➤ **What jobs do your parents do?**

➤ **What types of jobs interest you?**

Application Story

Read the following story to the students.

Faithful in Little Things

"Jordan, have you cleaned up your room yet?" Mom called.

Jordan lowered his book and glanced around. Glue and model airplane parts cluttered his desk. Flight magazines littered the floor.

"No, Mom. I'm trying to finish this book on jet planes."

"Your room's been a mess for over a week, and we're having company soon. You need to clean it today. I need your help with some other chores too—washing the windows, mowing the lawn, and painting the lawn furniture. Get started right away."

Jordan put his book down with a huge sigh. "Mom, couldn't I just finish this book? I've got only fifteen more pages to go."

"Now, Jordan. You can finish the book later."

Jordan trudged to the garage to find the can of white paint. *I hate doing these silly jobs around the house,* he thought. *I don't need to know how to do these things to be a pilot.*

Jordan began slapping paint on one of the lawn chairs. He imagined that it was his first day on the job as a commercial pilot. "Ladies and gentlemen," he said out loud in a low, calm voice, "we are now taxiing to the runway and looking good for takeoff in approximately seven minutes." Lost in his daydream, he dripped paint as he worked. When he was finished, large white splotches dotted the deck. Jordan shrugged and left the brushes lying on top of the paint can without bothering to clean them.

He found window cleaner and a cloth and started washing windows. In his mind he flew an aerobatic plane, zooming low over the ground, rocketing skyward, looping and turning. In his haste, he left streaks on each window, and he even forgot one row of windows completely.

Almost done, Jordan thought. *Then I can get back to my book.* He sloshed gasoline into the power mower, hardly noticing that he'd spilled some on the garage floor. He was too busy picturing himself scanning the instrument panel and talking on his radio in the cockpit of a fighter plane.

He mowed the yard hurriedly, leaving crooked rows and missed patches of grass. On his last row, he failed to notice the rock border around his mom's flower beds. He ran the mower up on a rock and heard a loud grinding sound. Quickly he shut it off.

"Oh, great," he muttered.

Dad came around the corner of the house. "What happened, Jordan?"

"I ran up on that rock and broke one of the blades, Dad," he said. "Sorry."

Without a word Dad bent and examined the broken blade. He stood and looked Jordan in the eye. "Were you looking where you were going?" he asked.

Jordan squirmed. "Well, I—I was sort of . . ." His voice trailed off.

Dad watched him. "Jordan, you want to be a pilot, don't you?"

"Yeah."

"Do you know what flying requires? Not just skill. But accuracy. Thoroughness. Carefulness. Pilots are responsible for people's lives, Jordan. I just finished talking to your mom about how your chores have gone today, and I wouldn't call your work careful."

Jordan just stared down at his shoe.

"Do you remember the parable of the talents in the Bible?" Dad asked.

"You mean the one about the guys who got money from their boss to invest?"

Dad smiled a little. "That's the one I mean. And when the boss returned, he told the two faithful servants that because they were faithful in a few things, he would make them ruler over many things. Remember that?"

"Yes." Jordan frowned.

"God wants to be able to say the same to you, Jordan. He wants to see that you're faithful in the little things—the things Mom and I ask of you—before He gives you bigger things to do."

"Like flying planes?"

Dad nodded. "Like flying planes." He removed his work gloves. "Let's get in the car, Son," he said. "You can think about this while you ride with me to the shop to get this mower repaired."

- ➤ **What did Jordan want to be when he grew up?** *(a pilot)*
- ➤ **Why did Jordan not want to clean his room?** *(He wanted to finish reading his book about jet planes.)*
- ➤ **What problem did Jordan have?** *(He was careless and had an attitude problem.)*
- ➤ **Is carelessness a sin? Why?** *(Yes. Because carelessness does not bring glory to God, it is sin. Also, the careless person is not being faithful to others.)*
- ➤ **How can you keep from carelessness?** *(Ask God to help when you have to do something you may not enjoy and keep your mind on your work.)*

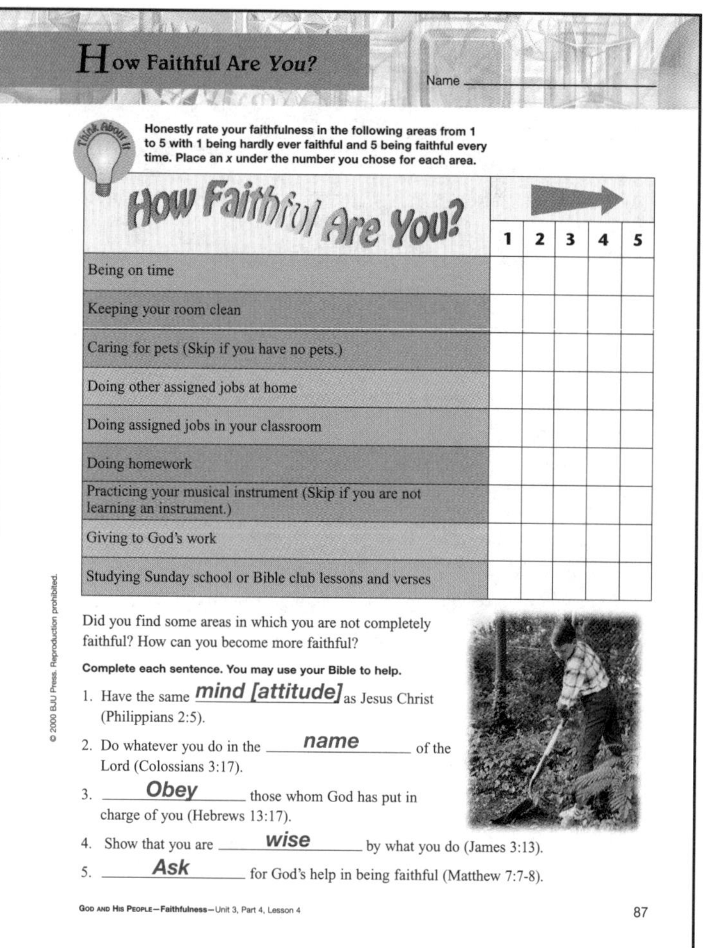

How Faithful Are *You?*

Name ______________________

Honestly rate your faithfulness in the following areas from 1 to 5 with 1 being hardly ever faithful and 5 being faithful every time. Place an *x* under the number you chose for each area.

How Faithful Are You?	1	2	3	4	5
Being on time					
Keeping your room clean					
Caring for pets (Skip if you have no pets.)					
Doing other assigned jobs at home					
Doing assigned jobs in your classroom					
Doing homework					
Practicing your musical instrument (Skip if you are not learning an instrument.)					
Giving to God's work					
Studying Sunday school or Bible club lessons and verses					

Did you find some areas in which you are not completely faithful? How can you become more faithful?

Complete each sentence. You may use your Bible to help.

1. Have the same mind [attitude] as Jesus Christ (Philippians 2:5).
2. Do whatever you do in the name of the Lord (Colossians 3:17).
3. Obey those whom God has put in charge of you (Hebrews 13:17).
4. Show that you are wise by what you do (James 3:13).
5. Ask for God's help in being faithful (Matthew 7:7-8).

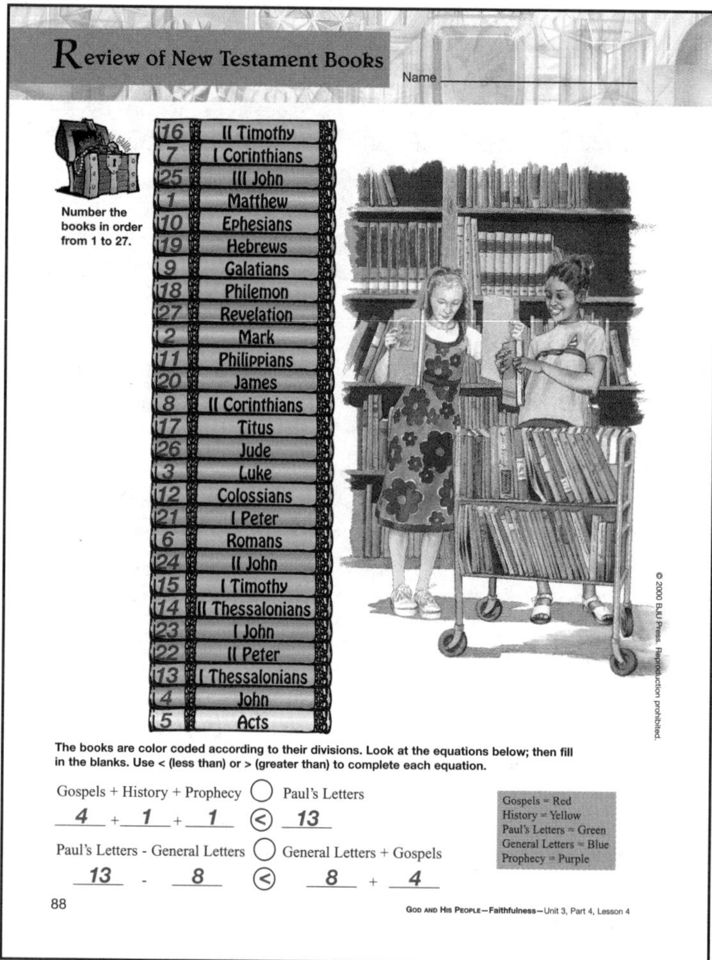

Review of New Testament Books

Name ______________________

Number the books in order from 1 to 27.

16 II Timothy
7 I Corinthians
25 III John
1 Matthew
10 Ephesians
19 Hebrews
9 Galatians
18 Philemon
27 Revelation
2 Mark
11 Philippians
20 James
8 II Corinthians
17 Titus
26 Jude
3 Luke
12 Colossians
21 I Peter
6 Romans
24 II John
15 I Timothy
14 II Thessalonians
23 I John
22 II Peter
13 I Thessalonians
4 John
5 Acts

The books are color coded according to their divisions. Look at the equations below; then fill in the blanks. Use < (less than) or > (greater than) to complete each equation.

Gospels + History + Prophecy ◯ Paul's Letters
4 + 1 + 1 < 13

Paul's Letters - General Letters ◯ General Letters + Gospels
13 - 8 < 8 + 4

Gospels = Red
History = Yellow
Paul's Letters = Green
General Letters = Blue
Prophecy = Purple

Worktext page 87

Apply Bible knowledge to everyday life. Explain the rating scale and encourage each student to rate himself on the responsibilities listed.

Locate information in Scripture. Challenge the students to evaluate their faithfulness based on the checklist; then direct them to use Scripture to complete the statements.

Song: "Books of the New Testament"

Sing the song (Worktext page 288). Give each student a New Testament Divisions Bookmark. Lead in reading together the names of the New Testament books. Play the recording and lead in singing "Books of the New Testament."

Bible Study Skills

Review the New Testament divisions. Divide the students into three or four teams. Line up the teams. Show a New Testament Bible Book Card to the student at the front of each line. The student who first calls out the division where the book is located receives a point for his team. Let each student in front go to the end of his line after his turn.

One-on-One: Give the student the New Testament Bible Book Cards to sequence correctly. Then mix up the cards and show one at a time, challenging the student to identify in which division it belongs.

Bible Study Skills, Worktext page 88

Sequence the books of the New Testament and identify their divisions.

Going Beyond

Enrichment

Set a goal. Challenge each student to set a goal to be faithful in an activity. They should be faithful for a week if it is a daily activity or for a month if it is a weekly activity. Challenge the students to do an activity that they are not already doing. Possible goals may include:

- Each week meet with a friend to read Scripture together and pray.
- Choose a chore you could do for someone in your family, and do it daily or weekly.
- Read to a younger brother, sister, or neighbor.
- Pray daily for a missionary.
- Get permission from your teacher to do a classroom job.

Unit 3 Review

Name ____________________

Match the Bible character with the description by putting the correct letter on the line.

B 1. Ahab and Jezebel
F 2. Hosea and Gomer
C 3. Elisha
D 4. Joash
A 5. Jehoiada
E 6. Naboth

A. He was a priest who faithfully protected and trained Joash, God's choice for king.
B. They were judged for their unfaithfulness to God.
C. He was faithful to trust the Lord for protection in times of battle and famine.
D. His life reminds us to follow godly advice and to be careful to remain faithful to God.
E. He was faithful to God's command and did not sell his vineyard.
F. Their marriage was a picture of God's faithfulness to faithless Israel.

Start with the first letter and skip every other letter in order to answer number 7. Start with the second letter and skip every other letter in order to answer number 8.

PRREOWTAERCDTSPJRUODVGIEDSE

7. The Lord is faithful to p r o t e c t and p r o v i d e for His servants.

8. God r e w a r d s those who are faithful to Him, but He j u d g e s those who are unfaithful to Him.

Use a word from the word bank below to complete the paragraph.

9. God provided [jar] for a widow and her two sons. God provided [bread] for the prophets. God protected Elisha with [chariots of fire]. The Israelites faithfully gave [money bag] for God's work. God used angels and lepers to provide [food] for the Israelites.

angels and lepers	widow and her two sons	
Elisha	Israelites	prophets

Use your Bible to review the order of the books in the New Testament.

God and His People — Use after completing Unit 3 — S57

Unit Review

Materials

- Copy of Supplement page S57, "Unit 3 Review," for each student

Guide a review of Unit 3. Review the people and events in preparation for the Unit 3 Test (optional).

Christmas: Announced by Angels

Overview

Preparing the Teacher

"Fear not for, behold, I bring you good tidings of great joy. . . ." God was made flesh. God is with us. Great joy! Christmas joy! All that God is—in Jesus Christ. He is altogether lovely, perfect in His plan and purpose for our lives. Yet we often fret, and we sometimes fear. We forget that in His perfection, He wants what is best for us. We forget that in His perfect power He promises to work out all things in our lives for our good and His glory. Praise God for His Son—our Christmas joy. Read the following references and consider anew the gift of this joy. He is our joy in salvation **(Psalm 51:12);** our joy in His strength **(Nehemiah 8:10);** our joy in His eternal presence **(Psalm 16:11);** our joy in trials **(James 1:2);** our joy in answered prayer **(John 16:24);** our joy in the fruit of our Christian ministry **(III John 4);** and our joy in the hope of His soon return **(John 14:28).** May the remembrances of these promises ring out "Christ our Joy" in our hearts and lives during this Christmas season and throughout the coming year!

Preparing the Lessons

Part 1 Lesson 1 Materials—two small pieces of magnetic tape for each student

Part 1 Lesson 3 Materials—two instruments (toy or real), one usable and one unusable (e.g., without a mouthpiece, without a reed, or with a broken string) (optional)

Part 1 Lesson 4 Materials—*Young Person's Guide to the Orchestra* by Benjamin Britten (optional)

Part 1 Going Beyond Materials—a wrapped Christmas gift box with a removable lid

Part 2 Lesson 1 Materials—an adult-sized coat and/or shoes (optional)

Part 2 Lesson 3 Materials—scale and yardstick or meter stick (optional)

Part 2 Lesson 4 Materials—a Christmas card

Part 2 Going Beyond Materials—an 18" strip of adding machine paper for each student

Unit 4 Christmas: Announced by Angels

Hymn: "There's a Song in the Air"

Part	Lesson number	Lesson pages	Worktext pages	Supplement pages	Bible Account	Application
Part 1: God's Chosen Instruments	1	127	89-92	S69	God's Chosen Man (Matthew 1:18-25)	
	2	129	93		God's Chosen Woman (Luke 1:26-56)	
	3	130	94-96			"A Usable Instrument" (Part 1)
	4	133	97-98			"A Usable Instrument" (Part 2)
Part 2: The Birth and Childhood of a King	1	135	99-100	S70	The Birth of a King (Matthew 2:1-12; Luke 2:1-20)	
	2	137	101		The Childhood of a King (Matthew 2:13-16; Luke 2:41-52)	
	3	138	102			**Hero of the Faith:** Jean Henri Merle d'Aubigné
	4	140	103-4			**Picture the Point:** God's Omniscience

Connections	Memory Verses and Principles	Bible Doctrines	Skills/Applications
   Music	Luke 1:37-38 *God can do anything; He is omnipotent.*	**The Doctrine of the Bible** **Proofs for inspiration:** The Bible is accurate in its history (John 17:17). The Bible is accurate in its prophecy (Num. 23:19). **The Doctrine of God** **Existence of God:** God has shown Himself in the Bible (John 5:39). **Nature of God:** The Son is God (Heb. 1:8). **The Doctrine of Man** **Original State of Man:** He has a will (I Tim. 2:14). **The Doctrine of Salvation** **Provision of God:** Christ became man (incarnation) (John 1:14). **The Doctrine of Angels and Satan** **Organization:** Angels reveal God's will to man (Luke 1:13).	**Foundational:** • Realize that with God nothing is impossible • Realize that Jesus, the Son of God, became man • Realize that the Bible is accurate **Practical:** • Recall facts and details • Locate information in Scripture • Learn the divisions of the Old Testament • Match dialogue with the correct character **Personal:** • Develop a Bible reading habit • Develop a desire to be an instrument used by God • Apply Bible knowledge to everyday life
TimeLine: Birth of Christ History **TimeLine: Jean Henri Merle d'Aubigné**	Luke 2:52 *Jesus is our example.*		

Preparing the Unit 4 Bulletin Board

Cover the bulletin board with blue background paper or fabric. Attach piano keys or another musical motif in black and white as the border. Use black letters for the title: "When God Chooses the Instruments . . . the Songs Are Heavenly." Arrange musical instruments as shown. (*Note:* Patterns for some musical instruments are available on Supplement page S69.)

God's Chosen Instruments

Unit 4, Part 1

Preview

Doctrines

- The Bible is accurate in its prophecy (Numbers 23:19)—Lesson 1
- The Bible is accurate in its history (John 17:17)—Lesson 1
- Angels reveal God's will to man (Luke 1:13)—Lessons 1-2
- Man has a will (I Timothy 2:14)—Lesson 2
- Christ became man (incarnation) (John 1:14)—Lesson 2

Skills and Applications

- Learn Luke 1:37-38
- Recall facts and details
- Locate information in Scripture
- Match dialogue with the correct character
- Realize that with God nothing is impossible
- Realize that the Bible is accurate
- Develop a Bible reading habit
- Develop a desire to be an instrument used by God
- Apply Bible knowledge to everyday life

Lesson 1

Materials

- Chart 14: "God Chose a Family for Jesus"
- Song: "The Bible Reading Habit"
- Two small pieces of magnetic tape for each student
- Unit 4 Bookmark for each student
- Highlighter for each student (optional)

Draw or cut out a large paper Christmas tree. Display the tree. Cut out a gold or silver paper star for the top of the tree with the reference Luke 1:37-38 written on it. Prepare approximately thirty instrument ornaments, using the patterns from Supplement page S69.

Worktext pages 89-90

Develop a Bible reading habit. Read and discuss page 89 with the students. Explain the four-week Bible reading activity. Encourage each student to complete the Bible reading, coloring the ornaments after each day's reading. Lead in singing the song "The Bible Reading Habit" from Worktext page 271.

Background Information

Public Example—*Jewish law at this time stated that if a woman was found pregnant while she was betrothed or engaged, she could be taken before all the people of the city and stoned.*

Introducing the Bible Account

Discuss Joseph. Point out the location of Nazareth on the map on Worktext page 91. Read aloud the information about carpenters.

Bible Account

Read the following Bible account or read Matthew 1:18-25. Direct attention to Worktext page 91 as indicated in the account.

God's Chosen Man

Joseph and Mary were engaged to be married. As was the custom during New Testament times, the couple were to be engaged for one year before the wedding could take place. (Read about betrothal from Worktext page 91.)

During this betrothal time, Mary was found to be with child. The Bible says, "Joseph . . . being a just man," did not make an example out of Mary. The Bible also tells us that an angel of the Lord appeared to Joseph in a dream and said, "Fear not to take unto thee Mary thy wife; for that which is conceived in her is of the Holy Ghost. And she shall bring forth a son, and thou shalt call his name JESUS: for he shall save his people from their sins." This is what had been said many years before by Isaiah the prophet. "Therefore the

Lord himself shall give you a sign; Behold, a virgin shall conceive, and bear a son, and shall call his name Immanuel" (Isaiah 7:14). *Immanuel* means "God with us."

Christmas Is Coming! Christmas Has Come!
Christmas Preparations
Name
You and your family probably are making many preparations for celebrating Christmas. There are presents to wrap and secrets to keep, cards to write and parties to plan, carols to sing and cookies to bake. Do not become so busy that you forget the habit of opening God's Word every day to find the wonderful gifts He has for you there. As you spend quiet times with Him, you will discover that celebrating the birth of the Savior is not limited to a few weeks each year.
You might like to share with someone what you have learned about getting the H.A.B.I.T. of having a quiet time every day.
Use the guide on page 89 to help you practice the Bible reading H.A.B.I.T. as you read these Scriptures. Color the tree decoration in the box after you read each one.
God chose prophets to tell that He would give His Son. Isaiah 9:6-7
God chose the time when His Son would be born as well as the place of His birth. Luke 2:1-6
God chose to announce the birth of the Savior to those nearby. Luke 2:8-14
God chose to announce the birth of the Savior to those far away. Matthew 2:1-11
God chose to place the Savior in the line of David. Jeremiah 23:5-6
God chose to send a messenger before the Savior. Luke 1:13-17
God chose a mother for Jesus. Luke 1:26-33
God chose a godly man to look after Jesus and His mother. Matthew 1:18-25
God chose to have fellowship with man. I John 1:1-7
God allows us to choose to believe in Jesus Christ and be saved. I John 5:9-12
© 2000 BJU Press. Reproduction prohibited.
90
God and His People—Christmas: Announced by Angels—Unit 4, Part 1, Lesson 1

Joseph was awakened from his dream and did as the angel from God had told him and took Mary as his wife. Joseph trusted and obeyed God. God chose Joseph to be the earthly father of our Lord because he was a man of godly character.

InfoScene: "God Chose a Family for Jesus"
Display Chart 14 for reference throughout this unit. Review and discuss the Bible account as time permits.

➤ **What does *just* mean, and how did Joseph display this character trait?** Direct the students to look up *just* in the glossary (optional). *(fair and honest; Joseph was fair and honest.)*

➤ **How did Joseph find out what was expected of him?** *(The angel of the Lord appeared to him in a dream and told him to take Mary as his wife.)*

➤ **What Old Testament prophecy was being fulfilled?** *(that a virgin would bring forth a son and call his name Immanuel [Isaiah 7:14])*

➤ **What does *Immanuel* mean?** *(God with us)*

Memory Verses—Luke 1:37-38

Principle: God can do anything; He is omnipotent. Locate **Luke 1:37-38** and read the verses aloud as the students read silently.

➤ **What is the word for God's ability to do anything?** *(omnipotence)*

➤ **How did we know that Mary was willing to obey God?** *(She said that she was willing to go through whatever God said.)*

➤ **What kind of response should you have when God has something for you to do?** *(one of willingness and obedience)*

Choose volunteers to read the verses aloud. Assign each student a different word from the verses to write on an instrument ornament. Attach the ornaments on the Christmas tree. Instruct the students to highlight the verses in their Bibles (optional).

Give each student a Unit 4 Bookmark to mark the location of the verses. Point out the Christmas scene. Direct the students to attach the pieces of magnetic tape to their bookmark and then to place it over the page.

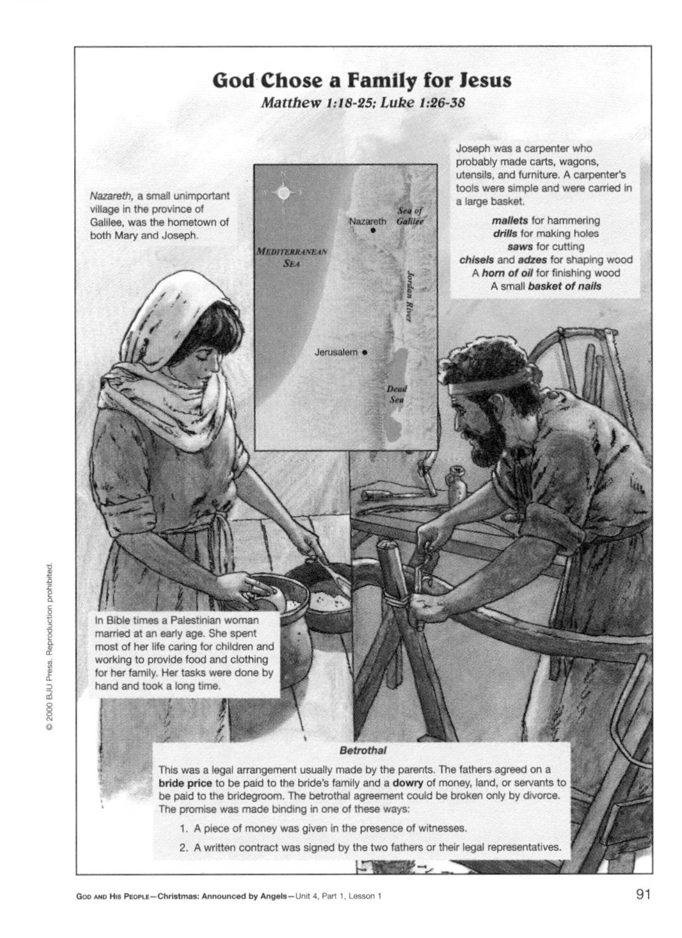
God Chose a Family for Jesus
Matthew 1:18-25; Luke 1:26-38

Nazareth, a small unimportant village in the province of Galilee, was the hometown of both Mary and Joseph.

Joseph was a carpenter who probably made carts, wagons, utensils, and furniture. A carpenter's tools were simple and were carried in a large basket.

mallets for hammering
drills for making holes
saws for cutting
chisels and ***adzes*** for shaping wood
A ***horn of oil*** for finishing wood
A small ***basket of nails***

In Bible times a Palestinian woman married at an early age. She spent most of her life caring for children and working to provide food and clothing for her family. Her tasks were done by hand and took a long time.

Betrothal

This was a legal arrangement usually made by the parents. The fathers agreed on a **bride price** to be paid to the bride's family and a **dowry** of money, land, or servants to be paid to the bridegroom. The betrothal agreement could be broken only by divorce. The promise was made binding in one of these ways:

1. A piece of money was given in the presence of witnesses.
2. A written contract was signed by the two fathers or their legal representatives.

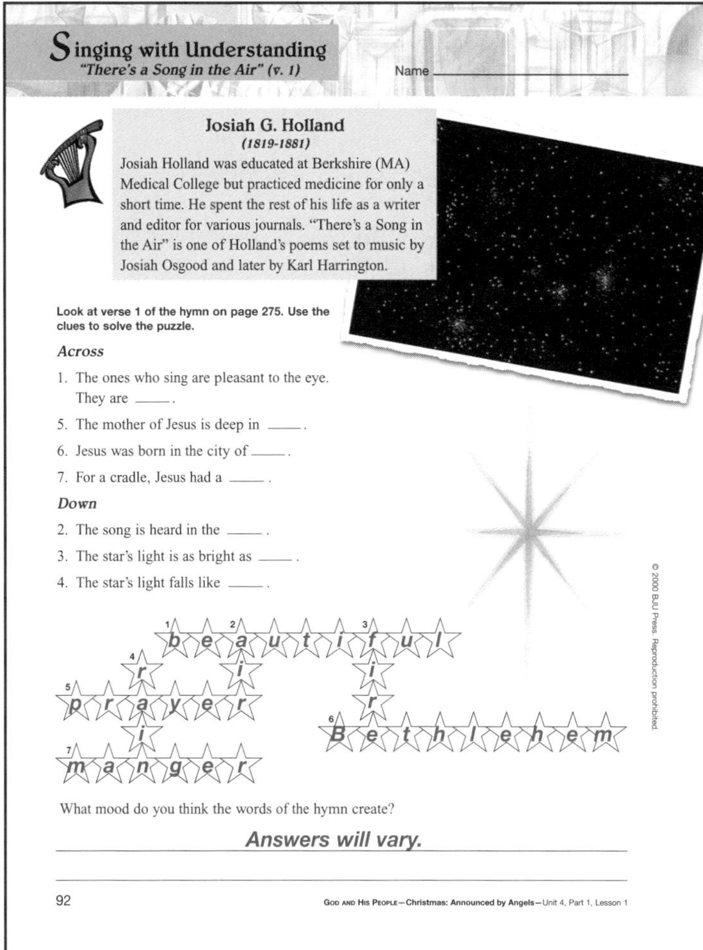
Singing with Understanding
"There's a Song in the Air" (v. 1)

Name ______________

Josiah G. Holland
(1819-1881)
Josiah Holland was educated at Berkshire (MA) Medical College but practiced medicine for only a short time. He spent the rest of his life as a writer and editor for various journals. "There's a Song in the Air" is one of Holland's poems set to music by Josiah Osgood and later by Karl Harrington.

Look at verse 1 of the hymn on page 275. Use the clues to solve the puzzle.

Across
1. The ones who sing are pleasant to the eye. They are ____.
5. The mother of Jesus is deep in ____.
6. Jesus was born in the city of ____.
7. For a cradle, Jesus had a ____.

Down
2. The song is heard in the ____.
3. The star's light is as bright as ____.
4. The star's light falls like ____.

What mood do you think the words of the hymn create?

Answers will vary.

Hymn: "There's a Song in the Air!"
Teach the first verse (Worktext page 275). Play the recording for the students as they follow along.

- **What does the word *rain* mean when the writer is talking about the star?** *(It is shining down its light while the angels are speaking.)*
- **Who are *the beautiful* that the hymn mentions singing?** *(probably angels)*
- **Do we know for sure whether the angels actually sang their glad tidings to the shepherds?** *(We do not know whether angels actually sang their message, but we do know that they were praising God.)*

Worktext page 92
Singing with understanding, verse 1.

Lesson 2

Hymn: "There's a Song in The Air!"
Sing the first verse (Worktext page 275). Play the recording, directing one group to sing the first line and another group the second line. Lead in singing the last two lines together. Sing the hymn again and direct the students to reverse the parts they sang the first time.

Background Information
Virgin Birth—*This was an impossible event made possible by God. The Bible does not present the virgin birth of Christ as myth, but as fact. The virgin birth of Christ is the basis of Christian belief.*

Mary—*She was not what people would have expected for the woman chosen to carry the Christ child. She was of a lower class—poor and not of royalty—but she was submissive to God. During New Testament times, if an engaged woman was pregnant, she could be stoned or be put away from her family to live on the streets. In spite of knowing this, Mary accepted what the angel said with a heart of love and obedience, yielding to God's will.*

Introducing the Bible Account
Define *incarnate.* Direct the students to find *incarnate* in the glossary. Discuss the definition.

Bible Account

Read the following Bible account or read Luke 1:26-56.

God's Chosen Woman

The angel Gabriel was sent by God to the city of Nazareth to Mary, a virgin engaged to a man named Joseph, a descendant of David. The angel came to Mary and said, "Hail, thou that art highly favoured, the Lord is with thee: blessed art thou among women."

Mary was troubled, because she did not understand what the greeting by the angel meant. The angel spoke again and told Mary not to be afraid, because what he was going to tell her was from God. Gabriel told Mary that she would conceive, and have a son, and would call his name Jesus. He told her that Jesus would reign over the house of Jacob and that His kingdom would not end.

Mary asked the angel how this would all happen, since she was not married, nor had she lived with a man. The angel told her it would be a work of the Holy Ghost and that "with God nothing shall be impossible." Mary responded to the angel, "Behold the handmaid of the Lord; be it unto me according to thy word." And the angel went away from Mary.

Mary hurried to the town in the hills where her cousin Elisabeth lived. Elisabeth greeted Mary as the mother of the Savior. Mary responded with words of praise.

Read **Luke 1:46-55** to the students, explaining that this is called "The Magnificat," a song of praise by Mary to God.

- ➤ **What was Mary's first reaction when she saw the angel Gabriel?** *(She was troubled and afraid.)*
- ➤ **What did the angel tell Mary?** *(that she would have a son, that she was to call His name Jesus, and that His kingdom would last forever)*
- ➤ **What was Mary's response to what the angel told her?** *(She wondered how this would happen but was willing to be used of the Lord.)*
- ➤ **Do you have a willing heart to be used of God?**

Memory Verses—Luke 1:37-38

Practice the memory verses. Locate **Luke 1:37-38** and read the verses aloud as the students follow along. Direct the students to read verse 37 aloud after you read each question.

- ➤ **How can God be everywhere?** Read verse 37 together.
- ➤ **How can God know what we need before we pray?** Read verse 37 together.

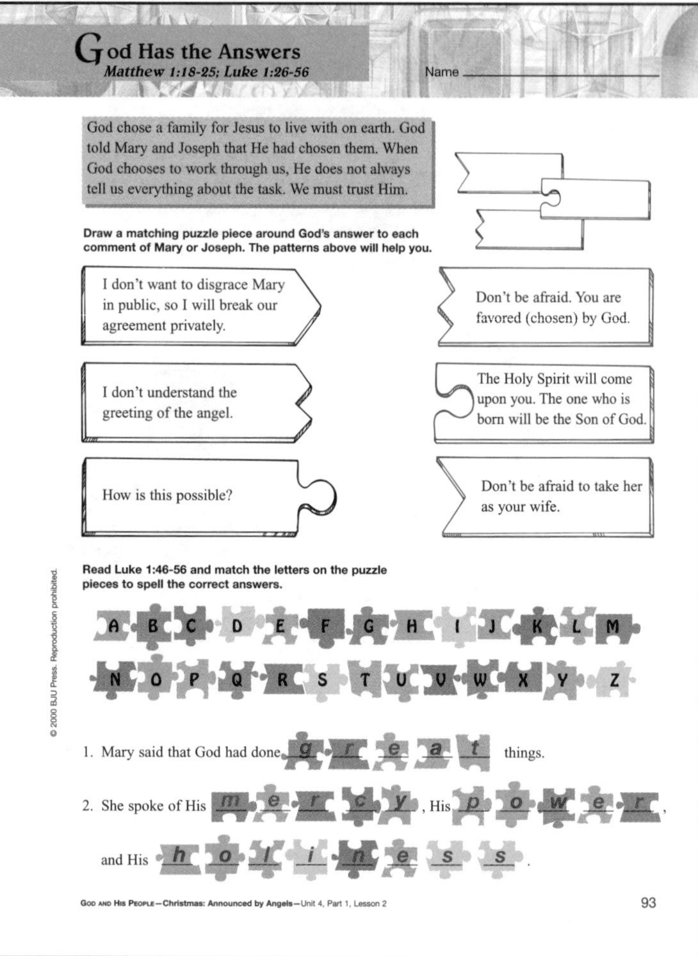

God Has the Answers
Matthew 1:18-25; Luke 1:26-56

Name

God chose a family for Jesus to live with on earth. God told Mary and Joseph that He had chosen them. When God chooses to work through us, He does not always tell us everything about the task. We must trust Him.

Draw a matching puzzle piece around God's answer to each comment of Mary or Joseph. The patterns above will help you.

I don't want to disgrace Mary in public, so I will break our agreement privately.

Don't be afraid. You are favored (chosen) by God.

I don't understand the greeting of the angel.

The Holy Spirit will come upon you. The one who is born will be the Son of God.

How is this possible?

Don't be afraid to take her as your wife.

Read Luke 1:46-56 and match the letters on the puzzle pieces to spell the correct answers.

A B C D E F G H I J K L M

N O P Q R S T U V W X Y Z

1. Mary said that God had done g r e a t things.
2. She spoke of His m e r c y, His p o w e r, and His h o l i n e s s.

- ➤ **Why should Christians not worry about their problems?** Read verse 37 together; then read both verses together.

Worktext page 93

Recall details about Mary and Joseph.

Lesson 3

Materials

- Cellophane tape
- Two instruments, one usable and one unusable (e.g., without a mouthpiece, without a reed, or with a broken string) (optional)

Hymn: "There's a Song in the Air!"

Teach the second verse (Worktext page 275). Read through the second verse, explaining that a *tumult* is a loud noise. Explain that this probably refers to the "multitude of the heavenly host praising God" (Luke 2:13). Play the recording and sing verse 2, paying close attention to dynamics. (e.g., Sing "For the virgin's sweet boy is the Lord of the earth" with a soft, quiet voice and "Ay! the star rains its fire while the beautiful sing" with a louder voice.) Sing verses 1-2 together.

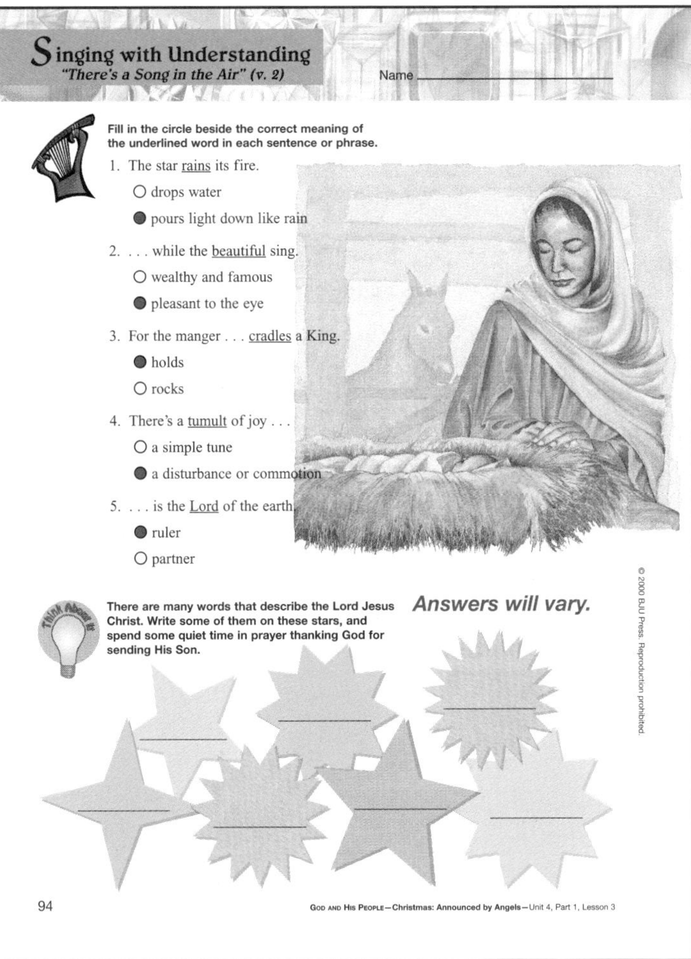
Singing with Understanding
"There's a Song in the Air" (v. 2)

Name ______________________

Fill in the circle beside the correct meaning of the underlined word in each sentence or phrase.

1. The star rains its fire.
   - ○ drops water
   - ● pours light down like rain
2. . . . while the beautiful sing.
   - ○ wealthy and famous
   - ● pleasant to the eye
3. For the manger . . . cradles a King.
   - ● holds
   - ○ rocks
4. There's a tumult of joy . . .
   - ○ a simple tune
   - ● a disturbance or commotion
5. . . . is the Lord of the earth.
   - ● ruler
   - ○ partner

There are many words that describe the Lord Jesus Christ. Write some of them on these stars, and spend some quiet time in prayer thanking God for sending His Son.

Answers will vary.

© 2000 BJU Press. Reproduction prohibited.

94 God and His People—Christmas: Announced by Angels—Unit 4, Part 1, Lesson 3

Worktext page 94

Singing with understanding, verse 2.

Introducing the Application Story

Demonstrate usable and unusable instruments. Display the two instruments. Explain that one instrument can fulfill its job or function, whereas the other instrument cannot.

Application Story

Read the following story to the students.

A Usable Instrument (Part 1)

Brad lay across the bed with his hands behind his head and his eyes closed. *This classical piano music is great! One day,* he thought, *I will play like this.* He sat up in his bed and played an imaginary piano in front of him.

Brad jumped at the sound of his mother's voice. "Why can't I get you to do that on a real piano?" she asked. She stood in the doorway, holding his bag of piano books.

Brad turned off the CD. "Oh, Mom, it's no fun to practice," he said. "I just want to play the way Piano Pete does." Brad held up one of his CDs. Piano Pete, whose real name was Peter Harris, was the best pianist in the world in Brad's eyes. He could play *anything* on the piano.

Mom smiled, "Do you think he got to be that good without practicing?" Brad sighed. He took the bag from his mother and went downstairs to the car.

By the end of Brad's piano lesson, he could not even look at his teacher, Mr. Sabbadino. Obviously, Brad had not done his piano practice every day.

Mr. Sabbadino shook his head, "Bradley, you must practice, practice, practice." Brad said nothing. "I'm not sure I should tell you about the Christmas concert."

Mr. Sabbadino had taken him to Christmas concerts every year since he began taking lessons three years ago. Brad's mind raced to think of a good reason he had not practiced the past week, but nothing came to mind.

"The great classical pianist Claudio Focaccio is coming to town," said Mr. Sabbadino. "He's a friend of mine from the old country." Mr. Sabbadino was from Italy, which he always called "the old country."

Brad determined that he would practice for an hour every day for the next two weeks. But after three days of it, he gave up. The two weeks went by faster than he thought, and before he knew it, it was the night of the concert.

Brad put in his favorite Piano Pete CD to listen to as he got ready. As Mr. Sabbadino turned in the driveway, Mom straightened Brad's tie and gave him his final instructions. "Now stay with Mr. Sabbadino," she said. "And sit quietly throughout the concert."

Sitting still was no problem for Brad. He loved piano concerts—and Claudio Focaccio was no disappointment. Brad waited patiently for the other artists and the orchestra to finish playing. Then Claudio played his piece. His hands danced across the keyboard, creating an echo of beauty in the large auditorium. *He's no Piano Pete,* thought Brad, *but he's great.*

At the end of the concert, Brad turned to follow the crowd out the door. A hand caught his shoulder. "Wait," said Mr. Sabbadino. "There's someone I want you to meet." Brad followed his teacher to the stage and paused before following him through a small door. "It's all right," said Mr. Sabbadino. Brad continued to follow and found himself standing in front of the great pianist he had just heard.

"Bradley," said Mr. Sabbadino, "This is Mr. Claudio Focaccio."

Claudio shook Brad's hand. "It's very nice to meet you," said Brad.

"It is a pleasure to meet you," said Claudio. "I've heard much about you from your teacher."

Claudio invited Brad to sit down in the small room. "You have a very good teacher," said Claudio. "*This* man," he said, pointing to Mr. Sabbadino, "was also *my* teacher." Brad stared.

"Claudio has something he would like to share with you," said Mr. Sabbadino. "He has some advice." Brad looked at Claudio. *What advice would this great man have for him?*

"When I play the piano," said Claudio. "I want to play my best for the Lord. Is that why you play?"

Brad nodded. I really do, he thought. I want to bring glory to God in everything I do—especially playing the piano.

Claudio took a piece of paper out of his pocket. "There is one thing God had to teach me before I could play as I do now. I have written it on this piece of paper. Read it when you are ready."

Brad thanked the man and took the piece of paper. He carefully put it in his shirt pocket. Mr. Sabbadino said goodbye to Claudio, and he and Brad left quietly. Nothing was said on the way home, but as Mr. Sabbadino pulled up in front of Brad's house, they shook hands as Brad muttered, "Thank you."

Once inside the house, Brad called, "I'm home. Had a good time." Then he raced up to his room, took the piece of paper out of his pocket, and slowly unfolded it.

- ➤ **What did Brad want to be able to do?** *(play the piano like Piano Pete)*
- ➤ **What was Brad's biggest problem with the piano, and why was this a problem?** *(He did not practice as he should. Accept any reasonable answer.)*
- ➤ **What surprise did Mr. Sabbadino have for Brad after the Christmas concert?** *(to meet Claudio Focaccio, the pianist)*
- ➤ **What was Claudio's reason for playing his best?** *(so he would bring glory to God in whatever he did)*
- ➤ Mary and Joseph were willing and usable servants of God. **Do you have a desire to bring glory to God in whatever you do?** Ask yourself whether you are a usable instrument for God.

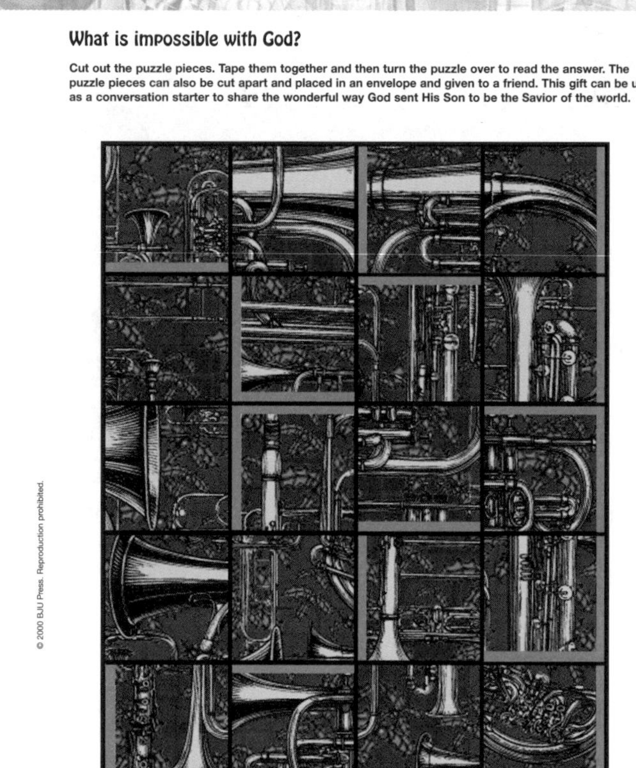
With God . . .
Luke 1:37-38

Name ______________________

What is impossible with God?

Cut out the puzzle pieces. Tape them together and then turn the puzzle over to read the answer. The puzzle pieces can also be cut apart and placed in an envelope and given to a friend. This gift can be used as a conversation starter to share the wonderful way God sent His Son to be the Savior of the world.

God and His People—Christmas: Announced by Angels—Unit 4, Part 1, Lesson 3 95

Memory Verses—Luke 1:37-38

Practice the memory verses. Direct attention to the Christmas tree, decorated with the instrument ornaments. Read the verses together. Direct the students to close their eyes or to put their heads down on their desks. Call on a student to choose two ornaments from the tree. When the students open their eyes, select a student to identify which words are missing. Read the verses together without those words. Continue in this way until all the ornaments are off the tree.

Worktext pages 95-96

Apply the memory verse to everyday life.

Lesson 4

Materials

- *Young Person's Guide to the Orchestra* by Benjamin Britten (optional)

Reattach the instrument ornaments to the Christmas tree in verse order.

Hymn: "There's a Song in the Air!"

Sing the first two verses (Worktext page 275). Play the recording and sing together verses 1 and 2.

Memory Verses—Luke 1:37-38

Practice the memory verses. Direct attention to the Christmas tree decorated with the instrument ornaments. Read the verses together. Direct the students to close their eyes or to put their heads down on their desks. Call on a student to choose two ornaments from the tree. When the students open their eyes, select a student to identify which words are missing. Read the verses together without those words. Continue in this way until all the ornaments are off the tree.

Introducing the Application Story

Review Part 1 of the application story. Discuss what might be written on the paper that Claudio Focaccio gave to Brad.

Application Story

Read the following story to the students.

A Usable Instrument (Part 2)

Brad stared at the piece of paper and the five words on it. *An instrument cannot play itself.* "That's it?" Brad asked aloud.

His father stepped into the doorway. "How was the concert?" he asked.

"Good," said Brad. He was still looking at the piece of paper.

"Nothing special about it?" Dad asked. It took a few seconds for Brad to hear the question.

"Oh, yeah," he said. "I met Claudio Focaccio. And he gave me this piece of paper." Dad took the paper and read it.

"What do you think about it?" he asked.

"I don't get it," said Brad. "Everyone knows that my piano isn't going to play itself. Do *you* know what it means?"

Dad smiled, "Why don't you take off your suit before it gets wrinkled and then get your Bible. I think I know what he means."

Brad hung up his suit coat and sat on the bed next to his father. "Have you heard anything called an instrument besides a musical instrument?"

"Well, Grandpa uses instruments to fly his plane." Brad thought for a moment. "And doctors use instruments to do operations."

Dad looked over at Brad. "What do those instruments all have in common?"

"They are used to get some kind of job done."

"Maybe Claudio wasn't just talking about pianos, or planes, or scalpels." Dad paused. "Who has the greatest work to do with His instruments—greater than any pianist, pilot, or doctor—greater than any person on earth?"

"God does." Brad wrinkled his forehead, then began to smile. "Do you mean that I'm God's instrument?"

"That's right," said Dad. "God has chosen each Christian to do a special part of His work for His glory. Can you think of a task God has given you to do right now in a way that will bring glory to Him?"

Brad looked sideways at Dad. "Oh—practice the piano." He sighed. "But it's so hard to keep at it. I mean to, and then . . ."

"Turn to Philippians 2 and read verse 13."

Brad read the verse, "For it is God which worketh in you both to will and to do of His good pleasure." Then Brad picked up the piece of paper from Claudio. *An instrument cannot play itself.*

Dad leaned forward and said, "I think perhaps you are trying to practice faithfully all by yourself. God will not only help you want to do what pleases Him—He will help you carry through and do it too. Why don't you ask Him to help you?"

Brad flattened out the folded piece of paper and put it next to his bed. The next day he put the piece of paper on the piano. He continued to practice every day for the next week. By the time Christmas Eve came, Brad had his piece well memorized.

"Why don't you play it for us tonight?" suggested Mom. Mom and Dad followed Brad to the piano, where he played his piece for them. Then Dad asked Brad whether he would like to open one Christmas gift.

Brad chose a small one under the tree—just the perfect size to be Piano Pete's new CD. When Brad opened it, he found that it was something more meaningful. It was a plaque which read the words he had come to understand: *An instrument cannot play itself.*

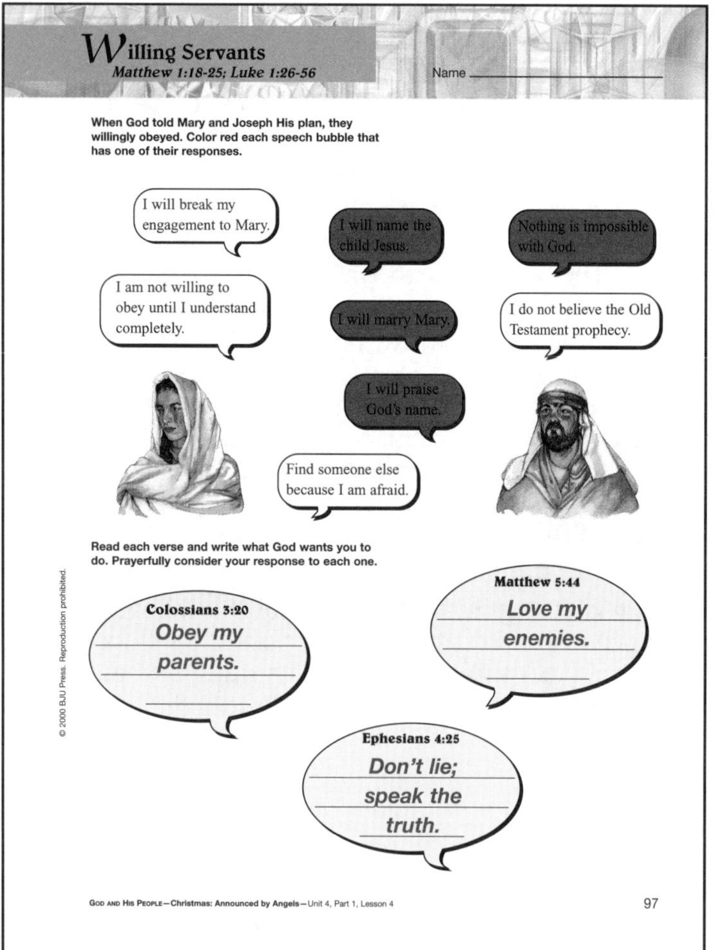

Willing Servants
Matthew 1:18-25; Luke 1:26-56

Name ____________

When God told Mary and Joseph His plan, they willingly obeyed. Color red each speech bubble that has one of their responses.

I will break my engagement to Mary.

I will name the child Jesus.

Nothing is impossible with God.

I am not willing to obey until I understand completely.

I will marry Mary.

I do not believe the Old Testament prophecy.

I will praise God's name.

Find someone else because I am afraid.

Read each verse and write what God wants you to do. Prayerfully consider your response to each one.

Colossians 3:20 — *Obey my parents.*

Matthew 5:44 — *Love my enemies.*

Ephesians 4:25 — *Don't lie; speak the truth.*

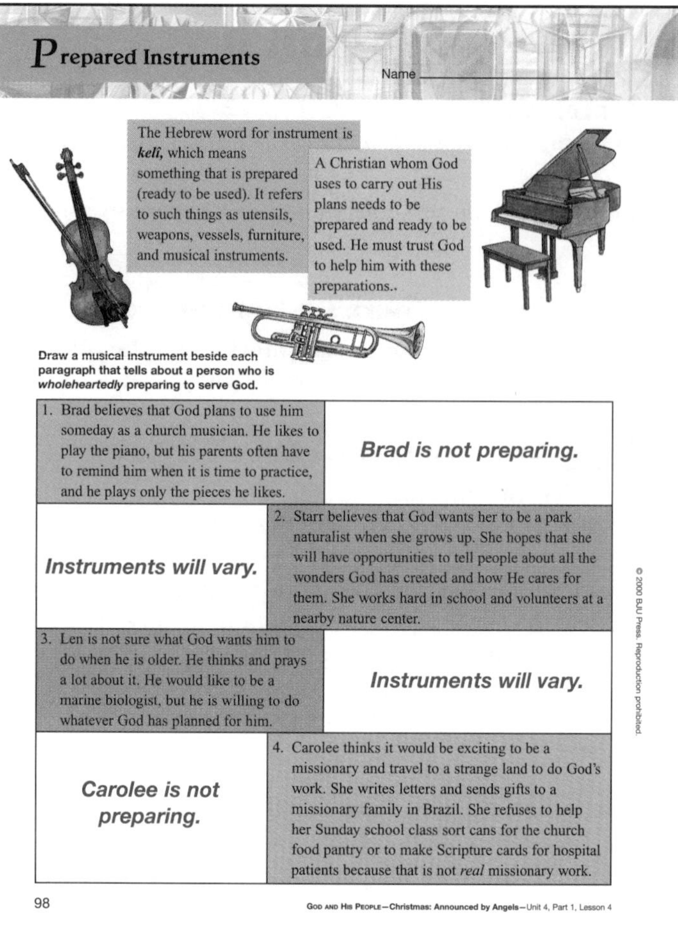

Prepared Instruments

Name ____________

The Hebrew word for instrument is *keli,* which means something that is prepared (ready to be used). It refers to such things as utensils, weapons, vessels, furniture, and musical instruments.

A Christian whom God uses to carry out His plans needs to be prepared and ready to be used. He must trust God to help him with these preparations..

Draw a musical instrument beside each paragraph that tells about a person who is *wholeheartedly* preparing to serve God.

1. Brad believes that God plans to use him someday as a church musician. He likes to play the piano, but his parents often have to remind him when it is time to practice, and he plays only the pieces he likes.	*Brad is not preparing.*
Instruments will vary.	2. Starr believes that God wants her to be a park naturalist when she grows up. She hopes that she will have opportunities to tell people about all the wonders God has created and how He cares for them. She works hard in school and volunteers at a nearby nature center.
3. Len is not sure what God wants him to do when he is older. He thinks and prays a lot about it. He would like to be a marine biologist, but he is willing to do whatever God has planned for him.	*Instruments will vary.*
Carolee is not preparing.	4. Carolee thinks it would be exciting to be a missionary and travel to a strange land to do God's work. She writes letters and sends gifts to a missionary family in Brazil. She refuses to help her Sunday school class sort cans for the church food pantry or to make Scripture cards for hospital patients because that is not *real* missionary work.

➤ **What was written on the piece of paper?** *("An instrument cannot play itself.")*

➤ **Why did Brad say he was an instrument?** *(because he was a Christian, and because God chooses each Christian to do a special part of His work)*

➤ **What did the message on the paper mean?** *(Believers cannot do the work God has chosen them to do without God's help.)*

➤ Brad had a difficult time practicing the piano. **Is there anything God wants you to do that seems difficult? If so, what can you do about it?** *(Pray and ask God for help.)*

Worktext page 97

Match dialogue with the correct character and locate information in Scripture.

Worktext page 98

Identify situations in which Christians are preparing to serve God.

Music Connection (optional)

Introduce an orchestra. If possible, play a recording which features various instruments of the orchestra, such as *Young Person's Guide to the Orchestra* by Benjamin Britten. Explain that an orchestra can symbolize all believers: each instrument is unique with its own sound and its own part, but all the instruments playing together create beautiful harmony. In God's plan each Christian is unique with special talents given by God. Each Christian has a special job to do, but all Christians working together accomplish God's work and bring glory to Him.

Going Beyond

Materials

- A wrapped Christmas gift box with a removable lid
- Art supplies: construction paper, glitter, felt-tip pens, etc.

Enrichment

Discuss giving your best to Christ. Show the wrapped box, explaining that this box will represent the students' gift to Christ. Give each student some art supplies to make a paper ornament; then challenge him to write on the ornament something that he can give or do for others that will bring glory to God (e.g., bake some cookies for an unsaved neighbor, offer to sweep the walkway for an elderly person, or plan to play a song on the piano for children's church). After each student has written his gift on the ornament, allow him to share his plans with the class and then to place the ornament in the gift box. (*Note:* As a follow-up, you may wish to ask the students how their gift-giving experiences went.)

The Birth and Childhood of a King

Preview

Doctrines

- Christ became man (incarnation) (John 1:14)—Lesson 1
- God has shown Himself in the Bible (John 5:39)—Lesson 1
- The Son is God (Hebrews 1:8)—Lesson 2

Skills and Applications

- Learn Luke 2:52
- Learn the divisions of the Old Testament
- Recall facts and details
- Realize that Jesus, the Son of God, became man
- Apply Bible knowledge to everyday life

Lesson 1

Materials

- TimeLine and picture: *Birth of Christ*
- An adult-sized coat and/or shoes (optional)
- A copy of Supplement page S70, "Taking a Census" for each student. (optional)
- Highlighter for each student (optional)

Memory Verse—Luke 2:52

Principle: Jesus is our example. Locate **Luke 2:52** and read it aloud as the students read silently. Choose a student to put on the adult-sized coat and/or shoes. Explain that someday the student will most likely fit into these clothes, but right now the items are too large for him. Point out that believers need to grow not only physically, or in stature, but also spiritually and socially. Choose volunteers to read the verse aloud; then direct the students to highlight the verse in their Bibles (optional) and to mark the location with the Unit 4 Bookmark.

Background Information

Census—*The Roman governor called for everyone to be registered and to be taxed. Each man was commanded to go to the city of his birth. When he registered, the census takers listed his name, his occupation, who his relatives were, how many lived in his home, and what he owned (such as a donkey or a house). All of these things determined how much money in taxes he owed.*

Caesar Augustus (63 B.C.–A.D. 14)—*Gaius Julius Caesar Octavianus (Octavian) was given the title "Augustus," meaning "the exalted," by the Roman Senate in 27 B.C. when he came to the throne as Rome's first emperor. (*Note: *He was the great-nephew and adopted son of Julius Caesar.) He became ruler along with Julius Caesar's chief lieutenant, Mark Anthony, when Julius Caesar was assassinated. Caesar Augustus became sole ruler after Mark Anthony's suicide and ruled Rome until his death in A.D. 14. He maintained peace and prosperity throughout the spreading empire. God had announced many years before that the Christ child would be born in Bethlehem. Caesar's decree that everyone go to his city of birth was part of God's plan.*

King Herod the Great—*He was the ruler over an area of Judea that became part of the Roman Empire. He made a name for himself with the Romans, who valued peace and order, by putting down a Galilean rebellion. In gratitude the Roman Senate gave Herod the title "King of the Jews." The Jews did not willingly accept Herod because he was an outsider, an Idumean (from Edom) whose family was among those forcibly converted to Judaism during the period after the Maccabean revolt. He ruled ruthlessly and maintained control over all the major institutions of the Jews. He renovated his capital, Jerusalem, and built the third temple there. He died shortly after the birth of Christ.*

Introducing the Bible Account

Explain census. Share the background information about the census and about Caesar Augustus (optional).

Bible Account

Read the following Bible account or read Matthew 2:1-12 and Luke 2:1-20.

The Birth of a King

There came a decree from Caesar Augustus that each Roman citizen was to go to the city of his heritage in order to be counted and taxed. God had said through the prophet Micah that the Christ child would be born in Bethlehem (Micah 5:2). Joseph and Mary lived in Galilee. God used a Roman emperor, Caesar Augustus, to continue His perfect plan. At the appointed time everyone went to his own city to be taxed.

Joseph, who was living in the city of Nazareth in Galilee, took Mary, his espoused wife, who was about to give birth to a child, and they traveled the long, rugged way to the city of David, which is called Bethlehem. While they were in Bethlehem, Mary came to the time when her child would be born. Joseph looked all over Bethlehem, but the city was so crowded because of the census taking that he could not find a place for them to stay. Finally an innkeeper offered them shelter that was meant for the animals of the people staying in his inn.

Mary "brought forth her firstborn son, and wrapped him in swaddling clothes, and laid him in a manger."

Not far from Bethlehem a group of shepherds were out in the field, watching over their sheep. Suddenly, the angel of the Lord appeared before the shepherds. The shepherds were afraid, but the angel said, "Fear not: for, behold I bring you good tidings of great joy, which shall be to all people. For unto you is born this day in the city of David a Saviour, which is Christ the Lord." Then appeared a large group of angels, praising God. When the angels went away, the shepherds went quickly into the city of Bethlehem to see whether they could find the Christ child that the angel had told them about. They found Mary and Joseph and the Christ child just as the angel had said. The shepherds went and told others about what they had seen and believed. Mary remembered all these things and thought about them, keeping them in her heart.

Before the Lord Jesus was two years of age, wise men came to Jerusalem and went to King Herod and asked him, "Where is he that is born King of the Jews? for we have seen his star in the east, and are come to worship him." Herod told the wise men to come back to him and to report where they had found this next king of the Jews so he could also go and worship Him. Now Herod really did not intend to go worship the Christ child. Herod was upset that there was a king born; he wanted to find this child so that he could get rid of Him.

The wise men did find the Christ child. They followed a special star from Jerusalem to Bethlehem and then to the house where the child was. They worshiped Him, and they gave Him gifts. God warned them in a dream not to return to Herod, so they went back to their country another way.

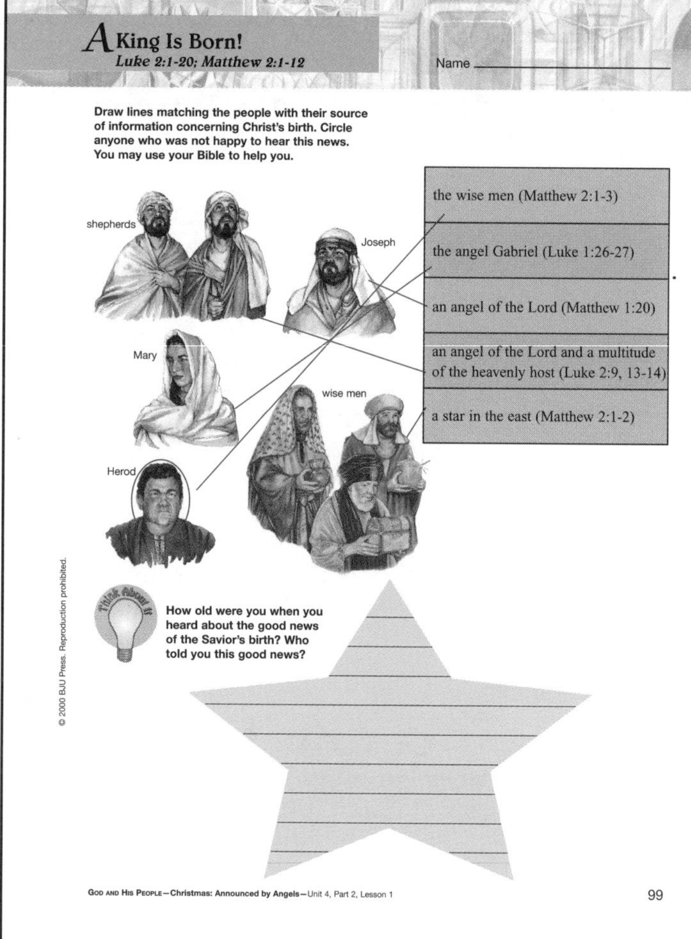
A King Is Born!
Luke 2:1-20; Matthew 2:1-12

Name ____________

Draw lines matching the people with their source of information concerning Christ's birth. Circle anyone who was not happy to hear this news. You may use your Bible to help you.

How old were you when you heard about the good news of the Savior's birth? Who told you this good news?

God and His People—Christmas: Announced by Angels—Unit 4, Part 2, Lesson 1 99

➤ **Why did Joseph and Mary have to go from Nazareth of Galilee to Bethlehem?** *(to obey the law that everyone go to the city of his birth to be counted and taxed)*

➤ **Who told the shepherds about the Christ child, and what did the shepherds do?** *(The angel told the shepherds, who went to worship the Christ child.)*

➤ **How did King Herod find out that the Christ child had been born, and why was he not told where the child was?** *(The wise men [Magi] told him about Christ's birth but were warned by an angel of God in a dream to return home another way.)*

TimeLine

Place the *Birth of Christ* on the TimeLine. Choose a student to attach the card for the *Birth of Christ* onto the TimeLine as you guide the students in gluing their picture onto their individual TimeLines. Explain the way we mark time changes at the birth of Jesus—B.C. ("before Christ") from A.D. (*Anno Domini,* "in the year of the Lord").

Worktext page 99

Recall facts about the Bible account.

Singing with Understanding
"There's a Song in the Air" (v. 3)

Name ______________________

In the light of that star
Lie the ages impearled,

Impearled means "adorned as if with pearls." Circle the words that could be used to describe pearls.

UGLY shining dull

valuable beautiful

... In the homes of the nations
That Jesus is King!

Think About It

Is Jesus the King in *every* home? Has *everyone* heard how God sent His Son to be the Savior of the world? What would you tell someone who has never heard this good news? Write your answer on the lines below.

100 God and His People—Christmas: Announced by Angels—Unit 4, Part 2, Lesson 1

Hymn: "There's a Song in the Air!"

Teach the third verse (Worktext page 275). Play the recording of the third verse as the students follow along.

➤ **What is a *hearth?*** *(a fireplace floor)* Explain that sometimes *hearth* refers to "home" or "family life."

Sing verse 3 together; then sing verses 1-3.

Worktext page 100

Singing with understanding, verse 3.

History Connection (optional)

Conduct a census. Explain that generally a census in America is a counting of the population, or people, in a given area. In the United States a census has been taken every ten years since 1790. Give each student a copy of Supplement page S70, "Taking a Census," encouraging them to take part in a class census. Explain also that the census determines the number of representatives a state or county has in the government of the United States.

One-on-One: Give a copy of Supplement page S70 to each family member to complete. Give a copy to friends and relatives living nearby to complete (optional).

Lesson 2

Memory Verse—Luke 2:52

Practice the memory verse. Locate **Luke 2:52** and read the verse aloud as the students read silently.

➤ **What are four ways that people grow?** *(physically, spiritually, mentally, and socially)*

➤ **How can you grow better physically?** *(Possible answers include exercising, eating the right foods, and getting plenty of rest.)*

➤ **How can you grow mentally?** *(Possible answers include going to school, reading, and studying.)*

➤ **How can you grow socially?** *(Possible answers include having a variety of friends; being involved in church, clubs, and teams; and using good manners.)*

➤ **How can you grow spiritually?** *(Possible answers include going to church, reading the Bible, and praying.)*

Read the verse throughout the day for practice.

Hymn: "There's a Song in the Air!"

Sing the hymn. Play the recording and lead in singing verses 1-3 together.

Introducing the Bible Account

Describe family reunions and celebrations.

➤ **Have you ever attended a family reunion?**

➤ **What did the people do there?**

➤ **What other family celebrations have you attended?**

➤ **What did the people do at the celebrations?**

Tell the students that in the following Bible account they will hear about a time when Jesus went to celebrate the Feast of the Passover.

Bible Account

Read the following Bible account or read Matthew 2:13-16, 19-23 and Luke 2:41-52.

The Childhood of a King

King Herod discovered that the wise men had found the Christ child but had left the country without returning to him. King Herod was angry and ordered the killing of all the children two years old and younger that were in Bethlehem and in all Judea.

At the direction of God, Joseph and Mary took Jesus to Egypt to escape Herod's anger and jealousy. They returned when God's messenger told them it was safe. They settled in Nazareth, a city of Galilee.

Every year the people of Nazareth and other Jewish families would celebrate the Feast of the Passover. This celebration began when God led the Israelites out of Egypt. Joseph and Mary had been to this feast many times before. Jesus was twelve years old at this time. During the journey home after the long day, the men would walk together and the women would walk together until they arrived at a place to lodge for the night. When Mary and Joseph came together, they realized that Jesus was not with either of them. They looked everywhere and asked their relatives and friends. Finally, they went back into Jerusalem, and after three days they were able to find Jesus. He was in the temple court, talking with the teachers of Jerusalem. Mary asked Jesus, "Son, why hast thou thus dealt with us? behold, thy father and I have sought thee sorrowing."

Jesus answered His mother with these words, "How is it that ye sought me? wist [knew] ye not that I must be about my Father's business?" Jesus was in the temple, learning all He could and teaching the teachers and doctors by His answers to their questions. The teachers were amazed that this young boy knew so much about the Scriptures. Jesus left the temple with Joseph and Mary, and He grew in wisdom (true understanding), in stature (physical development), and in favor with God and men (pleasing God and getting along with others).

➤ **When did the angel of the Lord appear to Joseph in dreams?** *(when he was told to marry Mary, when he was told to take Mary and Jesus to Egypt to avoid King Herod, and when he was told to return from Egypt after the death of King Herod)*

➤ **Why did Mary and Joseph go to Jerusalem to celebrate the Feast of the Passover?** *(to thank God for leading the Israelites out of their bondage in Egypt)*

➤ **Where did Joseph and Mary eventually find Jesus?** *(in the temple)*

➤ **What was Jesus doing?** *(teaching others and asking questions so that He could learn more about the Scriptures)*

➤ **How can Christians learn more about their heavenly Father?** *(Possible answers include reading the Bible and attending church.)*

Worktext page 101

Complete sentences about Mary, Joseph, and Jesus at the Passover Feast.

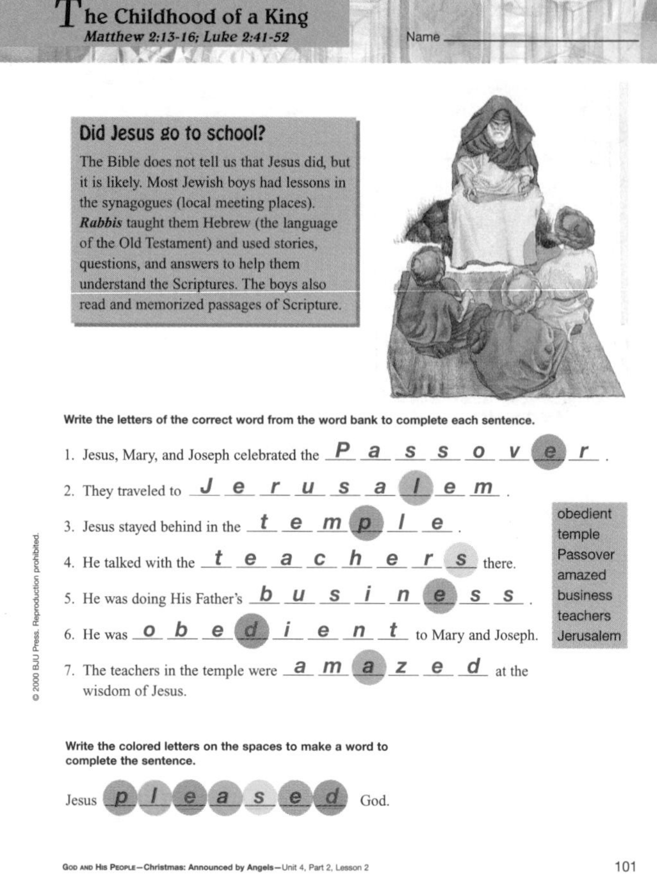

The Childhood of a King
Matthew 2:13-16; Luke 2:41-52

Name ____________

Did Jesus go to school?
The Bible does not tell us that Jesus did, but it is likely. Most Jewish boys had lessons in the synagogues (local meeting places). ***Rabbis*** taught them Hebrew (the language of the Old Testament) and used stories, questions, and answers to help them understand the Scriptures. The boys also read and memorized passages of Scripture.

Write the letters of the correct word from the word bank to complete each sentence.

1. Jesus, Mary, and Joseph celebrated the P a s s o v e r.
2. They traveled to J e r u s a l e m.
3. Jesus stayed behind in the t e m p l e.
4. He talked with the t e a c h e r s there.
5. He was doing His Father's b u s i n e s s.
6. He was o b e d i e n t to Mary and Joseph.
7. The teachers in the temple were a m a z e d at the wisdom of Jesus.

Word bank: obedient, temple, Passover, amazed, business, teachers, Jerusalem

Write the colored letters on the spaces to make a word to complete the sentence.

Jesus p l e a s e d God.

Lesson 3

Materials

- TimeLine and picture: *Jean Henri Merle d'Aubigné*
- Scale and yardstick or meter stick (optional)

Hymn: "There's a Song in the Air!"

Sing the hymn (Worktext page 275). Play the recording and sing all three verses together.

Hero of the Faith

Read the following story based on the life of Jean Henri Merle d'Aubigné.

Jean Henri Merle d'Aubigné

Jean Henri Merle d'Aubigné (Dō•bēn•yā) was born in Geneva, Switzerland, in 1794. When Jean Henri was five years old, his father was sent on a mission for the government and never returned home. Jean Henri and his two brothers were left without a father. However, God was watching out for Jean Henri, even though he had never accepted Christ as his Savior.

As an adult Merle d'Aubigné surprised his family by going into the ministry rather than the business world. During this time God was working in Merle d'Aubigné's heart.

In 1813 Merle d'Aubigné entered the Geneva Academy, which meant that he would not fight in the wars that were taking place. During his stay at the Geneva Academy, he rarely studied the Bible and was taught very little about God and His Word. God continued working in his heart and continued preparing him for the day when he would hear the truth of the gospel.

One day in Geneva, Merle d'Aubigné met a businessman named Robert Haldane. Haldane conducted some Bible studies, and Merle d'Aubigné attended. His heart was challenged with what he was learning from the Bible. Jean Henri Merle d'Aubigné had thought all his life that man was basically good, but Robert Haldane showed him from the Bible that this was not true. Merle d'Aubigné accepted Christ as his Savior. As he began to study the Bible more, he realized that his old religious beliefs were false.

Merle d'Aubigné studied a great deal about the life of Martin Luther. He visited Martin Luther's birthplace, as well as the castle where Luther had been a prisoner and had done much of the translation work for the German Bible. Merle d'Aubigné later wrote a book about Martin Luther called *The Triumph of Truth.*

Merle d'Aubigné enrolled in the University of Berlin, and as he grew older, he realized that God could use him to make a difference in the lives of other people. He went back to Geneva in 1831 and became the president of a new theological school and a professor of church history. Whenever he did any writing, which was what he loved best, he strove to be accurate. Even today people read the books he wrote. It took Merle d'Aubigné thirty-eight years to research and write thirteen books about church history. He taught and tried to do his best for God at this school until he died.

➤ **Because Merle d'Aubigné learned very little Bible at the Geneva Academy, what was his opinion about man?** *(He thought that man was basically good.)*

➤ **What did Robert Haldane do for Merle d'Aubigné?** *(He taught him the Bible, especially the truth that man is not basically good but is born with a sin nature.)*

➤ **Whom did Merle d'Aubigné study and write about a great deal?** *(Martin Luther)*

Jean Henri Merle d'Aubigné
(1794-1872)

Name ____________________

Imagine that you are a young man who has gone to college to become a Christian minister. You have chosen this career just as you might have chosen a career in business, or law, or some other field. You believe that man is good, so you do not see the need for a Savior. You have many other beliefs that are false, but you do not recognize your errors because you do not read your Bible. This is exactly how Jean Henri Merle d'Aubigné began his studies at Geneva Academy (Switzerland) in 1813, but God was working in his life to bring him to salvation.

One day Merle d'Aubigné met a businessman named Robert Haldane. The young scholar went to some Bible study sessions taught by Mr. Haldane and was challenged by what he heard. Merle d'Aubigné realized that his beliefs were wrong and that he needed to be saved. He accepted Christ and began to faithfully study God's Word.

Merle d'Aubigné enrolled in the University of Berlin (Germany) and completed his studies. He returned to Geneva and became the president of a new theological school and a professor of church history. He continued to learn and teach all of his life. He thoroughly researched the life of Martin Luther. He visited Luther's birthplace and the castle where Luther had translated much of the German Bible while a prisoner. Merle d'Aubigné wrote *The Triumph of Truth,* a book that is still regarded as an excellent source of information about Luther's life and work. His other books also remain helpful to those studying church history.

In all his studying, teaching, and writing, Merle d'Aubigné tried to do his best to the glory of God.

Answer the questions.

1. What was wrong with Merle d'Aubigné's life when he began his studies at Geneva Academy?
   He was not saved.
2. What was different when he began his studies at the University of Berlin?
   He had accepted Christ as his Savior.
3. What subject did Merle d'Aubigné study and teach?
   church history

➤ **What is Merle d'Aubigné most known for?** *(his research and writing about church history)*

TimeLine

Place *Jean Henri Merle d'Aubigné* on the TimeLine. Choose a student to attach the picture of *Merle d'Aubigné* onto the TimeLine at 1794-1872. Guide the students in gluing the picture of *Merle d'Aubigné* onto their individual TimeLines.

Worktext Supplement page 305

Review Hero of the Faith, Jean Henri Merle d'Aubigné.

Memory Verse—Luke 2:52

Practice the memory verse. Locate and read **Luke 2:52.** Write the verse on an erasable board, erasing a few key words; read the verse together. Continue erasing words and reading the verse together until all the words are erased and the students can say the verse from memory.

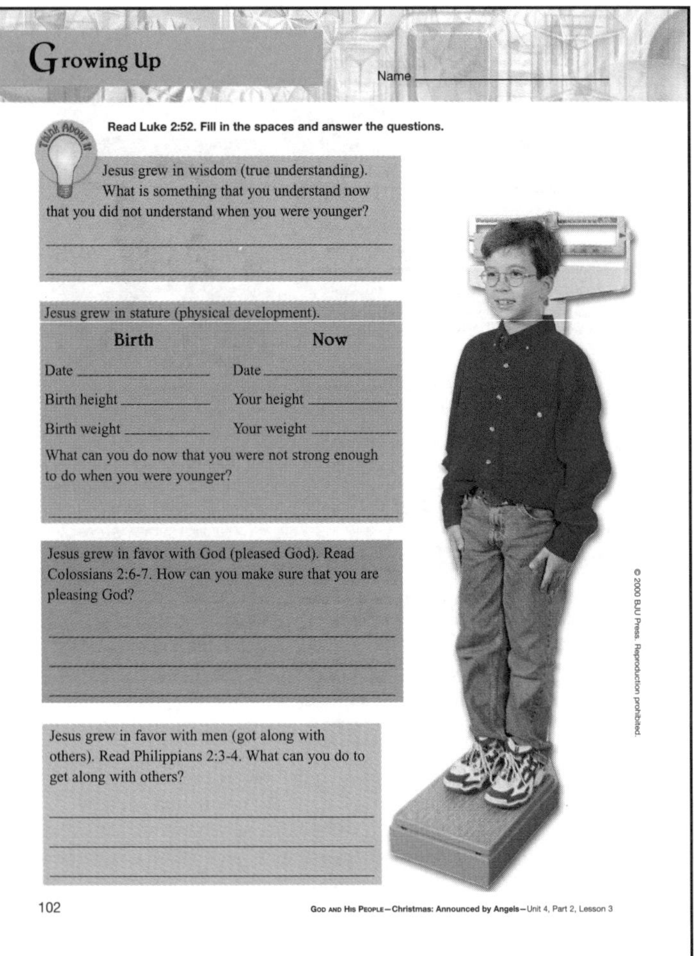

Growing Up

Name ____________________

Read Luke 2:52. Fill in the spaces and answer the questions.

Jesus grew in wisdom (true understanding). What is something that you understand now that you did not understand when you were younger?

Jesus grew in stature (physical development).

Birth	Now
Date ______	Date ______
Birth height ______	Your height ______
Birth weight ______	Your weight ______

What can you do now that you were not strong enough to do when you were younger?

Jesus grew in favor with God (pleased God). Read Colossians 2:6-7. How can you make sure that you are pleasing God?

Jesus grew in favor with men (got along with others). Read Philippians 2:3-4. What can you do to get along with others?

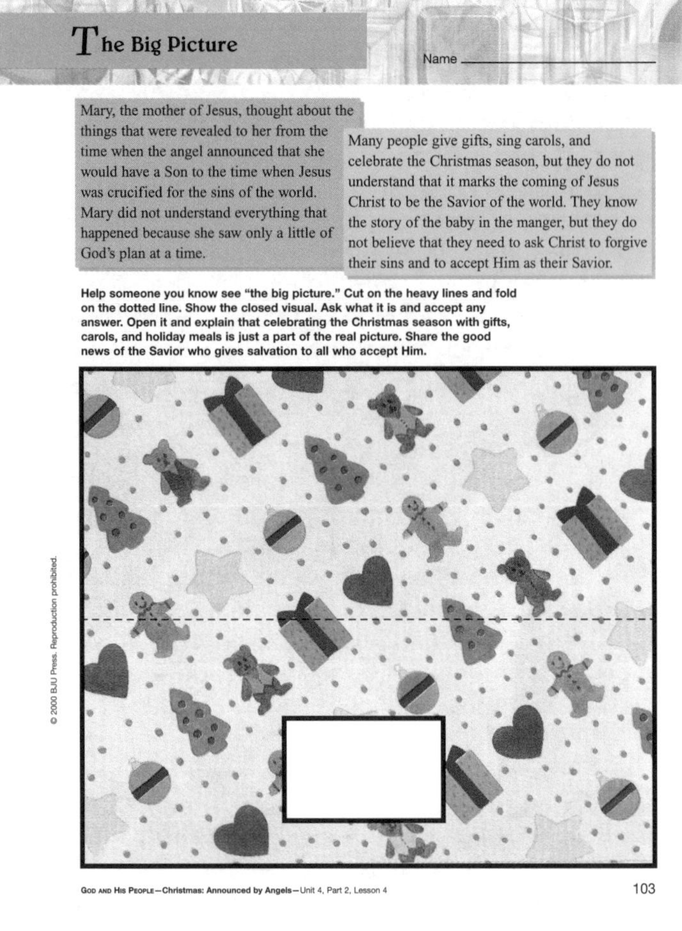

The Big Picture

Name ____________________

Mary, the mother of Jesus, thought about the things that were revealed to her from the time when the angel announced that she would have a Son to the time when Jesus was crucified for the sins of the world. Mary did not understand everything that happened because she saw only a little of God's plan at a time.

Many people give gifts, sing carols, and celebrate the Christmas season, but they do not understand that it marks the coming of Jesus Christ to be the Savior of the world. They know the story of the baby in the manger, but they do not believe that they need to ask Christ to forgive their sins and to accept Him as their Savior.

Help someone you know see "the big picture." Cut on the heavy lines and fold on the dotted line. Show the closed visual. Ask what it is and accept any answer. Open it and explain that celebrating the Christmas season with gifts, carols, and holiday meals is just a part of the real picture. Share the good news of the Savior who gives salvation to all who accept Him.

Worktext page 102

Apply the memory verse to personal life. (*Note:* This page may be completed at home.)

Lesson 4

Materials

- Old Testament Bible Book Cards
- Christmas card and one sheet of construction paper

Punch one hole in the center of a sheet of construction paper.

Hymn: "There's a Song in the Air!"

Sing the hymn (Worktext page 275). Play the recording and sing the hymn. Divide the students into groups and allow each group to sing a verse.

Memory Verse—Luke 2:52

Practice the memory verse. Locate and read together **Luke 2:52.** Allow students to practice saying the verse from memory.

➤ **What would happen if a child were to remain the same physically?** *(Answers will vary, but point out that he would not become like most adults.)*

➤ **What would happen if a child were to remain the same mentally?** *(Possible answers include he might never drive a car, work at a job, or have a family.)*

➤ **What happens if a Christian remains a spiritual child?** *(Possible answers include God may not be able to use him for what He had planned and he does not gain understanding of God.)*

Bible Study Skills

Review the Old Testament divisions. Divide the students into teams. Line up the teams. Show a Bible Book Card to the students at the front of each line. The student who first calls out the name of the division receives a point for his team. Let the students in front go to the end of their lines. Continue playing until all the Old Testament books have been reviewed.

One-on-One: The teacher shows a Bible Book Card to the student, and he answers with the name of the correct division.

Picture the Point

Illustrate God's omniscience. Cover the Christmas card with the construction paper. Direct the students to look through the hole and to offer suggestions of what is behind

The Big Picture (continued)

104 God and His People—Christmas: Announced by Angels—Unit 4, Part 2, Lesson 4

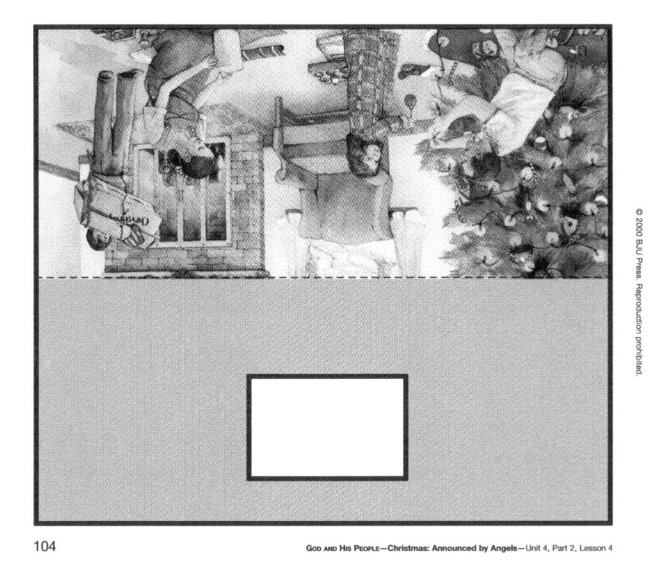

the construction paper. After allowing several guesses, show the students the Christmas card. Explain that they cannot tell exactly what is behind the construction paper because they cannot see the whole picture.

Explain to the students that God can see our entire lives before Him; we can only see from our birth to the present. We cannot see the future, but God can. God can guide us through each day, each hour, and each moment if we allow Him to be in control of our lives. Sometimes people make wrong choices and decisions and do what they want to do. It is important for Christians to follow God and to choose to do things that are pleasing to Him.

➤ **Which of the following people allowed God to guide them: Mary, Joseph, the shepherds, the wise men, King Herod?** *(all except King Herod)*

➤ **Do you choose to do things that will please God?**

➤ **Do you allow God to guide you throughout the day?**

Worktext pages 103-104

Make a visual to use in sharing the good news of the Savior, who brought salvation. Ask the following questions and then read the information about Mary seeing only a small part of God's plan. Explain the visual.

➤ **What do you see in the window?**

➤ **Who is pictured?**

➤ **Where is she?**

➤ **What is she doing?**

Going Beyond

Materials

- An 18" strip of adding machine paper for each student

Write the following Bible references for display: **Matthew 2:1-11; Matthew 2:19-24; Matthew 2:13-14; Luke 2:15-16; Luke 2:41-42; Luke 2:7**.

Enrichment

Make a time line for the childhood of Jesus. Give each student a strip of adding machine paper and direct him to divide it into six sections. Guide the students in placing the events (and drawing simple illustrations) in the correct sequence on the time line. Direct them to read the following passages and determine where to place each event on the time line.

Luke 2:7—birth of Christ

Luke 2:41-42—celebrated the Feast of the Passover in Jerusalem

Matthew 2:1-11—visited by wise men

Matthew 2:13-14—moved to Egypt

Luke 2:15-16—visited by shepherds

Matthew 2:19-24—moved to Nazareth

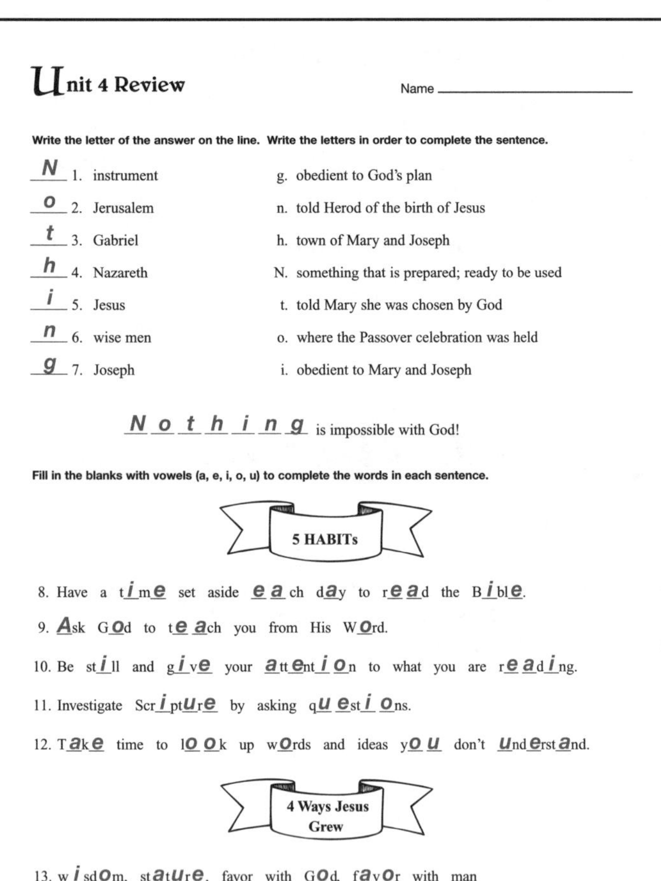

Unit 4 Review

Name ____________________

Write the letter of the answer on the line. Write the letters in order to complete the sentence.

N	1. instrument	g.	obedient to God's plan
o	2. Jerusalem	n.	told Herod of the birth of Jesus
t	3. Gabriel	h.	town of Mary and Joseph
h	4. Nazareth	N.	something that is prepared; ready to be used
i	5. Jesus	t.	told Mary she was chosen by God
n	6. wise men	o.	where the Passover celebration was held
g	7. Joseph	i.	obedient to Mary and Joseph

N o t h i n g is impossible with God!

Fill in the blanks with vowels (a, e, i, o, u) to complete the words in each sentence.

5 HABITs

8. Have a time set aside each day to read the Bible.
9. Ask God to teach you from His Word.
10. Be still and give your attention to what you are reading.
11. Investigate Scripture by asking questions.
12. Take time to look up words and ideas you don't understand.

4 Ways Jesus Grew

13. wisdom, stature, favor with God, favor with man

S58 Use after completing Unit 4 God and His People

Unit Review

Materials

- Copy of Supplement page S58, "Unit 4 Review," for each student

Guide a review of Unit 4. Review the people and events in preparation for the Unit 4 Test (optional).

Victory

Overview

Preparing the Teacher

In the Book of Romans, Paul tells us that the "flesh" is not subject to the law of God. Our flesh does not get any better in our Christian experience. We cannot fight sin in our own strength. Only as we *daily* feed on God's Word can we grow spiritually to fight Satan's attacks and to be perfected or matured, having all aspects of our lives properly adjusted spiritually. Our days often do not go as we planned them. Frustration is not the answer. Only God's Word can change the atmosphere of the world around us and increase our ability to believe God's promises and obey His commands. Christ quoted the Scriptures to Satan when He was tempted. He used the Word as a weapon to show us that we should do likewise. We should fill our lives with God's Word to push out evil. God's Word assures us of God's presence in all our trials. The lives of the martyrs are a reminder that God's Word could not be burned out of His people. Determine anew to allow God to engrave His Word in your heart. Read **II Timothy 3:16-17** and **II Corinthians 4:16.**

Preparing the Lessons

Part 1 Lesson 1 Materials—two small pieces of magnetic tape for each student

Part 1 Lesson 4 Materials—a blindfold

Part 1 Going Beyond Materials—drawing paper for each student, Bible dictionary or a set of encyclopedias

Part 3 Going Beyond Materials—drawing paper for each student, Bible dictionary or a set of encyclopedias

Part 4 Going Beyond Materials—drawing paper for each student, Bible dictionary or a set of encyclopedias

UNIT 5 VICTORY

Hymn: "Faith Is the Victory"

Part	Lesson number	Lesson pages	Worktext pages	Supplement pages	Bible Account	Application
PART 1: **JESUS CONQUERS TEMPTATION**	1	147	105-108		Jesus Tempted in the Wilderness (Matthew 4:1-11)	
	2	150	109-110		**Bible Study:** Temptation	
	3	151	111			"Keith Says 'No' "
	4	152	112			**Picture the Point:** Faith
PART 2: **JESUS CONQUERS DEATH**	1	154	113-14		Centurion's Servant Healed (Luke 7:1-10)	
	2	156	115-16		A Young Man Raised (Luke 7:11-17)	
	3	157	117-18			"The Victory Service"
	4	158	119-20		Jesus Restores Two Lives (Mark 5:21-43)	
PART 3: **JESUS GIVES VICTORY OVER SATAN**	1	161	121-22		Demoniac of Gadara Healed (Mark 5:1-20)	
	2	163	123-24			"The Shield of Faith"
	3	165	125		Boy Healed of Demons (Mark 9:14-29)	
	4	166	126			**Missionary Story:** Gladys Aylward
PART 4: **JESUS GIVES VICTORY OVER ETERNAL DEATH**	1	168	127-28		**Prophet Focus:** Haggai	**Picture the Point:** Gifts Are Free
	2	170	129-30		Lost Things Found (Luke 15:4-10)	
	3	171	131-32		Rich Man and Lazarus (Luke 16:19-31)	
	4	173	133-34			"The Greatest Victory"

Connections	Memory Verses and Principles	Bible Doctrines	Skills/Applications
	James 1:12-13 *Jesus Christ, our example, overcame temptation.*	**The Doctrine of the Bible** **Proofs for inspiration:** The Bible provides for man's physical and spiritual needs (Phil. 4:19). **The Doctrine of God** **Attributes of God:** God is all-knowing (omniscient) (Ps. 94:11). God is all-powerful (omnipotent) (Matt. 19:26). God is faithful (I Cor. 1:9). God is love (John 3:16). **The Doctrine of Man** **Original State of Man:** Man has immortality (I Cor. 15:54). **Final State of Man:** Unredeemed man experiences the second death (Rev. 20:14). Redeemed man experiences eternal life (Rev. 22:3-5). **The Doctrine of Salvation** **Provision of God:** Christ did not yield to temptations in His nature (Heb. 4:15). **Elements of Salvation:** Faith is turning to Christ (John 1:12). God restores the believer to His favor (adoption) (Rom. 5:1-2). **The Doctrine of Angels and Satan** **Organization of Angels:** Demons inflict men with evil (Matt. 17:15, 18). **Work of Satan:** He can control unbelievers (Luke 22:3). He tempts believers (Luke 22:31).	**Foundational:** • Realize that Jesus Christ overcame temptations • Be aware that Satan tempts Christians to sin • Realize that God is faithful in helping Christians overcome temptation • Realize that Jesus has the power to conquer death **Practical:** • Recall facts and details • Locate information in Scripture • Learn the divisions of the books of the Bible • Identify the correct title • Identify similarities and differences • Determine cause and effect • Use cross-references **Personal:** • Develop an understanding of Scripture • Develop a Bible reading habit • Know what to do when tempted to do wrong • Allow God to help in overcoming temptation • Apply Bible knowledge to everyday life
	James 1:14-15 *The result of sin is spiritual death.*		
	I Corinthians 10:13 *God is faithful in helping believers overcome temptation.*		
TimeLine: Haggai	Ephesians 2:8-9 *God's gift of eternal life is free.*		

Preparing the Unit 5 Bulletin Board

Cover the bulletin board with white paper and border it in blue. Center a large gold trophy with the title "Jesus Christ Gives Victory." Place ribbons in each corner and label as shown with the Unit 5 part titles.

Jesus Conquers Temptation

Unit 5, Part 1

Preview

Doctrines

- The Bible provides for man's physical and spiritual needs (Philippians 4:19)—Lesson 1
- Christ did not yield to temptations in His nature (Hebrews 4:15)—Lesson 1
- Satan tempts believers (Luke 22:31)—Lesson 1

Skills and Applications

- Learn James 1:12-13
- Recall facts and details
- Use cross-references
- Locate information in Scripture
- Be aware that Satan tempts Christians to sin
- Develop a Bible reading habit
- Realize that Jesus Christ overcame temptation
- Allow God to help you overcome temptation
- Apply Bible knowledge to everyday life

Lesson 1

Materials

- Chart 15, "Jesus Tempted in the Wilderness"
- Song: "The Bible Reading Habit"
- Two small pieces of magnetic tape for each student
- Unit 5 Bookmark for each student
- Highlighter for each student (optional)

Bible Study Skills, Worktext pages 105-106

Develop a Bible reading habit. Read the top part of page 105 to the students. Select students to read aloud the Bible reading guidelines, emphasizing that God is speaking to Christians from His Word and we should be listening with a ready heart and mind. Explain the four-week Bible reading activity on page 106. Encourage each student to complete the Bible reading, coloring the trophy after each day's reading. Lead in singing together the song "The Bible Reading Habit" from Worktext page 271.

Background Information

Satan—*God's enemy has many names, one of which is "tempter." The name Satan means "adversary" or "enemy." Every believer must be constantly on guard against Satan and realize that Satan is working to tempt man in every way possible.*

Fasting—*The term used in Jewish law is "afflicting the soul." It is the sacrificing of one's personal will. Fasts varied in strictness. Abstinence, or going without food, was often accompanied by wearing of sackcloth or tearing the garments and putting ashes on the head. Fasting did not necessarily mean observance of religious rites. Abstinence from food might simply mean that food was not available.*

Time Frame—*Jesus' baptism and temptation marked the beginning of His earthly ministry. The temptation demonstrates the meaning as well as the method of the gospel ministry. The temptation illustrates that we can triumph over temptation and sin. The method used reminds us that Satan is one who provokes us to sin and temptation.*

Introducing the Bible Account

Discuss temptation. Share the background information about Satan and fasting.

➤ **What does it mean to be tempted?** *(encouraged by someone or something to do that which is contrary to God's will)*

➤ **In what two areas is a person tempted?** *(need and/or desire)*

➤ **Who tempts you to sin?** *(Satan; flesh; world)*

Explain to the students that in the following Bible account they will hear how Christ was tempted.

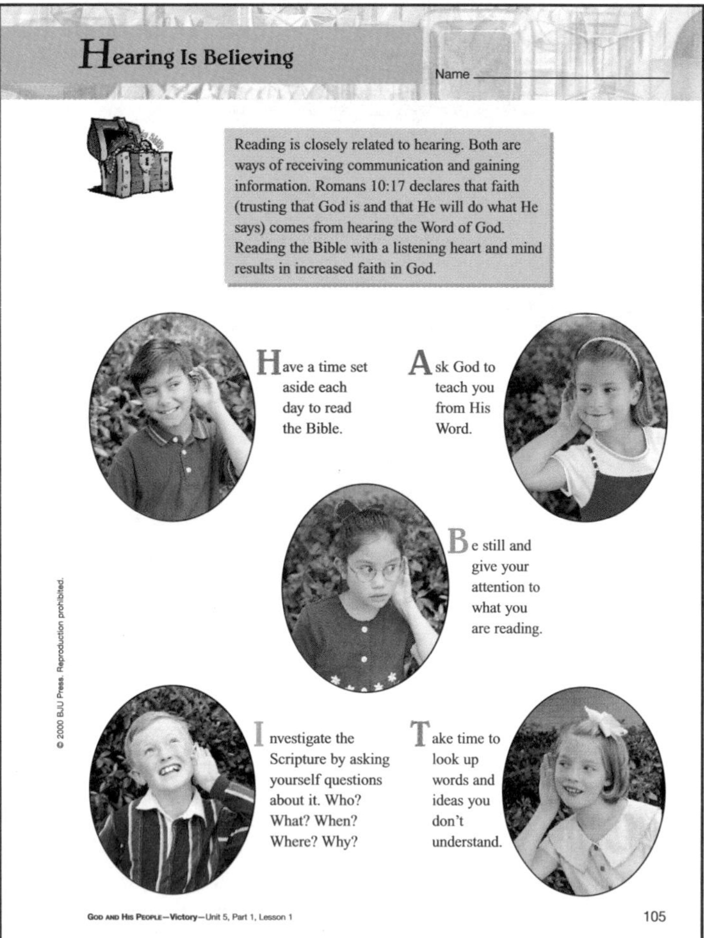
Hearing Is Believing

Name ______________

Reading is closely related to hearing. Both are ways of receiving communication and gaining information. Romans 10:17 declares that faith (trusting that God is and that He will do what He says) comes from hearing the Word of God. Reading the Bible with a listening heart and mind results in increased faith in God.

Have a time set aside each day to read the Bible.

Ask God to teach you from His Word.

Be still and give your attention to what you are reading.

Investigate the Scripture by asking yourself questions about it. Who? What? When? Where? Why?

Take time to look up words and ideas you don't understand.

© 2000 BJU Press. Reproduction prohibited.

God and His People—Victory—Unit 5, Part 1, Lesson 1 105

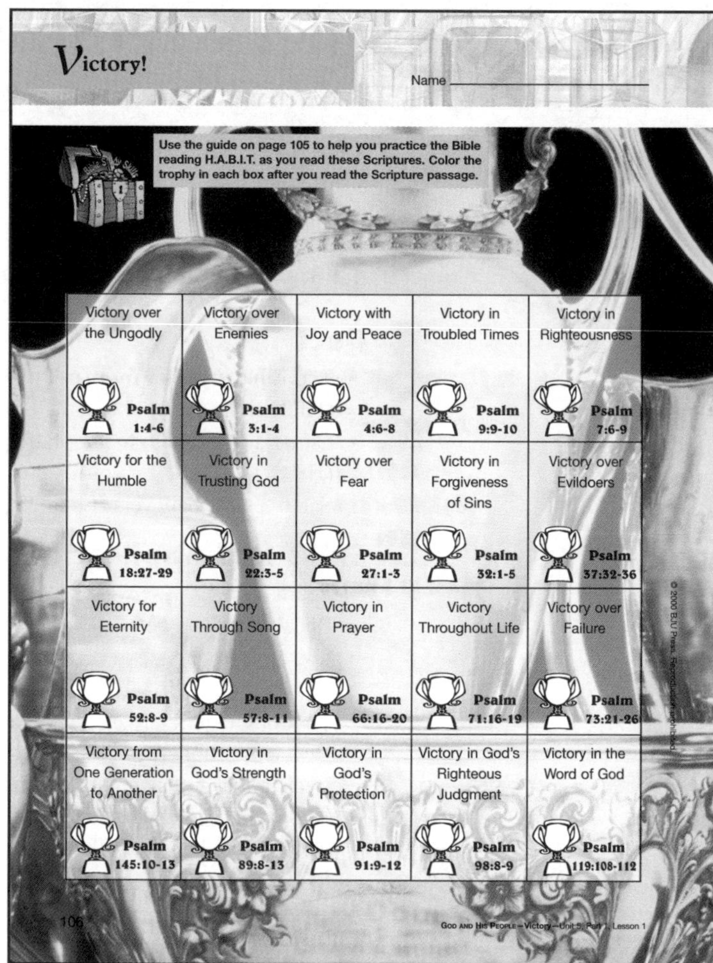
Victory!

Name ______________

Use the guide on page 105 to help you practice the Bible reading H.A.B.I.T. as you read these Scriptures. Color the trophy in each box after you read the Scripture passage.

Victory over the Ungodly Psalm 1:4-6	Victory over Enemies Psalm 3:1-4	Victory with Joy and Peace Psalm 4:6-8	Victory in Troubled Times Psalm 9:9-10	Victory in Righteousness Psalm 7:6-9
Victory for the Humble Psalm 18:27-29	Victory in Trusting God Psalm 22:3-5	Victory over Fear Psalm 27:1-3	Victory in Forgiveness of Sins Psalm 32:1-5	Victory over Evildoers Psalm 37:32-36
Victory for Eternity Psalm 52:8-9	Victory Through Song Psalm 57:8-11	Victory in Prayer Psalm 66:16-20	Victory Throughout Life Psalm 71:16-19	Victory over Failure Psalm 73:21-26
Victory from One Generation to Another Psalm 145:10-13	Victory in God's Strength Psalm 89:8-13	Victory in God's Protection Psalm 91:9-12	Victory in God's Righteous Judgment Psalm 98:8-9	Victory in the Word of God Psalm 119:108-112

© 2000 BJU Press. Reproduction prohibited.

106 God and His People—Victory—Unit 5, Part 1, Lesson 1

Bible Account

Read the following Bible account or read Matthew 4:1-11. Display Chart 15, "Jesus Tempted in the Wilderness." Direct the students to look at the picture and the map on Worktext page 107 as you read the account.

Jesus Tempted in the Wilderness

Jesus Christ, the Son of man as well as the Son of God, had just been baptized by John the Baptist. The Holy Spirit took Jesus up into the wilderness. While in the wilderness, Jesus fasted—He did not eat for forty days and nights. (Point out the wilderness on the map and read the background information if desired.)

Satan, also called the tempter, came and said to Jesus, "If thou be the Son of God, command that these stones be made bread." Jesus answered the tempter by quoting Old Testament Scripture. "Man shall not live by bread alone, but by every word that proceedeth out of the mouth of God."

Satan then took Jesus up to sit on the pinnacle or highest point of the temple in Jerusalem. (Point out the picture of the pinnacle [from a model of the temple] and read the background information if desired.)

Satan again said, "If thou be the Son of God, cast thyself down: for it is written, He shall give his angels charge concerning thee: and in their hands they shall bear thee up, lest at any time thou dash thy foot against a stone."

Jesus again responded to Satan with Old Testament Scripture. Using Deuteronomy 6:16, He said, "Thou shalt not tempt the Lord thy God." During this time of physical weakness, Satan had come to tempt Him. Jesus, however, did not give in to Satan; Jesus did not sin.

Satan tempted Jesus a third time. Satan took Jesus up into a high mountain. Once on the mountain, Satan began to point out to Jesus all the different kingdoms of the world. Satan said to Jesus, "All these things will I give thee, if thou wilt fall down and worship me." Satan was telling Jesus that He could be ruler over kingdoms that Jesus was already the ruler over. Jesus then responded to Satan, "Get thee hence, Satan: for it is written, Thou shalt worship the Lord thy God, and him only shalt thou serve." With that, Satan left Jesus alone, and the angels came to Jesus to "minister unto" Him.

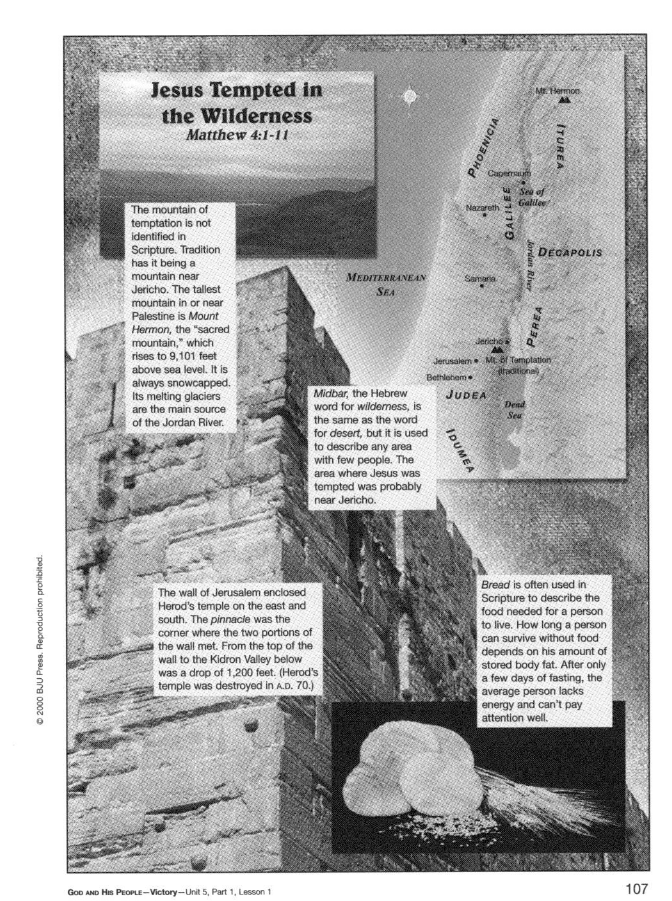

Jesus Tempted in the Wilderness

Matthew 4:1-11

The mountain of temptation is not identified in Scripture. Tradition has it being a mountain near Jericho. The tallest mountain in or near Palestine is *Mount Hermon*, the "sacred mountain," which rises to 9,101 feet above sea level. It is always snowcapped. Its melting glaciers are the main source of the Jordan River.

Midbar, the Hebrew word for *wilderness*, is the same as the word for *desert*, but it is used to describe any area with few people. The area where Jesus was tempted was probably near Jericho.

The wall of Jerusalem enclosed Herod's temple on the east and south. The *pinnacle* was the corner where the two portions of the wall met. From the top of the wall to the Kidron Valley below was a drop of 1,200 feet. (Herod's temple was destroyed in A.D. 70.)

Bread is often used in Scripture to describe the food needed for a person to live. How long a person can survive without food depends on his amount of stored body fat. After only a few days of fasting, the average person lacks energy and can't pay attention well.

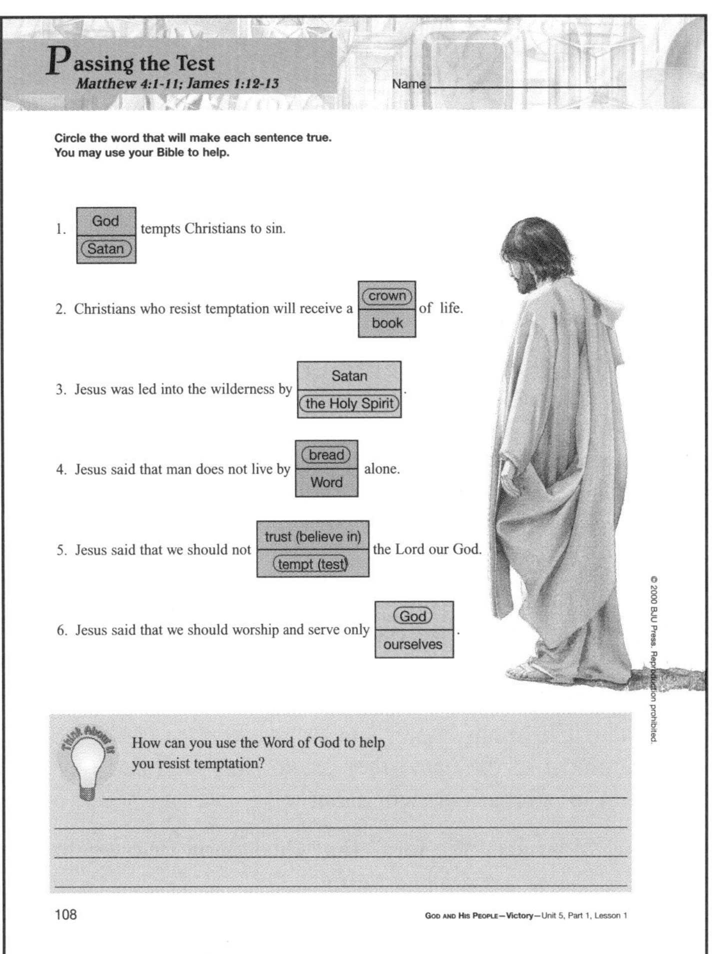

Passing the Test

Matthew 4:1-11; James 1:12-13

Name ____________________

Circle the word that will make each sentence true. You may use your Bible to help.

1. [God / (Satan)] tempts Christians to sin.
2. Christians who resist temptation will receive a [(crown) / book] of life.
3. Jesus was led into the wilderness by [Satan / (the Holy Spirit)].
4. Jesus said that man does not live by [(bread) / Word] alone.
5. Jesus said that we should not [trust (believe in) / (tempt (test))] the Lord our God.
6. Jesus said that we should worship and serve only [(God) / ourselves].

Think About It

How can you use the Word of God to help you resist temptation?

Point out that Jesus used two defenses against temptation—Scripture and prayer. Both of these defensive weapons are available to every Christian. The Lord has promised to believers that they will receive a crown of life for enduring trials and for doing the right thing in the midst of temptations.

InfoScene: "Jesus Tempted in the Wilderness"
Display Chart 15 for reference throughout this unit. Review and discuss the Bible account as time permits.

- ➤ **With what did Satan first tempt the Lord, and why could this have been tempting?** *(turning a stone into bread; Jesus had not eaten for forty days and nights and would have been hungry.)*
- ➤ **What was the second temptation, and why could this have been tempting?** *(jumping off the pinnacle of the temple and letting the angels catch Him; Jesus could have allowed this to happen to prove His power over angels.)*
- ➤ **What was the third temptation, and why could this have been tempting?** *(power over the world; Jesus could have received His earthly kingdom immediately without following God's plan for Him to go to the cross.)*
- ➤ **Why did God allow Jesus to be tempted?** *(to show that Jesus was human and can understand our temptations; to be an example to believers that they, through Christ's help, can overcome temptation)*
- ➤ **What are we demonstrating when we choose to sin?** *(that we prefer our way over God's way)*

Memory Verses—James 1:12-13

Principle: Jesus Christ, our example, overcame temptation. Locate **James 1:12-13** and read the verses aloud as the students read silently; choose volunteers to read the verses aloud while the other students follow along in their Bibles.

- ➤ **Why does God allow believers to be tempted?** *(God permits temptations so that we may learn to trust and obey Him more.)*
- ➤ **What tool does God give believers to defend themselves from Satan?** *(the Bible)*

Direct the students to highlight the verses in their Bibles (optional). Give each student a Unit 5 Bookmark to mark the location of the verses. Point out the illustration of the trophies, telling the students that often trophies are given to the winners, or victors, in competitions. Remind them that God wants believers to be victorious over temptations just like Christ was victorious. Direct the students to attach the pieces of magnetic tape onto the bookmarks and to place the Unit 5 Bookmark over the page.

Worktext page 108

Recall facts about the Bible account and apply the memory verse to everyday life.

Lesson 2

Preparation of Materials

Write the following examples of sins for display:

stealing	being unkind
lying	disobeying parents
gossiping	thinking wrong thoughts
cheating	

Memory Verses—James 1:12-13

Practice the memory verses. Direct the students to locate and read **James 1:12-13**; then let each student read one word aloud until both verses have been read. Repeat the procedure, encouraging the students to try to say their words without looking at their Bibles.

Hymn: "Faith Is the Victory"

Teach the first verse (Worktext pages 276-77). Read the words aloud as the students read silently. Explain that Christians are in a spiritual war—a battle between God and Satan. Christians know that God will win the battle, but in the midst of the battle they are to trust God and rely on Him for strength to fight Satan.

➤ **Who are "the foes" that Christians fight against?** *(Satan, world, and flesh)*

➤ **How long are Christians to fight in the battle against Satan?** *(until the Lord returns and defeats Satan)*

➤ **What will give us victory over sin and the world?** *(faith in God and knowing and using God's Word)*

Play the recording and sing verse 1 together.

Worktext page 109

Singing with understanding, verse 1.

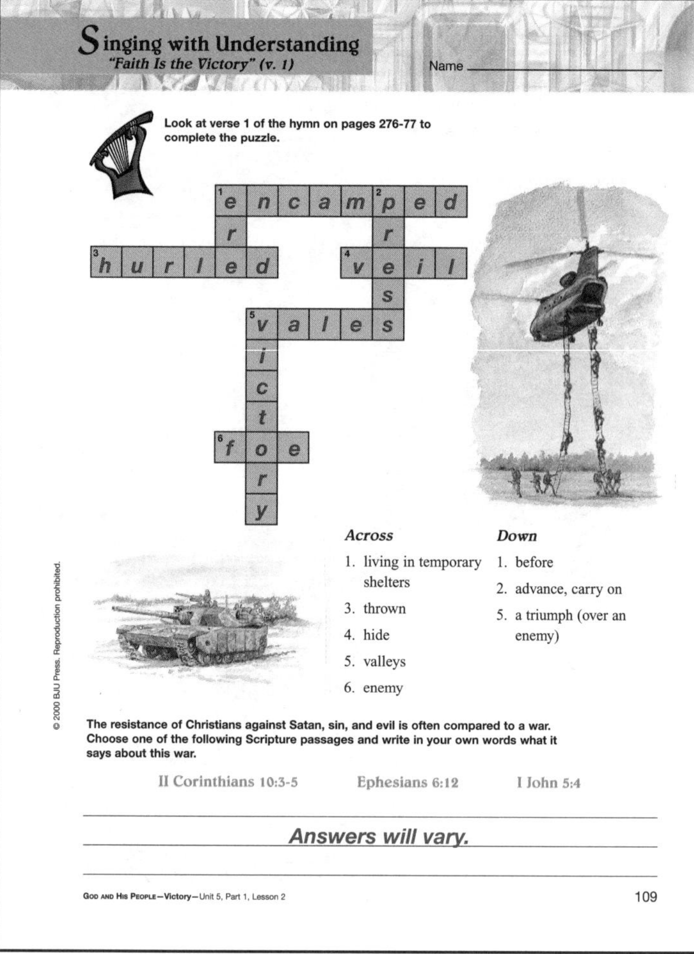

Singing with Understanding
"Faith Is the Victory" (v. 1)

Name ____________________

Look at verse 1 of the hymn on pages 276-77 to complete the puzzle.

Across
1. living in temporary shelters
3. thrown
4. hide
5. valleys
6. enemy

Down
1. before
2. advance, carry on
5. a triumph (over an enemy)

The resistance of Christians against Satan, sin, and evil is often compared to a war. Choose one of the following Scripture passages and write in your own words what it says about this war.

II Corinthians 10:3-5 Ephesians 6:12 I John 5:4

Answers will vary.

God and His People—Victory—Unit 5, Part 1, Lesson 2 109

Bible Study

Direct a Bible study about temptation. Remind the students of the importance of knowing God's Word in order to be able to fight temptation. Assign any of the following Scriptures to different students to read aloud and then to identify the temptations that are being discussed in the verses.

Exodus 20:15—stealing, cheating (stealing someone else's work)

Leviticus 19:11—stealing, lying, cheating

Deuteronomy 5:16—disobeying parents

Psalm 15:1-3—lying, gossiping, being unkind

Psalm 34:13—lying

Psalm 120:2—lying

Proverbs 12:22—lying

Matthew 5:44—being unkind

Romans 12:17—being unkind

II Corinthians 10:5—thinking wrong thoughts

Ephesians 4:25, 28, 32—lying, stealing, being unkind

Ephesians 6:1-2—disobeying parents

Philippians 4:8—thinking wrong thoughts

Hebrews 12:15—thinking wrong thoughts

Encourage the students to think about which of these areas they struggle with most often. Challenge them to copy the references listed in that category, write out or memorize the verses, and read or quote those verses to themselves the next time they are tempted.

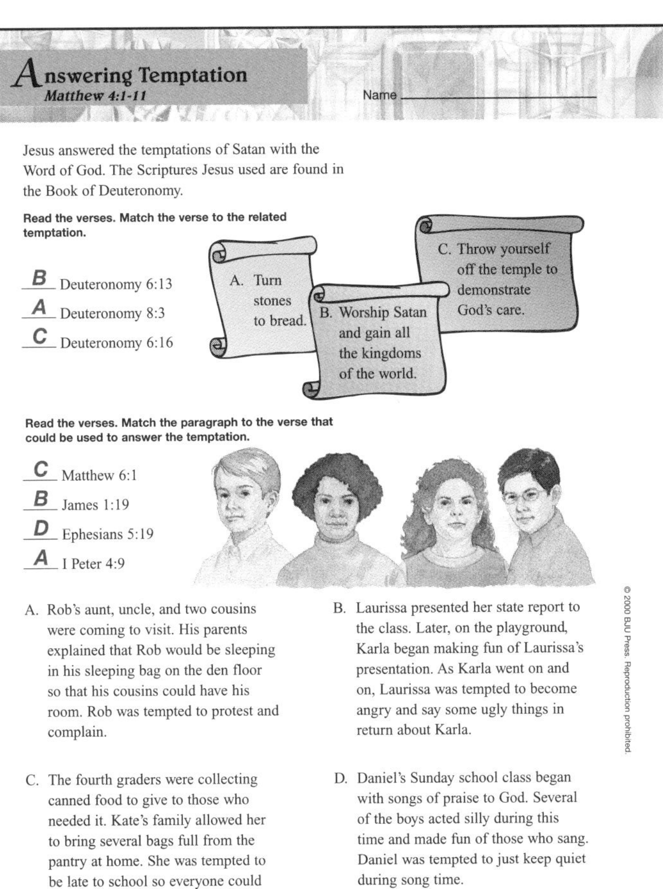

Answering Temptation

Matthew 4:1-11

Name ____________________

Jesus answered the temptations of Satan with the Word of God. The Scriptures Jesus used are found in the Book of Deuteronomy.

Read the verses. Match the verse to the related temptation.

B Deuteronomy 6:13
A Deuteronomy 8:3
C Deuteronomy 6:16

A. Turn stones to bread.
B. Worship Satan and gain all the kingdoms of the world.
C. Throw yourself off the temple to demonstrate God's care.

Read the verses. Match the paragraph to the verse that could be used to answer the temptation.

C Matthew 6:1
B James 1:19
D Ephesians 5:19
A I Peter 4:9

A. Rob's aunt, uncle, and two cousins were coming to visit. His parents explained that Rob would be sleeping in his sleeping bag on the den floor so that his cousins could have his room. Rob was tempted to protest and complain.

B. Laurissa presented her state report to the class. Later, on the playground, Karla began making fun of Laurissa's presentation. As Karla went on and on, Laurissa was tempted to become angry and say some ugly things in return about Karla.

C. The fourth graders were collecting canned food to give to those who needed it. Kate's family allowed her to bring several bags full from the pantry at home. She was tempted to be late to school so everyone could see her carrying in all that food.

D. Daniel's Sunday school class began with songs of praise to God. Several of the boys acted silly during this time and made fun of those who sang. Daniel was tempted to just keep quiet during song time.

110 God and His People—Victory—Unit 5, Part 1, Lesson 2

Worktext page 110

Identify Scriptures to combat temptations.

Lesson 3

Hymn: "Faith Is the Victory"

Sing the first verse (Worktext pages 276-77). Play the recording, directing the students to sing along. Assign groups, with each group singing a phrase; then change the order, with each group singing a different phrase.

Memory Verses—James 1:12-13

Practice the memory verses. Direct the students to read **James 1:12-13** silently; then close their Bibles to quietly say the verses to themselves; then reread the verses as a check.

Introducing the Application Story

Discuss temptation. Elicit from the students what to do when temptation comes and ways that they can avoid that temptation in the future. Tell the students to listen to find out what Keith does to avoid temptation.

Application Story

Read the following story to the students.

Keith Says "No"

Keith grinned as he heard the bell ring on the last day of school. It was time to go visit Grandmother! He hurried to the parking lot. Mom had his suitcase and was waiting to take him to Grandmother's house.

A few miles from Grandmother's, Keith suddenly remembered what had happened the last time he had been there. He had taken cookies from Grandmother's cookie jar and had gotten very sick. Knowing Keith's diabetes could make him sick if he ate too many sweets, Grandmother had reminded Keith not to eat the cookies unless she gave them to him. But the cookies looked so good that Keith had sneaked four of them out of the jar when Grandmother wasn't looking. Not only had Keith been punished for disobeying; he had also been sick for the rest of the day.

But this summer is going to be different, thought Keith. *I've accepted Jesus as my Savior.* Keith had begun reading his Bible and praying every night. *God will help me show Grandmother I'm different now,* he thought.

The morning after Keith's arrival at Grandmother's, he awoke to the delicious smell of baking cookies. When he came down to the kitchen, Grandmother was just filling the cookie jar with freshly baked oatmeal cookies. She set the jar on the shelf above the stove.

"Keith," she said, "I made these cookies for us, but your mom said no sweets between meals. You may have some at lunch but not until then. We don't want you to get sick again. Understand?"

Keith nodded.

Grandmother pulled on her sweater. "I'm going to a meeting up at church now. There's some cereal and toast here for your breakfast." She opened the door and then turned back and added, "Oh, I almost forgot. Mr. Clayton is coming to fix the refrigerator—he may come while I'm gone. You'll see his red truck in the driveway. Just ask him to come in. He knows what to do. And if you need anything, Grandfather's working in the barn—just holler for him."

Just as Keith was finishing his cereal, he heard a knock on the back door. He glanced out, saw the red truck, and went to the door. "Good morning," said the repairman. "I'm Mr. Clayton. I'm here to fix the refrigerator."

"May I watch you?" Keith asked as the man laid out some tools on the table.

"Sure thing. I'd be glad for some company." The man whistled softly while he worked.

Keith watched with interest for a while, but then his eyes strayed to the cookie jar on the shelf. He remembered the wonderful smell he had awakened to. *Mr. Clayton's almost finished,* he thought. *And Grandmother won't be back for at least an hour. I could take just one or two. They'd never be missed.*

Immediately James 4:7 came to Keith's mind: *Submit yourself therefore to God. Resist the devil, and he will flee from you.*

Keith stomped his foot hard. Mr. Clayton turned and looked at him, frowning. "Did you see a bug or something?" he asked.

Keith felt his ears grow warm. "I'm just telling Satan that I won't take any of Grandmother's cookies," he said.

Mr. Clayton laughed. "Sometimes that's the only way to deal with Satan," he said. "Just face him straight out, and he'll leave you alone. Well, I think I've got this thing working now." He gathered up his tools.

Keith walked out to the truck with Mr. Clayton and waved as he drove away. As soon as the red truck disappeared, he thought of the cookie jar again. "No," he said out loud. "I won't even go back in the house." He played with the kittens near the barn until Grandmother came home a few minutes later.

When Grandmother's car turned in the drive, Keith dusted himself off and ran over to the car. "I stopped at the store for a few things after our meeting," Grandmother said. "Want to help me with these? Then we'll plan our day and discuss our lunch menu— with cookies for dessert, of course."

As Keith took a sack of groceries, his heart was glad. God *had* helped him with temptation.

➤ **What had happened the year before when Keith stayed at Grandmother's?** *(He had stolen cookies and gotten sick.)*

➤ **What was different about Keith this time?** *(Keith had gotten saved.)*

➤ **What did Keith do to avoid the temptation?** *(He quoted Scripture to himself, stomped his foot, and told Satan "no." He also went outside so he would be away from the temptation.)*

I Just Couldn't Help It

Name ____________________

You might have said or heard someone say, "I just couldn't help it." But Christians *can* resist temptation. God's Word tells how.

Multiply each number by 6. You may use a separate sheet of paper to solve the problems.

A	B	C	D	E	F	G	H	I	J	K	L	M
11	9	3	10	7	5	13	2	8	1	4	12	6
66	*54*	*18*	*60*	*42*	*30*	*78*	*12*	*48*	*6*	*24*	*72*	*36*

Multiply each number by 4. You may use a separate sheet of paper to solve the problems.

N	O	P	Q	R	S	T	U	V	W	X	Y	Z
5	10	8	4	1	7	11	0	13	20	100	50	2
20	*40*	*32*	*16*	*4*	*28*	*44*	*0*	*52*	*80*	*400*	*200*	*8*

Follow the directions to complete the code. Use the code to spell each answer. You may use your Bible to help.

1. Consider it a *j* (6) *o* (40) *y* (200) to be tried (James 1:2).
2. Remember that God knows how to *r* (4) *e* (42) *s* (28) *c* (18) *u* (0) *e* (42) you (II Peter 2:9).
3. Ask God to *l* (72) *e* (42) *a* (66) *d* (60) you away from temptation (Matthew 6:13).
4. *W* (80) *a* (66) *t* (44) *c* (18) *h* (12) and *p* (32) *r* (4) *a* (66) *y* (200) (Matthew 26:41).
5. Make sure that you have the *s* (28) *h* (12) *i* (48) *e* (42) *l* (72) *d* (60) of faith (Ephesians 6:16).
6. Remember that *J* (6) *e* (42) *s* (28) *u* (0) *s* (28) was tempted in every way that you are tempted (Hebrews 4:15).

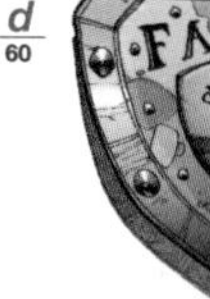

➤ **What can you do to avoid daily temptation?** *(Ask Jesus to help you when temptation comes, memorize Scripture, and avoid places and people where temptation is likely.)*

Worktext page 111

Apply Bible knowledge to everyday life.

Lesson 4

Materials

- A blindfold
- Old Testament and New Testament Student Bible Book Cards for each pair of students

Hymn: "Faith Is the Victory"

Sing the first verse (Worktext pages 276-77). Play the recording and lead in singing verse 1 together. Place the students in two groups, with one group singing the chorus, everyone singing verse 1, and the other group singing the chorus again.

Memory Verses—James 1:12-13

Practice the memory verses. Read and study **James 1:12-13** in pairs. Allow the students to explain what the verses mean, then read the verses or say them from memory.

Picture the Point

Illustrate faith. Blindfold a student; then let another student hold his arm and carefully lead him around the room. Blindfold another student and direct him to walk around the room—this time with no one leading him. Let the student walk only a few feet; then direct him to stop and take the blindfold off. Point out that the blindfolded student without a leader bumped into things while trying to find his own way—a picture of those who do not know Christ. They have no direction. Explain that the student who was led is a picture of a Christian who has faith in God to lead him. Faith requires obedience. If the blindfolded person had been told to turn right and had turned left, he could have been hurt. Avoiding temptation involves obedience to God and following the example that Jesus Christ gave.

- ➤ **What did the first blindfolded person need in order to follow the directions of the leader?** *(faith or trust)*
- ➤ **To follow Jesus Christ, what does a Christian need?** *(faith that Jesus Christ will do what He says He will do)*

Bible Study Skills

Practice the order of the books of the Bible. Explain that a good swordsman practices fighting with his sword. Challenge the students to sharpen their skills in locating the books of the Bible.

Divide the students into pairs, directing them to mix up one set of Old Testament and New Testament Bible Book Cards and to turn them face down. Tell each student to take turns choosing a Bible Book Card, identifying Old Testament or New Testament, and telling the name of the book that comes before and after the book named on the card. If he answers correctly, he receives a point. The person with more points at the end of the game time wins. (*Note:* Students may use the table of contents in their Bibles to check their partner's answers.)

Bible Study Skills, Worktext page 112

Use cross-references to learn more about Scripture.

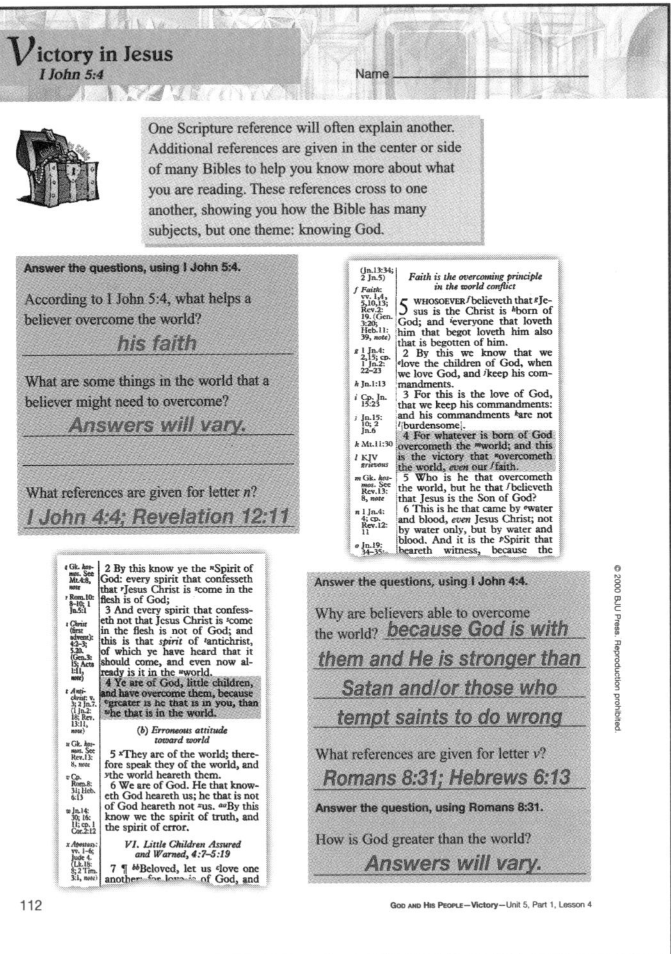

Victory in Jesus
I John 5:4

Name ____________________

One Scripture reference will often explain another. Additional references are given in the center or side of many Bibles to help you know more about what you are reading. These references cross to one another, showing you how the Bible has many subjects, but one theme: knowing God.

Answer the questions, using I John 5:4.

According to I John 5:4, what helps a believer overcome the world? *his faith*

What are some things in the world that a believer might need to overcome? *Answers will vary.*

What references are given for letter *n*? *I John 4:4; Revelation 12:11*

(Jn.13:34; 2 Jn.5)
f Faith: vv. 1,4, 5,10,13; Rev.2: 19. (Gen. 3:20; Heb.11: 39, note)
g 1 Jn.4: 2,15; cp. 1 Jn.2: 22–23
h Jn.1:13
i Cp. Jn. 15:23
j Jn.15: 10; 2 Jn.6
k Mt.11:30
l KJV grievous
m Gk. kosmos. See Rev.13: 8, note
n 1 Jn.4: 4; cp. Rev.12: 11
o Jn.19: 34–35;

Faith is the overcoming principle in the world conflict

5 WHOSOEVER [f]believeth that [g]Jesus is the Christ is [h]born of God; and [i]everyone that loveth him that begot loveth him also that is begotten of him.
2 By this we know that we [e]love the children of God, when we love God, and [j]keep his commandments.
3 For this is the love of God, that we keep his commandments: and his commandments [k]are not [l][burdensome].
4 For whatever is born of God overcometh the [m]world; and this is the victory that [n]overcometh the world, *even* our [f]faith.
5 Who is he that overcometh the world, but he that [f]believeth that Jesus is the Son of God?
6 This is he that came by [o]water and blood, *even* Jesus Christ; not by water only, but by water and blood. And it is the [p]Spirit that beareth witness, because the

q Gk. kosmos. See Mt.4:8, note
r Rom.10: 8–10; 1 Jn.5:1
s Christ (first advent): 4:2–3; 5:20. (Gen.3: 15; Acts 1:11, note)
t Antichrist: v. 3; 2 Jn.7. (1 Jn.2: 18; Rev. 13:11, note)
u Gk. kosmos. See Rev.13: 8, note
v Cp. Rom.8: 31; Heb. 6:13
w Jn.14: 30; 16: 11; cp. 1 Cor.2:12
x Apostasy: vv. 1–6; Jude 4. (Lk.18: 8; 2 Tim. 3:1, note)

2 By this know ye the [n]Spirit of God: every spirit that confesseth that [r]Jesus Christ is [s]come in the flesh is of God;
3 And every spirit that confesseth not that Jesus Christ is [s]come in the flesh is not of God; and this is that *spirit* of [t]antichrist, of which ye have heard that it should come, and even now already is it in the [u]world.
4 Ye are of God, little children, and have overcome them, because [v]greater is he that is in you, than [w]he that is in the world.

(b) Erroneous attitude toward world

5 [x]They are of the world; therefore speak they of the world, and [y]the world heareth them.
6 We are of God. He that knoweth God heareth us; he that is not of God heareth not [z]us. [aa]By this know we the spirit of truth, and the spirit of error.

VI. Little Children Assured and Warned, 4:7–5:19

7 ¶ [bb]Beloved, let us [c]love one another: for love is of God, and

Answer the questions, using I John 4:4.

Why are believers able to overcome the world? *because God is with them and He is stronger than Satan and/or those who tempt saints to do wrong*

What references are given for letter *v*? *Romans 8:31; Hebrews 6:13*

Answer the question, using Romans 8:31.

How is God greater than the world? *Answers will vary.*

112

God and His People—Victory—Unit 5, Part 1, Lesson 4

Going Beyond

Materials

- Bible dictionary or a set of encyclopedias
- Drawing paper for each student

Enrichment

Discuss and research swords. Read **Ephesians 6:10-17** to the students. Focus their attention on the "sword . . . which is the Word of God." Discuss how a sword is used in battle—not just in offense against the enemy, but also in defense. Using Scripture as Jesus Christ did with Satan in the wilderness is how believers are to use the "sword" that God has given to them.

Direct the students to use a Bible dictionary or a set of encyclopedias to find out about different kinds of swords, countries that had their own types of swords, and dates of usage. Direct each student to divide his paper in half, drawing a picture of his favorite type of sword on one part and designing his own sword on the other part.

Jesus Conquers Death

Preview

Doctrines

- God is all-powerful (omnipotent) (Matthew 19:26)—Lessons 1-2
- God is all-knowing (omniscient) (Psalm 94:11)—Lesson 2
- Man has immortality (I Corinthians 15:54)—Lesson 4
- God restores the believer to His favor (adoption) (Romans 5:1-2)—Lesson 4

Skills and Applications

- Learn James 1:14-15
- Recall facts and details
- Compare similarities and differences between Bible characters
- Realize that Jesus has the power to conquer death
- Allow God to help you overcome temptation
- Apply Bible knowledge to everyday life

Lesson 1

Materials

- Chart 33, "Palestine in the Time of Christ"

Introducing the Bible Account

Discuss sickness and death.

➤ **What happened to Adam and Eve when they ate from the tree of the knowledge of good and evil?** *(Possible answers include they sinned against God, they were sent out of the Garden of Eden, they would endure hardships in living, and they would eventually die.)*

➤ **When did sickness and death enter into the world?** *(when Adam and Eve sinned)*

Bible Account

Read the following Bible account or read Luke 7:1-10. Point out Capernaum on Chart 33, "Palestine in the Time of Christ."

Centurion's Servant Healed

In the town of Capernaum there lived a Roman centurion (a leader of about one hundred soldiers). The centurion had many servants. One day one of his servants became very sick. The centurion had heard that Jesus was on His way to Capernaum and that Jesus could heal people. So the centurion asked the Jewish leaders in the synagogue to tell Jesus about his servant's sickness. Even though this centurion was a Roman, he was special in that he still had dealings with the Jews. He believed in Jesus and had paid to have a synagogue built for the Jews. This was not common for someone in his position.

The Jewish leaders told Jesus of the sick servant and went with Jesus to the home of the centurion. When they were close to the centurion's home, the centurion, believing he was not worthy to speak to Jesus, sent friends out to meet Him with a message: "Lord, trouble not thyself: for I am not worthy that thou shouldest enter under my roof." The friends said that the centurion had asked Jesus to heal the servant from where Jesus was so He would not have to come into the house. Now the centurion was a powerful man. Whatever he said, his servants would do, but the centurion knew that Jesus had far greater power—that Jesus could heal his servant with the spoken word.

Jesus' response to the centurion was, "I have not found so great faith, no, not in Israel." When those that had been sent returned to the centurion's household, they found the servant healed of his sickness!

➤ **What was unusual about the centurion?** *(He was a Roman leader who associated with the Jews and believed in Jesus.)*

➤ **What did the centurion request of Jesus and why didn't he request it in person?** *(He asked for Jesus to heal his servant; he felt unworthy to ask Jesus personally.)*

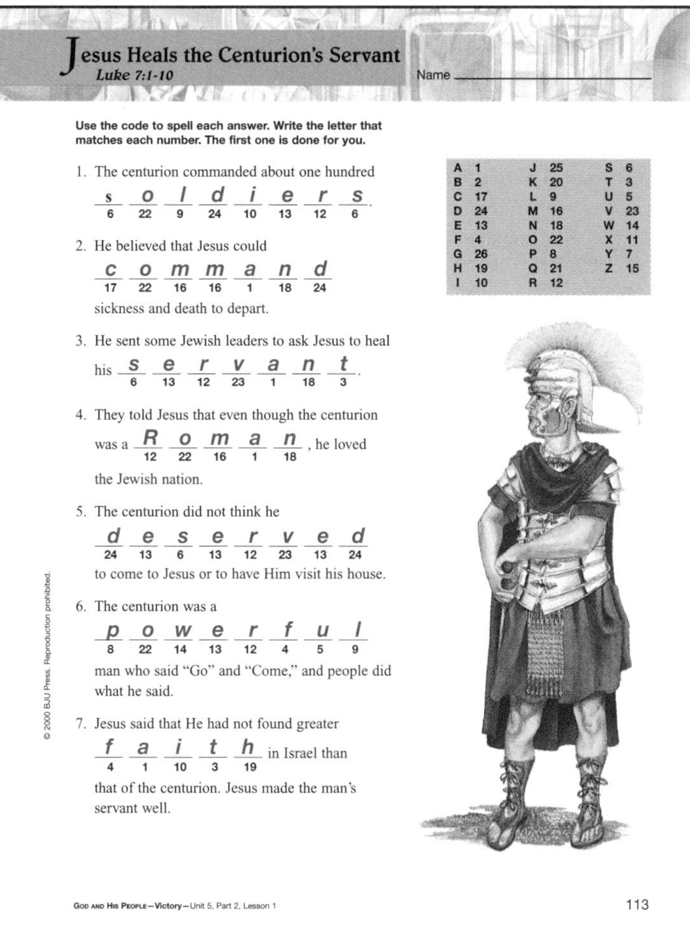

Jesus Heals the Centurion's Servant
Luke 7:1-10

Name ____________

Use the code to spell each answer. Write the letter that matches each number. The first one is done for you.

A 1	J 25	S 6
B 2	K 20	T 3
C 17	L 9	U 5
D 24	M 16	V 23
E 13	N 18	W 14
F 4	O 22	X 11
G 26	P 8	Y 7
H 19	Q 21	Z 15
I 10	R 12	

1. The centurion commanded about one hundred s o l d i e r s (6 22 9 24 10 13 12 6).
2. He believed that Jesus could c o m m a n d (17 22 16 16 1 18 24) sickness and death to depart.
3. He sent some Jewish leaders to ask Jesus to heal his s e r v a n t (6 13 12 23 1 18 3).
4. They told Jesus that even though the centurion was a R o m a n (12 22 16 1 18), he loved the Jewish nation.
5. The centurion did not think he d e s e r v e d (24 13 6 13 12 23 13 24) to come to Jesus or to have Him visit his house.
6. The centurion was a p o w e r f u l (8 22 14 13 12 4 5 9) man who said "Go" and "Come," and people did what he said.
7. Jesus said that He had not found greater f a i t h (4 1 10 3 19) in Israel than that of the centurion. Jesus made the man's servant well.

God and His People—Victory—Unit 5, Part 2, Lesson 1 113

- ➤ **How did the centurion demonstrate the faith that Christians should have?** *(He believed Jesus had the power of God and could heal his servant just by speaking.)*
- ➤ **Why is understanding the power Jesus has important to Christians?** *(Answers may vary.)*

Worktext page 113

Recall facts from the Bible account.

Hymn: "Faith Is the Victory"

Sing the first verse (Worktext pages 276-77). Lead in singing verse 1 together.

Memory Verses—James 1:14-15

Principle: The result of sin is spiritual death. Locate **James 1:14-15** and read the verses aloud as the students read silently.

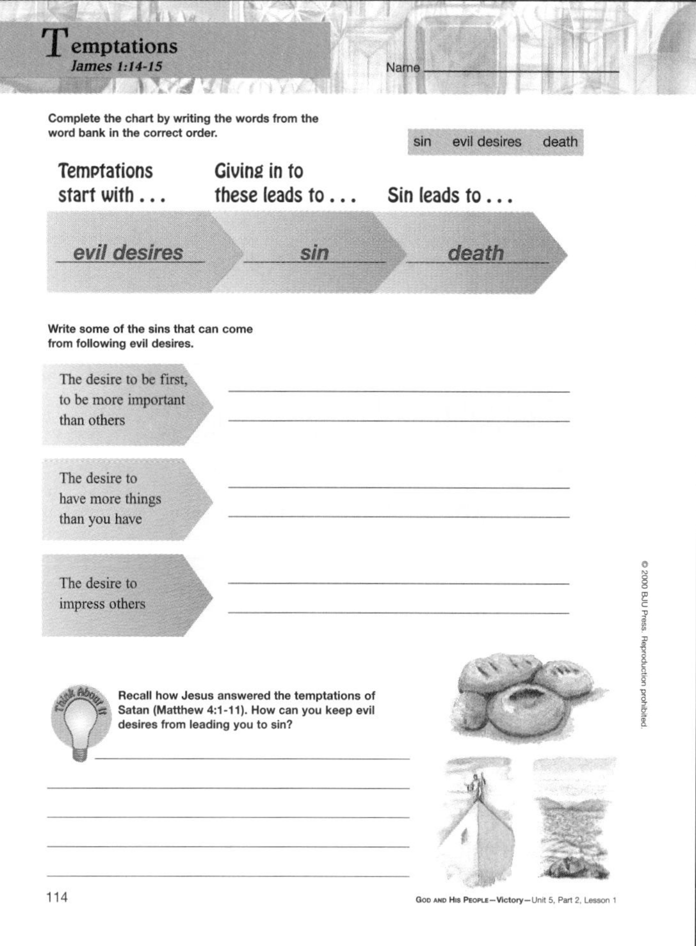

Temptations
James 1:14-15

Name ____________

Complete the chart by writing the words from the word bank in the correct order.

sin evil desires death

Temptations start with . . .	Giving in to these leads to . . .	Sin leads to . . .
evil desires	sin	death

Write some of the sins that can come from following evil desires.

The desire to be first, to be more important than others ____________

The desire to have more things than you have ____________

The desire to impress others ____________

Think About It: **Recall how Jesus answered the temptations of Satan (Matthew 4:1-11). How can you keep evil desires from leading you to sin?**

____

114 God and His People—Victory—Unit 5, Part 2, Lesson 1

- ➤ **Who is tempted?** *(everyone)*
- ➤ **Who does the tempting?** *(God does not tempt us but allows Satan to tempt us in order for our faith to be tested.)*
- ➤ **How does a believer resist temptation?** *(Ask God for help to overcome the temptation, memorize Scripture, choose to obey God's Word concerning the temptation, and avoid places where temptation is likely and people who are likely to cause it.)*

Direct the students to highlight the verses in their Bibles (optional) and to mark the location with their Unit 5 Bookmarks.

Worktext page 114

Develop understanding of the memory verses.

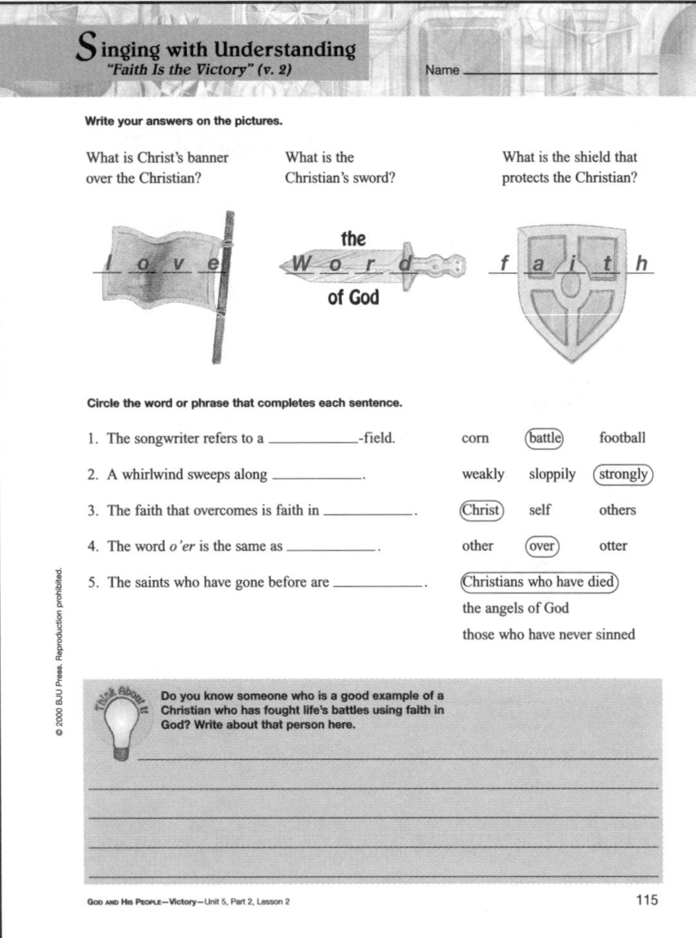

Singing with Understanding
"Faith Is the Victory" (v. 2)
Name
Write your answers on the pictures.
What is Christ's banner over the Christian?
What is the Christian's sword?
What is the shield that protects the Christian?
l o v e
the W o r d of God
f a i t h
Circle the word or phrase that completes each sentence.
1. The songwriter refers to a ________-field. corn battle football
2. A whirlwind sweeps along ________. weakly sloppily strongly
3. The faith that overcomes is faith in ________. Christ self others
4. The word o'er is the same as ________. other over otter
5. The saints who have gone before are ________. Christians who have died / the angels of God / those who have never sinned
Do you know someone who is a good example of a Christian who has fought life's battles using faith in God? Write about that person here.
© 2000 BJU Press. Reproduction prohibited.
God and His People—Victory—Unit 5, Part 2, Lesson 2
115

Lesson 2

Materials

- Chart 33, "Palestine in the Time of Christ"

Memory Verses—James 1:14-15

Practice the memory verses. Direct the students to locate and study **James 1:14-15** while you write the verses on an erasable board. Erase a word or phrase and select a student to read the verses. Continue erasing words and select students to read the verses until all the words have been erased and the students can say the verses from memory.

One-on-One: Prepare a copy of the memory verses with some of the words missing. Direct the student to use his Bible to complete the verses.

Hymn: "Faith Is the Victory"

Teach the second verse (Worktext pages 276-77). Play the recording, directing the students to read verse 2 silently. Explain that the saints are believers who have lived before them and have preached or witnessed for the Lord. Those believers who are doing the same today are following in the same path as these saints. Believers of the past, present, and future need to have this same faith. Lead in singing verses 1 and 2.

Worktext page 115

Singing with understanding, verse 2.

Background Information

Traditional Jewish Funerals—*Following the death of a relative, a person would wail loudly so everyone in the town would be aware that someone had died. Due to warm temperatures of the region, the body of the dead person would be buried within twenty-four hours. The body was washed, wrapped in strips of cloth, and carried on a bier (wooden stretcher) to the burial place outside the city or village. The family would make a procession through the city, and any onlookers were expected to join the procession, wailing and lamenting with the family and friends out of respect for the person who had died.*

Introducing the Bible Account

Discuss death. Using the background information, discuss with the students the differences between traditional Jewish funerals and modern funerals.

Bible Account

Read the following Bible account or read Luke 7:11-17. Using Chart 33, "Palestine in the Time of Christ," point out Capernaum, where the previous Bible account took place; then point out Nain, where the following Bible account takes place.

A Young Man Raised

After Jesus left Capernaum, He traveled along with His disciples and many other people.

When he arrived at the gate of the city of Nain, the body of a young man was being carried out to be buried. His mother, a widow, was following the body, and many people of the city were following behind.

When Jesus saw the widow, He had compassion on her, for she had no husband, and now her son was dead. Jesus said to her, "Weep not." Then He approached the stretcher that the body was lying on and touched it, and the people that were carrying the body stood still. Jesus said, "Young man, I say unto thee, Arise." The young man sat up and began to speak, and he was presented to his mother.

The people around became fearful. They said, "A great prophet is risen up among us . . . God hath visited his people." The people of Nain praised God, for they had seen a miracle. Jesus showed His power over death. The people told everyone they saw what had happened.

➤ **Who was with Jesus when He traveled from Capernaum to Nain?** *(his disciples and other followers from Capernaum)*

*S*tronger than Death
Luke 7:11-17

Name ____________________

If the statement is *true*, color the squares with the corresponding number *purple*. If the statement is *false*, color the squares *yellow*. The completed puzzle will show you what Jesus Christ gives to Christians. They do not need to fear their own deaths or the deaths of loved ones who are saved.

1. Jesus was traveling from Nain to Capernaum.
2. Jesus and His followers saw a funeral procession at the gate of the city.
3. Jesus restored the widow's son because the widow would not stop asking Him to help.
4. The young man's brothers also asked for help.
5. With her son dead, the woman would be left alone.
6. Jesus told the woman to stop weeping.
7. Jesus touched those who were carrying the young man's body, and they stopped walking.
8. Jesus told them to help the young man to sit up.
9. Jesus told the young man to rise.
10. The young man sat up and spoke.
11. Jesus presented the young man to the Pharisees.
12. Everyone who was there was afraid and glorified God.
13. They spoke about it to no one.
14. The power of God is stronger than death.

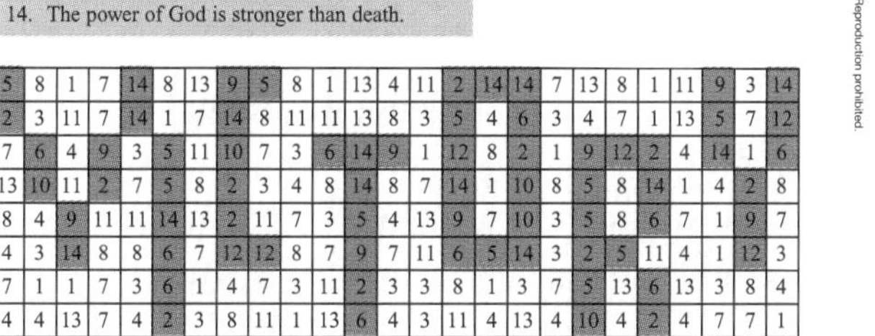

5	8	1	7	14	8	13	9	5	8	1	13	4	11	2	14	14	7	13	8	1	11	9	3	14
2	3	11	7	14	1	7	14	8	11	11	13	8	3	5	4	6	3	4	7	1	13	5	7	12
7	6	4	9	3	5	11	10	7	3	6	14	9	1	12	8	2	1	9	12	2	4	14	1	6
13	10	11	2	7	5	8	2	3	4	8	14	8	7	14	1	10	8	5	8	14	1	4	2	8
8	4	9	11	11	14	13	2	11	7	3	5	4	13	9	7	10	3	5	8	6	7	1	9	7
4	3	14	8	8	6	7	12	12	8	7	9	7	11	6	5	14	3	2	5	11	4	1	12	3
7	1	1	7	3	6	1	4	7	3	11	2	3	3	8	1	3	7	5	13	6	13	3	8	4
4	4	13	7	4	2	3	8	11	1	13	6	4	3	11	4	13	4	10	4	2	4	7	7	1

➤ **Why were the circumstances worse for the woman now that her son had died?** *(She had no husband, and now that her son had died she would have no one to support her. She might possibly have to beg in order to have food.)*

➤ **Why did Jesus command the widow not to weep?** *(because He had compassion on her and was going to raise her son from the dead)*

➤ **What did the people do after Jesus raised the man?** *(They were afraid, praised God, and reported to other people what had happened.)*

Worktext page 116

Distinguish between true and false statements.

Lesson 3

Hymn: "Faith Is The Victory"

Sing the first and second verses (Worktext pages 276-77). Play the recording and sing verses 1 and 2 together.

Memory Verses—James 1:14-15

Practice the memory verses. Locate **James 1:14-15** and choose a student to read or say the verses from memory. Study verses 14 and 15. Choose students to explain what the verses mean. Read **Romans 6:23** aloud.

➤ **What are both of these Scriptures telling us about sin?** *(that the penalty for sin is death)*

Introducing the Application Story

Discuss victory.

➤ **What is *victory?*** *(success, winning over an opponent, usually in a competition)*

➤ **How does a person or team feel when they are victorious?** *(joyful, happy)*

Tell the students that the following story is about a special type of victory.

Application Story

Read the following story to the students.

The Victory Service

Laura was just opening the back door of her car as Juanita coasted by on her skates. "Hey," Juanita called, "where are you going all dressed up?"

Laura smiled at her. "We're going to Grandmother's victory service," she said.

"A victory service? What's that?" Juanita coasted down the driveway toward Laura.

"Well, remember me telling you that Grandmother Thorsell died?" asked Laura. Juanita nodded as Laura continued, "Grandmother was a Christian—always caring about others. She talked about heaven a lot and how she wanted to see the Lord, so for Grandmother, dying wasn't a bad thing—it was a time of rejoicing.

"How can dying be so happy?" asked Juanita.

Laura said, "We know Grandmother's happy and healthy in heaven. She's with the Lord Jesus whom she loves—so we're having a special service to remember Grandmother and her love for the Lord."

"Why do you call it a victory service? A victory is when you win something, isn't it?" asked Juanita.

Laura smiled and said, "Oh, Grandmother would probably say that now in heaven she's won the greatest victory of all—victory over sin. In heaven God gave Grandmother a new and perfect body. And since there's no sin in heaven, Grandmother will never be tempted to sin again."

Juanita looked down at her skates. "I'll miss your grandmother too. She was always nice to me—and she made the best peanut butter cookies. I can't imagine her sinning—*ever.*

Laura walked toward the porch swing, motioning for Juanita to join her. "Juanita, we've talked about this before. The Bible says that *all* have sinned. That means our parents, the preacher, Grandmother, me—and you too. But God sent His only Son, Jesus, to die on the cross to pay for our sins. God offers the free gift of salvation to all who ask for it."

Juanita nodded thoughtfully. *Yes, they had talked about this before. Maybe she should learn more.* "Are you going to talk more about God's gift at the victory service?" Juanita asked.

"Sure we are. We'll sing, read the Bible, and pray—just the things Grandmother loved most. Hey, I've got an idea. Would you like to go to the victory service too? I know Grandmother prayed for you.

"She prayed for me? I never knew she cared so much."

Laura smiled. "She did. But I know someone who cares even more. God."

Juanita sat quietly for a moment, then stood up. "I'll go ask my mom if I can go," she said.

"Great! We can pick you up on the way."

Juanita waved and whisked away on her skates. She could hardly wait to hear more.

➤ **Why was going to heaven a victory for Grandmother?** *(In heaven she would have victory over sin and would be happy and healthy.)*

➤ **How did Laura describe a victory service?** *(a time to sing, read the Bible, pray, and honor Grandmother and the God she loved)*

➤ **Why do you think Grandmother prayed for Juanita?** *(for Juanita to be saved)*

➤ **What does God require of a person before he can go to heaven?** *(No one can enter heaven unless his heart is changed through salvation in Jesus Christ.)*

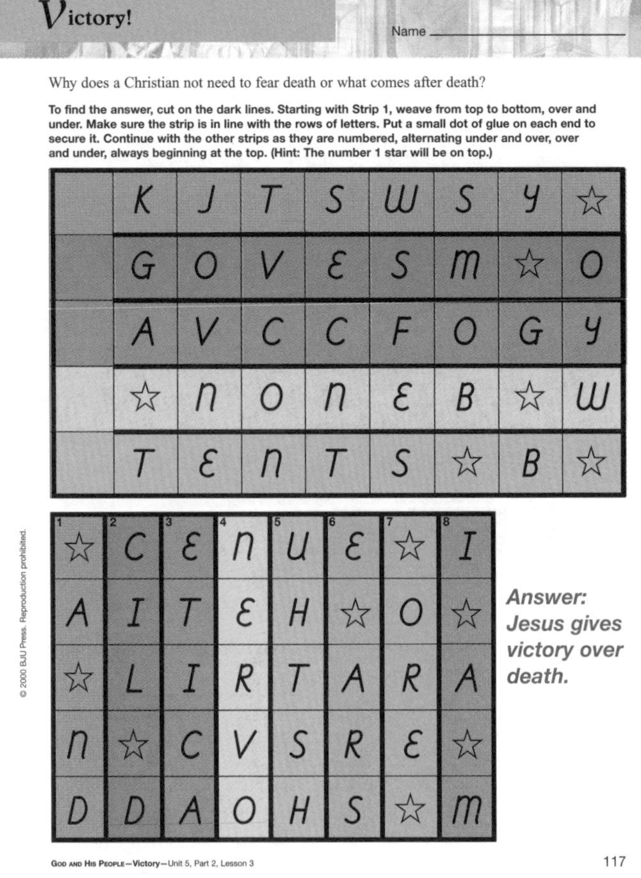

Victory! Name ____________

Why does a Christian not need to fear death or what comes after death?

To find the answer, cut on the dark lines. Starting with Strip 1, weave from top to bottom, over and under. Make sure the strip is in line with the rows of letters. Put a small dot of glue on each end to secure it. Continue with the other strips as they are numbered, alternating under and over, over and under, always beginning at the top. (Hint: The number 1 star will be on top.)

	K	J	T	S	W	S	y	☆
	G	O	V	E	S	m	☆	O
	A	V	C	C	F	O	G	y
	☆	n	O	n	E	B	☆	W
	T	E	n	T	S	☆	B	☆

1	2	3	4	5	6	7	8
☆	C	E	n	U	E	☆	I
A	I	T	E	H	☆	O	☆
☆	L	I	R	T	A	R	A
n	☆	C	V	S	R	E	☆
D	D	A	O	H	S	☆	m

Answer: Jesus gives victory over death.

God and His People—Victory—Unit 5, Part 2, Lesson 3 117

Worktext pages 117-18

Apply Bible knowledge to everyday life.

Lesson 4

Materials

- Chart 16 "Jesus Restores Two Lives"

Memory Verses—James 1:14-15

Practice the memory verses. Locate and read **James 1:14-15** as the students follow along in their Bibles. Select different groups of students to stand and read or recite the verses from memory.

Background Information

Jairus—*He was a ruler in a synagogue and was responsible for taking care of the services and different activities that took place there. Generally, those in leadership at the synagogue had close ties with the Pharisees, who did not support what Jesus did or who He is. It was unusual for someone of Jairus's position to bow and worship Jesus.*

Introducing the Bible Account

Discuss the public ministry of Jesus. Explain that the public ministry of Jesus lasted about three years. During that time Jesus traveled in Judea, Samaria, and Galilee, teaching and ministering to the people. Scripture tells us about some of His work during these three years. Explain to the students that they are learning about only a few of the miracles that Jesus performed during that time.

Bible Account

Read the following Bible account or read Mark 5:21-43. Direct the students to look at the picture on Worktext page 119.

Jesus Restores Two Lives

Jesus had crossed over the Sea of Galilee by ship. Many people gathered around Him. Upon seeing Jesus, a man came and fell down in front of Him and worshiped Him. This man was Jairus, a ruler of the local synagogue (place of worship). Jairus said to the Lord pleadingly, "My little daughter lieth at the point of death: I pray thee, come and lay thy hands on her, that she may be healed; and she shall live."

As Jesus and Jairus made their way to the home where the daughter was sick, the crowd followed. In the crowd there was a woman with a blood disease. She had been sick for many years and had spent all she had, going from one doctor to another, trying to find a cure. She had heard that Jesus was coming and believed that if she could just touch Jesus' clothes, she would be healed. The woman tried to get closer and closer, and finally she was close enough to touch His clothes. Immediately, she was healed of her disease.

Jesus turned around in the crowd and asked, "Who touched my clothes?" The disciples who were with Jesus were surprised that He would ask such a question, since the people crowded on every side of them. Many people probably touched Him as they moved along.

The woman came forward and fell down before the Lord and told Him of her disease. She admitted that she was the one who had touched Him and had been healed. Jesus told the woman, "Thy faith hath made thee whole."

While Jesus was speaking with the woman, someone from Jairus's house came running, saying, "Thy daughter is dead: why troublest thou the Master any further?" When Jesus heard these words, He told Jairus not to be afraid, but to believe. Jesus told the crowd to wait there. Then Jesus took Peter, James, and John, the brother of James, with Him to the home of Jairus. Many people were crying in the house. Jesus told those in the house that the girl was not dead, but rather sleeping.

They laughed at Him, but He had the people leave the house. Then Jesus took Jairus, Jairus's wife, and the three disciples with Him to the place where the daughter was lying. Jesus took the girl by the hand and said, "Damsel, I say unto thee, arise." The daughter, who was twelve years old, arose and walked. Jesus then asked those who had seen the miracle not to tell anyone but to give the girl something to eat.

InfoScene: "Jesus Restores Two Lives"

Display Chart 16 for reference throughout this unit. Review and discuss the Bible account as time permits.

➤ **Why did Jairus believe Jesus could heal his daughter?** *(because he had faith in the power of God)*

➤ **In what two ways was the woman healed, and why did she believe she would be healed by touching Jesus?** *(She was healed both physically and spiritually because she had faith in the Lord.)*

➤ **What did Jesus say about the daughter of Jairus?** *(She was asleep, not dead.)*

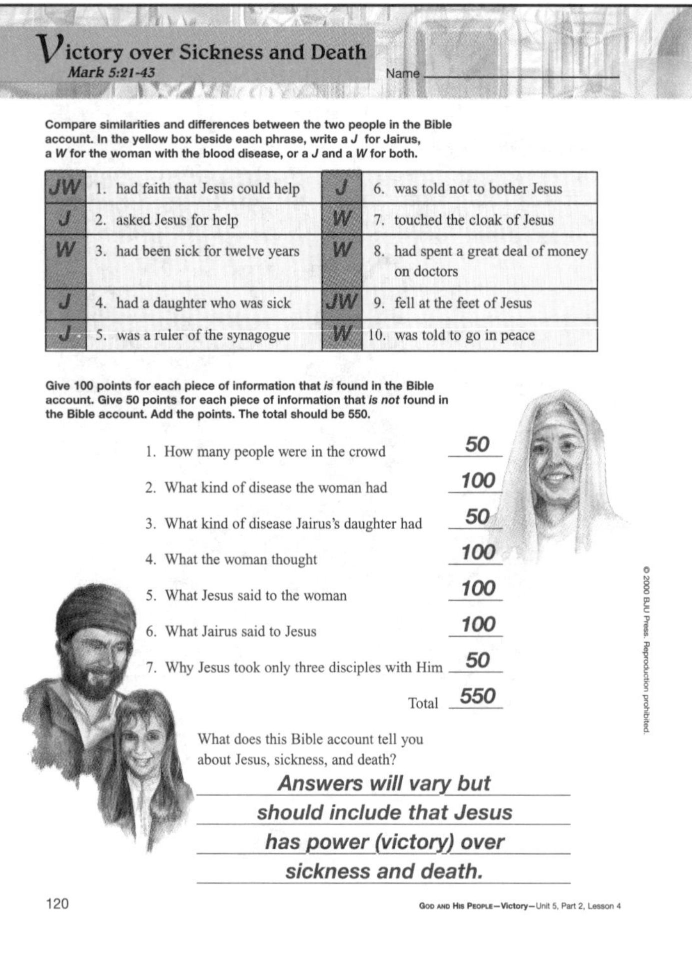

Victory over Sickness and Death

Mark 5:21-43

Name ______________________

Compare similarities and differences between the two people in the Bible account. In the yellow box beside each phrase, write a *J* for Jairus, a *W* for the woman with the blood disease, or a *J* and a *W* for both.

JW	1. had faith that Jesus could help	*J*	6. was told not to bother Jesus
J	2. asked Jesus for help	*W*	7. touched the cloak of Jesus
W	3. had been sick for twelve years	*W*	8. had spent a great deal of money on doctors
J	4. had a daughter who was sick	*JW*	9. fell at the feet of Jesus
J	5. was a ruler of the synagogue	*W*	10. was told to go in peace

Give 100 points for each piece of information that *is* found in the Bible account. Give 50 points for each piece of information that *is not* found in the Bible account. Add the points. The total should be 550.

1. How many people were in the crowd *50*
2. What kind of disease the woman had *100*
3. What kind of disease Jairus's daughter had *50*
4. What the woman thought *100*
5. What Jesus said to the woman *100*
6. What Jairus said to Jesus *100*
7. Why Jesus took only three disciples with Him *50*

Total *550*

What does this Bible account tell you about Jesus, sickness, and death?

Answers will vary but should include that Jesus has power (victory) over sickness and death.

120 GOD AND HIS PEOPLE—Victory—Unit 5, Part 2, Lesson 4

➤ **What are some possible reasons that Jesus asked Jairus, his wife, and the disciples not to tell others about the miracle?** *(Discuss the following reasons: Jesus wanted people to hear His words more than to see His works, because His words were far more important. Another reason might be that the miracles being performed would create a stir among the religious leaders of the day.)*

➤ **What do you feel like doing when you have something good happen to you?** *(Possible answers include telling others, rejoicing, and thanking God.)*

Worktext page 120

Compare similarities and differences between two Bible characters.

Going Beyond

Enrichment

Discuss breastplates. Read **Ephesians 6:14** aloud. Explain that the breastplate protects the heart, a vital organ. Read **Proverbs 4:23** aloud and explain that a Christian must protect his heart, needs, and desires from the temptations that Satan will throw his way. Read aloud the following verses that deal with specific sins and how Christians are to respond. Encourage the students to strengthen their breastplates by memorizing the verses listed.

Lying—Psalm 119:29
Stealing—Ephesians 4:28
Wrong thoughts—Philippians 4:8
Disobedience—Hebrews 13:17
Pride—Psalm 36:11

Jesus Gives Victory over Satan

Unit 5, Part 3

Preview

Doctrines

- God is all-powerful (omnipotent) (Matthew 19:26)—Lesson 1
- Faith is turning to Christ (John 1:12)—Lesson 1
- Demons inflict men with evil (Matthew 17:15, 18)—Lesson 3
- Satan can control unbelievers (Luke 22:3)—Lesson 3

Skills and Applications

- Learn I Corinthians 10:13
- Learn the divisions of the books of the Bible
- Recall facts and details
- Locate information in Scripture
- Be aware that Satan tempts Christians to sin
- Know what to do when you are tempted to do wrong
- Allow God to help you overcome temptations
- Apply Bible knowledge to everyday life

Lesson 1

Memory Verse—I Corinthians 10:13

Principle: God is faithful in helping believers overcome temptation. Locate **I Corinthians 10:13** and read it aloud as the students read silently. Choose volunteers to read the verse aloud; then choose a student to look up and read aloud the definition of *temptation* from the glossary. Explain that temptation is sometimes referred to as a trial or test. Direct the students to highlight the verse in their Bibles (optional) and mark the location with the Unit 5 Bookmark.

➤ **What is Satan's chief purpose?** *(to get men to sin, which takes away from the glory of God)*

➤ **Why does God allow Christians to be tempted by Satan?** *(so that their faith in God will grow)*

➤ **According to the verse, what does God provide in the midst of temptation?** *(a way of escape, an alternative to the temptation, a way to overcome and to do the right thing)*

Hymn: "Faith Is the Victory"

Teach the third verse (Worktext pages 276-77). Read the words of verse 3 aloud. Explain that everywhere a Christian turns there is sin and temptation. Play the recording and lead in singing the third verse. Read **Ephesians 6:10-17** aloud and explain that this is the armor that Christians must use to fight against sin and temptation. Lead in singing verses 1-3.

Worktext page 121

Singing with understanding, verse 3.

Background Information

Demons—*Demons ("devils") are mentioned throughout the New Testament. Scripture refers to Satan as the prince of the demons (Matthew 9:34). Satan's demons are many, and they are in many places. Demons are capable of entering into the bodies of animals as well as unbelievers. Satan has a strong hold on those who are possessed by demons, and only the Holy Spirit can conquer the forces of Satan.*

Introducing the Bible Account

Discuss demons. Share the background information about demons (optional). Explain that a Christian cannot have a demon living in him. However, a Christian must be prepared to use his shield of faith—the Word of God—to fight against the temptation and sin ("fiery darts") that Satan brings his way. Stress with the students that Jesus Christ, the Son of God, is far more powerful than Satan. Jesus Christ is the captain in our battle with Satan.

Bible Account

Read the following Bible account or read Mark 5:1-20.

Demoniac of Gadara Healed

Jesus and His disciples arrived at the shore of the Gadarenes on the other side of the Sea of Galilee. As Jesus came up out of the ship, a man with an unclean spirit came to Him. The man had been living in tombs. No one wanted to have any contact with him, be-

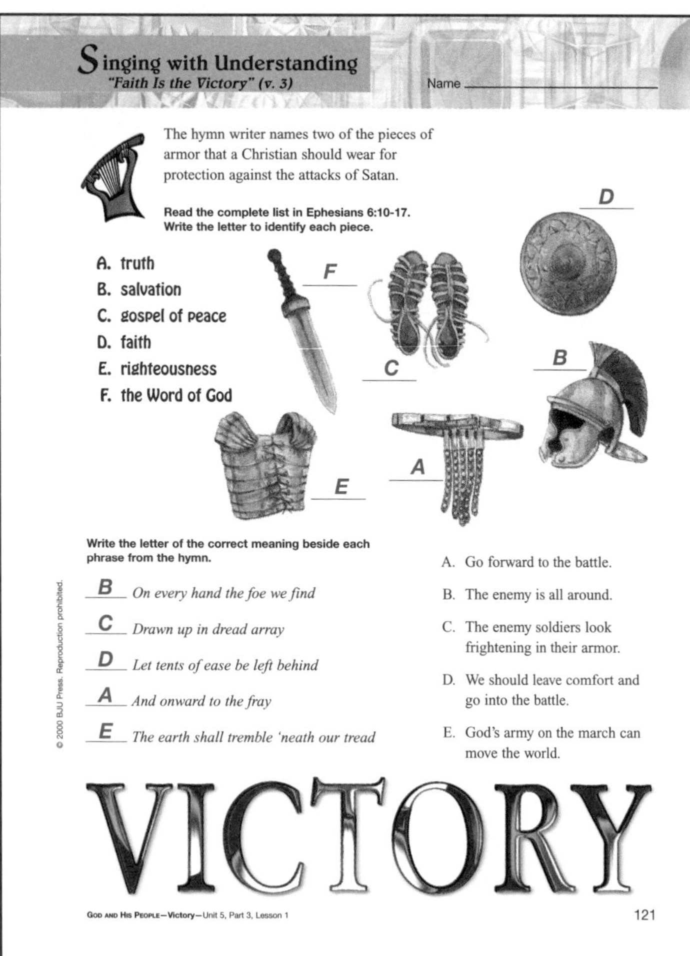

Singing with Understanding

"Faith Is the Victory" (v. 3) Name ____________

The hymn writer names two of the pieces of armor that a Christian should wear for protection against the attacks of Satan.

Read the complete list in Ephesians 6:10-17. Write the letter to identify each piece.

A. truth
B. salvation
C. gospel of peace
D. faith
E. righteousness
F. the Word of God

Write the letter of the correct meaning beside each phrase from the hymn.

B *On every hand the foe we find*
C *Drawn up in dread array*
D *Let tents of ease be left behind*
A *And onward to the fray*
E *The earth shall tremble 'neath our tread*

A. Go forward to the battle.
B. The enemy is all around.
C. The enemy soldiers look frightening in their armor.
D. We should leave comfort and go into the battle.
E. God's army on the march can move the world.

VICTORY

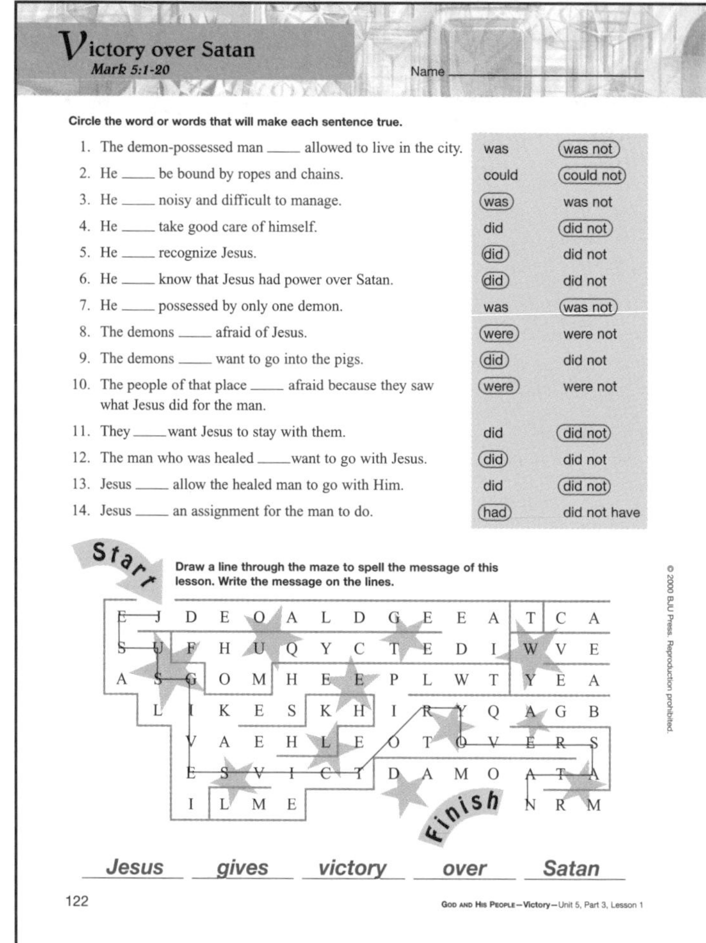

Victory over Satan

Mark 5:1-20 Name ____________

Circle the word or words that will make each sentence true.

1.	The demon-possessed man ____ allowed to live in the city.	was	**(was not)**
2.	He ____ be bound by ropes and chains.	could	**(could not)**
3.	He ____ noisy and difficult to manage.	**(was)**	was not
4.	He ____ take good care of himself.	did	**(did not)**
5.	He ____ recognize Jesus.	**(did)**	did not
6.	He ____ know that Jesus had power over Satan.	**(did)**	did not
7.	He ____ possessed by only one demon.	was	**(was not)**
8.	The demons ____ afraid of Jesus.	**(were)**	were not
9.	The demons ____ want to go into the pigs.	**(did)**	did not
10.	The people of that place ____ afraid because they saw what Jesus did for the man.	**(were)**	were not
11.	They ____ want Jesus to stay with them.	did	**(did not)**
12.	The man who was healed ____ want to go with Jesus.	**(did)**	did not
13.	Jesus ____ allow the healed man to go with Him.	did	**(did not)**
14.	Jesus ____ an assignment for the man to do.	**(had)**	did not have

Draw a line through the maze to spell the message of this lesson. Write the message on the lines.

Jesus *gives* *victory* *over* *Satan*

cause of the unclean spirit that possessed him. Men in the city had tried to tie him up with rope and chains, but he would simply tear them all off. Day and night the man could be heard crying and cutting himself with stones. When the man saw Jesus off in the distance coming out of the ship, he ran over to worship Him. The man then said with a loud voice, "What have I to do with thee, Jesus, thou Son of the most high God? I adjure [beg] thee by God, that thou torment me not."

Jesus had said to the man, "Come out of the man, thou unclean spirit." Jesus then asked, "What is thy name?" and the demon replied, "My name is Legion: for we are many." And he begged Jesus that He would not send them away out of the country.

Over in the distance, there was a herd of pigs feeding on the mountain. The spirits begged to be sent into the pigs, and Jesus cast them into the pigs. The herd began to run violently and went over the side of the mountain into the sea below and were drowned. The people who owned the pigs went and told everyone what had happened. People from all over came to see the man who had been possessed of the unclean spirits. They saw this man clothed, sitting with Jesus, and in his right mind. The people of the city were so afraid of what they saw that they begged Jesus to depart from them. The man wanted to go with Jesus, but Jesus sent him home to tell his family what the Lord had done for him.

➤ **What did the man with the unclean spirit do and ask when he came to Jesus?** *(He bowed down and worshiped Jesus and asked Him not to torment him.)*

➤ **Why would the demons ask the Lord Jesus not to torment them?** *(They knew who Jesus was and recognized His power over them, even though they served Satan.)*

➤ **Do you think the people cared more about the man or about their possessions?** *(Accept any answer.)*

➤ **What did Jesus tell the healed man to do?** *(to go tell his family what Jesus had done for him)*

 **Worktext page 122**

Recall facts and details about the Bible account.

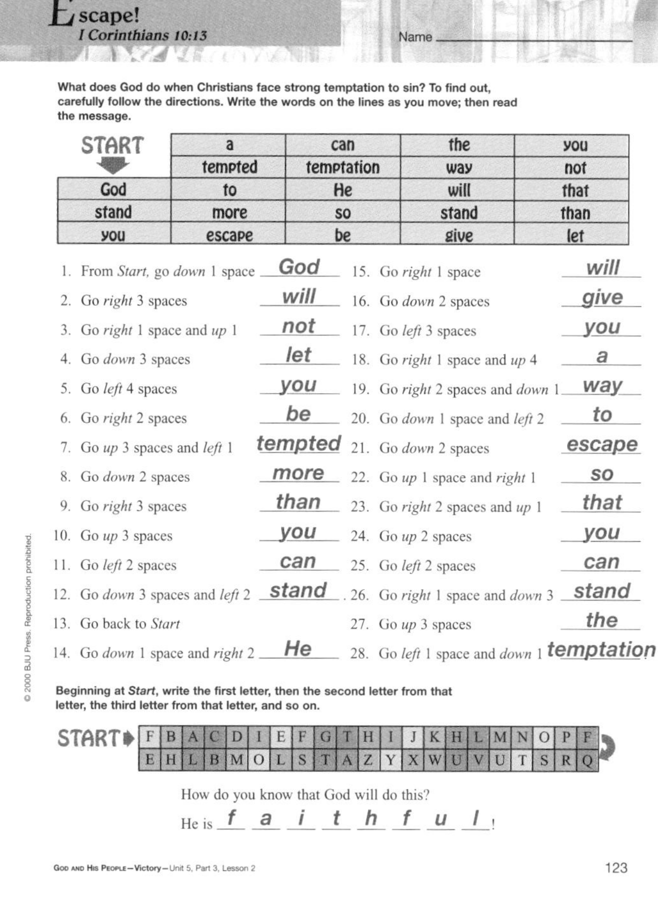

Escape!
I Corinthians 10:13

Name ____________

What does God do when Christians face strong temptation to sin? To find out, carefully follow the directions. Write the words on the lines as you move; then read the message.

START

	a	can	the	you
	tempted	temptation	way	not
God	to	He	will	that
stand	more	so	stand	than
you	escape	be	give	let

1. From *Start,* go *down* 1 space — God
2. Go *right* 3 spaces — will
3. Go *right* 1 space and *up* 1 — not
4. Go *down* 3 spaces — let
5. Go *left* 4 spaces — you
6. Go *right* 2 spaces — be
7. Go *up* 3 spaces and *left* 1 — tempted
8. Go *down* 2 spaces — more
9. Go *right* 3 spaces — than
10. Go *up* 3 spaces — you
11. Go *left* 2 spaces — can
12. Go *down* 3 spaces and *left* 2 — stand
13. Go back to *Start*
14. Go *down* 1 space and *right* 2 — He
15. Go *right* 1 space — will
16. Go *down* 2 spaces — give
17. Go *left* 3 spaces — you
18. Go *right* 1 space and *up* 4 — a
19. Go *right* 2 spaces and *down* 1 — way
20. Go *down* 1 space and *left* 2 — to
21. Go *down* 2 spaces — escape
22. Go *up* 1 space and *right* 1 — so
23. Go *right* 2 spaces and *up* 1 — that
24. Go *up* 2 spaces — you
25. Go *left* 2 spaces — can
26. Go *right* 1 space and *down* 3 — stand
27. Go *up* 3 spaces — the
28. Go *left* 1 space and *down* 1 — temptation

Beginning at *Start,* write the first letter, then the second letter from that letter, the third letter from that letter, and so on.

START ➧ F B A C D I E F G T H I J K H L M N O P F
E H L B M O L S T A Z Y X W U V U T S R Q

How do you know that God will do this?

He is f a i t h f u l !

God and His People—Victory—Unit 5, Part 3, Lesson 2 123

Lesson 2

Hymn: "Faith Is the Victory"

Sing the first three verses (Worktext pages 276-77). Divide the students into three groups, allowing each group to sing a verse. Lead in singing verses 1-3 together.

Memory Verse—I Corinthians 10:13

Practice the memory verse. Read and study **I Corinthians 10:13.** Divide the students into four to six groups. Assign each group a phrase to read. Continue until each group has read each phrase of the verse.

Worktext page 123

Develop an understanding of the memory verse.

Introducing the Application Story

Discuss the memory verse.

➤ **How does I Corinthians 10:13 apply to your life?** *(Answers will vary.)*

Remind the students that the word *temptation* could be changed to *trial.* Tell the students to think about any temptations or trials that they may face; then listen to find out what temptation Jimmy gave in to and how he should have responded to the situation. *(wrong attitude and unkindness, right attitude and kindness)*

Application Story

Read the following story to the students.

The Shield of Faith

"Now we will vote for the team captain," the gym teacher said. Jimmy Wilson closed his eyes and held his breath while the teacher called his name and counted the hands. Then the teacher called Scott Parker's name and counted the hands.

"Our new team captain is Scott Parker," the teacher said.

Jimmy's eyes flew open. Several boys were already giving Scott high fives. Jimmy turned away, feeling like he was going to choke. Scott—the team captain? Scott didn't even know the rules.

"He only won because he's smart and has nice clothes," Jimmy thought.

Jimmy kicked a rock along the sidewalk all the way home from school, scuffing up his shoes. When his mother asked him about his day, he just muttered, "Okay," and went straight to his room.

After supper his mother asked him to take out the trash and start his homework. Jimmy made a face. His dad clapped a firm hand on his shoulder.

"Come with me, young man," he said. "We need to have a talk."

Uh-oh, Jimmy thought as Dad led the way to Jimmy's room.

Dad sat in Jimmy's desk chair, and Jimmy sat with slumped shoulders on the bed, facing him. "Son, your attitude toward your mother was disrespectful just now. That kind of behavior won't be tolerated in this house. Is that clear?"

"Yes, sir," Jimmy mumbled.

"As soon as we leave this room, you will go apologize, and if this happens again, you can expect some painful consequences. Understood?"

Jimmy's voice was barely above a whisper. "Yes, sir."

"Now, would you like to tell me what's wrong?"

"Oh, nothing," muttered Jimmy.

"You'll have to do better than that. Unkindness isn't a normal way of life for you. What's eating you?" Dad leaned forward and waited.

Jimmy swallowed a huge lump in his throat so he could speak. "We had the election today for team captain. Dad, I was sure they would elect me."

"And they didn't?"

"They chose Scott Parker—because he's smart, and has nice clothes, and a swimming pool in his back yard. He doesn't know *anything* about soccer."

Dad waited a moment longer. "And did you think," he asked, "that being rude to Mom would help make life better for you somehow?"

"I don't know. I'm just mad."

Dad reached for the Bible on Jimmy's bookshelf. He turned pages quickly, found the spot he wanted, and handed the Bible to Jimmy. "Why don't you read this verse for me, Jimmy?" He pointed to the page.

Jimmy read the verse out loud. "There hath no temptation taken you but such as is common to man: but God is faithful, who will not suffer you to be tempted above that ye are able; but will with the temptation also make a way to escape, that ye may be able to bear it." Jimmy paused and looked up at Dad.

"Son, today you were tempted."

"What do you mean, Dad?"

"Well, today you were faced with a choice. Either you could be mean and nasty because Scott was chosen, or you could be kind to others no matter what happened. And, of course, you could try again next season for team captain."

Jimmy straightened his shoulders a little. He hadn't thought of that.

"Now, why don't you put on your shield of faith?"

"What does that have to do with being team captain?"

"Just what the verse says. God is faithful, no matter what temptation you face. You need to have faith in God. Believe that He has a purpose in not letting you be team captain this time—and that He can help you act in a way that pleases Him even though you're disappointed."

Jimmy let out a sigh. "That's not easy."

"You're right. It's hard for us humans to do," Dad said. "But remember, Jimmy—nothing is too hard for God."

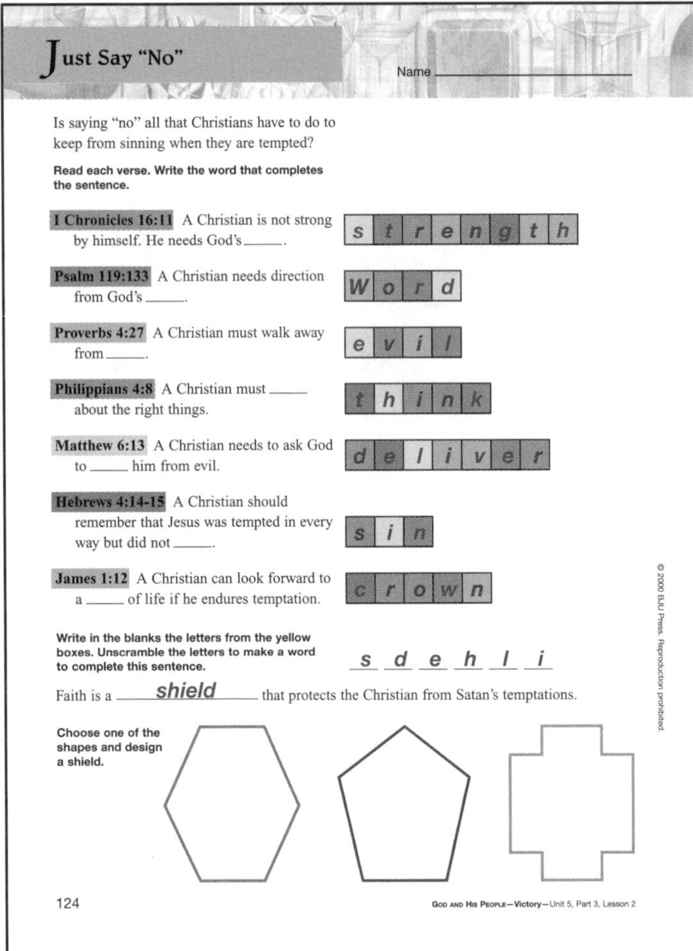

Just Say "No"

Name ____________

Is saying "no" all that Christians have to do to keep from sinning when they are tempted?

Read each verse. Write the word that completes the sentence.

I Chronicles 16:11 A Christian is not strong by himself. He needs God's ____. s t r e n g t h

Psalm 119:133 A Christian needs direction from God's ____. W o r d

Proverbs 4:27 A Christian must walk away from ____. e v i l

Philippians 4:8 A Christian must ____ about the right things. t h i n k

Matthew 6:13 A Christian needs to ask God to ____ him from evil. d e l i v e r

Hebrews 4:14-15 A Christian should remember that Jesus was tempted in every way but did not ____. s i n

James 1:12 A Christian can look forward to a ____ of life if he endures temptation. c r o w n

Write in the blanks the letters from the yellow boxes. Unscramble the letters to make a word to complete this sentence. s d e h l i

Faith is a shield that protects the Christian from Satan's temptations.

Choose one of the shapes and design a shield.

© 2000 BJU Press. Reproduction prohibited.

124 God and His People—Victory—Unit 5, Part 3, Lesson 2

➤ **Why did Jimmy think Scott was elected team captain?** *(Scott was more popular, had nicer clothes, and had a swimming pool in his back yard.)*

➤ **What temptation did Jimmy give in to?** *(being disrespectful and unkind)*

➤ **What did Jimmy learn from reading the Bible verse and talking with his father?** *(that he had given in to temptation but that God could help him overcome temptation in the future)*

➤ **What are some ways that you can overcome temptation?** *(Possible answers include reading God's Word, praying, and staying away from things that tempt you.)*

Worktext page 124

Locate information in Scripture that tells how a Christian should live.

Lesson 3

Hymn: "Faith Is the Victory"

Sing the first three verses (Worktext pages 276-77). Play the recording and lead in singing verses 1-3. Allow different groups to alternate singing each verse.

Memory Verse—I Corinthians 10:13

Practice the memory verse. Choose volunteers to locate and read **I Corinthians 10:13.** Allow students to work with partners to practice the verse together.

Background Information

Transfiguration—*Jesus took Peter, James, and John up the mountain, and there they saw the glory of the Lord. This was a special revelation from God of the divinity or divine nature of Jesus. It also reconfirmed to the disciples that everything that Jesus had done up to that point and was going to do was guided by God.*

Introducing the Bible Account

Discuss the transfiguration. Share the background information about the transfiguration.

Bible Account

Read the following Bible account or read Mark 9:14-29.

Faith Made It Possible
Mark 9:14-29

Name ________________

Write the letter to match the correct question with each answer.

J 1. the Mount of Transfiguration
I 2. possession by an evil spirit
U 3. the disciples
H 4. since childhood
F 5. He threw himself into the fire and into water.
A 6. "Come out and never enter him again."
T 7. nothing

A. What did Jesus say to the spirit who possessed the boy?
F. How did the possessed boy behave?
H. How long had the boy been troubled by the spirit?
I. What was wrong with the boy?
J. Where had Jesus and some of His disciples been?
T. What is impossible if one has faith?
U. Who was not able to cast out the spirit?

Use the letters that match these answer numbers to spell the correct word.

What did the disciples lack? F (5) a (6) i (2) t (7) h (4)

God and His People—Victory—Unit 5, Part 3, Lesson 3 125

Boy Healed of Demons

When Jesus came down from the Mount of Transfiguration with Peter, James, and John, there was a large group of people gathering around the other disciples. As Jesus came close, a man came and asked Him to heal his son. The man told the Lord that the boy could not control himself and was unable to speak. He would fall on the ground and foam at the mouth. He would sometimes throw himself into fire or water, not knowing what he was doing. The boy had been this way since he was a young child. The father told Jesus that he had brought his son to the other disciples, but they were unable to cast out the demon.

Jesus Christ rebuked his disciples for their lack of faith. Then He asked them to bring the boy to Him. The boy was brought to Jesus, and the father asked Jesus to "have compassion on us, and help us. Jesus said unto him, If thou canst believe, all things are possible to him that believeth. And straightway the father of the child cried out, and said with tears, Lord, I believe; help thou mine unbelief." Jesus rebuked the devil and commanded it to leave the boy. The child was left so limp that the crowd of onlookers said he was dead. Jesus took the boy by the hand and raised him up, and the father took the boy home.

Later when Jesus and the disciples were alone, the disciples asked Jesus why they were not able to drive out the demon. Jesus used this experience to teach the disciples that in their ministries they were going to need the Lord, for they could not have victory without Him. They must believe that God would help them to do the things that He had called them to do.

- ➤ **What was wrong with the man's son?** *(He was possessed by a demon.)*
- ➤ **What did Jesus do to heal the boy?** *(He spoke, and the demon came out.)*
- ➤ **What does every believer need in order to live a victorious Christian life?** *(faith in God)*

Worktext page 125

Recall facts and details about the Bible account.

Lesson 4

Materials

- Chart 28, "World Map," or a globe (optional)
- Old and New Testament Student Bible Book Cards for each group of students

Memory Verse—I Corinthians 10:13

Practice the memory verse. Read and study **I Corinthians 10:13.** Choose students to recite the verse from memory. Encourage all the students to try at least once. Say the verse together as a class.

Introducing the Missionary Story

Discuss living in a foreign country.

➤ **Have you ever visited a foreign country?**

➤ **Would you be able to understand the language of people in a foreign country?** *(Answers will depend upon the country.)*

➤ **Would you like the food?** *(Answers will vary.)*

➤ **Would you like to live in a foreign country? Why?** *(Answers will vary.)*

Allow any students who have lived in another country to tell about it. Point to China on Chart 28, "World Map," or on a globe. Explain that the missionary story takes place in China.

Missionary Story

Read the following story based on the life of Gladys Aylward. (*Note:* For more information, a biography about Gladys Aylward, *These Are My People,* is available through Journey Books, a division of Bob Jones University Press.)

The Chinese Mandarin

When missionary Gladys Aylward was in China, all the Chinese women still had their feet "bound," or tied up very tightly so that they could hardly walk. The Chinese felt that small feet were a sign of true beauty, so they bound the feet of baby girls to prevent their feet from growing.

The mayor of a Chinese town was called the *mandarin.* He was very wealthy and had a lot of power. He could have anyone killed if he wished. One day the mandarin came to visit Miss Aylward at the inn that she ran.

"The Chinese government has said that the women's feet must be unbound. I need a woman to travel into all the villages in this area and see that they unbind their feet. The woman will receive money and will have an escort of soldiers to make sure she is safe," he said.

"Sir, I don't know of any woman who could do this. All of the missionaries are busy."

"Then *you* do it! I appoint you Official Inspector of Women's Feet!"

Gladys Aylward did not know what to say. *Who would take care of her inn? She was already so busy!* But she was afraid to say no to the mandarin.

"Sir, may I tell them the story of Jesus Christ?"

"You may say anything you wish, so long as you see that their feet are unbound."

The order was not so bad after all. Gladys went into the country villages and told people about Jesus. Without the job as Official Inspector of Women's Feet, she never could have done this.

As time went on, Gladys and the mandarin became friends. The mandarin was grateful for Gladys' help, and she was respected in the country. At one point, Gladys was even called upon to stop a prison riot.

Several years passed, and a terrible war began. The mandarin ordered the people of the town to carry away all their belongings and hide them in the hills. They were going to tear down all the town buildings so that the enemy would have nothing to occupy. The last night before everyone was to leave the city, the mandarin held a great feast and invited Miss Aylward. Gladys was surprised—the Chinese did not usually invite women to their feasts. At the end of the feast, the mandarin made a speech. He thanked all those who had helped him. Then he named all the things Gladys Aylward had done—how she had stopped the prison riot and how she had unbound women's feet.

"No one else could have done these things—only a woman in whom lives the Spirit of the living God. Miss Aylward, I have listened to you and argued with you. I have seen how you live, and now I know that the Bible is true. I want to become a Christian," said the mandarin.

People know God's Word is true when they see its power in the lives of Christians. Many times Christians are the only "Bible" another person may read.

➤ **What did the Chinese mandarin ask Gladys Aylward, a missionary to the Chinese people, to do?** *(Go to the women and make sure that all the women's feet were unbound.)*

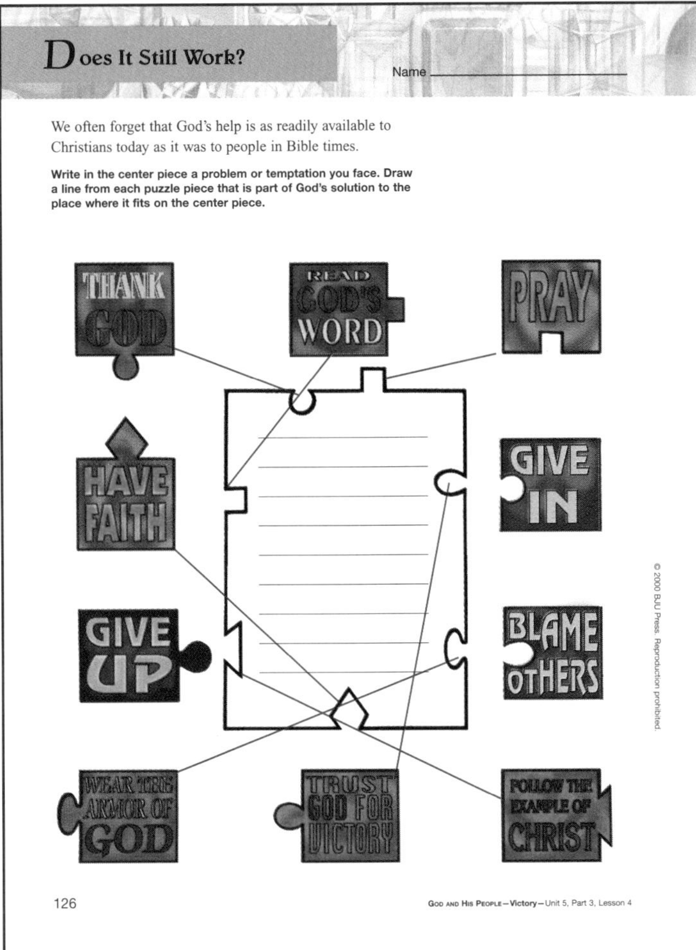
Does It Still Work?

Name ____________________

We often forget that God's help is as readily available to Christians today as it was to people in Bible times.

Write in the center piece a problem or temptation you face. Draw a line from each puzzle piece that is part of God's solution to the place where it fits on the center piece.

➤ **What did Gladys ask permission of the mandarin to do, and how did the mandarin respond?** *(She asked to be allowed to tell the women about the Lord; the mandarin said that as long as she did her job of making sure that the women unbound their feet, she could say whatever she wanted.)*

➤ **In this story, how did God use an unbeliever to accomplish His purpose?** *(He caused the mandarin to give Gladys this job so that she could take the gospel to people who had never heard it.)*

➤ **What influenced the mandarin to want to become a Christian?** *(He watched Gladys Aylward's life and listened as she taught about God's Word.)*

➤ **What enabled Gladys to live a victorious Christian life, doing what God wanted her to do?** *(her faith in God)*

➤ **What can help Christians today live victorious lives?** *(having faith in God)*

Worktext page 126

Become aware of God's solutions to personal temptations.

Bible Study Skills (optional)

Study the divisions of the Bible. Divide the students into groups of two, three, or four. Explain the following game directions. (*Note:* The game uses one set of the Old and New Testament Student Bible Book Cards from the Student Materials Packet for each group.)

1. Distribute six cards to each player.
2. Place the remainder of the cards face down in a pile.
3. Allow players time to see whether they have any matches: two books from the same division.
4. Player 1 asks another player whether he has a book from the division of . . . (e.g., Minor Prophets, Old Testament History).
5. If the player has a book from that division, he gives the card to Player 1. If the player does not have a card from that division, Player 1 draws a card from the pile.
6. Follow the same procedure with each player taking turns.
7. The player with the most matches at the end of the time wins.

Going Beyond

Materials

- Bible dictionary or a set of encyclopedias
- Drawing paper for each student

Enrichment

Discuss and research shields. Read **Ephesians 6:10-17** to the students. Focus their attention on the "shield of faith." Discuss how a shield is used in battle—to protect the soldier from the weapons of the enemy. Christians are to use their shields of faith in God to ward off the daily attacks of Satan.

Direct the students to use a Bible dictionary or encyclopedia to find out about different kinds of shields, when people began to use shields in battle, and what the symbols on shields mean. Direct each student to divide his paper in half, drawing a picture of his favorite type of shield on one part, and designing his own shield on the other part.

Jesus Gives Victory over Eternal Death

Unit 5, Part 4

Preview

Doctrines

- God is faithful (I Corinthians 1:9)—Lesson 2
- God is love (John 3:16)—Lesson 2
- Redeemed man experiences eternal life (Revelation 22:3-5)—Lessons 2-3
- Unredeemed man experiences the second death (Revelation 20:14)—Lesson 3

Skills and Applications

- Learn Ephesians 2:8-9
- Recall facts and details
- Illustrate a Bible account
- Identify the correct title
- Identify similarities and differences between two accounts
- Develop an understanding of Scripture
- Determine cause and effect
- Apply Bible knowledge to everyday life

Lesson 1

Materials

- TimeLine and picture: *Haggai*

Write the reference **Ephesians 2:8-9** on a card. Place the card inside a box and gift-wrap the box, or place the card inside a gift bag.

Picture the Point

Illustrate that gifts are free. Display the wrapped package or gift bag.

➤ **Who would like to have this gift?**

➤ **Who would like to buy this package for ten dollars?** *(Answers will vary.)*

➤ **Why would more people want to have the package when it was offered for free than when it was priced at ten dollars?**

Memory Verses—Ephesians 2:8-9

Principle: God's gift of eternal life is free. Choose a student to open the package and to read the card aloud. Locate **Ephesians 2:8-9,** reading the verses aloud as the students read silently. Choose several students to read the verses aloud. Guide the students to highlight the verses in their Bibles (optional) and to mark the location with the Unit 5 Bookmark.

➤ **What does *grace* mean?** *(unmerited favor)*

➤ **What do we need to be saved from?** *(eternal death)*

➤ **What is God's gift to everyone?** *(Answers will vary, but should include God's Son, Jesus, salvation, and eternal life.)*

Hymn: "Faith Is the Victory"

Teach the fourth verse (Worktext pages 276-77). Play the recording of verse 4.

➤ **How can someone be protected from harm?** *(Possible answers include with a gun, knife, sword, guard dog, or police.)*

➤ **Will these weapons, tools, people, and animals always be able to protect you? Why not?** *(No. Answers will vary.)*

➤ **What protection do believers have that unbelievers do not have?** *(Jesus Christ)*

Play the recording and lead in singing verse 4; then sing verses 1-4 together.

Singing with Understanding
"Faith Is the Victory" (v. 4)

Name ____________

Connect the numbers and write the letters that each line goes through. (You may choose to use a ruler.)

The hymn writer based the first two phrases of verse 4 on Revelation 3:5.

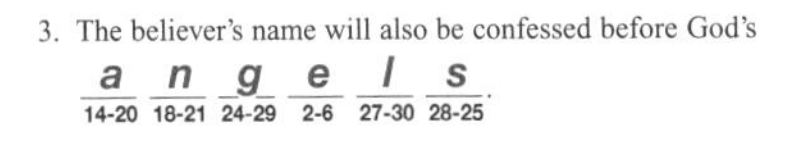

1. Those who overcome will wear *w* (1-8) *h* (4-10) *i* (7-5) *t* (3-9) *e* (2-6) clothing (raiment).
2. Each one who overcomes will hear his name confessed (acknowledged) before the heavenly *F* (11-12) *a* (14-20) *t* (3-9) *h* (4-10) *e* (2-6) *r* (16-19).
3. The believer's name will also be confessed before God's *a* (14-20) *n* (18-21) *g* (24-29) *e* (2-6) *l* (27-30) *s* (28-25).
4. The names of those who overcome will never be blotted out (erased) from the *B* (32-35) *o* (26-31) *o* (26-31) *k* (34-37) of Life.
5. Jesus said that He is the Light of the *W* (1-8) *o* (26-31) *r* (16-19) *l* (27-30) *d* (38-40).
6. He said that the ones who follow Him will not walk in *d* (38-40) *a* (14-20) *r* (16-19) *k* (34-37) *n* (18-21) *e* (2-6) *s* (28-25) *s* (28-25).
7. The name of Jesus is *a* (14-20) *b* (32-35) *o* (26-31) *v* (41-39) *e* (2-6) every name.

The name of Jesus is the name that conquers (Philippians 2:9).

The source for the phrase "hills of light" is not certain, but Christ referred to Himself as Light: His people march and battle in that Light (John 8:12).

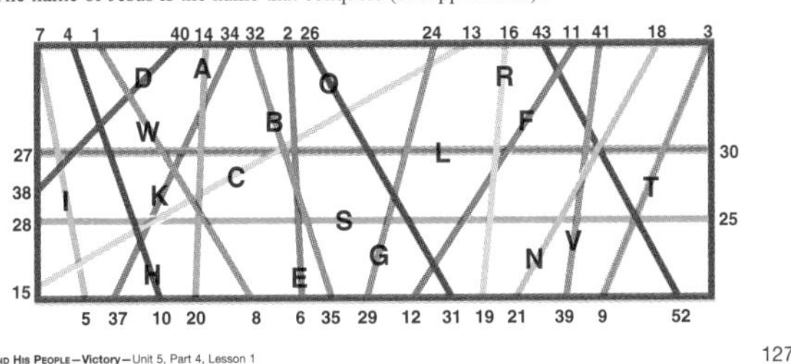

Worktext page 127

Singing with understanding, verse 4.

Background Information

Prophets—*A prophet is someone who communicates God's message to His people. Prophets were chosen by God, and their messages varied. Some messages were warnings, instructing the people to repent of their wrongdoing; other messages were prophesies of the future. Whatever the message, the people knew that it came from God Himself, because the prophets usually began with, "Thus saith the Lord."*

Post-exilic—*This means after the exile in Babylon. There were three post-exilic prophets: Zechariah, Malachi, and Haggai.*

Introducing the Prophet Focus

Discuss the ministry of prophets. Share the background information about prophets. Explain that there were only three prophets after the Jews' release from exile (captivity). Explain that Haggai was the first of these prophets.

TimeLine

Place *Haggai* on the TimeLine. Choose a student to place *Haggai* onto the TimeLine ca. 520 B.C. Guide the students in placing *Haggai* onto their individual TimeLines.

Prophet Focus

Read about the message of Haggai to the students.

Haggai

The Jews were taken captive by the Babylonians in 586 B.C., and the temple at Jerusalem was destroyed. While the Jews were in captivity, Babylon was overthrown by Cyrus. In 538 B.C., the Jews were freed and were allowed to go back to Jerusalem. When they returned to Jerusalem, they were determined to rebuild the temple.

As time went on, there were delays in the rebuilding process. The people began to use excuses—building houses for themselves—for not helping to rebuild the temple. The people also experienced problems of opposition from their neighbors in nearby Palestine.

God was not pleased that His temple was not being rebuilt, so He raised up Haggai, a prophet, to instruct the people.

The people decided that the time had come for them to rebuild the temple.

Haggai encouraged the leaders and the people to continue the rebuilding of the temple. Haggai told the people to do first things first. God—nothing else—was to come first in their lives. The leadership of the people began to listen to Haggai, and the rebuilding process continued. Haggai encouraged the people to "consider their ways" and not to be bothered by planting, or eating and drinking, but to continue doing God's work first. By rebuilding the temple, the people would be blessed by God.

- ➤ **What happened to the temple in Jerusalem?** *(It was destroyed by the Babylonians.)*
- ➤ **Why was the rebuilding of the temple in Jerusalem slow?** *(The people were more concerned about building their own homes, and they had opposition from neighboring people.)*
- ➤ **What was Haggai's message to the Jews?** *(Put God first, and continue to rebuild the temple.)*
- ➤ **How does Haggai's message apply to Christians?** *(They should put God first and others second in their lives; they should turn to God when they are tempted, show love and kindness toward others, and be faithful and obedient to God.)*

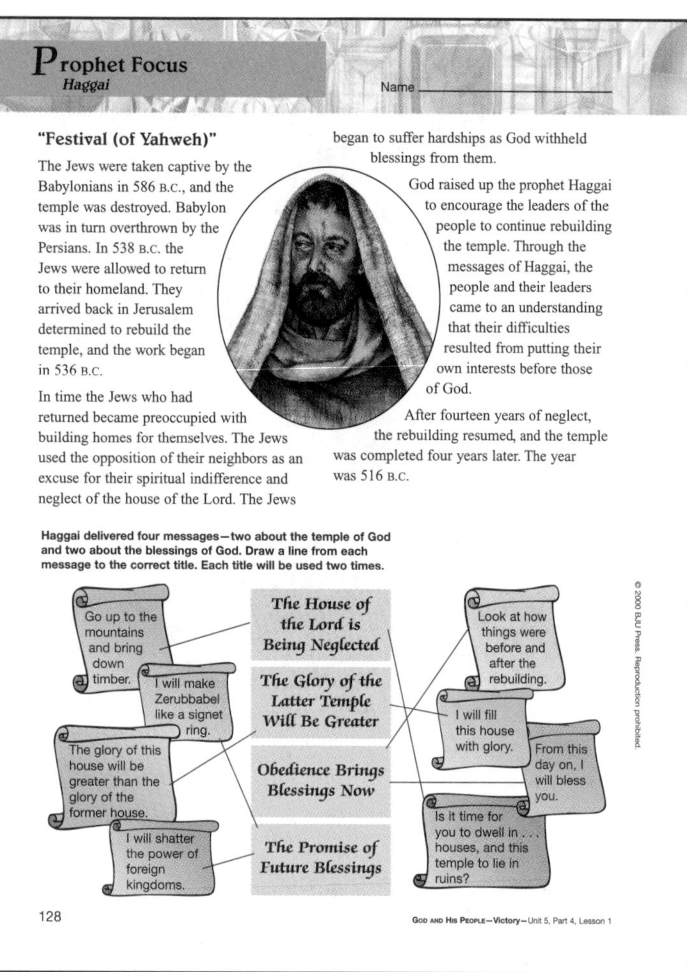

Prophet Focus
Haggai

Name ______________________

"Festival (of Yahweh)"

The Jews were taken captive by the Babylonians in 586 B.C., and the temple was destroyed. Babylon was in turn overthrown by the Persians. In 538 B.C. the Jews were allowed to return to their homeland. They arrived back in Jerusalem determined to rebuild the temple, and the work began in 536 B.C.

In time the Jews who had returned became preoccupied with building homes for themselves. The Jews used the opposition of their neighbors as an excuse for their spiritual indifference and neglect of the house of the Lord. The Jews began to suffer hardships as God withheld blessings from them.

God raised up the prophet Haggai to encourage the leaders of the people to continue rebuilding the temple. Through the messages of Haggai, the people and their leaders came to an understanding that their difficulties resulted from putting their own interests before those of God.

After fourteen years of neglect, the rebuilding resumed, and the temple was completed four years later. The year was 516 B.C.

Haggai delivered four messages—two about the temple of God and two about the blessings of God. Draw a line from each message to the correct title. Each title will be used two times.

128 GOD AND HIS PEOPLE—Victory—Unit 5, Part 4, Lesson 1

Worktext page 128

Review the messages of the prophet Haggai.

Lesson 2

Hymn: "Faith Is The Victory"

Sing the hymn (Worktext pages 276-77). Review the meaning of the fourth verse. Explain that Christians overcome the foes or conflicts brought on by Satan only with the Lord's help. When Christians are actually taken to heaven, the battle will be won. Play the recording and lead in singing verses 1-4.

Background Information

Coins—*During the time of Jesus, there were many different kinds of coins. Generally, a coin would have a caesar or king pictured on one side and his symbol on the other side. When people came to the temple to sacrifice an offering, they would have to exchange their monies, because foreign currency was not accepted.*

Introducing the Bible Account

Discuss losing an object.

➤ **Have you ever lost something important to you?** Encourage the students to tell about it.

➤ **Was the object ever found?**

➤ **How did you feel?**

Direct a student to read aloud the definition of a *parable* from the glossary.

Bible Account

Read the following Bible account or read Luke 15:4-10.

Lost Things Found

What would you do if you had one hundred sheep to care for, and you discovered that one sheep was lost? In one of the parables Jesus told, this is exactly what happened. The man responsible for the sheep left the ninety-nine who were safe and went out to look for the one sheep that was lost.

He probably had to search in many places, perhaps for many hours. How do you think he felt when he finally found that lost sheep? Jesus said that he laid the sheep across his shoulders and carried it home, rejoicing. He wanted to tell all of his friends what had happened. "Rejoice with me," he called to them, "for I have found my sheep which was lost."

Jesus told another parable about a woman who had ten pieces of silver. One day this woman realized she had only nine pieces of silver; she had lost one! She immediately lit a candle so that she would be able to see every part of her house clearly. Then she began to sweep the floor, searching for the lost coin.

Finally the woman found the coin. She went immediately to the homes of her friends and neighbors, asking them to rejoice with her that she had found the coin she had lost.

Jesus told these two stories to illustrate a truth about salvation. The two lost things—the sheep and the coin—represent a person's lost soul. Jesus said that just as the shepherd and the woman and their friends rejoiced over finding the lost things, the angels in heaven rejoice over each sinner who repents of his sin and accepts the Lord Jesus as His Savior.

➤ **Whom do you think the shepherd and the woman might represent in the parables?** *(Possible answers include Jesus, because He "looks" for those who are lost or unsaved.)*

➤ **In the parables, who represents the angels in heaven, rejoicing when a lost sinner comes to Jesus Christ?** *(the friends and neighbors)*

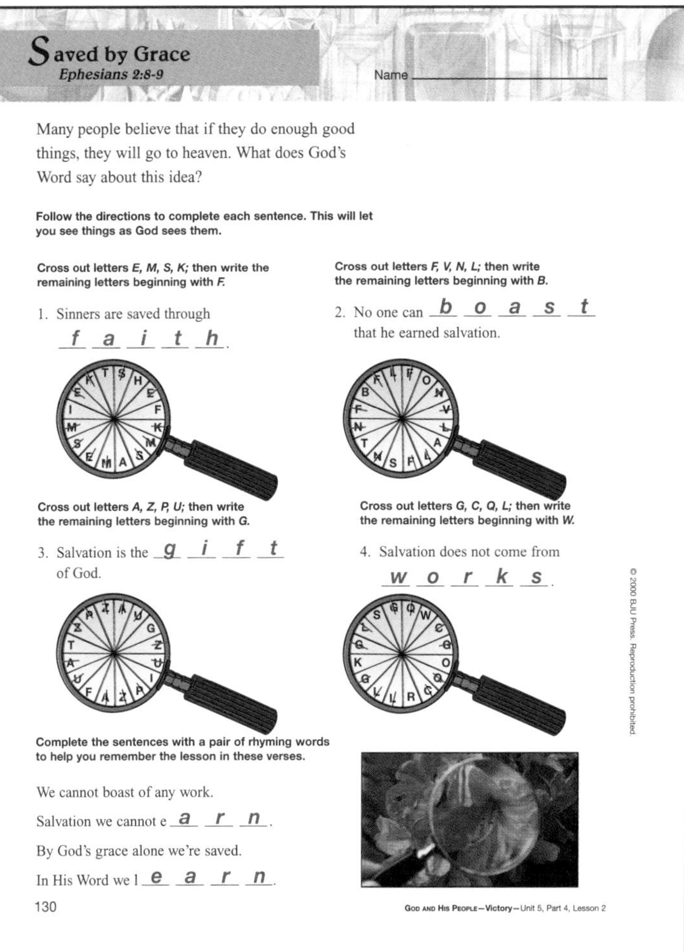

Worktext page 129

Identify similarities and differences between two parables.

Memory Verses—Ephesians 2:8-9

Practice the memory verses. Tell the students to read and study **Ephesians 2:8-9.** Direct them in reading the verses responsively. Begin by reading the first word, letting the students read the second word, and so on. If time allows, let pairs of students read the verses together, taking turns reading every other word.

Worktext page 130

Develop an understanding of the memory verses.

Lesson 3

Materials

- Chart 17, "The Rich Man and Lazarus"

Hymn: "Faith Is the Victory"

Sing the hymn (Worktext pages 276-77). Play the recording and lead in singing verse 4 together. Divide the students into three groups, each group singing a verse of the hymn and then all the students singing verse 4 together again.

Memory Verses—Ephesians 2:8-9

Practice the memory verses. Choose several students to read **Ephesians 2:8-9.** Write the verses on an erasable board; then erase a word or phrase and read the verses. Continue erasing words and reading the verses until all the words have been erased and the students can say the verses from memory.

One-on-One: Prepare a copy of the memory verses with some of the words missing. Direct the student to use his Bible to complete the verse.

Background Information

Lazarus—*He should not be confused with Lazarus, the brother of Mary and Martha, whom Jesus raised from the dead. The name Lazarus was a common name among Jews in the time of the Lord. The name was probably a symbolic name meaning "God has helped."*

Abraham's bosom—*This was considered a place of security or significance. We do not know for sure whether this is a reference to heaven, but it does seem to be a permanent or fixed location because of the answers and denials to the rich man's requests.*

Introducing the Bible Account

Discuss ideas about getting to heaven. Explain that some people believe that there are many ways to get to heaven.

➤ **How do some people think they can get to heaven?** *(by doing good things; being kind to others; going to church; giving money to the church or to the needy)*

➤ **According to God's Word, what is the only way to get to heaven?** *(by receiving God's gift of eternal life)* Select a student to read aloud or say from memory **Ephesians 2:8-9.**

Bible Account

Read the following Bible account or read Luke 16:19-31. Direct the students to look at the picture on Worktext page 131.

Rich Man and Lazarus

Jesus told a story about a rich man and a beggar. The beggar's name was Lazarus, and he was laid at the gate of the home of the rich man. The Bible says that Lazarus had sores all over his body, and every day the dogs, which were considered unclean by the Jews in that day, came and licked his sores. Every day Lazarus desired just the crumbs that were dropped from the rich man's table, but he was not even given those.

Lazarus died, and the angels carried him to Abraham's bosom. The rich man died too and was buried. In hell the rich man was in great torment and looked up and saw Lazarus in Abraham's bosom. The rich man pleaded for mercy and a drop of water to cool him from the flames that were tormenting him.

Abraham answered the rich man saying, "Son, remember that thou in thy lifetime receivedst thy good things, and likewise Lazarus evil things: but now is he comforted, and thou art tormented." Abraham continued to say that there was a great gulf between them so that they could not come to one another.

The rich man, realizing his situation, asked another favor, ". . . send him [Lazarus] to my father's house: For I have five brethren; that he may testify unto them, lest they also come into this place of torment." Abraham again answered the rich man, telling him that his brothers could hear from Moses or the prophets about how to avoid the torment. But the rich man said that they would repent if they heard from someone that came to them from the dead.

Abraham told the rich man this was not so and explained that if they would not repent by what they heard from Moses or the prophets, they would not repent because of one coming from the dead. (Read aloud the information from Worktext page 131.)

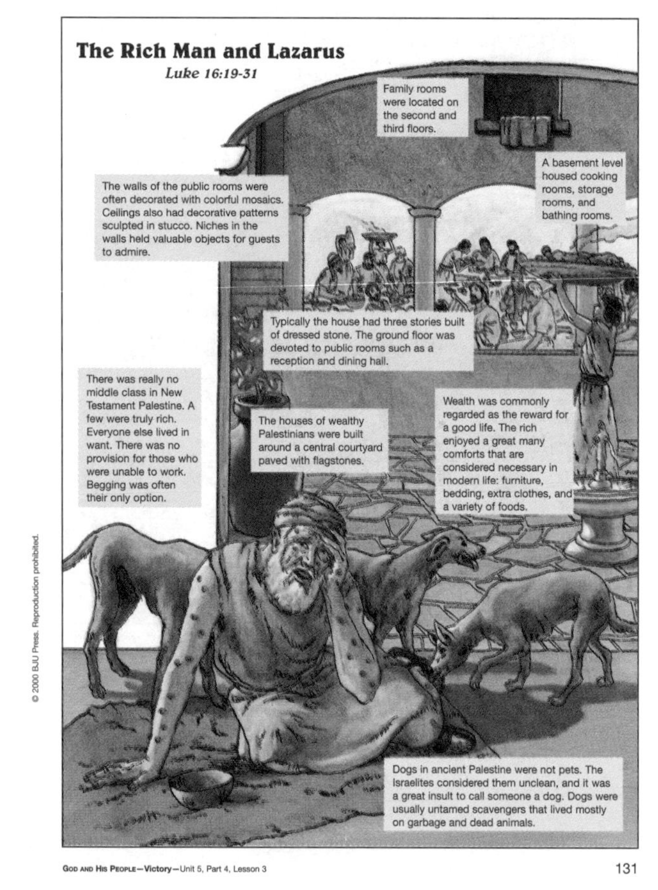

InfoScene: "The Rich Man and Lazarus"
Display Chart 17 for reference throughout this unit. Review and discuss the Bible account as time permits.

➤ **What is the difference between the two men in the account?** *(One is poor, and one is rich.)*

➤ **Where did Lazarus go when he died, and where is this place?** *(to Abraham's bosom which is thought to be heaven)*

➤ **Why did the rich man go to hell?** *(because he did not repent of his sin and believe on the Lord Jesus Christ)*

➤ **Why did Lazarus go to heaven?** *(because he asked for forgiveness and believed on the Lord Jesus Christ)*

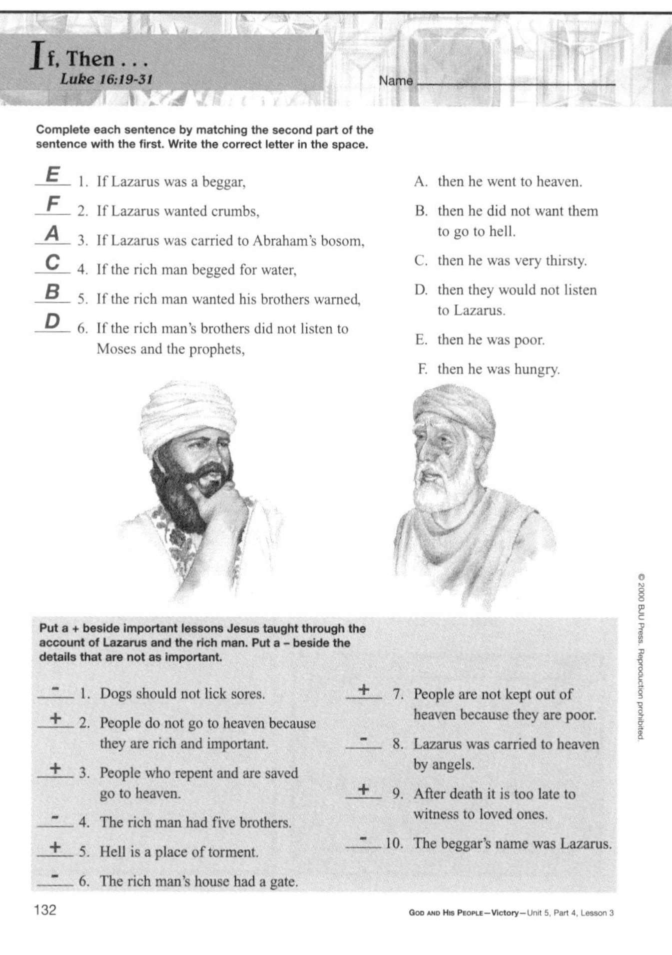

If, Then . . .
Luke 16:19-31

Name________________

Complete each sentence by matching the second part of the sentence with the first. Write the correct letter in the space.

E 1. If Lazarus was a beggar,
F 2. If Lazarus wanted crumbs,
A 3. If Lazarus was carried to Abraham's bosom,
C 4. If the rich man begged for water,
B 5. If the rich man wanted his brothers warned,
D 6. If the rich man's brothers did not listen to Moses and the prophets,

A. then he went to heaven.
B. then he did not want them to go to hell.
C. then he was very thirsty.
D. then they would not listen to Lazarus.
E. then he was poor.
F. then he was hungry.

Put a + beside important lessons Jesus taught through the account of Lazarus and the rich man. Put a – beside the details that are not as important.

\- 1. Dogs should not lick sores.
\+ 2. People do not go to heaven because they are rich and important.
\+ 3. People who repent and are saved go to heaven.
\- 4. The rich man had five brothers.
\+ 5. Hell is a place of torment.
\- 6. The rich man's house had a gate.
\+ 7. People are not kept out of heaven because they are poor.
\- 8. Lazarus was carried to heaven by angels.
\+ 9. After death it is too late to witness to loved ones.
\- 10. The beggar's name was Lazarus.

132 GOD AND HIS PEOPLE—Victory—Unit 5, Part 4, Lesson 3

➤ **What was Jesus trying to teach with this story?** *(Wealth will not get you to heaven; there is a future judgment for the decisions made in this life.)*

Worktext page 132

Determine cause and effect.

Lesson 4

Hymn: "Faith Is the Victory"

Sing the hymn (Worktext pages 276-77). Divide the students into four groups, allowing each group to sing a verse of the hymn.

Memory Verses—Ephesians 2:8-9

Practice the memory verses. Direct the students to locate and read **Ephesians 2:8-9** silently. Allow any students who wish to say the verses from memory.

➤ **What are we not saved by?** *(our own works)*

➤ **What are some good works people may do to try to earn eternal life?** *(Possible answers include going to church, giving money to the poor, and being kind.)*

➤ **Why is man not saved by works?** *(because he would be proud in himself, not in God; man is a sinner, and none of his works would be enough to pay the penalty for his sin and give him the righteousness he needs)*

➤ **How are we saved?** *(by faith)*

Read the memory verses throughout the day for practice.

Introducing the Application Story

Discuss salvation experiences. Choose several students to tell about their salvation experiences. Explain that salvation is the most important decision they will make in their lives.

Application Story

Read the following story to the students.

The Greatest Victory

Tony stood twisting his hands inside the pockets of his jacket. His stomach churned—but not because of the motion of the elevator. He glanced up at his mom. She was staring at the panel of buttons with no expression on her face. When he caught her eye, she gave him a tiny smile.

"Remember, Tony—you don't want to upset Nathan," she said. "He's very sick. Just talk a few minutes. Maybe tell him what's going on at school and on the baseball team. Then we'll leave."

The elevator doors swung open, and they walked down the hospital corridor. Tony's feet made no sound on the carpeted floor. They stopped at the nurse's desk, and Mom gave them Nathan's name.

"He's in the room right around the corner," said the nurse, smiling at Tony. "Go on in. He's just finished lunch, and he'll be glad to have some company."

Tony's hands felt cold, and he kept them in his pockets as he followed Mom to Nathan's room.

Mom pushed open the door. "Hey, there!" she said in a voice Tony hardly recognized. It sounded too cheerful somehow.

Nathan was sitting up in bed. He had on a funny little cap. Tony knew Nathan had lost his hair during the radiation treatments. "Hi, Nate," he said, trying not to stare at the cap.

Nathan's face looked whiter than usual, and his eyes looked tired. But he smiled.

"Hey, Tony. I got your e-mail," he said. "Thanks for keeping me posted on the baseball scores."

Suddenly Tony felt better. Mom's hand squeezed his shoulder, and it gave him courage. "No problem," he said. "Man, you should have seen us in the game against Oakdale. Justin and Julio both hit grand slams. It was great."

Nathan pushed himself a little higher on his pillows. "Awesome!" he said.

After about ten minutes of talking, Mom edged toward the door. "I'll be there in a minute, Mom," said Tony. There was something he had to ask Nathan.

Mom moved out into the hall, and Tony sat down in the chair beside the bed. "Hey, Nate." His voice sounded tense. "Are you scared? I mean, because of what the doctors said . . ."

Nathan interrupted, "Scared to die, you mean?"

Tony nodded, unable to say any more.

Nathan leaned back on his pillows. "When they first told me I had leukemia, I was a little scared," he said. "And I guess it still scares me a little because I don't know what dying will be like." He looked straight at Tony. "But you know what? I have this kind of calm feeling deep down—because I know Jesus has saved me."

Tony leaned forward. "Are you sure? How do you know?"

"Because I asked Him to forgive my sin, and the Bible says He did. When you know Jesus, dying isn't so scary, Tony. In fact, it's sort of happy to think about, because it's the way to get to Jesus."

"Can anyone ask Jesus to save him?" Tony heard his voice shaking. "Anyone? Even if they're not sick?"

Nathan laughed. "You can ask Him today," he said. "Right here." He reached for the Bible on his bedside table. "I'll help you."

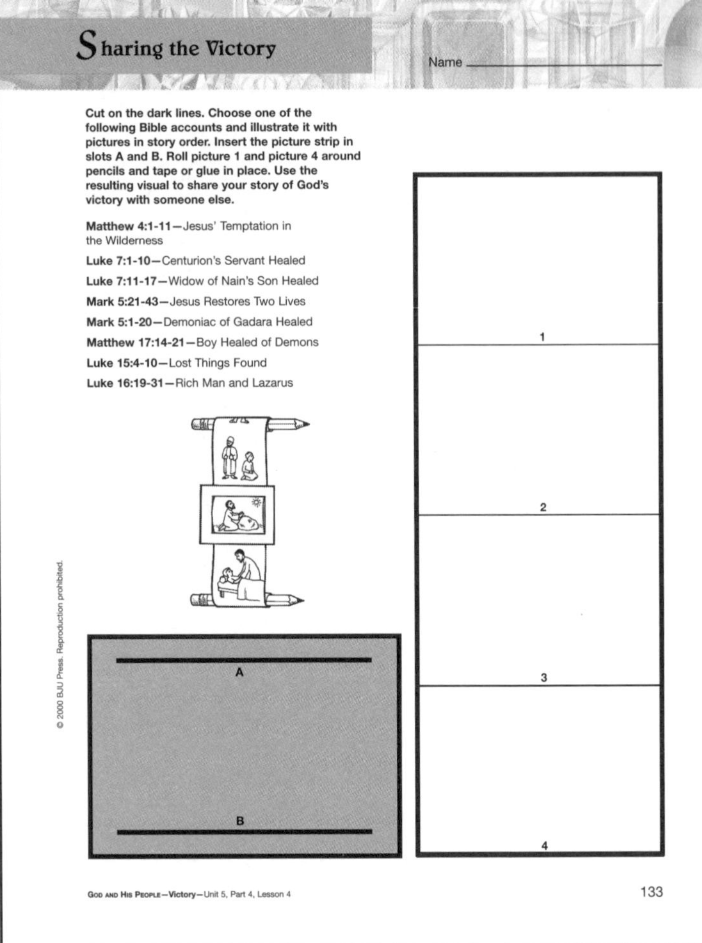

Sharing the Victory

Name ____________________

Cut on the dark lines. Choose one of the following Bible accounts and illustrate it with pictures in story order. Insert the picture strip in slots A and B. Roll picture 1 and picture 4 around pencils and tape or glue in place. Use the resulting visual to share your story of God's victory with someone else.

Matthew 4:1-11—Jesus' Temptation in the Wilderness
Luke 7:1-10—Centurion's Servant Healed
Luke 7:11-17—Widow of Nain's Son Healed
Mark 5:21-43—Jesus Restores Two Lives
Mark 5:1-20—Demoniac of Gadara Healed
Matthew 17:14-21—Boy Healed of Demons
Luke 15:4-10—Lost Things Found
Luke 16:19-31—Rich Man and Lazarus

A

B

1

2

3

4

God and His People—Victory—Unit 5, Part 4, Lesson 4 133

Nathan began to tell Tony about a victory far greater than any baseball game—a victory over death itself. Tony listened with an eager heart.

➤ **Why was Tony nervous about seeing Nathan?** *(because Nathan was sick and was not expected to live)*

➤ **What did Tony ask Nathan?** *(whether he was scared to die)*

➤ **How did Nathan respond to Tony's question about being scared?** *(He said he was a little scared because he was not sure what death would be like, but he had a calm feeling down inside that everything would be okay.)*

➤ **Why did Nathan say that dying would be okay—even happy?** *(because he had accepted Jesus as his Savior)*

➤ **Why is the victory of going to heaven greater to Nathan than winning a ballgame?** *(because this victory lasts for eternity—Nathan can go to heaven to live with Jesus for eternity)*

 **Worktext pages 133-34**

Illustrate a Bible account in sequence.

Going Beyond

Materials

- Bible dictionary or a set of encyclopedias
- Drawing paper for each student

Enrichment

Discuss helmets and foot armor. Read **Ephesians 6:10-17** to the students. Explain verse 15 and the "helmet of salvation." Discuss how a helmet and foot armor are necessary in battle—to protect the soldier from the weapons of the enemy. Christians are to use their helmets and foot armor—protection for soldiers—to ward off the daily attacks of Satan.

Direct the students to use a Bible dictionary or encyclopedia to find out about different kinds of helmets and when people began to use helmets in battle. Direct each student to divide his paper in half, drawing a picture of his favorite type of helmet on one part, and designing his own helmet on the other part.

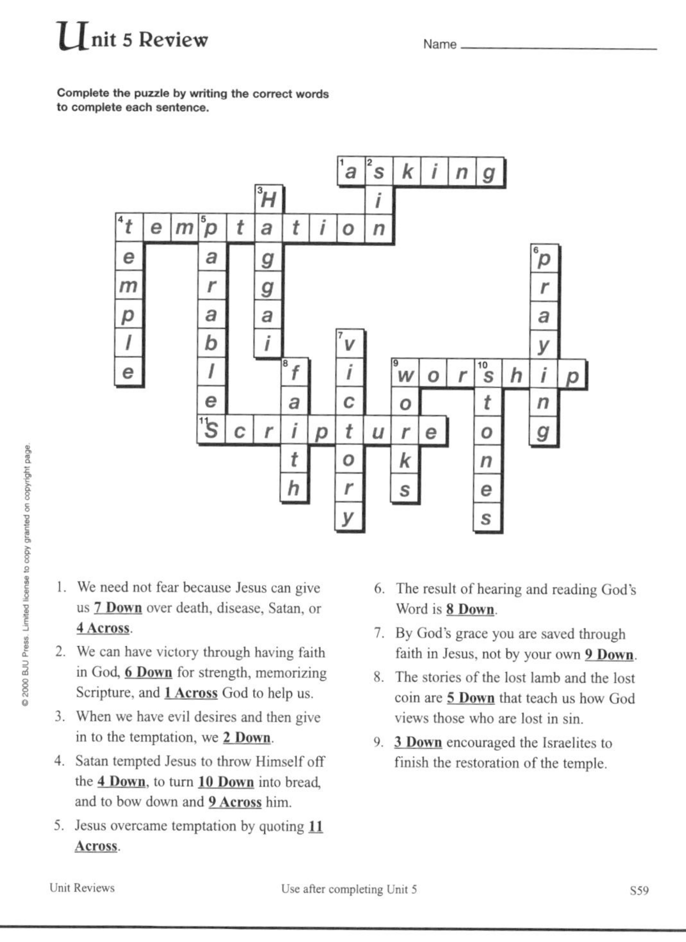

Unit 5 Review Name ____________

Complete the puzzle by writing the correct words to complete each sentence.

1. We need not fear because Jesus can give us **7 Down** over death, disease, Satan, or **4 Across**.
2. We can have victory through having faith in God, **6 Down** for strength, memorizing Scripture, and **1 Across** God to help us.
3. When we have evil desires and then give in to the temptation, we **2 Down**.
4. Satan tempted Jesus to throw Himself off the **4 Down**, to turn **10 Down** into bread, and to bow down and **9 Across** him.
5. Jesus overcame temptation by quoting **11 Across**.
6. The result of hearing and reading God's Word is **8 Down**.
7. By God's grace you are saved through faith in Jesus, not by your own **9 Down**.
8. The stories of the lost lamb and the lost coin are **5 Down** that teach us how God views those who are lost in sin.
9. **3 Down** encouraged the Israelites to finish the restoration of the temple.

Unit Reviews — Use after completing Unit 5 — S59

Unit Review

Materials

- Copy of Supplement page S59, "Unit 5 Review," for each student

Guide a review of Unit 5. Review the people and events in preparation for the Unit 5 Test (optional).

Contentment

Overview

Preparing the Teacher

"The steps of a good man are ordered by the Lord: and he delighteth in his way" (Ps. 37:23). In a society where the prevailing philosophy is "Get all you can get—you deserve it," contentment is very rare. For the Christian, contentment stems from trust in every circumstance that our Lord is working in and through us for His glory. God's Word admonishes us not to set our affections and expectations on the comforts of this world. Yet we are often tempted to argue with what He has called us to do, where He has placed us to serve, how people respond to our actions, and the means He has given us to accomplish His work. Read again and meditate on **I Timothy 6:6-12.**

Preparing the Lessons

Part 1 Lesson 1 Materials—two small pieces of magnetic tape for each student

Part 1 Lesson 2 Materials—several magnets and several pieces of string to attach to the magnets

Part 1 Lesson 3 Materials—art paper for each student (optional)

Part 1 Lesson 4 Materials—a thermometer

Part 2 Lesson 3 Materials—a small piece of carob candy for each student (optional)

Part 2 Lesson 4 Materials—magazine pictures (optional)

Part 3 Lesson 3 Materials—magazines to be cut (optional)

Part 4 Lessons 1-3 Materials—map marker (e.g., dried bean, small candy, dry cereal) for each student

Unit 6 Contentment — Hymn: "Count Your Blessings"

Part	Lesson number	Lesson pages	Worktext pages	Supplement pages	Bible Account	Application
Part 1: I Have Everything That I Need to Serve God	1	181	135-38			**Hero of the Faith:** Bernard of Clairvaux
	2	185	139-40		God Uses Fishermen (Matthew 4:18-22; 14:22-23; 17:24-27; Luke 9:57-58; John 6:1-13; 19:26-27; Acts 12:1-2)	
	3	188	141		God Uses a Tax Collector (Matthew 9:9-13)	
	4	189	142			**Picture the Point:** Contentment
Part 2: God Put Me in My Family	1	191	143		**Character Focus:** Timothy, a Gentile Believer	
	2	193	144-46			**Hymn History Story:** "Count Your Blessings"
	3	195	147-48		A Merciful Father (Luke 15:11-32)	
	4	197	149-50			"God's Answer Is Best"
Part 3: God Gave Me What I Have	1	199	151-52			"Clay He Can Use"
	2	202	153-54		The Martyrdom of Stephen (Acts 6:8–8:4)	
	3	203	155-56	S71	**Bible Study:** Contentment	
	4	206	157-58		Saul's Conversion (Acts 9:1-31; 11:19-30)	
Part 4: God Will Take Care of My Future	1	209	159-60		Paul's First Missionary Journey (Acts 11:19-26; 13:1–14:28; 15:1-29)	
	2	212	161-62		Paul's Second Missionary Journey (Acts 15:30–18:22)	
	3	215	163-64		Paul's Third Missionary Journey (Acts 18:23–23:11)	
	4	218	165		Paul's Journey to Rome (Acts 27:1–28:31)	

<table>
<tr><th>Connections</th><th>Memory Verses and Principles</th><th>Bible Doctrines</th><th>Skills/Applications</th></tr>
<tr><td>TimeLine:
Bernard of Clairvaux</td><td rowspan="4">Hebrews 13:5

Only God can give contentment.</td><td rowspan="16">The Doctrine of God
Attributes of God:
God is all-knowing (omniscient) (Job 42:2).
The Doctrine of Man
Redemption of Man:
Man faces a struggle between the two natures (Rom. 7:23-25).
The Doctrine of Salvation
Reception by Man:
Man must turn away from everything else, including works, for salvation (Eph. 2:8-9).
Elements of Salvation:
God calls men through men (Rom. 10:14-15).
God calls men through providence (Rom. 2:4).
The Doctrine of the Church
Organization of the Local Church:
The apostles served in the establishment of the church (Eph. 4:11).
Function of the Local Church:
Christians should evangelize the lost (Matt. 28:19-20).</td><td rowspan="16">Foundational:
• Realize that Christians should not worry
• Realize that God provides for all our needs
• Realize that Christians should praise God
• Know that contentment comes from God
Practical:
• Recall facts and details
• Locate information in Scripture
• Read a map
• Read a time line
• Take notes
Personal:
• Develop an understanding of contentment
• Choose to be content with good and bad circumstances
• Be content with the family God gave you
• Be content with the possessions God has allowed you to have
• Develop a Bible reading habit
• Apply Bible knowledge to everyday life</td></tr>
<tr><td></td></tr>
<tr><td></td></tr>
<tr><td></td></tr>
<tr><td></td><td rowspan="4">I Timothy 6:6-8

God provides for all of our needs.</td></tr>
<tr><td>History</td></tr>
<tr><td></td></tr>
<tr><td>Art</td></tr>
<tr><td>Science</td><td rowspan="4">Matthew 6:25-26

Worrying is sin.</td></tr>
<tr><td></td></tr>
<tr><td>Art</td></tr>
<tr><td>TimeLine:
Paul (Saul)
TimeLine:
The Life of Paul</td></tr>
<tr><td>TimeLine:
The Life of Paul</td><td rowspan="4">Philippians 4:11

Contentment is a decision.</td></tr>
<tr><td>TimeLine:
The Life of Paul</td></tr>
<tr><td>Math
TimeLine:
The Life of Paul</td></tr>
<tr><td>TimeLine:
The Life of Paul</td></tr>
</table>

Preparing the Unit 6 Bulletin Board

Prepare the bulletin board with the background, border, and colors of your choice. Mount the title, "Contented Christians Count Blessings, Not Circumstances," vertically down the side of the board. (*Note:* Place numerals as indicated between lines of the title.) Direct students to draw pictures of blessings (e.g., food, family, house, school) to be displayed on the board.

I Have Everything That I Need to Serve God

Preview

Doctrines

- God calls men through men (Romans 10:14-15)—Lessons 2-3
- Christians should evangelize the lost (Matthew 28:19-20)—Lessons 2-3

Skills and Applications

- Learn Hebrews 13:5
- Read a time line
- Locate information in Scripture
- Recall facts and details
- Realize that God has given the believer everything he needs
- Realize that Christians should praise God
- Know that contentment comes from God
- Develop a Bible reading habit
- Apply Bible knowledge to everyday life

Lesson 1

Materials

- Song: "The Bible Reading Habit"
- TimeLine and picture: *Bernard of Clairvaux*
- Two small pieces of magnetic tape for each student
- Unit 6 Bookmark for each student
- Highlighter for each student (optional)

Background Information

Monasticism—*Bernard's choice of a monastic life may puzzle the modern believer. Monasticism is based on a misunderstanding of several Bible passages (e.g., Matthew 19:21; 22:30; Luke 20:35; Revelation 14:4) and the equally mistaken notion that bodily discipline results in spiritual holiness. In Bernard's time, the more earnest a man was in seeking salvation, the more likely he was to become a monk. The rituals that these monks practiced increased their burden of sin rather than freeing them from it. Monasticism often clouded the way of salvation.*

Hero of the Faith

Read the following story based on the life of Bernard of Clairvaux (klĕr•vō´).

Bernard of Clairvaux

Few people have had a time in history named after them. The time that Bernard of Clairvaux lived, from A.D. 1090 to 1152, is sometimes called "The Age of Bernard."

Bernard was born into a noble family in France. He had six brothers and sisters. When he was fifteen, both of his parents died. Because his mother had been such a godly woman, Bernard decided that he wanted to serve the Lord. He thought the best way to do that was to join a monastery.

Most people who joined monasteries during that time were looking for salvation. But Bernard knew the Lord already, and he was so convinced that this place was best that he brought thirty other men—four of whom were his brothers—with him. The monastery that they joined was humble and was no more than a large cabin made of logs with a dirt floor. The monks slept in the attic on beds of straw and dry leaves with logs for pillows. They woke at 2:00 A.M. and spent the day in services, silent prayer, study, and work in the fields. They ate plain meals and were in bed by 8:00 P.M.

One of the tasks that the monks had was copying the Bible in the Latin language. There were no printing machines, so each copy of the Bible had to be written by hand, causing mistakes over hundreds of years of copying. Bernard was known for his excellent work in correcting errors. He had a great desire to do things right, even to the smallest details.

Bernard acted as a sort of pastor in his monastery. He supervised the work in the fields, did much of the preaching, and taught the other monks. He also wrote to other monasteries to help them with their problems. He became well known because of his ministry of helping others.

Over time, the monastery that Bernard joined became too large. Twelve men were chosen to go out and begin new monasteries. Bernard was one of these men, and he chose to go to Clairvaux, a place whose name means "valley of light." Bernard and his followers did all the work in getting the land ready and building the monastery. It was difficult at times, but Bernard believed that this type of work could teach them.

In his preaching, teaching, and writing, Bernard emphasized Christ. He spoke of the divine Christ and the believer's union with Him, and he also taught Christians the importance of imitating the life of Christ. Bernard's love for God's Word prompted the desire for self-discipline and godliness in his own life and helped him influence others toward Christlikeness. Bernard was considered the greatest preacher of his time.

Bernard is best remembered for his writing. He wrote several hymns, including "Jesus, the Very Thought of Thee" and "Jesus, Thou Joy of Loving Hearts." Bernard's hymns reveal his deep love for and dedication to his Lord.

➤ **In what country was Bernard born?** *(France)*

➤ **Why did Bernard join a monastery?** *(His parents died when he was fifteen. Bernard decided this was the best way for him to serve the Lord.)*

➤ **Why was Bernard well suited for the job of correcting errors as he copied the Latin Bible?** *(He desired to do everything right—even small details.)*

➤ **Why do you think that Bernard helped other monasteries with their problems?** *(Possible answers include that he liked helping others and that he followed Christ's example.)*

➤ **Why is Bernard called Bernard of Clairvaux?** *(He started a new monastery in Clairvaux.)*

➤ **What is Bernard known for?** *(great preaching, writing of hymns, writing to believers and teaching them to imitate the life of Christ)*

Read aloud the following words to Bernard's hymn "Jesus, the Very Thought of Thee."

Jesus, the very thought of Thee
With sweetness fills my breast;
But sweeter far Thy face to see,
And in Thy presence rest.

Nor voice can sing, nor heart can frame,
Nor can the memory find
A sweeter sound than Thy blest name,
O Savior of mankind.

Bernard of Clairvaux
(1090-1152)

Name ______________________

What is most important to you? Do you think you need a car, a house, a toy, or clothes? Temporary things were not important to Bernard of Clairvaux. He knew the joy and contentment of serving God.

Bernard was born into a noble family in France. When he was fifteen years old, both of his parents died. He had seen the godly example of his mother as he grew, so he decided to serve the Lord in a monastery.

Life in the monastery was not a life of ease and comfort. Can you imagine sleeping on a bed of straw and dry leaves? Each day began at 2:00 A.M. and included services, silent prayer, study, and work in the fields. Bernard did not do these things to earn salvation. His desire was to do what he could for God. He thought of what was important to God, not what he wanted.

Bernard's love and dedication for the Lord showed up in his preaching, teaching, and writing. Through his study of God's Word, he sought self-discipline and godliness. His writing focused on teaching Christians to imitate the life of Christ. Bernard loved God's Word and became known for his excellent work as he carefully copied the Bible into the Latin language.

We also remember Bernard for his ministry of helping others. As the monasteries grew, men were chosen to go and to build more monasteries. Bernard was chosen to go to Clairvaux, which means *valley of light,* where he continued his service to God.

Today, we sing hymns that Bernard wrote to show love and praise for God. One such hymn is "Jesus, the Very Thought of Thee."

Answer the questions.

How did Bernard of Clairvaux show his love for God?

____

____

____

Can you sing praise to God today and mean it from your heart? How can you show your love to God now?

____

____

Our word **service** *comes from the Latin word* **servus,** *which means "slave." A Christian serves the Lord in submission because of love.*

306 GOD AND HIS PEOPLE—Heroes of the Faith—Unit 6, Part 1, Lesson 1

O Hope of every contrite heart,
O Joy of all the meek,
To those who fall, how kind Thou art!
How good to those who seek!

But what to those who find? Ah! this
Nor tongue nor pen can show;
The love of Jesus, what it is
None but His loved ones know.

TimeLine

Add *Bernard of Clairvaux* to the TimeLine. Attach the picture of *Bernard of Clairvaux* (A.D. 1090-1152) to the TimeLine. Remind the students that this time period is sometimes referred to as "The Age of Bernard." Guide the students in gluing their pictures onto their TimeLines. Point out the amount of time that has passed from Bernard until today.

Worktext Supplement page 306 (optional)

Recall details about Bernard of Clairvaux.

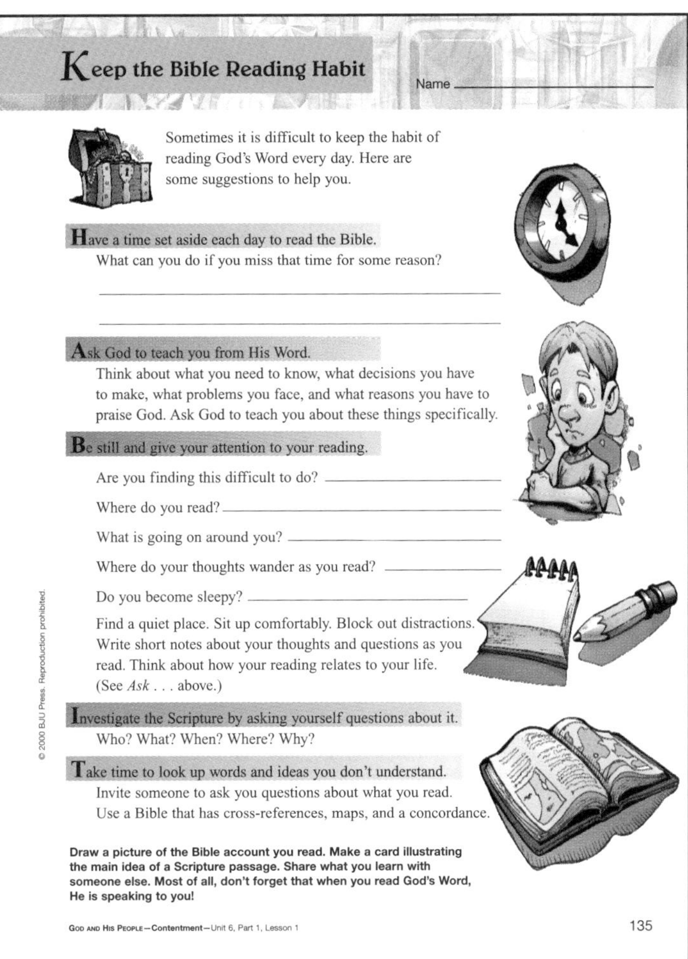

Keep the Bible Reading Habit

Name ____________________

Sometimes it is difficult to keep the habit of reading God's Word every day. Here are some suggestions to help you.

Have a time set aside each day to read the Bible.
What can you do if you miss that time for some reason?

____

____

Ask God to teach you from His Word.
Think about what you need to know, what decisions you have to make, what problems you face, and what reasons you have to praise God. Ask God to teach you about these things specifically.

Be still and give your attention to your reading.

Are you finding this difficult to do? ____________

Where do you read? ____________

What is going on around you? ____________

Where do your thoughts wander as you read? ____________

Do you become sleepy? ____________

Find a quiet place. Sit up comfortably. Block out distractions. Write short notes about your thoughts and questions as you read. Think about how your reading relates to your life. (See *Ask* . . . above.)

Investigate the Scripture by asking yourself questions about it.
Who? What? When? Where? Why?

Take time to look up words and ideas you don't understand.
Invite someone to ask you questions about what you read.
Use a Bible that has cross-references, maps, and a concordance.

Draw a picture of the Bible account you read. Make a card illustrating the main idea of a Scripture passage. Share what you learn with someone else. Most of all, don't forget that when you read God's Word, He is speaking to you!

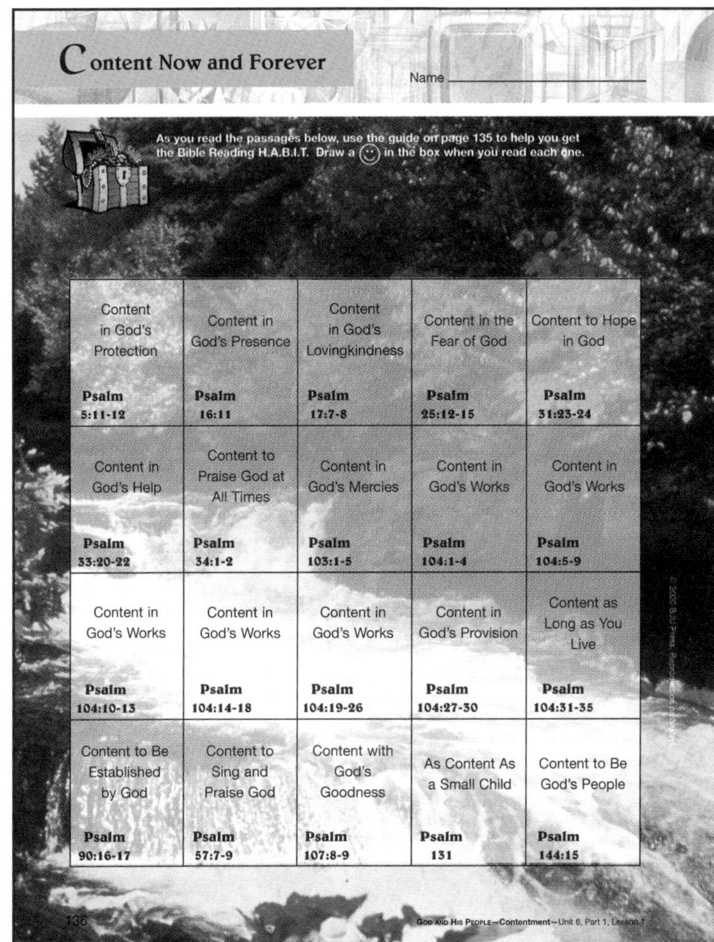

Content Now and Forever

Name ____________________

As you read the passages below, use the guide on page 135 to help you get the Bible Reading H.A.B.I.T. Draw a ☺ in the box when you read each one.

Content in God's Protection **Psalm 5:11-12**	Content in God's Presence **Psalm 16:11**	Content in God's Lovingkindness **Psalm 17:7-8**	Content in the Fear of God **Psalm 25:12-15**	Content to Hope in God **Psalm 31:23-24**
Content in God's Help **Psalm 33:20-22**	Content to Praise God at All Times **Psalm 34:1-2**	Content in God's Mercies **Psalm 103:1-5**	Content in God's Works **Psalm 104:1-4**	Content in God's Works **Psalm 104:5-9**
Content in God's Works **Psalm 104:10-13**	Content in God's Works **Psalm 104:14-18**	Content in God's Works **Psalm 104:19-26**	Content in God's Provision **Psalm 104:27-30**	Content as Long as You Live **Psalm 104:31-35**
Content to Be Established by God **Psalm 90:16-17**	Content to Sing and Praise God **Psalm 57:7-9**	Content with God's Goodness **Psalm 107:8-9**	As Content As a Small Child **Psalm 131**	Content to Be God's People **Psalm 144:15**

Worktext pages 135-36

Develop a Bible reading habit. Read and discuss the page with the students, allowing time for them to answer the questions. Select students to read aloud the highlighted Bible reading guidelines, emphasizing that God's Word is spiritual food for Christians. Explain the four-week Bible reading activity on page 136. Lead in singing together the song "The Bible Reading Habit" from Worktext page 271.

Memory Verse—Hebrews 13:5

Principle: Only God can give contentment. Locate **Hebrews 13:5** and read the verse aloud as the students read silently. Explain that being *content* means "being pleased with what you have." Point out that no one is truly satisfied without knowing Christ as his Savior.

- ➤ **What should your way of life be without?** *(covetousness, the love of money)*
- ➤ **Why should Christians be content with what they have?** *(because they have God)*
- ➤ **How did Bernard of Clairvaux show that he obeyed what God said in this verse?** *(He lived his life without loving money but instead loved and served the Lord.)*

Allow volunteers to read the verse aloud. Direct the students to highlight the verse in their Bibles (optional). Give each student a Unit 6 Bookmark to mark the location of the verse. Point out the illustration of the fish net with fish as a reminder that God provided for His disciples who became fishers of men, and God provides for Christians today. They should learn to be content with what they have. Direct the students to attach the pieces of magnetic tape and to place the Unit 6 Bookmark over the page.

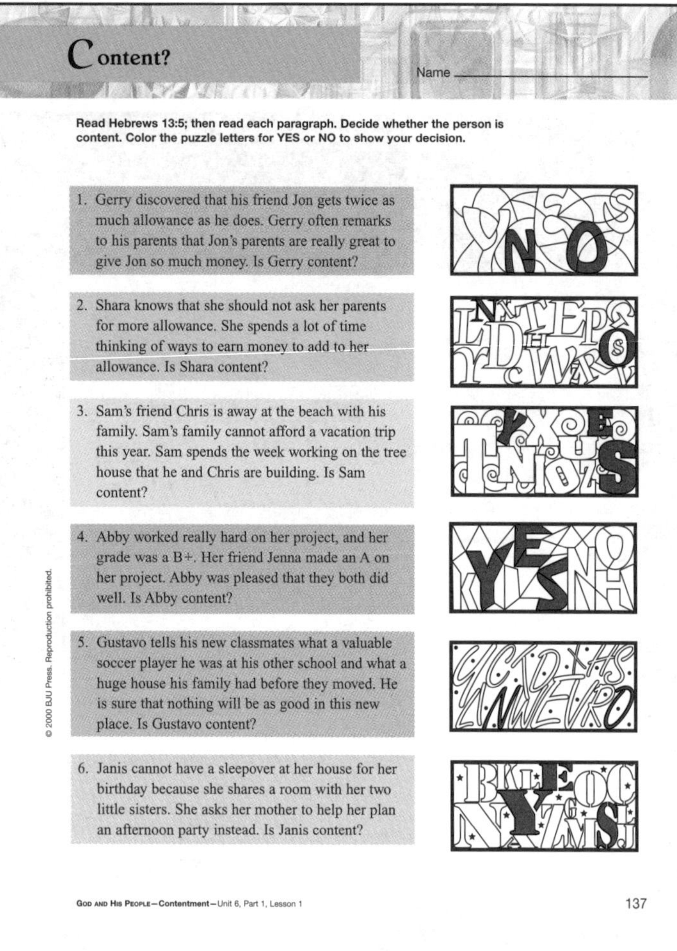

Content?

Name ____________

Read Hebrews 13:5; then read each paragraph. Decide whether the person is content. Color the puzzle letters for YES or NO to show your decision.

1. Gerry discovered that his friend Jon gets twice as much allowance as he does. Gerry often remarks to his parents that Jon's parents are really great to give Jon so much money. Is Gerry content?
2. Shara knows that she should not ask her parents for more allowance. She spends a lot of time thinking of ways to earn money to add to her allowance. Is Shara content?
3. Sam's friend Chris is away at the beach with his family. Sam's family cannot afford a vacation trip this year. Sam spends the week working on the tree house that he and Chris are building. Is Sam content?
4. Abby worked really hard on her project, and her grade was a B+. Her friend Jenna made an A on her project. Abby was pleased that they both did well. Is Abby content?
5. Gustavo tells his new classmates what a valuable soccer player he was at his other school and what a huge house his family had before they moved. He is sure that nothing will be as good in this new place. Is Gustavo content?
6. Janis cannot have a sleepover at her house for her birthday because she shares a room with her two little sisters. She asks her mother to help her plan an afternoon party instead. Is Janis content?

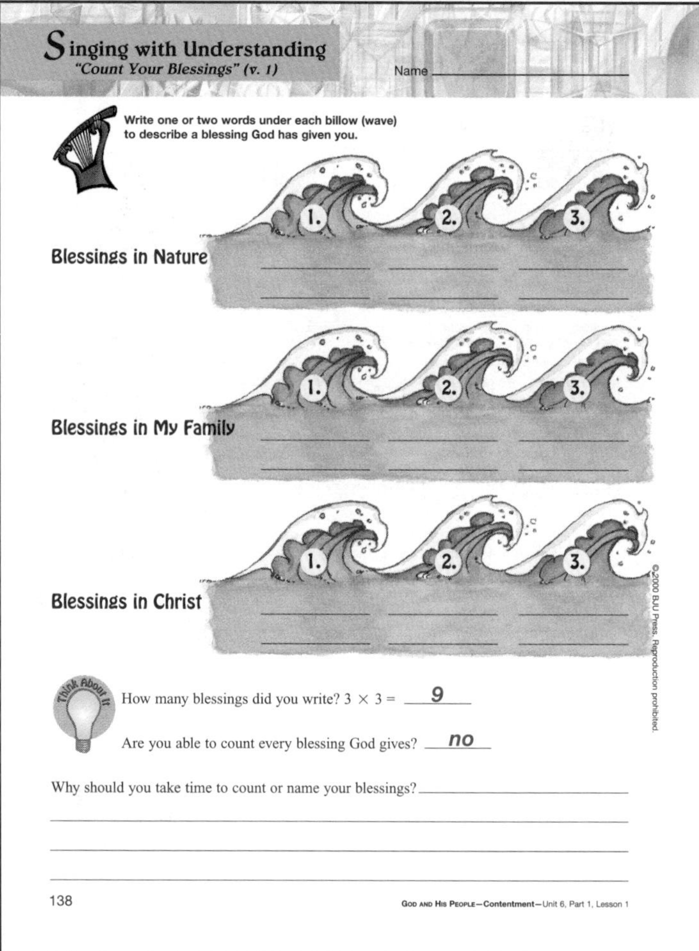

Singing with Understanding

"Count Your Blessings" (v. 1)

Name ____________

Write one or two words under each billow (wave) to describe a blessing God has given you.

Blessings in Nature 1. 2. 3.

Blessings in My Family 1. 2. 3.

Blessings in Christ 1. 2. 3.

Think About It

How many blessings did you write? 3 × 3 = 9

Are you able to count every blessing God gives? no

Why should you take time to count or name your blessings? ____________

Worktext page 137

Identify children showing contentment in real-life situations.

Hymn: "Count Your Blessings"

Teach the first verse (Worktext pages 278-79). Read the words aloud as the students follow along. Play the recording and lead in singing verse 1 together.

Discuss storms.

➤ **What is a *tempest?*** *(a rough, stormy, violent windstorm)*

➤ **What are *billows?*** *(the high points of waves in water)*

Explain that *tempest* can also mean "confusion and trouble." Times of large problems in our lives are like billows on the water during a storm.

➤ **What are the dangers of high waves in water?** *(Possible answers include swimmers drowning and boats flooding.)*

➤ **What is a *blessing?*** *(a gift from God)*

➤ **What does the hymn writer say to do when you are discouraged, and how will this help?** *(Count your blessings, and you will see what the Lord has done.)*

➤ **What are some blessings that Christians can count?** *(Possible answers include the gift of salvation, answered prayer, the Bible, family, friends, houses, food, and clothes.)*

Worktext page 138

Singing with understanding, verse 1.

Lesson 2

Materials

- Chart 18, "Jesus Called Fishermen"

Prepare nine memory-verse cards by cutting simple fish patterns out of paper. Write a few words from **Hebrews 13:5** on each fish. Attach a paper clip to each fish.

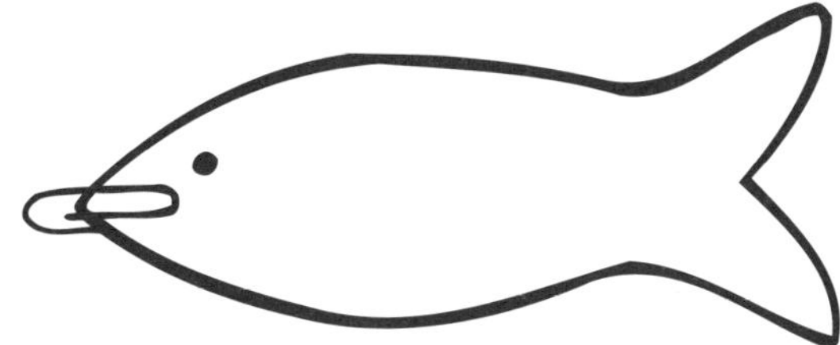

Cut several pieces of string (approximately six feet each). Tie a magnet on one end of the string and make a loop on the other end.

Hymn: "Count Your Blessings"

Sing the first verse (Worktext pages 278-79). Play the recording and sing the first verse together. Review the meanings of the words *billows* and *tempest.* Explain that when we are in a tough situation, we think *all is lost;* when we are sad, we sometimes lose *hope.*

➤ **What does it mean to hope for something?** *(Many answers are acceptable, and students will probably associate the word with wishing for something.)*

Explain that in the Bible, *hope* is not merely a wish for something, but rather a confident expectation—knowing without a doubt that something is coming.

Background Information

The First Disciples—*The first year of the Lord's ministry in Galilee was almost unknown; then Jesus began to choose disciples who would learn from Him. This was not the first time these men had had contact with Jesus. Over a year earlier, John the Baptist had preached, "Behold the Lamb of God."*

Disciple	Background
Simon	• named **Peter** (John 1:40) • caught fish in Bethsaida before Jesus called him (Luke 5) • walked on water to Jesus (Matthew 14) • called both "a stone" and "Satan" by Jesus (Matthew 16) • denied knowing Jesus (Matthew 26) • spoke for/led the disciples • crucified for his faith (John 21) • wrote I and II Peter • was the brother of Andrew (John 1)
Andrew	• taught by John the Baptist (John 1) • caught fish in Bethsaida before Jesus called him (Matthew 4) • brought Peter to Christ (John 1) • brought Jesus five loaves and two fishes to feed five thousand men (John 6)
John	• called "the disciple whom Jesus loved" (John 13) • caught fish with his brother James before following Jesus (Mark 1) • took care of Jesus' mother after His crucifixion (John 19) • wrote the Gospel of John; I, II, and III John; and Revelation • was the brother of James and the son of Zebedee (Mark 1) • called a "Son of Thunder"
James	• suffered and died for his faith in Christ (Acts 12:1-2)
Levi	• called **Matthew** • wrote the Book of Matthew • was a publican [tax collector] before Jesus called him (Matthew 9) • considered a traitor by the Jews because he taxed them • Jesus was criticized for eating with him
Philip	• lived in Bethsaida as did Peter and Andrew (John 1) • called by Jesus' saying, "Follow me" (John 1) • told Nathanael about Jesus (John 1) • asked by Jesus where to get bread to feed five thousand people • asked Jesus to let the disciples see God, not grasping that Jesus was God (John 14)
Nathanael	• called **Bartholomew** • believed that Jesus was the Son of God and King of Israel (John 1) • called an honest man by Jesus (John 1)
Thomas	• also called **Didymus,** which means "twin" • suggested that the disciples die with Jesus (John 11) • doubted that Jesus had risen until he could touch the holes in His hands (John 20)
James	• known as the **son of Alphaeus, James the Less,** and **James the younger** • obeyed and followed Jesus
Thaddaeus	• known as **Judas, son of James; Judas, not Iscariot;** and **Lebbaeus**
Simon	• called **the Canaanite,** which is a transliteration of the Aramaic term meaning "zealous" (Luke 6)
Judas	• called **Iscariot** • was the son of a Simon (John 6) • identified as the betrayer and one of the twelve • returned betrayal money and hanged himself (Matthew 27)

Introducing the Bible Account

Discuss fishing during Bible times. Direct the students' attention to Worktext page 139. Select students to read the information aloud as the students look at the picture.

Bible Account

Read the following retelling of several Bible accounts or tell about these fishermen's lives in your own words.

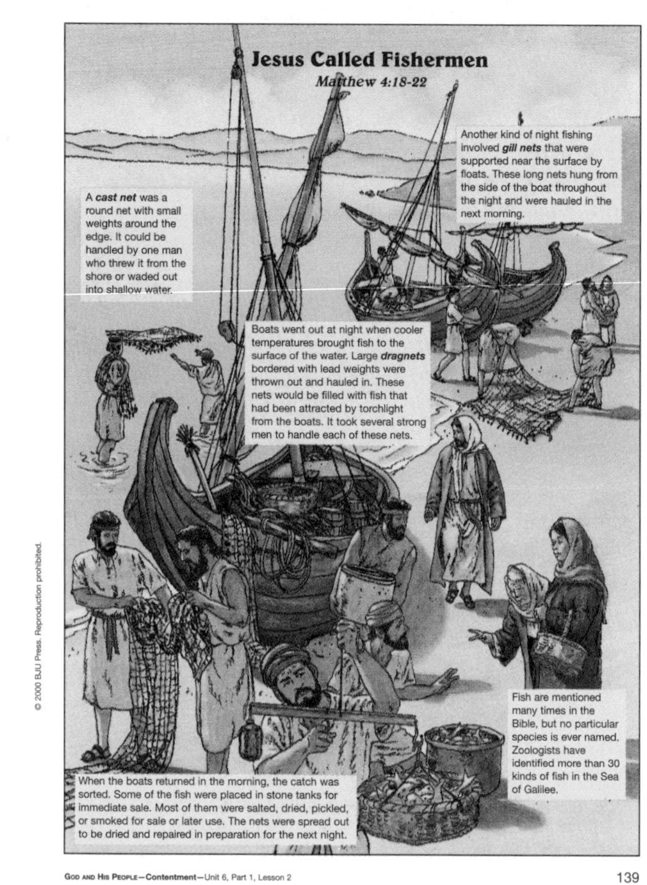

God Uses Fishermen

Simon, who was also called Peter, and his brother Andrew were casting their nets into the Sea of Galilee to catch fish. As Jesus was walking by, He said to them, "Follow me, and I will make you fishers of men." They had seen Jesus before and knew that He was the Son of God. Right away, Peter and Andrew left their nets and followed Jesus (Matthew 4:18-20).

Jesus continued on and saw two more men—James and John—who also were brothers. They were in a fishing boat with their father, Zebedee, mending their broken nets. Jesus called to them, and they immediately left their ship and their father to follow Jesus (Matthew 4:21-22).

Simon Peter became one of Jesus' disciples as well as a close friend of Jesus. One time when the disciples were on a ship in the middle of a sea, Jesus came to them, walking on the water. Peter asked whether he could come to Jesus on the water, and the Lord allowed Peter to walk on the water to Him (Matthew 14:22-33).

When Peter needed money, Jesus told him to go to the sea, cast a hook, and open the mouth of the first fish that he caught. Inside the fish's mouth was a piece of money that Peter used to pay the taxes (Matthew 17:24-27).

Peter became a fisher of men's souls, as the Lord had said that he would. Peter preached and witnessed to people throughout his life and wrote the books of I and II Peter in the Bible.

Andrew, Simon Peter's brother, was a fisher of men too. When John the Baptist told Andrew that Jesus Christ was the promised Messiah from the Old Testament, Andrew believed it. Then Andrew went to his brother and brought him to Jesus Christ. When Jesus fed more than five thousand people, Andrew was the disciple who brought him the boy with five loaves and two fishes. Andrew brought others to Christ (John 6:1-13).

John became known as "the disciple whom Jesus loved." John left his job of fishing to follow Jesus and to tell others about the Lord. Right before he died on the cross, Jesus Christ left His mother, Mary, in the care of John (John 19:26-27). John later wrote the books of John; I, II, and III John; and Revelation. John was exiled to the island of Patmos because of his faith. People today still come to know Christ because of John's writings.

James was one of the three disciples closest to Jesus, along with John and Peter. James died for his faith in Christ. Herod, king of Jerusalem, killed James with a sword (Acts 12:1-2).

One time a man told Jesus that he would follow Him wherever Jesus went. Jesus replied to the man, "Foxes have holes, and birds of the air have nests; but the Son of man hath not where to lay his head." This man did not follow Jesus (Luke 9:57-58).

The four fishermen did not have high-paying or important jobs, but they had the right hearts. Each one willingly left what he had to follow Jesus. They did not have much, but they had everything that they needed to serve God. These ordinary men led extraordinary lives because they were content to be followers of Jesus anywhere in any circumstance.

Share additional information about the disciples from the background information (optional).

InfoScene: "Jesus Called Fishermen"
Display Chart 18 for reference throughout this unit. Review and discuss the Bible account as time permits.

- ➤ **How was the Lord able to use Simon Peter?** *(Accept any incident in Peter's life, including walking on water to Jesus Christ, catching a fish with tax money in its mouth, witnessing to others, and writing part of the Bible.)*
- ➤ **How did the Lord use Andrew?** *(Accept any incident in Andrew's life, including bringing Peter to Christ, bringing the lad's lunch to Jesus to feed a multitude, and witnessing to others.)*
- ➤ **How did the Lord use John?** *(Accept any incident in John's life, including taking care of Jesus' mother, witnessing to others, being exiled for his faith, and writing part of the Bible.)*
- ➤ **How did the Lord use James?** *(Accept any incident in James's life, including being close to Jesus and dying for his faith.)*
- ➤ **How can God use Christians today?** *(Answers will vary.)* Guide a discussion about ways that Christians can witness for God and be a good testimony to others.
- ➤ **If you are saved, what more must you have before you can begin serving God?** *(nothing)*

Memory Verse—Hebrews 13:5

Practice the memory verse. Locate and read **Hebrews 13:5** together. Spread the nine verse fish out on the floor. Distribute the strings with magnets to the students. Allow them to loop the string around their fingers or on a pencil and try to hook part of the verse. When they are able to pick up one of the fish, direct them to display it so that the verse is in order when all the fish are picked up. Read the verse; then scatter the fish on the floor and repeat the activity as time allows.

One-on-One: Place the fish in an empty fishbowl (optional) or on the floor. Direct the student to catch each fish and to place it in the correct order.

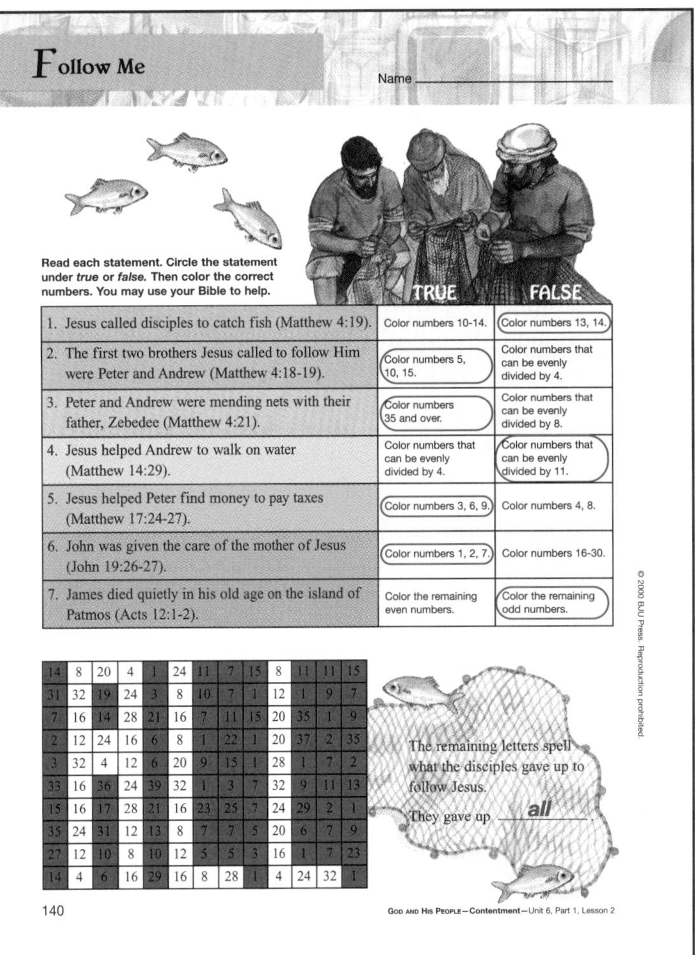

Follow Me

Name ____________________

Read each statement. Circle the statement under *true* or *false*. Then color the correct numbers. You may use your Bible to help.

	TRUE	FALSE
1. Jesus called disciples to catch fish (Matthew 4:19).	Color numbers 10-14.	(Color numbers 13, 14.)
2. The first two brothers Jesus called to follow Him were Peter and Andrew (Matthew 4:18-19).	(Color numbers 5, 10, 15.)	Color numbers that can be evenly divided by 4.
3. Peter and Andrew were mending nets with their father, Zebedee (Matthew 4:21).	(Color numbers 35 and over.)	Color numbers that can be evenly divided by 8.
4. Jesus helped Andrew to walk on water (Matthew 14:29).	Color numbers that can be evenly divided by 4.	(Color numbers that can be evenly divided by 11.)
5. Jesus helped Peter find money to pay taxes (Matthew 17:24-27).	(Color numbers 3, 6, 9.)	Color numbers 4, 8.
6. John was given the care of the mother of Jesus (John 19:26-27).	(Color numbers 1, 2, 7.)	Color numbers 16-30.
7. James died quietly in his old age on the island of Patmos (Acts 12:1-2).	Color the remaining even numbers.	(Color the remaining odd numbers.)

14	8	20	4	1	24	11	7	15	8	11	11	15
31	32	19	24	3	8	10	7	1	12	1	9	7
7	16	14	28	21	16	7	11	15	20	35	1	9
2	12	24	16	6	8	1	22	1	20	37	2	35
3	32	4	12	6	20	9	15	1	28	1	7	2
33	16	36	24	39	32	1	3	7	32	9	11	13
15	16	17	28	21	16	23	25	7	24	29	2	1
35	24	31	12	13	8	7	7	5	20	6	7	9
27	12	10	8	10	12	5	5	3	16	1	7	23
14	4	6	16	29	16	8	28	1	4	24	32	1

The remaining letters spell what the disciples gave up to follow Jesus.

They gave up ___all___.

140

God and His People—Contentment—Unit 6, Part 1, Lesson 2

Worktext page 140

Recall facts about the Bible account.

Lesson 3

Materials

- Memory-verse cards (fish) and string from the previous lesson (optional)
- Piece of art paper for each student (optional)

Hymn: "Count Your Blessings"

Teach the second verse (Worktext pages 278-79). Read the second verse aloud as the students read silently. Play the recording and lead in singing verse 2.

➤ **What does it mean to be *burdened*?** *(weighed down or troubled)*

➤ **What loads of care, or worries, do people sometimes have?** *(Possible answers include sick family members, needing money, getting good grades, or not having friends.)*

➤ **What does the hymn writer mean by "does the cross seem heavy you are called to bear"?** *(Possible answers include "are you going through difficult situations?" or "Do you have hard burdens or worry?")*

➤ **Who will carry our burdens for us?** *(the Lord Jesus Christ)*

Explain that Jesus carried the cross to Calvary where He was crucified. Similarly, Christians are to bear their burdens with Christ's help. Read **Matthew 16:24** aloud. When the disciples lived, following Christ meant possible death. Following Christ for believers today means dying to self, obeying God, and telling others how they can get to heaven. Sing verses 1-2 together.

Memory Verse—Hebrews 13:5

Practice the memory verse. Locate and read **Hebrews 13:5** aloud while the students read silently. Divide the students into four groups. Direct Group 1 to say the first phrase from memory, Group 2 to say the second phrase, and so on. Practice the verse in this way; then assign different phrases to different groups. Continue until every group has practiced saying each phrase from memory. Explain that God says that He will never forsake—give up or turn away from—us.

➤ **What did Bernard give up when he entered the monastery?** *(Possible answers include expensive foods, a comfortable home, an easier job, and nice clothes.)*

➤ **What did Bernard need to be content?** *(to know the Lord Jesus as his Savior)*

➤ **What do we need to have in order to be content?** *(to know the Lord Jesus as our Savior and trust Him to bring into our lives what is best for us)*

One-on-One: Direct the student to "fish" for the verse cards, place them in the correct order, and read the verse aloud. Tell him to remove a card and read the verse aloud again, continuing as long as there are cards to read.

Background Information

Tax Collectors—*During Jesus' day, the Romans controlled Palestine. The Roman government hired tax collectors, or publicans, to collect taxes from the Jews. These publicans were also Jews, which increased the other Jews' hatred of them. Many of these publicans used the position of tax collector to make themselves rich. Matthew was a tax collector before he became a disciple of Jesus. To the Jewish leaders, tax collectors or publicans were sinful people, collecting extra money as profit and cheating the people. The Pharisees viewed anyone who refused to follow the law of Moses as a sinner (Mark 2:16). Their religion promised the grace of God only to those who obeyed the law. Jesus said He did not come to call self-righteous people—those who try to gain salvation by carrying out the details of the law—but sinners, those who realized they needed God to change their lives.*

Introducing the Bible Account

Discuss tax collectors. Choose a student to read the definition for *publican* from the glossary. Share the background information about tax collectors.

Bible Account

Read the following Bible account or read Matthew 9:9-13.

God Uses a Tax Collector

As Jesus was walking by a tax office, he saw a man named Matthew (also called Levi) sitting inside. Christ said to him, "Follow me," and Matthew got up and followed. Jesus and His disciples went home with Matthew to eat at his house. While they were eating, other tax collectors and sinners came and sat down with Jesus and His disciples.

The Pharisees who saw this said to Christ's disciples, "Why eateth your Master with publicans and sinners?"

Jesus heard what they had said and replied, "They that be whole need not a physician, but they that are sick." People who are sick need a doctor, and people who are sinners need Jesus Christ.

Matthew was a sinner like all people. He believed on Jesus Christ and was saved. God used Matthew to tell others about Jesus. He became a disciple of Christ and showed that Jesus accepts everyone who comes to Him. Matthew was once a tax collector and a record keeper of money; he became a record keeper of Jesus. Matthew wrote the Gospel of Matthew, which is the first book in the New Testament. This book contains more of the words spoken by the Lord Jesus than any of the other Gospels.

Matthew did not need to become a good person before he believed on the Lord Jesus Christ. After becoming a believer, he left his job to follow Christ.

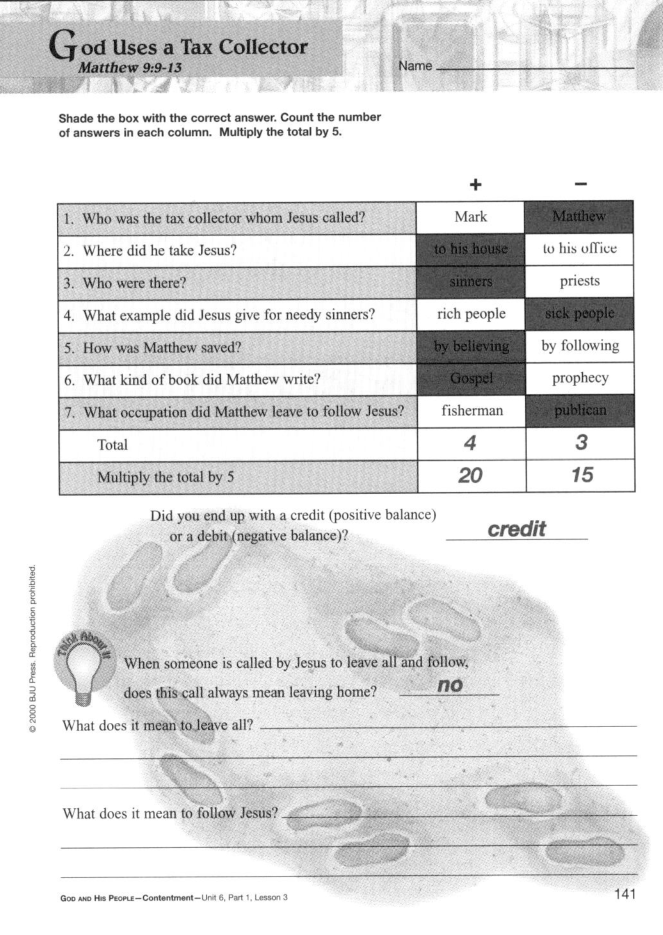

God Uses a Tax Collector
Matthew 9:9-13

Name ___________

Shade the box with the correct answer. Count the number of answers in each column. Multiply the total by 5.

	+	–
1. Who was the tax collector whom Jesus called?	Mark	Matthew
2. Where did he take Jesus?	to his house	to his office
3. Who were there?	sinners	priests
4. What example did Jesus give for needy sinners?	rich people	sick people
5. How was Matthew saved?	by believing	by following
6. What kind of book did Matthew write?	Gospel	prophecy
7. What occupation did Matthew leave to follow Jesus?	fisherman	publican
Total	4	3
Multiply the total by 5	20	15

Did you end up with a credit (positive balance) or a debit (negative balance)? credit

Think About It

When someone is called by Jesus to leave all and follow, does this call always mean leaving home? no

What does it mean to leave all? ___________

What does it mean to follow Jesus? ___________

God and His People—Contentment—Unit 6, Part 1, Lesson 3 141

➤ **What was Matthew's job?** *(tax collector)*

➤ **Where did Jesus go with Matthew?** *(to his house for a meal)*

➤ **How did Jesus respond to the people who asked Him why He ate with sinners?** *(Just as sick people need a doctor, sinners need Jesus Christ.)*

➤ **What did Matthew do to be saved?** *(believed on the Lord Jesus Christ)*

➤ **How did God use Matthew?** *(Possible answers include that Matthew became a disciple of Jesus and that he wrote the Gospel of Matthew.)*

➤ **Do you think that Matthew was worried about what he would do to make money after he left his job?**

Worktext page 141

Recall facts and details and apply Bible knowledge to everyday life.

Lesson 4

Materials

- A thermometer
- Memory-verse cards (fish) and string from Unit 6, Part 1, Lesson 2
- Student Bible Book Cards for each pair of students

(*Note:* If there is no visible thermostat in your room, draw a simple one for display.)

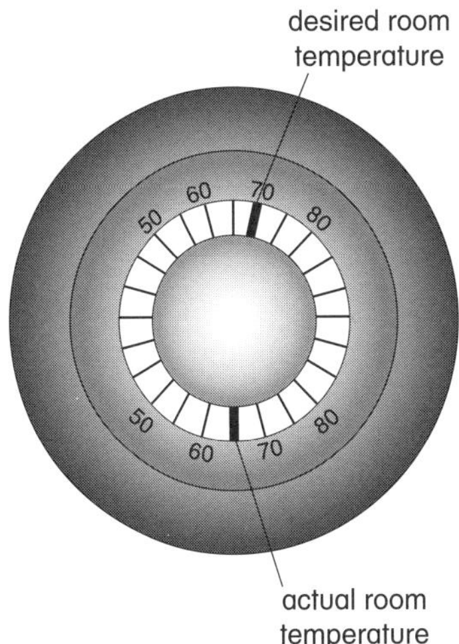

Picture the Point

Illustrate contentment. Remind the students that the love of money is wrong, but with Christ comes contentment. Explain that there are times when Christians will be tempted to want things that they do not have. Instead of letting their desires control what they think, they should use their minds to control their desires. Display the thermometer.

➤ **What does a thermometer do?** *(tells the temperature of a person or room)*

➤ **Does a thermometer stay the same, or does it change?** *(It changes with the temperature around it.)*

Refer to the thermostat in the room or the drawing of one on display. Explain that a thermostat keeps a room or several rooms at a desired temperature. It can also keep an oven at a hot temperature and a refrigerator at a cold temperature.

➤ **What can a thermostat do that a thermometer cannot?** *(control the heat of a heater or the coolness of an air conditioner so that the temperature can stay the same or be changed)*

Explain that when Christians get discouraged, they can control how they feel by remembering that the Lord gives them everything they need. God loves His children and will never leave them. Christians should not let their trials control their "temperature," or temper, but instead choose to be content.

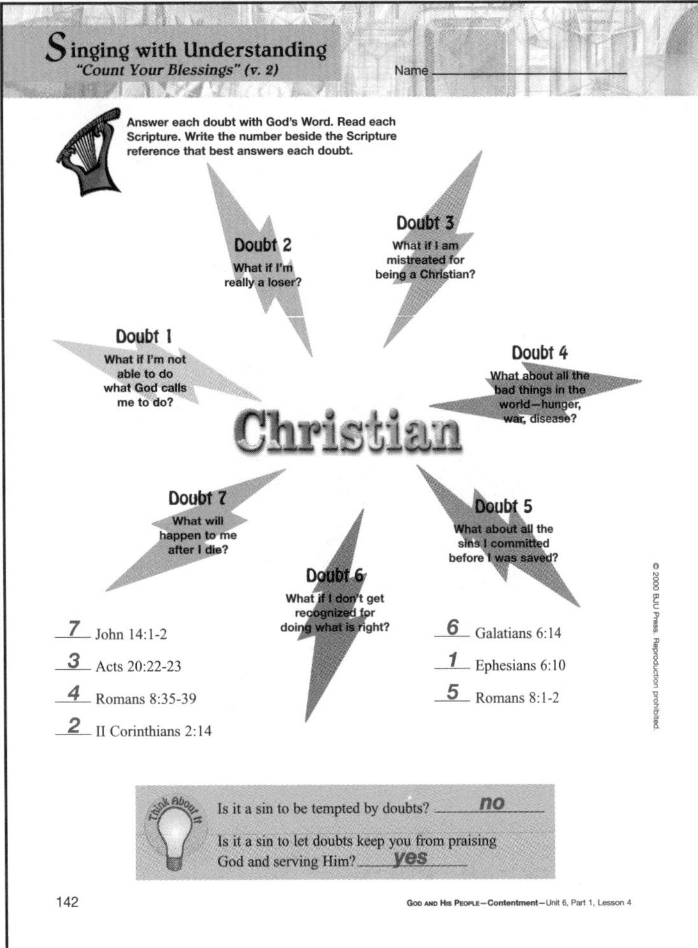

Singing with Understanding
"Count Your Blessings" (v. 2)

Name ____________

Answer each doubt with God's Word. Read each Scripture. Write the number beside the Scripture reference that best answers each doubt.

Christian
Doubt 1
What if I'm not able to do what God calls me to do?
Doubt 2
What if I'm really a loser?
Doubt 3
What if I am mistreated for being a Christian?
Doubt 4
What about all the bad things in the world—hunger, war, disease?
Doubt 5
What about all the sins I committed before I was saved?
Doubt 6
What if I don't get recognized for doing what is right?
Doubt 7
What will happen to me after I die?

7 John 14:1-2
3 Acts 20:22-23
4 Romans 8:35-39
2 II Corinthians 2:14
6 Galatians 6:14
1 Ephesians 6:10
5 Romans 8:1-2

Think About It

Is it a sin to be tempted by doubts? no

Is it a sin to let doubts keep you from praising God and serving Him? yes

142 God and His People—Contentment—Unit 6, Part 1, Lesson 4

Memory Verse—Hebrews 13:5

Practice the memory verse. Locate and read **Hebrews 13:5**. Direct the verse fishing activity, reading the verse together after all of the words are caught and arranged in the correct order. Pass the thermometer to students throughout the day as an indication to say the verse together.

Hymn: "Count Your Blessings"

Sing the first two verses (Worktext pages 278-79). Play the recording and lead in singing verses 1 and 2 together. Explain that Christians can be a blessing to others who may be discouraged. Direct each student to draw a picture (optional), showing a way that he can be a blessing to someone else. Encourage the students to pray for an opportunity to be a blessing to someone.

Worktext page 142

Singing with understanding, verse 2.

Bible Study Skills

Play Bible Concentration. Place the students in pairs. Tell them to place their Bible Book Cards face down in rows. Direct the players to take turns turning two cards over, trying to make a match with both cards being in the same division. (*Note:* Odd numbers of books in a division will cause some cards not to have matches.) The winner is the player with the most matches at the end of the allotted time.

Going Beyond

Enrichment

Make a blessings calendar.

➤ **What is a *blessing?*** *(a gift from God)*

Direct the students to write down one or two specific blessings for which they can thank the Lord. Collect their blessings and make a calendar by typing one blessing in each calendar square (*Note:* You may wish to add your own general blessings that all students share.) Distribute a copy of the completed calendar to each student. Use the calendar throughout the month to thank God for something specific each day.

God Put Me in My Family

Unit 6, Part 2

Preview

Doctrines

- God is all-knowing (omniscient) (Job 42:2)—Lesson 1
- Members of the local church should evangelize the lost (Acts 1:8)—Lesson 1
- Man faces a struggle between the two natures (Romans 7:23-25)—Lesson 3

Skills and Applications

- Learn I Timothy 6:6-8
- Recall facts and details
- Be content with the family that God gave you
- Be content with the possessions that God has allowed you to have
- Realize that God provides for all our needs
- Apply Bible knowledge to everyday life

Lesson 1

Memory Verses—I Timothy 6:6-8

Principle: God provides for all of our needs. Locate and read **I Timothy 6:6-8** aloud as the students read silently. Tell them that Paul wrote these words to Timothy.

➤ **What does the word *gain* mean?** *(Elicit that it is to profit or end up with more than was had at the beginning.)*

Call on two students to read aloud **Mark 8:36** and **Philippians 1:21.**

➤ **What is more important than gaining the whole world?** *(not losing your soul, spending eternity with God)*

➤ **What must a person do to save his soul?** *(Ask the Lord Jesus to save him.)*

➤ **According to Philippians 1:21, what did the author (Paul) live for?** *(Christ—to glorify Him by love and obedience)*

Direct the students to highlight the verses in their Bibles (optional), marking the location with the Unit 6 Bookmark.

Hymn: "Count Your Blessings"

Teach the third verse (Worktext pages 278-79). Play the recording of verse 3; then read the words aloud.

➤ **According to the hymn, what should Christians do when they are jealous of what others have?** *(Remember that Christ has promised Christians His wealth.)*

Explain that the hymn speaks of Christ's wealth *untold* because we cannot even imagine what heaven will be like, but it will be more joyful than anything we can imagine here on earth. Salvation is worth more than any amount of money or possessions that anyone can have on earth. Christians can spend eternity in heaven with Christ. Lead in singing the third verse; then sing verses 1-3 together.

Background Information

Dissension Between the Jews and Samaritans—*In 409 B.C. Nehemiah expelled the tribe of Manasseh for unlawful marriages. The tribe of Manasseh built the Samaritan temple on Mt. Gerizim. Samaritans rejected all of the Old Testament except the books of Moses, called the Pentateuch. They claimed to observe the precepts of these books better than the Jews. The Samaritans knew that the Messiah was coming but had few other biblical beliefs. The Jews would not admit that Samaritans were Jews by birth. They cursed them in the synagogues and would not allow them to witness in their courts. If possible, the Jews avoided them altogether, sometimes going miles out of their way to avoid Samaritans.*

Samaritans—*The Bible account of the good Samaritan is given in Luke 10:30-37. The Samaritans were of mixed ancestry and thus were hated by the Jews. When the Jews of Israel were defeated in 721 B.C., they intermarried with foreigners, who were Gentiles moved into Israel by Assyria. Timothy was also of mixed ancestry and would be hated by the Jews in the same way.*

Introducing the Character Focus

Discuss the good Samaritan. Choose a student to tell what he remembers about the good Samaritan.

➤ **Why was it unusual that a Samaritan would help this wounded man?** *(The man was a Jew.)*

➤ **Why was there hatred between the Jews and the Samaritans?** *(Accept any answer.)*

Share the background information about Samaritans.

Character Focus

Read the following retelling of several Bible accounts or summarize the life of Timothy in your own words.

Timothy, a Gentile Believer

Timothy's name means "honoring God," and that is what Timothy did with his life. His mother was a Jew and a believer, but his father was a Greek. Timothy and his mother were from Lystra. Timothy had good instruction in the Scripture from his mother and grandmother (II Timothy 1:5; 3:15-16). When Timothy was a young man, two missionaries named Paul and Silas came to Lystra. Timothy was saved during this time. The missionaries left, and Timothy became a leader in the church (Acts 16:1-5).

Being part Greek, Timothy would have problems being accepted by Jews and preaching about Jesus Christ. Paul helped Timothy and taught him Jewish customs. Even though witnessing to Jews was more difficult for Timothy, his family background gave him an advantage in witnessing to Greeks. He knew the customs of Greeks, and they more easily accepted him because he was one of them.

When Paul left Lystra the second time, Timothy went along. Although Timothy was young, he became one of Paul's most trusted helpers.

Throughout the rest of his life, Timothy was a missionary. He traveled to Philippi (Philippians 1:1), Thessalonica in Macedonia (I Thessalonians 3:2), and Corinth in Greece (I Corinthians 4:17).

Paul referred to Timothy as "my workfellow" (Romans 16:21), "brother" (II Corinthians 1:1), and "servant of Jesus Christ" (Philippians 1:1). Most of all, Paul was a spiritual father to Timothy. He called him "my beloved son" (I Corinthians 4:17), "my own son in the faith" (I Timothy 1:2), and "my dearly beloved son" (II Timothy 1:2).

Paul encouraged and loved Timothy as a father would his son. When Paul left Timothy to minister in Ephesus, he continued to encourage him by writing letters. First and Second Timothy are two letters written by Paul to Timothy.

God gave Timothy an earthly family and also gave him Paul as a "second" father to help him serve God. God places us in our families, and He makes no mistakes.

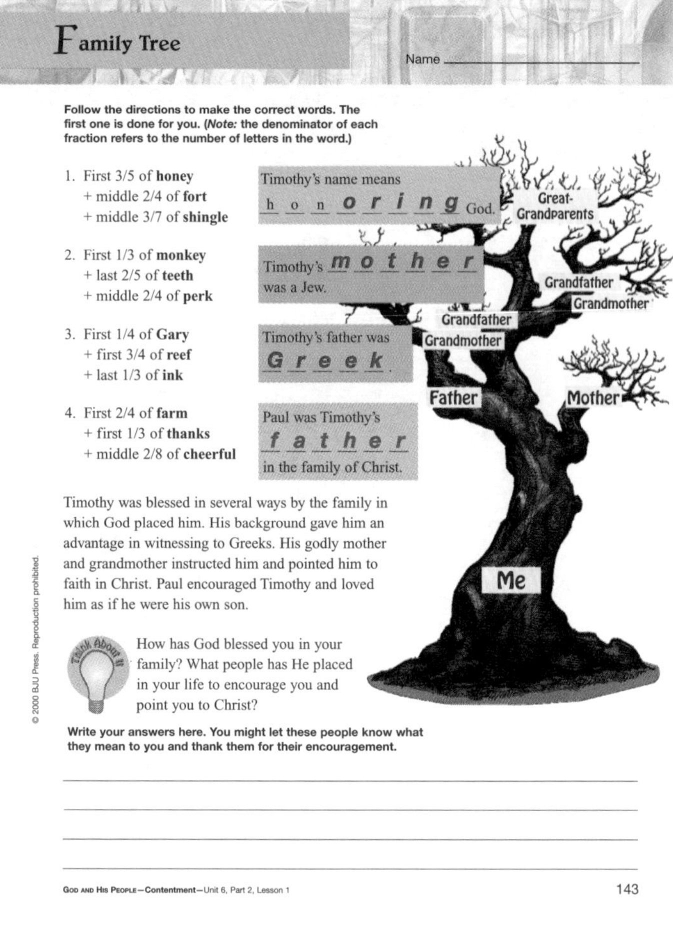

Family Tree Name ____________

Follow the directions to make the correct words. The first one is done for you. (*Note:* the denominator of each fraction refers to the number of letters in the word.)

1. First 3/5 of **honey** + middle 2/4 of **fort** + middle 3/7 of **shingle** — Timothy's name means h o n o r i n g God.
2. First 1/3 of **monkey** + last 2/5 of **teeth** + middle 2/4 of **perk** — Timothy's m o t h e r was a Jew.
3. First 1/4 of **Gary** + first 3/4 of **reef** + last 1/3 of **ink** — Timothy's father was G r e e k.
4. First 2/4 of **farm** + first 1/3 of **thanks** + middle 2/8 of **cheerful** — Paul was Timothy's f a t h e r in the family of Christ.

Timothy was blessed in several ways by the family in which God placed him. His background gave him an advantage in witnessing to Greeks. His godly mother and grandmother instructed him and pointed him to faith in Christ. Paul encouraged Timothy and loved him as if he were his own son.

How has God blessed you in your family? What people has He placed in your life to encourage you and point you to Christ?

Write your answers here. You might let these people know what they mean to you and thank them for their encouragement.

GOD AND HIS PEOPLE—Contentment—Unit 6, Part 2, Lesson 1 143

➤ **What does the name *Timothy* mean?** *("honoring God")*

➤ **How did Timothy meet Paul?** *(Paul came to Timothy's homeland, Lystra, as a missionary.)*

➤ **How did Timothy honor God with his life?** *(Many answers are acceptable but elicit that he witnessed to others for God.)*

➤ **Why was it harder for Timothy to witness to the Jews than for Paul?** *(Timothy's mother was a Jew, but his father was a Greek; Paul was a Jew.)*

➤ **How can Christians be like Timothy?** *(Possible answers include following Timothy's example and honoring God with their lives and being willing to witness to anyone who will listen.)*

Worktext page 143

Recall details and apply Bible knowledge. (*Note:* You may wish to work this page with the students.)

Lesson 2

Materials

- Charts 5-6: "Old Testament Library" and "New Testament Library"

Memory Verses—I Timothy 6:6-8

Practice the memory verses. Locate and read **I Timothy 6:6-8** aloud as the students follow along.

- ➤ **What did we bring with us at birth?** *(nothing)*
- ➤ **What do we need while we are in this world?** *(food and clothing)*
- ➤ **Who provides for all of our needs?** *(God)*
- ➤ **What will happen to all of our possessions when we die?** *(Accept any answer but elicit that we cannot take them with us.)*

Read the verses throughout the day for practice.

Background Information

Mummies—*The embalming process could take up to seventy days. The richer a person was, the more elaborate the embalming. First, the brain was removed by pulling it through the nose by a hook. Other organs in the body, excluding the kidney and heart, were removed surgically, and the space was stuffed with material or wood. The body was put in chemicals to dry out, then wrapped in bandages.*

History Connection (optional)

Read the following story about a man who tried to carry treasures out of this world. (*Note:* You may wish to use the TimeLine to further explain when these events took place.)

King Tutankhamen (to͞ot´•äng•kä´•mən)

King Tutankhamen (better known as King Tut) became pharaoh at age nine and ruled Egypt from 1347 B.C. to 1339 B.C. Like all Egyptian leaders, King Tut was to be buried in a special tomb. When he died, his body was made into a mummy. (Share the background information about mummies if desired.) King Tut's body was put into a beautiful gold coffin inside an underground chamber.

King Tut's coffin was not the only thing placed in the chamber. Like other Egyptian rulers, King Tut believed that he could take his possessions with him after death; he was not content to leave them behind.

In 1922 a British archaeologist, Howard Carter, discovered King Tut's tomb. King Tutankhamen's four-room tomb contained more than five thousand objects, many made of gold and beautifully carved. Among the items discovered were clothes, food, paintings, jewelry, toys and games, beds and other furniture, gold cups, chariots, swords and other weapons, musical instruments, gold statues, jars of precious oils, thrones, and ostrich-feather fans. (*Note:* Most of the items found in King Tut's tomb are on display in the Egyptian Museum in Cairo.) This ruler, who died at about age eighteen, tried to take his treasures with him into eternity. There was only one thing that was never recovered from this tomb—King Tut's soul.

- ➤ Read **Matthew 6:19-20** to the students. **When we die, will we be able to take earthly treasures with us? What did King Tut try to take with him when he died?** *(No. He tried to take clothes, art, furniture, sculptures, chariots, weapons, food, and jewelry with him.)*
- ➤ **What was never recovered from King Tut's tomb?** *(his soul)*
- ➤ **What heavenly treasures will Christians be able to lay up for themselves?** *(obeying God's commands, salvation, telling others about Jesus Christ, worshiping God in His house, etc.)*
- ➤ **What is the first command that people must obey before they can lay up treasures?** *(the command to be saved)*

Hymn History Story

Read the following story about the writing of "Count Your Blessings."

When Joseph Oatman Jr. was a boy, he always tried to sit next to his father in church. He liked to hear his father's strong voice ringing out as the hymns were sung. Perhaps this early interest in singing hymns prepared Joseph for his later career as a hymn writer.

When Joseph grew older, his father gave him a partnership in the family's merchant business. After a while, Joseph felt that the Lord wanted him in a church ministry. He was ordained as a preacher and ministered in a church in New Jersey. Later, he became a traveling preacher, visiting many different churches and giving the gospel. Though he was not a talented speaker, Joseph was willing for the Lord to use him, and many people accepted Christ through his ministry.

At the age of thirty-six, Joseph Oatman discovered that he had a talent for writing hymns. He found that he could give the gospel through a hymn even more effectively than through speaking. Oatman wrote more than five thousand hymns, including "Higher Ground" and "No, Not One."

In 1897 Edwin Excell—a brick mason, song leader, and music teacher—composed the

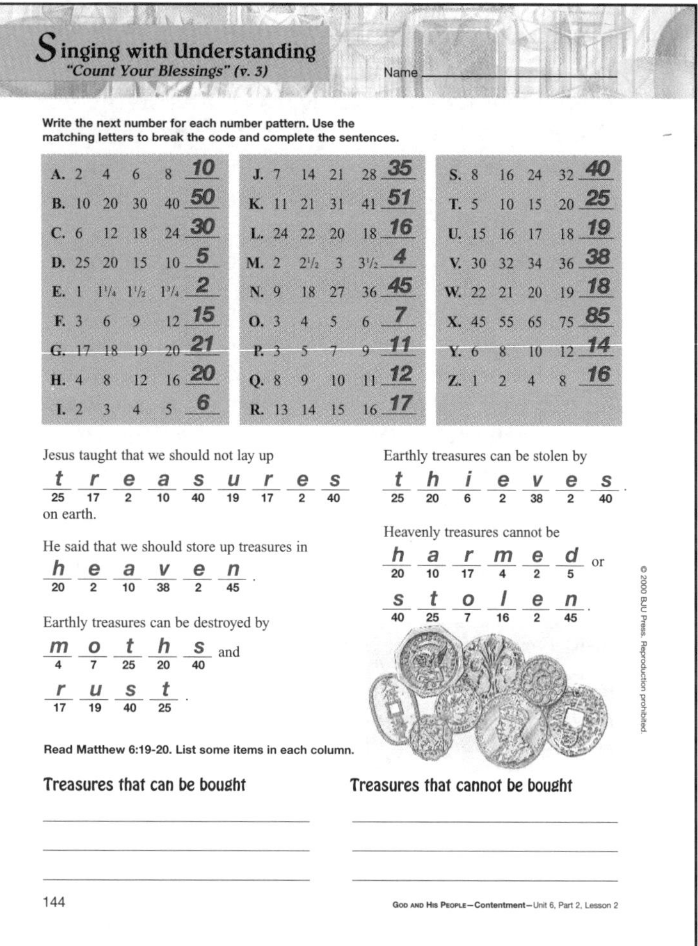

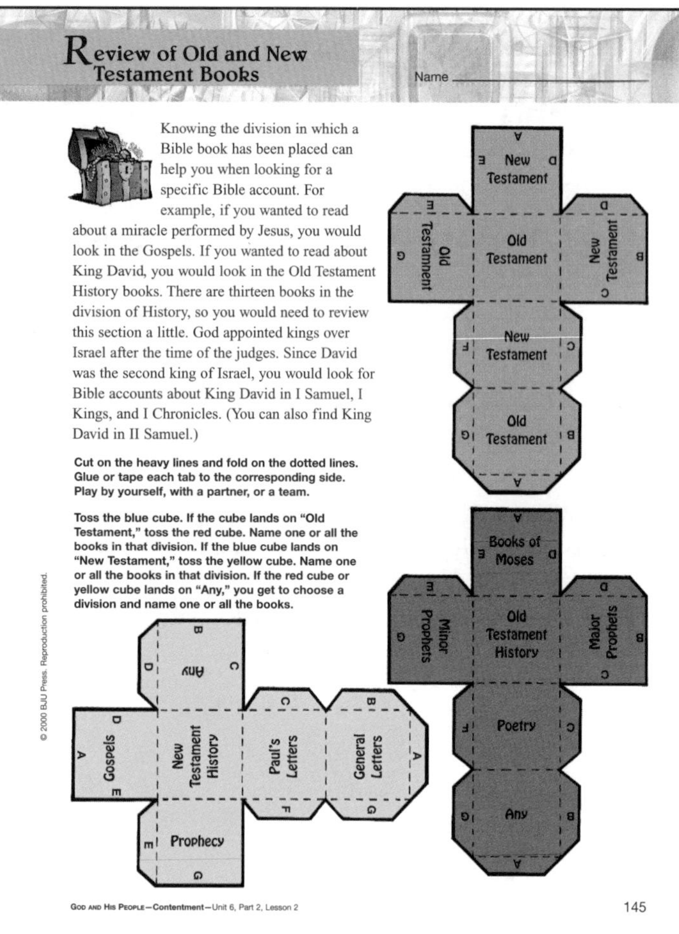

music to Oatman's hymn "Count Your Blessings." Sometimes Excell traveled with the well-known preacher Gipsy Smith and sang at his evangelistic meetings. "Count Your Blessings" was very popular in Great Britain, especially in London. Gipsy Smith said of this hymn, "The men sing it, the boys whistle it, and the women rock their babies to sleep to it." Today the hymn is sung in many different languages all over the world.

- **What were some jobs that Joseph Oatman Jr. had?** *(a partner in his family's merchant business, a preacher at a church, a traveling preacher, and a hymn writer)*
- **Why do you think "Count Your Blessings" is such a well-loved hymn?** *(Possible answers include that it reminds Christians of the blessings of God.)*

Hymn: "Count Your Blessings"

Sing the first three verses (Worktext pages 278-79). Lead in singing the first three verses of the hymn. Encourage the students to write down as many blessings as they can in one minute. Allow three students with the most blessings listed to each lead the singing of a verse (optional).

Worktext page 144

Singing with understanding, verse 3.

Bible Study Skills

Review the divisions of the books of the Bible. Display Chart 5, "Old Testament Library" and Chart 6, "New Testament Library." Choose students to read the names of the books in each division.

Worktext pages 145-46

Review the Old Testament and New Testament divisions. (*Note:* Students may refer to Charts 5 and 6 or to their bookmarks to check each other's answers.)

Lesson 3

Materials

- Small piece of carob candy for each student (optional)

Hymn: "Count Your Blessings"

Teach the fourth verse (Worktext pages 278-79). Read the words of the fourth verse aloud.

➤ **What is a *conflict?* How should you respond to conflict?** *(a battle or problem; Do not be discouraged but trust God.)*

➤ **Whom does God send to help Christians in times of trouble?** *(His angels)*

➤ **What do God and His angels give you whenever you have need?** *(help and comfort)*

Lead in singing the fourth verse; then sing together verses 1-4.

Background Information

Husks—*Husks referred to in the Bible were not corn husks. Maize, or corn as we call it, was unknown in Bible times. These husks were probably carob-tree fruit pods, which grow six to ten inches long. They were usually fed to animals (pigs).*

Introducing the Bible Account

Discuss hunger.

➤ **What are some of your least favorite foods?** *(Accept any answer.)*

➤ Pretend that you skipped lunch and sat down to supper. **How would you feel if you were served your least favorite food?**

➤ Pretend that for some reason you had not eaten for several days. **How would you feel if you were served your least favorite food?**

Explain that when people have gone without food and are starving, they will eat food that they would not normally eat.

Bible Account

Read the following Bible account or read Luke 15:11-32.

A Merciful Father

A certain father lived with his two sons. The older son was obedient to the father, but the younger son was discontented with his life and wanted to leave home. He asked his father for his inheritance—the money that he was to receive when his father died.

While the older son stayed at home with the father, the younger son gathered together all his possessions and traveled to a far country. There he spent all the inheritance that he had. He was a prodigal, or a wasteful son who had spent all of his money on worldly pleasures. A famine arose in the country where he was living, and he found himself with no money and no food.

The younger son found a pig farmer who hired him to feed his pigs. He was so hungry that he considered eating the husks intended for the pigs' food.

One day the prodigal son realized how foolish he had been. "How many hired servants of my father's have bread enough and to spare!" he said. The father's servants had no needs, yet one of the father's sons was starving.

The young man planned how he could return home to his loving father and say to him, "Father, I have sinned . . . and am no more worthy to be called thy son: make me as one of thy hired servants." The son knew that he had sinned against his father and against God and that he must ask for forgiveness.

The young man left the pig farm for home. When he was still far away, his father saw him, ran to him, and kissed him. The son began to tell his father that he had sinned, but before he could finish, his father stopped him and called out to his servants, "Bring forth the best robe, and put it on him; and put a ring on his hand, and shoes on his feet." The father called for a celebration with food and music.

The older son, who had been working in the field, walked toward the house and saw all the excitement. He called to one of the servants and asked him what the celebration was about.

When the servant told the older brother that his younger brother had returned and the father was celebrating because of it, the older son grew angry. He would not even go into the feast. When his father learned that his older son had stayed outside, he came out to speak to him.

The older son told the father that he had always been a good son; he had never run away or disobeyed. But he complained that his father had never given him a celebration with food and friends.

The father said that the older son was always with him, and everything that belonged to him belonged to this son. The father explained that it was right to celebrate because the younger son had been lost but now was found.

➤ **According to I Timothy 6:8, why should the youngest son have been content at home?** *(He had food and clothing.)*

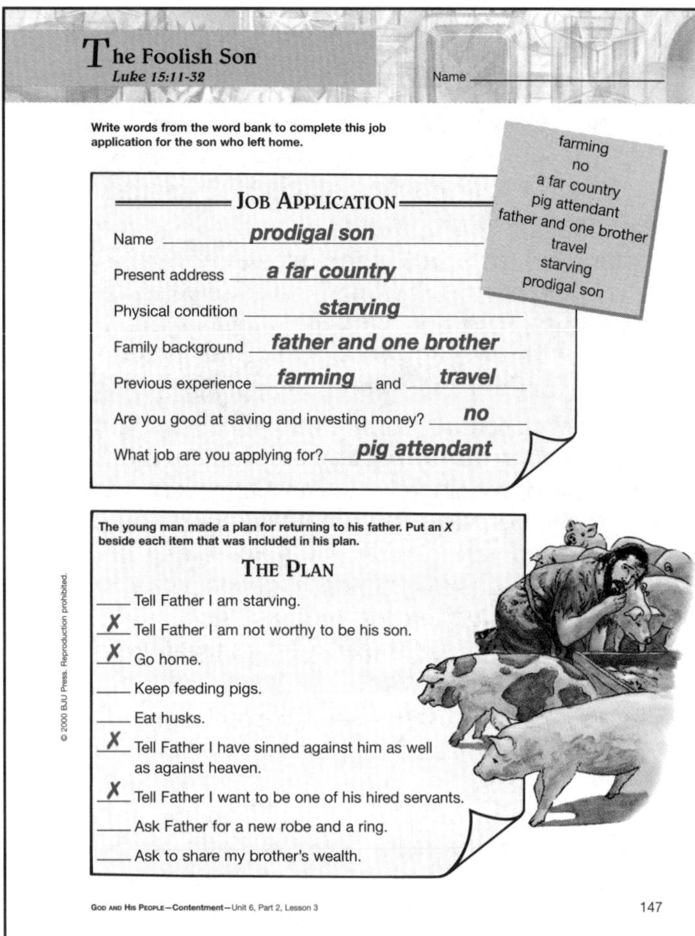

The Foolish Son
Luke 15:11-32

Name ______

Write words from the word bank to complete this job application for the son who left home.

farming
no
a far country
pig attendant
father and one brother
travel
starving
prodigal son

Job Application

Name ***prodigal son***

Present address ***a far country***

Physical condition ***starving***

Family background ***father and one brother***

Previous experience ***farming*** and ***travel***

Are you good at saving and investing money? ***no***

What job are you applying for? ***pig attendant***

The young man made a plan for returning to his father. Put an *X* beside each item that was included in his plan.

The Plan

___ Tell Father I am starving.
_X_ Tell Father I am not worthy to be his son.
_X_ Go home.
___ Keep feeding pigs.
___ Eat husks.
_X_ Tell Father I have sinned against him as well as against heaven.
_X_ Tell Father I want to be one of his hired servants.
___ Ask Father for a new robe and a ring.
___ Ask to share my brother's wealth.

God and His People—Contentment—Unit 6, Part 2, Lesson 3 147

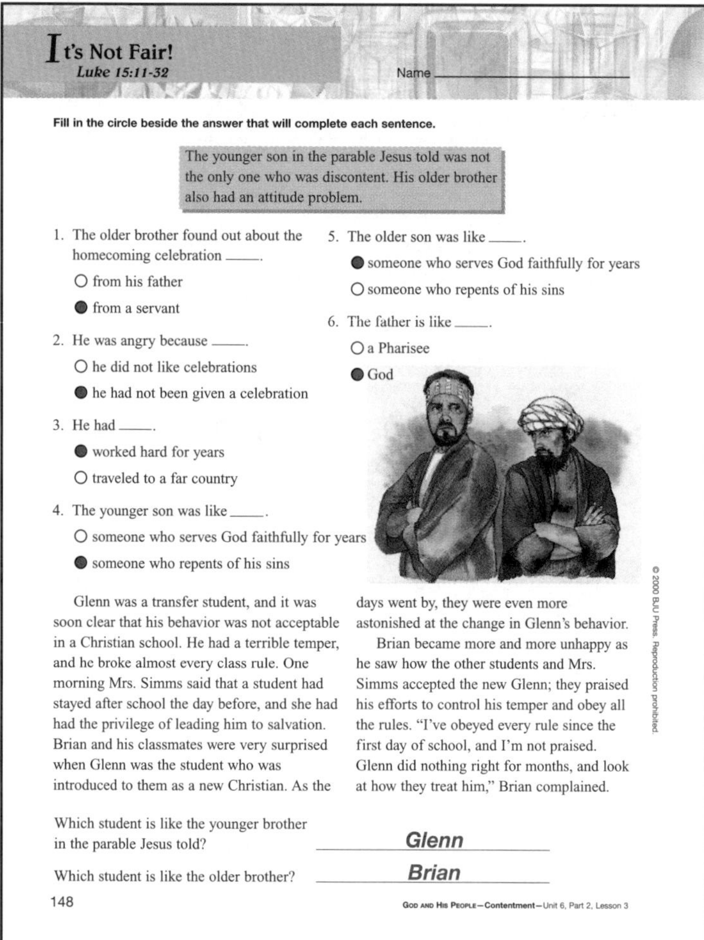

It's Not Fair!
Luke 15:11-32

Name ______

Fill in the circle beside the answer that will complete each sentence.

The younger son in the parable Jesus told was not the only one who was discontent. His older brother also had an attitude problem.

1. The older brother found out about the homecoming celebration ___.
   - ○ from his father
   - ● from a servant
2. He was angry because ___.
   - ○ he did not like celebrations
   - ● he had not been given a celebration
3. He had ___.
   - ● worked hard for years
   - ○ traveled to a far country
4. The younger son was like ___.
   - ○ someone who serves God faithfully for years
   - ● someone who repents of his sins
5. The older son was like ___.
   - ● someone who serves God faithfully for years
   - ○ someone who repents of his sins
6. The father is like ___.
   - ○ a Pharisee
   - ● God

Glenn was a transfer student, and it was soon clear that his behavior was not acceptable in a Christian school. He had a terrible temper, and he broke almost every class rule. One morning Mrs. Simms said that a student had stayed after school the day before, and she had had the privilege of leading him to salvation. Brian and his classmates were very surprised when Glenn was the student who was introduced to them as a new Christian. As the days went by, they were even more astonished at the change in Glenn's behavior.

Brian became more and more unhappy as he saw how the other students and Mrs. Simms accepted the new Glenn; they praised his efforts to control his temper and obey all the rules. "I've obeyed every rule since the first day of school, and I'm not praised. Glenn did nothing right for months, and look at how they treat him," Brian complained.

Which student is like the younger brother in the parable Jesus told? ***Glenn***

Which student is like the older brother? ***Brian***

148 God and His People—Contentment—Unit 6, Part 2, Lesson 3

- ➤ **What other blessings did the youngest son have?** *(Possible answers include a loving father, a brother, and servants.)*
- ➤ **Why was each brother discontent?** *(The younger son was discontent to live at home, and the older was discontent with the way that the father celebrated the return of his brother.)*
- ➤ **Did the younger son find contentment after leaving home? Where did the younger son become content?** *(No. He found contentment at home where he was to begin with.)*
- ➤ **What does the word *prodigal* mean?** *(wasteful and careless)* If no one knows the meaning, choose a student to look up *prodigal* in the glossary and read the definition aloud.
- ➤ **How does God expect us to treat what He gives us?** *(He expects us to take care of it, being good stewards.)*
- ➤ **How could this account be a picture of salvation?** *(The father represents the heavenly Father, the younger son represents sinners, and the older son represents the Pharisees.)*

Memory Verses—I Timothy 6:6-8

Practice the memory verses. Locate **I Timothy 6:6-8** and read it aloud as the students follow along. Point out that the younger son was not content at home with his family, and he was not content with the pigs. Share the background information about husks. Explain that the carob tree produces fruit similar to peas inside the husks of brown leathery pods. Gum from these pods is often roasted and ground and can be used as a substitute for chocolate. Call the students forward in small groups to say the memory verse; then give each member of the group a piece of carob candy (optional).

Worktext page 147

Recall details about the Bible account.

Worktext page 148

Apply Bible knowledge to everyday life.

Lesson 4

Materials

- Magazine pictures (optional)

Introducing the Application Story

Discuss disappointments.

➤ **Have you ever been looking forward to something for a long time only to have it canceled for some reason?**

➤ **What was your reaction to the change in plans?**

➤ **Who is in control of all things?** *(God)*

Application Story

Read the following story to the students.

God's Answer Is Best

"Lord, please let me go water-skiing this weekend," Louie prayed. "I want so much to learn how." Louie was already a good swimmer. He and his Uncle Melvin had spent many Saturdays at the lake. Louie liked to watch the skiers skimming the surface in a white spray of water. Uncle Melvin had just bought a new boat and had promised to teach Louie how to ski.

This Saturday would be the perfect time, thought Louie. All week he kept praying for good weather. But when Saturday came, it was cloudy. Uncle Melvin frowned at the sky.

"Louie, there could be danger if a storm should come up. I don't think we'd better go today."

Louie tried to smile, but he couldn't. He went back to his room and flopped down by his bed. "Dear Lord," he prayed, "I don't think that You answered my prayer, but help me to give thanks in everything and learn to be content."

Louie kept busy that morning. His dad had some jobs for him to do around the house, and he didn't miss the lake much—until the sun came shining through the windows of the house.

"Oh, Uncle Melvin was wrong; we could have gone out today. Look how nice it is," said Louie.

"There was no way Uncle Melvin could have known the sun would come out," said Dad. "The Lord had a good reason for keeping you home today."

That happened right before lunch. About two o'clock the sky became overcast again, and it began to rain. The wind swept the rain against the windows.

That night, Louie was setting the table when his mom called him into the living room to see the news on television.

"We have just had a report that although this afternoon's rain and wind were light in town, there was a storm out on the lake, endangering the lives of all who were out boating. Memorial Hospital reports four emergency patients this afternoon from boating injuries."

Louie's dad turned off the television. "The Lord did have a reason for keeping me home today," said Louie.

He hurried back to his room before supper and bowed his head. "Dear Jesus, thank You for keeping me safe. Help me to accept *all* the answers You give to my prayers, and not just the ones that I like. Amen."

➤ **Why did Uncle Melvin decide not to go water-skiing on Saturday?** *(He thought a storm might come.)*

➤ **Was Louie content to not go water-skiing?** *(not when the sun came out and there was no storm)*

➤ **Did God know that there would be a storm?** *(yes)*

➤ **If God does not give us a "yes" to our prayers, what other answer may He give us?** *(Possible answers include "no" or "wait.")*

➤ **Have you ever prayed to God, had Him answer "wait," and later answer "yes"?** Tell us about it.

 Memory Verses—I Timothy 6:6-8

Practice the memory verses. Locate **I Timothy 6:6-8** and read the verses aloud as the students read silently. Explain that in order to understand these verses and live believing them, a person must be saved. A person cannot be godly if God is not the ruler of his life.

Read **John 1:40-42*a*** to the students. Explain that these verses happened when John the Baptist was preaching about Christ. Point out that when Andrew heard about Christ, the *first* thing that he did was tell his brother. Encourage the students to make sure that they themselves are saved and then to think of their family. Believers need to be good examples of Christians for their families. A good way for Christians to be an example is to be content. Call on students to say the verses from memory.

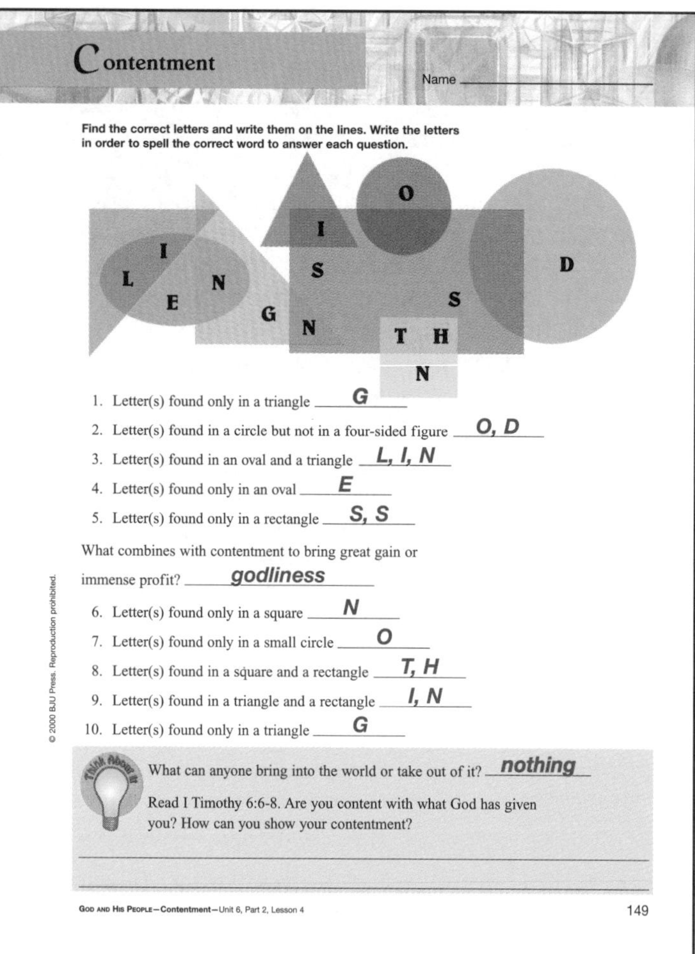

Contentment

Name ______

Find the correct letters and write them on the lines. Write the letters in order to spell the correct word to answer each question.

1. Letter(s) found only in a triangle **G**
2. Letter(s) found in a circle but not in a four-sided figure **O, D**
3. Letter(s) found in an oval and a triangle **L, I, N**
4. Letter(s) found only in an oval **E**
5. Letter(s) found only in a rectangle **S, S**

What combines with contentment to bring great gain or immense profit? **godliness**

6. Letter(s) found only in a square **N**
7. Letter(s) found only in a small circle **O**
8. Letter(s) found in a square and a rectangle **T, H**
9. Letter(s) found in a triangle and a rectangle **I, N**
10. Letter(s) found only in a triangle **G**

Think About It

What can anyone bring into the world or take out of it? **nothing**

Read I Timothy 6:6-8. Are you content with what God has given you? How can you show your contentment?

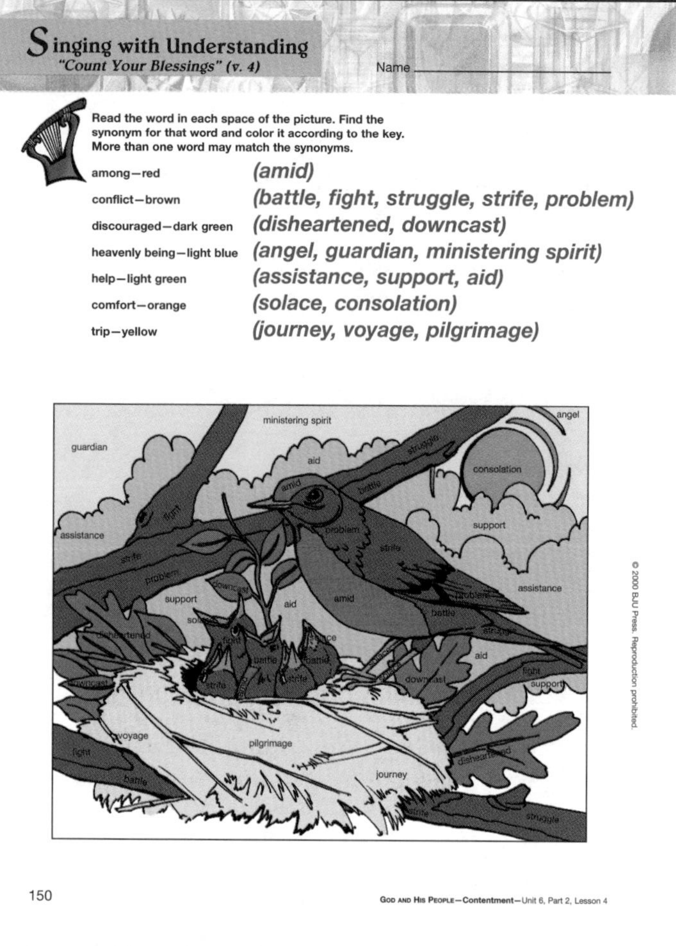

Singing with Understanding

"Count Your Blessings" (v. 4)

Name ______

Read the word in each space of the picture. Find the synonym for that word and color it according to the key. More than one word may match the synonyms.

among—red	(amid)
conflict—brown	(battle, fight, struggle, strife, problem)
discouraged—dark green	(disheartened, downcast)
heavenly being—light blue	(angel, guardian, ministering spirit)
help—light green	(assistance, support, aid)
comfort—orange	(solace, consolation)
trip—yellow	(journey, voyage, pilgrimage)

Worktext page 149

Develop an understanding of the memory verse.

Hymn: "Count Your Blessings"

Sing the hymn (Worktext pages 278-79). Play the recording and lead in singing the hymn together.

Art Connection (optional)

Create a collage of blessings. Distribute the magazine pictures among the students. Allow each student to choose one picture of something that is a blessing to him. Choose a wall on which students may display pictures of their blessings. Allow students to tell about their blessings; then sing the refrain of "Count Your Blessings" together.

Worktext page 150

Singing with understanding, verse 4. (*Note:* You may wish to work this page with the students or allow them to use a dictionary or a thesaurus.)

Going Beyond

Enrichment

Learn about who sang to God. Assign students to look up the following verses to read aloud. Tell the students to listen as the verse is read to decide who sang the song and why.

Verse	Who sang?	Why did they sing?
Exodus 15:1	Moses and the children of Israel	God gave them victory in crossing the Red Sea.
II Chronicles 29:28	The singers in the congregation (the people)	They were worshiping God during the burnt offering.
Ezra 3:11	The Israelites	They were praising the Lord.
Psalm 106:12	They (the Israelites)	They believed His (God's) words.
Acts 16:25	Paul and Silas	They were praising God.

Explain that these people counted their blessings and, as a result, sang to God. God gave us music so that we can glorify Him. When we get angry or sad about something, we should focus on what God has done for us, and our sadness will turn to joy. Sing several hymns, encouraging the students to sing joyfully.

God Gave Me What I Have

Unit 6, Part 3

Preview

Doctrines

- God is faithful (II Timothy 2:13)—Lesson 2
- God calls men through men (Romans 10:14-17)—Lesson 4
- God calls men through providence (Romans 2:4)—Lesson 4
- Christians should evangelize the lost (Matthew 28:19-20)—Lesson 4

Skills and Applications

- Learn Matthew 6:25-26
- Take notes
- Recall facts and details
- Read a time line
- Locate information in Scripture
- Read a map
- Develop an understanding of contentment
- Realize that Christians need not worry
- Apply Bible knowledge to everyday life

Lesson 1

Materials

- Song: "The Journeys of Paul"

Memory Verses—Matthew 6:25-26

Principle: Worrying is sin. Locate **Matthew 6:25-26** and read the verses aloud as the students read silently. Explain that Jesus spoke these words during the Sermon on the Mount. Tell the students that the word *raiment* means "clothing."

➤ **According to verse 25, what should we not worry about?** *(our lives, what we will eat or drink, what will happen to our bodies, and what we will wear)*

➤ **What are some things that we sometimes do worry about?** *(Possible answers include our tests in school, having money to buy something, how we look, and safety of our family.)*

Remind the students that Christians should pray and trust God for all things. Prayer will not stop hard situations from occurring, but it will help Christians to be content with everything God gives them.

Practice the verses. Call on students to read the verses according to their favorite foods (e.g., pizza, doughnuts, etc.), and then by what colors they are wearing (optional). Direct the students to highlight the verses in their Bibles (optional) and to mark the location with their Unit 6 Bookmarks.

Hymn: "Count Your Blessings"

Sing the hymn (Worktext pages 278-79). Play the recording and lead in singing verses 1-4. Allow individuals or small groups of students to sing a verse for the rest of the students (optional).

Song: "The Journeys of Paul" (optional)

Teach the chorus (Worktext pages 280-81). Explain that the words to this chorus come from Philippians 4, in which Paul talks about the importance of contentment. Play the recording and sing the chorus together. (*Note:* The first verse is taught in Unit 6, Part 3, Lesson 4.)

Introducing the Application Story

Discuss playing games.

➤ **What games do you like to play?**

➤ **Do you need skill to play this game?**

➤ **How do you feel when you play with someone who has more skill than you?**

Application Story

Read the following story to the students.

Clay He Can Use

Jerome walked home slowly. Baseball practice had been a failure—at least for him. He was not wearing his glasses because he hated the way they always slid down his nose when he ran. But without the glasses he could not see the ball. After Jerome had made his fifth out, the boys had started calling him "Squinty."

He kicked every piece of gravel in his path as he walked home. *Why can't I be like Joel?* he thought. Joel was the biggest kid in the fourth grade. He was also the strongest and the fastest. Joel won first place in the fitness awards every year. Joel didn't have short, scrawny legs like Jerome's, nor did he wear glasses.

Jerome turned onto the street where he lived. As he got closer to his house, he noticed the broken-down porch, the small yard, the peeling paint, and a big crack in one of the front windows. Jerome thought about the birthday party at Joel's house last summer: *a nice big house with a swimming pool and a basketball court.*

Jerome walked into his house and looked around at all the old furniture. By the time he reached the kitchen, he was angry. Mom closed the refrigerator door and smiled. "How was the game?" she asked.

Jerome told her about the game, and the longer he talked, the angrier he grew. Mom listened until he was finished and then said, "Let's go for a ride."

"Where?" asked Jerome.

"You'll see," said Mom.

- ➤ **Why did Jerome want to be like Joel?** *(Joel was bigger, was better at sports, did not wear glasses, and lived in a nicer house.)*
- ➤ **Why was Jerome angry?** *(He had not played a good baseball game, and his family did not have things as nice as the things that Joel's family had.)*
- ➤ **What could Jerome have done to help himself not get angry?** *(Possible answers include praying, controlling his thoughts, doing something for someone else, and counting his blessings.)*
- ➤ **What blessings does Jerome have that he could have been content with?** *(Possible answers include a house to live in, his parents, two legs to run with, and the opportunity to play baseball.)*

Jerome stood in front of the pottery store with Mom. "What are we doing here?" he asked. Mom just smiled.

Inside, the store was dim and cool and smelled of clay. Shelves holding vases of all shapes and sizes lined the walls. But Mom did not stop to look. She walked through the store to a back door. She knocked, and a voice inside said, "Come in."

Mom and Jerome entered the small room. Jagged scraps of pottery lay on the floor in huge piles. In one corner sat a bin of clay, and in the center of the room was a man, sitting at a large wheel. He smiled.

"Jerome," said Mom. "This is Mr. Adams. He is a potter. I thought you would like to see what he does for a living."

Jerome tried to smile politely. But he was still confused as to why Mom had brought him here. "I would shake your hand," said Mr. Adams, "but it's a little dirty." Jerome laughed. The man's whole body was covered with gray powder.

"How do you decide what you are going to make?" asked Jerome.

"I have a special purpose for each piece," said Mr. Adams. "I design it with that purpose in mind. Take this one, for example." Mr. Adams picked up a short, sturdy vessel. "This will be a sugar bowl, so it must be strong and have a wide top." He chose another—a tall, fragile piece. "This is to be a beautiful flower vase." The potter dipped his hands in water and sat down at the wheel again.

Mr. Adams began to work the clay on the wheel. As he formed the vessel, it began to look crooked. After a few more turns of the wheel, Mr. Adams stopped it, took a knife, and scraped the clay off the wheel. He held it in his hand and looked at Jerome. "This one," he said, "doesn't seem content to be the way I want it to be."

Mom looked at Jerome, who turned a little red. *Content,* he thought, *to wear glasses and not be the best in sports and not live in the best house.*

"I cannot use this," said Mr. Adams. He put the misshapen clay aside and reached for new clay.

"No," said Jerome. "Maybe I—I mean, it—just needs more work. Don't give up on it yet." Mr. Adams picked up the clay that he had cast aside. He put some water on it, kneaded it, and placed it back on the wheel. Slowly, the clay smoothed and straightened under the pressure of Mr. Adam's hands.

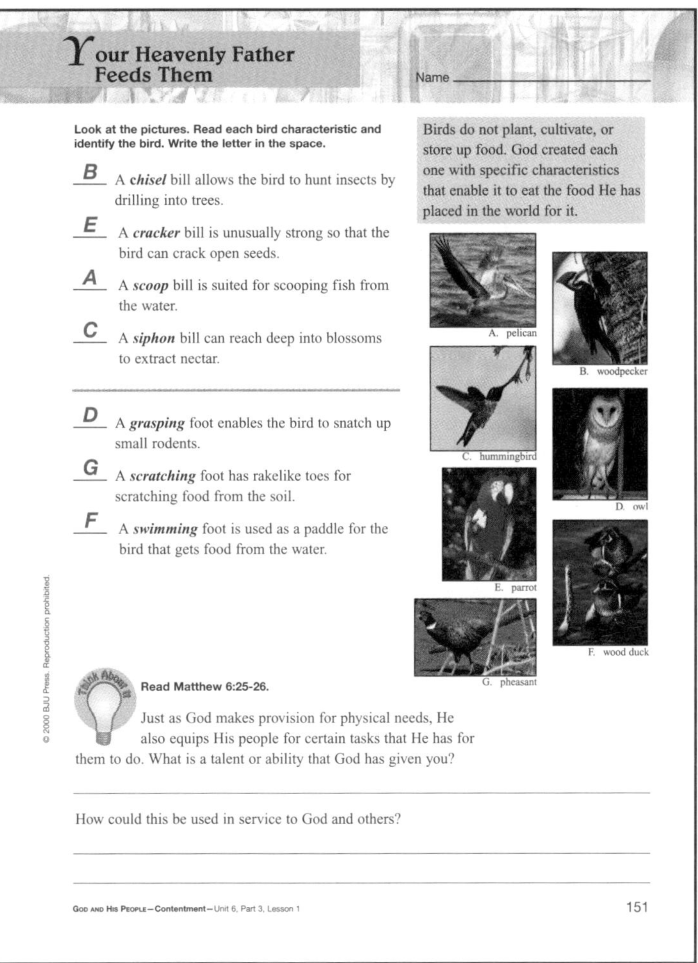

Your Heavenly Father Feeds Them

Name ____________________

Look at the pictures. Read each bird characteristic and identify the bird. Write the letter in the space.

Birds do not plant, cultivate, or store up food. God created each one with specific characteristics that enable it to eat the food He has placed in the world for it.

B A *chisel* bill allows the bird to hunt insects by drilling into trees.

E A *cracker* bill is unusually strong so that the bird can crack open seeds.

A A *scoop* bill is suited for scooping fish from the water.

C A *siphon* bill can reach deep into blossoms to extract nectar.

D A *grasping* foot enables the bird to snatch up small rodents.

G A *scratching* foot has rakelike toes for scratching food from the soil.

F A *swimming* foot is used as a paddle for the bird that gets food from the water.

A. pelican

B. woodpecker

C. hummingbird

D. owl

E. parrot

F. wood duck

G. pheasant

Think About It

Read Matthew 6:25-26.

Just as God makes provision for physical needs, He also equips His people for certain tasks that He has for them to do. What is a talent or ability that God has given you?

How could this be used in service to God and others?

God and His People—Contentment—Unit 6, Part 3, Lesson 1 151

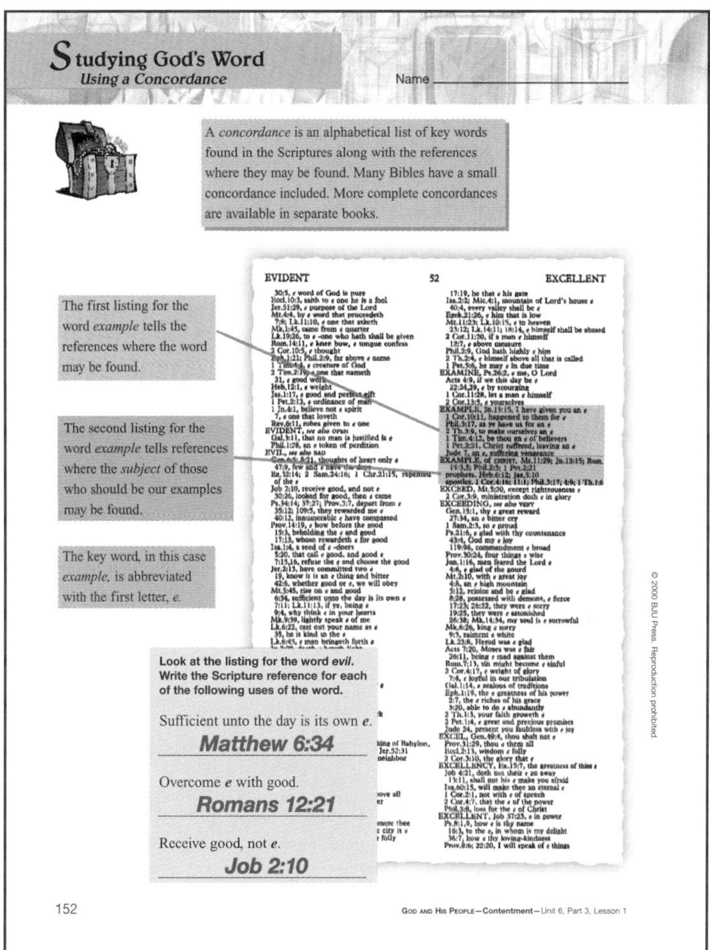

Studying God's Word
Using a Concordance

Name ____________________

A *concordance* is an alphabetical list of key words found in the Scriptures along with the references where they may be found. Many Bibles have a small concordance included. More complete concordances are available in separate books.

The first listing for the word *example* tells the references where the word may be found.

The second listing for the word *example* tells references where the *subject* of those who should be our examples may be found.

The key word, in this case *example*, is abbreviated with the first letter, *e*.

EVIDENT 52 EXCELLENT

Look at the listing for the word *evil*. Write the Scripture reference for each of the following uses of the word.

Sufficient unto the day is its own *e*. **Matthew 6:34**

Overcome *e* with good. **Romans 12:21**

Receive good, not *e*. **Job 2:10**

152 God and His People—Contentment—Unit 6, Part 3, Lesson 1

"Now," said Mr. Adams, looking at the beautiful vase that was forming, "it is letting me form it. This is clay that I can use."

➤ **How did Mr. Adams, the potter, decide what each lump of clay would become?** *(He had a purpose for each one and knew what it should look like.)*

➤ **Who made us and why?** *(God made us for His own glory.)*

➤ **How can we glorify God?** *(by loving Him and doing what He commands)*

➤ Read **Isaiah 64:8** aloud. **How is God like a potter?** *(Through His Word and through prayer, He molds Christians to be usable for Him.)*

➤ **How can Jerome and other Christians be usable clay to God?** *(by obeying His commands and being content with what He gives them, where He places them, and whatever happens to them)*

Science Connection (optional)

Discuss God's provision for birds.

➤ **What do birds eat?** *(Possible answers include seeds, bugs, worms, or fish.)*

➤ According to Matthew 6:26, birds do not have to plant their food, pick it, and store it in barns. **Where does their food come from?** *(God created all the things that they eat.)*

Explain that God created each bird specifically for the tasks that it would need to do.

➤ **What would happen if a robin had webbed feet like a duck?** *(Elicit that the robin would be unable to hang onto branches of trees.)*

Worktext page 151

Match birds with their characteristics and answer questions about God's provision for each person.

Bible Study Skills, Worktext page 152

Use a concordance.

Lesson 2

Materials

- Song: "The Journeys of Paul"

Hymn: "Count Your Blessings"

Sing the hymn (Worktext pages 278-79). Lead in singing all the verses, directing the students to stand when they sing the word *you* or *your.* Explain that the words could also be *I* and *my.*

Song: "The Journeys of Paul"

Sing the chorus (Worktext pages 280-81). Play the recording and lead in singing the chorus.

➤ **What reasons does this song give for being content?** *(The Lord supplies all of our needs; His love for us is unchanging.)*

➤ **What needs has God supplied for you this week?**

Memory Verses—Matthew 6:25-26

Practice the memory verses. Locate **Matthew 6:25-26** and select a student to read the verses aloud as the other students follow along. Divide the students into groups of two. Tell each student to read the verses silently and then to his partner.

Background Information

The meaning of *Stephen*—*The name* Stephen *comes from a word meaning "crown."*

Memorials to Stephen—*Two churches in or near Jerusalem have been built as memorials to Stephen, the first Christian to die for his testimony for Jesus Christ. One memorial is a Greek Orthodox church, which is said to stand on the spot where Stephen was killed. It lies at the foot of the southern tip of the western slope of the Mount of Olives, north of the garden of Gethsemane on the Jericho Road. About twenty miles south of Jerusalem on the way to Beersheba is a small church that also claims to be the location of Stephen's death. This church has mosaics dating back to the fifth and sixth centuries.*

Introducing the Bible Account

Discuss Christian martyrs. Explain that a *martyr* is a person who chooses to suffer or die rather than give up his faith in Christ. Our English word *martyr* comes from the Greek word for "witness." A true witness tells the truth about what he has seen, regardless of the cost. Tell the students that the following Bible account is about the first Christian martyr.

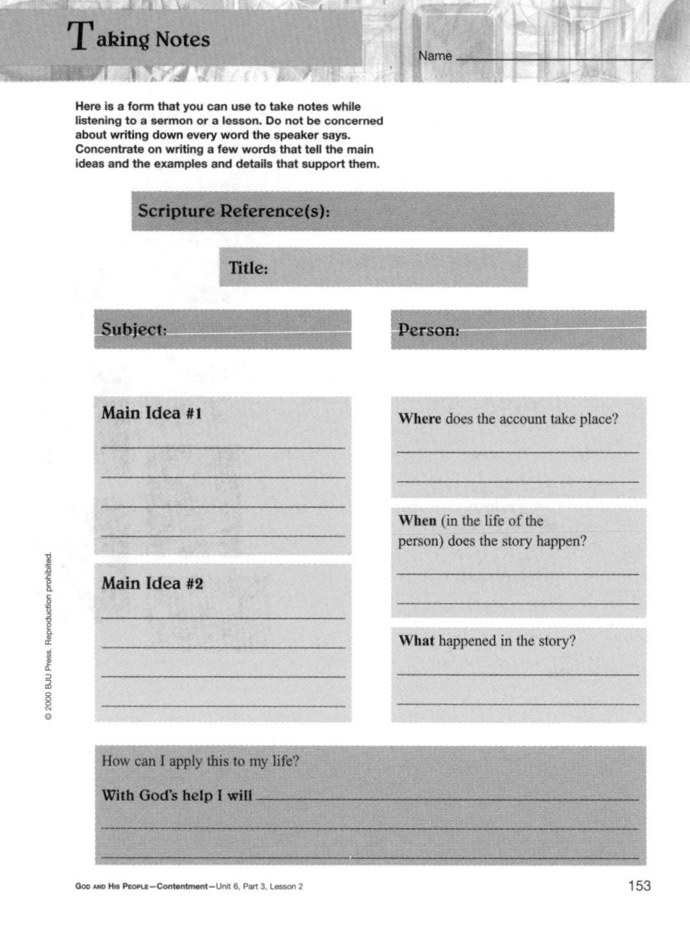

Taking Notes

Name ______

Here is a form that you can use to take notes while listening to a sermon or a lesson. Do not be concerned about writing down every word the speaker says. Concentrate on writing a few words that tell the main ideas and the examples and details that support them.

Scripture Reference(s):

Title:

Subject:

Person:

Main Idea #1

Where does the account take place?

When (in the life of the person) does the story happen?

Main Idea #2

What happened in the story?

How can I apply this to my life?

With God's help I will ______

© 2000 BJU Press. Reproduction prohibited.

God and His People—Contentment—Unit 6, Part 3, Lesson 2 153

Bible Account

Read the following Bible account or retell Acts 6:8–8:4 in your own words. (*Note:* Worktext page 153 teaches students how to take notes. It can be completed while students listen to this account, a different account, or a sermon that they hear at church.)

The Martyrdom of Stephen

When the apostles of the Lord Jesus became busy with witnessing, the church in Jerusalem appointed certain Christian men to be their leaders—to take care of administration so that the apostles could focus on preaching. Stephen, a man "full of faith and power," one who "did great wonders and miracles among the people," was chosen. Stephen not only served food to needy Christians and helped to provide housing and clothing for them, but he also preached and testified about Jesus outside the church.

One day Stephen was speaking to some religious men. Having heard Stephen's words, they paid men to say that Stephen had said wicked things about God so that they could charge Stephen and bring him before the Sanhedrin, the Jewish religious council. At the council false witnesses made accusations against Stephen. As the men in the council watched Stephen, they saw that his face was like the face of an angel.

The high priest asked Stephen whether the charges against him were true. In answer, Stephen gave a long sermon, reminding them of how God had worked in the lives of their ancestors: Abraham, Isaac, Jacob, and Joseph. He reminded them of how God had kept His promise to give Abraham a son and how He had brought him into this land. He reminded them of how God had used Joseph to feed his family in the time of famine. He reminded them of how God had led the Israelites out of Egypt under the leadership of Moses. Stephen also reminded them of how their fathers had persecuted God's prophets and told them that now they, too, were rebelling against the truth that the Holy Spirit had revealed through Christ. "Ye do always resist the Holy Ghost:" he said, "as your fathers did."

The council was furious and began gnashing their teeth at Stephen. But Stephen, full of the Holy Spirit, looked up toward heaven and said, "Behold, I see the heavens opened, and the Son of man standing on the right hand of God."

When the religious leaders heard him say that, they clapped their hands over their ears so that they would not hear any more. The angry men formed a mob and took Stephen outside the city and threw stones at him to kill him.

As Stephen was being stoned, he prayed and asked the Lord Jesus to receive his spirit. Then Stephen kneeled down and asked the Lord not to blame the men who were stoning him. As Stephen finished praying, he fell asleep and went to see Jesus in heaven.

During the stoning of Stephen, the men had laid their coats at the feet of Saul. Saul was a Pharisee who wanted to persecute everyone who believed in the Lord Jesus Christ. He disrupted the church by going to the houses of believers and sending the men and women to prison. As a result, believers were forced to scatter away from Jerusalem. Wherever they went, Christians preached the gospel and saw many people saved.

➤ **What was Stephen doing before the council?** *(preaching about Jesus Christ and reminding them how God had cared for the men of old)*

➤ **What did the religious leaders do when Stephen said that he saw Jesus in heaven standing at the right hand of God?** *(They covered their ears, formed a mob, seized Stephen, and took him outside the city to stone him to death.)*

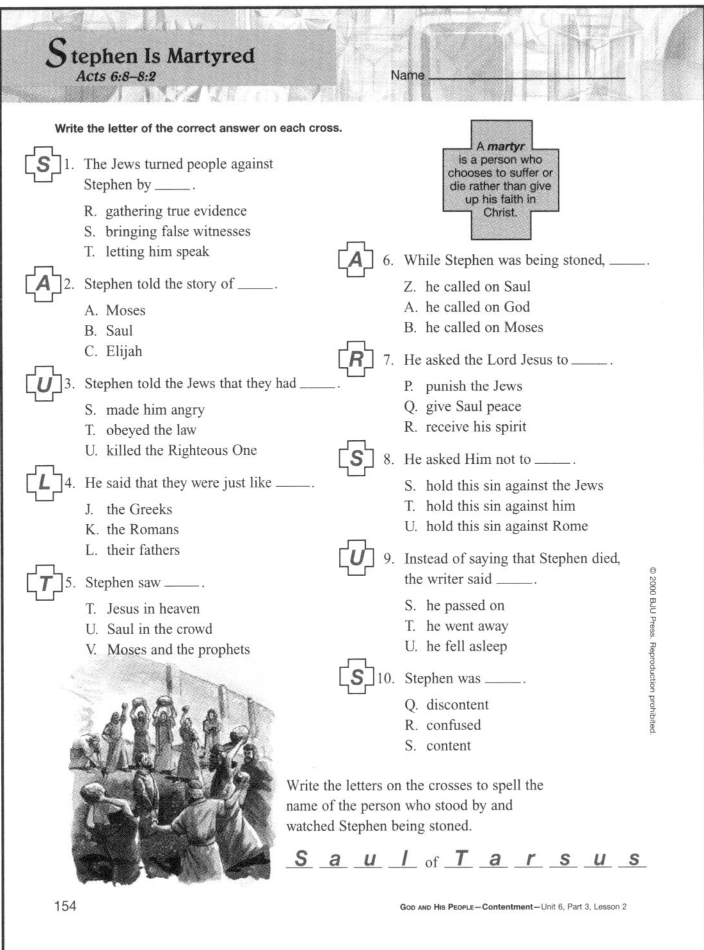

Stephen Is Martyred
Acts 6:8–8:2

Name ____________

Write the letter of the correct answer on each cross.

A *martyr* is a person who chooses to suffer or die rather than give up his faith in Christ.

S 1. The Jews turned people against Stephen by ____.
R. gathering true evidence
S. bringing false witnesses
T. letting him speak

A 2. Stephen told the story of ____.
A. Moses
B. Saul
C. Elijah

U 3. Stephen told the Jews that they had ____.
S. made him angry
T. obeyed the law
U. killed the Righteous One

L 4. He said that they were just like ____.
J. the Greeks
K. the Romans
L. their fathers

T 5. Stephen saw ____.
T. Jesus in heaven
U. Saul in the crowd
V. Moses and the prophets

A 6. While Stephen was being stoned, ____.
Z. he called on Saul
A. he called on God
B. he called on Moses

R 7. He asked the Lord Jesus to ____.
P. punish the Jews
Q. give Saul peace
R. receive his spirit

S 8. He asked Him not to ____.
S. hold this sin against the Jews
T. hold this sin against him
U. hold this sin against Rome

U 9. Instead of saying that Stephen died, the writer said ____.
S. he passed on
T. he went away
U. he fell asleep

S 10. Stephen was ____.
Q. discontent
R. confused
S. content

Write the letters on the crosses to spell the name of the person who stood by and watched Stephen being stoned.

S a u l of T a r s u s

154 God and His People—Contentment—Unit 6, Part 3, Lesson 2

➤ **Who was with Stephen throughout the whole ordeal, and how do we know?** *(Jesus was with him, because Stephen talked to Jesus and could see Him.)*

➤ **Was Stephen content to die for his faith? How did his death help to spread the gospel to other places?** *(Yes. Christians were forced to leave and took the gospel wherever they went.)*

➤ **How could Jesus Christ save someone like Saul?** *(Jesus offers salvation to all who call upon Him—Hebrews 7:25; John 6:37; Romans 10:13.)*

Worktext page 154

Recall details about the martyrdom of Stephen.

Lesson 3

Materials

- Song: "The Journeys of Paul"
- Magazines to cut (optional)
- A half-sheet copy of Supplement page S71, "Contentment Is . . . ," for each student

Song: "The Journeys of Paul" (optional)

Sing the chorus (Worktext pages 280-81). Play the recording and lead in singing the chorus.

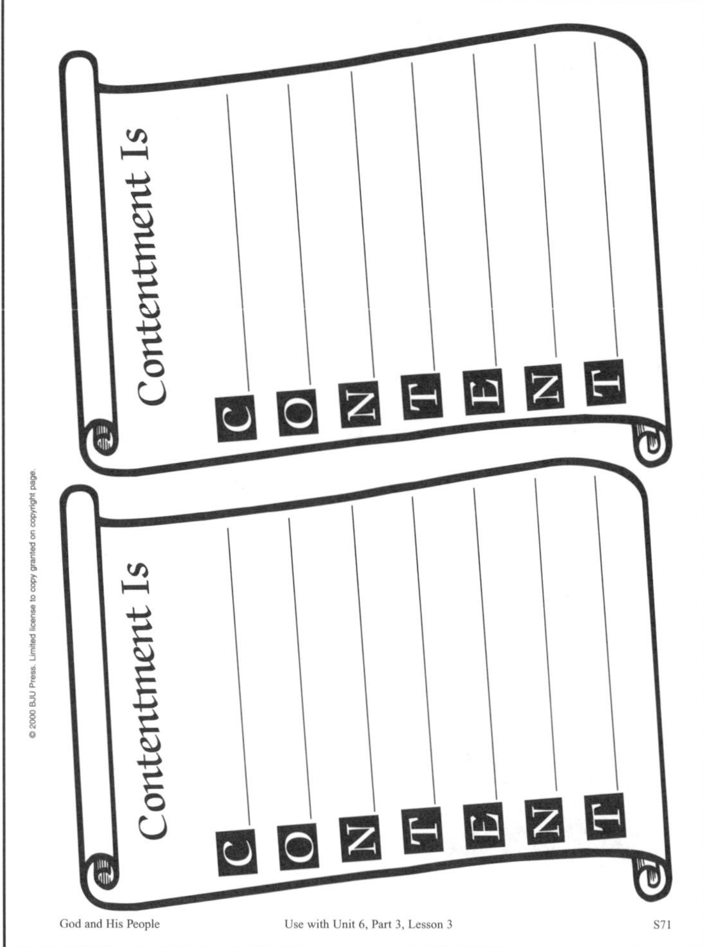

- **Is this a song that Peter, Andrew, James, or John could have sung? Why?** *(Yes. They were content to follow Jesus, even though they had to leave everything to do so.)*
- **How do you think they survived since they did not earn money by fishing anymore?** *(Jesus met all of their needs.)*

Sing the chorus again.

Bible Study

Read the following study about contentment. Distribute a half-sheet copy of Supplement page S71, "Contentment Is . . .," to each student. If you wish, write the bold headings on the chalkboard for the students to copy onto their papers as you conduct the Bible study.

Contentment Means

Communicating with God (II Kings 19:11-37). When King Sennacherib and his armies invaded the Southern Kingdom of Judah and mocked King Hezekiah and his trust in God, Hezekiah prayed for God to save his land and people so that "all the kingdoms of the earth may know that thou art the Lord God, even thou only." God heard King Hezekiah's prayer and assured him of His protection. And just as God had said, that night the angel of the Lord came into the camp of the Assyrians and killed 185,000 soldiers and caused King Sennacherib to return to his own land. **When Christians face a hard situation, they should pray for God's guidance and encouragement.** *(Unit 2, Part 4, Lesson 1.)*

Obeying God's commands (Exodus 3:1-22; 4:1-17; 5:1–12:36). While Moses was a shepherd in Midian, God spoke to him from a burning bush. God told Moses to go to Egypt to command Pharaoh to let the Israelites go. God showed Moses His great power and promised that Moses would succeed if he obeyed. So Moses obeyed and went to Pharaoh and said and did all that God had told him. **Christians should obey God always, knowing that His way is perfect.** *(Unit 1, Part 1, Lessons 1-3.)*

Not being lazy (Luke 15:8-10). In the parable of the lost coin, the woman did not become discontent, but neither did she sit around and wait for God to show her the coin. She was *active*—searching for the coin. **Christians should pray about their trials and needs, but they should also think about what God wants them to do about their needs.** *(Unit 5, Part 4, Lesson 2.)*

Trusting God to supply needs (II Kings 4:1-6). The widow had to trust God to help her and her two sons when they did not have enough money to pay their debts. The widow had to have faith to believe Elisha and to borrow many vessels before she saw what would be done with them. The widow was content to let God fulfill her needs as He desired. **Christians should trust God to supply all their needs.** *(Unit 3, Part 3, Lesson 2.)*

Exemplifying Jesus Christ (Mark 1:12-13). The Lord Jesus Christ lived on earth as a man and was tempted with all of the same temptations that we are. Instead of becoming discontent, He focused on God's Word and used it to fight against Satan. **When Christians are tempted to become discontent, they should follow Christ's example.** *(Unit 5, Part 1, Lesson 1.)*

Not always wanting more (I Kings 3:4-28). One night God appeared to Solomon in a dream and promised to give him whatever he asked. Solomon praised God and asked only for wisdom to lead and serve others. God was pleased with Solomon's request and granted him wisdom—*and* riches, long life, and victory over his enemies. **Christians should be satisfied with God's plan and provision for them, for His way is perfect.** *(Unit 2, Part 1, Lesson 2.)*

Thanking God for his blessings (Luke 1:46-55). Mary spoke these words after she was told that she would be the mother of Jesus. The news was frightening for Mary be-

Who Was Content?

Name ____________________

Read each verse. Write the name of the person in the verse(s); put an *X* under *content* or *discontent* to show the attitude of that person.

Scripture	Person	Attitude	
		Content	Discontent
I Kings 21:4	*Ahab*		✗
II Kings 6:16-17	*Elisha*	✗	
Luke 1:38	*Mary*	✗	
Matthew 2:1-3	*Herod*		✗
Luke 16:22*a*	*Lazarus*	✗	
Luke 16:22*b*-23	*the rich man*		✗
Matthew 1:24	*Joseph*	✗	

Choose one of the people who was content and answer the following questions.

1. How was the person serving God?

2. Was the person satisfied to trust God no matter what happened?

3. What do you think makes a person content?

4. Are you content? Why or why not?

Worried About Worms?

Name ____________________

Jesus taught that worry does not profit anything. The example that He used is that birds do not worry about their next meal because they are fed by the heavenly Father. God's children, who are certainly more valuable than birds, will be provided for, so is there any cause for Christians to worry?

Read Matthew 6:25-26. Use the code on the birds to spell what should take the place of worry in the life of a Christian.

cause she was young and not married. Instead of becoming discontent in her difficult situation, she praised God in song for her calling to be used for His glory. **Christians should praise God for His daily blessings.** *(Unit 4, Part 1, Lesson 2.)*

Encourage the students to memorize the acronym CONTENT and to keep the study in their Bibles.

Hymn: "Count Your Blessings"

Sing the hymn (Worktext pages 278-79). Recount the blessings that the Bible characters in the Bible study had. Play the recording and lead in singing verses 1-4.

Worktext page 155

Locate information in Scripture.

Memory Verses—Matthew 6:25-26

Practice the memory verses. Locate and study **Matthew 6:25-26** together.

➤ **What did Jesus say Christians should have little care or worry for?** *(food, drink, clothing)*

Worktext page 156

Develop an understanding of the memory verses.

Art Connection (optional)

Illustrate Matthew 6:25-26. Place the students in groups. Give each group some magazines to cut and a sheet of construction paper or poster board. Tell them to find pictures to illustrate parts of the verses (food, drink, body, clothes, birds, barns, etc.). Direct each group to use the pictures to make a verse collage to use in saying the verses together.

Lesson 4

Materials

- Chart 34, "Mediterranean in the Time of Paul"
- TimeLine and picture: *Paul (Saul)*
- The Life of Paul TimeLine
- TimeLine Cards 1-2: *Martyrdom of Stephen* and *Saul's Conversion*
- Song: "The Journeys of Paul"

(*Note:* The last five lessons of Unit 6 consist of five Bible accounts, periodically interrupted by putting cards on the TimeLine for the life of Paul, located in the Visual Packet. Using this "magnified TimeLine" will help students follow the accounts as well as gain an understanding of the sequence of events. All dates of Paul's life are approximate. A completed copy of the Life of Paul TimeLine is on Supplement pages S78-79 for use with individual students and small groups.)

Memory Verses—Matthew 6:25-26

Practice the memory verses. Write the verses on an erasable board and lead the students in reading them together. Erase some words or phrases and read the verses again. Continue in this way, erasing words or phrases and reading the verses until all the words have been erased and the students can say the verses from memory.

TimeLine

Place Paul (Saul) on the TimeLine. Choose a student to attach the picture of Paul (Saul) onto the large TimeLine (5 B.C.–A.D. 67). Guide the students as they glue their pictures of Paul onto their individual TimeLines.

Background Information

Damascus—*The city of Damascus is about 175 miles northeast of Jerusalem in Syria. It is probably the oldest continuously inhabited city in the world. Others are older, but they have fallen to ruins or been unoccupied for periods of time. The road from Jerusalem to Damascus was a well-traveled trade route, but the journey was not easy because it led over hills and rough terrain near the desert.*

Introducing the Bible Account

Explain the magnified TimeLine. Display The Life of Paul TimeLine. Point to Paul on the large TimeLine. Remind the students that this TimeLine shows over four thousand years. Explain that they will be studying about Paul in the following lessons. To get a better understanding of the order and time of events for the approximately seventy-two years of Paul's life, we magnified or enlarged this time with a separate TimeLine about the life of Paul.

➤ **What do you remember about Paul, or Saul, in the Bible account about the death of Stephen?** *(Those who stoned Stephen laid down their cloaks at the feet of Saul.)*

TimeLine: The Life of Paul

Place Card 1, *Martyrdom of Stephen* on the TimeLine at A.D. 32. Explain that this is the first time we hear about Paul (Saul).

Introducing the Bible Account

Discuss Saul (Paul). Tell the students that when the persecution of those who believed in Christ increased in Jerusalem, many of the disciples went to preach the gospel in the cities in outlying places like Damascus. Tell them that the following account is about one who was saved on the road to Damascus.

Bible Account

Read the following Bible account or read Acts 9:1-21. Point out the location of Jerusalem and Damascus on Chart 34, "Mediterranean in the Time of Paul."

Saul's Conversion: The Road to Damascus

Because the believers scattered, Saul asked the high priest to send letters to the Jews in Damascus. These letters said that if Saul found any believers on his travels through that area, he had permission to arrest them and bring them bound to Jerusalem.

Saul took his letters from the high priest and left Jerusalem for Damascus with two servants. On the way Saul had a blinding vision of the Lord. "Lord, what wilt thou have me to do?" asked Saul. After the vision Saul could not see anything. The Lord told Saul to go to Damascus, where a disciple named Ananias would help him.

The Lord also came to Ananias in a vision and said to him, "Arise, and go into the street which is called Straight, and inquire [ask] . . . for one called Saul of Tarsus." God told Ananias that he would lay his hands on Saul "that he might receive his sight."

Ananias had heard about Saul, the man who killed and imprisoned people who believed in Jesus Christ. Ananias knew that Saul could harm anyone he wanted to. The Lord said that Saul was a "chosen vessel." The Lord said, "I will shew him how great things he must suffer for my name's sake."

For three days Saul could not see. He did not eat or drink anything. Ananias obeyed God and went to the house in Damascus where Saul was. He greeted Saul as a brother and restored his sight. Saul got up and was baptized and ate some food.

Saul met the Lord on the road to Damascus that day. He accepted Jesus as his Savior and was saved. Saul joined other believers at Damascus. He also began to witness to others about the Lord Jesus Christ.

People who heard Saul preach were amazed. Saul was a man who had done wicked things to believers, and now he was urging people to accept Christ. Saul continued to preach everywhere that he went.

➤ **What happened to Saul on the road to Damascus?** *(He was blinded by the Lord.)*

➤ **How did this affect Saul?** *(He accepted the Lord as his Savior.)*

➤ **What was surprising to those who heard Saul preach?** *(He used to persecute Christians, and now he was preaching that people might become Christians.)*

The Life of Paul TimeLine

Place Card 2, *Saul's Conversion* on the TimeLine at A.D. 33. (*Note:* You may wish to use this opportunity to invite students who have never been saved to talk with you.

Bible Account

Read the following Bible account or read Acts 9:20-31. Display Chart 34, "Mediterranean in the Time of Paul," pointing out where Saul traveled.

Saul's Conversion: Beginning of Ministry

Saul was just as determined to preach the gospel as he had been to persecute believers of the gospel before he was saved. After Saul was saved, the Jews in Damascus wanted to kill him, just as he had tried to kill believers. Saul's preaching in Damascus made the Jews angry. "They watched the gates day and night to kill him." Saul heard about what the Jews wanted to do to him, so he planned an escape. One night, the disciples "let him down by the wall in a basket," and he went on to Jerusalem.

From Jerusalem, Saul visited many cities and preached the gospel everywhere he went. He usually went first to the Jewish synagogues, where he taught that the Messiah had come to the Jews. Many of the people would believe in Jesus, but most would not. Soon, the leaders would tell Saul that he could no longer preach in the city. Those who had believed on Jesus would leave the synagogue and make their own assemblies. Often then Saul would be told to leave or he would be arrested or he would be beaten and thrown out of the city.

Barnabas, however, had heard about all the work Saul had done in Damascus, and Barnabas presented Saul to the apostles and disciples. Barnabas told them of the testimony and witness for Jesus Christ that Saul had been in Damascus. As Saul began to teach with the apostles, the Jews who had supported Saul's persecution of believers plotted to kill him. When the Lord allowed the disciples to hear of their plot, they secretly took Saul to Caesarea during the night, and from there he took a boat to his home city of Tarsus.

➤ **What happened when Saul's life was threatened?** *(The Lord allowed the disciples to find out about the plan and to help Saul escape.)*

➤ **How did God take care of Saul's future?** *(The Lord redeemed Saul, and He saved Saul's life twice from those who would have killed him.)*

➤ **Will God take care of our futures like Saul's?** *(If we seek Him, the Lord will save us; and if we give him control of our lives, He will lead us in our futures.)*

Bible Account

Read the following Bible account or read Acts 11:19-30. Point out the distance between Tarsus and Antioch of Syria on Chart 34, "Mediterranean in the Time of Paul."

Saul's Conversion: Coming to Antioch

After Saul fled from Jerusalem to Tarsus, he continued to teach and witness for about six years in the cities and towns around his home area. During this time Saul had many trials. Scripture does not reveal which trials took place during this time, but in II Corinthians 11:23-27, he mentions five lashings—a common form of discipline of the synagogues. Saul was certainly preaching that Jesus was the Messiah and Redeemer, which made the unbelieving Jews furious. These trials must have been difficult, but the Lord protected Saul and guided his future.

Meanwhile, the believers who had been driven out of Jerusalem in the early persecutions had moved to the other big cities of the Roman Empire. And Barnabas, who had introduced Saul to the apostles, was sent to the believers at Antioch of Syria, the third largest city in the Roman Empire.

Barnabas soon saw the need for qualified help to take advantage of the open door for evangelism. So Barnabas went to Tarsus, searching for Saul to come and help with all the new believers at Antioch. When Saul and Barnabas left Tarsus, they went to Antioch and preached for over a year. In Antioch the believers were first called *Christians.*

➤ **Why did Saul keep preaching even after being punished with lashings?** *(He knew God wanted him to preach; he feared God more than men.)*

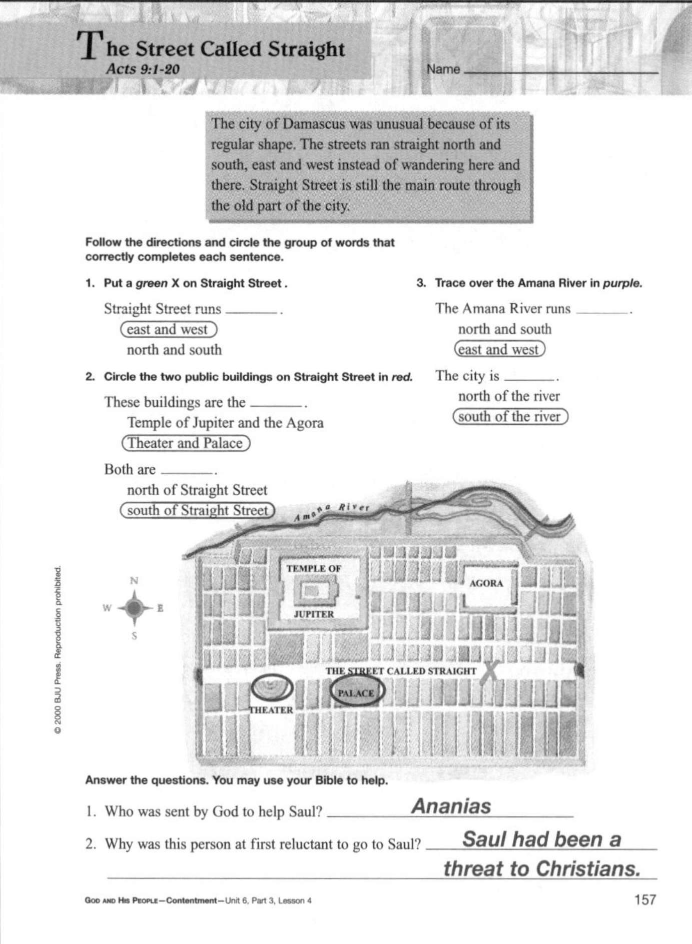

The Street Called Straight
Acts 9:1-20

Name ____________

The city of Damascus was unusual because of its regular shape. The streets ran straight north and south, east and west instead of wandering here and there. Straight Street is still the main route through the old part of the city.

Follow the directions and circle the group of words that correctly completes each sentence.

1. **Put a *green* X on Straight Street.**

   Straight Street runs ______.
   - (east and west) [circled]
   - north and south

2. **Circle the two public buildings on Straight Street in *red*.**

   These buildings are the ______.
   - Temple of Jupiter and the Agora
   - (Theater and Palace) [circled]

   Both are ______.
   - north of Straight Street
   - (south of Straight Street) [circled]

3. **Trace over the Amana River in *purple*.**

   The Amana River runs ______.
   - north and south
   - (east and west) [circled]

   The city is ______.
   - north of the river
   - (south of the river) [circled]

Answer the questions. You may use your Bible to help.

1. Who was sent by God to help Saul? ***Ananias***
2. Why was this person at first reluctant to go to Saul? ***Saul had been a threat to Christians.***

God and His People—Contentment—Unit 6, Part 3, Lesson 4 157

The New Saul
Acts 9:20-31; 11:19-30

Name ____________

Draw a [star] around every *true* statement.

1. It was not surprising that Saul would become a preacher of the gospel.
2. Saul left Damascus by the city gates.
3. The disciples at Jerusalem did not want Saul to join them. [starred]
4. Saul taught for some years in his hometown of Tarsus. [starred]
5. The high priest recommended Saul to the disciples.
6. From Jerusalem Saul went to Caesarea. [starred]
7. Saul and Barnabas taught in the church at Antioch. [starred]
8. It was at Jerusalem that the followers of Christ were first called Christians.
9. The Lord chose Saul to carry His name to the Gentiles. [starred]
10. Barnabas never preached again after he met Saul.

158 God and His People—Contentment—Unit 6, Part 3, Lesson 4

➤ **How did God use Barnabas to help Saul find a new ministry?** *(Barnabas went and found Saul and brought him to help the church in Antioch.)*

Song: "The Journeys of Paul"

Teach the first verse (Worktext pages 280-81). Explain that the chorus they have sung in earlier lessons is about the life of Paul. Each verse talks about a different journey in the life of Paul. Sing the first verse along with the recording. Explain that the meaning of the words will become clearer as they continue to study Paul's life.

Worktext page 157

Read a map.

Worktext page 158

Recall details about Saul's conversion and the beginning of his ministry.

Going Beyond

Enrichment

Conduct a sword drill. Briefly review the story, "Clay He Can Use" on pages 200-201. Tell the students that you will call out a reference to a verse in the Bible that talks about making pottery. Direct the students to stand when they have found where the verse mentions pottery. Call on the first student standing to read the verse aloud and to tell what part of the verse refers to making pottery. Discuss the verses. Suggested verses include **Job 10:9; Psalm 2:9; Isaiah 29:16; Isaiah 45:9; Isaiah 64:8; Jeremiah 18:6;** and **Romans 9:21.**

God Will Take Care of My Future

Preview

Doctrines

- Man must turn away from everything else, including works, for salvation (Ephesians 2:8-9)—Lesson 1
- The apostles served in the establishment of the church (Ephesians 4:11)—Lesson 2
- God calls men through men (Romans 10:14-15)—Lesson 4

Skills and Applications

- Learn Philippians 4:11
- Read a map
- Recall facts and details
- Locate information in Scripture
- Choose to be content with good and bad circumstances
- Apply Bible knowledge to everyday life

Lesson 1

Materials

- Charts 19 and 35: "Paul's First Missionary Journey" and "Paul's Route—First Journey"
- The Life of Paul TimeLine
- TimeLine Cards 3-5: *The Calling of Saul and Barnabas, Paul's First Missionary Journey,* and *The First Apostolic Council*
- Map marker (e.g., dried bean, small candy, or dry cereal) for each student
- Song: "The Journeys of Paul"

Memory Verse—Philippians 4:11

Principle: Contentment is a decision. Read **Philippians 4:11** aloud as the students read silently. Explain that this was written in a letter that Paul wrote to the church members in Philippi. Paul was in prison, and the church had been sending him money. Paul thanked them for supporting him and told them that he was thanking them with a contented heart. Choose volunteers to read the verse aloud. Direct the students to highlight the verse in their Bibles (optional) and to mark the location with the Unit 6 Bookmark.

Background Information

The Church in Antioch—*Antioch of Syria was located fifteen miles from the coast of the Mediterranean Sea. A city of 500,000 people, Antioch boasted a boulevard built by Herod the Great. The Christian church began here when men from Cyprus and Cyrene came and preached to the Gentiles. A great number of people in Antioch believed and turned to the Lord, and the church grew quickly. The disciples of Christ were first called Christians in Antioch, and the Antioch church became the sending church of Saul and Barnabas when they left on their first missionary journey. After the destruction of Jerusalem in A.D. 70, Antioch became the leading city of Christianity.*

Introducing the Bible Account

Read a map. Explain that the church Paul and Barnabas had been helping was an important church in the history of Christianity. Throughout his ministry, Paul considered Antioch his home church, just as missionaries today have home churches. Point out Antioch in Syria and Antioch in Pisidia on Chart 35, "Paul's Route—First Journey." Direct each student to mark the location of Antioch in Syria on Worktext page 297 by placing his map marker on it. Share the background information about the church in Antioch. Tell the students to move their markers to the other cities mentioned as the Bible account progresses.

Bible Account

Read the following Bible account or read Acts 11:19-26 and 13:1-3.

Paul's First Missionary Journey: The Calling

Persecution drove Christians from Jerusalem into Judea, Samaria, and other parts of the world. Barnabas came from *Jerusalem* to help the church in *Antioch* and to encourage Saul to help too.

After Barnabas and Saul had been helping in the church for a while, the Holy Spirit spoke to the church leaders and said, "Separate me Barnabas and Saul for the work whereunto I have called them." After praying and fasting, the leaders laid their hands on Barnabas and Saul. Then they sent them away to do God's work.

The Life of Paul TimeLine

Place Card 3, *The Calling of Saul and Barnabas,* on the TimeLine at A.D. 43.

Background Information

First Missionary Journey—*Paul and Barnabas visited nine cities during their first missionary journey: Antioch in Syria, Seleucia, Salamis, Paphos, Perga, Antioch in Pisidia, Iconium, Lystra, and Derbe.*

Cyprus—*This island is off the shore of Syria, where the cities of Salamis and Paphos were located. It was also the home of Barnabas.*

John Mark—*John Mark, Barnabas's nephew, wrote the Gospel of Mark. His mother Mary, a Christian, was the one in whose home the believers were praying when Peter was released from prison (Acts 12:12). Since Mary's home is thought to have been a frequent gathering place for Christians, John Mark was probably acquainted with many of the apostles and heard their teachings.*

Bible Account

Read the following Bible account or read Acts 13:1–14:28. Remind the students to move their map markers to the cities mentioned.

Paul's First Missionary Journey: Traveling and Preaching

Paul and Barnabas's first stop was the island of *Cyprus.* While they preached in the city of *Salamis,* John Mark helped them and then traveled with them to *Paphos,* another city on the island. A false prophet named Bar-Jesus in the city tried to turn one of Paul's converts away from his new faith. Paul looked at Bar-Jesus and called him a child of the Devil and an enemy of righteousness. Paul told the man that he would become blind for a while, and immediately Bar-Jesus was blind.

Paul and Barnabas headed for Asia Minor. Shortly after they arrived in the city of *Perga,* John Mark left them and returned to Jerusalem.

Paul and Barnabas went on through the regions of Pamphylia and Galatia, preaching Christ. In the city of *Lystra,* the Lord gave Paul power to heal a crippled man. When the people of Lystra saw the miracle, they thought that Paul and Barnabas were gods and tried to worship them. Paul and Barnabas would not let the people perform their worship ceremonies. Later, some Jews came to the city and persuaded the Lystrans to stone Paul. Paul was left for dead outside the gates of Lystra, but God restored his health, and the next day Paul left with Barnabas for *Derbe.*

Whenever Paul reached a new city, he went straight to the Jewish synagogues, where natural-born Jews gathered, along with Gentiles who had converted to the Jewish faith. People were saved when Paul preached Christ. Paul appointed leaders over these new congregations and encouraged them in the Christian faith. Later in his ministry, Paul wrote the Book of Galatians to Christians in Galatia. At the end of their preaching tour, Paul and Barnabas returned to their church in *Antioch* of Syria to report their results.

The Life of Paul TimeLine

Place Card 4, *Paul's First Missionary Journey,* on the TimeLine at A.D. 46-48.

Background Information

Judaizers—*Those who were troubling the Gentile believers were part of a sect called Judaizers. These were Jewish Christians who believed that keeping certain aspects of the Mosaic law, especially circumcision, was necessary for salvation.*

The Apostolic Council—*The Apostolic Council was held in Jerusalem around A.D. 48 or 49. Many scholars believe that the account Paul gives in Galatians 2:1-10 also refers to this meeting.*

Bible Account

Read the following Bible account or read Acts 15:1-29.

Paul's First Missionary Journey: The Jerusalem Council

While Paul and Barnabas were in Antioch, some Jewish Christians came to the city and began teaching false doctrine. They told the new Gentile believers that they had to practice certain Jewish rituals in order to be saved. Paul and Barnabas were disturbed by this teaching, because they had preached the gospel of salvation by faith in Christ alone. After an argument between the two sides, everyone agreed that Paul, Barnabas, and some others should go to the apostles and church elders at Jerusalem to settle the dispute.

When the question was presented at this council, there was much debate and discussion about it. Finally Peter stood to speak to the council. He reminded the people that God had commanded the apostles to preach His gospel to the Gentiles. God had placed His divine seal of acceptance on the Gentile believers by giving them the Holy Spirit. "Why tempt ye God," Peter asked the Jewish Christians, "to put a yoke upon the neck of the [Gentile] disciples, which neither our fathers nor we were able to bear?" Forcing Gentiles to keep the Jewish law would place them under the same bondage that the Jews had been under before they had believed on Christ and been freed from the law.

"We believe," Peter continued, "that through the grace of the Lord Jesus Christ we shall be saved, even as they." Salvation had been given to the Jewish Christians, not because they kept certain rituals, but because the Lord Jesus had been gracious to them.

The people were silent after Peter's speech. They listened as Paul and Barnabas gave testimonies about the many Gentiles God had saved.

James was the next speaker. He agreed with Peter that God's clear instructions had been to preach the gospel to Gentile nations. He believed God intended to save many of these Gentile people. He did not think it was necessary for these believers to practice Jewish customs. But he saw a need to set certain standards for all believers to follow to set them apart from the unbelievers around them.

James recommended that the Gentile Christians stay away from four things: eating meat that had been offered to idols, fornication, eating meat of animals that been strangled, and drinking blood. Avoiding these things would not only set the believers apart from the unbelievers but would also help them get along well with their Jewish brothers and sisters. These suggestions satisfied the council. They sent men to the Gentile churches carrying letters that explained the decision.

The Life of Paul TimeLine

Place Card 5, *The First Apostolic Council,* on the TimeLine at A.D. 49.

InfoScene: "Paul's First Missionary Journey"
Display Chart 19 for reference throughout this unit. Review and discuss the Bible account as time permits.

- ➤ **Why do you think the Gentiles were often more ready to believe than the Jews?** *(Answers may vary, but explain that the Jews knew that they were God's chosen people and were trying to keep the law.)*
- ➤ **Why did Paul later write letters to the people in the churches he had started?** *(to encourage them, to answer their questions, and to help them grow)*
- ➤ **Why do you think some people believed that Gentiles needed to practice the law to be saved?** *(Many answers are acceptable, but point out that many Jews thought the law of Moses should still apply to everyone.)*

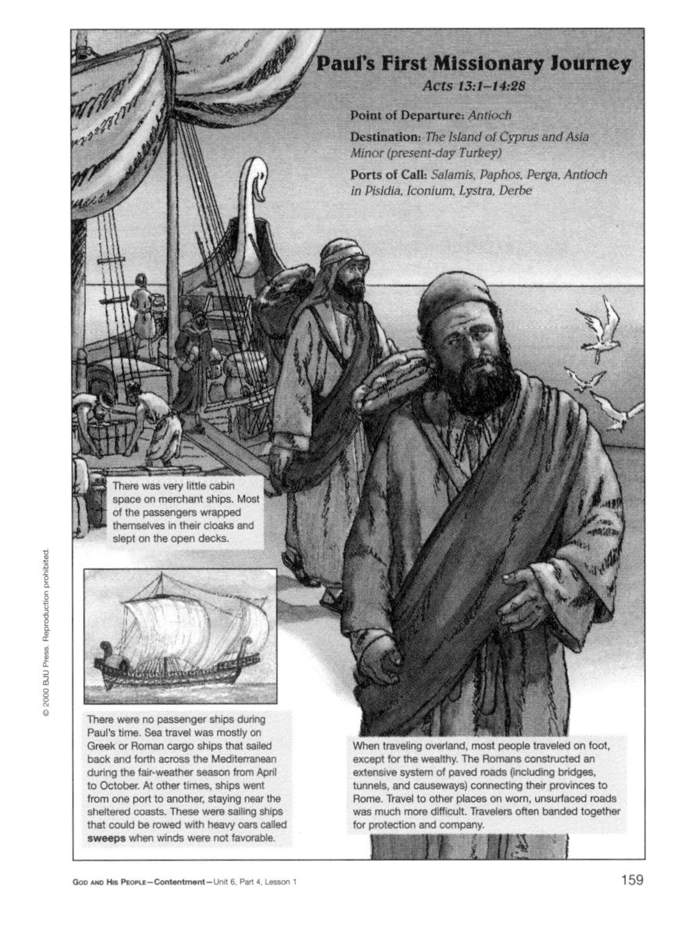

Paul's First Missionary Journey
Acts 13:1–14:28

Point of Departure: *Antioch*

Destination: *The Island of Cyprus and Asia Minor (present-day Turkey)*

Ports of Call: *Salamis, Paphos, Perga, Antioch in Pisidia, Iconium, Lystra, Derbe*

There was very little cabin space on merchant ships. Most of the passengers wrapped themselves in their cloaks and slept on the open decks.

There were no passenger ships during Paul's time. Sea travel was mostly on Greek or Roman cargo ships that sailed back and forth across the Mediterranean during the fair-weather season from April to October. At other times, ships went from one port to another, staying near the sheltered coasts. These were sailing ships that could be rowed with heavy oars called **sweeps** when winds were not favorable.

When traveling overland, most people traveled on foot, except for the wealthy. The Romans constructed an extensive system of paved roads (including bridges, tunnels, and causeways) connecting their provinces to Rome. Travel to other places on worn, unsurfaced roads was much more difficult. Travelers often banded together for protection and company.

GOD AND HIS PEOPLE—**Contentment**—Unit 6, Part 4, Lesson 1 159

- ➤ **In what other ways do people *try* to get salvation?** *(Possible answers include trying to live a good life, going to church, reading the Bible, saying prayers, giving to the poor, and being kind to people.)*
- ➤ **Who can save us?** *(The only Savior of men is the Lord Jesus Christ.)*
- ➤ **Who will be saved?** *(Whoever repents and believes on the Lord Jesus Christ will be saved.)*

Song: "The Journeys of Paul"

Sing the first verse (Worktext pages 280-81). Play the recording and lead in singing verse 1.

- ➤ **What was the first stop for Paul and Barnabas?** *(the island of Cyprus)*

Worktext page 159

Read for information.

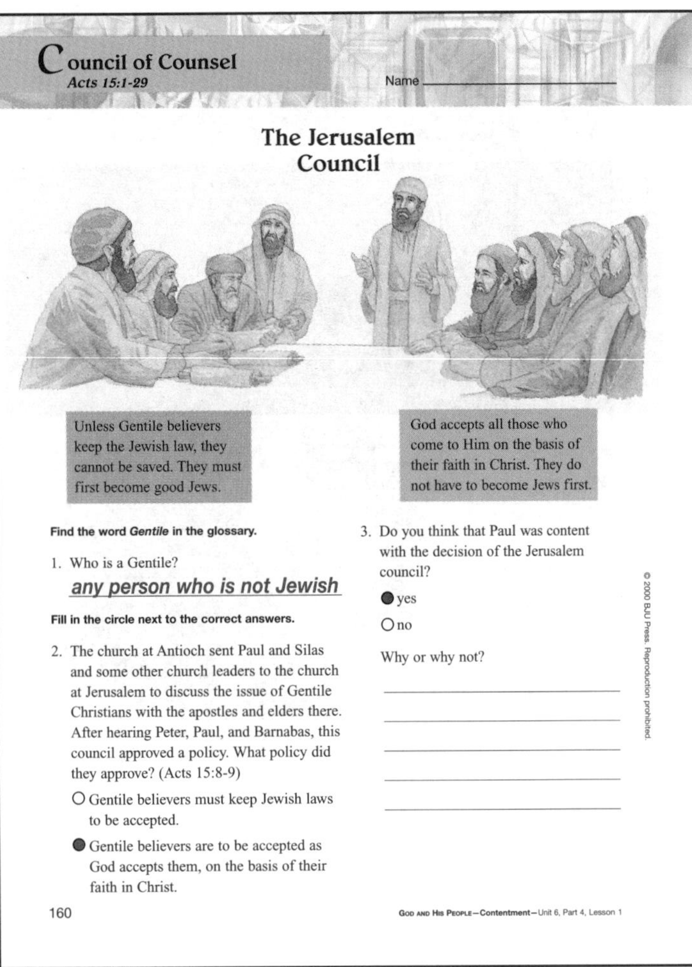

Council of Counsel
Acts 15:1-29

Name ______________________

The Jerusalem Council

Unless Gentile believers keep the Jewish law, they cannot be saved. They must first become good Jews.

God accepts all those who come to Him on the basis of their faith in Christ. They do not have to become Jews first.

Find the word *Gentile* in the glossary.

1. Who is a Gentile?
   any person who is not Jewish

Fill in the circle next to the correct answers.

2. The church at Antioch sent Paul and Silas and some other church leaders to the church at Jerusalem to discuss the issue of Gentile Christians with the apostles and elders there. After hearing Peter, Paul, and Barnabas, this council approved a policy. What policy did they approve? (Acts 15:8-9)
   - ○ Gentile believers must keep Jewish laws to be accepted.
   - ● Gentile believers are to be accepted as God accepts them, on the basis of their faith in Christ.

3. Do you think that Paul was content with the decision of the Jerusalem council?
   - ● yes
   - ○ no

   Why or why not?

160 God and His People—Contentment—Unit 6, Part 4, Lesson 1

Worktext page 160

Recall facts about the Jerusalem Council.

Lesson 2

Materials

- Charts 20 and 36: "Paul's Second Missionary Journey" and "Paul's Route—Second Journey"
- The Life of Paul TimeLine
- TimeLine Cards 6-7: *Paul's Second Missionary Journey* and *The Epistles of the End Times*
- Song: "The Journeys of Paul"
- Map marker for each student

Introducing the Bible Account

Discuss helping missionaries.

➤ **What are some ways that Christians can help missionaries?** *(Possible answers include giving, praying, and writing to them.)*

Explain that sometimes people go to a foreign country to help missionaries living there. This Bible account will give the names of two men who went with missionaries Paul and Barnabas to help them.

Bible Account

Read the following Bible account or read Acts 15:30-39.

Paul's Second Missionary Journey: Choosing a Helper

Paul and Barnabas returned to Antioch and delivered the letters from the apostles about the council's decision. Two men from Jerusalem, Judas and Silas, went with them. The Christians in the Gentile churches were greatly comforted by the news in the letters. As Paul and Barnabas made plans to visit the churches that were started on their first preaching tour, they had a disagreement. Barnabas wanted to take John Mark again, but Paul refused because Mark had left them on the first trip. So Barnabas took Mark and went to Cyprus, and Paul chose Silas for a helper.

Background Information

Second Missionary Journey—*Paul visited the following cities during his second missionary journey: Antioch in Syria, various cities in Syria and Cilicia, Derbe, Lystra, Iconium, Troas, Neapolis, Philippi, Amphipolis, Apollonia, Thessalonica, Berea, Athens, Corinth, Cenchrea, Ephesus, Caesarea, and Jerusalem.*

Purple Dye—*Lydia, a "seller of purple," made and sold purple dye from the murex shellfish. She probably learned the trade in her hometown, Thyatira (now in Turkey), which was famous for its purple dye. Purple was a favorite color of the Romans, but few people could afford much of the dye. It was expensive because it took much work to get the dye from the shellfish.*

Corinth—*The city of Corinth was well known for its people's wickedness. In Paul's day,* to corinthianize *meant "to sin." The results of Paul's preaching the gospel in Corinth show that even in the most difficult areas, people can be saved when the Word is preached.*

Judgment Seat—*Paul was brought before the "judgment seat" at Corinth. The Greek word is* bema. *Roman officials heard cases brought before them at this judgment seat. Excavations at ancient Corinth show ruins of the judgment seat where Paul stood before Gallio.*

Bible Account

Read the following Bible account or retell Acts 16:1–18:22. Use Chart 36, "Paul's Route—Second Journey," to help students visualize where Paul went. Direct the students to move their map markers on Worktext page 298 to each city mentioned as the Bible account progresses. (*Note:* Unit 6, Part 4, Going Beyond suggests a Bible walk of Paul's Second Missionary Journey. You may wish to go on the walk after telling this account.)

Paul's Second Missionary Journey: Traveling and Preaching

After leaving *Antioch,* Paul stopped first at *Derbe* and *Lystra,* where he had preached on the first journey. He and Silas were joined here by a young believer named Timothy. Paul followed the leading of the Holy Spirit to *Troas,* just across the Aegean Sea from Greece. At Troas, Paul had a vision of a man from Macedonia calling, "Come over into Macedonia, and help us."

Arriving in the city of *Philippi* in Macedonia, Paul was greeted by a woman named Lydia. God had touched her heart already, and she received the gospel. While at Philippi, Paul cast an evil spirit out of a girl misused by the townspeople, who were making money through her fortunetelling. Angry that the girl could no longer earn money for them, her masters started a riot. The mob beat Paul and Silas and threw them into jail. But while they were there, a great earthquake shook the prison and opened all the doors. The frightened jailer asked Paul and Silas, "What must I do to be saved?" They told him, "Believe on the Lord Jesus Christ, and thou shalt be saved." The jailer and his whole family believed. A church was started from the small group of believers in Philippi. Later in his ministry, Paul wrote to these Philippians to remind them to "rejoice in the Lord."

When Paul preached to the Jews in the Thessalonian synagogue, "some of them believed" (Acts 17:4). In *Thessalonica,* Paul and Silas had the reputation as "these that have turned the world upside down" (Acts 17:6) because of their exciting testimony for Christ. The unbelievers, however, turned the city into an uproar against them and forced Paul and Silas to leave. Later on this same journey, Paul wrote from Corinth to the Thessalonians. His two letters to them are called I and II Thessalonians.

Paul also preached in the synagogue in *Berea,* where the people received the word more readily than in Thessalonica. The unbelieving Jews from Thessalonica went to Berea and forced Paul to leave once again. Silas and Timothy stayed in Berea until Paul sent for them a little later.

When Paul arrived by boat in *Athens* from Macedonia, he was troubled to find the people there worshiping idols. The Athenians even had an altar to the unknown god. To the Athenians, Paul was just another voice, asking them to worship another God.

On Mars' Hill Paul showed the Athenians that the unknown God that they worshiped could be known. Paul preached the one true God who will one day judge the world through His Son, Jesus Christ, whom He raised from the dead.

When the people heard Paul's preaching, some made fun of Paul, but others said they would listen to him speak more. Some people accepted what Paul said and believed on Jesus Christ as their Savior.

Paul traveled on to *Corinth.* (Share the background information about Corinth here if desired.) The unbelieving Jews there opposed Paul's preaching, but God was working. Crispus, the chief ruler of the synagogue, was converted. Many others were saved too, and God assured Paul through a vision that He was with him and that He had many people in Corinth.

Paul ministered in Corinth for eighteen months, staying and working with Priscilla and Aquila, who were tentmakers. After a change in the government of the province, the Jews stirred up trouble again. Paul was brought before the judgment seat, but Gallio (brother of the Roman orator Seneca), the new official, did not want to hear the case. Paul left Corinth and stopped briefly at *Ephesus* and *Caesarea* before returning to his home church at *Antioch* in Syria to report God's blessing on his missionary journey.

InfoScene: "Paul's Second Missionary Journey"
Display Chart 20 for reference throughout this unit. Review and discuss the Bible account as time permits.

- ➤ **Why did Paul and Barnabas split up on this second journey?** *(because they disagreed over taking John Mark with them)*
- ➤ **Would you want to go back to a place where you had been stoned? What do you think made Paul return to Lystra?** *(Possible answers include to encourage the believers there and to preach to those who were still unsaved.)*
- ➤ **How did God turn the experience of being in prison into something good for Paul and Silas?** *(Because of their testimony while in prison, the jailer and his whole family were saved.)*
- ➤ **How do you think Paul felt when he was forced to leave city after city?** *(Many answers are acceptable. Lead the students to conclude that God gave Paul grace to go on without giving in to discouragement.)*
- ➤ **How should Christians be like Paul when they have difficult experiences?** *(be content)*

The Life of Paul TimeLine

Place Card 6, *Paul's Second Missionary Journey,* on the TimeLine at A.D. 49-52.

Paul's Second Missionary Journey
Acts 16:1–18:22

Point of Departure: *Antioch*

Destination: *The churches established on the first journey and certain other cities of Asia Minor*

Ports of Call: *Tarsus, Derbe, Lystra, Antioch in Pisidia, Iconium, Troas, Neapolis, Philippi, Amphipolis, Apollonia, Thessalonica, Berea, Athens, Corinth, Cenchrea, Ephesus, Rhodes*

Athens was a center for culture and learning, but it was also a center for idol worship. Everywhere Paul looked he must have seen temples and statues dedicated to false gods.

The Greeks were proud of their capital city, Athens. Their poets called it the most beautiful city in the world. The Parthenon crowning the Acropolis was a temple dedicated to Athena, the Greek goddess of truth and justice for whom the city was named.

Paul preached about Jesus Christ in the ***Areopagus***, the original meeting place of the Athenian court of law.

Greece was conquered by the Romans in 146 B.C. and became the province of Achaia in the Roman Empire.

God and His People—Contentment—Unit 6, Part 4, Lesson 2 161

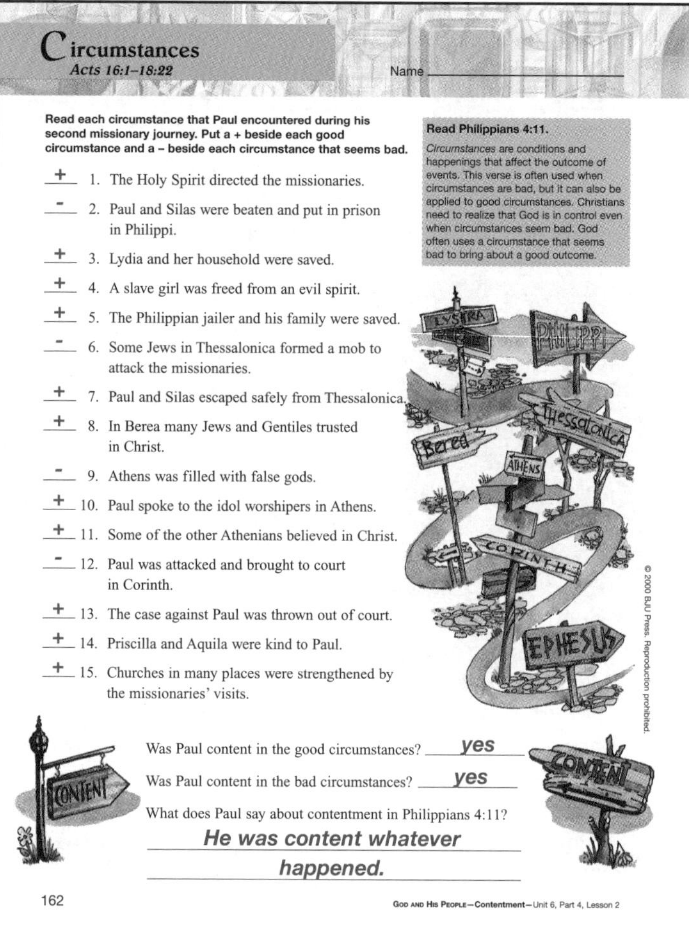
Circumstances
Acts 16:1–18:22

Name ____________________

Read each circumstance that Paul encountered during his second missionary journey. Put a + beside each good circumstance and a – beside each circumstance that seems bad.

Read Philippians 4:11.
Circumstances are conditions and happenings that affect the outcome of events. This verse is often used when circumstances are bad, but it can also be applied to good circumstances. Christians need to realize that God is in control even when circumstances seem bad. God often uses a circumstance that seems bad to bring about a good outcome.

+ 1. The Holy Spirit directed the missionaries.
– 2. Paul and Silas were beaten and put in prison in Philippi.
+ 3. Lydia and her household were saved.
+ 4. A slave girl was freed from an evil spirit.
+ 5. The Philippian jailer and his family were saved.
– 6. Some Jews in Thessalonica formed a mob to attack the missionaries.
+ 7. Paul and Silas escaped safely from Thessalonica.
+ 8. In Berea many Jews and Gentiles trusted in Christ.
– 9. Athens was filled with false gods.
+ 10. Paul spoke to the idol worshipers in Athens.
+ 11. Some of the other Athenians believed in Christ.
– 12. Paul was attacked and brought to court in Corinth.
+ 13. The case against Paul was thrown out of court.
+ 14. Priscilla and Aquila were kind to Paul.
+ 15. Churches in many places were strengthened by the missionaries' visits.

Was Paul content in the good circumstances? *yes*

Was Paul content in the bad circumstances? *yes*

What does Paul say about contentment in Philippians 4:11? *He was content whatever happened.*

162 God and His People—Contentment—Unit 6, Part 4, Lesson 2

The Life of Paul TimeLine

Place Card 7, *The Epistles of the End Times,* on the TimeLine at A.D. 50-51.

Worktext page 161

Read for information.

Memory Verse—Philippians 4:11

Practice the memory verse. Locate **Philippians 4:11** and select a student to read the verse aloud as the others follow along. Explain that Paul was saying that he needed nothing but was content in Christ.

- ➤ **Where was Paul when he wrote this verse?** *(in prison)*
- ➤ **What does it mean to *learn* something?** *(Elicit that it means to gain knowledge about something and be able to put it into practice.)*

Explain that learning always takes time. Students may remember learning how to ride a bicycle. They had to learn how to stay balanced on the bike, steer with the handlebars, and use the brakes. Some places are harder to ride a bike than others. It takes practice to ride up a hill or on a rough road. At first they might have fallen or crashed, but eventually they learned how to ride without thinking about all the details—it came naturally. Paul learned to be content in the same way. It was probably difficult to be content in prisons or in shipwrecks, and sometimes he "fell." In this verse Paul tells us that he learned to be content in all situations. Practice memorizing by choosing students to read the verse throughout the day.

Song: "The Journeys of Paul"

Teach the second verse (Worktext pages 280-81). Play the recording of verse 2. Briefly review the account of the vision Paul had of a man asking him to come to Macedonia. Remind the students that Priscilla and Aquila were the tentmakers. Sing together verse 2; then sing verses 1-2.

Worktext page 162

Recall facts about Paul's second missionary journey.

Lesson 3

Materials

- Charts 21 and 37: "Paul's Third Missionary Journey" and "Paul's Route—Third Journey"
- The Life of Paul TimeLine
- TimeLine Cards 8-10: *Paul's Third Missionary Journey, The Major Epistles,* and *Paul's Arrest in Jerusalem*
- Map marker for each student
- Song: "The Journeys of Paul"

Memory Verse—Philippians 4:11

Practice the memory verse. Locate and read **Philippians 4:11.** Write the memory verse on an erasable board, leaving out five key words. Choose students to read the verse, filling in the missing words.

Background Information

Third Missionary Journey—*Paul visited the following cities during his third missionary journey: Antioch in Syria; various cities in Galatia and Phrygia; Ephesus; various cities in Macedonia, Achaia, and Asia; Troas; Assos; Mitylene; Miletus; Patara; Tyre; Ptolemais; Caesarea; and Jerusalem.*

Ephesus—*In the days of Paul, Ephesus was a center for the occult. It was also the center of worship for Diana (or Artemis, as she was called in Greek), a goddess of fertility. In Diana's temple at Ephesus was a statue of Diana that the Ephesians believed had fallen from Jupiter, the king of the gods. Her beautiful temple was considered one of the wonders of the ancient world. Artists crafted miniatures of Diana's temple for people to buy to take home and use in worship of the goddess. Outlines of the statue and her temple are clearly visible on coins recovered from that time.*

The School of Tyrannus—*Paul probably used the school building of a local philosopher as a place to teach.*

Introducing the Bible Account

Discuss saying goodbye.

➤ **Have you ever had to be separated from a parent or family member for a long period of time?**

➤ **What was it like to say goodbye to someone you wouldn't see again for a while?**

Explain that in the following Bible account, Paul says goodbye to his friends in the church in Ephesus, knowing that he will never see them again. Encourage the students to imagine how Paul felt.

Bible Account

Read the following Bible account or retell Acts 18:23–23:11 in your own words. Display Chart 37, "Paul's Route—Third Journey" and tell the students to move their map markers on Worktext page 299 to the locations mentioned as the Bible account progresses.

Paul's Third Missionary Journey: Ministry in Ephesus

After reporting to his home church in Antioch of Syria, Paul started his third journey. He had promised the Ephesians that he would return, but he traveled first through Galatia and Phrygia to strengthen the new churches there. When Paul arrived in *Ephesus,* he found that the believers there had been baptized, believing in John the Baptist's message of repentance but not knowing about Jesus. Then Paul said, "John verily baptized with the baptism of repentance, saying unto the people, that they should believe on him which should come after him, that is, on Christ Jesus."

Paul ministered in the synagogue at Ephesus for three months, but enemies made him leave. He moved his place of ministry to the school of Tyrannus, where he witnessed daily for the Lord. Paul's ministry at Ephesus lasted two years, during which he had many battles with satanic power. On one occasion after people were converted, they burned their witchcraft books in public. On another occasion an idol-maker named Demetrius stirred up the entire city against Paul. A city official finally put a stop to the riot.

On this third journey Paul traveled through Macedonia and back. While at *Troas,* Paul met with the believers "upon the first day of the week" for the breaking of bread and preaching of the Word. During the service, a young man named Eutychus, who was sitting in a window, fell asleep and fell to the ground three stories below. Paul went to Eutychus, embraced him, and said, "Trouble not yourselves, for his life is in him." Paul raised Eutychus from the dead and then continued preaching until dawn and then departed.

Knowing that as he returned he must witness in Jerusalem and that he would be put in prison, Paul met one last time with the Ephesian elders at *Miletus* (Acts 20:17-38). These men were Paul's dear friends, and they wept when Paul told them that he would not be able to come to see them again. Later in his ministry while in prison, Paul wrote a letter to the church at Ephesus. It is now the Book of Ephesians.

- ➤ **How was Satan defeated at Ephesus while Paul was there?** *(The people were converted and they burned their witchcraft books.)*
- ➤ **Does Satan leave Christians alone after they are saved? Explain.** *(No. He tempts them to sin.)*
- ➤ **How can Christians resist Satan?** *(Possible answers include by drawing near to God, by obeying God, by praying, and by spending time in God's Word.)*
- ➤ **How do we know that Paul loved the people of Ephesus?** *(He sorrowed at having to leave them; he wrote the Book of Ephesians to them later from prison.)*
- ➤ **How could Paul be content when he knew that he would not see his friends again on earth?** *(Possible answers include that he would see them in heaven and that he was doing the will of God.)*

The Life of Paul TimeLine

Place Card 8, *Paul's Third Missionary Journey,* on the TimeLine at A.D. 53-58.

The Life of Paul TimeLine

Place Card 9, *The Major Epistles,* on the TimeLine at A.D. 56-57.

Background Information

Sadducees—*The Sadducees were a religious group in Israel who believed and taught differently from the Pharisees. One of the major differences between the two groups was that the Pharisees believed in the resurrection of the dead, while the Sadducees denied the resurrection and the idea of an afterlife.*

Bible Account

Read the following Bible account or retell Acts 21:1–23:11 in your own words. Direct the students' attention to Worktext page 163.

Paul's Third Missionary Journey: Witnessing at Jerusalem

Paul's burden for his own people made him go to Jerusalem to witness. His friends warned him not to go because they thought the Jews would try to kill him at Jerusalem. Paul responded, "I am ready not to be bound only, but also to die at Jerusalem for the name of the Lord Jesus" (Acts 21:13). After Paul arrived in Jerusalem, unbelieving Jews from Asia Minor falsely accused him and formed a mob to seize him. But he was rescued by the Roman army. As Paul was led away to safety, he asked to speak to the Jewish mob. When the centurion gave him permission, Paul told how God had saved him and called him to preach the gospel.

The mob became angry when Paul spoke of his ministry to the Gentiles, so the Roman of-

ficial called a council to let the Jews make their accusations against Paul. Knowing that the council was made up of Pharisees and Sadducees, Paul began his defense by saying that he believed in the resurrection. Since the Sadducees denied the resurrection, they began arguing with the Pharisees instead of with Paul. The argument became so heated that Paul had to leave the room to save his life.

Paul's Third Missionary Journey
Acts 18:23–23:11
Point of Departure: Antioch
Destination: The areas he visited before, including Ephesus (for a longer stay) and Palestine
Ports of Call: Tarsus, Iconium, Ephesus, Mitylene, Thessalonica, Corinth, Philippi, Troas, Assos, Miletus, Cos, Rhodes, Patara, Paphos, Tyre, Ptolemais, Caesarea, Jerusalem
Roman Citizenship
Rights and Privileges
➤ Only a citizen may wear a white toga.
➤ Only a citizen may vote or hold office.
➤ Citizens receive the best seats in theaters.
➤ Citizens may have first place in line.
➤ Other people must make way for citizens in the streets.
➤ A citizen may not be punished without trial.
➤ A citizen may not be tortured during questioning.
➤ A citizen accused of a crime for which the penalty is death may appeal to Caesar.
➤ If a citizen is sentenced to death, he is to be killed quickly with the sword rather than suffering slow death by crucifixion.
Paul was held in protective custody in the Tower of Antonia (the Antonia Fortress) which stood on Zion, Jerusalem's highest hill. It was joined to the temple enclosure by two stairways and an underground tunnel. This is probably the place where Pontius Pilate sentenced Jesus.
Paul was protected from his fellow Jews by a cohort of Roman soldiers who were members of the Roman Tenth Legion stationed in Caesarea to keep order.
© 2000 BJU Press. Reproduction prohibited.
GOD AND HIS PEOPLE—Contentment—Unit 6, Part 4, Lesson 3
163

Fearing for Paul's safety in Jerusalem, the Roman officials placed Paul in protective custody until he could be sent to Caesarea. That night the Lord appeared to Paul to reassure him: "Be of good cheer, Paul: for as thou hast testified of me in Jerusalem, so must thou bear witness also at Rome" (Acts 23:11).

InfoScene: "Paul's Third Missionary Journey"
Display Chart 21 for reference throughout this unit. Review and discuss the Bible account as time permits.

- ➤ **Why did Paul go to Jerusalem even when he knew bad things would happen to him there?** *(He was burdened to witness to his own people there.)*
- ➤ **How could Paul be content when he knew that he would not see his friends again on earth?** *(Possible answers include that he would see them in heaven and that he was doing the will of God.)*

➤ **How did the Lord encourage Paul?** *(He appeared to him in prison, assuring Paul that He was with him to help him.)*

➤ **How can Christians be encouraged in the Lord?** *(Possible answers include spending time in prayer and reading God's Word, fellowshiping with other Christians, and singing praises to God.)*

The Life of Paul TimeLine

Place Card 10, *Paul's Arrest in Jerusalem,* on the TimeLine at A.D. 58-59.

Background Information

Roman Roads—*Paul's traveling often took him over roads built to link the Roman provinces with the capital at Rome. From the center of Rome, where an official measurement marked the beginning of all Roman roads, twenty-nine different roads extended so that "all roads led to Rome." Although the Romans were not the first to construct roads, the network they built stretched over thousands of miles—a remarkable engineering undertaking at the time.*

Typical Roman Road Construction—*First, the roadway was marked out, ditches were dug alongside, and curbstones were placed on the inner side of the ditches. Next, the area inside the curbstones was dug deeper and then refilled with foundation materials, such as sand and small stones. Finally, large, flat stones were laid for the top surface. A high point at the center of the road allowed water to drain into the ditches at the sides of the road.*

Math Connection (optional)

Discuss distances. Share the background information about Roman roads. Explain that as Paul walked along the Roman roads, he found "milestones," which provided information about the next towns. The Roman "mile" measured one thousand paces, *mille passum.* A "pace" was actually a double step measuring about five feet, so the Roman mile was about five thousand feet. The standard mile today measures 5,280 feet.

Calculate the number of paces in a mile. Mark a distance of ten feet. Allow several students to walk the ten feet while you count the number of paces (double steps). Determine the average number of student paces in ten feet and multiply by 528. The result is the number of student paces in 1 mile.

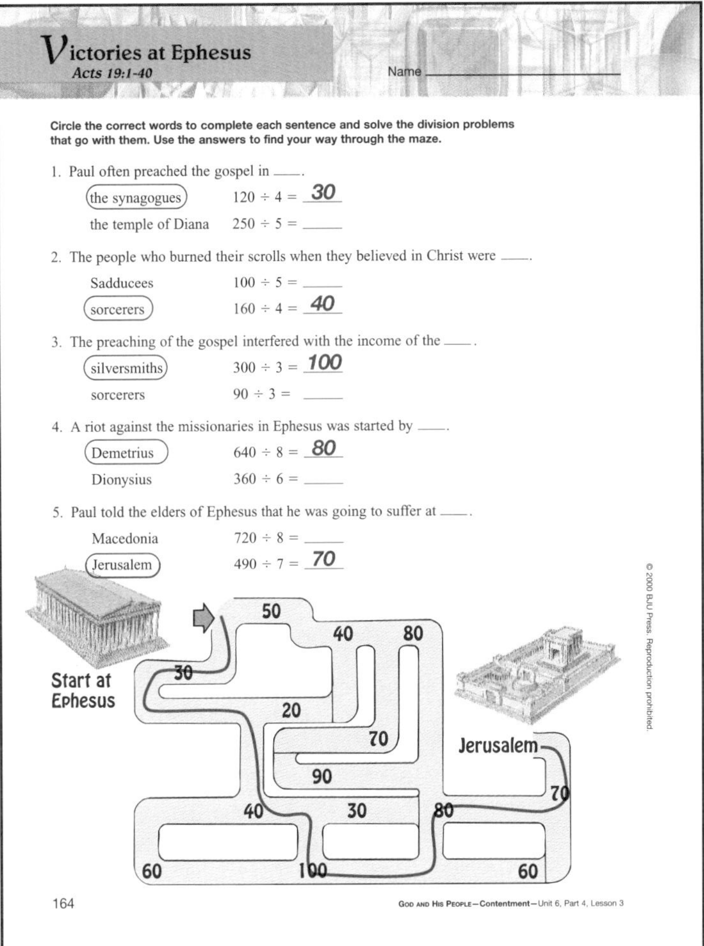

Victories at Ephesus
Acts 19:1-40

Name ____________________

Circle the correct words to complete each sentence and solve the division problems that go with them. Use the answers to find your way through the maze.

1. Paul often preached the gospel in ___.
   (the synagogues) 120 ÷ 4 = 30
   the temple of Diana 250 ÷ 5 = ___
2. The people who burned their scrolls when they believed in Christ were ___.
   Sadducees 100 ÷ 5 = ___
   (sorcerers) 160 ÷ 4 = 40
3. The preaching of the gospel interfered with the income of the ___.
   (silversmiths) 300 ÷ 3 = 100
   sorcerers 90 ÷ 3 = ___
4. A riot against the missionaries in Ephesus was started by ___.
   (Demetrius) 640 ÷ 8 = 80
   Dionysius 360 ÷ 6 = ___
5. Paul told the elders of Ephesus that he was going to suffer at ___.
   Macedonia 720 ÷ 8 = ___
   (Jerusalem) 490 ÷ 7 = 70

164 God and His People—Contentment—Unit 6, Part 4, Lesson 3

Song: "The Journeys of Paul"

Teach the third verse (Worktext pages 280-81). Play the recording and lead in singing the first two verses. Sing verse 3 together with the recording.

Worktext page 164

Recall details about Paul's ministry in Ephesus.

Lesson 4

Materials

- Chart 38, "Paul's Route—Journey to Rome"
- The Life of Paul TimeLine
- TimeLine Cards 11-14: *Journey to Rome, The Prison Epistles, The Pastoral Epistles,* and *Martyrdom of Paul*
- Song: "The Journeys of Paul"

Memory Verse—Philippians 4:11

Practice the memory verse. Locate and read **Philippians 4:11**; then call on students to say the verse from memory.

The Life of Paul TimeLine

Place Card 11, *Journey to Rome,* on the TimeLine at A.D. 59-60.

Background Information

Felix—*Antonius Felix became governor of Judea as a result of his brother Pallas's influence. Felix married Drusilla, the daughter of Herod Agrippa I, after convincing her to leave her husband. Felix was known for his cruelty and corruption, and he was eventually removed from his seat of government by Nero around A.D. 60.*

Festus—*Porcius Festus replaced Felix when Nero removed him (Acts 24:27). Festus held the office for only two years and died in A.D. 62. Historically, Festus had a much better reputation as a governor than Felix.*

Herod Agrippa II—*Marcus Julius Agrippa II was the last in the line of rulers named Herod that held positions in Palestine between 40 B.C. and A.D. 100. He often used his power to help the Jews. Since he had been given power to appoint the Jewish high priest, he was probably considered an authority on the Jewish religion in Rome. Bernice, mentioned in Acts 25:13, was Agrippa's younger sister who lived with Agrippa.*

Introducing the Bible Account

Share the background information. Point out that because Paul was willing for God to use him, he was able to give the gospel to these important leaders. Encourage the students to notice the responses of these men to the gospel as you read the following Bible account.

Bible Account

Read the following Bible account or retell Acts 23:9–28:31 in your own words. Direct the students' attention to Chart 38, "Paul's Route—Journey to Rome," as you tell the following account.

Paul's Journey to Rome

The Jews in Asia brought false charges against Paul, causing him to be imprisoned at Caesarea under Roman guard. During these two years of imprisonment, Paul witnessed to several important people, including Felix, Festus, and Herod Agrippa II. Felix trembled as Paul preached "righteousness, temperance, and judgment to come" (Acts 24:25), but he put Paul off. "Go thy way for this time; when I have a convenient season, I will call for thee," Felix said. Felix sent for Paul and talked with him often. He hoped that Paul would pay him a bribe, and then he would release him from prison. We have no record that Felix ever accepted Christ as his Savior. Festus accused Paul of being insane after hearing his testimony (Acts 26:24). King Agrippa asked to hear Paul. After Agrippa heard Paul's words about Christ, he exclaimed, "Almost thou persuadest me to be a Christian" (Acts 26:28), but the Scriptures never tell us that Agrippa received Christ.

Paul went to Rome because as a Roman citizen he had a right to appeal to Caesar and to have his case tried in the highest courts. On the way to Rome, there was a terrible storm, and the ship wrecked. During the storm, however, the Lord's angel again reassured Paul, "Fear not, Paul; thou must be brought before Caesar" (Acts 27:24). The guards wanted to kill the prisoners to keep them from escaping. God spared not only Paul's life but also the lives of all the other men on the ship. When Paul finally arrived in Rome, he was placed under Roman guard, but he lived in his own rented house and was free to preach the gospel. Even members of Caesar's own household were converted (Philippians 4:22).

While under house arrest, Paul wrote letters to the Colossians, the Ephesians, the Philippians, and Philemon.

During a short release from prison, he also wrote I Timothy and Titus.

Just before Paul was martyred during his second imprisonment at Rome, he wrote his "last will and testament" in II Timothy. Paul fought a good fight, he finished the course, and he kept the faith.

➤ **Why do you think Felix put off accepting Christ, even though he was troubled by Paul's words about judgment? Why is putting off salvation unwise?** *(Possible answers include that he was embarrassed, he didn't want to change his sinful lifestyle, or he didn't believe Paul was telling the truth. We never know when we will die; after death, it is too late to receive Christ.)*

➤ **What did Festus think about Paul? Did this attitude discourage Paul and cause him to stop witnessing?** *(Festus thought that Paul was insane, but Paul continued to witness for Christ.)*

➤ **How did God encourage Paul during the shipwreck?** *(He sent an angel to comfort him.)*

➤ **How did Paul spend his time during his house arrest?** *(preaching, writing to churches)*

Content Anywhere

Acts 23:9–28:31

Name ______________________

Paul preached the kingdom of God and taught about the Lord Jesus Christ at every possible opportunity. Paul preached while he was being escorted to Rome, while he was under house arrest in Caesarea, and while he was imprisoned in Rome.

Read each statement. Circle the letter under TRUE or FALSE. You may use your Bible to help.

	TRUE	FALSE
1. Tertullus was the governor of Caesarea before whom Paul was tried (Acts 24:1).	T	(S)
2. Felix allowed Paul to speak of Christ (Acts 24:24).	(B)	O
3. Festus kept Paul in Caesarea to be judged (Acts 25:4-6).	(O)	M
4. Paul thought that he should not be tried before Caesar's court.	N	(T)
5. Festus agreed to send Paul to Caesar (Acts 25:12).	(L)	D
6. King Agrippa asked to hear Paul (Acts 25:22).	(D)	K
7. King Agrippa was familiar with Jewish customs (Acts 26:3).	(L)	M
8. Festus said Paul had become insane due to lack of learning (Acts 26:24).	H	(Y)
9. Paul lived in his own house in Rome for two years and preached the gospel there (Acts 28:30).	(Y)	E

Write in order the letters you circled in the TRUE column to spell a word that tells how Paul witnessed.

Paul preached and taught

b o l d l y

(Acts 28:31).

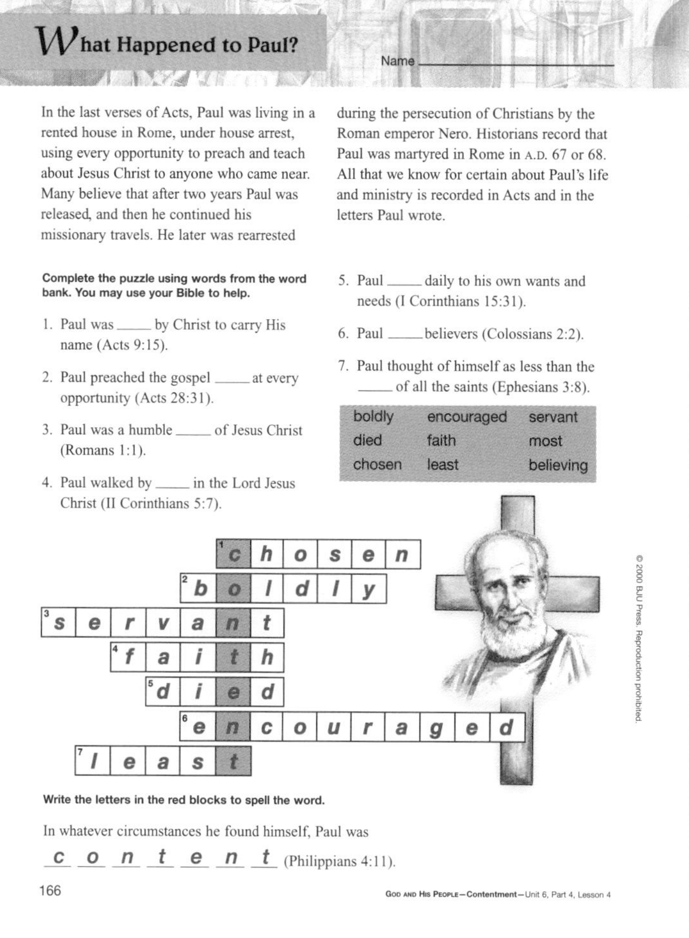

What Happened to Paul?

Name ______________________

In the last verses of Acts, Paul was living in a rented house in Rome, under house arrest, using every opportunity to preach and teach about Jesus Christ to anyone who came near. Many believe that after two years Paul was released, and then he continued his missionary travels. He later was rearrested during the persecution of Christians by the Roman emperor Nero. Historians record that Paul was martyred in Rome in A.D. 67 or 68. All that we know for certain about Paul's life and ministry is recorded in Acts and in the letters Paul wrote.

Complete the puzzle using words from the word bank. You may use your Bible to help.

1. Paul was ____ by Christ to carry His name (Acts 9:15).
2. Paul preached the gospel ____ at every opportunity (Acts 28:31).
3. Paul was a humble ____ of Jesus Christ (Romans 1:1).
4. Paul walked by ____ in the Lord Jesus Christ (II Corinthians 5:7).
5. Paul ____ daily to his own wants and needs (I Corinthians 15:31).
6. Paul ____ believers (Colossians 2:2).
7. Paul thought of himself as less than the ____ of all the saints (Ephesians 3:8).

boldly	encouraged	servant
died	faith	most
chosen	least	believing

1 c h o s e n
2 b o l d l y
3 s e r v a n t
4 f a i t h
5 d i e d
6 e n c o u r a g e d
7 l e a s t

Write the letters in the red blocks to spell the word.

In whatever circumstances he found himself, Paul was *c o n t e n t* (Philippians 4:11).

➤ **Do you think Paul was fearful when he learned that he would be martyred for Christ? How do you know?** *(Many answers are acceptable.)* Direct the students' attention to such passages as **Romans 8:38-39, I Corinthians 15:54-57,** or **Philippians 1:21-23.**

The Life of Paul TimeLine

Place Card 12, *The Prison Epistles,* on the TimeLine at A.D. 61-62. Place Card 13, *The Pastoral Epistles,* on the TimeLine at A.D. 65-67. Place Card 14, *Martyrdom of Paul,* on the TimeLine at A.D. 67.

Song: "The Journeys of Paul"

Teach the fourth verse (Worktext pages 280-81). Play the recording and lead in singing the fourth verse; then sing verses 1-4 together. Allow the students to sing the song without the recording (optional).

Worktext page 165

Locate information in Scripture.

Worktext page 166

Recall details about the ministry of Paul.

Going Beyond

Preparation of Materials

Make posters with the following city names: Lystra, Troas, Philippi, Thessalonica, Berea, Athens, Corinth, and Ephesus. Using the diagram provided, place the cities in the proper areas on a soccer field before class or as you take the walk. (*Note:* Posters may be attached to wooden stakes and placed in the ground.)

Bible Walk:
Paul's Second Missionary Journey

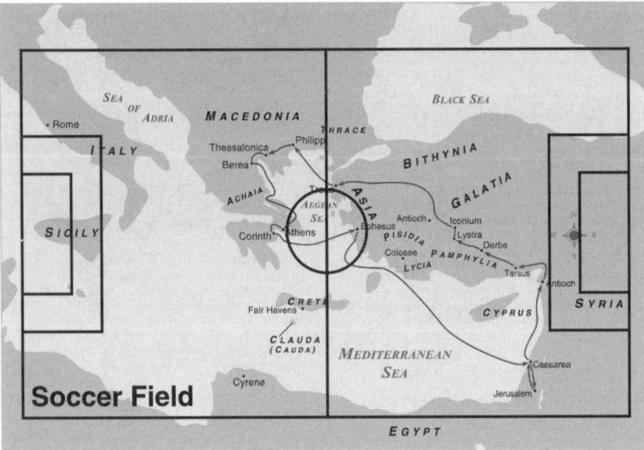

Enrichment

Lead a Bible walk of Paul's second journey. Explain to the students that you will be making Paul's second journey on a smaller scale outside. Lead the students to the soccer field and walk through the cities, pausing at each one and commenting on the events that took place there. Begin at Antioch in Syria and make the "missionary journey," traveling from city to city in numerical order. (*Note:* If you have no access to a soccer field, you may wish to use a playground area.)

Lystra—Timothy joined Paul and Silas.

Troas—Paul had a vision of the man from Macedonia; Luke joined them.

Philippi—Conversion of Lydia and the jailer; church started

Thessalonica—Preaching and the people persecuted them; church started

Berea—Preaching and the people received the Word

Athens—Paul's sermon on Mars' Hill

Corinth—Paul stayed for eighteen months; church founded; trial before Gallio; Paul wrote I and II Thessalonians.

Ephesus—Short stay before returning to Antioch by way of Caesarea and Jerusalem

Unit 6 Review Name ______________

Write the letter of the correct answer on the line.

A. Rome	C. concordance	F. Timothy	I. Philippi
B. Barnabas	D. Stephen	G. Matthew	J. rich man
	E. martyr	H. Peter	

__E__ 1. one who chooses to suffer or die rather than give up his faith in Christ

__B__ 2. Paul's partner on his first missionary journey

__F__ 3. His mother was a Jew, his father was a Greek

__H__ 4. a fisherman called to follow Jesus along with his brother

__C__ 5. an alphabetical list of key words with Scripture references

__I__ 6. city where Paul and Silas led a jailer to the Lord

__G__ 7. a tax collector called to follow Jesus

__A__ 8. city where Paul was a witness while under house arrest

__D__ 9. while being stoned by Jews he asked Jesus not to hold their sin against them

__J__ 10. His life of greed is compared with Lazarus' life of contentment

Complete the sentences by writing the missing words.

content
faithful
family
forgave
future
older
position
prodigal son
wealth
younger

The parable of the __prodigal son__ reminds us to be __content__ with the service we are called to, the __family__ into which we are born, the __wealth__ and __position__ we are blessed with, and the __future__ that God has for us. The __older__ brother was __faithful__ but not content; he desired recognition for his service.

Although the __younger__ brother was not faithful or content, his father __forgave__ him.

S60 Use after completing Unit 6 God and His People

Unit Review

Materials

- Copy of Supplement page S60, "Unit 6 Review," for each student

Guide a review of Unit 6. Review the people and events in preparation for the Unit 6 Test (optional).

Love

Overview

Preparing the Teacher

God is perfect in His nature. He is therefore perfect in His love, which is based on His truth and holiness. God is love **(I John 4:8, 16).** God's love is manifest in His provision for our salvation even though we are unlovely **(I John 3:1; 4:10).** When we receive God's love into our lives through Jesus Christ **(I John 4:9),** we are to manifest His love to fellow believers **(I John 4:21)** and to the unsaved in the world around us **(I John 4:14).** To know God is to show love. Love cannot be separated from obedience to God's commands **(I John 2:3, 5; 3:23-24).** As you consider the theme of love during this unit, determine to develop more fully this fruit of the Spirit, maturing in God's love, as you meditate on these verses from the Epistle of I John.

Preparing the Lessons

Parts 1-4 Lesson Materials—a copy of *With Daring Faith* for the teacher

Part 1 Lesson 1 Materials—two small pieces of magnetic tape for each student

Part 1 Lesson 4 Materials—picture of a comet (optional

Part 2 Lesson 2 Materials—a missionary prayer card for each student or pair of students (optional)

Part 2 Lesson 3 Materials—classified section of a newspaper with employment opportunities (optional)

Part 2 Lesson 4 Materials—jewelry, coins, plastic animal, and a work-related item (e.g., briefcase, toy tractor, or stethoscope)

Part 2 Going Beyond Materials—classified section of a newspaper with employment opportunities

Part 3 Lesson 3 Materials—a hat for each student (*Note:* Request that each student bring a hat from home.)

Part 4 Lesson 3 Materials—a telegram (optional), pictures of a caterpillar and a butterfly or moth (optional)

Part 4 Going Beyond Materials—travel brochure, books or encyclopedias about India

Unit 7 Love

Hymn: "O to Be Like Thee!"

Part	Lesson number	Lesson pages	Worktext pages	Supplement pages	Bible Account	Application
PART 1: **LOVING GOD**	1	225	167-70		**Character Focus:** John the Baptist (Matthew 3-4; Mark 6; Luke 1, 3)	
	2	228	171-72		Martha and Mary Welcome Jesus (Luke 10:38-42)	
	3	230	173-74, 322			**Missionary Biography:** *With Daring Faith*
	4	232	175-76, 323			**Missionary Biography:** *With Daring Faith*
PART 2: **LOVING THE BRETHREN**	1	235	177		Prayer for Peter (Acts 12:1-19)	
	2	236	178-79, 324			**Missionary Biography:** *With Daring Faith*
	3	238	180-81, 325			**Missionary Biography:** *With Daring Faith*
	4	240	182-84, 326			**Missionary Biography:** *With Daring Faith*
PART 3: **LOVING THE UNSAVED**	1	243	185		Jesus Forgives the Unfaithful Woman (John 8:1-11)	
	2	245	186, 327			**Missionary Biography:** *With Daring Faith*
	3	246	187-88, 328			**Missionary Biography:** *With Daring Faith*
	4	248	189-90		Peter and Cornelius (Acts 10)	
PART 4: **LOVING YOUR ENEMIES**	1	251	191		**Bible Study:** Responses to Enemies	
	2	253	192		**Bible Study:** Christlikeness Demonstrated	
	3	254	193-95, 329			**Missionary Biography:** *With Daring Faith*
	4	256	196, 330			**Hero of the Faith:** Amy Carmichael (optional) **Missionary Biography:** *With Daring Faith*

<table>
<tr><th>Connections</th><th>Memory Verses and Principles</th><th>Bible Doctrines</th><th>Skills/Applications</th></tr>
<tr><td>Science</td><td>Mark 12:29-30

Believers are to love God before all else.</td><td rowspan="4">The Doctrine of God
Attributes of God:
God is love (John 3:16).
The Doctrine of Man
Fall of Man:
Man is guilty before God (Rom. 3:10-12).
Redemption of Man:
Man by faith receives Christ's righteousness (Phil. 3:9).
Man faces a struggle between the two natures (Rom. 7:23-25).
The Doctrine of Salvation
Reception by Man:
Man must repent of his sins (Rom. 2:4).
Elements of Salvation:
God calls men through the Holy Spirit (John 16:7-11).
Repentance is turning away from sin (II Cor. 7:9-10).
Sanctification includes dying to sin and living to righteousness (Rom. 8:13).
The Doctrine of the Church
Definitions:
The universal church, an organism, is the mystical body of Christ composed of all true believers (I Cor. 12:13).
Functions of the Local Church:
Pray (Acts 12:5).
The Doctrine of Angels and Satan
Organization:
They reveal God's will to man (Luke 1:13).
They assist mankind (Acts 12:5-11).</td><td rowspan="4">Foundational:
• Realize that Christians should love God above all else
• Understand the meaning of repentance
• Understand the importance of prayer
• Recognize that showing kindness is the key to love
• Understand proper reactions to enemies
Practical:
• Recall facts and details
• Use a glossary
• Locate information in Scripture
• Sequence the books of the Bible
• Identify the location of Bible accounts
• Compare Bible characters
• Identify character traits
• Read a time line
• Use cross-references
• Learn the abbreviations of the books of the Bible
Personal:
• Develop a Bible reading habit
• Develop Christlike character traits
• Be Christlike in words and actions
• Put the needs of others before your own
• Recognize ways to demonstrate love
• Realize that God helps you to love your enemies
• Apply Bible knowledge to everyday life</td></tr>
<tr><td>Culture</td><td>Mark 12:31

Believers are to love others.</td></tr>
<tr><td></td><td>Ephesians 4:31-32

The key to love is kindness.</td></tr>
<tr><td>TimeLine:
Amy Carmichael</td><td>Matthew 5:43-44

Love your enemies.</td></tr>
</table>

Preparing the Unit 7 Bulletin Board

Cover the bulletin board with dark red and border it with gold. Mount the title, "With Christ It Is Possible!" in white. Cut four large hearts and place them around the white caption, "Love," as shown. Place the part titles of Unit 7 in gold on the hearts:

God
Fellow Christians
The Unsaved
Enemies

Preview

Doctrines

- Angels reveal God's will to man (Luke 1:13)—Lesson 1
- Repentance is turning away from sin (II Corinthians 7:9-10)—Lesson 1
- Man must repent of his sins (Romans 2:4)—Lesson 1
- Sanctification includes dying to sin and living to righteousness (Romans 8:13)—Lesson 2

Skills and Applications

- Learn Mark 12:29-30
- Locate information in Scripture
- Recall facts and details
- Develop a Bible reading habit
- Sequence the books of the Bible
- Learn the abbreviations for the books of the Bible
- Use a glossary
- Realize that Christians should love God above all else
- Understand the meaning of repentance
- Apply Bible knowledge to everyday life

Lesson 1

Materials

- Song: "The Bible Reading Habit"
- Two small pieces of magnetic tape for each student
- Unit 7 Bookmark for each student
- Highlighter for each student (optional)

Memory Verses—Mark 12:29-30

Principle: Believers are to love God before all else. Locate **Mark 12:29-30** and read the verses aloud as the students read silently. Choose students to read the verses aloud.

➤ **What four ways are believers commanded to love God?** *(with all their heart, soul, mind, and strength)*

➤ **What is the first of all commandments, and how can a believer demonstrate this?** *(to love God; Possible answers include praying, attending church, witnessing, reading the Bible to learn more about God, thinking about God's Word and what pleases God, and hating sin.)*

➤ **If a believer loves God the way the Bible says, will sin be a problem in his life?** *(Accept any answer, but explain that a believer will still sin because of his sinful nature but his desire should be to do what is right and to avoid sin at all times.)*

Direct the students to highlight the verses in their Bibles (optional). Give each student a Unit 7 Bookmark to mark the location of the verses. Direct attention to the sign language symbols for *I love you.* Direct the students to attach the magnetic tape and to place the Unit 7 Bookmark over the page.

Hymn: "O to Be Like Thee!"

Teach the first verse (Worktext pages 282-83). Read through the first verse and play the recording.

➤ **Whom do you want to be like when you grow up and why?** *(Answers will vary.)*

➤ **Can a believer be exactly like God? Why?** *(No. Possible answers include that God is perfect and without sin, all-knowing, all-powerful, and unchangeable.)*

➤ **If a believer cannot be exactly like God, why did the hymn writer choose this title for the hymn?** *(A believer's desire should be to be like God and to strive for holiness in word, thought, and actions.)*

➤ **What are some ways that believers are to demonstrate their desire to please God and therefore be like Him?** *(Possible answers include being kind to those who are unkind toward us, putting others first, loving God, and asking for God's help to have an obedient, submissive attitude.)*

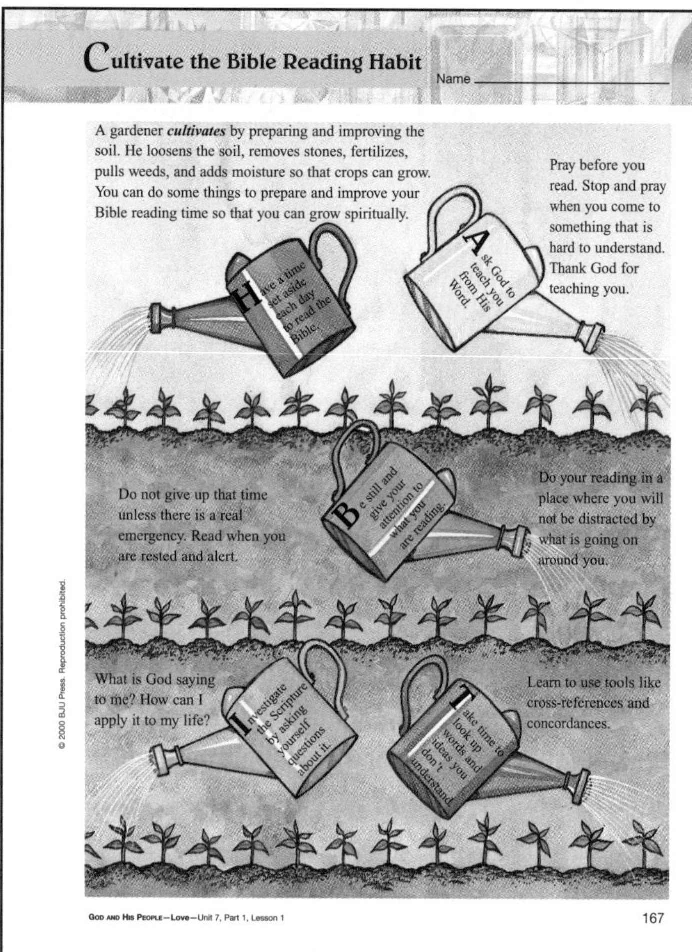
Cultivate the Bible Reading Habit

Name ____________________

A gardener *cultivates* by preparing and improving the soil. He loosens the soil, removes stones, fertilizes, pulls weeds, and adds moisture so that crops can grow. You can do some things to prepare and improve your Bible reading time so that you can grow spiritually.

Have a time set aside each day to read the Bible.

Do not give up that time unless there is a real emergency. Read when you are rested and alert.

Ask God to teach you from His Word.

Pray before you read. Stop and pray when you come to something that is hard to understand. Thank God for teaching you.

Be still and give your attention to what you are reading.

Do your reading in a place where you will not be distracted by what is going on around you.

Investigate the Scripture by asking yourself questions about it.

What is God saying to me? How can I apply it to my life?

Take time to look up words and ideas you don't understand.

Learn to use tools like cross-references and concordances.

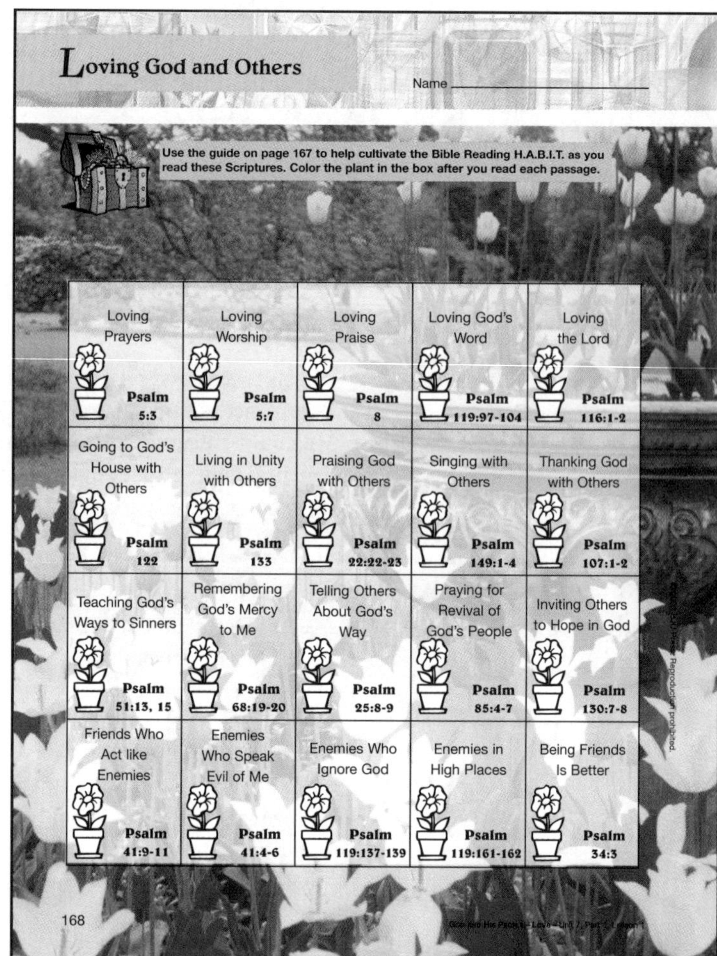
Loving God and Others

Name ____________________

Use the guide on page 167 to help cultivate the Bible Reading H.A.B.I.T. as you read these Scriptures. Color the plant in the box after you read each passage.

Loving Prayers Psalm 5:3	Loving Worship Psalm 5:7	Loving Praise Psalm 8	Loving God's Word Psalm 119:97-104	Loving the Lord Psalm 116:1-2
Going to God's House with Others Psalm 122	Living in Unity with Others Psalm 133	Praising God with Others Psalm 22:22-23	Singing with Others Psalm 149:1-4	Thanking God with Others Psalm 107:1-2
Teaching God's Ways to Sinners Psalm 51:13, 15	Remembering God's Mercy to Me Psalm 68:19-20	Telling Others About God's Way Psalm 25:8-9	Praying for Revival of God's People Psalm 85:4-7	Inviting Others to Hope in God Psalm 130:7-8
Friends Who Act like Enemies Psalm 41:9-11	Enemies Who Speak Evil of Me Psalm 41:4-6	Enemies Who Ignore God Psalm 119:137-139	Enemies in High Places Psalm 119:161-162	Being Friends Is Better Psalm 34:3

Bible Study Skills, Worktext pages 167-68

Develop a Bible reading habit. Read the top part of page 167 to the students. Select students to read aloud the Bible reading guidelines, emphasizing that God's Word helps Christians to grow spiritually. Explain the four-week Bible reading activity on page 168. Lead in singing the song "The Bible Reading Habit" from Worktext page 271.

Background Information

Old Testament Prophecy About John the Baptist—*Both Malachi and Isaiah prophesied that someone would come to prepare the way of the Lord (Malachi 4:5; Isaiah 40:3). The New Testament revealed that John the Baptist was the one sent from God to prepare the way of the Lord and to preach the message of repentance (Luke 1:17).*

Baptism by John—*Jewish baptisms were ceremonial cleansings and were quite common before the time of Christ and the establishment of the church. The baptism of John was Jewish and was to show repentance for sin and preparation for the coming of the Messiah.*

Introducing the Character Focus

Discuss repentance. Write the word *repentance* for display.

➤ **What is the root word or base word in *repentance?*** *(repent)*

➤ **What does it mean to repent?** *(to be sorry for and ask forgiveness of sin)*

Direct each student to locate the word *repentance* in his glossary. Choose a student to read the definition aloud. Explain that in turning *away* from sin, a person who truly repents must turn *to* God.

➤ **How many times does a person need to repent?** *(Answers will vary.)*

Explain that to become a Christian, every man, woman, and child must come before God, repent of his sins, and place his trust in Jesus Christ to save him from the penalty of eternal death.

➤ **After a person becomes a Christian, does he ever need to repent again? Why?** *(Yes. Because of his sinful nature, a Christian will sin after he is saved. He should confess his sin, ask for forgiveness for sin, and turn away from his sin.)*

Explain that repentance after salvation is important for close fellowship with God.

Character Focus

Read the following about the life of John the Baptist (Matthew 3-4, Mark 6, and Luke 1-3).

The Ministry of John the Baptist

Zacharias was a priest who served God in the temple at Jerusalem. His wife, Elisabeth, was also born into a family of the priestly line of Israel. Zacharias and Elisabeth were both godly people who loved and served the Lord faithfully. Although they had prayed for a child for a long time, the Lord had never given them any children.

One day, when Zacharias was performing the priestly duty of burning incense in the temple at Jerusalem, the angel Gabriel appeared to him to give him some astonishing news. Gabriel told Zacharias that God was giving him a son that he was to name John. The angel said that this son would grow up to love and serve the Lord. He would be great in the sight of the Lord and would preach repentance, turning many Israelites back to the Lord their God. Gabriel said that John's preaching was to prepare the people for the ministry, death, and resurrection of the promised Messiah. Zacharias did not believe the angel, for he and Elisabeth were too old to have children. The angel told Zacharias that he had come from the very presence of God to give him this news, but because Zacharias doubted God's Word and His power, he would be unable to speak until the baby was born.

Soon after Gabriel's visit to Zacharias, this same heavenly messenger came to Mary to tell her that she was to give birth to the long-awaited Messiah of Israel—the Son of God. Mary and Elisabeth were cousins. Luke tells us that Mary visited Elisabeth in the country while they both were with child.

When John was born, the neighbors and relatives of Zacharias and Elisabeth rejoiced with them that the Lord had given them a son. When John was eight days old, his parents dedicated him to the Lord. Everyone thought that the baby would be named after his father, but Zacharias wrote down on a tablet that his son was to be called John. Immediately after Zacharias had written this, he was able to speak again. Zacharias praised God for His love and mercy. The people who were there were astonished and wondered what kind of child John was and what kind of man he was to become.

The Bible tells us that John grew up to be strong both physically and spiritually. And then he began the ministry that God had sent him to do in the hill country of Judea.

John lived a very simple life. He wore clothes like the poor people of his day—a rough garment made of camel's hair with a leather belt to bind up his loose outer cloak. He ate locusts and wild honey that he found in the countryside where he lived and preached. (*Note:* No one knows for sure whether the locusts were insects or locust beans.)

John's ministry took place in the wilderness. He preached a simple but most important message that people should repent, be sorry for their sins and turn from living their own way to living in obedience to God and His Word. John told the people that they should get ready for the coming of the Messiah by repenting and being baptized.

John's lifestyle was so strange and his message was so powerful that many people, even the religious leaders from Jerusalem and Judea in the region around the Jordan River, came to see and hear him. Many of these people asked John who he was. Some thought that he might be the Christ that they were looking for, or Elijah, or another prophet raised from the dead. John answered, "I am the voice of one crying in the wilderness, Make straight the way of the Lord." John told the people that he was the one that Isaiah had prophesied about—that he had come to introduce Christ (Isaiah 40:3).

Many of these people repented—confessed their sins—and were baptized in the Jordan River. John said that he could baptize them with water as a symbol of their salvation, but the Messiah was coming soon to baptize them with the Holy Spirit.

Soon after that, the Lord Jesus Himself came to John to be baptized. John said that he was not worthy to baptize the Son of God but that instead, the Lord should baptize him.

Some of John's disciples became disciples of Jesus. Later when Jesus preached, He spoke of John's ministry.

With great boldness, John preached his message to all. He even reproved King Herod for his wickedness. Herod became so angry that he had John shut up in prison and later beheaded. John the Baptist loved the Lord God so much that he gave up all worldly comforts to tell others about Jesus Christ. John's love for Christ was proclaimed during his lifetime as well as in his death.

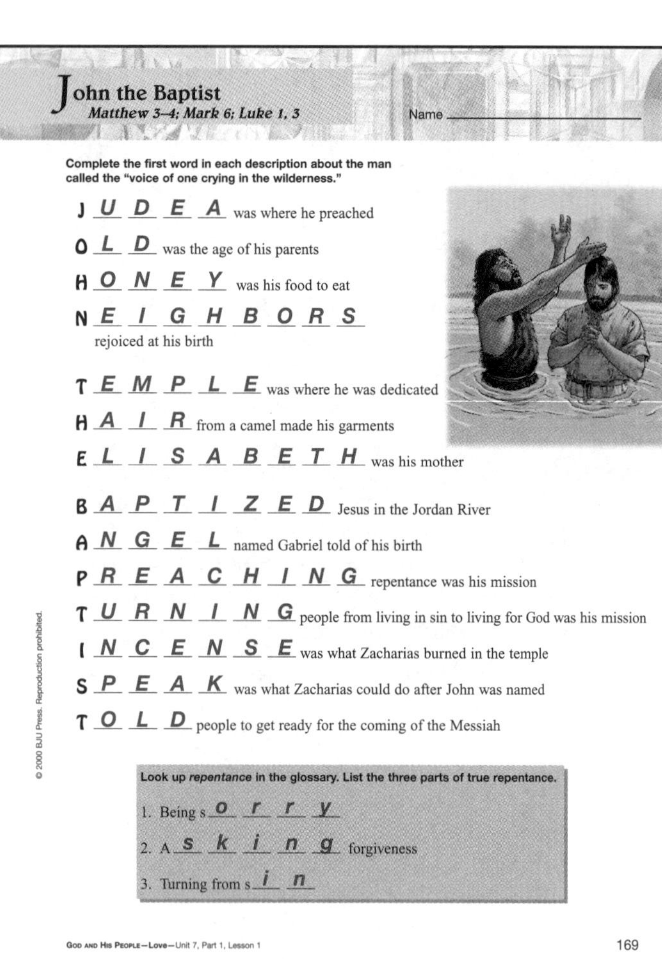

John the Baptist

Matthew 3–4; Mark 6; Luke 1, 3 Name ______________

Complete the first word in each description about the man called the "voice of one crying in the wilderness."

J U D E A was where he preached

O L D was the age of his parents

H O N E Y was his food to eat

N E I G H B O R S rejoiced at his birth

T E M P L E was where he was dedicated

H A I R from a camel made his garments

E L I S A B E T H was his mother

B A P T I Z E D Jesus in the Jordan River

A N G E L named Gabriel told of his birth

P R E A C H I N G repentance was his mission

T U R N I N G people from living in sin to living for God was his mission

I N C E N S E was what Zacharias burned in the temple

S P E A K was what Zacharias could do after John was named

T O L D people to get ready for the coming of the Messiah

Look up *repentance* in the glossary. List the three parts of true repentance.

1. Being s o r r y
2. A s k i n g forgiveness
3. Turning from s i n

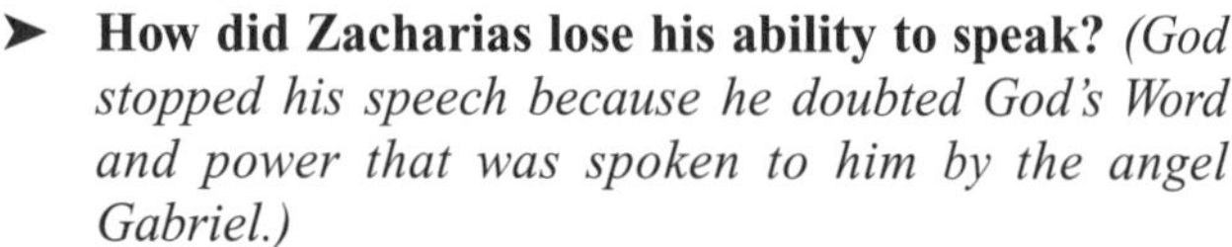

➤ **How did Zacharias lose his ability to speak?** *(God stopped his speech because he doubted God's Word and power that was spoken to him by the angel Gabriel.)*

➤ **What plan did God have for John's life? Did John follow God's plan?** *(He preached repentance and told the people to prepare for the coming Messiah. Yes. John loved and obeyed God.)*

➤ **Was John the Baptist a martyr? Why?** *(Yes. John was killed for preaching Christ.)* Remind the students that a *martyr* is a person who chooses to suffer or die rather than to give up his faith in Christ.

➤ **Would you be willing to die for doing what God told you to do?**

Worktext page 169

Recall details about John the Baptist.

Worktext page 170

Find information in Scripture.

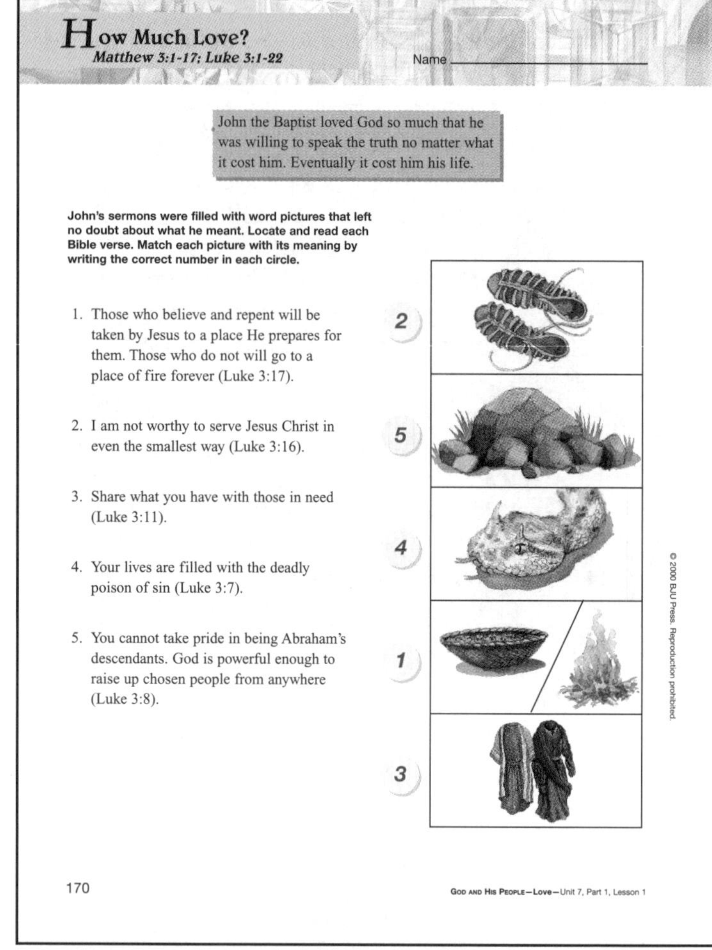

How Much Love?

Matthew 3:1-17; Luke 3:1-22 Name ______________

John the Baptist loved God so much that he was willing to speak the truth no matter what it cost him. Eventually it cost him his life.

John's sermons were filled with word pictures that left no doubt about what he meant. Locate and read each Bible verse. Match each picture with its meaning by writing the correct number in each circle.

1. Those who believe and repent will be taken by Jesus to a place He prepares for them. Those who do not will go to a place of fire forever (Luke 3:17).
2. I am not worthy to serve Jesus Christ in even the smallest way (Luke 3:16).
3. Share what you have with those in need (Luke 3:11).
4. Your lives are filled with the deadly poison of sin (Luke 3:7).
5. You cannot take pride in being Abraham's descendants. God is powerful enough to raise up chosen people from anywhere (Luke 3:8).

Circles: 2, 5, 4, 1, 3

Lesson 2

Materials

- Charts 22 and 33: "Mary and Martha" and "Palestine in the Time of Christ" (optional)

Memory Verses—Mark 12:29-30

Practice the memory verses. Locate **Mark 12:29-30** and select a student to read the verses aloud as the other students follow along.

➤ **Why did God make you and all things?** *(for His own glory)*

➤ **How can you glorify God?** *(by loving Him and doing what He commands)*

➤ **Why ought you to glorify God?** *(because He made me and takes care of me)*

➤ **Where do you learn how to love and obey God?** *(in the Bible alone)*

Hymn: "O to Be Like Thee!"

Sing the first verse (Worktext pages 282-83). Play the recording and lead in singing verse 1.

Mary and Martha

Luke 10:38-42

Guests in the home meant adding a meat dish and some side dishes to the family meal of bread and vegetable stew. Meat (except for the Passover lamb that was roasted) was usually boiled in a pot over the fire. Fresh fish were cooked over an open fire; salted or dried fish were eaten as they were or cooked like fresh fish.

Most families owned a goat that had to be milked twice a day to provide fresh milk and cheese.

Because there were few reliable ways of preserving food, a daily trip to the village market was necessary for those who did not grow their own food.

For special occasions cakes or pastries were baked. There was no refined sugar. Sweetening was added in the form of honey or a syrup made by boiling together dates and locust beans.

Bread had to be baked fresh daily. The grain (usually barley or wheat) first had to be ground between two stones to make a coarse flour, which was then mixed with salt, water, or olive oil, and a small amount of fermented dough (leaven) saved from the day before. This was kneaded and left to rise for several hours before it was shaped into round, flat loaves and baked.

Only wealthy homes had ovens. Other people baked items over an open fire in the middle of the floor or outdoors. Sometimes an earthenware pot was inverted over the fire to conduct the heat more evenly. Baking was done on smooth stones or on the bottom of the pot.

A cistern (cone-shaped pit) might catch rainwater from the gutters for cleaning and bathing, but not for cooking and drinking. Water for these latter purposes had to be carried from the village well in earthenware jars, balanced on the head or shoulder.

God and His People—Love—Unit 7, Part 1, Lesson 2 171

Background Information

Bethany—*This small town is located a short distance east of Jerusalem. Jesus' friends—Lazarus and his sisters, Martha and Mary—lived in Bethany.*

Mary—*This is the same Mary who broke the bottle of alabaster to pour the expensive ointment on the Lord Jesus to show her love and devotion to Him.*

Foot Washing—*It was a custom in Old and New Testament homes for the host or hostess to offer water to guests to wash their tired feet. People wore simple sandals or even went barefoot if they were very poor. They always removed their sandals before entering a home, the temple, or other holy places.*

Introducing the Bible Account

Discuss food preparation in Bible times. Direct the students' attention to Worktext page 171. Read aloud or choose students to read aloud the information. Tell them that in the following Bible account, Jesus and His disciples eat a meal at the home of friends. Point out that many of the things that they read about took place in order to prepare the meal, although they are not mentioned specifically in the Bible.

Bible Account

Read the following Bible account or read Luke 10:38-42. Point out Bethany on Chart 33, "Palestine in the Time of Christ" (optional).

Martha and Mary Welcome Jesus

Jesus and His followers had been traveling from town to town. When they arrived at Bethany, they were welcomed into the home of Jesus' friends, Lazarus and his two sisters, Mary and Martha. Martha served as hostess, welcoming the Lord and His disciples into their home. As a hostess, Martha had many duties to perform. She probably offered them food and drink and attended to any other special needs that they might have had. (Share the background information about foot washing.)

Mary could have helped her sister Martha, but she chose to sit at the feet of the Lord Jesus along with His disciples to hear the teachings of the Lord. Perhaps Martha also wished that she could hear the Lord's words, but she had the responsibility of serving the guests. Martha went to the Lord Jesus and complained about Mary's leaving her to do all the work. Martha wanted the Lord to tell Mary to help her.

The Lord answered her, "Martha, Martha, thou art careful and troubled about many things: But one thing is needful: and Mary hath chosen that good part, which shall not be taken away from her."

Jesus knew what Martha was thinking. Both Mary and Martha loved their Lord, and He loved them. The Lord wanted Martha to know that loving the Lord and taking the time to fellowship with Him by hearing His words and talking to Him was the most important thing she could do.

InfoScene: "Mary and Martha"

Display Chart 22 for reference throughout this unit. Review and discuss the Bible account as time permits.

- ➤ **Where did Lazarus and his sisters live?** *(in Bethany)*
- ➤ **Who served as hostess in their home when Jesus and His disciples came?** *(Martha)*
- ➤ **What was Mary doing while Martha was serving their guests?** *(sitting at the feet of the Lord Jesus, listening to His teaching)*
- ➤ **What did Martha want the Lord to tell Mary?** *(to help her sister)*
- ➤ **What did the Lord want Martha to learn?** *(that to love Him and to fellowship with Him is the most important duty)*

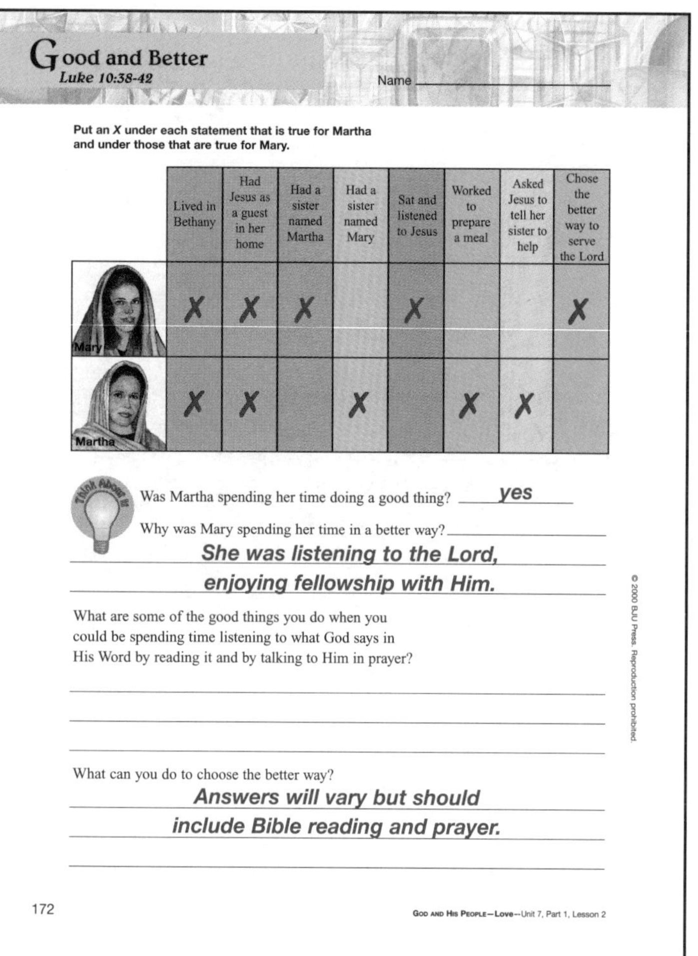
Good and Better
Luke 10:38-42

Name ____________

Put an *X* under each statement that is true for Martha and under those that are true for Mary.

	Lived in Bethany	Had Jesus as a guest in her home	Had a sister named Martha	Had a sister named Mary	Sat and listened to Jesus	Worked to prepare a meal	Asked Jesus to tell her sister to help	Chose the better way to serve the Lord
Mary	X	X	X		X			X
Martha	X	X		X		X	X	

Was Martha spending her time doing a good thing? *yes*

Why was Mary spending her time in a better way? *She was listening to the Lord, enjoying fellowship with Him.*

What are some of the good things you do when you could be spending time listening to what God says in His Word by reading it and by talking to Him in prayer?

What can you do to choose the better way? *Answers will vary but should include Bible reading and prayer.*

172 GOD AND HIS PEOPLE—Love—Unit 7, Part 1, Lesson 2

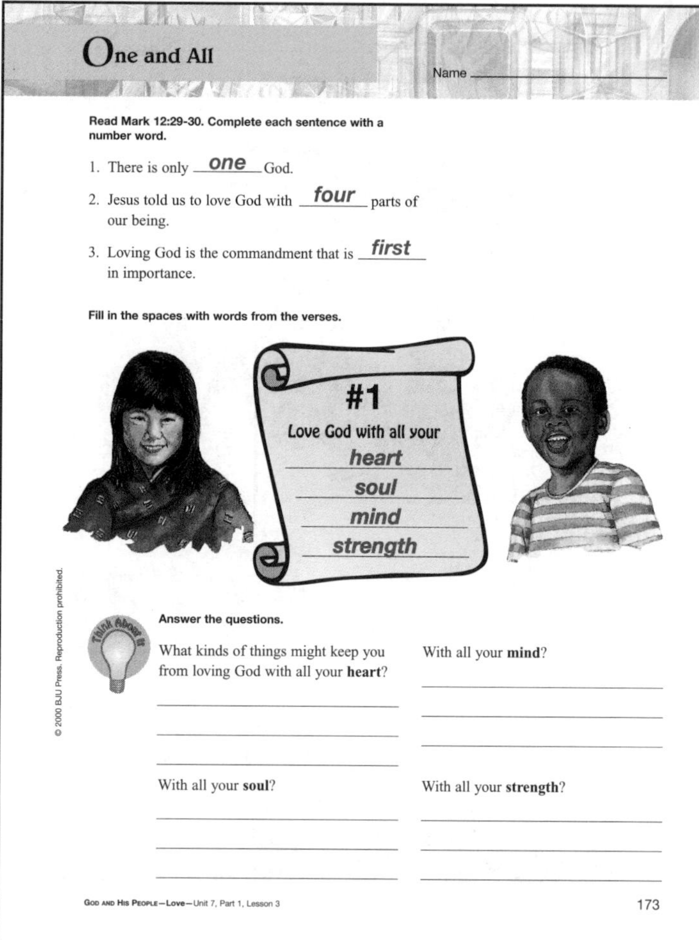
One and All

Name ____________

Read Mark 12:29-30. Complete each sentence with a number word.

1. There is only *one* God.
2. Jesus told us to love God with *four* parts of our being.
3. Loving God is the commandment that is *first* in importance.

Fill in the spaces with words from the verses.

#1
Love God with all your
heart
soul
mind
strength

Answer the questions.

What kinds of things might keep you from loving God with all your **heart**?

With all your **mind**?

With all your **soul**?

With all your **strength**?

GOD AND HIS PEOPLE—Love—Unit 7, Part 1, Lesson 3 173

➤ **What lesson can you learn from this account?** *(Although Christians cannot listen and talk to Jesus like Mary did, they should not get so busy in serving the Lord that they do not spend time studying His Word and praying.)*

Worktext page 172

Recall facts about Mary and Martha and then make application personally.

Lesson 3

Materials

- Chart 28, "World Map" (or globe)
- Bible Book Cards: Old Testament abbreviations
- Copy of *With Daring Faith* for the teacher

(*Note: With Daring Faith* is longer than many of the application novels and missionary stories used in the Bible curriculum. This book is read and discussed in nine lessons in Unit 7. You may choose to read the biography on Day 5 of each week as a read-aloud book.)

Hymn: "O to Be Like Thee!"

Sing the first verse (Worktext pages 282-83). Select a student to identify a name for Jesus in the first verse. *(Blessed Redeemer)* Explain that a redeemer is one who buys back something that was lost. Jesus is the Redeemer because He bought the freedom of sinners from their bondage to sin by His death on the cross.

➤ **What does it mean to be *constant?*** *(continuous, never stopping)*

➤ **How can a believer be constant about wanting to have the holiness of God in his life?** *(A believer is to have a continuous desire for holiness.)*

➤ **What in a believer's life may not encourage him to be holy?** *(Answers will vary.)*

➤ **What would you be willing to give up in order to please God with your life?** *(Possible answers include money, fame, and friends and family by going to a foreign mission field or into full-time Christian service.)*

Memory Verses—Mark 12:29-30

Practice the memory verses. Locate **Mark 12:29-30** and select different students to read the verses aloud as the other students read silently. Practice saying the verses from memory.

Worktext page 173

Develop an understanding of the memory verses.

Shortened Forms—Old Testament

Name________________

The Bible books are color coded to show how their abbreviations are written: yellow shows those that are written as the first few letters; green shows those that are not written in abbreviated form. Complete each abbreviation as indicated. Finish numbering the books in order. You may use your Bible to help.

No.	Book	Abbreviation	No.	Book	Abbreviation
5	Deuteronomy	Deut.	27	Daniel	Dan.
2	Exodus	Exod.	26	Ezekiel	Ezek.
1	Genesis	Gen.	23	Isaiah	Isa.
3	Leviticus	Lev.	24	Jeremiah	Jer.
4	Numbers	Num.	25	Lamentations	Lam.
14	II Chronicles	II Chron.	30	Amos	Amos
13	I Chronicles	I Chron.	35	Habakkuk	Hab.
17	Esther	Esther	37	Haggai	Hag.
15	Ezra	Ezra	28	Hosea	Hos.
6	Joshua	Josh.	29	Joel	Joel
7	Judges	Judg.	32	Jonah	Jon.
12	II Kings	II Kings	39	Malachi	Mal.
11	I Kings	I Kings	33	Micah	Mic.
16	Nehemiah	Neh.	34	Nahum	Nah.
8	Ruth	Ruth	31	Obadiah	Obad.
9	I Samuel	I Sam.	36	Zephaniah	Zeph.
10	II Samuel	II Sam.	38	Zechariah	Zech.
21	Ecclesiastes	Eccles.			
18	Job	Job			
19	Psalms	Ps.			
20	Proverbs	Prov.			
22	Song of Solomon	Song of Sol.			

174 God and His People—Love—Unit 7, Part 1, Lesson 3

Bible Study Skills

Teach the abbreviations of Old Testament books. Explain that most of the names of the books of the Bible are abbreviated with the first several letters of the name. Some books are not abbreviated when writing the reference. A few of the abbreviations are different according to the publisher of a particular Bible (e.g., Deuteronomy—Deut. or Dt.). Mix up the Bible Book Cards so that they are not in the correct order. Display the card with an abbreviation and let the students call out the name of the book that it represents.

After displaying the cards one time, play a game with four teams for additional practice (optional). Hold up an abbreviation card; the first person to say the name of the book receives a point for his team. Continue in this way until all the cards are shown or until time is up.

Bible Study Skills, Worktext page 174

Sequence and abbreviate Old Testament books.

Background Information

Amy Carmichael—*Amy Carmichael was born on December 16, 1867, in Ireland. The family then moved to England in 1889. Amy went to India as a missionary in 1895 and was there for over fifty years. She sought to rescue children from being sold as slaves in the Hindu temples. She also wrote many books during her last twenty years, as she was unable to walk. The secret to her unwavering love for her children was her unwavering love for the Lord. This love led her to pray as she sought the Lord's direction in the work.*

Setting—*India is located on a peninsula in the Indian Ocean above the equator. The temperature is usually above 70 degrees Fahrenheit. The land is varied with mountains, plains, and desert. Among the Himalayan Mountains to the north is the tallest mountain in the world, Mount Everest. The Indus, Ganges, and Brahmaputra Rivers water the northern plains. Some places in India may get over four hundred inches of rain in a year, while the deserts may get less than ten inches in the same year.* Monsoons *are an important weather factor in India. These winds bring wet air in the summer and dry air in the winter. If the rains are little or late, drought and famine may occur.*

Introducing the Missionary Biography

Introduce the biography. Explain that a *biography* is the story one person writes about another person's life. Point out that *With Daring Faith* is a missionary biography about Amy Carmichael.

➤ **What do you think someone would write about you?** *(Answers will vary.)*

Read about the author, Rebecca Henry Davis, from the back of the book. Point to Ireland and India on Chart 28, "World Map," or on a globe. Share the background information about the setting.

Missionary Biography: *With Daring Faith*

Read Chapters 1 and 2. Direct the students to listen to find out what it was that Amy did not like about herself. *(She had brown eyes, but she wanted blue eyes.)*

➤ **Why do you think God did not answer Amy's prayer the way she wanted?** *(Answers will vary.)*

Remind the students that God knows what is best. He made each of us just the way He wanted. Point out that later in her life Amy could see why it was best to have brown eyes.

➤ **What did Amy know for sure about Jesus?** *(Jesus loved her, and she loved Him.)*

➤ **What was on Amy's sampler?** *(the date 1876 and the verse "Rejoice evermore.")* Explain that a *sampler* is a piece of fabric with many types of embroidery stitches.

➤ **What does the verse mean?** *(Be thankful at all times for everything, whether it is good or bad.)*

➤ **How did Amy's parents show their desire to help others in need?** *(They gave away their horse and carriage.)* Point out that this was the way people traveled at this time.

➤ **What did Amy say about this?** *(She said her parents were noble and that the Lord would bless them.)*

➤ **Should believers do things for God just so He will "bless" them? Why or why not?** *(No. Christians should serve God with a willing spirit because they love Him for what He has done for them.)*

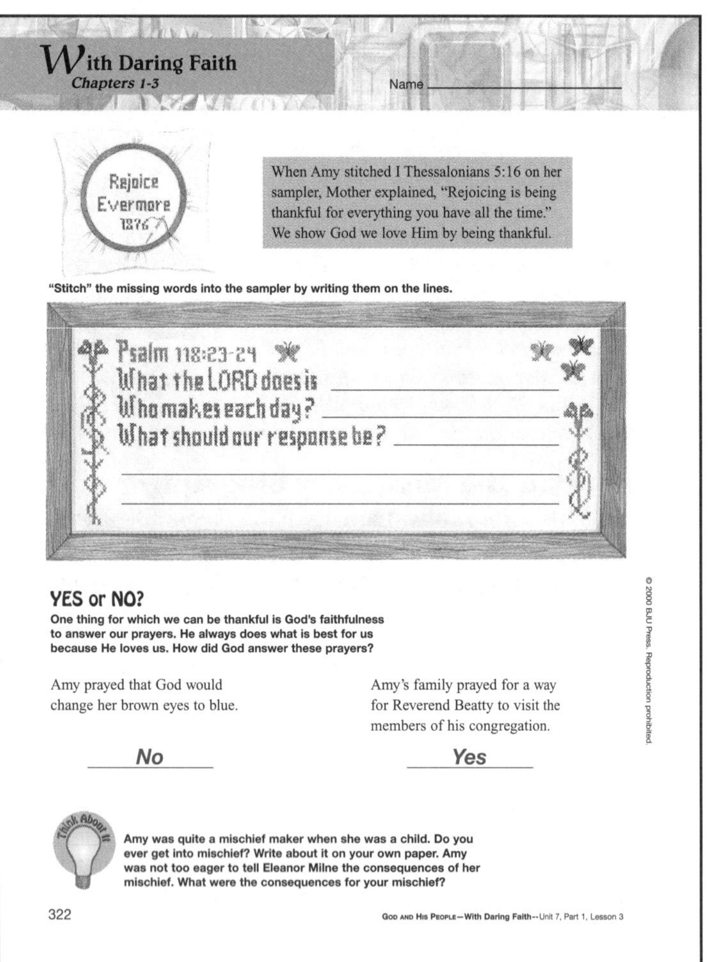

With Daring Faith
Chapters 1-3

Name ____________

Rejoice Evermore 1876

When Amy stitched I Thessalonians 5:16 on her sampler, Mother explained, "Rejoicing is being thankful for everything you have all the time." We show God we love Him by being thankful.

"Stitch" the missing words into the sampler by writing them on the lines.

Psalm 118:23-24
What the LORD does is ____________
Who makes each day? ____________
What should our response be? ____________
____
____

YES or NO?
One thing for which we can be thankful is God's faithfulness to answer our prayers. He always does what is best for us because He loves us. How did God answer these prayers?

Amy prayed that God would change her brown eyes to blue.

No

Amy's family prayed for a way for Reverend Beatty to visit the members of his congregation.

Yes

Think About It

Amy was quite a mischief maker when she was a child. Do you ever get into mischief? Write about it on your own paper. Amy was not too eager to tell Eleanor Milne the consequences of her mischief. What were the consequences for your mischief?

322 GOD AND HIS PEOPLE—With Daring Faith—Unit 7, Part 1, Lesson 3

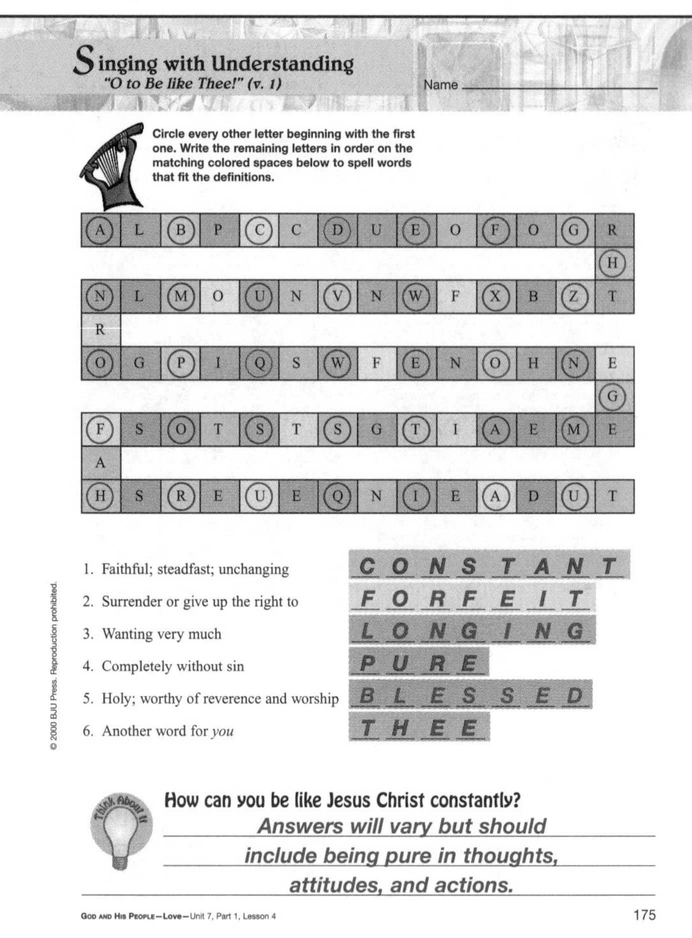

Singing with Understanding
"O to Be like Thee!" (v. 1)

Name ____________

Circle every other letter beginning with the first one. Write the remaining letters in order on the matching colored spaces below to spell words that fit the definitions.

(A) L (B) P (C) C (D) U (E) O (F) O (G) R (H)
(N) L (M) O (U) N (V) N (W) F (X) B (Z) T
R
(O) G (P) I (Q) S (W) F (E) N (O) H (N) E (G)
(F) S (O) T (S) T (S) G (T) I (A) E (M) E
A
(H) S (R) E (U) E (Q) N (I) E (A) D (U) T

1. Faithful; steadfast; unchanging — *C O N S T A N T*
2. Surrender or give up the right to — *F O R F E I T*
3. Wanting very much — *L O N G I N G*
4. Completely without sin — *P U R E*
5. Holy; worthy of reverence and worship — *B L E S S E D*
6. Another word for *you* — *T H E E*

Think About It

How can you be like Jesus Christ constantly?
Answers will vary but should include being pure in thoughts, attitudes, and actions.

GOD AND HIS PEOPLE—Love—Unit 7, Part 1, Lesson 4 175

Read Chapter 3. Direct the students to listen to find out who told Amy stories about India. *(Mrs. Beatty)*

- ➤ **How did Amy meet Mr. and Mrs. Beatty?** *(They were missionaries to India who moved in next door.)*
- ➤ **What is a *martyr*?** *(a person who chooses to suffer or die rather than to give up his faith in Christ)*
- ➤ **What events during Amy's childhood show her boldness and daring sense of adventure?** *(Answers may include when she walked on the roof, ate laburnum pods, or was rescued by the coastguard.)* (*Note:* A laburnum tree has pods with seeds in them similar to a pea pod.)

Point out how God kept Amy safe and used the stories about India later to accomplish His will in Amy's life.

Worktext Supplement page 322

Develop an understanding of Scripture and prayer.

Lesson 4

Materials

- Bible Book Cards: New Testament abbreviations
- Copy of *With Daring Faith* for the teacher
- Picture of a comet (optional)

Hymn: "O to Be Like Thee!"

Sing the first verse (Worktext pages 282-83). Sing the first verse, alternating between the lines for different groups.

Worktext page 175

Singing with understanding, verse 1.

Memory Verses—Mark 12:29-30

Practice the memory verses. Locate **Mark 12:29-30** and direct the students to read the verses silently. Write the first letter of each word for display. Choose a student to complete a word without using his Bible if possible. Continue this until the verses are complete. Allow the students to use their Bibles if necessary. Direct the students to read the verses to themselves in a quiet whisper.

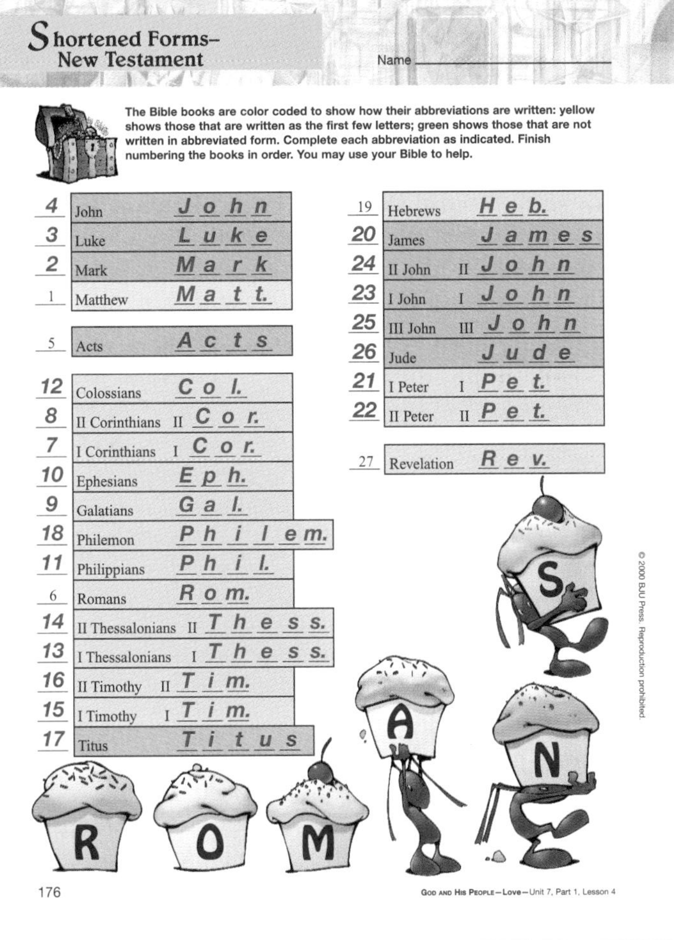

Shortened Forms–New Testament

Name ____________________

The Bible books are color coded to show how their abbreviations are written: yellow shows those that are written as the first few letters; green shows those that are not written in abbreviated form. Complete each abbreviation as indicated. Finish numbering the books in order. You may use your Bible to help.

No.	Book	Abbreviation
4	John	John
3	Luke	Luke
2	Mark	Mark
1	Matthew	Matt.
5	Acts	Acts
12	Colossians	Col.
8	II Corinthians	II Cor.
7	I Corinthians	I Cor.
10	Ephesians	Eph.
9	Galatians	Gal.
18	Philemon	Philem.
11	Philippians	Phil.
6	Romans	Rom.
14	II Thessalonians	II Thess.
13	I Thessalonians	I Thess.
16	II Timothy	II Tim.
15	I Timothy	I Tim.
17	Titus	Titus

No.	Book	Abbreviation
19	Hebrews	Heb.
20	James	James
24	II John	II John
23	I John	I John
25	III John	III John
26	Jude	Jude
21	I Peter	I Pet.
22	II Peter	II Pet.
27	Revelation	Rev.

176 God and His People—Love—Unit 7, Part 1, Lesson 4

One-on-One: Direct the student to copy the verses, drawing pictures for as many words as possible (e.g., heart: love).

Bible Study Skills

Teach the abbreviations of New Testament books. Mix up the cards so that they are not in the correct order. Display the card with an abbreviation and let the students call out the name of the book that it represents.

After displaying the cards one time, play a game with four teams for additional practice (optional). Hold up an abbreviation card; the first person to say the name of the book receives a point for his team. Continue until all the cards are shown or until time is up.

Bible Study Skills, Worktext page 176

Sequence and abbreviate New Testament books.

Introducing the Missionary Biography

Review Chapters 1-3.

- ➤ **What kind of child was Amy Carmichael?** *(bold, daring, sickly, played tricks)*
- ➤ **How did Amy's parents show compassion?** *(They gave away their horse and carriage.)*
- ➤ **How did Amy hear stories about India?** *(from missionaries who lived next door)*

Missionary Biography: *With Daring Faith*

Read Chapter 4. Direct the students to listen to find out the turning point in Amy's life. *(her salvation)*

- ➤ **Where did Amy go to school when she was young and then when she turned thirteen?** *(A governess taught the children at home; then Amy went to a boarding school called Marlborough House.)*
- ➤ **Why did Amy not like her name, and what did she do about it?** *(She wanted a grown-up name, so she called herself Beatrice—her middle name—while at boarding school.)*
- ➤ **Why did the girls want to stay up?** *(to see the Great Comet)*
- ➤ **Did Amy and the other girls choose to obey or disobey?** *(They chose to disobey and to stay up to watch the Great Comet.)*
- ➤ **What did Amy realize at school?** *(that she needed a Savior; She knew God loved her, and she thought she loved God; but this was not enough.)*

Point out that all people sin. Sin separates us from God. We deserve God's everlasting punishment for our sin. The only way to come to God is through faith, believing God sent Jesus Christ to die as the penalty for sin.

Read Chapters 5 and 6. Direct the students to listen to find out what disease affected Amy. *(neuralgia, which affects the nerves)*

- ➤ **What tragedy struck the Carmichael home?** *(Amy's father died.)*
- ➤ **Why did Amy return home from boarding school and move with her family to Belfast?** *(Her family no longer had the money for her to attend.)*
- ➤ **What did Amy decide to do?** *(to serve the Lord Jesus because she wanted the things she did to count for eternity)*
- ➤ **How did Amy serve the Lord in Belfast?** *(She began to teach a children's Bible study, a prayer meeting, and a Sunday morning class; and she worked with the "shawlies.")*
- ➤ **Who were the "shawlies"?** *(poor girls who wore shawls to church because they could not buy hats)*
- ➤ **Why did Amy not want a new dress?** *(Material things were not important to her. Amy knew that living a holy life was more important.)*
- ➤ **Why did Amy decide to go to the mission field?** *(She could trust God to take care of everything.)*

Emphasize that a believer shows love to God by obeying what he knows God wants him to do.

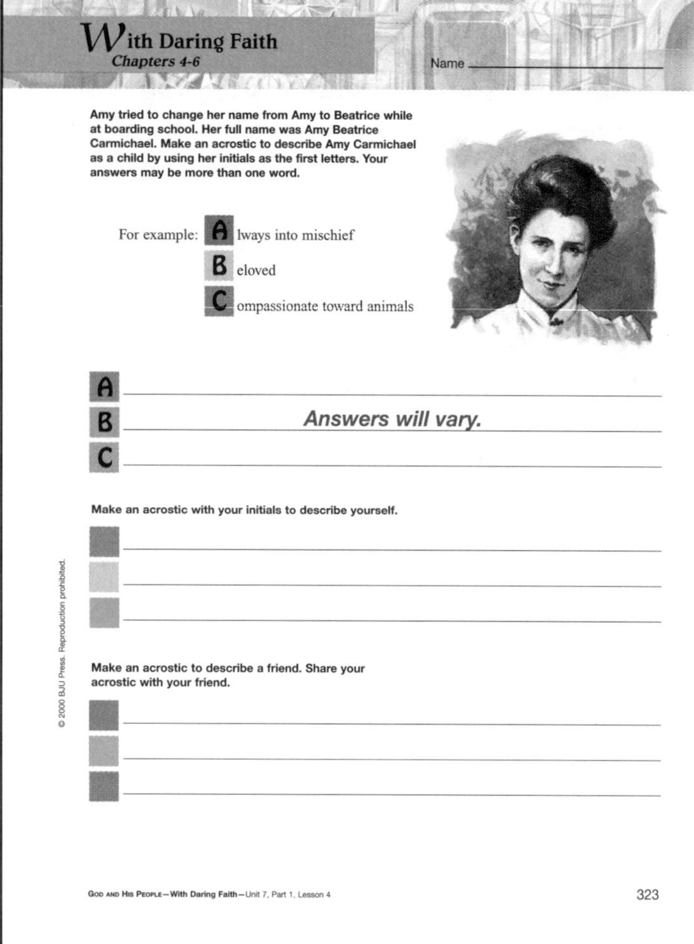

With Daring Faith
Chapters 4-6

Name ____________

Amy tried to change her name from Amy to Beatrice while at boarding school. Her full name was Amy Beatrice Carmichael. Make an acrostic to describe Amy Carmichael as a child by using her initials as the first letters. Your answers may be more than one word.

For example: **A** lways into mischief
B eloved
C ompassionate toward animals

A ____________
B *Answers will vary.*
C ____________

Make an acrostic with your initials to describe yourself.

____
____
____

Make an acrostic to describe a friend. Share your acrostic with your friend.

____
____
____

God and His People—With Daring Faith—Unit 7, Part 1, Lesson 4 323

Worktext Supplement page 323

Use descriptive words.

Science Connection (optional)

Discuss Comets. Show a picture of a comet, pointing out its parts as you give the following information.

> Seen from earth, a comet usually looks like a long bright streak. The *head,* which may be as large as ten miles wide, is actually made up of frozen gases, ice, and dust. As the comet orbits closer to the sun, the ice in the head melts and makes a cloud called a *coma.* As the particles are pushed away from the head, a *tail* forms, which may extend up to one million miles long. The brightness of the comet comes from the sun's light reflecting off the comet's frozen particles.

Tell the students that the Great Comet of 1882 was photographed by the Scottish astronomer Sir David Gill. His photographs showed so many stars that the idea of using photographs to catalog the stars was begun.

➤ **Who made the stars?** *(God)* Read aloud **Genesis 1:16.** Point out that long before man thought to try to catalog the stars, God knew them all by name. Read aloud **Psalm 147:4** and **Isaiah 40:26.**

➤ **Why do you think God made the stars and other heavenly bodies?** *(for times and seasons and for His own glory)* Read aloud **Psalm 19** and **Romans 1:20,** pointing out that even without God's Word, a missionary, or a preacher, people everywhere can see creation and know of God and His great power.

Explain that for hundreds of years, people thought that comets signaled the coming of major disasters, such as wars, epidemics, or famines. If a tragic event *did* occur, they would think back and blame it on the comet. Remind the students that the Scriptures teach against believing the signs in the skies that the unsaved believe. Read aloud **Jeremiah 10:2** and remind the students that Christians are to trust in the Lord as the Bible says.

Going Beyond

Enrichment

Guide a role-playing activity. Choose groups of two students to role-play typical situations that occur at home and school. Direct Student 1 to role-play the situation and Student 2 to react in a Christlike manner. Sample situations include:

1. Student 1 takes the biggest piece of cake.
2. Student 1 cuts in line in front of Student 2.
3. Student 1 bumps into Student 2, causing him to spill his drink.
4. Student 1 brags about how easy it is to get all *A*s.
5. Student 1 leaves the lid off of the toothpaste tube and does not put the tube away.

Preview

Doctrines

- Members of the local church should pray (Acts 12:5)—Lesson 1
- Angels assist mankind (Acts 12:5-11)—Lesson 1

Skills and Applications

- Learn Mark 12:31
- Recall facts and details
- Locate information in Scripture
- Identify the location of specific accounts in the Bible
- Understand the importance of prayer
- Recognize ways to demonstrate love
- Apply Bible knowledge to everyday life

Lesson 1

Memory Verse—Mark 12:31

Principle: Believers are to love others. Locate **Mark 12:31** and read the verse aloud as the students read silently.

➤ **According to the verse, how are believers to love others?** *(the same way they love themselves)*

➤ **What are some ways to love others as you love yourself?** *(Possible answers include being kind to others, sharing, or helping or encouraging others.)*

Direct the students to take turns reading the verse to a partner. Guide them to highlight the verse in their Bibles (optional) and to mark the location with their Unit 7 Bookmark.

Hymn: "O to Be Like Thee!"

Teach the second verse. Play the recording and lead in singing verse 2; then sing verses 1-2 together.

Background Information

Herod Agrippa I—*He was a proud man whose pride seems to have been inherited. His grandfather ordered the children in Bethlehem to be murdered. His father, Herod Antipas, had John the Baptist beheaded. Herod Agrippa I had James killed, and now he was holding Peter to be killed. After Peter's escape, Herod left Jerusalem and went to Caesarea to stay. It was here that Herod dressed in his royal clothes and sat on his throne to give a speech. After the speech, the people called Herod a god. Because proud Herod did not give God any of the glory, he was eaten of worms and died.*

Rhoda—*She was a family servant. This is the only account where she is mentioned in Scripture. Rhoda is recorded to have been at a prayer meeting for Peter.*

Passover Feast—*This was an eight-day Jewish feast in remembrance of the Israelites' escape from Egypt. It was the tenth plague when God killed the firstborn children of the Egyptians and spared (passed over) the firstborn of the Jews.*

Introducing the Bible Account

Discuss praying for others.

➤ **What is *prayer*?** *(talking to God)*

➤ **In whose name should we pray?** *(Jesus Christ, our intercessor)*

➤ **What is a prayer list?** *(a reminder to pray for specific needs)*

Explain that one way to show love for others is to pray for them. Encourage students to give personal prayer requests; then guide a time of prayer.

Bible Account

Read the following Bible account or read Acts 12:1-19.

Prayer for Peter

Herod Agrippa I, the king of the Palestinian regions, arrested some church members. He had James, the brother of John, killed with the sword. When he saw how pleased the Jews were by this, he had Peter arrested. It was the week of Passover, so Herod imprisoned Peter, intending to try him publicly after the festival.

The night before Peter was to be condemned to die, he was bound with two chains between two soldiers. Suddenly, an angel of the Lord appeared and woke up Peter. When the angel told Peter to get up, his chains fell off from his hands. The angel told Peter to put on his sandals and his robe. Peter did as he was told and followed the angel. They passed one guard and then another; and when they came to the iron gate, it opened by itself. At first Peter thought it was a dream, but once they were outside the prison, Peter realized that an angel of the Lord had come to deliver him.

During Peter's time of imprisonment, his family and fellow believers were praying for his release.

When Peter realized he was free, he went to the house of Mary, the mother of John Mark. Peter knocked on the door, and the servant girl Rhoda came to see who was there. After recognizing Peter's voice, Rhoda was so excited that she left Peter standing outside and went and told the others that Peter was at the door. Those in the house, who had been praying most of the night for Peter, did not believe Rhoda. They said that she was out of her mind and that she had seen an angel. Peter knocked again, and others came and opened the door. The people could not believe it! God had answered their prayers! Peter told the people how God sent an angel to him. Peter told them to tell others what God had done, and then he left them.

The next morning the soldiers awoke and realized that Peter was missing. They searched all over for him so that he could be put to death, but they could not find him.

- ➤ **Whom had Herod Agrippa already killed?** *(James, the brother of John)*
- ➤ **Why was Peter not killed immediately?** *(because the Passover was in progress)*
- ➤ **Why were the Jewish leaders pleased with Herod for having James killed and Peter arrested?** *(Possible answers include that they were preaching about salvation through Jesus Christ and pointing out the Jews' errors.)*
- ➤ **How did Peter get out of prison?** *(The angel of the Lord woke him and opened all the doors for him to leave.)*
- ➤ **What were the group of believers doing all night long? Why?** *(They were praying for Peter because they loved him and were concerned for his well-being.)*
- ➤ **What can you do for others to show your love to them?** *(Accept any reasonable answer.)*

Worktext page 177

Review the Bible account.

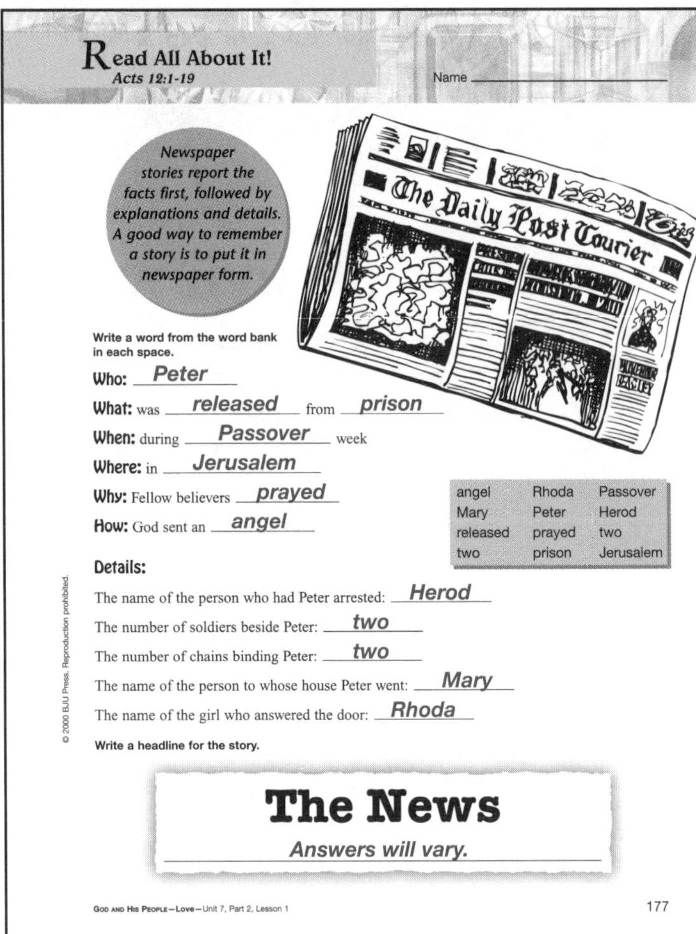

Read All About It!
Acts 12:1-19

Name ______________

Newspaper stories report the facts first, followed by explanations and details. A good way to remember a story is to put it in newspaper form.

Write a word from the word bank in each space.

Who: Peter

What: was released from prison

When: during Passover week

Where: in Jerusalem

Why: Fellow believers prayed

How: God sent an angel

angel	Rhoda	Passover
Mary	Peter	Herod
released	prayed	two
two	prison	Jerusalem

Details:

The name of the person who had Peter arrested: Herod

The number of soldiers beside Peter: two

The number of chains binding Peter: two

The name of the person to whose house Peter went: Mary

The name of the girl who answered the door: Rhoda

Write a headline for the story.

The News

Answers will vary.

Lesson 2

Materials

- Copy of *With Daring Faith* for the teacher
- Missionary prayer card for each student or pair of students (optional)

Memory Verse—Mark 12:31

Review the memory verse. Locate **Mark 12:31** and select a student to read the verse aloud. Challenge the students to think of something they could do that day to put this verse into action (e.g., let someone go in front of them in line, give their neighbor a pencil or piece of paper). Practice the verse by reading it throughout the day.

As Yourself

Name ____________

Read Mark 12:30-31. Answer the questions.

1. What did Jesus say was the most important commandment? *Answers may vary but should include loving God above all else–with your heart, soul, mind, and strength.*
2. What did Jesus say was the second most important commandment? *Answers may vary but should include loving others as you love yourself.*

Complete the chart.

	Check One. Yes	No	What should this cause you to do if you love your neighbor as yourself?
1. Do you treat yourself kindly?			
2. Do you make sure you have what you need?			
3. Do you keep from hurting yourself?			
4. Do you think and say good things about yourself?			

178 GOD AND HIS PEOPLE—Love—Unit 7, Part 2, Lesson 2

Singing with Understanding
"O to Be like Thee!" (v. 2)

Name ____________

There are two parts to *compassion:* being deeply aware that someone is suffering, and wanting very much to relieve that suffering. The hymn writer names several ways that compassion and love are demonstrated by the Lord Jesus Christ.

Read the Bible verses and answer the questions.

1. **"Helping the helpless"**—Jesus has compassion when He sees how helpless people are (Matthew 9:35-36). What did the crowds of people seem like to Him? *sheep without a shepherd*
2. **"Cheering the fainting"**—Jesus has compassion on those who have no other hope (Mark 5:24-34). What did He do for the woman whom many doctors had been unable to help? *healed her*
3. **"Seeking the wand'ring sinner to find"**—Jesus has compassion on sinners and seeks to save them (Acts 9:1-5). Who is this sinner? How did Jesus get his attention? *Saul/Paul; a light from heaven blinded Saul*

Do you know someone who does not know how loving, gentle, forgiving, and kind Jesus Christ is? How can you show that person what the Lord is like? *Answers will vary but should include being loving, gentle, forgiving, and kind toward the person.*

GOD AND HIS PEOPLE—Love—Unit 7, Part 2, Lesson 2 179

Worktext page 178

Develop understanding of the memory verse.

Hymn: "O to Be Like Thee!"

Sing the first and second verses (Worktext pages 282-83). Play the recording and lead in singing verses 1-2.

Worktext page 179

Singing with understanding, verse 2.

Background Information

Buddhism—*Siddhartha Gautama began the religion of Buddhism in India near the end of the sixth century. Although he had many luxuries of this world, he sought a remedy for his unhappiness. He believed that a person found happiness in doing good and ignoring personal desires. According to Buddhism, people earn salvation by suffering and doing good works. The religion of Buddhism spread to China and Japan, where it was more widely accepted.*

Introducing the Missionary Biography

Discuss missionaries. Write a list of questions for display similar to those provided. Discuss the differences in language, food, and customs that a missionary might face. Distribute the prayer cards, allowing time for the students to read them before asking the questions.

- **Which missionaries live in countries close to the equator?**
- **Which missionaries have children?**
- **How would life be different in that country?**
- **What should we pray for concerning these missionary families?** *(Possible answers include safety; health, daily food, and provisions; boldness; faithfulness to God, their family, and those to whom they minister; and for people to be saved.)*

Missionary Biography: *With Daring Faith*

Read Chapter 7.

- **How long did Amy expect to be away when she went to Japan as a missionary?** *(many years)*
- **How did Amy respond to living with bugs and rats while on the ship?** *(She decided to be thankful.)*
- **What happened on the ship because of Amy's testimony?** *(The captain of the ship accepted Christ.)*
- **How did Amy respond to the difficulty of not knowing the Japanese language upon her arrival at the dock?** *(She laughed, almost cried, and then prayed.)*
- **What was the common religion in Japan?** *(Buddhism)* Share the background information about Buddhism (optional).

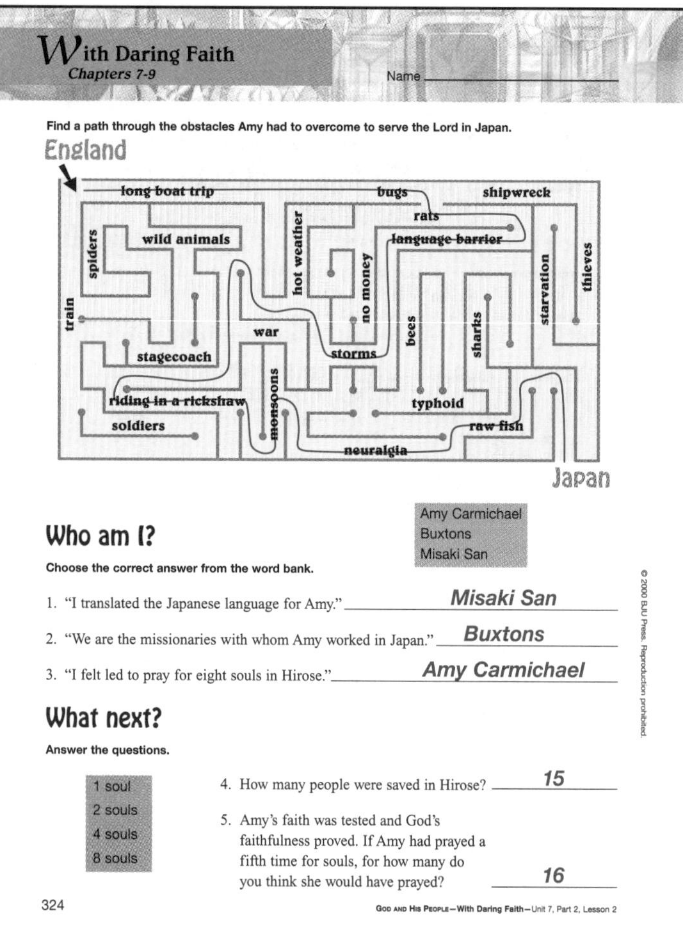

With Daring Faith
Chapters 7-9

Name ______________________

Find a path through the obstacles Amy had to overcome to serve the Lord in Japan.

England

long boat trip, bugs, shipwreck, rats, language barrier, wild animals, spiders, hot weather, no money, starvation, thieves, train, war, bees, sharks, stagecoach, storms, riding in a rickshaw, monsoons, typhoid, soldiers, raw fish, neuralgia

Japan

Who am I?

Choose the correct answer from the word bank.

Amy Carmichael
Buxtons
Misaki San

1. "I translated the Japanese language for Amy." *Misaki San*
2. "We are the missionaries with whom Amy worked in Japan." *Buxtons*
3. "I felt led to pray for eight souls in Hirose." *Amy Carmichael*

What next?

Answer the questions.

1 soul
2 souls
4 souls
8 souls

4. How many people were saved in Hirose? *15*
5. Amy's faith was tested and God's faithfulness proved. If Amy had prayed a fifth time for souls, for how many do you think she would have prayed? *16*

324

God and His People—With Daring Faith—Unit 7, Part 2, Lesson 2

Read Chapter 8. Tell the students to listen to find out what Amy decided to change about her appearance. *(her clothing)*

➤ **Why did Amy decide to wear a kimono when witnessing?** *(Her clothes distracted the Japanese women when she witnessed to them.)*

➤ **How did Amy show boldness during the situation with the wild man?** *(Amy and Misaki San believed God's promises and prayed for the wild man. God delivered the man by casting out the evil spirit, and the man became a Christian.)*

Read Chapter 9. Read aloud the title for Chapter 9, "Just Four Souls, Lord." Direct the students to listen to find out what else was special about the day Amy and Misaki San led four people to Christ. *(The day was Amy's birthday.)*

➤ **What words describe Amy's witnessing?** *(boldness and faithfulness)*

➤ **Why did Amy pray for a specific number of people to be saved?** *(She believed God wanted her to trust Him, and she believed that God would provide the four souls.)*

Point out that Amy prayed to know the will of God and that His will would be done. Amy realized that people were not saved through her own strength. People are saved by God's Spirit convicting them of sin and showing them the need of a Savior.

➤ **Why did some of the Christians think it was foolish to pray for eight souls?** *(The missionaries did not usually see eight people saved in a whole year.)*

Worktext Supplement page 324

Recall facts about Chapters 7-9, *With Daring Faith*.

Lesson 3

Materials

- Copy of *With Daring Faith* for the teacher
- Classified section of a newspaper with employment opportunities

List job opportunities with salaries specified from the newspaper section for display.

Hymn: "O to Be Like Thee!"

Sing the first two verses (Worktext pages 282-83). Play the recording of verses 1-2.

➤ **How is Jesus described in these verses?** *(blessed, perfect, pure, compassionate, loving, forgiving, tender, kind, helping)*

Sing verses 1-2 together.

Memory Verse—Mark 12:31

Practice the memory verse. Locate **Mark 12:31** and choose a student to read the verse aloud.

➤ **How can you apply this verse to how you treat others?** *(Possible answers include putting others before yourself by being kind and generous.)*

➤ **Has anyone ever treated you this way?**

Allow students to share examples of how others have treated them as Jesus said. Explain how Christ is the perfect example of a servant. He taught that love is shown to others by our attitudes and actions. A believer is to be a servant to others. Read **Philippians 2:5-8** several times throughout the day for practice.

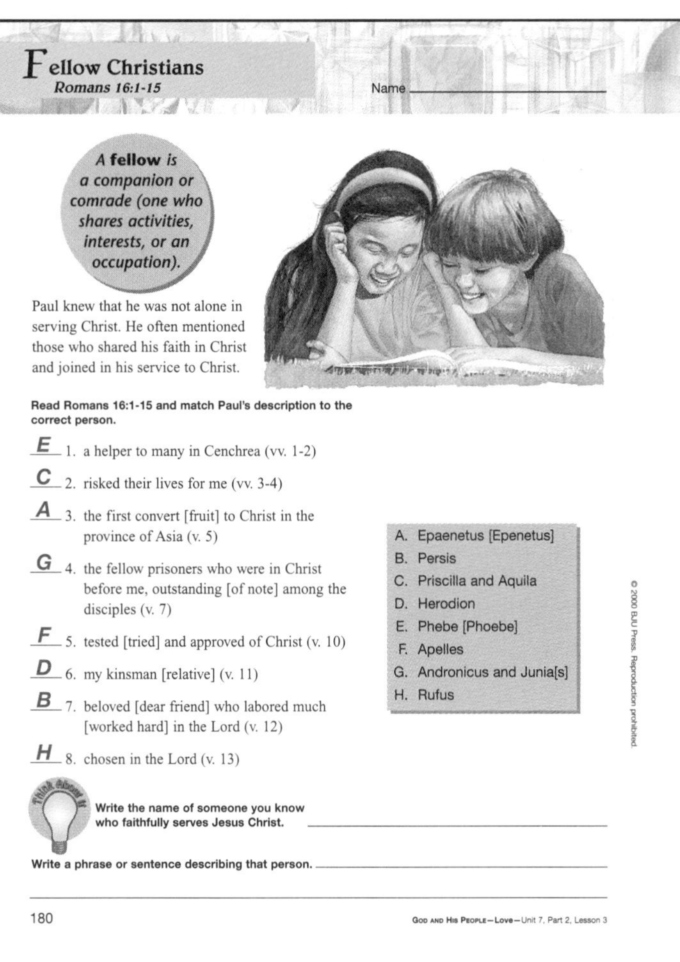

Fellow Christians
Romans 16:1-15

Name ______________________

A **fellow** is a companion or comrade (one who shares activities, interests, or an occupation).

Paul knew that he was not alone in serving Christ. He often mentioned those who shared his faith in Christ and joined in his service to Christ.

Read Romans 16:1-15 and match Paul's description to the correct person.

E 1. a helper to many in Cenchrea (vv. 1-2)
C 2. risked their lives for me (vv. 3-4)
A 3. the first convert [fruit] to Christ in the province of Asia (v. 5)
G 4. the fellow prisoners who were in Christ before me, outstanding [of note] among the disciples (v. 7)
F 5. tested [tried] and approved of Christ (v. 10)
D 6. my kinsman [relative] (v. 11)
B 7. beloved [dear friend] who labored much [worked hard] in the Lord (v. 12)
H 8. chosen in the Lord (v. 13)

A. Epaenetus [Epenetus]
B. Persis
C. Priscilla and Aquila
D. Herodion
E. Phebe [Phoebe]
F. Apelles
G. Andronicus and Junia[s]
H. Rufus

Think About It

Write the name of someone you know who faithfully serves Jesus Christ. ______________________

Write a phrase or sentence describing that person. ______________________

180 God and His People—Love—Unit 7, Part 2, Lesson 3

Review Old and New

Name ______________________

Circle the name of the Bible book where each account may be found.

Account	Book
1. God sent plagues on Egypt.	Matthew/**Exodus**
2. Solomon asked God for wisdom.	Ephesians/**I Kings**
3. Mary, the mother of Jesus, obeyed God.	**Luke**/Ruth
4. God punished Ahab and Jezebel.	I Timothy/**II Kings**
5. Jesus grew in wisdom, in stature, and in favor with God and men.	Exodus/**Luke**
6. God provided for Paul's journeys.	**Acts**/Job
7. Jesus told the parable of the lost son.	**Luke**/Ezra
8. Elisha's servant saw chariots of fire.	Romans/**II Kings**
9. God's people dedicated the temple Solomon had built.	Revelation/**II Chronicles**
10. Stephen was stoned because he preached Jesus Christ.	**Acts**/Genesis
11. Jesus was tempted in the wilderness.	I Samuel/**Matthew**
12. Rahab helped the Israelite spies.	**Joshua**/John
13. Jairus' daughter was raised from the dead.	Numbers/**Mark**
14. The story of Lazarus and the rich man was told.	**Luke**/Judges
15. Hezekiah's life was extended because he prayed to God.	**II Kings**/I Peter

God and His People—Love—Unit 7, Part 2, Lesson 3 181

Worktext page 180

Locate information in Scripture.

Bible Study Skills, Worktext page 181

Identify the location of specific accounts in the Bible. (*Note:* You may wish to allow the students to work in groups to complete this page.)

Background Information

Dowry—*A dowry is something of value from the bride's family given to the groom at marriage. It could include land, money, or jewels. A bride's dowry reflects the wealth of the family.*

Caste System—*There are four main classes of Indian society: (1) priests, (2) warriors and rulers, (3) farmers, traders, and laborers, and (4) servants. From the highest level (priests) to the lowest (servants), caste rules determine one's job, marriage, clothing, and eating habits. The* untouchables *were outside the caste system. Traditionally, the untouchables held unclean jobs and were required to use noisemakers to warn others of their approach. Modern Hindus associate with members of other castes in the workplace but maintain a much stricter separation in their homes.*

Reincarnation—*The idea that people can live more than once in different bodies, even in bodies of animals, is called* reincarnation. *Other Hindu practices include worship at temples and shrines, sacrifices and money given to the priest, prayers, and rituals to perform. A Hindu hopes to earn salvation by his good works. The Bible clearly refutes reincarnation (Ecclesiastes 9:4-6; Hebrews 9:27).*

Introducing the Missionary Biography

Review previous chapters. (*Note:* You may want to display books or items representing India.)

- **What was Amy like as a child?** *(Possible answers include mean, daring, and compassionate.)*
- **How was Amy Carmichael serving God?** *(as a missionary in Japan)*

Missionary Biography: *With Daring Faith*

Read Chapter 10. Direct the students to listen to find out Amy's motto. *("Nothing too precious for Jesus.")*

- **Why did Amy leave Japan?** *(Her health was poor, and Mr. Wilson, or D.O.M., had a stroke.)*
- **What happened when Amy arrived in India?** *(She was very sick.)*
- **What problem came between the Christian Indians and God?** *(money)* Explain that the money was not evil, but the problem was that money became more important to them than serving God.

Read Chapter 11. Direct the students to listen to find out who the Starry Cluster were. *(Indian believers who traveled to teach women and children about the Lord)*

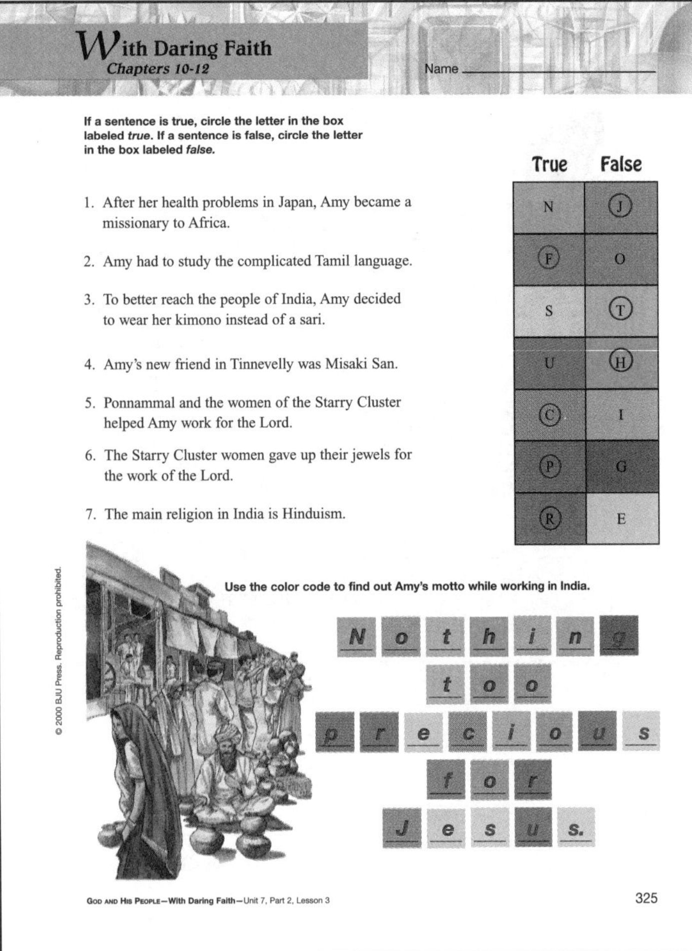

With Daring Faith
Chapters 10-12

Name ______________________

If a sentence is true, circle the letter in the box labeled *true.* If a sentence is false, circle the letter in the box labeled *false.*

	True	False
1. After her health problems in Japan, Amy became a missionary to Africa.	N	(J)
2. Amy had to study the complicated Tamil language.	(F)	O
3. To better reach the people of India, Amy decided to wear her kimono instead of a sari.	S	(T)
4. Amy's new friend in Tinnevelly was Misaki San.	U	(H)
5. Ponnammal and the women of the Starry Cluster helped Amy work for the Lord.	(C)	I
6. The Starry Cluster women gave up their jewels for the work of the Lord.	(P)	G
7. The main religion in India is Hinduism.	(R)	E

Use the color code to find out Amy's motto while working in India.

N o t h i n g
t o o
p r e c i o u s
f o r
J e s u s.

GOD AND HIS PEOPLE—With Daring Faith—Unit 7, Part 2, Lesson 3 325

➤ **How did God answer Amy's prayer that the Christian workers not let anything, including money, come before the Lord?** *(The women known as the Starry Cluster were willing to give up their pay and jewelry for the Lord and let God provide.)*

➤ **Why were jewels important to the Indian women?** *(They showed the husband's wealth.)* Share the background information about a dowry.

➤ **How did it help the Starry Cluster not to have jewels?** *(They could travel at night and not be robbed.)*

➤ **How were the Christian women showing fruit as true believers?** *(Answers will vary.)*

Challenge the students to think about what the Lord expects of them. Point out that a Christian should seek to live to honor and obey God. A believer shows a life that is changed by the power of God.

➤ **Would you be willing to give up something valuable to follow the Lord?**

Read Chapter 12. Point out that the next chapter explains how life is different in India because of the *caste system.* Share the background information about the caste system. Tell the students to listen to find out whether they would like to live under these expectations.

➤ **What were some other differences Amy observed?** *(Possible answers include language, travel, cows in the huts, clothing, and worship of idols.)*

➤ **What is the main religion in India?** *(Hinduism)*

➤ **Why would a Hindu not kill a fly or a cow?** *(He thinks that it might be a dead relative.)*

Refer to the background information to explain reincarnation. Explain that God's plan has no second chance for salvation after death. Read aloud **Hebrews 9:27-28.** Remind the students that God provides salvation through the blood of Jesus on the cross. Once a person repents and accepts Jesus as Savior, he should show his love for God through obedience to Him.

Point out that God's love has no boundaries. Read **John 3:16** aloud. Remind the students that Jesus Christ came to die for all people. No person's social or economic background, race, or nationality prevents God from loving him. Just as God demonstrated His great love to all people, a Christian should show godly love to others. Read aloud **I John 4** as time allows.

Culture Connection

Assign jobs to explain the caste system. Explain that a worker in India already has a job decided for him. Direct attention to the job opportunities and salaries on display. Read aloud five job opportunities and randomly assign these jobs to students. Continue until all students have been given a job. Tell them that if they were in India, they could talk and eat only with certain students. Explain that their job would be determined by their father's job. Discuss how this system would tend to make people proud, thinking themselves better than others.

Worktext Supplement page 325

Identify true and false statements about Chapters 10-12.

Lesson 4

Materials

- Copy of *With Daring Faith* for the teacher
- Jewelry, coins, plastic animal, and a work-related item (e.g., briefcase, toy tractor, or stethoscope)

Hymn: "O to Be Like Thee!"

Sing the first two verses (Worktext pages 282-83). Play the recording and lead in singing verses 1-2.

Memory Verse—Mark 12:31

Review the memory verse. Locate **Mark 12:31** and select a student to read it aloud. Encourage volunteers to read the verse or to say it from memory.

➤ **How have you shown love to your neighbor?**

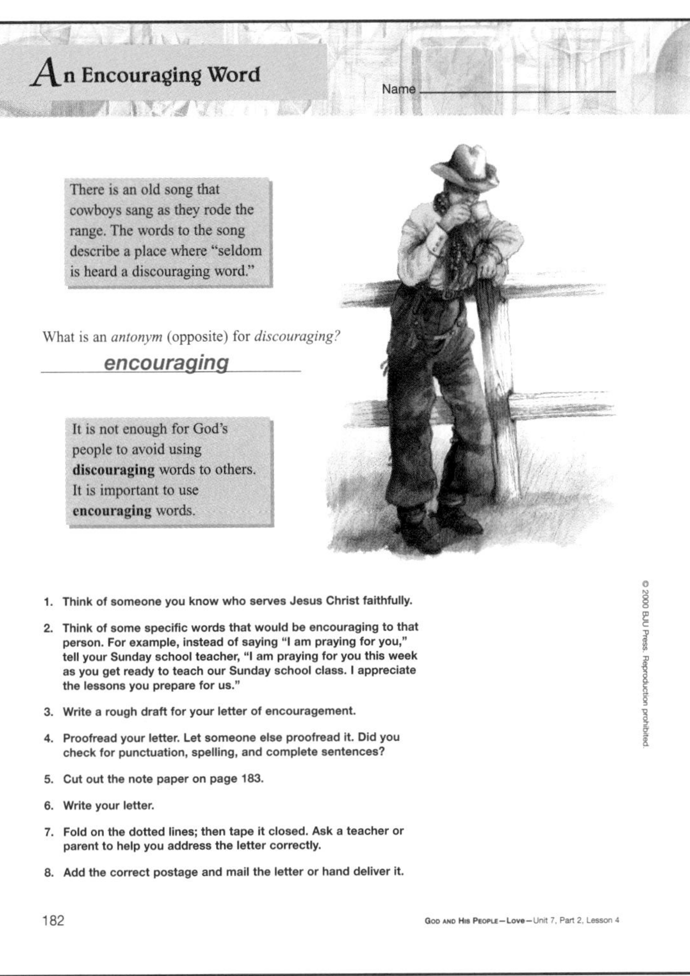

An Encouraging Word

Name ____________________

There is an old song that cowboys sang as they rode the range. The words to the song describe a place where "seldom is heard a discouraging word."

What is an *antonym* (opposite) for *discouraging?*

encouraging

It is not enough for God's people to avoid using **discouraging** words to others. It is important to use **encouraging** words.

1. Think of someone you know who serves Jesus Christ faithfully.
2. Think of some specific words that would be encouraging to that person. For example, instead of saying "I am praying for you," tell your Sunday school teacher, "I am praying for you this week as you get ready to teach our Sunday school class. I appreciate the lessons you prepare for us."
3. Write a rough draft for your letter of encouragement.
4. Proofread your letter. Let someone else proofread it. Did you check for punctuation, spelling, and complete sentences?
5. Cut out the note paper on page 183.
6. Write your letter.
7. Fold on the dotted lines; then tape it closed. Ask a teacher or parent to help you address the letter correctly.
8. Add the correct postage and mail the letter or hand deliver it.

182 God and His People—Love—Unit 7, Part 2, Lesson 4

An Encouraging Word (continued)

Name ____________________

Dear ____________,

I have been studying about loving others and encouraging fellow Christians. I would like to offer you the following encouraging words:

Your friend,

God and His People—Love—Unit 7, Part 2, Lesson 4 183

Writing Connection, Worktext pages 182-84 (optional)

Write a letter of encouragement. Review the parts of a letter. Discuss the meaning of *encouragement,* "giving hope and confidence to; inspiration." Elicit from students words that are encouraging. Write their list of words so that all can see. Explain how to complete Steps 1-3. Offer assistance in checking the students' rough drafts. (*Note:* Students may bring addresses, envelopes, and stamps to school, or the letters may be sent home for the parents to help address before mailing.)

Background Information

Hinduism—*Hinduism is a religion teaching that many gods exist in plants and animals. Hinduism teaches that man achieves holiness by suffering and doing good deeds. It teaches that a man dies many times and lives again in different bodies, even in the bodies of animals. The sacred books of Hinduism are called the Vedas.*

Foundation of Religions—*Essential elements of any religion deal with the following questions:*

Who is God?
What is the source of truth?
Who is Jesus Christ?
What is the nature of man?

The foundation of Christianity is an infinite, eternal, and holy God. The Bible is God's inspired and infallible Word. Man is sinful. Jesus Christ is the sinless Son of God who lived, died, and rose again to take the penalty for the sins of mankind.

You will notice that the common feature of false religions is that they assume man can somehow save himself through his own works. The Bible makes it clear that this is not possible and sets forth the true way of salvation through accepting God's perfect sacrifice for sins (Romans 3:24-25).

(*Note:* You may also want to review the Catechism questions, "Do I Know About God?" on page xxii.)

Scripture to Refute Hinduism—*You may want to read the following Scriptures to your students.*

Isaiah 45:5-6 (one God)
Genesis 1:1, Colossians 1:16-17 (creation by God)
Hebrews 9:27 (man dies once)
Ephesians 2:8-9 (man is saved only by faith)

Introducing the Missionary Biography

Review previous chapters. Display the jewelry, coins, plastic animal, and work-related item. Call on students to tell how each item relates to the biography.

jewelry—*The Christian women (called the Starry Cluster) were willing to sell their jewelry.*
coins—*The believers were willing to work without pay and let God provide for them.*
animal—*Hindus would not kill animals because of their belief in reincarnation.*

work-related item—*The caste system in India determines one's work, marriage, clothing, and eating habits.*

Point out that Amy Carmichael tried to understand the culture and people in India in order to present the gospel clearly. Remind the students that in any culture true salvation means turning by faith to Jesus Christ as the only Savior from sin.

Missionary Biography: *With Daring Faith*

Read Chapter 13. Explain that the next two chapters tell more about the beliefs of Hinduism. Challenge the students to listen as you read aloud to find out whether Hinduism teaches there is one God or many gods. *(many gods)*

- ➤ **Why did Amy and Ponnammal not enter a hut at meal time?** *(The Indians believed that if a white woman looked at their food, they would have to throw it away and cook some more food.)*
- ➤ **How did the women respond when Amy told them about the love of Jesus Christ?** *(Answers include that they listened but were indifferent, were polite but insincere, or were afraid to turn from the caste.)*
- ➤ **Who had shown Amy by her life that God's power could change an Indian woman's heart?** *(Ponnammal)*

Read Chapter 14.

- ➤ **Who stopped Amy and Ponnammal to ask questions?** *(an old man)*
- ➤ **Did the men understand that there is only one true God?** *(No. They used some of the same words, but they did not mean the same thing.)* Share the background information about Hinduism.

Explain that many false religions may sound similar to what the Bible says, but each one is a lie. Share the background information about the foundations of religions.

- ➤ **Why did Amy not enter the houses in the higher-caste village?** *(Their caste rules did not allow white women to enter their houses.)*
- ➤ **How did Amy and Ponnammal get the people to come and hear the gospel?** *(They sang.)*

Read Chapter 15. Read the title of Chapter 15, "A Festival and a Funeral."

- ➤ **What activities went on at the festivals?** *(People sold cakes, rugs, saris, or jewels; and some worshiped idols and made animal sacrifices.)*
- ➤ **What were some of the burial customs?** *(Possible answers include that the men bathed in the river before the ceremony, food and light were given to the dead man, and the priest chanted.)*
- ➤ **What did Amy realize about those at the funeral?** *(These people had no hope.)*

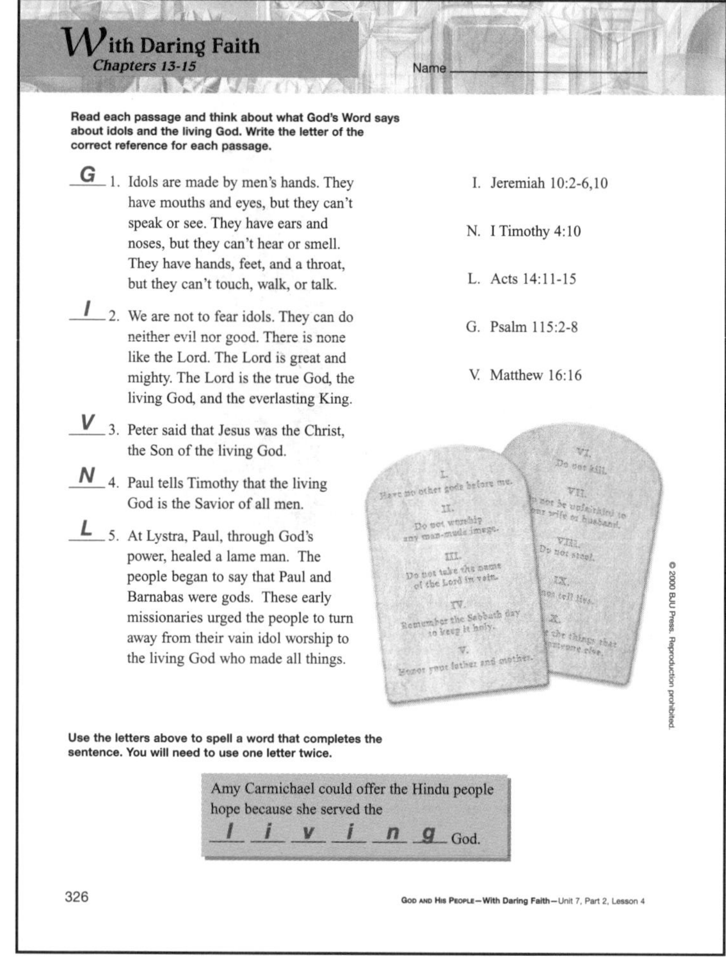

With Daring Faith
Chapters 13-15
Name ______________________

Read each passage and think about what God's Word says about idols and the living God. Write the letter of the correct reference for each passage.

G	1. Idols are made by men's hands. They have mouths and eyes, but they can't speak or see. They have ears and noses, but they can't hear or smell. They have hands, feet, and a throat, but they can't touch, walk, or talk.	I. Jeremiah 10:2-6,10
I	2. We are not to fear idols. They can do neither evil nor good. There is none like the Lord. The Lord is great and mighty. The Lord is the true God, the living God, and the everlasting King.	N. I Timothy 4:10
V	3. Peter said that Jesus was the Christ, the Son of the living God.	L. Acts 14:11-15
N	4. Paul tells Timothy that the living God is the Savior of all men.	G. Psalm 115:2-8
L	5. At Lystra, Paul, through God's power, healed a lame man. The people began to say that Paul and Barnabas were gods. These early missionaries urged the people to turn away from their vain idol worship to the living God who made all things.	V. Matthew 16:16

Use the letters above to spell a word that completes the sentence. You will need to use one letter twice.

Amy Carmichael could offer the Hindu people hope because she served the l i v i n g God.

326

GOD AND HIS PEOPLE—With Daring Faith—Unit 7, Part 2, Lesson 4

© 2000 BJU Press. Reproduction prohibited.

- ➤ **Why did Amy love these people?** *(God loved them, and Amy wanted to show God's love to them through her example and life.)*

Explain that although the people did not want to hear the gospel, the message of salvation is like a seed that is planted and later bears fruit. Point out that each person makes a decision to turn to Christ or to reject His offer of salvation. There is also an eternal consequence to each decision made.

- ➤ **What becomes of man at death?** *(The body returns to dust, and the soul goes to either heaven or hell.)*

Worktext Supplement page 326

Locate information in Scripture.

Going Beyond

Materials

- Classified section of a newspaper with employment opportunities

Enrichment

Write a classified ad. Allow students to read over the ads about employment opportunities. Direct them to write an ad for the "job" of a missionary. Remind them to include the qualifications of a missionary and to specify job responsibilities.

Loving the Unsaved

Preview

Doctrines

- God is love (John 3:16)—Lesson 1
- Man is guilty before God (Romans 3:10-12)—Lesson 1
- God calls men through the Holy Spirit (John 16:7-11)—Lesson 4
- The universal church, an organism, is the mystical body of Christ composed of all true believers (I Corinthians 12:13)—Lesson 4

Skills and Applications

- Learn Ephesians 4:31-32
- Recall facts and details
- Locate information in Scripture
- Compare Bible characters
- Recognize that showing kindness is the key to love
- Develop a love for all mankind
- Put the needs of others before self
- Be Christlike in words and actions
- Apply Bible knowledge to everyday life

Lesson 1

Hymn: "O to Be Like Thee!"

Teach the third verse (Worktext pages 282-83). Read the words of verse 3 aloud as the students read silently. Explain that this verse tells characteristics of Jesus that should be in a Christian's life. Explain that *lowly* means "humble, not having pride." Play the recording and lead in singing verse 3.

➤ **What do the words *holy* and *harmless* mean?** *(without sin and free from causing pain to someone else)*

➤ **How can you be holy and harmless?** *(Confess sin and be kind rather than hurtful to others.)*

➤ **How did Jesus respond to cruel reproaches or mean things that people said about Him or did to Him?** *(He did not say anything but responded with love and kindness.)*

➤ **How should Christians respond to mean words or actions toward them?** *(with kindness and love)* Play the recording and lead in singing verses 1-3.

Memory Verses—Ephesians 4:31-32

Principle: The key to love is kindness. Locate and read aloud **Ephesians 4:31-32.** Explain that just as we exchange dirty clothes for clean ones, so we are to put off, or put away, things that do not please God. Remind the students of the hymn "O to Be Like Thee!" and that in order to be like Christ, Christians may need to change their attitudes and actions. Direct the students to highlight the verses in their Bibles (optional) and to mark the location with their Unit 7 Bookmark.

➤ **What happens when you lose your temper?** *(You become angry with someone.)*

➤ **If we are angry with someone and we stay angry for several days, what does the anger turn into?** *(bitterness)*

➤ **Since God made you, should you, His creation, say mean things to someone or about someone? What *should* come out of a Christian's mouth?** *(no; words of kindness)*

Background Information

Courts of the Temple—*There were four different courts in the temple. There was an outer court where anyone—both Jews and Gentiles—could come. There was a court of women where women were allowed. The men could go farther into the court of Israel and sometimes into the Priest's Court. We do not know for sure where Jesus was when the unfaithful woman was brought to Him, but it seems probable that He was in the Gentile Court since Jesus preached there on many occasions.*

Scribes—*Their job was to make copies of the Scriptures and to teach the law to the people.*

Pharisees—*The name* Pharisee *means "separated one," but the Pharisees of Jesus' day practiced a separation that followed their own rules rather than those in the Word of God. God's chosen people, the Jews, were to be separate, or distinct from others, but* *the Pharisees were so busy keeping every detail of the law that they ended up doing things that were against the real purpose of the law. The Pharisees became enemies of the Lord Jesus because of their hypocrisy, their lack of true repentance, and their zeal for putting their traditions above the revealed Word of God. Their hatred for Jesus caused them to call for His crucifixion.*

Types of Law—*There are three main types: ceremonial, civil, and moral. Ceremonial law pertains to the Jews and their offerings or sacrifices. This law no longer applies because of Jesus' death and resurrection, which is the payment for the sin of all mankind. Civil law refers to daily living. This guided the Jews in their response to others and how they were to treat one another. The moral law refers to those laws regarding right and wrong that have been given to us directly by God. The Ten Commandments are of this type. It is important, however, to remember that obedience to the law does not bring salvation. The law referred to in the following Bible account would be moral law.*

Introducing the Bible Account

Define *faithfulness.* Explain that to be *faithful* a person must be consistent, or reliable to a particular cause or belief. Faithfulness is a characteristic of the Lord Jesus Christ. If Christians are going to be like Christ, they are to be faithful.

➤ **How can you be faithful at home or school?** *(Possible answers include turning homework in on time, telling friends about the Lord, studying for tests to do your best, and showing kindness to others.)*

Explain that in the Bible account, a woman was brought to Jesus because of her unfaithfulness.

Bible Account

Read the following Bible account or read John 8:1-11.

Jesus Forgives the Unfaithful Woman

Early one morning Jesus went into the temple in Jerusalem to teach the people. As He was teaching, the scribes and Pharisees brought a woman to Him. They told Jesus that this woman had been unfaithful to her husband and to the promises that she had made to him at their marriage. The scribes and Pharisees reminded Jesus that in the law Moses commanded them to stone those who were found to be unfaithful to their marriage promises. Then they asked Jesus what He thought they should do.

The scribes and Pharisees were trying to trick Jesus because the law said an unfaithful wife should be put to death by stoning. Jesus bent down and wrote on the ground as though He did not hear their question. The scribes and Pharisees continued asking Jesus what to do, and finally Jesus stood up and said to them, "He that is without sin among you, let him first cast a stone at her."

Jesus bent back down and continued writing on the ground. Then one by one the scribes and Pharisees recognized their own sin and left the temple. Jesus once again raised Himself up from the ground, and the only person left was the woman who had been accused. Jesus asked the woman where her accusers had gone and if any had condemned her, and she answered, "No man, Lord." Jesus then said to the woman, "Neither do I condemn thee: go, and sin no more."

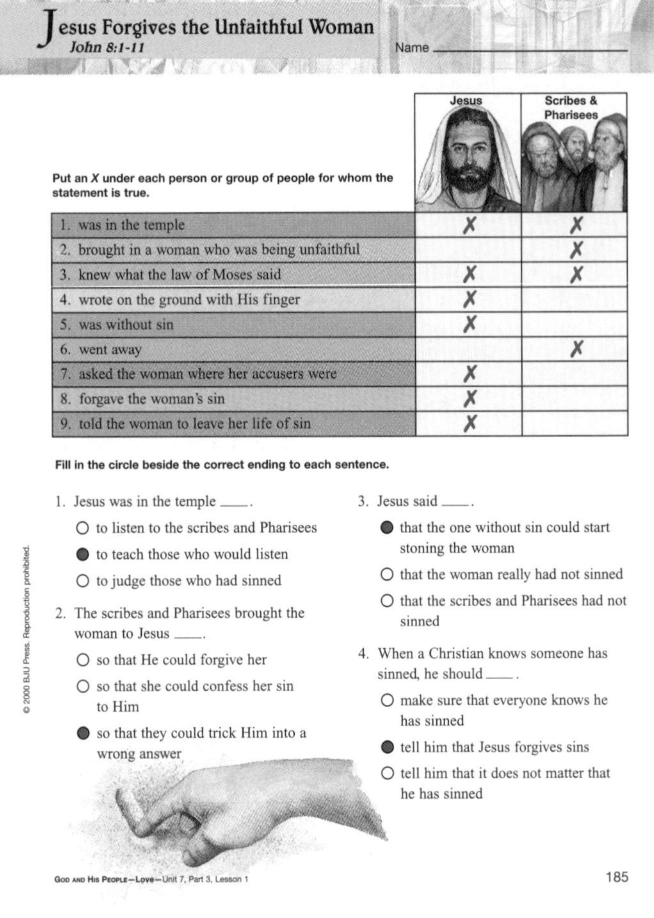

Jesus Forgives the Unfaithful Woman
John 8:1-11

Name ____________

Put an *X* under each person or group of people for whom the statement is true.

	Jesus	Scribes & Pharisees
1. was in the temple	✗	✗
2. brought in a woman who was being unfaithful		✗
3. knew what the law of Moses said	✗	✗
4. wrote on the ground with His finger	✗	
5. was without sin	✗	
6. went away		✗
7. asked the woman where her accusers were	✗	
8. forgave the woman's sin	✗	
9. told the woman to leave her life of sin	✗	

Fill in the circle beside the correct ending to each sentence.

1. Jesus was in the temple ____.
   - ○ to listen to the scribes and Pharisees
   - ● to teach those who would listen
   - ○ to judge those who had sinned
2. The scribes and Pharisees brought the woman to Jesus ____.
   - ○ so that He could forgive her
   - ○ so that she could confess her sin to Him
   - ● so that they could trick Him into a wrong answer
3. Jesus said ____.
   - ● that the one without sin could start stoning the woman
   - ○ that the woman really had not sinned
   - ○ that the scribes and Pharisees had not sinned
4. When a Christian knows someone has sinned, he should ____.
   - ○ make sure that everyone knows he has sinned
   - ● tell him that Jesus forgives sins
   - ○ tell him that it does not matter that he has sinned

© 2000 BJU Press. Reproduction prohibited.

God and His People—Love—Unit 7, Part 3, Lesson 1 185

➤ **Why was Jesus in the temple?** *(to teach those who had come to listen)*

➤ **Whom did the scribes and Pharisees bring before Jesus, and why did they bring her?** *(They brought an unfaithful woman in order to trick Jesus.)*

➤ **What was Jesus' answer to their question about what to do with the woman?** *("He that is without sin among you, let him first cast a stone at her.")*

➤ **What happened to the woman?** *(Jesus forgave her, and she went away.)*

➤ **How are Christians to treat those who sin against them?** *(forgive them and show them love and kindness as well as encourage them to do what is right)*

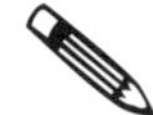

Worktext page 185

Recall details from the Bible account.

Lesson 2

Materials

- Bible Book Cards: New and Old Testament abbreviations
- Copy of *With Daring Faith* for the teacher

Memory Verses—Ephesians 4:31-32

Practice the memory verses. Locate **Ephesians 4:31-32,** choosing two volunteers to stand and read aloud one verse each. Remind the students that Jesus was a servant to others.

➤ **How does verse 31 say Christians should not treat others?** *(with anger and bitterness)*

➤ **How does verse 32 say Christians should treat others?** *(with kindness, forgiving others)*

Read the verses several times throughout the day for practice and as a reminder of how to act.

Hymn: "O to Be Like Thee!"

Sing the first three verses (Worktext pages 282-83). Play the recording and lead in singing verses 1-3.

Worktext page 186

Singing with understanding, verse 3.

Bible Study Skills

Practice abbreviations for the books of the Bible. Remind the students that there are differences in how people abbreviate some of the books of the Bible when writing a Bible reference (e.g., Matthew: Matt. or Mt.; Exodus: Exod. or Ex.). The important skill is being able to identify the correct book.

Draw a baseball diamond for display. Divide the students into two teams. Show the abbreviation to the student up at bat; if he tells the name of the correct book of the Bible, he can advance to first base. Continue in this manner with students advancing a base with each correct answer until runs are scored. For each incorrect answer, an out is called. After three outs, the next team is up to bat, trying to score runs. At the end of the time allotted, the team with more runs (points) wins.

One-on-One: Use the Bible Book Abbreviation Cards for the teacher and student to play a game similar to "Go Fish" (See page 167 for directions.), or "Concentration" (See page 190 for directions.).

Introducing the Missionary Biography

Discuss a salvation experience. Tell about your salvation experience. Select students to tell about themselves and when they accepted Christ as their Savior.

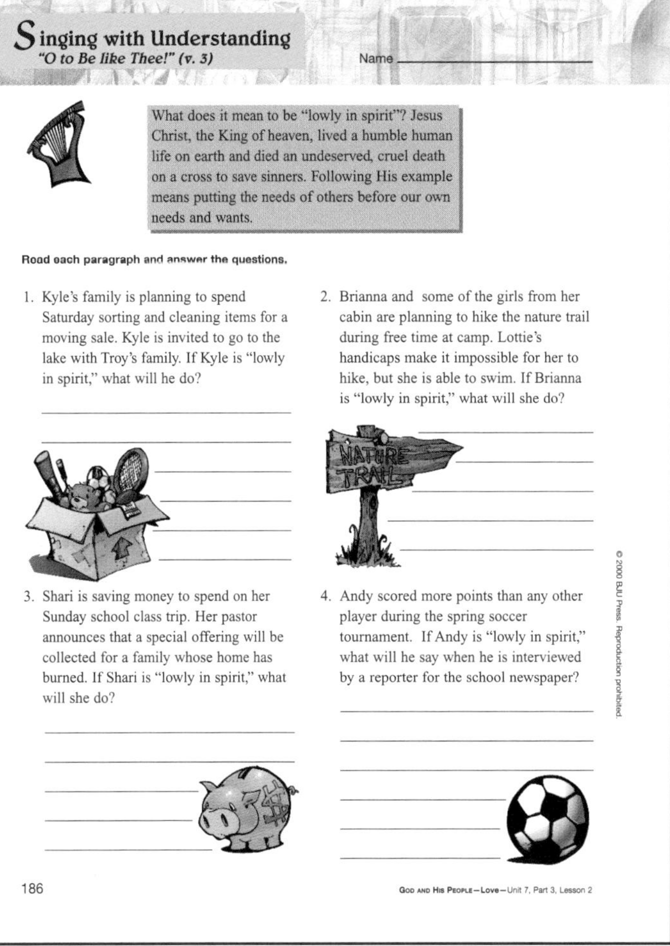

Singing with Understanding
"O to Be like Thee!" (v. 3)

Name ______________

What does it mean to be "lowly in spirit"? Jesus Christ, the King of heaven, lived a humble human life on earth and died an undeserved, cruel death on a cross to save sinners. Following His example means putting the needs of others before our own needs and wants.

Read each paragraph and answer the questions.

1. Kyle's family is planning to spend Saturday sorting and cleaning items for a moving sale. Kyle is invited to go to the lake with Troy's family. If Kyle is "lowly in spirit," what will he do?
2. Brianna and some of the girls from her cabin are planning to hike the nature trail during free time at camp. Lottie's handicaps make it impossible for her to hike, but she is able to swim. If Brianna is "lowly in spirit," what will she do?
3. Shari is saving money to spend on her Sunday school class trip. Her pastor announces that a special offering will be collected for a family whose home has burned. If Shari is "lowly in spirit," what will she do?
4. Andy scored more points than any other player during the spring soccer tournament. If Andy is "lowly in spirit," what will he say when he is interviewed by a reporter for the school newspaper?

186 God and His People—Love—Unit 7, Part 3, Lesson 2

Missionary Biography: *With Daring Faith*

Read Chapter 16.

➤ **Why do you think Arulai was trying to find the greatest god?** *(Answers may vary, but point out that the true and living God was working in her heart.)*

➤ **Why did Arulai's mother punish her when she came home?** *(She had been listening to the low-caste people or missionaries.)*

➤ **What two answers to prayer did Arulai receive?** *(Fruit from a tree fell so that she would have something to eat and would not have to steal. Her mother did not punish her.)*

Read Chapter 17. Tell the students to listen to find out how God worked it out for Arulai to stay with Amy. *(Possible answers include that the power of God was shown to her father and he allowed her to stay.)*

➤ **Why do you think Arulai prayed to God that she be allowed to go to the *ammal* (Amy)?** *(so that she could learn more)*

➤ **What did God provide for Arulai while she was on her way to see Amy?** *(a coin)*

➤ **What happened to Arulai that day at the temple?** *(Arulai accepted the Lord as her Savior.)*

With Daring Faith
Chapters 16-18

Name ____________

Who am I?

Choose the correct name to identify the person described.

Arulai 1. I prayed that the living God would show Himself to me.

Jewel of Victory 2. I accepted Christ as my Savior at a mission school.

Jewel of Life 3. I was the second teenage girl to run to the mission house for refuge.

Preena 4. I was given to the temple women for service by my mother.

Servant of Jesus 5. I brought a temple child to Amy to care for.

Child-stealing Woman 6. I was given this nickname by the Hindu women because I gave refuge to girls fleeing the Hindu religion.

Ponnammal 7. I am Amy's fellow laborer at the mission.

Arulai
Preena
Jewel of Life
Servant of Jesus
Child-stealing Woman
Ponnammal
Jewel of Victory

GOD AND HIS PEOPLE—With Daring Faith—Unit 7, Part 3, Lesson 2 327

➤ **Why was Amy afraid for Arulai?** *(It was likely that Arulai would be beaten or even killed for following the missionaries.)*

➤ **What amazing thing happened for Arulai?** *(Her parents allowed her to go back and see the* ammal.*)*

Read Chapter 18. Tell the students to listen to find out why mothers would give their little girls to the temple woman. *(Possible answers include that it was considered honorable, that the family did not have the money to care for them, or that there were too many children in the family.)*

➤ **Why did Jewel of Victory come running to the mission in the middle of the night?** *(She came because God told her to.)*

➤ **How did the mission school burn?** *(Jewel of Victory's family became angry and set it on fire.)*

➤ **Who came to Amy at the mission after Jewel of Victory?** *(Jewel of Life)*

➤ **Why did Preena's mother give her to the temple woman?** *(She believed it would help her and her daughter. She also believed she was doing something wonderful for the gods.)*

Worktext Supplement page 327

Identify the correct character.

Lesson 3

Materials

- Copy of *With Daring Faith* for the teacher
- A hat for each student (*Note:* Request that each student bring a hat from home.)

Hymn: "O to Be Like Thee!"

Sing the first three verses (Worktext pages 282-83). Play the recording of verses 1-3 and sing them together.

Memory Verses—Ephesians 4:31-32

Practice the memory verses. Locate **Ephesians 4:31-32** and tell the students to read the verses silently, to say the verses to themselves in a whisper, and then to read them silently again.

➤ **Is it possible to put away something and not replace it with something else?** Explain that it might be possible, but it still may be hard to keep from doing whatever it is that has been put away.

➤ **How can Christians be tenderhearted to one another?** *(Possible answers include being kind, helpful, and sympathetic.)*

Guide the students in reading verse 31 and then in saying it from memory. Then direct them to read verse 32 and to say it from memory.

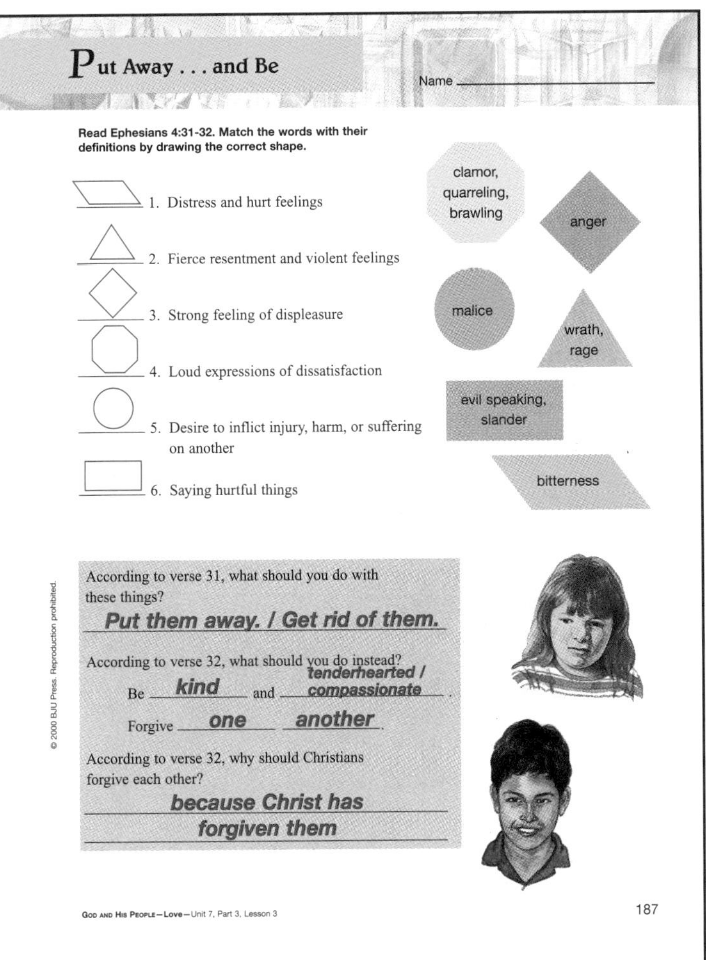

Put Away . . . and Be

Name ____________

Read Ephesians 4:31-32. Match the words with their definitions by drawing the correct shape.

1. Distress and hurt feelings
2. Fierce resentment and violent feelings
3. Strong feeling of displeasure
4. Loud expressions of dissatisfaction
5. Desire to inflict injury, harm, or suffering on another
6. Saying hurtful things

clamor, quarreling, brawling

anger

malice

wrath, rage

evil speaking, slander

bitterness

According to verse 31, what should you do with these things?
Put them away. / Get rid of them.

According to verse 32, what should you do instead?
Be *kind* and *tenderhearted / compassionate*.
Forgive *one another*.

According to verse 32, why should Christians forgive each other?
because Christ has forgiven them

God and His People—Love—Unit 7, Part 3, Lesson 3 187

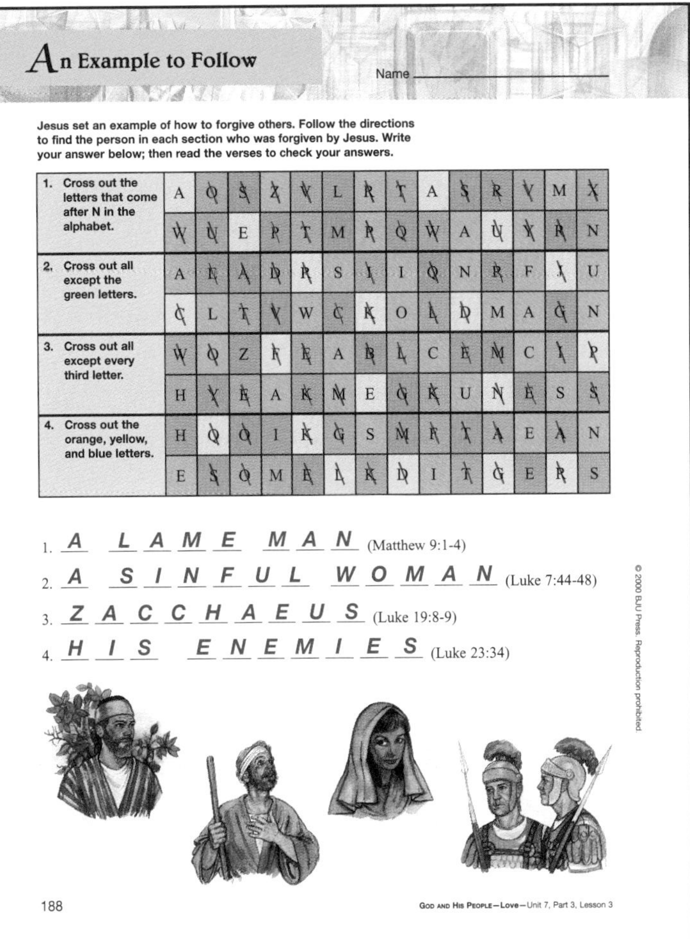

An Example to Follow

Name ____________

Jesus set an example of how to forgive others. Follow the directions to find the person in each section who was forgiven by Jesus. Write your answer below; then read the verses to check your answers.

1. Cross out the letters that come after N in the alphabet.	A	Q	S	X	V	L	R	T	A	S	R	V	M	X
	W	U	E	R	T	M	R	Q	W	A	U	Y	R	N
2. Cross out all except the green letters.	A	E	A	D	R	S	L	I	Q	N	R	F	X	U
	C	L	T	V	W	C	K	O	L	D	M	A	G	N
3. Cross out all except every third letter.	W	Q	Z	K	E	A	B	L	C	E	M	C	X	P
	H	Y	E	A	K	M	E	G	K	U	N	E	S	S
4. Cross out the orange, yellow, and blue letters.	H	Q	Q	I	K	G	S	M	R	T	A	E	A	N
	E	S	Q	M	E	L	K	D	I	T	G	E	R	S

1. *A LAME MAN* (Matthew 9:1-4)
2. *A SINFUL WOMAN* (Luke 7:44-48)
3. *ZACCHAEUS* (Luke 19:8-9)
4. *HIS ENEMIES* (Luke 23:34)

188 God and His People—Love—Unit 7, Part 3, Lesson 3

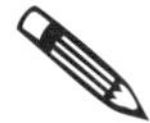

Worktext page 187

Develop an understanding of the memory verses.

Worktext page 188

Identify people forgiven by Jesus.

Introducing the Missionary Biography

Discuss being different. Allow one student to wear his hat. Ask him how it feels to be the only one wearing a hat. Ask the other students how they feel not wearing hats. Now tell all the students except one to put on their hats. Ask the students wearing hats how they feel to be wearing hats. Ask them how they think the hatless student feels; then ask the hatless person how he feels to be the only person not wearing a hat. Tell the students that in the following chapters, Amy feels different and tries to be more like the ones around her.

Missionary Biography: *With Daring Faith*

Read Chapter 19.

➤ **Why was Amy staining her skin with coffee?** *(so she would look like an Indian and be able to enter the temple and find out what took place there)*

➤ **What did Arulai say that made Amy realize her eyes *were* the right color?** *(She would not have been able to blend in if she had had blue eyes.)*

➤ **What did Amy find out about the Hindu people and their relationship to the temple?** *(that the Hindu people were really unaware of what took place inside the temple)*

➤ **How long did Amy work to find out what was really taking place in the temple?** *(three years)*

Read Chapter 20. Tell the students to listen to find out what Amy and the girls had allowed to come in and eat breakfast with them. *(a squirrel)*

➤ **Why did Amy pray for more children?** *(because she did not want them to become temple servants and live in the temple for the rest of their lives)*

➤ **Whom did God provide to help Amy in rescuing the girls from the temple woman?** *(an elderly Christian Indian woman named Old Devai)*

➤ **Why was Old Devai better at getting the children than Amy?** *(Possible answers include that she was Indian, so the people were more likely to trust her; and she was older.)*

➤ **After two years, how many children did Amy have?** *(seventy)*

➤ **What blessing did God send to Amy?** *(Her mother was able to come for a visit.)*

Read Chapter 21.

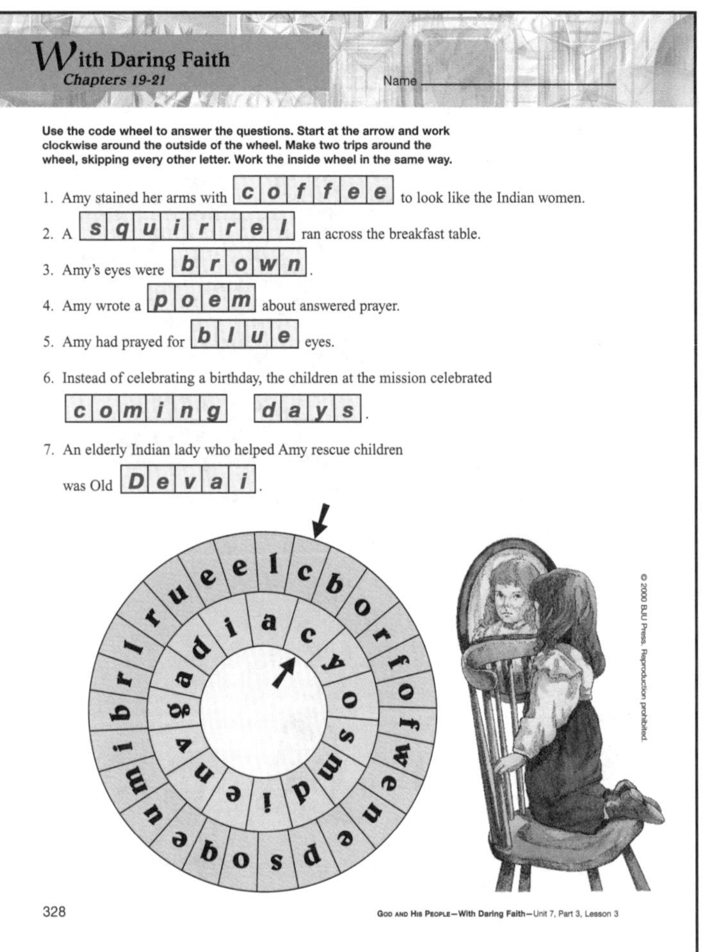

With Daring Faith
Chapters 19-21

Name ______________________

Use the code wheel to answer the questions. Start at the arrow and work clockwise around the outside of the wheel. Make two trips around the wheel, skipping every other letter. Work the inside wheel in the same way.

1. Amy stained her arms with c o f f e e to look like the Indian women.
2. A s q u i r r e l ran across the breakfast table.
3. Amy's eyes were b r o w n.
4. Amy wrote a p o e m about answered prayer.
5. Amy had prayed for b l u e eyes.
6. Instead of celebrating a birthday, the children at the mission celebrated c o m i n g d a y s.
7. An elderly Indian lady who helped Amy rescue children was Old D e v a i.

© 2000 BJU Press. Reproduction prohibited.

328 GOD AND HIS PEOPLE—With Daring Faith—Unit 7, Part 3, Lesson 3

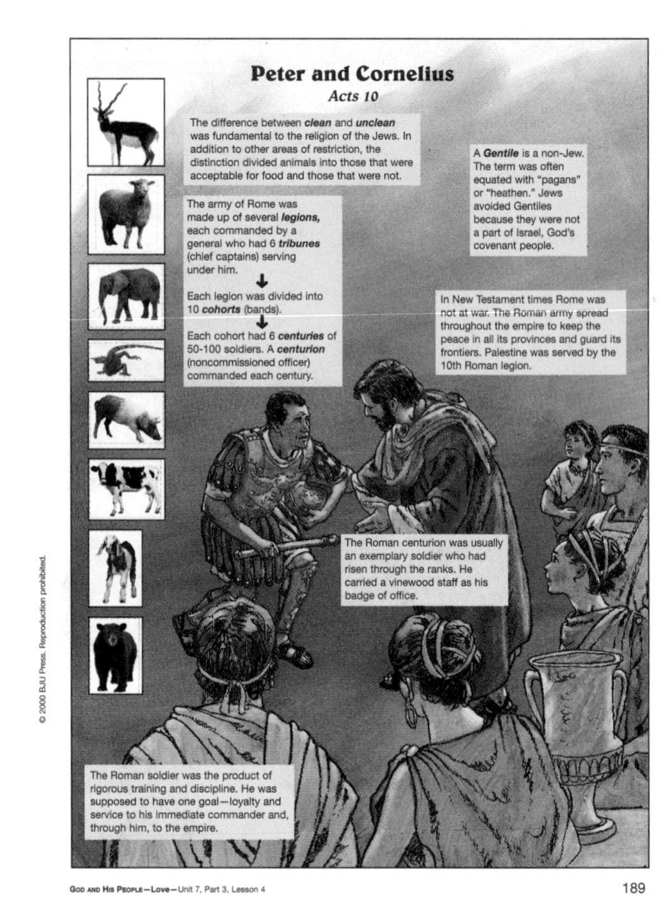

Peter and Cornelius
Acts 10

The difference between ***clean*** and ***unclean*** was fundamental to the religion of the Jews. In addition to other areas of restriction, the distinction divided animals into those that were acceptable for food and those that were not.

A ***Gentile*** is a non-Jew. The term was often equated with "pagans" or "heathen." Jews avoided Gentiles because they were not a part of Israel, God's covenant people.

The army of Rome was made up of several ***legions,*** each commanded by a general who had 6 ***tribunes*** (chief captains) serving under him.

Each legion was divided into 10 ***cohorts*** (bands).

Each cohort had 6 ***centuries*** of 50-100 soldiers. A ***centurion*** (noncommissioned officer) commanded each century.

In New Testament times Rome was not at war. The Roman army spread throughout the empire to keep the peace in all its provinces and guard its frontiers. Palestine was served by the 10th Roman legion.

The Roman centurion was usually an exemplary soldier who had risen through the ranks. He carried a vinewood staff as his badge of office.

The Roman soldier was the product of rigorous training and discipline. He was supposed to have one goal—loyalty and service to his immediate commander and, through him, to the empire.

© 2000 BJU Press. Reproduction prohibited.

GOD AND HIS PEOPLE—Love—Unit 7, Part 3, Lesson 4 189

➤ **Why was Muttammal brought to Amy?** *(so her uncle would not marry her off and take the land that had been given to Muttammal by her father)*

➤ **Who came and took Muttammal away from Amy?** *(her mother)*

➤ **Does God always work things out the way we think He should?** *(No. Sometimes God's plan is different, but it is always best.)*

Worktext Supplement page 328

Recall facts and details from Chapters 19-21.

Lesson 4

Materials

- Charts 23 and 33: "Peter and Cornelius" and "Palestine in the Time of Christ"

Hymn: "O to Be Like Thee!"

Sing the first three verses (Worktext pages 282-83). Play the recording and lead in singing verses 1-3. Divide the students into three groups, allowing each group to sing a different verse of the hymn.

Memory Verses—Ephesians 4:31-32

Practice the memory verses. Locate **Ephesians 4:31-32** and read them responsively two times, switching parts. Choose volunteers to stand and say the verses, using their Bibles if necessary.

Background Information

Common/Unclean—*Jewish law made certain foods forbidden. Some of the foods Gentiles ate were those things that were often forbidden to a Jew. This is one of the many reasons that the association of Jews and Gentiles was undesirable, or at least inconvenient.*

Introducing the Bible Account

Explain the setting. Direct the students' attention to Worktext page 189. Read and discuss the information with the students.

Bible Account

Read the following Bible account or read Acts 10. Direct the students to look at the picture on Worktext page 189.

Peter and Cornelius

Cornelius, a Roman centurion, lived in the town of Caesarea. (Point out Caesarea near the Mediterranean Sea on Chart 33, "Palestine in the Time of Christ.") The Bible tells us that Cornelius was a devout, religious Gentile who feared God; however, Cornelius had never accepted Christ as his personal Savior.

One night while Cornelius was sleeping, he had a dream, or a vision. In the dream an angel of the Lord appeared and told Cornelius to send some servants to Joppa to find a man named Simon Peter. (Point out Joppa on Chart 33, "Palestine in the Time of Christ.")

When the angel of the Lord departed, Cornelius called two of his servants and one soldier to come to him. Cornelius told them about the angel of the Lord and what he had said; then he sent the three men to Joppa to find Peter.

As the servants were nearing Joppa, Peter was praying on the roof of his house. During his prayer, Peter became very hungry and had a dream. In his dream Peter saw heaven open and a vessel that looked like a large sheet with four corners fastened together coming down. Inside the sheet were four-footed beasts and all types of animals. A voice said to Peter, "Rise, Peter; kill and eat." Peter answered, "Not so Lord; for I have never eaten any thing that is common or unclean." The voice again spoke saying, "What God hath cleansed, that call not thou common." This happened three times.

Peter was confused about what his dream might mean. The Spirit spoke to Peter saying, "Behold, three men seek thee. Arise therefore, and get thee down, and go with them, doubting nothing: for I have sent them."

The servants and soldiers of Cornelius came and knocked at the door of Peter's house. Peter went down and met the three men and asked why they had come. The men answered, "Cornelius the centurion, a just man, and one that feareth God, and of good report among all the nation of the Jews, was warned from God by an holy angel to send for thee into his house, and to hear words of thee."

Peter welcomed the three men to stay in his home overnight. The next morning the men took Peter with them to Caesarea to meet Cornelius. With Cornelius were his relatives and friends, all awaiting the arrival of Peter. When Cornelius met Peter, he fell down to worship Peter. Peter said to Cornelius, "Stand up; I myself also am a man."

Peter and Cornelius talked about the fact that Peter was a Jew and Cornelius a Gentile. They discussed why normally Jews and Gentiles did not associate with each other.

Cornelius told Peter that four days before while he was praying, he saw a vision of an angel telling him to send for Peter. Peter answered Cornelius, saying, "Of a truth I perceive that God is no respecter of persons: But in every nation he that feareth him, and worketh righteousness, is accepted with him." Peter continued speaking in Cornelius's home, explaining that Jesus was crucified and resurrected for everyone, not just the Jews. Those in Cornelius's house received Peter's message and believed on Jesus and were baptized.

InfoScene: "Peter and Cornelius"
Display Chart 23 for reference throughout this unit. Review and discuss the Bible account as time permits.

- ➤ **What words were used to describe Cornelius?** *(a Roman centurion who was devout and feared God)*
- ➤ **How did Cornelius know whom to send for?** *(An angel of the Lord told him in a dream.)*
- ➤ **Why did Peter, a Jew, choose to go with the three Gentile men that Cornelius had sent?** *(The Spirit of God told him to go.)*
- ➤ **What did Peter realize about God's relationship with all men?** *(God provides salvation for all who believe.)*
- ➤ **What is the most important thing a Christian can tell an unsaved person? Why?** *(about the gospel of Jesus Christ; because if they never accept Christ, they will go to hell)*
- ➤ **How are Christians to treat those who are different from them?** *(kindly and lovingly, just as God does)*

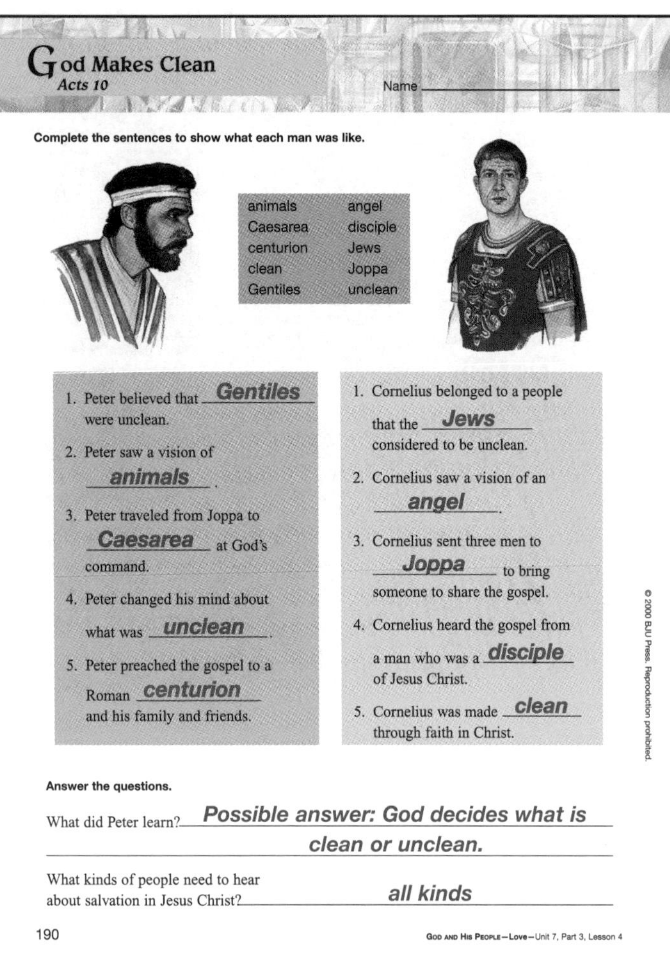

God Makes Clean
Acts 10

Name ______________________

Complete the sentences to show what each man was like.

animals	angel
Caesarea	disciple
centurion	Jews
clean	Joppa
Gentiles	unclean

1. Peter believed that **Gentiles** were unclean.
2. Peter saw a vision of **animals**.
3. Peter traveled from Joppa to **Caesarea** at God's command.
4. Peter changed his mind about what was **unclean**.
5. Peter preached the gospel to a Roman **centurion** and his family and friends.

1. Cornelius belonged to a people that the **Jews** considered to be unclean.
2. Cornelius saw a vision of an **angel**.
3. Cornelius sent three men to **Joppa** to bring someone to share the gospel.
4. Cornelius heard the gospel from a man who was a **disciple** of Jesus Christ.
5. Cornelius was made **clean** through faith in Christ.

Answer the questions.

What did Peter learn? **Possible answer: God decides what is clean or unclean.**

What kinds of people need to hear about salvation in Jesus Christ? **all kinds**

190 God and His People—Love—Unit 7, Part 3, Lesson 4

Worktext page 190

Compare Peter and Cornelius.

Going Beyond

Enrichment

Guide a writing activity. Direct the students to write an explanation of how a person is saved or to write their own personal testimony about how they were saved. Collect the students' writings to read privately. Take this opportunity to explain again how a person is saved. Follow through with individual students needing personal counseling.

Loving Your Enemies

Unit 7, Part 4

Preview

Doctrines

- God is love (John 3:16)—Lesson 1
- Man by faith receives Christ's righteousness (Philippians 3:9)—Lesson 2
- Man faces a struggle between the two natures (Romans 7:23-25)—Lesson 2

Skills and Applications

- Learn Matthew 5:43-44
- Recall facts and details
- Read a time line
- Use cross-references
- Develop Christlike character traits
- Identify character traits
- Realize that God helps us to love our enemies
- Understand proper reactions to enemies
- Apply Bible knowledge to everyday life

Lesson 1

Hymn: "O to Be Like Thee!"

Teach the fourth verse (Worktext pages 282-83). Read aloud the words of verse 4. Explain that part of being like Christ is "the indwelling of the Holy Spirit." The Holy Spirit guides each Christian and instructs his conscience to do what is right in every circumstance. The Holy Spirit is saddened, or grieved, when a Christian allows sin to enter his heart and life. This is why when a believer sins and realizes his sin, he needs to ask for forgiveness immediately.

➤ **In what ways should a Christian desire to be like Christ?** *(in everything—actions, words, and thoughts)*

➤ **Who owns our bodies? Why?** *(The Lord Jesus Christ owns our bodies because He created us.)*

Play the recording and lead in singing verse 4 together; then lead in singing all of the verses.

Memory Verses—Matthew 5:43-44

Principle: Love your enemies. Locate and read aloud **Matthew 5:43-44** as the students read silently. Explain that verse 43, which is what had been said in the Old Testament, had been understood by the Pharisees to mean that you were to be kind to those who have been kind to you. Jesus was explaining the true meaning of the Scripture: to overcome evil with good. Choose volunteers to read the verses aloud. Direct the students to highlight the verses in their Bibles (optional) and to mark the location with the Unit 7 Bookmark.

➤ **Who helps us to love our enemies?** *(Jesus Christ or the Holy Spirit)*

➤ **If *bless* means to honor, how can you bless those that curse you or say mean things to you?** *(Possible answers include not saying mean things back, giving them a compliment, and saying only nice things to them.)*

➤ **In what ways can you show love to your enemies?** *(Pray for them, ask God to help you to love them, and then be kind to them when you see them.)*

Introducing the Bible Study

Discuss enemies.

➤ **Has there ever been someone you just couldn't get along with?**

➤ **What can you do if you have an enemy or someone who seems to hate you and wants to upset you?**

Bible Study

Read the following reviews about Bible characters and how they responded to their enemies. Discuss the proper response by Christians.

Responses to Enemies

Moses/Pharaoh—God chose Moses to go and lead the children of Israel out of Egypt. Moses went before Pharaoh and asked for God's people to be freed. It took ten plagues and the death of the firstborn in each Egyptian household before Pharaoh would let the Israelites go. God was in control in spite of the many hard things that the Israelites went through during their time in Egyptian captivity. *(God is there to help us in the midst of trouble with the enemy.)* (Unit 1, Part 1, Lesson 3)

David/Saul—God chose David to be the king over the Israelites after King Saul sinned against God and lied to Samuel, the priest, about his sin. David, "the man after God's own heart," tried to honor God with his life. King Saul became angry with David and wanted him dead so that David could not be the next king. David went into hiding and prayed for God's protection. There were several times when David could have killed Saul, but he did not. *(Allow God to take care of your enemy rather than taking things into your own hands.)* (Unit 2, Part 1, Lesson 1)

Hezekiah/King Sennacherib—When Hezekiah was king of Israel, he brought the Word of God back to the people and had the temples reopened so that the people could worship God. One day Hezekiah received word that Sennacherib and his people, the Assyrians, were going to attack Israel. Hezekiah immediately fell down before God and prayed, asking God how to deal with this enemy. God told Hezekiah not to fear because He would take care of Israel. Hezekiah prayed and God took care of the enemy by killing many of the Assyrians. *(God takes care of His own.)* (Unit 2, Part 4, Lesson 1)

Naboth/Ahab & Jezebel—Naboth was a man who honored God and followed God's law. One such law said that if a man received something by inheritance, he was not to sell it. King Ahab, a wicked king over Israel, wanted Naboth's vineyard and began to pout over it. Jezebel, Ahab's wife, who was even more wicked than Ahab, developed a scheme to have Naboth killed so that Ahab could have the vineyard. Both Ahab and Jezebel were later killed by God for their wickedness. Naboth obeyed God's law instead of giving in to his enemy. *(Sometimes God allows things to happen to His people, but the wicked are always punished for their sin.)* (Unit 3, Part 1, Lesson 1)

Christ/Many Enemies—(Read **I Peter 2:21-24** aloud.) The enemies of Christ did many things to Him during His life. Christ showed love for His enemies. *(Follow the example of Christ and love your enemies.)*

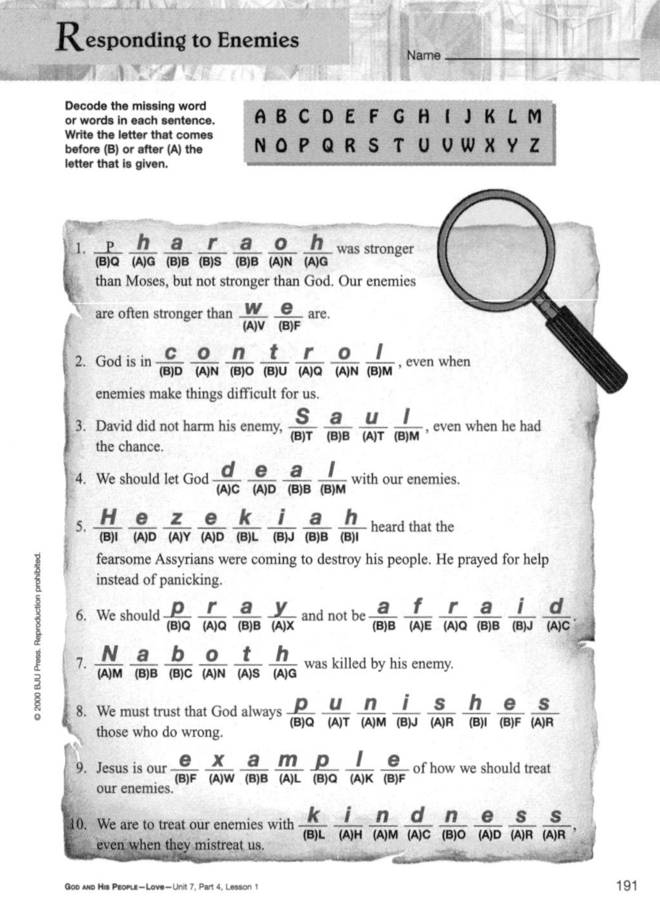

Responding to Enemies

Name ______________

Decode the missing word or words in each sentence. Write the letter that comes before (B) or after (A) the letter that is given.

A B C D E F G H I J K L M
N O P Q R S T U V W X Y Z

1. p h a r a o h [(B)Q (A)G (B)B (B)S (B)B (A)N (A)G] was stronger than Moses, but not stronger than God. Our enemies are often stronger than w e [(A)V (B)F] are.

2. God is in c o n t r o l [(B)D (A)N (B)O (B)U (A)Q (A)N (B)M], even when enemies make things difficult for us.

3. David did not harm his enemy, S a u l [(B)T (B)B (A)T (B)M], even when he had the chance.

4. We should let God d e a l [(A)C (A)D (B)B (B)M] with our enemies.

5. H e z e k i a h [(B)I (A)D (A)Y (A)D (B)L (B)J (B)B (B)I] heard that the fearsome Assyrians were coming to destroy his people. He prayed for help instead of panicking.

6. We should p r a y [(B)Q (A)Q (B)B (A)X] and not be a f r a i d [(B)B (A)E (A)Q (B)B (B)J (A)C].

7. N a b o t h [(A)M (B)B (B)C (A)N (A)S (A)G] was killed by his enemy.

8. We must trust that God always p u n i s h e s [(B)Q (A)T (A)M (B)J (A)R (B)I (B)F (A)R] those who do wrong.

9. Jesus is our e x a m p l e [(B)F (A)W (B)B (A)L (B)Q (A)K (B)F] of how we should treat our enemies.

10. We are to treat our enemies with k i n d n e s s [(B)L (A)H (A)M (A)C (B)O (A)D (A)R (A)R], even when they mistreat us.

God and His People—Love—Unit 7, Part 4, Lesson 1 191

Worktext page 191

Recall facts about how to respond to our enemies.

Lesson 2

Memory Verses—Matthew 5:43-44

Practice the memory verses. Locate **Matthew 5:43-44**, directing the students to read silently and then to read in a quiet whisper.

➤ **What does *persecute* mean?** *(to be mean to, to annoy)*

Encourage the students to avoid persecuting brothers and sisters as well as classmates. Guide the students in reading the verses responsively two times, alternating parts.

Hymn: "O to Be Like Thee!"

Sing the hymn (Worktext pages 282-83). Play the recording and lead in singing the fourth verse together. Divide the students into four groups, allowing each group to sing a verse of the hymn with all groups joining together to sing the chorus each time.

Introducing the Bible Study

Discuss daily devotions. Explain to the students that if they desire to know a friend better, they want to spend time with that friend. The same is true with a Christian developing a relationship with Christ. If a Christian is to be more like Christ, he needs to spend time with Christ to get to understand and know Him.

➤ **How can Christians spend time with Christ?** *(through prayer and Bible reading)*

Bible Study

Read some of the following reviews about Bible characters previously studied. Tell the students to listen to find out how these people tried to live their lives to please the Lord. These people were not perfect, but they demonstrated traits in their lives that Christians can follow as examples.

Christlikeness Demonstrated

Moses—*Patient;* Moses went before Pharaoh to ask for the release of God's people, the Israelites. Moses waited through ten plagues including the death of the firstborn in each of the Egyptian homes before the Israelites were released. Once out of Egypt, the Israelites complained and disobeyed God, but Moses was patient with the people. *(Patience is a trait that we can learn from the life of Moses.)* (Unit 1, Part 1, Lesson 2)

Rahab—*Willing to be used;* Although Rahab was a Canaanite, she hid the spies in her home. Rahab trusted the Lord as her Savior. She and her family were saved when Jericho was destroyed. God used a Canaanite to accomplish His purpose. *(Christians need to be ready to be used for whatever purposes God may have for them.)* (Unit 1, Part 4, Lesson 2)

David—*Confident;* David was confident that God would deliver him when he fought Goliath. Throughout his life, David was confident of the Lord's protection during danger. *(Christians must be confident that God will protect them.)* (Unit 2, Part 1, Lesson 1)

Hezekiah—*Trusting;* Hezekiah prayed to the Lord when his enemy was going to attack. *(Christians must trust God in all situations.)* (Unit 2, Part 4, Lesson 1)

Elisha—*Compassionate;* Elisha helped fellow believers in good times and in bad times. Elisha helped a believer when a borrowed ax fell into the water. He helped a poor widow and her two sons when they needed money to pay a debt. When others were in need, Elisha was there to help them and to encourage them to follow the Lord. *(Christians are to encourage others to do what is right, especially if they are heading a direction that is wrong.)* (Unit 3, Part 3, Lesson 2)

Joseph—*Humble;* God chose Joseph, a carpenter, to be the earthly father of Jesus. God wanted to use Joseph, and because Joseph was willing, God received the glory for the miracle that took place at the birth of Christ. *(Christians are to be humble, not wanting others' attention or needing praise from others in order to do what is right.)* (Unit 4, Part 1, Lesson 1)

Mary—*Obedient;* In spite of her limited knowledge and youth, Mary was willing to be used by God to bear His Son. Though she did not understand the miracle of this special birth, Mary was obedient to God. *(God wants Christians to be obedient and to trust Him in all circumstances of life.)* (Unit 4, Part 1, Lesson 2)

Paul—*Servant;* God had a plan for Paul and prepared him for the plan. God used Paul to travel to many places and to preach the gospel. Paul said many times that he wanted others to see Christ and that he was willing to die for Christ. *(God may not call you to die for Him, but He does want you to be willing to be a servant.)* (Unit 6, Part 4, Lessons 1-4)

➤ **Who are some other Bible characters that tried to do their best for the Lord?** *(Possible answers include Peter, James, John, Matthew, and Timothy.)*

➤ **What is another trait, not part of the Bible Study, that you could work on to be more like Christ?** *(Possible answers include love, generosity, and obedience.)*

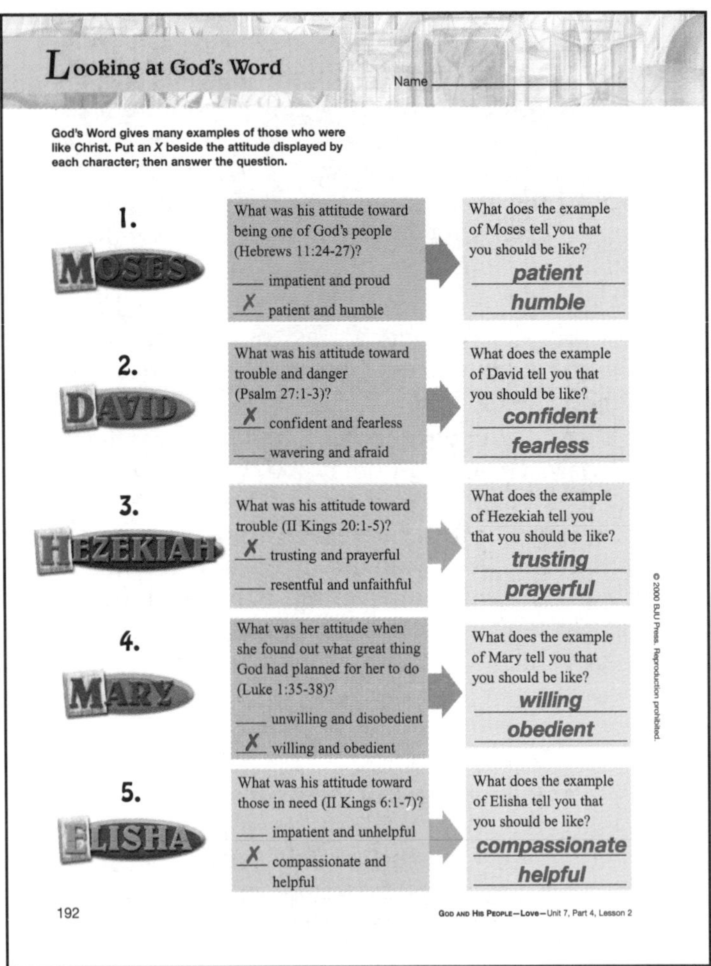

Looking at God's Word

Name ____________

God's Word gives many examples of those who were like Christ. Put an *X* beside the attitude displayed by each character; then answer the question.

1. MOSES	What was his attitude toward being one of God's people (Hebrews 11:24-27)? ___ impatient and proud _X_ patient and humble	What does the example of Moses tell you that you should be like? patient humble
2. DAVID	What was his attitude toward trouble and danger (Psalm 27:1-3)? _X_ confident and fearless ___ wavering and afraid	What does the example of David tell you that you should be like? confident fearless
3. HEZEKIAH	What was his attitude toward trouble (II Kings 20:1-5)? _X_ trusting and prayerful ___ resentful and unfaithful	What does the example of Hezekiah tell you that you should be like? trusting prayerful
4. MARY	What was her attitude when she found out what great thing God had planned for her to do (Luke 1:35-38)? ___ unwilling and disobedient _X_ willing and obedient	What does the example of Mary tell you that you should be like? willing obedient
5. ELISHA	What was his attitude toward those in need (II Kings 6:1-7)? ___ impatient and unhelpful _X_ compassionate and helpful	What does the example of Elisha tell you that you should be like? compassionate helpful

192 God and His People—Love—Unit 7, Part 4, Lesson 2

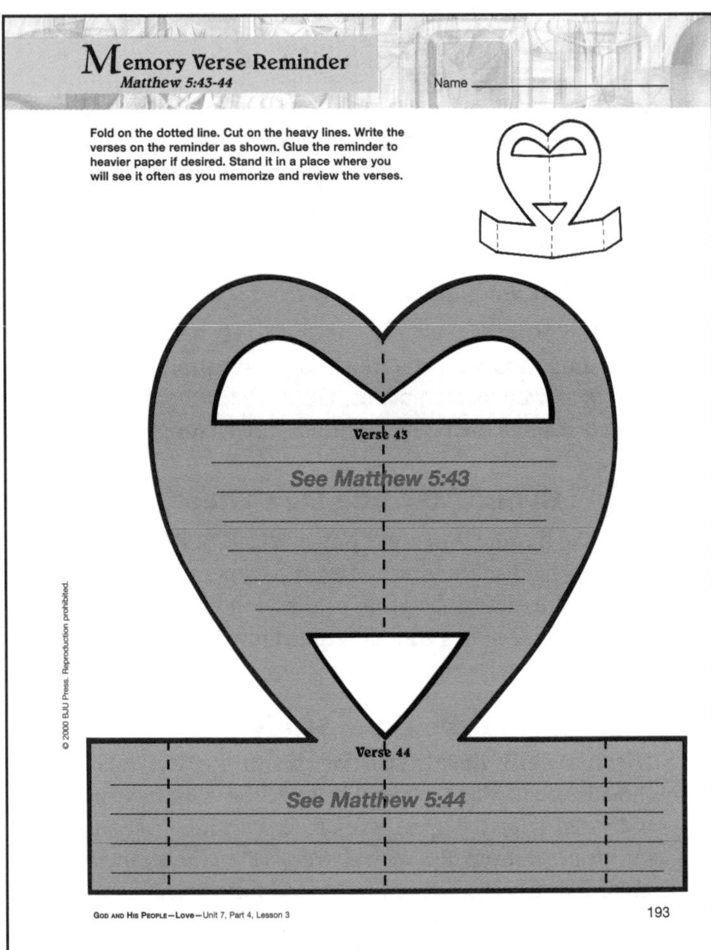

Memory Verse Reminder
Matthew 5:43-44

Name ____________

Fold on the dotted line. Cut on the heavy lines. Write the verses on the reminder as shown. Glue the reminder to heavier paper if desired. Stand it in a place where you will see it often as you memorize and review the verses.

God and His People—Love—Unit 7, Part 4, Lesson 3 193

Worktext page 192

Apply Scripture to your life.

Lesson 3

Materials

- Copy of *With Daring Faith* for the teacher
- A telegram (optional)
- Pictures of a caterpillar and a butterfly or moth (optional)

Memory Verses—Matthew 5:43-44

Practice the memory verses. Locate **Matthew 5:43-44** and select a student to read the verses aloud. Divide the students into four groups to play a game. Give each group a sheet of paper, telling the first person in each group to write the first word of the memory passage and to pass the paper to the second person to write the second word, and so on until the entire passage has been written. Direct a student in each group to read his group's paper aloud to check for accuracy.

Worktext pages 193-94

Make a memory verse reminder.

Hymn: "O to Be Like Thee!"

Sing the hymn (Worktext pages 282-83). Tell the students to think about the words of the hymn, realizing that becoming more like Christ is a daily process. Play the recording and lead in singing the hymn together.

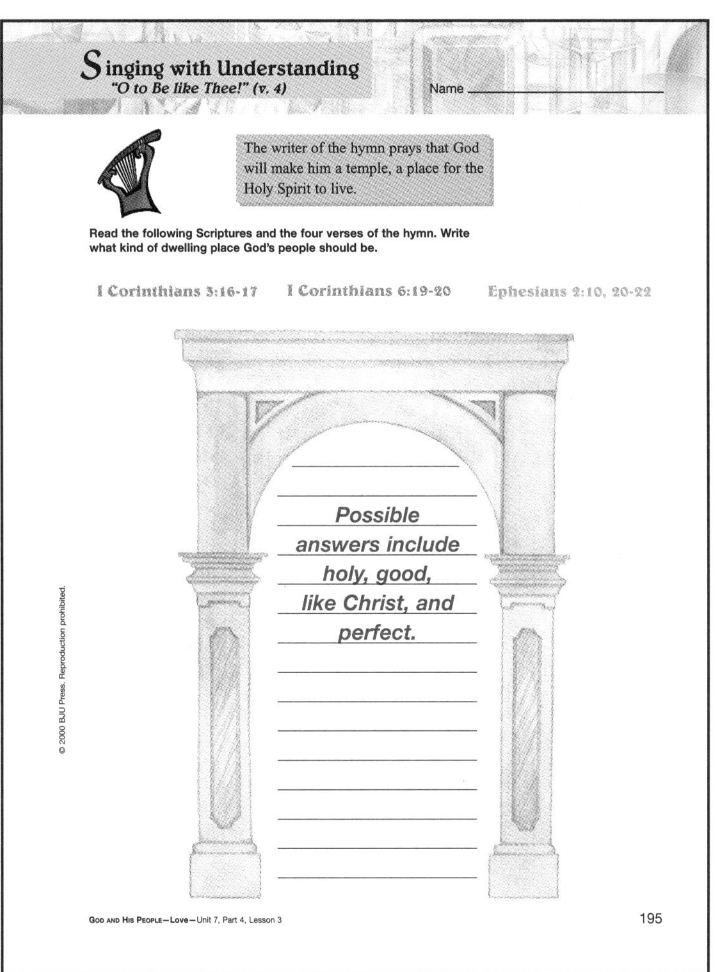

Singing with Understanding
"O to Be like Thee!" (v. 4)

Name ____________________

The writer of the hymn prays that God will make him a temple, a place for the Holy Spirit to live.

Read the following Scriptures and the four verses of the hymn. Write what kind of dwelling place God's people should be.

I Corinthians 3:16-17 | I Corinthians 6:19-20 | Ephesians 2:10, 20-22

Possible answers include holy, good, like Christ, and perfect.

© 2000 BJU Press. Reproduction prohibited.

GOD AND HIS PEOPLE—Love—Unit 7, Part 4, Lesson 3 195

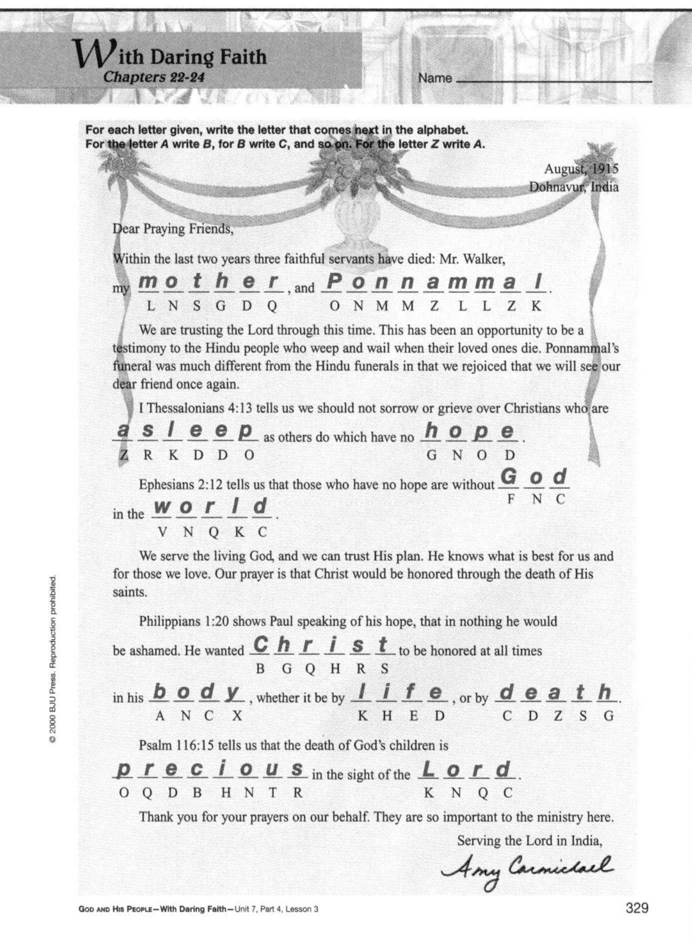

With Daring Faith
Chapters 22-24

Name ____________________

For each letter given, write the letter that comes next in the alphabet. For the letter *A* write *B*, for *B* write *C*, and so on. For the letter *Z* write *A*.

August, 1915
Dohnavur, India

Dear Praying Friends,

Within the last two years three faithful servants have died: Mr. Walker, my *mother* (L N S G D Q), and *Ponnammal* (O N M M Z L L Z K).

We are trusting the Lord through this time. This has been an opportunity to be a testimony to the Hindu people who weep and wail when their loved ones die. Ponnammal's funeral was much different from the Hindu funerals in that we rejoiced that we will see our dear friend once again.

I Thessalonians 4:13 tells us we should not sorrow or grieve over Christians who are *asleep* (Z R K D D O) as others do which have no *hope* (G N O D).

Ephesians 2:12 tells us that those who have no hope are without *God* (F N C) in the *world* (V N Q K C).

We serve the living God, and we can trust His plan. He knows what is best for us and for those we love. Our prayer is that Christ would be honored through the death of His saints.

Philippians 1:20 shows Paul speaking of his hope, that in nothing he would be ashamed. He wanted *Christ* (B G Q H R S) to be honored at all times in his *body* (A N C X), whether it be by *life* (K H E D), or by *death* (C D Z S G).

Psalm 116:15 tells us that the death of God's children is *precious* (O Q D B H N T R) in the sight of the *Lord* (K N Q C).

Thank you for your prayers on our behalf. They are so important to the ministry here.

Serving the Lord in India,
Amy Carmichael

© 2000 BJU Press. Reproduction prohibited.

GOD AND HIS PEOPLE—With Daring Faith—Unit 7, Part 4, Lesson 3 329

Worktext page 195

Singing with understanding, verse 4.

Introducing the Missionary Biography

Discuss telegrams. Show the telegram to the students.

➤ **What is this, and why is it used?** *(a telegram; used to send a short message quickly at a distance)*

➤ **Have you or any family members ever received a telegram? If so, what was the important message?** Point out that telegrams are not used as often today as they were long ago before telephones and computers.

Missionary Biography: *With Daring Faith*

Read Chapter 22. Tell the students to listen to find out why Amy got two telegrams. *(The first telegram told her that Mr. Walker was sick, and the second told her that he had died.)*

➤ **Why did those working at Dohnavur not receive pay?** *(There was no money to pay the workers. The workers did their jobs out of love for the Lord and the people.)*

➤ **What attitude did Amy want to show when a believer died?** *(the hope of the believer even in death; When a Christian dies, the loved one is in heaven with Jesus and will be seen again.)*

Read Chapter 23.

➤ **What trick did Amy play on the children?** *(She pretended to be a bear in the bushes.)*

➤ **How did the Dohnavur family overcome the need for the workmen to work faster on their new building in the Grey Jungle?** *(All the children pitched in to help the workmen and to be a testimony that a Christian does his work well.)*

Read Chapter 24.

➤ **What happened to the little boys if their family did not want them?** *(They were wanted by drama companies, which were just as bad as the temples for the girls.)*

➤ **How did God answer the prayer of the Dohnavur families to save the rice crop?** *(God sent birds to eat the caterpillars so that the caterpillars would not eat the rice.)*

➤ **What did Amy begin praying for?** *(a hospital)*

Worktext Supplement page 329

Recall details about Chapters 22-24.

Science Connection (optional)

Discuss caterpillars. Show pictures of a caterpillar. Read the following information to the students:

> A caterpillar is the larva, the second stage in the life cycle of a butterfly or moth. While the insect is in this larva stage, it continues to grow. As it grows, its skin becomes tight and eventually splits, causing the caterpillar to crawl out and become larger, wearing its new soft "skin." The process is repeated many times as the caterpillar grows. To have the energy to do all of this changing, the caterpillar must eat almost constantly. It prefers to eat the tender leaves and stems of plants. If there are many caterpillars in an area, whole fields can become stripped of vegetation, leaving only small pieces of stems where plants had been. Once the caterpillar has grown big enough and stored enough nutrients, it will transform into a butterfly or moth. (Show a picture of a butterfly or moth.)

Lesson 4

Materials

- Copy of *With Daring Faith* for the teacher

Hymn: "O to Be Like Thee!"

Sing the hymn (Worktext pages 282-83). Play the recording and lead in singing the hymn together. (*Note:* Arrange to sing the hymn for an audience—another class, parents, or nursing home residents [if desired]).

Memory Verses—Matthew 5:43-44

Practice the memory verses. Locate **Matthew 5:43-44** and direct the students to read silently. Choose volunteers to stand and say the verses from memory. Give help as needed.

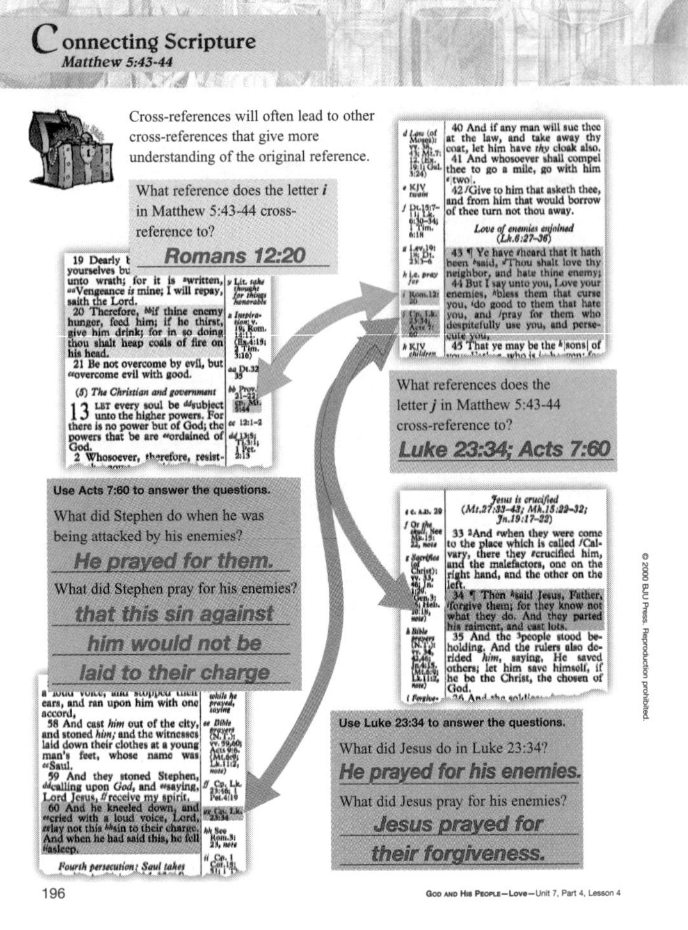

Connecting Scripture
Matthew 5:43-44

Cross-references will often lead to other cross-references that give more understanding of the original reference.

What reference does the letter *i* in Matthew 5:43-44 cross-reference to?
Romans 12:20

What references does the letter *j* in Matthew 5:43-44 cross-reference to?
Luke 23:34; Acts 7:60

Use Acts 7:60 to answer the questions.
What did Stephen do when he was being attacked by his enemies?
He prayed for them.
What did Stephen pray for his enemies?
that this sin against him would not be laid to their charge

Use Luke 23:34 to answer the questions.
What did Jesus do in Luke 23:34?
He prayed for his enemies.
What did Jesus pray for his enemies?
Jesus prayed for their forgiveness.

196 God and His People—Love—Unit 7, Part 4, Lesson 4

© 2000 BJU Press. Reproduction prohibited.

Bible Study Skills, Worktext page 196

Use cross-references.

TimeLine

Place *Amy Carmichael* on the TimeLine. Choose a student to attach the picture of *Amy Carmichael* on the TimeLine at 1867-1951. Guide the students in gluing the picture of Miss Carmichael onto their individual TimeLines.

Hero of the Faith (optional)

Read the following story, based on the life of Amy Carmichael. (*Note:* If you have been reading *With Daring Faith*, the biography of Amy Carmichael's life, you will want to finish reading the book in this lesson instead of reading aloud the following summary.)

Amy Carmichael

In Northern Ireland on December 16, 1867, David and Catherine Carmichael welcomed their first child into the world and named her Amy. As a child, Amy was known for her playful ways. Sometimes, even in her best clothes, she would run to the shore to play and return covered in sea spray. Amy liked to eat fruit, but she didn't always take time to spit out the seeds. Attempting to stop Amy from swallowing plum stones, or seeds, one lady told Amy that a plum tree would grow in her head for every plum stone she swallowed. Amy decided that she would like twelve trees in her head, so she quickly found and swallowed twelve plums—stones and all. When Amy was scolded, she responded, "If only you knew how much naughtier I could be, you wouldn't think I'm naughty at all."

Amy wanted something; she wanted it so badly that every night she prayed, "God, please change my brown eyes to blue; I want my eyes to be the color of the sky. Please give me blue eyes." When Amy awoke, she would rush to the mirror to see her new blue eyes. Her reflection would reveal the same old brown eyes—filled with sadness at what she thought was unanswered prayer.

Amy's mother told her, "God *does* hear us when we pray, Amy. He *does* answer us; His answer this time was *no.* God knows what is best."

Later in her life as a missionary to India, Amy would need her brown eyes when she disguised herself as one of the natives. Blue eyes would have given her away. God gave her the eyes she needed with His perfect plan in mind.

As she grew, Amy's love for others also grew. She helped the poor and took care of the sick whenever she could. She was also concerned about their salvation. Amy knew that the Lord wanted her to become a missionary. She desired to go tell people what Christ had done for them.

In 1892, at the age of twenty-five, Amy Carmichael packed for China. She was ready to leave when her doctors told her, "You are too weak to go to China. You'll have to stay here." Amy Carmichael knew better; she knew that God wanted her to go to some foreign land as a missionary.

A year later, Miss Carmichael was able to go to Japan. She learned the Japanese language right away so that she would be able to tell the Japanese people the gospel. Because of poor health, Amy Carmichael stayed in Japan only a year. Her friends said, "Go back to England. You are too weak to be a missionary." Miss Carmichael answered, "Yes, *I* may be too weak, but my *God* is not." She knew that God would provide a way for her to continue her mission work.

In 1895 Amy Carmichael traveled to India—her home for the rest of her life. Her first job was to learn the language. Then she changed the way she dressed so that she would blend in with the people. She colored her skin with coffee to make it dark like that of the natives. She prayed, "Lord, *now* I know why you gave me brown eyes. I understand your plan for me. Thank you for my brown eyes."

Amy Carmichael became known as the "Defender of Children." She saved many, many children from terrible futures—being sold to the temple, being given to passersby to use however they wanted. Miss Carmichael discovered these horrors and began to raise the money so that she herself could buy the children and give them their freedom. In the first two years, *Missie Amma,* meaning "mother," rescued seventy children, many of whom stayed in Miss Carmichael's family. Before her death, Amy Carmichael had kept one thousand children in her home.

Amy Carmichael spent most of the last twenty years of her life too weak to leave her bed. She had prayed often, "Lord, please don't let me stay when it's time for me to go. Please just take me." She wanted either to work for the Lord or to be with Him. In God's perfect plan, He kept her here on earth to write many books so that today we can read about her life—both her joys and her sorrows.

Amy Carmichael gave up everything she had to become a missionary. She knew she was not very healthy, but that did not keep her from going to India. She also knew that she would have to leave her family behind, but that, too, did not keep her from going. The choices she made in her life teach us how important it is to do what God wants us to do, no matter the cost.

➤ **As a child, what did Amy pray for every night?** *(for blue eyes)*

Amy Carmichael
(1867-1951)

Name ______________________

There are many ways to show love for others. Have you ever prayed for those who are sick? Has your family sent food and clothing to those in need? Sometimes you can share God's Word to encourage other Christians. Love gives of oneself to help others.

Even as a child, Amy Carmichael learned compassion at home. Amy joined her parents in unselfishly giving to others. Amy also cared for the spiritual needs of others and willingly shared the gospel of Christ. She knew God wanted her to be a missionary. Her first missionary assignment was to Japan. However, she was able to stay only a year because of health problems.

Later, she went to India, where she served God for over fifty years. She quickly learned the language and grew to love the people. In India she discovered why God allowed her to have brown eyes, and not the blue eyes she had prayed for as a child. The dark eyes and native clothing made it easier for Amy to work among the people of India.

Amy soon noticed the suffering of many children in India; she saw parents selling children to the temples or giving children away. Amy raised money and began to rescue the children of India. Through her determination, boldness, and faith in God, Amy established a mission to teach and to care for the children. Over and over she saw the faithfulness of God as lives were changed for eternity.

In her last twenty years, Amy was unable to leave her bed. Her desire was that in her physical pain she might help others. She wrote many books during this time to encourage and to teach others. She continued to pray, and God continued to use Amy Carmichael to show the power of the living God.

Answer the questions.

What did Amy pray for as a child? *blue eyes*

Did Amy get what she asked for? *no*

Did God answer her prayers? *yes*

What are the three ways God answers prayer? *yes; no; wait*

Fill in the prayer list. Remember to pray each day. You may want to send a note to tell each person that you are praying for him or her.

Prayer List

The person I am praying for: ______________________

How I can help: ______________________

God and His People—Heroes of the Faith—Unit 7, Part 4, Lesson 4 307

With Daring Faith
Chapters 25-26

Name ______________________

Color the spaces that have only one dot. Write the hidden word in the sentences.

Amy Carmichael was a *f a i t h f u l* servant of the Lord in India.

God is *f a i t h f u l* to those who answer His call (I Thessalonians 5:24).

330 God and His People—With Daring Faith—Unit 7, Part 4, Lesson 4

➤ **As an adult, why did Amy thank God for giving her brown eyes?** *(She could blend in better in India and therefore present the gospel more freely there.)*

➤ **Are you thankful for the way God made you? Are you serving Him with your life?**

Worktext Supplement page 307

Recall facts about Hero of the Faith, Amy Carmichael. (*Note:* If you are reading the missionary biography, this page does not need to be completed.)

Missionary Biography: *With Daring Faith*

Read Chapters 25 and 26. Direct the students to listen to find out what Amy wished she could do. *(meet Jambulingam and tell him about Jesus)*

➤ **What did Amy get Red Tiger (Jambulingam) to promise her?** *(that he would use his gun only to protect his life)*

➤ **Did Red Tiger (Jambulingam) keep his promise?** *(yes)*

➤ **Why did Amy not think she should ask Godfrey and Murray to stay and work in India?** *(because she believed God had called them to China)*

➤ **When telling a stranger that Dohnavur was paid for and owed no money, what did the man and Amy say?** *(God does the impossible.)*

➤ **Why did Amy Carmichael go to Japan and then India?** *(because of her love for God and those who did not know Him)*

Read the epilogue. Tell the students that an *epilogue* is a summary. This epilogue summarizes the life of Amy Carmichael.

➤ **Why do you think Matthew 25:21 was read at Amy Carmichael's funeral?** *(Accept any answer; then read aloud* **Matthew 25:21.***)* Read aloud the conclusion of the book.

➤ **What request did Amy make that she later surrendered to whatever God wanted to do with her life?** *(She had asked that God would take her right away when she was unable to do His work anymore.)*

➤ **What was Amy able to do while confined to bed for twenty years?** *(She wrote many books and prayed for the work at Dohnavur.)*

➤ **Whom did Amy plan to take over the work at Dohnavur after her death?** *(Arulai, Godfrey, Murray, and Dr. Powell)*

➤ **Is that what happened? Explain.** *(No. God raised up others to help.)*

Worktext Supplement page 330

Apply the Bible to everyday life.

Going Beyond

Materials

- Travel brochure
- Books or encyclopedias about India

Enrichment

Make a travel brochure for India. Display a travel brochure, explaining that it was designed to make someone want to visit this particular place. Direct the students to make a travel brochure about India. Remind them to include information about the climate, the people, and interesting places to visit. Display the completed travel brochures.

Unit Review

Materials

- Copy of Supplement pages S61-S62, "Unit 7 Review," for each student

Guide a review of Unit 7. Review the people and events in preparation for the Unit 7 Test (optional).

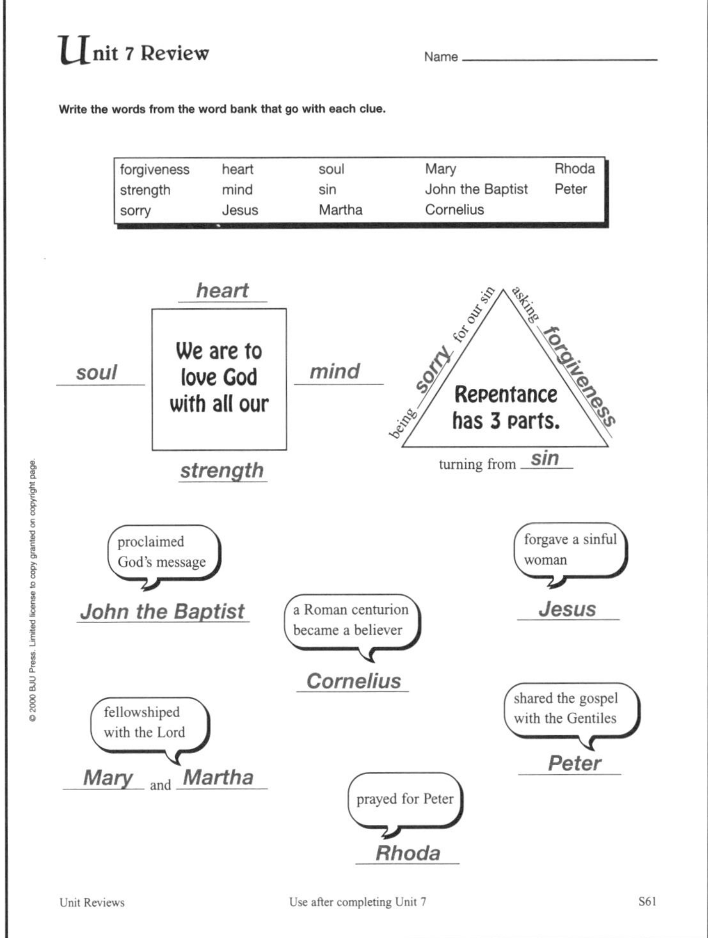

Unit 7 Review

Name ______________

Write the words from the word bank that go with each clue.

forgiveness	heart	soul	Mary	Rhoda
strength	mind	sin	John the Baptist	Peter
sorry	Jesus	Martha	Cornelius	

We are to love God with all our: *heart*, *soul*, *mind*, *strength*

Repentance has 3 parts.: being *sorry* for our sin; asking *forgiveness*; turning from *sin*

proclaimed God's message: *John the Baptist*

a Roman centurion became a believer: *Cornelius*

forgave a sinful woman: *Jesus*

fellowshiped with the Lord: *Mary* and *Martha*

shared the gospel with the Gentiles: *Peter*

prayed for Peter: *Rhoda*

Unit Reviews | Use after completing Unit 7 | S61

Unit 7 Review (continued)

Name ______________

Color the heart red if it shows a loving heart.

(r) kind	angry	(r) forgiving
bitter	(r) compassionate	(r) encouraging
quarreling	full of wrath	gossiping

Match the letter of the principle that the situation illustrates.

A. Loving God	B. Loving the believer
C. Loving the unsaved	D. Loving your enemies

A 1. Ryan sang his best during chapel even though the other boys weren't singing.

C 2. Michael told his cousin about Jesus at their summer family reunion.

B 3. Sasha prayed for her pastor's mother who was hurt in a car accident.

C 4. Zach helped his dad pass out church invitations in a nearby neighborhood.

D 5. Sam prayed for his next-door neighbor Keith when his dog died, even though Keith bullied Sam every time he played outside.

B 6. Ellen made cookies for an elderly lady in her church who wasn't well.

S62 | Use after completing Unit 7 | God and His People

Easter: Victory over Death

Overview

Preparing the Teacher

When Christ gave up His spirit on the cross, the veil of the temple was torn in two. The Word—Christ—became flesh and through the rending of His flesh—Christ's death—we have direct access to the throne of God. We have the privilege of coming into God's presence, of worshiping Him. We as believers become members of the priesthood.

We have access to the presence of God the Father through the work of His Son Jesus Christ at Calvary. Think on it! Meditate on this great truth. Praise God for this great transaction. Take a few minutes to read and reflect on **Hebrews 10:19-22.**

Meditate on these words from the hymn "The Unveiled Christ" by N. B. Herrell:

Once our blessed Christ of beauty
  Was veiled off from human view;
But through suff'ring, death, and sorrow
  He has rent the veil in two.
O behold the Man of Sorrows,
  O behold Him in plain view;
Lo! He is the mighty Conq'ror,
  Since He rent the veil in two.

Preparing the Lessons

Part 1 Lesson 1 Materials—two small pieces of magnetic tape for each student

Part 2 Going Beyond Materials—graph paper for each student

Unit 8 Easter: Victory over Death						**Hymn: "It Is Finished"**
Part	Lesson number	Lesson pages	Worktext pages	Supplement pages	Bible Account	Application
Part 1: **The Passover Week**	1	265	197-200		Plotting and Feasting (Matthew 26:1-5, 14-30; Luke 22:1-23)	
	2	268	201-2		Betrayed and Arrested (Matthew 26:30-56; Luke 22:39-53)	
	3	269	203-4		Falsely Accused and Denied (Matthew 26:57–27:5; John 18:12-40)	
	4	272	205-6			"More Important than a Race"
Part 2: **Suffering Savior! Risen Lord!**	1	275	207-8		God's Begotten Son (Matthew 27:27-56; Luke 23:26-49; John 19:16-37)	
	2	277	209-10		Thine Be the Glory! (Matthew 27:57–28:15; John 19:38–20:18)	
	3	279	211-12			"A Lesson of the Dogwood"
	4	281	213-14			**Hero of the Faith:** Charles Albert Tindley

Connections	Memory Verses and Principles	Bible Doctrines	Skills/Applications
	Isaiah 53:3-4 *Jesus was rejected by man.*	**The Doctrine of God** **Existence of God:** God is eternal (Ps. 90:2). God is all-knowing (omniscient) (Ps. 94:11). God is love (John 3:16). **The Doctrine of Salvation** **Provision of God:** Christ died for man (atonement) (I Cor. 15:3). Christ arose from the dead (resurrection) (I Cor. 15:3-8).	**Foundational:** • Realize that Christ died for the sins of all men • Understand that Jesus was rejected by men • Know that Christ rose from the dead **Practical:** • Recall facts and details • Locate information in Scripture • Identify the correct Bible character • Write captions for pictures • Read a time line • Use a concordance **Personal:** • Realize that Christ died for my sins. • Develop a Bible reading habit • Apply Bible knowledge to everyday life
TimeLine: The Crucifixion	Isaiah 53:5-6 *Jesus paid the penalty for the sins of the world.*		
Science			
TimeLine: Charles Albert Tindley			

Preparing the Unit 8 Bulletin Board

Cover the bulletin board with pale yellow and border it with purple. Mount a large brown paper cross on the left and caption it "Suffering Savior." Place a bare tree branch on the right with the caption "Risen Lord!" under it as shown. Allow students to cover it with dogwood blossoms that they have made. (*Note:* The dogwood blossom consists of four white bracts [modified leaves] with a cluster of yellow flowers in the center.)

To make dogwood blossoms:

Start with four bracts cut from thin white paper (e.g., origami paper, tissue paper).
Shade around the indentation in the broad end of each bract with red.
Pleat each bract at the narrow end.
Glue or staple the four bracts together in the center.
Glue a cluster of yellow dots (made with a hole puncher) in the center of each grouping of bracts.

The Passover Week

Unit 8, Part 1

Preview

Doctrines

- God is love (John 3:16)—Lesson 1
- God is all-knowing (omniscient) (Psalm 94:11)—Lesson 2
- God is eternal (Psalm 90:2)—Lesson 3

Skills and Applications

- Learn Isaiah 53:3-4
- Read a map
- Recall facts and details
- Identify the correct Bible characters
- Locate information in Scripture
- Understand that Jesus was rejected by men
- Develop a Bible reading habit
- Apply Bible knowledge to everyday life

Lesson 1

Materials

- Song: "The Bible Reading Habit"
- Two small pieces of magnetic tape for each student
- Unit 8 Bookmark for each student
- Highlighter for each student (optional)

Memory Verses—Isaiah 53:3-4

Principle: Jesus was rejected by man. Locate **Isaiah 53:3-4,** reading the verses aloud as the students read silently. Explain that in Isaiah 53 the prophet Isaiah foretells details of Christ's death.

➤ **How is the Lord described?** *(despised, hated, rejected, refused, grieved, afflicted, sorrowed)*

➤ Jesus was "a man of sorrows." **What does this phrase mean?** *(During His life on earth, Christ was observed by others to be a man who had great sorrow or trouble.)*

➤ **Why did men hide their faces from Christ on the cross?** *(His physical appearance was terrible to look upon.)*

➤ **How do we know that Jesus wasn't thought to be important?** *(Jesus was not esteemed by man.)*

Direct the students to highlight the verses in their Bibles (optional). Give each student a Unit 8 Bookmark to mark the location of the verses. Direct attention to the illustration of the lamb and the cross as reminders that Christ's death on the cross paid the final sacrifice for our sins. Guide the students in attaching a piece of magnetic tape to both ends of the Unit 8 Bookmark and in placing it over the page.

Bible Study Skills, Worktext pages 197-98

Develop a Bible reading habit. Read the top part of page 197 to the students. Select students to read aloud the Bible reading guidelines, emphasizing that God's Word helps Christians to grow spiritually. Explain the four-week Bible reading activity on page 198. Lead in singing the song "The Bible Reading Habit" from Worktext page 271.

Hymn: "It Is Finished"

Teach the first verse (Worktext page 284). Play the recording of the first verse.

➤ **What word tells who took our shame upon Himself on the cross?** *(Savior)*

➤ **Why do you think the hymn writer was touched with sorrow?** *(because Jesus died for him)*

Explain that *stead* means "place." Select a student to read the first verse aloud.

➤ **How was God's plan for the sins of men accomplished?** *(through the death of Jesus Christ on the cross)*

Lead in singing the first verse together with the recording.

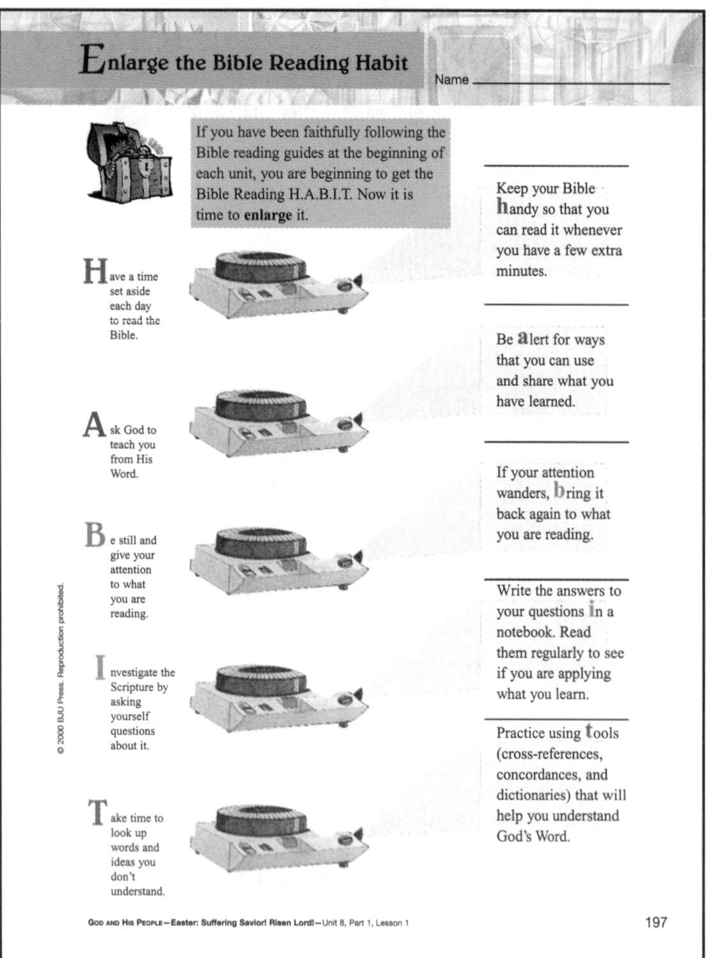

Enlarge the Bible Reading Habit

Name ______________

If you have been faithfully following the Bible reading guides at the beginning of each unit, you are beginning to get the Bible Reading H.A.B.I.T. Now it is time to **enlarge** it.

Have a time set aside each day to read the Bible.

Keep your Bible **h**andy so that you can read it whenever you have a few extra minutes.

Ask God to teach you from His Word.

Be **a**lert for ways that you can use and share what you have learned.

Be still and give your attention to what you are reading.

If your attention wanders, **b**ring it back again to what you are reading.

Investigate the Scripture by asking yourself questions about it.

Write the answers to your questions **i**n a notebook. Read them regularly to see if you are applying what you learn.

Take time to look up words and ideas you don't understand.

Practice using **t**ools (cross-references, concordances, and dictionaries) that will help you understand God's Word.

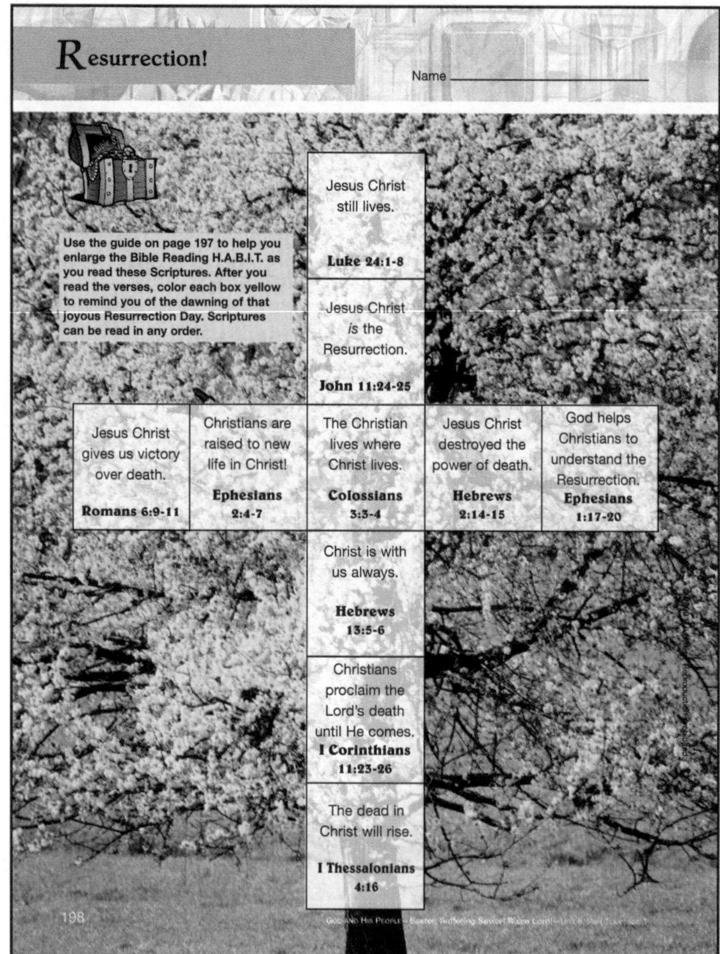

Resurrection!

Name ______________

Use the guide on page 197 to help you enlarge the Bible Reading H.A.B.I.T. as you read these Scriptures. After you read the verses, color each box yellow to remind you of the dawning of that joyous Resurrection Day. Scriptures can be read in any order.

Jesus Christ still lives. **Luke 24:1-8**

Jesus Christ *is* the Resurrection. **John 11:24-25**

Jesus Christ gives us victory over death. **Romans 6:9-11**

Christians are raised to new life in Christ! **Ephesians 2:4-7**

The Christian lives where Christ lives. **Colossians 3:3-4**

Jesus Christ destroyed the power of death. **Hebrews 2:14-15**

God helps Christians to understand the Resurrection. **Ephesians 1:17-20**

Christ is with us always. **Hebrews 13:5-6**

Christians proclaim the Lord's death until He comes. **I Corinthians 11:23-26**

The dead in Christ will rise. **I Thessalonians 4:16**

Worktext page 199

Singing with understanding, verse 1.

Background Information

Animosity of the Chief Priests, Scribes, and Elders—*Jesus was a threat to the power of the chief priests, scribes, and elders. Other reasons they did not like Jesus were*

- *Jesus rebuked them publicly in front of a multitude of people (Matthew 23:13).*
- *Jesus warned the people about the religious leaders' hypocrisy (Mark 12:38-40).*

Thirty Pieces of Silver—*The amount of money paid for recovering a slave from his owner was thirty pieces of silver. Exodus 21:32 tells us that this was the sum paid for a slave who was accidentally gored to death by an ox. Zechariah prophesied this transaction showing how lightly the Lord was thought of (Zechariah 11:12-13).*

The Cup—*In ancient times, cups were made of pottery or metal, various shapes and sizes, some having handles and some with none. A cup could denote blessing or punishment in the Old Testament, and fellowship with Christ or suffering in the New Testament.*

The Passover and the Lord's Supper—*The Passover was a special day that was set aside to recall the Israelites' delivery from slavery in Egypt. An observance of this feast took place the night before the Crucifixion. As part of the Passover observance, Christ ate a meal with His disciples. This has been called the Last Supper. At this meal Christ established what has become known as the Lord's Supper, a memorial of the death of Christ for the deliverance from sin and a looking forward to His coming back to earth again.*

The Passover Hymn—*A hymn was sung at the Last Supper; then the disciples went out into the Mount of Olives. At the Passover the Jews traditionally sang Psalms 114-118 antiphonally, meaning that the leader sang the lines and the others responded with "Hallelujah."*

Introducing the Bible Account

Discuss feasts.

➤ **What is a *feast?*** *(a large meal for many people)*

➤ **On what occasions do families gather for a feast?** *(Possible answers include Thanksgiving, Christmas, and reunions.)*

Bible Account

Read the following Bible account or retell Matthew 26:1-5, 14-30 and Luke 22:1-23 in your own words.

Plotting and Feasting

Two days before the Passover, Jesus told His disciples that He would be arrested and put to death. Meanwhile, the chief priests, the scribes, and the elders gathered together at the palace of Caiaphas, the high priest, to adopt a plan for arresting Jesus. To avoid a dis-

Singing with Understanding
"It Is Finished" (v. 1)

Name ______

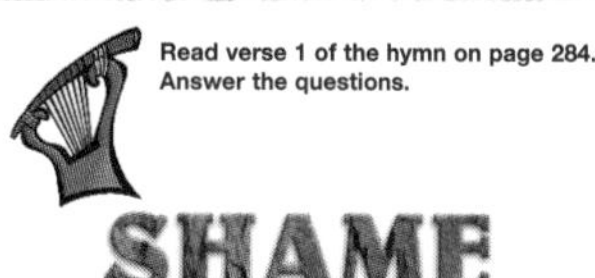

Read verse 1 of the hymn on page 284. Answer the questions.

SHAME

Painful feeling

Knowing that one has done something dishonorable, disgraceful, or wrong

Who deserves to feel shame for the sins that we have committed?

We do.

Who did not deserve to feel shame because He never sinned?

Jesus

STEAD

The place of another

Substitution for another

Who deserves to be punished for the sins that we have committed?

We do.

Who was punished in the place of sinners?

Jesus

FINISHED

Over; ended

Perfectly complete

Who is unable to complete a perfect work of salvation from sin?

We are.

Who was able to complete a perfect work of salvation for all mankind?

Jesus

Why did Jesus Christ suffer and die for sinners though He had no sin and deserved no punishment?

He loves us.

GOD AND HIS PEOPLE—Easter: Suffering Savior! Risen Lord!—Unit 8, Part 1, Lesson 1 199

turbance among the people, the plan had to be carried out when the crowd had gone home. (Share the background information about the animosity of the chief priests, scribes, and elders.)

Judas Iscariot went to the chief priests and offered to point out Jesus to the arresting officers and to be a witness against Jesus when He was brought to trial. Judas asked what he would be given for performing this service for the chief priests. The chief priests agreed to pay Judas thirty pieces of silver. Judas began to look for a chance to betray Jesus. (Share the background information about thirty pieces of silver, optional.)

On the first day of the Passover week, Jesus told Peter and John, "Go and prepare us the passover, that we may eat." The Passover pointed back to the deliverance of the Israelites out of Egypt and forward to the coming of Christ as the sacrificial Lamb. The disciples asked Jesus where to go to prepare the feast. He told them to follow a man carrying a jar of water to a certain house in the city of Jerusalem. The men were directed to a large upper room, or guest room, where they prepared the Passover feast.

In the evening, as Jesus and His disciples were at the table eating, Jesus said, "One of you shall betray me." The disciples were greatly troubled and asked, "Lord, is it I?" Jesus knew Judas would betray Him and that great sorrow would come to Judas, for Jesus said, "It had been good for that man if he had not been born."

While Jesus and the disciples were eating, Jesus took the bread, prayed, and shared it with His disciples. Jesus used the bread to represent the death of His body. After giving thanks, Jesus shared the cup with His disciples. (Share background information about the cup, optional.) The wine represented the blood that Jesus would shed for man's sins. Following the singing of a hymn, Jesus and His disciples went out into the Mount of Olives to pray.

- ➤ **What were the religious leaders discussing at the home of Caiaphas, the high priest?** *(a plan for arresting Jesus)*
- ➤ **How would you describe Judas when he volunteered to point out Jesus to the arresting officers?** *(Possible answers include selfish, deceitful, dishonest, crafty, and evil.)*
- ➤ **What was the Passover?** *(a celebration pointing back to the deliverance of the Israelites out of Egypt and pointing forward to the coming of Christ as the sacrificial Lamb)* (Share background information about the Passover, optional.)
- ➤ **What special meaning did Jesus give to the eating of the bread and the drinking of the wine?** *(The bread represented the death of His body, and the wine represented His blood that would be shed for the sins of men.)*
- ➤ **What did Jesus and the disciples do after eating the Passover feast?** *(sang a hymn and went to the Mount of Olives to pray)* Share the background information about the Passover hymn (optional).
- ➤ **Why do Christians celebrate the Lord's Supper today?** *(as a reminder of Christ's death on the cross and a looking forward to the time when He comes again)*

New Meaning for a Special Meal
Matthew 26:14-30

Name ____________________

Complete the sentences. You may use your Bible.

The last and most important meaning of the meal was given by Jesus as He and His disciples ate the Passover feast together.

The Passover looked back to the time when God brought His people out of ***Egypt*** (Exodus 12:17).

The Passover looked ahead to the coming of Christ, the perfect ***Lamb*** of God (John 1:29).

He said that the bread represents His ***body***, which was given as a sacrifice for sin (Matthew 26:26).

He said that the cup represents His ***blood***, which was shed for the forgiveness of sins (Matthew 26:28).

Read I Corinthians 11:23-26.

Why is the Lord's Supper (the special meal that Jesus described) still celebrated?

Answers should include the purpose of remembering Christ's death until He comes again.

200 GOD AND HIS PEOPLE—Easter: Suffering Savior! Risen Lord!—Unit 8, Part 1, Lesson 1

The Garden of Gethsemane
Matthew 26:30-56; Luke 22:39-53
Bethphage
Bethany
Temple
Gethsemane
Mount of Olives
Kidron Valley
Jerusalem
The Mount of Olives is a ridge about a mile long that curves around the entire eastern side and part of the western side of Jerusalem. For part of that distance it is separated from the city by the Kidron Valley.
Several sites are claimed today as the place where Jesus prayed in agony on the night of His arrest, but the exact location has not been determined. Gethsemane means olive press, and there probably was such a machine for extracting oil from the olives that grew there. Today a number of ancient olive trees grow in the area, but they probably do not date from the time of Christ.
© 2000 BJU Press. Reproduction prohibited.
GOD AND HIS PEOPLE—Easter: Suffering Savior! Risen Lord!—Unit 8, Part 1, Lesson 2
201

Worktext page 200

Recall facts and details.

Lesson 2

Materials

- Chart 24, "The Garden of Gethsemane"

Hymn: "It Is Finished"

Sing the first verse. (Worktext page 284). Direct the students to read the words silently. Play the recording and lead in singing verse 1.

Background Information

The Kiss—*A kiss of greeting was a tradition in the Near East. Children of a Jewish family kissed older people on the beard or hand. A husband or father kissed his wife or children on the forehead. Usually a disciple did not kiss his master on the face as Judas chose to do.*

Introducing the Bible Account

Discuss gardens.

➤ **What are some different kinds of gardens?** *(Answers may vary. Elicit that there are rock gardens, vegetable gardens, flower gardens, small gardens, and large gardens).*

➤ **In what garden did man first live?** *(in the Garden of Eden)*

➤ **In what garden was sin first committed?** *(in the Garden of Eden)*

Explain that the Garden of Gethsemane was a garden of olive trees, with clusters of beautiful blooms in the spring. Jesus and His disciples went to the garden after the Passover meal. Direct the students' attention to Worktext page 201. Discuss the location of the Garden of Gethsemane and read the information together.

Bible Account

Read the following Bible account or read one of the following passages: Matthew 26:31-56 or Luke 22:39-53. Tell the students to listen to find out who the unwelcome visitor was in the garden while Jesus was praying. *(Judas)*

Betrayed and Arrested

As Jesus and His disciples entered into the Garden of Gethsemane, He instructed them to sit and wait while He took Peter and the sons of Zebedee, James and John, with Him to a private place to pray. Filled with sorrow, Jesus told the three disciples to watch while He went to be alone to pray. As He prayed, Jesus cried out to God saying, "O my Father, if it be possible, let this cup pass from me: nevertheless not as I will, but as thou wilt." Returning to the three disciples, Jesus found them asleep. Jesus was troubled that they could not stay awake to watch for just one hour. Two more times Jesus went to pray and returned to find His disciples sleeping.

While Jesus was still speaking, Judas arrived with a mob of Roman soldiers and temple guards carrying weapons. Judas had told the men that the man he would kiss was the person to be arrested. The moment Judas greeted Jesus and kissed Him, the men grabbed Jesus to arrest Him.

When Peter struck the ear of a servant with his sword, Jesus told Peter to put away his sword. Then Jesus touched the servant's ear and healed him. Jesus then asked the chief priest and elders from the temple why they came out at night with swords to take Him instead of taking Him in the temple where He sat daily teaching the people. But all this was done so that writings of the prophets would be fulfilled. Then the disciples deserted Jesus.

InfoScene: "The Garden of Gethsemane"
Display Chart 24 for reference throughout this unit. Review and discuss the Bible account as time permits.

- ➤ **Why had Peter, James, and John gone with Jesus to the Garden of Gethsemane?** *(to pray)*
- ➤ **When Jesus went alone to pray, what did He tell His disciples to do? What did He find them doing when He returned?** *(He told them to watch, but He found them sleeping.)*
- ➤ **Why was Jesus grieved with His disciples?** *(The disciples could not stay awake for one hour while Jesus went to pray.)*
- ➤ **How might Christians today grieve God?** *(Possible answers include not reading the Bible, not being a witness to others, disobeying parents, not being kind to others, and displaying an ungrateful spirit.)*
- ➤ **How did the officers know which man was Jesus, the one they were to arrest?** *(He was the man Judas kissed.)* Share the background information about the kiss (optional).
- ➤ **Why was it necessary for Jesus to die on the cross?** *(God sent Jesus to be the Savior of mankind. Jesus Christ took upon Himself the sins of all men when He died on the cross.)*

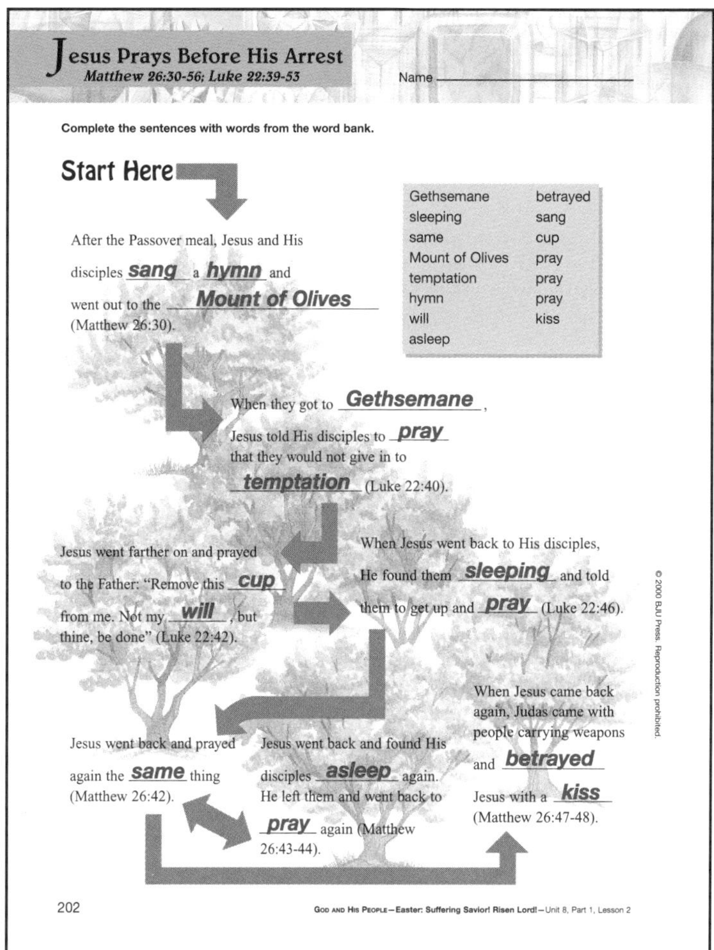

Jesus Prays Before His Arrest
Matthew 26:30-56; Luke 22:39-53

Name ____________

Complete the sentences with words from the word bank.

Start Here

Gethsemane	betrayed
sleeping	sang
same	cup
Mount of Olives	pray
temptation	pray
hymn	pray
will	kiss
asleep	

After the Passover meal, Jesus and His disciples __sang__ a __hymn__ and went out to the __Mount of Olives__ (Matthew 26:30).

When they got to __Gethsemane__, Jesus told His disciples to __pray__ that they would not give in to __temptation__ (Luke 22:40).

Jesus went farther on and prayed to the Father: "Remove this __cup__ from me. Not my __will__, but thine, be done" (Luke 22:42).

When Jesus went back to His disciples, He found them __sleeping__ and told them to get up and __pray__ (Luke 22:46).

Jesus went back and prayed again the __same__ thing (Matthew 26:42).

Jesus went back and found His disciples __asleep__ again. He left them and went back to __pray__ again (Matthew 26:43-44).

When Jesus came back again, Judas came with people carrying weapons and __betrayed__ Jesus with a __kiss__ (Matthew 26:47-48).

202 God and His People—Easter: Suffering Savior! Risen Lord!—Unit 8, Part 1, Lesson 2

Worktext page 202

Review the Bible account.

Memory Verses—Isaiah 53:3-4

Practice the memory verses. Locate **Isaiah 53:3-4** and select students to read the verses aloud. Explain that Jesus took upon Himself our sicknesses, our diseases, and our pain of punishment. Read **Matthew 8:17** aloud. Point out that Isaiah prophesied that Jesus would suffer the punishment for our sins.

Lesson 3

Preparation of Materials:

Write Isaiah 53:3-4 on an erasable board.

Memory Verses—Isaiah 53:3-4

Practice the memory verses. Direct attention to the verses on the board. Read the verses aloud together. Erase a phrase, then say the verses. Continue to erase a phrase and say the verses until both verses have been completely erased.

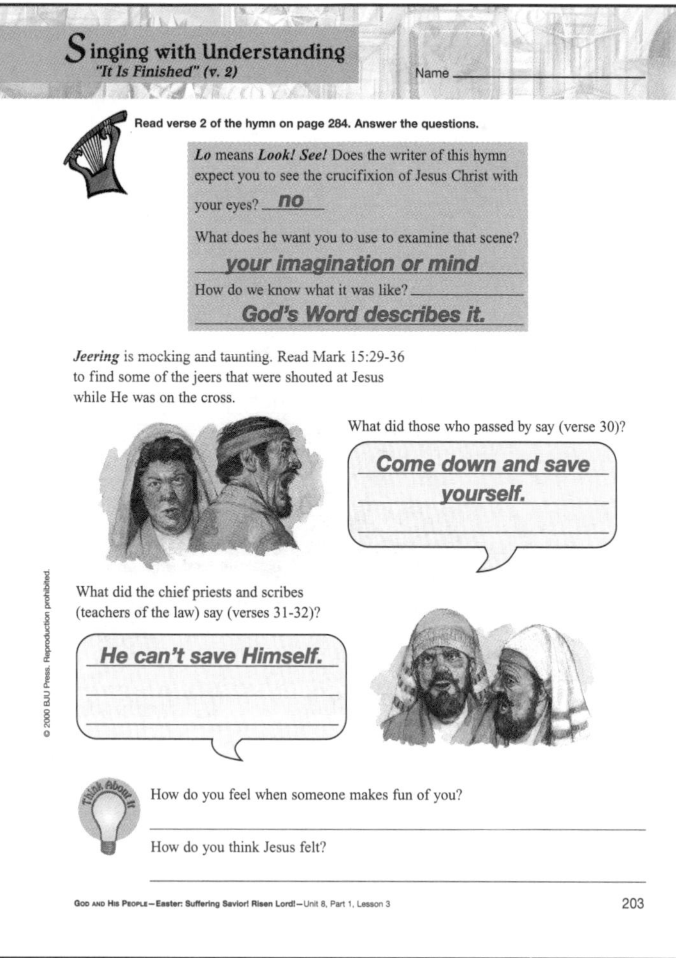

Singing with Understanding
"It Is Finished" (v. 2)

Name ____________

Read verse 2 of the hymn on page 284. Answer the questions.

Lo means ***Look! See!*** Does the writer of this hymn expect you to see the crucifixion of Jesus Christ with your eyes? **no**

What does he want you to use to examine that scene? **your imagination or mind**

How do we know what it was like? **God's Word describes it.**

Jeering is mocking and taunting. Read Mark 15:29-36 to find some of the jeers that were shouted at Jesus while He was on the cross.

What did those who passed by say (verse 30)? **Come down and save yourself.**

What did the chief priests and scribes (teachers of the law) say (verses 31-32)? **He can't save Himself.**

Think About It

How do you feel when someone makes fun of you? ____________

How do you think Jesus felt? ____________

God and His People—Easter: Suffering Savior! Risen Lord!—Unit 8, Part 1, Lesson 3 203

Hymn: "It Is Finished"

Teach the second verse. (Worktext page 284). Play the recording and lead in singing the first verse.

➤ **What are the events that took place the day Christ was crucified?** *(There was darkness, the earth shook, and the crowd was mocking Jesus.)*

Lead in singing verse 2; then sing verses 1-2 together.

Worktext page 203

Singing with understanding, verse 2.

Background Information

Barabbas—*The Bible tells us little about Barabbas. According to the Gospel writers, Barabbas was a notorious prisoner, arrested with a group of murderers during an uprising. His father may have been a rabbi, a teacher skillful in interpreting the Jewish law.*

Introducing the Bible Account

Discuss that honesty is always right. Read the following situation to the students.

Brian's dad told him to rake the leaves before he went skating with his best friend. But Brian chose to go skating first, intending to rake the leaves later. Before Brian returned home, it began to rain.

➤ **When Brian's dad asked him whether he raked the leaves, what should Brian tell him?** *(Be honest and tell his father that he had disobeyed.)*

➤ **What punishment should he receive?** *(Answers will vary.)*

➤ **Why is it wrong to disobey?** *(Answers may vary. Point out that disobedience is sin.)*

➤ **Are there ever consequences for being honest? If so, what are they?** *(Answers will vary.)*

Bible Account

Read the following Bible account or read one of the following passages: Matthew 26:57–27:5 or John 18:12-40.

Falsely Accused and Denied

Roman soldiers, along with Jewish officials, bound Jesus and arrested Him. They brought Jesus to the house of Annas, a high priest and the father-in-law of Caiaphas. Annas, the ruling high priest, had Jesus sent to the house of Caiaphas where the council of chief priests, scribes, and elders was gathered. Caiaphas questioned Jesus about His teachings in the synagogue and in the temple. A number of false witnesses were called to testify against Jesus. Jesus did not argue against these witnesses, but He did suggest that Caiaphas ask the people who heard His teaching to be a witness to what He had said. An officer became angry by Jesus' response and hit Jesus. Caiaphas asked Jesus whether He was "the Christ, the Son of God." Jesus replied, "Thou hast said: nevertheless I say unto you, Hereafter shall ye see the Son of man sitting on the right hand of power, and coming in the clouds of heaven." After hearing the answer given by Jesus, the council found Jesus guilty of blaspheming God and decided to put Him to death.

When Jesus had been delivered to Caiaphas, Peter, keeping his distance, followed the crowd into the fire-lit courtyard to watch what would happen to Jesus. As Peter sat down among the people, a servant girl said she had seen him with Jesus. Peter told her that he did not know Jesus. Two more people said that they had seen Peter with Jesus, but Peter insisted that he had not been with Jesus. Immediately a rooster crowed. Jesus turned from where He was and looked at Peter (Luke 22:61). Then Peter remembered that Jesus had said Peter would deny Him three times before the rooster crowed. Peter left the courtyard and wept bitterly.

➤ **Why did Peter follow the crowd to Caiaphas's house?** *(to observe the questioning of Jesus)*

➤ **Do you think Peter was expecting anyone to recognize him as having been with Jesus?** *(Answers will vary. Point out that it was dark and that the only light was from the fire in the courtyard.)*

➤ **What response should Peter have given instead of denying Christ each time?** *(admit that he was a follower of Jesus)*

When the early morning had come, all the chief priests and elders of the people decided to put Jesus to death. Jesus was bound and led to Pontius Pilate, the Roman governor of Judea. Hearing this news, Judas grieved over his horrible deed of betraying Christ and took the bag of silver coins back to the religious leaders and cried out, "I have sinned in that I have betrayed the innocent blood." The leaders replied, "What is that to us?" Judas threw down the money "in the temple, and departed, and went and hanged himself."

As Jesus stood before Pilate, the chief priests accused Jesus of undermining the nation, opposing taxes, and calling Himself King. Pilate asked Jesus if He was the Son of God. Jesus answered that He was. After Pilate questioned Jesus, he said, "I find no fault in this man." Hearing this, the chief priests accused Jesus of stirring up all the Jews from Galilee to Jerusalem.

When Pilate found out that Jesus was from Galilee, he decided to send Jesus to Herod. Pilate knew that Herod, the governor of Galilee, was in Jerusalem for the Passover. Herod was pleased to see Jesus, thinking that He would perform a miracle. When Herod questioned Him, Jesus remained silent. Herod and his men accused Jesus, mocked Him, put a beautiful robe on Him, and sent Him back to Pilate.

Later at the feast, Pilate was expected to release a prisoner. The crowd cried out, "Away with this man, and release unto us Barabbas." Barabbas had been in prison for rebelling against authority. Pilate attempted to convince the crowd to release Jesus since He had done no wrong. But the crowd cried out, "Crucify Him, crucify Him."

When Pilate realized he was defeated, "he took water, and washed his hands before the multitude, saying, I am innocent of the blood of this just person."

All the people answered, "His blood be on us, and on our children."

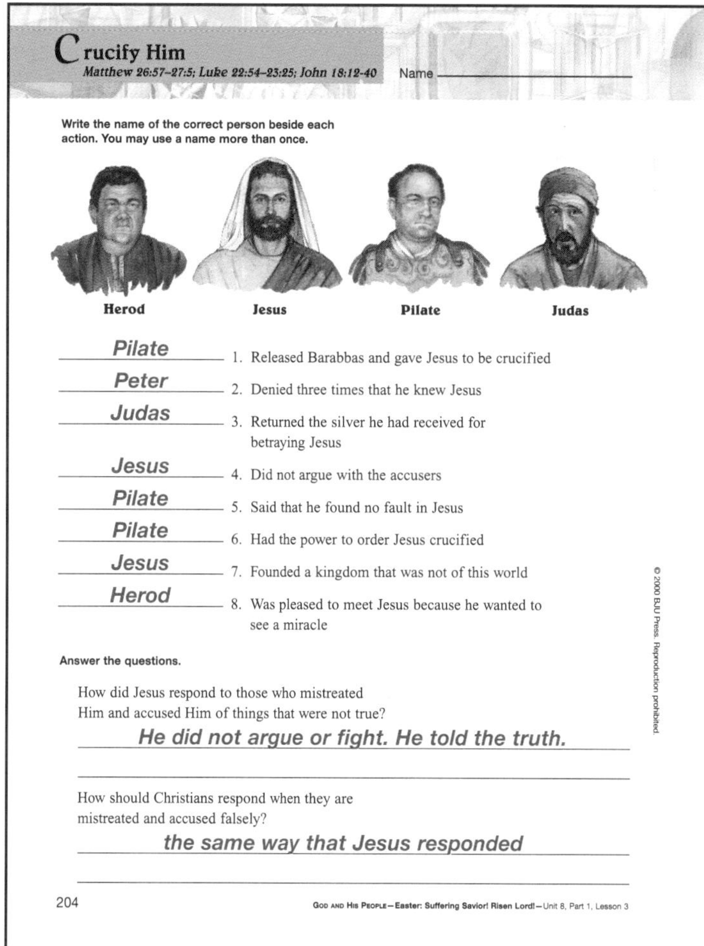

Crucify Him

Matthew 26:57–27:5; Luke 22:54–23:25; John 18:12-40

Name ______________

Write the name of the correct person beside each action. You may use a name more than once.

Herod Jesus Pilate Judas

Pilate 1. Released Barabbas and gave Jesus to be crucified

Peter 2. Denied three times that he knew Jesus

Judas 3. Returned the silver he had received for betraying Jesus

Jesus 4. Did not argue with the accusers

Pilate 5. Said that he found no fault in Jesus

Pilate 6. Had the power to order Jesus crucified

Jesus 7. Founded a kingdom that was not of this world

Herod 8. Was pleased to meet Jesus because he wanted to see a miracle

Answer the questions.

How did Jesus respond to those who mistreated Him and accused Him of things that were not true?

He did not argue or fight. He told the truth.

How should Christians respond when they are mistreated and accused falsely?

the same way that Jesus responded

204 God and His People—Easter: Suffering Savior! Risen Lord!—Unit 8, Part 1, Lesson 3

➤ **What did Judas do when he heard the news that Jesus was condemned to die?** *(threw the money down in the temple and went out and hanged himself)*

➤ **What did Herod do when Jesus refused to answer his questions?** *(He accused Jesus, mocked Him, put a beautiful robe on Him, and sent Him back to Pilate.)*

➤ **What was Pilate expected to do at the feast?** *(release a prisoner to gain acceptance with the Jews)*

➤ **Why did the crowd choose Barabbas to be released rather than Jesus?** *(The religious leaders wanted to get rid of Jesus. The crowd believed the lies about Jesus.)*

Worktext page 204

Identify the correct Bible characters.

Lesson 4

Hymn: "It Is Finished"

Sing the first two verses (Worktext page 284). Play the recording and lead in singing verses 1-2. Divide the students into two groups. Lead Group 1 in singing the first verse and Group 2 in singing the second verse. Direct the students to sing the chorus together.

Introducing the Application Story

Discuss running in a race.

- ➤ **Have you ever run in a race? If so, what kind of shoes and clothes did you wear?** *(Answers will vary.)*
- ➤ **How often did you practice?** *(Answers will vary.)*
- ➤ **What was used to signal the runner to begin running?** *(Possible answers include a whistle, a starter pistol, a flag, etc.)*
- ➤ **What was used to record the running time?** *(a stopwatch)*

Application Story

Read the following story aloud. Direct the students to listen to find out whether Eric took a Christian stand. *(yes)*

More Important Than a Race

"Will that festival ever get here?" Eric ran along beside his best friend, Reggie, the lines on the track whizzing by beneath his shoes.

"Only four more days," Reggie said between carefully measured breaths. "Think we're in pretty good shape for the hundred?"

"We ought to be by now." Eric thought about the many mornings their feet had pounded the track as they practiced together for the Valley Hill County Festival. The festival had many attractions—rides, games, cotton candy, and fireworks—but for Eric and Reggie, the highlight was the 100-yard dash. Reggie had won it three years ago, but for the last two years, Eric had edged over the line just ahead of him.

"Let's go full speed on this last lap," said Reggie.

Eric picked up speed. He felt the wind rush past his ears.

The boys crossed the finish line exactly at the same time. They both threw their arms up in a victory sign. "Yes!" Reggie yelled. "We'll have to watch that replay, ladies and gents, but I think Reggie Clayton is the winner by a nose."

"No way." Eric jabbed Reggie in the ribs. The boys continued circling the track at a walk.

Eric's thoughts went back to his father's prayer at breakfast that morning. "Dear God, help us to speak a word for You today whenever we can." Eric had tried to speak to Reggie before. But maybe it was time to try again.

Eric took an extra-deep breath. "Hey, Reggie, guess what I found when I was reading my Bible today?"

Reggie kept his eyes down. "I don't know. What?" he said.

"I found a verse about running," Eric said.

"Oh, yeah? What'd it say—*thou shalt let thy best friend win at the hundred?*" Reggie said with a chuckle.

"No, it talked about how lots of people run in a race, but only one person wins, and we're supposed to try our best to win. It was talking about being a Christian."

"Hey, that sounds like good advice," said Reggie. "I just might follow what that Book says, 'cause I really want to beat you in the hundred."

They reached the gate that led to the locker rooms. "See you same time tomorrow, Eric?" asked Reggie.

"See you later." Eric waved and watched Reggie dash off. "Dear God," he prayed, "I really want to tell Reggie about You, but he's always clowning around. Please help me show him I'm really serious about serving You."

The next day, Eric's dad met him at the bottom of the stairs, holding the newspaper.

"What's up, Dad?" said Eric.

"Son," said Dad, "there's no easy way to tell you this. Mayor Kirby was killed in a boating accident last night. The funeral's on Saturday, and the festival has been postponed until Sunday."

Eric's mouth dropped open. "Sunday?" He stared at Dad for a moment; then he sat down on the lowest step. "But I can't run on a *Sunday.*"

"That's the right decision, Eric," Dad said quietly. "It's the Lord's Day, and I think He'll honor your decision to honor Him."

Eric hurried to the track right after breakfast, wondering how he was going to explain to Reggie. He was on the bleachers, pulling on his running shoes when Reggie came up and slapped him on the back. "Hey, Eric, did you hear the news? Festival's not till Sunday. That gives me an extra day to practice so I can set the new record for the hundred."

"Reggie," Eric said. "I won't be running."

Reggie just looked at him for a moment. "You're kidding, right?"

"No, I'm not. My parents—and, well, me too—we believe Sunday's the Lord's Day. We

Avoiding Temptation

Name ______________________

What two things does Jesus Christ tell Christians to do so that they will not give in to temptation? Find out by coloring the multiples of 2 blue and the multiples of 5 red.

Jesus said to ___watch___ and ___pray___ (Matthew 26:41).

For Me

Name ______________________

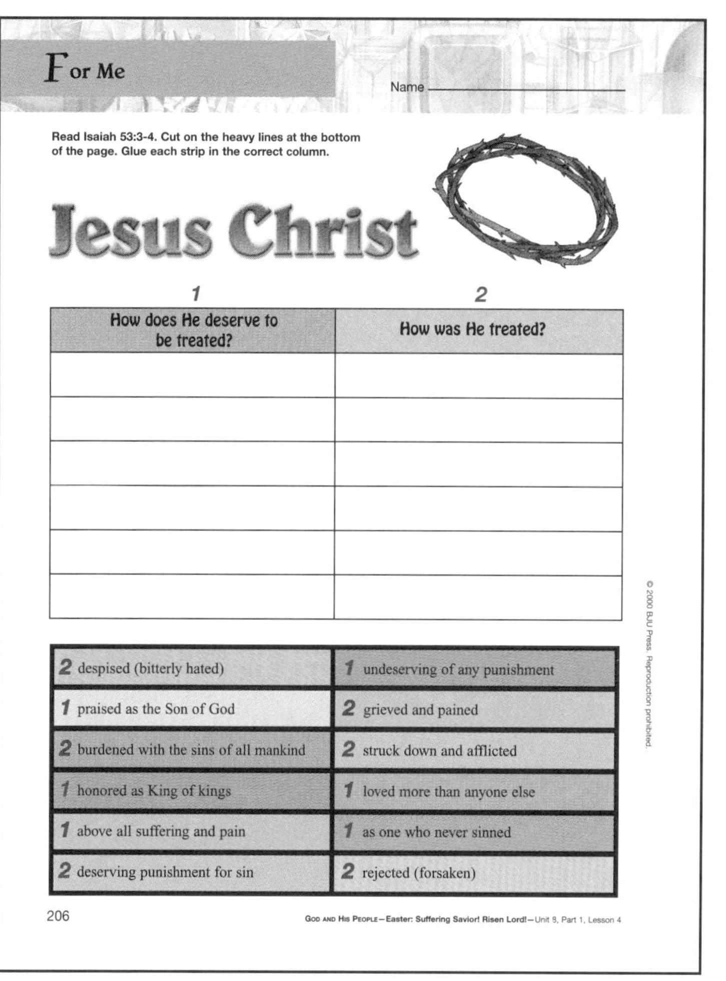

Read Isaiah 53:3-4. Cut on the heavy lines at the bottom of the page. Glue each strip in the correct column.

Jesus Christ

1 How does He deserve to be treated?	2 How was He treated?

2 despised (bitterly hated)	1 undeserving of any punishment
1 praised as the Son of God	2 grieved and pained
2 burdened with the sins of all mankind	2 struck down and afflicted
1 honored as King of kings	1 loved more than anyone else
1 above all suffering and pain	1 as one who never sinned
2 deserving punishment for sin	2 rejected (forsaken)

go to Sunday school and church and try to keep that day for God. I just can't run on a Sunday."

"Whoa," said Reggie. "You really *are* serious." He sat down next to Eric. Eric didn't know what else to say, so he just waited.

"So let me get it straight," Reggie said. "This being a Christian stuff is so important to you that you'd give up a race for it?"

Eric met Reggie's eyes. "Yeah, it *is* that important."

"Wow," Reggie said. "All this time, I thought you were kind of faking that Bible stuff. Like trying to get points for Sunday school or something. But I guess I was wrong. Man, the hundred won't be much fun without you."

Eric kept quiet, but inside he felt like a spotlight had just come on in a dark stadium. Maybe God was going to use this thing to open the door—just a crack—to Reggie's heart.

➤ **What yearly activity were Eric and Reggie anticipating?** *(the 100-yard dash at the Valley Hill County Festival)*

➤ **In previous years, how had Eric done in the 100-yard dash?** *(won for the past two years)*

➤ **What had Eric recalled his dad praying about?** *(remembering to speak for the Lord whenever possible)*

➤ **Why was it important for Eric to be a good testimony to Reggie?** *(Reggie was not saved.)*

➤ **How did the death of Mayor Kirby influence Eric's participation in the 100-yard dash?** *(Eric did not participate because the festival was postponed until Sunday.)*

➤ **Do you think Reggie became a Christian?** *(The story doesn't tell us. But the testimony of Eric was a good influence on Reggie.)*

Worktext page 205

Apply Bible knowledge to everyday life.

Memory Verse—Isaiah 53:3-4

Practice the memory verses. Locate **Isaiah 53:3-4** and direct the students to read the verses silently and then to say the verses from memory to themselves. Choose two students to each explain one of the verses.

Worktext page 206

Develop an understanding of the memory verses.

Going Beyond

Enrichment

Direct a time-keeping chart activity. Tell each student to keep track of what he does from 4:00 P.M. to 7:00 P.M.

Make bar graphs. The next day, discuss the results.

➤ **What activity did you do from 4:00 to 4:30?** *(Answers will vary.)*

➤ **Who did chores from 4:30 to 5:00?** *(Answers will vary.)*

➤ **What did you do from 5:00 to 5:30?** *(Answers will vary.)*

➤ **What did you do from 5:30 to 6:00?** *(Answers will vary.)*

➤ **What did you do from 6:00 to 6:30?** *(Answers will vary.)*

➤ **What activity did you do from 6:30 to 7:00?** *(Answers will vary.)*

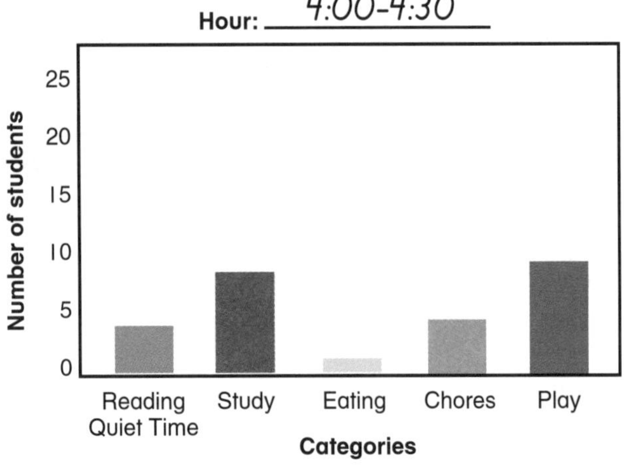

red = play

green = chores

yellow = eating

blue = study

orange = reading and quiet time

Make bar graphs, showing the number of students who participated in each category 4:00-4:30, 4:30-5:00, etc. Remind the students that Jesus asked His three disciples to watch for one hour, and they fell asleep. Challenge the students to use their time for God.

Suffering Savior! Risen Lord!

Unit 8, Part 2

Preview

Doctrines

- Christ died for man (atonement) (I Corinthians 15:3)—Lesson 1
- Christ arose from the dead (resurrection) (I Corinthians 15:3-8)—Lesson 2

Skills and Applications

- Learn Isaiah 53:5-6
- Read a time line
- Recall facts and details
- Write captions for pictures
- Use a concordance
- Understand that Christ died for the sins of all men
- Know that Christ rose from the dead
- Apply Bible knowledge to everyday life

Lesson 1

Materials

- TimeLine and picture: *The Crucifixion*

Memory Verses—Isaiah 53:5-6

Principle: Jesus paid the penalty for the sins of the world. Locate and read aloud **Isaiah 53:5-6** as the students read silently. Explain that verse 5 is a continuation of the details of Christ's death. Both verses tell how Jesus paid the penalty for all of man's sins.

➤ **What is *sin?*** *(the transgression of the law of God)*

➤ **What is meant by *transgression?*** *(failing to do what God commands or doing what He forbids)*

Explain that God used the physical suffering of Christ to bring the spiritual healing in salvation.

Background Information

Scourging—*In Bible times, people convicted of criminal or religious offenses were punished with the severe use of a whip. The most brutal form of scourging was called* flagellation. *Knots and pieces of metal or bone were tied into the whip, making a club of knotted cord with metal beads and twelve separate lashes.*

Veil to the Holy of Holies—*The inner veil that was made to hang at the entrance to the holy of holies for the Hebrew tabernacle and later the temple was a type of Christ's human body (Hebrews 10:19-20). Only the high priest was to pass through this veil to offer sacrifices for the sins of the people. When Jesus Christ died, the veil in the temple was torn in two (Matthew 27:51), giving all believers access to God through faith in His Son and His work on the cross. Second Corinthians 3:14 tells us this "vail is done away in Christ."*

Breaking of Bones—*Because the Sabbath began at 6:00 P.M. on the day of the Crucifixion, the Jews asked Pilate to have the legs of the men broken so that they would die more quickly. They did not want the bodies to remain on the crosses during the Sabbath. With broken legs, the men could not push themselves up to breathe.*

Introducing the Bible Account

Identify a prophecy about Christ's death. Read **Psalm 34:19-20** to the students.

➤ **What does David say about the bones of Christ?** *(They would not be broken.)*

Explain that in Bible times it was a custom for the leg bones to be broken to hasten death, but David, who reigned from 1020 to 975 B.C., prophesied that Christ's bones would not be broken. Tell the students to listen to see whether David's prophecy was fulfilled. *(yes)*

Bible Account

Read the following Bible account or read one of the following passages: Matthew 27:27-56; Luke 23:26-49; or John 19:16-37.

God's Begotten Son

The soldiers took Jesus into the palace, stripped Him of His clothes, and put a scarlet robe on Him. On His head they placed a crown of thorns, and they put a staff in His right hand. The soldiers knelt before Jesus and said, "Hail, King of the Jews!" They spit upon Him, hit Him, took the robe off His body, put His own clothes on Him, and led Him away to be crucified.

As they left the hall, they found Simon of Cyrene and forced him to carry the cross piece for Jesus. Many people followed Jesus to Golgotha, "a place of a skull." Jesus was given vinegar mixed with gall to drink. But when Jesus tasted it, He refused to drink it. While Jesus was on the cross, the soldiers divided His clothes among them. His outer garment had no seams, which made it very special, so they cast lots for it. This fulfilled the prophecy of David in Psalm 22:18. "They part my garments among them and cast lots upon my vesture." A sign over the head of Jesus read, "This is Jesus, the King of the Jews." Two thieves were crucified with Jesus, one on either side of Him. The chief priests, scribes, and elders mocked Jesus. They said they would believe He was the Son of God if Jesus came down from the cross.

Darkness covered the earth from the sixth hour (noon) until the ninth hour (3:00 P.M.). At the ninth hour Jesus cried with a loud voice, "Eli, Eli, lama sabachthani? that is to say, My God, my God, why hast thou forsaken me?" Some of the people thought Jesus was calling for Elijah. They watched to see whether Elijah would come to save Jesus from death.

A sponge filled with vinegar was offered to Jesus. Then Jesus shouted out in a loud voice saying, "Father, into thy hands I commend my spirit." Then He gave up His life.

Immediately the curtain in the temple was torn in two from top to bottom. The earth shook, and the rocks split. Many believers who had died and been buried were brought to life.

When the centurion saw what had happened, he said, "Truly this was the Son of God."

Because the Sabbath would begin in a few hours, the Jews asked Pilate if the legs of the crucified men could be broken. Pilate agreed, so the soldiers came and broke the legs of the thieves. But Jesus had already died, so the soldiers did not break His legs.

- **What kind of death did Jesus die?** *(Jesus died the shameful and painful death of being nailed to the cross.)*
- **Where was Jesus taken to be crucified?** *(to Golgotha)*
- **What is meant by "they parted my garments among them, and upon my vesture did they cast lots"?** *(The soldiers divided Christ's clothing among themselves. His coat was special because it had no seams, so they cast lots to see who would get it.)* Point out that another prophecy of David had been fulfilled.
- **Why was it unusual for darkness to cover the earth?** *(It was the middle of the day.)*
- **What happened immediately when Christ gave up His life?** *(The curtain of the temple was torn in two from the top to the bottom; the earth shook, and rocks split. Life was restored to some believers who were dead.)*
- **What did the centurion say about Jesus?** *(Jesus was the Son of God.)*
- **What does Jesus' death provide for us?** *(the way of salvation—we no longer have to die for our sins. If we accept this gift of salvation, Jesus cleanses us and gives us eternal life.)*

TimeLine

Add *The Crucifixion* to the TimeLine. Select a student to place *The Crucifixion* on the TimeLine at A.D. 30. Remind the students that through the death of Jesus, the penalty for the sins of mankind was paid. Jesus rose from the grave and lives in heaven. Jesus is preparing a place in heaven for those who have asked His forgiveness for their sins. Guide the students in gluing their pictures onto their individual TimeLines.

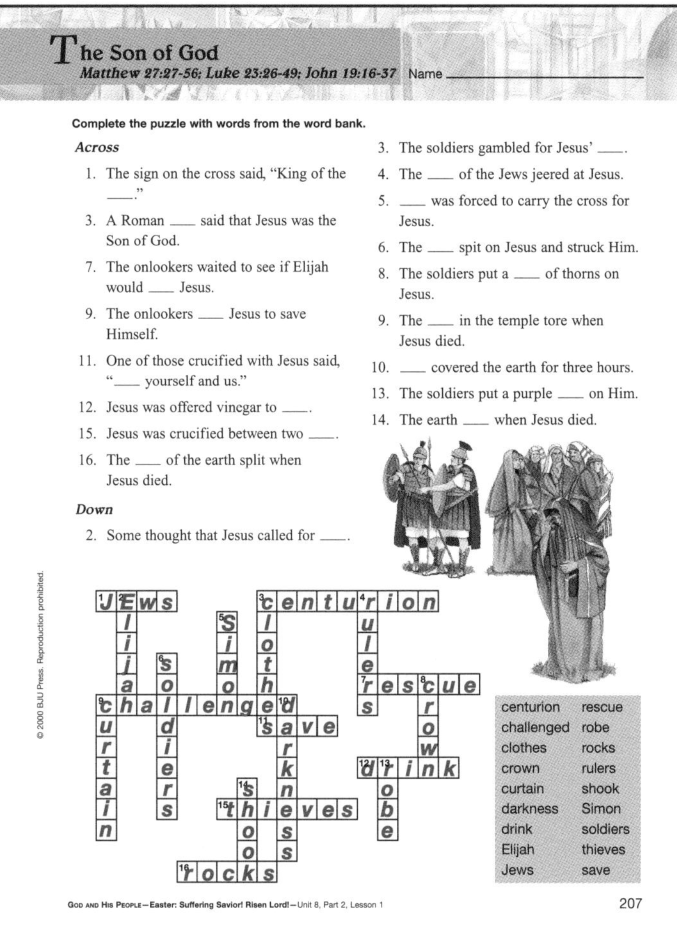

Worktext page 207

Recall details about the Bible account.

Hymn: "It Is Finished"

Teach the third verse (Worktext page 284). Lead in singing together verses 1-2. Play the recording of verse 3. Discuss the meaning of verse 3; then lead in singing it together.

➤ **Who called to heaven?** *(my Savior)*

➤ **What did Jesus ask His heavenly Father to do?** *(to forgive the crowd, for they did not know what they were doing)*

Worktext page 208

Singing with understanding, verse 3.

Lesson 2

Materials

- Chart 25, "Thine Be the Glory!"

Hymn: "It Is Finished"

Sing the first three verses (Worktext page 284). Play the recording and lead in singing verses 1-2. Divide the students into three groups. Direct Group 1 to stand to read the first phrase of verse 3, Group 2 to stand and read the second phrase, and Group 3 to stand and read the third phrase. Repeat the procedure until all of verse 3 has been read aloud. Play the recording and lead in singing the third verse.

Background Information

Burial Place—*Throughout history people have buried their dead in various ways—a hole in the ground, intricate burial caves, mausoleums, or pyramids. The communal grave was a burial place shared by a group of people.* Dolmens, *house-shaped tombs, were constructed of two upright stone slabs, capped with a flat stone slab. Caves, both man-made and natural, were popular sites for tombs. Burial of cherished objects with the deceased was practiced in ancient and in biblical times.*

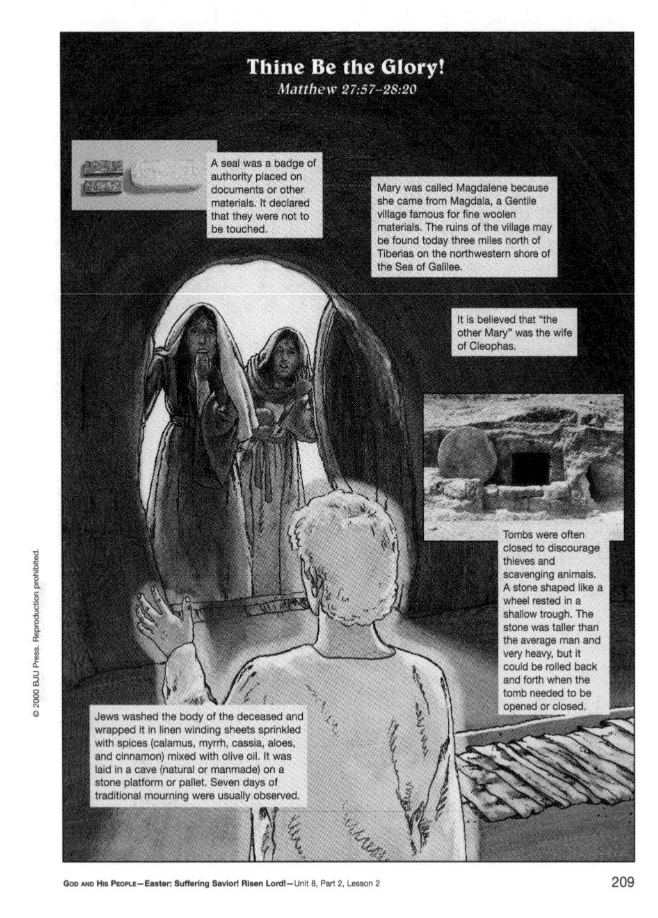

Introducing the Bible Account

Discuss the preparations of a burial (optional).

➤ **When a person has died, how is the body prepared for burial?** *(Answers will vary.)* Explain that in the United States the body is taken to the mortuary, where it is prepared for burial.

Bible Account

Read the following Bible account or read Matthew 27:57–28:15 or John 19:38–20:18 (optional). Direct the students' attention to the picture on Worktext page 209. Tell them to listen to find out how Jesus' body was prepared for burial. *(It was wrapped in strips of linen cloth and spices.)*

Thine Be the Glory!

Joseph of Arimathea was a disciple of Jesus, but he kept it a secret because he feared the Jews. He came to Pilate and asked for the body of Jesus. Joseph was granted the authority to take the body of Jesus. Nicodemus, a ruler of the Jews who had visited with Jesus earlier, helped Joseph prepare the body for burial. Nicodemus brought a mixture of myrrh and aloes, weighing about one hundred pounds (John 19:38-42). According to Jewish custom, the men wrapped Jesus' body with strips of linen cloth and spices. Then the body of Jesus was put in the new tomb that Joseph of Arimathea had had cut from the rock. Joseph and the men rolled a stone to the entrance of the tomb and went away. Mary Magdalene and "the other Mary" sat nearby.

The next day, the chief priests and Pharisees reminded Pilate that Jesus had said, "After three days I will rise again." The tomb was sealed, and a guard stood at the entrance. Now no one could come steal the body and say that Jesus had risen.

On the first day of the week, Mary Magdalene and the other Mary came to the tomb of Jesus. There had been a great earthquake and an angel from heaven had come and rolled the stone away. His face was like lightning, and His clothes white as snow. The soldiers guarding the tomb had been so scared that they fainted. The angel told the women not to be frightened. He knew that they had come looking for Jesus. The angel told them, "He is not here: for He is risen, as he said. Come, see the place where the Lord lay. And go quickly, and tell his disciples that He is risen from the dead."

Mary Magdalene and the other Mary went to Galilee to share the good news with the disciples. Some of the guards reported to the chief priests, who decided to pay the soldiers to keep quiet. The soldiers were told to say that Jesus' disciples had stolen the body during the night while the guards slept.

InfoScene: "Thine Be the Glory!"

Display Chart 25 for reference throughout this unit. Review and discuss the Bible account as time permits.

➤ **Why was Joseph of Arimathea a secret disciple of Jesus?** *(He was afraid of the Jews.)* Read the definition of *disciple* from the glossary (optional).

➤ **Why do you think Joseph requested the body of Jesus, and what did he do with it?** *(Answers will vary. He had it wrapped in strips of linen cloth and spices.)* Explain that Joseph wanted to show his love for Christ by placing the body of Christ in his own new tomb.

➤ **What was done to the tomb when Pilate was reminded that Jesus had said He would rise again after three days?** *(The stone was sealed, and a guard was placed at the entrance.)*

➤ **What good news did the angel tell Mary Magdalene and the other Mary, and how do you know that they did not keep this news a secret?** *(Jesus was risen just as He had said. They went to Galilee to tell the disciples.)*

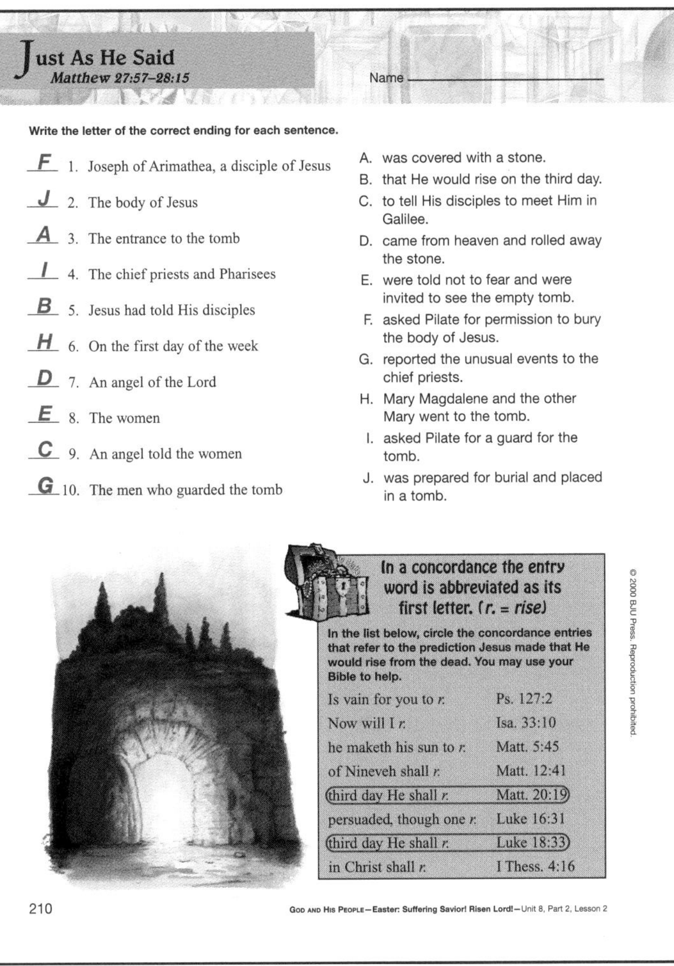

Just As He Said
Matthew 27:57–28:15

Name ____________

Write the letter of the correct ending for each sentence.

F 1. Joseph of Arimathea, a disciple of Jesus
J 2. The body of Jesus
A 3. The entrance to the tomb
I 4. The chief priests and Pharisees
B 5. Jesus had told His disciples
H 6. On the first day of the week
D 7. An angel of the Lord
E 8. The women
C 9. An angel told the women
G 10. The men who guarded the tomb

A. was covered with a stone.
B. that He would rise on the third day.
C. to tell His disciples to meet Him in Galilee.
D. came from heaven and rolled away the stone.
E. were told not to fear and were invited to see the empty tomb.
F. asked Pilate for permission to bury the body of Jesus.
G. reported the unusual events to the chief priests.
H. Mary Magdalene and the other Mary went to the tomb.
I. asked Pilate for a guard for the tomb.
J. was prepared for burial and placed in a tomb.

In a concordance the entry word is abbreviated as its first letter. (*r.* = *rise*)

In the list below, circle the concordance entries that refer to the prediction Jesus made that He would rise from the dead. You may use your Bible to help.

Is vain for you to *r.*	Ps. 127:2
Now will I *r.*	Isa. 33:10
he maketh his sun to *r.*	Matt. 5:45
of Nineveh shall *r.*	Matt. 12:41
(third day He shall *r.*	Matt. 20:19)
persuaded, though one *r.*	Luke 16:31
(third day He shall *r.*	Luke 18:33)
in Christ shall *r.*	I Thess. 4:16

210 God and His People—Easter: Suffering Savior! Risen Lord!—Unit 8, Part 2, Lesson 2

➤ **Why do you think the chief priests and elders wanted the soldiers to lie about the tomb being empty?** *(Answers will vary.)* Point out that the chief priests and elders did not want the people to believe that Jesus is the Son of God.

Worktext page 210

Recall facts and details and use a concordance.

Memory Verses—Isaiah 53:5-6

Practice the memory verses. Locate **Isaiah 53:5-6** and direct the students to read the verses silently.

➤ **According to verse 6, with what animal is man compared?** *(a sheep)*

➤ **How are men like sheep?** *(They do things their own way.)*

Explain that sheep travel in a flock, following the lead sheep. When the leader gets off the path, it can be dangerous for all of the sheep. Men, apart from God, are doomed to eternal separation. Christ's death on the cross paid for all the sins of mankind. Read **Isaiah 53:5-6** throughout the day for practice.

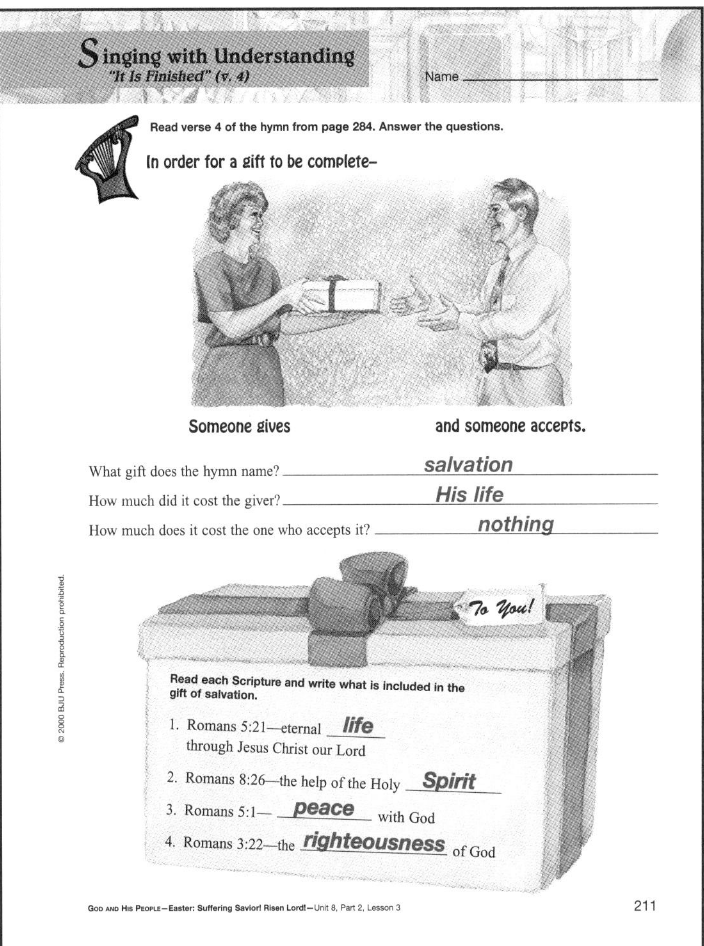

Singing with Understanding
"It Is Finished" (v. 4)

Name ____________

Read verse 4 of the hymn from page 284. Answer the questions.

In order for a gift to be complete–

Someone gives and someone accepts.

What gift does the hymn name? salvation
How much did it cost the giver? His life
How much does it cost the one who accepts it? nothing

Read each Scripture and write what is included in the gift of salvation.

1. Romans 5:21—eternal life through Jesus Christ our Lord
2. Romans 8:26—the help of the Holy Spirit
3. Romans 5:1—peace with God
4. Romans 3:22—the righteousness of God

God and His People—Easter: Suffering Savior! Risen Lord!—Unit 8, Part 2, Lesson 3 211

Lesson 3

Hymn: "It Is Finished"

Teach the fourth verse (Worktext page 284). Play the recording of verse 4.

➤ **What does God offer to us?** *(free salvation)*

➤ **What price did Jesus pay for our free salvation?** *(He died on the cross.)*

Instruct the students to read verse 4; then lead the singing of verse 4; then sing verses 1-4 together.

Worktext page 211

Singing with understanding, verse 4.

Memory Verses—Isaiah 53:5-6

Practice the memory verses. Locate **Isaiah 53:5-6** and direct the students to read the verses silently, recall them in a quiet whisper, and then read them silently again. Tell the students that you will say the first word aloud and each student in turn will pop up and say the next word until both verses have been said aloud.

Introducing the Application Story

Discuss creation.

- ➤ **Have you ever looked up in the sky and thought that the clouds had formed a shape? What shapes did you see?** *(Answers will vary.)*
- ➤ **Have you ever thought about the different shapes and colors of flowers? Describe some of the flowers you have seen.** *(Answers will vary.)*
- ➤ **Why did God make you and all things?** *(for His own glory)*

Application Story

Read the following story aloud. Listen to find out which creation can remind us of Christ's Crucifixion. *(the dogwood tree)*

A Lesson of the Dogwood

"Easter vacation! No school for a week!" Damian Finley jumped out of bed early Saturday morning.

Each year at this time, the Finley family got up early, packed a picnic lunch, threw on their hiking shoes, and hopped into the car for a day at Grove Creek Gardens. Damian glanced out the window. "Great day for a picnic!" he said. The sun was peeping out above the trees. The birds were singing in the giant oak tree outside the back door. Damian saw squirrels scamper across the dew-covered lawn.

After breakfast, Damian and his twin sister LaTrisha raced each other to the car. Mom arrived with her purse over one arm, a bag of snacks and CDs over the other arm, and her hands full of books. Dad helped her in with a smile.

"Everyone ready now?" he asked.

"Ready!" answered Mom and the twins together.

The two-hour drive went by quickly. Soon they reached the winding bumpy road that led to the gate of Grove Creek Gardens. Inside the gate sat Mr. Coggins, the kind old gentleman who cared for the gardens. He was busy digging in a bed of tulips. Not wanting to disturb him, Dad, Mom, and the children went on to the welcome center.

"Dad! Mom! May we hear one of Mr. Coggins's stories?" asked the twins. Mr. Coggins loved to chat with the visitors who traveled to view the acres of trees and flowers. Damian and LaTrisha loved to hear his stories.

"Yes, we'll listen to a story before we leave," answered Dad.

The Finley family strolled through the gardens, looking at the flowers and trees. When LaTrisha stopped to take a picture of the rhododendron, they noticed Mr. Coggins ambling along the path toward them.

"Gardens are beautiful as usual, Mr. Coggins," Mom called out. "You've done a wonderful job."

Mr. Coggins smiled and rested his hand on a nearby dogwood tree. "I do my part, and the Lord does the rest," he said.

"I think the dogwood trees are my favorite," said Dad.

Mr. Coggins looked up at the pink and white flowers above his head for a long moment. He took off his cap and rubbed his gray hair. "There are some important spiritual lessons we can learn from the dogwood." He pulled at a branch. "The wood reminds me of the cross where Jesus died for all the sins of the world. The wood of the dogwood is pretty durable. Won't break under the stress of strong winds." He replaced his cap. "The Lord Jesus is an example of strength too. Think how He withstood Satan's temptations, took abuse from the Pharisees, and suffered agonizing pain on the cross."

Damian fixed his eyes on Mr. Coggins's face. He'd heard this story before, but never like this.

Mr. Coggins continued, "The dogwood's white flower reminds me of the purity and sinlessness of Jesus. Look—"

He bent a branch down close to where they stood. Damian and LaTrisha stepped forward. "The bracts form the shape of a cross. See that small crown in the center? Those are the actual flowers. They look kind of like the crown of thorns the Lord Jesus wore."

Damian could only nod his head in silence and stare.

"Look at the tips of the bracts. See that reddish color? What does that remind you of?"

"The blood?" LaTrisha asked.

Mr. Coggins nodded. "The blood of Christ."

His fingers moved to the green leaf. "Does the leaf remind you of something too?" asked Damian.

Mr. Coggins looked down at him, his gray eyes twinkling. "Well, I might just turn the question on you, young man. What does it make you think of?"

Damian thought for a moment. "Maybe green stands for the new life a person gets when he accepts Jesus' death for his sins!"

Mr. Coggins tipped his cap. "Right you are."

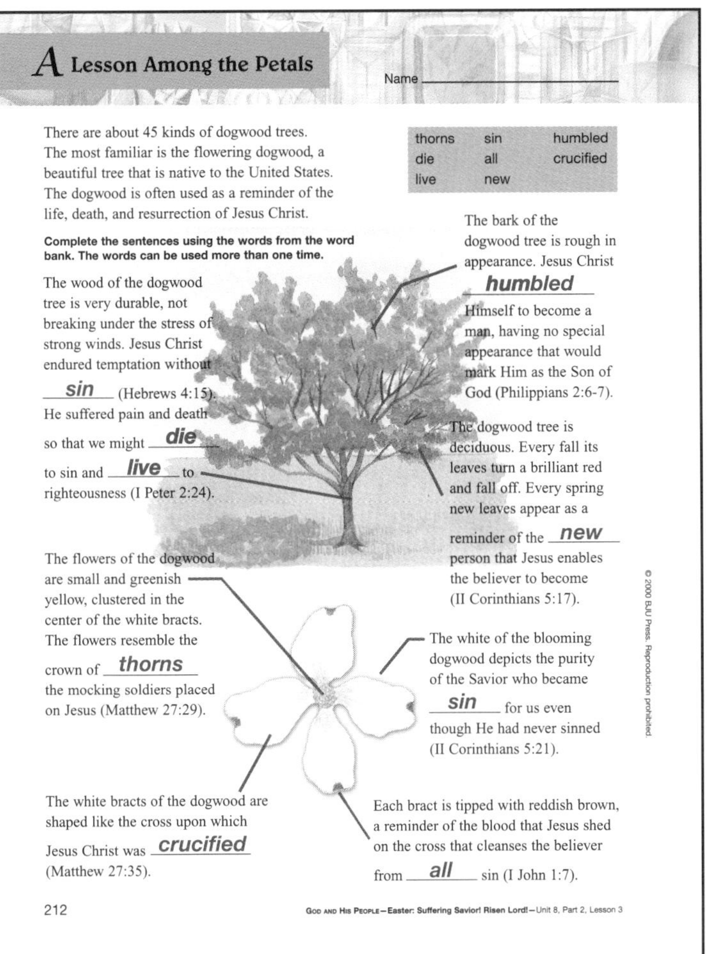

A Lesson Among the Petals

Name ______

thorns	sin	humbled
die	all	crucified
live	new	

There are about 45 kinds of dogwood trees. The most familiar is the flowering dogwood, a beautiful tree that is native to the United States. The dogwood is often used as a reminder of the life, death, and resurrection of Jesus Christ.

Complete the sentences using the words from the word bank. The words can be used more than one time.

The wood of the dogwood tree is very durable, not breaking under the stress of strong winds. Jesus Christ endured temptation without __sin__ (Hebrews 4:15). He suffered pain and death so that we might __die__ to sin and __live__ to righteousness (I Peter 2:24).

The bark of the dogwood tree is rough in appearance. Jesus Christ __humbled__ Himself to become a man, having no special appearance that would mark Him as the Son of God (Philippians 2:6-7).

The dogwood tree is deciduous. Every fall its leaves turn a brilliant red and fall off. Every spring new leaves appear as a reminder of the __new__ person that Jesus enables the believer to become (II Corinthians 5:17).

The flowers of the dogwood are small and greenish yellow, clustered in the center of the white bracts. The flowers resemble the crown of __thorns__ the mocking soldiers placed on Jesus (Matthew 27:29).

The white of the blooming dogwood depicts the purity of the Savior who became __sin__ for us even though He had never sinned (II Corinthians 5:21).

The white bracts of the dogwood are shaped like the cross upon which Jesus Christ was __crucified__ (Matthew 27:35).

Each bract is tipped with reddish brown, a reminder of the blood that Jesus shed on the cross that cleanses the believer from __all__ sin (I John 1:7).

212 God and His People—Easter: Suffering Savior! Risen Lord!—Unit 8, Part 2, Lesson 3

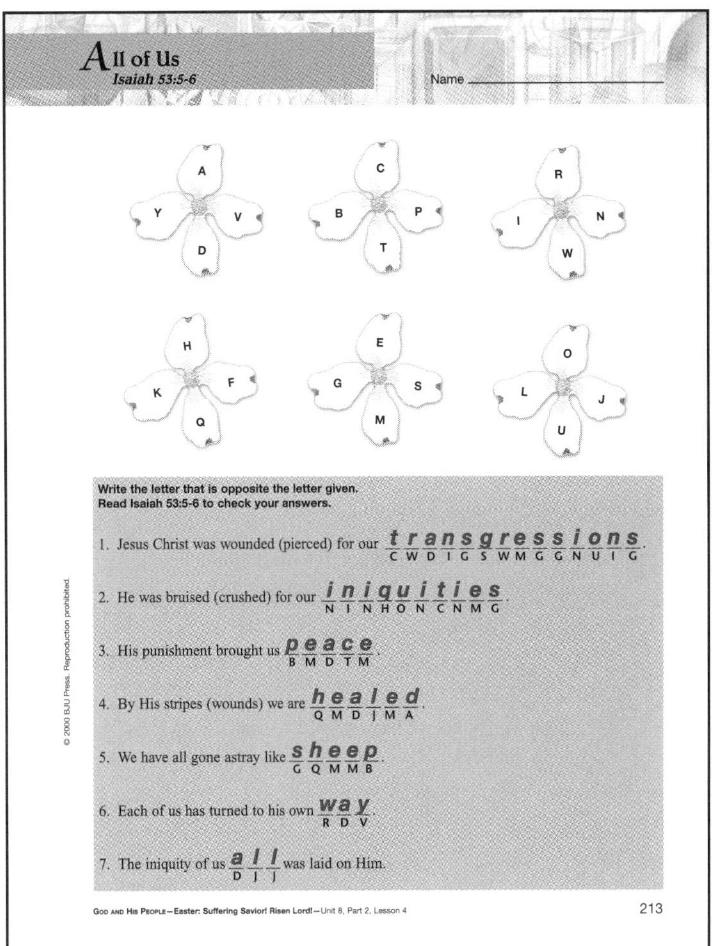

All of Us
Isaiah 53:5-6

Name ______

Write the letter that is opposite the letter given. Read Isaiah 53:5-6 to check your answers.

1. Jesus Christ was wounded (pierced) for our __transgressions__.
   C W D I G S W M G G N U I G
2. He was bruised (crushed) for our __iniquities__.
   N I N H O N C N M G
3. His punishment brought us __peace__.
   B M D T M
4. By His stripes (wounds) we are __healed__.
   Q M D J M A
5. We have all gone astray like __sheep__.
   G Q M M B
6. Each of us has turned to his own __way__.
   R D V
7. The iniquity of us __all__ was laid on Him.
   D J J

God and His People—Easter: Suffering Savior! Risen Lord!—Unit 8, Part 2, Lesson 4 213

"We have a dogwood tree in our yard at home," Mom said quietly. "Did you ever look at it closely?"

"I have. But I've never thought of all those things," LaTrisha said.

"Neither have I," said Damian. "When I get home, I'm going to tell all my friends about the lessons of the dogwood."

➤ **What additional attraction drew the visitors each year to the Grove Creek Gardens?** *(Mr. Coggins telling his stories)*

➤ **How was Mr. Coggins's story different from former stories he had told?** *(He told how one of God's creations can remind us what Jesus did on the cross for the sins of men.)*

Worktext page 212

Apply Bible knowledge to everyday life.

Science Connection (optional)

Classify trees. Tell the students that simply stated a *tree* is a tall plant with one long stem. Trees can be *conifers, monocots,* or *dicots. Conifers* are cone-producing trees whose leaves can be needle-like in clusters or flattened needles. *Monocots* are flowering plants with soft hollow stems, one-seed leaves, and petals in groups of three. *Dicots* are flowering plants with woody stems, two-seed leaves, and flowers in groups of fours or fives. Tell the students that the flowering dogwood tree is a dicot, native to eastern and central United States.

Lesson 4

Materials

- TimeLine and picture: Charles Tindley

Hymn: "It Is Finished"

Sing the hymn (Worktext page 284). Play the recording and sing all the verses together. Choose a different leader to lead each verse.

Memory Verses—Isaiah 53:5-6

Practice the memory verses. Locate and read aloud **Isaiah 53:3-6.** Place the students into four groups. Assign each group a different verse to say from memory. Continue the activity by switching verses until each group has said all four verses. A student may be selected to say all the verses or just verses 5-6.

Worktext page 213

Develop further understanding of the memory verses.

Introducing the Hero of the Faith

Discuss heroes.

➤ **According to the world's standards, what qualities make a hero?** *(Possible answers include physical characteristics or abilities, musical abilities, art skills, accumulation of wealth, and the ability to invent.)*

➤ **What qualities does God look for in His heroes?** *(Answers will vary.)* Explain that God looks at man's heart, not at his outward appearance or abilities.

Hero of the Faith

Read the following story based on the life of Charles Albert Tindley.

Nothing Between

Have you ever noticed who wrote the hymns you sing in church? Most great hymns came from men and women dedicated to God. Charles Albert Tindley was such a man.

Charles's mother died when he was two years old. Charles's father loved him, but he could not afford to take care of Charles or send him to school. Charles was hired out to work for different families. Some of the families were cruel. Charles could not go to school, so he found pieces of newspaper on the streets. Carefully he studied the letters on those little scraps and taught himself how to read. While everyone was asleep, Charles lit pine knots as a lamp to read by and used charcoal to write.

One time as Charles finished his chores early and was on his way to church, he looked down at his dirty feet and stopped to wash them. He sat down in the back of the church, but all the children were called forward to read from the Bible. Immediately Charles stood up and walked forward. Some people snickered and whispered because Charles had bare feet. At that moment, Charles determined: "I don't want to be poor like this my whole life. Nothing is going to keep me from getting an education."

Charles often plowed all day in the field; then at night he walked or ran fourteen miles to have lessons with the school teacher.

Charles Tindley was a teenager when the Civil War ended. After he married, Charles continued to work all day and attend school in the evenings.

One day while visiting a church, Tindley realized that a life without Christ was a true life of poverty. Charles Tindley put his trust in Christ that day, and he became truly rich.

Tindley became the church janitor and continued his education by taking correspondence courses while attending an institute. He wanted to buy every book that had something he needed to know. Finally Tindley went to take the examination to enter the ministry. He found that all the other candidates had diplomas. "How do you expect to pass your examination?" one man asked. Charles Tindley not only passed the exam, but he had the second highest score.

For fifteen years, Tindley served as pastor to several churches. He also helped provide meals and a place to stay for the hungry and homeless. One day the pastoral position in the same church where Tindley had served as a janitor was vacant. Tindley became the pastor.

The church grew so large that the members could not attend both services on Sunday. The Lord allowed the church to construct a new building that seated 3,200. But when the first service was held in the new building, Charles Tindley was not there. His wife had passed away suddenly that morning.

God strengthened Tindley and helped him continue preaching and witnessing whenever there was an opportunity. God also helped him to write over forty songs to share with other believers. Tindley wanted people to learn through his hymns that God is sovereign. God controls every detail of the lives of His children. One of Tindley's hymns is "Nothing Between." Nothing should come between the Christian and his Savior.

➤ **Even though Charles did not go to school, how did he learn to read?** *(He gathered scraps of newspaper and read them by the light of pine knot lamps after everyone had gone to bed.)*

➤ **How did God honor Tindley's effort when he went to take the examination for entering the ministry?** *(He made the second highest score on the exam.)*

➤ **Do you think the death of Charles Tindley's wife stopped his ministry? Why not?** *(No. God strengthened Tindley to continue preaching, witnessing, and writing songs.)*

➤ **What is God doing in your life to make you more like Christ?** *(Answers will vary.)*

TimeLine

Place *Charles Tindley* on the TimeLine. Select a student to place *Charles Tindley* onto the TimeLine at 1851-1933. Guide the students in gluing the figure of *Charles Tindley* onto their individual TimeLines.

Charles Albert Tindley
(1851-1933)

Name ______________________

"Nothing between my soul and the Savior . . ." is the opening line of one of the many hymns written by Charles Albert Tindley. It was also the creed by which Tindley lived. He wanted nothing between him and service to the Savior he loved.

After the death of his mother, Charles Albert Tindley went from one family to another, working for his keep. Most of the time he was ill fed and mistreated. He could not go to school, so he learned to read from scraps of newspapers he found on the streets. To write, he used charcoal for ink. After plowing all day in the fields, he walked fourteen miles for lessons with a teacher.

As an adult, Tindley continued to work all day and attend school in the evenings. He heard the gospel in a church he visited and trusted Christ as his Savior. He became the custodian of that church. From then on his goal was to become a minister. When he went to take the examination to enter the ministry, all the other candidates had diplomas. He was asked how he hoped to pass the test without a degree. By the grace of God, Tindley scored the second highest mark on the test.

For fifteen years Tindley served as pastor to several churches. Along with preaching the gospel, he led the churches in providing meals and shelter for the hungry and homeless. The church where Tindley had been custodian called him as its pastor, and under his leadership it grew to several thousand members. He continued serving, preaching, and witnessing until God called him to "Triumph at last! With nothing between!" The hymns he wrote live on as testimony to the faith by which he lived.

Answer the questions.

What trials did Charles Albert Tindley face in growing up?

His mother died, and he had to work for a living. He could not go to school. He had only scraps of newspapers to read.

How did God honor Tindley's efforts to become educated and serve Him?

He made the second highest score on a test. He became a pastor. He wrote hymns.

What is God doing in your life to make you more like Christ?

____

____

____

____

Worktext Supplement page 308

Hero of the Faith, Charles Tindley.

I Believe

Name ______________________

You have studied what God's Word tells about the life, death, and resurrection of the Lord Jesus Christ. In order to be saved, a person must believe that these things were planned and took place *for him or her personally.* Do you believe this? In order to make it meaningful to you, write your first name on each line.

I believe that God sent His only Son into the world to save ______________.

I believe that Jesus Christ rose again the third day to give ______________ victory over death and hell.

I believe that Jesus Christ took on Himself the sins of ______________ and suffered and died for them.

I believe that ______________ can find salvation only in Jesus Christ.

If you believe these things and have asked Jesus Christ to save you, spend some time thanking Him for the wonderful gift of your salvation.

If you believe these things and have not asked Jesus Christ to save you, talk with your parent, teacher, or pastor about your need for salvation.

Worktext page 214

Realize that salvation is meant for all men.

Going Beyond

Materials

- Graph paper for each student

Enrichment

Make a puzzle activity about Easter. Instruct each student to make his own crossword puzzle using graph paper. Direct the students to brainstorm about Easter words; then write the words on a chart or a chalkboard. Challenge each student to design his own puzzle, choosing the Easter words from the list and writing his own clues. After the puzzles are complete, allow students to exchange puzzles to solve or make copies so students can solve all of the puzzles.

Unit 8 Review Name ____________

Complete the sentences.

body	Christ	cup	Egypt
Gethsemane	Judas	Lamb	Passover
perfect	pray	sleeping	watch

The last supper Jesus ate with His disciples was the **Passover** meal. At the time of Passover, the Jews looked back to the Israelites' deliverance from **Egypt** and forward to the coming of **Christ**. Jesus gave the meal a new meaning when he explained that the bread would represent His **body** and the **cup** would represent His blood. Today Christians remember Christ's death as the **perfect** **Lamb** of God and look forward to His return.

Afterward, Jesus and His disciples entered **Gethsemane**, the garden where Jesus was betrayed by **Judas** with a kiss. When Jesus returned, He found His disciples **sleeping**. He instructed the disciples to **watch** and **pray** to avoid temptation.

Arimathea	Barabbas	Galilee
Magdalene	Peter	Pilate
	Simon	

When Jesus was arrested, **Peter** denied knowing the Lord. At the trial **Pilate** found Jesus innocent but condemned Him to death to please the Jews. He released a criminal named **Barabbas** instead. A man named **Simon** was ordered to carry the cross of Christ to the place of crucifixion.

After Jesus was crucified, Joseph of **Arimathea** buried the body of Jesus in a tomb sealed by a great stone. Pilate ordered soldiers to guard the tomb. Three days after His death, Jesus arose as He had said He would. Mary **Magdalene** saw the empty tomb. She and other women were told to tell the disciples that Jesus was alive and that He would meet them in **Galilee**.

God and His People   Use after completing Unit 8   S63

Unit Review

Materials

- Copy of Supplement page S63, "Unit 8 Review," for each student

Guide a review of Unit 8. Review the people and events in preparation for the Unit 8 Test (optional).

Christ and His People

Overview

Preparing the Teacher

The English word *church* comes from a Greek word that means "belonging to the Lord." It is usually defined as a body of people called out from the world and belonging to the Lord. We teach our students that the reason God made us was for His own glory. We bring glory to the Lord not only in prayer and praise but also in exhibiting Christlikeness in our lives. **Titus 2:10** admonishes the church to "adorn the doctrine of God . . . in all things," and **I Peter 2:9** tells us to "show forth [His] praises."

Do your students see your life bearing the fruit of the Spirit? Only as we allow the Holy Spirit to produce His fruit in our own lives can we expect to develop these graces in the lives of our students. Remember that they will not only hear your words; they will also see your actions and reactions. "Herein is my Father glorified, that ye bear much fruit; so shall ye be my disciples" **(John 15:8).**

Preparing the Lessons

Part 1 Lesson 1 Materials—two small pieces of magnetic tape for each student

Part 3 Lesson 1 Materials—ten pennies, ten one-dollar bills, a calculator for each student (optional)

Part 3 Lesson 3 Materials—four packages of seeds

Part 4 Lesson 1 Materials—a branch from a tree or shrub, cut and withered

Unit 9 Christ and His People

Hymn: "The Church's One Foundation"

Part	Lesson number	Lesson pages	Worktext pages	Supplement pages	Bible Account	Application
PART 1: **THE FOUNDATION OF THE CHURCH**	1	289	215-18		Peter's Confession of Christ (Matthew 16:13-17)	
	2	291	219-20		Peter's First Sermon (Acts 2:1-47)	
	3	294	221-22			"Seeking for God"
	4	295	223-24	S72	**Bible Study:** Names of Jesus	
PART 2: **THE CHURCH LEADERS**	1	298	225-26		Aquila, Priscilla, and Apollos (Acts 18:1-3, 18–19:1)	
	2	300	227-28		Helpers Needed (Acts 6:1-7)	
	3	302	229			**Hymn History Story:** "The Church's One Foundation"
	4	303	230			**Hero of the Faith:** John Knox
PART 3: **THE CHURCH MEMBERS**	1	306	231-32		Tithing (Malachi 3:8-12)	
	2	308	233-34		Giving to the Ministry (Acts 11:27-30; II Corinthians 8:1-12)	
	3	310	235-36			"Make Me Willing" **Picture the Point:** Giving to God
	4	312	237-38		Edifying the Saints (Hebrews 10:19-25)	
PART 4: **THE WORK OF BELIEVERS**	1	315	239-40		Believers Are the Branches (John 15:1-8)	
	2	317	241-42			"Abide in Me"
	3	319	243	S73	The Ministry of Believers (Acts 20:17-35)	
	4	320	244			"Repairs"

Connections	Memory Verses and Principles	Bible Doctrines	Skills/Applications
	Matthew 16:15-16 *Jesus is God.*	**The Doctrine of God** **Attributes of God:** God is unchanging (immutable) (Mal. 3:6). **The Doctrine of Man** **Redemption of Man:** Man by faith receives Christ's righteousness (Phil. 3:9). **The Doctrine of Salvation** **Reception by Man:** Man must turn to Christ alone for salvation (John 14:6). **Elements of Salvation:** God calls men through men (Rom. 10:14-15). Sanctification is the work of God's Spirit which enables Christians more and more to die to sin and to live unto righteousness (Rom. 8:13). **The Doctrine of the Church** **Definitions:** The universal church, an organism, is the mystical body of Christ composed of all true believers (I Cor. 12:13). The local church, an organization, is a group of professing believers gathered together for the purposes of God (Acts 2:41, 42). **Organization of the Local Church:** The apostles served in the establishment of the church (Eph. 4:11). Officers should preach the Word (II Tim. 4:2). Officers should teach members (Eph. 4:11-16). Officers should care for those having special needs (Acts 6:1-7). Members should exhort one another (Heb. 10:25). Members should pray (Acts 2:42). Members should evangelize the lost (Matt. 22:1-14). Members should contribute financially (I Cor. 16:1-2).	**Foundational:** • Know that Jesus is God • Realize that the church is composed of all true believers • Understand that God planned that Christians should do good works to bring honor and glory to Him • Understand the role of deacons in the church • Realize that God wants believers to willingly contribute to His work **Practical:** • Recall facts and details • Locate information in Scripture • Use Bible reference tools—cross-reference, concordance • Use a glossary • Define words • Read a map • Use a map scale • Read a time line • Order words in a sentence • Complete the plan of salvation • Determine the extent of a Scripture reference • Make a false statement true • Identify character qualities of a Christian **Personal:** • Develop a Bible reading habit • Realize that Christians are to encourage each other • Realize that Christians are to pray for one another • Realize that God wants Christians to be His witnesses • Apply Bible knowledge to everyday life
TimeLine: John Knox	Ephesians 3:20-21 *Let the church glorify Jesus Christ now and forever.*		
Math	II Corinthians 9:6-7 *Give generously and cheerfully to God.*		
	Ephesians 2:10 *We are God's workmanship, and God wants Christians to do good works to honor and glorify Him.*		

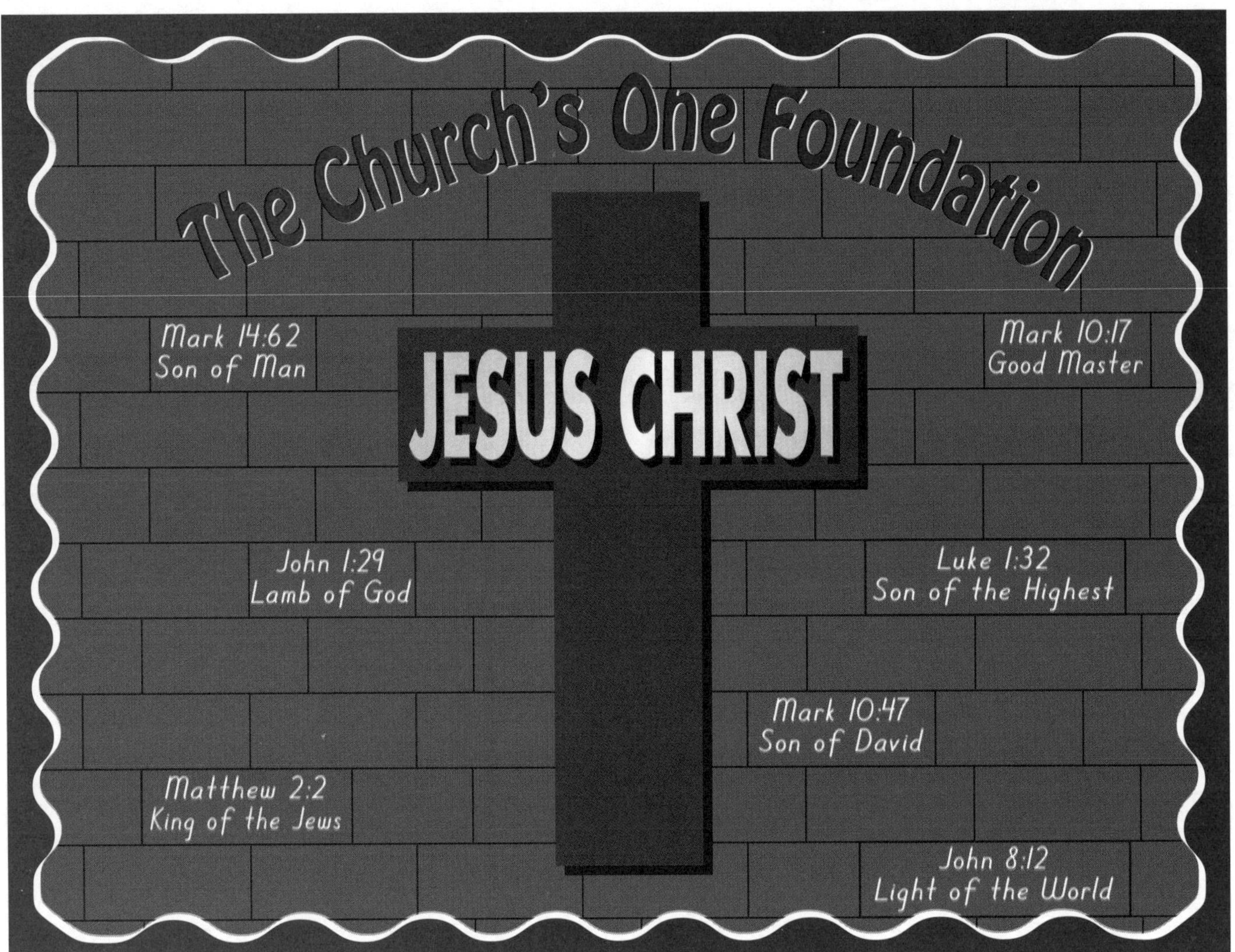

Preparing the Unit 9 Bulletin Board

Cover the bulletin board with brick patterned paper and border it in white or black. Make the top caption "The Church's One Foundation" in black. Make the center caption "Jesus Christ" within a cross outline. After the students complete the Bible Study in Part 1, Lesson 4, allow them to place their "bricks" of references and names for Jesus over the bulletin board bricks to form a foundation.

The Foundation of the Church

Unit 9, Part 1

Preview

Doctrines

- Man by faith receives Christ's righteousness (Philippians 3:9)—Lesson 1
- Man must turn to Christ alone for salvation (John 14:6)—Lesson 1
- The universal church, an organism, is the mystical body of Christ composed of all true believers (I Corinthians 12:13)—Lesson 2
- The local church, an organization, is a group of professing believers gathered together for the purposes of God (Acts 2:41, 42)—Lesson 2

Skills and Applications

- Learn Matthew 16:15-16
- Use a glossary
- Locate information in Scripture
- Read a map
- Use a map scale
- Recall facts and details
- Make a false statement true
- Realize that the church is composed of all true believers
- Know that Jesus is God
- Develop a Bible reading habit
- Apply Bible knowledge to everyday life

Lesson 1

Materials

- Chart 33, "Palestine in the Time of Christ"
- Song: "The Bible Reading Habit"
- Two pieces of magnetic tape for each student
- A copy of a test
- Unit 9 Bookmark for each student
- Highlighter for each student (optional)

Background Information

Caesarea Philippi—*In the foothills of Mount Hermon, where the Jordan River begins, is the little village of Caesarea Philippi. The town was formerly named in honor of Pan, the Greek god of nature. Philip, the son of Herod who was a ruler at the time of Jesus' birth, rebuilt and enlarged the village. Philip renamed it to honor his emperor Caesar and added his name to distinguish it from the city of Caesarea on the coast.*

Messiah—*The word* Messiah *comes from the Hebrew word* mashiah, *which means "anointed." The Greek word* Christ, *used in the New Testament, means the same thing. The Jewish people waited centuries for their Messiah, their "Anointed One," to come and declare Himself to be King.*

Introducing the Bible Account

Discuss tests. Display the copy of a test.

➤ **Why do teachers give tests?** *(Accept any answer.)*

➤ **What do most school tests contain?** *(questions)*

Explain that in the following Bible account, Jesus gave His disciples a test.

Bible Account

Read the following Bible account or read Matthew 16:13-17. Point out Caesarea Philippi on Chart 33, "Palestine in the Time of Christ," and read the background information about Caesarea Philippi.

Peter's Confession of Christ

Jesus had been teaching His disciples for two years. He had taught them a great deal about who He was and what He had come to earth to do. Jesus' disciples had seen Him heal the sick, cast out demons, feed multitudes, and raise the dead. They had heard the wonderful sermons Jesus had preached and had heard the parables He had told. They had witnessed Jesus confronting the religious leaders of the day. Now it was time to determine whether they had learned the lessons Jesus had taught them or whether they would fail to see Him as the Messiah (the one sent from God).

One day Jesus went out with His disciples into the village of Caesarea Philippi. On the way He asked His disciples who the people

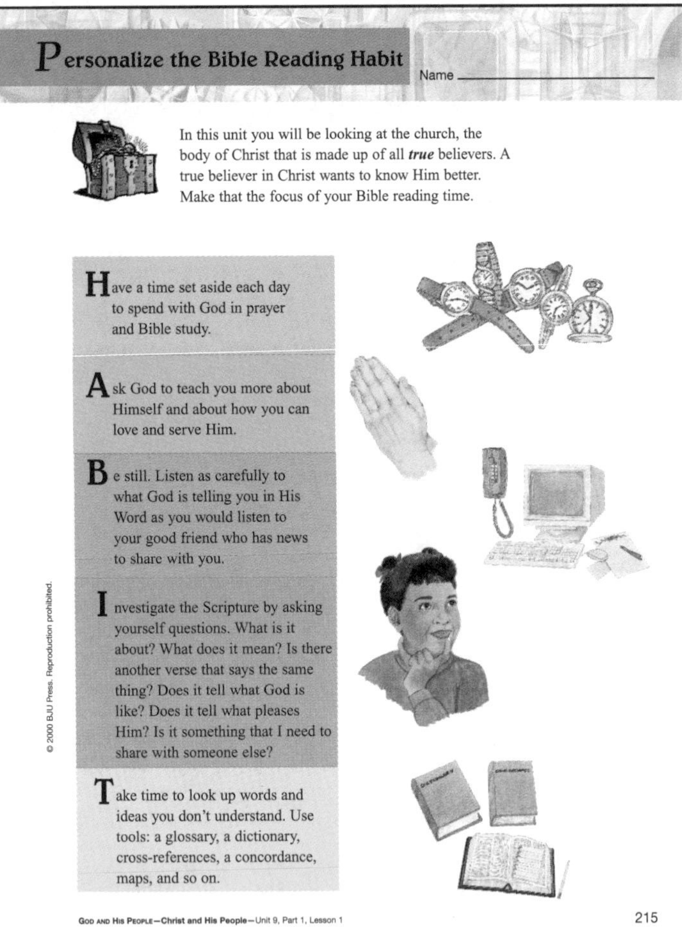

Personalize the Bible Reading Habit

Name ____________________

In this unit you will be looking at the church, the body of Christ that is made up of all ***true*** believers. A true believer in Christ wants to know Him better. Make that the focus of your Bible reading time.

Have a time set aside each day to spend with God in prayer and Bible study.

Ask God to teach you more about Himself and about how you can love and serve Him.

Be still. Listen as carefully to what God is telling you in His Word as you would listen to your good friend who has news to share with you.

Investigate the Scripture by asking yourself questions. What is it about? What does it mean? Is there another verse that says the same thing? Does it tell what God is like? Does it tell what pleases Him? Is it something that I need to share with someone else?

Take time to look up words and ideas you don't understand. Use tools: a glossary, a dictionary, cross-references, a concordance, maps, and so on.

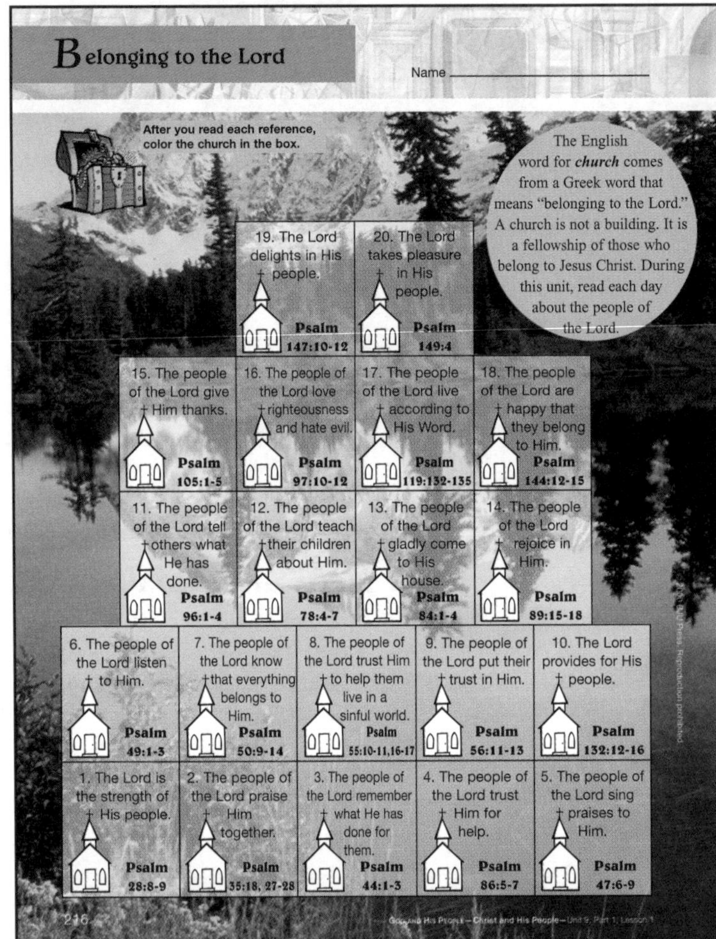

Belonging to the Lord

Name ____________________

After you read each reference, color the church in the box.

The English word for *church* comes from a Greek word that means "belonging to the Lord." A church is not a building. It is a fellowship of those who belong to Jesus Christ. During this unit, read each day about the people of the Lord.

19. The Lord delights in His people. Psalm 147:10-12
20. The Lord takes pleasure in His people. Psalm 149:4
15. The people of the Lord give Him thanks. Psalm 105:1-5
16. The people of the Lord love righteousness and hate evil. Psalm 97:10-12
17. The people of the Lord live according to His Word. Psalm 119:132-135
18. The people of the Lord are happy that they belong to Him. Psalm 144:12-15
11. The people of the Lord tell others what He has done. Psalm 96:1-4
12. The people of the Lord teach their children about Him. Psalm 78:4-7
13. The people of the Lord gladly come to His house. Psalm 84:1-4
14. The people of the Lord rejoice in Him. Psalm 89:15-18
6. The people of the Lord listen to Him. Psalm 49:1-3
7. The people of the Lord know that everything belongs to Him. Psalm 50:9-14
8. The people of the Lord trust Him to help them live in a sinful world. Psalm 55:10-11,16-17
9. The people of the Lord put their trust in Him. Psalm 56:11-13
10. The Lord provides for His people. Psalm 132:12-16
1. The Lord is the strength of His people. Psalm 28:8-9
2. The people of the Lord praise Him together. Psalm 35:18, 27-28
3. The people of the Lord remember what He has done for them. Psalm 44:1-3
4. The people of the Lord trust Him for help. Psalm 86:5-7
5. The people of the Lord sing praises to Him. Psalm 47:6-9

thought He was. The disciples told Jesus that some people were saying He was John the Baptist or Elijah. Others said that He was one of the other prophets come back to life.

Then Jesus asked another question, wanting a personal response from His disciples. He asked them who *they* thought He was. Peter, often the spokesman for the disciples and who sometimes spoke hastily, gave a great confession. He answered, "Thou art the Christ, the Son of the living God." This was not a man's opinion. Peter's answer was from God. God had revealed to Peter that Jesus was God. Peter knew that Jesus was anointed of God. Peter had passed the test! He understood the miracles, sermons, and daily contacts with the Lord. The disciples recognized that Christ was sent by the Father to fulfill His will.

Explain that God wants Christians to be personally responsible for what they hear, just as Jesus wanted His disciples to be personally responsible for their knowledge of Christ. Explain that Peter's answer came from God because Peter was in fellowship with God. The more time Christians spend with God and His Word, the more Christ will be revealed.

➤ **What had Jesus taught and shown His disciples during the two years He had been with them?** *(Jesus taught them who He was and what He had come to do. He healed the sick, cast out demons, fed the multitudes, and raised the dead.)*

➤ **According to the disciples, who did the people say Jesus was?** *(John the Baptist, Elijah, or one of the other prophets come back to life)*

➤ **How did Peter answer Jesus' question?** *(He told Jesus, "Thou art the Christ, the Son of the living God.")*

➤ **What did Peter mean by his answer?** *(He recognized that Jesus was God and that He was anointed of God.)*

➤ **How do you think the Pharisees would have answered the question Peter was asked?** *(They would have denied that Jesus was God no matter what evidence they had.)*

Explain that God asks Christians today that same question about Jesus: "Who do you think Jesus is?" Allow students to voluntarily share their testimonies at this time.

Bible Study Skills, Worktext pages 215-16

Develop a Bible reading habit. Read the top part of page 215 aloud. Select students to read aloud the Bible reading guidelines, emphasizing that because a true believer wants

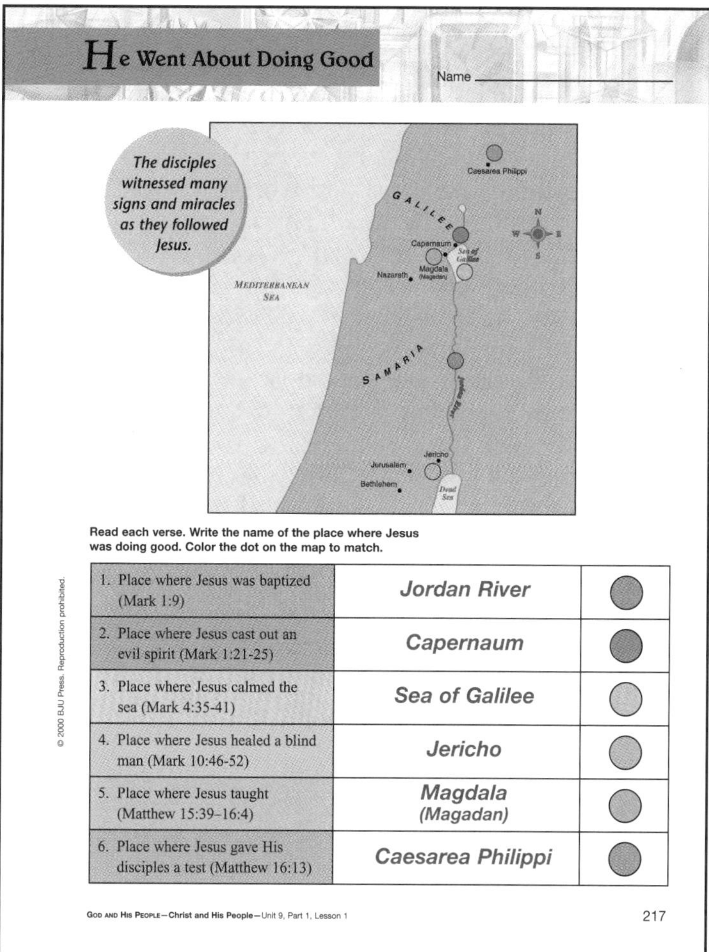

He Went About Doing Good

Name ______________________

Read each verse. Write the name of the place where Jesus was doing good. Color the dot on the map to match.

1. Place where Jesus was baptized (Mark 1:9)	*Jordan River*	
2. Place where Jesus cast out an evil spirit (Mark 1:21-25)	*Capernaum*	
3. Place where Jesus calmed the sea (Mark 4:35-41)	*Sea of Galilee*	
4. Place where Jesus healed a blind man (Mark 10:46-52)	*Jericho*	
5. Place where Jesus taught (Matthew 15:39-16:4)	*Magdala (Magadan)*	
6. Place where Jesus gave His disciples a test (Matthew 16:13)	*Caesarea Philippi*	

GOD AND HIS PEOPLE—Christ and His People—Unit 9, Part 1, Lesson 1 217

to know God better, he studies God's Word. Explain the four-week Bible reading activity on page 216. Lead in singing the song "The Bible Reading Habit" from Worktext page 271.

Worktext page 217

Locate information in Scripture and read a map.

Memory Verses—Matthew 16:15-16

Principle: Jesus is God. Locate and read **Matthew 16:15-16** aloud as the students read silently.

➤ **Who asks the question in verse 15?** *(Jesus)*

➤ **What did Jesus ask His disciples?** *(Who did they think He was?)*

➤ **In verse 16, who answers the question?** *(Simon Peter)*

➤ **How does Peter answer?** *(He says that Jesus is the Christ, the Son of the living God.)*

Remind the students that Peter recognized Jesus as the promised Messiah. Divide the students into two groups with Group 1 reading verse 15 and Group 2 reading verse 16; then reverse their roles to read the verses again. Direct the students to highlight the verses in their Bibles (optional). Give each student a Unit 9 Bookmark. Direct attention to the illustration of the seed and its growth as an

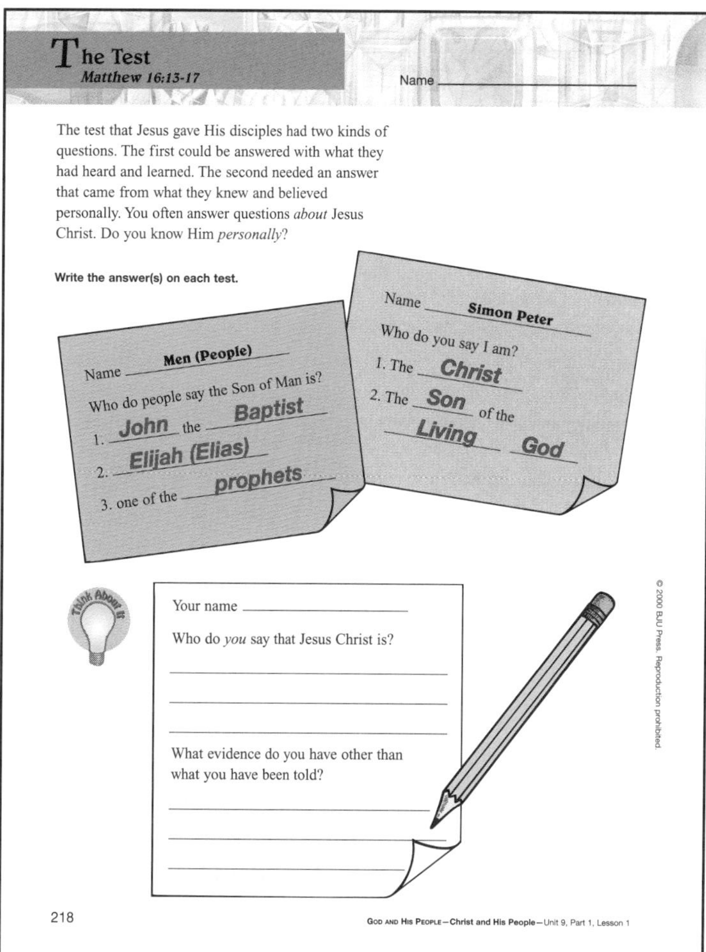

The Test
Matthew 16:13-17

Name ______________________

The test that Jesus gave His disciples had two kinds of questions. The first could be answered with what they had heard and learned. The second needed an answer that came from what they knew and believed personally. You often answer questions *about* Jesus Christ. Do you know Him *personally*?

Write the answer(s) on each test.

Name **Men (People)**
Who do people say the Son of Man is?
1. *John* the *Baptist*
2. *Elijah (Elias)*
3. one of the *prophets*

Name **Simon Peter**
Who do you say I am?
1. The *Christ*
2. The *Son* of the *Living God*

Your name ______________________
Who do *you* say that Jesus Christ is?
____
What evidence do you have other than what you have been told?
____

218 GOD AND HIS PEOPLE—Christ and His People—Unit 9, Part 1, Lesson 1

example of Christ's wanting Christians to grow spiritually. Direct the students to attach a piece of magnetic tape to each end and to place the Unit 9 Bookmark over the page.

Worktext page 218

Recall facts about the Bible account and apply the Bible personally.

Lesson 2

Preparation of Materials

Make four memory-verse cards by writing half of each memory verse (Matthew 16:15-16) on a piece of tagboard or poster board.

Memory Verses—Matthew 16:15-16

Practice the memory verses. Locate **Matthew 16:15-16** and select students to read the verses aloud. Give the cards to four students. Instruct the students to stand holding the cards in order so that they can be read. Direct the students at their seats to close their eyes. Tap one of the four students, instructing him to hide his card behind his back. Instruct the students to open their eyes and call on students to read the verses. Continue this procedure as time permits.

One-on-One: Direct the student to arrange the memory-verse cards in the correct order. Tell him to practice reading the verses, removing one card at a time and rereading the verses.

Background Information

Pentecost—*The word Pentecost comes from the root word* penta *meaning "five" and* konta *meaning "ten times." In the Old Testament it was a Jewish feast to celebrate the harvest and the giving of the law of Moses. Pentecost was observed fifty days (seven weeks) after Passover. In the New Testament, the occasion of the receiving of the Holy Spirit by the apostles and early Christians is called Pentecost.*

Coming of the Holy Spirit—*On the day of Pentecost, God used three signs to show that the coming of the Holy Spirit was the work of God: the sound of a mighty rushing wind, the tongues of fire, and the voice of the Holy Spirit speaking through the disciples in many languages. The way the Holy Spirit came at Pentecost was never repeated. The Holy Spirit was given to several groups under different conditions but never twice in the same way. For example, the split tongues of fire never appeared again. Later, the gift of tongues was given to individuals but never to all believers as at Pentecost. After the first century, all the signs ceased.*

The Church—*After Christ ascended into heaven, His plan was to form a new group of believers called the church. He sent the Holy Spirit to indwell all believers and to give them power to do what the Lord Jesus had commanded.*

Introducing the Bible Account

Discuss churches. Encourage the students to share information about what church they attend and any special project or activity of their church that they may have been involved in.

Bible Account

Read the following Bible account or read Acts 2:1-47.

Peter's First Sermon

The disciples were gathered together in one place on the day of Pentecost. While they were sitting in the house, God showed His power to the disciples by filling them with His Holy Spirit. Suddenly, there was a great noise. It sounded like the sound of a mighty rushing wind. As the disciples looked around, they saw tongues of fire that settled on each of them. All of the disciples were filled with the Holy Spirit and spoke in foreign languages. The Jews, who were in Jerusalem from every nation to observe the Feast of the Ingathering at the end of the harvest, heard the noise and gathered together. They were amazed that each one of them was hearing the disciples speak in his own language about God's mighty works.

Some of the Jews thought it was strange that the disciples were speaking in foreign tongues and said that the disciples were drunk. Peter stood and declared in a loud voice that they were not drunk. He explained that this miracle of the disciples' being filled with the Holy Spirit fulfilled prophecy spoken by Joel (Joel 2:20). Peter preached to the Jews, addressing them as men of Israel. He told them to listen to what he had to say. He reminded them that God had worked miracles and signs through Jesus, which they had seen. He told them that Christ had been crucified by those now present. Peter said that Christ had risen from the dead and that David had predicted this many years before. He explained that Christ's rising from the dead proved that Christ was God. Peter said that he and the other disciples were witnesses to Christ's resurrection. He said that Christ ascended into heaven and is there now, exalted before the throne of God. He said that they had just witnessed God's outpouring of the Holy Spirit, which Christ had promised.

When the Jews heard Peter's preaching, "they were pricked in their heart, and said unto Peter and to the rest of the apostles, Men and brethren, what shall we do?" Peter told them to repent, or turn from their sin, and then be baptized in Jesus' name to show that they had accepted Christ as Savior. Peter told them that when they repented they would receive the gift of the Holy Spirit.

Peter's sermon produced a great harvest of souls. Three thousand people repented and were baptized. God's Holy Spirit had convicted these Jews of their sin and saved them. God's Holy Spirit, now present in their lives, brought unity to the early believers, for "they continued stedfastly in the apostles' doctrine and fellowship and in breaking of bread, and in prayers." The believers rejoiced in each other's company. They practiced self-sacrificial love, selling their goods and giving to those among them who were in need. The believers praised God and found favor with all the people. God continued to work among them, and day by day people were saved and added to the church.

➤ **As the disciples were filled with the Holy Spirit, who heard the noise and how did they react?** *(The Jews that had come to Jerusalem from every nation heard and were amazed that the disciples could speak of God in their language; some mocked, saying that the disciples were drunk.)*

➤ **What did Peter preach about Christ, and how did the Jews react to this?** *(He preached that Christ had died for their sins, was buried, and rose again. Three thousand souls were saved that day.)*

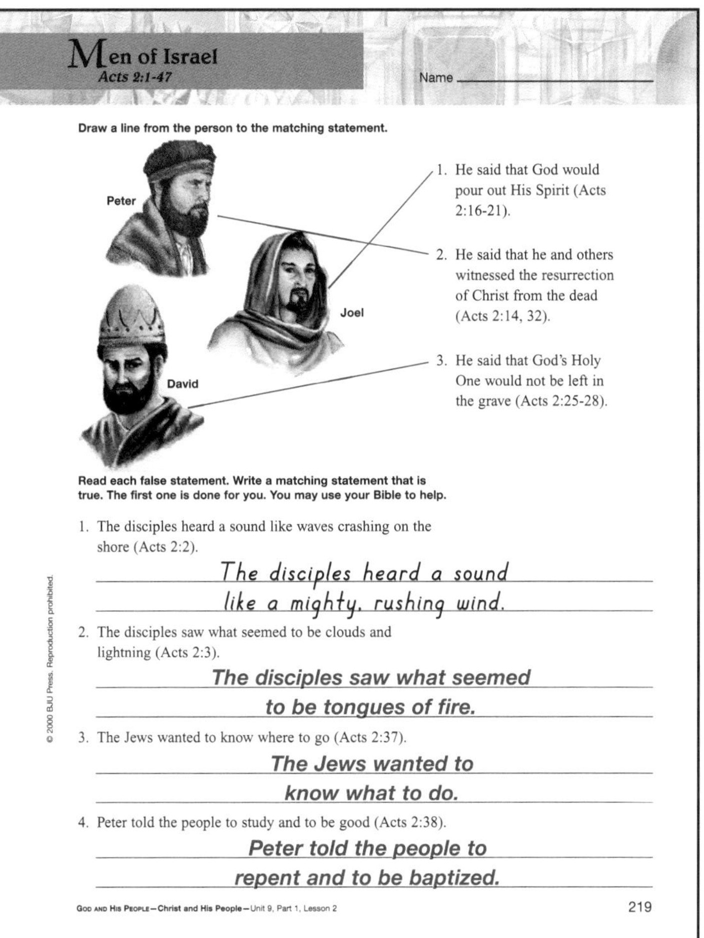

Men of Israel
Acts 2:1-47

Name ______________

Draw a line from the person to the matching statement.

Peter

Joel

David

1. He said that God would pour out His Spirit (Acts 2:16-21).
2. He said that he and others witnessed the resurrection of Christ from the dead (Acts 2:14, 32).
3. He said that God's Holy One would not be left in the grave (Acts 2:25-28).

Read each false statement. Write a matching statement that is true. The first one is done for you. You may use your Bible to help.

1. The disciples heard a sound like waves crashing on the shore (Acts 2:2).
   The disciples heard a sound like a mighty, rushing wind.
2. The disciples saw what seemed to be clouds and lightning (Acts 2:3).
   The disciples saw what seemed to be tongues of fire.
3. The Jews wanted to know where to go (Acts 2:37).
   The Jews wanted to know what to do.
4. Peter told the people to study and to be good (Acts 2:38).
   Peter told the people to repent and to be baptized.

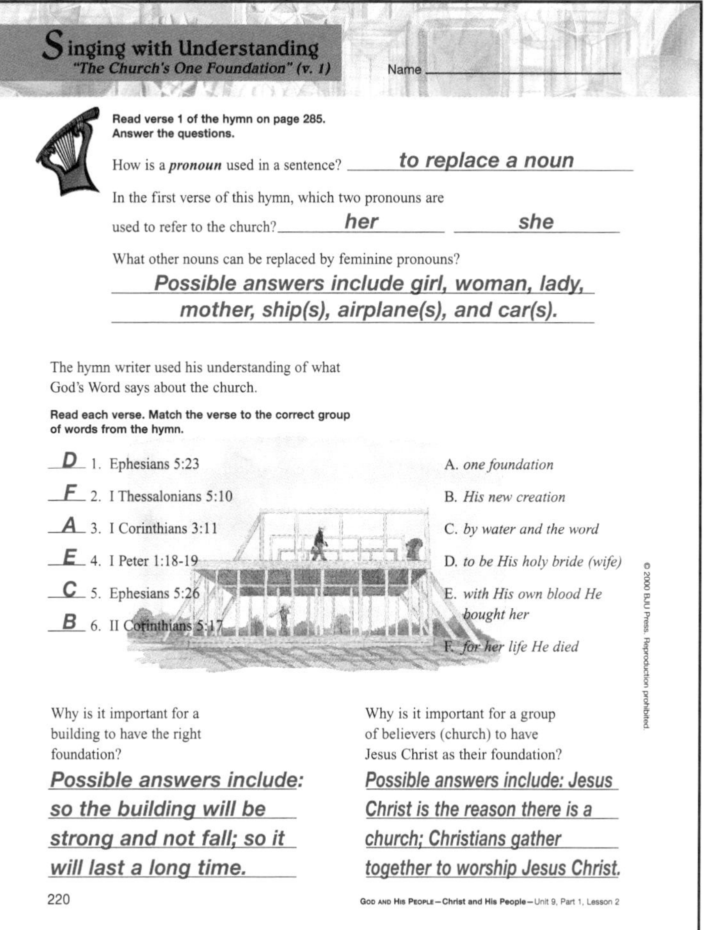

Singing with Understanding
"The Church's One Foundation" (v. 1)

Name ______________

Read verse 1 of the hymn on page 285. Answer the questions.

How is a ***pronoun*** used in a sentence? *to replace a noun*

In the first verse of this hymn, which two pronouns are used to refer to the church? *her* *she*

What other nouns can be replaced by feminine pronouns?
Possible answers include girl, woman, lady, mother, ship(s), airplane(s), and car(s).

The hymn writer used his understanding of what God's Word says about the church.

Read each verse. Match the verse to the correct group of words from the hymn.

D 1. Ephesians 5:23
F 2. I Thessalonians 5:10
A 3. I Corinthians 3:11
E 4. I Peter 1:18-19
C 5. Ephesians 5:26
B 6. II Corinthians 5:17

A. *one foundation*
B. *His new creation*
C. *by water and the word*
D. *to be His holy bride (wife)*
E. *with His own blood He bought her*
F. *for her life He died*

Why is it important for a building to have the right foundation?
Possible answers include: so the building will be strong and not fall; so it will last a long time.

Why is it important for a group of believers (church) to have Jesus Christ as their foundation?
Possible answers include: Jesus Christ is the reason there is a church; Christians gather together to worship Jesus Christ.

➤ **What happened as a result of the people accepting Christ?** *(They continued in the instruction they received from the apostles and fellowshiped together; they continued in the breaking of bread and in prayer.)*

➤ God added to the church daily. **Are souls being added to the church every day in your community? Why or why not?** *(Accept any answer but discuss the need for all Christians to witness faithfully.)*

Worktext page 219

Identify characters with dialogue and make false statements true.

Hymn: "The Church's One Foundation"

Teach the first verse (Worktext page 285). Read the first verse of the hymn aloud.

➤ **What is a *foundation*?** *(a support on which other parts rest)*

➤ **What is the church's one foundation?** *(Jesus Christ, her Lord)*

➤ **What is the *church*?** *(It is the believers themselves.)*

Explain that the church (a body of believers) is resting on its foundation, the Lord Jesus Christ. The church is God's creation because He made the people (physical birth) and then grants them spiritual birth when they receive Christ as Savior. Play the recording and lead in singing verse 1 together.

➤ **Who came from heaven to seek and to save those who are lost?** *(Jesus Christ)*

➤ **What will Christ make His church?** *(His holy bride)*

➤ **How did Christ establish the church?** *(through shedding His blood on the cross)*

➤ **Why can the church have life?** *(because Christ died for the church)*

Worktext page 220

Singing with understanding, verse 1.

Lesson 3

Materials

- Memory-verse cards from the previous lesson

Hymn: "The Church's One Foundation"

Sing the first verse (Worktext page 285). Review the meaning of *foundation* (a support on which other parts rest). Play the recording and lead in singing verse 1 together. Call one group to sing the first two lines and another group to sing the last two lines; then sing verse 1 together again.

➤ **How was the church created?** *(God made man [physical birth] and then when man accepts Christ as Savior, he is born spiritually.)*

➤ **How did Christ "buy" the church?** *(with His own blood)*

Introducing the Application Story

Discuss the words *rabbi* and *Messiah.* Write the words *rabbi* and *Messiah* for display. Allow the students to tell what they think the words mean and then guide them in finding the definitions in the glossary to see whether they are correct. Tell them to listen for these words in the following story.

Application Story

Read the following story to the students.

Seeking for God

Many years ago a little Jewish girl named Judith lived in Russia. Her family was very religious and had many ceremonies that they thought would please God. But they did not read God's Word and did not really know much about God. Judith asked her father many questions about God, but he could not answer. Still, Judith longed in her heart to know more about God.

Judith's family was amazed at all the questions she asked. Finally, they told her to ask these questions to her grandfather, who was a rabbi and knew many things. "Grandfather," Judith asked, "couldn't Jesus have been the Messiah that God promised would come to save our nation?"

Her grandfather became very angry. "You are asking too many questions for a little girl! It is not good for you. You should think about other things!"

I wonder what I said to make him so angry, Judith thought.

That night, two other rabbis came to see her grandfather. They stayed all night, talking in the room downstairs. Sometimes their voices would rise in argument. Instead of going to bed, Judith stayed by the window where she could hear what the men were saying. "Jesus Christ really *is* the Messiah—I'm *sure* of it!" she heard one of the men say.

Judith's heart pounded. "Please, dear God," she prayed, "I do not know much about You. But I want to know more so I can please and obey You. Please send me someone to tell me about Jesus, the Messiah."

Several years passed, and it might have seemed that God had not heard Judith's prayer. But He had. One day, Judith saw a poster in a restaurant window, advertising a meeting of some Christians. Jewish people especially were invited. Judith went to the meeting. There she heard about salvation in Christ, and she asked Jesus to save her. God had put a longing in her heart to know more about Him, and He had heard and answered her prayer.

➤ **How did Judith's grandfather, a rabbi, react to the question "Was Jesus the Messiah that God promised to save the Jewish nation?"** *(He was angry and told her she asked too many questions; he told her to think about other things.)*

➤ **What did one of the rabbis who came to visit Judith's grandfather tell him?** *(that Jesus was the Messiah)*

➤ **What did Judith pray?** *(She asked God to send her someone who would tell her about Jesus, the Messiah.)*

➤ **How did God answer her prayer?** *(Judith saw a poster advertising a meeting; there she heard the gospel and asked Jesus to save her.)*

➤ **How were the people who were having the meeting pleasing God?** *(They were trying to reach others with the gospel.)*

➤ **Do you think that God could use you to show someone more about God? Why or why not?**

What Do You Say?

Name ________________

Are you always ready to tell others about Jesus Christ, but you are not quite sure how to begin? Perhaps this tract will help.

1. Pray sincerely that God will cause people to want to know about Christ and that God will use you to witness to those people.
2. Complete and color the banner on the front of the tract.
3. Sign your name on the inside of the tract.
4. Be ready for God to lead you to someone to whom you should show the tract.
5. When you hand it to someone and he asks about it, be ready to do the following:

   Briefly tell the story about Peter's witnessing to the Jews (Acts 2:14-42).

   Say Matthew 16:15-16 from memory.

   Invite the person to repent of his sins and accept Jesus Christ as his Savior.

   Pray with the person if he wants to be saved.

   Read Acts 2:21 aloud.

Important: To be a witness for Jesus Christ, you must first know Him personally. Have you made this important decision?

I Say That Jesus Christ Is

Possible answers include the living God, the Savior of the world, God's Son, and the Messiah.

Acts 2:21

Memory Verses—Matthew 16:15-16

Practice the memory verses. Give the memory-verse cards to four students, telling them to arrange themselves in the correct order at the front of the room and to read the verses aloud. Direct the students to read the verses silently; then tell one of the four students to be seated and direct the students to read the verses aloud. Continue practicing the verses each time a student is seated.

Worktext page 221-22

Use the memory verse for witnessing. (*Note:* Use the tract as an opportunity to present the plan of salvation to unsaved students as well as to teach students how to witness.)

Lesson 4

Materials

- Student Bible Book Cards: Old Testament, New Testament, Old and New Testament abbreviations for each group of students

Make a red construction paper "brick" for each student. Write a Bible reference on each "brick." Use verses from the list provided:

Matthew 2:2	King of the Jews
Mark 10:47	Son of David
Mark 14:62	Son of man
John 1:1	the Word
John 1:29	Lamb of God
John 4:42	Savior of the world
John 8:12	Light of the world
John 8:58	I AM
John 15:5	the vine
Acts 10:42	judge
I Corinthians 2:8	Lord of glory
I Corinthians 15:45	the last Adam
Titus 3:4	our Savior
Hebrews 4:14	Son of God
Revelation 19:16	King of kings, Lord of lords

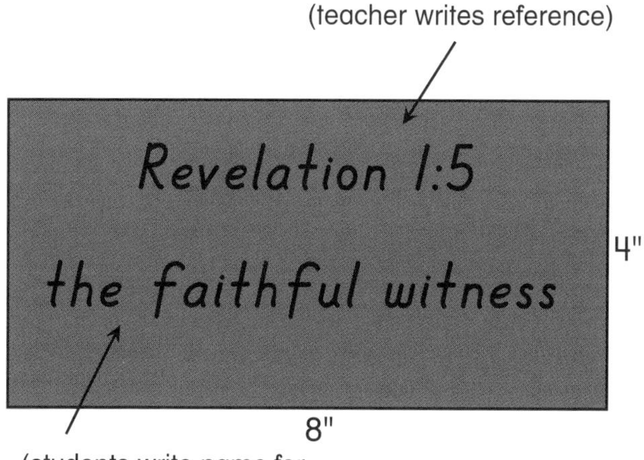

(teacher writes reference)

Revelation 1:5

the faithful witness

4"

8"

(students write name for Jesus found in verse)

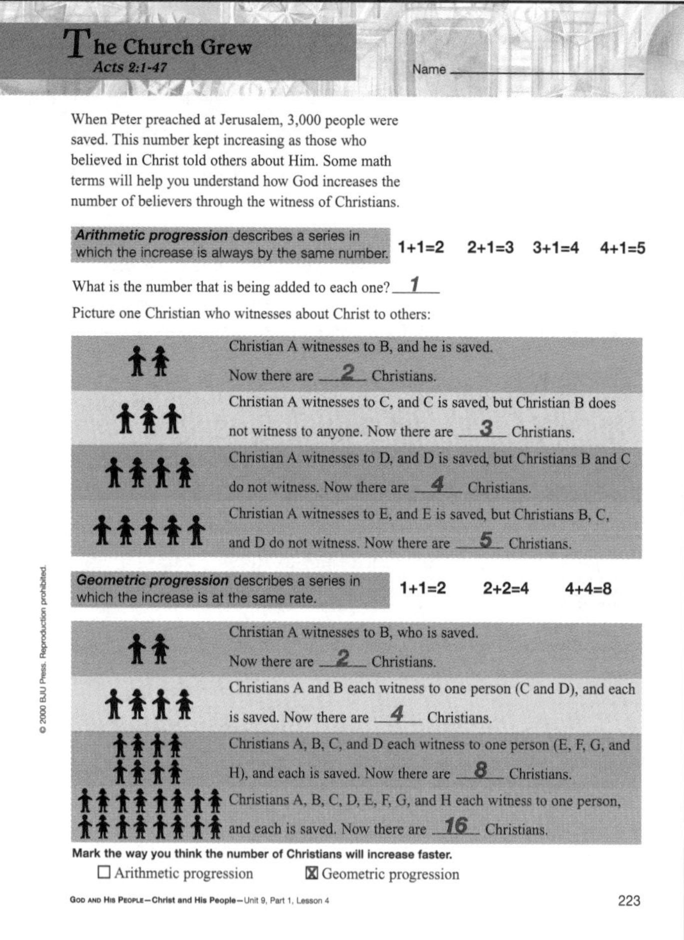

The Church Grew
Acts 2:1-47

Name ______________________

When Peter preached at Jerusalem, 3,000 people were saved. This number kept increasing as those who believed in Christ told others about Him. Some math terms will help you understand how God increases the number of believers through the witness of Christians.

Arithmetic progression describes a series in which the increase is always by the same number. 1+1=2 2+1=3 3+1=4 4+1=5

What is the number that is being added to each one? __1__

Picture one Christian who witnesses about Christ to others:

Christian A witnesses to B, and he is saved. Now there are __2__ Christians.

Christian A witnesses to C, and C is saved, but Christian B does not witness to anyone. Now there are __3__ Christians.

Christian A witnesses to D, and D is saved, but Christians B and C do not witness. Now there are __4__ Christians.

Christian A witnesses to E, and E is saved, but Christians B, C, and D do not witness. Now there are __5__ Christians.

Geometric progression describes a series in which the increase is at the same rate. 1+1=2 2+2=4 4+4=8

Christian A witnesses to B, who is saved. Now there are __2__ Christians.

Christians A and B each witness to one person (C and D), and each is saved. Now there are __4__ Christians.

Christians A, B, C, and D each witness to one person (E, F, G, and H), and each is saved. Now there are __8__ Christians.

Christians A, B, C, D, E, F, G, and H each witness to one person, and each is saved. Now there are __16__ Christians.

Mark the way you think the number of Christians will increase faster.

☐ Arithmetic progression ☒ Geometric progression

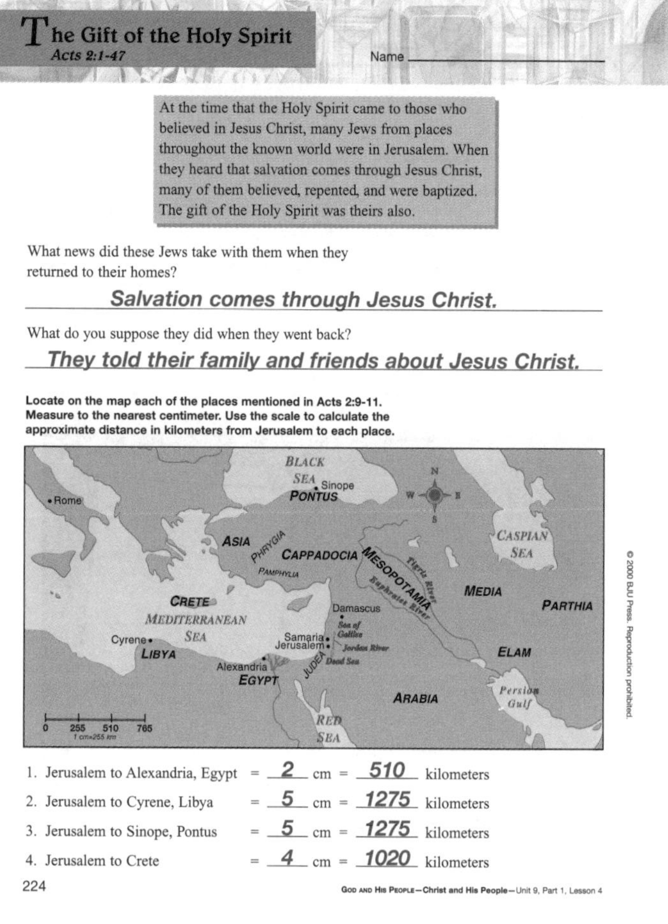

The Gift of the Holy Spirit
Acts 2:1-47

Name ______________________

At the time that the Holy Spirit came to those who believed in Jesus Christ, many Jews from places throughout the known world were in Jerusalem. When they heard that salvation comes through Jesus Christ, many of them believed, repented, and were baptized. The gift of the Holy Spirit was theirs also.

What news did these Jews take with them when they returned to their homes?

Salvation comes through Jesus Christ.

What do you suppose they did when they went back?

They told their family and friends about Jesus Christ.

Locate on the map each of the places mentioned in Acts 2:9-11. Measure to the nearest centimeter. Use the scale to calculate the approximate distance in kilometers from Jerusalem to each place.

1. Jerusalem to Alexandria, Egypt = __2__ cm = __510__ kilometers
2. Jerusalem to Cyrene, Libya = __5__ cm = __1275__ kilometers
3. Jerusalem to Sinope, Pontus = __5__ cm = __1275__ kilometers
4. Jerusalem to Crete = __4__ cm = __1020__ kilometers

Hymn: "The Church's One Foundation"

Sing the first verse (Worktext page 285). Play the recording and lead in singing verse 1 together.

Memory Verses—Matthew 16:15-16

Practice the memory verses. Call on volunteers to say the verses aloud.

➤ **What does it mean that Jesus is the Son of the *living* God?** *(Possible answers include that God is alive, but idols and other gods are made or formed by man and without power.)*

Worktext page 223

Apply Bible knowledge to everyday life.

Worktext page 224

Read a map scale.

Bible Study

Guide a Bible study of the names of Jesus.

➤ **Where is the church's foundation?** *(in Jesus Christ)*

Give each student a prepared paper "brick," telling him to locate the reference and to write the name for Jesus given in the verse. Explain each name; then allow the student(s) with that brick to attach their brick onto a wall or onto the Unit 9 bulletin board.

King of the Jews—Old Testament prophecy told that a ruler of Israel would one day come from Bethlehem of Judea. Jesus came to be the spiritual King of the Jews and will come again to reign on earth in righteousness. At the crucifixion of Christ, Pilate had the soldiers place a sign which read, "The King of the Jews."

Son of David—Old Testament prophecy told that the Messiah would be born in the family of David. Both Mary and Joseph were descendants of David.

Son of man—This is the name used by the Lord for Himself. It refers to the Lord's humanity—He became like us to bear our sins on the cross.

The Word—This name emphasizes Christ's deity. He is the living Word. Jesus is all of God's wisdom in thoughts and word.

Lamb of God—This name refers to Jesus as the sacrifice that God provided to atone for the sins of the world.

Savior of the world—Jesus came not just to save the Israelites but to save the world. Saving faith in Jesus brings everlasting life.

Light of the world—This name refers to Jesus' exposing the darkness and falsehood of sin and showing the way to eternal life.

I AM—This name emphasizes that Jesus is the eternal God. He has always existed, even before creation.

The vine—This name is a reminder that we can have eternal life only through Jesus. We get our life through God the Son. Believers can be productive and bear fruit only as they obey and depend upon God.

Judge—Jesus is Savior to those who accept Him, but He is judge to the unsaved who reject Him. He will decide man's eternal destiny according to whether the person has accepted Christ as Savior.

Lord of glory—This name refers to the deity of the Lord Jesus, to whom all praise and honor is due.

The last Adam—The first Adam gave human life, which is brief. The last Adam, who *is* life, gives spiritual life, which is eternal.

Our Savior—Christians are saved from the penalty of sin through Christ. In eternity, Christians will be changed into His likeness.

Son of God—This name refers to Christ as the Messiah King begotten of God. He has all the attributes of God. He intercedes for believers.

King of kings, Lord of lords—Christ will someday come back in glory to rule the earth in righteousness.

One-on-One: Give the student ten construction paper bricks or put the bricks in a learning center. Tell the student to complete each brick by locating the reference and writing the name for Jesus given. Allow the student to make a foundation by attaching his ten bricks onto a wall or bulletin board. Explain the ten names to the student.

Bible Study Skills

Play a matching game. Divide the students into groups of two, three, or four. Explain the following game directions for using all of the student Bible Book Cards:

1. Mix up all of the cards. Distribute six cards to each player.
2. Place the remainder of the cards facedown in a pile.
3. Allow the players time to see whether they have any matches: two books from the same division or book names and abbreviations.
4. Player 1 asks another player whether he has a book from the division of . . . (e.g., Minor Prophets, Old Testament History) or does he have the abbreviation of . . . .
5. If the player has the card for the book requested, he gives the card to Player 1. If the player does not have the card, Player 1 draws a card from the pile.
6. Follow the same procedure with each player taking turns.
7. The player with the most matches at the end of the time wins.

Answering Questions

Name ____________

Jesus often taught His followers by asking questions. Read the following Bible references to find the questions Jesus asked; then look for possible reasons why He asked the questions.

Question Asked	Purpose for the Question
Matthew 26:8-12 Jesus asked? (v. 10) *See Matthew 26:10.*	*To help the disciples realize Mary's actions were honorable*
Mark 5:25-34 Jesus asked? (v. 30) *See Mark 5:30.*	*So the woman would show her faith*
Luke 2:46-50 Jesus asked? (v. 49) *See Luke 2:49.*	*Jesus explained His purpose in the form of a question, so Mary and Joseph would understand.*
Luke 22:44-46 Jesus asked? (v. 46) *See Luke 22:46.*	*Encourage the disciples to be faithful in prayer*
John 9:13-38 Jesus asked? (v. 35) *See John 9:35.*	*Jesus' question helped the blind man to know Christ better.*

S72 Use with Unit 9, Part 1, Going Beyond God and His People

Going Beyond

Materials

- A copy of Supplement page S72 "Answering Questions," for each student

Enrichment

Discuss questions Jesus asked. Give each student a copy of Supplement page S72, "Answering Questions." Direct the students to look up the references, read them, write the questions that Jesus asked, and give the reasons for the questions. Discuss the questions and their purposes together.

The Church Leaders

Unit 9, Part 2

Preview

Doctrines

- Officers of the local church should preach the Word (II Timothy 4:2)—Lesson 1
- Members of the local church should evangelize the lost (Matthew 22:1-14)—Lesson 1
- The apostles served in the establishment of the church (Ephesians 4:11)—Lesson 2
- Officers of the local church should care for those having special needs (Acts 6:1-7)—Lesson 2

Skills and Applications

- Learn Ephesians 3:20-21
- Locate information in Scripture
- Use a glossary
- Read a time line
- Complete the plan of salvation
- Recall facts and details
- Use Bible reference tools—cross-reference, concordance
- Realize that God wants Christians to be His witnesses
- Understand the role of deacons in the church
- Apply Bible knowledge to everyday life

Lesson 1

Materials

- Charts 26 and 36: "The Tentmakers" and "Paul's Route—Second Journey"

Memory Verses—Ephesians 3:20-21

Principle: Let the church glorify Jesus Christ now and forever. Locate **Ephesians 3:20-21** and read the verses aloud as the students read silently.

➤ **What is the church referred to in verse 21?** *(all believers)*

➤ The Scripture says "to Him be glory." **What does it mean to *glorify*?** *(Accept any answer, but direct the students to look up the word in their glossaries.)*

➤ **Who is the church supposed to glorify?** *(God)*

➤ **How are we to glorify God and for how long?** *(through Jesus Christ; forever)*

Direct the students to take turns reading the verses to a partner. Guide them to highlight the verses in their Bibles (optional) and to mark the location with the Unit 9 Bookmark.

Hymn: "The Church's One Foundation"

Teach the second verse (Worktext page 285). Read verse 2 aloud, pointing out that believers who make up the church are the *elect,* chosen by God from every nation. Play the recording and lead in singing the second verse. Explain that the church's *charter* of salvation is the principles upon which believers stand.

➤ **What are three principles upon which the church stands?** *(one Lord—the Lord Jesus Christ, who is God; one faith—the only way to heaven is to believe in the Lord Jesus Christ; one birth—the new birth is a spiritual birth experienced when one accepts Christ as Savior)*

➤ **What is the "one holy name" that the church blesses?** *(the Lord Jesus Christ)*

➤ **What is the church's "holy food"?** *(the Word of God)*

Explain that by God's grace the church presses toward that one assured hope, that Christ will return for His bride (the church). Sing verses 1-2.

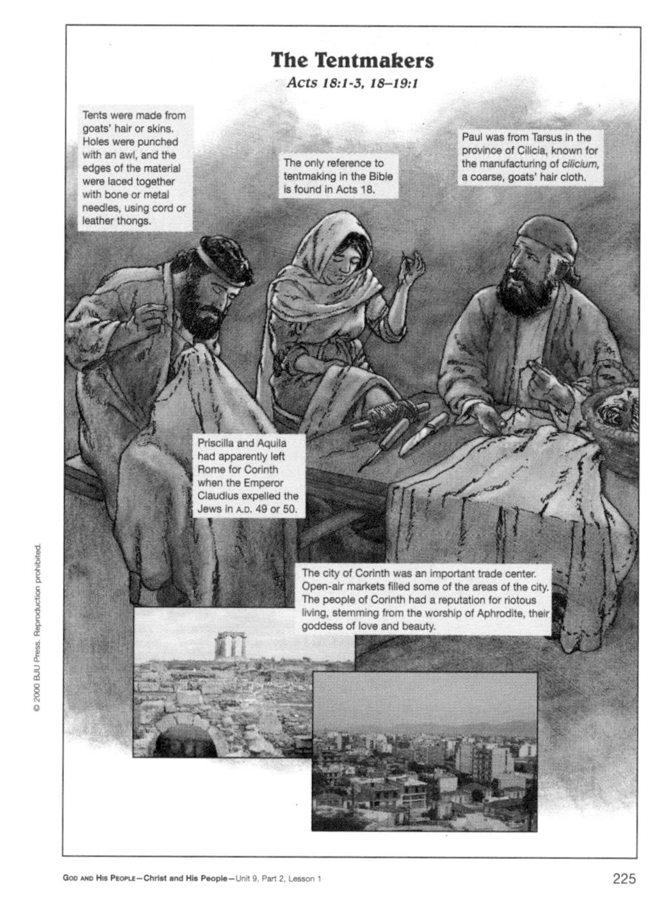

Background Information

Corinth—*Corinth was a center for shipping and commerce. Because sailing around the southern tip of Greece was a perilous trip, many people went to the two ports at Corinth first. Today Corinth is a city in the south of modern Greece. It is located northeast of the ancient Corinth of Bible times.*

Synagogues—*The synagogues of the New Testament were the centers of religious and public education for the Jews. Jesus regularly attended the synagogue when He grew up. He taught in several synagogues during His public ministry. Paul the Apostle preached the gospel in synagogues. Many Jews still meet in synagogues on the Sabbath.*

Introducing the Bible Account

Discuss tentmaking. Direct the students' attention to Worktext page 225 and read the information together.

Bible Account

Read the following Bible account or retell Acts 18:1-3, 18–19:1. Display Chart 36, "Paul's Route—Second Journey," pointing out the italicized cities and areas.

Aquila, Priscilla, and Apollos

When the apostle Paul left *Athens,* he went to *Corinth* where he met a man and his wife, Aquila and Priscilla. Aquila and Priscilla had recently come to Corinth from Italy because the emperor Claudius had ordered the Jews to leave Rome. Paul visited this couple and stayed with them because they shared a common faith and a common occupation—tentmaking. Paul stayed in Corinth for eighteen months, preaching the Word of God. Priscilla and Aquila were dedicated to God's work and helped Paul in his ministry. Paul called them his "helpers in Christ" (Romans 16:3). The church met in Aquila and Priscilla's home (I Corinthians 16:19). Paul was thankful to Aquila and Priscilla, as were all the Gentile churches, because Aquila and Priscilla had risked their lives for him (Romans 16:4, 5).

When Paul left for Syria, Priscilla and Aquila went with him. When they arrived in *Ephesus,* Priscilla and Aquila stayed, but Paul sailed on to *Caesarea.* He then went to *Jerusalem* to keep the feast before traveling on to *Antioch.*

Priscilla and Aquila continued to be a witness for God. While they were in Ephesus, a Jew named Apollos, from Alexandria, came to Ephesus. He had excellent speaking skills and good knowledge of the Scriptures. He spoke of Jesus but did not teach about Christ's crucifixion and resurrection. Because of this, when Aquila and Priscilla heard Apollos speak, they took him aside and explained God's way to him more accurately. Apollos accepted Jesus Christ as the Messiah, the one sent from God to save him.

Apollos now went to the synagogues in Ephesus and preached Jesus as the Messiah. Then when Apollos wanted to go to the believers in *Achaia,* the believers in Ephesus recommended him. When Apollos arrived in Achaia, he was a great help to the believers. He refuted the wrong teachings of the Jews in public, declaring that Jesus was the Christ. God used Apollos to turn many unbelieving Jews to Christ.

Acts 19:1 tells us that Apollos had preached to the church at Corinth. The people there were arguing among themselves, some saying they followed Paul and some saying they follow Apollos. Paul told the Corinthians that both he and Apollos were only God's servants through whom they came to believe. Paul referred to himself as having been used by God to plant the Word of God, Apollos as having watered what was planted, but God as the one who saved them and caused them to grow as Christians.

InfoScene: "The Tentmakers"
Display Chart 26 for reference throughout this unit. Review and discuss the Bible account as time permits.

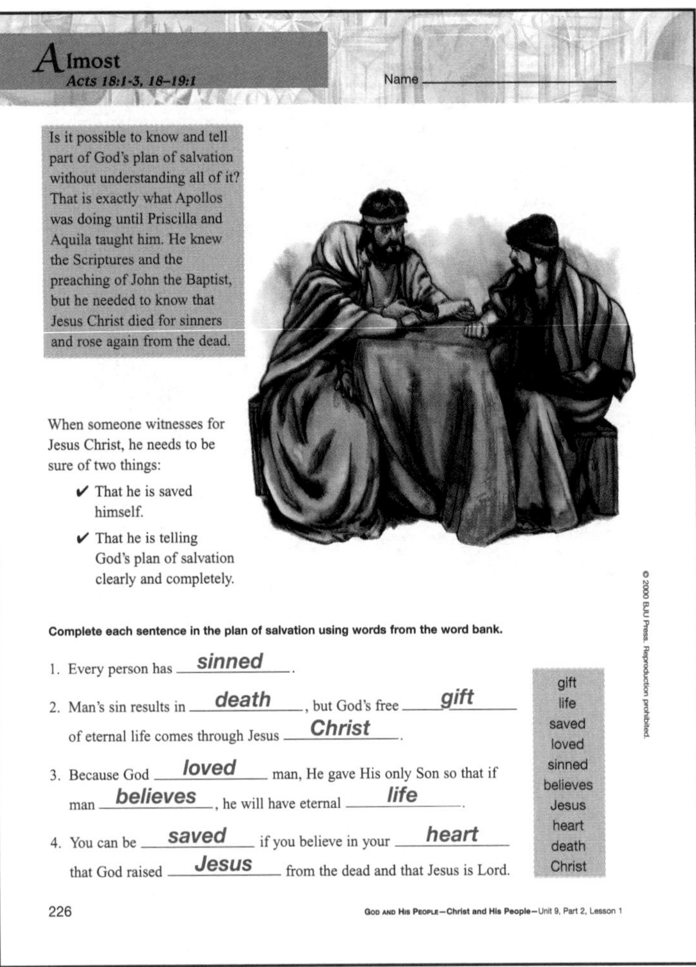

Almost
Acts 18:1-3, 18–19:1

Name ________________

Is it possible to know and tell part of God's plan of salvation without understanding all of it? That is exactly what Apollos was doing until Priscilla and Aquila taught him. He knew the Scriptures and the preaching of John the Baptist, but he needed to know that Jesus Christ died for sinners and rose again from the dead.

When someone witnesses for Jesus Christ, he needs to be sure of two things:

- ✔ That he is saved himself.
- ✔ That he is telling God's plan of salvation clearly and completely.

Complete each sentence in the plan of salvation using words from the word bank.

1. Every person has *sinned*.
2. Man's sin results in *death*, but God's free *gift* of eternal life comes through Jesus *Christ*.
3. Because God *loved* man, He gave His only Son so that if man *believes*, he will have eternal *life*.
4. You can be *saved* if you believe in your *heart* that God raised *Jesus* from the dead and that Jesus is Lord.

Word bank: gift, life, saved, loved, sinned, believes, Jesus, heart, death, Christ

226 GOD AND HIS PEOPLE—Christ and His People—Unit 9, Part 2, Lesson 1

- ➤ **What did Paul have in common with Aquila and Priscilla?** *(They shared a common faith and were tentmakers.)*
- ➤ **Why had Aquila and Priscilla left Rome?** *(The ruler, Claudius, had ordered the Jews to leave.)*
- ➤ **How do you know that Apollos was not a Christian when Aquila and Priscilla first met him in Ephesus?** *(He was not preaching Christ's crucifixion and resurrection.)*
- ➤ **After he was saved, what did Apollos preach in the synagogues?** *(that Jesus was the Christ)*
- ➤ **What did Paul explain to the Corinthians concerning his ministry and Apollos's ministry?** *(He told them that he and Apollos were only God's servants and that God was the one who saved them and caused them to grow.)*

Worktext page 226

Complete the plan of salvation.

Lesson 2

Memory Verses—Ephesians 3:20-21

Practice the memory verses. Locate **Ephesians 3:20-21** and direct the students to read the verses.

- ➤ **To whom is the pronoun *he* referring in verse 20?** *(God)* Read **Ephesians 3:19** aloud.
- ➤ **How much power does God have?** *(Answers may vary. Be sure students understand that God is all-powerful.)*
- ➤ **What does it mean that God can do "exceeding abundantly above all that we ask or think"?** *(Our minds are finite, or limited. God can do more than we can imagine Him doing.)*

Pair the students with partners, telling them to read the verses aloud to each other.

Hymn: "The Church's One Foundation"

Sing the first two verses (Worktext page 285).

- ➤ **What is the foundation of the church built on?** *(Jesus Christ)*
- ➤ **How did Jesus Christ buy the church?** *(by His blood shed on the cross)*

Play the recording and sing together verses 1-2.

Background Information

Deacon—*The word* deacon *(I Timothy 3:8) means "servant" or "minister" (in the sense of helper, not pastor, whom we sometimes call "minister" today). The first deacons were appointed when there was a need for the early church to provide helpers or servants to free the apostles for prayer and teaching of the Word of God.*

Grecians and Hebrews—*During the New Testament era, Jews were scattered all over the Roman world. The Jews living in Palestine learned to speak Aramaic, while those living elsewhere learned Greek. Often these Greek-speaking Jews returned to live in Jerusalem, and members of both groups of Jews became Christians. Conflicts arose when the Aramaic-speaking Christians ("Hebrews") neglected the Greek-speaking Christians in distributing food to widows. The apostles appointed deacons to take care of the matter.*

Martyr—*Our English word* martyr *comes from the Greek word for* "witness." *A true witness tells the truth about what he has seen, regardless of the cost. Stephen, one of the first deacons, witnessed for the Lord, and it cost him his life.*

Introducing the Bible Account

Discuss church leaders.

- ➤ **Who are the leaders in your church?** *(Possible answers include pastors, deacons, and elders.)*

Explain that God has specified certain qualifications that the leaders in the local church should have. God also wants all believers to live a godly life and to serve Him.

- ➤ Read **I Timothy 3:8** aloud. **What qualifications are given for a deacon in this verse?** *(He should be worthy of respect, sincere, honest, not a cheater, and not given to wine.)*
- ➤ Read **I Timothy 3:9-10** aloud. **What qualifications are given in these verses?** *(He must live his Christianity and not just speak it. He should be living a Christlike life before he serves as a deacon.)*
- ➤ Read **I Timothy 3:11** aloud. **What does this verse say about a deacon's wife?** *(She should be trustworthy, respectable, and faithful.)*
- ➤ Read **I Timothy 3:12** aloud. **What else does the Bible say about a deacon?** *(He should have only one wife, and he should manage his children and household well.)*

Explain that God says when a deacon serves well, he has confidence in his Christian faith and good standing before other Christians.

Bible Account

Read the following Bible account or read Acts 6:1-7.

Helpers Needed

God was blessing the early church, and it was growing rapidly. In one congregation, however, the Grecian Jews had a complaint against the Hebrew Jews. The Grecian widows were being neglected in the daily distribution of food.

The apostles gathered the church people together and told the church people that it would not be right for them to neglect their responsibilities of prayer and preaching to serve tables. The size of the congregation was increasing, and they needed help. The apostles told the people, "Look ye out among you seven men of honest report, full of the Holy Ghost and wisdom, whom we may appoint over this business; But we will give ourselves continually to prayer, and to the ministry of the word."

The church people chose seven men to be put in charge of serving the widows. They chose "Stephen, a man full of faith and of the Holy Ghost, and Philip, and Prochorus, and Nicanor, and Timon, and Parmenas, and Nicolas a proselyte of Antioch." The apostle Paul later referred to these servants in the church as deacons (Philippians 1:1).

The deacons, who had been chosen by the church, were now presented to the apostles, who prayed and laid their hands on them. God's Word continued to spread, and the number of Christians in Jerusalem increased.

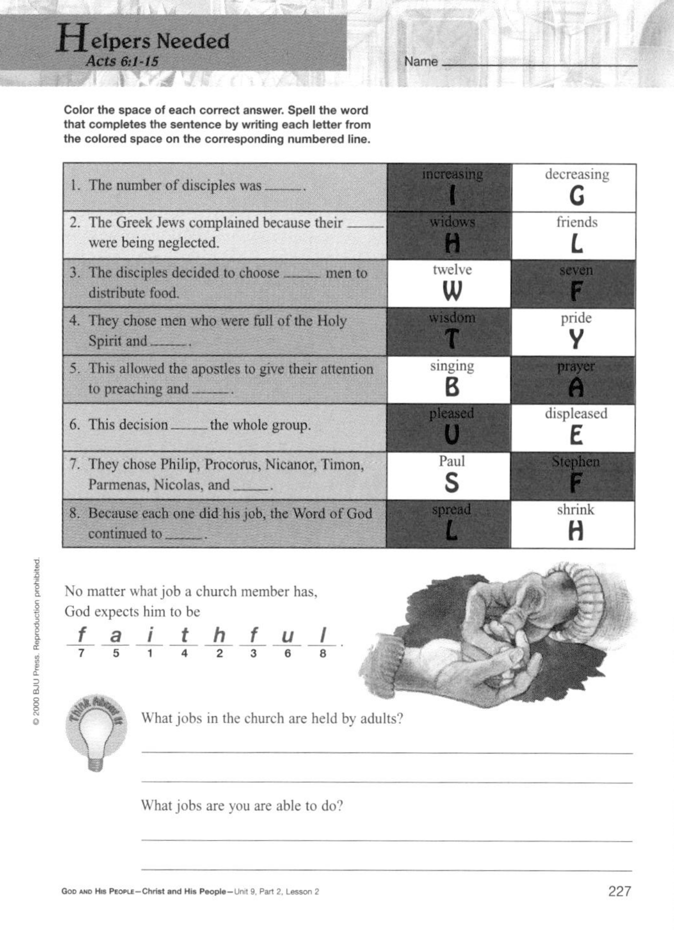

Helpers Needed
Acts 6:1-15

Name ____________

Color the space of each correct answer. Spell the word that completes the sentence by writing each letter from the colored space on the corresponding numbered line.

1. The number of disciples was ____.	increasing I	decreasing G
2. The Greek Jews complained because their ____ were being neglected.	widows H	friends L
3. The disciples decided to choose ____ men to distribute food.	twelve W	seven F
4. They chose men who were full of the Holy Spirit and ____.	wisdom T	pride Y
5. This allowed the apostles to give their attention to preaching and ____.	singing B	prayer A
6. This decision ____ the whole group.	pleased U	displeased E
7. They chose Philip, Procorus, Nicanor, Timon, Parmenas, Nicolas, and ____.	Paul S	Stephen F
8. Because each one did his job, the Word of God continued to ____.	spread L	shrink H

No matter what job a church member has, God expects him to be f a i t h f u l (7 5 1 4 2 3 6 8).

Think About It

What jobs in the church are held by adults?

What jobs are you are able to do?

God and His People—Christ and His People—Unit 9, Part 2, Lesson 2 227

- ➤ **What problem arose in the early church?** *(The church was growing, and the apostles did not have time to meet the needs of the widows.)*
- ➤ **How does God want His people to solve problems among themselves?** *(Possible answers include discussion, prayer, guidance from the Scripture, and follow-up on plans that they make.)*
- ➤ **How was the problem in the first church solved?** *(The apostles had the people choose seven men to help serve the widows.)*
- ➤ **What qualifications did these seven men need to have?** *(They were to be controlled by the Holy Spirit, full of wisdom, and respected by all.)*
- ➤ **Who referred to these men as deacons?** *(the apostle Paul)*
- ➤ **What does God expect, not only of church leaders, but of all Christians?** *(He expects us to live godly lives as explained in the Scriptures.)*

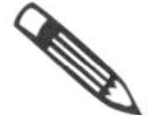

Worktext page 227

Recall facts about the Bible account.

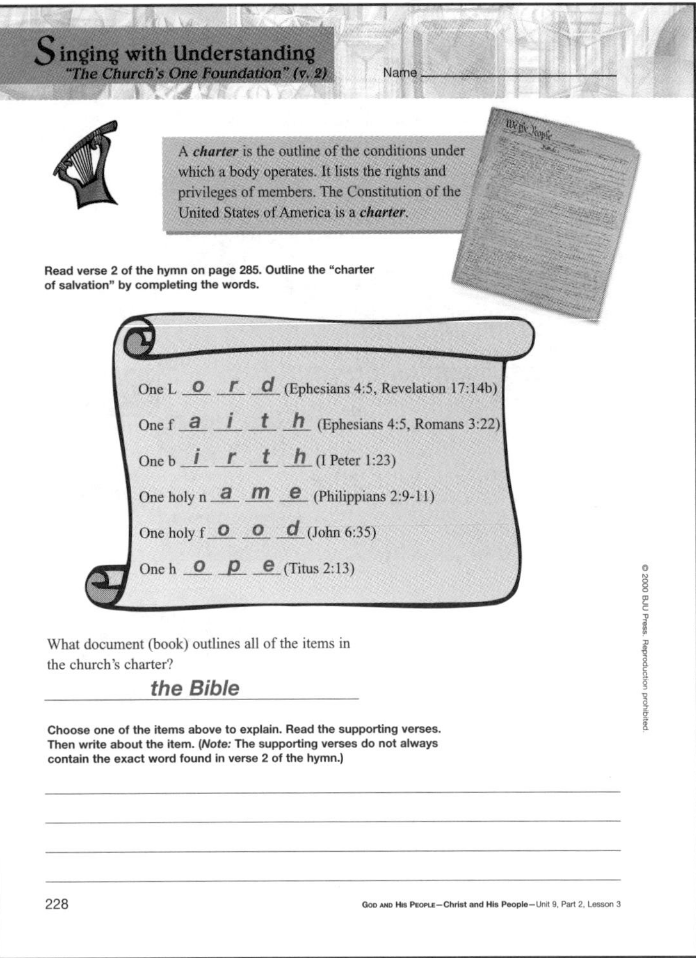

Singing with Understanding
"The Church's One Foundation" (v. 2)   Name ____________________

A *charter* is the outline of the conditions under which a body operates. It lists the rights and privileges of members. The Constitution of the United States of America is a *charter*.

Read verse 2 of the hymn on page 285. Outline the "charter of salvation" by completing the words.

One L o r d (Ephesians 4:5, Revelation 17:14b)

One f a i t h (Ephesians 4:5, Romans 3:22)

One b i r t h (I Peter 1:23)

One holy n a m e (Philippians 2:9-11)

One holy f o o d (John 6:35)

One h o p e (Titus 2:13)

What document (book) outlines all of the items in the church's charter?

the Bible

Choose one of the items above to explain. Read the supporting verses. Then write about the item. (*Note:* The supporting verses do not always contain the exact word found in verse 2 of the hymn.)

228   God and His People—Christ and His People—Unit 9, Part 2, Lesson 3

Hymn: "The Church's One Foundation"

Sing the first two verses (Worktext page 285). Play the recording and lead in singing verses 1-2 together.

Worktext page 228

Singing with understanding, verse 2

Lesson 3

Hymn History Story

Read the following story about the writing of "The Church's One Foundation."

To Know the Truth

Samuel Stone, a twenty-seven-year-old pastor of a parish in London, sat down to write. He wanted to write a hymn that would explain a doctrinal truth to his church people. He wanted to explain that Christ was the head of the church—not just of their parish in London, but of all the Christians who had ever lived in the world.

It was important to Mr. Stone that his people know what the Bible taught. At that time, a pastor in South Africa named John Colenso had been promoting false ideas among Christians, claiming that not everything in the Bible was true. This false teacher had caused great division among Christians in South Africa. "The Book of Joshua is a myth," Colenso had taught, "and many of the sayings of Christ recorded in the New Testament are not what He really said." People had begun to doubt that the Bible is God's Word.

Mr. Stone wanted his people to believe that every word of the Bible was inspired, so he wrote twelve hymns to explain the major teachings held by the Christian church. The one he wrote about the headship of Christ became known as "The Church's One Foundation." (*Note:* Although the original hymn had seven stanzas with three more added later, most hymnals today include only four or five.)

Samuel Stone had graduated from Oxford, where he excelled in both studies and sports. He was strong and athletic, and he won awards in boating competitions. For a while, he had planned to spend his life in the army. But the Lord led him into the ministry, and soon he became pastor of the parish where his father had ministered.

Mr. Stone was so widely known for his concern for the poor people of London that people called him "the poor man's pastor." He held a special early service in the mornings at 6:30 for poor people who arrived in town early for their jobs. After the service, the poor people could rest or read in the church building until time to start work.

Mr. Stone wrote seven books of poetry, and many of his poems became hymns. He always based his hymns on Scripture. In 1909 he served on a committee to select hymns for a famous English hymnal. "The Church's One Foundation" was included in this hymnal and continues to be sung today.

➤ **What was Samuel Stone's purpose in writing the hymn?** *(to teach the doctrine that Christ is the head of the church)*

➤ **Why was it especially important at that time for people to know what the Bible taught?** *(A false teacher in South Africa had been saying that the Bible was not really God's Word, and he was causing people to doubt.)*

➤ **What other talents and interests did Stone have besides hymn writing?** *(athletics, boating, preaching, writing poetry)*

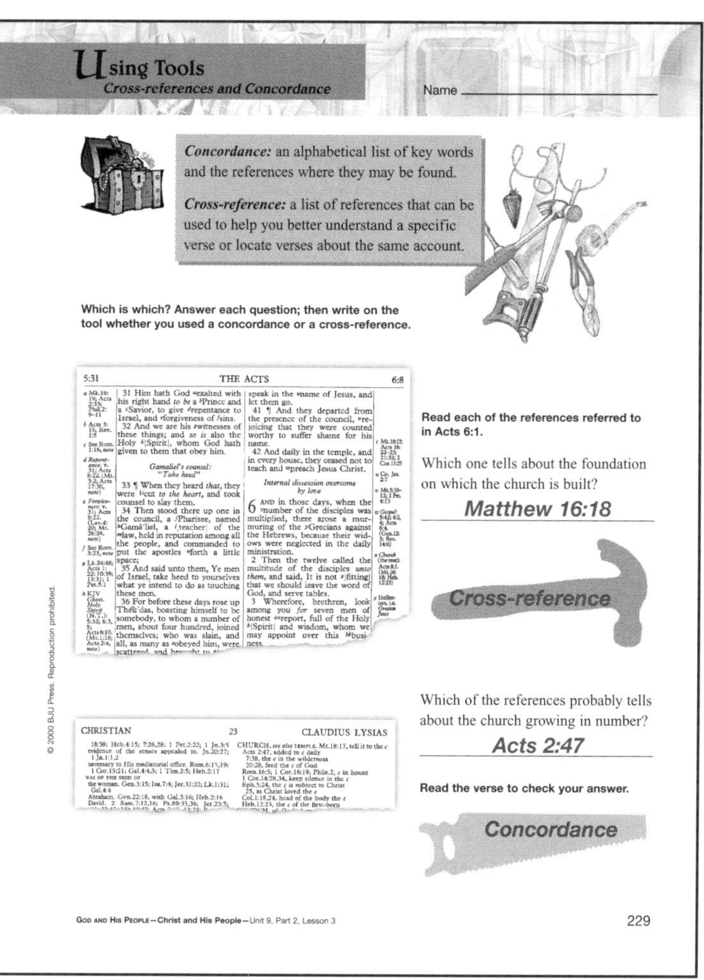

Using Tools
Cross-references and Concordance

Name ______________

Concordance: an alphabetical list of key words and the references where they may be found.

Cross-reference: a list of references that can be used to help you better understand a specific verse or locate verses about the same account.

Which is which? Answer each question; then write on the tool whether you used a concordance or a cross-reference.

5:31 THE ACTS 6:8

Read each of the references referred to in Acts 6:1.

Which one tells about the foundation on which the church is built?

Matthew 16:18

Cross-reference

CHRISTIAN 23 CLAUDIUS LYSIAS

Which of the references probably tells about the church growing in number?

Acts 2:47

Read the verse to check your answer.

Concordance

God and His People—Christ and His People—Unit 9, Part 2, Lesson 3 229

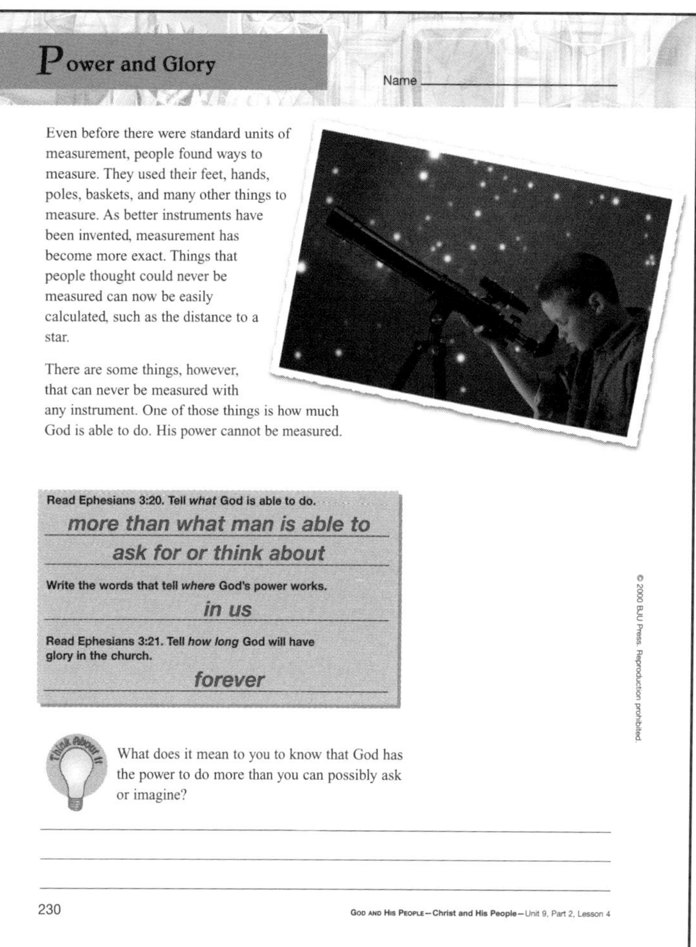

Power and Glory

Name ______________

Even before there were standard units of measurement, people found ways to measure. They used their feet, hands, poles, baskets, and many other things to measure. As better instruments have been invented, measurement has become more exact. Things that people thought could never be measured can now be easily calculated, such as the distance to a star.

There are some things, however, that can never be measured with any instrument. One of those things is how much God is able to do. His power cannot be measured.

Read Ephesians 3:20. Tell *what* God is able to do.

more than what man is able to ask for or think about

Write the words that tell *where* God's power works.

in us

Read Ephesians 3:21. Tell *how long* God will have glory in the church.

forever

Think About It!

What does it mean to you to know that God has the power to do more than you can possibly ask or imagine?

230 God and His People—Christ and His People—Unit 9, Part 2, Lesson 4

➤ **What did Stone do for the poor in London?** *(held a special early service for them; allowed them to stay in the church to rest before going to their jobs)*

➤ **What kind of person do you think Samuel Stone was?** *(kind; compassionate; he cared about people's physical needs as well as their spiritual needs)*

Hymn: "The Church's One Foundation"

Sing the first two verses (Worktext page 285). Place the students in two groups. Play the recording, allowing each group to sing a verse.

Memory Verses—Ephesians 3:20-21

Practice the memory verses. Write the verses on an erasable board and select a student to read them aloud. Erase a few words or phrases and select another student to read the verses aloud. Continue erasing words or phrases and calling on students to read the verse aloud until all the words have been erased and the students can say the verses from memory.

Bible Study Skills, Worktext page 229

Use Bible reference tools—cross-references and a concordance.

Lesson 4

Materials

- TimeLine and picture: *John Knox*

Hymn: "The Church's One Foundation"

Sing the first two verses (Worktext page 285). Play the recording, allowing a volunteer or small group to sing a verse to the students (optional).

Memory Verses—Ephesians 3:20-21

Practice the memory verses. Locate and read aloud **Ephesians 3:20-21.** Allow any students who wish to say the verses from memory to do so.

Worktext page 230

Develop an understanding of the memory verses.

Background Information

Reformation—*This spiritual revival swept across Europe during the sixteenth century. The brave men of this movement who held to the Bible as the sole authority for the Christian faith were called* reformers. *They rejected the authority of the pope, believing that Christ was the only head of the church. The key doctrines of this movement were "Scripture alone, faith alone, grace alone!"*

Protestant—*The term dates back to the early days of the Reformation when representatives of the German states (1529) "protested" that they would agree with "nothing contrary to His Word." Today the word refers to anyone who holds to the biblical teachings of the Reformation in opposition to Roman Catholicism.*

Introducing the Hero of the Faith

Explain the terms *Reformation* and *Protestant*. Share the background information with the students.

Hero of the Faith

Read the following account based on the life of John Knox.

Candle in Darkness

Have you ever seen a candle placed in a completely dark room? All it takes is one small flame to give light. The life of John Knox has been compared to a candle flame, burning in darkness.

John Knox was born in Haddington, Scotland, around 1513. The Roman Catholic Church ruled the country at that time. Scotland was involved in almost constant warfare with England. Education and trade were disorganized, and only a small group of noblemen had any wealth.

When John was a teenager, a young Scottish nobleman named Patrick Hamilton was burned at the stake for teaching "heresy." He had taught Martin Luther's views about salvation by faith alone. John Knox never forgot that young man's sacrifice for his belief in Christ.

As a young man, Knox became the bodyguard for George Wishart, a gentle teacher and preacher who needed protection from those who disagreed with him. Wishart had angered the church by reading the Greek New Testament with his students. He taught them that Scripture, not the church, was the only test of truth. For this, he too, was branded a heretic, arrested, and placed on trial. As John Knox watched Wishart's steadfast refusal to change his beliefs, his respect for him grew. Knox, too, wanted to join this battle for the cause of the gospel.

Wishart was sentenced to be burned at the stake. "Let me go with you to the place of execution," John Knox begged. But Wishart shook his head and said quietly, "One is sufficient for one sacrifice." Wishart was burned exactly eighteen years after Patrick Hamilton's death.

These burnt sacrifices kindled a flame in John Knox that burned until his own light was put out. His country—Scotland—was the darkness in which his candle burned.

Shortly after the death of Wishart, a group of noblemen murdered the cardinal who had condemned him to be burned. They fled to a seaside castle called St. Andrews and claimed John Knox as their chaplain. Knox stayed with them while they awaited help from England. He studied and became such a fiery preacher of God's Word that he was called "the thundering Scot."

But at last, the French Catholics arrived at St. Andrews. They captured John Knox along with his parishioners, and he became a galley slave on a ship for nineteen months.

After his release, John Knox went to England, where he pastored several churches. When Mary Tudor, a Catholic queen, took the throne, Knox fled to Switzerland. There he met and worked with John Calvin. He learned about other men's work to promote the truth of the gospel and speak out against Catholicism. These men were called *reformers*.

John Knox returned to Scotland in 1555. As he preached, many Scottish noblemen banded together to stand against the false teaching of the Catholic Church and to hold fast to the Word of God. They drew up a document that stated what they believed. The Scottish Parliament read the document and accepted it, and the Presbyterian Church was established. For a little while, the struggle against the Catholic Church appeared to be over. But one more battle remained.

Mary, Queen of Scots, became the new ruler of Scotland. She was a Roman Catholic queen, entering a country that was trying to overthrow the false teaching of her church. She wanted to revive Catholicism, and this brought her into conflict with John Knox.

Five records remain of conversations between the queen and John Knox. Queen Mary was no match for this master of words and faithful man of God. Five years after arriving in Scotland, Mary, Queen of Scots, fled to England, leaving her son to rule.

John Knox continued building the nation of Scotland for five more years. He gave Scotland God's truth and led it into the modern world.

The birth date of John Knox is uncertain, but all of Scotland remembers his life and death. His grave is marked with his initials on a simple stone. No monument stands as his memorial, but it has been said that "Scotland is his monument."

John Knox
(ca. 1514-1572)

Name ____________________

"This little light of mine, I'm going to let it shine." Some would say that this simple song defines the life of John Knox.

John Knox grew up in Haddington, Scotland, in the early 1500s. As a teenager, Knox saw Patrick Hamilton burned at the stake for daring to oppose the Roman Catholic Church. John followed Hamilton's teaching of salvation by faith alone, not by approval of any church. He later became a bodyguard for George Wishart, who preached the same. For preaching this message, Wishart was also convicted of heresy and burned at the stake.

God placed a desire in Knox's heart to continue the teaching and preaching his friends had started. John began studying the Scriptures and became a mighty preacher of God's Word, for which he was later called "the thundering Scot." Because of his preaching, John was put into prison for nineteen months. Many times he fled Scotland in order to preserve his life, but he never lost sight of his burden for how the people of Scotland needed the light of God's Word.

In 1555, Knox returned to Scotland and formed the Presbyterian church. Shortly after, Mary, Queen of Scots, came to rule Scotland and wanted to revive Catholicism. Records show that Knox confronted the queen about her faith. After five years, Queen Mary fled to England, leaving her son to rule. God was working in Scotland!

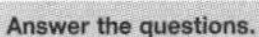

Answer the questions.

1. Why were Patrick Hamilton and George Wishart burned at the stake?
   because they opposed the Catholic church
2. What message did Hamilton, Wishart, and Knox preach?
   Answers will vary but should include salvation by faith alone.
3. John Knox had a burden for the people of Scotland. Do you have a burden for someone you know?
   ____
4. What are some ways you could be a light to that person?
   ____

GOD AND HIS PEOPLE—Heroes of the Faith—Unit 9, Part 2, Lesson 4 309

➤ **Where was John Knox born?** *(Scotland)*

➤ **What did John Knox do when he was in England?** *(He pastored several churches.)*

➤ **Why do you think John Knox had to flee to Switzerland when England was no longer ruled by a Protestant?** *(Answers will vary but should include that he was no longer free to preach the Word of God in England, so he went to a country where he had more freedom.)*

➤ **What happened in Scotland as a result of John Knox's leadership?** *(Scotland left Roman Catholicism and became a Protestant nation. The Presbyterian Church was established.)*

➤ **How is Scotland John Knox's monument?** *(He brought the gospel message to Scotland, which forever changed people's lives.)*

TimeLine

Add *John Knox* to the TimeLine. Place the figure of *John Knox* onto the TimeLine (ca. 1514-1572), reminding the students that Knox influenced the country of Scotland for the Lord. Guide the students as they glue the picture of *John Knox* onto their TimeLines.

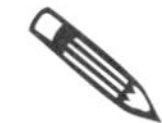

Worktext Supplement page 309

Review the Hero of the Faith, John Knox.

Going Beyond

Enrichment

Play a game of "Who Am I?"

➤ **Who are some of the Bible characters and Heroes of Faith studied so far in this unit?** Write the names on the chalkboard. *(Possible names include Jesus, Aquila, Priscilla, Apollos, Stephen, Paul, Philip, John Knox, John Calvin, Patrick Hamilton, and George Wishart.)*

Select a volunteer to come to the front of the classroom and give a description of or quote from one of the characters. Instruct the student to then say, "Who am I?" Allow the student to choose a volunteer from the class to answer the question. Continue this as time permits. (*Note:* If students need help, prepare the descriptions or quotes on strips of paper. Allow volunteers to select a paper and read the information to the other students.)

The Church Members

Unit 9, Part 3

Preview

Doctrines

- God is unchanging (immutable) (Malachi 3:6)—Lesson 1
- Members of the local church should contribute financially (I Corinthians 16:1-2)—Lesson 2
- Officers of the local church should teach members (Ephesians 4:11-16)—Lesson 2
- Members of the local church should exhort one another (Hebrews 10:25)—Lesson 4

Skills and Applications

- Learn II Corinthians 9:6-7
- Recall facts and details
- Use a glossary
- Define words
- Order words in a sentence
- Determine the extent of a Scripture reference
- Realize that God wants believers to willingly contribute to His work
- Realize that Christians are to encourage one another
- Apply Bible knowledge to everyday life

Lesson 1

Materials

- Ten pennies
- Ten one-dollar bills
- A calculator for each student (optional)

Hymn: "The Church's One Foundation"

Sing the first two verses (Worktext page 285). Review the meaning of the first and second verses; then lead the students in singing with the recording.

Memory Verses—II Corinthians 9:6-7

Principle: Give generously and cheerfully to God. Locate **II Corinthians 9:6-7** and read the verses aloud as the students read silently.

➤ **What does God's Word say about giving in verse 6?** *(If we give a small part of what we have, we will be rewarded a little; if we give generously, we will be rewarded generously.)*

➤ **What should your attitude be when you give?** *(You should do it cheerfully, not grudgingly or reluctantly. You should give because you want to, not because you are forced to give.)*

➤ **Whom does God love?** *(a cheerful giver, one who gives from the heart)*

➤ **What can you give God besides money?** *(your time and your talents)*

Select a student to read the verses aloud. Direct the students to highlight the verses in their Bibles (optional) and mark the location with the Unit 9 Bookmark.

Background Information

Tithe—*The Hebrew and Greek words translated* tithe *mean "a tenth part of something." Abraham presented a tenth, or tithe, to Melchizedek after victory in battle (Genesis 14:20). Jacob promised God a tithe of all that God gave to him (Genesis 28:22). In the law, God also commanded tithes from Israel—the tenth given to God provided a living for the priests. God wanted the Jews to learn the spiritual lesson that all they had came from God. Christians today should give from the same spiritual devotion, realizing that all their blessings, even their material goods, are from God.*

Introducing the Bible Account

Demonstrate the tithe. Share the background information. Display the ten pennies and elicit from the students that one-tenth of the pennies would be one of the ten pennies. Display the ten one-dollar bills and elicit that one-tenth of the ten dollars would be one dollar.

➤ **What is one-tenth of $100?** *($10)*

➤ **What is one-tenth of $200?** *($20)*

➤ **What is one-tenth of $50?** *($5)*

Bible Account

Read the following Bible account or read Malachi 3:8-12.

Tithing

Malachi was preaching to God's chosen people, the Israelites. He asked the people a question, "Will a man rob God?" Malachi told God's people that they were robbing God by not bringing their tithes and offerings into God's storehouse.

Malachi told the nation of Israel that in withholding their tithes and offerings, they were robbing God by not giving back to Him what was already His. The Israelites were supposed to be giving God a *tithe*—a tenth of their crops, flocks, and cattle. This tithe was to be used for the priests for their services. The Lord, through Malachi, told the people to test Him to see whether He would not "open you the windows of heaven, and pour you out a blessing, that there should not be room enough to receive it."

Malachi told the people that God would bless them if they would return to Him and give God what was due Him. God said that He would keep their crops from being destroyed and that all nations would bless them because their land would be delightful.

➤ **How had the Israelites been robbing God?** *(They were not bringing their tithes and offerings into God's storehouse.)*

➤ **What is the difference between a *tithe* and an *offering*?** Direct the students to find and read the definition of *tithe* and *offering* from the glossary. *(Answers will vary, but explain that a* tithe *is what God expects His people to give, and an* offering *is an additional gift, freely given.)*

➤ **What promise did God make to the people if they would return to Him and give what was due Him?** *(He promised them that their crops would not be destroyed and that all nations would bless them because their land would be delightful.)*

➤ **What does God want you to do about giving to Him?** *(Answers will vary, but elicit that God wants us to give of our time, talent, and money because He has given these things to us.)*

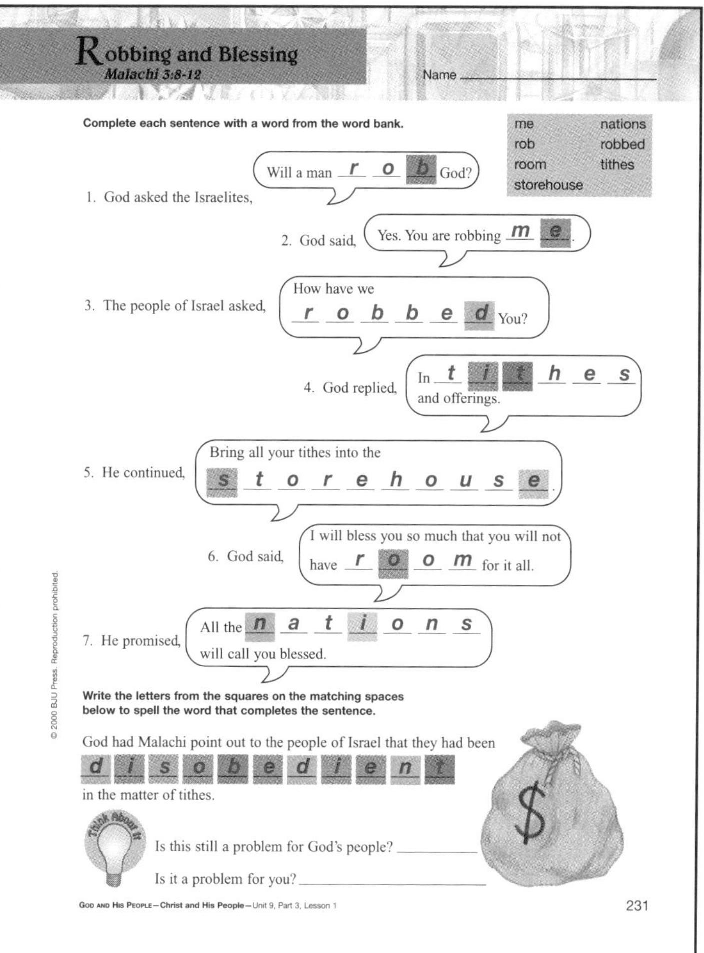

Robbing and Blessing
Malachi 3:8-12

Name ____________

Complete each sentence with a word from the word bank.

me	nations
rob	robbed
room	tithes
storehouse	

1. God asked the Israelites, "Will a man r o b God?"
2. God said, "Yes. You are robbing m e."
3. The people of Israel asked, "How have we r o b b e d You?"
4. God replied, "In t i t h e s and offerings."
5. He continued, "Bring all your tithes into the s t o r e h o u s e."
6. God said, "I will bless you so much that you will not have r o o m for it all."
7. He promised, "All the n a t i o n s will call you blessed."

Write the letters from the squares on the matching spaces below to spell the word that completes the sentence.

God had Malachi point out to the people of Israel that they had been d i s o b e d i e n t in the matter of tithes.

Think About It

Is this still a problem for God's people? ____________

Is it a problem for you? ____________

© 2000 BJU Press. Reproduction prohibited.

God and His People—Christ and His People—Unit 9, Part 3, Lesson 1 231

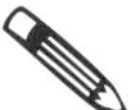

Worktext page 231

Recall details.

Math Connection (optional)

Find one-tenth of a number.

➤ **How much is a tithe?** *(a tenth)*

Explain that if a man grew 10 ephahs of wheat in Bible times, he would give 1 ephah to the Lord. If 100 lambs were born into his flock of sheep, he would give 10 lambs to the Lord.

Explain that one-tenth is 10 percent and that 10 percent can be represented as a decimal *(0.10)*. Using a calculator, show the students how to find 10 percent of a number (multiply the number by .10 or .1). Allow students to use calculators to solve the problems. Encourage the students to make up their own math problems.

John earned $62.50 in one month mowing lawns. If he gives the Lord a tithe, how much will he give? *($6.25)*

Mr. Smith earns $28,600 a year. If he gives the Lord a tithe, how much does he give? *($2,860)*

John's sister earns $60 each week working after school. How much will she have left after she gives her tithe to the Lord? *($60-$6=$54)*

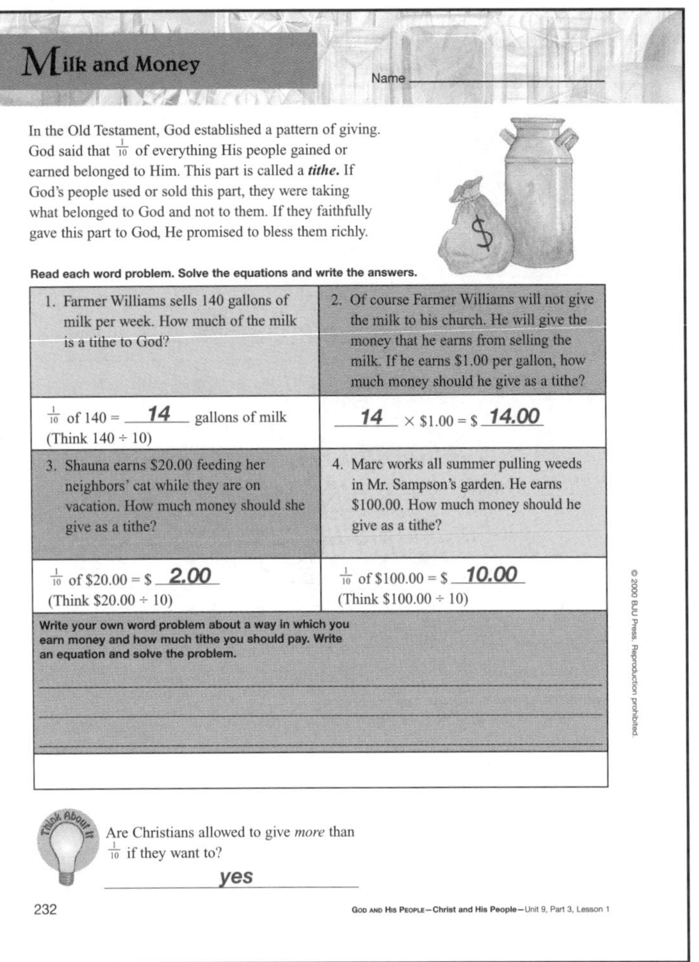

Milk and Money

Name ____________________

In the Old Testament, God established a pattern of giving. God said that $\frac{1}{10}$ of everything His people gained or earned belonged to Him. This part is called a ***tithe.*** If God's people used or sold this part, they were taking what belonged to God and not to them. If they faithfully gave this part to God, He promised to bless them richly.

Read each word problem. Solve the equations and write the answers.

1. Farmer Williams sells 140 gallons of milk per week. How much of the milk is a tithe to God?	2. Of course Farmer Williams will not give the milk to his church. He will give the money that he earns from selling the milk. If he earns $1.00 per gallon, how much money should he give as a tithe?
$\frac{1}{10}$ of 140 = __14__ gallons of milk (Think 140 ÷ 10)	__14__ × $1.00 = $ __14.00__
3. Shauna earns $20.00 feeding her neighbors' cat while they are on vacation. How much money should she give as a tithe?	4. Marc works all summer pulling weeds in Mr. Sampson's garden. He earns $100.00. How much money should he give as a tithe?
$\frac{1}{10}$ of $20.00 = $ __2.00__ (Think $20.00 ÷ 10)	$\frac{1}{10}$ of $100.00 = $ __10.00__ (Think $100.00 ÷ 10)

Write your own word problem about a way in which you earn money and how much tithe you should pay. Write an equation and solve the problem.

Think About It: Are Christians allowed to give *more* than $\frac{1}{10}$ if they want to?

__yes__

232 GOD AND HIS PEOPLE—Christ and His People—Unit 9, Part 3, Lesson 1

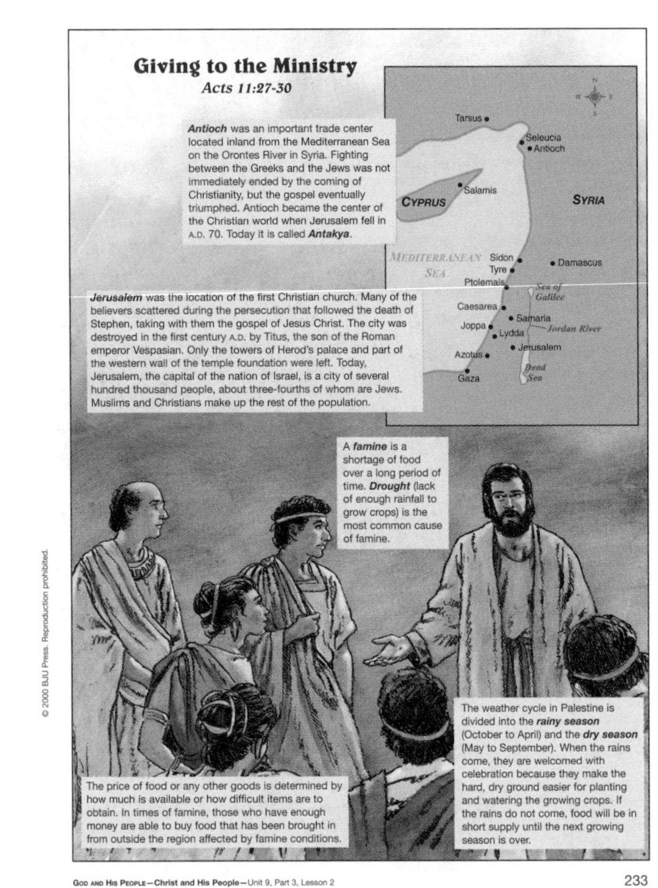

Worktext page 232

Apply Bible knowledge to everyday life.

Lesson 2

Materials

- Chart 27, "Giving to the Ministry"

Hymn: "The Church's One Foundation"

Teach the third verse (Worktext page 285). Play the recording and lead in singing verse 3 together. Explain that *consummation* means "fulfillment, completion."

➤ **What is the consummation that the church is waiting for?** *(Christ's return to earth, bringing peace forever)*

➤ **What conditions exist on earth while Christians wait for Christ's return?** *(troubles, afflictions, and wars; man is in the middle of these things and he is toiling—working hard)*

➤ **What glorious vision do you think the church waits for?** *(Christ's return for His bride, the church)*

➤ **Who or what is the church?** *(all true believers)*

Point out that after Christ's return, the church will be blessed and at rest. Lead in singing verses 1-3.

Background Information

The New Testament Prophet—*Both in the Old Testament and in the New, a prophet functioned as a "mouthpiece" for God, one who received God's message and proclaimed it. On occasion the prophet was able to predict the future. Thus, Agabus foresaw the famine of Acts 11:28.*

Agabus's Famine—*Secular sources reveal that the reign of Claudius (A.D. 41-54) was marked by crop failures and bad famines.*

Introducing the Bible Account

Discuss *stewards.* Choose a volunteer to read **I Corinthians 4:2** aloud. Elicit from the students that Christians are called *stewards.* Explain that in Bible times, wealthy people used stewards to manage their household and financial matters. A steward's job was to manage his master's money, run the house efficiently, and see that all the servants did their work. Explain that the Lord has entrusted us with possessions and talents, which He expects us to use for Him.

➤ **How should Christians use their possessions and talents?** *(for the Lord)*

Bible Account

Read the following Bible account or read Acts 11:27-30 and II Corinthians 8:1-12. Direct the students to look at the map on Worktext page 233.

Giving to the Ministry

A prophet named Agabus visited Antioch with some other prophets from Jerusalem. While Agabus was in Antioch, he prophesied that a severe famine would spread throughout the Roman world during the reign of the emperor Claudius. Of course, the Antioch believers could not stop the famine, but they could help those in need. The Jewish believers in Jerusalem had brought the gospel to Antioch, and now the Christians in Antioch could help the Christians in Jerusalem. Immediately, believers in Antioch *wanted* to provide help for the believers living in Jerusalem. Unselfishly, the Antioch believers took an offering and sent their gift to the elders in Jerusalem by the hands of Barnabas and Paul.

Paul also encouraged churches in Asia, Macedonia, and Achaia to give money to help the believers in Jerusalem. Paul wanted the Christians to show compassion to their fellow believers, and he wanted to promote unity between the Jews and the Gentiles.

The believers in Corinth had promised to help, but they had not given anything yet. Paul reminded them that some Christians, such as those in Macedonia, gave willingly when they had very little to give. He said that their giving was a result of God's grace. Paul used the testimony of the Macedonians to encourage the Corinthians to keep their promise. He told them that he was testing the sincerity of their love for others by comparing it to what other Christians had done. Paul told the believers that the supreme example in giving is the Lord Jesus. Paul told the Corinthians that "ye know the grace of our Lord Jesus Christ, that, though he was rich, yet for your sakes he became poor, that ye through his poverty might be rich." Paul told the Corinthian believers that when they *did* give they should do it *willingly*.

InfoScene: "Giving to the Ministry"
Display Chart 27 for reference throughout this unit. Review and discuss the Bible account as time permits.

➤ **How did the Christians in Antioch react to the prophecy by Agabus?** *(They wanted to provide help for the believers in Jerusalem, so they sent an offering by way of Barnabas and Paul.)*

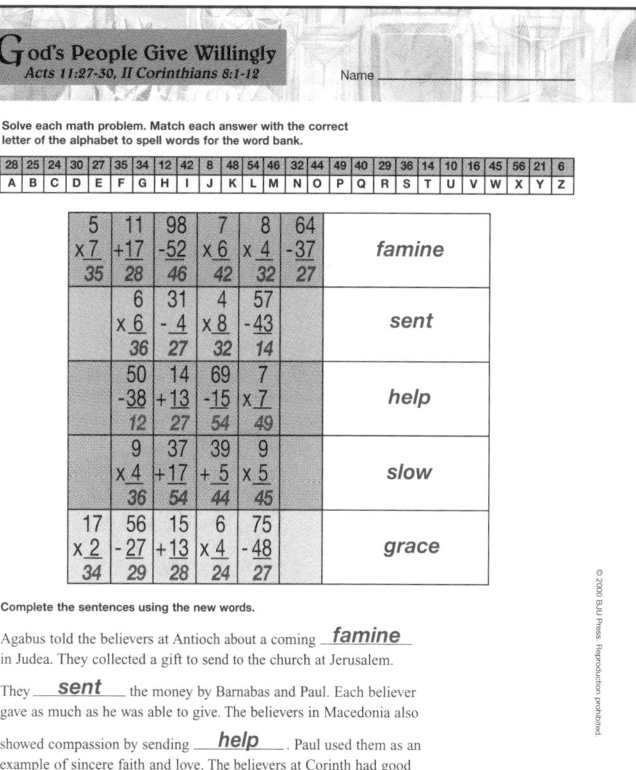

God's People Give Willingly
Acts 11:27-30, II Corinthians 8:1-12

Name ____________________

Solve each math problem. Match each answer with the correct letter of the alphabet to spell words for the word bank.

28	25	24	30	27	35	34	12	42	8	48	54	46	32	44	49	40	29	36	14	10	16	45	56	21	6
A	B	C	D	E	F	G	H	I	J	K	L	M	N	O	P	Q	R	S	T	U	V	W	X	Y	Z

5 x 7 = *35*	11 + 17 = *28*	98 - 52 = *46*	7 x 6 = *42*	8 x 4 = *32*	64 - 37 = *27*	*famine*
	6 x 6 = *36*	31 - 4 = *27*	4 x 8 = *32*	57 - 43 = *14*		*sent*
	50 - 38 = *12*	14 + 13 = *27*	69 - 15 = *54*	7 x 7 = *49*		*help*
	9 x 4 = *36*	37 + 17 = *54*	39 + 5 = *44*	9 x 5 = *45*		*slow*
17 x 2 = *34*	56 - 27 = *29*	15 + 13 = *28*	6 x 4 = *24*	75 - 48 = *27*		*grace*

Complete the sentences using the new words.

Agabus told the believers at Antioch about a coming ***famine*** in Judea. They collected a gift to send to the church at Jerusalem.

They ***sent*** the money by Barnabas and Paul. Each believer gave as much as he was able to give. The believers in Macedonia also showed compassion by sending ***help***. Paul used them as an example of sincere faith and love. The believers at Corinth had good intentions, but they were ***slow*** to give. Paul advised them to make their gift match their willingness to give. If a person is willing, his gift is judged by what he has, not by what he does not have. Jesus Christ by His ***grace*** gives salvation to poor sinners.

➤ **What had the Jewish Christians done for the believers in Antioch?** *(They were the ones who had brought them the gospel.)*

➤ **Why did Paul encourage the churches in Asia, Macedonia, and Achaia to give also?** *(He wanted them to show compassion to their fellow believers, and he wanted to promote unity between the Jews and Gentiles.)*

➤ **What did Paul tell the Corinthians in order to encourage them to keep their promise of giving to the Jerusalem church?** *(He told them that the Macedonian church, although they did not have much, had given willingly to the Jerusalem church; he also told them that Christ had been the supreme example because He was rich and became poor so that we who are poor could become rich.)*

➤ Paul said that giving was a result of God's grace. **How do we know whether our giving is because of God's grace?** *(It will be done willingly and cheerfully even when we do not have much to give.)*

Worktext page 234

Review the Bible account.

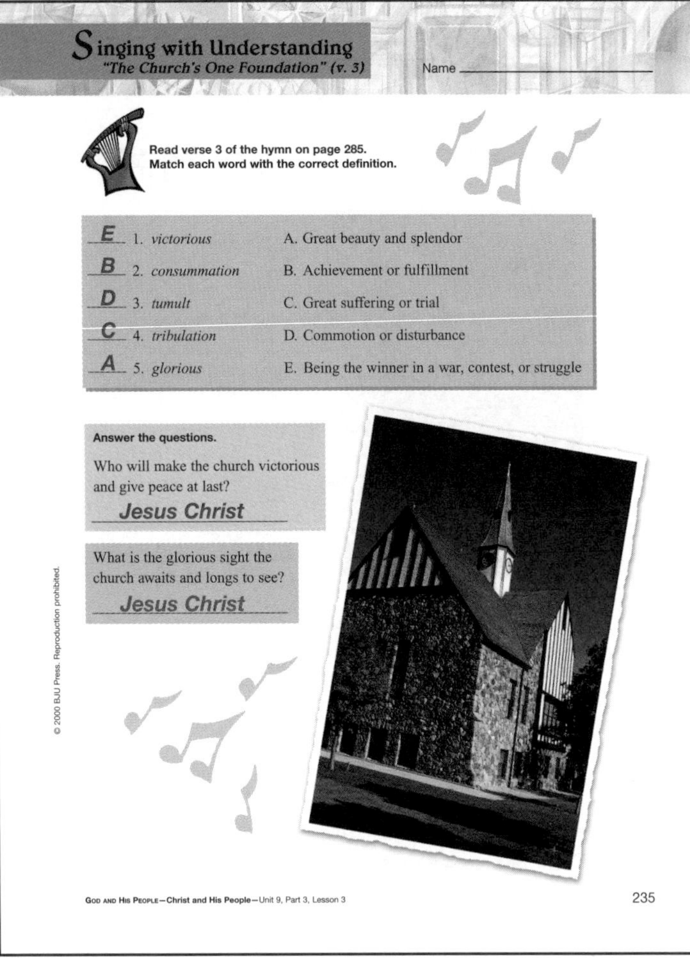

Singing with Understanding
"The Church's One Foundation" (v. 3)
Name ____________

Read verse 3 of the hymn on page 285.
Match each word with the correct definition.

Answer	Word	Definition
E	1. *victorious*	A. Great beauty and splendor
B	2. *consummation*	B. Achievement or fulfillment
D	3. *tumult*	C. Great suffering or trial
C	4. *tribulation*	D. Commotion or disturbance
A	5. *glorious*	E. Being the winner in a war, contest, or struggle

Answer the questions.

Who will make the church victorious and give peace at last?
Jesus Christ

What is the glorious sight the church awaits and longs to see?
Jesus Christ

GOD AND HIS PEOPLE—Christ and His People—Unit 9, Part 3, Lesson 3 235

Memory Verses—II Corinthians 9:6-7

Practice the memory verses. Locate and read **II Corinthians 9:6-7** aloud. Place the students with partners, directing each student to take turns reading the verses.

Lesson 3

Materials

- Four packages of seeds

Hymn: "The Church's One Foundation"

Sing the first three verses (Worktext page 285). Play the recording and lead in singing verses 1-3.

Worktext page 235

Singing with understanding, verse 3.

Introducing the Application Story

Discuss I Chronicles 29:14. Read the verse aloud, explaining that it comes from David's prayer of thanksgiving after the people willingly gave an offering for the Lord's house.

➤ **Have you ever given something away without really wanting to? How did you feel afterwards?** *(Accept any answer.)*

Point out that willingness to give to the Lord is a result of His working in our hearts.

Application Story

Read the following story to the students.

Make Me Willing

Marcus swept the last step of the porch and leaned the broom against the wall. "Anything else I can do for you, Mr. Mills?" he asked.

Mr. Mills hobbled over to a porch chair and sat down. "You've been a good worker, Marcus," he said. "It would've taken me three times as long as you to pull all those weeds from my garden. Here's something for all your help today."

He handed Marcus a ten-dollar bill. "Wow! Thanks, Mr. Mills!"

"Thank you, young man. See you at church tomorrow?"

"See you then!"

Ten dollars! Marcus pedaled his bike faster than he ever had before. *Wait'll I tell Dad,* he thought. *I won't have to borrow any more from him—I'm a working man now!*

Marcus found Dad in the garage. He waved the ten-dollar bill in front of him. Dad smiled. "That's great, Son. I'm proud of you—you must have done good work today. What are you going to do with the money?"

"I'm not sure. I have some stuff I'd like to buy, but . . . how much do you think I should give to God?"

Dad looked thoughtful. "Well, maybe you should ask God how much He wants," he said.

"I know I ought to give Him at least a dollar," said Marcus. "Our Sunday school teacher said a tithe is one-tenth. But how will I know if God wants more?"

Dad put a hand on Marcus's shoulder. "Why don't you pray this way, Marcus: 'Lord, make me willing to give You however much of this money You'd like me to give.' Then see what God does."

Marcus asked his mother to change his ten-dollar bill for ten ones. He went to church the next morning with all of the money in his pocket. "Lord," he prayed in the car, "make me willing to give however much You want me to give."

In Sunday school, Marcus's teacher read from Mark 12 about the poor widow who gave all that she had as an offering. *All that she had,* Marcus thought. *Whew! I would never do that. I need to keep some money.*

But as Marcus left the Sunday school room and went to the church service, the words *all that she had* kept echoing in his mind. He found his parents and sat down in their row. *All that she had. All that she had.* He couldn't seem to stop thinking about those words.

"All right, Lord," he prayed. "If you want me to put in all of it, make me willing." When the offering plate was passed, Marcus reached into his pocket. He counted out three ones. He hesitated and added two more. The plate was coming. He thought for a moment more. Then he quickly added the other five bills to his stack. He dropped the stack into the plate as it passed. *There it went,* he thought. *All I had.* But then he felt Mom reach over and squeeze his hand. He didn't wonder about his decision anymore.

After the service, Marcus felt a hand on his shoulder. He turned around and looked up to see Mr. Wess. "Marcus, Mr. Mills tells me you did some good work for him in his garden yesterday," Mr. Wess said in his big, booming voice.

Marcus looked down, not sure what to say.

"I could use some help myself," Mr. Wess said. "Could you come tomorrow after school?"

Marcus looked up at his mother. She nodded.

"Sure, Mr. Wess," Marcus said. "I think that would be fine."

"Guess that settles it then," Mr. Wess boomed. He leaned forward and lowered his voice to a whisper. "And since I'm making you come on a weekday, I'll make you a special offer," he said. "You tell me how much Mr. Mills paid you, and I'll double it." He winked.

Marcus's eyes grew wide. "Really?"

Mr. Wess straightened up, and his voice boomed once more. "Good help is hard to find, young man," he said. "That's what I always say." He slapped Marcus on the shoulder. "See you tomorrow."

"Wow, Mom," Marcus whispered. He watched Mr. Wess walk away. "Last night I had ten dollars. Today I have nothing. But tomorrow I'll have twenty!"

Mom smiled. "God always blesses," she said, "when we're willing."

- ➤ **What did Marcus's dad tell him to do?** *(Ask God to make him willing to give however much He wanted him to give.)*
- ➤ **How did God show Marcus what He wanted him to do?** *(through the verse in Sunday school about the widow giving all that she had)*
- ➤ **Does God always ask us to give *all* our money to the Lord's work?** *(no)*
- ➤ **How do you think Marcus felt about giving all his money?** *(a little hesitant, but then glad because he had prayed and asked God to show him how much to give and God impressed upon Marcus to give it all)*
- ➤ **How did God bless Marcus?** *(Mr. Wess gave him a job and offered to pay him double.)*
- ➤ **In what other ways does God bless us for obedience, besides providing money or material things?** *(He gives us joy and peace inside; sometimes He allows us to see how our obedience aided His work on earth, influenced the life of another person, or brought us closer to Himself.)*

Memory Verses—II Corinthians 9:6-7

Practice the memory verses. Locate **II Corinthians 9:6-7** and select a student to read the verses aloud. Direct the students to read the verses silently, to read them in a quiet whisper to themselves, and then to read them to a partner.

Picture the Point

Illustrate giving to God. Give one package of seeds to one student (student A) and three packages of seeds to a second student (student B). Tell the class to pretend that both students are farmers who sow their seeds at the same time and under the same conditions.

- ➤ **What does it mean to sow seed?** *(plant it)*
- ➤ **What does *reap* mean?** *(to cut or gather a crop; to earn a reward or punishment)*
- ➤ **Why will farmer B reap more?** *(He planted more.)*
- ➤ **Does it matter *how* or *where* farmer B sows his seed? Why or why not?** *(Yes. Most seeds need to be placed several inches into good soil and covered; then with the proper sunlight and watering, they will grow well.)*

Point out that the soil must be fertile and the planting conditions right for the seeds to grow well. If a farmer digs a hole one-foot deep and plants the seeds, they will not grow. If he throws the seeds into a river, they will not grow to maturity. Explain that God's Word tells us how God wants Christians to *sow* (give) generously and how they will *reap* (be rewarded) accordingly. Choose a volunteer to read **II Corinthians 9:6-7** aloud.

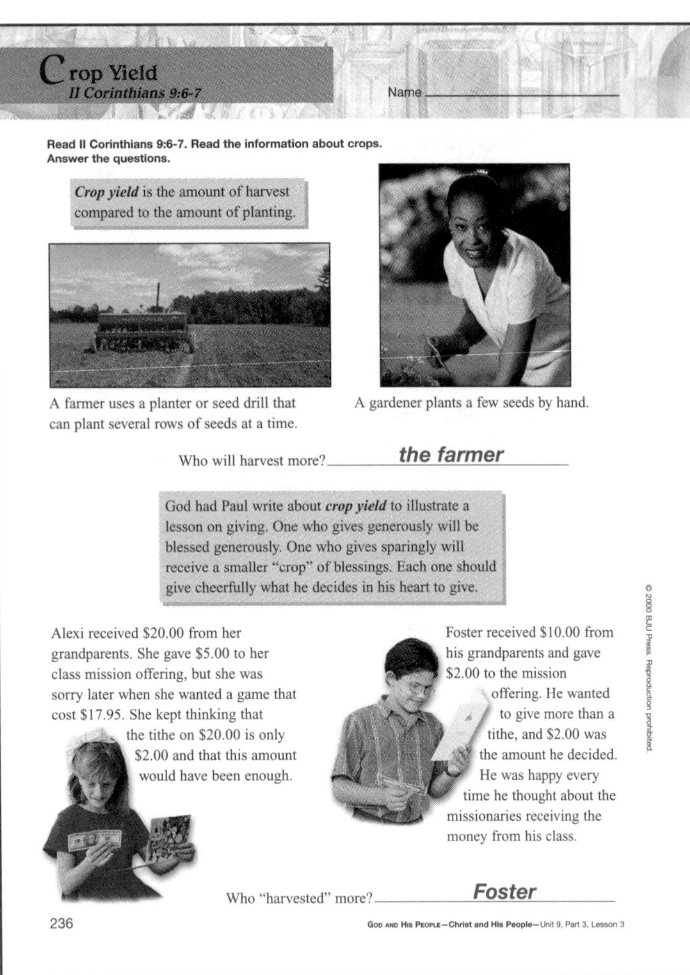

Crop Yield
II Corinthians 9:6-7

Name ________________

Read II Corinthians 9:6-7. Read the information about crops. Answer the questions.

Crop yield is the amount of harvest compared to the amount of planting.

A farmer uses a planter or seed drill that can plant several rows of seeds at a time.

A gardener plants a few seeds by hand.

Who will harvest more? *the farmer*

God had Paul write about ***crop yield*** to illustrate a lesson on giving. One who gives generously will be blessed generously. One who gives sparingly will receive a smaller "crop" of blessings. Each one should give cheerfully what he decides in his heart to give.

Alexi received $20.00 from her grandparents. She gave $5.00 to her class mission offering, but she was sorry later when she wanted a game that cost $17.95. She kept thinking that the tithe on $20.00 is only $2.00 and that this amount would have been enough.

Foster received $10.00 from his grandparents and gave $2.00 to the mission offering. He wanted to give more than a tithe, and $2.00 was the amount he decided. He was happy every time he thought about the missionaries receiving the money from his class.

Who "harvested" more? *Foster*

236 GOD AND HIS PEOPLE—Christ and His People—Unit 9, Part 3, Lesson 3

Worktext page 236

Apply Bible knowledge to everyday life.

Lesson 4

Hymn: "The Church's One Foundation"

Sing all three verses (Worktext page 285). Play the recording and lead in singing verses 1-3. Divide the students into three groups, directing each group to sing a verse of the hymn.

Memory Verses—II Corinthians 9:6-7

Practice the memory verses. Call on volunteers to say the verses from memory.

Background Information

The Writer of Hebrews—*No one knows for certain who wrote the Book of Hebrews. The author does not name himself as do Paul (Romans 1:1), James (James 1:1), and Peter (I Peter 1:1). However, many people believe that Paul wrote Hebrews because of the reference to Timothy (Hebrews 13:23) and the Paul-like closing to the book. Peter said that Paul wrote things that were "hard to be understood" (II Peter 3:16). Hebrews certainly fits that description. Others note that most of the book sounds very unlike Paul's style. Whoever the author was, he knew the Old Testament Scriptures and the Levitical system of sacrifice. He showed conclusively how the Old Testament types and shadows were fulfilled in Jesus Christ.*

Covenant—*A* covenant *is a promise made between two or more people. Sometimes the New Testament uses the word* testament *to mean the same thing. The New Testament speaks of the "new" and the "old" covenants. The old covenant of the law was called "old," not because it was outdated or replaced, but because it was fulfilled in the new. Christ established the new covenant of grace through which the righteousness of the law can now be fulfilled through the work of Christ.*

The Priesthood—*In the Old Testament, the high priest came into the holy of holies once each year on the Day of Atonement to sprinkle blood on the mercy seat atop the ark of the covenant. In the New Testament, Christ's blood is the atonement for our sin. Specific responsibilities of the priests included representing the people before God. Now every believer has the privilege of coming directly to God in worship, prayer, and praise.*

Introducing the Bible Account

Use a glossary. Direct the students to use their glossaries to find the definitions of *edify, intercede,* and *saint.* Select students to read the definitions aloud.

➤ **How can Christians edify one another?** *(Possible answers include to say and do things that would encourage each other in the Lord.)*

Point out that Jesus *intercedes* on the Christian's behalf to God.

Bible Account

Read the following Bible account or read Hebrews 10:19-25.

Edifying the Saints

The writer of Hebrews encourages his fellow believers to enter boldly into the very presence of God through the blood of the Lord Jesus Christ. He tells Christians that Christ gave His body on the cross and provided a new way for people to come into God's presence. The Old Testament way of salvation—the sacrifice of an animal by the high priest—has been replaced. The old covenant of the law was only a "picture" of salvation. It showed what salvation was like, but it was not reality. Christians now have Christ—the complete reality of salvation, not just its picture or type.

Christians come to God through Jesus, who "ever liveth to make intercession for us" (Hebrews 7:25). The priests were Israel's intercessors. The Christians are reminded that now Jesus is the High Priest, the intercessor, and He is over the house of God. Under the old covenant, the priest had to offer sacrifices every year. Christ is the great sacrifice for sin offered once for all. Therefore, Christians should come to God with a "true heart and in

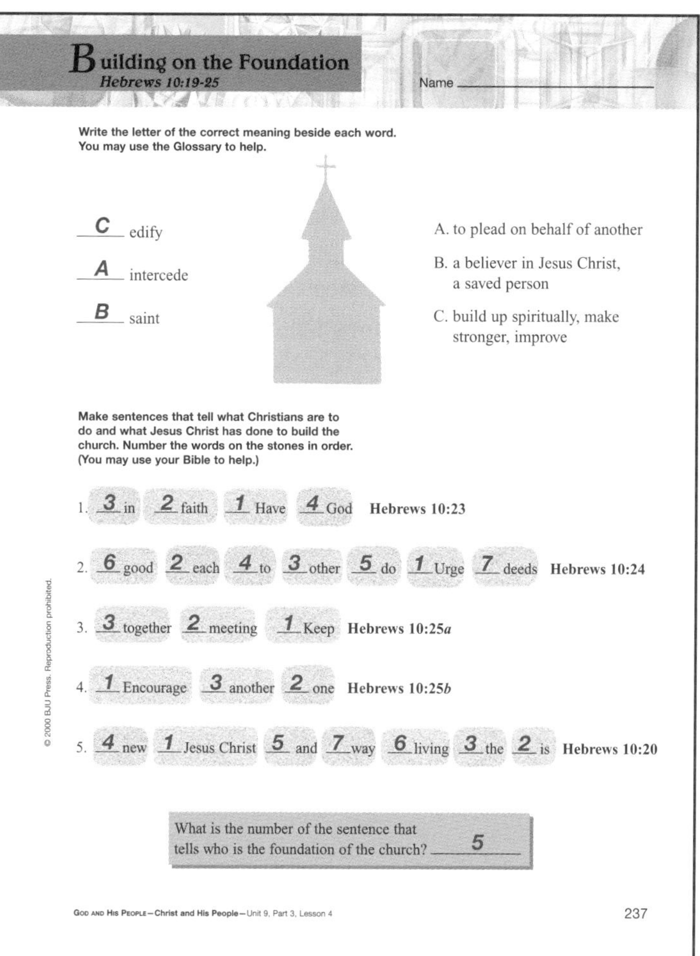

Building on the Foundation
Hebrews 10:19-25

Name ____________

Write the letter of the correct meaning beside each word. You may use the Glossary to help.

C edify
A intercede
B saint

A. to plead on behalf of another
B. a believer in Jesus Christ, a saved person
C. build up spiritually, make stronger, improve

Make sentences that tell what Christians are to do and what Jesus Christ has done to build the church. Number the words on the stones in order. (You may use your Bible to help.)

1. 3 in 2 faith 1 Have 4 God **Hebrews 10:23**
2. 6 good 2 each 4 to 3 other 5 do 1 Urge 7 deeds **Hebrews 10:24**
3. 3 together 2 meeting 1 Keep **Hebrews 10:25*a***
4. 1 Encourage 3 another 2 one **Hebrews 10:25*b***
5. 4 new 1 Jesus Christ 5 and 7 way 6 living 3 the 2 is **Hebrews 10:20**

What is the number of the sentence that tells who is the foundation of the church? 5

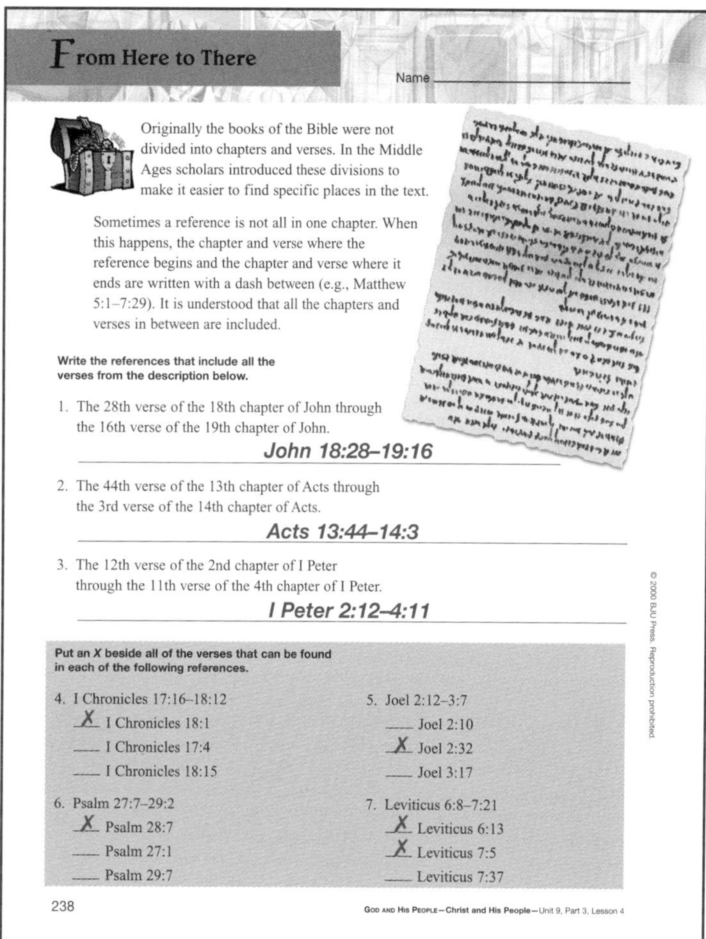

From Here to There

Name ____________

Originally the books of the Bible were not divided into chapters and verses. In the Middle Ages scholars introduced these divisions to make it easier to find specific places in the text.

Sometimes a reference is not all in one chapter. When this happens, the chapter and verse where the reference begins and the chapter and verse where it ends are written with a dash between (e.g., Matthew 5:1–7:29). It is understood that all the chapters and verses in between are included.

Write the references that include all the verses from the description below.

1. The 28th verse of the 18th chapter of John through the 16th verse of the 19th chapter of John.
   John 18:28–19:16
2. The 44th verse of the 13th chapter of Acts through the 3rd verse of the 14th chapter of Acts.
   Acts 13:44–14:3
3. The 12th verse of the 2nd chapter of I Peter through the 11th verse of the 4th chapter of I Peter.
   I Peter 2:12–4:11

Put an *X* beside all of the verses that can be found in each of the following references.

4. I Chronicles 17:16–18:12
   X I Chronicles 18:1
   ___ I Chronicles 17:4
   ___ I Chronicles 18:15
5. Joel 2:12–3:7
   ___ Joel 2:10
   X Joel 2:32
   ___ Joel 3:17
6. Psalm 27:7–29:2
   X Psalm 28:7
   ___ Psalm 27:1
   ___ Psalm 29:7
7. Leviticus 6:8–7:21
   X Leviticus 6:13
   X Leviticus 7:5
   ___ Leviticus 7:37

full assurance of our faith." In the Old Testament, Aaron's sons were sprinkled with blood and washed in water, but under the new way, Christians are cleansed by the blood of the Lamb—the Lord Jesus Christ. Believers are encouraged to be obedient to God and to serve Him because of what Jesus Christ has done for them.

The writer of Hebrews encourages believers not to waver in the hope (confidence) they have of Christ returning for His bride, the church. Christians should hold fast and trust God, knowing that He is faithful and will keep His promises. Jesus said, "And if I go and prepare a place for you, I will come again, and receive you unto myself; that where I am, there ye may be also" (John 14:3).

The Book of Hebrews also tells Christians what they can do to grow spiritually. They are told to encourage, strengthen, and care for each other. They should encourage one another to do good works. They should continue to meet together in God's house as an encouragement to one another. This is even more necessary as the day of Christ's return for His church gets nearer.

➤ **How did people in the Old Testament times enter into God's presence?** *(The high priest went into the holy of holies for them once a year.)*

➤ **How do we enter into God's presence today?** *(The Lord Jesus Christ shed His blood in sacrifice for our sins.)*

➤ **What is the hope that believers have?** *(that Christ will return for His bride, the church)*

➤ **Why should Christians meet together?** *(to encourage, strengthen, and care for one another—they should encourage one another to do good works and encourage one another about Christ's soon return.)*

Worktext page 237

Define words.

Bible Study Skills, Worktext page 238

Determine the extent of a Scripture reference.

Going Beyond

Preparation of Materials

Prepare one piece of white poster board as shown. Center the word *GIVING.* Cut a "window" in the second piece of white poster board, centering the "window" so that when the pieces of poster board are attached, the back piece will flip over onto the front piece to reveal the word *GIVING.*

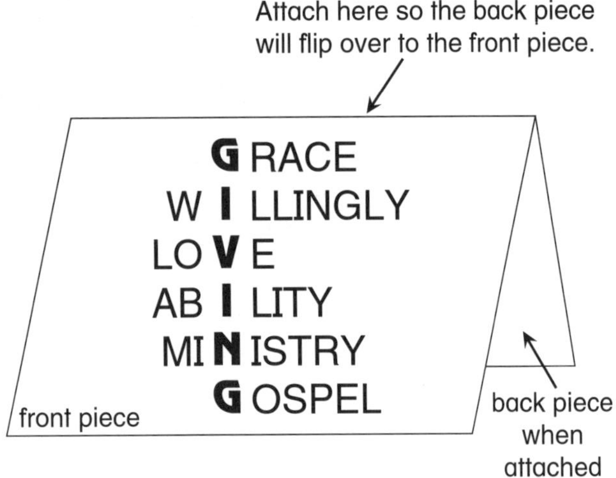

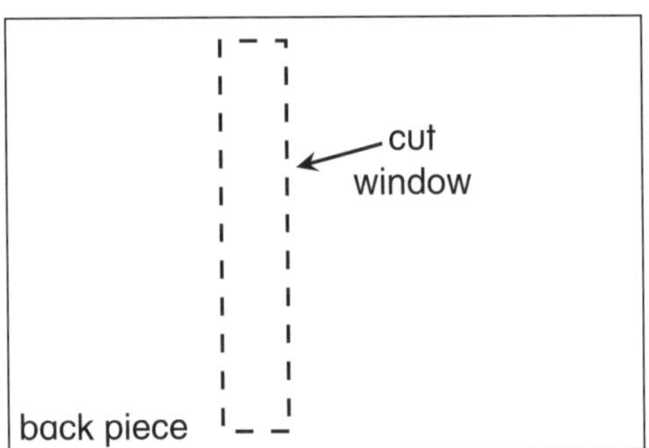

Enrichment

Teach the principle of giving. Display the posterboard "wallet" so that the words written on the front piece are showing.

- ➤ **What is giving a result of?** *(God's grace)*
- ➤ **How does God want Christians to give?** *(willingly)*
- ➤ **What should our heart attitude be when we give?** *(We should give out of a heart of love.)*
- ➤ **On what did the Antioch believers base their giving?** *(It was according to their ability to give.)*

Elicit from the students that a Christian can further the ministry of another Christian and help to spread the gospel when he gives willingly, out of a heart of love, and according to his ability.

Flip the back piece of the chart onto the front piece as you tell the students that God is pleased with our giving when we follow these principles.

The Work of Believers

Unit 9, Part 4

Preview

Doctrines

- Members of the local church should exhort one another (Hebrews 10:25)—Lesson 1
- Members of the local church should pray (Acts 2:42)—Lesson 1
- God calls men through men (Romans 10:14-15)—Lesson 3
- Sanctification is the work of God's Spirit which enables Christians more and more to die to sin and to live unto righteousness (Romans 8:13)—Lesson 3

Skills and Applications

- Learn Ephesians 2:10
- Recall facts and details
- Locate information in Scripture
- Identify character qualities of a Christian
- Realize that Christians are to encourage one another
- Realize that Christians are to pray for one another
- Understand that God planned that Christians should do good works to bring honor and glory to Him
- Apply Bible knowledge to everyday life

Lesson 1

Preparation of Materials

Cut a branch from a tree or shrub and allow the leaves to wither.

Background Information

Illustration of the Vine and the Branches—*John 15:1-8 was taught by Jesus to His disciples after the Lord's Supper was celebrated for the first time. It is likely that the path they followed after leaving the city on their way to the Garden of Gethsemane (John 14:31) influenced the illustration Jesus had chosen, since vineyards grew on the hillsides.*

Introducing the Bible Account

Discuss abiding. Display the withered branch.

➤ **What happens when a branch is cut from a tree?** *(It withers and dies.)*

➤ **What does it mean for a Christian to abide in Christ?** *(Possible answers include accepting and obeying Christ and walking in fellowship with Him.)*

Direct the students to listen to find out what happens to Christians who do not abide in Christ. *(They bear no fruit.)*

Bible Account

Read the following Bible account or read John 15:1-8.

Believers Are the Branches

Jesus wanted to teach His disciples about living the Christian life. He used a vine and its branches and the husbandman, or gardener, to illustrate what He wanted to teach them.

Jesus told His disciples that He was the "true vine" and that God the Father was the gardener. He told His disciples that they were like the branches that grow from the vine. Jesus told them that they would be taken away if they did not make themselves useful to the Lord. But if they were useful, God would purge and cleanse them so that they could become *more* useful to Him. The disciples were aware that a branch cannot live apart from the vine—that it withers and dies. They also knew that a gardener prunes or cuts back the branches on a plant so that they will grow even more. God had sent Jesus to cleanse them and to continue to cleanse them so that they could grow in Him. He cleanses through His Word as it is read and obeyed.

Christ told the disciples that they could be fruitful only by abiding in or depending on Him. Jesus told His disciples that faithfulness to

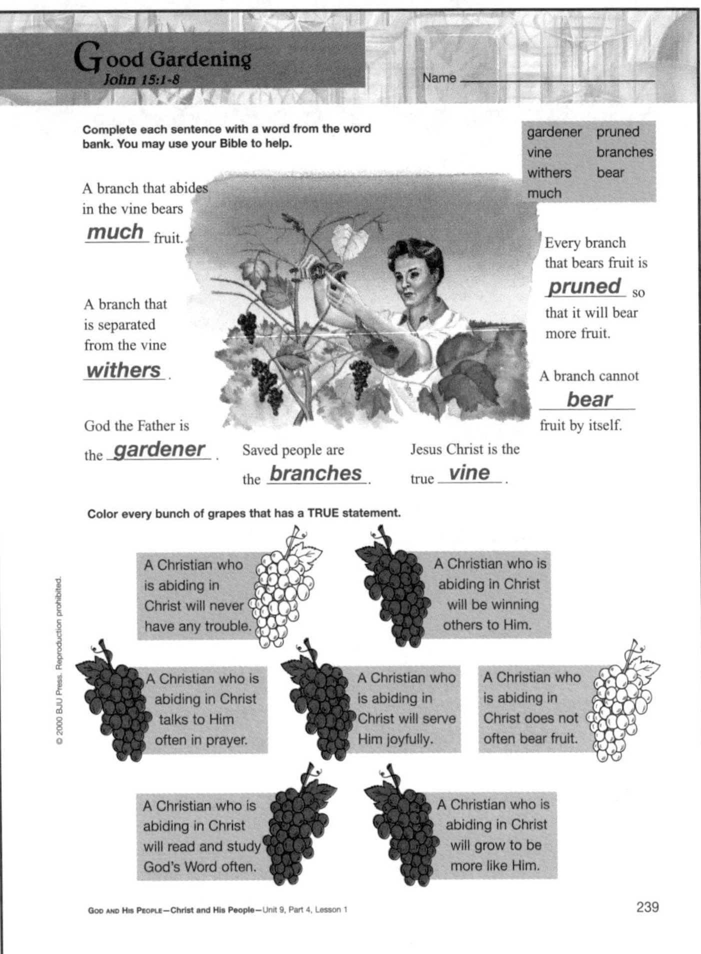

A branch that abides in the vine bears much fruit.
Every branch that bears fruit is pruned so that it will bear more fruit.
A branch that is separated from the vine withers.

Color every bunch of grapes that has a TRUE statement.

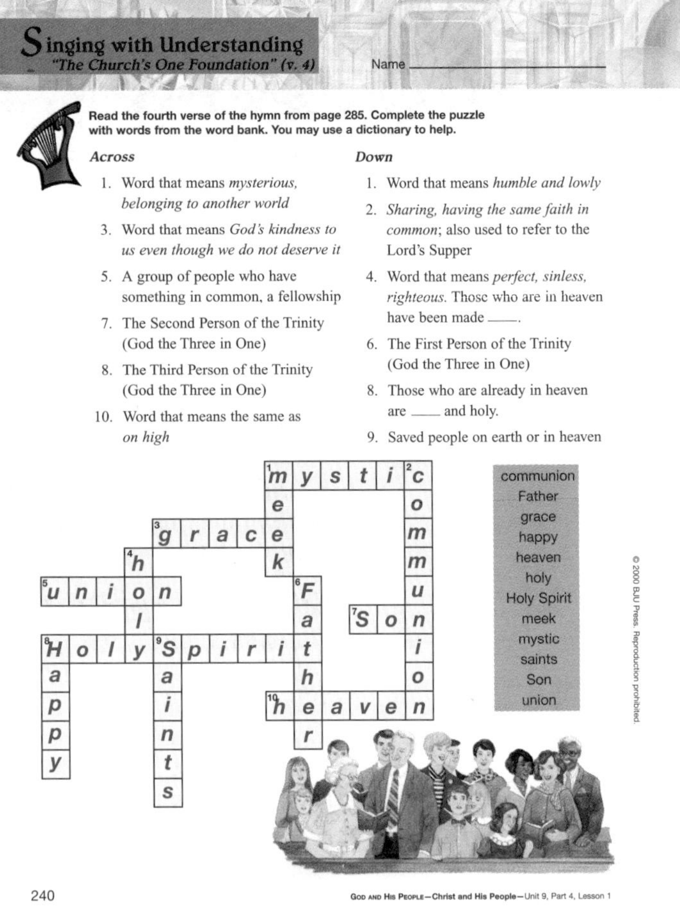

Him depends on obedience to His Word and prayer. As they ask God for help to serve Him, He will provide it. Christ said that reading God's Word and praying to Him will bring fruitfulness and glory to God.

Singing with Understanding
"The Church's One Foundation" (v. 4)
Good Gardening
Name
withers bear
Read the fourth verse of the hymn from page 285. Complete the puzzle with words from the word bank. You may use a dictionary to help.
Across
1. Word that means mysterious, belonging to another world
3. Word that means God's kindness to us even though we do not deserve it
5. A group of people who have something in common, a fellowship
7. The Second Person of the Trinity (God the Three in One)
8. The Third Person of the Trinity (God the Three in One)
10. Word that means the same as on high
Down
1. Word that means humble and lowly
2. Sharing, having the same faith in common; also used to refer to the Lord's Supper
4. Word that means perfect, sinless, righteous. Those who are in heaven have been made ___.
6. The First Person of the Trinity (God the Three in One)
8. Those who are already in heaven are ___ and holy.
9. Saved people on earth or in heaven
communion
Father
grace
happy
heaven
holy
Holy Spirit
meek
mystic
saints
Son
union
240

- ➤ **What did Jesus use to illustrate a principle about living the Christian life?** *(the illustration of a vine and its branches)*
- ➤ **In Christ's illustration of the vine and the branches, what did the vine, branches, and husbandman represent?** *(The branches are believers, the vine is Christ, and the husbandman is God the Father.)*
- ➤ **What will happen to believers if they do not abide in Christ?** *(They will not be fruitful; they will be useless.)*
- ➤ **What will Christ do when we abide in Him and bear fruit?** *(He will cleanse or prune us and cause us to bear more fruit.)*
- ➤ **What does faithfulness and fruitfulness for the Lord depend on?** *(obedience to God's Word and prayer, abiding in Christ)*

Worktext page 239

Recall details and apply Scripture to your life.

Memory Verse—Ephesians 2:10

Principle: We are God's workmanship, and God wants Christians to do good works to honor and glorify Him. Locate and read **Ephesians 2:10** aloud. Elicit from the students that God had it planned that we should be born into His family through the blood of Jesus Christ and that we should do good works. Direct the girls to read the verse and then the boys to read it. Direct the students to highlight the verse (optional) and mark the location with the Unit 9 Bookmark.

- ➤ **Whose workmanship are we?** *(We are God's.)*
- ➤ **Why did God save us?** *(so that we might do good works that would bring God glory)*
- ➤ **What had God planned beforehand?** *(that we should walk in good works; that we should live the life that He has planned for us)*
- ➤ **Will these good works save us? How are we saved?** *(No. We are saved only by the grace of God through faith in Jesus Christ.)*

Hymn: "The Church's One Foundation"

Teach the fourth verse (Worktext page 285). Play the recording and lead in singing the fourth verse. Explain that the hymn writer is speaking about the fellowship the church has with God the Father, God the Son, and God the

Holy Spirit as the church awaits its eternal home. The hymn writer asks God for grace as he waits for that time that he, too, will be in heaven with the Lord and the other saints already there. Lead in singing verses 1-4.

Worktext page 240

Singing with understanding, verse 4.

Lesson 2

Hymn: "The Church's One Foundation"

Sing the hymn (Worktext page 285). Play the recording and sing verse 4 together.

➤ In verse 4, the hymn writer speaks about having fellowship or communion together. **Whom is he referring to?** *(the fellowship that the body of believers, the church, has with God the Father, Son, and Holy Spirit)* Choose several students to lead the singing of verses 1-4.

Introducing the Application Story

Discuss abiding in Christ.

➤ **What kinds of attitudes would not be part of your life if you were abiding in Christ?** *(Possible answers include anger, bitterness, hatred, fear, worry, and jealousy.)*

Application Story

Read the following story to the students.

Abide in Me

Rachel slammed the door, hoping her sister would hear it. A few minutes before, Rachel had left Emily's room and slammed *that* door as well. Emily's parting words still echoed through Rachel's mind. "The only reason they picked you to be in the play is because you can't sing."

Mom was waiting in the driveway to take Rachel to church for the final play rehearsal. She climbed into the car and slammed one last door. "Careful," Mom said. "Your attitude is showing."

"I can't help it. Emily makes me so mad!" said Rachel.

Mom sighed, "Honey, I heard the things Emily said to you. Daddy's going to have a talk with her while we're gone. Her feathers are a little ruffled because you were chosen to be in the play and she was only chosen for the choir. But *both* are important jobs for the Lord. I wish you girls could understand that."

Rachel stared out at the spring blossoms on the cherry trees and was silent.

Rachel joined her friends in the church auditorium. Two of the older boys from the youth group were setting up the stage with furniture and background scenery. Mr. Michaels, the director, played a loud chord on the piano to get their attention.

"Before we begin today, I would like to read a verse," he said. "It's found in John 15:4. 'Abide in me, and I in you. As the branch cannot bear fruit of itself, except it abide in the vine; no more can ye, except ye abide in me.' We would really like for this play to bear fruit—for people to be blessed and encouraged by it. For some people watching, it may be the first time they ever hear the gospel presented.

"But our play won't amount to anything—won't bear any fruit—if we're not abiding in Christ. That means we can't do it with a wrong attitude in our hearts. We can't be proud or bitter or envious of others and their talents. We must do this for the Lord Jesus and trust Him to use us—just as we are. Let's pray."

They all bowed their heads, but Rachel's thoughts went straight to Emily. *Emily's attitude is really wrong,* she thought. *She's jealous of me. Who cares if she does sing better than me? I'm the one who gets to be in the play.*

Rehearsal started, and Rachel walked up onto the stage with the others in the first scene. She noticed Mom sitting near the back of the auditorium, her head bowed slightly. Rachel wondered just for a moment if Mom was sad because of her attitude.

The practice did not go well for Rachel. She kept thinking about how wrong Emily was. Then she started thinking about how sad Mom looked. Several times Rachel was so lost in thought that she missed the cues where she was supposed to speak. And once she forgot a whole section of her lines.

Mr. Michaels walked over to her after the rehearsal. "Try to practice a little bit at home this afternoon, Rachel," he said. "We need you to be nice and sharp with those lines. Tomorrow's the big day!"

Rachel's face felt hot as she hurried back to Mom. "Can we go home now?" she asked.

"What happened, Rachel?" Mom asked as they drove out of the church parking lot. "You knew those lines so well last night."

Rachel felt tears burning her eyes. "It was just like Mr. Michaels said. Mom, I can't do anything right when my attitude is bad." She

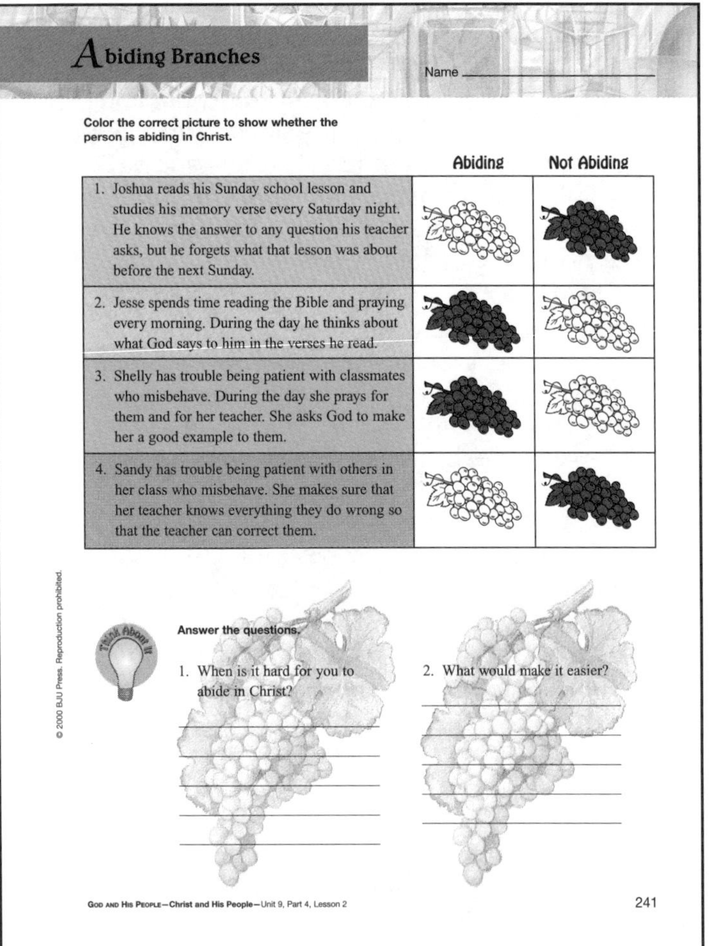

Abiding Branches

Name ____________

Color the correct picture to show whether the person is abiding in Christ.

	Abiding	Not Abiding
1. Joshua reads his Sunday school lesson and studies his memory verse every Saturday night. He knows the answer to any question his teacher asks, but he forgets what that lesson was about before the next Sunday.		(colored)
2. Jesse spends time reading the Bible and praying every morning. During the day he thinks about what God says to him in the verses he read.	(colored)	
3. Shelly has trouble being patient with classmates who misbehave. During the day she prays for them and for her teacher. She asks God to make her a good example to them.	(colored)	
4. Sandy has trouble being patient with others in her class who misbehave. She makes sure that her teacher knows everything they do wrong so that the teacher can correct them.		(colored)

Think About It

Answer the questions.

1. When is it hard for you to abide in Christ?
2. What would make it easier?

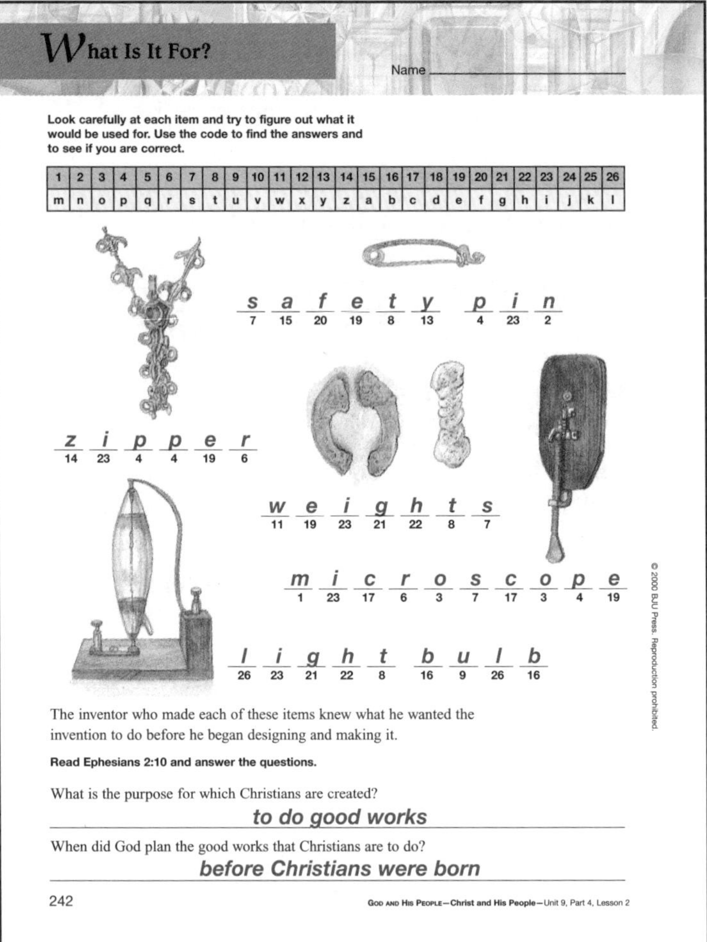

What Is It For?

Name ____________

Look carefully at each item and try to figure out what it would be used for. Use the code to find the answers and to see if you are correct.

1	2	3	4	5	6	7	8	9	10	11	12	13	14	15	16	17	18	19	20	21	22	23	24	25	26
m	n	o	p	q	r	s	t	u	v	w	x	y	z	a	b	c	d	e	f	g	h	i	j	k	l

safety pin (7 15 20 19 8 13 4 23 2)

zipper (14 23 4 4 19 6)

weights (11 19 23 21 22 8 7)

microscope (1 23 17 6 3 7 17 3 4 19)

light bulb (26 23 21 22 8 16 9 26 16)

The inventor who made each of these items knew what he wanted the invention to do before he began designing and making it.

Read Ephesians 2:10 and answer the questions.

What is the purpose for which Christians are created?
to do good works

When did God plan the good works that Christians are to do?
before Christians were born

paused. "Do you think that's what that verse about abiding in Christ means?"

"I think that's exactly what it means," Mom said, "because we need Christ's help to have a good attitude." Rachel heard a smile in Mom's voice. "When we get home, Emily might like to help you practice your lines. You think so?"

"I'll ask her," Rachel said. She watched out the window, noticing the cherry blossoms again. They were just blossoms now—but one of these days, they would be fruit.

➤ **What was wrong with Rachel's attitude?** *(She was angry with Emily; she was focused on the wrong Emily had done instead of on her own wrongdoing.)*

➤ **What was wrong with Emily's attitude?** *(She was jealous of Rachel's having a part in the play; she was unkind.)*

➤ **How would abiding in Christ change either kind of attitude?** *(Christ would give the strength needed to have a kind, gracious spirit.)*

➤ **What did Mr. Michaels say would not take place if the actors in the play did not abide in Christ?** *(The play would not bear fruit—would not be an encouragement and a witness to others.)*

➤ **What do you think Rachel should do if Emily continues to treat her unkindly when she gets home?** *(ask the Lord's help to be kind to Emily anyway; pray for her)*

Worktext page 241

Apply Bible knowledge to everyday life.

Memory Verse—Ephesians 2:10

Practice the memory verse. Locate and read **Ephesians 2:10** aloud. Direct the students to read the verse responsively—you reading one word and the students reading one word.

Worktext page 242

Develop an understanding of the memory verse.

Lesson 3

Materials

- A copy of Supplement page S73, "Taking Notes," for each student
- Chart 37, "Paul's Route—Third Journey" (optional)

Hymn: "The Church's One Foundation"

Sing the hymn (Worktext page 285). Lead the students in singing all four verses.

Memory Verse—Ephesians 2:10

Practice the memory verse. Select a student to read **Ephesians 2:8-9** aloud; then select a student to read **Ephesians 2:10** aloud.

➤ **Why does God want Christians to do good works?** *(to honor and glorify Him)*

➤ **What would the unsaved think of a Christian who lived for himself and did not do good works?** *(Possible answers include that he is just like them so there is no need for them to be saved; it would be a poor testimony.)*

Direct the students to read the memory verse to a partner.

Background Information

Paul's Travels—*He tried to leave Corinth and sail directly to Syria, but some Jews tried to kill him; therefore, he returned by land to Philippi and then back to Troas. Paul was in Troas for a week and from there traveled to Miletus. While in Miletus, Paul called for the Ephesian elders to meet him.*

Elders—*Paul addresses the Ephesian elders, referred to in the New Testament as bishops, overseers, pastors or shepherds, and teachers.*

Introducing the Bible Account

Review Paul's third missionary journey. Share the background information. Trace the route on Chart 37, "Paul's Route—Third Journey" (optional).

Bible Account

Read the following Bible account or read Acts 20:17-35. Give each student a copy of Supplement page S73, "Taking Notes," directing him to take notes of the main ideas of the following Bible account.

The Ministry of Believers

From Troas, Paul sailed to Miletus. While there he sent for the Ephesian elders and spoke with them. "Ye know, from the first day that I came into Asia, after what manner I have been with you at all seasons." Paul was reminding the elders that he had been consistently *faithful* in his service to the Lord. He said he had served the Lord with "all humility of mind." Paul was a *humble* servant of Christ in spite of the fact that he had a brilliant mind, that he had preached all over the known world, and that he had seen many converts come to Christ.

In his service for Christ, Paul had shared in the sufferings, the griefs, and the cares of the Ephesians. Paul had shown he had a servant's heart—a *compassionate* heart.

Then Paul spoke to the Ephesian elders about his zeal in witnessing and proclaiming the gospel. He warned the elders of dangers confronting them. He told them to be on their guard, preaching the Word of God to the people in the churches and reminding them that God had purchased them with His own blood. Paul was *enthusiastic* in preaching God's Word "from house to house" to all who would listen.

Paul knew that the opposition he faced from some of the Jews would increase. But physical dangers did not discourage Paul. He was a *courageous* servant of the Lord.

Finally, Paul told the elders that his only desire was to give of himself in his service for Christ. Paul was *unselfish.* He had not coveted another man's silver, gold, or clothing. He hoped that his example of working hard to support himself and others would remind his brothers in Christ that Jesus said, "It is more blessed to give than to receive," and would inspire them, too, to live unselfishly.

➤ **How was Paul a *faithful* servant of the Lord?** *(He reminded the elders that from the first day they met him until the present time he had been serving the Lord.)*

➤ **Why can we say that Paul was an *enthusiastic* servant of the Lord?** *(His main interest was to see others come to Christ, and he eagerly pursued this goal.)*

Wanted: A Good Example
Acts 20:17-35

Name ____________

Paul encouraged the Christians at Ephesus to follow his example.

Read the classified ad.

WANTED: ZOO SERVICES FOOD DIRECTOR

Requires strong leadership and technical skills. Knowledge of the dietary preferences of large mammals necessary. Experience with persuading tigers to eat the food instead of the food provider is preferred. Benefits include full medical coverage and an attractive salary. Please send resumé to Zoo Services, 118 Tiger Trail, Growlville.

Think about each of the questions below and then write an ad for a good example of what a Christian should be.

What character traits does a Christian example need?
What does a Christian need to know in order to be an example?
What kind of previous experience does a Christian example need?
What are the benefits of being a Christian example?

WANTED: CHRISTIAN EXAMPLE

God and His People—Christ and His People—Unit 9, Part 4, Lesson 3 243

- ➤ **What made Paul a *humble* servant of Christ?** *(He gave God the credit and knew he was a sinner saved by God's grace.)*
- ➤ **Why can we say that Paul was a *compassionate* servant of Christ?** *(He was a caring person who suffered for and with the believers.)*
- ➤ **How was Paul a *courageous* servant of the Lord?** *(He continued to preach Christ even though others sought to kill him.)*
- ➤ **How was Paul an *unselfish* servant of Christ?** *(He worked to help others and put their needs before his own.)*

Discuss the notes taken by the students.

- ➤ **How can these character qualities be a part of your lives also?** *(Answers will vary.)*

Worktext page 243

Identify character qualities of a Christian.

Lesson 4

Materials

- Bible Book Cards: Old Testament and New Testament

Hymn: "The Church's One Foundation"

Sing the hymn (Worktext page 285).

- ➤ **Who is the foundation of the church?** *(Jesus Christ)*
- ➤ **According to verse 2, through salvation in Christ, what do Christians have?** *(one Lord, one faith, one birth)*
- ➤ **When will the church be victorious and at rest?** *(when Christ returns)*

Play the recording and lead in singing verses 1-4.

Memory Verse—Ephesians 2:10

Practice the memory verse. Call on a student to say the verse. Continue this procedure until all volunteers have been given the opportunity to say the verse from memory.

Bible Study Skills

Review the Old Testament and the New Testament. Mix up the Bible Book Cards for the Old and New Testaments. Arrange the students in several teams. Display the flash cards one at a time, directing the first student on each team to identify Old Testament or New Testament and to name the book that comes before and the book that comes after the book on the card. The student receives a point for his team for each correct answer. Continue showing cards, allowing the students to answer until all the cards have been shown or the time allotted for playing is complete.

One-on-One: Tell the student to sequence the Old Testament and New Testament Bible Book Cards correctly.

Application Story

Read the following story to the students.

Repairs

Bernie watched the neighbor boy, Will, whiz away on his bike. He yelled something over his shoulder that Bernie couldn't hear.

"What'd he say, Max?" Bernie asked his friend.

"He called us a bad name. You don't want to know." Max shrugged. "He's just stupid, like I said."

Bernie frowned. "I don't think you should've called him stupid, Max. That's what made him mad."

Max folded his arms. "Anyone that doesn't get saved is stupid," he said. "Will's going to go to hell if he doesn't trust Christ. Now that would be a stupid move, don't you think?"

Bernie hesitated. "Yeah, but—maybe you shouldn't have said—"

"We're supposed to be bold when we witness, remember? Like Paul was. I believe in telling it straight." Max swung his leg over the seat of his bike. "Gotta go. See you at church tomorrow, Bernie."

Bernie wandered into the garage. Dad looked up from the workbench. Engine parts were spread out before him. "What are you doing?" Bernie asked.

"Hoping to fix the lawnmower," said Dad.

Bernie looked at the scattered parts and thought of Will. He hoped Dad might be able to fix more than just the lawnmower. "Dad, Max and I just messed up," he said. "Big time." He hopped up on a stool beside Dad.

"Does this have anything to do with Will?" Dad asked. "I heard you guys talking."

"Yeah. Max and I invited Will to church. He said his dad thinks Christians believe a bunch of fairy tales. And then Max got mad and called him stupid for not believing the gospel."

"That must have been the point when Will took off on his bike."

Bernie nodded. "But Max says we're supposed to be bold like Paul was."

Dad picked up several parts, one by one, and examined them. Bernie waited. Finally, Dad pushed the parts aside and turned to face him. "I'm going to have to get some help with that engine," he said. "But about your problem: let me remind you of some things Paul said in his letters."

Dad wiped his hands on a cloth and pulled his New Testament out of his pocket. He found a place in Acts and read aloud. " 'Serving the Lord with all humility of mind . . . ' " He turned some pages. " 'Now I Paul myself beseech you by the meekness and gentleness of Christ . . .' " He flipped some more pages. " 'But speaking the truth in love . . .' 'But we were gentle among you, even as a nurse cherisheth her children . . .' 'And the servant of the Lord must not strive; but be gentle unto all men . . . in meekness instructing those that oppose themselves . . .' 'To speak evil of no man, to be no brawlers, but gentle, shewing all meekness unto all men . . .' " He looked up. "Are you getting my point here, Bernie?"

Bernie looked down. "Yes, sir. We're supposed to be meek and humble with people."

"Right. And does that mean we are not to be bold?"

Bernie paused. "Well, we *are* supposed to be bold."

"Being bold means to give someone all the information they need to understand truth," Dad said. "It doesn't mean responding in anger to their attacks on your faith. That is not boldness, Son. That's pride."

Bernie shoved his hands into his pockets. "But Max already ruined everything, Dad."

Dad nodded thoughtfully. "Max definitely did some damage," he said. "But perhaps you boys could help smooth things over by talking to Will—in the right spirit. Which means you would need to apologize first."

Bernie sighed. "That'll be hard to do," he said.

Dad closed his Bible and ran his fingers over the binding a few times. He looked up at Bernie. "Humility," he said, "doesn't come as easily as pride, does it?"

Bernie stared at Dad for a moment; then he stood up. "Thanks, Dad," he said. "I guess Max and I have some fixing to do."

➤ **Why did Max call Will stupid?** *(He was angry with Will for attacking his faith in Christ.)*

➤ **What was right about Max's witness to Will?** *(He spoke truthfully when he told Will that he would go to hell if he didn't accept Christ.)*

➤ **What was wrong with Max's witness?** *(His spirit was wrong: he responded in anger and pride; he lost Will's friendship by attacking him personally.)*

➤ **What would have been a better way to respond?** *(Many answers are acceptable; guide the students to understand that Max should have responded in meekness.)*

➤ **How did Bernie's dad define *boldness?*** *(giving someone all the information he needs to understand truth)*

➤ **How can a person be bold and meek at the same time?** *(by speaking the truth in love)*

Read **I Peter 2:7-8,** explaining that often people become offended at the gospel because it convicts them of their disobedience.

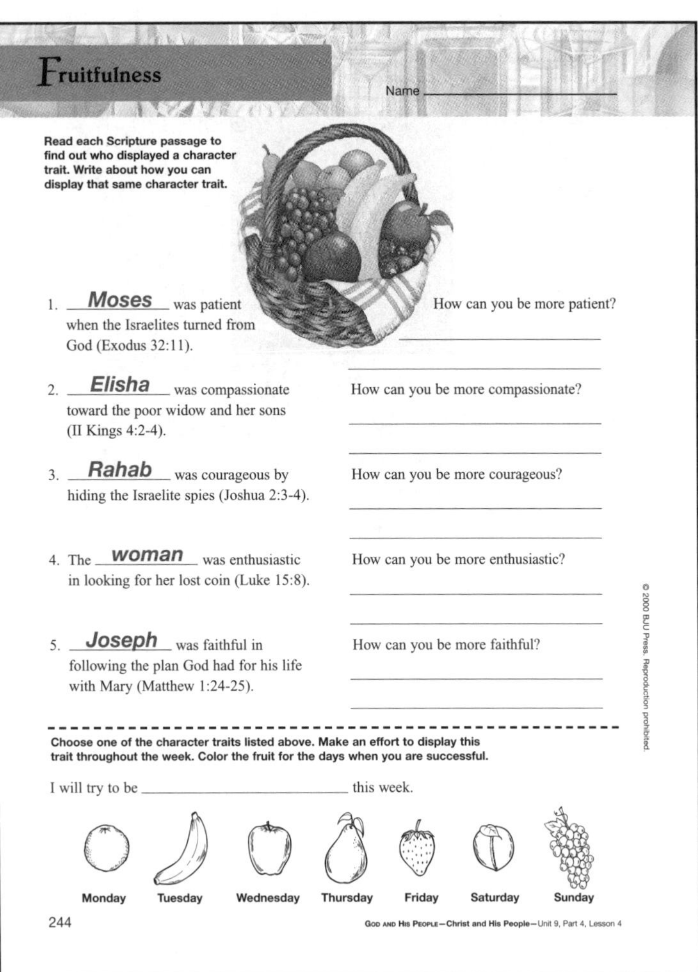

Fruitfulness

Name ____________________

Read each Scripture passage to find out who displayed a character trait. Write about how you can display that same character trait.

1. **Moses** was patient when the Israelites turned from God (Exodus 32:11). How can you be more patient? ____________________
2. **Elisha** was compassionate toward the poor widow and her sons (II Kings 4:2-4). How can you be more compassionate? ____________________
3. **Rahab** was courageous by hiding the Israelite spies (Joshua 2:3-4). How can you be more courageous? ____________________
4. The **woman** was enthusiastic in looking for her lost coin (Luke 15:8). How can you be more enthusiastic? ____________________
5. **Joseph** was faithful in following the plan God had for his life with Mary (Matthew 1:24-25). How can you be more faithful? ____________________

Choose one of the character traits listed above. Make an effort to display this trait throughout the week. Color the fruit for the days when you are successful.

I will try to be ____________________ this week.

Monday Tuesday Wednesday Thursday Friday Saturday Sunday

244 GOD AND HIS PEOPLE—Christ and His People—Unit 9, Part 4, Lesson 4

Worktext page 244

Locate information in Scripture and apply Scripture to everyday life.

Going Beyond

Enrichment

Direct a role-playing activity. Display the list of character traits used in the Bible account on pages 319-20: faithful, humble, compassionate, enthusiastic, courageous, unselfish. Divide the students into six groups, assigning each group to act out a situation in which one of the character traits can be revealed. Allow the groups to perform their skits with the other students guessing which character trait is being portrayed. Challenge them to be like Paul in their daily Christian lives.

Unit Review

Materials

- Copy of Supplement pages S64-65, "Unit 9 Review," for each student

Guide a review of Unit 9. Review the people and events in preparation for the Unit 9 Test (optional).

Unit 9 Review

Name ____________

Draw a line to match the beginning of each sentence to the correct ending.

Have a time set aside to — spend with the Lord in Bible reading and prayer.
Ask Jesus to — teach you about Himself.
Be still and — listen carefully to what God is telling you.
Investigate Scripture as you — ask yourself questions about its meaning.
Take time to — look up words and ideas you don't understand.

Draw a line matching the items that belong together.

God — gardener
Jesus — vine
Christians — branches

edify — build up spiritually
saint — a saved person
intercession — pleading on another's behalf
church — belonging to the Lord
tithe — one tenth of our income

Draw a line matching the three parts that make each sentence.

Abiding in Christ means to — live in obedience to the Lord's will or — be filled with the Holy Spirit.
Peter said, — "Thou art the Christ," — "the Son of the Living God."
Christians should — give cheerfully — and generously.
We can edify the saints — by meeting together — and encouraging each other.

S64 Use after completing Unit 9 God and His People

Unit 9 Review (continued)

Name ____________

Complete the chart by writing the missing names, events, and places.

Apollos	Aquila	Corinth	deacons
famine	Macedonia	Pentecost	Priscilla

WHO	WHAT	WHERE
1. Agabus	foretold the *famine* that would come to	Jerusalem and the surrounding regions.
2. *Apollos*	didn't fully understand the Gospel in	Ephesus.
3. *Aquila* and *Priscilla* were	tentmakers who discipled Apollos in the city of	Ephesus.
4. Barnabas and Paul	transported an offering from the believers in	*Macedonia*.
5. Believers	sent help to Jerusalem from	*Corinth*.
6. Peter	preached at *Pentecost*, and thousands of people were saved in	Jerusalem.
7. Philip, Nicolas, and Stephen	were chosen as *deacons* in	Jerusalem.

God and His People Use after completing Unit 9 S65

Eternal Promises

Overview

Preparing the Teacher

Even though **Revelation 22:10** admonishes, "Seal not the sayings of the prophecy of this book: for the time is at hand," most of us shy away from studying and teaching this final book of God's Word. Yet the Book of Revelation begins with a blessing for those who read and keep its words. As you ponder God's promises to believers in relationship to future events, remember **Matthew 5:8,** "Blessed are the pure in heart, for they shall see God." And pray with the apostle John, "Even so, come, Lord Jesus!"

Preparing the Lessons

Part 1 Lesson 1 Materials—two small pieces of magnetic tape for each student

Part 1 Lesson 4 Materials—recording of "Worthy Is the Lamb That Was Slain" from *Messiah* by George Frederick Handel (optional)

Part 2 Going Beyond Materials—dictionaries, thesauruses

Part 3 Lessons 1 and 3 Materials—recording of "For Unto Us a Child Is Born" from *Messiah* by George Frederick Handel (optional)

Part 4 Going Beyond Materials—3" × 5" cards, tagboard, or construction paper (optional); a small file box, an old recipe box, an empty check box, or a small manila envelope for each student (optional)

Unit 10 Eternal Promises — Hymn: "It Is Well with My Soul"

Part	Lesson number	Lesson pages	Worktext pages	Supplement pages	Bible Account	Application
Part 1: **Jesus Christ Protects His Own**	1	329	245-48		**Bible Study:** God's Promise of Eternal Protection (John 10)	
	2	332	249		**Prophet Focus:** Amos	
	3	334	250		**Bible Study:** The Lamb Opens the Seals (Revelation 5)	
	4	336	251-52			**Picture the Point:** Lambs
Part 2: **Jesus Christ Will Conquer and Judge**	1	339	253-54		Christ, the Faithful and True Judge (Revelation 6-19)	
	2	341	255		**Bible Study:** The Wrath of God	
	3	343	256			"As the Stars Forever" (Part 1)
	4	345	257-58			"As the Stars Forever" (Part 2)
Part 3: **Jesus Christ Will Rule and Reign**	1	347	259-60		The Promise of God's Rule (Isaiah 9:6-7)	
	2	349	261-62		**Bible Study:** The Millennium	
	3	351	263		A Kingdom of Righteousness (Revelation 20)	
	4	353	264			Application Activity
Part 4: **Jesus Christ Gives Life Eternal**	1	355	265		**Bible Study:** God's Promise of Eternal Life (I John)	
	2	357	266			"Mark It with a *P*"
	3	359	267			**Hymn History Story**: "It Is Well with My Soul"
	4	361	268		God's Promise of an Eternal Home (Revelation 21)	

Connections	Memory Verses and Principles	Bible Doctrines	Skills/Applications
TimeLine: Amos Music	John 10:27-28 *Christians can trust God to keep them for Himself as He has promised.*	**The Doctrine of the Bible** The Bible is accurate in its prophecy (Num. 23:19). **The Doctrine of God** God is all-powerful (omnipotent) (Jer. 32:27). God is unchanging (immutable) (James 1:17). God is faithful (I Cor. 1:9), righteous (Ps. 145:17), and love (I John 4:8). **The Doctrine of Man** The final state of unredeemed man is eternal separation from God (Rev. 20:14-15). **The Doctrine of Salvation** Man must turn to Christ alone for salvation (John 14:6). Man turns to God through repentance and faith (conversion) (II Cor. 7:9-10). **The Doctrine of Angels and Satan** Cherubim guard God's throne, possessions, and holiness (Gen. 3:24). Angels worship God (Rev. 5:11). **The Doctrine of the End Times** **The Tribulation:** The Antichrist will rise (Rev. 13:1-8). The False Prophet will exalt the Antichrist (Rev. 13:11-15). Christ will appear gloriously (Rev. 19:11-16). The Antichrist and the False Prophet will be cast into the lake of fire (Rev. 19:20–20:10). **The Millennium:** The saints will rule with Christ (Rev. 20:6). There will be worldwide peace with other men and animals (Isa. 65:25). Earth will be filled with the knowledge of the Lord, although not all will be saved (Isa. 2:3). **Ages to Come:** There will be the judgment of sin and punishment in the lake of fire (Rev. 20:13-15).	**Foundational:** • Understand the spiritual application of Jesus Christ, the Good Shepherd and the Lamb • Realize that God promises to give eternal life to believers • Appreciate God's plan and promises for provision for His children **Practical:** • Recall facts and details • Locate information in Scripture • Learn the divisions for the books of the Bible • Use a glossary • Use a concordance • Distinguish between characteristics • Complete an outline web • Complete an outline map • Identify definitions • Sequence events of the end times • Complete an analogy • Identify promises of God **Personal:** • Develop a Bible reading habit • Understand how to have assurance of salvation • Realize the need to be ready to meet God • Develop an understanding of the end times • Grow in an appreciation of God's eternal plan and provision for Christians • Apply Bible knowledge to everyday life
	Revelation 19:11 *God's judgment is righteous, in keeping with the faithfulness and truth of His character.*		
	Isaiah 9:6-7 *Jesus Christ, the Son of God and Savior of men, will someday come as King to rule the world in righteousness.*		
	I John 5:11-13 *God has given us the assurance of salvation in His Word.*		

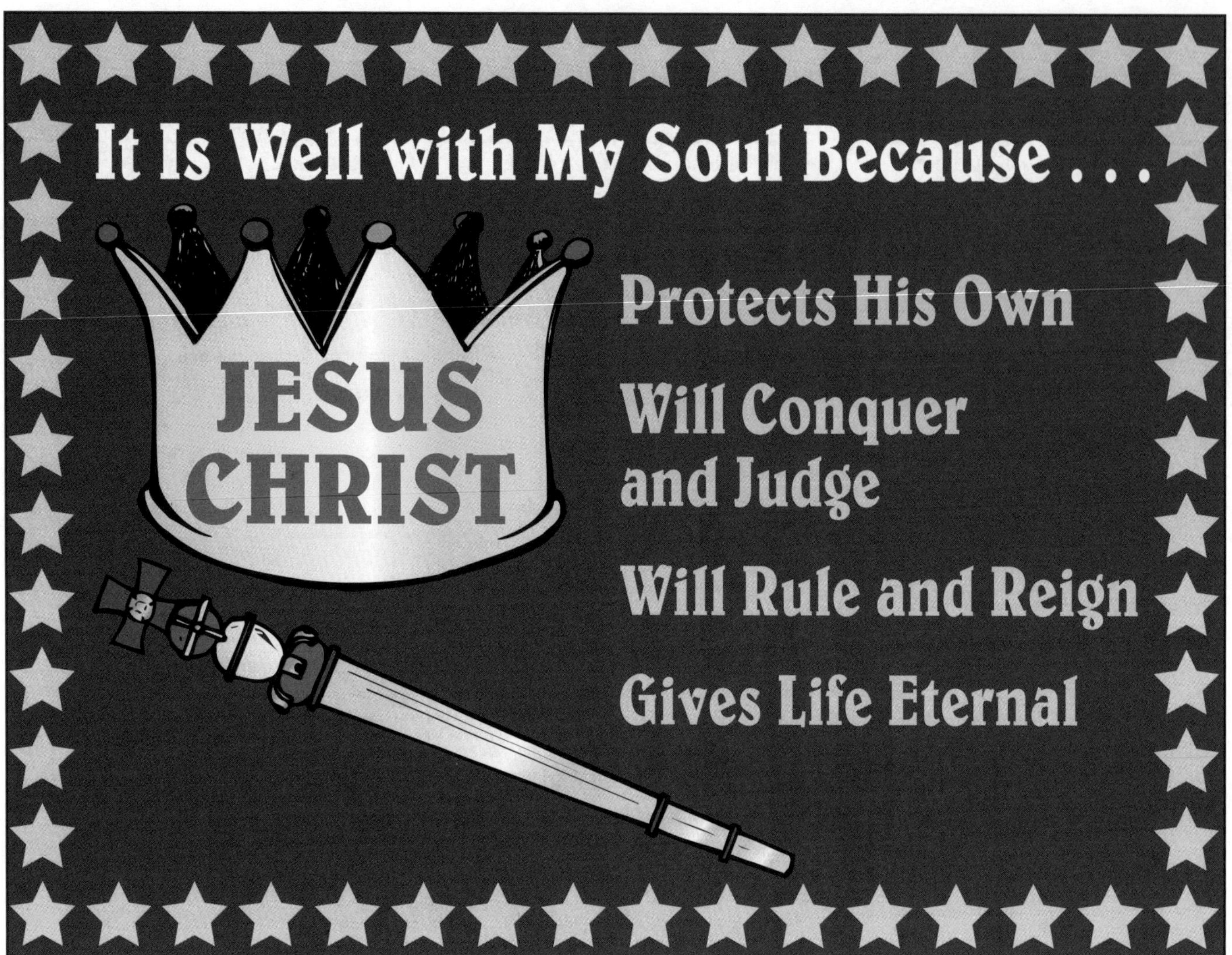

Preparing the Unit 10 Bulletin Board

Cover the bulletin board with deep purple or blue background paper and border it with gold stars. Prepare gold lettering and mount as shown: "It Is Well with My Soul Because . . . Jesus Christ Protects His Own, Will Conquer and Judge, Will Rule and Reign, and Gives Life Eternal." Prepare a gold crown and a scepter as a background to the name *Jesus Christ*. Sprinkle the background with tiny stars or brush the border and the crown, scepter, and name with gold glitter (optional).

Jesus Christ Protects His Own

Unit 10, Part 1

Preview

Doctrines

- God is all-powerful (omnipotent) (Jeremiah 32:27)—Lesson 1
- Man must turn to Christ alone for salvation (John 14:6)—Lesson 1
- God is righteous (Psalm 145:17)—Lesson 3
- Cherubim guard God's throne, possessions, and holiness (Genesis 3:24)—Lesson 3
- Angels worship God (Revelation 5:11)—Lesson 3

Skills and Applications

- Learn John 10:27-28
- Learn the divisions for the books of the Bible
- Recall facts and details
- Complete an analogy
- Locate information in Scripture
- Distinguish between characteristics
- Understand the spiritual application of Jesus Christ, the Good Shepherd and the Lamb
- Realize that God promises to give eternal life to believers
- Develop an understanding of the end times
- Develop a Bible reading habit
- Apply Bible knowledge to everyday life

Lesson 1

Materials

- Song: "The Bible Reading Habit"
- Two small pieces of magnetic tape for each student
- Unit 10 Bookmark for each student
- Highlighter for each student (optional)

Write the following references for display: **John 10:1-2, John 10:3-5, John 10:6, John 8:39, John 10:7-10, John 10:11-15, John 10:16-17, Galatians 3:26,** and **John 10:27-28.**

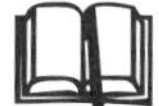

Memory Verses—John 10:27-28

Principle: Christians can trust God to keep them for Himself as He has promised. Locate and read **John 10:27-28** to the students. Guide them in highlighting the verses in their Bibles (optional). Give each student a Unit 10 Bookmark to mark the location of the verses. Point out that the illustration of the clocks and watches should remind them that they should be using their time wisely for the Lord since His coming can be at any time. Direct the students to attach the magnetic tape and to place the Unit 10 Bookmark over the page.

➤ **What does it mean to promise someone something?** *(to say you will do or not do something)*

➤ **Do you always keep your promises? Why?** *(Answers will vary. Sometimes illness or bad weather or other things may prevent you from keeping a promise.)*

➤ **Does God always keep His promises? Why?** *(Yes. God's Word is true, pure, faithful, and powerful; God knows what will happen from the beginning to the end.)*

➤ **What does God promise to those who accept His Son?** *(He will give them eternal life, and they will never die.)*

Bible Study Skills, Worktext pages 245-46

Develop a Bible reading habit. Read the top part of page 245 to the students. Select students to read aloud the Bible reading guidelines, emphasizing that because a true believer wants to know God better, he studies God's Word. Explain the four-week Bible reading activity on page 246, pointing out that this is a survey. Encourage the students to evaluate how well they have developed the Bible reading habit during the school year. (*Note:* You may want to compile the survey results and advise individual students.)

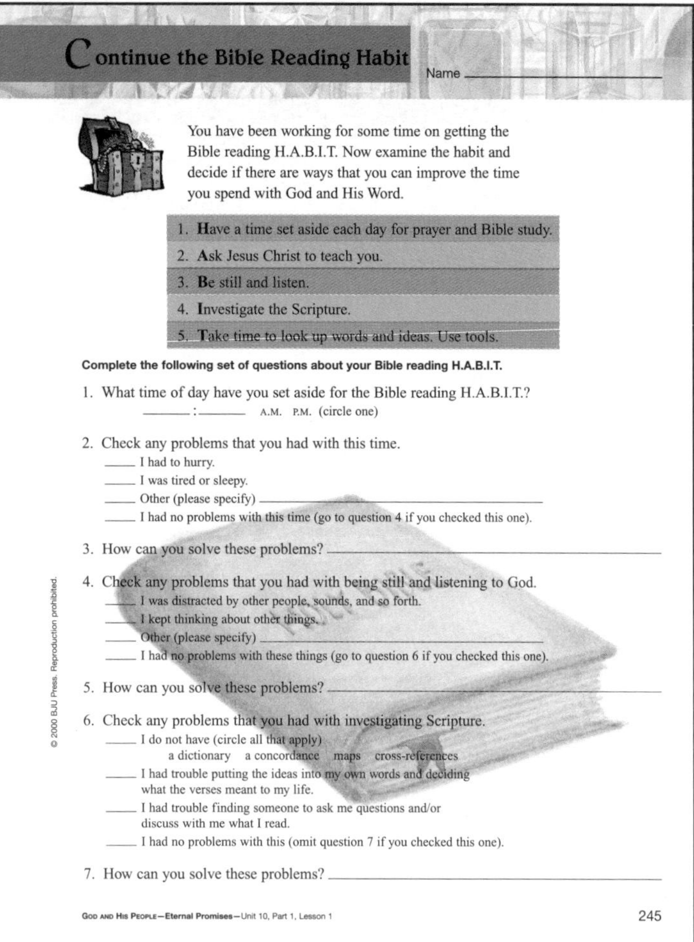

Continue the Bible Reading Habit

Name ______________________

You have been working for some time on getting the Bible reading H.A.B.I.T. Now examine the habit and decide if there are ways that you can improve the time you spend with God and His Word.

1. **H**ave a time set aside each day for prayer and Bible study.
2. **A**sk Jesus Christ to teach you.
3. **B**e still and listen.
4. **I**nvestigate the Scripture.
5. **T**ake time to look up words and ideas. Use tools.

Complete the following set of questions about your Bible reading H.A.B.I.T.

1. What time of day have you set aside for the Bible reading H.A.B.I.T.?
   ______:______ A.M. P.M. (circle one)
2. Check any problems that you had with this time.
   ____ I had to hurry.
   ____ I was tired or sleepy.
   ____ Other (please specify) ______________________
   ____ I had no problems with this time (go to question 4 if you checked this one).
3. How can you solve these problems? ______________________
4. Check any problems that you had with being still and listening to God.
   ____ I was distracted by other people, sounds, and so forth.
   ____ I kept thinking about other things.
   ____ Other (please specify) ______________________
   ____ I had no problems with these things (go to question 6 if you checked this one).
5. How can you solve these problems? ______________________
6. Check any problems that you had with investigating Scripture.
   ____ I do not have (circle all that apply)
   a dictionary a concordance maps cross-references
   ____ I had trouble putting the ideas into my own words and deciding what the verses meant to my life.
   ____ I had trouble finding someone to ask me questions and/or discuss with me what I read.
   ____ I had no problems with this (omit question 7 if you checked this one).
7. How can you solve these problems? ______________________

God and His People—Eternal Promises—Unit 10, Part 1, Lesson 1 245

God Rules Eternally

Name ______________________

Christians have security in knowing that nothing on earth or in heaven is outside the knowledge and control of God. He is stronger than any of His enemies, and His kingdom will prevail. God loves His people and is able to keep those who belong to Him in perfect peace and safety now and forever.

Color each scroll after you read the verses for that day.

God's wrath is directed against those who challenge Him. Psalm 2:1-6	God delivers those who turn to Him in repentance and faith. Psalm 6:1-4, 8-10	God's love is unfailing, even when enemies seem to triumph. Psalm 13	God will not allow the one who walks in His righteous ways to be shaken. Psalm 15	When God appears, His enemies will be destroyed. Psalm 21:8-13
The one who trusts in God does not need to fear. Psalm 56:1-4	God is King forever. He is worshiped in holiness. Psalm 29:1-2, 10-11	God rules forever in justice and righteousness. Psalm 45:6-7	God rules over the nations of the earth. Psalm 22:27-28	God is a refuge for those who trust Him. Psalm 62:5-8
God will scatter His enemies and will make His people to rejoice. Psalm 68:1-3	God chooses the appointed time for everything. Psalm 46	God hides His people from all harm. Psalm 91:1-8	God protects those who trust Him. Psalm 18:30-32	God reigns eternally. Psalm 93
God's power and glory are seen by all. Psalm 97:1-6	God will keep His people from harm forever. Psalm 121	God's people praise Him every day and forever. Psalm 145:1-2	There is no limit to God's power and understanding. Psalm 147:4-5	Let everything that has breath praise the Lord. Psalm 150

246 God and His People—Eternal Promises—Unit 10, Part 1, Lesson 1

Lead in singing the song "The Bible Reading Habit" from Worktext page 271.

Hymn: "It Is Well with My Soul"

Teach the first verse (Worktext page 286). Direct the students to read the words of the first verse silently.

➤ **What is the hymn writer telling us in this hymn?** *(Answers will vary. Lead students to understand that whether everything is going peacefully in our lives or whether we experience sorrow, we can know all is well if we are trusting in the Lord.)*

➤ **What can keep us from having peace in our heart?** *(unconfessed sin that we are practicing)*

➤ **How can we have peace restored to our hearts?** *(We must confess our sins and turn from them. Christians must say the same thing about sin that God does.)* Read **I John 1:9-10** to the students.

Play the recording and lead in singing the first verse.

Worktext page 247

Singing with understanding, verse 1.

Background Information

Sheep in the Holy Land—*Sheep were very common in the part of the world where Jesus was born and lived during His earthly ministry. It is common even today in the Holy Land to see shepherds with their flocks grazing on the countryside. Many of the great men of the Old Testament—such as Moses, David, and Amos—were shepherds. Therefore, when the Lord used the shepherding analogy to teach the principles of Christ's relationship to His people, those who heard Him could understand the illustration. They did, however, have difficulty understanding the spiritual application.*

Analogy—*This is a comparison of one thing to another because the two things are alike in some way.*

Sheepfold—*The sheep were kept in this enclosure made of rocks. An opening in the rock wall served as a door. The flocks of several shepherds were kept in the same sheepfold. A shepherd would come to the fold and call for his flock; his sheep would recognize his voice and come when he called.*

Hireling—*This term refers to a worker who works only for the money he is paid and usually has no interest or pride in doing his work well. Jesus uses this term to refer to the religious leaders of the day who were supposed to lead the Jewish people spiritually but who were actually more concerned about themselves than their "sheep."*

Introducing the Bible Study

Discuss the shepherd and his sheep.

➤ **Why do sheep need a shepherd?** *(to lead them to food and water and to protect them from danger)*

Share the background information about sheep in the Holy Land.

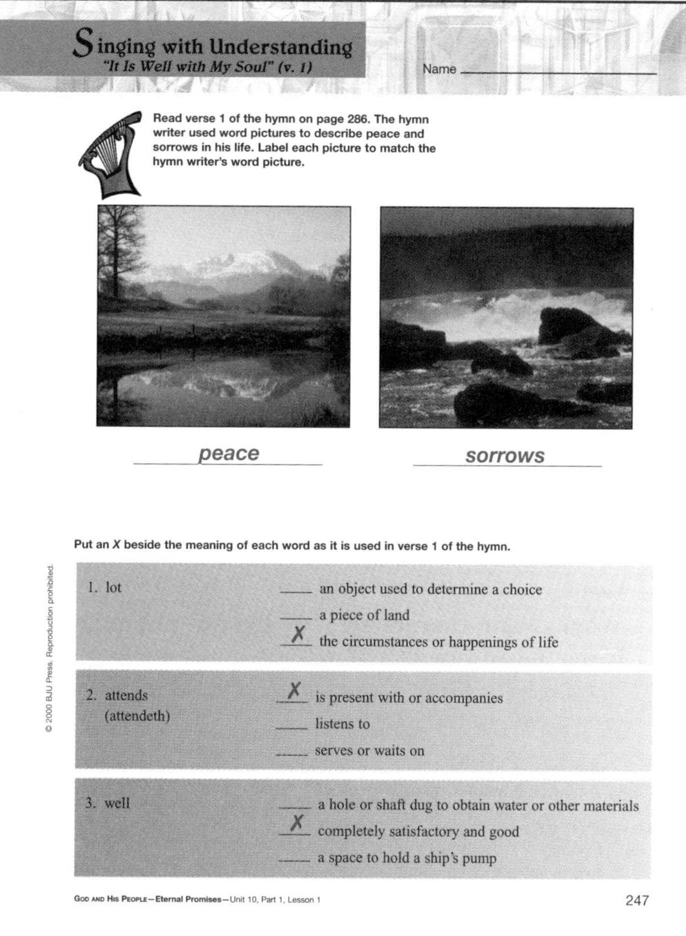
Singing with Understanding
"It Is Well with My Soul" (v. 1)

Name ______________________

Read verse 1 of the hymn on page 286. The hymn writer used word pictures to describe peace and sorrows in his life. Label each picture to match the hymn writer's word picture.

peace — sorrows

Put an X beside the meaning of each word as it is used in verse 1 of the hymn.

1. lot
- ___ an object used to determine a choice
- ___ a piece of land
- X the circumstances or happenings of life

2. attends (attendeth)
- X is present with or accompanies
- ___ listens to
- ___ serves or waits on

3. well
- ___ a hole or shaft dug to obtain water or other materials
- X completely satisfactory and good
- ___ a space to hold a ship's pump

God and His People—Eternal Promises—Unit 10, Part 1, Lesson 1 247

Bible Study

Study John 10 about God's promise of eternal protection. Explain that this chapter makes an *analogy:* it compares people to sheep and Christ to a good shepherd. Share the meaning of *analogy* from the background information.

Point out the list of nine Scripture references. Assign each student one of the references to read silently. Choose a student to read the passage aloud when you are ready for it in the lesson. After each passage is read, share the information that follows and discuss the question.

John 10:1-2—The opening phrase in the chapter is used several times in the Gospel of John to tell what Jesus Christ came to earth to do. By assuring the people that He was telling the truth, Christ declared that what He was about to say was very important. These first six verses of John 10 tell about a sheepfold. (Share the background information about the sheepfold.)

➤ **How is being a Christian like being in a sheepfold?** *(Just as there is only one entrance to the sheepfold, the only way to become a Christian is through Jesus Christ.)*

John 10:3-5—The shepherd knows each of his sheep and calls them by name. In turn, the sheep know their shepherd's voice and listen to and follow him. They refuse to listen to another shepherd or to a stranger. If a sheepfold holds flocks belonging to more than one shepherd, each shepherd can separate his sheep by calling them. Each shepherd goes before his flock, guiding them to the best pasture for food and water to drink. He guards them against danger. The sheep would not follow a stranger because his voice is unfamiliar. They would hear the difference in the voice and run away in panic.

➤ **In what way is Jesus Christ like a shepherd?** *(The shepherd is the only one who can enter the sheepfold. Jesus is the only way to heaven [John 14:6]. Jesus likens Himself to the Good Shepherd who knows each of his sheep—those who believe on Him—and calls them by name. Jesus guides His sheep and provides for them.)*

John 10:6; John 8:39—Even though the Jewish people understood the story about the shepherd and the sheep, some of them still did not understand the spiritual meaning of the lesson the Lord was teaching them. These Jews thought that because they were Jews—God's special chosen people, the children of Abraham—they would automatically go to heaven.

➤ **What did the Jews really need in order to go to heaven?** *(They needed to trust in the Lord Jesus Christ for salvation and eternal life.)*

John 10:7-10—The Lord compares Himself to the door of the sheepfold. At night when the shepherd led his sheep into the pen, he would stand in the doorway and inspect each sheep as it passed through. He poured oil on their scratches, gave them water to drink, and counted them to make sure that they were all there. Then he would actually lie down across the doorway to protect his flock. The Lord reminded these Jews about the many false leaders who had come before Him who had promised to deliver them politically as a nation. But Jesus told them that He had come to deliver them from sin, to heal them spiritually, and to offer them eternal life.

➤ **How is Jesus Christ like the door to the sheepfold of Christianity?** *(A person can enter heaven only through Christ, who protects His sheep from Satan's attacks and secures them by guarding the entrance.)*

The Good Shepherd
John 10:1-28

Name ______________________

Analogies point out relationships between things that are not generally alike.

Complete each analogy.

1. *Driver* is to *car* as **pilot** is to *plane.*
2. *Day* is to *week* as *month* is to **year**.
3. *Story* is to **read** as *song* is to *sing.*
4. *Tear* is to *paper* as **break** is to *glass.*

Write an analogy of your own here.

5. __________ is to __________ as __________ is to __________.

Complete the analogy; then answer the questions. You may use your Bible to help.

6. *Jesus Christ* is to *Christians* as a *shepherd* is to **sheep**.

The shepherd provides for the needs of his sheep. How does Jesus Christ provide for the needs of those who belong to Him?

Answers will vary.

The shepherd goes ahead of the sheep to lead them. What kind of guidance does Jesus Christ give to those who belong to Him?

Answers will vary.

The shepherd protects the sheep. From what dangers does Jesus Christ protect those who belong to Him?

Answers will vary.

248 GOD AND HIS PEOPLE—Eternal Promises—Unit 10, Part 1, Lesson 1

John 10:11-15—(Share the background information about the hireling.) When danger comes, the hireling deserts the flock. He is concerned only about his pay for doing the job. But our Good Shepherd, who has laid down His life for His sheep and knows them by name, has promised never to desert them. The Lord tells us many times in the Bible that He will always be with His sheep.

➤ **What is the difference between a hireling and a good shepherd?** *(A good shepherd will never desert his sheep; he cares about what will happen to them. The hireling cares only about his pay for doing the job.)*

John 10:16-17; Galatians 3:26—These very important verses tell about Gentiles—people who are not Jewish—who trust Christ and come into His spiritual sheepfold. Galatians tells us that we are *all* the children of God by faith in Christ Jesus. Jesus revealed that God was the one who gave Him His authority as the shepherd of all believers.

➤ **How does God view Gentile believers in comparison to Jewish believers?** *(He views them both the same; all are members of the same sheepfold under the leadership of the Good Shepherd, Jesus Christ.)*

John 10:27-28—This is a great promise of God's protection for His spiritual sheep. No one is strong enough to snatch God's sheep from Him. The omnipotent God is our eternal protector.

➤ **What psalm tells us about the Lord as our Shepherd?** *(Psalm 23)* Read Psalm 23 to the students (optional).

➤ **What are the characteristics of the sheep in this study?** *(Possible answers include that they listen to their Shepherd, they know Him, they recognize His voice, and they follow Him.)*

➤ **What should characterize our lives when the Lord is our Good Shepherd?** *(Possible answers include reading His Word, loving and obeying Him, and growing more Christlike.)*

Worktext page 248

Complete analogies.

Lesson 2

Memory Verses—John 10:27-28

Practice the memory verses. Locate **John 10:27-28** and select a student to read them aloud.

➤ **Who do you think might want to pluck or snatch the Lord's sheep out of His hand?** *(Possible answers include Satan, false teachers, or unbelievers.)*

➤ **What characteristics of God can we rely upon to make it impossible for anyone to do this?** *(Possible answers include God's omnipotence, His faithfulness, His love for us, and His integrity in keeping His promises.)*

Direct the students to read the verses silently, then to read them to themselves in a quiet whisper, and then to read them to a partner.

Hymn: "It Is Well with My Soul"

Sing the first verse (Worktext page 286).

➤ **Can you think of a time when everything was happy, peaceful, and smooth in your life—when you did not seem to have any problems?** Let several students share experiences.

➤ **Can you remember a time when you were upset or unhappy with a situation in your life?** Let several students share experiences.

- ➤ **How do you feel right now?** Allow the students to answer the question silently in their hearts.

Encourage the students to remember that no matter how they feel, no matter what circumstances God allows in their lives, no matter what problems they face, they can trust in an all-powerful God who has promised to take care of them forever. Lead in singing verse 1 as a prayer of thanksgiving.

Background Information

Amos—*Amos was a shepherd from Tekoa, a town about ten miles south of Jerusalem in Judah. He cared for sycamore-fig trees. His writings are full of analogies to the natural world that he encountered in his work. While his prophecy includes warnings of judgment against several nations, including the Southern Kingdom of Judah, his writings are directed primarily against the Northern Kingdom of Israel.*

Introducing the Prophet Focus

Introduce the time period in which Amos lived. Explain to the students that Amos prophesied around 765 B.C. Both Northern and Southern Kingdoms were prospering financially and politically, but because they were worshiping idols and living in sin, their moral and social foundations were crumbling.

Prophet Focus

Read the following account based on the life of Amos.

Amos

Amos took care of sheep and raised figs. Does that sound like a prophet's job to you? God used an ordinary man to do an extraordinary task. God used Amos to take His message to the Israelites. Amos was from Judah in the south, and God asked him to speak to the Israelites in the north.

The nation of Israel was wealthy and had powerful leaders. But the people were not right with God. They had time for everything except God; they worshiped idols. The Israelites were selfish; they took care of their own wants but ignored the poor and needy. God had taken them out of Egypt and had led them through the wilderness to possess the Promised Land. But they broke God's commandments and rejected His messengers. The Israelites had forgotten from where they came and who could satisfy their needs.

God reminded Israel that He had punished them before. God had brought famine, drought, crop failure, pestilence, and war. Yet the Israelites would not return to Him. So God said, "Prepare to meet thy God, O Israel." Israel had rejected the Lord, the God of hosts, the Creator and Sustainer of all things. God despised Israel's empty worship—their days set apart for remembering what God had done, their offerings and songs.

God showed Amos how He would destroy Israel, and Amos asked God to forgive His people. God answered Amos's plea, but judgment was sure to come. God showed Amos a plumbline—an instrument used by builders to make sure they built the wall straight. If a wall was built crooked, it would soon fall. God said that He would put a plumbline in the middle of His people. God would show how crooked they were, for they had allowed sin to make them crooked before God, the Holy and Righteous One.

Jeroboam, the king of Israel, had a priest named Amaziah. The priest told the king that Amos was conspiring against him. Amaziah tried to remove Amos from his land. Amaziah told Amos to go back home and prophesy in his *own* land, Judah.

"I was no prophet," Amos said, "neither was I a prophet's son; but I was an herdman, and a gatherer of sycomore fruit: And the Lord took me as I followed the flock, and the Lord said unto me, Go, prophesy unto my people Israel." God judged Amaziah the priest because he had told Amos to disobey God.

God said that He would punish His people. They would mourn. God would take His words away from Israel. The Israelites would wander from their land and seek God's words, but they would not find them.

But God also gave the Israelites hope. "Seek ye me, and ye shall live," He said. "Hate the evil, and love the good." God promised that He would not totally destroy Israel. He would sift them as grain and destroy the bad. God promised to plant Israel once again on their land, nevermore to be pulled up.

God used an ordinary man to carry a powerful message to a backsliding nation. Amos simply obeyed, and God worked through him. God delights in using simple and weak things that He might be glorified.

- ➤ **Why do you think God used Amos?** *(Amos was willing to obey God.)*
- ➤ **What did the Lord call Amos to do?** *(speak to Israel about their sin and God's judgment)*
- ➤ **What had Israel done to displease the Lord?** *(worshiped idols, broken laws, forgotten God, been unconcerned about the poor)*
- ➤ **Why did God punish Amaziah?** *(because he had told Amos to disobey God by going home to his own land)*

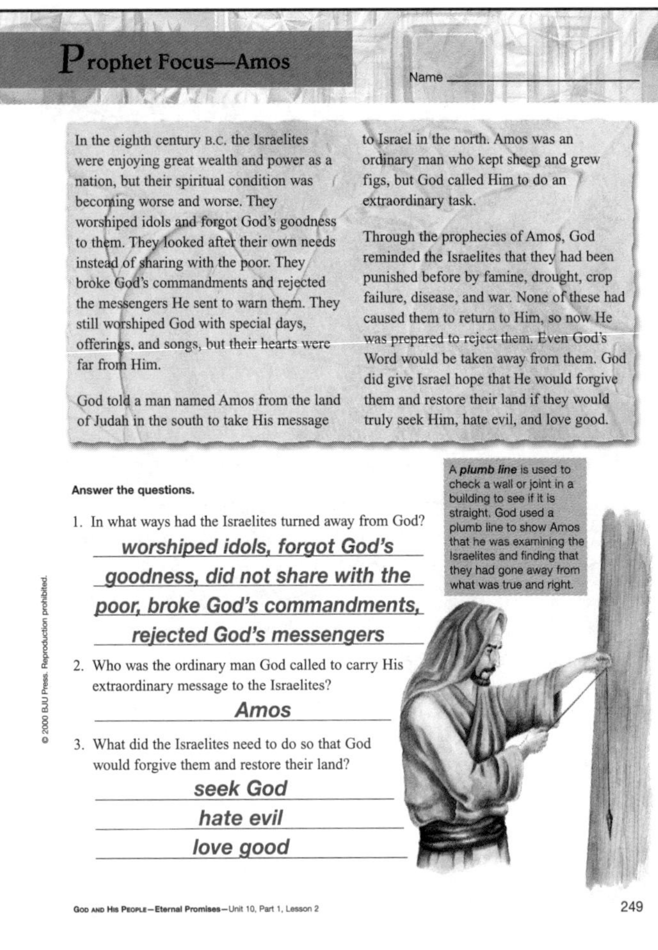

Prophet Focus—Amos

Name ______________________

In the eighth century B.C. the Israelites were enjoying great wealth and power as a nation, but their spiritual condition was becoming worse and worse. They worshiped idols and forgot God's goodness to them. They looked after their own needs instead of sharing with the poor. They broke God's commandments and rejected the messengers He sent to warn them. They still worshiped God with special days, offerings, and songs, but their hearts were far from Him.

God told a man named Amos from the land of Judah in the south to take His message to Israel in the north. Amos was an ordinary man who kept sheep and grew figs, but God called Him to do an extraordinary task.

Through the prophecies of Amos, God reminded the Israelites that they had been punished before by famine, drought, crop failure, disease, and war. None of these had caused them to return to Him, so now He was prepared to reject them. Even God's Word would be taken away from them. God did give Israel hope that He would forgive them and restore their land if they would truly seek Him, hate evil, and love good.

A *plumb line* is used to check a wall or joint in a building to see if it is straight. God used a plumb line to show Amos that he was examining the Israelites and finding that they had gone away from what was true and right.

Answer the questions.

1. In what ways had the Israelites turned away from God?
   worshiped idols, forgot God's goodness, did not share with the poor, broke God's commandments, rejected God's messengers
2. Who was the ordinary man God called to carry His extraordinary message to the Israelites?
   Amos
3. What did the Israelites need to do so that God would forgive them and restore their land?
   seek God
   hate evil
   love good

➤ **What hope did God offer Israel?** *(If they sought Him, they would live; He would not totally destroy them; He would plant them and never allow them to be pulled up.)*

➤ **What hope is there for Christians when they sin against God?** *(If they confess their sin and turn from it, God will forgive them.)*

TimeLine

Place *Amos* on the TimeLine. Choose a student to place *Amos* onto the large classroom TimeLine at ca. 765 B.C. Allow the students to place *Amos* onto their individual TimeLines.

Worktext page 249

Recall details about the prophecy of Amos.

Lesson 3

Materials

- Charts 34 and 39-40: "Mediterranean in the Time of Paul" and "Revelation of the End Times" (A copy of "Revelation of the End Times" is on Supplement page S80 for use with students and small groups.)

(*Note:* Lessons on the end times present the premillennial, pretribulational position.)

Hymn: "It Is Well with My Soul"

Sing the first verse (Worktext page 286). Play the recording and lead in singing verse 1. Encourage the students to sing parts on the echoed phrases in the chorus.

Memory Verses—John 10:27-28

Practice the memory verses. Locate and read aloud **John 10:27-28.** Instruct the students to practice saying the verses aloud to a partner.

Background Information

The Rapture—*It is Christ's return for Christians. Although we do not know when the Rapture will take place, God says to be ready all the time. In I Thessalonians 4:16-18, Christ tells us that He will descend from heaven with a shout, with the voice of the archangel, and with the trump of God. The saved people who have died will rise from their graves and meet the Lord in the air. Then Christians who are alive will rise to meet the Lord.*

The Judgment Seat of Christ—*It will take place in heaven and will include only saved people—those who have accepted Christ's payment for their sins by the shedding of His blood on the cross. They will be judged and rewarded according to their faithfulness in serving God, and crowns will be given to the redeemed.*

The Tribulation—*Christians will not go through the Tribulation. The seven years following the Rapture will be a time of great trouble upon the earth. During this time, the Antichrist, who claims to be God, will command everyone to worship him. God's chosen people, the Jews, will be greatly persecuted. Many will believe on Christ during the Tribulation and will be called the Tribulation saints.*

The Second Coming—*At the end of the Tribulation, a great battle will take place at Armageddon. As the nations turn to fight one another, Christ will return—coming in glory. The wicked armies will all turn against Him. God will bind Satan and cast the Antichrist into the lake of fire.*

The Millennium—*Christ will usher in the Millennium with His coming in glory (Matthew 16, Matthew 24, Matthew 25, Mark 8, Luke 17, Luke 21, John 14). Jesus Christ will reign on earth for one thousand years of peace. At the end of the Millennium, Satan will be released for a short period of time and will organize a rebellion against Christ and the saved. God will send fire down to destroy all those who follow Satan. Satan will be defeated and cast into the lake of fire forever. God will create a new heaven and a new earth (Revelation 20). The earth will be new, beautiful, and peaceful.*

The Great White Throne Judgment—*After the Millennium, the unbelievers will be judged for their sin and will be punished eternally in the lake of fire. The Book of Life will be opened. Those who have rejected Christ will not find their names written in the Lamb's book and will be forever separated from God (John 5; Revelation 20).*

The Book of Revelation—*While John was a prisoner on the isle of Patmos, he had a vision from Christ. This vision was given to John about one hundred years after Christ's birth here on earth. It was an unveiling of Christ—a vision of prophecy, or things to come. The Lord showed him many unusual things relating to Christ's return and God's eternal kingdom. We have an account of these things in the Book of Revelation. The Book of Revelation contains more promises of blessing than any other book in the Bible—promises to those who read the book, blessings for all those who have trusted in the Lord, eternal life in an eternal home, and many more.*

The Seven-Sealed Scroll (Roll)—*The "book" in John's vision was actually a scroll or rolled-up parchment, probably sheepskin. Scrolls were sealed with wax, and then a ring was impressed on them to protect them from being opened by anyone other than the owner. This scroll had seven seals, indicating that after it was written, it was rolled up partway and sealed, then rolled up further and sealed, and so on until the seventh seal closed the entire book. This scroll represented the plan of God for the world. Since Christ alone could open the book, He alone possessed the right to consummate the plan of God for the world.*

Twenty-four Elders—*The twenty-four elders are symbolic of the redeemed (Christians). In I Chronicles 24, King David appointed twenty-four divisions of Levites to rotate in performing the ceremonial duties in the temple, representing all of the Levitical priesthood. These twenty-four elders mentioned in Revelation represent the whole heavenly priesthood who are the redeemed saints—those who have died in the Lord or who were caught up at the Rapture of the church. Revelation says that these redeemed will be dressed in white and crowned. These crowns are representative of victory, and the elders will cast these crowns before the throne and worship the Lamb.*

Cherubim—*The cherubim are symbolic of God's holy presence. Some Bible teachers believe these celestial beings guard the righteousness of God. When God banished Adam and Eve from the Garden of Eden after they sinned, He placed cherubim there to guard the tree of life (Genesis 3:24). In the Old Testament tabernacle, God's glory dwelt between the cherubim in the holy of holies (Exodus 25).*

Introducing the Bible Study

Discuss the Rapture. Read **I Thessalonians 4:13-18** aloud. Explain that this passage describes the Rapture, an event that could occur at any time. Point out the Rapture on Charts 39-40, "Revelation of the End Times," and share the background information about it.

➤ **In what way are these words about the Rapture meant to be comforting to Christians today?** *(Believers will one day be reunited with Christians who have died; they have the promise of seeing the Lord and living forever with Him.)*

➤ **When will the Rapture occur?** *(at any time)*

➤ **What will happen at the Rapture?** *(At the Rapture, Christ will bring to life all Christians who have died, change those who are living, and give all an incorruptible body.)*

➤ **How can we be certain that we are ready for the Rapture?** *(We are ready if we have confessed our sin and we have saving faith in Jesus Christ.)*

Explain that the following Bible account tells of events that will take place in heaven after Christians have been raptured to be with the Lord forever.

Review the sequence of events in prophecy. Display Charts 39-40, "Revelation of the End Times," briefly explaining the background information on the Judgment Seat of Christ, the Tribulation, the Second Coming, the Millennium, and the Great White Throne Judgment. Share the background information about the Book of Revelation and lead the students to locate Patmos on Chart 34, "Mediterranean in the Time of Paul" (optional). (*Note:* These events were introduced in Unit 10 in *Following Christ, BIBLE TRUTHS 3 for Christian Schools.* Some teachers may prefer to spend an entire lesson reviewing these events. In that case, it is suggested that you use the Bible study of Revelation 5 for the next lesson and skip Lesson 4 or teach Lesson 4 on the fifth day of this week.)

Bible Study

Study Revelation 5 about John's vision of Christ's return and God's eternal kingdom. Read each passage aloud; then share the information that follows. Choose students to read the Old Testament passages that connect with the events being described in Revelation (optional).

Revelation 5:1-4—While in exile as a prisoner on the isle of Patmos, John saw a vision of heaven. God was sitting on His throne, holding in His right hand a sealed book or scroll. Around him sat twenty-four elders and four living creatures (Revelation 4:4-11). (Share the background information about the seven-sealed scroll and the twenty-four elders.)

A mighty angel called out, "Who is worthy to open the book, and to loose the seals thereof?" Who could be worthy enough to open such a book—the book that represented the completion of God's plan for the world? Because all men have sinned, there was no one worthy of the privilege. John was so sad that he wept because no man was good enough to open and read the book.

Old Testament Connection: *Isaiah 59:16 speaks of this same idea—that there was no man found worthy, that God had to send His own righteous Son to bring salvation.*

Revelation 5:5-7—One of the elders told John not to cry. He encouraged John to look and see the Lion of the tribe of Judah, who was going to open the book. When John looked he saw not a lion but a Lamb standing in the middle of the redeemed. The Lord Jesus was called both "the Lion of the tribe of

Juda[h]" and "the Lamb that was slain." In heaven Jesus will have a glorified body, but Christians will still recognize Him as the slain Lamb because they will see on His body the reminders of His death—the nail prints and the mark of the Roman spear.

In John's vision, the Lamb had seven horns and seven eyes. (Point out that the number seven in Scripture symbolizes completion and perfection.)

Only the Lord Jesus, who created the world, could complete God's plan for the world. Christ went to the cross to pay the debt for the sins of everyone, to redeem us and free us from Satan's power.

Old Testament Connection: *Daniel also describes this scene in 7:13-14.*

Revelation 5:8-10—When the Lamb of God took the scroll, John saw the four living creatures—the cherubim—falling down before the Lamb to worship Him. (Share the background information about cherubim.)

John also saw the twenty-four elders falling down in worship of the Lamb. The elders had harps and bowls of incense, which symbolizes the prayers of Christians. John reveals that he heard all the redeemed sing a new song. The Lord has also made believers priests, and they shall reign on the earth with Him.

Revelation 5:11-12—The angels and cherubim around the throne also praised their God, saying, "Worthy is the Lamb." (Reread the sevenfold adoration in verse 12 and point out again the number of complete and perfect praise—seven.)

Revelation 5:13-14—Finally, all living creatures everywhere repeated the adoration and fell down on their knees, worshiping their Creator and everlasting Lord.

➤ **What was John describing in this chapter in Revelation?** *(the Lamb of God in heaven with seven horns and seven eyes)*

➤ **What do the four living creatures (beasts), holding harps and bowls, symbolize?** *(heavenly beings who guard the righteous presence of God)*

➤ **Of whom are the twenty-four elders symbolic?** *(the redeemed saints—Christians who had died or who were caught up in the Rapture)*

➤ **What was the seven-sealed scroll?** *(the plan of God for the world)*

➤ **Why did one of the elders tell John not to weep?** *(because the Lion of Judah—Jesus Christ, the Lamb of God—could open the scroll)*

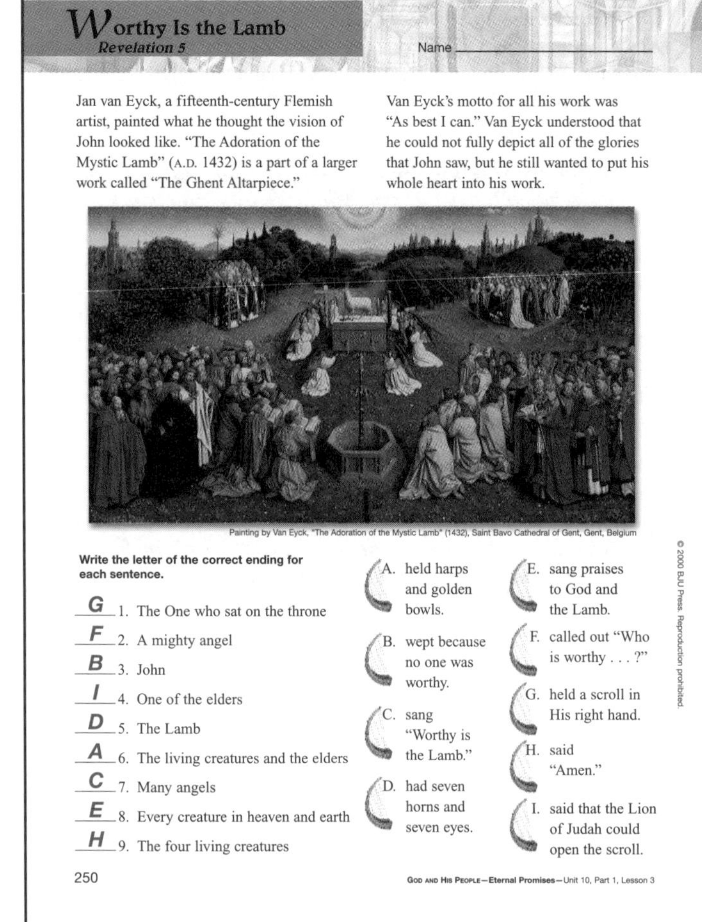

Worthy Is the Lamb
Revelation 5

Name ______________________

Jan van Eyck, a fifteenth-century Flemish artist, painted what he thought the vision of John looked like. "The Adoration of the Mystic Lamb" (A.D. 1432) is a part of a larger work called "The Ghent Altarpiece."

Van Eyck's motto for all his work was "As best I can." Van Eyck understood that he could not fully depict all of the glories that John saw, but he still wanted to put his whole heart into his work.

Painting by Van Eyck, "The Adoration of the Mystic Lamb" (1432), Saint Bavo Cathedral of Gent, Gent, Belgium

Write the letter of the correct ending for each sentence.

G 1. The One who sat on the throne
F 2. A mighty angel
B 3. John
I 4. One of the elders
D 5. The Lamb
A 6. The living creatures and the elders
C 7. Many angels
E 8. Every creature in heaven and earth
H 9. The four living creatures

A. held harps and golden bowls.
B. wept because no one was worthy.
C. sang "Worthy is the Lamb."
D. had seven horns and seven eyes.
E. sang praises to God and the Lamb.
F. called out "Who is worthy . . . ?"
G. held a scroll in His right hand.
H. said "Amen."
I. said that the Lion of Judah could open the scroll.

250

God and His People—Eternal Promises—Unit 10, Part 1, Lesson 3

Explain to the students that it can be disturbing for some to think of all the things that are to happen when Jesus Christ returns.

➤ **How can you keep from being confused or worried about what the end times will bring?** *(Know Jesus Christ as your personal Savior—the Lamb who paid the price for your sins and the Shepherd who leads you, watches over you, and cares for you.)*

Worktext page 250

Recall details about John's heavenly vision. (*Note:* You may wish to assist the students in completing this page.)

Lesson 4

Materials

- Student Bible Book Cards: Old Testament and New Testament
- Recording of "Worthy Is the Lamb That Was Slain" from *Messiah* by George Frederick Handel (optional)

Hymn: "It Is Well with My Soul"

Sing the first verse (Worktext page 286).

➤ **What are things in your lives that could be called "sorrows"?** *(Answers will vary.)*

Challenge the students to picture those sorrows as heavy burdens that they carry on their backs. Remind them that God wants to bear those burdens for them; He wants them to trust Him completely about those things in their lives. Allow a few moments for the students to pray silently and to give those burdens to the Lord, expressing to Him their trust that He is doing all things well in their lives. Play the recording of the first verse and lead in singing it together, adding the echoed parts in the chorus.

Picture the Point

Discuss lambs.

➤ **Have you ever seen a lamb?** Describe your experience.

➤ **What kind of temperament or "personality" does a lamb have?** *(usually gentle, quiet, peaceable)*

Explain that the Lord Jesus Christ is compared not only to a Good Shepherd in John 10 but also to a lamb. Direct the students to read **Isaiah 53:7** and **Exodus 12:3-13** silently.

➤ **What does Isaiah say a lamb does when it is being sheared?** *(It is quiet; it doesn't speak.)*

Read **Matthew 26:63; Mark 15:2-5; Luke 23:9;** and **John 19:9** aloud to the students.

➤ **How did Jesus fulfill this prophecy of Isaiah during His trial before His crucifixion?** *(When Jesus was accused and questioned by the religious leaders and the governor, He answered nothing.)*

➤ **What event is being described in Exodus 12:3-13?** *(preparations for the Passover; God withheld the tenth plague, death of the firstborn, from the homes of the Israelites who displayed the lambs' blood on their doorways.)*

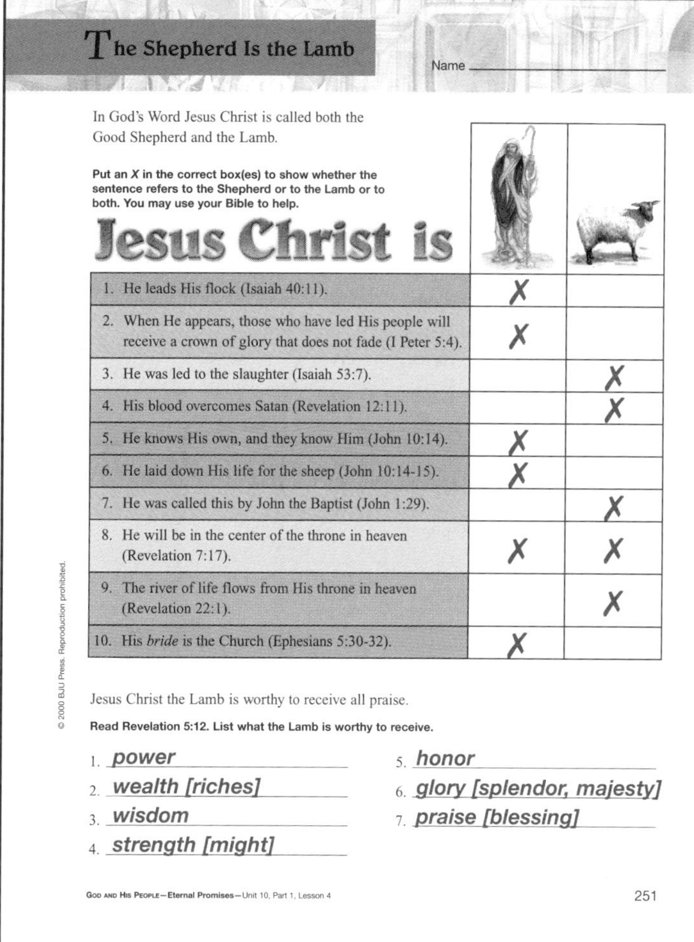

The Shepherd Is the Lamb

Name ______________________

In God's Word Jesus Christ is called both the Good Shepherd and the Lamb.

Put an X in the correct box(es) to show whether the sentence refers to the Shepherd or to the Lamb or to both. You may use your Bible to help.

Jesus Christ is

	Shepherd	Lamb
1. He leads His flock (Isaiah 40:11).	X	
2. When He appears, those who have led His people will receive a crown of glory that does not fade (I Peter 5:4).	X	
3. He was led to the slaughter (Isaiah 53:7).		X
4. His blood overcomes Satan (Revelation 12:11).		X
5. He knows His own, and they know Him (John 10:14).	X	
6. He laid down His life for the sheep (John 10:14-15).	X	
7. He was called this by John the Baptist (John 1:29).		X
8. He will be in the center of the throne in heaven (Revelation 7:17).	X	X
9. The river of life flows from His throne in heaven (Revelation 22:1).		X
10. His *bride* is the Church (Ephesians 5:30-32).	X	

Jesus Christ the Lamb is worthy to receive all praise.

Read Revelation 5:12. List what the Lamb is worthy to receive.

1. *power*
2. *wealth [riches]*
3. *wisdom*
4. *strength [might]*
5. *honor*
6. *glory [splendor, majesty]*
7. *praise [blessing]*

God and His People—Eternal Promises—Unit 10, Part 1, Lesson 4 251

Explain that the Passover was observed every year by the Israelites as a reminder of God's saving the Israelites from their bondage in Egypt and as a symbol of the death of the coming Messiah. Jesus Christ, the spotless Lamb of God, would shed His blood for the remission of the sins of the whole world. When a person places his trust fully in Christ's sacrificial death and resurrection, God withholds His judgment from him and saves him.

Worktext page 251

Distinguish between characteristics of Jesus Christ as Shepherd and as Lamb.

Memory Verses—John 10:27-28

Practice the memory verses. Select a student to read **John 10:27-28** aloud. Then choose volunteers to say the verses from memory.

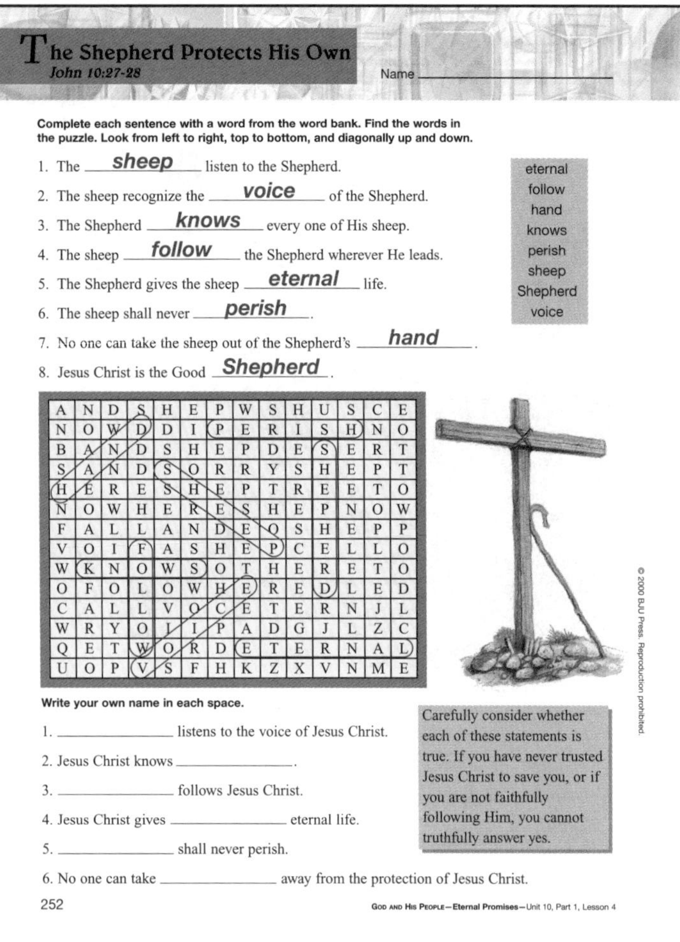

The Shepherd Protects His Own
John 10:27-28

Name ____________________

Complete each sentence with a word from the word bank. Find the words in the puzzle. Look from left to right, top to bottom, and diagonally up and down.

1. The **sheep** listen to the Shepherd.
2. The sheep recognize the **voice** of the Shepherd.
3. The Shepherd **knows** every one of His sheep.
4. The sheep **follow** the Shepherd wherever He leads.
5. The Shepherd gives the sheep **eternal** life.
6. The sheep shall never **perish**.
7. No one can take the sheep out of the Shepherd's **hand**.
8. Jesus Christ is the Good **Shepherd**.

eternal
follow
hand
knows
perish
sheep
Shepherd
voice

A	N	D	S	H	E	P	W	S	H	U	S	C	E
N	O	W	D	D	I	P	E	R	I	S	H	N	O
B	A	N	D	S	H	E	P	D	E	S	E	R	T
S	A	N	D	S	O	R	R	Y	S	H	E	P	T
H	E	R	E	S	H	E	P	T	R	E	E	T	O
N	O	W	H	E	R	E	S	H	E	P	N	O	W
F	A	L	L	A	N	D	E	Q	S	H	E	P	P
V	O	I	F	A	S	H	E	P	C	E	L	L	O
W	K	N	O	W	S	O	T	H	E	R	E	T	O
O	F	O	L	O	W	H	E	R	E	D	L	E	D
C	A	L	L	V	O	C	E	T	E	R	N	J	L
W	R	Y	O	I	I	P	A	D	G	J	L	Z	C
Q	E	T	W	O	R	D	E	T	E	R	N	A	L
U	O	P	V	S	F	H	K	Z	X	V	N	M	E

Write your own name in each space.

1. ______________ listens to the voice of Jesus Christ.
2. Jesus Christ knows ______________.
3. ______________ follows Jesus Christ.
4. Jesus Christ gives ______________ eternal life.
5. ______________ shall never perish.
6. No one can take ______________ away from the protection of Jesus Christ.

Carefully consider whether each of these statements is true. If you have never trusted Jesus Christ to save you, or if you are not faithfully following Him, you cannot truthfully answer yes.

252 GOD AND HIS PEOPLE—Eternal Promises—Unit 10, Part 1, Lesson 4

Worktext page 252

Develop understanding of the memory verses.

Bible Study Skills

Study the divisions for the Bible. Divide the students into groups of two, three, or four. Explain the following game directions for using the student Bible Book Cards:

1. Distribute six cards to each player.
2. Place the remainder of the cards facedown in a pile.
3. Allow players time to see whether they have any matches: two books from the same division.
4. Player 1 asks another player whether he has a book from the division of . . . (e.g., Minor Prophets, Old Testament History).
5. If the player has a book from that division, he gives the card to Player 1. If the player does not have a card from that division, Player 1 draws a card from the pile.
6. Follow the same procedure with each player taking turns.
7. The player with the most matches at the end of the time wins.

Music Connection (optional)

Discuss Handel's *Messiah*. Read **Revelation 5:12** aloud. Tell the students that the words of this verse are used in a well-known musical work, *Messiah,* by George Frederick Handel. Explain that *Messiah* is an *oratorio*—a lengthy musical composition often based on Scripture. It contains pieces for soloists, ensembles, and choir and is usually accompanied by an orchestra. Many oratorios tell a story. Handel's *Messiah* is the most well known oratorio ever written. The words to *Messiah* come directly from Scriptural prophecies about Jesus Christ.

Play the chorus "Worthy Is the Lamb That Was Slain" from Part III of *Messiah.* Direct the students to follow along in their Bibles as the choir sings, explaining that the words come from Revelation 5:9 and 5:12.

- ➤ **Why were the words from this passage in Revelation included in an oratorio about the Messiah?** *(The passage is speaking about the Messiah, the Lord Jesus Christ, who was slain on the cross for our sins.)*
- ➤ **What does the music make you think about?** *(Answers will vary. Elicit that the music sounds glorious and majestic, fit to be sung to a king. It is full of rejoicing for what the Lamb of God has accomplished.)*

Going Beyond

Enrichment

Lead a Bible drill. Explain that the verses in this Bible drill reflect the frequent use of the number seven as the number of perfection in the Bible. Use the following verses in this drill:

Genesis 2:2	Genesis 29:18
Leviticus 4:6	Leviticus 23:15
Numbers 8:2	Numbers 29:2
Ruth 4:15	II Kings 5:10
Psalm 12:6	Proverbs 24:16
Isaiah 30:26	Daniel 3:19
Matthew 18:21-22	

Direct the students to begin the drill with their Bibles closed and upraised. After you read each reference aloud or write the reference for display, the students may lower their Bibles and find the passage. The first person to find the verse and be ready to tell how the number seven is used should stand to read it aloud. If desired, make the drill competitive by dividing the students into teams, giving a point to the team member that locates each passage first and offering a small prize to the team that scores the most points.

Jesus Christ Will Conquer and Judge

Unit 10, Part 2

Preview

Doctrines

- The Antichrist will rise (Revelation 13:1-8)—Lesson 1
- The False Prophet will exalt the Antichrist (Revelation 13:11-15)—Lesson 1
- Christ will appear gloriously (Revelation 19:11-16)—Lesson 1
- The Antichrist and the False Prophet will be cast into the lake of fire (Revelation 19:20–20:10)—Lesson 1
- The final state of unredeemed man is eternal separation from God (Revelation 20:14-15)—Lesson 2
- Man turns to God through repentance and faith (conversion) (II Corinthians 7:9-10)—Lesson 2

Skills and Applications

- Learn Revelation 19:11
- Locate information in Scripture
- Use a concordance
- Complete an outline web
- Understand the sequence of the end times
- Appreciate God's plan and promises of provision for His children
- Apply Bible knowledge to everyday life

Lesson 1

Materials

- Charts 39-40, "Revelation of the End Times"

Hymn: "It Is Well with My Soul"

Teach the second verse (Worktext page 286). Direct the students to read the words of verse 2 silently.

➤ **What does *buffet* mean?** *(to repeatedly strike against or to attack)*

➤ **How does Satan buffet Christians?** *(He tempts them to sin; causes them to doubt their salvation; tempts them to forget the commandments, promises, and warnings in God's Word; and tries to get them to turn aside from God's Word and follow false teachers.)*

Emphasize that Satan is the enemy of God. Satan is called "the tempter" in Scripture.

➤ **Where do Christians get assurance of their relationship with God?** *(from the Bible)* Read **I John 5:11-13** to the students.

Worktext page 253

Singing with understanding, verse 2.

Background Information

The Judgment Seat of Christ—*After the Rapture, Christians will be judged in heaven before God to give an account of the way that they have used the time, talents, and opportunities that God gave them on earth. Since all sin is covered by the blood of Christ for those who have accepted His payment, this will be a judging and rewarding according to faithfulness (Romans 14:10; I Corinthians 3:10-15; II Corinthians 5:10).*

Jews During the Tribulation—*Today most Jews do not accept Jesus as the Messiah who was promised in the Old Testament. They do not recognize that the Savior has already come to earth; they are still looking for Him to be born. Jews reject the New Testament and explain away Old Testament passages such as Isaiah 53 that Jesus Christ fulfilled in His first coming. But during the Tribulation, many Jews will repent and will believe on Christ. Revelation 7:3-8 speaks of 144,000 Jews who are "sealed" as the servants of God. Jeremiah 30:7-9 reveals that the conversion of these Jewish people is one of the main purposes for the Tribulation period.*

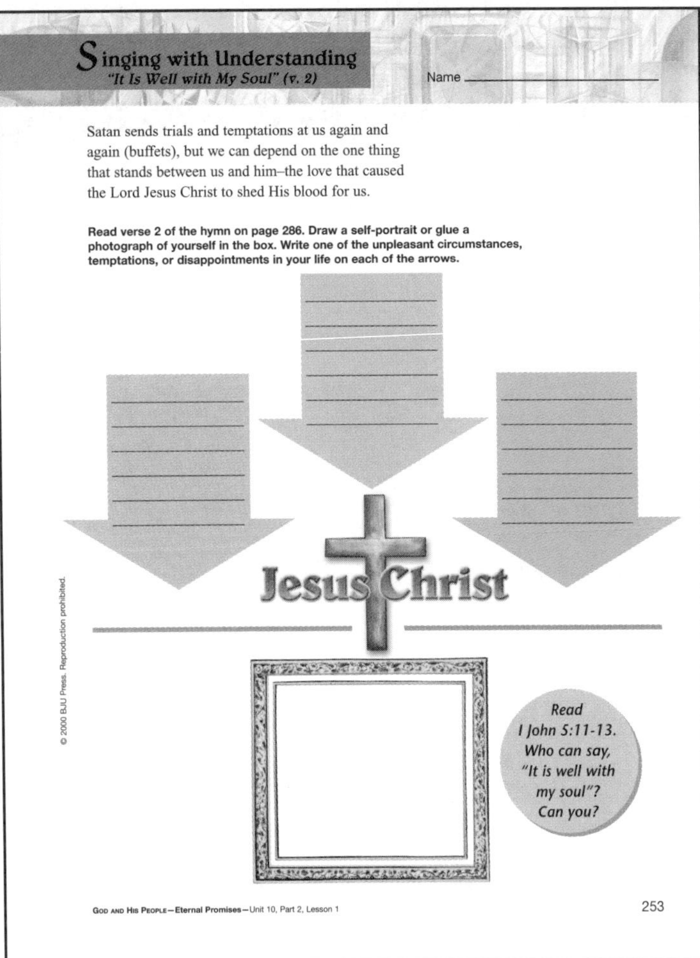

Singing with Understanding
"It Is Well with My Soul" (v. 2)

Name ______________________

Satan sends trials and temptations at us again and again (buffets), but we can depend on the one thing that stands between us and him–the love that caused the Lord Jesus Christ to shed His blood for us.

Read verse 2 of the hymn on page 286. Draw a self-portrait or glue a photograph of yourself in the box. Write one of the unpleasant circumstances, temptations, or disappointments in your life on each of the arrows.

Jesus Christ

Read I John 5:11-13. Who can say, "It is well with my soul"? Can you?

God and His People—Eternal Promises—Unit 10, Part 2, Lesson 1 253

The Battle of Armageddon—*The battle between the armies of Christ and the armies of the Antichrist will take place at Armageddon (Revelation 16:16). Many nations will participate in this warfare, siding with Satan. All of these united world powers will be no match for Christ and His army of redeemed saints.*

Introducing the Bible Account

Review the background for the Book of Revelation from page 334 (Unit 10, Part 1, Lesson 3).

- **Where was John when he wrote the Book of Revelation?** *(He was a prisoner on the isle of Patmos.)*
- **What is the Book of Revelation?** *(John's vision of things to come concerning Christ and His kingdom)*

Bible Account

Read the Bible account or summarize events from Revelation 6-19 in your own words. Display Charts 39-40, "Revelation of the End Times," as you read the account.

Christ the Faithful and True Judge

After the saints (Christians) have been raptured, the Lamb will begin to open the seals of the scroll. The crowns on the heads of the redeemed elders seem to indicate that rewards have been given. (Share the background information about the Judgment Seat of Christ.)

As the Lamb breaks each new seal of the scroll, a fearful judgment on the world will come during the Tribulation. The saints (Christians) will be safe from these judgments since they will be in the presence of Christ.

The judgments that Jesus Christ described when He was on earth are named again in Revelation: war, famine, and sickness resulting in death. Although the Christians of today will be gone, some people who are left on earth will be saved. These new Christians will be persecuted, and many will be martyred for their faith in Christ.

There will be natural disasters—earthquakes and disturbances in the heavens. John saw the sun becoming dark, the moon becoming like blood, stars falling like ripe figs, and the heaven vanishing like a scroll rolling up. People will be so frightened by these obvious acts of God's judgment that they will cry out to the mountains and rocks, "Fall on us, and hide us from the face of him that sitteth on the throne, and from the wrath of the Lamb."

During this Tribulation time a powerful, evil ruler will claim to be Christ and demand to be worshiped. He is called the Antichrist, a "beast" (Revelation 13), because he receives power from Satan and is the opposite of Christ. For a time, the entire world will be under the rule of the Antichrist. The Antichrist will persecute believers, both Gentiles and Jews, who are saved during the Tribulation.

The Antichrist will be supported by a secondary ruler, referred to as both a "beast" and a "false prophet." The role of this false prophet is to promote the worship of Antichrist (Revelation 13).

One of the angels in John's vision promised judgment to any who worship the Antichrist during the Tribulation. He promises that such people will "drink of the wine of the wrath of God." John saw this promise fulfilled in Revelation 16:2 when an angel pours out a terrible physical illness on all those who have worshiped the Antichrist.

God will bring the Tribulation to an end (Revelation 19) when Jesus Christ comes to earth again, leading an army of saints clothed in white. John describes Christ as sitting on a white horse, with eyes as flames of fire. On His head are many crowns, and His clothing has been dipped in blood—a sign of the bloodshed to come as He judges His enemies. Inscribed on Christ's clothing are the words "King of kings, and Lord of lords." Jesus Christ will make war with the Antichrist and his followers. Christ will gloriously triumph and will send the Antichrist and the False Prophet to their just punishment in a lake of fire.

Two names in Revelation 19:11 refer to the Lord Jesus Christ: *True*—Christ must bring judgment on all that is false, and *Faithful*—Christ will never fail to protect His own through any fearful event. Jesus Christ is to be trusted to do what is right and to protect His own. Those who have been redeemed through the blood of Christ truly belong to Him and are not to be fearful of the future.

- ➤ **Where and for what purpose will Christians of today be judged?** *(in heaven at the Judgment Seat of Christ; for the way they have used the time, talents, and opportunities that God gave them on earth)*
- ➤ **In what ways will Christ judge the earth during the Tribulation?** *(war, famine, sickness, death, natural disasters, and subjection of the world to the Antichrist)*
- ➤ **Who will be martyred during the Tribulation?** *(Jews and Gentiles who have trusted Christ during that time)*
- ➤ **What will happen to end the Tribulation?** *(Christ will return to earth with an army to defeat the Antichrist and his army.)*
- ➤ **What characteristics of Christ help us know that He will do what is right as He judges?** *(He is faithful and true.)*
- ➤ **What ought to be the attitude of Christians when they think about these future events?** *(They should trust Christ to protect them; they should be seeking to win the lost to Christ so that they will be spared from God's wrath.)*

Memory Verse—Revelation 19:11

Principle: God's judgment is righteous, in keeping with the faithfulness and truth of His character. Locate and read aloud **Revelation 19:11.**

- ➤ **Who is called Faithful and True?** *(Jesus Christ)*
- ➤ **What is Christ preparing to do?** *(make war against the armies of the Antichrist)*
- ➤ **What kind of judgments would a faithful and true judge give out?** *(He would do what was right and just; he would punish evil and reward good.)*
- ➤ **What would a faithful and true judge do for those who trust him?** *(protect them)*

Direct the students to read the verse silently. Tell them to highlight the verse in their Bibles (optional) and to mark the location with their Unit 10 Bookmarks. Read the verse for practice throughout the day.

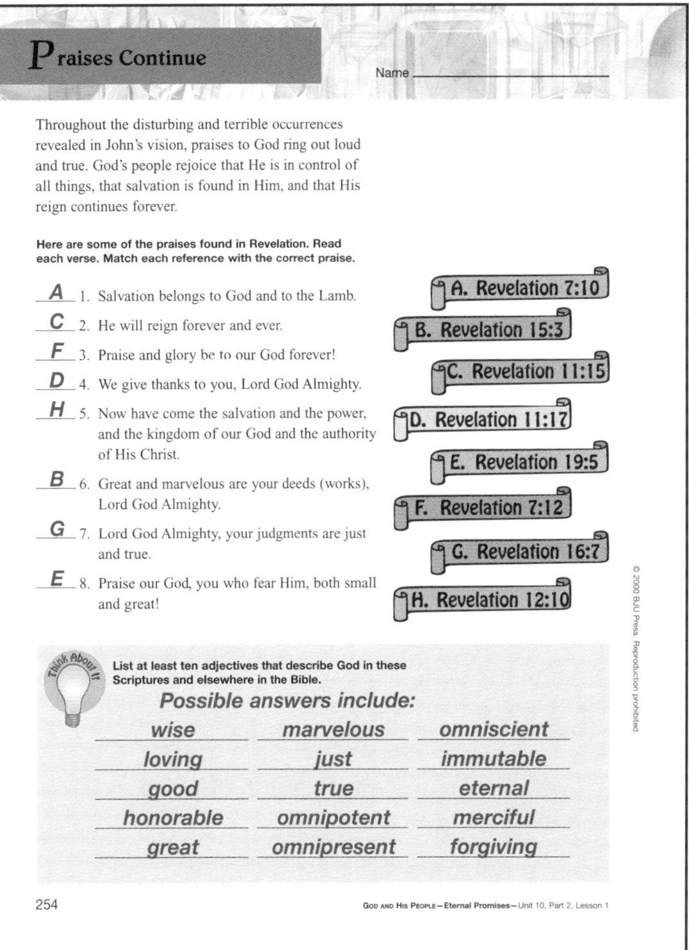

Praises Continue

Name ____________________

Throughout the disturbing and terrible occurrences revealed in John's vision, praises to God ring out loud and true. God's people rejoice that He is in control of all things, that salvation is found in Him, and that His reign continues forever.

Here are some of the praises found in Revelation. Read each verse. Match each reference with the correct praise.

__A__ 1. Salvation belongs to God and to the Lamb.
__C__ 2. He will reign forever and ever.
__F__ 3. Praise and glory be to our God forever!
__D__ 4. We give thanks to you, Lord God Almighty.
__H__ 5. Now have come the salvation and the power, and the kingdom of our God and the authority of His Christ.
__B__ 6. Great and marvelous are your deeds (works), Lord God Almighty.
__G__ 7. Lord God Almighty, your judgments are just and true.
__E__ 8. Praise our God, you who fear Him, both small and great!

A. Revelation 7:10
B. Revelation 15:3
C. Revelation 11:15
D. Revelation 11:17
E. Revelation 19:5
F. Revelation 7:12
G. Revelation 16:7
H. Revelation 12:10

Think About It

List at least ten adjectives that describe God in these Scriptures and elsewhere in the Bible.

Possible answers include:

wise	marvelous	omniscient
loving	just	immutable
good	true	eternal
honorable	omnipotent	merciful
great	omnipresent	forgiving

254 GOD AND HIS PEOPLE—Eternal Promises—Unit 10, Part 2, Lesson 1

Worktext page 254

Locate information in Scripture.

Lesson 2

Hymn: "It Is Well with My Soul"

Sing the first two verses (Worktext page 286). Play the recording and lead the students in singing verses 1-2.

Background Information

God's Attributes—*All of God's attributes, including His wrath, exist in Him in a state of perfection. The wrath, or anger, of God is in perfect harmony with His other attributes, such as His longsuffering, compassion, goodness, mercy, and righteousness. Attributes such as longsuffering and compassion make God "slow to anger" (Nehemiah 9:17; Psalm 103:8; 145:8; Joel 2:13; Jonah 4:2; Nahum 1:3). By his persistence in sin, man provokes God to wrath and essentially brings judgment upon himself. When God's wrath falls, it is always well deserved and something to be greatly feared.*

Introducing the Bible Study

Discuss the wrath of God.

➤ **What are some attributes, or characteristics, of God?** *(Possible answers include omnipotence, omnipresence, omniscience, holiness, love, righteousness, mercy, and faithfulness.)*

Point out that one of God's characteristics that we often avoid discussing is His wrath—His anger or hot displeasure that causes Him to punish and chasten people. (Share the background information about God's attributes.)

Explain that God's wrath is perfect and righteous, and it can fall on believers (through chastening for sin) and unbelievers (through judgment or punishment for sin). In the end times, God's wrath will rest on the leaders of the evil world system and on their followers who have rejected Christ. The following study will teach about people's attitudes and actions that stir up the wrath, or anger, of God.

Bible Study

Study the wrath of God. Read aloud the starred portions of Scripture as teaching examples. Discuss with the students the three questions about each passage.

➤ **Against whom is God's wrath directed in this passage?**

➤ **What was the reason for God's wrath?**

➤ **What were the consequences of God's wrath?**

* **Exodus 32:7-14, 27-28, 35**—The Lord's wrath came against the Israelites in the wilderness after they broke God's law against idolatry and worshiped the golden calf. God's wrath was partially turned away because Moses pled with Him on behalf of the people. But God still allowed three thousand Israelites to be killed by the Levites, and He sent a plague on the people who were left. **Application:** *God's wrath comes on those who rebel and put idols in the place of God.*

* **Joshua 7:1, 7-15, 20-22, 25-26**—God's wrath came on all the congregation of Israel because of Achan's sin of stealing. God allowed Israel to be defeated by Ai in battle, and He also commanded that Achan and all His family be stoned to death. **Application:** *God's wrath comes on those who disobey Him. Sometimes others have to suffer the consequences for one person's sin.*

Direct attention to Worktext page 255. Explain to the students that they are to choose a reference and read the verses; then they are to complete page 255, answering the three questions about their passage. Allow students to share their answers with the other students.

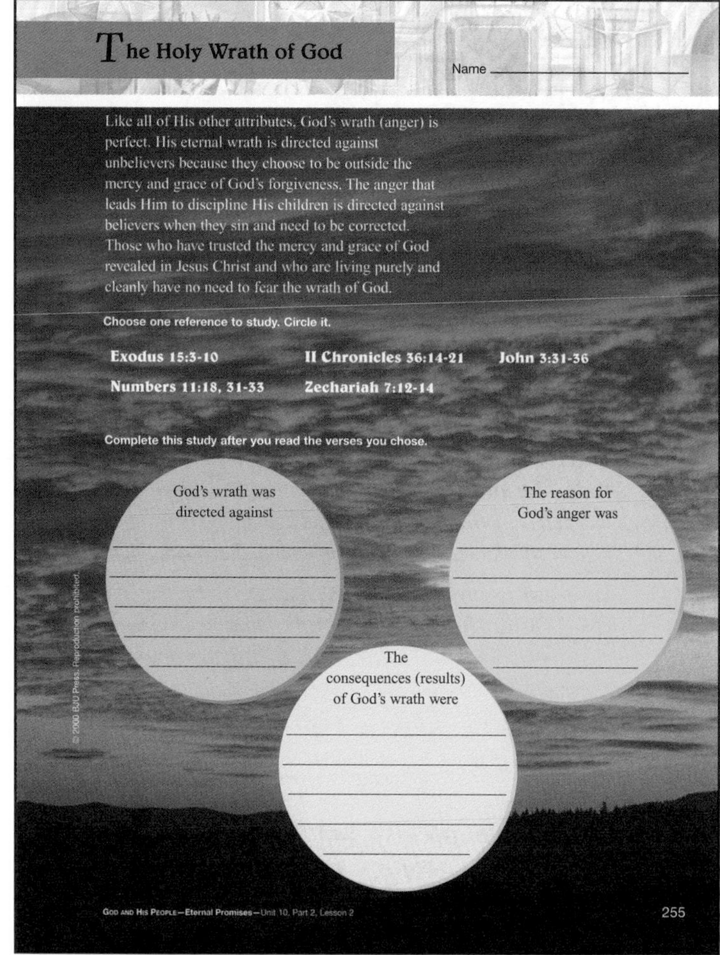

The Holy Wrath of God

Name ______________________

Like all of His other attributes, God's wrath (anger) is perfect. His eternal wrath is directed against unbelievers because they choose to be outside the mercy and grace of God's forgiveness. The anger that leads Him to discipline His children is directed against believers when they sin and need to be corrected. Those who have trusted the mercy and grace of God revealed in Jesus Christ and who are living purely and cleanly have no need to fear the wrath of God.

Choose one reference to study. Circle it.

Exodus 15:3-10 **II Chronicles 36:14-21** **John 3:31-36**
Numbers 11:18, 31-33 **Zechariah 7:12-14**

Complete this study after you read the verses you chose.

God's wrath was directed against ______________________

The reason for God's anger was ______________________

The consequences (results) of God's wrath were ______________________

Exodus 15:3-10—God's wrath fell on the Egyptians after they tried to pursue and destroy God's people, the Israelites. The consequence of God's wrath was the drowning of the entire Egyptian army in the Red Sea. **Application:** *God's wrath comes on those who are enemies of His people; He defends His own.*

Numbers 11:18, 31-33—God's wrath fell on the Israelites after they had complained that they had no meat. God sent quail to them, but He also sent a very great plague. **Application:** *God's wrath comes on those who complain and are ungrateful for His provision.*

II Chronicles 36:14-21—God's wrath fell on the Israelites who mocked His messengers and despised His words. God allowed Israel to be conquered and taken captive by Babylon. **Application:** *God's wrath comes on those who do not have respect for His message and His messengers.*

Zechariah 7:12-14—God's wrath came on Israel because they hardened their hearts and refused to hear God's Word. As a consequence, God scattered the Israelites among foreign nations and left their land empty. **Application:** *God's wrath comes on those whose hearts are hard and cold to His Word.*

John 3:31-36—God's wrath comes on anyone who does not believe on Jesus Christ for salvation. The consequence is that God's wrath "abides" on that one for as long as he refuses to believe. **Application:** *Whoever refuses to believe on Christ is in constant danger of God's punishment of hell for eternity.*

Explain that God's wrath is something we can avoid. Read aloud each of the following Scripture passages or assign the passages to volunteers to read. Discuss what is learned about avoiding God's wrath.

II Kings 22:15-20—Josiah avoided God's wrath because he listened to God's Word with a tender heart and humbled himself before God. Josiah wept for his sins and the sins of the people. God promised peace for him and for Israel during his lifetime. **Application:** *God responds in mercy to a tender heart and a humble spirit. Christians should not try to make excuses for their sin, but confess their sin openly and humbly to God.*

Romans 5:9—God promises that those who are justified by the blood of Christ will be saved from wrath through Christ. **Application:** *If we trust Christ as our Savior from sin, we will be saved from God's wrathful judgment. God's wrath will not come on Christians in the end times, but they will live safely with Him in heaven.* Read aloud **I Thessalonians 1:10** and **5:9-10**, which repeats this promise.

- ➤ **What kind of attitudes provoke God's anger?** *(rebellion, disrespect, ingratitude, pride, hardness)*
- ➤ **What kind of attitudes please Him and cause Him to be merciful?** *(humility, tenderness of heart, belief on His Son)*

Memory Verse—Revelation 19:11

Practice the memory verse. Locate and read aloud **Revelation 19:11** as the students read silently.

- ➤ **What words come to your mind as you picture this scene that John saw?** *(Answers will vary.)*
- ➤ **How could thinking about this scene help you when you feel afraid?** *(Elicit that thinking about God's power, faithfulness, and righteousness can encourage us and assure us of His ability to keep and protect us.)*

Write the verse on an erasable board, leaving several blanks for words or phrases. Select volunteers to read the verse aloud, filling in the missing words.

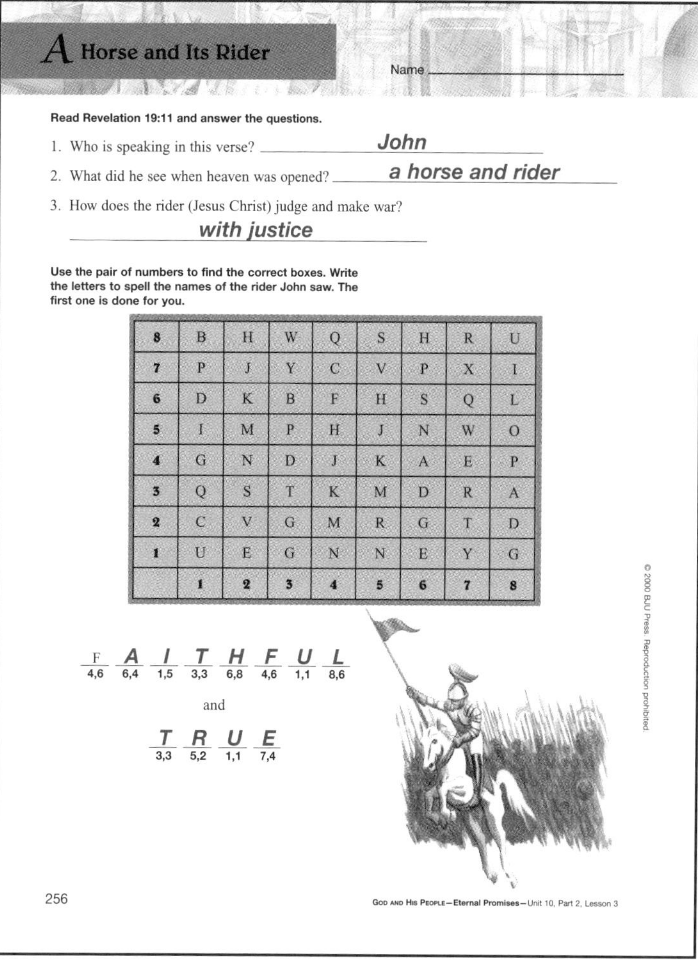

A Horse and Its Rider

Name ____________

Read Revelation 19:11 and answer the questions.

1. Who is speaking in this verse? *John*
2. What did he see when heaven was opened? *a horse and rider*
3. How does the rider (Jesus Christ) judge and make war? *with justice*

Use the pair of numbers to find the correct boxes. Write the letters to spell the names of the rider John saw. The first one is done for you.

8	B	H	W	Q	S	H	R	U
7	P	J	Y	C	V	P	X	I
6	D	K	B	F	H	S	Q	L
5	I	M	P	H	J	N	W	O
4	G	N	D	J	K	A	E	P
3	Q	S	T	K	M	D	R	A
2	C	V	G	M	R	G	T	D
1	U	E	G	N	N	E	Y	G
	1	**2**	**3**	**4**	**5**	**6**	**7**	**8**

F (4,6) *A* (6,4) *I* (1,5) *T* (3,3) *H* (6,8) *F* (4,6) *U* (1,1) *L* (8,6)

and

T (3,3) *R* (5,2) *U* (1,1) *E* (7,4)

256

God and His People—Eternal Promises—Unit 10, Part 2, Lesson 3

Lesson 3

Memory Verse—Revelation 19:11

Practice the memory verse. Locate and read **Revelation 19:11** aloud as the students read silently. Direct the students to take turns reading the verse to a partner and then to read it responsively with their partners.

Worktext page 256

Develop an understanding of the memory verse.

Introducing the Application Story

Discuss summer camp.

- ➤ **Have you ever been to a summer camp?**
- ➤ **What kinds of activities did you enjoy at camp?**
- ➤ **If you attended a Bible camp, did you make any important decisions while you were there?** Allow any students who wish to share these decisions with the class to do so.

Application Story

Read the following story to the students.

As the Stars Forever (Part 1)

Joanna hurled the basketball at the hoop. It bounced off the rim. "Ohhh!" She looked over at her brother Craig and scowled. "I'll *never* learn to do this."

"Sure you will. Try it again. Keep your eye on the basket while you shoot. Like this."

Craig loped to the hoop and tossed up the ball. It sank through the basket. "Sweet," he said. "Nothing but net."

Joanna sighed and watched Craig dribble the ball smoothly to the end of the driveway. True, Craig was much older than she was—almost a senior in high school—but he had already shown promise as a basketball player when he was her age. Here she was—going into fifth grade—and still unable to sink an easy layup. "Maybe talent doesn't always run in the family," she said aloud.

"What are you talking about?" Craig stopped dribbling and spun the ball on his finger. "You've got the old Nelson touch buried in there somewhere. You just need a little more practice."

"You make it look so easy," Joanna said. "Craig, how does it feel to be a star?" she asked.

Everyone knew that Craig Nelson was the best player on the varsity team at his high school. A few of his games had been highlighted on the local news. Joanna had seen the stack of mail from local college recruiters piling up in Craig's room. Dad had said once that Craig could probably go to a big state university on a basketball scholarship.

But now Craig had a funny, faraway expression on his face. "A star?" he asked. "Am I?"

"The newspapers say you are."

Craig flopped down in the grass at the edge of the driveway. "Let's take a break, Jo," he said. "I've got something to tell you."

Joanna let the ball roll into the grass and sat down where she could see Craig. His face had that serious expression she had often seen on it since he'd returned from Bible camp earlier that summer.

"You know how I've always been sort of—well, you know, how I've always sort of aimed my whole life at going to a state school and playing basketball?"

Joanna nodded. "You're good enough to do that!"

"Well, when I was at camp, I started doing some thinking." Craig reached for the basketball and tossed it back and forth in his fingertips.

"About basketball?"

"Kind of. Toward the end of the week, we had this speaker in one of the services. He's been a missionary in Cambodia."

Joanna frowned, trying to remember her geography. "Where's that?"

"The Far East. Somewhere south of China. Anyway, he talked a lot about the people all over the world who need the gospel. People are *dying,* Jo. People who've never even heard the name of Jesus Christ. They're going to hell because there's no one to tell them. I guess that wasn't a new idea to me, but for some reason—it just never hit me like that before."

Craig paused, and Joanna waited, wondering what this had to do with basketball.

"They had this invitation and all kinds of people went forward to tell the Lord they'd go wherever. But I was scared to do that. I was afraid God would make me give up my dream." Craig let the basketball rest in his lap. "But all the rest of that evening, I was miserable. I knew I had said no to God because I wanted my own way—my own plans. So when I got back to my cabin, I told God right then and there that I would go."

Joanna's eyes grew wide. "To Cambodia?" she asked.

Craig laughed. "Well, anywhere, really. Anywhere people need the gospel. But all this means I have to tell Dad sometime soon that . . . I won't be going to a state college."

"You won't?"

Craig lifted his chin a little. His face was still serious, but Joanna could see a sparkle in his eyes. "I'm going to go to Bible college," he said.

- ➤ **What did Joanna want to do?** *(play basketball well like her brother Craig)*
- ➤ **What has Craig wanted to do for most of his life?** *(play basketball at a state college)*
- ➤ **What decision did Craig make at camp?** *(to go wherever God led him and give the gospel to unsaved people)*
- ➤ **What did Craig realize the Lord wanted him to do instead of going to a state college?** *(study at a Bible college)*
- ➤ **How do you think Craig feels about the decision he has made?** *(Possible answers include excited, serious, and determined.)*

Hymn: "It Is Well with My Soul"

Sing the first two verses (Worktext page 286). Play the recording and lead in singing verses 1-2.

- ➤ **In what way were we helpless?** *(We were helpless to save ourselves; we were lost in our sins; there was nothing we could do about our sinfulness.)*
- ➤ **What did Christ do to help us when we were in this helpless condition?** *(shed His own blood for our souls)*
- ➤ **How should this make you feel?** *(Possible answers include grateful, thankful, and happy.)*

Lesson 4

Hymn: "It Is Well with My Soul"

Sing the first two verses (Worktext page 286). Play the recording as you lead in singing verses 1-2.

Introducing the Application Story

Review "As the Stars Forever," Part 1.

- ➤ **What did Craig tell Joanna at the end of the story in the previous lesson?** *(that he had decided to go to Bible college)*
- ➤ **Why does Craig plan to go to Bible college instead of a state college?** *(He made a decision at camp to serve the Lord as a missionary.)*
- ➤ **Whom does Craig still need to tell about his plans?** *(his dad)*

Application Story

Read the following story to the students. Explain that this is the conclusion of the story from the previous lesson.

As the Stars Forever (Part 2)

Joanna stood up and brushed some grass off her clothes. She bounced the basketball on the edge of the driveway but kept her eyes on Craig. "Why haven't you told Dad about your decision?" she asked. "Don't you think he'll be glad?"

Craig sighed. "I don't know. Dad wanted so much for me to get a basketball scholarship."

"When are you going to tell him?"

Craig chewed on a blade of grass for a moment. "I think I'll tell him tonight at dinner," he said. He stood up. "Hey, thanks for listening, Jo. You're not bad—for a little sister."

That night at dinner, Joanna kept glancing across the table at Craig. She thought he looked nervous. He didn't say much, and he didn't even eat his usual second piece of Mom's homemade bread.

Craig waited until Dad pushed back his plate before speaking. "Uh, Dad? I've got something to tell you—it's about college next year, and well, kind of about camp last month too."

Dad looked puzzled, but he didn't say anything.

In a rush of words, Craig poured out the story he had told Joanna earlier that day. "I just knew I had to go out and tell the world, Dad," he finished. "You know how I love to play basketball. But when I think about people spending eternity in a lake of fire, basketball doesn't seem so important anymore."

Dad stared at his water glass. He jiggled it a little, and the ice cubes clinked loudly in the silence. Mom reached over and squeezed Craig's hand.

"I know you wanted me to get a scholarship to a big school, Dad," Craig hurried on. "But maybe I could get a decent job next school year to help pay for Bible school. And it wouldn't be like I'd quit basketball all together. Christian colleges have teams. And maybe I could even use it on the mission field—as a way to reach teenagers."

Dad studied Craig's face for a long moment. "Son," he said quietly, "I'm convinced. You've chosen a far better thing for your life than I'd ever dreamed of."

Before she could stop herself, Joanna let out a huge sigh of relief. But Craig was speaking again. "Well, that's the funny thing, Dad," he said. "A couple months ago, I wouldn't have even considered this. It was kind of like God just chose it for me. Just a second—I'll show you something."

He jumped up from the table and came back a moment later with his Bible. "That night at camp," he said, looking from Mom to Dad, "I really had a struggle with giving up my dream of a basketball career. You know—wanting to be a star, and all." He swallowed. "But then the next morning, I was reading in Daniel, and God had me read this verse."

He flipped quickly through the pages. "Daniel 12:3. 'And they that be wise shall shine as the brightness of the firmament; and they that turn many to righteousness as the stars for ever and ever.' So I guess in God's eyes—I'll be a star anyway. And that's what's important."

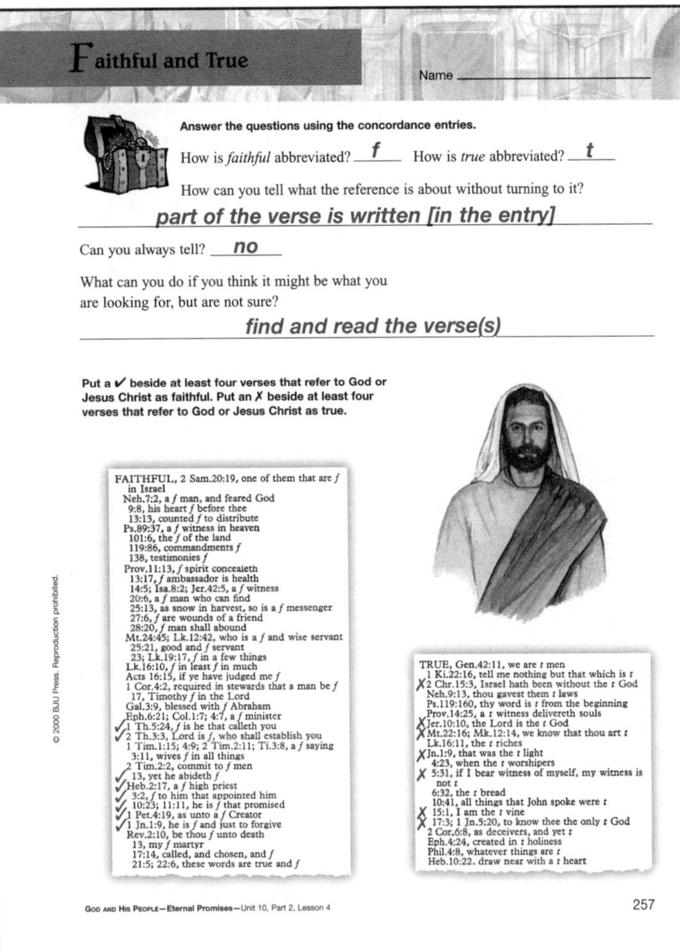

Faithful and True

Name ____________________

Answer the questions using the concordance entries.

How is *faithful* abbreviated? __f__ How is *true* abbreviated? __t__

How can you tell what the reference is about without turning to it?

__part of the verse is written [in the entry]__

Can you always tell? __no__

What can you do if you think it might be what you are looking for, but are not sure?

__find and read the verse(s)__

Put a ✓ beside at least four verses that refer to God or Jesus Christ as faithful. Put an ✗ beside at least four verses that refer to God or Jesus Christ as true.

FAITHFUL, 2 Sam.20:19, one of them that are *f* in Israel
Neh.7:2, a *f* man, and feared God
9:8, his heart *f* before thee
13:13, counted *f* to distribute
Ps.89:37, a *f* witness in heaven
101:6, the *f* of the land
119:86, commandments *f*
138, testimonies *f*
Prov.11:13, *f* spirit concealeth
13:17, *f* ambassador is health
14:5; Isa.8:2; Jer.42:5, a *f* witness
20:6, a *f* man who can find
25:13, as snow in harvest, so is a *f* messenger
27:6, *f* are wounds of a friend
28:20, *f* man shall abound
Mt.24:45; Lk.12:42, who is a *f* and wise servant
25:21, good and *f* servant
23; Lk.19:17, *f* in a few things
Lk.16:10, *f* in least *f* in much
Acts 16:15, if ye have judged me *f*
1 Cor.4:2, required in stewards that a man be *f*
17, Timothy *f* in the Lord
Gal.3:9, blessed with *f* Abraham
Eph.6:21; Col.1:7; 4:7, a *f* minister
✓ 1 Th.5:24, *f* is he that calleth you
✓ 2 Th.3:3, Lord is *f*, who shall establish you
1 Tim.1:15; 4:9; 2 Tim.2:11; Ti.3:8, a *f* saying
3:11, wives *f* in all things
2 Tim.2:2, commit to *f* men
✓ 13, yet he abideth *f*
✓ Heb.2:17, a *f* high priest
✓ 3:2, *f* to him that appointed him
✓ 10:23; 11:11, he is *f* that promised
✓ 1 Pet.4:19, as unto a *f* Creator
✓ 1 Jn.1:9, he is *f* and just to forgive
Rev.2:10, be thou *f* unto death
13, my *f* martyr
17:14, called, and chosen, and *f*
21:5; 22:6, these words are true and *f*

TRUE, Gen.42:11, we are *t* men
1 Ki.22:16, tell me nothing but that which is *t*
✗ 2 Chr.15:3, Israel hath been without the *t* God
Neh.9:13, thou gavest them *t* laws
Ps.119:160, thy word is *t* from the beginning
Prov.14:25, a *t* witness delivereth souls
✗ Jer.10:10, the Lord is the *t* God
✗ Mt.22:16; Mk.12:14, we know that thou art *t*
Lk.16:11, the *t* riches
✗ Jn.1:9, that was the *t* light
4:23, when the *t* worshipers
✗ 5:31, if I bear witness of myself, my witness is not *t*
6:32, the *t* bread
10:41, all things that John spoke were *t*
✗ 15:1, I am the *t* vine
✗ 17:3; 1 Jn.5:20, to know thee the only *t* God
2 Cor.6:8, as deceivers, and yet *t*
Eph.4:24, created in *t* holiness
Phil.4:8, whatever things are *t*
Heb.10:22. draw near with a *t* heart

GOD AND HIS PEOPLE—Eternal Promises—Unit 10, Part 2, Lesson 4 257

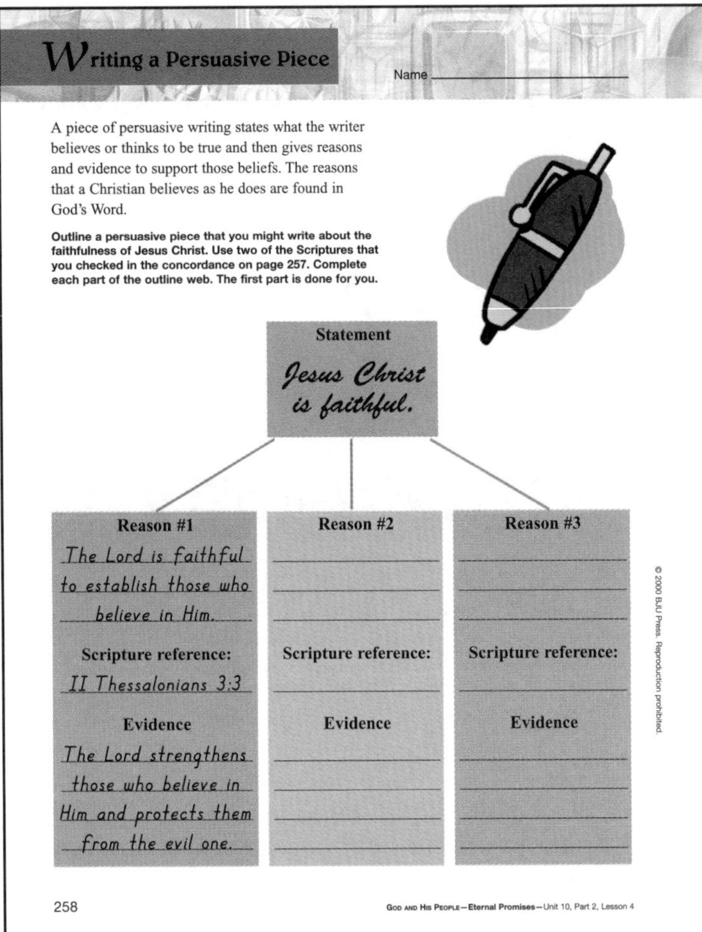

Writing a Persuasive Piece

Name ____________________

A piece of persuasive writing states what the writer believes or thinks to be true and then gives reasons and evidence to support those beliefs. The reasons that a Christian believes as he does are found in God's Word.

Outline a persuasive piece that you might write about the faithfulness of Jesus Christ. Use two of the Scriptures that you checked in the concordance on page 257. Complete each part of the outline web. The first part is done for you.

Statement
Jesus Christ is faithful.

Reason #1	Reason #2	Reason #3
The Lord is faithful to establish those who believe in Him.		
Scripture reference: II Thessalonians 3:3	**Scripture reference:**	**Scripture reference:**
Evidence The Lord strengthens those who believe in Him and protects them from the evil one.	**Evidence**	**Evidence**

258 GOD AND HIS PEOPLE—Eternal Promises—Unit 10, Part 2, Lesson 4

➤ **Why was Craig nervous about telling his dad he had decided to go to Bible college?** *(He knew his dad wanted him to get a basketball scholarship and play on a state college team.)*

➤ **What did Craig say was more important than basketball?** *(warning unsaved people about an eternity in the lake of fire)*

Memory Verse—Revelation 19:11

Practice the memory verse. Locate and read aloud **Revelation 19:11** as the students read silently. Select volunteers to say the verse from memory.

Bible Study Skills, Worktext page 257

Use a Bible concordance.

Worktext page 258

Use a concordance to study the Bible and complete an outline web.

Going Beyond

Materials

- Dictionaries
- Thesauruses

Enrichment

Direct a Scripture meditation activity. Instruct the students to write two column headings at the top of a sheet of paper: "Faithful" and "True." Beneath each heading, tell them to list other words or phrases that come to mind when they think about those words. Allow them to use dictionaries or thesauruses to find synonyms for these words.

Suggest that they ask themselves questions such as: "What would a faithful person do? What would he not do? What would a true person be like?" After several minutes, allow the students to share some of the words or phrases that they listed. Encourage them to continue meditating on these qualities of God and applying them to their own lives and circumstances. For example,

➤ God is faithful. **What does that mean to me when I am lonely or sad?**

➤ God is true. **What does that mean to me when someone disappoints or betrays me?**

Read aloud the promise in **Psalm 1:2-3** for those who meditate on God's Word.

Jesus Christ Will Rule and Reign

Unit 10, Part 3

Preview

Doctrines

- The Bible is accurate in its prophecy (Numbers 23:19)—Lesson 1
- During the Millennium there will be worldwide peace with other men and animals (Isaiah 65:25)—Lesson 2
- During the Millennium the earth will be filled with the knowledge of the Lord, although not all will be saved (Isaiah 2:3)—Lesson 2
- During the Millennium the saints will rule with Christ (Revelation 20:6)—Lesson 3
- In the ages to come, there will be the judgment of sin and punishment in the lake of fire (Revelation 20:13-15)—Lesson 3

Skills and Applications

- Learn Isaiah 9:6-7
- Use a glossary
- Complete an outline map
- Identify definitions
- Locate information in Scripture
- Gain an understanding of the sequence of the end times
- Develop an understanding of prophetic foreshortening
- Grow in an appreciation of God's eternal plan and provision for Christians
- Apply Bible knowledge to everyday life

Lesson 1

Materials

- Charts 39-40, "Revelation of the End Times"
- Recording of "For Unto Us a Child Is Born" from *Messiah* by George Frederick Handel (optional)

Hymn: "It Is Well with My Soul"

Sing the first two verses (Worktext page 286). Divide the students into two groups. Direct one group to sing verse 1 and the second group to sing verse 2.

Background Information

Prophetic Foreshortening—*One way that God hid the full meaning of these prophecies from centuries of readers and sometimes from the prophets themselves was by using the principle of* prophetic foreshortening. *A prophecy might describe two events, one that would happen soon and another that would happen much later. The nearer event would only partially fulfill the prophecy, while the later event would complete the fulfillment. For example, in Matthew 24:2 Christ described the destruction of the temple by the Romans in A.D. 70. But when His disciples asked Him to describe the time surrounding this event, He spoke not only of the Roman invasion but also of the end times, which are yet to occur. Matthew 24:4-13 could apply to either the first century or the end times, while verses 14 and following have not yet been fulfilled and rightly apply to the last days.*

This principle is called "prophetic foreshortening" because it is similar to the photographic principle of foreshortening. From the camera's lens, distances are sometimes distorted so that objects that are far apart appear to be close together.

The prophets of the Old Testament did not always perceive the distances between the events that God revealed to them. They often saw the first and second coming of Christ together, although they will actually be far apart in their fulfillment. First Peter 1:10-12 tells us that the Old Testament prophets did not always understand what they were writing. Daniel was told that his words were to be "shut up," or hidden, so that they could not be fully understood until much later when his prophecies began to be fulfilled (Daniel 12:4-10).

Introducing the Bible Account

Explain prophetic foreshortening. Direct the students to look at the illustration of photographic foreshortening on Worktext page 259 as you read aloud the background information about prophetic foreshortening.

Bible Account

Read the following Bible account or read Isaiah 9:6-7. Point to each event on Charts 39-40, "Revelation of the End Times," as it is mentioned in the lesson.

The Promise of God's Rule

Even though we quote Isaiah 9:6-7 at Christmas, this passage goes beyond the birth of the Christ child. Verse 7 refers to the second coming of the Lord Jesus Christ and gives no indication of a gap in time between His birth as a child and the setting up of His government on earth during the Millennium. From God's point of view, these two events are both certain and are parts of the same action.

Isaiah looked on the life and work of Christ as a whole. He described different parts of that whole without always following the order in which they would happen. In this passage Isaiah saw both the first and second coming of Christ. Yet much later, Isaiah described Christ's first coming in more detail. Isaiah told how Christ came to bear the sins of the whole world as a suffering servant on the cross (Isaiah 53).

When we read in Isaiah 9 "a child is born; unto us a son is given," we see the birth of Christ—His first coming. But the rest of verse 6 and verse 7 look forward to His second coming, which is still to come in the future. Verse 6 lists four names given to the Lord Jesus that prove He is God.

Wonderful Counsellor—These two names should be read as one title. *Wonderful* means "exceptional" or "distinguished." *Counsellor* means "the authoritative one, to whom the people will listen." The Lord Jesus needs no counselor, for He already knows all things. The Wonderful Counsellor is coming to reign on earth during the Millennium and for eternity.

Mighty God—This name refers to the omnipotent God to whom all power is given. The mighty God is coming to reign for one thousand years during the Millennium and for eternity.

Everlasting Father—This title reminds us that Christ is the eternal Creator of the universe. He is called the "Ancient of Days" (Daniel 7:9). The Everlasting Father is coming to reign forever.

Prince of Peace—This name reflects Christ's role as a ruler—one who will rule peacefully. There have always been wars on earth. Nations have tried to make peace by means of peace treaties and organizations such as the League of Nations and the United Nations. Man cannot make peace happen apart from God. Lasting peace will come only when the Prince of Peace reigns.

Verse 7 reminds us of the promise that the Messiah would come through David's descendants—through his family line. Jesus has already fulfilled this promise in His first coming. When He comes the second time, there will be no end to His peaceful reign from David's throne. His kingdom will be eternal, and His reign will be characterized by righteousness and justice.

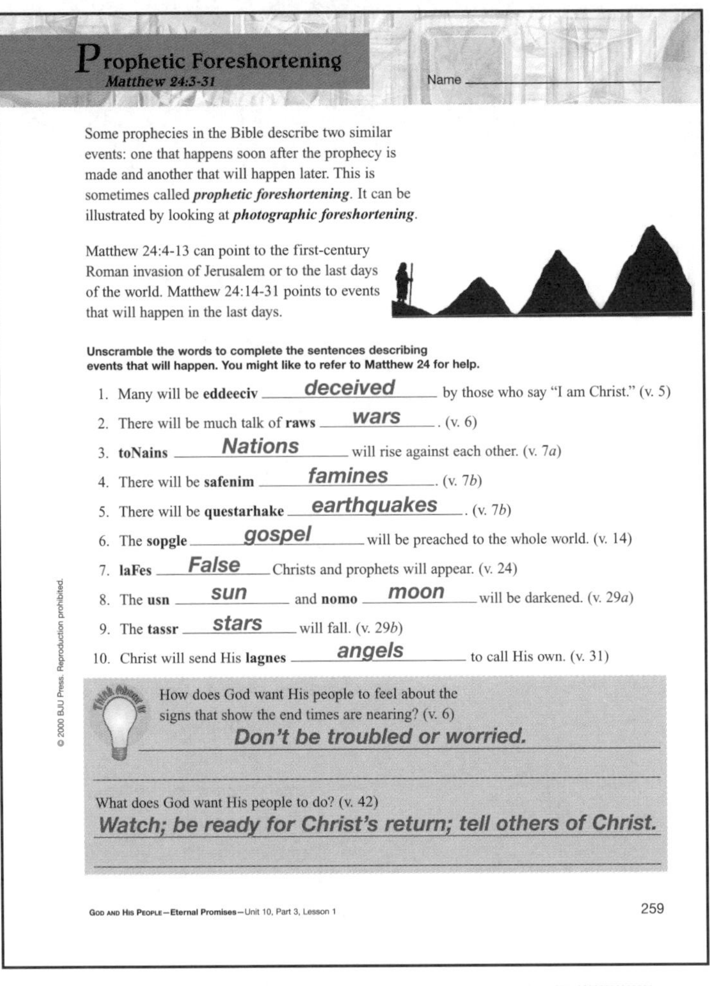

Prophetic Foreshortening
Matthew 24:3-31

Name ____________

Some prophecies in the Bible describe two similar events: one that happens soon after the prophecy is made and another that will happen later. This is sometimes called ***prophetic foreshortening***. It can be illustrated by looking at ***photographic foreshortening***.

Matthew 24:4-13 can point to the first-century Roman invasion of Jerusalem or to the last days of the world. Matthew 24:14-31 points to events that will happen in the last days.

Unscramble the words to complete the sentences describing events that will happen. You might like to refer to Matthew 24 for help.

1. Many will be **eddeeciv** __deceived__ by those who say "I am Christ." (v. 5)
2. There will be much talk of **raws** __wars__. (v. 6)
3. **toNains** __Nations__ will rise against each other. (v. 7*a*)
4. There will be **safenim** __famines__. (v. 7*b*)
5. There will be **questarhake** __earthquakes__. (v. 7*b*)
6. The **sopgle** __gospel__ will be preached to the whole world. (v. 14)
7. **laFes** __False__ Christs and prophets will appear. (v. 24)
8. The **usn** __sun__ and **nomo** __moon__ will be darkened. (v. 29*a*)
9. The **tassr** __stars__ will fall. (v. 29*b*)
10. Christ will send His **lagnes** __angels__ to call His own. (v. 31)

Think About It

How does God want His people to feel about the signs that show the end times are nearing? (v. 6)

Don't be troubled or worried.

What does God want His people to do? (v. 42)

Watch; be ready for Christ's return; tell others of Christ.

➤ **Through what people did God promise that all other people would be blessed?** *(through David's descendants) Point out that these descendants make up the nation of Israel.*

➤ **What is the period when the Lord will reign on earth from David's throne for a thousand years?** *(the Millennium)*

➤ **What will characterize the reign of Christ?** *(Possible answers include righteousness, peace, knowledge, power, and eternality.)*

Christmas and Beyond

Name ____________

These verses are another example of prophetic foreshortening. Isaiah 9:6 tells of the coming of Jesus Christ to earth as Savior. Isaiah 9:7 describes His second coming and the government He will establish on earth.

Read Isaiah 9:6-7 and answer the questions.

1. Who is born and given to us?	*a child, a Son [Jesus Christ]*
2. What will He carry on His shoulders?	*the government*
3. What will He be called?	*Wonderful Counselor, mighty God, everlasting Father, Prince of Peace*
4. Of what will there be no end?	*the increase of His government and peace*
5. Over what will He reign?	*David's kingdom*
6. How will He reign?	*with justice and righteousness*
7. What will accomplish this?	*the zeal of the Lord of hosts [Lord Almighty]*

© 2000 BJU Press. Reproduction prohibited.

260 God and His People—Eternal Promises—Unit 10, Part 3, Lesson 1

The Millennium

Name ____________

Millennium, the word for the thousand years in which Christ will reign on the earth after the Tribulation, is formed from *mill(e),* the Latin word for "thousand."

Read the verses. Complete the outline map to show what the Millennium will be like. In an outline, only a few important words stand for the idea.

Isaiah 32:15, Isaiah 35:1, Isaiah 55:13, Isaiah 65:25

The Natural World

fruitful crops and forests
desert will bloom
no thorns or briars
animals will be at peace

Psalm 2:7-9, Psalm 72:1-3

The Reign of Christ

rule with a rod of iron
righteousness
peace

the millennium

Isaiah 10:21, Isaiah 11:11-12

The Nation of Israel

will return
will be recovered
will be gathered together

Isaiah 11:9, Ezekiel 37:23, Zechariah 8:22

People

will be God's people
will pray
no one will hurt or destroy

© 2000 BJU Press. Reproduction prohibited.

God and His People—Eternal Promises—Unit 10, Part 3, Lesson 2 261

Worktext page 259

Find information in Scripture and develop an understanding of prophetic foreshortening.

Memory Verses—Isaiah 9:6-7

Principle: Jesus Christ, the Son of God and Savior of men, will someday come as King to rule the world in righteousness. Locate **Isaiah 9:6-7** and select students to read the verses aloud. Direct the students to read the verses silently, then in a quiet whisper, and then to a partner. Direct the students to highlight the verses in their Bibles (optional) and to mark the location with the Unit 10 Bookmark. Review the meanings of the four names for God.

Play "For Unto Us a Child Is Born" from the oratorio *Messiah,* which quotes **Isaiah 9:6** (optional).

➤ **Have you previously heard this music?**

➤ **When do we usually hear this part of *Messiah* sung?** *(at Christmas)*

➤ **What do we celebrate at Christmas?** *(Christ's first coming to earth as a baby)*

Worktext page 260

Develop an understanding of the memory verses.

Lesson 2

Background Information

"That Day"—*Old Testament prophecies often use the phrase "that day" to refer to Christ's second coming and millennial reign on the earth.*

Introducing the Bible Study

Use a glossary. Direct the students to find and read the definition of *Millennium* in their glossaries.

Bible Study

Study the Millennium. Direct the students' attention to the list of references on Worktext page 261. Explain that these are only some of the many promises and prophecies concerning the millennial rule of Christ on earth. Assign each student a passage to read silently. (*Note:* More than one student may read a passage, or you may allow students to work together in groups.) Give each student or group of students an opportunity to share the promise or prophecy about the Millennium found in the passage. Direct the students to complete the outline map on Worktext page 261 as you discuss the passages.

- **Isaiah 32:15**—*The land will be fruitful with crops and forests.*
- **Isaiah 35:1**—*The desert will blossom like a rose.*
- **Isaiah 55:13**—*There will be no more thorns and briars on the earth, a sign that the curse of sin will have been removed.*
- **Isaiah 65:25**—*The animal world will be at peace.*
- **Psalm 2:7-9**—*Christ will mightily defeat His foes with a rod of iron. He will break the rule of evil as a piece of pottery is broken.*
- **Psalm 72:1-3**—*Christ's earthly reign will be a rule of righteousness and peace.*
- **Isaiah 10:21**—*A remnant of Israel will repent and return to the Lord.*
- **Isaiah 11:11-12**—*Christ will regather His people Israel and restore them as a nation under His rule.*
- **Isaiah 11:9**—*No one will hurt or destroy one another; the earth will be full of the knowledge of the Lord.*
- **Ezekiel 37:23**—*The people of Israel will be cleansed from their sin; they will no longer take part in idolatry or rebellion against the Lord.*
- **Zechariah 8:22-23**—*People from all the nations of the earth will worship Christ.*

➤ **When will these promises and prophecies be fulfilled?** *(during the Millennium)*

➤ **What will happen to the nation of Israel during the Millennium?** *(It will be judged, cleansed, restored, and reunited as a nation to rule and preach righteousness to all other nations.)*

➤ **What will Christ's rule be like?** *(righteous, peaceful; He will be worshiped by all nations.)*

Background Information

Jesus Lived in Galilee—*Isaiah 9:1-2 is quoted in the New Testament (Matthew 4:13-17). Galilee was the region that the tribes Zebulun and Naphtali inhabited. Jesus grew up in the town of Nazareth in Galilee and spent most of His earthly ministry there. He was the "great light" that shone on the people living in that region.*

Memory Verses—Isaiah 9:6-7

Practice the memory verses. Locate and read aloud **Isaiah 9:6-7.** Remind the students that these verses speak of the coming of Christ as a child and then go on to tell of Christ's rule from the throne of David. (*Note:* See background information about Jesus living in Galilee.) Direct the students to read and study the verses. Read the verses throughout the day for practice.

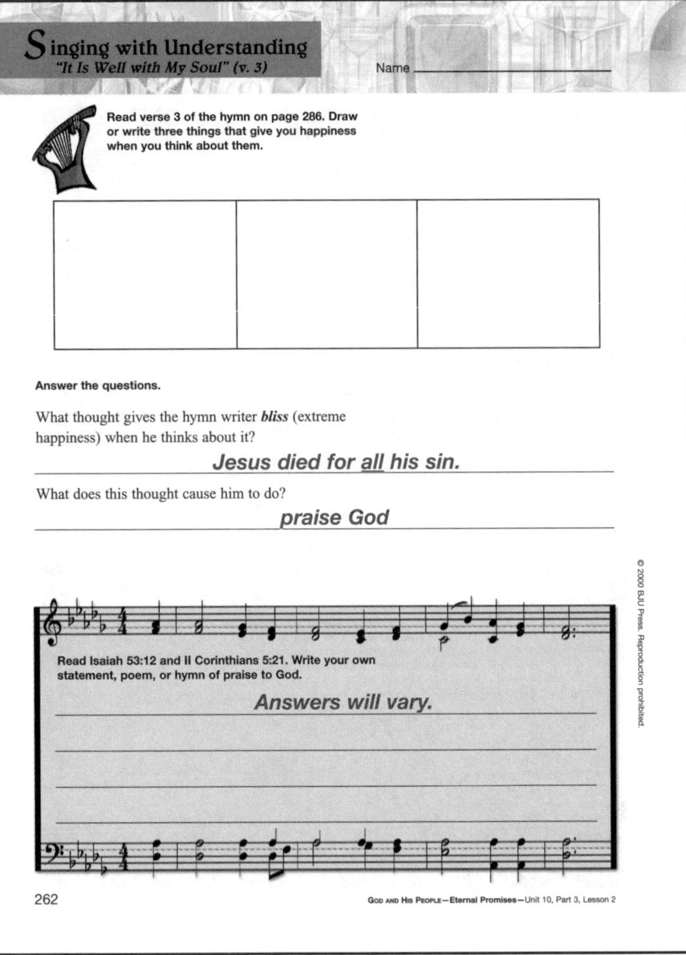

Singing with Understanding
"It Is Well with My Soul" (v. 3)

Name ____________________

Read verse 3 of the hymn on page 286. Draw or write three things that give you happiness when you think about them.

Answer the questions.

What thought gives the hymn writer *bliss* (extreme happiness) when he thinks about it?

Jesus died for all his sin.

What does this thought cause him to do?

praise God

Read Isaiah 53:12 and II Corinthians 5:21. Write your own statement, poem, or hymn of praise to God.

Answers will vary.

262

God and His People—Eternal Promises—Unit 10, Part 3, Lesson 2

Hymn: "It Is Well with My Soul"

Teach the third verse (Worktext page 286). Sing verses 1-2 together. Read the third verse to the students.

➤ **What does the word *bliss* mean?** *(happiness, joy)*

➤ **What is the hymn writer joyful about?** *(His sin is nailed to the cross; he bears it no more.)*

➤ **How much of our sin did Jesus bear on the cross?** *(all of it)*

➤ **What can we gain from the work of Christ?** *(salvation through saving faith in Christ)*

➤ **What should our response be to Christ if He has truly saved us?** *(thankfulness, praise)*

Play the recording and lead in singing the third verse.

Worktext page 262

Singing with understanding, verse 3.

Lesson 3

Materials

- Charts 39-40, "Revelation of the End Times"
- Recording of "For Unto Us a Child Is Born" from *Messiah* by George Frederick Handel (optional)

Background Information

The Second Coming—*The first part of Christ's second coming (the Rapture) is to be private, seen only by believers. The second part of His second coming will be public, for all to see. Christ will come in the air at the Rapture (I Thessalonians 4:17); He will come to the earth in glory later on (Zechariah 14:4).*

Battle of Armageddon—*The powers of Satan and his followers will prepare to make war on the Son of God at His second coming. Zechariah prophesied that Christ's "feet shall stand in that day upon the mount of Olives" (Zechariah 14:4). All the soldiers of the nations on earth will fight against the God of heaven (Revelation 19:19). God will defeat all these armies with His Word, which we are told is sharper than any two-edged sword. Then the Antichrist and the False Prophet will be cast into the lake of fire.*

Millennium—*Following the Tribulation period and the Battle of Armageddon, the Lord will set up His kingdom of righteousness on earth. He will rule with a rod of iron, and His saints will reign with Him during a thousand years of peace. The word* millennium *is derived from a Latin word meaning "thousand." It is used to refer to the thousand years of the kingdom age when the Lord will reign on earth. This type of government with God as the head is called a* theocracy.

Kingdom of God—*Throughout the New Testament we are told that the kingdom of God will have no end. That was God's plan from Creation when He told Adam to have dominion over the earth (Genesis 1:28). God's kingdom is not only an earthly kingdom to come in the future, but it also exists right now in the hearts of His people as they yield to His rule (Psalm 110:1-3).*

Introducing the Bible Account

Review the sequence of events of the end times. Use Charts 39-40, "Revelation of the End Times," to review the background information about the second coming of Christ and the Battle of Armageddon.

Bible Account

Read the following Bible account or read Revelation 20.

A Kingdom of Righteousness

Following the Battle of Armageddon, John saw an angel unlock a bottomless pit, bind Satan with a chain, and cast him into it. Satan will be bound in this pit during the thousand years of Christ's earthly kingdom—but not forever.

In his vision, John saw many thrones occupied by saints around the throne of God. The redeemed from all ages will be on earth during this millennial rule—all those who have trusted in the Lord Jesus Christ. Those who have died during the Tribulation for their worship and witness of Christ will be there as well. And there will be another group of believers who did not die for their belief during the Tribulation. Many Jews and Gentiles will have hidden and escaped martyrdom by the Antichrist.

All those on earth at the beginning of the Millennium will be believers. Everyone will be under the rule of God. The believers John describes are enthroned as judges. This is especially important to each of us who have accepted God's Son as our Savior from sin. Not only can we know that we will be with Christ on earth during the Millennium, but we can also know that we will reign, or rule, with Him.

There will be no other political system and no man-made religions. God alone will be worshiped in fulfillment of the Lord's prayer, "Thy kingdom come. Thy will be done." All believers will serve God, and their service for Him will continue forever after this point.

Not everyone on earth at the end of this thousand-year rule will be a believer in Christ. New generations will be born and will grow up during the Millennium. At the end of a thousand years, Satan will be loosed on the earth again, and he will deceive many of the people of these new generations. The Book of Revelation compares the number of those who will follow Satan at this time to the sands of the sea.

This rebellion led by Satan will be doomed from its beginning. No sooner will Satan's army encircle the city of Jerusalem than fire will fall from heaven and destroy every person in the army. Satan, the great deceiver, will be thrown into the lake of fire, where the Beast and False Prophet are, to be tormented and punished forever. This will be the end of Satan's power.

Next, Christ will sit on a great white throne and judge all those who have died without Christ—before, during, and after the Tribulation. Christ will have the Book of Life, in which all the names of those who have put their trust in Him as Savior will appear. Because the names of the dead do not appear in this book, they also will be thrown into the lake of fire, where they will spend eternity.

Just before this Great White Throne Judgment, heaven and earth will flee away. The last two chapters of Revelation tell us a new heaven and a new earth will replace the present ones. Believers will spend eternity there with Christ.

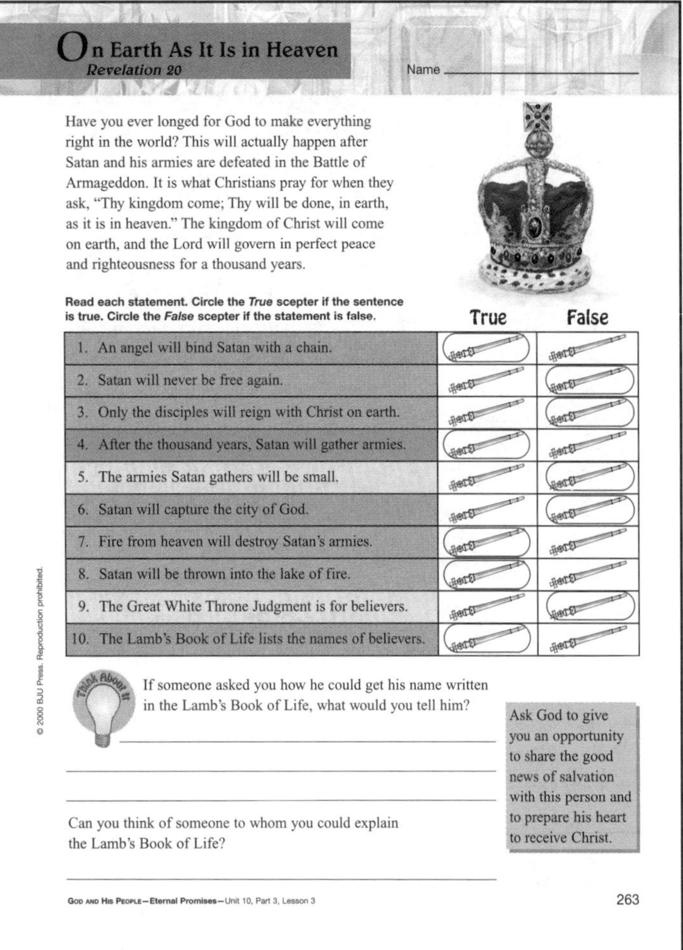

On Earth As It Is in Heaven

Revelation 20

Name ____________________

Have you ever longed for God to make everything right in the world? This will actually happen after Satan and his armies are defeated in the Battle of Armageddon. It is what Christians pray for when they ask, "Thy kingdom come; Thy will be done, in earth, as it is in heaven." The kingdom of Christ will come on earth, and the Lord will govern in perfect peace and righteousness for a thousand years.

Read each statement. Circle the *True* scepter if the sentence is true. Circle the *False* scepter if the statement is false.

Statement	True	False
1. An angel will bind Satan with a chain.	(circled)	
2. Satan will never be free again.		(circled)
3. Only the disciples will reign with Christ on earth.		(circled)
4. After the thousand years, Satan will gather armies.	(circled)	
5. The armies Satan gathers will be small.		(circled)
6. Satan will capture the city of God.		(circled)
7. Fire from heaven will destroy Satan's armies.	(circled)	
8. Satan will be thrown into the lake of fire.	(circled)	
9. The Great White Throne Judgment is for believers.		(circled)
10. The Lamb's Book of Life lists the names of believers.	(circled)	

Think About It

If someone asked you how he could get his name written in the Lamb's Book of Life, what would you tell him?

____

Can you think of someone to whom you could explain the Lamb's Book of Life?

____

Ask God to give you an opportunity to share the good news of salvation with this person and to prepare his heart to receive Christ.

God and His People—Eternal Promises—Unit 10, Part 3, Lesson 3 263

- ➤ **Where will Satan be during the Millennium?** *(bound in a bottomless pit)*
- ➤ **What will believers be doing during this earthly millennial reign?** *(sitting on thrones, judging and reigning with the Lord, serving the Lord [Isaiah 1:26; Daniel 7:22; Matthew 19:28; I Corinthians 6:2-3])*
- ➤ **What will Satan be permitted to do at the end of a thousand years?** *(He will be released on the earth and deceive many into rebelling against Christ.)*
- ➤ **What will happen to Satan and his army of rebels?** *(They will be destroyed with fire from heaven.)*
- ➤ **Where will Satan and all unbelievers spend eternity?** *(in the lake of fire)*
- ➤ **Who will escape the lake of fire?** *(all those whose names appear in the Book of Life; all those who have trusted Christ as their Savior from sin)*

Hymn: "It Is Well with My Soul"

Sing the first three verses (Worktext page 286). Before singing, challenge the students to think about the following questions without responding.

- ➤ **Has your sin been "nailed to the cross"?**
- ➤ **Is your name written in Christ's Book of Life?**
- ➤ **Will you reign with Christ on earth and escape His judgment in the lake of fire?**

Explain that if each student can answer "yes" to all three questions, he has every reason to say, "It is well with my soul." Invite any students who cannot answer "yes" to come and talk with you at a specific time. Play the recording and lead in singing verses 1-3.

Memory Verses—Isaiah 9:6-7

Practice the memory verses. Select a student to read the verses aloud. Then play Handel's "For Unto Us a Child is Born" and invite the students to try to sing along (optional).

Worktext page 263

Recall details about the Bible account.

Lesson 4

Memory Verses—Isaiah 9:6-7

Practice the memory verses. Locate and read the verses aloud as the students read silently; then select volunteers to say the verses from memory.

- ➤ **What is the Old Testament prophecy in Isaiah 9:6-7 referring to?** *(The first part of the prophecy refers to Christ's first coming to earth as Savior; the second part refers to Christ's reign over man during the Millennium.)*
- ➤ **How long will this Millennium period last?** *(a thousand years)*
- ➤ **What will Christ be doing during the Millennium?** *(reigning in righteousness and peace)*

Direct the students to read the verses silently, then to read them in a quiet whisper to themselves, and then to read or say them from memory to a partner.

Hymn: "It Is Well with My Soul"

Sing the first three verses (Worktext page 286). Play the recording of the first three verses and lead in singing them together. Encourage some of the students to sing the echoed parts on the chorus.

Application Activity

Apply the principle of "seeking first the kingdom of God" to daily life. Students will be reading or listening to Bible verses and situations. Discuss each situation with the students. (*Note:* You may choose to share a true situation that has influenced your students, school, or family.)

Read **Matthew 6:31-33** to the students and remind them of the things they have just learned about the coming kingdom of God on earth. Challenge them to think about what it means to "seek first the kingdom of God" as you read the following stories.

Situation 1

Mom told Adam that he could invite one friend to go with him to the Sunday school picnic on Saturday. Adam has been planning to invite Kyle, one of his Christian friends from school who goes to another church in town. He knows Kyle would fit in well with the kids at the picnic. But there is one other possibility. Last night, Adam rode bikes with Ethan, the boy who lives down the street. Adam doesn't think Ethan is saved; his family doesn't go to church, and Ethan said once that he believes in evolution. Ethan probably wouldn't fit in very well with the kids at the picnic—he might say something about evolution or use some swear words. Adam would feel more comfortable taking Kyle with him, but he also realizes that taking Ethan might give him an opportunity to talk to him about the Lord.

➤ **Whom do you think Adam should invite—Kyle or Ethan? Why?** *(Lead the students to conclude that "seeking first the kingdom" means to place greater priority on seeking a lost soul than on "fitting in" and having fun with friends.)*

Situation 2

Krischa has been earning money by taking care of a dog whose owner is out of town. After the owner returns and pays her, Krischa thinks about how she will spend the money after she has given her tithe. She would really like to have a new CD, but she suddenly remembers that her cousin Staci still needs some money for her mission trip this summer. Krischa thinks the Lord might want her to give Staci some of the money. Should she buy the CD first and then give whatever is left over to Staci? Or should she set aside some money to give to Staci *before* shopping for the CD?

➤ **What do you think Krischa should do? Why?** *(Lead the students to understand that Krischa should pray first and ask the Lord how much of her money He would like her to give to Staci. Her gift to Staci should come first because that money is going toward the "kingdom of God"—giving out the gospel to the lost. Perhaps after setting aside a certain amount for Staci, she could look for a CD that she can afford with the leftover money.)*

Situation 3

Carl has the opportunity to go rafting with a group from his church this weekend. But his friend Ramon has invited him to come over to his house that same Saturday. Ramon has just been saved a few weeks, but he lives with his grandmother, who is unsaved. Ramon told Carl that he really hopes the two of them can explain to his grandmother what the Lord has done in his life. Ramon is praying every day that his grandmother might be saved. Carl wants to help Ramon, but he thinks rafting sounds like a lot more fun.

➤ **What do you think Carl should do? Why?** *(Lead the students to understand that while there is nothing wrong with a rafting trip, a person's soul is much more important in the light of eternity. If Carl makes his choice based on which of the two activities is more important to God, he should choose helping Ramon witness to his grandmother.)*

➤ **What does it mean to "seek first the kingdom of God"?** *(to give our first priority to those things that will count for eternity; doing all that we can to bring souls into the kingdom of God)*

➤ **How much time does God want Christians to spend witnessing, praying, or reading their Bibles?** *(God doesn't expect Christians to spend all of their time doing these things, but He wants them to place their highest priority on doing things that count for eternity.)*

Explain that Christians need times of relaxation to keep their bodies healthy. Christians should pray and seek God's direction about the way they use their time.

➤ **What can you do this week to obey this command to seek first the kingdom of God?**

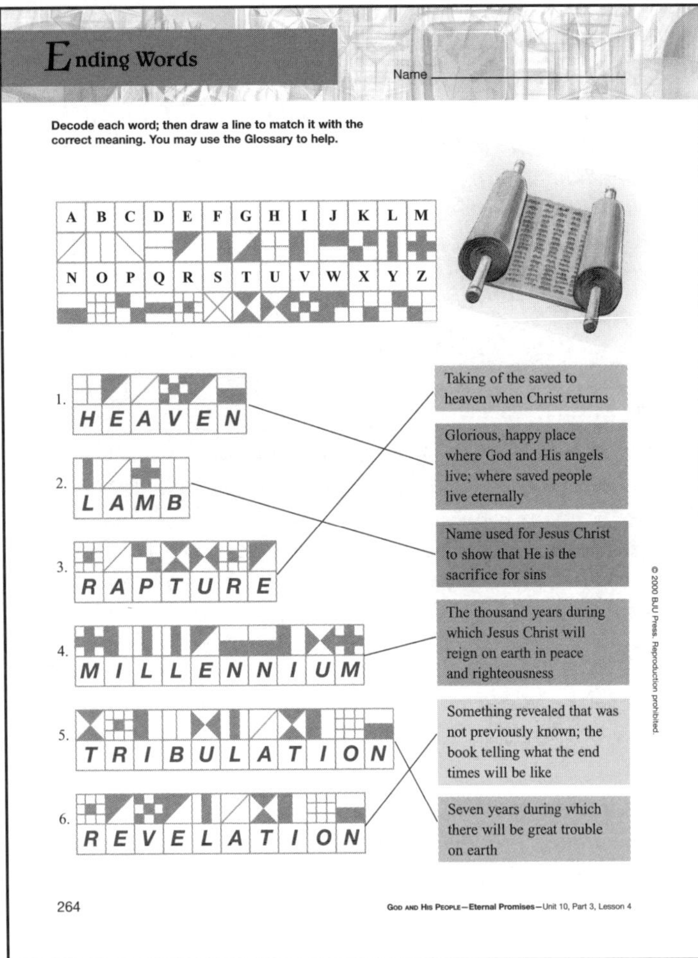
Ending Words

Name ____________

Decode each word; then draw a line to match it with the correct meaning. You may use the Glossary to help.

A B C D E F G H I J K L M

N O P Q R S T U V W X Y Z

1. HEAVEN
2. LAMB
3. RAPTURE
4. MILLENNIUM
5. TRIBULATION
6. REVELATION

Taking of the saved to heaven when Christ returns

Glorious, happy place where God and His angels live; where saved people live eternally

Name used for Jesus Christ to show that He is the sacrifice for sins

The thousand years during which Jesus Christ will reign on earth in peace and righteousness

Something revealed that was not previously known; the book telling what the end times will be like

Seven years during which there will be great trouble on earth

Worktext page 264

Identify definitions of words about the end times.

Going Beyond

Enrichment

Guide a creative writing activity. Encourage the students to write another situation in which a boy or girl has to choose whether to seek first the kingdom of God. As time permits, allow any students who wish to read their situations to the class to do so.

Jesus Christ Gives Life Eternal

Unit 10, Part 4

Preview

Doctrines

- God is love (I John 4:8)—Lesson 1
- God is unchanging (immutable) (James 1:17)—Lesson 1
- God is faithful (I Corinthians 1:9)—Lesson 1
- God is righteous (Psalm 145:17)—Lesson 1
- There will be a new heaven and a new earth (Isaiah 65:17)—Lesson 3

Skills and Applications

- Learn I John 5:11-13
- Locate information in Scripture
- Gain an understanding of the sequence of the end times
- Identify promises of God
- Realize the need to be ready to meet God
- Understand how to have assurance of salvation
- Apply Bible knowledge to everyday life

Lesson 1

Preparation of Materials

Write the following Scripture references for display: **John 3:16; I John 2:25; I John 5:11-12; I John 4:8-9; Ephesians 2:8; I John 2:3-5; I John 2:9-10; I John 5:13; Psalm 16:11;** and **Hebrews 13:8.**

Background Information

Promises of God—*God's Word is full of promises. When God makes a promise, He is certain to fulfill it, because His promises are based on His character. God is omnipotent and immutable. Sending Jesus Christ into the world to redeem lost sinners was the fulfillment of God's centuries-old promise to the Jews that a Messiah would come to them. Through Christ, God made it possible for Gentiles also to be "partakers of his promise in Christ by the gospel" (Ephesians 3:6). Believers can know for certain, just as if God had said it aloud to them, that He will keep His promises (II Corinthians 1:20). God's ability to keep His promises brings Him glory; therefore, Christians can be assured that He will do exactly what He says.*

Letter of I John—*John did not address this letter to any particular church; it was probably circulated to many different congregations. False teachers had entered the church, claiming that Jesus was not really God in human form and trying to change God's Word. As these teachers spread their heresies, questions and doubts formed in the minds of believers. An eyewitness of Christ's life and ministry, John wrote this letter to disprove the false teachings from his perspective as one who knew and believed all of Christ's claims. John reminded the believers that the message of the gospel is from the beginning of time because it is of God, and "eternal life" refers to the very character of the life that is of God. John also stressed the importance of assurance of salvation for Christians, and throughout the letter he gives doubting readers many ways to "test" their lives for evidences that they truly possess eternal life in Christ.*

Introducing the Bible Study

Guide a discussion. Encourage the students to answer the first two questions honestly in their hearts.

➤ **Do you ever think, "How can I know that I am really on my way to heaven?"**

➤ **Do you ever doubt your salvation?**

➤ **Have you ever heard or read an explanation of how to get to heaven that did not agree with what God's Word says?** Allow students to tell about these false ideas.

Bible Study

Study God's promise of eternal life. Direct the students' attention to the list of references. Assign each student or group of students a Scripture passage to locate and read silently. Call on the student to read the passage aloud; then discuss the question that follows.

- **John 3:16; I John 2:25—What has God promised?** *(eternal life to all who accept Christ)*

  Eternal life is the greatest promise ever given, and God is the greatest keeper of promises. God alone has the authority to promise eternal life.

- **I John 5:11-12—Where does this eternal life come from?** *(It is in God's Son.)*

God has the power to fulfill His promise because He Himself is life.

- **I John 4:8-9—What attribute of God do these verses show?** *(God is love.)*

Christians can trust God to keep His promise because He loves them and desires them to be with Him. Love is the basis of His promise of eternal life—the love that sent His own Son to die for our sins.

- **Ephesians 2:8—By what means does God save us, or give us eternal life?** *(grace)*

Our eternal life begins when we recognize that we are sinners and cannot save ourselves, when we confess our sins and accept God's Son as our Savior from sin. We immediately begin to live in God's presence.

- **I John 2:3-5—What do these verses say that a saved person, a person with eternal life, will not make a habit of doing?** *(sinning)*

One of the ways we can tell that we are truly saved is that we will not continually commit sin. Because God is righteous, He cannot have fellowship with sin. Sin hurts our fellowship with God. God's Spirit will convict us when we have sinned. A saved person who does sin should confess that sin to God, and Christ's blood will cleanse him from it. God will be faithful to cleanse us each time we ask Him.

- **I John 2:9-10—What do these verses say that a person with eternal life will do?** *(love his brother)*

Brother is another word for a fellow Christian. If we are truly saved, we will have a love for other Christians and a desire to fellowship with them.

- **I John 5:13—Why did John write about these things?** *(so that we would know we have eternal life)*

God wants true believers to be sure of their salvation. He does not want them to be doubtful and sad but to have confidence that they possess eternal life. If we doubt whether we have truly been saved, we should examine our lives for evidence that we are true Christians. Confessing sin and loving other Christians are two things that will characterize the life of a true Christian.

- **Psalm 16:11—How should living in God's presence and having the assurance of eternal life make us feel?** *(joyful, happy)*

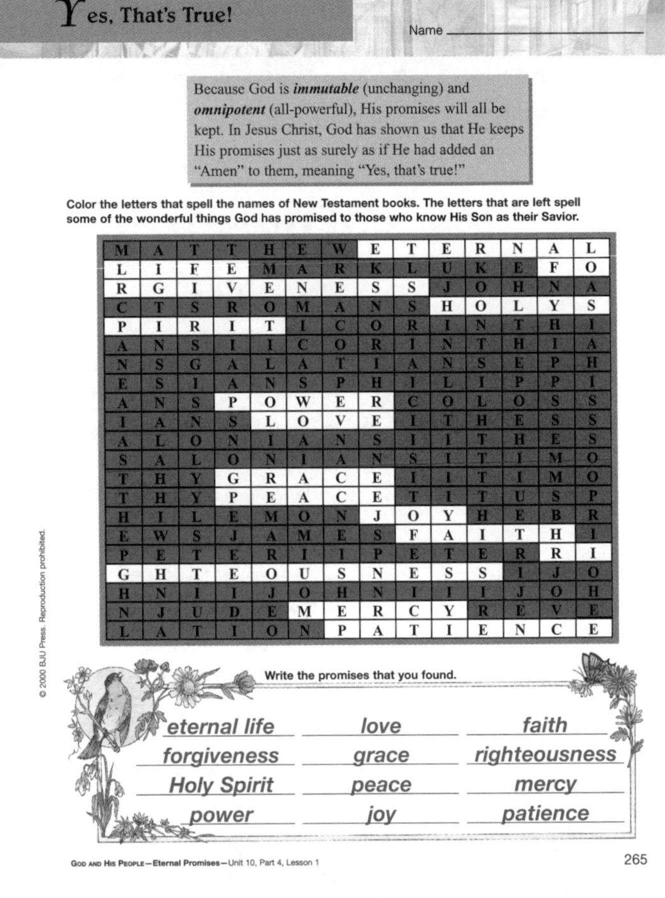

Yes, That's True!

Name ____________

Because God is ***immutable*** (unchanging) and ***omnipotent*** (all-powerful), His promises will all be kept. In Jesus Christ, God has shown us that He keeps His promises just as surely as if He had added an "Amen" to them, meaning "Yes, that's true!"

Color the letters that spell the names of New Testament books. The letters that are left spell some of the wonderful things God has promised to those who know His Son as their Savior.

M	A	T	T	H	E	W	E	T	E	R	N	A	L
L	I	F	E	M	A	R	K	L	U	K	E	F	O
R	G	I	V	E	N	E	S	S	J	O	H	N	A
C	T	S	R	O	M	A	N	S	H	O	L	Y	S
P	I	R	I	T	I	C	O	R	I	N	T	H	I
A	N	S	I	I	C	O	R	I	N	T	H	I	A
N	S	G	A	L	A	T	I	A	N	S	E	P	H
E	S	I	A	N	S	P	H	I	L	I	P	P	I
A	N	S	P	O	W	E	R	C	O	L	O	S	S
I	A	N	S	L	O	V	E	I	T	H	E	S	S
A	L	O	N	I	A	N	S	I	I	T	H	E	S
S	A	L	O	N	I	A	N	S	I	T	I	M	O
T	H	Y	G	R	A	C	E	I	I	T	I	M	O
T	H	Y	P	E	A	C	E	T	I	T	U	S	P
H	I	L	E	M	O	N	J	O	Y	H	E	B	R
E	W	S	J	A	M	E	S	F	A	I	T	H	I
P	E	T	E	R	I	I	P	E	T	E	R	R	I
G	H	T	E	O	U	S	N	E	S	S	I	J	O
H	N	I	I	J	O	H	N	I	I	I	J	O	H
N	J	U	D	E	M	E	R	C	Y	R	E	V	E
L	A	T	I	O	N	P	A	T	I	E	N	C	E

Write the promises that you found.

eternal life	*love*	*faith*
forgiveness	*grace*	*righteousness*
Holy Spirit	*peace*	*mercy*
power	*joy*	*patience*

The promise of eternal life is not just for the future; it is for right now. Thinking about it each day will give Christians great joy.

- **Hebrews 13:8—What attribute of God does this verse show us?** *(He is immutable, unchanging.)*

Because the character of God never changes, His promises can never change. Because God is righteous and true, we can depend upon Him to keep His promise of eternal life. This basic teaching of salvation by faith has existed from the beginning, and it will not change because it is from God.

➤ **Christians, do you remember when you believed God's promise of eternal life and accepted His Son as your personal Savior?** Allow students to share their testimonies.

➤ **Have you ever quoted John 3:16 to someone so that he would know about God's great promise?** Give opportunities for responses. Emphasize that it is God's plan for us to share the gospel of Jesus Christ.

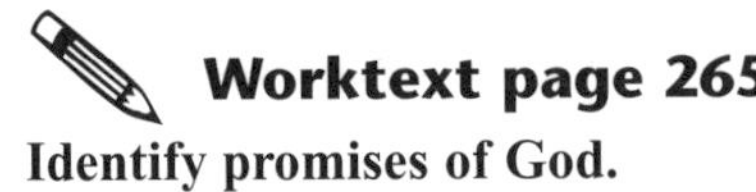

Worktext page 265

Identify promises of God.

Memory Verses—I John 5:11-13

Principle: God has given us the assurance of salvation in His Word. Locate **I John 5:11-13** and read it aloud as the students read silently. Direct the students to highlight the verses in their Bibles (optional) and to mark the location with the Unit 10 Bookmark.

- ➤ **What has God recorded, or written, in His Word?** *(that God has given us eternal life in His Son)*
- ➤ **When do we receive this eternal life?** *(when we accept God's Son as our Savior)*
- ➤ **Can we rely on the promises of God? Why?** *(Yes. God is true, perfectly holy, and unchanging.)*
- ➤ **How do we know what God has promised to His children?** *(by reading what He has recorded in His Word)*
- ➤ **What is the condition to this promise?** *(We must believe that Jesus died for our sins and accept Him as our Savior. We must be born again. Christ has promised us His personal and eternal protection.)*
- ➤ **How can we earn our salvation?** *(We can't; salvation is the gift of God [Romans 6:23].)*

Practice by reading the verses throughout the day.

Hymn: "It Is Well with My Soul"

Teach the fourth verse (Worktext page 286). Explain that the word *haste* means "hurry" and *trump* refers to "trumpet."

- ➤ **What event is the fourth verse describing?** *(the second coming)*

Play the recording and lead the singing of verses 1-4.

Lesson 2

Hymn: "It Is Well with My Soul"

Sing the hymn (Worktext page 286). Play the recording and lead in singing verses 1-4 together.

Introducing the Application Story

Discuss the unreliability of our feelings.

- ➤ **Do you ever have days when you don't "feel like" you are saved? What causes those feelings?** *(Answers will vary; elicit that such things as difficult circumstances, health problems, and unconfessed sin might cause us to feel separated from God.)*
- ➤ **What should we base our salvation on—our feelings or what God's Word teaches?** *(what God's Word teaches)*

Remind the students that Satan would like to defeat Christians by discouraging them about their relationship with God. Christians sometimes forget that they can come to God at *any* time for forgiveness or comfort, regardless of how they feel. God promises to hear and receive them. The following story reminds us that once we are saved, our relationship with God never changes, even when our circumstances or our feelings change.

Application Story

Read the following story to the students.

Mark It with a *P*

Charmaine opened the door of Number 22 Walnut Street and stepped out onto the porch. She smiled as she saw the mailman coming up the street. Her family had moved here only four days ago, but already Charmaine searched each day's mail for letters from her friends back in Ohio.

The mailman had just reached Number 20, the little white house next door. "Morning, Miss Sarah. Getting kind of cold out, isn't it?" he called to the lady in the white rocker.

Even from a distance, Charmaine could see Miss Sarah flash her bright smile. "Yes, yes, but then—the Lord always keeps His promises," the gray-haired lady said. "Right in Genesis. 'While the earth remaineth, seedtime and harvest, and cold and heat, and summer and winter, and day and night shall not cease.'"

"Yup. I'll be seeing you, Miss Sarah."

"Thanks for the mail, Sam. Oh, and when you get to the next house, please tell that little girl on the porch I'm expecting her for tea in five minutes. Just as soon as she runs in and tells her mother."

Four minutes later, Charmaine climbed Miss Sarah's porch and sat on the big wicker love seat next to the rocker. Miss Sarah handed her a cup of tea with lots of milk. "Here, have a cookie too, Charmaine."

Charmaine's hand stopped midway to the plate of cookies. She stared at Miss Sarah.

Miss Sarah chuckled. "Well, now, Charmaine, you needn't look so surprised that I know your name! This is your mother's hometown, you know. I taught your mother in Sunday school when she was just about your age. I've made it a point to keep up with my children—and their children."

Charmaine smiled. She munched a ginger cookie, trying to imagine what her mother had looked like when she was her age.

"Charmaine, I have a very important question I'd like to ask you—a question I've asked all my Sunday school children. Do you know Jesus Christ as your Savior?"

Charmaine looked down and brushed some crumbs off her hands. "Well, yes, I think I do," she said.

Miss Sarah peered at her over the top of her glasses. "You think?" she asked.

Charmaine hesitated. "Well, I asked Him to save me from my sins when I was six. But sometimes He seems so far away." Charmaine spoke quietly, almost afraid to say the words. "I wonder sometimes if I really know God at all."

Miss Sarah picked up the large Bible on the table between them. "Charmaine, when you asked God to save you, did you believe you were a sinner?"

"Yes, ma'am."

"And did you believe Christ died for your sins and rose again?"

Charmaine thought only a moment before nodding her head. "Yes, and I still believe that," she said.

"Well then, look here in my Bible. Read this verse to me. It's a promise, you know."

Charmaine leaned over to see the verse in Romans 10. Miss Sarah had marked a red *p* in the margin beside verse nine. (Read **Romans 10:9** to the students.)

"Good. Now let me read another verse to you."

As Miss Sarah turned the pages of her Bible, Charmaine caught glimpses of more red *p*'s on the pages.

"Ah, here it is. John 6:37. (Read **John 6:37** to the students.) That's a promise too. And for those times when God seems far away, how about this one—Hebrews 13:5? (Read **Hebrews 13:5** to the students.)

"Miss Sarah, what are all those red *p*'s for in your Bible? Does that stand for promise?"

"Well, not exactly. It stands for *proved.* Whenever I see one of God's promises worked out in my own life, I mark it with a *p*. You might try it, Charmaine."

Charmaine walked home with a light step. She peeked into the mailbox. No letters from Ohio. She sighed.

She looked over at the house next door. *But God did give me a new friend today,* she thought. *What was it Miss Sarah had read? "I will never leave thee nor forsake thee."*

"I'm going to go find that in my Bible," Charmaine said out loud, "and mark it with a *p*." She glanced over and waved at Miss Sarah. The little gray-haired lady waved back.

➤ **Why was Charmaine unsure that she really knew Christ?** *(God seemed far away; being in a new place far from her friends made her feel lonely.)*

➤ **What did the red *p*'s in Miss Sarah's Bible stand for?** *("proved"; God had worked out those promises in her life.)*

➤ **What caused Charmaine to feel sad for a moment when she got home?** *(She didn't receive any letters from her friends in Ohio.)*

➤ **How did God fulfill a promise in her life that day?** *(He gave her Miss Sarah as a friend—a reminder to Charmaine that He would never leave her.)*

➤ **What promises has God fulfilled in your own life?** *(Answers will vary.)*

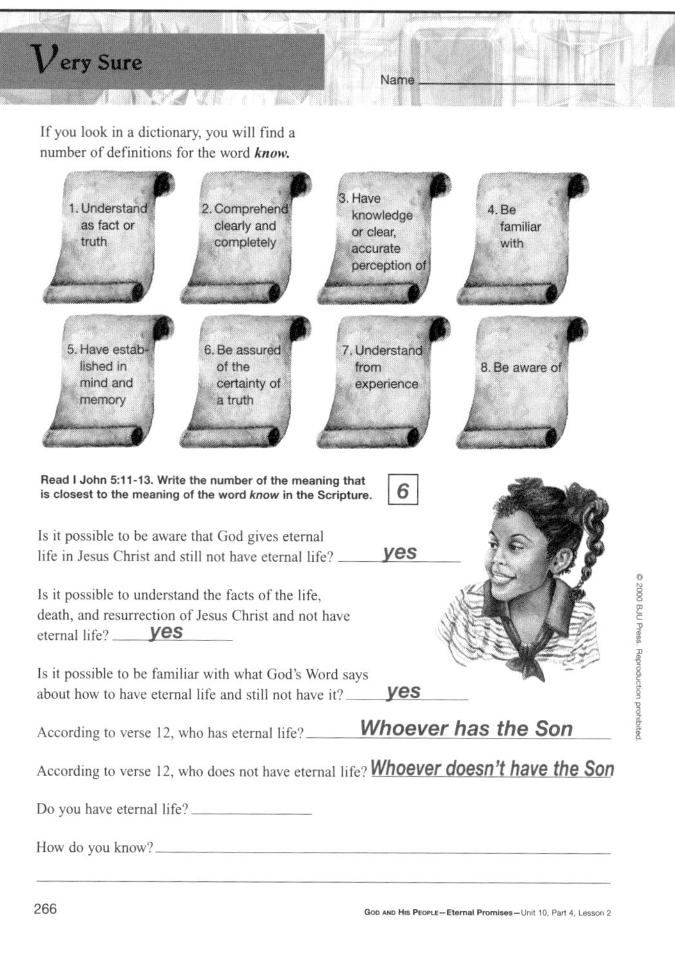

Very Sure

Name____________________

If you look in a dictionary, you will find a number of definitions for the word ***know.***

1. Understand as fact or truth
2. Comprehend clearly and completely
3. Have knowledge or clear, accurate perception of
4. Be familiar with
5. Have established in mind and memory
6. Be assured of the certainty of a truth
7. Understand from experience
8. Be aware of

Read I John 5:11-13. Write the number of the meaning that is closest to the meaning of the word *know* in the Scripture. 6

Is it possible to be aware that God gives eternal life in Jesus Christ and still not have eternal life? *yes*

Is it possible to understand the facts of the life, death, and resurrection of Jesus Christ and not have eternal life? *yes*

Is it possible to be familiar with what God's Word says about how to have eternal life and still not have it? *yes*

According to verse 12, who has eternal life? *Whoever has the Son*

According to verse 12, who does not have eternal life? *Whoever doesn't have the Son*

Do you have eternal life?____________

How do you know?________________________________

266 GOD AND HIS PEOPLE—Eternal Promises—Unit 10, Part 4, Lesson 2

Memory Verses—I John 5:11-13

Practice the memory verses. Locate and read **I John 5:11-13** aloud as the students read the verses silently. Discuss assurance of salvation.

- ➤ **What does God want us to know?** *(that we have eternal life)*
- ➤ **What kind of people have eternal life?** *(those who believe on the name of the Son of God)*
- ➤ **What do we need to believe God's Son has done for us to have eternal life?** *(We need to believe that Christ died to pay the price for our sin and to reconcile us to God and that He rose from the dead to give us eternal life.)*

Choose students to read the verses aloud, emphasizing the words *believe* and *know.*

Worktext page 266

Develop an understanding of the memory verses.

Lesson 3

Memory Verses—I John 5:11-13

Practice the memory verses. Write the memory verses on an erasable board, leaving blank spaces where the words *believe* and *know* should be. Choose a student to say the verses aloud, filling in the blanks. Erase several more key words from the verse and choose another student to say the verses. Repeat this process until the verse has been entirely erased and the students can say the verses from memory.

Hymn: "It Is Well with My Soul"

Sing the hymn (Worktext page 286). Read the words to all four verses aloud as a poem.

- ➤ **Do you think the writer of this hymn was going through a sorrowful time or a peaceful time when he wrote the words?** *(Accept any answer.)*

Play the recording of the entire hymn and lead in singing it together.

Hymn History Story

Read the following story based on the writing of "It Is Well with My Soul."

It Is Well

Horatio Spafford stood on the deck of the ship, watching the rise and fall of the gray waves. Soon, the captain had said, they would reach the spot he was looking for.

Mr. Spafford's thoughts went back to the events of several days ago. He had been looking over some legal documents in his office when a man brought him the news. "Mr. Spafford, word has reached us that the *Ville du Havre* was struck by another ship the very day it sailed. We haven't heard specific reports about any of the passengers, but—it is likely all were lost." The man shuffled his feet awkwardly. "I know your family was aboard, and I thought you'd want to . . ." His voice trailed off. "I'm terribly sorry, sir."

Mr. Spafford rose from his chair. "My wife," he murmured. "My wife and my four daughters!" He turned his face to the window. "O dear God, if they're still alive—please help them."

Mr. Spafford had booked passage for his wife and daughters to sail to Europe aboard the *Ville du Havre.* They were planning to help his friend the Reverend D. L. Moody in his evangelistic campaign, and Mr. Spafford intended to join them in Europe when his business matters were finished.

Later, when a friend dined with Mr. Spafford in his home, a knock came at the door, Mr. Spafford rose from the table. "Henry, if you'll excuse me."

A servant stood nervously at the door. "A cablegram for you, sir—from Wales."

Mr. Spafford's hands shook as he took the cablegram. A lump filled his throat as he read the two words from his wife: "Saved alone."

"Father, thank you that my wife is safe," he whispered.

Mr. Spafford's friend appeared in the doorway. "Good news, Horatio?" he asked.

"My wife is safe, Henry," said Mr. Spafford.

"And the girls?"

Mr. Spafford waited a moment before speaking. "Lost at sea." He looked up. "But not eternally lost, Henry. All four of my girls trusted Christ at Mr. Moody's meetings in Chicago."

Henry nodded and said nothing.

Mr. Spafford paced the floor a few times; then he turned to face his friend again. "Henry, I am glad to trust Christ when it costs me something."

Mr. Spafford's time of remembering the last few days was interrupted by the gentle touch of a hand on his shoulder. "Mr. Spafford, sir." The captain was still standing on the ship's deck beside him. His eyes were kind. "It was about here that the *Ville du Havre* sank."

"Thank you, sir."

The captain stood there a moment longer—then left Mr. Spafford alone with his thoughts.

Propping his elbows on the rail, Mr. Spafford lowered his face into his hands. He spoke out loud, his voice covered by the sounds of the sea. "Father, thank you that my wife is safe and that I'm on my way to meet her. Thank you that my daughters are in heaven and that I will see them again someday. Lord, it is well with my soul."

Shortly afterward, Mr. Spafford wrote four stanzas of a poem, calling it by that title: "It Is Well with My Soul." The words were set to music by Philip P. Bliss, and the hymn has remained a favorite for over a century.

➤ **Why was the news about the sinking of the *Ville du Havre* shocking to Mr. Spafford?** *(His wife and four daughters were aboard.)*

➤ **Where had his family been going aboard the ship?** *(to Europe to help in Moody's campaign)*

Singing with Understanding

"It Is Well with My Soul" (v. 4)

Name ____________

Horatio G. Spafford

(1828-1888)

Horatio Spafford and his wife and four young daughters were scheduled to sail for France. Mr. Spafford was delayed by business, so his family went on ahead of him. On November 22, 1873, the ship carrying Spafford's wife and children collided with a large sailing vessel and sank. Mrs. Spafford was rescued, but all four daughters perished along with most of the other passengers. When Mr. Spafford received his wife's message that read "Saved alone," he crossed the Atlantic to comfort her. When the ship on which he was traveling passed over the place where the tragedy had occurred, he stood silently on deck for a few moments and then went to his cabin and wrote a poem, "It Is Well with My Soul." Three years later Philip P. Bliss, an evangelistic singer, set the poem to music and sang it publicly for the first time at Farwell Hall in Chicago.

Read the Scriptures. Draw a line to match each group of words from the hymn with the correct Scripture reference.

D	1. "haste the day" (come quickly)	**A. I Corinthians 13:12**
A	2. "faith shall be sight"	**B. I Corinthians 15:52**
C	3. "clouds be rolled back as a scroll"	**C. Revelation 6:14**
B	4. "trump shall resound"	**D. Revelation 22:20**

Do you know someone who praises God and tells others of His goodness even though he has had great trouble or sorrow in his life? Write about that person here.

____

____

____

____

➤ **What message came from Mr. Spafford's wife a few days later?** *("saved alone")*

➤ **What comforted Mr. Spafford in the death of his daughters?** *(They were not eternally lost; they had been saved, and he would see them in heaven.)*

➤ **What did Mr. Spafford say he was glad to do after hearing the news?** *(trust Christ when it cost him something)*

➤ **What was Mr. Spafford's attitude toward God when the ship passed over the spot where the *Ville du Havre* had sunk?** *("It is well with my soul"; he had peace because he was trusting God to do what was best.)*

➤ **How can Christians be comforted when they experience hurtful situations and problems?** *(Possible answers include by having peace from God and by knowing that He is in control of all things.)*

Worktext page 267

Singing with understanding, verse 4.

Lesson 4

 **Hymn: "It Is Well with My Soul"**

Sing the hymn. Divide the students into four groups, allowing each group to sing a verse of the hymn.

 **Memory Verses—I John 5:11-13**

Practice the memory verses. Choose volunteers to say **I John 5:11-13** from memory.

Background Information

River of Life—*This river flowing from the throne of God is also described in Ezekiel 47 and referred to in Psalm 46:4-5. The Lord Jesus Himself is the water of life (John 4:14).*

Tree of Life—*The tree of life in the Garden of Eden represented eternal life (Genesis 3:22, 24). When Adam and Eve ate the forbidden fruit from the tree of the knowledge of good and evil, they forfeited the privilege of eating from the tree of life. After they sinned, God drove them out of the garden and set the cherubim with a flaming sword to guard the way to the tree of life. It is only through faith in the death and resurrection of God's Son that man can be restored to fellowship with God.*

Alpha and Omega—*Christ refers to Himself as Alpha and Omega (Revelation 22:13). Alpha is the name for the first letter in the Greek alphabet, and Omega is the name of the last letter. Jesus asserts that He is God from before the beginning, the absolute source of all truth, the God of Creation and all history. He is and will be the eternal God.*

Root and Offspring of David—*The Lord introduces Himself by His personal name, Jesus, and also by His title in connection with Israel—"root," meaning He was David's Creator, that David sprang from Him; and "offspring," meaning that the Lord was born to a daughter of David in the family of Judah (Revelation 22:16).*

Introducing the Bible Account

Discuss heaven.

➤ **Have you ever heard someone say, "Oh, that sounds heavenly!" or "That would be paradise"? What do they mean?** *(They are describing a thing, an event, or a person as very desirable.)*

Tell the students that in the last two chapters of Revelation, John describes a place to be greatly desired—heaven, the true paradise that awaits Christians. John calls it "the holy city." Because God will be there, no sin can be there. Those whose names are written in the Lamb's Book of Life will live there forever with their God.

Bible Account

Read the following Bible account or read Revelation 21.

God's Promise of an Eternal Home

John describes heaven as the city of God, or the New Jerusalem. The city, as John saw it in his vision, has walls of jasper and twelve gates of pearl. The foundations of the walls are decorated with many precious stones. The twelve gates are inscribed with the names of the twelve Old Testament patriarchs, and the twelve foundations are inscribed with the names of the New Testament apostles. The streets are pure gold. No temple will be needed there because the Lord Himself will be the temple.

John saw in this city a pure river of life coming out of the throne on which God the Father and God the Son sit. This crystal clear water, a symbol of God's holiness and purity, is a reminder of the presence of God in the Holy City. It will be part of the New Jerusalem in the new earth. It will flow in the middle of a great street paved with gold. This great river will give life wherever it flows.

The Lord showed John that God's curse on Adam in the Garden of Eden and on all mankind would no longer exist in this city (Genesis 3:17-19). Jesus Christ removed that curse of sin by His death on the cross.

The city that John saw must have been filled with bright light, for John writes that there will be no need for artificial light in heaven. The glory of God and the Lamb are all the light the city will need. John writes that the saints—those who have accepted Jesus Christ God's Son as Savior from sin—will rule with God in this bright city forever and ever. Can you imagine what a great joy it will be for those who are saved to serve the Lord throughout eternity?

John was so overcome with what he heard and saw that he fell down to worship the angel messenger. The angel rebuked him and said that angels are not to be worshiped because they are God's servants, just as people are. "Worship God," the angel said.

We often consider the last words of a person we love to be very important. How much more important are the last words of God in the Bible! The angel left John with one last message from God. This message to us includes four things:

(1) **A final assurance** is given to the saved that the Lord Jesus will come quickly, bringing rewards for those who have served Him. "Behold, I come quickly" is repeated three times (Revelation 22:7, 12, 20). This phrase sums up the theme of Revelation—the promise of Christ's return. We will be happy if we read and meditate on these things which are to come and if we consider this book's promises and warnings.

(2) **A final invitation** is given for the unsaved to come to Him for salvation. Some people will hear the words of this prophecy and continue to live wickedly. This group of people are the unsaved—those who have not accepted Christ as their Savior. Others will hear, repent, and live for God. This group of people are the saved, those who have been set apart by God's redemption and have had their robes washed in the blood of the Lamb. There will be only these two types of people—the saved and the unsaved—until the Lord comes.

(3) **A final warning** is given not to tamper with the revelation of God in this book. God warns of punishments for those who do: plagues to those who add to the book and eternity in hell for those who take away from the words of this prophecy.

(4) **God's final promise,** "I am coming quickly." John closes with a prayer, "Amen, even so, come, Lord Jesus." All Christians should pray this prayer with John.

➤ **What has God promised Christians besides eternal life if they believe on His Son?** *(an eternal home)*

➤ **Who is called the water of life in the New Testament?** *(Jesus Christ)* Share the background information about the river of life.

➤ **Where do we first read about the tree of life in the Bible?** *(Genesis)* Share the background information about the tree of life.

➤ **Who does the Book of Revelation tell us is the tree of life?** *(the Lord Jesus Christ)*

➤ **What is the *final assurance* and also the theme of the Book of Revelation?** *(Jesus Christ will come again.)*

➤ **To whom is a *final invitation* given?** *(to the unsaved)*

➤ **What is the *final warning* of the book?** *(not to add to or subtract from what is written in the book)*

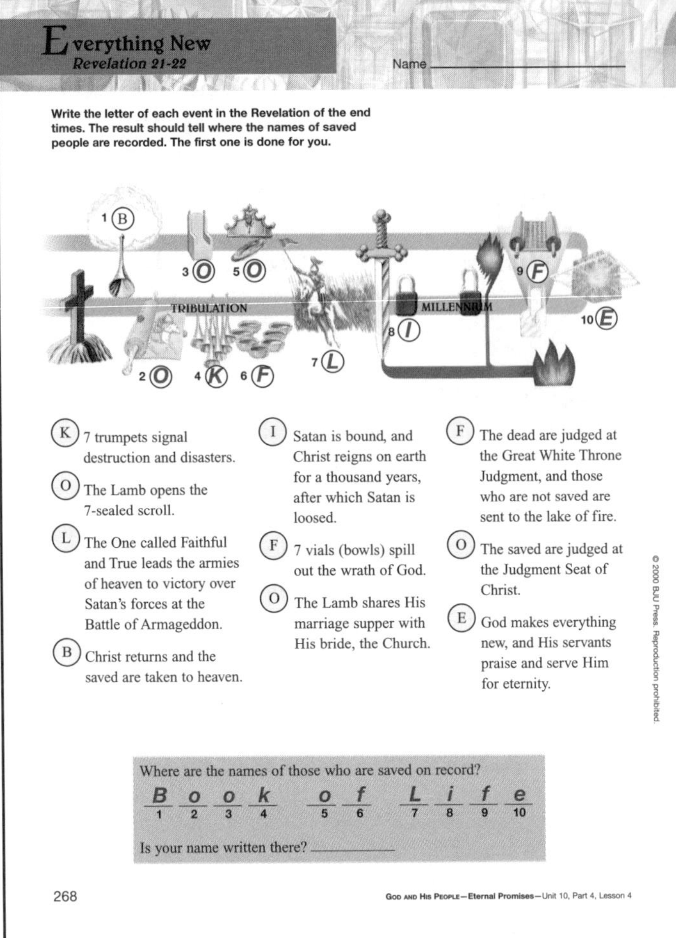

Everything New
Revelation 21-22

Name ____________

Write the letter of each event in the Revelation of the end times. The result should tell where the names of saved people are recorded. The first one is done for you.

(K) 7 trumpets signal destruction and disasters.

(O) The Lamb opens the 7-sealed scroll.

(L) The One called Faithful and True leads the armies of heaven to victory over Satan's forces at the Battle of Armageddon.

(B) Christ returns and the saved are taken to heaven.

(I) Satan is bound, and Christ reigns on earth for a thousand years, after which Satan is loosed.

(F) 7 vials (bowls) spill out the wrath of God.

(O) The Lamb shares His marriage supper with His bride, the Church.

(F) The dead are judged at the Great White Throne Judgment, and those who are not saved are sent to the lake of fire.

(O) The saved are judged at the Judgment Seat of Christ.

(E) God makes everything new, and His servants praise and serve Him for eternity.

Where are the names of those who are saved on record?

B o o k   o f   L i f e
(1 2 3 4   5 6   7 8 9 10)

Is your name written there? ____________

268 — God and His People—Eternal Promises—Unit 10, Part 4, Lesson 4

Read **Revelation 22:21** aloud and emphasize that it is only by God's grace in offering us salvation through Jesus Christ that Christians can enter the Holy City of God, where He promises that they shall reign with Him forever (Ephesians 2:8).

➤ **Do you have a saving faith in Jesus Christ so that you can pray with John, "Even so, come, Lord Jesus"?**

Worktext page 268

Sequence events of the end times. (*Note:* You may wish to assist the students in completing this page.)

Going Beyond

Materials

- Five slips of paper for each student (optional)
- 3" × 5" cards, tagboard, or construction paper (optional)
- A small file box, an old recipe box, an empty check box, or a small manila envelope for each student (optional)

Enrichment

Make a promise box. Distribute five slips of paper to each student. Instruct each student to find five of his favorite promises in the Bible and to write each promise with its reference on a slip of paper. Compile the promises, type them, and make photocopies on large sheets of paper. Distribute the copies so that each student has a complete collection of favorite promises from his classmates and himself. Instruct the students to cut the promises apart; to glue each one on an index card, tagboard, or construction paper; and to place it in the box.

Explain that this is a "promise box" from which they may draw a promise card each day. Encourage them to keep that card in a visible place throughout the day in order to memorize and remember that promise. Allow the students to decorate the outside of the boxes as desired.

One-on-One: After the student has compiled his own collection of favorite promises, encourage him to ask family members and friends to add their favorites to his collection.

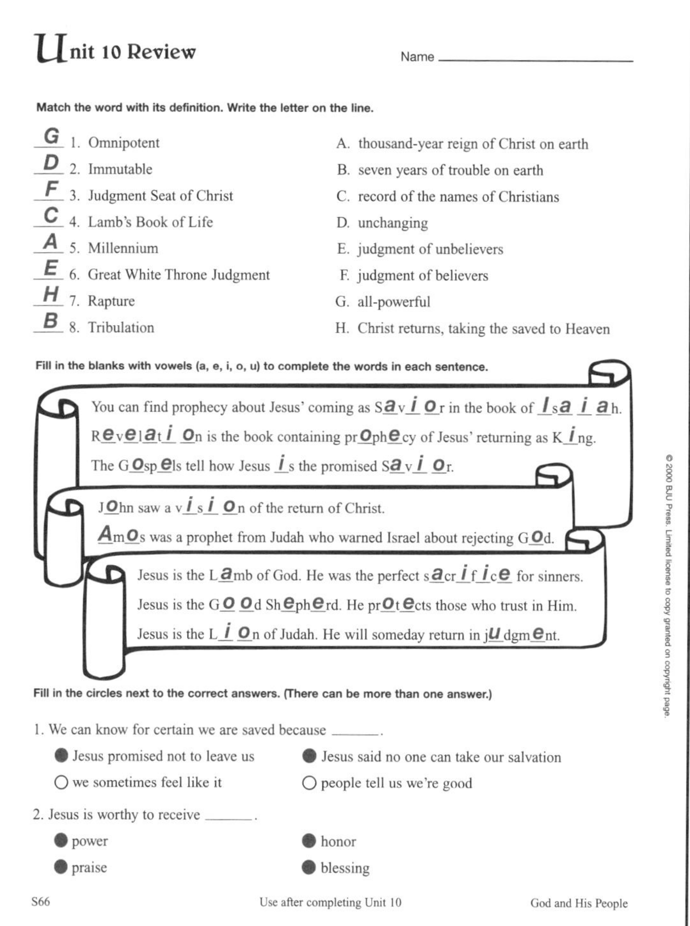

Unit 10 Review   Name ____________

Match the word with its definition. Write the letter on the line.

G 1. Omnipotent   A. thousand-year reign of Christ on earth
D 2. Immutable   B. seven years of trouble on earth
F 3. Judgment Seat of Christ   C. record of the names of Christians
C 4. Lamb's Book of Life   D. unchanging
A 5. Millennium   E. judgment of unbelievers
E 6. Great White Throne Judgment   F. judgment of believers
H 7. Rapture   G. all-powerful
B 8. Tribulation   H. Christ returns, taking the saved to Heaven

Fill in the blanks with vowels (a, e, i, o, u) to complete the words in each sentence.

You can find prophecy about Jesus' coming as Savior in the book of Isaiah.
Revelation is the book containing prophecy of Jesus' returning as King.
The Gospels tell how Jesus is the promised Savior.
John saw a vision of the return of Christ.
Amos was a prophet from Judah who warned Israel about rejecting God.
Jesus is the Lamb of God. He was the perfect sacrifice for sinners.
Jesus is the Good Shepherd. He protects those who trust in Him.
Jesus is the Lion of Judah. He will someday return in judgment.

Fill in the circles next to the correct answers. (There can be more than one answer.)

1. We can know for certain we are saved because ______.
   - ● Jesus promised not to leave us
   - ● Jesus said no one can take our salvation
   - ○ we sometimes feel like it
   - ○ people tell us we're good

2. Jesus is worthy to receive ______.
   - ● power
   - ● honor
   - ● praise
   - ● blessing

S66   Use after completing Unit 10   God and His People

Unit Review

Materials

- Copy of Supplement page S66, "Unit 10 Review," for each student

Guide a review of Unit 10. Review the people and events in preparation for the Unit 10 Test (optional).

Hymns

Students have a copy of the unit hymns and those songs indicated above with boldface type in the supplement of their worktext.

*Permission is granted for the teacher to make a photocopy for each student in the class.
**Permission is granted for the teacher to make one overhead transparency for classroom use.

I Sing the Mighty Power of God

Isaac Watts

From *Gesangbuch der Herzogl*,
Württemberg, 1784

O God, Our Help in Ages Past

From Psalm 90
Isaac Watts

Ascribed to William Croft
"Supplement to the New Version," 1708

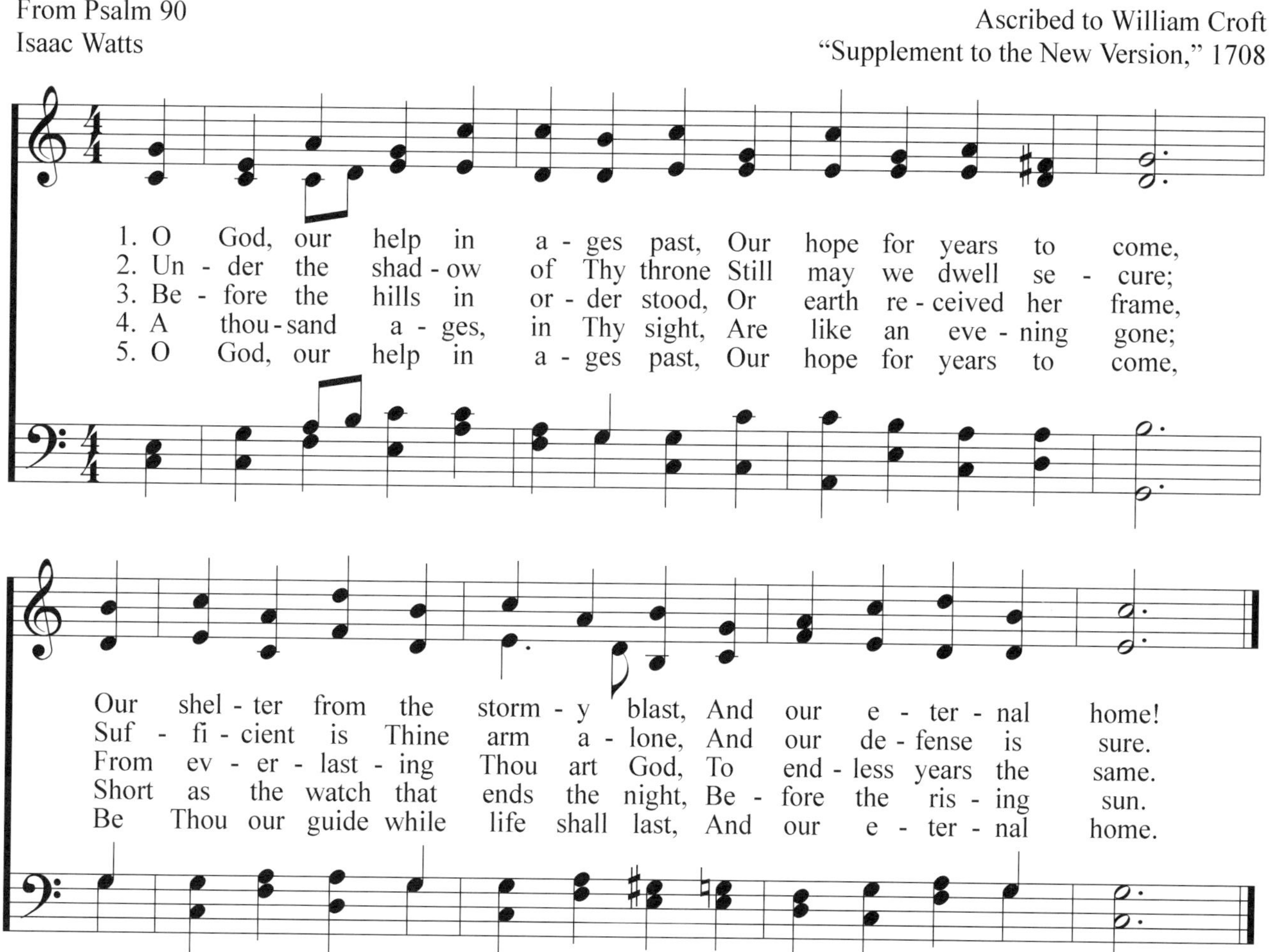

With God All Things Are Possible

ear - nest-ly seek shall be found; If we but ask in prayer, be-liev-ing, He will
bless; For He who sees the spar - row fall to the
ground Shall sure - ly give to us, His chil-dren, what is best.

Break Thou the Bread of Life

Mary Ann Lathbury

William F. Sherwin

Take Time to Be Holy

Be Thou My Vision

Ancient Irish
Trans. by Mary E. Byrne
Versed by Eleanor H. Hull

Traditional Irish melody

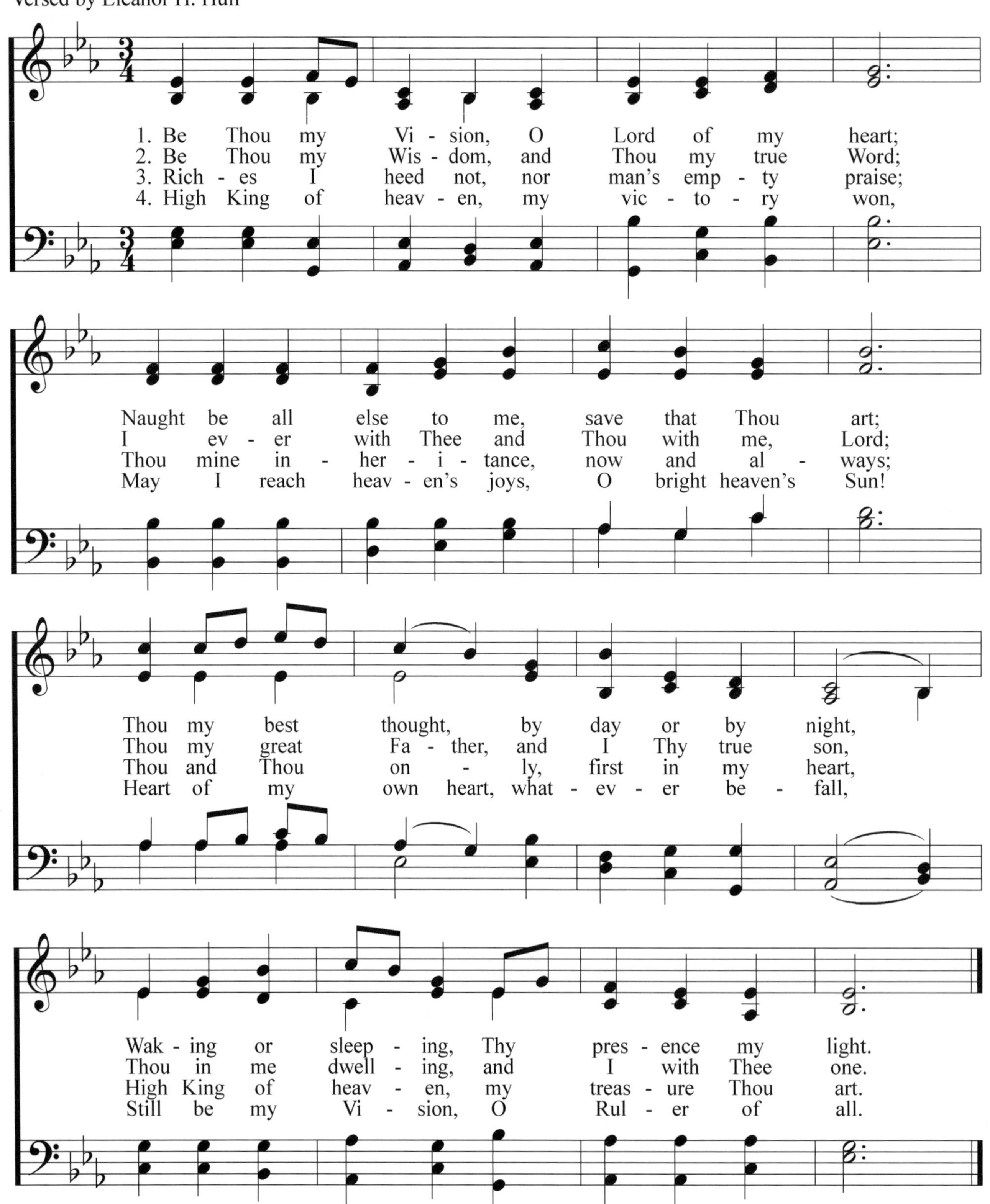

I Would Be True

Howard A. Walter

Joseph Yates Peek

Great Is Thy Faithfulness

Thomas O. Chisholm

William M. Runyan

GREAT IS THY FAITHFULNESS
Words: Thomas O. Chisholm
Music: William M. Runyan

Jesus Never Fails

There's a Song in the Air!

Josiah G. Holland

Karl P. Harrington

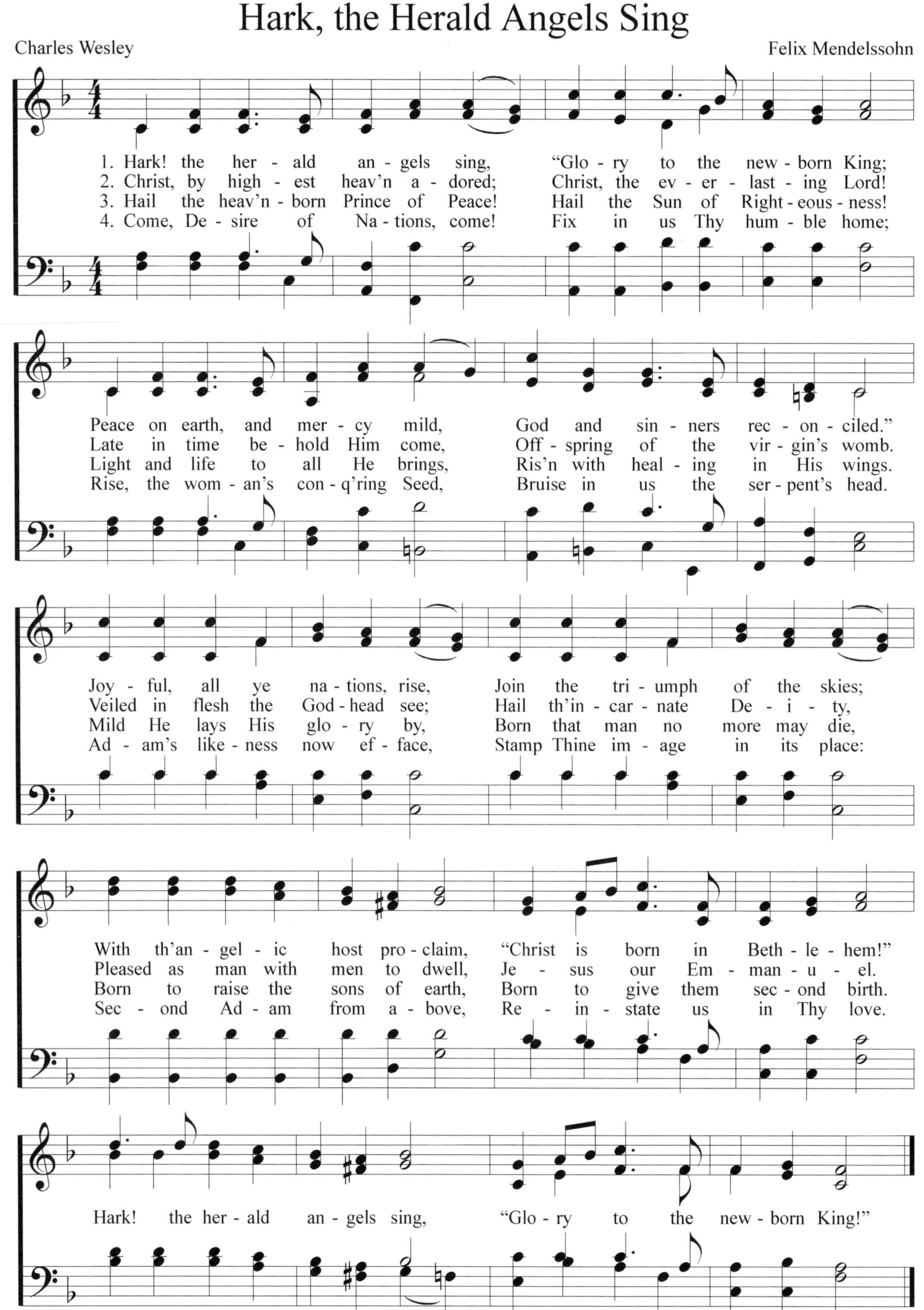
Hark, the Herald Angels Sing
Charles Wesley
Felix Mendelssohn
1. Hark! the her - ald an - gels sing, "Glo - ry to the new - born King;
2. Christ, by high - est heav'n a - dored; Christ, the ev - er - last - ing Lord!
3. Hail the heav'n - born Prince of Peace! Hail the Sun of Right - eous - ness!
4. Come, De - sire of Na - tions, come! Fix in us Thy hum - ble home;
Peace on earth, and mer - cy mild, God and sin - ners rec - on - ciled."
Late in time be - hold Him come, Off - spring of the vir - gin's womb.
Light and life to all He brings, Ris'n with heal - ing in His wings.
Rise, the wom - an's con - q'ring Seed, Bruise in us the ser - pent's head.
Joy - ful, all ye na - tions, rise, Join the tri - umph of the skies;
Veiled in flesh the God - head see; Hail th'in - car - nate De - i - ty,
Mild He lays His glo - ry by, Born that man no more may die,
Ad - am's like - ness now ef - face, Stamp Thine im - age in its place:
With th'an - gel - ic host pro - claim, "Christ is born in Beth - le - hem!"
Pleased as man with men to dwell, Je - sus our Em - man - u - el.
Born to raise the sons of earth, Born to give them sec - ond birth.
Sec - ond Ad - am from a - bove, Re - in - state us in Thy love.
Hark! the her - ald an - gels sing, "Glo - ry to the new - born King!"

Channels Only

Mary E. Maxwell

Ada Rose Gibbs

Faith Is the Victory

Faith is the vic - to - ry! Faith is the vic - to - ry!
O glo - ri - ous vic - to - ry That o - ver - comes the world.

Complete in Thee

Aaron R. Wolfe
Refrain, James M. Gray

Talmadge J. Bittikofer

1. Com - plete in Thee! no work of mine May take, dear Lord, the place of Thine;
2. Com - plete in Thee! no more shall sin, Thy grace hath con - quered, reign with - in;
3. Com - plete in Thee—each want sup - plied, And no good thing to me de - nied;
4. Dear Sav - ior! when be - fore Thy bar All tribes and tongues as - sem - bled are,

Thy blood hath par - don bought for me, And I am now com - plete in Thee.
Thy voice shall bid the tempt - er flee, And I shall stand com - plete in Thee.
Since Thou my por - tion, Lord, wilt be, I ask no more, com - plete in Thee.
A - mong Thy cho - sen will I be, At Thy right hand, com - plete in Thee.

Yea, jus - ti - fied! O bless - ed thought! And sanc - ti - fied! Sal - va - tion wrought!

Thy blood hath par - don bought for me, And glo - ri - fied, I too, shall be!

Soldiers of Christ, Arise

Charles Wesley

George J. Elvey

Count Your Blessings

Count your bless-ings— name them one by one;
Count your bless-ings— see what God hath done;
Count your bless-ings— name them one by one;
Count your man - y bless-ings— see what God hath done.

The Journeys of Paul

The Lord sup - plies all that I need, Wher - ev - er I am sent.
And in His great, un - chang - ing love, I've learned to be con - tent.

Why Worry When You Can Pray?

John W. Peterson

John W. Peterson and
Alfred B. Smith

Jesus, Thou Joy of Loving Hearts

Bernard of Clairvaux
Trans. by Ray Palmer

Henry Baker

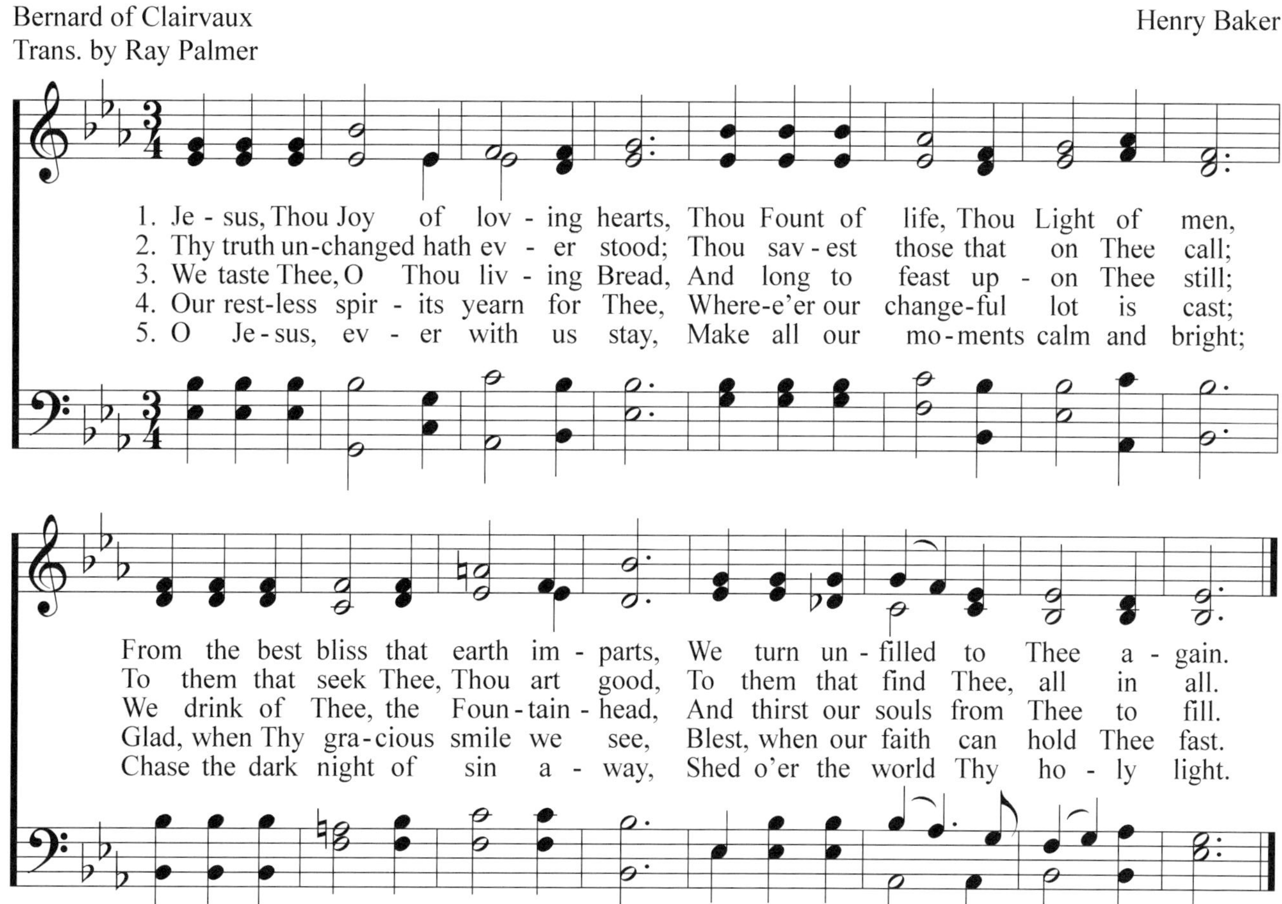

O to Be Like Thee!

deem - er, pure as Thou art! Come in Thy sweet - ness, come in Thy
full - ness; Stamp Thine own im - age deep on my heart.

Something for Thee

I Love Thee

Anonymous
Ingall's *Christian Harmony,* 1805
1. I love Thee, I love Thee, I love Thee, my Lord;
2. I'm hap - py, I'm hap - py, oh, won - drous ac - count!
3. O Je - sus, my Sav - ior, with Thee I am blest,
4. Oh, who's like my Sav - ior? He's Sa - lem's bright King;
I love Thee, my Sav - ior, I love Thee, my God:
My joys are im - mor - tal, I stand on the mount:
My life and sal - va - tion, my joy and my rest:
He smiles and He loves me and helps me to sing:
I love Thee, I love Thee, and that Thou dost know;
I gaze on my treas - ure and long to be there,
Thy name be my theme, and Thy love be my song;
I'll praise Him, I'll praise Him with notes loud and clear,
But how much I love Thee my ac - tions will show.
With Je - sus and an - gels and kin - dred so dear.
Thy grace shall in - spire both my heart and my tongue.
While riv - ers of pleas - ure my spir - it shall cheer.

It Is Finished

Easter's Dawning Light

Were You There

Traditional spiritual

Adapt. John W. Work Jr.
and Frederick J. Work

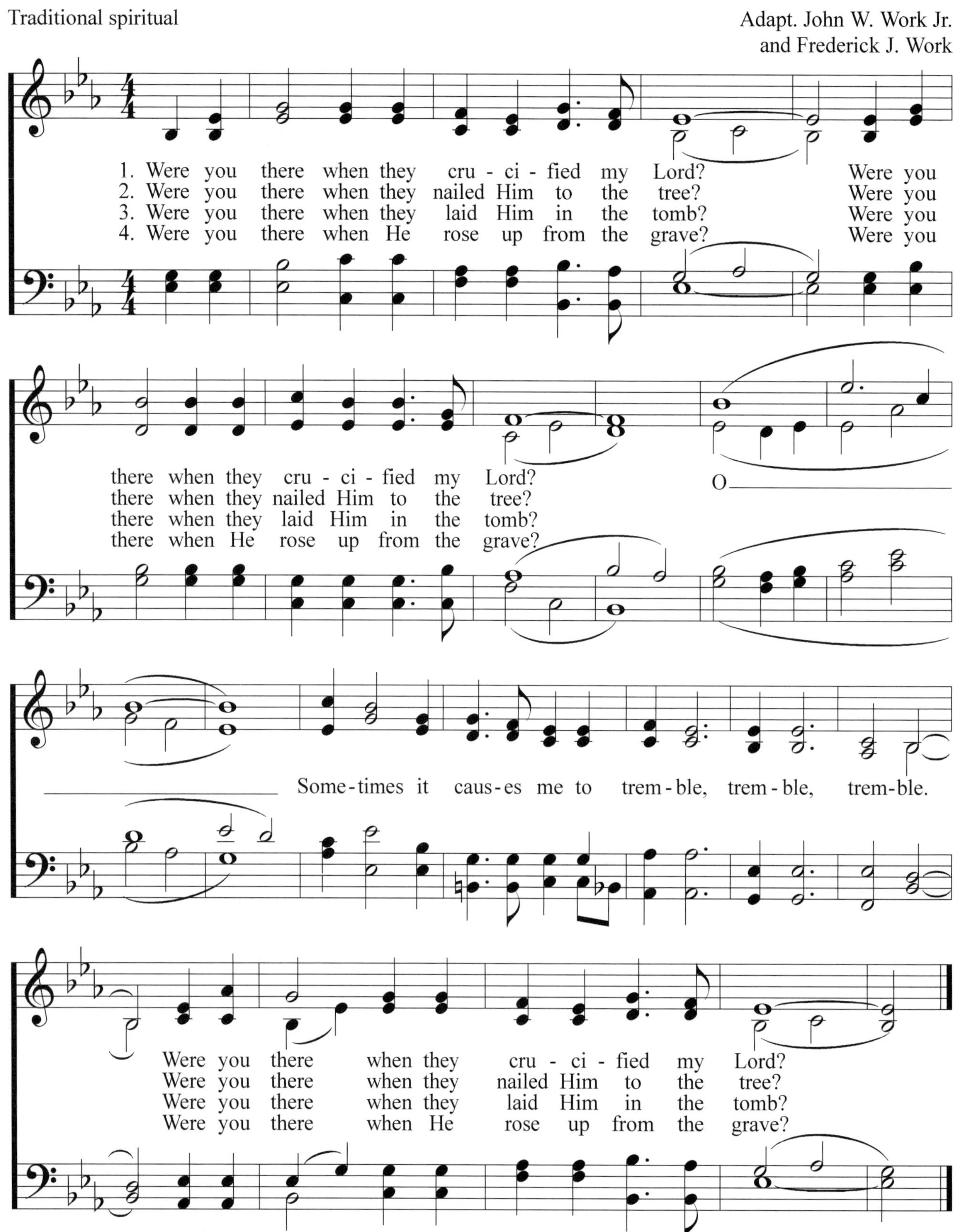

The Church's One Foundation

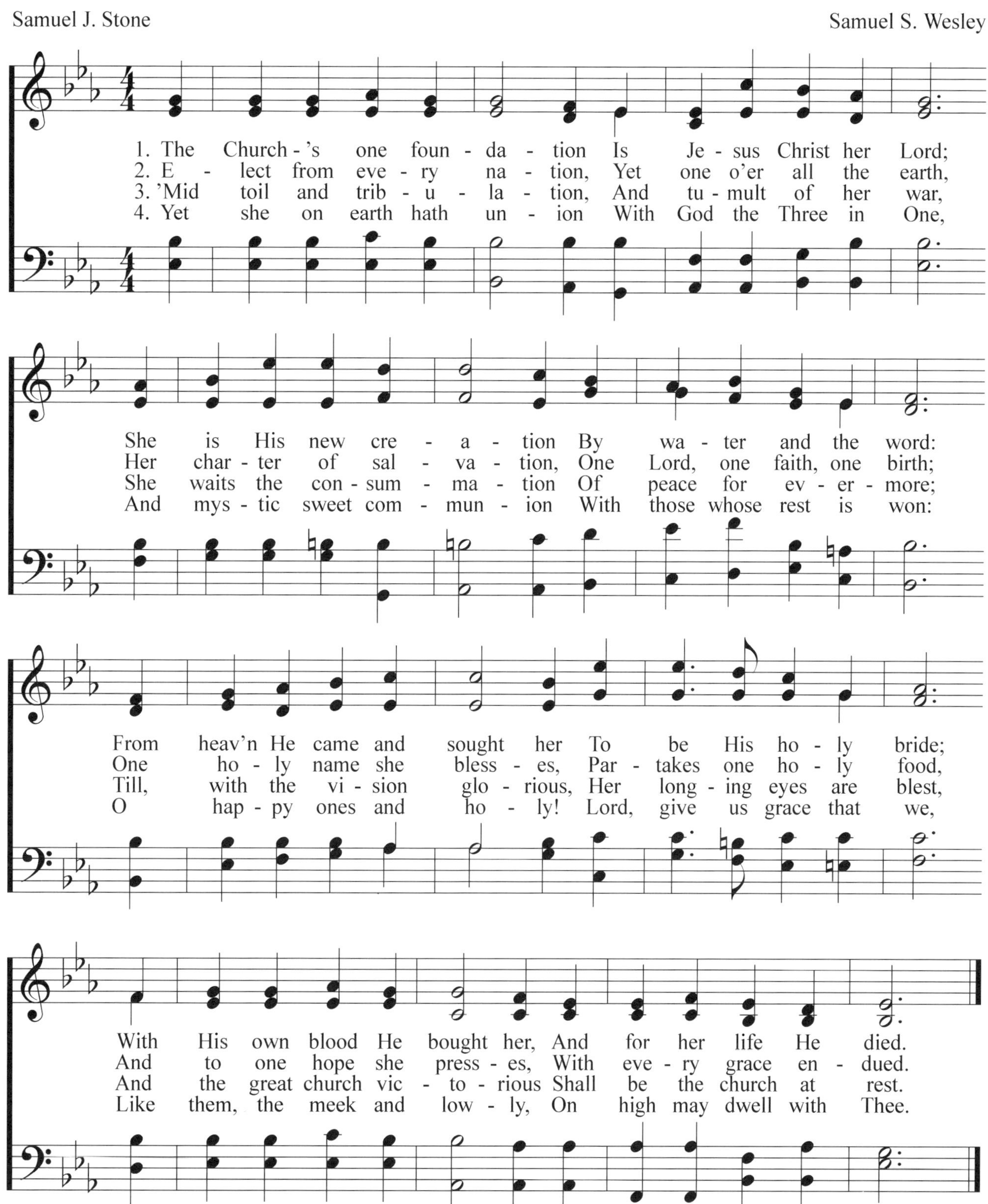

Onward, Christian Soldiers
Sabine Baring-Gould
Arthur S. Sullivan
1. On - ward, Chris - tian sol - diers, March - ing as to war, With the cross of
2. Like a might - y ar - my Moves the Church of God; Bro - thers, we are
3. Crowns and thrones may per - ish, King - doms rise and wane, But the Church of
4. On - ward, then, ye peo - ple, Join our hap - py throng, Blend with ours your
Je - sus Go - ing on be - fore: Christ the roy - al Mas - ter
tread - ing Where the saints have trod; We are not di - vid - ed,
Je - sus Con - stant will re - main; Gates of hell can nev - er
voic - es In the tri - umph song; Glo - ry, laud, and hon - or
Leads a - gainst the foe; For - ward in - to bat - tle,
All one bod - y we, One in hope and doc - trine,
'Gainst that Church pre - vail; We have Christ's own pro - mise,
Un - to Christ the King; This through count - less a - ges
See, His ban - ners go.
One in char - i - ty.
And that can - not fail.
Men and an - gels sing.
On - ward, Chris - tian sol - diers,
March - ing as to war, With the cross of Je - sus Go - ing on be - fore.

How Firm a Foundation

"K" in Rippon's *Selection of Hymns,* 1787

American melody
From Caldwell's *Union Harmony,* 1837

It Is Well with My Soul
Horatio G. Spafford
Philip P. Bliss
1. When peace, like a riv - er, at - tend - eth my way,
2. Though Sa - tan should buf - fet, though tri - als should come,
3. My sin— oh, the bliss of this glo - ri - ous thought,
4. And, Lord, haste the day when the faith shall be sight,
When sor - rows like sea - bil - lows roll; What - ev - er my
Let this blest as - sur - ance con - trol, That Christ has re -
My sin— not in part, but the whole, Is nailed to the
The clouds be rolled back as a scroll, The trump shall re -
lot, Thou hast taught me to say, "It is well, it is
gard - ed my help - less es - tate, And hath shed His own
cross and I bear it no more, Praise the Lord, praise the
sound and the Lord shall de - scend, "E - ven so"— it is
well with my soul."
blood for my soul.
Lord, O my soul!
well with my soul.
It is well with my
It is well
soul,
with my soul,
It is well, it is well with my soul.

Amazing Grace

St. 1-3, John Newton
St. 4, Anonymous

Virginia Harmony, 1851
Arr. by Edwin O. Excell

Original concluding verse by John Newton:

The earth shall soon dissolve like snow,
The sun forbear to shine;
But God, who call'd me here below,
Will be forever mine.

The Lord Is My Shepherd

Based on Psalm 23

Unknown

I Will Sing of the Mercies of the Lord
Psalm 89:1
J. H. Fillmore
I will sing of the mer - cies of the Lord for - ev - er, I will
sing, I will sing. I will sing of the mer - cies of the
Lord for - ev - er, I will sing of the mer - cies of the Lord.
Fine
With my mouth will I make known Thy faith-ful - ness, Thy faith-ful - ness. With my
D.C. al Fine
mouth will I make known Thy faith - ful-ness to all gen - er - a - tions.

Books of the Old Testament

Author unknown

German Folksong

Books of the New Testament

Jo Hall and Lisa Marie Massato

German Folksong

The Bible Reading Habit

God's People Thank Him for His Mercies

Thanksgiving MiniUnit

Preview

Doctrines

- God is righteous (Psalm 116:5)—Lessons 1-2
- God is merciful (Psalm 86:15)—Lessons 1-2
- God is unchanging (immutable) (Malachi 3:6)—Lesson 2

Skills and Applications

- Write a poem of praise
- Speak God's praises in a choral reading
- Demonstrate an awareness of God's protection and provision
- Demonstrate a thankful attitude toward God
- Learn about how God's people praised Him in Bible times

Lesson 1

Preparation of Materials

Prepare an overhead transparency or chart of Supplement page S39, "I Will Sing of the Mercies of the Lord."

Prepare an overhead transparency or chalkboard drawing of the semantic map from Supplement page S48, "The First Thanksgiving in America."

Prepare a copy of Supplement page S49, "God's Mercies to Me," for each student.

Hymn: "I Will Sing of the Mercies of the Lord"

Teach the hymn. Display a copy of the hymn. Lead in reading the words together phrase by phrase.

➤ **What are *mercies?*** *(Accept any answer.)* Explain that mercies are loving kindnesses toward those in need, no matter how undeserving they are.

➤ **What are some of the mercies God extends to mankind?** *(Possible answers include forgiveness, salvation, protection, and provision for daily needs.)*

➤ **What is a *generation?*** *(all the people born in a certain time period)*

Demonstrate the meaning of generations by drawing a simple family tree and designating the generations (grandparents, parents, children). Explain that God's mercies extend to all generations. Play the recording and lead in singing the song together.

Background Information

Passover—*God used a series of plagues on the Egyptians to deliver His people from slavery in Egypt. The final plague was death of all the firstborn in the land. God commanded that His protection from this judgment and deliverance from slavery be celebrated by His people from generation to generation. God gave very specific commands concerning this observance. It was so important that the whole calendar was to be adjusted so that the month in which the Passover occurred became the first month of the year.*

Passover Through the Centuries—*Passover was observed the second year after the Israelites left Egypt and then not again until they reached the Promised Land. For seven days in the first month of each year, Passover was kept. These seven days, called the* Feast of Unleavened Bread, *began and ended with a holy convocation. Except for serving meals, no work was done on these days. No leavened bread was eaten, and no leaven was kept in the house. A meal of the same foods as those eaten at the original Passover was shared by each household. So that the meaning of the Passover would not be forgotten, it became customary for the youngest child in the family to ask a set of questions about why this time was set apart; the questions were answered by the head of each family.*

Passover During the Time of Christ—*Jews traveled from all over Palestine, from Babylonia, and from every part of the Roman Empire to observe the Passover in Jerusalem. They stayed in rented rooms and even on rooftops during the festival. The women bought herbs, wine, and bread to prepare for the meal. The men went to the temple to buy the lamb and have it sacrificed by the priests. The blood of the lamb was splashed on the altar, the entrails and fat were burned, and the meat was wrapped in the skin and returned to the owner to be roasted and eaten at home. During the remaining days of the Passover week, men usually visited the temple several more times to worship.*

Passover in Modern Times—*A service, called the* Seder, *is held in the home, taking the place of the sacrifice and the accompanying paschal [sacrificial] meal. All leaven is carefully removed from the house. At nightfall the day before the Seder, the head of the family uses a candle to light all corners and search the house for any leaven that might have been overlooked. At the traditional meal, the following items are placed on the table in front of the head of the family:*

- *Three cakes of unleavened bread, called* matzah, *commemorating the bread eaten prior to the flight from Egypt*

- *Bitter herbs, symbolizing the bitter treatment the Israelites endured in Egypt*
- Haroseth *(a mixture of chopped apple, nuts, raisins, and cinnamon), symbolizing the mortar the Israelites were forced to tread during their slavery in Egypt*
- *A roasted egg, symbolizing the special sacrifice offered in the temple on Passover*
- *The shankbone of a lamb, symbolizing the paschal sacrifice*
- *Parsley or radishes, the usual side dishes of ancient banquets*
- *Four, sometimes five, cups of wine. A large goblet of wine is also set in the center of the table for the prophet Elijah, precursor of the Messiah.*

The traditional questions are asked by the youngest child, and the story of the going forth from Egypt is recited in hymns and prayers. The meal is concluded with the Aphikomen *(after dish), a piece of unleavened cake.*

Introducing the Bible Account

Discuss the first American Thanksgiving. Display the semantic map from Supplement page S48, "The First Thanksgiving in America." Ask the following question and record students' responses in one or two words on each of the ears of Indian corn.

➤ **What were some of the mercies for which the Pilgrims probably thanked God?** *(Possible answers include safety in travel, provision of food, shelter, safety in a new land, friendship with others, and the freedom to worship Him as they wished.)*

Explain that God's people, the Israelites, held two separate harvest festivals—the Feast of Weeks and the Feast of Booths (Tabernacles). They also celebrated with a thanksgiving feast that was not connected to the harvest—the Feast of the Passover. In the Feast of the Passover, the Israelites were commanded by God to celebrate their deliverance from the Egyptians and from the judgment of death that came upon them. This special thanksgiving celebration was to continue generation after generation.

Bible Account

Read the following Bible account or read Exodus 12:1-28.

Feast of the Passover

God sent nine terrible plagues to show His power and purpose to the Egyptians. Still they would not release the Israelites. Now God prepared to strike the Egyptians and their stubborn ruler with the tenth plague, the worst plague of all—the death of all firstborn.

Before this happened, God gave Moses and Aaron instructions for His people to obey. In the middle of all their preparations for leaving the land of their slavery, the Israelites were to do everything *exactly* right so that it would be remembered when they were safe in the Promised Land. Each household was to choose a healthy, unmarked lamb. On the evening of the fourteenth day of the month of Nisan, the lamb was to be killed and its blood painted on the sides and top of the door with a brush made of hyssop twigs. The meat was to be roasted and eaten quickly with unleavened bread and bitter herbs.

In years to come, when the Jewish children asked what the special thanksgiving celebration meant, the heads of the families were to reply, "It is the sacrifice of the Lord's passover, who passed over the houses of the children of Israel in Egypt, when he smote the Egyptians, and delivered our houses." When they put the blood of the lamb on the sides and top of the door, and when they ate the roasted meat, they remembered that Israel was God's firstborn among the nations and that He protected and provided for them. When they ate the bitter herbs, they remembered that though their suffering in Egypt had been bitter, God had not forgotten them. The unleavened bread was a reminder of the haste of their departure when God delivered them from Egypt.

➤ **How did God show His power and purpose to the Egyptians?** *(He sent terrible plagues.)*

➤ **What preparations did God tell Moses and Aaron to have His people make before the tenth plague?** *(Kill a healthy, unmarked lamb, paint its blood on their doors, roast the lamb, and eat it with bitter herbs and unleavened bread.)*

➤ **What did God tell the Israelites to answer when their children asked why they observed the Passover?** *(God passed over their houses, smote the Egyptians, and delivered the Israelites [from slavery].)*

➤ **What did the roasted meat and the blood on the doors help the Jews remember?** *(that Israel was God's firstborn, and that He protected and provided for them)*

➤ **What did the bitter herbs help them remember?** *(Even though their suffering had been bitter, God had not forgotten them.)*

➤ **What did the unleavened bread remind them of?** *(the haste of their departure when God delivered them)*

➤ **What must God's people do in order to offer Him true worship and thanksgiving?** *(remember His mercies to them in the past)*

Emphasize that it is just as important for God's people today to remember what He has done for them and to honor and thank Him as it was for the Israelites. In fact, it is *more* important because Christians today have been given the finished work of salvation in Christ. Read **II Corinthians 9:15** to the students.

Writing Connection (optional)

Discuss God's mercies. Give each student a copy of Supplement page S49, "God's Mercies to Me." Direct him to list on the handwriting lines some of God's mercies to him and his family; then tell him to color and cut out the corn. Display each student's corn on the bulletin board. See page S47 (optional).

Lesson 2

Materials

- Hymn: "I Will Sing of the Mercies of the Lord"

Prepare a copy of Supplement page S50, "Write a Praise Poem," for each student.

Prepare an overhead transparency or chart of Supplement page S51, "Choral Reading."

Hymn: "I Will Sing of the Mercies of the Lord"

Sing the hymn. Play the recording and lead in singing the hymn together. Then divide the students into two or three groups to sing as a round. Select a student to be the leader of each group, telling him to motion for his group to begin singing at the appropriate time. Each group should begin singing after the previous group has finished singing the first line ("I will sing of the mercies of the Lord forever").

Background Information

Singing Psalms—*When the Israelites worshiped, they sang the psalms that we read in God's Word. By about 250 B.C., a special psalm had been assigned to each day of the week in temple worship. The singing was accompanied by musical instruments—harps, lyres, horns, and cymbals. We do not know what melodies were used. There were three ways of singing.* Directed singing *meant that a leader chanted the words and a selected group or the whole congregation repeated the same words (Psalm 124:1-2).* Antiphonal (responsive) singing *involved one group singing a verse or phrase at a time and another group repeating a refrain after each one (Psalm 136).* Unison singing *involved everyone singing the same words at the same time (Psalm 122).*

The Hallel and the Great Hallel—*Other psalms were added to the psalms of daily worship when festivals were celebrated. Psalms 113-118 were called "The Hallel" because they usually began with "Hallelujah" ["Praise the Lord"]. Psalms 120-136, called "The Great Hallel," were sometimes sung as a conclusion to the Passover meal.*

Choral Reading

Guide a choral reading. Explain to students that a choral reading is performed as a choir would perform a piece of music, attention being given to when to speak and when to be silent. Like singing, choral reading is a way of praising and worshiping God. Encourage clear, pleasant speech and a worshipful attitude and posture.

Display the "Choral Reading" from Supplement page S51. Explain that the phrase on the bottom is to be repeated with enthusiasm after each line.

Practice with one or two lines. Assign the solos (or duets if there is a large number of students).

Direct the students in the choral reading of Psalm 136:1-15, 23-26. This may be prepared for performance as part of a Thanksgiving program.

Bible Account

Read the following Bible account or read II Kings 21:19–22:2; 23:3, 21-25. Direct the students to listen to find out about the greatest Passover ever celebrated by any of the kings of Israel and Judah.

Keep the Passover

Amon, the king of Judah, had led God's people away from worshiping and serving Him to follow false gods. They had forgotten God's Word and His way. They no longer remembered to thank God for His great mercies toward them. When Amon was killed by his own servants, his eight-year-old son, Josiah, became the sixteenth king of Judah. Josiah "did that which was right in the sight of the Lord, and walked in all the way of David his father [ancestor], and turned not aside to the right hand or to the left."

In the eighteenth year of his reign, Josiah ordered the temple of God to be repaired. The book of the law was found there, and Josiah read it to all the residents of Jerusalem. Together they made a covenant to "walk after the Lord, and to keep his commandments and his testimonies and his statutes with all their heart and all their soul."

Josiah commanded that the Passover would be kept as God's Word had stated it should be. It is recorded that there had not been such a keeping of the Passover from the days of the judges up to that time. Once they had been reminded by God's Word, the people of Judah showed their thankfulness and worship as it had not been shown for many years.

- ➤ **Why did God command the Israelites to celebrate the Passover?** *(so that they would not forget what God had done for them when He delivered them from Egypt)*
- ➤ **What had happened between the first Passover and the time when Josiah became king?** *(God's people had forgotten the great things God had done for them.)*
- ➤ **What kind of king was Josiah?** *(He did what was right in God's sight; he was like David; he had the temple repaired.)*
- ➤ **What covenant did Josiah and the people of Judah make?** *(to walk after the Lord and keep His commandments [laws, statutes])*

➤ **How did Josiah and the people of Judah show their thankfulness and worship?** *(They kept the Passover.)*

➤ **Why should we remember the things God has done for us?** *(so that we will thank Him and worship Him)*

Emphasize that reading God's Word helps us to remember His mercies to us.

Writing Connection (optional)

Discuss the form of David's poetry. Read **Psalm 136** aloud.

➤ **What phrase was repeated in each verse?** *("for his mercy endureth for ever")*

Point out that David, the author of this psalm, or poem, wrote of great things God had done and then repeated a phrase of praise and worship.

Write a praise poem. Give each student a copy of Supplement page S50, "Write a Praise Poem." Read the instructions aloud, encouraging each student to write a poem of praise. As time permits, allow any student who wishes to read his poem aloud.

Lesson 3

Materials

- Hymn: "I Will Sing of the Mercies of the Lord"
- A keepsake or memory box
- A copy of the Choral Reading from the previous lesson
- Two square pieces of wrapping paper (at least 6" × 6" and 7" × 7") for each student
- Several small slips of paper for each student

Prepare a copy of Supplement page S52, "Make a Thanksgiving Box," for each student.

Hymn: "I Will Sing of the Mercies of the Lord"

Sing the hymn. Display a copy of the hymn. Play the recording and lead in singing together.

Choral Reading

Practice the choral reading from Psalm 136.

Introducing the Application Story

Discuss a keepsake box. Show a keepsake box, explaining that some people call this a *memory box.*

➤ **What would you expect to find in a memory box?** *(Accept any answer.)*

Show what you keep in your keepsake box (e.g., photographs, a lock of hair, jewelry, letters).

Application Story

Read the following story to the students.

Thanksgiving in a Box

Kirk's class was visiting the residents of a nursing home. They sang some songs and did a choral reading. Afterwards they were supposed to visit with the people who lived there and give them some flowers they had made from ribbon.

Kirk's teacher, Miss Nicol, had given the class many instructions about visiting, but all that Kirk could remember was "smile." He looked around for someone who did not have a visitor. Slowly he walked over to a lady sitting in a wheelchair. Kirk smiled and handed the lady his flower. Before he could think what to say, the lady spoke in a voice that was so quiet that Kirk could hardly hear. "Thank you, young man. God is good."

Kirk couldn't think what to say. He stood in embarrassed silence until his eyes fell on a small box sitting on the lady's tray. "What's in the box?" he asked.

"It's my thanksgiving box," said the lady. Kirk leaned close and listened as the lady told him about the things that she lifted from the box—a card that her great grandson had made, a napkin from her 95th birthday party, and a small Bible that her Sunday school teacher had given her when she was nine years old. She explained that when she looked at these special things, they reminded her to thank God for giving her a wonderful family, a long and happy life, and salvation in Christ. "And now I will add this beautiful flower you gave me," she said. "It will remind me to thank God for young people like you who are kind enough to come and visit us. Remember, God is good."

➤ **What did Kirk's class do when they visited the nursing home?** *(sang, did a choral reading, gave the flowers they had made)*

➤ **What did the lady have on her tray?** *(a small box that she called her thanksgiving box)*

➤ **Why did the lady keep these things in the box?** *(to remind her to thank God for His blessings to her)*

➤ **What would the ribbon flower remind her to be thankful for?** *(young people like Kirk who were kind enough to visit)*

➤ **Why is it important to remember the good things God has given us?** *(so we will praise and thank Him)*

Art Connection (optional)

Make a memory box. Give each student a square of wrapping paper, several small slips of paper, and a copy of Supplement page S52, "Make a Thanksgiving Box." Guide the students in following the directions to make a box. When the boxes are completed, suggest that they use them to store reminders of God's blessings, written on small slips of paper. Allow time for the students to write some blessings on the slips of paper to include in their memory boxcs. If time permits, allow any students who wish to share some of their blessings.

Going Beyond

Materials

- Items for memory game: tray, cloth, small commonplace objects

Enrichment

Visit a nursing home. Make arrangements to visit a nursing home to perform a simple program and take small gifts to the residents.

Play the Memory Game. Place several small, commonplace objects on a tray and cover them with a cloth. Uncover them and allow students to concentrate on them for about thirty seconds. Cover the objects and challenge the students to write what they saw. Uncover the items again and allow the students to compare their lists with the actual items. Congratulate the student(s) who remembered all of the items.

Preparing the Thanksgiving Bulletin Board

Make a centerpiece on the bulletin board, using a pumpkin and several gourds made from a variety of paper textures (e.g., crumpled, corrugated, pleated) in fall colors. Arrange the students' Indian corn writings around the centerpiece *(See Writing Connection in Lesson 1).* Add the title: "O Give Thanks unto the Lord, For His Mercy Endureth Forever."

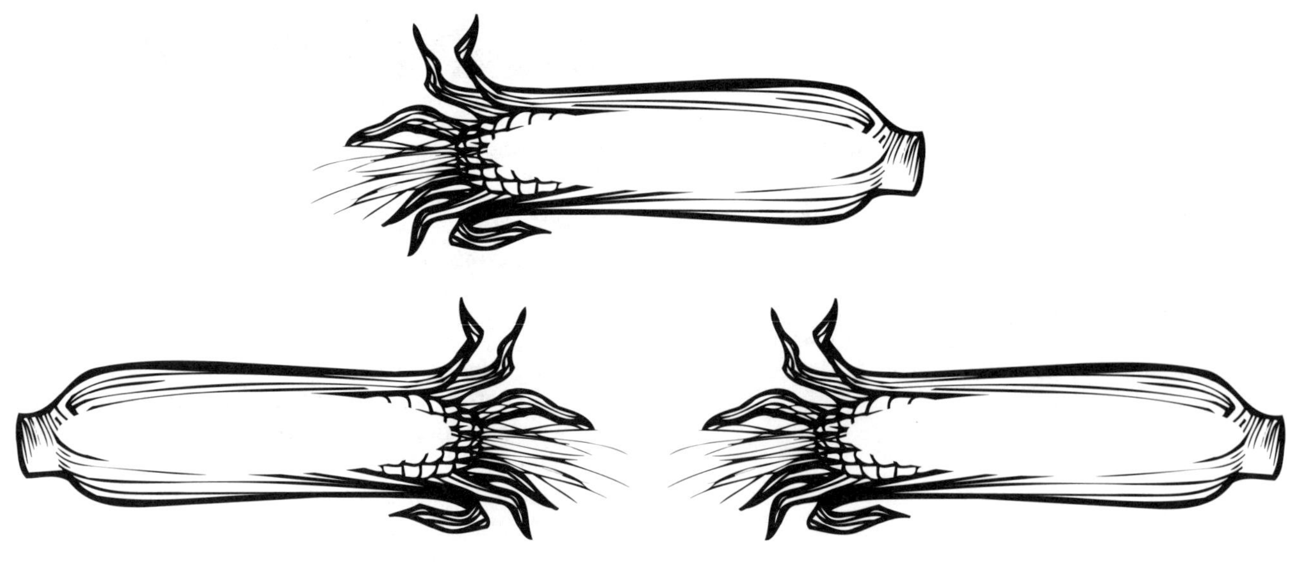

The First Thanksgiving in America

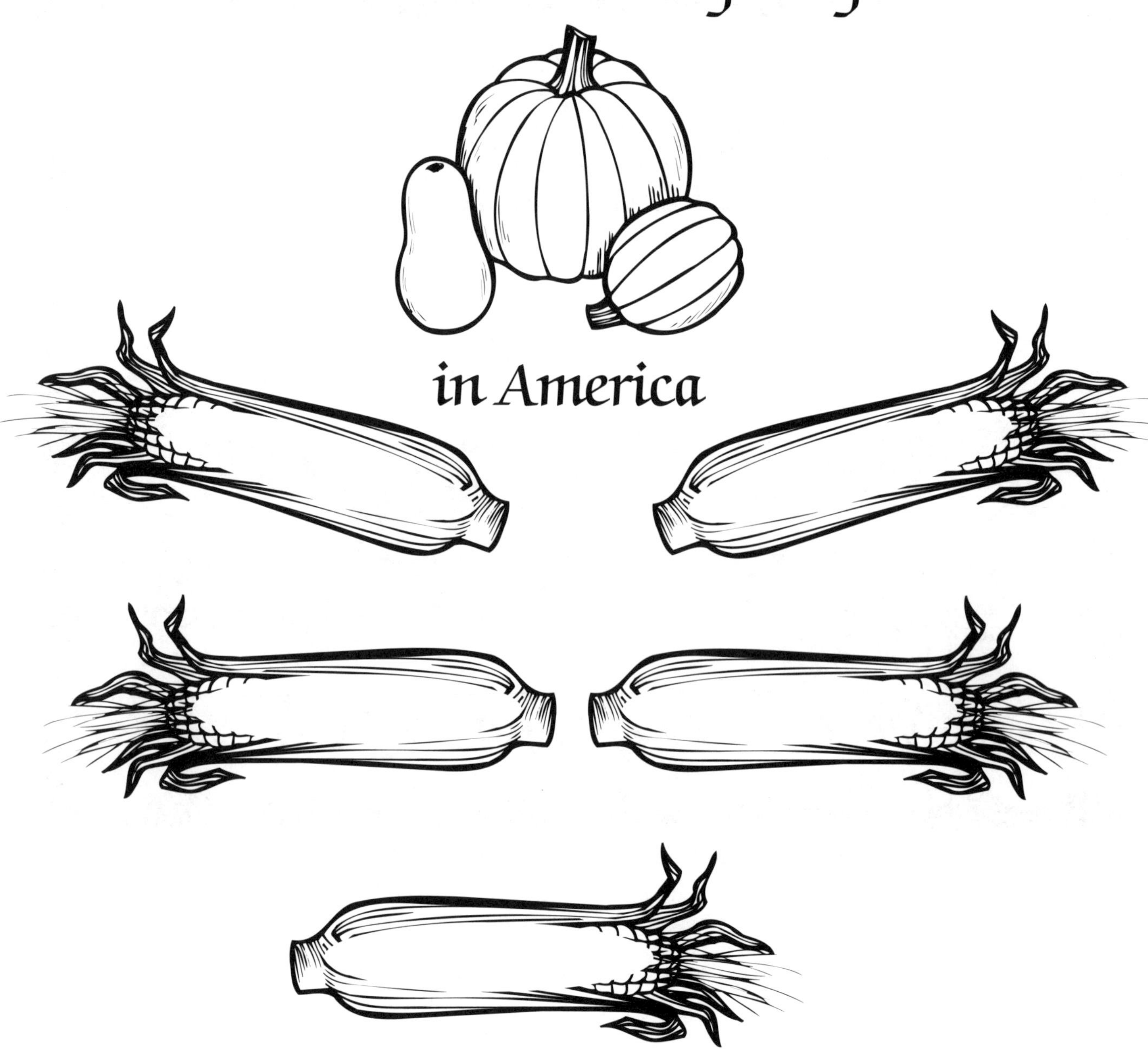

God's Mercies to Me

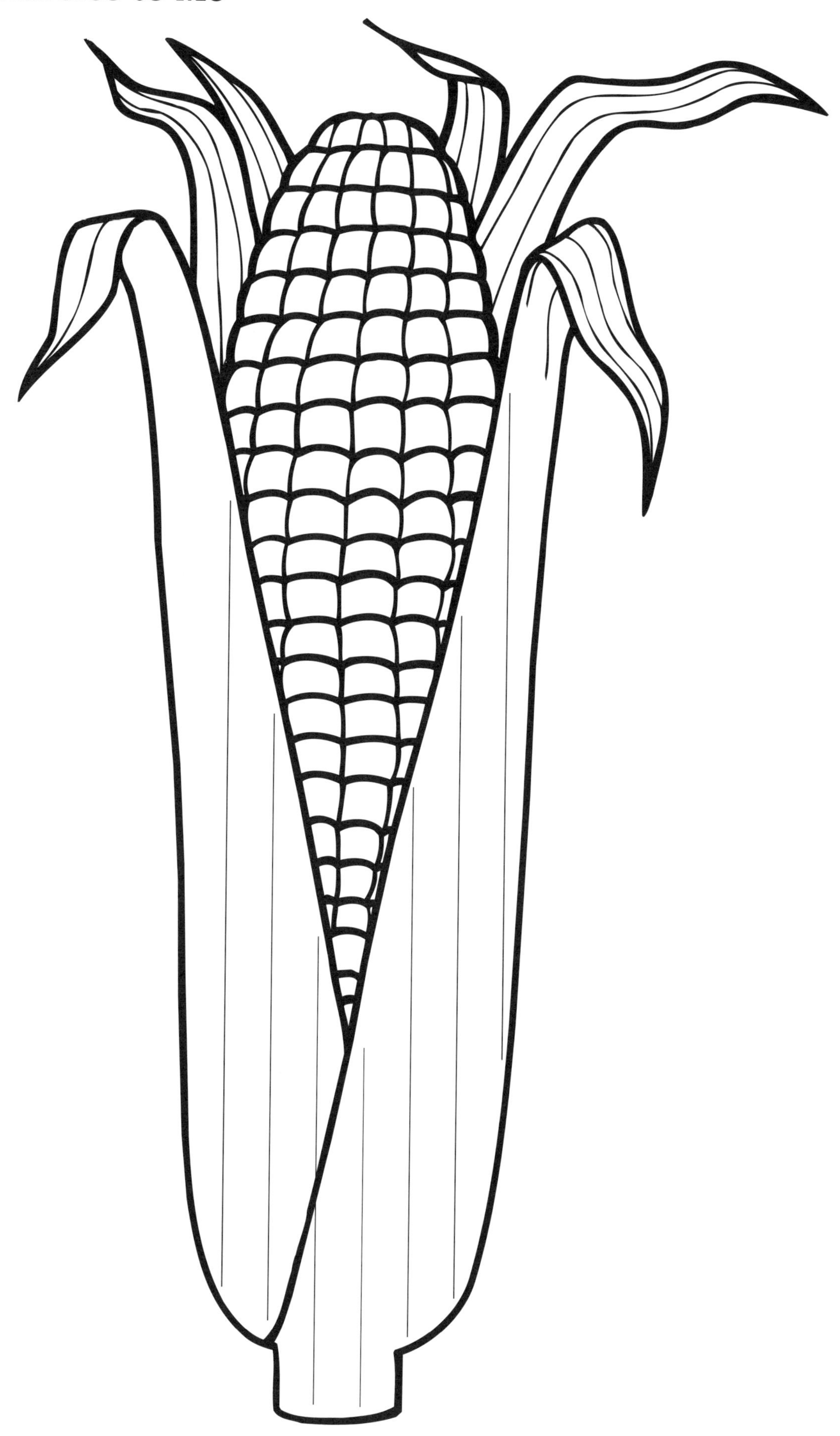

Write a Praise Poem

Name ____________________

Write some things God has done for you on lines 1-5.

Write your own praise phrase on line 6.

Fold back and forth on the dotted lines so that only line 1 is showing.

Read line 1 and then the praise phrase on line 6; unfold and read line 2, and so on.

You might like to share the poem with a friend or use it in a private time of praise to God.

6.

5.

4.

3.

2.

1.

Choral Reading

Psalm 136:1-15, 23-26
From the Great Hallel

All:	O give thanks unto the Lord; for he is good: O give thanks unto the God of gods: O give thanks to the Lord of lords:
Solo or Duet 1:	To him who alone doeth great wonders:
Solo or Duet 2:	To him that by wisdom made the heavens:
Solo or Duet 3:	To him that stretched out the earth above the waters:
Solo or Duet 4:	To him that made great lights:
Solo or Duet 5:	The sun to rule by day:
Solo or Duet 6:	The moon and stars to rule by night:
Solo or Duet 7:	To him that smote Egypt in their firstborn:
Solo or Duet 8:	And brought Israel from among them:
All:	With a strong hand, and with a stretched out arm:
Solo or Duet 9:	To him which divided the Red Sea into parts:
Solo or Duet 10:	And made Israel to pass through the midst of it:
Solo or Duet 11:	But overthrew Pharaoh and his host in the Red Sea:
Solo or Duet 12:	Who remembered us in our low estate:
Solo or Duet 13:	And hath redeemed us from our enemies:
Solo or Duet 14:	Who giveth food to all flesh:
All:	O give thanks unto the God of heaven:

For his mercy endureth for ever!

Make a Thanksgiving Box

Name ______________________________

1. Start with a square of wrapping paper (at least 6" x 6"). Fold into fourths and sharply crease as shown. Open.

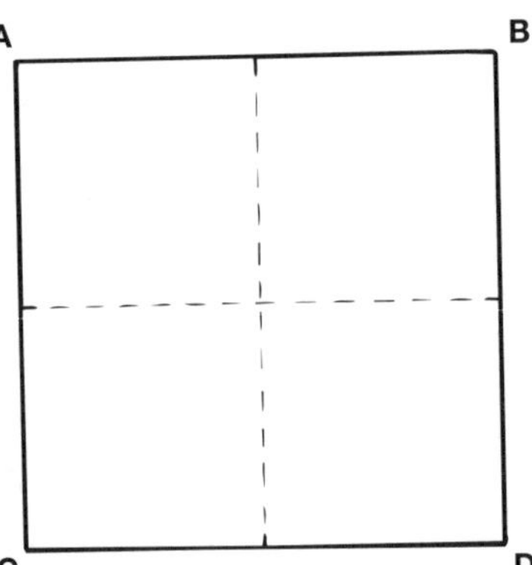

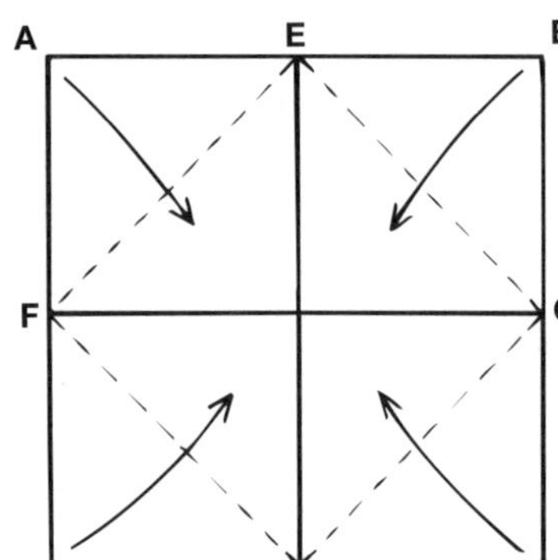

2. Fold the four corners to the center.

3. Fold each edge to the center.

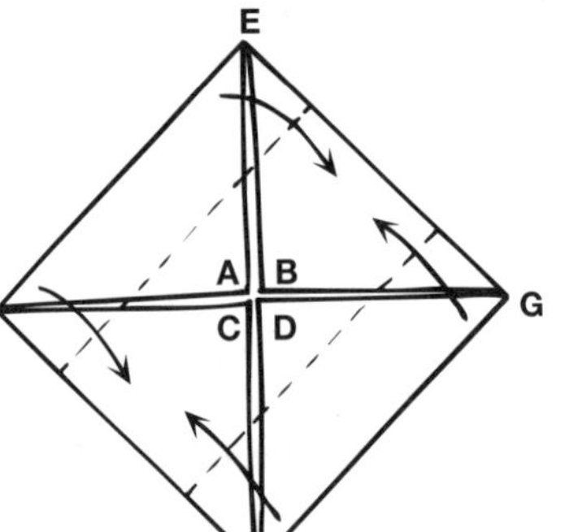

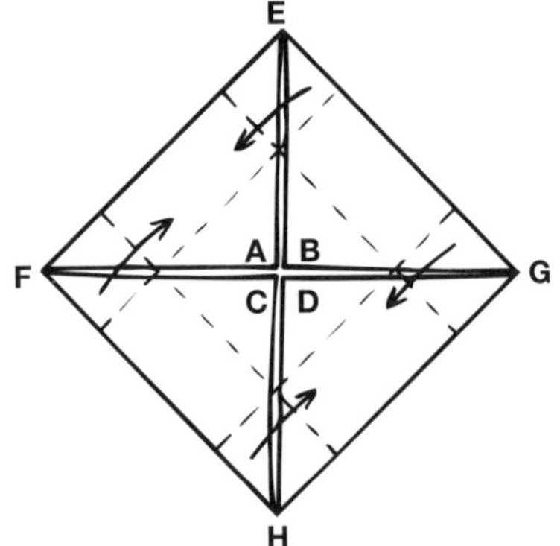

4. Pull open corners A and D.

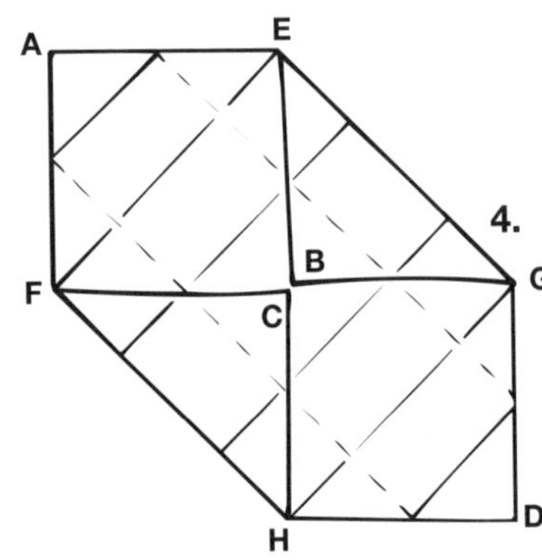

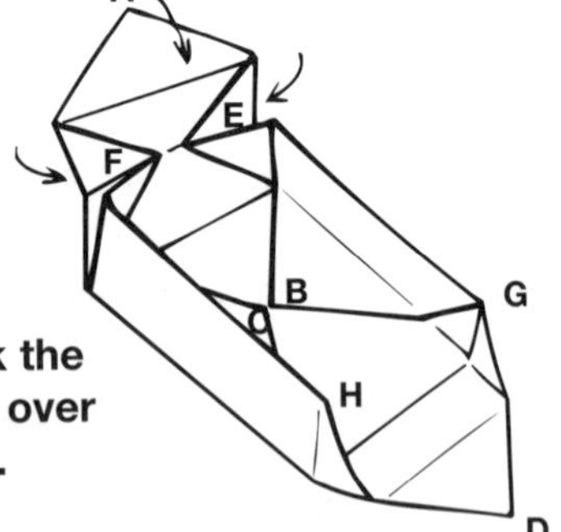

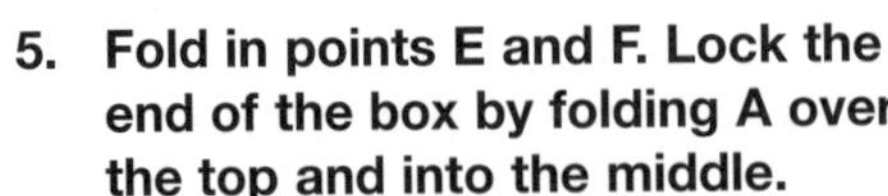

5. Fold in points E and F. Lock the end of the box by folding A over the top and into the middle.

6. Repeat Step 5 with H and G, folding D over the top to lock.

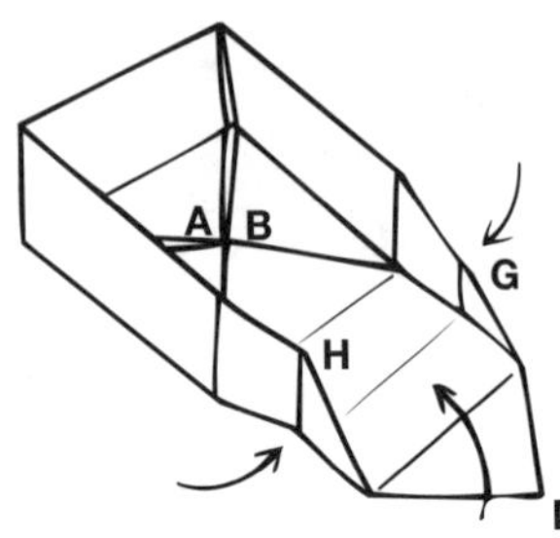

7. To make a lid, start with a slightly larger piece of paper and repeat Steps 1-6.

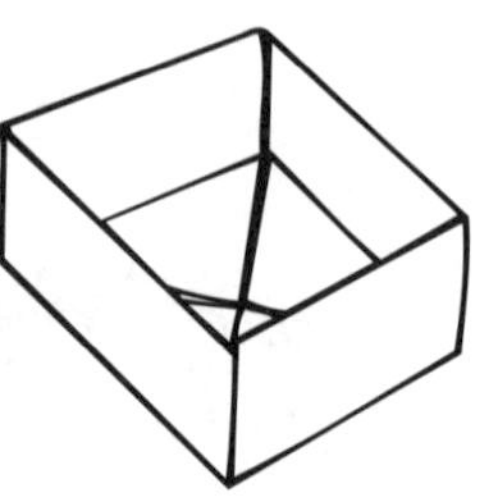

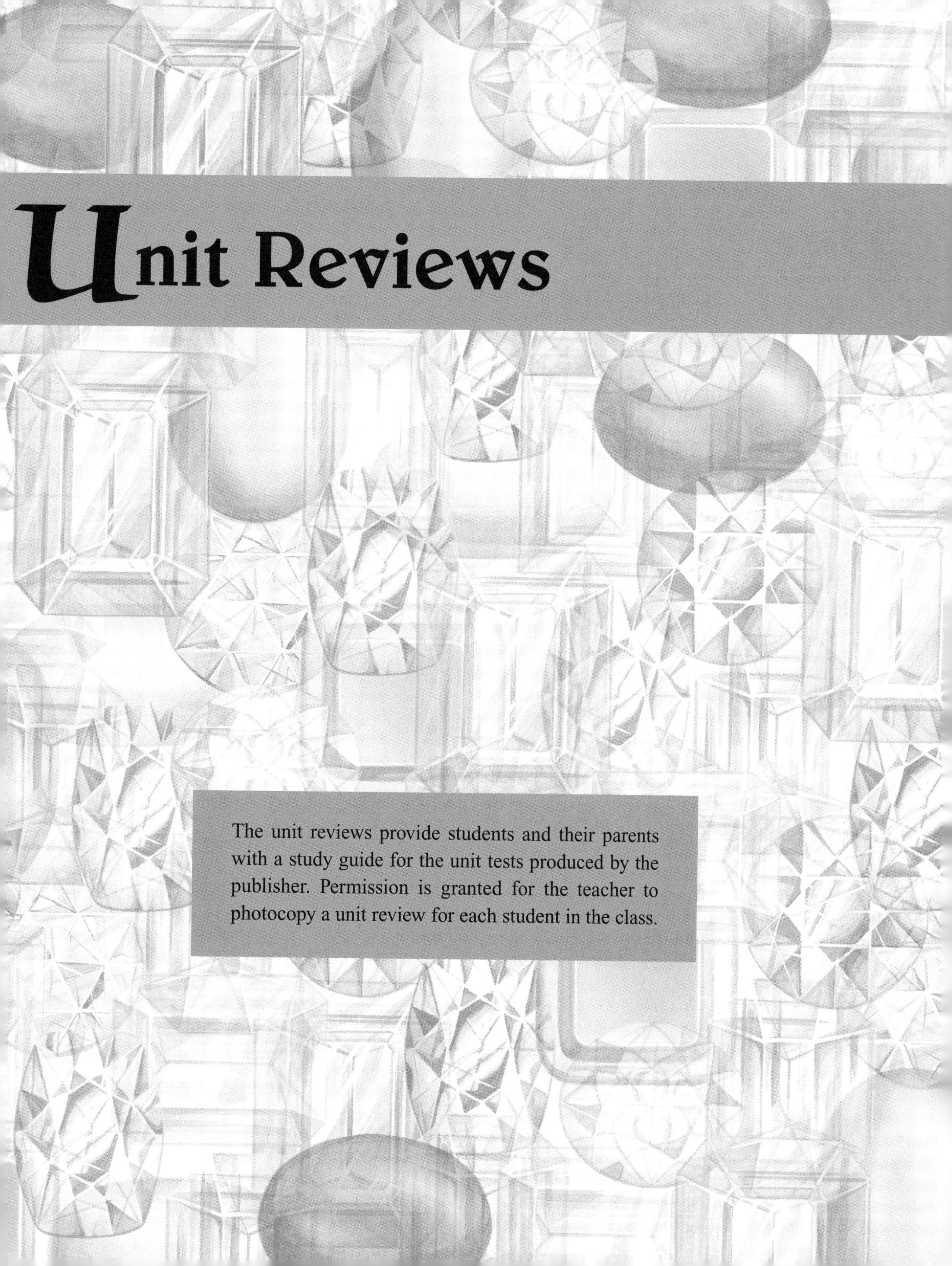

Unit Reviews

The unit reviews provide students and their parents with a study guide for the unit tests produced by the publisher. Permission is granted for the teacher to photocopy a unit review for each student in the class.

Unit 1 Review

Name ______________________

Fill in each box with one letter to spell the word that matches the definition. Use the code to complete the sentences, working from left to right if there are two letters for one code symbol.

✱	h	o		y	1. God is without sin.							
♥	l	o	v		n	g	2. God is caring toward His creation.					
➔	m	e	r		i	f	u	l	3. God is kind to the undeserving.			
■	i	m	m	u	t		b	l		4. God is always the same.		
◆		i	g	h	t	e	o		s	5. God is completely good and right.		
★	s	o	v	e			i	g	n	6. God rules over everything.		
●	o	m	n	i			i	e	n	t	7. God is all-knowing.	
▲	o	m	n	i		o		e	n	t	8. God is all-powerful.	
✖	o	m		i	p		e	s	e	n	t	9. God is everywhere.

God's nature is revealed to us in ___ ___ ___ ___ ___ ___ ___ ___ ___.
● ● ◆ ♥ ▲ ▲ ◆ ★ ★

A ___ ___ ___ ___ ___ d a ___ is helpful for starting a daily Bible reading habit.
➔ ■ ✱ ■ ✖ ✖

Complete the words in each sentence.

Five good Bible reading HABITs: Have a set t________ each day.

A__________ God to teach you. Be still and a____________________.

Investigate by asking q________________. Take time to look up w__________ you don't understand in a dictionary.

Unit 1 Review (continued)

Name ______________________________

Compare the Israelites with people today. Write the letter on the line. Use each answer only one time.

Israelites		**People today**
______	A. Slaves to sin	______
______	B. Slaves to Pharaoh	______
	C. Moses, through God's power, frees from slavery.	
	D. Jesus Christ frees from the bondage of sin.	

Write *T* if the sentence is true and *F* if it is false. If a sentence is false, change it to make it true. Draw a line through the word that is false, and write what will make it true on the line.

_____ The bronze snake on the pole was a picture of what it is like to look to Jesus in faith and be saved from sin and death. ______________________________

_____ Pharaoh let the Israelites go after the plague of hail. ______________________________

_____ The last four commandments teach our duty to God. ______________________________

Unit 2 Review

Name ______________________________

Write the letter of the correct answer on the line.

King ____ followed God. → result → He wanted his people to hear and know God's Word. → result → God sent peace and prosperity to the land of ____.

____ brought a message that Hezekiah would die. → result → Hezekiah prayed for mercy and healing. → result → God gave Hezekiah ____ years to live.

David looked away from God and sinned. → result → David ____ for forgiveness for his sin. → result → God sent ____ and forgiveness of sin.

God was pleased with ____ and asked what he desired. → result → Solomon asked God for ____. → result → God gave Solomon wisdom.

King Sennacherib threatened Hezekiah's kingdom. → result → ____ prayed for God's ____. → result → The kingdom was safe. Sennacherib's soldiers died.

We study the ____ and pray. → result → We learn to know God and ____ Him.

The Israelites held a ____ service to set apart the Lord's temple as a special, holy place. → result → Music was played, ____ were made, people fellow-shiped, and they held a solemn assembly.

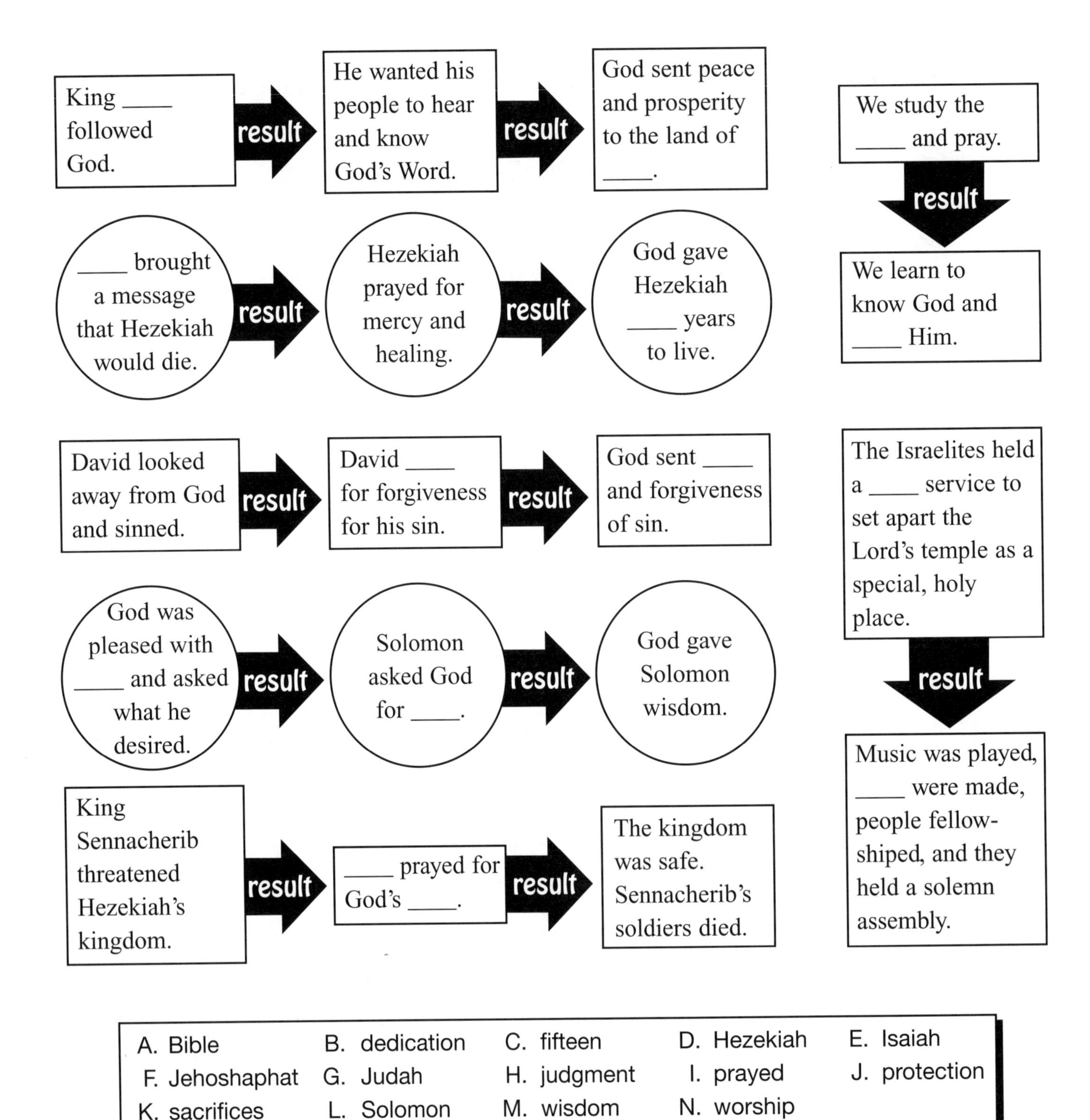

A. Bible	B. dedication	C. fifteen	D. Hezekiah	E. Isaiah
F. Jehoshaphat	G. Judah	H. judgment	I. prayed	J. protection
K. sacrifices	L. Solomon	M. wisdom	N. worship	

Use your Bible to review the order of the books in the Old Testament.

Unit 3 Review

Name ______________________

Match the Bible character with the description by putting the correct letter on the line.

____ 1. Ahab and Jezebel

____ 2. Hosea and Gomer

____ 3. Elisha

____ 4. Joash

____ 5. Jehoiada

____ 6. Naboth

A. He was a priest who faithfully protected and trained Joash, God's choice for king.

B. They were judged for their unfaithfulness to God.

C. He was faithful to trust the Lord for protection in times of battle and famine.

D. His life reminds us to follow godly advice and to be careful to remain faithful to God.

E. He was faithful to God's command and did not sell his vineyard.

F. Their marriage was a picture of God's faithfulness to faithless Israel.

Start with the first letter and skip every other letter in order to answer number 7. Start with the second letter and skip every other letter in order to answer number 8.

PRREOWTAERCDTSPJRUODVGIEDSE

7. The Lord is faithful to __ __ __ __ __ __ __ and __ __ __ __ __ __ __ for His servants.

8. God __ __ __ __ __ __ __ those who are faithful to Him, but He __ __ __ __ __ __ those who are unfaithful to Him.

Use a word from the word bank below to complete the paragraph.

9. God provided for a ______________________. God provided for the ______________________. God protected ______________________ with . The ______________________ faithfully gave for God's work. God used ______________________ to provide for the Israelites.

angels and lepers	widow and her two sons
Elisha Israelites	prophets

Use your Bible to review the order of the books in the New Testament.

Unit 4 Review

Name ______________________________

Write the letter of the answer on the line. Write the letters in order to complete the sentence.

_____ 1. instrument	g. obedient to God's plan
_____ 2. Jerusalem	n. told Herod of the birth of Jesus
_____ 3. Gabriel	h. town of Mary and Joseph
_____ 4. Nazareth	N. something that is prepared; ready to be used
_____ 5. Jesus	t. told Mary she was chosen by God
_____ 6. wise men	o. where the Passover celebration was held
_____ 7. Joseph	i. obedient to Mary and Joseph

___ ___ ___ ___ ___ ___ ___ is impossible with God!

Fill in the blanks with vowels (a, e, i, o, u) to complete the words in each sentence.

8. Have a t__m__ set aside __ __ch d__y to r__ __d the B__bl__.

9. __sk G__d to t__ __ch you from His W__rd.

10. Be st__ll and g__v__ your __tt__nt__ __n to what you are r__ __d__ng.

11. Investigate Scr__pt__r__ by asking q__ __st__ __ns.

12. T__k__ time to l__ __k up w__rds and ideas y__ __ don't __nd__rst__nd.

13. w__sd__m, st__t__r__, favor with G__d, f__v__r with man

Unit 5 Review

Name ______________________________

Complete the puzzle by writing the correct words to complete each sentence.

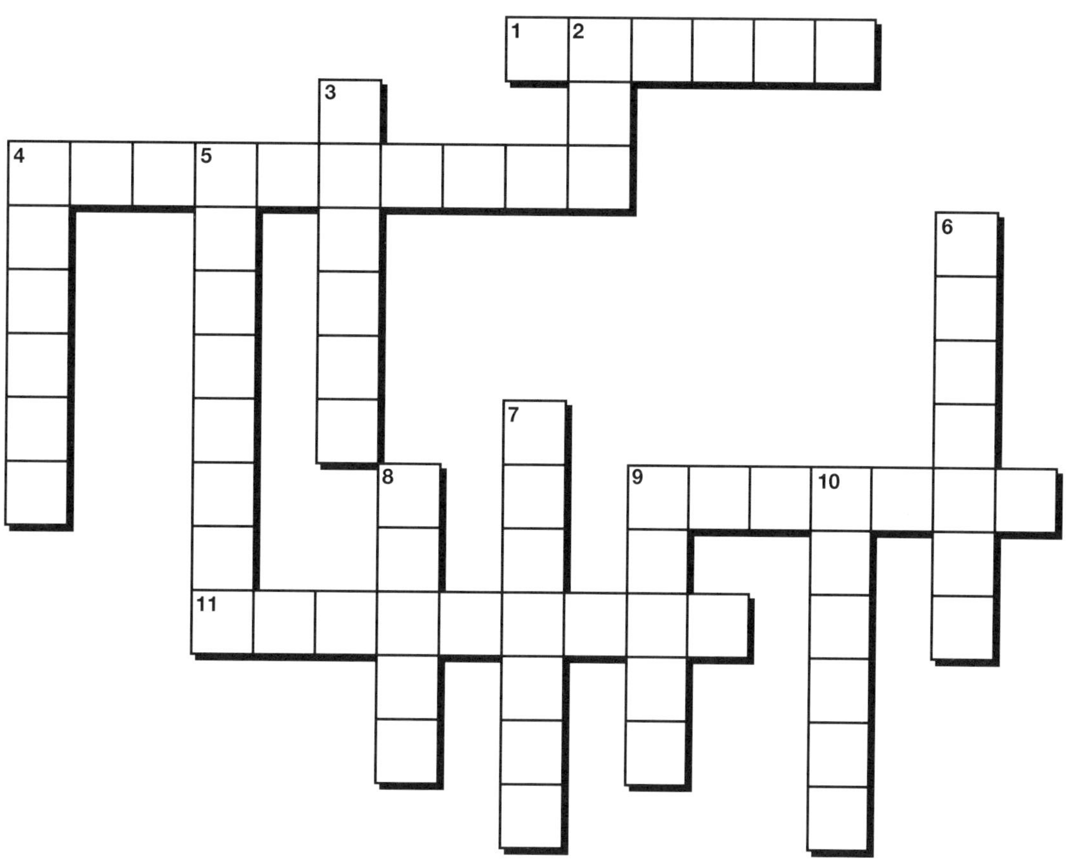

1. We need not fear because Jesus can give us **7 Down** over death, disease, Satan, or **4 Across**.
2. We can have victory through having faith in God, **6 Down** for strength, memorizing Scripture, and **1 Across** God to help us.
3. When we have evil desires and then give in to the temptation, we **2 Down**.
4. Satan tempted Jesus to throw Himself off the **4 Down**, to turn **10 Down** into bread, and to bow down and **9 Across** him.
5. Jesus overcame temptation by quoting **11 Across**.
6. The result of hearing and reading God's Word is **8 Down**.
7. By God's grace you are saved through faith in Jesus, not by your own **9 Down**.
8. The stories of the lost lamb and the lost coin are **5 Down** that teach us how God views those who are lost in sin.
9. **3 Down** encouraged the Israelites to finish the restoration of the temple.

Unit 6 Review

Name ______________________

Write the letter of the correct answer on the line.

A. Rome	C. concordance	F. Timothy	I. Philippi
B. Barnabas	D. Stephen	G. Matthew	J. rich man
	E. martyr	H. Peter	

____ 1. one who chooses to suffer or die rather than give up his faith in Christ

____ 2. Paul's partner on his first missionary journey

____ 3. His mother was a Jew, his father was a Greek

____ 4. a fisherman called to follow Jesus along with his brother

____ 5. an alphabetical list of key words with Scripture references

____ 6. city where Paul and Silas led a jailer to the Lord

____ 7. a tax collector called to follow Jesus

____ 8. city where Paul was a witness while under house arrest

____ 9. while being stoned by Jews he asked Jesus not to hold their sin against them

____10. His life of greed is compared with Lazarus' life of contentment

Complete the sentences by writing the missing words.

content
faithful
family
forgave
future
older
position
prodigal son
wealth
younger

The parable of the ______________ reminds us to be ______________ with the service we are called to, the ______________ into which we are born, the ______________ and ______________ we are blessed with, and the ______________ that God has for us. The ______________ brother was ______________ but not content; he desired recognition for his service.

Although the ______________ brother was not faithful or content, his father ______________ him.

Unit 7 Review

Name ______________________

Write the words from the word bank that go with each clue.

forgiveness	heart	soul	Mary	Rhoda
strength	mind	sin	John the Baptist	Peter
sorry	Jesus	Martha	Cornelius	

____

______________ **We are to love God with all our** ______________

____

being ______________ for our sin

asking ______________

Repentance has 3 parts.

proclaimed God's message

____

a Roman centurion became a believer

____

forgave a sinful woman

____

fellowshiped with the Lord

______________ and ______________

shared the gospel with the Gentiles

____

prayed for Peter

____

Unit 7 Review (continued)

Name ____________________

Color the heart red if it shows a loving heart.

kind
angry
forgiving
bitter
compassionate
encouraging
quarreling
full of wrath
gossiping

Match the letter of the principle that the situation illustrates.

A. Loving God	B. Loving the believer
C. Loving the unsaved	D. Loving your enemies

_____ 1. Ryan sang his best during chapel even though the other boys weren't singing.

_____ 2. Michael told his cousin about Jesus at their summer family reunion.

_____ 3. Sasha prayed for her pastor's mother who was hurt in a car accident.

_____ 4. Zach helped his dad pass out church invitations in a nearby neighborhood.

_____ 5. Sam prayed for his next-door neighbor Keith when his dog died, even though Keith bullied Sam every time he played outside.

_____ 6. Ellen made cookies for an elderly lady in her church who wasn't well.

Unit 8 Review

Name ______________________

Complete the sentences.

body	Christ	cup	Egypt
Gethsemane	Judas	Lamb	Passover
perfect	pray	sleeping	watch

The last supper Jesus ate with His disciples was the ______________ meal. At the time of Passover, the Jews looked back to the Israelites' deliverance from ______________ and forward to the coming of ______________. Jesus gave the meal a new meaning when he explained that the bread would represent His ______________ and the ______________ would represent His blood. Today Christians remember Christ's death as the ______________ ______________ of God and look forward to His return.

Afterward, Jesus and His disciples entered ______________, the garden where Jesus was betrayed by ______________ with a kiss. When Jesus returned, He found His disciples ______________. He instructed the disciples to ______________ and ______________ to avoid temptation.

Arimathea	Barabbas	Galilee
Magdalene	Peter	Pilate
	Simon	

When Jesus was arrested, ______________ denied knowing the Lord. At the trial ______________ found Jesus innocent but condemned Him to death to please the Jews. He released a criminal named ______________ instead. A man named ______________ was ordered to carry the cross of Christ to the place of crucifixion.

After Jesus was crucified, Joseph of ______________ buried the body of Jesus in a tomb sealed by a great stone. Pilate ordered soldiers to guard the tomb. Three days after His death, Jesus arose as He had said He would. Mary ______________ saw the empty tomb. She and other women were told to tell the disciples that Jesus was alive and that He would meet them in ______________.

Unit 9 Review

Name ______________________________

Draw a line to match the beginning of each sentence to the correct ending.

Have a time set aside to •	• teach you about Himself.
Ask Jesus to •	• listen carefully to what God is telling you.
Be still and •	• spend with the Lord in Bible reading and prayer.
Investigate Scripture as you •	• look up words and ideas you don't understand.
Take time to •	• ask yourself questions about its meaning.

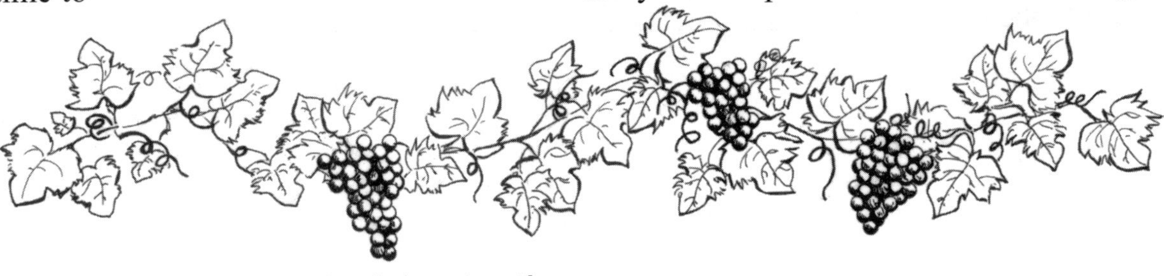

Draw a line matching the items that belong together.

God •	• branches	edify •	• a saved person
Jesus •	• gardener	saint •	• build up spiritually
Christians •	• vine	intercession •	• belonging to the Lord
		church •	• one tenth of our income
		tithe •	• pleading on another's behalf

Draw a line matching the three parts that make each sentence.

Abiding in Christ means to •	• "Thou art the Christ," •	• and generously.
Peter said, •	• give cheerfully •	• "the Son of the Living God."
Christians should •	• by meeting together •	• and encouraging each other.
We can edify the saints •	• live in obedience to the Lord's will or •	• be filled with the Holy Spirit.

Unit 9 Review (continued)

Name ____________________

Complete the chart by writing the missing names, events, and places.

Apollos	Aquila	Corinth	deacons
famine	Macedonia	Pentecost	Priscilla

WHO	WHAT	WHERE
1. Agabus	foretold the ____________ that would come to	Jerusalem and the surrounding regions.
2. ____________	didn't fully understand the Gospel in	Ephesus.
3. ____________ and ____________ were	tentmakers who discipled Apollos in the city of	Ephesus.
4. Barnabas and Paul	transported an offering from the believers in	____________ .
5. Believers	sent help to Jerusalem from	____________ .
6. Peter	preached at ____________, and thousands of people were saved in	Jerusalem.
7. Philip, Nicolas, and Stephen	were chosen as ____________ in	Jerusalem.

Unit 10 Review

Name ______________________

Match the word with its definition. Write the letter on the line.

____ 1. Omnipotent	A. thousand-year reign of Christ on earth
____ 2. Immutable	B. seven years of trouble on earth
____ 3. Judgment Seat of Christ	C. record of the names of Christians
____ 4. Lamb's Book of Life	D. unchanging
____ 5. Millennium	E. judgment of unbelievers
____ 6. Great White Throne Judgment	F. judgment of believers
____ 7. Rapture	G. all-powerful
____ 8. Tribulation	H. Christ returns, taking the saved to Heaven

Fill in the blanks with vowels (a, e, i, o, u) to complete the words in each sentence.

You can find prophecy about Jesus' coming as S__v__ __r in the book of __s__ __ __h.

R__v__l__t__ __n is the book containing pr__ph__cy of Jesus' returning as K__ng.

The G__sp__ls tell how Jesus __s the promised S__v__ __r.

J__hn saw a v__s__ __n of the return of Christ.

__m__s was a prophet from Judah who warned Israel about rejecting G__d.

Jesus is the L__mb of God. He was the perfect s__cr__f__c__ for sinners.

Jesus is the G__ __d Sh__ph__rd. He pr__t__cts those who trust in Him.

Jesus is the L__ __n of Judah. He will someday return in j__dgm__nt.

Fill in the circles next to the correct answers. (There can be more than one answer.)

1. We can know for certain we are saved because ______.

   ○ Jesus promised not to leave us
   ○ Jesus said no one can take our salvation
   ○ we sometimes feel like it
   ○ people tell us we're good

2. Jesus is worthy to receive ______.

   ○ power
   ○ honor
   ○ praise
   ○ blessing

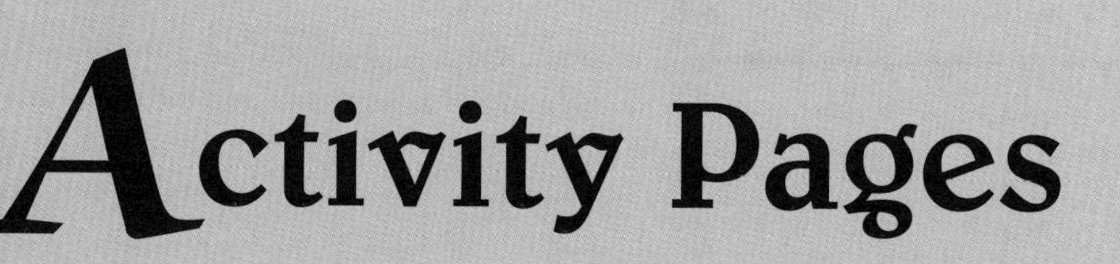

Activity Pages

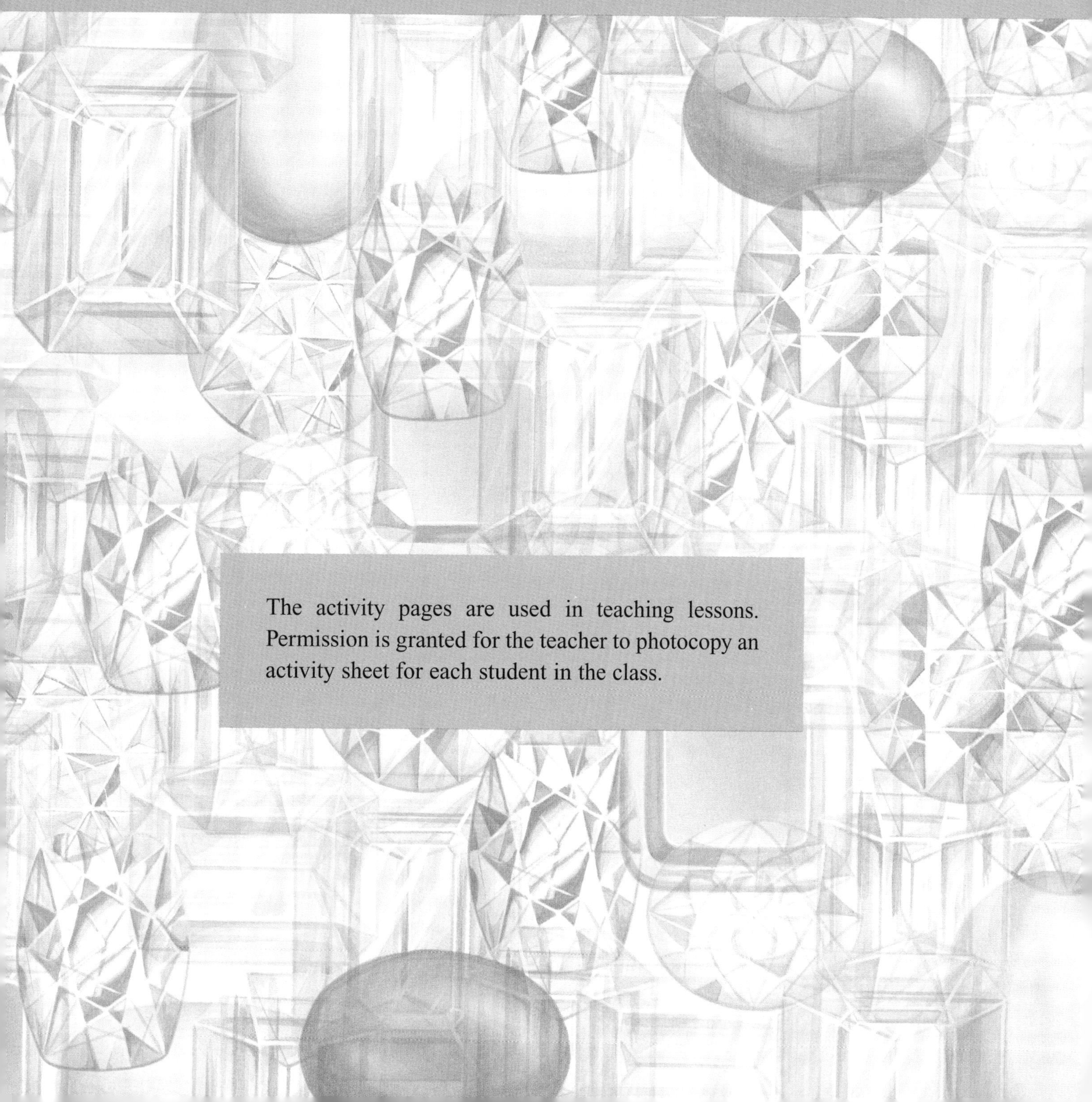

The activity pages are used in teaching lessons. Permission is granted for the teacher to photocopy an activity sheet for each student in the class.

Shape and Tell

Name ____________________

Cut on the dark lines. Place pieces as shown and join them at each X with a metal brad. Use the resulting story visual to retell a Bible account.

A D E B C

(snake) (cross) (Moses)

o

X X X X X X X

A B C D E

Taking a Census

Name ________________________

A *census* is an official count of population. A census survey also gathers information about where people live, what kinds of jobs they have, how the population is changing, and so on. The information gathered in a census is useful for determining such things as government plans and decisions, representation in government, and environmental needs.

Fill out this sample census form. Use the information on the forms to make bar graphs that record the results of the class census.

Please print clearly.

Family Name (last name) ________________________

Complete the following information for each member of the household.

First and middle names	Age (under 18 only)	Occupation	Country of citizenship	Relationship to head of household (son, niece, etc.)

Address: House number______ Apartment number______ Street name ________________

City ________________ State ______ Zip Code __________

Fill in the circle beside each answer.

1. Your residence is a ○ house ○ apartment ○ mobile home ○ other
2. Have you moved in the last 6 months? ○ Yes ○ No (If No, proceed to question 4.)
3. The move was ○ within the same state ○ state to state ○ to or from another country
4. How many licensed drivers are in the household? ○ 0 ○ 1 ○ 2 ○ 3 or more

Number of times family members have traveled by each type of transportation in the last 6 months.

Plane	○ 0	○ 1-5	○ 6-10	○ 11 or more
Train between cities	○ 0	○ 1-5	○ 6-10	○ 11 or more
City bus	○ 0	○ 1-5	○ 6-10	○ 11 or more
Subway or elevated railway	○ 0	○ 1-5	○ 6-10	○ 11 or more

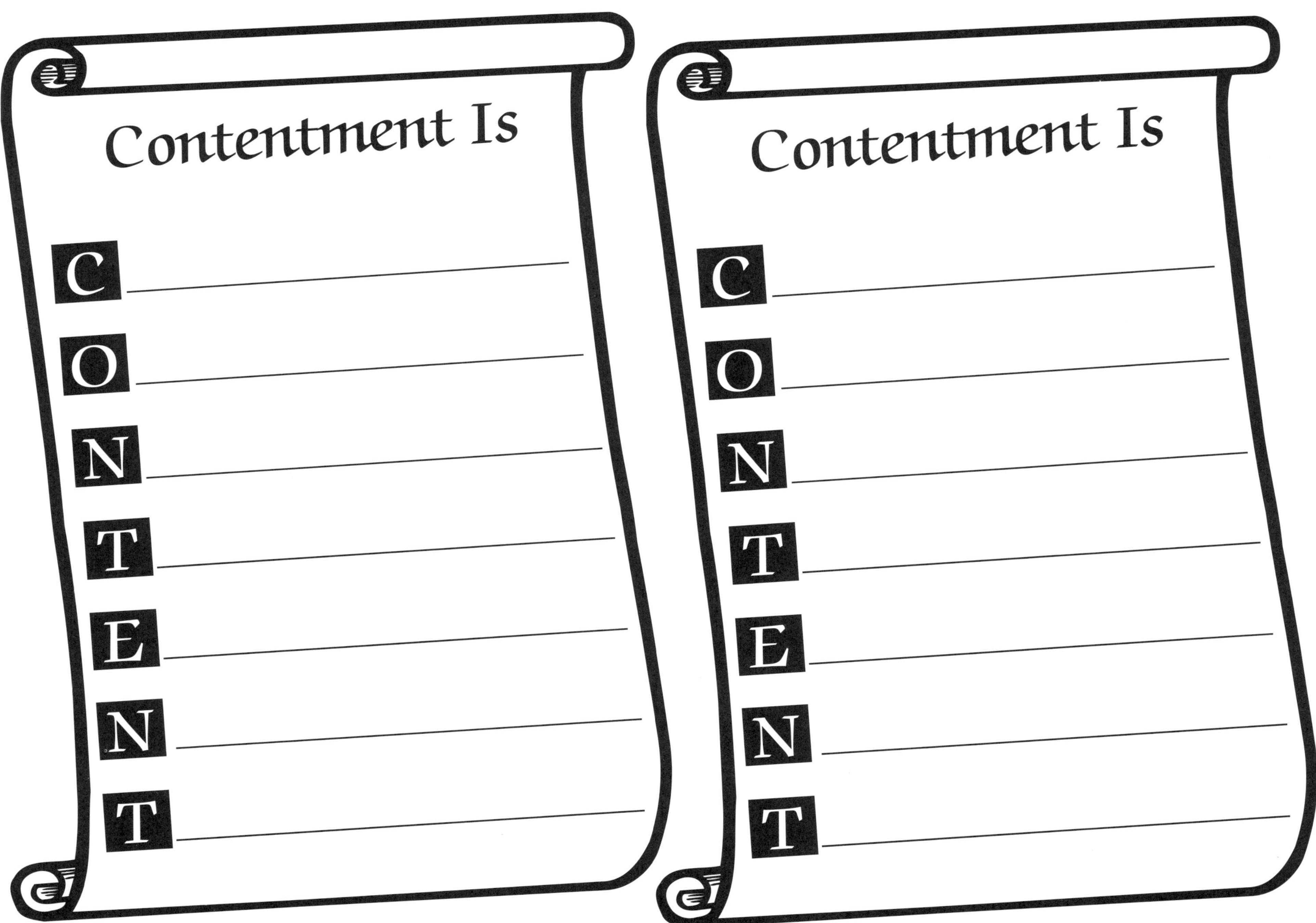
Contentment Is
C
O
N
T
E
N
T
Contentment Is
C
O
N
T
E
N
T

Answering Questions

Name ______________________

Jesus often taught His followers by asking questions. Read the following Bible references to find the questions Jesus asked; then look for possible reasons why He asked the questions.

Question Asked		Purpose for the Question
Matthew 26:8-12 Jesus asked? (v. 10) ______________________ ______________________ ______________________	⇨	______________________ ______________________ ______________________
Mark 5:25-34 Jesus asked? (v. 30) ______________________ ______________________ ______________________	⇨	______________________ ______________________ ______________________
Luke 2:46-50 Jesus asked? (v. 49) ______________________ ______________________ ______________________	⇨	______________________ ______________________ ______________________
Luke 22:44-46 Jesus asked? (v. 46) ______________________ ______________________ ______________________	⇨	______________________ ______________________ ______________________
John 9:13-38 Jesus asked? (v. 35) ______________________ ______________________ ______________________	⇨	______________________ ______________________ ______________________

Taking Notes

Name ______________________

Here is a form that you can use to take notes while listening to a sermon or lesson. Do not be concerned about writing down every word the speaker says. Concentrate on writing a few words that tell the main ideas and the examples and details that support them.

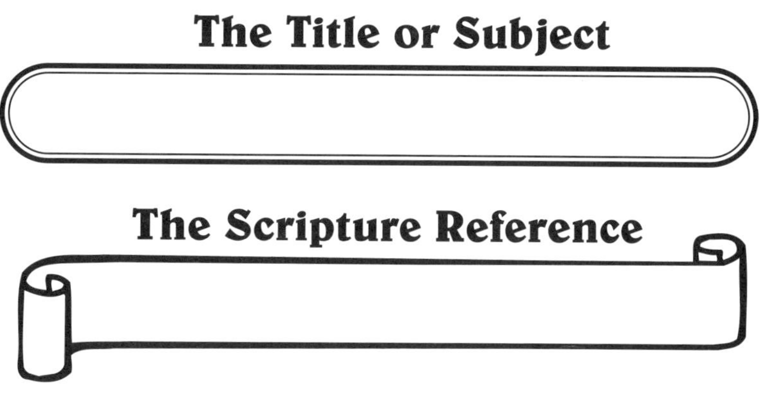

Examples and Supporting Details

Main Idea #1

Main Idea #2

Main Idea #3

What did I learn?

How can this be applied to my life?

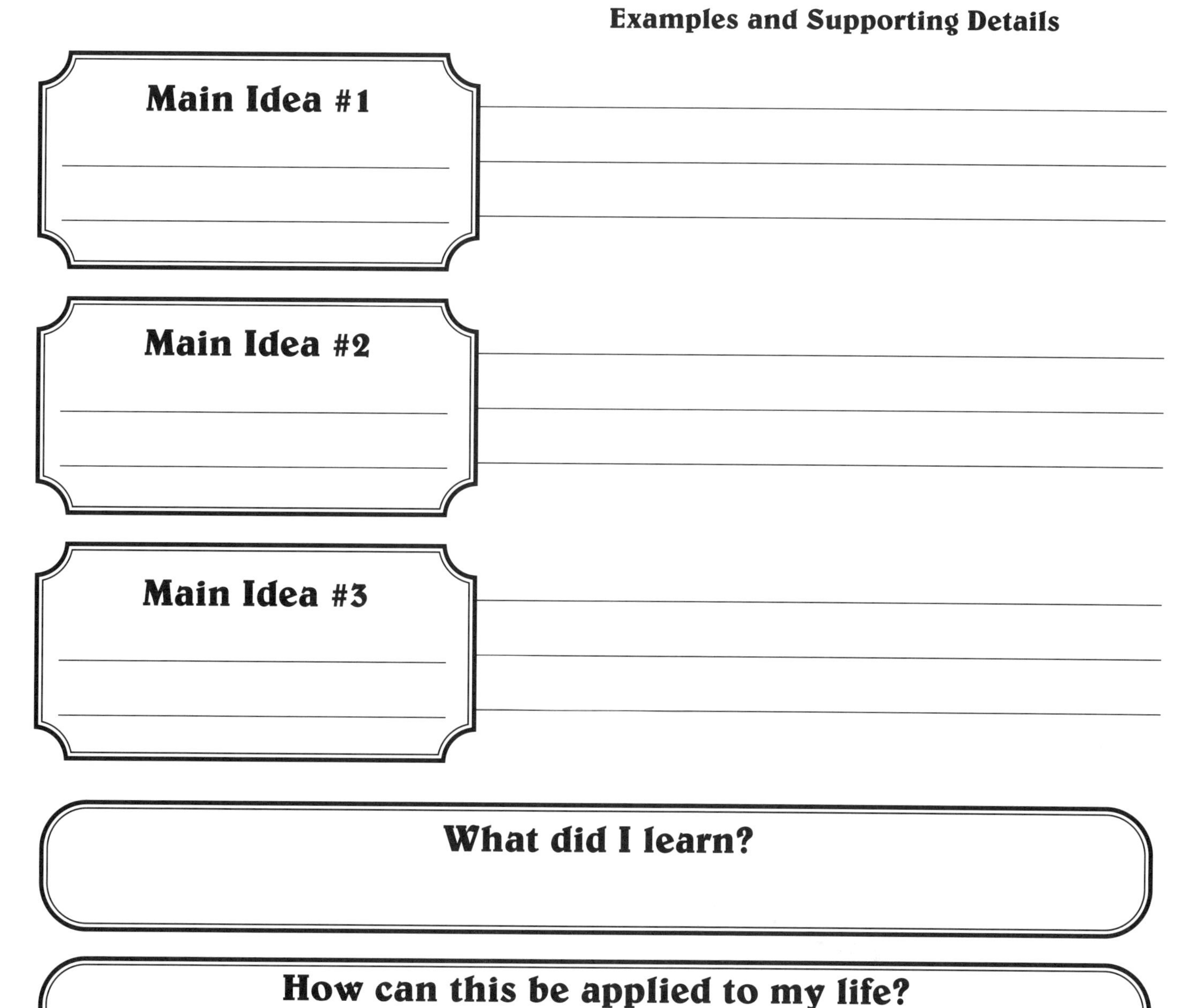

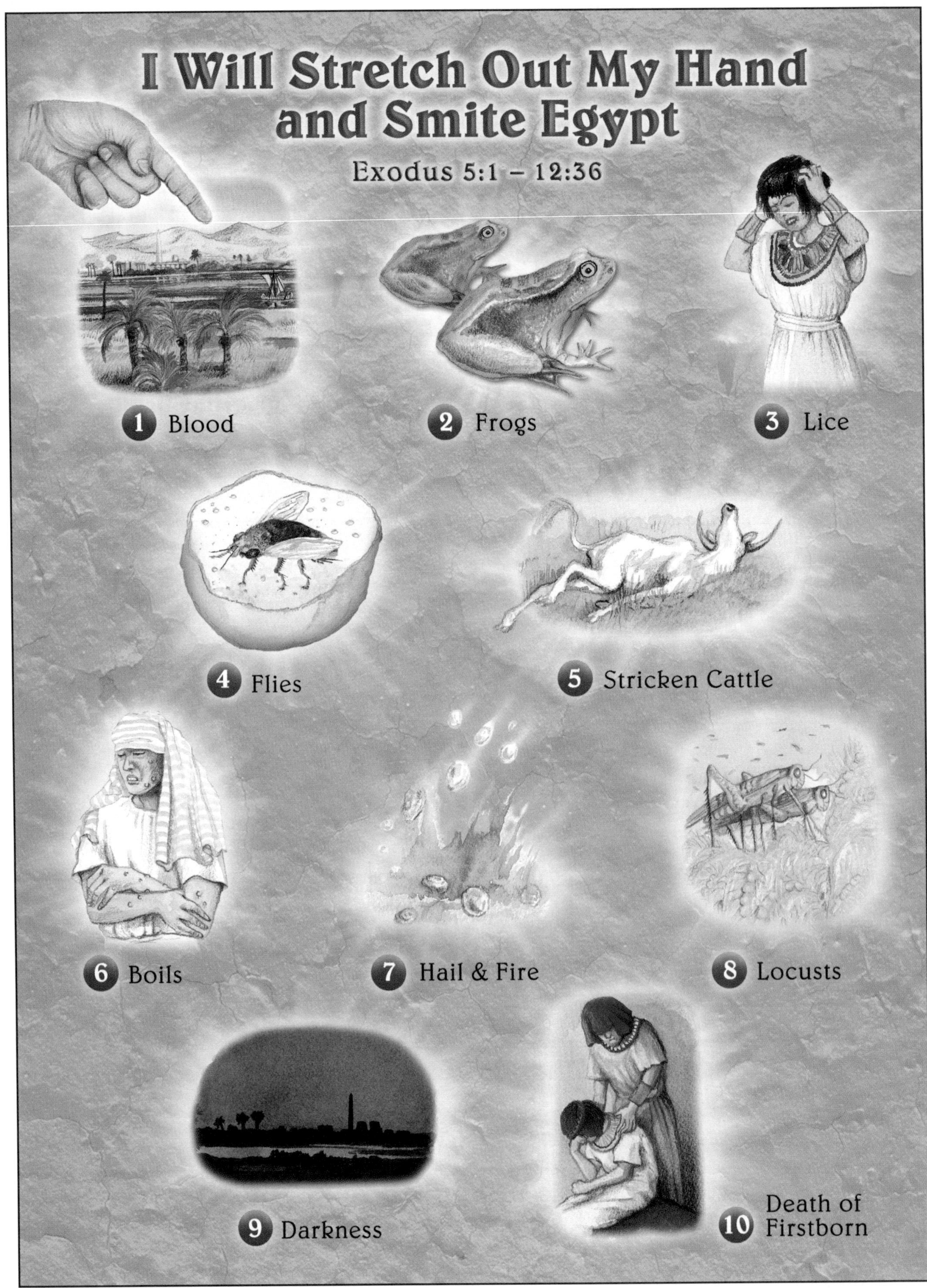
I Will Stretch Out My Hand and Smite Egypt
Exodus 5:1 – 12:36
1 Blood
2 Frogs
3 Lice
4 Flies
5 Stricken Cattle
6 Boils
7 Hail & Fire
8 Locusts
9 Darkness
10 Death of Firstborn

I.
Have no other gods before me.

II.
Do not worship
any man-made image.

III.
Do not take the name
of the Lord in vain.

IV.
Remember the Sabbath day
to keep it holy.

V.
Honor your father and mother.

VI.
Do not kill.

VII.
Do not be unfaithful to
your wife or husband.

VIII.
Do not steal.

IX.
Do not tell lies.

X.
Do not desire the things that
belong to someone else.

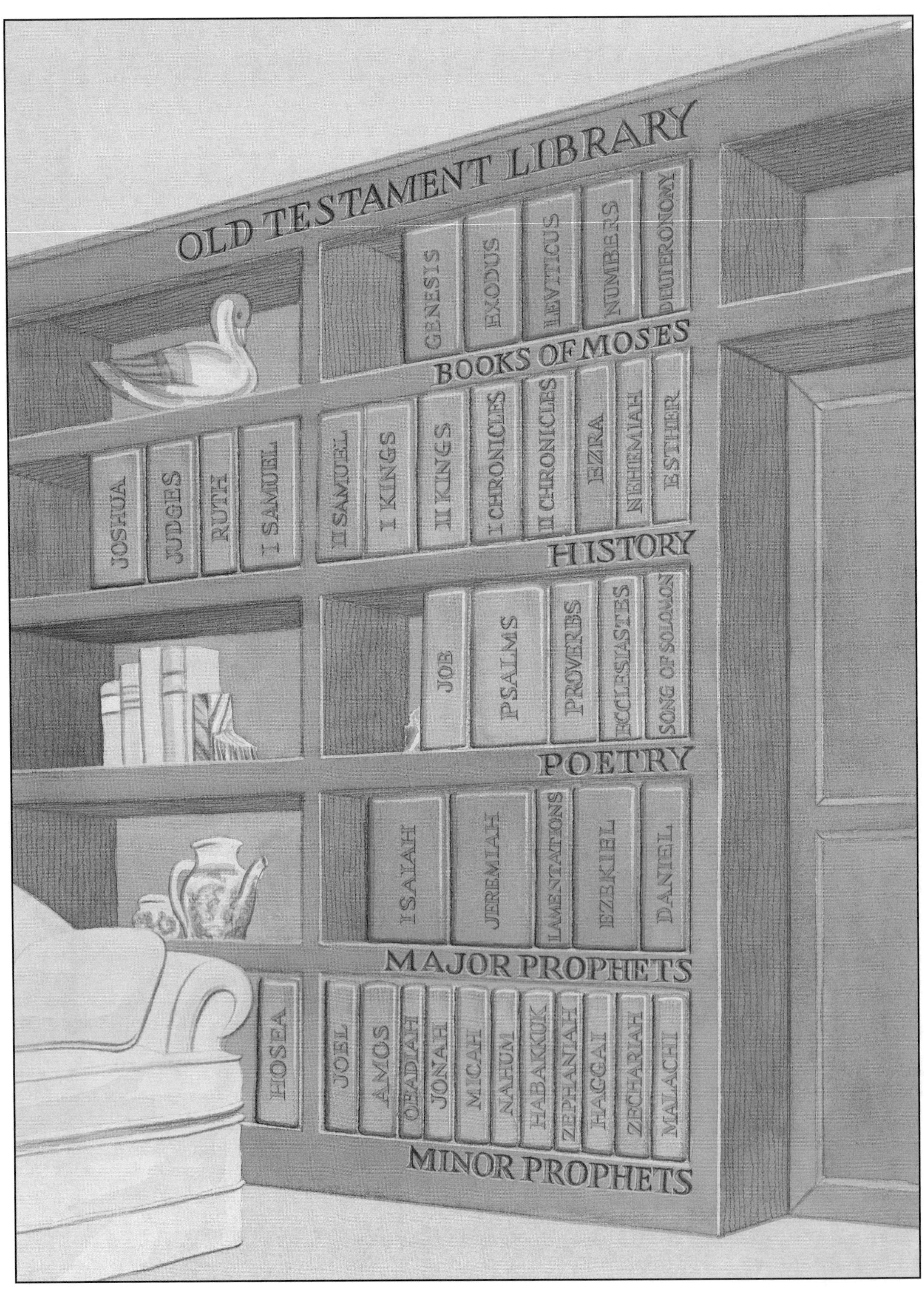
OLD TESTAMENT LIBRARY
GENESIS
EXODUS
LEVITICUS
NUMBERS
DEUTERONOMY
BOOKS OF MOSES
JOSHUA
JUDGES
RUTH
I SAMUEL
II SAMUEL
I KINGS
II KINGS
I CHRONICLES
II CHRONICLES
EZRA
NEHEMIAH
ESTHER
HISTORY
JOB
PSALMS
PROVERBS
ECCLESIASTES
SONG OF SOLOMON
POETRY
ISAIAH
JEREMIAH
LAMENTATIONS
EZEKIEL
DANIEL
MAJOR PROPHETS
HOSEA
JOEL
AMOS
OBADIAH
JONAH
MICAH
NAHUM
HABAKKUK
ZEPHANIAH
HAGGAI
ZECHARIAH
MALACHI
MINOR PROPHETS

NEW TESTAMENT LIBRARY
MATTHEW
MARK
LUKE
JOHN
THE GOSPELS
ACTS
HISTORY
ROMANS
I CORINTHIANS
II CORINTHIANS
GALATIANS
EPHESIANS
PHILIPPIANS
COLOSSIANS
I THESSALONIANS
II THESSALONIANS
I TIMOTHY
II TIMOTHY
TITUS
PHILEMON
PAUL'S LETTERS
HEBREWS
JAMES
I PETER
II PETER
I JOHN
II JOHN
III JOHN
JUDE
GENERAL LETTERS
REVELATION
PROPHECY

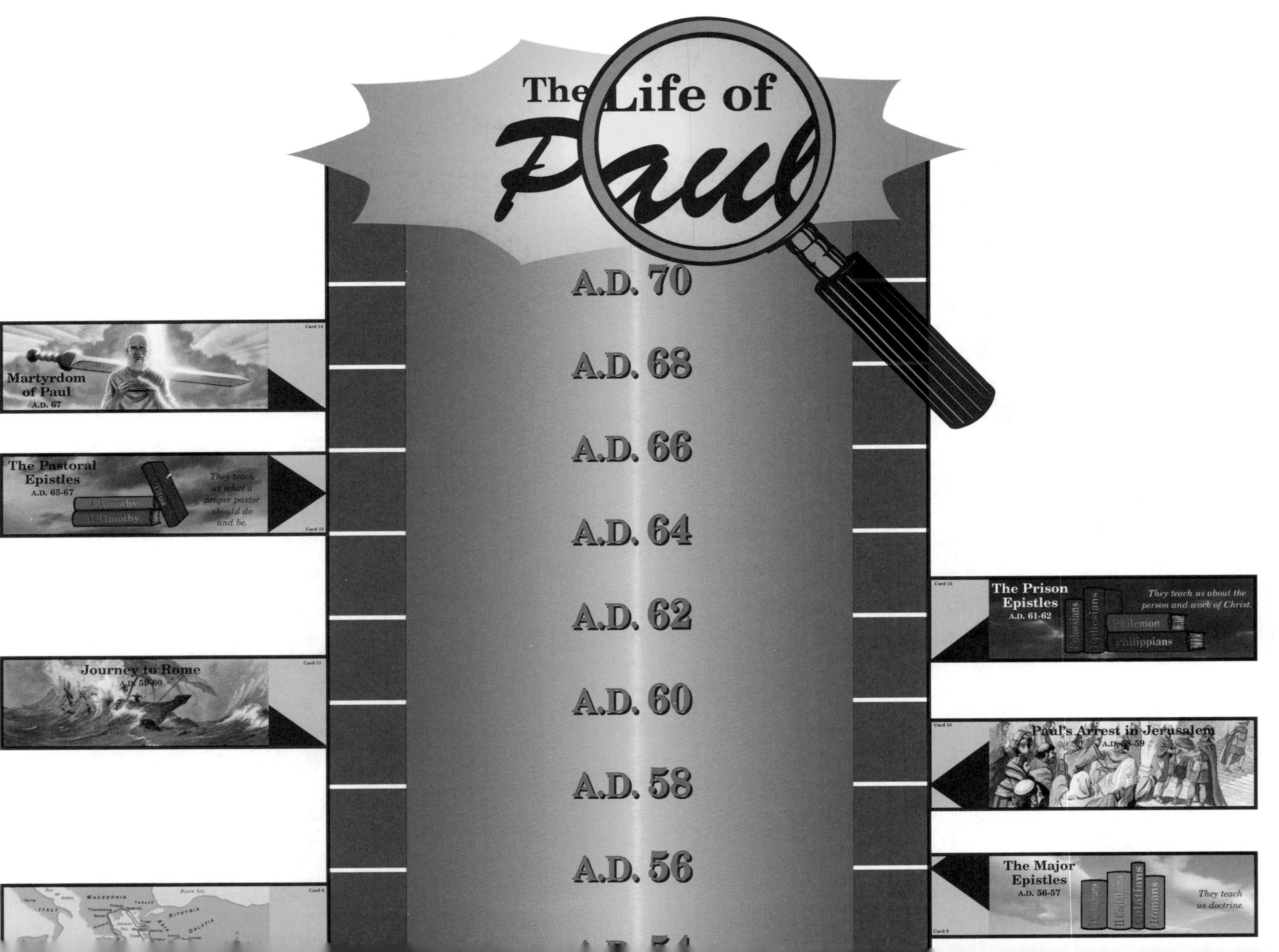
The Life of Paul
A.D. 70
A.D. 68
A.D. 66
A.D. 64
A.D. 62
A.D. 60
A.D. 58
A.D. 56
Martyrdom of Paul
A.D. 67
The Pastoral Epistles
A.D. 65-67
They teach us what a proper pastor should do and be.
Journey to Rome
The Prison Epistles
A.D. 61-62
They teach us about the person and work of Christ.
Philemon
Philippians
Paul's Arrest in Jerusalem
The Major Epistles
A.D. 56-57
They teach us doctrine.
Romans

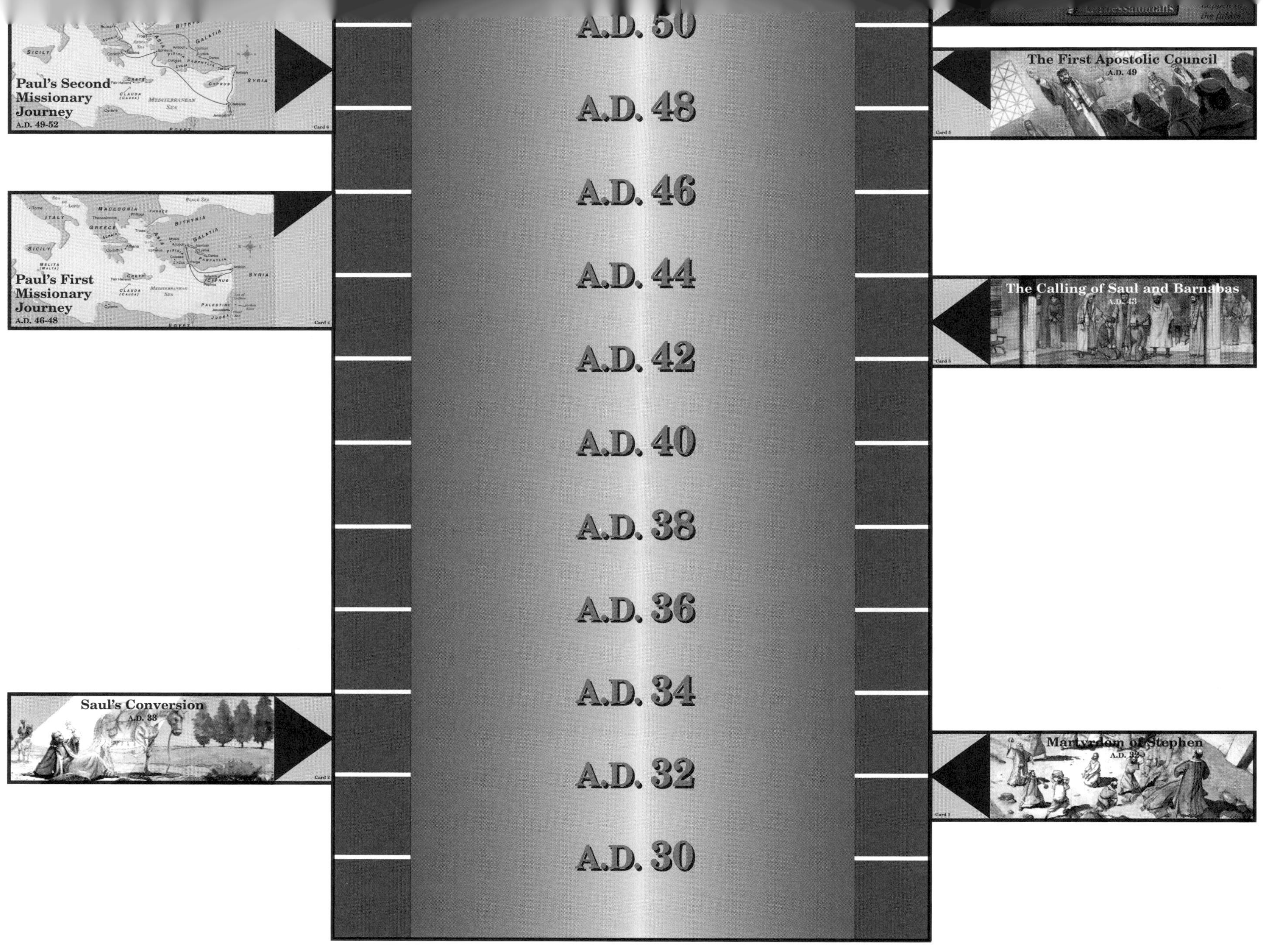

Paul's Second Missionary Journey
A.D. 49-52
Card 6
The First Apostolic Council
A.D. 49
Card 5
A.D. 50
A.D. 48
A.D. 46
A.D. 44
A.D. 42
A.D. 40
A.D. 38
A.D. 36
A.D. 34
A.D. 32
A.D. 30
Paul's First Missionary Journey
A.D. 46-48
Card 4
The Calling of Saul and Barnabas
A.D. 43
Card 3
Saul's Conversion
A.D. 33
Card 2
Martyrdom of Stephen
Card 1

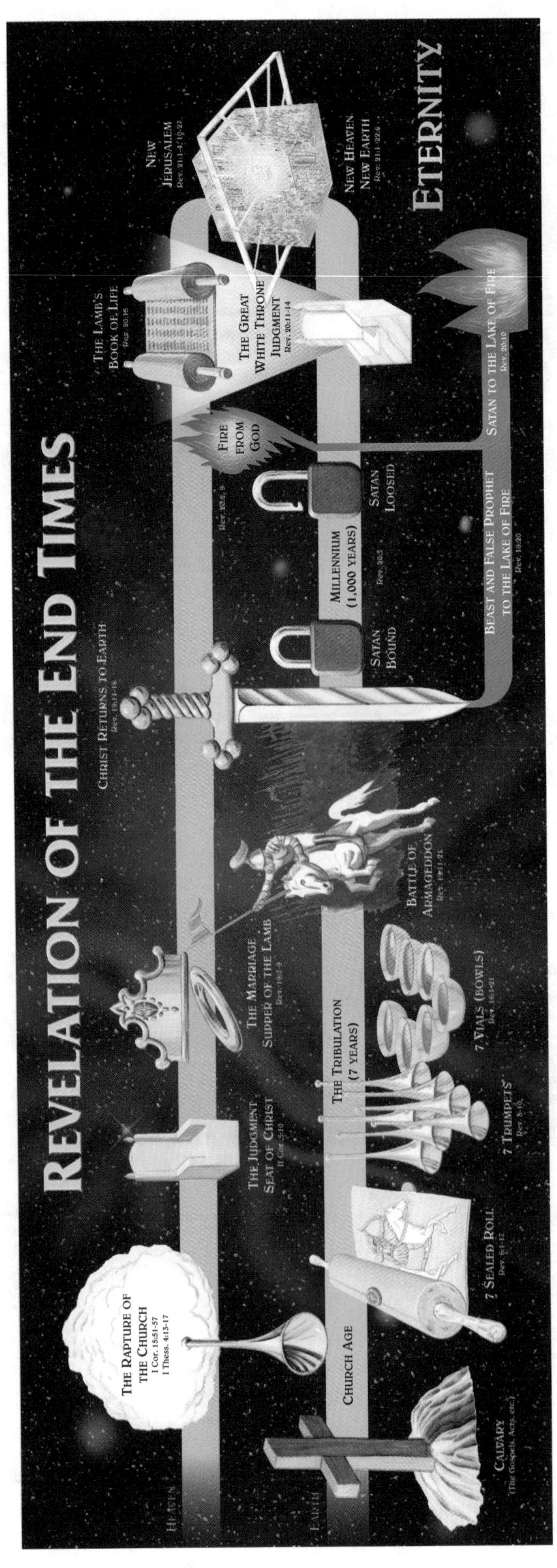
REVELATION OF THE END TIMES
HEAVEN
EARTH
THE RAPTURE OF THE CHURCH
I Cor. 15:51-57
I Thess. 4:13-17
CALVARY
(The Gospels, Acts, etc.)
CHURCH AGE
7 SEALED ROLL
Rev. 6:1-17
THE JUDGMENT SEAT OF CHRIST
II Cor. 5:10
THE MARRIAGE SUPPER OF THE LAMB
Rev. 19:7-9
THE TRIBULATION
(7 YEARS)
7 TRUMPETS
Rev. 8-10
7 VIALS (BOWLS)
Rev. 16:1-21
BATTLE OF ARMAGEDDON
Rev. 19:11-21
CHRIST RETURNS TO EARTH
Rev. 19:11-16
SATAN BOUND
MILLENNIUM
(1,000 YEARS)
Rev. 20:3
SATAN LOOSED
Rev. 20:8, 9
FIRE FROM GOD
BEAST AND FALSE PROPHET TO THE LAKE OF FIRE
Rev. 19:20
SATAN TO THE LAKE OF FIRE
Rev. 20:10
THE LAMB'S BOOK OF LIFE
Rev. 20:15
THE GREAT WHITE THRONE JUDGMENT
Rev. 20:11-14
NEW JERUSALEM
Rev. 21:1-4, 10-27
NEW HEAVEN NEW EARTH
Rev. 21:1-22:6
ETERNITY

Glossary

A

almighty (ôl mī′ tē) all-powerful; one of God's names

angel (ān′ jəl) heavenly messenger sent by God to earth; spirit who lives with God in heaven

apostle (ə pŏs′ əl) man chosen by Jesus to see the events of His life and His Resurrection and to tell others of Him

ark (ärk) large boat built by Noah

ark of the covenant (ärk′ ŭv THə kŭv′ ə nənt) the sacred box in which the Ten Commandments, a pot of manna, and Aaron's rod were kept

ascension (ə sĕn′ shən) Christ's going upward into heaven forty days after His Resurrection

assurance (ə shŏŏr′ əns) condition of knowing for sure; certainty

atone (ə tōn′) to give a satisfactory payment for a sin, wrongdoing, or injury

B

baptize (băp′ tīz′) to wash with water as a sign of a believer's following after Christ

begotten (bĭ gŏt′ tən) being the child of

beseech (bĭ sēch′) to beg or plead with

blasphemy (blăs′ fə mē) attributes evil to God; denies good that should be attributed to God; gives God's attributes to something or someone other than God

blessed (blĕs′ ĭd) holy; having God's favor

blessing (blĕs′ ĭng) a gift from God

born again (bôrn′ ə gĕn′) referring to one who has experienced the new birth (See *new birth.*)

Bread of Heaven (brĕd′ ŭv hĕv′ ən) a name for Christ, who provides physical and spiritual food

burnt offering (bûrnt′ ô′ fər ĭng) any Old Testament offering to God that was burned on an altar

C

caesar (sē′ zər) a title given to Roman emperors

Calvary (kăl′ vər ē) "the place of the skull"; the place near Jerusalem where Jesus was crucified; Golgotha

Canaan (kā′ nən) the land that God promised to give to the Israelites in the Old Testament; a name symbolizing heaven

centurion (sĕn tŏŏr′ ē ən) Roman commander of about one hundred soldiers

charity (chăr′ ĭ tē) love

cherubim (chĕr′ ə bĭm) more than one angel of the class called cherubs

Christian (krĭs′ chən) a person who believes in and accepts Christ as his Savior

church (chûrch) all of those who believe in Christ and are saved

cleanseth (klĕnz′ əth) frees from guilt; purges or clears

Comforter (kŭm′ fər tər) the Holy Spirit

commandment (kə mănd′ mənt) an order

commend (kə mĕnd′) to give to someone for safekeeping

compassion (kəm păsh′ ən) deep feeling for another person's problems or sorrows; sympathy

condemn (kən dĕm′) to declare guilty of wrongdoing

confess (kən fĕs′) to admit to doing wrong; to admit one's guilt; saying what God says about sin

corrupt (kə rŭpt′) evil and dirty; wicked; sinful

countenance (koun′ tə nəns) expression of a person's face; the face itself

covenant (kŭv′ ə nənt) promise or agreement made between two or more persons

covet (kŭv′ ĭt) to have a great want for something belonging to someone else; to wish something was yours

create (krē āt′) to make something from nothing

creator (krē ā′ tər) one that makes something new; Creator God

crucify (kro͞o′ sə fī′) to put to death by nailing or binding to a cross

D

Day of Atonement (dā′ ŭv ə tōn′ mənt) a day once a year when the high priest entered the holy of holies to offer sacrifices as payment for the people's sins

death (dĕth) separation of the body and spirit; separation from God

demon (dē′ mən) an evil spirit

descend (dĭ sĕnd′) to come down; to pass down from parent to child

devil (dĕv′ əl) an evil spirit; a demon; another name for Satan

disciple (dĭ sī′ pəl) one who follows and serves Jesus; a follower of a certain belief

divine (dĭ vīn′) having to do with God; holy and sacred

doctrine (dŏk′ trĭn) what a certain group of people believe and teach; a belief or principle

draught (drăft) drawing in of fish in a net

E

edify (ĕd′ ə fī′) to build up spiritually

Elohim (ĕl′ ō hĭm) a Hebrew name for God, indicating His power and authority

Emmanuel (ĭ măn′ yo͞o ĕl) a name of Jesus, meaning "God with us"

epistle (ĭ pĭs′ əl) letter or written work

eternal (ĭ tûr′ nəl) without end

eternity (ĭ tûr′ nĭ tē) time without beginning or end

eunuch (yo͞o′ nək) man in charge of a royal household

evangelize (ĭ văn′ jə līz) to spread the gospel

everlasting (ĕv′ ər lăs′ tĭng) without end; going on forever

exalt (ĭg zôlt′) to speak highly of; to praise and glorify

exhort (ĭg zôrt′) to try to convince

F

faith (fāth) trust in God; firm belief without physical proof

false prophet (fôls′ prŏf′ ĭt) man who preaches or teaches religious ideas against those found in God's Word; deceiver

fellowship (fĕl′ ō shĭp′) being together as friends; enjoying each other's company

firmament (fûr′ mə mənt) sky between the heavens and the earth

fisher of men (fĭsh′ ər ŭv mĕn′) person who leads others to be saved

follower (fŏl′ ō ər) one who serves another; one who believes and lives by another's teachings; disciple

foreknowledge (fôr′ nŏl′ ĭj) knowledge of something before it exists or happens

forerunner (fôr′ rŭn′ ər) person who goes before to prepare the way for another or to tell of another's coming

foretold (fôr tōld′) predicted; told about future happenings

forgiveness (fər gĭv′ nĭs) act of excusing or pardoning someone for a wrongdoing

fornication (fôr′ nĭ kā′ shən) immoral or evil behavior; idolatry

frankincense (frăng′ kĭn sĕns′) gum from certain trees that gives off a spicy, sweet odor when burned

fruit (fro͞ot) anything yielded or produced

furlough (fûr′ lō) period of time off from one's regular job or duties

G

genealogy (jē′ nē ŏl′ ə jē) record of ancestral descent; family tree

generation (jĕn′ ə rā′ shən) all the people born in a certain time period

Gentile (jĕn′ tīl) any person who is not Jewish

girdle (gûr′ dl) belt worn at the waist around a loose-fitting, thigh-length shirt

glorify (glôr′ ə fī) to praise or worship

Good Shepherd (go͝od′ shĕp′ ərd) a name for Christ, showing He leads and guides us

gospel (gŏs′ pəl) the truth of the good news of Christ's coming to earth, dying for our sins, and rising from the tomb

grace (grās) God's kindness to us even though we do not deserve it

Great Commission (grāt′ kə mĭsh′ ən) Christ's command to His disciples to teach the gospel (Matthew 28:19-20)

guilty (gĭl′ tē) having done wrong and deserving punishment

H

harlot (här′ lət) bad or immoral woman

heart (härt) innermost center of the natural condition of man; center of man's thought life and emotions

heathen (hē′ THən) person who does not know of or believe in God

heaven (hĕv′ ən) glorious and happy place where God and His angels live; where saved people will live eternally

Hebrew (hē′ bro͞o) Jewish language; Jewish person

hell (hĕl) place of dreadful and endless torment where the unsaved are punished after death

high priest (hī′ prēst′) head or chief of the Jewish priests with the responsibility of overseeing the temple and administering religious ceremonies

holy (hō′ lē) attribute of God: sinless, perfect, and righteous

holy of holies (hō′ lē ŭv hō′ lēz) the holiest place; place in the tabernacle where the ark of the covenant was kept

Holy Spirit (hō′ lē spĭr′ ĭt) the third Person of the Trinity who lives in the hearts of Christians; the Holy Ghost

homage (hŏm′ ĭj or ŏm′ ĭj) special respect shown to honor someone

honor (ŏn′ ər) *n.* glory and praise; honesty; *vb.* to treat with love, admiration, and respect

hospitality (hŏs′ pĭ tăl′ ĭ tē) kind or friendly treatment of guests; the art of being friendly and generous to others

household of faith (hous′ hōld′ ŏv fāth) believers born into the family of God through faith in Jesus Christ; born-again Christians

humble (hŭm′ bəl) not proud of oneself or boastful; meek or modest

humility (hyo͞o mil′ i tē) state of being without self-pride and boastfulness

I

I Am (ī′ ăm′) one of the names for God, showing His eternal existence "apart from" creation

idol (īd′ l) statue worshiped as a god; person or thing loved more than God

image (ĭm′ ĭj) likeness; something that is like another in form or nature; idol

impute (ĭm pyo͞ot′) to transfer (righteousness or guilt) from one person to another

incarnate (ĭn kär′ nĭt) the Son of God in human flesh

incense (ĭn′ sĕns′) substance that gives off a sweet smell when it is burned

incorruptible (ĭn′ kə rŭp′ tə bəl) clean and perfect; without error

infallible (ĭn făl′ ə bəl) incapable of error; perfect

infinite (ĭn′ fə nĭt) very great; without boundary; endless

iniquity (ĭ nĭk′ wĭ tē) sin and wickedness

inspiration (ĭn′ spə rā′ shən) God's breathing (of the Scriptures) into holy men

intercede (ĭn′ tər sēd′) to plead on behalf of another

interpret (ĭn tûr′ prĭt) to explain the meaning of

Israel (ĭz′ rē əl) God's chosen people; the Jews; the land of the Jews

J

Jehovah (jĭ hō′ və) the personal name of God in the Old Testament, meaning "the Eternal One who reveals Himself"

Jew (jo͞o) a person of the Hebrew race, God's chosen people

Jubilee Year (jo͞o′bə lē yîr′) a celebration the Jews observed every fifty years

judgment (jŭj′ mənt) act of hearing and deciding a case; decision given by a judge

just (jŭst) right, fair, and honest; good and righteous

justify (jŭs′ tĭ fī′) to declare righteous

L

Lamb (lăm) name used for Jesus Christ; it shows that by His death He paid the sacrifice for our sins, just as a lamb was sacrificed in the Old Testament for the sins of the Israelites.

laver (lā′ vər) large bowl used in washing sacrifices in the Jewish tabernacle or temple

law (lô) rule made by God or human authority

leaven (lĕv′ ən) substance such as yeast that causes dough to rise; often considered a symbol of sin in the Bible

leper (lĕp′ ər) person who has leprosy

leprosy (lĕp′ rə sē) skin disease that attacks the nerves, causes weakening and wasting away of muscles, and is characterized by white, scaly scabs; a picture of sin

Levite (lē′ vīt) member of the tribe of Levi from which the Jewish priests were chosen

longsuffering (lông′ sŭf′ ər ĭng) patience in pain or trouble

Lord (lôrd) God; Jesus Christ

Lord's Supper (lôrdz′ sŭp′ ər) communion; a church service by which we remember Christ's sacrifice on the cross; the last meal that Jesus had with His disciples

lots (to cast) (lŏtz) using bits of paper or wood to decide the outcome or determine the portion of something given to each person

Lucifer (lo͞o′ sə fər) Satan's name before he was cast out of heaven

M

magistrate (măj′ ĭ strāt′) officer of a government, such as a judge or president

malefactor (măl′ ə făk′ tər) one who does evil; criminal

Man of Sorrows (măn′ ŭv sŏr′ ōz) a name for Jesus, showing His sorrow and suffering for the sins of the world

mediator (mē′ dē ā′tər) person who acts as a go-between

mercy (mûr′ sē) God's withholding of the punishment we deserve

mercy seat (mûr′ sē sēt′) the gold plate covering the ark of the covenant on which the high priest sprinkled the blood for a sin offering; the throne of God

Messiah (mə sī′ ə) the Old Testament name for the promised Redeemer; Christ

might (mīt) power

Millennium (mĭ lĕn′ ē əm) period of one thousand years when Christ will reign on earth following the Tribulation

millstone (mĭl′ stōn′) one of two round, flat stones used for grinding grain

miracle (mĭr′ ə kəl) supernatural event done by the power of God that shows His works

missionary (mĭsh′ ə nĕr′ ē) person who goes out to tell the story of Jesus and God's plan of salvation

moneychanger (mŭn′ ē chān′ jər) person who exchanges one kind of money for another kind

myrrh (mûr) fragrant extract from the wood and bark of a common Palestinian bush

N

Nazarene (năz′ ə rēn′) a person from Nazareth; another name for Jesus

Nazarite (năz′ ər īt) a Hebrew who had taken certain religious vows; he could not drink wine, cut his hair, or touch an unclean thing

new birth (no͞o bûrth) occasion, upon confession and belief in the gospel, that God gives eternal life to a sinner

new heaven and new earth (no͞o hev′ ən and no͞o ûrth) future heaven and earth that will be created by God

O

obey (ō bā′) to do what one is told to do

observance (əb zûr′ vəns) act of keeping customs, laws, or religious ceremonies

offering (ô′ fər ĭng) giving of something as an act of worship to God

omnipotent (ŏm nĭp′ ə tənt) all-powerful; almighty

omnipresent (ŏm′ nə prĕz′ ənt) always present; existing everywhere at the same time

omniscient (ŏm nĭsh′ ənt) all-knowing; having complete knowledge of everything

ordinance (ôr′ dn əns) rule, especially one given by God

P

palsy (pôl′ zē) loss of power to feel or move

parable (păr′ ə bəl) short story that teaches a lesson; earthly story with a heavenly meaning

paradise (păr′ ə dīs′) heaven; dwelling place of God and His angels and where the saved will dwell in eternity

pardon (pär′ dn) forgiveness

Passover (păs′ ō′vər) the death angel's passing over the Hebrew homes that had blood sprinkled on the doorposts (Exodus 12:13)

Passover Feast (păs′ ō′vər fēst′) an eight-day Jewish feast in remembrance of the Israelites' escape from Egypt

patriarch (pā′ trē ärk′) father, ruler, or founder of a family, tribe, or group

Pentecost (pĕn′ tĭ kôst′) a Jewish celebration (feast) held fifty days after Passover to remember the harvest and the giving of the Ten Commandments; the giving of the Holy Spirit to the apostles and early Christians

persecution (pûr′ sĭ kyo͞o′ shən) harmful or cruel treatment

pharaoh (fâr′ ō) title given to the kings of ancient Egypt

Pharisee (făr′ ĭ sē′) member of a Jewish group that was strict in keeping Jewish law

Philistines (fĭ lĭs′ tēnz; fĭl′ ĭ stēnz′) enemies of the Jews who lived in the Holy Land during Old Testament times

plague (plāg) suffering or trouble sent from God; rapid spreading of a deadly disease

potter's field (pŏt′ ərz fēld′) cemetery for poor or friendless people

praise (prāz) to express the worth or value of something through words or songs

prayer (prâr) act of speaking to God

priest (prēst) Old Testament servant of God chosen by God to offer sacrifices

proclaim (prō klām′) to make known to the public

prodigal (prŏd′ ĭ gəl) wasteful and careless

prophecy (prŏf′ ĭ sē) the telling of future events

prophesy (prŏf′ ĭ sī′) to tell about future events; to proclaim God's will

prophet (prŏf′ ət) a Bible preacher who told of God's will and future events

propitiation (prō pĭsh′ ē ā′ shən) act of appeasing wrath; our means of salvation through Christ's death

proud (proud) feeling pleased over something done, made, or owned; honored; dignified

providence (prŏv′ ĭ dəns) divine acts of God in making all things to work out His purpose and plan

province (prŏv′ ĭns) section of a kingdom or an empire; in Roman times, a section of the empire ruled by a governor

psalm (säm) religious song, poem, or hymn of praise to God

publican (pŭb′ lĭ kən) tax collector of ancient Rome

pure (pyo͝or) not mixed with anything else; not having fault or guilt; clean

R

rabbi (răb′ ī) "teacher" or "master"; a Jewish religious leader

ram's horn (rămz′ hôrn′) trumpet made of a curly horn from a male sheep

ransom (răn′ səm) price paid to free captives

Rapture (răp′ chər) taking of the saved to heaven when Christ returns

reconcile (rĕk′ ən sīl′) to bring together again in peace and friendship after being separated

redeemer (rĭ dē′ mər) one who buys back something that was lost; one who saves or sets free; Jesus Christ

redemption (rĭ dĕmp′ shən) act of being rescued or freed from sin; our salvation

regeneration (rĭ jĕn′ ə rā′ shən) act of receiving a new spiritual life; salvation; new birth

remission (rĭ mĭsh′ ən) forgiveness of sin

repent (rĭ pĕnt′) to be sorry for and ask forgiveness for sin

repentance (rĭ pĕn′ təns) act of being sorry for, asking forgiveness for, and turning away from sin

resurrection (rĕz′ ə rĕk′ shən) act of coming to life again

revelation (rĕv′ ə lā′ shən) what God has made known to man

right (rīt) correct; true; just

righteous (rī′ chəs) doing that which is right in the sight of God; hatred of sin and love of good

S

Sabbath (săb′ əth) the seventh day of the week; the biblical day used for worship and rest

sackcloth (săk′ klôth′) rough cloth made from the hair of goats and camels and worn as a sign of sadness

sacrifice (săk′ rə fīs′) offering to God for the forgiveness of sin

Sadducees (săj′ ə sēz′) group of Jews who did not believe in angels or resurrection

saint (sānt) person who is saved

salvation (săl vā′ shən) God's saving us from the punishment of sin

sanctification (săngk′ tə fī kā′ shən) making holy in heart and behavior by God and the Holy Spirit after salvation

sanctuary (săngk′ cho͞o ĕr′ ē) holy place set apart for the worship of God

Sanhedrin (săn′ hē drĭn) the Jews' seventy-member supreme court for religious and government cases

Satan (sāt′ n) another name for the Devil; an evil spirit who is the enemy of God and of all Christians

saved (sāvd) description of one who has believed the gospel and asked forgiveness for sins; set free from sin and its results

savior (sāv′ yər) one who saves others from trouble or disaster

Savior (sāv′ yər) Jesus Christ our Lord

scapegoat (skāp′ gōt′) one who takes the blame for others; in Old Testament times a goat was taken into the wilderness yearly, symbolically taking the blame for the sins of the people; Jesus took the blame for our sins

Scripture (skrĭp′ chər) holy writings of God; the Bible

separation (sĕp′ ə rā′ shən) being set apart; living differently from the unsaved in a total and noticeable way

sepulchre or sepulcher (sĕp′ əl kər) tomb or cave used for burial

seraph (sĕr′ əf) angel of important position described in Isaiah 6:2 as having six wings and believed to lead in the worship of God

servant (sûr′ vənt) person who works for someone else

Sheol (shē′ ōl) a Hebrew name for hell

shofar or shophar (shō′ fär) ancient Hebrew trumpet made of a ram's horn and used for giving signals

sin (sĭn) disobedience to the law of God

slothful (slôth′ fəl) lazy

smite (smīt) to hit or slap; to destroy or kill

sojourn (sō′ jərn) to stay in one place for a time

soothsayer (so͞oth′ sā ər) one who tells the future, or pretends to; a fortuneteller

sorcerer (sôr′ sər ər) person who practices magic and claims to have the help of evil spirits

soul (sōl) part of the person that thinks, acts, feels, and lives forever

sow (sō) to spread or plant seed

surety (sho͞or′ ĭ tē) person who agrees to be responsible for the debts or faults of another

swaddling clothes (swŏd′ lĭng klōz′) strips of cloth used to wrap around a newborn baby

synagogue (sĭn′ ə gŏg′) Jewish congregation or a place to meet for worship

T

tabernacle (tăb′ ər năk′ əl) tent used by the Israelites as a place of worship while they were wandering in the wilderness

tablet (tăb′ lĭt) small flat sheet of stone used for writing

talent (tăl′ ənt) unit of weight for gold or silver; ability to do something well

tares (târz) harmful weeds that grow in grain fields

temple (tĕm′ pəl) building used for the worship of God or of false gods

temptation (tĕmp tā′ shən) act of trying to make a person do something wrong; attraction

Ten Commandments (tĕn′ kə mănd′ mənts) the ten rules for living that God gave to Moses on Mount Sinai (Exodus 20)

testament (tĕst′ tə mənt) will or promise; divisions of the Bible

testify (tĕs′ tə fī′) to give evidence for; to tell about what one has seen or heard

testimony (tĕs′ tə mō′ nē) open statement of one's beliefs or faith in God

thresh (thrĕsh) to separate the grain or seeds from a plant such as wheat

till (tĭl) to plow or cultivate the ground

tithe (tīTH) small part; small tax; offering to God of one-tenth of all that a person earns

transfiguration (trăns fĭg′ yə rā′ shən) the changed appearance of Christ on the mountain (Matthew 17:1-13)

transform (trăns fôrm′) to change the appearance, shape, or nature of a thing

transgression (trăns grĕsh′ ən) sin; act of doing what God forbids

translate (trăns′ lāt) to take to heaven without death; to make something understandable in another language

trespass (trĕs′ păs′) to disobey; to sin

tribe (trīb) any one of the twelve groups of the Hebrews, each of which descended from one of the sons of Jacob

Tribulation (trĭb′ yə lā′ shən) a period of seven years of great trouble and misery on earth during the End Times

tribute (trĭb′ yo͞ot′) tax; expression of thanks or respect

Trinity (trĭn′ ĭ tē) God the Father, God the Son, and God the Holy Spirit, in one divine nature

trust (trŭst) *n.* firm, unchanging belief in the power, love, or truthfulness of a person or thing; faith and confidence; *vb.* to have faith in

twinkling (twĭng′ klĭng) quick wink of the eye; very short time; moment

U

unbelief (ŭn′ bĭ lēf′) lack of thinking that something is true

undefiled (ŭn′ dĭ fīld′) clean and pure; not corrupted or made dirty

unfaithful (ŭn fāth′ fəl) not to keep one's promises

ungodly (ŭn gŏd′ lē) sinful and wicked

unrighteousness (ŭn rī′ chəs nĭs) wickedness; sinfulness

V

vainglory (vān′ glôr′ ē) great pride in oneself; boastful display or "showing off "; arrogance; opposite of humility

vengeance (vĕn′ jəns) punishment or injury in return for a wrong

vessel (vĕs′ əl) large boat or ship; container for holding liquids; person made or used for some purpose

viper (vī′ pər) type of poisonous snake

virgin (vûr′ jĭn) pure, unmarried female

W

watchtower (wŏch′ tou′ ər) high tower or high place from which to watch for enemy ships, forces, etc.

wayside (wā′ sīd′) side of a path or road

wilderness (wĭl′ dər nĭs) region of land with no people; dry, bare land

wise men (wīz′ mĕn′) men who gain knowledge, especially from the heavens; the men who followed the star from the East to Bethlehem where Jesus was born

witness (wĭt′ nĭs) *n.* person who tells about an event he has seen; *vb.* to tell others about Christ and the way of salvation

Word (wûrd) the way God speaks to man; in Scripture, referring to both the Bible (the written Word) and Jesus Christ (the living Word)

worship (wûr′ shĭp) to show honor, love, and respect

Y

yoke (yōk) wooden frame that fastens two oxen or horses together for pulling a plow or heavy load

Z

Zion (zī′ ən) heaven; a name for Jerusalem; a hill in Jerusalem that represents the whole city

Cumulative Index

	Grade 2	Grade 3	Grade 4
Israelites			
released from Egypt			unit 1
cross the Red Sea			unit 1
receive manna from heaven		unit 2	
receive quail from heaven		unit 2	unit 1
receive the Ten Commandments from God through Moses		unit 2	unit 1
worship a golden calf			unit 1
receive instructions for the tabernacle			unit 1
send forty spies to Canaan			unit 1
Jehoiada			
raises Joash to please God			unit 3
helps Joash become king			unit 3
Jehoshaphat			
leads the Israelites in obedience to God's Word			unit 2
Jeremiah			
See Prophet Focus			
Jesus			
birth	unit 4	unit 4	unit 4
teaches in the temple			unit 4
baptism	unit 9		
temptation by Satan	unit 9		unit 5
calls the disciples		unit 9	unit 6
talks to the woman at the well		unit 5	
teaches the Beatitudes in the Sermon on the Mount		unit 5	
tells about the rich man and Lazarus			unit 5
teaches about prayer, using the Lord's Prayer		unit 5	
loves the little children		unit 6	
sends the seventy missionaries		unit 5	
questioned about the unfaithful woman			unit 7
triumphal entry	unit 9		
cleansing the temple		unit 8	
foretells His death		unit 5	
tells why He came		unit 5	
betrayed by Judas			unit 8
arrested by the Romans			unit 8
stands trial			unit 8
Crucifixion	unit 8	unit 8	unit 8
death/burial	unit 8	unit 8	unit 8
Resurrection	unit 8	unit 8	unit 8
appearances after death		unit 8	unit 8
teaches the disciples			unit 9
Second Coming	unit 9		unit 10
Jezebel			
lies about Naboth			unit 3
punished for her wickedness			unit 3
Joash			
becomes king of Israel at a young age			unit 3
restores the temple of God			unit 3

	Grade 2	Grade 3	Grade 4
Job			
accepts trials		unit 3	
receives reward for righteousness		unit 3	
John Mark			
travels with Paul and Barnabas		unit 7	
John the Apostle			
sees Christ and receives Revelation		unit 10	unit 10
John the Baptist			
preaches about the coming Messiah	unit 9		unit 7
baptizes Jesus	unit 9		unit 7
dies as a martyr	unit 10		unit 7
Jonah			
See Prophet Focus			
Jonathan			
makes a covenant with David	unit 5		
Joseph, earthly father of Jesus			
obeys the angel of God and takes Mary as his wife			unit 4
journeys to Bethlehem			unit 4
Joshua			
gives a good report about Canaan			unit 1
leads Israel in battle with Jericho	unit 2		
Judson, Adoniram			
See Heroes of the Faith			
Korah			
rebels against Moses		unit 2	
dies by being swallowed by the earth		unit 2	
Knox, John			
See Heroes of the Faith			
Kuyper, Abraham			
See Heroes of the Faith			
Lathbury, Mary			
See Hymn History Stories			
Lazarus			
dies from illness	unit 9		
raised from the dead	unit 9		
Lot			
travels with Abraham	unit 1	unit 1	
pitches tent toward Sodom	unit 1	unit 1	
Luke			
journeys with Paul to Philippi		unit 7	
Lydia			
accepts Christ		unit 7	
Malachi			
teaches tithing			unit 9